MAINE BIOGRAPHIES

HARRIE B. COE

Reprinted in Two Volumes

Volume I

CLEARFIELD

Originally published as *Maine Resources, Attractions, and Its People.*
A History, 4 volumes, ed. Harrie B. Coe
New York, 1928

Volume III [Biographies] reprinted for Clearfield Company, Inc by
Genealogical Publishing Co , Inc.
Baltimore, Maryland, 2002

International Standard Book Number: 0-8063-5125-X
Set Number 0-8063-5124-1
Made in the United States of America

NOTE: The numerous illustrations originally included in this volume of
    Maine Resources, Attractions, and Its People· A History were
    not reproduced in the Clearfield Company reprint.

MAINE—A HISTORY

GEORGE ADDISON EMERY—The long life of George Addison Emery, unusually public spirited in inspiration and rich in accomplishment, has been a fine community asset to Saco, Maine. A remarkably able lawyer, he is, at eighty-nine years of age, the oldest living member of the York County bar. He retains an active connection with the outstanding educational institutions and progressive movements of the town and generously donates leadership which is as effective as ever.

George Addison Emery was born at Saco, Maine, November 14, 1839, son of Moses and Sarah Cutts (Thornton) Emery. The father, born in 1794, in Minot, Maine, was admitted to the Maine bar in 1836, after his graduation from Bowdoin College, and became a well-known attorney, enjoying wide success until his death in 1881 at the age of eighty-seven. His wife, mother to the subject of this record, was born in Saco and was the daughter of Thomas G. Thornton, in whose honor Thornton Academy was named. She died in 1889.

The son also attended Bowdoin College after completing the public school course, and graduated in 1863 with the degree of Bachelor of Arts. In 1866 he was admitted to the bar and began to practice law at once in Saco, in association with his father. When the father died fifteen years later, he continued his practice alone. His professional success has been attended by popular recognition of his qualities of leadership and public service. He was elevated to the bench as municipal judge in 1867, continuing in office until 1871, when he became recorder for a four-year term and proved so capable that he held the same office from 1878 to 1899. From 1881 to 1884, Judge Emery was a member of the State Legislature; from 1888 to 1891, he was Park Commissioner; and from 1890 to 1894, City Solicitor of Saco. He belonged to the York County Bar Association, of which he was president for a time, and to the Maine State and the American Bar associations. Along other lines, Judge Emery held office, for he was president of the York National Bank, secretary of the Saco Board of Trade and the Athenæum Society, and for twenty-five years secretary of the Saco Blue Lodge, Free and Accepted Masons. Formerly a member of several clubs and societies, he remains associated with the Maine Historical Society, a member of the standing committee. He is a communicant of the Unitarian church, and a member of the Maine State Executive Committee. He is a trustee and treasurer of Thornton Academy; treasurer of the York Institute, and a trustee of Laurel Hill Cemetery; president of the Thornton Alumni; and treasurer of the Dyer Public Library, of which he was an incorporator. For fifty-seven years he has been agent of the Provident Association of Saco, Maine. He is much interested in this society, which looks after the needy and unfortunate of the community. Thus in his vigorous and effective old age, he continues to serve, as throughout his life, the progressive and civilizing influences of Saco.

JUDGE BENJAMIN F. CLEAVES, one of the outstanding men of Portland, Maine, and at one time Judge of the District Court of Biddeford, Maine, was born January 14, 1866, at Waterborough, Maine, a son of Seth and Mary A. (Hamilton) Cleaves, both descendants of old and well-known New England families, particularly of Maine. Seth Cleaves, the father, also was born at Waterborough, in 1826. He was a millwright and lived in Maine during his lifetime. He died in January, 1880, a man beloved by everyone who knew him, and respected by all with whom he came in contact. Mary A. (Hamilton) Cleaves was born in Waterborough, in 1836. She died in December, 1878, a woman of much grace in her community.

Benjamin F. Cleaves received his early education in the public schools of Biddeford, and graduated from Biddeford High School with the class of 1885. Immediately after the completion of these courses of study, he entered newspaper work. In 1886 he became a member of the editorial staff of the Biddeford "Standard," and remained with this publication for approximately nine months. He spent the ensuing three months on the Biddeford "Times," after which he became a member of the staff of the Biddeford "Journal," a daily publication, with which he remained for two years. He then decided upon the law as a possible field of endeavor, entered the office of Hamilton & Haley, Biddeford attorneys, under whose competent preceptorship he studied until 1892, when he was formally admitted to practice at the bar of Maine. He formed a legal partnership with B. F. Hamilton, and this continued on a happy and successful basis until 1898, when the firm of Cleaves, Waterhouse & Emery was formed at Biddeford. As a partner in this widely-known concern, in 1914, Judge Cleaves was appointed chairman of the Maine Public Utilities Commission, serving in this capacity with honor to himself and satisfaction to the people until April, 1921, when he resigned to become executive secretary of the Associated Industries of Maine, a position which he is filling with ability and dispatch, in 1927. It should be made clear that Judge Cleaves did not rise to these high positions of trust quite as easily as it is given here. He is considered one of the most brilliant lawyers before the bar of Maine, and an executive of ability and integrity, and this distinction he won through hard work and perseverance. His high moral standards and his upright character naturally brought early recognition, and this is evidenced by the fact that, in 1898, while he was a comparatively young man, he was elevated to the bench as judge of the District Court of Biddeford. But the underlying depth of the respect he instilled is more clearly shown by the fact that he served as a judge of this court for more than sixteen years. This is a service for which Judge Benjamin F. Cleaves will long be remembered with pride in this community.

In his political views, he has ever been a staunch supporter of the Republican party; for more than two years he was a member of the Biddeford Board of Aldermen, and for more than three years was chairman of the Biddeford School Board. As a man and a citizen, he is noted for the fine manner in which he has stood behind any movement designed for the welfare or advancement of his community—indeed, it may be conservatively stated that this man has contributed his share, and more, toward the cause of Christianity and the progress of civilization in his part of our land. He has taken deep interest in the club and social life of his world, and in 1927 served as president of the Kiwanis Club of Portland, Maine. He is affiliated with Mavorshen Lodge, Free and Accepted Masons of Biddeford.

Benjamin F. Cleaves married, November 1, 1892, at Biddeford, Retta L. Foss, born December 5, 1868, in that community, a daughter of William A. and Elizabeth (Bradbury) Foss. William A. Foss was born in Holyoke, Massachusetts; Elizabeth (Bradbury) Foss was a native of Biddeford. Judge and Mrs. Cleaves are the parents of one son, Burton N. Cleaves, born at Portland, May 1, 1907. Judge Cleaves and his family maintain their principal residence at Biddeford, in which community they attend the Unitarian church.

ALEXANDER T. LAUGHLIN—The entire active career of Alexander T. Laughlin has been identified with the well-known firm which now operates under the name of the Milliken, Tomlinson Company, Incorporated, of Portland, Maine, of which he has been president and general manager since 1899. The corporation imports coffee, tea, molasses and other food products, and they are also coffee roasters and wholesale grocers.

Alexander T. Laughlin was born in Robbinston, Maine, November 21, 1856, son of Robert Laughlin, a native of Ireland, who was a shipsmith and who is now deceased, and of Elizabeth Porter (Stuart) Laughlin, of New Brunswick, Canada, also deceased. He received his education in the local public schools and, after completing his course in the Pembroke High School, began his business career in the employ of W. and C. R. Milliken, as office boy. In 1888, he was admitted to membership in the firm and when the merger with Cousins and Tomlinson was effected, in 1890, under the name of Milliken, Tomlinson Company, Incorporated, Mr. Laughlin was elected treasurer. He is well known as a business man of more than usual ability and his connection with the Milliken, Tomlinson Company, Incorporated, as chief executive and general manager, represents but a portion of the varied business connections which he maintains. He is a director of the E. T. Burrowes Company and a director of the Cumberland Loan & Building Association. In addition to his numerous business interests, Mr. Laughlin finds time for philanthropic and public service. He is a director of the Maine General Hospital and of the Children's Hospital, is a past president of the Portland Chamber of Commerce, was a director for three years, during the construction of the State Pier and, locally, served as a member and president of the Portland Common

Council, 1887-1888. Politically, Mr. Laughlin gives his support to the principles and the candidates of the Republican party. His religious affiliations are with the Chestnut Street Methodist Church, which he serves as a member of the board of trustees.

Alexander T. Laughlin was married, June 19, 1889, to Helen Emery and they are the parents of three children: 1. Dorothy, who is the wife of Kimball F. Frisbee. 2. Hilda, wife of Don J. Edwards, of Newton, Massachusetts. 3. Donald S., who is associated with the Thomas Laughlin Company.

The Millikin, Tomlinson Company, Incorporated, was established July 26, 1890, when the two firms of W. and C. R. Millikin and of Cousins and Tomlinson were merged into the present concern, with Weston F. Milliken as president, Edward Tomlinson as vice-president and manager, and Alexander T. Laughlin as treasurer. On October 10, 1898, Mr. Tomlinson died and he was succeeded as vice-president by Frank B. Milliken. On November 19, 1899, W. F. Milliken died and A. T. Laughlin became president and general manager, positions he now holds (1927). Charles O. Haskell was made treasurer at the same time and he held that position until 1913, when ill health made it necessary that he resign. At that time, Charles E. Baker (q. v.) was made treasurer. C. D. Merrill (q. v.) came into the firm in 1903, was made assistant manager a few years later, and in 1921 was elected vice-president, which official position he now holds. The concern maintains, in addition to the central plant at Portland, four branches, one at Presque Isle, one at Ellsworth, another at Belfast and a fourth at Milltown. The corporation also has a storehouse at Machias. The business has grown to proportions which require the services of one hundred and seventy-five people.

CLINTON D. MERRILL—One of the well-known business men of Portland is Clinton D. Merrill, vice-president of Milliken, Tomlinson Company, Incorporated, wholesale grocerymen, importers of coffees, teas, molasses, and other food products, and also coffee roasters. Mr. Merrill has been identified with the business since 1903, and has been vice-president for more than six years.

Clinton D. Merrill was born in Portland, Maine, May 25, 1885, son of Samuel Clinton Merrill, of Falmouth, Maine, now deceased, who was manager for the John B. Curtis Gum Factory, and of Elizabeth (Dewey) Merrill, a native of Lubec, Maine, also deceased. He attended the public schools of Portland and Phillips-Exeter Academy, and in 1903 became identified with Milliken, Tomlinson Company, Incorporated. A few years later he was made assistant manager, and in 1921 he was elected vice-president, a position he has continued to hold to the present time (1928). Politically, he gives his support to the principles and the candidates of the Republican party. He is a member of the Portland Athletic Club and of the Cumberland Club, and has a host of friends in Portland. His religious membership is with St. Lawrence Congregational Church.

Clinton D. Merrill was married, June 4, 1910, to Leona Curtis, of Portland, and they are the parents of three children: Elizabeth C., Barbara C., and Clinton D., Jr.

CHARLES E. BAKER—Since February, 1913, Charles E. Baker has been treasurer of the Milliken, Tomlinson Company, Incorporated, importers of tea, coffee, molasses, and other food products. His connection with one of the two concerns which were merged to form the Milliken, Tomlinson Company extends back to about 1889. He was president of the Wholesale Merchants' Association for a period of two years, and is well known in this section of the State as an able business man.

Charles E. Baker was born in Portland, Maine, August 15, 1863, son of Charles O. Baker, a native of Lancaster, New Hampshire, now deceased, who was in the employ of the Maine Central Railroad Company, and of Amanda M. (Byron) Baker, who was born in Maidstone, Vermont. He attended the public schools of Portland and Gray's Business College, in Portland, and then, at the age of sixteen, entered the employ of Woodbury and Latham, in their commercial department. That connection he continued for ten years, at the end of which time he became associated with the firm of Cousins and Tomlinson, as an employee. When the merger of that concern with the firm of W. and C. R. Milliken was effected in 1890, Mr. Baker remained with the new company, and on February 15, 1913, he was elected to the responsible position of treasurer of the company, an office he is still most efficiently filling. He is a member of the Portland Chamber of Commerce and of the Wholesale Merchants' Association, which he served as president for two years, and he is well known in this section of the State. Politically, he gives his allegiance to the Republican party. He is a member of the Independent Order of Odd Fellows and of the Knights of Pythias, and his religious interest is with the Congregational church, of which he is a member.

Charles E. Baker was married, March 4, 1897, to Lillian Jordan, of Mechanic Falls, Maine, and they are the parents of one child, Mary F.

NORMAN G. SMITH—The manufacture of feldspar has provided a lucrative business for Norman G. Smith, who since the death of his uncle in 1926 has been president of the Maine Feldspar Company. This firm was established in 1902, in Auburn, and in 1912 a large plant, which now is the company's main factory, was erected in Topsham, Maine.

The son of N. Newin and Clara (Hopkins) Smith, both natives of Maryland, Norman G. Smith was born in Conowingo, Maryland, February 13, 1873. His father, who is now deceased, was a farmer; his mother is still living (1928). As a boy, Norman G. Smith attended private school in Maryland and Westtown Friends School in Pennsylvania. Then he went into the paper business in Conowingo, Maryland, as an employee, and remained in this line of activity for ten years. In 1902 he came to Auburn, Maine, to establish the Maine Feldspar Company. This company, of which B. Gilpin Smith was president and Norman G. Smith was treasurer and general manager, started operations with a capacity of ten tons of feldspar daily. Later, the capacity was increased to thirty tons per day, which is its present capacity. B. Gilpin Smith, the late president of the Maine Feldspar Company, was born on February 12, 1853, in Conowingo, Maryland; was educated in the public schools; engaged in the flint-grinding and lumber business for many

years; was president of the Beaver Creek Lumber Company; was in the paper business, and directly connected with the power developing organization now known as the Conowingo Power Company; was a director of the York-Haven Paper Company, of Pennsylvania; purchased in the early nineties, while on a trip into Maine, two feldspar mines, which formed the nucleus of the present company; devoted the last ten years of his life almost entirely to the Maine Feldspar Company; and died in 1926. He was a member of the Free and Accepted Masons and of the Brunswick Club. He took for his wife, Rebekah Gould, of Hudson, New York, and had two children: Stanton G., who runs the Auburn plant of the Maine Feldspar Company; and Dorothy, who is the wife of Donald B. Abbott, of Yarmouth. When B. Gilpin Smith died in 1926, Norman G. Smith became president of the company; and Stanton G. Smith was made treasurer of the company and manager of the Auburn plant. The factory at Topsham, Maine, which is now the main plant of the company, having a daily capacity of forty tons, employing seventy-five persons, and shipping its product all over the United States, was built in 1912. Norman G. Smith, in addition to his presidency of the Maine Feldspar Company, has other business interests, being a director of the Ault-Williamson Shoe Company, of Auburn; and of the Brunswick Development Company; as well as of the Union Bank, of Brunswick. Politically, his affiliation is with the Republican party, as was his uncle's. He is a member of the Rotary Club, the Brunswick Club, the Town and College Club, and the Free and Accepted Masons. Religiously, he is identified, as was his uncle, with the Society of Friends.

In June, 1903, Norman G. Smith married Jane Brooke, of Montgomery County, Maryland. By this marriage there are the following children: 1. N. Brooke, who attends the University of Illinois. 2. Esther Newlin, who attends the Wheeler School, Providence, Rhode Island.

ROBERT COLE PLETTS, M. D.—One of the careful and successful physicians of Brunswick, Robert Cole Pletts, who is important in medical circles in this section, since 1916 has been conducting the general practice which he began in that year. His willingness to devote his time and talents freely to the work of caring for the ill and injured has brought to him the confidence and the esteem of the community in and near Brunswick.

The son of David Arthur Pletts, a native of Germany, also a physician, who came to the United States at an early age, and who died in 1903, and of Isabella Jane (Cole) Pletts, of Montreal, who is living, Robert Cole Pletts was born in Montreal, Province of Quebec, Canada, April 29, 1886. When he was only five years old he moved to Brunswick, Maine, with his family. As a boy he attended the public schools; then he went for his professional education to the Bowdoin Medical College, from which he was graduated in 1915 with the degree of Doctor of Medicine. After he had acquired experience as an interne at the Corporation Hospital, in Lowell, Massachusetts, and at the Malden Hospital, in Malden, Massachusetts, he started his general practice in Brunswick, Maine, November 11, 1916, and has continued it ever since that time. He is affiliated with the Cumberland County Medical Association, the Maine Medical Association, and the American Medical Association; the Phi Chi Fraternity; and the Independent Order of Odd Fellows. He is identified politically with the Republican party. He and his family are members of the Congregational church. When Dr. Pletts is not busy acting as physician and health adviser to the people of Brunswick, he finds time for his favorite hobby, which is horse racing. He always owns two or three horses, which he enters regularly in races on the tracks of Maine.

On September 22, 1915, Robert Cole Pletts married Sarah Van Stone of Fredericton, New Brunswick. They became the parents of the following children: Robert Cole, Jr., Harold Vincent, Donald Cole, Gilbert Oliver, all of whom attend the public schools in Brunswick; and Sarah Ellen, who died in 1927.

WILLIAM WARREN SMITH, M. D.—Widespread recognition of the professional ability of Dr. Smith, physician, of York County, Maine, has come to him as the result of over thirty years of successful practice. He has a large local clientele, which in summer is augmented by the many summer tourists. He was born at North Windham, Cumberland County, Maine, January 15, 1867, son of Andrew Francis Smith of Standish, and of Eunice L. (Skillen) Smith of Gray, both of whom are now deceased. Andrew Smith was a shoemaker, a man respected by all who knew him.

William Warren Smith received his early education in the common schools of Gorham, then attended Westbrook Seminary, and later matriculated at Dartmouth Medical College, from which institution he was graduated in 1894 with the degree of Doctor of Medicine. In that same year Dr. Smith began his practice at Shapleigh, remaining there until 1899, when he removed to Ogunquit, where he has engaged in his profession to the present (1928). In his political preference, Dr. Smith is an Independent, and has taken an active part in public affairs both in Shapleigh and in Ogunquit. Dr. Smith serves on the medical staff of York Hospital at Ogunquit, is a member of the County and State Medical associations, and of the American Medical Association. In his fraternal affiliations, he is a member of the Free and Accepted Masons. Dr. Smith retains the warm regard of the numerous families under his professional charge, the appreciation of the townspeople for sincere efforts toward community welfare, and the esteem of his confreres in medicine.

Dr. William Warren Smith married, December 25, 1894, at Shapleigh, Augusta S. Mann, and they are the parents of three children: 1. Kathryn, who graduated from Tufts College, and married William Ernest Brackett of Medford, Massachusetts; mother of two children: William Ernest, and Warren Richardson. 2. Roger W., a graduate of Bowdoin, class of 1919, Bachelor of Arts degree. 3. William W., Jr., graduate of Harvard University, Bachelor of Arts degree, and now connected with the Harvard University Press.

Mrs. Augusta S. Smith is an accomplished musician, and most gracious in her willingness to share her talent with others, particularly if a function is to be given in aid of some worthy charity. Her musical education began when she was but nine years of age, while she was still attending public school. Later, Mrs. Smith took special courses at Portland, Maine, for three years, and afterward attended the New England Conservatory of Music, and for many years has practiced her profession as teacher of music. Mrs. Smith is also prominent in club affairs, is a member of the Federation of Woman's Clubs and past president of Ogunquit Chapter, serving as a delegate to National and New England conventions of the organization. Along with these numerous activities, she finds time for civic interests, and serves as a trustee of York Hospital; is a former member of Ogunquit School Board; and both she and Dr. Smith are members of the Methodist Episcopal church.

HERBERT EDSON LOCKE—Among the prominent members of the legal profession in Augusta, Maine, is Herbert Edson Locke, who has been successfully engaged in general practice there since 1915. Mr. Locke is a Bowdoin College man, a graduate of Boston University Law School, and is well known in his city, not alone as a skilled practitioner, but also as a public-spirited citizen and as an active member of All Souls' Unitarian Church. His father, Edson Locke, was born at Locke's Corner, Mount Vernon, Maine. Later, he removed to Augusta, where he entered the grocery business and where he took an active part in civic affairs, serving as alderman of the city of Augusta. He married Ida Stevens, who was born in Norridgewock, Maine, and they were the parents of several children, among whom was Herbert Edson, of further mention.

Herbert Edson Locke, son of Edson and Ida (Stevens) Locke, was born in Augusta, Maine, April 6, 1891, and received his early and preparatory education in the public schools of his birthplace, graduating from Cony High School in 1908. The following year he matriculated at Bowdoin College, Brunswick, Maine, where he completed his course, with graduation in 1912, receiving at that time the degree of Bachelor of Arts. He had early decided upon the legal profession as his future field of achievement, and after completing his academic course began professional study in the Law School of Boston University, from which he was graduated in 1915, with the degree of Bachelor of Laws. He was admitted to the Maine bar that same year and opened an office in Augusta, where he has since been continuously and successfully engaged in practice. Mr. Locke is well known as a skilled and careful practitioner whose keen analytical powers and cogency in argument are factors to be reckoned with by his opponents. He is identified with the Augusta Trust Company, and is always ready to place his professional knowledge and experience at the service of the city. He served as City Solicitor, 1925-26, inclusive, and few projects planned for the advancement of the interests of Augusta fail to receive his earnest support. Fraternally, Mr. Locke is identified with the local York Rite bodies of the Masonic Order, Blue Lodge Chapter, Council, Commandery, and Kora Temple, and he is a member of the Abnaki Club (the Masonic club of Augusta), and of the Rotary International. He is also a member of Zeta Psi College Fraternity, and president of its Chapter House Corporation at Brunswick, Maine;

nebec and Maine State Bar associations; and of the also of Phi Delta Phi Legal Fraternity; of the Ken-Hoo Hoo Lumber Manufacturers' and Timberland Owners' Association. His religious affiliation is with All Souls' Unitarian Church of Augusta, which he has served as chairman of its standing committee; also a member of the Unitarian Laymen's League, and a member and secretary of the Maine Unitarian Association.

Herbert Edson Locke married, in Augusta, Maine, May 24, 1916, Marguerite Grosvenor Lowell, daughter of Harry Page and Bertha (Grosvenor) Lowell. Mr. and Mrs. Locke are the parents of one daughter, Nancy Locke.

JAMES H. KERR—One of the best-known contractors and builders in New England is James H. Kerr, of Rumford, Maine, head of a construction business which employs five hundred men and which is called on for many varieties of public and private building. One of the first concrete roads completed in Maine was the work of Mr. Kerr, who specializes in that line. Bridges, dams, and large buildings throughout New England have been erected under his skilled direction. He also participates in many departments of civic affairs.

James H. Kerr was born in Nova Scotia, March 7, 1874, son of Ephraim and Charlotte (Heather) Kerr. His education was acquired in the public schools, but his limited opportunities along formal lines have been amply supplemented by the rich and varied experience which has made up the years of his life since he left school. When he was twelve years old, he went to sea as cabin boy. By the time he was eighteen, he was master of a ship. His love of the sea has remained with him, but a life of unusual strenuousnes has prevented his seafaring very much. He has found his chief recreation in work. It was in 1897 that he began a business of his own as a general contractor in Rumford. Now his services are in demand all over New England. Besides the roads he has constructed, and the emphasis he lays on that character of construction, Mr. Kerr has completed many other big jobs. He built industrial structures for the Oxford Paper Company, vast, spreading buildings suitable to the magnitude of that plant. He erected the bank at Norway, Maine, a five-story garage in Haverhill, Massachusetts, the Hancock and Sullivan Bridge, an ornate and beautiful structure, several theatres, and many dams. He is now (1927) building a fine theatre in Portland, Maine. All this varied work is personally supervised by Mr. Kerr, whose experience gives him a quick mastery over the myriad details of each job and whose enthusiasm directs the perfection of its entire execution. Mr. Kerr is vice-president, general manager, and director of the Mt. Zircon Spring Water Company of Rumford and president of the Rumford Ice Company.

His broad interest in public welfare enlists Mr. Kerr's support of many organizations. He belongs to the Rumford Business Men's Association and the Republican party. His fraternal affiliations are with the Free and Accepted Masons, in which order he has risen to prominence as Past Commander of Rumford Commandery, Knights Templar, with the Independent Order of Odd Fellows, and Encampment, of which he is Past Patriarch, and with the Knights of Pythias. He is a communicant of the Baptist church.

February 5, 1918, in Rumford, Maine, James H. Kerr was married, and he is the father of three children: Marjorie E., James H., Jr., and Charlotte J.

JOHN JOSEPH RYAN, assistant postmaster of the United States Post Office at Augusta, Maine, and one of the well-known citizens of that community, was born there, June 29, 1882. He is a son of Richard and Margaret (MacDonald) Ryan, who now reside in Augusta. Richard Ryan, who was born in Ireland, is now living retired, his principal vocation being as the caretaker of a large estate near Augusta. Margaret (MacDonald) Ryan was born in Charlottetown, Prince Edward Island.

John Joseph Ryan received his education in the public schools of the community in which he was born, and he later graduated from the Augusta (Maine) High School. Immediately after the completion of these courses of study, he entered the drygoods business in Augusta. He remained at this type of work for more than three years, after which he resigned to enter the United States Post Office at Augusta. He was appointed distribution clerk there on July 1, 1903, and was later promoted to register clerk. Still later he became money order clerk, assistant superintendent of mails, then cashier, and on January 1, 1923, he was promoted to assistant postmaster, a position which he now fills (1928).

Mr. Ryan has contributed generously to the civic and general affairs of his community. In his political preferences he is a Republican, and he is noted for the manner in which he supports any movement designed for the welfare or advancement of Augusta. He has also been active in the commercial life of that city, and is a member of the Augusta Chamber of Commerce. He is affiliated with Augusta Lodge, Knights of Columbus, and he holds membership in a number of local clubs and social organizations. John Joseph Ryan maintains his residence in Augusta, in which community he attends and is a devotee of St. Mary's Roman Catholic Church.

EDWARD E. SHAPLEIGH, M. D.—Native of Kittery, Kittery Township, York County, and there engaged in the practice of medicine since 1891, Dr. Edward E. Shapleigh is one of the best-known men in the county, and an eminent and public-spirited citizen of the community. Dr. Shapleigh was born March 3, 1868, son of Dennis M. and Annie E. (Peirce) Shapleigh, of Kittery, his father having been engaged for many years, and with honorable reputation, as machinist, deceased, 1921, and his mother also deceased, 1901. The family of Shapleigh was one of the first to settle in Maine, as the founder of the American branch came from England, and established his dwelling in Kittery, about 1630. Hence, the house of Shapleigh ranks with the oldest in the United States, and has contributed its share of able men to the pursuit of professions and trades.

Dr. Edward E. Shapleigh received his early education in the public schools of Kittery, and matriculated in Phillips-Exeter Academy, graduating in 1886. When he was only nineteen years of age, he enrolled in the medical department of Bowdoin College, at Brunswick, Maine, and graduated with the degree of Doctor of Medicine in 1890. In that year he began general practice, at North Conway, New Hampshire, and the year following removed to his native town. In Kittery he has since conducted an extensive practice. Politically, an Independent Re-

8 MAINE—A HISTORY

publican, he has taken a prominent part in public affairs. For twenty years he was a member of the Kittery Board of Health, in charge of public sanitation, quarantine, and emergency cases requiring immediate attention at police headquarters. For twelve years he was coroner, directing inquests with diligent and unbiased conduct; and during the World War, though too advanced in years for service overseas, performed to the utmost of his ability those exercises on boards and societies and in Liberty Loan drives which crowded the many months of the United States' participation. Dr. Shapleigh is a member of the York County Medical Association, the Maine State Medical Association, and the American Medical Association; he is active in Riverside Independent Order of Odd Fellows, and Dirigo Encampment of the order; also a member of the Improved Order of Red Men. His religious faith is evident in good works rather than in profession, and his contributions to worthy charitable causes have been substantial.

Dr. Edward E. Shapleigh married, February 18, 1891, during his first year as physician in Kittery, Mabel Humphreys, of Brunswick, Maine; and they are the parents of two sons: 1. Edward E., Jr., employed as electrical draughtsman at the Navy Yard, Kittery; married Myrtle Schoof, of Groveton, New Hampshire; father of two children: Ruth E., and Elizabeth A. 2. Lloyd P., deputy collector of internal revenue at Bangor; married Marie Gallant, of Augusta, father of one son, Lloyd P., Jr.

EDWIN W. MALLETT—For many years prominent in the public affairs of Topsham, Sagadahoc County, Edwin W. Mallett is accounted one of the leading citizens of the neighborhood, and is engaged in farming on the farm settled by John Mallett, in about 1700, located on either side of the Brunswick-Augusta Federal Road. His husbandry is of a general character; yields from the fertile soil are fulsome, and he markets the produce locally. The farm is well stocked with cattle, the Mallett herd being one of those most admired for its quality in the countryside.

Edwin W. Mallett was born at Topsham, July 1, 1861, son of Isaac E. and Melicia (Purinton) Mallett, his father having been a native of Topsham, deceased, and his mother of Bowdoin, also deceased. Isaac Mallett loved the soil, and, after Edwin W. had attended the public schools of Topsham, he too, decided to make a career of agriculture. For a while he worked for his father; then, in 1883, when he was twenty-two, went West, and farmed for four years, returning to Topsham in 1887. Since then he has taken a deep interest in all affairs of the community, and on the extensive farm, modernly equipped throughout, which he now (1928) occupies, has achieved a considerable success. He is well known in business circles of Topsham, and is as much admired by neighboring farmers for commercial ability as he is for his high character. Member of the Republican party, he is loyal to its principles, and wields an important influence in local matters of a political nature. For fifteen years he has served the public, as first member of the Board of Selectmen, of Topsham. He is a member of the Grange and attends the Baptist church. His contributions to charitable causes are many, and always considerable.

Edwin W. Mallett married, at Phillips, March 11, 1896, Alice Samson, of Phillips, Maine.

EDWARD C. COOK, M. D.—At York, Maine, Dr. Edward C. Cook is well known as one of the skillful and faithful physicians of this locality. He has been engaged in general practice here since 1895, and is a member of the medical staff of York Hospital and of Portsmouth Hospital.

Dr. Edward C. Cook was born at Vassalboro, Maine, August 30, 1869, a son of Edward Hansom Cook, who was born in Milo, Maine, and of Annie Louise (Hamblin) Cook, a native of Falmouth, Massachusetts, both of whom are now deceased. Dr. Cook's father was a well-known educator and served as principal of a number of preparatory schools, notably, Oakwood Seminary, at Ithaca, New York, and Oak Grove Seminary at Vassalboro.

Edward C. Cook received his early education in Oak Grove Seminary. When his preparation was completed he entered the Medical School at Bowdoin College, where he completed his course in 1894, receiving at that time the degree of Doctor of Medicine. Later, he added to his preparation by a postgraduate course at Harvard Medical School. During this time he served one year at the Maine General Hospital and then located at York, Maine, in 1895. Here he has been engaged in general practice to the present time (1928). He has made for himself a reputation for skill and for faithfulness to the interests of his patients. Dr. Cook has always been interested in the public welfare in York, and for five years served as superintendent of schools. Fraternally, he is identified with St. Aspinquid Lodge, Free and Accepted Masons, of which he is a Past Master, and is also a Past Patron of the Order of the Eastern Star. In relation to his profession he is a member of the American Medical Association, Maine State and York County, and Portsmouth Medical societies.

Dr. Edward C. Cook was married, November 27, 1895, to Sally Bragdon Moody, of York, Maine, daughter of Edward C. and Juliette (Marshall) Moody, of York. Mrs. Cook is active in public affairs, giving her support to the Republican party, and she has served as a member of the Town Committee for several years. She is a member of the Order of the Eastern Star, in York, and is now a member of the National Auxiliary to the American Medical Association. She was also first president of the Auxiliary of the American Legion, and is a member of the Piscataqua Garden Club. Her special hobby is the raising of police dogs, one of her dogs winning a ribbon for its class at the last Boston Dog Show. She also writes along historical lines. Dr. and Mrs. Cook are members of the Congregational church, which Dr. Cook serves as a member of the board of trustees of the parish. Dr. and Mrs. Cook have one son, Edward Moody, of further mention.

Dr. Edward Moody Cook, son of Dr. Edward C. and Sally Bragdon (Moody) Cook, was born in York, Maine, July 10, 1899, and after attending the local grade schools prepared for college in Oak Grove Seminary. He then entered Colby College, at Waterville, Maine, where he completed his course with graduation in 1920, receiving at that time the degree of Bachelor of Science. During his studies, in 1917, Dr. Cook left college to enlist for service in the

World War, completing his course after the Armistice was signed. As he had chosen his father's profession, he then matriculated in the Medical School of Harvard University, from which he was graduated in 1924 with the degree of Doctor of Medicine. After serving an interneship of two years at the City Hospital in Worcester, Massachusetts, Dr. Cook began general practice in York, in 1926, and has since been engaged in practice.

Dr. Edward M. Cook is a member of the American Legion, and served as Commander in 1926-27. In his fraternal affiliations, he is a member of the Free and Accepted Masons and a member of the Order of the Eastern Star. He is also a member of Phi Chi Medical Fraternity, and the Lambda Chi Alpha College Fraternity. Professionally, he is identified with the American Medical Association, Maine State Medical Society, the York County Medical Society, and the Portsmouth Medical Society. He is a member of the staff of York Hospital and Portsmouth Hospital. Dr. Cook is an actively-interested citizen of York, and serves as health officer. His religious interest is with the Congregational church, of which he is a member.

Dr. Edward Moody Cook married, June 27, 1922, Mae Greenlaw, daughter of Fred and Maude (Gray) Greenlaw, of Deer Isle, Maine, and they are the parents of one child, Edward M., Jr.

CARROLL H. CLARK—By the very nature of his close and vital connection with the social and business progress of the community, the postmaster of a town is one of its most prominent and powerful factors. This office Carroll H. Clark has filled efficiently and constructively in Ogunquit, Maine, for the past five years. He is a man of vision and public spirit, who brings to the office more than an ideal of routine performance, for he seeks to make the post office a real community service.

Carroll H. Clark was born in Ogunquit, Maine, October 9, 1897, son of Joseph B. and Nellie (Snow) Clark. The former, born in Lyman, Maine, and a resident of Wells for many years, is a restaurant owner and deputy sheriff. The mother is a native of Pownal, Maine. The education of the son was obtained in the public schools and at Westbrook Seminary, with a course at Bowdoin College, which was interrupted by his military service. He graduated from Bowdoin in the first semester of 1922, with the degree of Bachelor of Science. He was a member of the Delta Upsilon Fraternity.

While still a college student, Mr. Clark became a member of the Reserve Officers' Training Corps. At the present time he holds a commission as second lieutenant in the Reserve Corps. His political alignment is with the Republican party. He was appointed postmaster of Ogunquit in 1922 and has since held the office, performing its duties with conscientuous ability and loyalty. He also handles real estate as an avocation. Mr. Clark belongs to the Lodge, Free and Accepted Masons; the Chapter, Royal Arch Masons; the Council, Royal and Select Masters; the Commandery, Knights Templar, and Kora Temple, Ancient Arabic Order Nobles of the Mystic Shrine. His other affiliations are with the Knights of Pythias and the American Legion. He is a communicant of the Episcopal church.

June 28, 1922, Carroll H. Clark married Gladys A. Leonard of Taunton, Massachusetts, and they

are the parents of Jean Sabra Clark, and Carroll H. Clark, Jr.

FRED W. BAYLEY—A man of resourcefulness and ambition, Fred W. Bayley, of Wells, Maine, has attained a position of prominence in his community as a farmer and man of business. Mr. Bayley's farm has been a family possession since 1828. He was born at Newburyport, Massachusetts, March 30, 1863, son of Charles W. and Mary Bartlett (Donnel) Bayley, both of whom are now deceased. The father was a grocer of Newburyport. The mother was a native of Wells, Maine.

Fred W. Bayley completed the course of studies in the common schools, including Wells High School, and went to sea at the age of sixteen in search of adventure. For two years he was cook on a schooner. He then spent two years in the leather business, at Peabody, Massachusetts. He returned to Wells, in 1883, and began his long tenure of the family farm, which he has successfully operated for nearly half a century. During twenty-three of the forty-four years he has lived on his farm, Mr. Bayley and his wife took summer boarders into their home. In 1914, he began a small coal business of his own and has continued to conduct it with unflagging success. He is a Democrat and has been a candidate in his party for both the House and Senate, of Maine. He served as chairman of the Board of Selectmen in Wells, in 1913, and as food administrator during the World War. He is Past Master of the local Grange, Patrons of Husbandry, and for many years served as clerk of the Congregational church.

At Newburyport, Massachusetts, December 5, 1894, Fred W. Bayley married Mary I. Jackman, daughter of Nathan M. and Wealthy Jane (Spates) Jackman. Her father, a shipbuilder of Newburyport, and a veteran of the Civil War, serving in the Navy, is now deceased, while the mother, a native of Brewer, Maine, is also dead. Mr. and Mrs. Bayley have children: 1. Stephen E., who married Ella L. Knight and has four children: Edward Knight, Russell Wilfred, Paul, and Philip Kenneth. 2. Charles W., married Grace MacIntyre and has children; Charles W., Jr., and Edwin Ruthven. 3. Wilfred D., married Moyle Platts, and has a child, Doris Mae. 4. Doris May, married Millard L. Storer. 5. Eleanor G., who resides at home.

GEORGE WALTER NAUGLER—As a building contractor, George Walter Naugler, who with his brother, conducts the Naugler Brothers Contracting Company, in Brunswick, has to his credit the erection of many large structures in this vicinity of Maine, having put up some of the finest business, residential and fraternal buildings in the State. The Naugler firm is generally regarded as the leader in its line in this part of the State.

The son of Robert W. Naugler, a lumber dealer, and Phoebe (Pye) Naugler, both of Nova Scotia, and both now living, George Walter Naugler was born in Halifax, Nova Scotia, August 18, 1888, the oldest of a family of fourteen children, all but one of whom are still alive. He received his education in the public schools of Halifax. After he had finished school, he worked for two years with the Kitchin Railroad Construction Company, starting at the age of sixteen years as a laborer and advancing, by the time he was eighteen years old, to the position of foreman over fifty men. Then he went to the Canadian Northwest, where he engaged for two years in the mining of copper and silver; after which he came to Clinton, Maine, where, with Charles Braydon, he learned the blacksmith's trade; went with the Sawyer Lumber Company, of Bangor; returned to Halifax and learned the machinist's trade in the Silica Car Works; spent two years as foreman and master mechanic with the International Paper Company, and two years in the same capacity with the St. Croix Paper Company; and for one year was engaged in the jobbing business in Bangor with his brother. Then, in 1921, the Naugler Brothers Contracting Company started operations, employing four men. The company, which grew rapidly, and now employs regularly one hundred and fifty men, has erected some of the finest buildings in Maine. Among the buildings which stand as monuments to the Naugler building ability are the $150,000 Odd Fellows' Home and the new Nurses' Home, in Augusta. George Walter Naugler, in addition to his contracting business, has other interests, being president of the Brunswick Paint Company. He is active in the fraternal life of his community, being a member of the Free and Accepted Masons, in which order he is also affiliated with the Brunswick Chapter; the Independent Order of Odd Fellows; the Knights of Pythias; the Modern Woodmen of America; and the Grange, in which he has taken the Pomona degree. He is a member of the Rotary Club, and he and his family are members of the Baptist church.

On September 2, 1913, George W. Naugler married Chrystal Neoda Burpee, of Orono, Maine. Their children, all of whom attend the local schools in Brunswick, are: Reginald Whitfield, Walter Harris, Chrystal Neoda, Priscilla Agnes, and Patricia Evelyn.

ARTHUR B. JOHNSON—Originally a resident of New York City and vicinity, Arthur B. Johnson held several positions in that metropolis before 1918, when he came to work for the Pejebscot Paper Company, in Brunswick, Maine. Not only is he in charge of the purchasing department of this company, but he has several additional business interests in Brunswick, and holds an important place in the ranks of the Republican party in this section.

The son of Samuel E. Johnson, now deceased, who was a native of Maine and a lumber dealer by occupation, and of Joanna P. (Tebbetts) Johnson, who is still living and who at the time of writing was eighty-three years old, Arthur B. Johnson was born in Queens County, Long Island, September 2, 1876. He attended the public schools of New York City, and for two years held jobs as office boy and other minor positions in Wall Street. Then, after having been engaged for some time in the contracting business with his brother, he came, in November, 1898, to Brunswick to be stenographer for the Pejebscot Paper Company. He held several different positions with this company until 1914, when he was put in charge of the purchasing department, which was formed at that time. Since, he has held this position. He has other business interests, being a trustee of the Water Company, and president of the Maine Concrete Company. Active at all times in the affairs of the Republican

party and taking a keen interest in political affairs, both local and national, he is chairman of the Committee of Twelve, of Topsham, Maine. Prominent in the fraternal and club life of Brunswick, he is a member of the Free and Accepted Masons, in which order he is affiliated with the Chapter and the Council; the Royal Arcanum; the Brunswick Club, of which he is a past president; and the Rotary Club. He and his family are members of the Congregational church, in which he is an assessor.

On April 14, 1901, Arthur B. Johnson married Angela Hazelton, of New Jersey. They are the parents of five children: 1. Helen R., a graduate of Mount Holyoke; has her Master of Arts degree from Brown University, and is now instructor in Battle Creek College. 2. Clarence H., graduate of Bowdoin College, where he was elected a member of the honorary fraternity of Phi Beta Kappa. 3. Ruth W., who spent one year at Radcliffe College, two years studying with Felix Winternitz of Boston, and is now (1928) studying the violin at the University School of Music, Ann Arbor, Michigan. 4. Angela H., attending the local schools. 5. Mary E., also attending the local schools.

EDWIN E. DURAND—Sound and efficient business methods have made Edwin E. Durand's shoe manufacturing business one of the outstanding companies in Richmond and in this section of Maine. Since 1923 he has been president and treasurer of the Durand Shoe Company, which makes women's Flexible McKay comforts. Before that time he was engaged for many years in the manufacture of shoes, among other occupations. He is recognized as one of the ablest shoe manufacturers in the community, and his coöperation will be a dependable factor in the future development of the town of Richmond. He is the son of Mose E. Durand, of Plattsburg, New York, who died in 1887; and of Christie Brigard. of Montreal, Province of Quebec, who died in 1909. His father was a hotel proprietor.

Edwin E. Durand was born in Montreal, Province of Quebec, January 28, 1867, and received a public school and academy training. When he finished his education, he took up for a short time the business of lithographing. Then he moved to Lynn, Massachusetts, where he acquired a thorough knowledge of the shoe industry, which he was later to use in the work which for many years has engaged most of his time and attention. After he learned the details of shoe manufacturing and served for a time as foreman in Lynn, he accepted a position as superintendent of the Woodbury Shoe Company, of Beverly, Massachusetts, where he remained for eleven years.

In 1913, at Salem, Massachusetts, he formed the shoe manufacturing concern of Hodgdon, Durand Company. But two years later, when this business was destroyed by the great fire which visited that city, he came to Richmond. There he acquired an interest in the firm of which M. George Rowe was president; Melvin Woodbury, vice-president; and George A. Hawkes, treasurer. In 1919 this business underwent a change, by which G. A. Clouston became president, and Mr. Durand treasurer. In 1923 he bought out all other interests, and since that time has been president and treasurer of what is known as Durand Shoe Company, manufacturing women's shoes and slippers. This company employs two hundred and fifty workers, and distributes its products nationally. The factory contains more than 60,000 square feet of floor space. Under the efficient business methods employed by Mr. Durand, the business of the company has more than tripled since he took it over in 1923, and the plant largely expanded, It has a capacity production of 3,000 pairs of shoes daily.

Mr. Durand is keenly interested in the welfare of Richmond, and has done much in the past for the betterment of the community. He has many plans for the industrial improvement of Richmond in the future. He is a member of the Benevolent and Protective Order of Elks, and of various local clubs, as well as of the Roman Catholic church.

In 1889, Edwin E. Durand married Mary L. Mayhew, of Stanstead, Province of Quebec, by which marriage there are two children: 1. Blanche L., married Robert E. Dickerman. 2. Ruth A., married Clarence Lang.

EDGAR S. CATLIN—Although some years ago Edgar S. Catlin was associated with the shell-manufacturing industry and, during the World War, supervised the manufacture of certain munitions, he has been engaged since 1919 in the paper business. He is now resident manager of the Pejebscot Paper Company, in Brunswick, a company whose product is distributed all over the United States.

The son of Ashboul O. Catlin, a native of Vermont, and a banker by occupation, and of Anna (McDonald) Catlin, Edgar S. Catlin was born in Spencer, Iowa, August 19, 1893. He attended the public school, and the high school of Warsaw, Indiana, and then studied at the Case School of Applied Science, from which he was graduated in 1915 with the degree of Bachelor of Science. He started his professional career as a foreman of the shell department of the Shell & Steel Wheel Company, of MacKees Rocks, Pennsylvania, where he remained for a year; then he spent a year as foreman in the American Steel Foundry Company, Indiana Harbor, Indiana. He went to the first Officers' Training Camp, was commissioned first lieutenant in the Ordnance Department, and was in service from May, 1917, until July, 1919, being supervisor of artillery ammunition for the Rochester district of the Ordnance Department. Then he went into the paper business, working a year with the Fraser Company, in Edmundston, New Brunswick; then a year with the R. B. Wolf Company, consulting engineers. In March, 1921, he became associated with the Pejebscot Paper Company, and in 1924 was made resident manager of this company, which office he still holds. The company is owned by the Inter-Continental Development Company, employs six hundred persons, and distributes goods all over the United States. Although Mr. Catlin considers himself affiliated politically with the Republican party, he forms his opinions independently in matters of government and public office, and regards sound administration of city, State and nation as more important than partisanship. He is affiliated with the local Lodge of the Free and Accepted Masons; the Chapter, Royal Arch Masons; with the Brunswick Club, and with the Brunswick Golf Club. He and his family are members of the Congregational church.

On January 16, 1926, Edgar S. Catlin married Helen Merryman, of New York City, by which marriage there is a son, Edgar S., Jr.

ARTHUR FLINT BROWN—After having given considerable military service to his country in the Spanish-American War, Arthur Flint Brown engaged in the general electrical business until he came to Brunswick, Maine, in 1907, to become general manager of the Baxter Paper Box Company. He has remained ever since that time with the paper box company, although at the time of the World War he again served in the United States military forces.

The son of Edward Flint Brown, now deceased, who was a native of Maine, born in the Sebago Lake district, and who was an attorney in New York City, and of Eleanor (Bonney) Brown, of New York City, who is still living, Arthur Flint Brown was born in New York City, June 4, 1874. After having attended private schools in New York City, he entered the Sheffield Scientific School at Yale University, from which he received the degree of Bachelor of Philosophy, when he was graduated with the class of 1896. In the Spanish-American War he served as a private and commissary sergeant with Troop A, New York Volunteer Cavalry. In the World War, he was graduated from the first Plattsburg Officers' Training Camp, commissioned captain of Cavalry, and was assigned to the General Staff of the Seventy-sixth Division, National Army, training at Camp Devens. Early in 1918, after a course at the War College, Washington, District of Columbia, he was transferred to the American Expeditionary Forces, with which he was intelligence staff officer of the First Division, at division headquarters, and with which he remained six months, until his own division, the Seventy-sixth, was ordered to France; then he was made the intelligence officer of this division. He was the organizer and the first commander of the George T. Files Post, American Legion, in Brunswick.

He began his business career after the Spanish-American War, in the electrical construction field, in Buffalo, New York, where he continued to operate for three years. The following two years he spent with the American Telephone and Telegraph Company in Chicago. Then, because of ill health, he came to Brunswick, Maine, and shortly after became general manager of the Baxter Paper Box Company. He is a Republican in his political views. He is active in several organizations and clubs, including the Sons of the American Revolution, the Sons of Colonial Wars, the Brunswick Club, the Yale Club of New York, and the Yale Club of Boston. He and his family are members of St. Paul's Episcopal Church, of which he is Past Senior Warden. He still holds a commission as captain in the Army, and is an officer of the Ninety-sixth Reserve Division.

On October 8, 1902, Arthur Flint Brown married Florence Washburn Carpenter, of Portland, Maine

LAURENCE CLYDE ANDREW—Starting in business when a young man of only nineteen years, Laurence Clyde Andrew of Portland, Maine, has established for himself a growing business with an ever-increasing patronage. His father and grandfather before him were lumbermen, so that he really grew up in the business and naturally adopted for himself a similar line. Being progressive and keenly interested in all angles of the lumber industry, he has extended his territory over a large area about Portland.

Mr. Andrew was born in Lisbon, New Hampshire,

November 23, 1893, the son of Irving B. and Lilla Davis Andrew. He came to Maine when a very young man and has whole-heartedly adopted Portland as his home. On September 15, 1915, he married Helen E. Richardson, daughter of William H. and Mary (Huston) Richardson of Portland. Mr. and Mrs. Andrew have five children: Ruth, William Richardson, Laurence Clyde, Jr., David Kilton, and Jeanette.

Mr. Andrew began his business career as manager of the Deering Junction plant of the B. F. Andrew & Son Company, a concern engaged in the manufacture of box shook. He remained with this firm until the plant was sold to the DuPont interests, in 1916. He then established his own company, L. C. Andrew, Manufacturer of Box Shook and Packing Cases, operating a factory at South Windham, ten miles outside of Portland. When, in 1925, his plant was destroyed by fire, he continued to supply his customers by purchasing from several other mills throughout the State. In 1922, he had started, as a side line, a retail lumber and builders' supply department. Since the destruction of his box factory, Mr. Andrew has made this his leading enterprise. Because of its location and warehousing facilities, his plant has easy access, not only to the outlying lake and camp district, but also to the Portland and Westbrook trade.

Mr. Andrew is a member of the Woodfords Congregational Church and the Deering Lodge of Masons. He is also a member of the National Shook Manufacturers' Association, and the Maine Lumbermen's Association. His clubs include the Portland Club, the Woodfords Club, and the Lions Club.

WILLIAM PORTER KITTREDGE—A native of Vermont, William Porter Kittredge of Newfield, Maine, is today a retail merchant of this town. With the exception of a few years as owner and operator of a farm, Mr. Kittredge has devoted his entire business life to the retail grocery and kindred lines of business.

William Porter Kittredge was born at St. Albans, Vermont, December 26, 1870. In October, 1926, he purchased the Moulton store at Newfield, which he has been running ever since. He is a Free and Accepted Mason, Knight of Golden Eagle, and a member of the Sons of Veterans, his father having been captain of a Vermont company during the Civil War. He is also a member of the Baptist church.

JACOB L. MASON—In the history of the development of industry, mechanical devices and machine tools, one never fails to review with admiration the work done by the craftsmen of early years, before the skill of the individual was separated from the article he built. In the list of craftsmen, none stand out with more skill than the wheelwrights, and so it is that in the community of Porter, Maine, Jacob L. Mason is held in the highest esteem as one who, having learned his trade under the able teaching of his father, who was a wheelwright, has carried on the work of carriage and sleigh building, and progressed into handling the more recently made vehicle of transportation, the automobile. His father was the late Orris L. Mason, and his mother, who is still living, is Mary G. (Stanley) Mason.

Jacob L. Mason was born at Porter, Maine, May 2, 1879. He received his first education in the public school and then, with a determination to push on, he undertook a business course by correspondence with the American Correspondent Normal School, which he completed with graduation. He worked for his father in the carriage-making and sleighmaking business for a number of years, when he moved over to New Hampshire and worked in the hotel business. He remained in that business for four years and at the end of that time, came back to the old "stamping ground" to again enter the carriage-making business, which he has continued to carry on. He did not stop with one line of business, for he conducts a flourishing general store and a garage, and is agent for several popular makes of cars. Also, he is trustee of the Washington Toll Company. Being a public-spirited citizen, Mr. Mason has served as selectman, town treasurer, deputy sheriff, constable, and for five years he has been town collector. In politics he is a Democrat.

On April 14, 1912, Jacob L. Mason married Alta Merrifield, daughter of the late Chester Merrifield, a farmer of Hiram, Maine, and of Emma J. (Burbank) Merrifield. They have two children: 1. Evelyn Stanley. 2. Barbara Lee.

CHARLES J. BRAGDON—After twenty-three years of successful practice in the dental profession, Charles J. Bragdon has retired from the practice of his profession and has accepted the appointment as postmaster of Gardiner, Maine. He has served in the last mentioned capacity since 1922, and is giving faithful and efficient service in this branch of Uncle Sam's official business.

His father, Edward P. M. Bragdon, was born in Maine in 1839, and died in June, 1926. He was a stone-cutter by trade, but later was engaged in the shoe business. An able and loyal citizen, he was one of the many who promptly enlisted for service in the Civil War, in which conflict he served as sergeant, taking part in many battles and engagements, including the battles of Gettysburg and of Antietam. He was the last survivor of his G. A. R. post in South Windham, Maine. He married Elizabeth Brown, a native of Maine, who is now deceased.

Charles J. Bragdon, son of Edward P. M. and Elizabeth (Brown) Bragdon, was born in Gorham, Maine, February 8, 1870, and received his early and preparatory education in the public schools of his birthplace. When his high school course was completed he began professional study in the dental department of the University of Maryland, at Baltimore, Maryland, from which he was graduated with his dental degree in 1899. He at once came to Gardiner, Maine, and opened an office. Here he built up a large and important practice and here he continued for a period of twenty-three years, making for himself a reputation as a skilled dental surgeon, and also becoming well known in local public affairs. In March, 1922, he retired from the practice of his profession, and since that time he has been devoting himself to the duties of public office. He was appointed postmaster of Gardiner in 1922, and since that time has been serving Uncle Sam in such a manner as to win the warm commendation of the people of Gardiner and vicinity. He is a member of the board of trustees of the Gardiner Savings Institution, and is known as a man of ability and initiative. Politically, he gives his support to the principles and candidates of the Republican party, and from the beginning of his residence in Gardiner, he has been active in the affairs of the community. He served as mayor of Gardiner from 1917 to 1920, and at the present time (1928) in addition to being postmaster, is a trustee of the Public Library. He is a generous supporter of any project planned for the good of Gardiner, and is known as one of the progressive and public-spirited citizens of the place. He is well known in Masonic circles, being a member and Past Commander of the local Commandery, Knights Templar, also a member of Kora Temple, of Lewiston, and of the Shrine Club, of Gardiner; and he is also a member of the Sons of Veterans. His club is the Rotary, and his religious affiliation is with the Congregational church.

Charles J. Bragdon was married, in Hallowell, Maine, January 24, 1890, to Maud H. Dudley. Mr. and Mrs. Bragdon make their home in Gardiner.

ARTHUR H. LANDER—Practically the entire active career of Arthur H. Lander has been identified with the postal service of Gardiner, Maine, and since January 1, 1908, he has been assistant postmaster here. Mr. Lander is a native of this place, where he is well known as an efficient official and as a prominent member of the Masonic Order. He was born in Gardiner, Maine, November 1, 1878, son of John C. Lander, who was born in Gardiner, and who was engaged in the hardware business here for thirty-three years. John C. Lander was active in the affairs of the Republican party to the time of his death, which occurred in 1904. He is survived by his wife, Susanna S. (Wiley) Lander, a native of Hallowell, Maine.

Arthur H. Lander received his education in the public schools of Gardiner, including the high school, and then, on March 14, 1898, entered Government employ as general delivery clerk in the Gardiner Post Office. He gave to his responsibilities and duties the meticulous care which brings promotion, and eventually became mailing clerk, then money order clerk, and finally, on January 1, 1908, was made assistant postmaster, which position he has continued to fill to the present time (1928). Mr. Lander knows practically all of those whom he serves, and he is known by almost everyone in Gardiner. He is a Republican in his political sympathies. Fraternally, he is identified with the Blue Lodge, Free and Accepted Masons; being Past Master thereof; he is Past High Priest of the Chapter, Royal Arch Masons; a member of Council, Royal and Select Masters; Maine Commandery, No. 1, Knights Templar; and of Kora Temple, Ancient Arabic Order Nobles of the Mystic Shrine, and the Shrine Club. His religious affiliation is with the Methodist church.

Arthur H. Lander was married, in Gardiner, Maine, October 30, 1901, to Edna Johnson, who was born in Gardiner, daughter of John and Mary Johnson. They have a host of friends in Gardiner and vicinity.

JOHN ALBERT SNOW—During his active life in the profession of law in Biddeford, Maine, nothing was of greater importance to the late John Albert Snow than the upholding of the highest standard of legal honor and professional duty. He built his career upon the four cornerstones: diligence, earning his position in the community by the result of

hard labor, and merit; conscientiousness, never forgetting that at the bottom of every legal question was a moral one; gentlemanliness, winning the respect and confidence of his friends and clients, the approbation of the judges before whom he appeared for his character and deportment; and finally character, the most important of all other essentials, for this is the substance from which reputation and prestige emanate. His was a well-rounded character, for he avoided extremes, courage without rashness, caution without timidity, justice without vindictiveness, firmness without obstinacy and ambition without selfishness. With these was his faithful adherence to the motive that "Once a client, always a friend." In his practice of law for more than thirty years in Biddeford, Maine, he was recognized as one of the leading practitioners in the community and was identified with much of the important litigation brought in the city and in the State. At the same time he was prominently associated in advisory and directory capacities in a number of the important corporations and financial institutions of Biddeford, and he was likewise active in the civic administration of his city in both local and State posts.

John Albert Snow was born at Scarborough, Maine, September 16, 1871, a son of John S. and Anna A. (Leavitt) Snow, both of whom are now deceased. The father was a captain of a fishing boat and followed sea-faring pursuits during his active life. John Albert Snow attended the public and high schools and thereafter entered Williams College, but after a year transferred to Bates College in Lewiston, Maine, where he completed his scholastic training. At the end of that time he determined to study law, and in the accomplishment of this purpose, chose what is probably the hardest, but most ambitious way. He entered the law offices of Hamilton and Cleaves in Biddeford, Maine, where he served as clerk, and studied and read law during his spare moments. He possessed natural ability and a wide capacity for learning, and within a short time qualified for admission to the bar of the State of Maine. In 1895 he was admitted to the practice, and he continued in the active conduct of his profession until his untimely death in 1926. Mr. Snow became associated with Hon. John M. Goodwin of Biddeford, and the legal partnership continued with increasing success and honor during the many years which followed, but was terminated in 1926. In 1908, Mr. Snow was elected to the State of Maine Legislature and served his term until 1909 with skilful and able administrative and legislative talent. His recognition as a counselor and attorney brought him hosts of friends and the marked esteem of his colleagues and associates. For many years prior to the time of his death, he was judge of the Municipal Court of Biddeford. His professional affiliations included the York County Bar Association, the Maine State Bar Association and the American Bar Association. He was likewise president of the York County Savings Bank, and member of the board of directors of the First National Bank of Biddeford. He was also prominently enrolled in the membership lists of the leading local social and civic clubs of Biddeford. In religious activities, he was a communicant of the Unitarian faith, and with his family attended the church of that denomination in his community.

In 1896, Mr. Snow married Ella K. Litchfield, of

14   MAINE—A HISTORY

Portland, Maine, a daughter of Charles L. and Mary W. (Kelsey) Litchfield of that city. Mr. and Mrs. Snow were the parents of the following children: 1. Kathleyne S., a graduate of Tufts College with the degrees of Bachelor of Arts and Doctor of Medicine, and now a practicing physician in Boston, Massachusetts. 2. John Albert, Jr., who attended Boston University and is married to Annabelle Roberge. 3. Annabel K. 4. Clarence L. 5. Clara E. 6. Eva L.

Death cut short the career of John Albert Snow, Novemper 19, 1926, at the age of fifty-five years. His passing brought forth many fitting and touching tributes from his score of friends and associates in whose memories his life and activities will ever remain warm and be inspirations for those who seek and aspire to the higher rewards of illustrious careers and attainments. In the legal profession, his strict integrity and probity in all matters won for him an outstanding position among his colleagues; in the industrial and financial world, his natural ability and sterling devotion to his interests and of those associated with him brought substantial success and distinction to his efforts; in the civic affairs of the community, his public spirit and untiring efforts to promote the welfare of his community have earned for him a permanent niche in the archives of the leading citizens of Biddeford; in his social and home life, his thoughtful consideration and attention as a loving husband and inspiring father, and loyal neighbor and friend, gained for him the deep reverence and esteem of all with whom he came in contact; and in his sense of duty and citizenship, he has left behind him a record that few men have been able to achieve, and although man himself is but mortal, his deeds are immortal. So it is with Mr. Snow, and he will continue to live and cast his influence upon all those who come within the radius of his spirit.

MORRIS McDONALD—A leading figure in railroad management and one who has taken an important part in the development of the railroad industry in Maine is Morris McDonald, who is president of the Maine Central Railroad and also the head of several associated roads. He has been for many years a resident of Portland, Maine.

He was born August 20, 1865, in New Albany, Indiana. After he had completed his education in the public schools, he started to work with the engineering corps of the Kentucky & Indiana Bridge Company in 1883. Two years later he became paymaster for the Louisville, Evansville & Saint Louis Railway, and between 1885 and 1892 he was promoted successively to the positions of assistant treasurer, chief clerk to the superintendent, trainmaster and superintendent of transportation. His work brought him to the attention of railroad men in the South, so that he became associated with the Central Railroad of Georgia. With that company he made his headquarters in Savannah, where he acted as chief clerk to the superintendent and as assistant trainmaster in charge of the Savannah division of the company. He held these positions during 1893 and 1894. In 1896 and 1897 he was secretary to the general manager of the Maine Central Railroad, and then, in 1897, he was promoted to the position of general superintendent, where he remained until 1908. From 1908 to 1913 he was vice-president and general manager of Maine Central Railroad, when on July

9, 1913, he was elected president, which position he now holds. He was president of the Boston & Maine Railroad during 1913 and 1914. He is also president of the Portland Terminal Company and The Samoset Company.

JAMES C. HAMLEN—For fourscore years the honored name of Hamlen has been identified with the internationally known lumber manufacturing and ship trading house of J. H. Hamlen & Son, of Portland, Maine, of which James C. Hamlen, son of the founder, and for some time president of the concern, is the moving spirit. The present head of this firm, which does business on four continents, enjoys a world-wide and enviable reputation for the ability with which he manages his great business interests, in the United States and other countries of the globe, and for his public services by which trade relations with foreign governments have been happily and profitably cemented. He is esteemed one of the best-informed men of the United States on trade conditions existing between this country and the West Indies and South America. In this respect, as well as for his patriotic citizenship, he has the confidence of the Federal Administration.

James Hopkinson Hamlen, father of James C. Hamlen, was born in Gorham, Maine, and finished his education at Gorham Academy, a member of the class in which the late ex-Governor Robie was a graduate. In the youthful Hamlen's veins there flowed the blood of courageous and hardy pioneers such as gave to New England a goodly number of its most distinguished sons. Earlier in his career, he thought to follow the profession of educator, and for a time taught school in Buxton, Maine. The compensation of a country school teacher was, however, too limited to meet the necessaries of life, and thus it came about that he sacrificed his ambition to remain in the educational field to enter the sterner realities of the business world. In 1846 he began the manufacture of staves, laying the foundation of the great establishment which afterwards became known under its present style of J. H. Hamlen & Son, Incorporated. He married Anne C. P. Patten, daughter of Stephen Patten, and shortly after he had entered business, he formed with his father-in-law the firm of Patten & Hamlen, which continued in the cooperage business until the death of the senior member. With that change in the membership of the firm, Mr. Hamlen, in 1871, organized the house of J. H. Hamlen & Son, the junior member being James C. Hamlen, who was destined to become the head of the incorporated concern, he having been a member of the original firm and of the company, its successor, since 1871. An uninterrupted career has attended this, one of the oldest concerns engaged in the cooperage business in the United States, and it is to the credit of the present management that the house has successfully kept pace with changing maritime and economic conditions and met them, with the result that its volume of trade has increased with the passing of the years.

The lumbering operations of the Hamlen firm were originally confined to the area in the vicinity of Portland, and some twenty mills were maintained within a radius of fifty miles of that city. They manufactured staves and other lumber for the West Indies trade and shipment to other far-distant points,

In the "70's" they opened a plant in Campbellsville, Kentucky, and later a plant in Scottsville, that State, in order to obtain a timber supply not to be found in the North. A few years later the company established its principal plant at Little Rock, Arkansas. J. H. Hamlen & Son instituted commercial relations with the West Indies and France in 1873, opening offices at Martinique and Guadeloupe. Their interests in those countries were cared for by relatives resident in France and her colonies. About 1880, they established three stores in Senegambia, West Africa, to which they carried merchandise of great variety for sale to the natives. The West African trade was a development of the firm's plan to supplement the declining shook business in the north caused by the use of British substitute containers and the stiff competition encountered while southern coastline ports. Consequently the West Indian trade with Portland fell to a very low ebb, but it was eventually reëstablished while the African commercial relations were being profitably developed.

The Hamlens once maintained a fleet of some six sailing vessels in the West Indian and West African trade, but these ships were disposed of one by one, the "James C. Hamlen" being the last of the fleet, as the modern steam vessels took over the majority of the freight-carrying business between American ports and the West Indies and South America.

J. H. Hamlen & Son operate extensive plants in Nova Scotia as well as in Arkansas, its Canadian manufactures being favored by the preferential tariff between Canada and the British West Indies. It is only the executive offices that remain in Portland, and these will undoubtedly not be transferred elsewhere, since sentiment and a fine old family tradition are elements in favor of retaining the firm's headquarters in the city after their original establishment in 1846.

James C. Hamlen, president of J. H. Hamlen & Son, Incorporated, was born in Portland, Maine, June 9, 1852, son of James Hopkinson Hamlen and Anne C. P. Patten. Having received his education in public and private schools, he entered the firm of J. H. Hamlen & Son on attaining his majority. He steadily advanced in the knowledge of the business, both from the executive and the practical standpoints, and soon was actively concerned in the management of the widely scattered interests of the firm, which reached out to many quarters of the world. His training and native capacity admirably fitted him to assume the duties of president of the concern upon its incorporation, and his has since been the guiding hand that has shaped much of the eminently successful program of trade and manufacture that still is in process of execution.

Mr. Hamlen has employed his widely recognized knowledge of South American trade conditions and affairs in general on that continent for the benefit of various business interests of this country. Thus it came about that in 1914 a delegation of manufacturers from Illinois made Barbadoes a port of call to take Mr. Hamlen aboard its specially chartered vessel on a trip to South America to assist them in obtaining first-hand information on the ground. In company of ex-President and Mrs. Theodore Roosevelt he made a voyage to the West Indies in 1915. In 1922 and 1923 he served under appointment from the President of the United States as commissioner from Maine to the International Centennial Exposi-

tion at Rio Janeiro, Brazil. In 1926-27, he was, by appointment of President Calvin Coolidge, a member of the National Advisory Commission to the Sesqui-Centennial International Exposition at Philadelphia. He has the unique distinction of having been appointed a member of the staff, with the rank of colonel, on the staff of the late Thomas Riley Marshall, then governor of Indiana, and afterwards vice-president of the United States, in spite of the fact that the appointee thus honored has never been a resident of Indiana.

A lifelong member of the Democratic party, and esteemed one of its most loyal supporters, Mr. Hamlen has been at different times a candidate of his party for the United States Senate and House of Representatives and for Mayor of Portland. His willingness to stand or fall by his organization's political fortunes is but another demonstration of his desire to serve wherever possible. During the World War period he accomplished a distinctly patriotic service as Federal Fuel Commissioner for Maine.

The associated business interests of Portland have always commanded the cordial coöperation of Mr. Hamlen, and he is a member of long standing in the Chamber of Commerce of that city. He is one of the oldest living members of Ancient Landmark Lodge, Free and Accepted Masons; a member of the Cumberland Club, of which he has been president for many years; and the oldest living member of the Portland Yacht Club. He is an attendant of St. Luke's Protestant Episcopal Church, Portland.

Mr. Hamlen married, June 30, 1880, Caroline F. White, of Southborough, Massachusetts. They have children: 1. Joseph Rochemont, vice-president of J. H. Hamlen & Son, Incorporated. 2. James C., Jr., also a vice-president of the same concern. 3. Robert Cushing, who is engaged in the banking business in Boston, Massachusetts.

———

LEIGH DAMON FLYNT—One of the best-known men of the newspaper profession in Maine is Leigh Damon Flynt, treasurer and assistant manager of the Kennebec Journal Company, at Augusta. Mr. Flynt was born in Augusta, February 25, 1894, the son of Charles F. and Ida M. (Horton) Flynt.

Following his early education in Cony High School, Mr. Flynt entered Bowdoin College, Brunswick, from which institution he graduated in 1917 with his degree of Bachelor of Arts. He then returned to Augusta and took the post of assistant night editor of the Kennebec "Journal." This was in 1917, and from that year until 1919 he acted as advertising manager, giving up his position as assistant night editor. In 1919 he became circulation manager and in 1922 was appointed treasurer and assistant manager. Mr. Flynt is a member of the local Lodge of the Benevolent and Protective Order of Elks and his college fraternity is Beta Theta Pi. He is a Republican in politics, and is affiliated with the Congregational church. His office is at No. 331 Water Street, and he has a very pretty residence at No. 5 Lincoln Street, Augusta.

On June 25, 1917, shortly after his graduation from Bowdoin, Leigh D. Flynt married Marian K. Fisher. Mr. and Mrs. Flynt are the parents of one child, a son, William F. Flynt.

GEORGE FOSTER CARY—In Portland bank circles George Foster Cary is a recognized leader, while his collateral interests are so varied as to mark him as one of the most versatile men of this section. For nearly forty years he has been intimately connected with banking affairs, during which time he has been elected to numerous places of trust and responsibility. He has ably served Portland and vicinity in civic matters, and it is to him that many associates look for advice and counsel in their various undertakings. Possessed of keen foresight and admirable poise, he is the fit representative of a class whose superior knowledge of finance equips them to guide the course of commerce in the community.

Mr. Cary was born March 16, 1867, at East Machias, Maine, the son of Charles and Mary Elizabeth (Cary) Cary. After attending the grammar schools of East Machias, he graduated from Washington Academy in 1884, whereupon he entered Bowdoin College at Brunswick, Maine, from which institution he graduated in 1888 with the degree of Bachelor of Arts. In 1889 he married. He became cashier of the Machias Bank in 1889, and served with great ability in this capacity until 1902, when in a reorganization into the Machias Banking Company, Incorporated, he was made president. Meantime, in 1897, he had been elected treasurer of the Machias Savings Bank. In 1912 he resigned from both of these positions to become a director and treasurer of the Union Safe Deposit & Trust Company, which position he held until 1924, when he was elected president of the Casco Mercantile Trust Company, a post he has continued to hold ever since. During the World War, while he was director and treasurer of the Union Safe Deposit & Trust Company, he rendered essential service to the United States, and received the thanks of a grateful government. Since 1897 to the present Mr. Cary has served as an overseer of Bowdoin College. It was at this institution that he joined the Delta Kappa Epsilon Fraternity and on account of high scholarship standing was elected to Phi Beta Kappa; he maintains his membership and interest in each. Since 1913 he has been treasurer of the Congregational Conference and Missionary Society of Maine. He served as president of the Portland Club in 1926, and is a member of the Rotary Club and the Portland Chamber of Commerce. In religious circles he is a member of the Congregationalist faith, and in political affairs a devout Republican.

Mr. Cary married, May 18, 1889, Charlotte Coleman, of Hartford, Connecticut, and they have a son, Charles Austin Cary, who married Frances Campbell of Cherryfield, Maine, and is the father of three children: George F. (2), Mary C., and Campbell. Mr. and Mrs. Cary reside at No. 79 Highland Street, Portland, where they entertain their friends in charming fashion.

LINWOOD J. GOODWIN, representative to the Maine State Legislature, and a rising young lawyer of Springvale, Maine, who was born June 4, 1901, at Sanford, Maine, is a son of Judge George A. Goodwin, the well-known judge of the Municipal Court at Sanford, Maine.

Linwood J. Goodwin received his preliminary education in the public schools of Sanford, Maine. Upon the completion of these courses of study he entered Bowdoin College, where he remained for two years. He then transferred to Boston University, and graduated from there with the class of 1925, when he received his degree as Bachelor of Laws. He was admitted to the bar in that same year and he began the practice of his profession in association with his father, Judge George A. Goodwin. In the few years in which he has been practicing, Linwood J. Goodwin has shown marked ability and gives great promise for his attainments in the future. A strong supporter of the Republican party, he is (1928) representative to the Maine State Legislature. This is a notable achievement when it is considered that Mr. Goodwin is a man less than thirty years of age.

Despite the manifold duties which his profession entails, Mr. Goodwin has nevertheless found time to take a keen interest in many outside activities. He is fraternally affiliated with the Masons, the Independent Order of Odd Fellows, the Modern Woodmen of America, and the college fraternity, Chi Psi. He is also a member of the Sanford Town Club, and the York County Bar Association.

Linwood J. Goodwin married, in 1925, Arlene M. Fowler, born in Haverhill, Massachusetts, a daughter of Sanford and Lottie B. (Chisholm) Fowler. Mr. and Mrs. Goodwin are the parents of a son, Donald G., born April 4, 1927. Mr. and Mrs. Goodwin attend the Baptist church.

PERCY R. KELLER, assistant engineer in the Maine State Highway Commission, and a prominent civil engineer, was born May 28, 1880, in Rockport, Maine, a son of Joseph Z. and Marcia L. (Bryant) Keller, both natives of Rockport. Joseph Z. Keller, the father, who died in 1909, conducted a dairy farm at Rockport for many years. During the Civil War he served in the Ninth Maine Infantry. Marcia L. (Bryant) Keller died in 1907.

Percy R. Keller received his early education in the public schools of Rockport, and graduated from Rockport High School with the class of 1897. He studied at the University of Maine, and graduated from there in 1901, when he received his degree as Bachelor of Mechanical Engineering. Upon the completion of these courses of study he was engaged in various branches of engineering construction work, and hydro-electric developments throughout the Middle-Western and Southern States, and in California. He continued thus until 1914, when he returned to Maine and became identified with the Maine State Highway Commission as resident engineer, engaged in road construction. He has been associated with that body since. In 1925 he was made assistant engineer in charge of State aid and third class highway construction. Mr. Keller maintains his offices in the Engineering and State Highway Building, at Augusta, Maine.

Despite the many varied and often exacting duties of the work in which he has been engaged, Mr. Keller has nevertheless found time to take a keen interest in the life of his community. In his political preferences he is a Republican. He is fraternally affiliated with St. Paul's Lodge, No. 82, Free and Accepted Masons, at Rockport, Maine, and the college fraternity, Alpha Tau Omega. He is also a member of the Maine Society of Engineers.

Percy R. Keller married, September 22, 1911, at Washington, District of Columbia, Grace H. Andrews, who was born September 25, 1881, at Rockport, Maine, a daughter of Alward D. and Elvena Libby Andrews, both natives of Rockport. Mrs. Keller's father, Alward D. Andrews, died in 1913. Mrs. Andrews died in 1916. Mr. and Mrs. Keller are the parents of a daughter, Ruth Charlotte, who was born October 28, 1912, at Two Rivers, Wisconsin. Mr. Keller and his family reside in Augusta, Maine, where they attend the Universalist church.

VINCENT T. LATHBURY, M. D.—Since 1917 Vincent T. Lathbury has been engaged in medical practice in Augusta, his office at No. 304 Water Street being equipped with physio-therapy apparatus and radium. Before coming to Augusta, Dr. Lathbury had been engaged in the practice of his profession at Searsport and Pittsfield, Maine, for a period of thirteen years. He has shown a natural aptitude in the practice of medicine and has won the confidence and respect of the various members of the profession in his community. Dr. Lathbury takes an active interest in the civic affairs of Augusta, and is well known in Masonic circles.

Dr. Vincent T. Lathbury was born in Brooklyn, New York, January 14, 1879, son of Rev. Clarence, a clergyman of Cleveland, Ohio, and of Florilla (Tibbals) Lathbury. His early education was received in the public schools of East Bridgewater, Massachusetts. When his preparatory work was finished he entered the Medical School of Boston University, from which he was graduated with the class of 1904, receiving the degree of Doctor of Medicine. The same year he opened an office in Searsport, Maine, where he continued in general practice for a period of three years. In 1907 he removed to Pittsfield, Maine, and here he was established in general practice until 1917, when he came to Augusta, where he has ever since remained, building up a large and successful clientele. He has made for himself an assured place among his professional associates, and is generally known as one of the skilled physicians of the city, a profession which one philosopher has stated to be the highest and most noble calling of man. Certain it is that in the hearts of the world the physician comes first, for humanitarianism—the epitome of the medical profession—begets love, respect and regard. Dr. Lathbury is a member of the American Institute of Homeopathy; Maine Homeopathic Medical Association; American Medical Association; Maine Medical Association, and the Kennebec County Medical Society. His clubs are the Augusta Country and the Rotary, while his religious fellowship is with the Unitarian church. Dr. Lathbury is well known in Masonic circles, being a member of all the York Rite bodies, excepting the Commandery, and of the Consistory, in which he holds the thirty-second degree.

Vincent T. Lathbury married, in East Bridgewater, Massachusetts, Edith H. Lyon, daughter of Walter, a native of Halifax, Massachusetts, and of Josephine (Osborne) Lyon, a native of East Bridgewater. Dr. and Mrs. Lathbury are the parents of two children: 1. Vincent, Jr., born November 4, 1909, in Pittsfield, Maine. 2. Louise, born October 17, 1915, in Pittsfield.

AUGUSTUS FREEDOM MOULTON—Among the successful members of the legal profession who have devoted their active careers to the city of Portland, is Augustus Freedom Moulton, who has been

engaged in practice here since 1876, and whose offices are located at No. 98 Exchange Street, Portland. Mr. Moulton has been taking care of a large and important clientele here for many years, and has a record of a half-century of practically continuous service. In addition to his general practice he has specialized in corporation law, and has served as counsel for a large number of corporations in this section of the State.

Augustus Freedom Moulton was born in Jay, Franklin County, Maine, May 1, 1848, son of Freedom Moulton, born in Scarboro, Maine, October 31, 1808, died July 31, 1857, a teacher in Gorham and continued in the teaching profession all of his life, and of Shuah Coffin (Carter) Moulton, born December 20, 1811, and died June 19, 1905. The son received his earlier education in the public schools of Scarboro, Maine, and then continued study in Gorham Seminary. Later he was a student in Thornton Academy, Saco, his preparation for college being completed in Westbrook Seminary, from which he was graduated with the class of 1869. The following year he became a student in Bowdoin College, from which he was graduated with the class of 1873, receiving at that time the degree of Bachelor of Arts. The following year was spent as tutor in Bowdoin College, and he then began the study of law in the office of Judge William L. Putnam, at Portland, Maine. He was admitted to the Cumberland County (Maine) bar in 1876, and that same year received from Bowdoin College the degree of Master of Arts. Immediately after his admission to the bar he engaged in general practice in Portland. Like all beginners of those days, the first few months were months of more waiting than practice, but as time passed he gained a foothold on the ladder of success and built up an important practice. Along with his general practice he has devoted much time to corporation law, and is known as a specialist in that field. Politically, he gives his support to the Republican party, and in 1878 and 1879 was chosen to represent his district in the State Legislature, where he served on the Judiciary Committee. Fraternally, he is identified with the Masonic Order, being a member of Ancient Landmark Lodge, Free and Accepted Masons; Mount Vernon Chapter, Royal Arch Masons; and an Eminent Commander of Portland Commandery, Knights Templar. In connection with his profession he is a member of the Cumberland County Bar Association, and has served as president. His religious affiliation is with the State Street Congregational Church of Portland. The present residence of Mr. Moulton is at the Columbia Hotel, Portland.

J. MERRILL LORD, now deceased, was a man of wide interests and very great talent. By profession he was a lawyer specializing in power and real estate law, and it was said of him that in this field he was better informed than any other man in the State of Maine. He was a pioneer in the development of the telephone system in Maine, building the first telephone in Parsonsfield, and he devoted part of his time to an insurance company in which he was interested, and to the management of a large fruit farm, which he owned. Business did not absorb all of Mr. Lord's energy, for he was three times a member of the State Legislature and took an active part in all phases of community life.

He was born in Parsonsfield, Maine, where he en-

tered the public schools, and later he was graduated
from Boston University, with the degree of Bachelor of Laws. For several years he taught at Boston
University Law School, and then because of the ill
health of his parents, he returned to Parsonsfield and
commenced the practice of his profession, which he
continued until the time of his death. Soon after
his return to Maine he became the owner of a one
hundred and thirty-five acre farm in the town of Parsonsfield, which was devoted entirely to orchards.
Mr. Lord was always much interested in this farm
which is now run by his sons under the firm name
of J. Merrill Lord & Sons. About this time he
built the first telephone in Parsonsfield, a single wire
connection between two private homes, and he was
instrumental in the formation of the Ossipee Valley
Telephone Company, which he later sold to the
New England Telephone Company. It was also
about this time that he founded the Sokokis Lumber
Company, in association with Harvey D. Granville.
In 1899, in partnership with Frank D. Fenderson, he
founded the insurance company known as Lord and
Fenderson, and this arrangement continued until
1901, when Mr. Lord took over the entire control
of the company, which he continued to direct until
the time of his death. His sons have since carried
on the business.

By political inclination, Mr. Lord was a member
of the Republican party. In 1906 he was elected to
the Maine House of Representatives, and in 1917
and 1919 he served in the Maine State Senate. He
was affiliated, fraternally, with the Free and Accepted
Masons, having taken all the degrees of York Rite.
He was also a member of the Independent Order of
Odd Fellows, the Improved Order of Red Men, and
the Grange. He attended the local United Baptist
Church.

J. Merrill Lord married Sarah May Churchill, and
they became the parents of five children: Theresa
Churchill, Frank W., Myron O., Daniel B., and
Phyllis Evelyn.

Frank W. Lord was born January 3, 1897, at
Parsonsfield. He entered the local public schools,
and later attended the University of Maine for two
years, at the end of which time he enlisted in the
United States Navy. When he returned home he
took over the management of his father's farm, which
he still continues in association with his brothers.
He married Ruth D. Verbeck, and they are the parents of three children: Jay Merrill, Howard Verbeck,
and Phillip Wardleigh. Mr. Lord is a member of
the Free and Accepted Masons, Past Master (1927),
the Kappa Sigma Fraternity, and the Grange.

Myron O. Lord was born January 19, 1899, at
Parsonsfield. He attended the local public schools,
Tufts College, and Gray's Business College. In 1919
he left college to take over the management of his
father's insurance business, which he still continues,
while his two brothers manage the farm. He is a
member of the Free and Accepted Masons; the
Grange, a Past Patron; and the Town Club. On
August 9, 1924, he married Edith J. Sweeney, of
Phippsburg, Maine.

Daniel B. Lord was born September 17, 1902. He
was educated in the public schools, and at Parsonsfield Seminary, after which he began work on his
father's farm, where he has since remained. He is
a member of the Free and Accepted Masons, and of
the Grange.

Theresa Churchill Lord married Donald Libby,

an electrical engineer of the Cumberland County
Light and Power Company, and is the mother of:
Katheryn Churchill, and Joan Elizabeth.

Phyllis Evelyn Lord was graduated from the Parsonsfield Seminary and is now attending Nasson Institute. All five children graduated from Parsonsfield Seminary.

HENRY SPRINCE, M. D.—In the medical profession in Maine, one of the youngest and most
prominent physicians is Dr. Henry Sprince, of Lewiston, who opened his present office and engaged in
general medical practice on December 15, 1924. Dr.
Sprince was successful immediately and has ever
continued to attract a large and consistently-increas-
ing clientele, winning the confidence and esteem of
his patients by his profound knowledge of his profession and his skillful surgery. In the past few
years, there have been so many revolutionary ideas
introduced into the science of medicine, and so
much has been done to aid and alleviate the ills and
sufferings of humanity, that Lewiston is fortunate
to have in its midst a physician who has had the
advantage of the most modern and scientific training. He is ever alert to new discoveries and new
processes, and keeps abreast of the times in everything pertaining to medical progress, benefiting his
patients by his researches and studies, and at the
same time, ministering to them with a degree of
courtesy and consideration which has earned for him
a high place in their estimation.

Dr. Sprince was born in Paris, France, August
16, 1898, son of Morris Sprince, who is living (1928),
and Rose (Hinden) Sprince, who died, 1905. Both
parents were born in Russia, and Morris Sprince has
long been prominent in mercantile affairs, being a
leading clothing merchant of this community.

Henry Sprince was educated in the public and
high schools of Lewiston, graduating with honors,
1916, after which he entered Bowdoin College,
receiving his degree of Bachelor of Arts with the
class of 1920. While here, he was leader of the Banjo
Club for four years; sang in Glee Club and College
choir, and played a French horn in the College
Band, and violin in the orchestra. He later studied
at Bowdoin College Medical School, and at McGill
University from which latter institution of learning
he received the degrees of Doctor of Medicine and
Master of Surgery with the class of 1923. He
served his internship at the Kings Park State Hospital, Long Island, New York, and later was an
interne at the Central Maine General Hospital, at
Lewiston, for another year. Since opening his office
as a general practitioner, Dr. Sprince has advanced
to a high place in the popularity and acclaim of
his fellow-citizens, and in local affairs he is an active
supporter of all projects for municipal improvement and community welfare. In politics, he is
an Independent, preferring to judge the merits of
the various candidates for public office rather than
align himself with any particular party. His fraternal associations are with Ashler Lodge, No. 105,
Free and Accepted Masons; the Civitan Club, of
which he is past president, and the Sigma Alpha
Mu Fraternity. His social connections are with the
Calumet Club, of which he is an active member.
He sings tenor in the Parker Glee Club of Lewiston,
which is on the roster of associated glee clubs of
America. While in high school, he composed words
and music for "L. H. S. Forever," and while in

McGill University, he composed a fraternity song, "Hail to the Purple." He also composed several marches. His religious adherence is given to the Congregation Beth-Jacob. During the recent World War, Dr. Sprince was enrolled in the United States Army as a member of the Student Army Training Corps. He is a member of the surgical staff of Central Maine General Hospital; was county chairman of Citizens' Military Training Camps Association for two years, 1927-28. At present, he is a member of Androscoggin Alumni Association of Bowdoin College; the American, Maine, and Androscoggin County Medical associations, of which he is secretary and treasurer, and the Clinical Round Table Club, of which he is secretary and treasurer.

Dr. Henry Sprince married, December 10, 1924, at Montreal, Canada, Norma Rothschild, who was born in Sudbury, Ontario, Canada, February 6, 1904, daughter of Max and Rachel (Bernstein) Rothschild, and to this union has been born one son, Richard Hinden, born in Lewiston, November 21, 1925.

CHESTER H. STURTEVANT—After a short experience in the teaching profession, Chester H. Sturtevant mastered the principles and the practice of banking, and in 1895 helped to organize the Livermore Falls Trust & Banking Company, of which he has been president since 1927. Mr. Sturtevant is one of the active and progressive citizens of Livermore Falls, Maine, and he is well known in Masonic circles, being a thirty-second degree member, a Shriner, and a Past Patron of Washburn Chapter, Order of the Eastern Star.

Josiah H. Sturtevant, father of Mr. Sturtevant, was born in Fayette, Maine, received his education in the local public schools, engaged in farming, and later, for many years was connected with the United States Treasury Department, in Washington, District of Columbia. At the outbreak of the Civil War, he enlisted for service with the Seventeenth Maine Infantry, but later was transferred to the Department of the Gulf and commissioned a second lieutenant. He married Helen E. Ormsby, who was born in Augusta, Maine, and they became the parents of Chester H., of further mention.

Chester H. Sturtevant was born in Fayette, Maine, May 4, 1866, and received his early education in the public schools of his birthplace. He prepared for college in Kents Hill Preparatory School, and then entered Colby College, at Waterville, Maine, from which he was graduated with the class of 1892, receiving at that time the degree of Bachelor of Arts. The year following his graduation he taught in the high school at Madison, Maine, and during 1894-95 studied banking with the Portland Trust Company, of Portland, Maine. In 1895 he was one of the organizers of the Livermore Falls Trust & Banking Company, and his connection with this financial institution has been continuous since that time. He was made treasurer at the time of the organization of the company, has held the office continuously to the present time, and in 1922 he was also made vice-president, and in 1927, president. He has also been a member of the board of trustees of the bank since 1912. About 1902 he started in the insurance business, and later, with his father-in-law, Joseph G. Ham, established an agency. When Mr. Ham died, Mr. Sturtevant took over the general insurance business. Mr. Sturtevant

takes an active interest in civic and in political affairs. A Republican, he is serving in the State Legislature, his term ending in 1928. He is a member of committees of banks and banking and insurance and mercantile affairs. He is president of the Livermore Falls Library Association, and is well known in banking circles, the bank is a member of the American Bankers' Association. He is a deacon of the Baptist church; member of the State Board of the United Baptist Convention, and a trustee of Colby College.

Chester H. Sturtevant was married, in Livermore Falls, Maine, to Charlotte L. Ham, who was born in Portland, Maine, October 10, 1872, daughter of Joseph and Mary Emma (Chandler) Ham. Mrs. Sturtevant was for many years treasurer of the local Chapter, Order of the Eastern Star, and was first assistant Matron; also a member of the "Ramblers," a woman's club. Mr. and Mrs. Sturtevant are the parents of four children, all born in Livermore Falls: 1. Reginald H.; enlisted in April, 1917, for service in the Navy, was discharged in January, 1919, and served in the Naval Reserve until 1921. 2. Norman G. 3. Ronald W. 4. Eleanor M. Reginald H. Sturtevant is secretary and member of the board of trustees in the bank which his father has served so long. He is also a partner in his father's insurance business.

THOMAS SAMUEL SMITH — Since 1923, Thomas Samuel Smith has been rendering service of a high order as secretary of the Young Men's Christian Association of Augusta, Maine. Mr. Smith has had a long and notably successful experience in this field, having served both in this State and in Massachusetts, and also overseas for three years during the World War. His skill and his thorough knowledge of the work, together with his genuine interest in the young men and the boys whom he serves, have enabled him to render exceptionally valuable service, both in Augusta and in the various other cities in which he has been stationed.

Thomas Samuel Smith was born in Anangance, New Brunswick, Canada, December 12, 1887, son of Christopher Smith, who was born June 27, 1846, and was in the employ of the Canadian National Railways Company to the time of his death, August 22, 1911, and of Sarah J. (Chittick) Smith, who was born December 15, 1846, and died in 1922, both natives of Anangance, New Brunswick, Canada. Mr. Smith attended the public schools of New Brunswick, Canada, graduating from Petitcodiac High School with the class of 1904, and then became a student in the Provincial Normal School, at Fredericton, New Brunswick, from which he was graduated with the class of 1906. Later, he entered the Young Men's Christian Association College, at Springfield, Massachusetts, and completed his training there with graduation in 1911. In 1911 he began his long and successful career as a Young Men's Christian Association secretary, by accepting a position as secretary in Bar Harbor, Maine, where he remained from 1912 to 1914. He was transferred to North Attleboro, Massachusetts, and he remained there until 1916, when he engaged in war work, serving overseas with the Canadian Expeditionary Forces for three years. At the end of that period, in 1921, he returned to the United States and resumed his work, this time as secretary of the Young Men's Christian Association at Athol, Massachusetts, where he served with notable efficiency until 1923, when he came to Augusta, Maine, as secretary. Here he has served with most marked success, giving to his work the enthusiasm and the personal interest which, aided by his skill and varied experience, has built up and greatly extended the activities and the influence of the organization. Politically, Mr. Smith gives his support to no one party organization, preferring to cast his vote for those candidates who seem best qualified to faithfully discharge the duties of the offices to which they aspire, regardless of party affiliations. He is a member of the Augusta Chamber of Commerce and of the Rotary Club. Fraternally, he is identified with Augusta Lodge, No. 141, Free and Accepted Masons, and his religious affiliation is with the Green Street Methodist Church.

Thomas Samuel Smith was married, in Urbana, Illinois, September 9, 1912, to Beatrice Elizabeth Griffith, born in Carthage, Missouri, December 25, 1887, daughter of William A. and Mary C. (Berry) Griffith. Mr. and Mrs. Smith are the parents of three children: 1. Anna Louise, born in Bar Harbor, Maine, October 2, 1913. 2. William Griffith, born in North Attleboro, Massachusetts, February 8, 1915. 3. Jefferson Stanley, born in Augusta, Maine, July 14, 1926.

FREDERIC OSGOOD EATON—A progressive and highly respected financial leader of his section of Maine is Frederic Osgood Eaton, president of the Rumford National Bank for more than twenty years. He has also held many town offices and represented his district in the Maine House of Representatives and the Maine Senate. Mr. Eaton was born in Rumford Center, June 7, 1872, son of Cyrus Putnam and Mary Elsie (Howe) Eaton. His father was superintendent of the Rumford Falls Light & Water Company, at Rumford, Maine. The son received a well-rounded education in the Rumford public schools, at Kent's Hill Seminary, and at the Shaw Business College in Portland, Maine.

His business experience began with a clerkship in the employ of the Rumford Falls Power Company, where Mr. Eaton remained for sixteen years, until 1906. Since that time he has been cashier of this company. From 1892 to 1906, he also was clerk for the Rumford Falls Light & Water Company, of which he became cashier in 1906, continuing in office until 1916, when he was promoted to the position of general manager. He has served in that capacity since, finding time also to discharge most capably the responsible duties of the presidency of the Rumford National Bank, an office he has filled since 1907. He is also treasurer of the Rumford Community Hospital. A Republican in politics, Mr. Eaton was clerk of the town of Rumford from 1896 to 1906, member of the Maine Legislature from 1917 to 1920, and of the Maine Senate from 1921 to 1924. In 1908 he was president of the Rumford Board of Trade, and he is a member of the Rumford Business Men's Association and the Rotary Club. His other clubs are the Oakdale Country, of Rumford, and the Portland, of Portland, Maine. His fraternal associations are as prominent as his business activities. He is Past Master of Blazing Star Lodge, Free and Accepted Masons; Past High Priest, Rumford Chapter, Royal Arch Masons; Past Commander, Strathgloss Commandery, Knights Templar,

all of Rumford; and Past Grand High Priest, Grand Royal Arch Chapter of Maine. Mr. Eaton attends the Methodist Episcopal church.

September 14, 1904, at Auburn, Maine, Frederic Osgood Eaton married Mary Louise Grierson, daughter of Peter S. and Susie A. Grierson. Children: Mary Elizabeth, born February 8, 1906; and Margaret, born March 17, 1911.

JAMES BERNARD O'KANE—As head of the Rumford Publishing Company, Incorporated, of Rumford, Maine, and publisher of the weekly paper known as the "Rumford Falls Times," James Bernard O'Kane is one of the well-known and successful men of his section. He was born at Lewiston, Maine, October 12, 1892, son of Henry and Annie (Quinn) O'Kane. The father was employed at the Lewiston Bleachery and Dye Works, died in Lewiston, Maine, in 1908, and the mother, born at Liverpool, England, died in March, 1917. The son was educated in the public schools of Lewiston and graduated in 1909 from Lewiston High School.

His initiation into the publishing and printing industry came shortly after he finished school, for in 1909, Mr. O'Kane became identified with the Lewiston "Journal" as advertising manager, and remained in that position for seven years, until 1916. His energy and enterprise, as well as his faculty for getting on with all sorts of people, brought him great success. This experience he capitalized by starting in business for himself as partner to James P. McCarthy. McCarthy and O'Kane conducted a printing business in Lewiston in 1916-17. In 1920, Mr. O'Kane purchased the Rumford Publishing Company, Incorporated, at Rumford, Maine, of which he is general manager. Besides publishing an excellent weekly paper which has enjoyed a steady growth in circulation, he handles printing and related business. His business career has not prevented Mr. O'Kane's serving his country in time of need, for he was a member of the United States Navy during the World War. He is a member of the Republican party, the American Legion, Post No. 24, at Rumford, Maine; the Benevolent and Protective Order of Elks, Lewiston Lodge, No. 371; the Knights of Columbus; the Rotary Club, and Rumford Business and Professional Men's Association. His religious affiliation is with the Roman Catholic church of Rumford.

At Rumford, Maine, June 11, 1923, James Bernard O'Kane married Geraldine McMennamin, born in that town, daughter of George B. and Annie (McGivney) McMennamin, both natives of Fredericton, New Brunswick. Children: 1. James B. O'Kane, Jr., born in Rumford, May 1, 1924. 2. Barbara Louisa, born in Rumford, February 22, 1927.

ORIN B. FROST—As president and treasurer of the O. B. Frost Construction Company, of Augusta, Maine, Orin B. Frost is directing one of the best-known general contracting enterprises in this section of the State. He has had a long and varied experience in this field, and had charge of important government work during the World War. After the close of the war he organized the O. B. Frost Construction Company, which he has developed into its present prosperity and importance. Mr. Frost is active in local public affairs and at present is serving as treasurer and collector of the city of Augusta. He was born in Butte, Montana, August 12, 1883, son of Grafton N. Frost, a native of Winthrop, Maine, who went West and became a rancher in Montana, and who was identified with the Masonic Order, and of Annie B. (Mears) Frost, a native of Maine, who was postmistress of Grafton, Montana. She died in February, 1892, and was survived by her husband, whose death occurred in 1909.

Orin B. Frost attended the public schools of Augusta, Maine, graduating from Cony High School with the class of 1903. Upon the completion of his school training he became associated with Joseph Larrabee & Company, plumbing contractors, with whom he learned the trade. In 1905, he was made a junior member of the firm. That connection was maintained until 1914, when Mr. Frost became general inspector of construction for the State Hospital Trustees. In 1916 he became inspector of construction, in the employ of the United States Government, located at the Squantum Plant, but later he was made second assistant resident engineer, in charge of forty inspectors, covering all classifications of construction. In 1917 he was transferred to the United States Housing Corporation at Quincy, Massachusetts, as chief inspector, and this position he held until the project was completed in September, 1919. Soon after this he organized the O. B. Frost Company, general contractors, of which he is president and treasurer, having held those offices from the time of the organization of the concern. At the present time (1928) the O. B. Frost Construction Company is one of the leading concerns of its kind in the city, and has made a reputation for the uniform excellence of its work.

Politically, Mr. Frost gives his support to the Democratic party, and he takes an active interest in the public affairs of Augusta. He is a member of the Augusta Chamber of Commerce, and always ready to aid in forwarding any project planned for the advancement of the general welfare of the city. In 1908 he was made a member of the State Park Commission, in which capacity he served until 1914. In 1910 he was elected a member of the School Board of Augusta, and in this connection also he served until 1914. In 1923 he was elected treasurer and collector of the city of Augusta; was reëlected in 1925, and in 1927 was elected to serve a third term, which will expire in 1929. Fraternally, Mr. Frost is affiliated with Bethlehem Lodge, No. 35, Free and Accepted Masons; with Cushnock Chapter, Royal Arch Masons; and he is also a member of the Kiwanis Club. His religious affiliation is with the Methodist church.

Orin B. Frost was married, at Augusta, Maine, June 18, 1908, to Grace Harriman, born in Gardiner, Maine, November 8, 1886, daughter of Edward L., a native of Gardiner, Maine, and of Katherine (Rhude) Harriman, a native of Nova Scotia. Mr. and Mrs. Frost are the parents of three children, all born in Augusta, Maine: Barbara C., Anna Marie, and Helen S.

WILLIAM B. LENNAN, a well-known citizen of Gardiner, Maine, and the present Gardiner district superintendent of the Central Maine Power Company, was born May 26, 1869, in this community, son of Hosea H. and Ann (Foye) Lennan, the former of whom is now deceased. Ann (Foye) Lennan was

also born in Gardiner, and Hosea H. Lennan was born at Richmond, Maine; died in 1911. He was a meat cutter by trade, and he followed this type of endeavor for the major portion of his life. He was prominent in fraternal circles, having been affiliated with the Masonic Order and the Independent Order of Odd Fellows, both at Gardiner.

William B. Lennan received his education in the public schools of the community in which he was born, graduating from Gardiner High School. Immediately after graduation he became identified with the Gardiner Stoneware Company, with whom he remained from 1885 until 1887. He then worked for H. A. Billings, a well-known grocer and drygoods merchant of Gardiner, until 1889. From 1889 until 1911 he served as a steamfitter at the mills of the S. S. Warren Paper Company of Gardiner, after which he became identified with the Central Maine Power Company. So well did he succeed with this organization that he was soon promoted to the office of the Gardiner district superintendent of this public service company, and this is the office he was filling in 1928. In his political views he is a staunch supporter of the Republican party, and is noted for the excellent manner in which he stands behind any movement designed for the welfare and advancement of Gardiner. He has been unusually active in his club and social life, and is affiliated with all branches of the Independent Order of Odd Fellows; with Lodge No. 1293, Benevolent and Protective Order of Elks; Herman Lodge, No. 32, Free and Accepted Masons; the Chapter, Royal Arch Masons; Council, Royal and Select Masters; the Consistory, Ancient Accepted Scottish Rite; the Commandery, Knights Templar; the Temple, Ancient Arabic Order Nobles of the Mystic Shrine, and he is a member of the Shrine Club of Gardiner. He is also an active member of the Rotary Club of Gardiner, and of the Gardiner Board of Trade.

William B. Lennan married, June 17, 1902, at Gardiner, Maine, Cora M. Malcolm, born in June, 1868, at West Gardiner, daughter of James T. and Elizabeth (Withee) Malcolm, both natives of Maine. Mr. and Mrs. Lennan maintain their residence in Gardiner, in which community they attend the Universalist church.

PAUL DUDLEY SARGENT—Born in Machias, Washington County, Maine, May 8, 1873, the son of Ignatius M. and Helen M. (Campbell) Sargent, Paul Dudley Sargent entered upon his distinguished career as a civil engineer early in life. Following his preliminary education in the local public and high schools, he entered the University of Maine, graduating in 1896 with the degree of Bachelor of Civil Engineering. He was assistant engineer for the Washington County Railroad during the construction of that line in 1897 and 1898, and occupied the same position with that road in the maintenance of way department, from 1899 to 1903. In the latter year he became Registrar of Deeds for Washington County, relinquishing that position in 1905 in order to assume the duties of State Highway Commissioner. This post he held until 1911, when he became Assistant Director in the Office of Public Roads for the United States Department of Agriculture. In 1913 he gave up this last post and assumed the duties of Chief Engineer of the State Highway Commission, which post he held with great credit to himself and advantage to the State, until December 31, 1927. On that date Mr. Sargent resigned his position to enter business.

Mr. Sargent was an active member of the Maine National Guard from 1896 to 1899. He is a prominent member of the American Society of Civil Engineers, the American Society for Testing Materials, and the Maine Society of Civil Engineers. He is affiliated with the local chapter of the Sons of the American Revolution, and his college fraternity is Phi Gamma Delta. He also belongs to the Massachusetts Highway Association and the American Road Builders' Association; was one of the Executive Committee of the Federal Highway Council, and is a leading member of the American Association of State Highway Officials, having been president of that organization in 1922. He is affiliated with the Free and Accepted Masons; is a Universalist in his religious beliefs, and Republican in politics. His clubs include the Rotary, and the Augusta Country. Mr. Sargent is a life-member of the Permanent International Association of Road Congresses and in 1926 was one of five delegates appointed by President Coolidge to represent the United States at the fifth Congress, which was held at Milan, Italy.

On June 6, 1900, Mr. Sargent married, at Calais, Washington County, Sarah McAllister. Mr. and Mrs. Sargent reside in a very charming residence at No. 83 Western Avenue, Augusta.

CHARLES H. WENTWORTH—There has never been a citizen of South Berwick who was more fully identified with the interests of the community than was the late Charles H. Wentworth, who was born here, received his education in the local schools and in the Berwick Academy, and for thirty years was the most efficient and faithful treasurer of the South Berwick Savings & Trust Company, which is now a branch of the Casco Mercantile Trust Company, of Portland. It is stated by those who are in a position to know that Mr. Wentworth was one of the most important factors in the development and continued success of the bank, and his colleagues are among the first and the most earnest in affirming that statement. He was also treasurer of the Berwick Academy, which in early years he attended as a student, and his interest in the welfare of South Berwick was an abiding interest which continued throughout his life.

Charles H. Wentworth was born in South Berwick, Maine, December 15, 1866, son of Charles K. a native of South Berwick, who was a carpenter and builder, and whose death occurred in 1906, and of Ellen (Plumer) Wentworth. He attended the local public schools and Berwick Academy, and then entered the South Berwick National Bank as clerk. His ability and faithfulness brought promotion to the position of cashier, in which capacity he served for many years. About 1904 he was made treasurer of the bank, and in this office he served to the time of his death, a period of thirty years. The original bank of South Berwick was established during the days before Andrew Jackson came to full power in the councils of his party, in the days of the rapid spread of State banks throughout the country, and it was as a State Bank that this institution was established in 1823. In 1866 the Savings Bank was established, just after the close of the Civil War, and in 1917 the two were amalga-

mated under the name of the South Berwick Savings & Trust Company, which was its name and organization at the time of the death of Mr. Wentworth in 1924. The following year it was taken over as a branch of the Casco Mercantile Trust Company of Portland. Mr. Wentworth continued his able and devoted service to the bank to the time of his death, which occurred April 8, 1924. As a citizen Mr. Wentworth was, though modest and unassuming, one of the most trusted members of the community. His family was one of the pioneer families of South Berwick, his whole life was identified with its interests, and his capabilities and his character and personality were such that his associates gave to him the voluntary and unquestioning faith which only true and unpretentious worth can command. During the period of the World War Mr. Wentworth placed his skill and experience at the service of the community, and was the efficient and trusted treasurer of the Red Cross organization and of the various "drives" by which the home war work of South Berwick was achieved. Fraternally, he was identified with St. John's Lodge, Free and Accepted Masons, of which he was treasurer; and he was also identified with all the York Rite bodies of that order, and with the Maine Consistory, in which he held the thirty-second degree. He was a member of the Country Club and of other local bodies, also a member of the South Berwick Chamber of Commerce, and its treasurer to the time of his death. His religious affiliation was with the Congregational church.

Charles H. Wentworth was married, in October, 1905, to Florence E. Stevens, of Salmon Falls, New Hampshire, daughter of Edwin A., president of the Salmon Falls Bank, and Clara A. (Speed) Stevens, a native of Dover, New Hampshire, whose death occurred in 1924. Mr. and Mrs. Wentworth never had children, and Mrs. Wentworth, who survives him (1928), makes her home on School Street, in South Berwick.

ALBERT J. WIGGIN, Superintendent of Maintenance, Maine State Highway Department, and a prominent citizen of this State, was born October 14, 1870, at Exeter, New Hampshire, a son of Alvin and Mary (French) Wiggin, both natives of New Hampshire. Mary (French) Wiggin was born at Kingston, and Alvin Wiggin was born at Exeter. He was a school teacher and a farmer, and a man who held a position of marked respect in his community.

Albert J. Wiggin received his education in the public schools of Exeter; graduated from Exeter High School; and studied at the Massachusetts Institute of Technology. Immediately after the completion of these courses of study he entered the vocation he was destined to follow and in which he was to achieve his present success, that of maintenance engineering. He worked for various builders and contractors, eventually becoming the engineer and superintendent of construction. In 1908 he became identified with the Maine State Highway Department, and such was the success with which he met in this field of endeavor that, in 1913, he was appointed Superintendent of Maintenance, a position which he was filling in 1928. In his political views he is a staunch supporter of the Republican party, and is noted for his whole-hearted support of all movements designed for the welfare or advancement of

MAINE—A HISTORY 23

his county and his State. He has been prominent in club and social life; is affiliated, fraternally, with York Lodge, No. 22, Free and Accepted Masons; the Council, Royal and Select Masters; the Chapter, Royal Arch Masons; the Commandery, Knights Templar, and Kora Temple, Ancient Arabic Order Nobles of the Mystic Shrine. He is also a member of the Massachusetts Highway Association.

Albert J. Wiggin married, January 7, 1924, at Belfast, Maine, Margaret Keene, born at Belfast, a daughter of William Keene, of Klondike. Mr. and Mrs. Wiggin attend the Congregational church.

JAMES W. MURRAY—The career of James W. Murray has been identified with varied interests and with more than one public office, in all of which he has achieved success and fully satisfied those with whom he has been associated. Since 1923 he has been serving as sheriff of Androscoggin County, and in 1926 he was reëlected to serve his third term in that same office. Mr. Murray makes his home in Auburn, where he is well known about town and where he is identified with several of the local organizations.

Born in Webster, Maine, James W. Murray is a son of Dennis Murray, a native of Ireland, who came to this country as a young man and settled in Webster, Maine. Mr. Murray received a good, practical education in the public schools of Webster, and then entered the employ of the Webster Woolen Company of that place, working in various capacities and finally being made paymaster. He had always been actively interested in local public affairs, especially in the affairs of the Democratic party, and in 1912 he was made register of probate for Androscoggin County, in which office he served most efficiently until 1921, a period of nine years. At the end of that time he entered the real estate and insurance business at Lewiston, Maine, where he was successfully engaged until 1923, when he was elected to the office of sheriff of Androscoggin County. So well did he discharge the duties of that office that he was reëlected in 1924, 1925, and 1926, and in 1927 was serving his fourth year in that important public office. As a Democrat Mr. Murray is loyal and active, and as a citizen he is public spirited and a generous promoter of the common good. He is a member of the Auburn Chamber of Commerce, of the National Sheriffs' Association of America, and of the Lions Club.

CLYDE H. STEVENS—The city of Auburn, Maine, is well taken care of so far as its engineering problems are concerned, by its able and efficient city engineer, Clyde H. Stevens, who has been identified with the department since his graduation from high school, but who has served as city engineer since 1925. Mr. Stevens is one of the well-known and well-liked young men of Auburn, one of its native sons, and he is filling the important office which he holds most ably. He was born in Auburn, Maine, August 31, 1898, son of Calvert S. Stevens, a shoemaker, and of —— (Perry) Stevens, both natives of Maine; the last-mentioned died in 1915.

Clyde H. Stevens attended the public schools of Auburn, graduating from Edward Little High School there with the class of 1918, and immediately after graduation became identified with the engineering department of the city of Auburn. For some time previous to his appointment to his present office he served as assistant city engineer, assisting Edward M. True, and his total period of service in the engineering department of the city of Auburn is more than eight years. Politically, Mr. Stevens gives his support to the candidates of no one political party, but prefers to cast his vote for those whom he considers best qualified to efficiently discharge the duties of the offices to which they aspire. He is a member of the Androscoggin Society of Engineers, and of the Maine Society of Engineers, and his fraternal affiliation is with the Independent Order of Odd Fellows.

EDWARD FARRINGTON ABBOTT—That Auburn is known as a city of remarkable industry, as well as a progressive community as to the government of its city institutions, is directly due to the fact of the calibre of citizenship of that prominent group in which Edward Farrington Abbott has undoubted leadership. Naturally, Mr. Abbott is vitally interested in maintaining the place of excellence of the Cushman-Hollis Company, of which he is the president; but he is none the less active in the matter of the general business increase of Auburn through the influence of its Chamber of Commerce, and of good government matters through his own participation in civic affairs.

Edward Farrington Abbott was born April 3, 1882, at Lake City, Colorado, a son of Jacob J. and Jennie L. (Farrington) Abbott. He came to Auburn at the age of seven, and there attended the grammar and high schools. He pursued his studies at Bowdoin College, where he was graduated in 1903 with the degree of Bachelor of Arts. Upon graduation, Mr. Abbott became identified with the Cushman-Hollis Company, at Auburn, and he has engaged in shoe manufacture as an official of that plant since. He was made the company's superintendent in 1905, continuing in that position until 1914, when he was made vice-president of the concern, his presidency being accorded him in 1919.

The Republican party is Mr. Abbott's choice in political matters. He was a member of the Auburn School Committee from 1916 to 1919; and in 1918, he was elected to the Auburn City Council, continuing therein until 1924. His activities with the Chamber of Commerce have found him a leader therein, and he presided as its president in 1919-21. Fraternally, he is affiliated with the Free and Accepted Masons; and with the Theta Delta College Fraternity. His religious faith is that of the Congregational church.

Edward Farrington Abbott married, June 7, 1906, at Westbrook, Mary Hale Dana. Their children: Helen D., Margaret F., Edward F., Jr., Ruth L., Luther D., and John C.

GILBERT D. HARRISON—Having the progress and welfare of Lewiston ever in mind, Gilbert D. Harrison is one of this city's adopted sons who holds a high place in the commercial and civic life of this community. Mr. Harrison came to Lewiston in 1920 and became associated with the Lewiston Bleachery & Dye Works in the capacity of general manager, advancing steadily in the ranks of this important organization until he was elected to his present position of vice-president, in 1925. In addition to the affairs of his own company, he displays a deep and sincere interest in all local problems and activities, being a factor in the financial and civic life of the city, and acting as a leader in all projects which tend to municipal improvement and advancement. His popularity is attested by membership in the leading fraternal and social societies, which are proud to include him on their rosters.

Mr. Harrison was born in Pawtucket, Rhode Island, October 22, 1885, son of Gilbert V. Harrison, born in Providence, Rhode Island, and Christine (McNaughton) Harrison, born in Pictou County, Nova Scotia. Gilbert V. Harrison has been engaged in the mill business all during his business career.

Gilbert D. Harrison was educated in the public schools of Pawtucket, graduating from Pawtucket High School with the class of 1903. After completing his formal education, he became associated with the Sayles Bleacheries at Saylesville, Rhode Island, and remained with this organization from 1905 to 1910, familiarizing himself thoroughly with all the details of this industry and advancing steadily towards the top. In 1910, he accepted an offer of the New York Mills Bleachery at Utica, New York, to become assistant superintendent of that plant, where he remained for one year. Mr. Harrison's services were in demand by reason of his thorough knowledge of this work and the splendid reputation which he had earned in his previous connections, and he was then offered a position with the Dutchess Bleachery at Wappingers Falls, New York, which he held for a year, until 1912. He next spent four years with the firm of Joseph Bancroft & Sons Company, at Wilmington, Delaware, as superintendent of the Kantmere Division. In 1916, he transferred his activities to the Utica Willowvale Bleachery, Utica, New York, serving as superintendent of this large organization until 1920, at which time he came to Lewiston as aforementioned. He was general manager of the concern from 1920 to 1925, treasurer of the firm from 1922 to 1925, and elected vice-president in 1925, which office he continues to fill with the greatest efficiency and success. He is a director of the First National Bank of Lewiston, also a director of the local Chamber of Commerce, a member of the Rotary Club and of the Merchants' Club of New York. His fraternal connections are with the Free and Accepted Masons, the Knights Templar, and the Ancient Arabic Order Nobles of the Mystic Shrine. He is prominently identified with the Martindale Country Club; his political adherence is given to the Republican party, while his religious affiliations are with the Congregational church.

Gilbert D. Harrison married, January 20, 1912, at Utica, New York, Margery Young, born in Utica, October 14, 1887, daughter of George Young, a native of Utica, and Ida (Humbert) Young, born in Syracuse, New York. To this union have been born two children: 1. Gilbert D., Jr., born February 26, 1914, at Wilmington, Delaware. 2. John W., born January 26, 1917, at Utica, New York.

JOSEPH WILLIAM SCANNELL, M. D.—More than twenty years in the practice of medicine and surgery, with extensive experience in hospital work and emergency cases, has shown to the people of Maine, and particularly of Lewiston, where he is resident,

that in Dr. Joseph William Scannell they possess a man of rare skill in his profession, and a citizen of high worth.

He was born in Lewiston, Maine, March 22, 1883, a son of Daniel J. and Ellen (Connor) Scannell. He received his education in Nichol's Latin School, at Bowdoin College, and obtained his degree of Doctor of Medicine at the University of Maryland, in 1906. In that year he began the practice of medicine in his native city. From 1907 until 1923 he was assistant surgeon at Central Maine General Hospital, since which time he has been major operating surgeon. At present he is surgeon for the Androscoggin & Kennebec Railroad, surgeon for the Portland & Lewiston Interurban Railroad, and since 1922 has been surgeon for the Lewiston Fire Department. He was president of the Androscoggin County Medical Society during 1914 and 1915, is a member of the American Medical Association, Research Medical Club, and of the Benevolent and Protective Order of Elks.

Dr. Scannell married, in Lewiston, Maine, October 5, 1910, Therese Winn, daughter of John and Margaret (Boland) Winn.

WILLIAM J. FAHEY, M. D.—For three generations the name of Fahey has been identified with the activities of Maine, the grandfather of William J. Fahey, a native of Galway, Ireland, having founded it here, when he came as a young man to seek his fortune. Here he married Bridget Gahagan, and became the father of twelve children, whose descendants are carrying on the name in honor and respect. There is no representative of the family who has achieved greater renown as a servitor of mankind than William J. Fahey, of Lewiston, where he has practiced the medical profession continuously since 1911, and is one of the most popular and largely patronized physicians in the city. Since it is conceded that there is no more exacting or altruistic calling than that of medicine to the man or woman who enters it with high ideals, and no larger field for the accomplishment of service to humanity, the profession needs must contain in its ranks minds that are superior to the rewards that usually follow success in the science. It follows that there are many such minds and one of the best representatives is Dr. William J. Fahey. A man of wholesome cheerfulness, he radiates warmth and geniality in hospital or sick chamber, lifting the low-spirited patient into a buoyant condition of hope through the effect of his own inspiring optimism, and half winning the battle before he has brought to his aid the weapons with which he combats disease through the medium of drugs. To a man of the true humanitarianism of Dr. Fahey there are bound to be occasions on which he has left a home of sorrow to enter another where a human creature lies ill. Never does he take into a home any display of feeling that must have invaded his soul in such cases, but always does he come with hope radiating from his sympathetic nature. Such a man has thousands of friends, begotten of a reciprocal sympathy that cannot be exhibited in words. He is a most worthy representative of a sympathetic race, a standard citizen, a devoted friend, a rare exponent of the science of medicine of whom the State of Maine is justly proud.

He was born in Auburn, Maine, January 20, 1886,

a son of Edmond Francis, and Catherine (Flynn) Fahey, his father being a native of Gorham, New Hampshire, born June 26, 1857, and now living in Lewiston, of which city his mother is also a native, born June 25, 1857. They were the parents of five children, of whom all are deceased save William Joseph. He acquired his education in the public schools of Lewiston, to which community his parents had removed when he was an infant, completing his elementary studies in 1901 and being graduated from the high school in 1905. Upon leaving this school he at once matriculated at Bowdoin College, from which institution he was graduated with the class of 1910 and received the degree of Doctor of Medicine. He was for a time at the Lying-In Hospital in New York City, then returning to the Central Maine Hospital, where he served as an interne for one year. In 1911 he established himself in practice in Lewiston, at No. 101 Pine Street, where he has since continued, one of the leaders of his profession in this State. He is a member of the Maine State Medical Association and of the Androscoggin County Medical Society, and is fraternally affiliated with the Ancient Order of Hibernians. His religion is Roman Catholic and he attends, with his family, St. Patrick's Church, in Lewiston.

Dr. Fahey married, July 17, 1911, Margaret E. McKenney, of Auburn, daughter of Thomas N. and Honora (O'Hare) McKenney, residents of Haverhill, Massachusetts, where the marriage took place. They are the parents of four children: 1. William Edmond, born August 20, 1912. 2. Thomas John, born May 5, 1914. 3. Walter Joseph, born July 5, 1916. 4. Margaret Catherine, born January 11, 1920.

RALPH WILLIAM BICKNELL, M. D.—In Winthrop, Maine, Dr. Ralph William Bicknell has been engaged in general medical practice since 1924. Before coming to Winthrop he had followed thorough professional preparation with extended hospital and infirmary practice, and had also completed about eleven years of general practice in Canton, Maine. Dr. Bicknell is a graduate of Tufts College Medical School, and has long ago established a reputation as a skilled physician.

Born in Canton, Maine, October 18, 1886, Dr. Bicknell is a son of James William Bicknell, a native of Canton, Maine, now deceased, and of Lillian May (Wentworth) Bicknell. The father was for many years engaged in business as a merchant in Canton, and was an earnest supporter of the Republican party and a member of the Independent Order of Odd Fellows.

Dr. Ralph William Bicknell attended the public schools of his birthplace, and then began his college preparatory course in Westbrook Seminary, from which he was graduated with the class of 1906. He has chosen the medical profession as his life work, and later entered Tufts College Medical School, at Tufts College, Massachusetts, where he completed his course with graduation in 1912, receiving at that time the degree of Doctor of Medicine. Before engaging in general practice on his own account, he had the advantages of a somewhat extended hospital experience, serving as house surgeon in the Boston City Hospital, and in Roosevelt Hospital, New York City; also in the Portland Eye and Ear

Infirmary. In 1913 he engaged in general practice in his birthplace, Canton, Maine, and there he continued until 1924, when he made a change, coming to Winthrop, Maine, where he has since been taking care of a large practice. He is a member of the staff of the Winthrop Community Hospital, and holds membership in the Oxford County Medical Association, the Kennebec County Medical Association, the Maine State Medical Association, and the American Medical Association. In politics, he is a Republican. He is a member of Winthrop Chamber of Commerce, and fraternally, is identified with the Blue Lodge, Free and Accepted Masons; and with the Loyal Order of Moose, of which last he is also medical examiner. He is an attendant of the Congregational church.

Dr. Ralph William Bicknell was married (first), at Lewiston, Maine, June 16, 1916, to Alice Hargrave Nulty, who was born in Buckfield, Maine, and died in 1926, daughter of Henry Nulty, a native of Bridgeton, Maine, and of Bell (Bridgham) Nulty, who was born in Buckfield, Maine. He married (second), June 2, 1927, Mary McManus, who was born in Windsor, Maine, daughter of Frank and Delia McManus. To the first marriage twins were born, in Canton, Maine, July 3, 1917: Ralph William, Jr., and Thomas Bridgham.

ALFRED C. PARENT—From a beginning as a stenographer and clerk in the offices of Wade & Dunton Carriage Company, of Lewiston, Alfred C. Parent has risen to be general manager of Wade & Dunton Motors, Incorporated, a division of the Wade & Dunton Carriage Company, who have the Ford and Lincoln contract for Lewiston, a position he has held since 1921. He is a man of industry, tireless energy and a pleasing personality, having a high code of business and social honor which he never forsakes, a busy man and a commendable citizen of great value to the community.

He was born in Waterville, Maine, June 1, 1893, a son of Isaac, a native of Lewiston, who died in 1917, and of Mary Parent, who was born in Waterville. The boy was educated in the public schools of Waterville and graduated from the high school and Morgan's Business College. He at once entered business life in association with the Wade & Dunton Carriage Company. He rose steadily from 1913 to his present position, where he has charge of the entire plant of Wade and Dunton Motors, Incorporated, and some thirty-five hands in the repair shop and salesrooms. He is Independent in politics and has membership in the Lewiston Chamber of Commerce and in the Benevolent and Protective Order of Elks.

Alfred C. Parent married, in Lewiston, October 12, 1915, Lea La Montagne, who was born in Lewiston, daughter of J. B. and Mary La Montagne, of the Dominion of Canada. They have two children: 1. Lucille, born in Lewiston, Maine, April 28, 1919. 2. Juliette, born in Lewiston, Maine, April 18, 1921.

J. ALFRED BREARD, M. D.—Coming to the United States from Canada, which country he is a native, J. Alfred Breard in 1925, established himself in the practice of medicine in Waterville, a welcome addition to the professional ranks and to the population. He has quickly adapted himself

MAINE—A HISTORY

to the country of his adoption, a real American among the descendants of pioneer Americans.

Dr. Breard was born in the Province of Quebec, Canada, January 2, 1893, a son of Charles B. Breard, a native of that Province, and Lucie (Begin) Breard, also of Quebec. His education was obtained in the Canadian schools and at St. Anne College, Nova Scotia, from which he was graduated in 1918 with the degree of Bachelor of Science. He also attended Montreal Seminary of Philosophy, and took his degree of Doctor of Medicine from the University of Montreal, Canada, in 1925. He has taken the Democratic party as his political faith. His church is the Roman Catholic Notre Dame. He is a Fellow of the American Medical Association, a member of the Kennebec Medical Association and is on the staff of the Sisters' Hospital at Waterville and a member of the Society of St. John the Baptist.

J. Alfred Breard married, in Waterville, Maine, August 8, 1926, Mamie King, born in Waterville, July 27, 1892, daughter of William King, a native of Quebec, and Mary (Moreau) King, born in Oldtown, Maine.

GEORGE G. AVERILL, M. D., was born in Lincoln, Maine, December 5, 1869, a son of David F. and Leah S. (Lowell) Averill. He was educated in the public schools and at Lee Academy and obtained his degree of Doctor of Medicine from Tufts College in 1896. He is a member of the Massachusetts Medical Society, a member of the Rotary Club, of Waterville, where he is established in the the practice of his profession, and the Order of Free and Accepted Masons. From 1896 until 1910 he practiced in Cambridge, Massachusetts. He was treasurer and general manager of the Keyes Fibre Company. He has a residence in Los Angeles, California, where he spends his winters.

Dr. George G. Averill married (first) Mabel L. Keyes, of Fairfield, November 18, 1908, deceased; he married (second) Frances B. Mosher, at Bangor, February 2, 1921.

FRED ALBERT WEEKS—Probably no Maine resident has served his State and the general public in a greater variety of ways than has Fred Albert Weeks, holder of many public offices and sales manager of the Mt. Zircon Spring Water Company of Rumford, Maine. He is a man of wide interests and great energy. Mr. Weeks was born in Canton, Maine, June 14, 1875, son of Alanson Melen and Vesta E. (Soule) Weeks. He was educated in the studies included in the high school curriculum at Mexico, Maine, and Byron, Maine, continuing his schooling in night school at Providence, Rhode Island.

From 1890 to 1898, he worked in the lumber camps while continuing his education. From 1899 to 1900 he was with the Boston & Lynn Railroad, and during the next two years, from 1900 to 1902, employed by the State of Massachusetts at Danvers State Hospital. The next four years found him busy as an officer of the Rhode Island State Prison. In 1916-17, Mr. Weeks was connected with the post office in Providence. Returning to Maine, he became interested in real estate in 1917, and continued thus occupied in Oxford County until 1921, when he accepted his present position as sales manager for the Mt. Zircon Spring Water Company. Here his unre-

mitting application to work and his judgment and personality have brought him large personal success and his company a greatly increased business. Mr. Weeks was deputy sheriff of Oxford County, Road Commissioner at Mexico, Maine, and Sealer of Weights and Measures there. He is president of the Maine Bottlers of Carbonated Beverages and a member of the Business Men's Association in Rumford. His fraternal affiliations are with the Knights of Pythias and the Patrons of Husbandry. He belongs to the Republican party and to the Oakdale Country Club. His religious adherence is given to the Methodist Episcopal church.

On February 27, 1903, Fred Albert Weeks married Eva J. Bridges, at Brookline, Massachusetts, and they reside at Riverside Drive, Ridlonville, Maine.

FRANK McGOULDRICK—Long years of experience as an educator and as an executive in the educational field have fitted Frank McGouldrick admirably for his present work as superintendent of schools of the progressive town of Dixfield, Maine. His learning and intellectual outlook are in accord with the best modern pedagogical principles. Mr. McGouldrick was born April 15, 1876, son of Charles and Mary A. (Murphy) McGouldrick, the former a native of Cherryfield, Maine, and engaged in the livery business, the latter born in Oldtown, Maine.

Educated in the public schools of Cherryfield, Maine, and the Cherryfield Academy, from which he graduated in 1894, Mr. McGouldrick attended Yale University in 1898 and 1899. He began his professional career in his home town, later teaching at Harrington, Princeton, and Searsport, Maine, and North East Harbor, in the same State, for a period of twelve years, 1895 to 1907. He was then appointed superintendent of schools at Blue Hill, Maine, remaining in that position until 1912. During the next four years he was superintendent of schools at Fort Fairfield and Easton, and from 1916 to 1924, at Bar Harbor, Maine. After a year and a half of activity outside the realm of educational work, Mr. McGouldrick accepted, January 1, 1925, the appointment he now holds as superintendent of schools at Dixfield, Maine. A Republican, he was a member of the Board of Selectmen at Cherry Hill. He belongs to the Maine State Teachers' Association, of which he was president in 1920, and to the Congregational church. His fraternal affiliations are with the Independent Order of Odd Fellows; the Blue Lodge, Free and Accepted Masons; the Knights Templar; the Ancient Arabic Order Nobles of the Mystic Shrine; the Knights of Pythias; and the State Grange, Patrons of Husbandry.

At Bangor, Maine, July 22, 1908, Frank McGouldrick married Alice Mayo, born at Blue Hill, Maine, September 1, 1883, daughter of Eben W. and Mary E. (Johnson) Mayo, both natives of Blue Hill and both deceased in 1926.

RALPH DUMPHRY SIMONS, M. D.—For nearly thirty years the medical profession of Gardiner has been honored by the membership of Ralph Dumphry Simons, who not only has contributed to the general excellence of our medical reputation, but has also ably represented the population in the State Legislature. His unvarying interest in the progress of the community and in its social, religious, civic, and fraternal institutions, in addition to his activities in his profession have assured him a high place in the regard of his fellow-citizens. He was born in Stark, Maine, January 31, 1877. His father was Edwin William Simons, a Methodist minister, and his mother, Louise K. (Duley) Simons.

Ralph D. Simons was educated in the public schools and afterward at the Bowdoin Medical School, with post-graduate work at the Mayo Foundation, obtaining his first Doctor of Medicine degree in 1899, from Bowdoin. He started practice in Kingfield, Maine, the same year. Since 1903 he has been in constant practice in Gardiner. He is a member of the surgical staff of the Gardiner General Hospital and is on the consulting staff of the Augusta General Hospital. Deeply interested in surgery, he devotes most of his time to this department of his profession. He is a director in the Gardiner Trust Company, and has been a first lieutenant in the United States Army Medical Reserve Corps. In 1918 he was elected on the Republican ticket to a seat in the Lower House of the Maine Legislature. He is a thirty-second degree member of the Lodge, Free and Accepted Masons, and may wear the fez of the Ancient Arabic Order Nobles of the Mystic Shrine. His professional affiliations include membership in the American Medical Association, Maine State Medical Association, and the Kennebec County Medical Association. He belongs to the Shriners' Club of Gardiner and attends the Universalist church.

Dr. Ralph D. Simons married (first) Alice S. Hunnewell, June 29, 1898, at Madison, Maine, and to this marriage were born: 1. Edwin H., September 13, 1900. 2. Robert L., October 13, 1905. He married (second), July 13, 1915, Florence T. Hildreth, of Boston, who, by a previous marriage, is the mother of twins: Charles L. and Horace A. Hildreth, born December 2, 1902.

CHARLES A. SNOW—In the progress of education in this great commonwealth, Charles A. Snow, of Fryeburg, has taken a prominent and constructive part in various positions in the school system, serving as superintendent of the district schools of Fryeburg since 1923. Mr. Snow has devoted his entire career to the instruction of school children, recognizing to what a great extent the future of both State and country depends upon the proper scholastic training of its youth, the future citizens and leaders of the land. Under his careful supervision, the schools of this district are in an extremely flourishing condition, ranking high in scholastic circles of the county and State for the progress made in general education and for the brilliant intellectual results obtained by their students. Mr. Snow was born in Milo, September 3, 1884, son of Charles A. Snow, born in Milo, and Clara (Crockett) Snow, born in Abbot, both of whom are now deceased. Charles A. Snow was prominent in the agricultural industry of this State, taking a leading part in the political affairs of his vicinity, being a staunch supporter of the Republican party.

Charles A. Snow was educated in the public schools of Milo, and after high school, attended Maine Central Institute, graduating with the class of 1905. He then taught in the schools of this State for a number of years, gaining valuable experience and laying the foundation for his future executive leadership in the realm of education, receiving the commendation of all who knew him for his popularity with his pupils and the excellent results accomplished under his training. Entering the Uni-

versity of Maine for a course of study, he received the degree of Bachelor of Arts with the class of 1920, and in July of that year, received the appointment to the position of superintendent of schools of Richmond, remaining in that office until 1923. At that time Mr. Snow was induced to come to Fryeburg to accept the superintendency of the schools of this district, and in this capacity he has continued to give to the members of this community a system of scholastic training of which they are proud. By his earnest and sincere efforts to give the children of this district the very finest instruction possible, he has earned for the town an enviable reputation throughout the commonwealth. In politics, Mr. Snow is a follower of the principles of the Republican party, while in public affairs he is active as clerk of the Fryeburg Village Corporation. His fraternal connections are with the Free and Accepted Masons, in which he has attained the third degree, and he is also a member of the Order of the Eastern Star. He is a member of the Saco Valley Teachers' Association, the National Education Association, and the Maine Teachers' Association, also the Department of Superintendence, National Education Association. His religious adherence is given to the Universalist church. During the World War, Mr. Snow was actively associated with the Young Men's Christian Association, stationed in Virginia.

Charles A. Snow married, September 1, 1915, at Stockton Springs, Junita Ellis, born in Stockton Springs, daughter of Alston Ellis, who was a deep water seaman and is now deceased, and Lillian (Ginn) Ellis. Mr. and Mrs. Snow have one daughter, Sylvia J., born January 15, 1925.

G. ERNEST GODING—Descendant of generations of an ancestry who have shared in the upbuilding of the State of Maine in industrial and mercantile lines, G. Ernest Goding, miller and feed dealer, and general merchant in the flour and feed business at Dixfield, has continued in his calling and in this prosperous section of the State the traditions and the long-established policy of probity and upright dealing that have brought honor to the memory of his forebears. He is a representative citizen and merchant at Dixfield, where he is already a force in its civic and social interests. His grandparents, Daniel and Mary Goding, farming people of Livermore Township, were respected Maine families; his father was George W. Goding, a farmer, born in Livermore, and his mother was Florella (Bryant) Goding.

G. Ernest Goding was born January 21, 1879, at Hartford, Maine, and he attended the public schools there and at Livermore, graduating from Livermore High School. For a number of years he worked at farming with his father; and from 1904 to 1909 he was in partnership with his father and brothers in a general store business at West Peru, known as G. W. Goding & Son store, afterwards purchasing that business on his own account and continuing its operation until 1912. During 1916-17, Mr. Goding first began to interest himself in the grain business, and he was so engaged at Poland during those two years. In 1917 he built his present mill, and established himself in the business in which he has become a leader, at Dixfield, as a flour, feed, hay and grain merchant, G. E. Goding being the firm name.

Never having sought public office, Mr. Goding

nevertheless, has strong convictions of the usefulness of the Republican party, and he votes for its candidates for office. Fraternally, he is affiliated with Tuscan Lodge, No. 22, Independent Order of Odd Fellows, a Past Noble Grand; and with King Hiram Lodge, No. 57, Free and Accepted Masons; also Order of the Eastern Star, Patron in 1927. His religious faith is that of the Congregational church.

G. Ernest Goding married, August 1, 1909, at Dixfield, Mary E. Rowe, who was born September 2, 1888, at Peru, daughter of Henry Orvis, who was born at Peru, and Etta L. (Carter) Rowe, a native of Rumford, granddaughter of Henry and Lucy (Lovejoy) Rowe. Their children: 1. Walter E., born December 15, 1912, at West Peru. 2. Marion R., born July 20, 1915, at Dixfield. Mrs. Goding is a member of the Order of the Eastern Star, Worthy Matron in 1927; also a member and Past Noble Grand of the Daughters of Rebekah.

CLARENCE FAIRBANKS KENDALL, M. D., Commissioner of Health for the State of Maine, attained that position of responsibility due to his notable professional record, both in private practice of medicine, in prior services to the State, and as an officer in the National Army on overseas duty during the World War.

The father of Dr. Kendall, Lucius H. Kendall, a native of Biddeford, Maine, where he was born January 1, 1853, was engaged for many years in the merchant tailoring business and also as a realtor; represented his community in the State Senate in 1889; was a colonel of the First Maine Regiment for a period of eighteen years, member of the Maine National Guard from 1876 until 1906, and served during the Spanish-American War. Lucius H. Kendall married Adesta L. Hall, who was born at Lewiston, Maine, August 25, 1856.

Clarence Fairbanks Kendall, son of Lucius H. and Adesta L. (Hall) Kendall, was born at Biddeford, Maine, January 15, 1876. He received his rudimentary education in the public schools of his home town, was graduated from the Biddeford High School in the class of 1894, was graduated, in 1898, from Bowdoin College, with the Bachelor of Arts degree; afterward matriculated at the Maine Medical School, from which institution he was graduated as a member of the class of 1901, with the degree of Doctor of Medicine. In the year of his graduation from medical school, Dr. Kendall engaged in the practice of his profession at Biddeford, thus continuing for the following year. During the years 1902 and 1903, he was interne at the Maine General Hospital, at Portland, this State. From 1903 until 1905, he was engaged in practice at Jonesport, Maine, and from the latter year until 1917, was similarly engaged at Biddeford. Upon the declaration of war by our nation upon the Central Powers, Dr. Kendall proffered his services, was commissioned a major, assigned as chief surgeon of the coast defenses at Portland, Maine; then becoming identified with the medical department of the American Expeditionary Forces, served overseas for seven months as surgeon of the Seventy-second Coast Artillery. Dr. Kendall was City Physician at Biddeford in 1906, and in the previous year had been a member of the Board of Health of Jonesport. On January 1, 1920, he was chosen as District Health Officer of the State Department of Health, thus serving until October 7,

1921, at which time he accepted the appointment as Commissioner of Health of the Commonwealth of Maine, for a period of six years. He was reappointed in October, 1927, for another period of six years.

The following are the professional organizations of which Dr. Kendall is a member: The American Medical Association, the American Public Health Association, the Maine Medical Association, the York County (Maine) Medical Association, also the American Child Health Association. Actively identified with the Masonic bodies, Dr. Kendall is a thirty-second degree Mason; Past Master of Dunlap Lodge, No. 47, Free and Accepted Masons, and affiliated with the Scottish and York rites, and the Ancient Arabic Order Nobles of the Mystic Shrine. He also holds membership in the American Legion, Gamma Chapter of Delta Upsilon Fraternity, Phi Chi Medical Fraternity, and is an attendant of the Congregational church.

On December 30, 1903, at Biddeford, Dr. Clarence F. Kendall was united in marriage to Annie L. Norton, a native of Jonesport, Maine, and daughter of Thomas and Matilda (Putnam) Norton, the latter a native of Nova Scotia. The following are the children of Dr. and Mrs. Kendall: 1. Lucia A., born at Jonesport, November 29, 1904. 2. Otis A., born at Biddeford, November 23, 1905. The official address of Dr. Kendall is the State House, Augusta, Maine. Mrs. Kendall is a graduate nurse, and well known as a lecturer.

NEIL L. VIOLETTE, Commissioner of the Forestry Department of the State of Maine, has served the commonwealth in other responsible capacities, and has also been connected with the United States Department of Agriculture. The forebears of Mr. Violette settled in the State of Maine in the latter part of the eighteenth century. Ambrose Violette, father of Neil L. Violette, followed the vocation of farmer, and served his native town, Van Buren, Maine, as a member of its Board of Selectmen. Ambrose Violette married Marie Madore, likewise a native of the town of Van Buren, and he died in 1911.

Neil L. Violette, son of Ambrose and Marie (Madore) Violette, was born March 16, 1882, at Van Buren, Maine. He received his earlier education in the public schools of Van Buren, was graduated as a member of the class of 1899 from St. Mary's Preparatory School, with the Bachelor of Arts degree, then matriculated at the University of Maine, which institution bestowed upon him, in 1903, the degree of Bachelor of Laws. Mr. Violette began his career in forestry activities in the interests of private owners of large wooded tracts and estates. In 1906 and 1907, he was in charge of the operation of a lumber mill, situated at Edmundston, New Brunswick, following which employment he was retained by the United States Department of Agriculture, in the capacity of special agent in connection with the gipsy moth commission of the agricultural department, this activity continuing from 1909 until 1912. During the years 1912 and 1913, Mr. Violette was a member of the Legislature of the State of Maine, and also, in 1913, he was Deputy Forest Commissioner of the State. On October 24, 1924, Mr. Violette accepted the office of Commissioner of the Forestry Department of the Commonwealth, in which capacity he has rendered service of incalculable value. Mr.

Violette is a Republican in political belief. He is a member of the Society of American Foresters, and, with his family, is a member of the Roman Catholic church.

On May 8, 1907, Neil L. Violette was married to Miss Georgia Thibodeau, a native of Caribou, Maine, and daughter of Stephen Thibodeau. Two children have blessed this union. 1. Blanche L., born at Waterville, Maine, October 14, 1908. 2. Philip R., born at Van Buren, November 4, 1911. The offices of Mr. Violette are located in the State House, Augusta, Maine.

EDGAR M. BRIGGS, well-known lawyer and prominently identified with public affairs of the city of Lewiston, Maine, has served that community in the capacity of prosecuting attorney, and has been active in political circles. A native of Parkman, Maine, Edgar M. Briggs was born on May 28, 1860, in that town. He was a student in the public schools at Parkman, attended the Maine Central Institute, from which he was graduated in the class of 1875, and finally matriculated at Bates College, from which institution he was graduated as a member of the class of 1879, with the Bachelor of Arts degree.

His education completed, Mr. Briggs entered the law offices of two eminent practitioners of their day, Messrs. Hutchinson and Savage, under whose tutelage he perfected his knowledge of legal procedure. Following his admission to the bar, in 1884, Mr. Briggs engaged in the general practice of law at Lewiston, where he has since continued. He has in the past served Lewiston as city solicitor, and is favorable to the policies and candidates of the Republican party. Mr. Briggs is a member of the American Bar Association, the Maine Bar Association, and the Androscoggin County Bar Association. His offices are located at No. 64 Lisbon Street, and he resides at Lewiston, Maine.

GEORGE S. McCARTY, prominent member of the legal profession at Lewiston, Maine, has represented his community in the State lawmaking body, and has also served in responsible public offices at different times during his long and active career. George S. McCarty, son of Daniel A. and Katherine (Stanley) McCarty, both of whom were natives of Ireland, was born at Lewiston, Maine, March 11, 1872. He acquired his rudimentay education in the local public schools, was graduated from the Lewiston High School in the class of 1890; graduated from the Dean Academy in the class of 1892, and completed his collegiate studies at Niagara University. After completing his college studies, Mr. McCarty became associated with the law offices of Noble and Crockett, prominent members of the local bar in their generation, and in April, 1898, was admitted to practice before the bar in the State of Maine. Mr. McCarty engaged in legal practice on his own account in 1899, locating his offices at Lewiston, his present address being No. 46 Lisbon Street, this city.

During the Spanish-American War, Mr. McCarty was a member of Company I, First Regiment, Maine Volunteer Infantry. A Republican in political affiliation, he is most active and influential in the affairs of that party. Mr. McCarty was a member of the Maine Legislature from Lewiston in 1915, has served as city solicitor and also as fire commissioner of Lewiston. Mr. McCarty is a member of the American Bar Association, the Bar Association of the State of Maine, and the Androscoggin County Bar Association. He is affiliated with the local lodge of the Benevolent and Protective Order of Elks, and is a member of the Roman Catholic church at Lewiston.

WILLIAM BERTRAM SKELTON, of Lewiston, was born in Bowdoin, Maine, August 9, 1871, son of Thomas William and Mary Luella (Holbrook) Skelton. He was educated in the public schools of Bowdoin, and graduated from Bates College in 1892.

He read law in the office of Newell and Judkins, in Lewiston, and was admitted to the bar in 1893. He practiced law with Hon. William H. Newell, as Newell and Skelton, from January 1, 1894, to October 1, 1914, when he retired from the firm to become a member of the Public Utilities Commission of Maine. He resumed the practice of his profession at Lewiston, April 1, 1919, first as a member of the firm of White, Carter & Skelton, and is now associated with his son under the name of W. B. & H. N. Skelton. He is also a member of the firm of Woodman, Whitehouse, Skelton & Thompson with offices at Portland.

Mr. Skelton was county attorney of Androscoggin County from 1901 to 1905; mayor of Lewiston from 1903 to 1905; Bank Commissioner of Maine from 1906 to 1911; member of the Public Utilities Commission of Maine from 1914 to 1919.

Mr. Skelton is president of the First National Bank of Lewiston, the Lewiston Loan and Building Association, the Androscoggin & Kennebec Railway Company and the Lewiston Gas Light Company; trustee of the Androscoggin County Savings Bank; treasurer of the Union Water Power Company and the Androscoggin Reservoir Company; director of the Boston & Maine Railroad, the Central Maine Power Company and the Androscoggin Electric Company; member of the Board of Fellows and chairman of the Executive Board of Bates College.

William Bertram Skelton was married to Florence L. Larrabee, of Auburn, May 21, 1894, and has five children: William L., assistant treasurer of the Bath Trust Company; Harold N., now his law partner; Thomas R., Florence L., wife of Stuart E. Edgerly head of the English Department in Bridgeton Academy; and Ruth E. One son, John H., died at the age of seven.

CARL FOLSOM GETCHELL — Among graduates of Dartmouth College who have made good in Maine stands prominently Carl Folsom Getchell, of Auburn, a lawyer who has brought to his profession an unusual equipment of native ability, energy and keen judgment, and who served his city nine years very ably as solicitor. Mr. Getchell enjoys a high-class, lucrative practice, and is prominent in civic and fraternal circles. Having served as chairman of the Republican City Committee and kept in close touch with political affairs, he is potentially eligible for advancement in public office, for he enjoys not alone the prestige of position and influence but youth as well.

Mr. Getchell was born May 17, 1883, at Monmouth, Maine, the son of Mark L. Getchell and Augusta (Woodbury) Getchell. His father, head of the

M. L. Getchell Company makers of the well-known "Monmouth Moccasin," was a native of Monmouth and died in 1906. His mother, a daughter of Hugh Woodbury, of Litchfield, Maine, died in 1915; the family to which she belonged was composed of twelve children, each of whom was known for some particular merit or accomplishment. She had but the one son.

Mr. Getchell might have followed his father's business to advantage or that of his grandfather, who was a Baptist clergyman, but early decided to take up the profession of law. He graduated from Monmouth Academy, Edward Little High School at Auburn, and upon completing his preparatory courses, matriculated at Dartmouth College, Hanover, New Hampshire, from which institution he was graduated in the year 1905 with the degree of Bachelor of Arts. After three years of business, Mr. Getchell entered the law department of the University of Maine and was graduated from this institution in 1910 with the degree of Bachelor of Laws. Embarking upon the practice of law at Lewiston, he formed a partnership with Charles B. Hosmer at No. 64 Lisbon Street, which is still Mr. Getchell's office address; the firm name of Getchell & Hosmer was discarded in 1920 upon the withdrawal of Mr. Hosmer to enter the United States Consular Service, he being well-known throughout the service, particularly for his work as vice-consul at Havana, Cuba. Later the firm name became Getchell & Lancaster. Mr. Fred H. Lancaster is now serving his first term as county attorney. In 1911 and 1912 Mr. Getchell served as a member of the Auburn City Council, and acted for many years as chairman of the Republican City Committee. In 1915 he was elected solicitor of the city of Auburn; for several terms he capably represented Auburn in this position, placing not alone the police but the fire department under Civil Service regulation, and revising the city ordinances in 1922. During the World War he rendered essential service to his country as a member of the Auburn Draft Board. In addition to his multifarious activities he is vice-president of the Central Maine Loan and Building Association, of Lewiston-Auburn, an organization he aided in establishing several years ago, and which contains the names of numerous prominent citizens of the "twin cities" as directors and officers. He is a member of the Androscoggin County Bar Association, the American Bar Association and the Maine State Bar Association. As a member of the Free and Accepted Masons he has taken the different degrees from the Blue Lodge up to the thirty-second degree, serving as Commander of Lewiston Commandery. He has served as director and adviser for many charitable institutions and is a member of the Chamber of Commerce and the Rotary Club, being a charter member and the first president of the last-named organization. In religious affairs Mr. Getchell is affiliated with the Universalist church. He is a member of the Martindale Country Club, as well as several college fraternities, and the Temple, Ancient Arabic Order Nobles of the Mystic Shrine.

Carl F. Getchell married, at Auburn, October 6, 1909, Lillian Bearce, daughter of W. Chandler Bearce, one of Auburn's best-known shoe manufacturers, having one factory at Lewiston and the other across the Androscoggin River at Auburn, and director and secretary of the National Shoemakers' Corporation. Mr. Bearce died April 10, 1927, at Long Beach, Cal-

ifornia. The mother of Mrs. Getchell, Julia (Wood) Bearce, whose family was one of the oldest and best known in Auburn, died in 1914. The children of Mr. and Mrs. Getchell are: Betty Bearce, a student at Edward Little High School, born September 29, 1912, at Auburn; and Carl Folsom, Jr., born in the same city, October 1, 1920.

Mr. Getchell insists, with characteristic loyalty, that his principal interest in life, as well as that of Mrs. Getchell, now centers around these two children. Both Mr. Getchell and Mr. Lancaster, his law partner, are associated in a diversity of business interests not only in their home cities but elsewhere within and outside of Maine.

ROBERT JAMES WISEMAN, M. D., three times mayor of Lewiston, Maine, and one of the most prominent and highly esteemed men in that community, was born June 26, 1871, at Princeville, Province of Quebec, Dominion of Canada. He is a son of George A. and Mary (Thomas) Wiseman, both of whom were born in the "old country." Mary (Thomas) Wiseman was a native of Ireland; while the father, George A. Wiseman, was born in Scotland. He was a baker by trade, and a man who held a position of much esteem in his community.

Robert James Wiseman received his early education in the public schools of Lewiston, Maine, and graduated from Bates College. He sought his professional training at Bowdoin Medical College, and graduated from there in 1903, when he received his degree of Doctor of Medicine. Immediately after the completion of his training, Dr. Wiseman at once branched out for himself, beginning a general medical and surgical practice in Lewiston, where he has since remained. His practice has steadily increased, just as the community itself has steadily grown, until Dr. Wiseman has the honor to serve one of the largest and most aristocratic clienteles in his part of the State.

Dr. Wiseman, in his political views, is an Independent, in so far as local or city politics are concerned. On matters of national importance he is a supporter of the Democratic principles. He has served for many years as president of the staff of St. Mary's General Hospital in Lewiston; he also served for a long period as member, and for part of that time as president, of the Lewiston School Board; he is a past president of the Board of Aldermen; and in 1914 he was elected mayor of Lewiston. That he performed the duties of that office with honor to himself and satisfaction to the people is proven by the fact that he was reëlected mayor in 1925, and again in 1926. This bespeaks the deep respect and esteem in which he is held by the people of Lewiston. In connection with his own work as a physician and surgeon, Dr. Wiseman has continued his membership in a number of those learned organizations which pertain to his profession, among the more important of them being the American Medical Association, the Maine State Medical Association, and the Androscoggin Medical Society. He is also a registered druggist.

Robert James Wiseman married, May 15, 1893, at Lewiston, Rose Cyr, born in Lewiston, a daughter of Stanislas and Souphrenia (Marcous) Cyr, both natives of the Dominion of Canada. Dr. and Mrs. Wiseman have become the parents of five children: Robert James, Jr., Philip J., and Armand J., all of whom were born in Lewiston; Albert J., born in Portland, Maine; and Priscilla Ann, born in Lewiston. Dr. Wiseman and his family maintain their residence in Lewiston, in which community they attend St. Peter's Catholic Church.

GEORGE H. BARRON, a member of the firm of C. H. & G. H. Barron & Company, a general contracting, engineering and building concern of Lewiston, Maine, and one of the most highly esteemed citizens of that city, was born there, August 30, 1889, a son of Chandler H. and Olive (Sawyer) Barron, both now deceased. Olive (Sawyer) Barron, born at Cambridge, Maine, died at Lewiston on May 17, 1926; Chandler H. Barron, a native of Emden, Maine, died August 19, 1905. He was a railroad man, for many years connected with the Maine Central Railroad, and one of the very substantial men in his community.

George H. Barron received his early education in the public and high schools of the community in which he was born and reared, Lewiston, and he later studied for three years at Bates College. Immediately after leaving college he started in engineering work, at Lewiston. He later was identified with the Portland & Lewiston Inter-Electric Railway Company. With this concern he was first assistant engineer from 1911 until 1914, after which he resigned to form a business partnership with his brother, Chandler H. Barron, at Lewiston. This concern, operating under the style of C. H. & G. H. Barron & Company, carries on a thriving and prosperous business enterprise in general contracting, engineering and building. Such is the success with which they have met that it is considered one of the largest and most important organizations of its kind in this part of the State. Mr. Barron is a staunch supporter of the Republican party, and is noted for the manner in which he supports any movement designed for the welfare or advancement of his community. He has been active in club and social life, and is affiliated with Ashlar Lodge, No. 105, Free and Accepted Masons; King Hiram Chapter, No. 9, Royal Arch Masons; Dunlap Council, Royal and Select Masters, and the Lewiston Commandery, Knights Templar.

George H. Barron married, at Lewiston, Maine, Wheatie Claire Whitman, born in Lewiston, daughter of Oscar F. and Clara (Shaw) Whitman. Oscar F. Whitman was born in Bethel, Maine; while Clara (Shaw) Whitman was a native of Cambridgeport, Massachusetts. Mr. and Mrs. Barron are the parents of a daughter, Phyllis C., born July 28, 1926, at Lewiston. They maintain their residence in Lewiston, where they attend the Universalist church.

WALTER G. MORSE—For more than three decades Walter G. Morse, grain dealer, has been a substantial and prosperous business man of Rumford, Maine, and an outstanding citizen whose achievements in the public service have been notable. His firm is known as Walter G. Morse, dealer in flour, grain, feed and salt. Mr. Morse was born in Rumford, January 31, 1876, son of James S. and Lydia (Colby) Morse. The former, born in Rumford, is a prosperous farmer and grain dealer, associated in business in the latter capacity with his son. The mother, likewise a native of Rumford, died April 8, 1915.

After obtaining his education in the Rumford public schools and at Hebron Academy, Mr. Morse started in business as a grain dealer with his father, August 5, 1893, in Rumford. The two partners flourished as joint heads of the enterprise until 1919, since when the son has operated the business alone. A Republican, he has long been influential in his party, which he serves as State Committeeman from Oxford County. He was on the Rumford Board of Selectmen from 1900 to 1905, and a member of the Maine Legislature for two terms, 1913-15 and 1915-17. His interest in all progressive civic movements and whatever tends to the general betterment is unwearying. Mr. Morse belongs to the Rotary Club and the Business Men's Association, and to several fraternal orders, including: Blazing Star Lodge, of Rumford, Free and Accepted Masons; the Knights Templar; the Ancient Arabic Order Nobles of the Mystic Shrine; and the Independent Order of Odd Fellows; the Benevolent and Protective Order of Elks; and the Knights of Pythias. He is a communicant of the Methodist church.

In Rumford, Maine, December 19, 1903, Walter G. Morse married Nellie Stanwood, born in Canton, Maine, May 30, 1878, daughter of Dr. A. L. and Nellie (Kimball) Stanwood. Her father was born in Brunswick, Maine. Children: 1. Kathleen, born in Rumford, June 5, 1905. 2. James S., born in Rumford, February 6, 1907. 3. Barbara, born in Rumford, July 17, 1912.

JACOB H. BERMAN—For many years Jacob H. Berman has been successfully engaged in general legal practice in Portland, Maine, where he is known as an able attorney, a clear and cogent speaker, and resourceful advocate. His offices are located at No. 85 Exchange Street, Portland, where he is taking care of a large and important practice. He is also United States Commissioner. He was born in Portland, Maine, September 1, 1886, son of Herman I. Berman, a native of Russia, who came to this country and was a merchant in Lewiston, Maine, and of Belle (Markson) Berman, also a native of Russia. Jacob H. Berman attended the public schools of Lewiston, graduating from Lewiston High School with the class of 1906, and then matriculated at the Law School of Boston University, from which he was graduated with the class of 1909, receiving at that time the degree of Bachelor of Laws. He was admitted to the Massachusetts bar, and that same year was also admitted to the Maine bar and opened an office in Portland. Since that time he has been engaged in general practice in Portland, where he has made for himself an assured place in his profession. He is a member of the Cumberland County Bar Association, the Maine State Bar Association, and the American Bar Association, and keeps thoroughly abreast of the progress of general professional interests throughout the country. He gives his support to the Democratic party, and has always been interested in public affairs. He served as county attorney 1915-16, and at the present time (1928) is a United States Commissioner. During the World War he served as a "four-minute" speaker, and in the Intelligence Service. He is well known in fraternal circles, being a member of Portland Lodge, No. 188, Benevolent and Protective Order of Elks; Raboni Lodge, No. 150, Free and Accepted Masons, of Lewiston, Maine; and of the Knights of Pythias. He is a member of the

Fairview Country Club, and his religious affiliation is with the Hebrew church.

Jacob H. Berman was married, in Worcester, Massachusetts, October 6, 1912, to Marie Katz, born in Suncook, New Hampshire, daughter of Julius and Rachel (Saidel) Katz, both natives of Poland. Mr. and Mrs. Berman are the parents of two children, both born in Portland: 1. Charlotte L., born July 12, 1914. 2. Ruth A., born September 6, 1921.

CHARLES DUNBAR BOOTH, one of the foremost lawyers of Portland, Maine, and a member of the law firm of Verrill, Hale, Booth & Ives, of that city, was born November 17, 1871, at Ashtabula, Ohio, son of Charles C. and Sarah B. (Dunbar) Booth, both deceased.

Charles Dunbar Booth received his primary training in the public schools of the community in which he was born, and graduated from the Ashtabula High School with the class of 1888. He entered Phillips Academy at Exeter, and graduated with the class of 1892, after which he sought his higher academic education at Harvard University, graduating with the class of 1896, when he received the degree of Bachelor of Arts. He returned to the Law College of Harvard University, completing his legal training with the class of 1898, when he received the degree of Bachelor of Laws. He was formally admitted in 1899, to practice at the bar of Maine, and settling in Portland he laid the foundations for the success and honor he has since achieved. Mr. Booth is considered one of the most brilliant lawyers in this State. Shortly after he began work in Portland he became associated with Harry M. Verrill, and in 1900 he became a member of the firm, B. D. & H. M. Verrill & C. D. Booth and later of the firm now known as Verrill, Hale, Booth & Ives, one of the most substantial and influential groups of attorneys in Maine.

Mr. Booth has ever taken a profound interest in the civic and general affairs of his community. In his political views, he is a staunch supporter of the Republican party; and he is noted for the staunch manner in which he stands behind any movement designed for the welfare or advancement of Portland. He has long been an active member of the Portland Chamber of Commerce and he is identified with several organizations which pertain to his profession, including the American Bar Association, and the Cumberland County Bar Association. Mr. Booth has taken a fair share of the social responsibility of Portland. He now holds membership in the Portland Country Club, the Cumberland Club, the Portland Athletic Club, the Harvard Club of Maine, the Phillips-Exeter Club of Maine, and he is affiliated with the Maine Historical Society.

Charles Dunbar Booth married, in 1901, at Boston, Massachusetts, Florence J. Mack. Mr. and Mrs. Booth maintain their residence in Portland, in which community they attend St. Luke's Episcopal Church.

ROBERT HALE—Among the well-known members of the legal profession in Portland, Maine, is Robert Hale, whose offices are located at No. 57 Exchange Street. He was born in Portland, Maine, November 29, 1889, a son of Clarence and Margaret J. (Röllins) Hale, who was born in Berwick, Maine, June 12, 1856.

Mr. Hale received his early education in the public schools of his native city, graduating from the

high school in 1906. The following autumn he became a student in Bowdoin College, at Brunswick, Maine, from which he was graduated in 1910, with the degree of Bachelor of Arts. He then went to England and entered Oxford University, from which he received the degree of Bachelor of Arts in Jurisprudence in 1912, and the degree of Master of Arts in 1921. On Mr. Hale's return from Oxford in 1913, he studied for a year in the Law School of Harvard University, and in 1914 was admitted to the Massachusetts bar. He practiced in Boston with the firm of Choate, Hall & Stewart from 1914 to 1917. In 1917 he was admitted to the bar of Maine and became associated with the firm of Verrill, Hale, Booth & Ives, in which firm he became a partner in 1920. Mr. Hale is a member of the Cumberland County Bar Association, the Maine Bar Association, and the American Bar Association.

During the World War, Mr. Hale enlisted in August, 1917, was commissioned a lieutenant in the United States Army, served overseas with the American Expeditionary Forces from December, 1917, to August, 1919, and received his honorable discharge in September, 1919. After the Armistice Mr. Hale served as legal adviser to a commission sent by the American Commission to Negotiate Peace to Finland, Esthonia, Latvia, and Lithuania. Upon his return to civilian life he resumed the practice of law in Portland. Mr. Hale is a member of Psi Upsilon, American Legion, Veterans of Foreign Wars, Portland Yacht Club, Cumberland Club, Portland Club, and Purpoodock Club. He is also a member of the State Street Congregational Church of Portland. In his political affiliations Mr. Hale is a Republican and has represented the city of Portland in the House of Representatives of the State Legislature in the sessions of 1923, 1925 and 1927, being the majority floor leader during the 1927 session.

Robert Hale married, at Morristown, New Jersey, April 20, 1922, Agnes Burke, who was born in Morristown, November 23, 1890, daughter of Eugene S. and Margaret Burke, both natives of New Jersey.

JOHN FESSENDEN DANA was born in Portland, Maine, March 30, 1877, son of John Winchester Dana, now deceased, who was born in Kenosha, Wisconsin, and for many years was treasurer of the Portland & Ogdensburg Railroad Company, and also accountant, and of Martha Oliver (Fessenden) Dana, now deceased, a native of Portland. Mr. Dana attended the public schools of Portland and graduated from Portland High School with the class of 1894. The following fall he matriculated in Bowdoin College, at Brunswick, Maine, from which he was graduated with the class of 1898, receiving the degree of Bachelor of Arts. He had early decided upon the legal profession as his future field of activity, and after the completion of his regular college course began professional study in the Law School of Harvard University, from which he was graduated in 1901, with the degree of Bachelor of Laws. He was admitted to the bar the same year, and engaged in general practice in Portland. He continued alone until 1917, when he became a member of the firm of Verrill, Hale, Booth and Ives, which connection he still maintains (1928). He is a member of the Cumberland County Bar Association, Maine Bar Association, and American Bar Association. He gives his support to the principles and the candidates of the Re-

MAINE—A HISTORY 33

publican party, but has never sought or desired public office. He is a member of the Portland Club, Portland Athletic Club, Portland Country Club, Purpoodock Club, Rotary Club, Harvard Club of Maine, and Bowdoin Club of Portland. His religious affiliation is with the State Street Congregational Church of Portland. He is an overseer of Bowdoin College.

John Fessenden Dana was married, in Portland, Maine, June 24, 1905, to Helen H. Hunt, born in Portland, Maine, February 28, 1876, daughter of Dr. Charles O. Hunt, a native of Gorham, Maine, now deceased, and of Cornelia D. (Carson) Hunt, who was born in Lancaster, Pennsylvania. Mrs. Dana died in Portland, June 9, 1926. There are two children, both born in Portland, Maine: 1. Edward F., born March 8, 1908. 2. Mary H., born June 20, 1913.

CHARLES ALBERT ROBINSON—After an exciting and distinguished career as an officer in the American Army during the World War, Major Charles Albert Robinson took the office of postmaster of Portland, in which position he has given general satisfaction to the citizens of his community.

Major Robinson was born in Oxford, Oxford County, September 28, 1868, the son of Thomas L. and Louise (Weeks) Robinson. Following his education in the Fryeburg and Phillips academies, Mr. Robinson went into business for himself as a woolen manufacturer at Somersworth, Lowell, and South Windham, from 1887 to 1907. He became a wholesale coal merchant in Portland in 1910, retaining his interest in this business until 1917, when, the United States having entered the World War, he took up a course of training and received his commission. He received his promotion to major shortly before his discharge from the army, in 1919. In 1922 he received the appointment of postmaster to Portland, which post he still retains. Major Robinson is affiliated with the Free and Accepted Masons, and is an active member of the Portland Club, the Portland Country Club, the Rotary Club, and the Cumberland Club. He is a member of the Federal Business Association; in politics a Republican and in a religion a Congregationalist.

On June 30, 1892, Major Robinson married Edith Nute, at Somersworth, New Hampshire. Major and Mrs. Robinson are the parents of a daughter, Alberta.

ROBINSON VERRILL was born in Portland, Maine, August 22, 1896, son of Harry Mighels Verrill and Louise (Brown) Verrill. He was educated in the public schools of Portland and at Westminster School, Simsbury, Connecticut, after which he attended Yale College, leaving there in April, 1917, during his Junior year, for war service. In 1920 he received the degree of Bachelor of Arts *Honoris Causa* as of the class of 1918. In September, 1919, he entered Harvard Law School from which he graduated in 1922, with the degree of Bachelor of Laws. He was admitted to the Massachusetts bar, August 1, 1923, and to the Maine bar, November 2, 1926. From September 4, 1923, to September 1, 1926, he practiced law in the office of Herrick, Smith, Donald & Farley, in Boston, Massachusetts, and on October 1, 1926, became a member of the firm of Verrill, Hale, Booth & Ives, of Portland. On April 27, 1925, he was married to Agnes Walton Thompson in Brooklyn, New York.

Mr. Verrill attended the Plattsburg Camp in

Maine—3

1915, and in November of the same year enlisted in the so-called "Yale Batteries," the Tenth Field Artillery of the Connecticut National Guard, from which he received an honorable discharge in September, 1916. From May, 1917, to November, 1917, he served as a volunteer in the American Field Service in France and Serbia. At Paris, in November, he was commissioned a second lieutenant of Field Artillery in the American Expeditionary Forces. After completing the course at the Field Artillery School of Instruction at Saumur, France, he was stationed at La Courtine and Le Courneau, France, with the Field Artillery Replacement Division. Later he was assigned to the Three Hundred and Twenty-third Field Artillery and served as regimental intelligence officer, with the One Hundred and Fifty-eighth Artillery Brigade in the Army of Occupation. He was in active service during the battle of the Argonne and along the defense sector, and was honorably discharged at St. Aignan, France, April 19, 1919.

WALTER WALLACE MORSE—From drug clerk to the position of first vice-president and agency director of the Eastern Casualty Insurance Company, with offices at 312-13 Fidelity Building, Portland, is the record of Walter Wallace Morse. Mr. Morse entered the drug business soon after leaving school, and it was soon apparent to him that the insurance business was better suited to his particular talents; he made a change and from that day forward was successful, and has built up a clientele that has few equals in New England. He is actively interested in fraternal order work and in civic movements, and all in all, is one of the most prominent men in this section. Mr. Morse was born at Swans' Island, Maine, March 4, 1885, son of Byron Morse, a mariner, and Viola Ann (Rowe) Morse; his father, a native of Bristol, Maine, died August 28, 1897, while his mother, born on Swans' Island, died October 9, 1921.

Walter W. Morse received his education in the public and high schools of Swans' Island and in Portland; studied under private tutors and finally took commercial courses at two institutions. He first obtained employment with the G. I. Robinson Drug Company, at Thomaston, only a few months after leaving school. Then, in 1906, he was employed by the Metropolitan Life Insurance Company, with which concern he remained until 1907. In 1908 he was employed by the Portland Casualty Company, and in 1909, 1910 and 1911, by the Sagamore Insurance Company. In 1912 he formed a connection with the Eastern Casualty Insurance Company, first as special agent, then as State manager, then resident vice-president, vice-president, and finally the position he holds in 1927 of first vice-president and agency director. It will be seen from this statement that his advance was not only steady but rapid, and his youth indicates that still higher honors await him in the insurance world.

Mr. Morse is a member of the Cumberland County Board of Fire Underwriters, the Maine Life Underwriters, the Insurance Federation of Maine and the United States Health and Accident Underwriters' Conference. He is a leading member of the Chamber of Commerce, in civic affairs and in fraternal orders a member of the Improved Order of Red Men, the Knights of Pythias and the Free and Accepted Masons. In religious affairs he belongs to the Christian Science denomination. His clubs include the Lincoln, Economic, Woodfords, Willowdale Golf, Elks, Lions (president 1927-28), and Portland Country. In politics he gives his allegiance to the Republican party.

Walter W. Morse married, at Portland, January 8, 1911, Hattie Damon Griffin, born at East Boston, Massachusetts, October 16, 1880, daughter of Francis A. Griffin, native of Newburyport, and Grace (Wood) Griffin, of Boston, and their union has been blessed with a daughter, Norma Virginia Morse, born at Portland, August 22, 1913.

HON. JOHN H. MAXWELL—A man of unusual energy and ability is the Hon. John H. Maxwell. Beginning as a school teacher, he soon took up the study of law, and has conducted a very successful general practice at Livermore Falls since his admission to the Maine State bar in 1895. In addition to his legal work, he has acted as treasurer and general manager of the Livermore Falls Light & Power Company. His appointment to the bench of the Muncipal Court was in recognition of the high esteem in which he is held by his community.

His father, Davis Maxwell, was born at Webster, Maine, November 21, 1835. He was a farmer and engaged in this work until his death in 1915. His mother, Mary E. Davis, was born at Lisbon, Maine, April 3, 1838. Now, at ninety years of age, she is still most active and takes a great interest in current events, being a great reader.

John H. Maxwell was born at Webster, Maine, June 2, 1866. He entered the public schools of Wales, Maine, and later attended the Nichols Latin Preparatory School. In the year 1888, he was graduated from Bowdoin College with the degree of Bachelor of Arts. From 1890 to 1894, he taught school at Sanford, North Berwick, and Berwick, Maine. In 1894, he began the study of law with Tascus Atwood, at Auburn, Maine. He was admitted to the bar in 1895, and began the practice of law at Livermore Falls, which he has continued to the present time (1928). He has been treasurer and general manager of the Livermore Falls Light & Power Company since its incorporation in 1899. From 1899 to 1907 he served, also, as treasurer and general manager of the Livermore Falls Water Company. In May, 1923, he was appointed Judge of the Municipal Court of Livermore Falls for a term of four years.

By political inclination, Judge Maxwell is a member of the Republican party, and he is past chairman of his County Republican Committee, having served on that committee from 1902 to 1912. In 1921 he was elected to the Maine State Legislature, and during 1921 and 1922, he was a member of the Republican State Committee. He is affiliated with the Ancient Free and Accepted Masons; the Independent Order of Odd Fellows; the Knights of Pythias, of which order he has been Supreme Representative since 1908. In 1927 was again reëlected for his sixth consecutive term. He is a member of the American Bar Association, the Maine State Bar Association, and the County Bar Association. He attends the Universalist church.

On January 17, 1900, at Auburn, Maine, John H. Maxwell married Della D. Davis, the daughter of M. J. and Nancy E. Davis.

DANA CARROLL DOUGLASS—From stenographer to vice-president and general manager of an important Eastern railroad in twenty-six years is the somewhat unusual record attained by Dana Carroll Douglass, of Portland, whose abilities have long since won him recognition of a high order from his fellow transportation associates. In 1894, at seventeen years of age, Mr. Douglass applied for a position with the Maine Central Railroad. He did not appear to the manager of the passenger department to possess any quality beyond intelligence and a willingness to work, so he was assigned to a place behind a typewriter and told to take some dictation in shorthand, which at that time was just having a vogue. His work was of such a high order that he was soon advanced to the position of stenographer in the general manager's office, in which tasks he familiarized himself with every feature of the railroad business, to the extent that he often knew certain things that were not known to the officers of the road, and was consequently in great demand for the correspondence and the composition of new route plans, time tables and rates, to meet the demand of a greatly increasing business. In each position he so fortified himself with knowledge that his advancement became a matter of course. He was next made secretary to the general manager, and the president of the road, noticing that his organization contained a man whose encyclopedic storehouse was comparable to that of Noah Webster, drafted his services and made him his assistant. He continued as assistant to the president of the Maine Central until 1913, when he was advanced again, this time to the position of general manager. From 1913 to 1917 he and his co-workers greatly improved the service and facilities of the road, and then came the World War, with its kaleidoscopic changes and dislocation of personnel and industry. Mr. Douglass placed himself at the disposal of the Government and substantially contributed to that coördination of railroad effort which was so necessary to the winning of the war. In 1918, when further coördination of railroad activity was needed and Congress created the Railroad Administration, which was directed by William G. McAdoo, Mr. Douglass was made federal manager of the Maine Central Railroad. He served until 1920, through the administration of Walker D. Hines as well as Mr. McAdoo. On March 1, 1920, his war work and previous duties were recognized by his own company in his elevation to the position of vice-president and general manager in charge of operation, and he has capably filled this place to the present time.

Mr. Douglass is yet a young man and the future opens up gloriously before him. He was born at Leeds, Maine, February 2, 1877. As a boy he attended the public schools of his home town and made the most of limited opportunities. The family finances were not in such condition that he was able to take a college education, so while he was still in his teens he went out into the business world. How well he has succeeded is imperfectly told herein, and the years that are left to his purposes will undoubtedly see additional brilliant laurels added to his crown. His predecessor in the office of vice-president and general manager of the Maine Central was Morris McDonald (q. v.), who, in 1913, was promoted to the presidency of the Boston & Maine Railroad and its subsidiary, the Maine Central.

JOHN CALVIN STEVENS, architect, of Portland, has been prominent in all matters pertaining to the advancement of his home city, and has exercised a particularly strong influence in the development of the art of building in Portland. Among the important structures which he has designed are the Surgery Building at the Maine General Hospital, the Maine Medical School Building, The L. D. M. Sweat Memorial Art Museum, the Portland Athletic Club Building, the Eastern Maine Insane Hospital, the new Chamber of Commerce Building, the Maine State Sanitorium at Hebron; the Marshall House at York Harbor; as well as buildings in Hampton, Virginia, at the National Home for Disabled Volunteer Soldiers, and many others of importance. He was associated with Carrère and Hastings, of New York, in the building of the new Portland City Hall; and many of the finer residences in town and country stand as monuments to his skill. He has received honors for the quality of his work from his fellow craftsmen.

He was born October 8, 1855, in Boston, Massachusetts, a son of Leander and Maria Jane Hancock (Wingate) Stevens, and a descendant of Moses Stevens, of Wells, Maine, who was prominent there in 1700. John Calvin Stevens attended the public schools, and was graduated from the Portland High School in the class of 1873, in which year he entered the office of F. H. Fassett, architect. After several years of thorough application to his work, he was admitted to the firm in 1880, becoming the junior partner of the organization that then became known as Fassett and Stevens. The partnership lasted four years, two of which Mr. Stevens spent in Boston as the representative of the branch office in that city. Then he withdrew from the firm and opened an office of his own in 1883. In 1889 he entered into partnership with A. W. Cobb under the firm name of Stevens and Cobb. This relationship continued for two years, at the end of which time he engaged in work under his own name. His son, John Howard Stevens, became associated with him in the business, and since 1906 they together have built the firm into a large organization whose work extends throughout Maine and into several other States, mostly in New England.

Aside from his own business, Mr. Stevens has a number of other interests. He is an honorary trustee of the Maine Eye and Ear Infirmary; a member of the Boston Society of Architects; the Architectural League of New York; the Maine Society of Civil Engineers; the Portland Society of Art, of which he has been president since 1920; the Maine Genealogical Society; the Society for the Preservation of New England Antiquities; the Society for the Protection of New Hampshire Forests; the American Federation of Arts; the American Forestry Association; and the National Conservation Association. In 1890 and 1891 he was president of the Maine Charitable Mechanics' Association. In 1889 he was made Fellow of the American Institute of Architects. In his political affiliations he is a Republican. He is a member of the Free and Accepted Masons, including the Commandery, Knights Templar; and the Independent Order of Odd Fellows. He also holds membership in the Portland Chamber of Commerce, serving as president in 1923; the Salmagundi Club, of New York; the Portland Athletic Club, of which he was once president; the Portland Club, of which

he was president in 1921; the Cumberland Club; the Economic Club; and the Portland Yacht Club. In 1891, in collaboration with his partner of that time, A. W. Cobb, he became the author of a book entitled "Examples of Domestic Architecture," which won the esteem of his professional colleagues and was added to numerous libraries.

On December 25, 1877, John Calvin Stevens married Martha Louise Waldron, of Portland, and they have four children: 1. John Howard, referred to above, who works with his father as an architect. 2. Caroline Maria, now Mrs. Henry K. Fitts. 3. Margaret Louise, now Mrs. Neal W. Allen. 4. Dorothy Wingate.

ADAM PHILLIPS LEIGHTON, Jr., M. D.— When Dr. Adam Phillips Leighton, of Portland, was growing into manhood, he had an excellent opportunity to succeed his illustrious father in the business and political world, but preferring to enter different activities, he concentrated upon the medical profession, and is creating in it a most enviable position for himself. Dr. Leighton's father, Adam P. Leighton, Sr., was the originator of several business concerns which made a large success, including manufacturing, merchandising and banking, and served Portland twice as mayor. The avenues were open, therefore, for the son to step into going concerns; but a love of a profession that nobly serves mankind in the alleviation of suffering and a desire to contribute scientifically to the advancement of that profession led him into his present occupation, which his associates agree is the better for his having entered it. Dr. Leighton brings to the profession not only a love of the work but an equipment that is unusual, even for the best educated physicians of the day, since he spent some years in hospitals abroad, notably at Vienna and Dublin.

Dr. Leighton was born January 23, 1887, at Portland. His mother, Isadore M. Butler, daughter of Alonzo Butler, a prominent resident of Portland, was married to Mr. Leighton, June 30, 1873, and bore him four children; she died February 12, 1913. These children were: 1. Nettie May, born April 19, 1874, married Dr. Thomas W. Luce, of Portsmouth, New Hampshire, and died April 15, 1911, leaving her husband and two children: i. Isadore Leighton Luce. ii. Emily Elizabeth Luce. 2. Carlton Butler, born November 19, 1876, a dental surgeon, who enlisted in the World War in 1918 in the Dental Corps as a lieutenant and in recognition of his service in France was promoted to a captaincy. 3. Hugh Chisholm, born October 28, 1878, married, in 1908, Elizabeth F. Wilcox, of Janesville, Wisconsin, and they have four children: i. Hugh C., Jr. ii. Margaret Jane. iii. Elizabeth W. iv. Nancy B. Leighton. 4. Adam Phillips Leighton, Jr., of whom further. The paternal grandparents of Dr. Leighton, Adam and Julia Ann Leighton, were representatives of pioneer Maine families. His father was born on a farm at West Falmouth, April 6, 1851, and when Mr. Leighton's parents removed to Portland as he reached his tenth birthday, he accompanied them to the larger city, where he attended the public schools and Westbrook Seminary. On November 9, 1867, he entered the employ of Chisholm Brothers as a clerk in their bookstore on the main business street of Portland, and later when the firm acquired news agency privileges on the Grand Trunk Railway, he was placed in charge of the agents and the store in the Grand Trunk Railway Station. He became vice-president and general manager of this concern and held the position many years. His firm was the pioneer in putting newspapers and magazines on railway trains, and it controls the agencies on many of the railroads whose branch lines extend into Northern New England. The concern early entered the publishing business with the first picture post-cards and numerous books illustrating buildings and scenes in the United States and Europe. In 1898 Mr. Leighton purchased the pioneer chewing gum factory of the Curtis & Son Company in Portland, and conducted this plant until it was acquired by the Sen-Sen Chiclet Company, of which he later became president. Subsequently this firm was consolidated with the American Chiclet Company of New York, and Mr. Leighton was made a director. He served for four years as president of the Chapman National Bank, and at various times as a director in the Casco-Mercantile Trust Company and the Fidelity Trust Company. His political successes started in 1891 when he was successful in a contest for a seat in the Portland City Council, and he was reëlected twice. He served as Street Commissioner in 1894, and as Alderman in 1896 and 1897. In 1907 Mr. Leighton, a staunch Republican, overturned the Democratic administration by his election to the mayoralty by a substantial margin, and he was reëlected a year later by twice as big a vote. Six weeks after he had assumed office in his first term, the City Hall was destroyed by fire, and he became the head of a commission which erected a new structure in 1911 at a cost of $1,000,000. He was defeated in a move to erect this building in Lincoln Park so as to provide an ideal civic center. During the administration of Governor Plaisted and a Legislature controlled by Democrats, he successfully led a State-wide campaign against a proposed change in the Maine liquor prohibition laws. He was prominent in secret orders as a member of the Knights of Pythias and the Knights Templar.

Dr. Leighton attended the Holbrook School and Phillips-Exeter Academy at Exeter, New Hampshire. Entering the Medical School of Bowdoin College at Brunswick, he graduated in 1910 with the degree of Doctor of Medicine. In 1911 and 1912 he took post-graduate work in the University of Vienna, Vienna, Austria, after which he continued his practical work at the Rotunda Hospital at Dublin, Ireland. He was licensed to practice in Maine in 1910 and in New Hampshire in 1911, and during both of these years served as house doctor of the Maine General Hospital. He has specialized in obstetrics and gynecology, and has built up a most gratifying practice. In 1913 he opened the first private maternity hospital in Portland. In 1916 he became a member of the Maine State Board of Registration of Medicine, and since 1921 has served as secretary of the same. He is a member of the American Medical Association; the American Association of Obstetricians, Gynecologists and Abdominal Surgeons; the Maine Medical Society; the Portland Medical Club, of which he is secretary; the Aegis Medical Club, of which he is president; and the Association of Military Surgeons of the United States.

During the World War he enlisted as a lieutenant in the Medical Reserve Corps of the United States Navy, and in 1917 and 1918, while holding that posi-

tion, rendered patriotic civic service by sitting in the deliberations of the Portland City Council as an Alderman; he later became a member of the Common Council and was elected to the presidency of it. In business circles he is a director of the Chapman National Bank and the Cumberland County Loan & Building Association. He is the author of numerous articles on gynecology and obstetrics in various medical journals, and in these subjects he is regarded as an authority. His secret orders include the Free and Accepted Masons, the Knights Templar, the Scottish Rite, the Ancient Arabic Order Nobles of the Mystic Shrine, the Knights of Pythias, and the Benevolent and Protective Order of Elks. His medical fraternity is Alpha Kappa Kappa. Like his father, he is a Republican in politics, and in religion a member of the Congregational church. His lead in civic affairs is attested by the fact that he is president of the Kiwanis Club. Other clubs or organizations in which he maintains membership include the Cumberland Purpoodock Country, the Portland, Portland Country Bramhall League, American Legion, United States Naval Reserve Association, and the Economic Club. He is at present Illustrious Potentate of Kora Temple, Mystic Shrine, of Lewiston, Maine.

Dr. Leighton married, October 29, 1924, Anna Leahy, registered nurse of Worcester, Massachusetts. Dr. Leighton has one daughter, Eleanor Francesca, by a former marriage.

CHARLES GRANDISON ALLEN has been associated with the financial life of Portland continuously since 1877, advancing from the position of clerk in the Canal National Bank of Portland to that of president of The Portland National Bank with which bank he has been connected since 1889. In addition to this office, he also serves as president of the Union Safe Deposit & Trust Company, of Portland, being elected to this post in 1926, and he is a director in the Union Mutual Life Insurance Company, receiving this appointment in 1918.

Mr. Allen was born in Biddeford, Maine, May 30, 1859, son of John Howard and Martha A. (Goodspeed) Allen. John Howard Allen was engaged for many years in the mercantile trade and was a respected and esteemed member of his community.

Charles Grandison Allen was educated in Anson Academy, North Anson, Maine. He entered the employ of the Canal National Bank in January, 1877 and remained with that bank until 1889, when he became cashier of The Portland National Bank. In 1916, he was elected vice-president of The Portland National Bank and was vice-president and cashier until January, 1926, when he was elected president. His political principles are those of the Republican party, although he has never sought any political office. He is a member of the Cumberland Club, the Economic Club, the Portland Club, Portland Society of Art, the Rotary Club, and the Portland Athletic Club. His religious adherence is given to the Universalist church which he attends. His residence is at No. 273 Forest Avenue, Portland.

Mr. Allen married, October 20, 1887, in Deering, Annie Winslow Hersey, daughter of Elias and Harriette (Winslow) Hersey.

CARL MERRILL ROBINSON, M. D.—One of the well-known and very successful surgeons of

Portland, Maine, is Dr. Carl Merrill Robinson, whose offices are located at No. 188 State Street, in Portland. Dr. Robinson is a graduate of Bowdoin College and of Harvard Medical School, and since 1920, has been a Fellow of the American College of Surgeons. During the World War he served in France and in this country, and he is now (1928) a major in the Medical Reserve Corps of the United States Army. Dr. Robinson is also a thirty-second degree Mason.

Dr. Carl Merrill Robinson was born in Portland, Maine, July 4, 1886, son of Frederick William Robinson, who is engaged in business as a merchant, and who is vice-president of the firm of Loring, Short & Harmon, and of Alice Gertrude (Merrill) Robinson. After attending the excellent public schools of Portland, Dr. Robinson matriculated in Bowdoin College, where he finished his course in 1908, receiving at that time the degree of Bachelor of Arts. He then began professional study in the Medical School of Harvard University, where he completed his course with the class of 1911 and received the degree of Doctor of Medicine. During the following year, 1911-1912, he served as an interne in the Rhode Island Hospital, and this experience he followed with a year as surgical house officer in the Massachusetts General Hospital, 1912-1913. In June, 1916, he was commissioned a major in the Royal Army Medical Corps, Harvard Unit, British Expeditionary Forces. From December, 1916, to March, 1917, he was acting surgeon-in-chief of the Harvard Unit in the British Base Hospital No. 22, at Dannes-Camiers, France. He was captain in the Medical Corps, United States Army, from August, 1918, to December, 1918, and was then made instructor in military surgery at Fort Oglethorpe, Chickamauga Park, Georgia. He now ranks as major in the Medical Reserve Corps of the United States Army. Dr. Robinson is one of the well-known surgeons of this section. He is associate-surgeon of the Maine General Hospital, consulting surgeon of the Children's Hospital, and surgeon of St. Barnabas Hospital. He holds membership in the Cumberland County Medical Society and the American Medical Association, and he has the honor of being a Fellow of the American College of Surgeons, to which he was elected in 1920. Politically, he gives his support to the Republican party. He is a member of Delta Kappa Epsilon, of Phi Beta Kappa, and of Alpha Kappa Kappa College fraternities, and is also a member of the Masonic Order, in which he holds the thirty-second degree, being a member of the York Rite bodies, including St. Albans Commandery, Knights Templar. He is identified with the Cumberland Club, Portland Country Club, and the Rotary Club, and his religious membership is with the State Street Congregational church.

Dr. Carl Merrill Robinson was married, at Portland, Maine, September 20, 1917, to Grata Payson, daughter of Edgar Robinson and Harriet (Estabrook) Payson. Dr. and Mrs. Robinson are the parents of four children: 1. Ann Robinson, born August 31, 1919. 2. Martha Merrill, born December 13, 1920. 3. Grata, born July 30, 1922. 4. Mary Louise, born January 8, 1924. Dr. Robinson has his offices at No. 188 State Street, in Portland, and the family home is at No. 304 Spring Street, Portland.

FREDERICK WHEELER HINCKLEY—"The State of Maine must be developed industrially," was the slogan on which Frederick Wheeler Hinckley based his campaign for the Republican nomination for governor of Maine in the 1928 primaries. "Respect for the law is a pre-requisite to good government," he added, "law enforcement is a cardinal principle of any government. The prohibition law is an economic benefit to the human family. It is here to stay. It can and must be enforced." With these ringing words Mr. Hinckley launched his candidacy more than a year before the June primaries, and declared that if elected governor, his chief concern would be to build up and not tear down, to breed the spirit of love and not the spirit of hate, and by personal example, set a high moral standard for the people.

Born in Princeton, Washington County, May 26, 1878, the son of Adelbert E. and Sarah J. (McLaughlin) Hinckley, the family removed to Calais, Maine, while Frederick Wheeler Hinckley was still a child. His schooling was interrupted when he was thirteen years of age by the necessity of aiding in the support of the family, in which there were nine children. For four years he labored in the spinning room of a cotton mill, as weaver, or as laborer in the dyehouse, for a pittance of twenty-five cents a day for eleven hours' work. Then he went to work in a sawmill, piling boards. One Friday his employer called him to the office to ask if he knew how to survey lumber. Ambitious to earn a larger salary, and unabashed by the fact that he had never done such a thing in his life, he replied in the affirmative, and was told to report for his new job on Monday. Feverish study under the tutelage of an experienced timber man enabled him to make good, and he earned enough money in a year to be able to enter the Eastern Maine Conference Seminary at Bucksport. Once there, he earned his way by ringing the chapel bell, and bucksawing cordwood during the Christmas holidays. Upon completing his second term in this school, he entered the Coburn Classical Institute. After leaving school he traveled through Maine selling books. One of his first customers was Justice Fred Emery Beane, of Hallowell, whose purchase was a story of the Klondike gold fields. A year later Justice Beane himself journeyed to the Klondike. Other early patrons were Judge Charles F. Johnson, and Justice Warren C. Philbrook, in those days residents of Waterville.

Hon. Marshall N. McKusick, of Calais, Maine, invited him to enter his law office as a student, and three years later, at the age of twenty-two, the former bobbin boy was admitted to the bar. While reading law, he had taught elocution in Calais and St. Stephen, New Brunswick, having at one time fifty-seven pupils, including sixteen clergymen, one of whom, the Rev. Dr. McKenzie, then a pastor in Saint Stephen, became president of a college in California. Mr. Hinckley continued to practice law in Calais until 1904, when he removed to Portland. In 1912, his brother, George H. Hinckley, having been trained for the law at Dartmouth College and Harvard University, was taken into partnership, the firm being known as Hinckley & Hinckley.

Mr. Hinckley's public service began in 1913. Governor Haines appointed him a member of the board of trustees of Juvenile Institutions, and he was president of this board five years later, when elected to the Legislature. In 1919 he was elected mayor of South Portland, and the same year was again sent to the Legislature, and reëlected to that office. In 1923 and in 1925 he was State Senator from Cumberland County, and during his second term, was chairman of the committee on the judiciary, and of the committee on fees and salaries. During his second term he was also the Republican floor leader in the Senate. From his nineteenth year, Mr. Hinckley has devoted never less than two weeks to the Republican party's campaigns, and in close contests his services have been utilized in other States, notably Massachusetts, Louisiana and California. He opposed the sectarian issue in Maine in 1925, took an active part in the Kennebec Reservoir fight, was a volunteer counsel for the public in the Cumberland County Power & Light Company rate case; was of counsel for the State in the State Prisons investigation, and led the successful fight in the United States Senate on behalf of Senator Arthur R. Gould. Despite these public activities, his practice in general law has increased, and the firm, since 1926, having been proportionately enlarged, is now Hinckley, Hinckley & Sheshong. His hobby, if it can be called such, has been the designing and building of two hundred houses for a model community at South Portland Heights.

Mr. Hinckley is a member of the First Baptist Church of Portland, and active in the councils of the Free and Accepted Masons, the Benevolent and Protective Order of Elks, and the Independent Order of Odd Fellows, and of the Grange, Patrons of Husbandry. He also belongs to the Sons of the American Revolution, the Economic Club, the Lincoln Republican Club of Portland, the Boston City Club, and the Cape Shore Community Club. He has been brigadier-general, department commander of Maine, Order of Patriarchs Militant.

Mr. Hinckley married Blanche Richards, daughter of Enoch C. and Kate M. Richards, at Portland, Maine, October 23, 1907.

CHESTER MERRILL FOSS, member of the well-known firm of Chester M. Foss & Company, certified public accountants of Portland, Maine, was born July 2, 1888, at Hancock, Maine, a son of Ulmore E. and Lena H. (Sargent) Foss, both of whom were natives of this State.

Chester Merrill Foss received his early education in the public schools of the community in which he was born, and later graduated from Kents Hill Seminary. He then pursued his commercial training at Shaw's Business College at Portland. Immediately after the completion of these courses of study he began work in the bookkeeping departments of various corporations, meantime studying accountancy, a type of endeavor in which he has since remained and in which he has scored a very marked success. He became a certified public accountant, June 27, 1917, and such have been the heights to which he has risen in this work that in August, 1919, he founded the Chester M. Foss & Company organization, a concern devoted to the broad field of public accounting.

Despite the many exacting duties of his profession, Mr. Foss nevertheless was among the first to offer his services to his country during the emergency created by the entry of the United States

into the World War. In June, 1917, shortly after America's declaration of war, Mr. Foss entered Camp Devens as a field auditor of the construction division. He was later transferred to the Army Supply Base at Boston, and was there commissioned a captain, Quartermasters Corps, United States Army. This was on August 31, 1918, since which time, however, although discharged from regular line of duty at the close of hostilities, Mr. Foss has retained a commission in the United States Army Officers' Reserve Corps.

Since his return to civilian life, Mr. Foss has taken an increased interest in the civic and general affairs of Portland. He is treasurer of the Durgen Paper Box Company, and a director and treasurer of the Cumberland County Agricultural and Horticultural Society. He is a member of the American Society of Certified Public Accountants, the Kiwanis Club, the Economic Club, Willowdale Golf Club, the Portland Club, and he is fraternally affiliated with the Independent Order of Odd Fellows, Past Noble Grand of Beacon Lodge, No. 67; Ancient Landmark Lodge, Free and Accepted Masons; the Chapter, Royal Arch Masons; the Council, Royal and Select Masters; and St. Albans Commandery, Knights Templar.

Chester Merrill Foss married, October 18, 1910, at Portland, Maine, Flora M. Huston, a daughter of Walter and Lovina H. (Failes) Huston. Mr. and Mrs. Foss maintain their residence in Portland.

REV. JAMES F. SAVAGE is pastor at the Catholic Church of St. Francis, Belfast, Maine. He was ordained priest in 1913, and before that went through all the grades and studied philosophy and divinity in this country and in Ireland. He has held several important charges in Maine Diocese, and he became a pastor within a few years of his ordination. He is greatly respected in Belfast, not only by those who form his congregation, but also by individuals of different beliefs.

James F. Savage was born April 21, 1885, in Ireland, son of Jeremiah and Annie (Hannan) Savage. The father, who is living (1928), was a farmer and ranchman, born in Ireland, came to this country when young and was in the Civil War. The mother, who was also born in Ireland, is now deceased. Father Savage was educated at Boston College; at Villanova College, Pennsylvania, graduating in 1908 with the degree of Bachelor of Arts; in Dublin, Ireland, at Holy Cross College, and at Clonliffe Seminary, where he was ordained in 1913. In November, 1914, he was made assistant pastor at St. Dominic's Church, Portland, Maine. Then he went as assistant also to St. Mary's Church, Biddeford, Maine. In 1919, he was appointed pastor of St. Mary's Church, at Lincoln, Maine. In 1926, he came to St. Francis' Church, Belfast, Maine, as pastor, and he has been in that capacity since. Father Savage is an Independent in politics. He was chaplain in Lincoln of the Knights of Columbus.

GEORGE MOORS GRAFFAM, prominent citizen of Portland, Maine, and one of the very well-known certified public accountants of that city, was born September 3, 1873, at South Portland, Maine, a son of Ezra P. and Mary B. (Moors) Graffam. George Moors Graffam received his early education in the public schools of the community in which he was born, and he later attended South Portland High School. He then pursued further training at Shaw's Business College, after which he studied at the International Business University at Detroit, Michigan. He then branched out for himself, becoming a certified public accountant on February 1, 1915. Prior to this for fifteen years altogether, he had been in government service at Washington, District of Columbia. He has since served as an advisory member of the International Accountants' Society, at Chicago, Illinois, and he has been treasurer of the Baptist Church Convention in the State of Maine since 1916.

He is active in civic interests, and has been a member of the Portland Chamber of Commerce since 1915. In his political views he is a staunch supporter of the Republican party. He has taken a very marked interest in the club and social life of his world, and is a member of those organizations which pertain to his profession, such as the American Society of Certified Public Accountants, and the Maine State Society of Certified Public Accountants; likewise a member of the New England Water Works Association. He is affiliated, fraternally, with Lafayette Lodge, No. 19, Free and Accepted Masons, of Washington District of Columbia; Mount Vernon Chapter, Royal Arch Masons; Portland Council, Royal and Select Masters; Portland Commandery, Knights Templar; Kora Temple, Ancient Arabic Order Nobles of the Mystic Shrine, and the Shrine Club of Portland. He is also a member of the Woodsford Club.

George Moors Graffam married, December 22, 1897, at Brunswick, Maine, Amelia Ellen Pennell, daughter of Thomas and Eliza (Cook) Pennell. Mr. and Mrs. Graffam have one daughter, Marion, who married Fred Doucette, and they have two children, Ruth, and Barbara. Mr. and Mrs. Graffam maintain their residence in Portland.

JUDGE MAX L. PINANSKY—Though a native of Massachusetts, Judge Pinansky has been a resident of Maine since 1913 and in the decade and a half during which he has lived in the Pine Tree State he has succeeded to a remarkable degree in making an enviable position in his chosen profession and in the life of the city of his adoption, Portland. His achievements as a citizen, lawyer and judge are the more to his credit, because they are entirely the result of relentlessly hard work on his part. However, it is doubtful, if he could have reached his present prominence so early in his career, unless his unusual capacity for work had been complemented by several other outstanding characteristics, such as personal magnetism, extraordinary loyalty to friends and principles, exceptional unselfishness, strict adherence to the highest ideals and uncommonly broad vision and deep understanding of human relations.

Max Louis Pinansky was born in Boston, Massachusetts, December 11, 1887, the oldest son and child of Louis and Louisa (Birnbaum) Pinansky and brother of Samuel Pinansky, now engaged in the insurance business in Portland, and of Carrie (Pinansky) Turcot of Woodlynne, New Jersey. His father is a real estate operator in Boston, in which city several others of his kinsmen also occupy prominent positions in the business world. He received his preliminary education at the Lyman Grammar

School in Boston, after which he attended the Roxbury and the English High schools, as well as the Ballou and Hobigond Preparatory School. He was a member of the class of 1909 at Harvard University. During the greater part of the period which he devoted to obtaining an education, he also gave much time and effort to gaining a livelihood, so that the burden of these expenditures would not fall too heavily on his father's shoulders. While still attending college, he commenced to read law, first with Hon. Charles Innes of Boston, and later with Judge R. W. Gloag of South Boston, and with the late Colonel J. W. Spaulding of Boston. Admitted to the Massachusetts bar, March 5, 1909, it did not take him long to gain for himself a considerable reputation as an able and successful lawyer. He continued to practice his profession in Boston for three and a half years, during which period he frequently acted as counsel for different labor organizations. In 1913 he removed to Portland and on March 11 of that year he was admitted to the Maine bar. Since then and until he was appointed Judge of the Portland Municipal Court in 1927, he has been very successfully engaged in general practice, his offices being located at No. 97 Exchange Street. On February 10, 1927, Governor Ralph O. Brewster appointed him Judge of the Municipal Court of Portland for a term of four years. Not only did Judge Pinansky have the distinction of being the second lawyer of Jewish faith to become a member of the Maine bench, but the very large number of emphatic endorsements of his appointment, coming from all classes of people and from many sections of Maine, and even from other States, more clearly than anything else proved how greatly Judge Pinansky is respected and admired. This was also shown by the fact that the Governor's Council unanimously approved the appointment. Judge Pinansky took his seat on the bench for the first time on February 24, 1927, an occasion made memorable by many floral gifts from his large circle of friends, as well as by the receipt of numerous telegrams and letters of congratulation. Amongst those whose wishes came to Judge Pinansky on that day should be especially mentioned the following: Hon. Malcolm E. Nichols, a native of Maine and at that time mayor of Boston; Hon. James M. Curley, ex-mayor of Boston; Joseph B. Grossman, a member of the Massachusetts House of Representatives; Hubert C. Thompson, Assistant United States District Attorney at Boston; Elihu D. Stone, Assistant United States District Attorney at Boston and president of the New England region, Zionist Organization of America; Ely Rosenberg, president of the New York County Association of the Criminal Bar; Charles Hartman, prominent New York business man and member of the executive committee of the Grand Lodge, Independent Order of B'nai B'rith; Hon. Albert Ottinger, Attorney-General of the State of New York; Judge David A. Lourie, of the Superior Court of Massachusetts, and honorary president of the New England Region, Zionist Organization of America; Marcus M. Sperber, K. C., prominent Montreal lawyer; Lionel Covienski, president of the Montreal Lodge, Independent Order of B'nai B'rith; Charles E. Gurney, prominent Portland lawyer and chairman of the Maine Public Utilities Commission; James C. Furnival, secretary of the Portland City Manager; Leo F. O'Brien, United States Shipping

40   MAINE—A HISTORY

Commissioner at Portland; Henry F. Merrill, prominent Portland business man and civic and religious leader; Miss Pearl Rose Danforth, executive secretary of the Portland Chapter of the American Red Cross; and many other prominent lawyers, ministers, business men and private individuals in Maine, Massachusetts and other parts of the country. At the first anniversary of his elevation to the bench, Judge Pinansky entertained some twenty court attendants at a luncheon at the Congress Square Hotel, Portland. This manner of celebrating this occasion is typical of his geniality, a trait which, together with his untiring readiness to be of service to others and with an unblemished record for fair dealing, has made him one of the most popular men in the public life of Portland. This popularity extends to all classes and conditions of his fellow-citizens. Though always frankly and very actively interested in all phases of Jewish life, he has made a remarkably large number of sincere and loyal friends amongst the leaders of various Christian denominations. As a lawyer Judge Pinansky has appeared as counsel in many important criminal and civil cases and as the result of his great knowledge of the law and of his striking ability as a pleader he has to his credit many important victories. As a judge he has shown deep insight in and understanding of human nature and, though known as a firm believer in the authority and importance of law, he has understood how to temper justice with mercy and with a great deal of common sense. In spite of the fact that naturally his professional activities have at all times received the major share of his effort and attention, he has given much time to many other interests.

A supporter of the Republican party and its principles, he has been twice a candidate on the Republican ticket for the office of County Attorney of Cumberland County. He is widely and favorably known as a forceful and interesting public speaker. In this capacity he has addressed a very large number of organizations of all kinds in Portland and other parts of Maine, as well as in several Massachusetts cities, amongst which have been numerous churches and other religious organizations, various fraternal organizations, many Parent-Teachers' associations, and other organizations of a civic nature. In most of his public addresses he stresses the ideas and ideals of public service and community coöperation, closely following the lines along which the Permanent Conference for Better Understanding works. It is only natural that a man of Judge Pinansky's prominence and many-sided contacts should be actively interested in the work of numerous organizations, and he is a member of the following: Harvard Club of Maine; Economic and Lincoln clubs of Portland; Boston City Club; Cumberland County Bar Association; Maine State Committee, Boy Scouts of America; Executive Committee, Maine Conference of Social Welfare Workers; Executive Committee, Maine Association of Municipal Court Justices; Maine Juvenile Aid Society, which he was instrumental in founding in 1928 and of which Mrs. Pinansky is a trustee; 13 Class and Club of Portland; and North Deering Grange, Patrons of Husbandry. He is also very active in fraternal work and, indeed, it was largely due to his efforts that the Portland Lodge of the Independent Order of B'nai B'rith, Israel Lodge, No. 796, was organized, July 20, 1916. Of this he is a past president and since

1925 he has also been Chief Justice of the District Court of District No. I, comprising New York, the New England States and Canada, one of the highest offices of the Grand Lodge and carrying with it membership in the General Committee of the latter. He is also a member of Munjoy Lodge of Portland, Knights of Pythias; Ligonia Lodge, Independent Order of Odd Fellows; Pequawket Tribe, of Cumberland Mills, Improved Order of Red Men; and an honorary member of the Colby College Chapter of Gamma Phi Epsilon Fraternity. Ever since coming to Portland in 1913 he has been very active in Jewish affairs. As early as 1913 he served with much success as superintendent of the Sunday school of Temple Israel. In 1915 he formed, with the coöperation of the military authorities, an Army Young Men's Hebrew Association branch at Fort McKinley, Portland, the first of its kind in Maine. In 1917 he assumed the leadership in the organization of the first modern, English-speaking synagogue in Maine, which found its inception really in his own home. He is also greatly interested in Zionist activities. Since September 8, 1925, he has been president of the Maine State Zionist Association, the first to hold this office in Maine. For several years he has been a vice-president of the New England Region, Zionist Organization of America, and in 1927 he was a delegate to the American Jewish Congress. He is a member of the advisory board of the Portland Young Men's Hebrew Association. In 1927 he acted as Jewish chaplain at the Fort McKinley Citizens' Military Training Camp, in which capacity he organized a group of fifty young Hebrews into the first branch of the Jewish Brotherhood of the Citizens' Military Training Camp, a movement which bids fair to spread to other training camps. Recently he has been very active in bringing together the leaders of the various Jewish religious activities in Portland for the purpose of eventually forming a local Kehillah to centralize all these activities.

Judge Pinansky married, at Portland, January 5, 1913, Anna R. Bernstein, of Portland, a daughter of Robert and Rebecca Bernstein of Portland. Judge and Mrs. Pinansky are the parents of seven children: 1. Louisa, born February 22, 1914. 2. Irving M., born May 4, 1916, the youngest pupil in 1927 to enter Portland High School, of which he became a student shortly after passing his eleventh birthday and of which he has been an honor pupil ever since. 3. Harold, born February 10, 1918. 4. William D., born June 23, 1920. 5. Charlies Eliot, born December 23, 1921. 6. Mortimer M., born August 5, 1924. 7. Laura G. H., born November 28, 1925. Judge Pinansky and his family make their home at No. 462 Cumberland Avenue, Portland.

JOHN PICKERING THOMAS, prominent citizen of Portland, Maine, and a well-known architect of that city, was born there on March 30, 1880, a son of John Pickering and Susan C. (Ross) Thomas, of Portland.

The son, John Pickering Thomas, received his early education in the public schools of the community in which he was born, and attended Wilton Academy, graduating in 1905. He then entered Harvard University, and graduated from there with the class of 1909, after which he undertook a postgraduate course at the School of Arts and Sciences, graduating in 1912. After spending one year in

Italy, he returned to the United States and began his work as an architect in the office of C. Howard Walker of Boston. He was later with Welles Bosworth, still later with W. L. Howell, and again, with Wait & Copeland. This carried up to time of the entry of the United States into the World War, during which Mr. Thomas served as ensign, United States Navy, spending twenty months in overseas' duty. Upon his return, in 1919, he formed a business partnership with Charles Poor of Portland, and this carried on successfully until Mr. Poor's death in 1921, since which time Mr. Thomas has operated under his own name.

Mr. Thomas always found time in which to participate in the civic and general affairs of his community. In his political views he is a supporter of the Republican party, and is noted for the manner in which he stands behind any movement designed for the welfare or advancement of Portland. He has been active in his club and social life; for he is not only a member of those organizations which pertain to his profession, among the more important of which are the American Institute of Architects and the Boston Architectural Club, but he is also a member of the American Legion, the Kiwanis Club, the Cumberland Club, the Purpoopock Club, the Haylofters, the Harvard Club of Boston, and the Portland Chamber of Commerce.

John Pickering Thomas married, April 21, 1913, at St. Louis, Missouri, Alice K. McCandless, of that city. Mr. and Mrs. Thomas are the parents of three children: Mary Alice, Peter, and Susan J. Mr. Thomas and his family maintain their residence in Portland, Maine.

SIDNEY ST. F. THAXTER—Through the avenue of the law, of which Sidney St. F. Thaxter, of Portland, is an able exponent, he has attained important standing in this his native city. not only among the members of the bench and bar, but also in the financial and civic departments of the community life. During the score of years that he has been in practice he has built up one of the most desirable clientages known in legal fraternity circles locally, and his offices are sought out by those who esteem his counsel highly and pride themselves upon the sense of security they feel when acting upon his advice.

Sidney St. F. Thaxter was born in Portland, Maine, March 4, 1883, a son of Sidney W. and Julia St. F. (Thom) Thaxter. He attended the public schools of Portland, finishing his preparatory course at the high school, in 1900, in which year he entered Harvard University, whence he was graduated in the class of 1904 with the degree of Bachelor of Arts. Having made a choice of the legal profession, he took his training in Harvard Law School, receiving his degree of Bachelor of Laws on graduation in 1907. Shortly afterwards in that year he was admitted to the bar of the State of Maine.

Mr. Thaxter at once opened offices in Portland, and with characteristic enterprise and energy engaged in practice. He was widely acquainted in the community, and persons many years his senior, who had watched his school and college careers with sympathetic interest, were among the very first to help the rising young barrister not to regret his name and profession constituted the legend on his office door. Confining himself almost wholly

to general practice, he has been enabled to meet in a very large degree the demands placed upon his legal acumen and native capacity. Twenty years have now rolled by, and his standing in the community has advanced, as he has sought to serve his clients out of an enriched experience as the reinforcement of his learning in the law.

With the fidelity of the true lawyer, Mr. Thaxter has given much of his undivided attention to his practice, but he has not allowed himself to settle down to run in a groove. Other interests than the law have commanded his ability, and among the more important of these is the Chapman National Bank of Portland, of whose directorate he has been a member for some time. Politically, he is allied with the Republican party, and while he has not been persuaded to enter public office, he has stood, and so continues to do, four-square for the general welfare of the city of Portland. His high standing in the legal profession is definitely expressed by his election to membership in the American Bar Association and the Maine State Bar Association.

Mr. Thaxter married, June 25, 1913, at Portland, Maine, Marie Phyllis Schuyler, and they are the parents of four children: Sidney Warren, Hildegarde Schuyler, Phyllis St. F., and Mary Louise Reynaud. Mr. Thaxter and his family have their town house in Portland.

CHARLES FRED BERRY was born September 14, 1865, at Gorham, Maine, and moved to Portland, Maine, with his parents, in 1877. He attended the public schools of Gorham and Portland. He is the son of Charles J. and Sarah C. (Crockett) Berry, of Gorham, Maine.

In 1882 he entered the employ of the Portland Railroad Company, and in 1909 became its general manager and treasurer. In 1912 the Portland Railroad Company was absorbed by the Cumberland County Power & Light Company, and Mr. Berry was elected treasurer of that company. Through his connection with this industry he has seen it grow from a small horse-railroad, through the various stages of electrical development, to one of the largest and most successful public utilities in the State of Maine.

Mr. Berry is affiliated with the Masonic fraternity. He is a member of the Woodfords Club, the Kiwanis Club and the Economic Club. His religious preference is for the Congregational church. In politics, he is a Republican.

In 1890 Charles Fred Berry married Rachel E. Motley, who died in 1918. On September 14, 1922, he married Maud Macdonald. Mr. and Mrs. Berry reside at No. 45 Beacon Street, and his offices are at No. 443 Congress Street, Portland, Maine.

HERBERT ALONZO HARMON—More than forty-six years of experience in the fire insurance business has made Herbert Alonzo Harmon an expert in this line, and since the entire forty-six years have been spent in Portland, Mr. Harmon is thoroughly familiar with general conditions in this city. He is well known in fraternal circles, especially in the Masonic Order, being identified with both York and Scottish Rite bodies.

Born in Scarboro, Maine, February 29, 1864, Herbert Alonzo Harmon is a son of Alonzo F. and Cornelia M. (Merrill) Harmon. His parents removed to Portland, Maine, when he was four months of age, and he received his education in the public schools of this place. In 1881 he entered the fire insurance business in association with Warren Sparrow, and that connection was maintained for a period of five years, during which time he made himself thoroughly familiar with the business. After five years of experience he decided to establish an agency of his own, and since 1885 he has been continuously and successfully looking after a large and important enterprise in the city of Portland. He is well known in Portland and vicinity, and his office, located at No. 57 Exchange Street, has taken care of the writing of a vast number of policies during the past four decades. Fraternally, Mr. Harmon is identified with Deering Lodge, No. 183, Free and Accepted Masons; Mount Vernon Chapter, Royal Arch Masons; Portland Council, Royal and Select Masters; Portland Commandery, No. 2, Knights Templar; also with Yates Lodge of Perfection; Portland Council, Princes of Jerusalem; Dunlap Chapter, Rose Croix; and with Maine Consistory, Sublime Princes of the Royal Secret, in which he holds the thirty-second degree; and with Kora Temple, Ancient Arabic Order Nobles of the Mystic Shrine. He is also a member of Bramhall Lodge, No. 3, Knights of Pythias; Fraternity Lodge, No. 6, Independent Order of Odd Fellows; Samoset Tribe, No. 32, Improved Order of Red Men; and of Deering Grange, Patrons of Husbandry, of North Deering. He is a member of the Portland Club and a charter member of the Woodfords Club, and a member of the Chamber of Commerce and of the Venerable Cunner and Propeller Club, both of which he serves as treasurer; also Fern Park Association. Mr. Harmon is widely known in Portland.

Herbert Alonzo Harmon was married, in New York City, January 1. 1915, to Daisy Dean Gilmore.

FRANK L. AMESBURY—For forty-five years identified with the furniture industry of Gardiner, more than thirty of which have been devoted to establishments in which he is a leading partner, Frank L. Amesbury has made for himself a substantial place in the commerce of the town and region surrounding. His family is one of the pioneers of the State, his heritage of fealty to his native locality coming directly from his ancestors, who hewed their way into the wilderness and helped to erect the foundations upon which the commercial monument of today has been laid. He was far below the voting age when he began his life-work, since which time he has been one of the most active and energetic citizens. His success has been sound and the growth of his business constant, his friends are all who know him, their faith in his rectitude having often been demonstrated by calling him to public office as their representative in local government.

Frank L. Amesbury was born in Camden, Maine, December 16, 1865, a son of Captain Oliver Amesbury, of Rockport, and Lorinda (Hopkins) Amesbury, of Camden. Captain Oliver Amesbury was a master mariner and sea captain all his working life. He and his wife are now deceased. Frank L. Amesbury was educated in the public schools of Gardiner and attended the high school of that town. When he was seventeen years of age he began work in the furniture establishment of Wadsworth Brothers, of Gardiner, where he remained for ten years. He then became associated with the Adkin-

son Company, where he continued until 1895, when he established a partnership with Harry N. Wakefield, conducting a furniture establishment with him for eighteen years. In 1913 the house was incorporated as a stock company, the owners being Frank L. Amesbury, William E. Maxey and Herbert Twombly. In 1919 the concern admitted Bradford H. White as a shareholder, upon his purchase of the interest of Herbert Twombly. The firm has since been known as the Amesbury-White Company. The building it occupies was built in the year of Mr. Amesbury's birth (1865), by James Nash. Frank L. Amesbury is a Republican and has served two terms as alderman, in 1907 and in 1925. He is a vestryman of the Protestant Episcopal church of Gardiner, and a member of the local Rotary Club. He is Past Master of Lodge No. 37, Free and Accepted Masons, in which order he holds the thirty-second degree, and is Past Chancellor Commander of the Knights of Pythias.

Frank L. Amesbury married, January 15, 1891, at Gardiner, Julia M. Danforth, of Providence, Rhode Island. They have one child, Helen P., who married Bradford H. White, in 1921.

JAMES EARLE MOSHER—Adopting the modern business idea of chain store operation for standard commodities, thus increasing trade in the ratio of the links in the chain, James Earle Mosher, within seven years, has erected a commercial edifice of commanding importance, with headquarters at Gardiner. His operations in the automotive industry have attracted the attention of alert business men, who are quick to appreciate a virile personality within their circle. With no jealous enemies to combat, with friends in all circles and business fields, and with a sound knowledge of his profession, it is asserted that he has ahead of him a constantly-enlarging field for his operations, which it is certain he will be quite equal to cultivating.

James Earle Mosher was born in Mercer, Maine, July 17, 1898. His father was Edward H. Mosher, who conducted a general store in Belgrade for twenty-five years, was town clerk, by Democratic election, and treasurer for several terms, and also postmaster of that town. His mother was Nettie (Yeaton) Mosher, also a native of Belgrade. Both parents are still living, the father having retired from active business. James E. Mosher received his education in the Belgrade public schools and was graduated from the high school there. He afterward attended Bates College, from which he was graduated in 1920 with the degree of Bachelor of Science. In that year he established his first garage and automobile agency, in association with his father, at Gardiner, where they had the handling of the Dodge automobile. As business increased, branches were established, successively, at Pittsfield, Waterville, Skowhegan and Augusta. James Earle Mosher is Independent in politics and a Universalist in religion. During the participation of the United States in the World War, he served for two years in the Navy. He is a thirty-second degree Mason, holding membership in the Lodge, Free and Accepted Masons; the Commandery, Knights Templar; the Temple, Ancient Arabic Order Nobles of the Mystic Shrine; and he is also a member of the Benevolent and Protective Order of Elks; Gardiner

Rotary Club, and the local Grange, Patrons of Husbandry.

DR. GERTRUDE E. HEATH—Entering (the ranks of the early women medical practitioners, long before that day when equal suffrage for all American citizens became a constitutional fact, and at a time when the difficulties attending success in that profession for her sex seemed almost insurmountable, Gertrude E. Heath, of Gardiner, rose superior to a trying situation. Having a sound education in medicine and inheriting an abiding faith in rewards that must come with honesty of effort and intensity of purpose, she has reared for herself a professional edifice in the strength of which her great list of followers have shown themselves to be confident and proud. Her family line in Maine is long and honorable, the traditions of which she has faithfully observed during more than forty years of active professional labor among her people. She will be long remembered and ever honored in every rank of society where she is so well known and beloved.

Gertrude E. Heath was born in Gardiner, January 20, 1859. Her father was Alvan M. C. Heath, born in Windsor, Maine, and her mother, Sarah (Philbrook) Heath, a native of Fairfield. Alvan Heath was a son of Dr. Asa Heath, native of Windsor, and Margaret (Boynton) Heath, a native of this State and a graduate of Bowdoin College. Alvan M. C. Heath was the founder of the Gardiner "Home Journal" and lived in Gardiner for years. He was educated in the public schools and, upon the call for troops to put down the rebellion, enlisted in the Sixteenth Regiment, Maine Volunteer Infantry. This regiment went to the front at the opening of the Civil War, and engaged in many of the great battles of that conflict. Alvan Heath gave his life for his country, having been killed, December 16, 1862, at the battle of Fredericksburg. He had been, at the time of his tragic death, president of the Mechanics' Association of Gardiner. To do him honor, upon the organization of the Grand Army of the Republic, following the war, the first post in Gardiner was named "Heath Post," which it still remains.

Gertrude E. Heath received her early education in the public schools and the high school of Gardiner, afterward attending Hahnemann Medical College at Chicago, Illinois, taking special courses. She was graduated from this institution in 1883 with the degree of Doctor of Medicine, and began medical practice in Chicago in 1884. She returned to Gardiner that year and established herself in practice here, beginning with general work, but later confining herself to specialization. For seven years she was attached to the staff of the Maine State Hospital, at Augusta, and for a number of years served on the staff of the Gardiner Hospital. In politics she is a Republican and for four years was school physician of Gardiner. She also was a member of the Board of Health of Farmingdale, and, during the World War was a director of the local branch of the American Red Cross. She is a member of the Maine Homeopathic Society, and a member of the Gardiner Protestant Episcopal Church. She was the first president of the Gardiner Current Events Club, and is now a director in that organization. Her three brothers, all of whom are deceased, were Herbert M., a lawyer, of Augusta, head of the Maine

Bar Association at the time of his death; Willis K., for forty years a chief accountant, and Dr. Frederick C. Heath, a physician of Indianapolis, Indiana.

MATTHEW McCARTHY—An established factor in the business and professional progress of Rumford, Maine, is Matthew McCarthy, attorney-at-law, who enjoys a large general practice there. He is also associated with municipal affairs and served as Judge of the Municipal Court from 1910 to 1918. He was born at Glenburn, Maine, June 2, 1874, son of William and Mary (Gallagher) McCarthy, both natives of Ireland. The father was a prosperous farmer, who died when the son was an infant.

Matthew McCarthy was educated in the public schools of Glenburn and Bangor, Maine, at the East Maine Conference Seminary at Bucksport, at Higgins Classical Institute, and at the University of Maine, graduating from the last-named institution in 1900 with the degree of Bachelor of Laws. He worked at various pursuits during his early life in order to pay for his education.

His professional career began in 1900, when he was admitted to the bar and began an independent law practice at Bangor, Maine. Two years later, in 1902, Mr. McCarthy moved to Lewiston, where he formed a partnership with M. T. O'Brien and practiced law until 1905. In that year Mr. McCarthy opened an office of his own at Rumford, Maine, where he has prospered for twenty-two years and proved so successful in managing the legal affairs of individuals and business concerns, as well as the city, that he is highly regarded by his legal confreres and by the public-at-large. He is a director and treasurer of the Mt. Zircon Spring Water Company and attorney for the Rumford National Bank. A Democrat, he was municipal judge for eight years. He belongs to the Oxford County Bar Association, the American Bar Association, and the Merchants' Association; to the Rotary Club, a charter member thereof; and to several fraternal orders, including the Benevolent and Protective Order of Elks, the Loyal Order of Moose, and the Knights of Columbus, fourth degree. He is a communicant of the Roman Catholic church.

Matthew McCarthy married (first) Mildred Lynch, born in Orono, Maine, June 3, 1875, died in Rumford in 1911, seven years after their marriage in Orono, which occurred in 1904. He married (second), in Berlin, New Hampshire, Mabel Lavertu, born in that town, the wedding occurring in 1916. The children of the first marriage are: Mary E., Margaret, Francis, and Mildred, all born in Rumford. Those of the second are: Matthew and William McCarthy, also born in Rumford. Mary E., Margaret, and Francis McCarthy all graduated from Gorham Normal School the same year (1927), and are teaching in the Rumford schools.

EDWARD WINSLOW HANNAFORD—It has been well said that the fundamentals of every business lie at the bottom of the ladder, and that one must have experienced all of them before he can mount to the top. This essential principle has been abundantly borne out in the experience of Edward Winslow Hannaford of Portland, President of the Forest City Trust Company, who started his business career as an employee in a match factory and passed from this to a clerical position in a grocery store before he entered business with his two brothers, thus entering upon a period of unbroken success, and today he is recognized as one of the leaders in Portland's business and financial life and enjoys a standing among his contemporaries which is unsurpassed.

Mr. Hannaford was born April 23, 1863, in Cape Elizabeth, on the farm of his parents, Albert Francis Hannaford, and Mary Washburn (Jordan) Hannaford. Albert Francis Hannaford, a native of Portland, conducted a large farm in Cape Elizabeth, about four and one-half miles from Portland, and to him and Mrs. Hannaford ten children were born: 1. Arthur, deceased. 2. Edward Winslow, of whom further. 3. Isaiah, of Portland. 4. Howard C., of Cape Elizabeth. 5. Henry, of Portland. 6. William, of Cape Elizabeth. 7. Burton, who died in infancy. 8. Philip E., of South Portland. 9. Herbert, who died in infancy. 10. Jennie, who married Dr. George Hill, of Cape Elizabeth.

Edward W. Hannaford remained on his father's farm until he was seventeen years of age, learning the rudiments of farming, and having been in overalls often he was not afraid of work when he removed to Portland. He received a little schooling in the public school system, after which he attended Gray's Business College, having determined to enter business without a college education but equipped with energy, ambition, judgment and other tools which it is possible for a young man to acquire outside. He obtained a position with the Portland Star Match Company, which gave him his first insight into modern business methods. Next, he began clerking in a grocery store and for a period of about ten years he was engaged in various positions in Maine, New Hampshire and Massachusetts, and gained by experience and hard knocks a knowledge of the outside world and bided his time for the chance that was to mean his first big advance. This chance soon came in the form of a partnership agreement in 1888 with himself and his two brothers, to organize Hannaford Brothers, the brothers being Arthur M. and Howard C. In a short time the E. W. and H. C. Hannaford purchased the A. M. Hannaford interest and in 1903 they incorporated under the name of Hannaford Brothers Company, and took in several of their employees as stockholders. With this concern he has remained ever since as president. He has engaged in outside activities at various times and has seen the business grow from about ten thousand a year to two and one-quarter millions in 1926.

Before becoming president and general manager of the Forest City Trust Company he served in the position of vice-president, so that his advance was by the rules of fitness, integrity and efficiency. Mr. Hannaford is prominent in every activity with which he is connected, and is a substantial citizen in every sense of the word. Although he is absorbed in his commercial activities, he finds time to join in all movements for the advancement of the city and community, and to dispense a generous charity to all worthy enterprises. He is a charter member of the Portland Rotary Club, a member of the Round Table and Cumberland clubs, a member of the Portland Chamber of Commerce, member of the Portland Society of Arts, and also president of the Portland Boys' Club, thus giving him an opportunity to touch many young lives to their benefit. In

fraternal circles, he is a member of the Improved Order of Red Men. He is an enthusiastic devotee of outdoor life. His religious affiliation is with the Universalist church, in whose activities he enters with his characteristic zest and ability.

Mr. Hannaford was married September 20, 1892, to Sarah Parker, who, like himself, is a native of Cape Elizabeth, and who is a daughter of James and Mary Parker, representatives of old New England families, and both now deceased. Following their marriage they lived a short time in Cape Elizabeth and South Portland, then moved to Portland, and have since made it their home.

STEPHEN H. CROWLEY, assistant general manager of the Lewiston Bleachery & Dye Works, has worked his way upward in that company during thirty years, and is considered one of the substantial citizens of the city.

He was born in Lewiston, Maine, December 25, 1882, a son of John Crowley, a farmer and native of Halifax, Nova Scotia, and of Bridget (Deveney) Crowley, born in Washington, District of Columbia. His education was acquired in the elementary public schools of Lewiston, after which he went to work in the mills of the Lewiston Bleachery, in 1898. He worked in every department of the plant and in the offices, reached the grade of foreman and then of manager of the manufacturing office. He was then promoted to be superintendent, which he retained for six years. For about three years he made all purchases for the company. In 1922 he was appointed assistant general manager, a post he still holds. The company bleaches and dyes cotton goods. He is also a director in the Lewiston Bleachery and Dye Works. In politics he is a Republican, in religion a communicant of St. Patrick's Roman Catholic Church of Lewiston. He is a member of the Chamber of Commerce, the Knights of Columbus, and the Foresters of America.

Mr. Crowley married, in Lewiston, Maine, October 12, 1902, Lucy F. Collins, born in Lowell, Massachusetts, June 23, 1883, daughter of James Collins, a native of Lewiston, and of Katherine (O'Day) Collins, born in Ireland. They are the parents of seven children: Olive M., Mary Edith, Lucy P., Katherine, Elizabeth A., Helen, and Stephen.

GEORGE WASHINGTON MERRILL—Identified with several lines of successful business enterprises in Augusta, Maine, George Washington Merrill is among those who have been established in mercantile enterprises here for many years and have taken an important part in the growth and prosperity of the city. He is the son of Paul and Rebecca M. (Lee) Merrill, and his father was well known here as a practicing physician in the times when automobiles and telephones were unknown as conveniences for physicians and their patients.

George Washington Merrill was born in Augusta, Maine, October 2, 1864. He completed his school education with the grammar school and then set about to learn the printing business. For a time, he was employed in the office of "The Maine Farmer" and here, learning the trade of a printer he worked until 1898. In that year, Mr. Merrill became interested in the insurance business and established an agency of general insurance, which he still continues to manage. In 1914, he opened a stationery store which he has carried on with success, and in addition to this, Mr. Merrill conducts the Augusta Flower Shop, and operates a picture-finishing business. He is also a member of several fraternal organizations, being a Past Noble Grand in Asylum Lodge, No. 70, Independent Order of Odd Fellows, and is one of the trustees of this lodge at the present time. He is a Past Exalted Ruler of Augusta Lodge, No. 964, Benevolent and Protective Order of Elks, and is also a trustee of this lodge. He is a member of the Free and Accepted Masons and of the Knights of Pythias, and of the Elks' Club.

George Washington Merrill married (first) Helen Annette Couch, September 14, 1886, who died in 1895. They had five children: 1. Sara Helen, born June 30, 1888. 2. Harold Couch, born June 5, 1890 (deceased). 3. Paul Bemouth, born February 7, 1892. 4-5. Henry Madgett and Loring Crosby (deceased) (twins), born April 29, 1895. On June 10, 1908, George Washington Merrill married (second) Eunice Bangs Merrill.

LUCIUS D. BARROWS—Since leaving college, Lucius D. Barrows has been identified with the national and State highway departments, in various capacities, and in 1913 he was made assistant engineer of the State Highway Commission, which office he has continued to hold to the present time (1928). Mr. Barrows is an expert in his field and is rendering most efficient service to the public, especially to the traveling public. His offices are in the State House at Augusta.

Lucius D. Barrows was born in Dover Foxcroft, Maine, August 12, 1885, son of Fred D. Barrows, a printer, of Dover-Foxcroft, Maine, who was born in Guilford, Maine, May 6, 1854, and of Lulu (Dwelley) Barrows, a native of Boston, now deceased. After attending the public schools, Mr. Barrows prepared for college in Foxcroft Academy, from which he was graduated with the class of 1903, and then became a student in the University of Maine, at Orono, Maine, where he completed his course with graduation in 1907, receiving at that time the degree of Bachelor of Science. Soon after graduation he accepted a position in the United States Government office of public roads, at Washington, District of Columbia, where he remained from 1907 to 1910. In 1910 he became identified with the Maine State Highway Department, with his office at Augusta, serving as clerk. In 1911 he was made assistant State highway commissioner, which position he filled until 1913, when he was appointed to his present responsible position as assistant engineer of the State Highway Commission. Summer tourists in the State of Maine are often amazed at the improvements which have been made in the course of a year, and as year after year passes the great expanses of territory in this State are being made more and more accessible to motor vehicles. Macadam and asphalt roads are steadily replacing the old dirt roads, while the old poor dirt roads are being transformed into good dirt roads pending the time when they, too, may receive the transforming asphalt or macadam. In his political sympathies Mr. Barrow is a Republican. He is a member of the Maine Association of Engineers, and, fraternally, is identified with Sigma Alpha Epsilon College Fraternity, and with Augusta Lodge, Free and Accepted

Masons. His religious affiliation is with the Baptist church.

Lucius D. Barrows was married, in Readfield, Maine, September 13, 1913, to Blanche A. Gordon, who was born in Readfield, Maine, May 20, 1889, daughter of Nelson D., a native of Readfield, and of Mary H. (Henry) Gordon, who was born in Beverly, New Jersey.

RALPH WARDLAW CROCKETT—Descended from a distinguished line of ancestors, possessed of a finished education, acquired in college and university, a legal practitioner of established reputation, and a man of attractive personality, Ralph Wardlaw Crockett, of Lewiston, is one of the high lights of his profession and maintains an unassailable position at the bar and in the life of the community.

He was born in Lewiston, April 7, 1869, a son of George W. and Hannah B. (Sanborn) Crockett, and received his elementary scholastic training in the public schools of this city. He then attended Amherst College and received the degree of Bachelor of Arts upon his graduation therefrom in 1891. Three years later he was given the degree of Master of Arts from the same institution, following which he went to Boston University Law School, from which he was graduated in 1894 with the degree of Bachelor of Laws. In 1893 he was admitted to the bar and soon began the practice of law in the firm of Noble & Crockett, the firm continuing until the death of Mr. Noble in 1927. Since that time he has practiced independently. In 1909 he was admitted to practice before the Supreme Court of the United States. He is a member of the Maine State Bar Association, and was city solicitor of Lewiston from 1894 until 1897. He was a member of the School Board of this city from 1905 until 1909, whereon he served as its president in 1905-06. From 1917 until 1920 he was chairman of the Lewiston Police Commission and from 1920 to 1928 judge of the Lewiston Municipal Court. He holds the highest degree of Masonry—the thirty-third—and is affiliated with all grades of that order. He is a Republican in politics, and a member of the Congregational church.

Ralph W. Crockett married, November 27, 1912, Celia M. Choate, of Essex, Massachusetts, granddaughter of Rufus Choate. Their children are: Elisabeth C., and John S.

MERRILL SELDEN FREDERICK GREENE, M. D.—Although but a few years in the active practice of medicine, Merrill Selden Frederick Greene, of Lewiston, has had an unusually varied and profitable experience in hospital work in several States other than Maine prior to coming here to make his permanent location. Young men of his attainments and sound medical education are not so numerous as to give anxiety to the older practitioners, who have given to Dr. Greene a welcome and a whole-hearted coöperation. Endowed with a pleasing personality and equipped with a broad medical and scientific education, it is not unlikely that he will attain the highest reaches of his profession.

He was born in Athens, Maine, July 17, 1900, a son of Merrill G. Greene, a merchant of that town, and Myrtie Edna (Bush) Greene, a native of Athens. He attained his early education in the Athens public schools and was graduated from Somerset Academy with the class of 1916. He then attended Colby College and was graduated four years later with the degree of Bachelor of Science. This was followed by attendance at Tufts College, where he took special courses in chemistry. He then went to the Medical School of Harvard University, from which he was graduated and received his degree of Doctor of Medicine in 1924. During the remainder of that year and the following he was an interne in the Bridgeport Hospital, Bridgeport, Connecticut, and in 1925 and 1926 served as such in the Harper Hospital, Detroit, Michigan, and in the Children's Hospital of Michigan, in the same city. In 1926 and 1927 he was on the staff as resident physician at the hospital of the University of Michigan, Ann Arbor. Leaving that post, he came to Lewiston, where he established himself in general practice at No. 384 Main Street. Here, he is a member of the staff of the Central Maine General Hospital. During the participation of the United States in the World War, he was a student in the Army Medical Training Corps. He is a member of Keystone Lodge, No. 80, Order of Free and Accepted Masons; the Eastern Star; Modern Woodmen of America; American Legion; the American Medical Association; the State and the County Medical associations; and of the Grange, Patrons of Husbandry. His college fraternity is Lambda Chi Alpha. He is a member of the Pine Street Congregational Church of Lewiston.

Dr. Greene married, in Yarmouth, Maine, September 3, 1927, Harriet Lawrence Sweetser, daughter of William G. Sweetser, of Yarmouth.

DANIEL JOSEPH CONLEY—In his veins the sturdy blood of the Gaelic race, although he is of the second generation of his family having their nativity on American soil, Daniel Joseph Conley, of Lewiston, has long made himself one of our most progressive citizens. In large measure he possesses a delightful combination of Irish traditional courage and industry, associated with the vigorous enterprise of the pioneers of his and other races that founded civilization upon the American Continent. His is an estimable citizenship that takes a pride in all that is vital to the progress of the community and the maintenance of sound government, because of which he is held in the highest esteem by his fellows.

Daniel Joseph Conley was born in Lewiston, Maine, October 5, 1891, a son of Daniel J. Conley, also born in Lewiston, and Delia (Lyons) Conley, a native of Chatham, New Brunswick, Canada. The grandfather of the present Daniel Joseph was Daniel, born in County Cork, Ireland, in 1815, who emigrated to America when a young man and settled in Lewiston with his wife, whom he had married in Ireland. She was Mary Lucy Conley and they were among the first settlers of this region. He went to work in the Continental Mill and worked there for more than fifty-five years. He also was engaged in the construction of the Lewiston Canal and helped in building all the railroads that now operate about this section. He and his wife were the parents of fourteen children. Daniel Conley, Jr., was born August 18, 1856, at Lewiston, and lived here until his death, July 20, 1913. He was a farmer, whose widow for many years has been known as one of the fashionable modistes of Lewiston. She and her husband

were the parents of six children, of whom Daniel Joseph is the fourth.

The early ambition of Daniel Joseph Conley was to become an artist and, after his completion, in Lewiston, of the elementary school work and his graduation from high school, he went to Boston, where he studied art. Before that training he had painted at least one picture of merit, his "Madonna and Child," executed when he was but eleven years of age, having attracted the attention of renowned artists. Art as a life-work, however, did not appeal to him as he grew in years and when he returned to Lewiston from his studies in Boston he purchased the undertaking business of A. E. McDonough which he conducts today, later having purchased the Colonel Drew Homestead, which was converted into one of Maine's finest funeral homes. Determined to possess every whit of knowledge that modern science demands of the mortician, he took the course at the New England Institute of Sanitary Science and Embalming, graduating therefrom in February, 1915, and receiving his State license as a qualified embalmer. His establishment is one of the most complete in the State, equipped with every modern device for the conduct of the work, while its proprietor is admittedly in the front rank of his profession. In politics he is Independent; in religion a Roman Catholic, having membership in St. Joseph's Church in Lewiston. He is a member of the Civitans' Club and the Country Club; Knights of Columbus, and of the New England Order of Protection.

HOWARD A. TEAGUE—For more than forty years Howard A. Teague has been one of the prominent and progressive citizens of Lewiston, Maine, where he has continuously conducted an undertaking business since 1894. It may be truthfully said of him that the interests of the citizens of Lewiston are the interests of himself, for the city holds no more devoted representative of its citizenry, no one more calculated to use every bit of moral strength he possesses to advance any cause that he believes to be for the advantage of the whole body politic. His life has been spent in devotion to the business in which he so long ago established himself, as well as to the promotion of other commercial enterprises through an exchange of ideas and experiences in the field of daily labor. Rewards have come to him from his fellow-citizens, who have recognized his ability and substantial character, while his friends are as numerous as his acquaintances. In short, he is one of the most outstanding members of the community in which he has lived all his life.

Mr. Teague was born in Lewiston, Maine, December 4, 1866, a son of Greenleaf Teague, of Turner, Maine, and of Rebecca (Symons) Teague, a native of Skowhegan, Maine. Howard A. Teague was educated in the public schools of Lewiston and was graduated from the Lewiston High School. He then learned the undertaking business under the direction of F. E. Crane, of Lewiston, with whom he was associated from 1887 to 1894, in which last-named year he established himself in independent business in Lewiston. He later received into partnership William Russell Harlow, in 1923, who continues to share the responsibilities of the business. He is a Republican in politics and served as Councilman during 1886 and 1887, also as Coroner of Androscoggin County. He is a thirty-second degree member of the Free and Accepted Masons, belonging to all bodies of that organization including Kora Temple, Ancient Arabic Order Nobles of the Mystic Shrine; belongs to the Independent Order of Odd Fellows, is Frank H. George, and Modern Woodmen of America, also holding membership in the Maine Undertakers' Association.

Mr. Teague married, in Lewiston, Maine, August 25, 1898, Carrie W. Cole, a native of Old Town, Maine, daughter of William, born in Old Town, and of Sarah (Wadleigh) Cole, born in Boston, Massachusetts.

FRANK H. COOPER—One of the most prominent figures in the governmental affairs of Belfast, Maine, is Frank H. Cooper, at present sheriff of Waldo County, former selectman and tax collector of Searsmont, Maine, and a vigorous figure in Republican politics of his town and county. Mr. Cooper is at present operating a large farm, in addition to his other interests. He established an automobile business in Belfast, which he disposed of a year later. Mr. Cooper was born in Searsmont, Maine, September 24, 1887, the son of George N. and Lucy (Jackson) Cooper, also natives of Maine. Mr. Cooper's father also was born in Searsmont and spent his life there, also running a farm and serving the town as selectman.

Frank H. Cooper attended the grammar and high schools in Searsmont, then came home to help his father run the farm. The routine of farm life began to pall, after a few years, and he became interested in business, deciding to venture into this field on his own responsibility; which he did for a time, opening an automobile agency in Belfast. In 1923 he closed his business and went to Waldoboro, where he remained three and a half years. When he was elected sheriff, he returned to the farm. Since that time he has, in addition to his official duties, been extensively engaged in farming and timbering.

Having been elected, like his father, a selectman of Searsmont, Mr. Cooper was honored further by the Republican party by election to the office of sheriff of Waldo County in 1926 and took the oath of office January 1, 1927. He is a prominent Mason, being identified with the Lodge, Chapter, Council and Commandery of that Order. He is also a member of the Independent Order of Odd Fellows.

Frank H. Cooper married Bertha A. Woodbury, daughter of Andrew J. and Emma (Cushman) Woodbury, in Searsmont, October 9, 1914. They have two children: 1. Lucy Emma, born April 22, 1916. 2. George Andrew, born July 3, 1925.

WILLIAM RUSSELL HARLOW—One of the very active young citizens of Lewiston, Maine, as well as a business man of constantly developing powers, William Russell Harlow is also possessed of an attractive personality and sympathetic nature that makes friends in abundance. In the commercial life of Lewiston there is room for such citizens, whose reward is ever commensurate with their earnest endeavors to perform their business, civic and other public duties on the plane of their best ability. There is no question that these attributes are a part of the physical and mental composition of this young man.

He was born in Portland, Maine, June 21, 1892, a son of Edward, of Portland, and Nellie (Patterson) Harlow, of Vincennes, Indiana. His father was a locomotive engineer, who left that occupation and conducted a prosperous restaurant business. The son was educated in the public schools of Portland and was graduated from the high school in that city. He then graduated from the New England Institute of Embalming, at Boston, Massachusetts, and in February, 1914, became associated with the undertaking establishment of James A. Martin & Son, in Portland. In September, 1923, he formed a partnership with Howard A. Teague in the same character of enterprise, locating in Lewiston, where the firm of Teague & Harlow now is engaged in business. He is a Republican in politics and served in the Army during the World War, enlisting in June, 1917, and being attached to the Medical Corps of the Infantry. He was honorably mustered out February 5, 1919. He is a member of Lewiston Post, No. 22, American Legion; of the Free and Accepted Masons; the Chapter, Royal Arch Masons; the Council, Royal and Select Masters; also of the Independent Order of Odd Fellows.

Mr. Harlow married, in Portland, Maine, April 15, 1919, Lulu M. Currier, of Minot, Maine, daughter of George W. Currier, native of Minot, and Julia (Brann) Currier, born in Dover, Maine.

EDWIN WENTWORTH ADAMS—One of the very essential factors in many modern industries is the application of chemistry to production, a science in which all the world of higher education is constantly contributing discoveries. In none of the industries in which it is used is it of more importance than in dyeing, where colors must be permanent in order to be of full value. This branch of science is the work that has been taken up by Edwin Wentworth Adams, superintendent for the Lewiston Bleachery and Dye Works, of Lewiston, Maine, one of the younger of the active citizens whose rise to fame in his profession will be as certain as may be his contribution to the commercial industries of our State and country.

Edwin Wentworth Adams was born in Jackson, Maine, August 13, 1895, a son of John and Annie (Wentworth) Adams. He was educated in the local public schools and at Edward Little High School, from which he was graduated. Later he attended the University of Maine and Bates College, being graduated from the last-named institution with the degree of Bachelor of Science, in 1919. He became associated with the Lewiston Bleachery & Dye Works as assistant chemist, being promoted to chemist in 1919, and serving in that capacity until 1925, when he was again promoted, this time to be superintendent of the company, a position he now holds. His college fraternity is Phi Beta Kappa. He belongs to the American Chemical Society, to the National Geographic Society and to the American Association of Textile Chemists and Colorists; the Rotary Club; Free and Accepted Masons,—various bodies, including the Commandery. His politics are Republican, his religion the Methodist Episcopal.

WILLIAM A. WEDGE—Identified with the box manufacturing industry in Maine since 1901, William A. Wedge, of Lewiston, has made an enviable reputation as a man of great business ability and

48   MAINE—A HISTORY

a citizen of commendable character. Operating on
a code of business ethics that invariably makes
friends of all customers, his establishment has ever
been regarded as one of the models in a section
largely devoted to manufacturing in its varying
forms. Beginning his business career in Massachusetts, he gradually enlarged the scene of his
activities, eventually coming to this State and establishing himself in what is now a factory conducted by his individual authority. He is a man
of pleasing urbanity, a citizen of intensive quality,
a business power of strength in binding together
the many units of local commercial enterprises. His
success has been measured only by the demand for
his output, steadily growing in usefulness as one
of the many vigorous wheels of progress, while
his personal friends are limited only by his acquaintances.
    He was born in Brookfield, Massachusetts, Jan-
uary 10, 1877, a son of Israel and Sophia (Harper)
Wedge, both natives of the Dominion of Canada,
who removed to Massachusetts, where the elder
Wedge was long engaged in the manufacture of
boxes, at East Brookfield. Their son was educated
in the public schools of North Brookfield and was
graduated from the high school of East Brookfield.
Following a period of instructive occupation, he became associated with the Isaac Prouty Company, of
Spencer, Massachusetts, manufacturers of box
shooks, as superintendent of the plant. This he retained until 1906, when he accepted a similar position with the Studley Box and Lumber Company.
He remained in that post until 1909, when he went
to the Howe Lumber Company, at Marlborough,
changing again to become associated with the G. H.
Spring Lumber Company, at Milford, New Hampshire, where he remained for eighteen months as
superintendent. From 1922 until 1926, he was associated with the Rubair Arsenalt Company in the
manufacture of box shooks, this concern becoming
Wedge & Arsenalt and, in 1926, again to be trans-
posed into the William A. Wedge Company, operated
exclusively by Mr. Wedge, who employs between
twenty-five and thirty hands at his plant. He is a
member of the Masonic Order, being affiliated with
the Blue Lodge and the Chapter, Royal Arch Masons. His church is the Roman Catholic.
    Mr. Wedge married, in East Brookfield, Massachu-
setts, in 1898, Amelia Bedore, of Montreal, Province
of Quebec, Dominion of Canada. They have one child:
Leland B., born in North Brookfield, Massachusetts, in 1900.

CHARLES S. LUGRIN—Identified with the
furniture business in Maine from early manhood,
Charles S. Lugrin has risen in his work step by
step until he now is assistant treasurer of the Lewiston store and treasurer of the one in Portland.
For more than thirty years he has been associated
with this company, which operates stores in Maine
at Rockland, Waterville, Lewiston and Portland, and
nine stores scattered throughout New England. Mr.
Lugrin's work has been such as to commend him
to his associates and their large clientele of patrons,
while his citizenship is of the highest character and
his fraternal and social affiliations appreciated sincerely.
    He was born in New York City, November 18,

1884, a son of George and Eva (Atherton) Lugrin,
both natives of Fredericton, New Brunswick, Dominion of Canada. His father was a printer, the son
being educated in New York City, where his father
was engaged at his trade.
    Following his graduation from high school, Charles
S. Lugrin followed various lines of work, eventually
coming to Maine in 1898, where he entered the employ of the Atherton Furniture Company, in Portland. That was his first and only connection in
the business, it fitting him so well that his rise was
continuous and in direct ratio with the years of his
service. The four Maine stores employ an average
of one hundred and fifteen people, Le Barron Atherton being president of the corporation, with Charles
S. Lugrin in the positions noted. He is Independent
in politics and belongs to the Rotary Club, the Chamber of Commerce and the Martindale Country Club,
and is affiliated with the Commandery, Knights
Templar, and other bodies of the Free and Accepted
Masons.
    Mr. Lugrin married, in Lewiston, Maine, May 5,
1914, Grace E. Hammond, daughter of George Hammond, of Bristol, New Hampshire. They have one
child: Marjorie, born in Lewiston, July 1, 1925.

LACEY L. CADWALLADER—Associated with
the brick manufacturing and contracting house of
Horace Purinton Company, of Waterville, since
1923, Lacey L. Cadwallader has established himself
here additionally in real estate and insurance, a welcome addition to the commercial life of the town.
    He was born in Philadelphia, Pennsylvania, De-
cember 14, 1876, and educated in the public schools
there, graduating from high school. His father was
William Cadwallader, a carpenter, born in Phila-
delphia; his mother, Esther (Shetzlina) Cadwallader.
Mr. Cadwallader is a Republican in politics and a
City Councilman of Waterville. He belongs to the
Order of Free and Accepted Masons, Waterville
Lodge, No. 33, is a member of the Masonic Club of
Waterville, and of the Maine State Real Estate
Board. His church is the Baptist.
    Lacey L. Cadwallader married, in Philadelphia,
Pennsylvania, November 27, 1901, Carrie Preston,
a native of Pittsburgh, Pennsylvania, daughter of
John B. and Annie (Zane) Preston, of Pennsylvania
and Maryland, respectively. The children of the
union are: 1. William Preston, born in Philadelphia.
2. Jean, born in Philadelphia. 3. Mary, born in Salt
Lake City, Utah.

IRA LELAND BELYEA—Until a little more
than twenty years ago the drygoods and grocery
businesses were the occupation of Ira Leland Belyea,
lately become one of the leading members of the commercial family of Waterville. His climb has been
steady, as has been the growth of the automobile
industry, with which he is now solely associated.
Of popular personality and engaged qualities, his
advance has been due to a combination of unflagging
industry and a keen mentality. Injuring none and
with a desire to assist in all matters that affect the
business and social life of the community, his citizenship is sound, his continued success assured.
    Ira Leland Belyea was born in Saint Johns, New
Brunswick, Canada, November 18, 1878. His father was James Alexander Belyea, a sea captain

and a native of New Brunswick, as was his wife, Cecelia J. (Watson) Belyea. Ira L. Belyea received his education in the public schools of Bangor, Maine, and the Nichols Latin School, at Lewiston. Upon concluding his studies he entered the employ of the wholesale drygoods house of Milliken, Cousins & Short, of Portland, remaining with them until 1902, when he entered the employ of Twitchell, Champlin & Company, of Portland, wholesale grocers. He worked in the home office for two years and then became a salesman, in which occupation he continued until 1906, when the automobile business suggested a better opportunity and he established himself in that line in Waterville, under the name of the Waterville Motor Company, remaining in that company until 1913, when the Hudson-Essex Motors, Incorporated, of Waterville, was organized. Associated with him in this corporation are George Boyden, Errol Taylor, Irwin Gray, and Maynard Brown. In politics he is a Republican, in religion his church is the Waterville Congregational. He is a member of the Maine Automobile Dealers' Association, of which he was formerly secretary. He belongs to the Lodge, Free and Accepted Masons; to the Commandery, Knights Templar; and the Chapter, Royal Arch Masons; also to the Masonic Club and the Rotary Club.

Ira L. Belyea married, in Winslow, Maine, April 17, 1912, Helen Bassett, of Winslow, daughter of Alden and Katherine (Hayden) Bassett, both natives of Winslow. They have two children: 1. Alden Bassett, born December 25, 1914. 2. Helen, born November 22, 1919.

LEON WENTWORTH DRESSER, member of the well-known firm of Millett, Fish & Dresser, public accountants, of Portland, was born July 15, 1893, at Scarboro, Maine. He is a son of Wilber F. and Sarah E. (MacLaughlin) Dresser, both of whom were born in this State.

Leon Wentworth Dresser received his early education in the public schools of the community in which he was born, and attended the South Portland High School, graduating from there with the class of 1911. Immediately thereafter he entered the employ of the Chapman National Bank, an institution with which he remained, in various capacities, for more than eight years. He then became a public accountant, and later formed the organization of Millett & Dresser in 1922. In 1925, this firm became Millett, Fish & Dresser, and it is under this style that it is now operating, rated as one of the leading groups of public accountants in Portland. Mr. Dresser has been especially active in the commercial advancement of Portland, and he is a valued member of the Portland Chamber of Commerce. He is also a member of the Fish and Game Association of Maine; and he is fraternally affiliated with Hiram Lodge, No. 180, Free and Accepted Masons; Hiram Chapter, No. 70, Royal Arch Masons; the Council, Royal and Select Masters; the Consistory, Ancient Accepted Scottish Rite; St. Albans Commandery, No. 8, Knights Templar; Kora Temple, Ancient Arabic Order Nobles of the Mystic Shrine; the Benevolent and Protective Order of Elks; and he is also a member of the Willowdale Country Club.

Leon Wentworth Dresser married, June 14, 1916, at South Portland, Maine, Phyllis H. Trefethen, a daughter of Charles N. and Minnie (Ramsdell) Tre-

fethen. Mr. and Mrs. Dresser are the parents of one son, Richard W. He and his family maintain their residence in South Portland.

RICHARD MELVIN MILLETT, well-known citizen of Portland, Maine, and a member of the firm of Millett, Fish & Dresser, public accountants, of Portland, was born November 22, 1898, at South Paris, Maine. He is a son of James M. and Hattie (Clifford) Millett, both of whom are natives of this State.

Richard Melvin Millett received his early education in the public schools of the community in which he was born, and later attended South Paris High School, graduating from there with the class of 1914. He attended Boston University, graduating with the class of 1922. After graduating from high school, Mr. Millett entered the employ of the South Paris Trust Company, where he remained for about three years, before he resign to enroll at Boston University. Following his studies at that school, he entered the treasurer's office of Boston University, and there remained for a year, at the expiration of which he resigned to become a member of the firm of Millett and Dresser, at Portland, Maine. The name of this organization has since been changed to Millett, Fish & Dresser. With this concern he has since remained. In November, 1926, Mr. Millett passed the Certified Public Accountants examination in Maine, this being the test required by the American Institute of Accountants.

Mr. Millett is a member of the Maine Board of Accountancy, and he is also identified with the Maine State Society of Certified Public Accountants, the American Society of Certified Public Accountants and the National Association of Certified Public Accountants. He has been active in club and social life, and is affiliated with the Alpha Kappa Psi College Fraternity (Boston University), Paris Lodge, No. 94, Free and Accepted Masons; Greenleaf Chapter, No. 12, Royal Arch Masons; the Council, Royal and Select Masters; St. Albans Commandery, No. 8, Knights Templar; Kora Temple, Ancient Arabic Order Nobles of the Mystic Shrine; Maine Consistory, Sublime Princes of the Royal Secret, thirty-second degree; and he holds membership in the Portland Civitan Club, Willowdale Country Club, and the Cumberland County Fish and Game Association.

Richard Melvin Millett married, June 12, 1922, at South Paris, Maine, Marion Amo Clark, a daughter of Arthur E. and Francilla (Gerry) Clark. Mr. and Mrs. Millett are the parents of a son and a daughter: 1. Robert Hall, born October 29, 1923. 2. Dorothea, born July 18, 1925. Mr. Millett and his family maintain their residence at No. 16 Richards Street, South Portland, and they attend the Woodfords Congregational Church.

WALTER J. GLIDDEN—The manager of one of the principal factories in Belfast, Maine, and a recognized authority on the manufacture of shoes is Walter J. Glidden, superintendent of the Hazzard Shoe Company's plant and an active member of the American Legion Club in Belfast. Although not a native of Maine, Mr. Glidden has come to be regarded almost as a native son by his adopted city. He was born in Natick, Massachusetts, July 5, 1888, the son of Lester Leland Glidden and Annie Louise

(Bates) Glidden. He was educated in the public and high schools of his native town and upon graduation, was at times employed by several concerns as a clerk. He first became interested in the manufacture of shoes in 1908, when he became field man for Goodyear Welt Company. Later, he entered the employ of a shoe factory in Marlboro, Massachusetts, where he remained five years, and left there for employment in the Leonard-Stevens shoe factory in Belfast, Maine, where he stayed for six months. The Norway Shoe Company, learning of his increasing familiarity with the details of shoe manufacture, offered him an opportunity in its factory, which he accepted, and continued in its employ for the next four years. He came to the Hazzard Shoe Company in Belfast, in September, 1926, as the manager of the company's factory, and has remained in that position ever since.

Mr. Glidden has always been an Independent in politics. He holds membership in the Blue Lodge, Free and Accepted Masons; Norway Chapter, Royal Arch Masons; the Council, Royal and Select Masters; the Commandery, Knights Templar; the Temple, Ancient Arabic Order Nobles of the Mystic Shrine, and the Shrine Club. He is enrolled with the Norway American Legion Club, and is a communicant of the Unitarian church.

Walter J. Glidden married Anna R. MacDonald, daughter of James and Mary (Leonard) MacDonald, of Athol, Massachusetts, February 20, 1913, at Brattleboro, Vermont. They have two children: 1. Phyllis Muriel, born August 18, 1915. 2. Walter Lester, born November 3, 1916.

WALTER BARKER PILLSBURY—A substantial business man and leading citizen of Rumford, Maine, is Walter Barker Pillsbury, hardware merchant, of the firm of Clough and Pillsbury. For more than a decade this company has taken a prominent position in that section and has given the best of service to the community because of its complete assortment of commodities and the efficiency and integrity of its business principles. Mr. Pillsbury was born at Biddeford, Maine, August 8, 1882, son of Chester and Lizzie A. (Rines) Pillsbury. The father, a machinist, was born in Shapleigh, the mother, in Augusta, Maine. A sound education was accorded the son, who attended the Biddeford public schools and graduated from high school in 1900.

His business career began with the American Express Company at Biddeford, where Mr. Pillsbury was employed. From 1900 to 1913 he worked at various occupations and in various towns, although he spent more time in Portland, Maine, than elsewhere. In 1913 he became associated with Talbot, Brooks & Ayer, hardware merchants, in Portland, and thus got his start in the direction of the hardware trade and his experience in a line he determined to follow. After two years of that association, Mr. Pillsbury joined William Allen Clough in forming the hardware firm of Clough and Pillsbury in Rumford, Maine. They deal in a wide variety of commodities, (including hardware, cutlery, stoves, tinware, paints, oils and varnishes, sporting goods and fishing tackle, seeds and garden tools. Their standards are high, both in merchandise and service, and they have met with merited success. Mr. Pillsbury belongs to the Rumford Business and

Professional Men's Association, and to the Republican party. His fraternal affiliations are with Blazing Star Lodge, Free and Accepted Masons, and Strathglass Commandery, Knights Templar. He is a communicant of the Universalist church.

As Skowhegan, Maine, March 3, 1903, Walter Barker Pillsbury married Ethel L. Clough, born in that town, March 4, 1884, daughter of William A. Clough. They have a son, Walter B. Pillsbury, Jr., born in Portland, Maine, November 27, 1904.

JOHN CARROLL MARBLE—The genial and capable proprietor of one of the best-known and most popular hotels in that section is John Carroll Marble, of Dixfield, Maine, owner of Hotel Stanley, which has achieved an excellent reputation under his management. He is the son of William Smith and Leonora (Whittier) Marble, the former of whom was born in Dixfield, and the latter in Mount Vernon, Maine. The father, engaged throughout his prosperous career in the hotel business, died in April, 1924. He was a member of the Free and Accepted Masons, and various of its bodies including the Chapter, Royal Arch Masons; the Commandery, Knights Templar; and the Temple, Ancient Arabic Order Nobles of the Mystic Shrine. His wife died in 1909.

John Carroll Marble was born in Rangeley, Maine, March 24, 1895, and educated in the public schools of that town and Portland, Maine, graduating from Portland High School. He was employed from 1915 to 1917 by the Packard Auto Company of Boston, Massachusetts, and found his business career interrupted by his patriotic participation in the World War. He enlisted in the United States Army in April, 1917, in Company D, One Hundred and First Engineers, Twenty-sixth Division, and saw active service with the American Expeditionary Forces in the Aisne-Marne offensive, the St. Mihiel Sector, and the Meuse-Argonne offensive. In famous Belleau Woods Mr. Marble was wounded. He was mustered out of service in April, 1919, after two years of devotion to his country's cause. Returning then to Maine, he established himself in the hotel business at Dixfield. His hotel, the Stanley, has twenty-five rooms, is charmingly furnished and admirably run, catering to year-round guests. Mr. Marble belongs to Lyman K. Swazey Post No. 100, American Legion, and to King Hiram Lodge, Free and Accepted Masons. He is a member of the Congregational church.

In Cambridge, Massachusetts, June 2, 1917, John Carroll Marble married Roselle Harlow, born in Dixfield, Maine, April 13, 1894, daughter of John S. and Agnes (Doe) Harlow. Her father was a native of Dixfield, her mother of South Paris. Children: John C. Marble, Jr., born in Jamaica Plain, Massachusetts, June 16, 1918; and Mary Elizabeth, born in the same place, April 21, 1922.

JAMESON LEE FINNEY—For more than ten years Jameson Lee Finney has been the efficient superintendent of the Dixfield branch of the Rumford Falls Light & Water Company, and in that capacity he has rendered the community a distinct service. Mr. Finney has had a long experience in the business of giving light to the public, both on the construction end and in other departments, and he is giving to his present connection the full benefit of the experience gained in other localities.

Jameson Lee Finney was born in Bethel, Maine, March 2, 1884, son of William E., a native of St. Louis, Missouri, now deceased, who was engaged in the insurance and farm brokerage business, and was a member of the Masonic Order, and of Ava (Young) Finney, who was born in Bethel, Maine, also deceased. Mr. Finney received his education in Gould's Academy, and in the Norway High School, from which he was graduated with the class of 1902, and then became identified with the Oxford Light Company, at Norway, Maine. This connection he maintained during the year 1902-03, and then entered the employ of the Lewiston & Auburn Electric Light Company, of Lewiston, Maine, where he continued for eight years, from 1903 to 1911. During the following year, 1911-12, he was engaged in building the plant of the Bethel Electric Company, and in 1912 he engaged in the general contracting business for himself in Bethel. He continued his own business enterprise until 1914, and then associated himself with the Oxford Light Company, at Norway, Maine, where he remained until 1917, when he was made superintendent of the Dixfield branch of the Rumford Falls Light & Water Company, which position he was filling in 1928. Mr. Finney is one of the many progressive citizens who regard personal fitness for office as more important than party affiliations, and he casts his vote accordingly. He was a member of the Maine National Guard from 1902 to 1917, and served in both the infantry and artillery, also as a member of the Hospital Corps. Fraternally, he is identified with Bethel Lodge, No. 97, Free and Accepted Masons; with the Chapter, Royal Arch Masons; and with the Council, Royal and Select Masters; also with Kora Temple, Ancient Arabic Order Nobles of the Mystic Shrine. His religious affiliation is with the Union Congregational church.

Jameson Lee Finney was married, in Auburn, Maine, March 24, 1904, to Maude Allen, who was born in Buckfield, Maine, daughter of Allen and Francilia (Foster) Allen.

DUNCAN ROSS CAMPBELL—Descendant of expert lumbermen who for generations, both in the United States and Canada, have chosen the practical business of the lumber dealer and surveyor for their vocation, Ducan Ross Campbell, for a considerable period a surveyor and estimator of timberlands in the West, has entered upon a similar field of operations in Maine, a State where lumbering has always been one of the staple industries. Here he is a dealer in lumber and timberlands. A veteran of the World War, Mr. Campbell was in the service overseas with the vast body of Engineers, whose activities are recorded as among the leading events of that conflict. His grandfather, Duncan Campbell, who was born in Scotland, was also engaged in lumbering, and was a veteran of the Civil War; his parents were John Charles Campbell, born in Durham, Ontario, Canada, a lumberman and miner; and Mary Jane (Shepard) Campbell, a native of Holland Centre, Ontario.

Duncan Ross Campbell was born December 25, 1889, at Cloquet, Minnesota, and receiving his education in the public schools, he was graduated at the high school in 1908. Pursuing a college course,

he was also graduated at the University of Minnesota in 1913, with the degree of Bachelor of Arts. That year he began to operate in the lumber business, under his own name, at Cloquet. Continuing in the work of surveying and making estimates of timber, he made an increasing success therein to the time of his enlistment in the World War in 1917, resuming his logging and lumbering interests as formerly in the West, from 1919 to 1925. In 1925, Mr. Campbell established his present business at Dixfield. His political interests are those of the Republican party, though he has never at any time sought public office.

With the Three Hundred and Thirteenth Engineers in the Eighty-eighth Division, Mr. Campbell shared in the events of the World War, his enlistment taking place in August, 1917, and with the American Expeditionary Forces he served ten months overseas, receiving his discharge in June, 1919. He is a college fraternity man, a member of Beta Theta Pi. His religious faith is that of the Congregational church.

LUTHER M. IRISH—For more than a half century, the Irish Brothers Company, the manufacturing of die blocks, and Buckfield, have been practically synonymous both in the mind of the trade and upon a high plane of specific industry, the people, the product and the place having demonstrated such a combination of merit as might be secured in no other section of the State. Luther M. Irish is the efficient manager of two old consolidated partnerships that have become one in a widely recognized leadership in whatsoever factories throughout the country die blocks are in use. Skilled in his specialty, and master of its high-class manufacturing methods, Mr. Irish is an authority in this department of the producing world.

Luther M. Irish was born May 27, 1879, at Hartford, Maine, a son of Horace A. Irish, manufacturer of die blocks, also a native of Hartford, and Virginia A. (Mason) Irish, who was born in Frederick, Maryland. After attending the Buckfield grammar and high schools, Mr. Irish was graduated at Gray Business College, and he at once entered into business in the long-established concern that bears the family name.

The Irish Brothers Company, manufacturers of die blocks, is a noted firm that was organized as C. M. and H. A. Irish, at Buckfield, about 1875, for the production of die blocks and cutting boards, a concern that received its papers of incorporation as at present in 1911. In 1904 a partnership had been consummated with C. M. Irish, H. A. Irish, and H. H. Wardell and L. M. Irish; when the Cushman Mill at West Paris was bought, they consolidating in 1911, and with headquarters at Buckfield, and employing on an average of twenty people throughout the year. The concern is situated in the heart of the best rock maple growth in the United States, and having every facility for selecting the best lumber for their particular use, they produce kiln-dried stock that holds no secondary place in the market.

In the political field, Mr. Irish is a Republican, voting the ticket of that party, but never having sought public office. Fraternally, he is affiliated with Evening Star Lodge, Free and Accepted Masons, at Buckfield, and with the Independent Order of

Odd Fellows. He attends the Universalist church. Luther M. Irish married, November 30, 1904, at Buckfield, Elizabeth H. Withington, daughter of Charles C. Withington, born at Portland, Maine, and Hattie (Quincy) Withington, a native of Bridgeton. They have one daughter, Elizabeth V., born September 24, 1906, at West Paris.

CHARLES C. WITHINGTON—An old industry and a substantial one that has aided in making Buckfield foremost among townships that manufacture some of the most useful articles in the world, is that of Charles C. Withington, expert brush manufacturer, who has followed in his father's footsteps in making this plant one of ever-increasing value to special industry. Mr. Withington, whether in the direction of the affairs of his factory, or in his interests in civic and community welfare, has given his best to his native town, and he has a host of friends throughout the State who appreciate the thoroughnes of his lifework, and his fine qualities in citizenship and in workmanship.

Charles C. Withington, a son of Charles Withington, manufacturer, and a native of Portland, and Ursula (Thombes) Withington, a native of Gorham, was born August 18, 1857, at Buckfield, and he attended the public schools here and at Auburn. From the first he has given his undivided attention to continuing the success of the manufactory established by his father at Buckfield, and today he is one of the foremost men in the State engaged in his specialty. The firm of C. Withington & Sons, manufacturers of brushes, was established and organized in 1855 by Charles Withington, at Buckfield; he was a native of Portland, but he accepted here an unusual oportunity for success, and the concern has been operating continuously to the present. Charles C. Withington, the son, started in to work for his father, and with his brother, Frank P. Withington, after leaving school, in 1872, and since the death of his brother, in October, 1922, he has continued along in the same line, employing an average of fifteen people. Independent in his political convictions, Mr. Withington thus votes at the polls for his chosen candidates to office.

In fraternal matters, Mr. Withington is affiliated with Evening Star Lodge, Free and Accepted Masons; with the Commandery, Knights Templar; and with the Temple, Ancient Arabic Order Nobles of the Mystic Shrine. He is also a member of the Independent Order of Odd Fellows, a Past Noble Grand. His religious faith is that of the Universalist church.

Charles C. Withington married, November 9, 1880, at North Conway, New Hampshire, Hattie Quincy, who was born at Bridgton, a daughter of William and Sarah (Dodge) Quincy. Their children: Elizabeth, and Clara B., both born in Buckfield.

JOHN FRANK ELLINGWOOD—One of the successful manufacturers of Buckfield, Maine, is John Frank Ellingwood, of the Ellingwood Novelty Company, Incorporated. This concern is engaged in the manufacture of brush blocks and duster handles, and employs about twenty people.

John Frank Ellingwood was born in Upton, Maine, June 15, 1878, son of Samuel B. Ellingwood, a native of Paris, Maine, who is engaged in the lumbering business, and of Angelia (Cash) Ellingwood, who

was born in Casco, Maine. Mr. Ellingwood received his education in the public schools of West Paris, Maine, and then entered the employ of L. M. Man & Son, at West Paris, manufacturers of clothes-pins. He continued this connection for a period of four years, from 1893 to 1897, and then made a change, entering the employ of the West Paris Creamery, where he remained for a year. Being of a versatile turn of mind, and not yet having found the work which seemed to be his, he next engaged in carpenter work, which he continued for several years. In 1904 he entered the employ of Irish Brothers, manufacturers of die blocks, and this connection he maintained until 1910. In that year he became associated with Lewis M. Irish, of Rumford, Maine, and Luther M. Irish, of Buckfield, Maine, manufacturers of brush blocks and duster handles, and in 1914 this concern was incorporated under the name of the Ellingwood Novelty Company, Incorporated, under which name it has continued to the present time (1928). The output of the establishment has steadily grown until at the present time the services of twenty employees are necessary to meet the demand for the products manufactured. Mr. Ellingwood is a Republican in his political sympathies. Fraternally, he is identified with the Independent Order of Odd Fellows, and with the Order of Rebekah, of Buckfield; also with the Sons of Veterans of Buckfield, and his religious affiliation is with the Universalist church.

John Frank Ellingwood was married, in Buckfield, Maine, to Jennie A. Record, who was born in Turner, Maine, daughter of William and Harriet (Mitchell) Record, the last-mentioned of whom was born in Turner, Maine.

HARRY S. BOYD—The careers of men who have started in business at the bottom of the ladder and have reached the top through their energy and application are an inspiration to the youth of today. Of these men, Harry S. Boyd, cashier of the Chapman National Bank of Portland, stands out prominently as a man who has advanced to his present position by reason of his diligence and thoroughness in every branch of his work, having started with this bank as a messenger while attending high school. Mr. Boyd was born in Portland, August 3, 1877, son of James H. Boyd, who is deceased, and Jennie F. (Lane) Boyd, who resides in Portland. James H. Boyd was for many years engaged in the stevedore and rigging business.

Harry S. Boyd was educated in the public schools of Portland, and while attending high school acted as messenger for the bank. After finishing his course, he entered the bank with which he since has remained, progressing steadily and occupying almost every position in that institution until May 15, 1922, when he was promoted to his present office of cashier. Mr. Boyd is a prominent figure in the financial life of the city and was treasurer for the State of Maine Near East Relief Campaign. He was for many years on the executive committee of the old Portland Bank Men's Association; served as its secretary, and was its vice-president when the organization ceased to exist. He helped organize and was first president of the Portland Chapter of the American Institute of Banking. At the present time he is serving as treasurer of the Portland Bank Officers' Association, and is a member of the Maine Bankers'

Association. He is also treasurer of the National Plant and Fruit Guild. Active in the Chamber of Commerce, he was for four years a member of its board of managers, and is now serving on that body's educational committee, as chairman. In addition to the many positions of trust previously mentioned, Mr. Boyd serves as secretary to the Knights of the Round Table, and is a member of the Portland Club, the Economic Club, Lions Club, Maine Historical Society, and Maine Charitable and Mechanical Society. He devotes freely of his time to fraternal and club proceedings, and is known throughout the State for his zeal in behalf of public welfare.

He is a member of all the Masonic bodies, holding the thirty-second degree, and including the Temple, Ancient Arabic Order Nobles of the Mystic Shrine; he is Past Master of Ancient Landmark Lodge; Past President of Past Masters' Association of the Seventeenth Masonic District; Senior Warden of Dunlap Chapter, Rose Croix; Past Patron of the Chapter, Order of the Eastern Star; treasurer of the Charity and Home funds of the Grand Chapter of the State of Maine; organizer and director of the Masonic Temple Historical and Memorial Association; one of the organizers and a director of the Masonic Club of Portland. He is also a trustee of Laconia Lodge, Independent Order of Odd Fellows. In politics, he is a Republican, although he has never sought office. In religious circles, Mr. Boyd is a prominent member of the Congress Square Universalist Church, wherein he was for many years clerk of the church parish, and also is treasurer of the Congress Square Men's Club, and assistant superintendent of the Sunday school.

Harry S. Boyd married, in Portland, April 25, 1905, Alice S. Boyd.

JOSEPH CHANDLER HAM—Inheriting his inclination for his profession, as a pharmacist, and qualified by special training and preparation, as well as by long experience, to engage with success in his life-work, Joseph Chandler Ham continues that business at the landmark established by his father at Livermore Falls, maintaining its traditions of accuracy and of skill in all branches of the druggist's activities. In both the religious and social life of Livermore Falls, Mr. Ham is constructive in membership and in official capacity. He is a son of Joseph Gardner Ham, a druggist, who was born in Portland, member of the Chapter, Royal Arch Masons, and of Mary Emma Ham, a native of Portland, Maine.

Joseph Chandler Ham was born January 20, 1876, at Livermore Falls, where he attended grammar and high schools. He was graduated at Hebron Academy in 1894, and then took a year's course at the Massachusetts College of Pharmacy, starting upon his profession that year, and engaging in the retail drug business with B. F. Bradbury; afterwards, from 1896 to 1912, working for the wholesale drug firm of Cooke, Everitt & Pennell. In 1912, Mr. Ham took over the pharmacy in Livermore Falls, upon the death of his father in February of that year, the well-known Ham's Drug Store having been established in 1873.

The fraternal orders find in Mr. Ham a loyal friend and associate, his affiliations being those of all bodies of the Free and Accepted Masons, in the Ancient Accepted Scottish Rite, thirty-second degree;

and the Knights of Pythias, of which he is a Past Chancellor of Trinity Lodge, at Portland; and he is treasurer of the Livermore Falls Automobile Association. He has also held the office of treasurer of the Baptist church for fourteen years.

Joseph Chandler Ham married Bessie Ellen Leavitt, of Portland, Maine, born April 11, 1880, at East Harpswell, daughter of Mr. and Mrs. Charles W. Leavitt. Mr. and Mrs. Ham are the parents of two children, both born at Portland: Beatrice Emma, and Phyllis Marie.

EUGENE HAYES SEWALL—Both the development of the real estate and the lumber interests of Livermore Falls have occupied the expert attention of Eugene Hayes Sewall for by far the larger portion of his business career, this region having produced no better known factor in either line, or one who has more completely familiarized himself with the conditions relating to each line of business. He is a son of Eugene Sewall, long engaged in the lumber business, who was born December 29, 1831, and died December 3, 1906, and of Fannie (Weston) Sewall, who was born at Madison in September, 1848, and died in June, 1921.

Eugene Hayes Sewall was born December 21, 1891, at Livermore Falls, where he attended grammar and high schools, and then graduated at Williston Seminary in the class of 1910. With the exception of the years 1917-1921, while he was identified with the Pacific Board of Underwriters, at San Francisco, California, Mr. Sewall has given his entire attention to his lumber and real estate business at Livermore Falls.

In the political field, Mr. Sewall is an Independent voter. Fraternally, he is affiliated with Oriental Star Lodge, Free and Accepted Masons; with Androscoggin Chapter, Royal Arch Masons; Pilgrim Commandery, Knights Templar; and with Kora Temple, Ancient Arabic Order Nobles of the Mystic Shrine; and he holds the office of president of the Livermore Falls Automobile Dealers' Association. His religious faith is that of the Universalist church, of which he was formerly a trustee.

PHILIP QUINCY LORING, a prominent insurance man of Portland, Maine, and a descendant of an old New England family, was born March 30, 1869, in Portland, Maine, a son of Prentiss and Helen C. (McAllester) Loring, both natives of Maine. Prentiss Loring, born in Yarmouth, Maine, in 1834, was one of the foremost citizens of Portland. He established the firm of Prentiss Loring & Company, in 1865, was always keenly interested in the affairs of his city and State, and served for a number of years as a member of the Portland School Board, and a representative to the Maine State Legislature. He was an active member of the Independent Order of Odd Fellows. Helen C. (McAllester) Loring was born in Portland, Maine.

Philip Quincy Loring received his early education in public and private schools of the community in which he was born, later attending Portland High School. He entered Phillips-Exeter Academy, and graduated from there with the class of 1890. Upon the completion of these courses of study, Mr. Loring entered his father's office in 1891, and engaged in the insurance business. Four years later, in 1895, Mr. Loring became a partner of the firm. He continued working with his father, Prentiss Loring, until the time of the latter's death, which occurred in October, 1905. Since that time Mr. Loring has been sole proprietor of the business, retaining the firm name of Prentiss Loring, Son & Company. He has met with eminent success in this line of endeavor. Mr. Loring handles general insurance, and maintains his office in the Fidelity Building, Portland. In his political preferences he is a staunch supporter of the Republican party. He is vice-president of the Portland Chamber of Commerce; a member of the Lions Club, and of the Portland Country Club.

Philip Quincy Loring married, in Portland, Maine, Maud Pomeroy, who was born in Portland, a daughter of William York and Ethel (Babb) Pomeroy. Mrs. Loring's father, William York Pomeroy, was a native of Falmouth, Maine. Mr. and Mrs. Loring are the parents of one child, Dorothy Quincy, born in Portland, and now Mrs. Minus. Mr. and Mrs. Loring maintain their residence in Portland, where they attend the State Street Church.

DAN W. CONY—After some sixteen years of experience as a salesman, Dan W. Cony returned to his native city, Augusta, Maine, and established a general insurance business, which he has built up into a prosperous and steadily growing enterprise. Mr. Cony is active in the public affairs of Augusta, serving at the present time (1928) as City Clerk and Auditor. He was born in Augusta, Maine, February 6, 1882, son of Roger D. and Catherine (Ryan) Cony, the first-mentioned of whom was born in Ireland in 1833, and was engaged as a cotton worker to the time of his death, and the last-mentioned of whom was born in Ireland, May 16, 1844.

Dan W. Cony attended the public schools of Augusta, graduating from Augusta High School with the class of 1902, and matriculated in the University of Maine, where he continued his studies for two years. In 1904 he entered the employ of the International Correspondence Schools, of Scranton, Pennsylvania, as a traveling salesman, and maintained that connection for about seven years. At the end of that time he left the employ of the International Correspondence Schools and associated himself with a grocery firm in Maine. Later he was associated with two other grocery enterprises in Boston, as traveling representative, continuing in this line until 1920. In that year he returned to Augusta and engaged in a general insurance business under his own name. During the more than six years which have passed since he engaged in this line of business activity, Mr. Cony has built up a very large and important patronage and has made for himself an assured place among the business men of the city. Politically, he gives his support to the principles and the candidates of the Democratic party, in the affairs of which he takes an active part, serving as chairman of the Democratic State Committee. He is active in local public affairs, also, and in 1923 was elected city clerk and auditor. So well did he serve that he was reëlected in 1925, and in 1927 he was again chosen for the term expiring January 1, 1929. Mr. Cony is an interested member of the Augusta Chamber of Commerce, and is known as a public-spirited citizen. Fraternally, he is affiliated with the Knights of Co-

lumbus and with the Benevolent and Protective Order of Elks, and his religious affiliation is with the Roman Catholic church.

Dan W. Cony was married, at Ellsworth, Maine, January 23, 1912, to Mary Doyle, who was born in Ellsworth, Maine, July 19, 1886, daughter of Edward E. and Sabrina (Ford) Doyle, both natives of Ellsworth, Maine. Mr. and Mrs. Cony are the parents of two children: 1. Margaret F., born in Ellsworth, Maine, February 16, 1914. 2. Edward, born in Augusta, Maine, March 16, 1923. Mr. and Mrs. Cony make their home at No. 39 Western Avenue, Augusta, Maine.

ARTHUR J. CRATTY—One of the younger members of the legal profession in Waterville, Maine, is Arthur J. Cratty, who has been egaged in general practice there since June, 1920. Mr. Cratty is a Colby man; a graduate of Boston University Law School; a veteran of the World War, and has, during the more than six years of his practice here, made for himself an assured place in his profession.

Arthur J. Cratty was born in Waterville, Maine, April 3, 1891, son of Jerry M. Cratty, a native of Fairfield, Maine, born January 10, 1857, Street Commissioner of Waterville for seven years, now retired, and of Maria (McCarty) Cratty, who was born in Pittsfield, Maine. He received his early and preparatory education in the public schools of Waterville, and after graduation from the high school with the class of 1910, matriculated in Colby College, at Waterville. He had decided upon the legal profession as his future field of service, and in 1915, began the study of law in the Law School of Boston University, from which he was graduated with the class of 1918, receiving the degree of Bachelor of Laws. He was admitted to the Massachusetts bar, September 16, 1919, and in that year began practice with the Boston Legal Aid Society. In 1920 he was admitted to the Maine bar, passing the examinations and winning his admission in March, and in June of the same year he came to his native town, Waterville, Maine, and opened an office. Since that time he has been successfully engaged in legal practice here, and has made for himself a reputation as an able attorney and a wise counsellor. He has built up a very prosperous practice, and is well known in this section.

In December, 1917, he enlisted for service in the World War, and was with the Aviation Department of the Navy until December, 1918, when he received his discharge. Fraternally, he is identified with Lodge No. 905, Benevolent and Protective Order of Elks, Waterville, Maine. He is a member of the Maine Bar Association, of the Kennebec Bar Association, of the American Legion, and Lambda Chi Alpha Fraternity, Colby College, and his religious affiliation is with the Roman Catholic church of Waterville. Mr. Cratty has many friends in this community, and is one of the well-known and highly esteemed citizens of the place.

Arthur J. Cratty was married, in Wakefield, Massachusetts, October 24, 1920, to Katherine F. Sullivan, born in Wakefield, Massachusetts, March 26, 1897, daughter of Patrick J. Sullivan, a native of Colchester, Connecticut, and of Mary (Reddington) Sullivan. Mr. and Mrs. Cratty are the parents of one son, Bernard Reddington, born in Waterville, Maine, September 12, 1925.

ORLO DUDLEY MUDGETT—A period of twenty-three years represents the record of Orlo Dudley Mudgett in the electrical business, and that period of time includes his whole active career to the present year (1928). He is superintendent of the Western Division of the Central Maine Power Company, and that responsible position he has held for the past eight years. Mr. Mudgett is one of the very well-known men of Lewiston and Auburn, Maine, where he has his office and where he makes his home, and he has long ago made for himself an assured place in his profession. He is a graduate of the University of New Hampshire, and is prominent in Masonic circles.

Orlo Dudley Mudgett was born in Gilmanton, New Hampshire, August 8, 1881, son of Eugene L. and Ella F. (Judkins) Murgett, the last-mentioned of whom was born in Belmont, New Hampshire. The father, Eugene L., was born in Gilmanton, New Hampshire, and died in December, 1909, after an active and useful life as a successful blacksmith and also as a public official, serving as Commissioner of Belknap County, New Hampshire, and as a member of the Board of Selectmen of Gilmanton. Orlo Dudley Mudgett attended the public schools of Gilmanton, New Hampshire, and then prepared for college in Gilmanton Academy, from which he was graduated with the class of 1900. He then matriculated in the University of New Hampshire, where he completed his course with graduation in 1905, receiving at that time the degree of Bachelor of Science. In June of that same year, immediately after graduation, he identified himself with the Westinghouse Electric and Manufacturing Company, of Pittsburgh, Pennsylvania, as engineering apprentice, and remained in that capacity until 1906, when he was transferred to the Boston office of the company and assigned to electrical engineering work. In October, 1908, he was made superintendent of the Belfast Gas & Electric Company, of Belfast, Maine, and there he remained until 1910, when he became associated with the Lewiston & Auburn Electric Light Company as assistant superintendent. In October, 1914, the company was reorganized under the name of the Androscoggin Electric Company, and Mr. Mudgett was appointed superintendent of the Power Division. In 1920 the Androscoggin Electric Company was purchased by the Central Maine Power Company, and at that time Mr. Mudgett was appointed to his present position as superintendent of the Western Division of the Central Maine Power Company, which position he is efficiently filling in 1928. In his political convictions, Mr. Mudgett is a Republican. He is a member of the Lewiston and Auburn Chamber of Commerce, and in the Masonic Order is prominent, being identified with Phoenix Lodge, No. 24, Free and Accepted Masons, of Belfast, Maine, and with all the York Rite bodies up to and including the Consistory, in which he holds the thirty-second degree. He is also a member of Kora Temple, Ancient Arabic Order Nobles of the Mystic Shrine, and of the Lewiston and Auburn Rotary Club. His religious affiliation is with the High Street Congregational Church of Auburn.

Orlo Dudley Mudgett was married, in Lewiston, Maine, July 12, 1914, to Jessie Roberts, born in Parrsboro, Nova Scotia, November 17, 1883, daughter of Annie Roberts. Mr. and Mrs. Mudgett are the parents of one daughter, Pauline Ann, who was born in Lewiston, Maine, August 9, 1921.

ARTHUR STILPHEN—The greater part of the active career of Arthur Stilphen has been identified with the electrical business, and since 1906 he has been associated with the business of furnishing heat, light, and working power to the public. He is now (1928) superintendent of the Winthrop office of the Central Maine Power Company, which position he has filled since 1920.

Arthur Stilphen was born in Boston, Massachusetts, May 3, 1882, son of Stacy W. Stilphen, a physician, born in Dresden, Maine, died in 1891, and of Annette (Bradstreet) Stilphen, born in Pittston, Maine, died in 1891. After attending the public schools of Warren and of Rockport, Maine, and completing his course in the Warren High School, Mr. Stilphen obtained a position with the American Express Company in 1902, and remained with that concern until 1906, a period of four years, being located at that time at Gardiner, Maine. In 1906 he associated himself with the Kennebec Light & Heat Company, at Gardiner, Maine, and since has held various offices in that connection. When the Kennebec Light & Heat Company was reorganized as a subsidiary of the Central Maine Power Company, Mr. Stilphen was appointed superintendent of the Winthrop office, June 20, 1920, and that position he has continued to fill to the present date (1928). The Winthrop office is a branch of the Augusta, Maine, office of the Central Maine Power Company, which, as its name indicates, furnishes heat, light, and power to a large portion of the central section of the State. Mr. Stilphen is a member of Temple Lodge, No. 25, Free and Accepted Masons, of Winthrop; and Winthrop Chapter, No. 37, Royal Arch Masons. He is also a member of the Winthrop Chamber of Commerce, and his religious affiliation is with the Congregational church. Mr. Stilphen is one of the representative citizens of Winthrop, and both he and his wife have many friends here.

Arthur Stilphen was married, in Gardiner, Maine, May 15, 1909, to Florence Percival, born in Gardiner, Maine, November 12, 1891, daughter of M. E. and Sadie (McCurdy) Percival. Mr. and Mrs. Stilphen are the parents of one son, Ralph P., born at Gardiner, Maine, August 12, 1910. Their home is at No. 69 Main Street, Winthrop.

FRANK E. TRACY—For more than forty years Frank E. Tracy, of Augusta, Maine, has been engaged in the work of building; first as apprentice, then as carpenter, and finally, since 1909, as general contractor and builder. He is a member of the firm of Tracy and Metcalf, and is located at No. 11½ Oak Street, in Augusta.

Mr. Tracy was born in Rome, Maine, October 15, 1867, son of Stephen Tracy, a native of Rome, Maine, born May 2, 1836, now deceased, and of Violette (Yeaton) Tracy, who was born in Belgrade, Maine, January 12, 1838, also now deceased. The father was a carpenter and builder, and in his political faith was a Democrat.

Frank E. Tracy received a practical education in the excellent public schools of Augusta, Maine, and then followed the trade of his father, learning the carpenter's trade thoroughly, and following that occupation as a workman and an excellent craftsman, until 1909, when he was forty-two years of age. He then formed a partnership with Charles C. Metcalf, of Augusta, under the firm name of Tracy and Metcalf, and engaged in business for himself as a contractor and builder. During the more than eighteen years which have passed since that time, he has been successful and has established a reputation for skill and for sound business principles. He is careful in the matter of keeping contracts, both as to time and as to materials, and has long been known as one of the contractors whose word can be depended upon. In politics, he has not followed in the footsteps of his father, who was a Democrat, but gives his support to the principles and the candidates of the Republican party. He is actively interested in civic affairs, and has served as a member of the Board of City Councilmen for three terms, 1912, 1913, and 1914. Fraternally, he holds membership in the Knights of Pythias, and he is a charter member of the local Rotary Club. As an active member of the Augusta Chamber of Commerce, he keeps closely in touch with the general business conditions of the city and vicinity, and his business ability is unquestioned. Mr. Tracy is an attendant of the Episcopal church.

Frank E. Tracy was married, in Augusta, Maine, to Lily M. Trask, daughter of Charles W. Trask, a native of Sidney, Maine, and of Minnie A. (Sullivan) Trask, a native of Boston, Massachusetts. Mr. and Mrs. Tracy have one daughter, Louise Virginia, who was born in Augusta, Maine, June 19, 1910. The family home is at No. 28 Cushman Street, in Augusta.

ORA MILLER MAXIM—Prominent among the business men of Winthrop, Maine, is Ora Miller Maxim, who, as manager of the D. H. Maxim Estate is operating the D. H. Maxim Company's business, a wholesale and retail flour, grain, feed, lime, and cement concern. Mr. Maxim has been identified with this firm since leaving school, and has been its manager since the death of his father in 1917.

Mr. Maxim was born in Winthrop, Maine, October 22, 1889, son of Daniel Hezelton and Annie Laurie (Miller) Maxim, the last-mentioned of whom was born in Waldoboro, Maine. Daniel Hezelton Maxim was born in Wayne, Maine, and was one of the able and versatile business men of Winthrop. He was engaged in the building and contracting business, and was also the founder and the owner of the wholesale and retail flour, grain, feed, and building supply concern which is still operated under the name of the D. H. Maxim Estate. He served in the Union Army during the Civil War, was a public-spirited citizen and a successful business man. His death occurred February 20, 1917.

Ora Miller Maxim received his early education in the public schools of Winthrop, and after attending Winthrop High School continued study in Westbrook Seminary. When his education was completed he entered the employ of his father in the wholesale and retail flour and grain business, and continued that association from 1909 to the death of his father, February 20, 1917. After the death of his father he became manager of the D. H. Maxim Estate, and in that capacity has continued to operate the business most successfully. In addition to the usual line of flour, grain, and feed, the concern also

carries a stock of lime and cement. Sound business methods and a steady maintenance of the high standards set by the founder have enabled Mr. Maxim to maintain and increase the volume of business conducted by his father, and during the years in which he has been in control decided progress has been made. In his political sympathies Mr. Maxim is a Republican. He is treasurer of the Winthrop Community Hospital, president of the Winthrop Chamber of Commerce, and prominent in the Masonic Order, being a member of all the York Rites; Temple Lodge, of which he is a Past Master; Winthrop Chapter, Royal Arch Masons, of which he is Past High Priest; Alpha Council, No. 3, Royal and Select Masters; Trinity Commandery, Knights Templar; and of the Consistory, Ancient Accepted Scottish Rite, in which he holds the thirty-second degree; Kora Temple, Ancient Arabic Order Nobles of the Mystic Shrine. His religious affiliation is with the Congregational church of Winthrop.

Ora Miller Maxim was married, in Winthrop, Maine, March 15, 1909, to Nellie Louise Maxwell, born in Winthrop, Maine, July 8, 1891, daughter of Willard and Nellie (Kimball) Maxwell, natives of Maine. Mr. and Mrs. Maxim are the parents of two children: 1. Daniel Harold, born October 7, 1909, in Winthrop. 2. Donald Willard, born April 5, 1915.

CHARLES IRVING BAILEY—To that long-established line of industry for which he has had a lifelong inclination, the manufacture of floor-covering, Charles Irving Bailey has always devoted his business energies, and the business that his father founded at Winthrop nearly a century ago continues upon its old-time prosperous basis, through the maintenance of those sterling qualities that have always distinguished this firm. Mr. Bailey has that standing in the community that invariably distinguishes its upright and industrious citizenship.

Charles Irving Bailey was born March 13, 1860, at Winthrop, a son of Charles M. Bailey, a manufacturer, who was born in October, 1820, and died in 1917, at Winthrop, and Sophia D. (Jones) Bailey, also a native of Winthrop. Mr. Bailey attended the grammar schools, and also the high schools both at Winthrop and Skowhegan. He first became interested in the business in which he is engaged, in 1877, in partnership with his father; and in 1921 he became sole owner.

The firm of Charles M. Bailey's Sons & Company was established by Charles M. Bailey in 1844, for the manufacture of floor coverings, this plant at Winthrop producing about thirty thousand rolls of floor covering annually, and employing on an average about sixty-five people.

The Republican party has Mr. Bailey's political allegiance, his vote and influence being directed in its interest. Besides his affiliation with the Associated Industries of Maine, he is a member of the Winthrop Chamber of Commerce, and the Rotary Club; and his religious faith is that of the Friends' Meeting.

Charles Irving Bailey married, in Boston, Massachusetts, Eva A. King, born at North Monmouth, daughter of Joseph R. and Emeline (Dexter) King; and they have one son, Paul H., born October 6, 1897, at Winthrop.

VAUGHAN M. MAYO—Waterville's business associations are directed by men of recognized worth in the mercantile and industrial activities of the State, the qualities of enterprise and ability in the flour, grain and milling interests being eminently those of Vaughan M. Mayo, president of the firm of Merrill & Mayo Company, wholesale and retail dealers, at Waterville. He is a veteran and a thoroughly experienced factor in his line, and has the good will of his State-wide associates and his immediate patronage and friends in this part of the State.

Vaughan M. Mayo was born October 12, 1866, at Fairfield, a son of Edwin R. Mayo, a native of Waterville, and Mary D. (King) Mayo. Mr. Mayo attended the grammar and the high schools at Fairfield, and he began his business career as a hardware merchant in his own name at Fairfield, so continuing for several years. In 1899, he became identified with Albert F. Merrill in the grain business at Waterville, the firm name being A. F. Merrill; and in 1902, he joined in partnership in the firm of Merrill, Runnells & Mayo, in the same line of business. Upon the retirement of Mr. Runnells, the firm name was changed, as at present, to Merrill and Mayo, wholesale and retail dealers in flour, grain, mill-feed and sugar.

In the political field, Mr. Mayo has always staunchly favored the interests of the Republican party. Besides his affiliation with the Associated Industries of Maine, he is a member of Salaam Lodge, No. 92, Free and Accepted Masons; the Chapter, Royal Arch Masons; Mount Lebanon Council, Royal and Select Masters; St. Elmo Commandery, Knights Templar; Maine Consistory, Ancient Accepted Scottish Rite; Kora Temple, Ancient Arabic Order Nobles of the Mystic Shrine; Benevolent and Protective Order of Elks; Waterville Chamber of Commerce, and the Rotary Club. His religious faith is that of the Methodist Episcopal church.

WILLIAM ALLEN CLOUGH—For a decade William Allen Clough, a hardware merchant of broad training and long experience, has conducted the prosperous enterprise known as Clough and Pillsbury, of Rumford, Maine, in partnership with Walter Barker Pillsbury. As public spirited as he is businesslike, Mr. Clough has participated actively in all phases of community life and has served in executive capacity in municipal office and organizations. He was born in Skowhegan, Maine, March 20, 1879, son of William Allen and Mary Emma (Nutting) Clough, both born in Madison, Maine, where the father was a contractor and builder, and both now deceased. When the son completed the grammar school course in the Skowhegan schools, he graduated from high school in 1897, and from Broomfield Academy.

All his business life has been associated with the hardware trade. His first employment was with the J. D. Rawles Hardware Company, from 1897 to 1899. For the next thirteen years, until 1912, Mr. Clough worked for the King and Dexter Company at Portland, Maine, leaving them for a more advantageous position with Talbot, Brooks & Ayer, in the same city. In 1916, after four years of this

association and nineteen years of experience in hardware, Mr. Clough joined Walter Barker Pillsbury in establishing Clough and Pillsbury, hardware, in Rumford, Maine. For more than ten years the enterprise has prospered. Mr. Clough is a director of the Rumford National Bank and president of the Rumford Business and Professional Men's Association. He has served on the Board of Selectmen of Rumford and is a charter member of the Rotary Club. His fraternal affiliations are with Blazing Star Lodge, Free and Accepted Masons, of which he is Past Master; the Chapter, Royal Arch Masons, and Strathglass Commandery, Knights Templar. He belongs to the Universalist church of Rumford.

In Portland, Maine, August 20, 1903, William Allen Clough married Rose Ella Mason, of Bethel, Maine, and daughter of Moses Mason of Albany. Children: 1. Ruperta Mason, born in Portland, September 20, 1904. 2. Reginald William Clough, born in Portland, August 8, 1905.

ERNEST SAMUEL KNOWLTON—Among the successful business men of Dixfield, Maine, is Ernest Samuel Knowlton, junior partner of a prosperous drygoods business here, of Harlow and Knowlton. Mr. Knowlton is a member of one of the pioneer families of this section, his grandfather, Samuel S. Knowlton, having been a native of Knowlton Corners, Maine, and his father, William T. Knowlton, a contractor, was also born at Knowlton Corners. Mr. Knowlton is a thirty-second degree Mason, including Anna Temple, and has a host of friends in this section of the State.

Ernest Samuel Knowlton was born in North Chesterfield, Maine, August 13, 1893, son of William T. and Eunice C. (Whittemore) Knowlton, the last-named of whom is a native of Livermore Falls, Maine. He attended the public schools of Farmington, Maine, graduating from Farmington High School with the class of 1912, and then engaged in various pursuits until 1922 when he came to Dixfield, where he is still (1928) successfully engaged in business. Mr. Knowlton is a Republican in his political sympathies, and is active in local public affairs. He is chairman of the Board of Assessors of Dixfield, and during the period of the participation of the United States in the World War was a member of the One Hundred and Fifty-first Depot Brigade, Camp Devens, Ayer, Massachusetts. He enlisted August, 17, 1917, and was discharged in February, 1919, with the rank of first lieutenant. Previous to the entrance of the United States into the World War Mr. Knowlton was a member of the Maine National Guard from 1910 to 1912, and his discharge from service in 1919 he again became a member of the National Guard, serving from 1920 to 1922, inclusive. Mr. Knowlton is very well known in fraternal circles, being a member of all the bodies of the Masonic Order, both York and Scottish Rites, and of the Consistory, in which he holds the thirty-second degree. He is a member of the American Legion, and of the Officers' Reserve Corps, in which he holds a captain's commission. His religious affiliation is with the Congregational church.

Ernest Samuel Knowlton was married, in Waterville, Maine, May 20, 1918, to Virginia Boushard, who was born in Canada, July 2, 1896. Mr. and Mrs. Knowlton make their home in Dixfield.

ELMER R. LANE—To the business of building contractor and building supplies merchant, Elmer R. Lane, in partnership with his brother, Charles A. Lane, devotes his assiduous and successful attention at his West Peru plant and headquarters, carrying along a business that though established only in recent years, holds a place that has been made important and permanent through its capable and enterprising administration. Previous to this, Mr. Lane engaged in the hard experiences of a soldier at the front in the World War, when with the Field Artillery, he received wounds on the battlefields of France. His grandparents were Augustus and L. Lane, and he is a son of Carl Lane, a farmer and a veteran of the Civil War, who was born at Springfield, Vermont, and Luella (Bisby) Lane, a native of Rumford.

Elmer R. Lane was born September 5, 1894, at Rumford, where he attended the public schools. After his war service he became interested in building and contract work at West Peru, and in 1925, together with his brother, Charles A. Lane, he entered upon general contracting, and in retail lumbering and building supplies lines. His political convictions are those of the Independent voter.

Mr. Lane was in active service with the American Expeditionary Forces in the World War. Overseas, after his enlistment on June 1, 1917, he was a member of the Sixth Field Artillery, of the First Division, at St. Mihiel and the Argonne Forest, where he was wounded. At the time of his discharge on July 24, 1919, he was a member of the Two Hundred and Thirty-seventh Military Police. His fraternity is the Independent Order of Odd Fellows, and his religious faith is that of the Congregational church.

Elmer E. Lane married, August 5, 1919, at Lewiston, Mary Richardson, who was born March 15, 1896, at Canton, daughter of Charles Richardson, a native of Canton, and Edith (Hackett) Richardson, who was born at Oxford. Their children: 1. Richard, born May 31, 1920, at Casper, Wyoming. 2. Roger, born March 1, 1927, at West Peru.

HARRY B. MARSH—The greater part of the active career of Harry B. Marsh, of Dixfield, has been identified with the business of the embalmer and funeral director, in Dixfield. Mr. Marsh has established a reputation for scientific methods and honest business dealings, and is known as one of the thoroughly reliable men of his profession.

Harry B. Marsh was born in Dixfield, March 28, 1878, son of Albion P. Marsh, a farmer and merchant, born in Dixfield, Maine, and died in 1899, and of Matilda (Newton) Marsh, also a native of Dixfield. Mr. Marsh received his early education in the public schools of Dixfield, including Dixfield High School, and then continued his studies in Hebron Academy and in Westbrook Seminary. When his education was completed, he engaged in the hardware business, in which line he continued six years, and then, in 1912, engaged in the embalming and funeral directing business for himself in Dixfield. During the years that have passed he has built up a large and important patronage, and has made his establishment one of the best known in this section. He gives his support to the Republican party, and is well known in Masonic circles, being a member of King Hiram Lodge, No. 57, Free and Accepted Masons; of the Chapter, Royal Arch Masons; and of the Commandery, Knights Templar, of Rumford, Maine.

His religious affiliation is with the Congregational church.

Harry B. Marsh was married, in Dixfield, Maine, to Bessie M. Thompson, who was born in Dixfield, daughter of John N. and Ida J. Thompson, both natives of Dixfield.

CARL HERVEY STEVENS, M. D.—Native of Maine and practicing physician and surgeon in Belfast since 1913, Carl Hervey Stevens is not only prominent in his great humanitarian profession, but is accounted among the foremost of citizens of the community, constantly concerned in enterprises for its development. Dr. Stevens was born in Northport, October 18, 1885, a son of Mason I. and Emma J. (Abbott) Stevens, both of whom were natives of this State. Mason I. Stevens was a man of intellect, and for a number of years, while maintaining his farm, taught in nearby rural schools. In Northport he enjoyed the sincere respect of all who knew him, and took an active part in all progressive movements.

Carl Hervey Stevens received his early academic training in the schools of Northport and Belfast, his parents having removed to Belfast during his childhood. He attended the M. C. Institute, and, inasmuch as he decided early to take up the profession of medicine, he matriculated in the Medical School of Maine soon after attaining his majority. He graduated from the Medical School in 1911, with the degree of Doctor of Medicine, and with high scholastic standing. He then spent a year in study at Bowdoin Medical School, and another year in the same institution as instructor. Then he took up general practice, in Belfast, quickly coming to the fore in the professional circles of town and county. He has, since the beginning of his career, enjoyed a flourishing activity. During the first year of professional residence in Belfast he was appointed to the surgical staff of the Waldo County Hospital, and the following year was chosen to membership on the Board of Health. In 1915 he was named school physician, charged with the health supervision of all students in the grade schools of the community; and in this capacity as he had during the year preceding, as well as continuously since 1913, on the Waldo County Hospital staff, performed great good to Belfast through diligent charge of its health. Examinations of students were made periodically, and those having trouble of any kind, namely of the eyes, nose, ears, throat, heart and skin, were reported to their parents; recommendations were made for specific treatment, and numerous ills were cured or avoided. A school physician has a most responsible post, and this Dr. Stevens realized; his service to the youth under his supervision, and incidentally to their parents and to local society at large, was incalculable. After war had been declared between this country and Germany, Dr. Stevens lost no time in offering his skill to the United States, and he was put into service in the Medical Reserve Corps. In 1918 he was chairman of the Waldo County Medical Defense Committee, and in that direction distinguished himself, his associates and the county as a whole for the excellence of results attained. Moreover, Dr. Stevens was instrumental in securing subscriptions to the several Liberty Loan campaigns, and in every possible way he did his duty.

Dr. Stevens is a member of the Waldo County Medical Society, the Maine State Medical Association, and the American Medical Association; and fraternally, of the Free and Accepted Masons, and the Belfast Rotary Club. He is a Republican, loyal to the principles of government upheld by the party, and possessed of a considerable influence in matters of local question, which he exercises without fanfare, quietly, to best effect. In affairs of charity he is of large heart, contributing liberally and readily to every worthy appeal, regardless of race or creed. Those of Belfast who know Dr. Stevens are happy to acknowledge to him the position that he deserves so fully, as a physician and surgeon of proven skill and undoubted ethics, as a man of character most honorable, and as a citizen of country, State and community.

On June 26, 1912, the year after his graduation from medical college, Dr. Stevens was united in marriage to Eleanor G. Wescott, in Northport; and to this union were born two children: John W., and Alice M. Mrs. Stevens is a woman of charm and refinement, and she is popular in all circles in which she moves. The family resides at No. 1 Court Street, and here, in his residence, Dr. Stevens has his offices.

RICHARD I. PETERSON—Associated with the broadening activities of the Maine Hotel Men's Association, and backed up by comprehensive experience in the hotel-keeper's life in this State, Richard I. Peterson is highly rated in his profession, his popular methods in conducting the Hotel Rumford having secured for that hostelry its deserved place among the leading hotels of this part of New England. Travelers and regular visitors know this hotel and its proprietor through his consistent catering to the public demands, and Mr. Peterson also is very highly regarded throughout this section for his broad and practical interest in public welfare and civic progress.

Richard I. Peterson, a son of J. P. Peterson, who was a chief of police in Sweden, and Caroline (Svedberg) Peterson, also a native of Sweden, was born May 3, 1878, in Sweden, where he received his education in the public schools and at college. When he came to the United States in 1897, he at once became interested in the sort of work that was to become his calling, and held a position at the Bangor House, in Bangor, from 1897 to 1909, thus fitting himself for the yet more responsible place to follow, that of manager for the Government of a hotel at Togus, and that that he ably conducted from 1904 to 1914.

It was in 1914 that his present opportunity presented itself, when he became proprietor of Hotel Rumford, a fine house of eighty rooms, that he has continued to conduct to the present, with the assistance of a corps of eighteen people. His political allegiance has been given to the Republican party. Besides his membership with the Maine Hotel Men's Association, Mr. Peterson's fraternal affiliations are with St. Andrew's Lodge, Free and Accepted Masons; the Commandery, Knights Templar; Kora Temple, Ancient Arabic Order Nobles of the Mystic Shrine; Benevolent and Protective Order of Elks, Past Exalted Ruler, Rumford Lodge; Past Chancellor Commander, Knights of Pythias; Rumford Business Men's Association; and Oakdale Country Club; and his religious faith is that of the Methodist Episcopal church.

Richard I. Peterson married, December 25, 1908, at Attleboro, Massachusetts, Georgia I. Fuller, who was born at Tennant's Harbor, Maine, daughter of

John A. Fuller, a native of Appleton, and Mary E. Fuller, who was born at Calais. They have one son, John Frederic Peterson, who was born in February, 1921, at Bangor.

LUTHER FRED PIKE—As partner in an outstanding mercantile establishment of Norway and South Paris, Maine, the L. F. Pike Company, and president of the Norway Board of Trade, Luther Fred Pike is one of the well-known and progressive men of this section. He was born at Norway, September 9, 1877, son of Albert Luther Farrar and Ellen Rowena (Andrews) Pike. The father, born in Norway, Maine, October 8, 1848, has long been an important factor in business development and is partner with his son in the retail clothing store they operate. He is a member of the Independent Order of Odd Fellows and Past Grand Representative for the State of Maine. The mother is a native of Otisfield, Maine.

After completing the course of studies in the public schools of Norway and graduating from high school in the class of 1895, Mr. Pike attended Gray's Business College. From 1900 to 1920 he was associated with F. H. Noyes in the retail clothing business in Norway. He then entered on his present partnership with his father under the firm name of the L. F. Pike Company. This concern deals in clothing, furnishings, and tailoring, and operates two prosperous stores in Norway and South Paris, Maine. Mr. Pike is a member of the Kiwanis Club and the Independent Order of Odd Fellows, Norway Lodge, No. 16, and is an Independent Democrat. He is a communicant of the Congregational church.

In Norway, Maine, June 16, 1908, Luther Fred Pike married Florence May Cross, born in Kingfield, Maine, March 24, 1878, daughter of Thomas and Emma Cross. Children: 1. Miriam Rowena, born in Norway, August 16, 1909. 2. John Francis, born in Norway, May 7, 1911. 3. Robert Gordon, born in Norway, November 9, 1913.

HOWARD HUNTINGTON POTTER—Since 1923 Howard Huntington Potter has been engaged as a civil engineer in Norway, Maine, where he has his office at No. 193 Main Street. Mr. Potter is a graduate of the Thayer School of Civil Engineering, and has been following his profession since his graduation in 1915. He is also a graduate of Dartmouth College.

Howard Huntington Potter was born in Worcester, Massachusetts, January 2, 1891, son of Frank H. Potter, a native of Colchester, Connecticut, and of Edith Russell (Greene) Potter, who was born in New York City. Mr. Potter received his early and preparatory education in the public schools of Boston and the Mechanical Arts High School, and then matriculated in Dartmouth College, from which he was graduated with the class of 1914, receiving at that time the degree of Bachelor of Science. His first professional connection was with Stone and Webster of Boston, with whom he was associated from 1915 to 1917. Meantime, in June, 1916, he had enlisted in the Massachusetts National Guard, and, upon the entrance of the United States into the World War his National Guard company was inducted into the Federal Service as Company C, One Hundred and Second Machine Gun Battalion, with which unit he was sent overseas. On October 21, 1918, he was transferred to Headquarters Company, One Hundred and First Engineers, and was discharged April 28, 1919.

Upon his return to this country and to civilian life, he entered the employ of the Harry Hope Engineering Company, of Boston, where he remained 1919-1920. His next connection was with the United Fruit Company, in Cuba, where he was employed as engineer, 1920-21. From 1921 to 1923 he was associated with the Department of Public Works in the Republic of Haiti, and in 1923 he came to Maine and located in Norway, where he opened an office and engaged in business for himself as a civil engineer. He has continued in this line and in this location, with his office at No. 193 Main Street, to the present time (1928). Politically, Mr. Potter is one of the independent voters and casts his ballot for the man whom he deems most fit for the office rather than for the candidates of any one party. He is a member of the American Legion, and his religious affiliation is with the Episcopal church.

Howard Huntington Potter was married, in New York City, June 11, 1923, to Sarah Simpson Smith, daughter of David Smith.

PHILIP F. STONE—A man of well-rounded education and public spirit, Philip F. Stone has been postmaster of Norway, Maine, since 1922. He is prominent in other departments of local activity and prompt in his support of all forward-looking programs. Mr. Stone is the son of George F. and Elizabeth (Rice) Stone. The father, a photographer, was born at Leominster, Massachusetts, and died in 1924, while the mother was born in Waterford, Maine.

Educated in the public and high schools of Norway, Maine, graduating from the last-named in 1902, Philip F. Stone taught school in Maine and Massachusetts for eight years, from 1902 to 1910. He became identified with the Norway Post Office and was appointed postmaster, the first time in December, 1922. So capable did he prove that in December, 1926, he was reappointed for a term of four years. His political adherence is given to the Republican party. He is a member of the local Board of Trade and the Kiwanis Club, and of several fraternal organizations, including Oxford Lodge, No. 18, Free and Accepted Masons; Oxford Chapter No. 29, Royal Arch Masons; the Ark Mariners; Tennessee Lodge, No. 18, Knights of Pythias; Norway Grange, Patrons of Husbandry, and he is a communicant of the Second Congregational Church.

JOHN W. HILBERT—Travelers or visitors arriving in Gardiner are always assured of a sincere welcome and the finest service and attention at the Johnson House, one of the best-known and most important hotels in the State of Maine, which has achieved a remarkable reputation for superior and distinctive service through the efforts of its genial proprietor and owner, John W. Hilbert, who has had many years' experience in catering to the needs of the traveling public. Mr. Hilbert leaves nothing undone to facilitate the comfort of his guests, preserving the homelike atmosphere for which the hotel has ever been noted, and at the same time furnishing the conveniences and modern appurtenances of a progressive and advanced hostelry. In his position, he is a great factor in advertising and advancing the interests of the town by the splendid impression made upon all visitors through the courteous and refined attention received at the hands of his organization.

Mr. Hilbert was born in England, county of Halifax, Canada, March 11, 1880, son of John and

Mary Jane (Crosley) Hilbert, both natives of England, Halifax, now living at Gardiner. John Hilbert, Sr., had an active career in the import and export industry and was active in the political affairs of England, serving as alderman of the town for twenty years. During the World War, he was head of the Food Control Board in Hebden Bridge, England.

John W. Hilbert was educated in the public schools of England, Halifax, and in 1904 came to the United States and became associated with a large importing and exporting concern in New York City, where he advanced steadily by his thorough devotion to business and his keen ability in grasping the details of the business. In 1906, he entered the hotel business, starting as clerk in the hotel which he now owns, continuing in this position for ten years, during which time he familiarized himself thoroughly with the methods and practices of hotel management, making many friends among the patrons, for whose care and comfort he was always watchful. In 1916, he purchased the hotel from its owner and has continued to operate it successfully. It is one of the most fascinating and inviting places in Central Maine, having been built in 1827, originally known as the Cobbossee House, and later being named the Johnson House. Mr. Hilbert has remodeled entirely the interior of the hotel, installing running water in every room, and operates it on the European plan. In order to insure the quality and absolute freshness of all foodstuffs used in his house, he owns and operates a large, modern farm, which supplies the various needs of the hotel, this being one of the unusual and most pleasant features of his organization. He is an active factor in the life of the town, both socially and commercially, being a director in the Gardiner Trust Company and taking a prominent part in politics, being an ardent supporter of the Republican party, and serving in the capacity of Treasurer of the city for the past three years (1928). He is a leader in fraternal circles, being a member of the Lodge, Free and Accepted Masons, and the Temple, Ancient Arabic Order Nobles of the Mystic Shrine, while he is prominently identified in the activities of the Fish and Game Association of Gardiner, acting as treasurer of the organization, and is a member of the Shrine Club. His religious adherence is given to the Episcopal church.

HARRY STEARNS LASSELLE, D. M. D.—One of the leaders in his profession in the State of Maine, Harry Stearns Lasselle, Doctor of Medical Dentistry with offices in Gardiner, is one of the most popular and efficient dentists in this vicinity. The science of dentistry has made such remarkable advances in the past few decades that the people of this town are fortunate in having the services of Dr. Lasselle, who has had the advantages of the most modern and scientific training and is constantly alert to new discoveries, that will be of benefit to his clientele. He takes a prominent and active part in the civic affairs of the town and is ever willing and enthusiastic in lending his assistance to all projects for the furtherance of public welfare.

Dr. Lasselle was born in Norway, August 26, 1896, son of George E. Lasselle, who died in 1917, and Mary E. (Jones) Lasselle, who is still living, born in Lovell. George E. Lasselle was born in Norway, and was for many years associated with the Grand Trunk Railway System in the capacity of telegrapher, while he took an active part in local matters, being a prominent member of the Republican party.

Harry Stearns Lasselle received his early education in the public schools of Norway, and after high school, entered the University of Maine, where he remained for one year, after which he matriculated at Tufts Dental College. Applying himself to the arduous studies of dental surgery, he distinguished himself in his studies and graduated with the class of 1922, receiving his degree of Doctor of Medical Dentistry. He then commenced the practice of his profession at the State Hospital, Augusta, and was connected with this institution for two and a quarter years. In 1924, he opened his present offices in Gardiner and engaged in the general practice of dentistry, winning the confidence and regard of his fellow-citizens from the first by his courteous and considerate manner and his expert ability, having the happy faculty of producing the maximum amount of finished work with the minimum discomfort to his patients. His many splendid qualities have made him a favorite with his clients, who recognize his complete knowledge of his profession and his earnest and sincere desire to be of service to humanity. Dr. Lasselle is a member of the Kennebec Valley Dental Society and the Maine Dental Society. His fraternal connections are with the Delta Sigma Delta National Fraternity and the Phi Eta Kappa Fraternity of the University of Maine. In politics, he is a Republican, and his religious adherence is given to the Episcopal church. Dr. Lasselle has had an extensive military career, having served on the Mexican border in 1916 as a musician in the Second Maine Regiment Band, and during the World War he was of valuable assistance to the cause in his work as a hospital apprentice in the Hospital Corps of the United States Naval Reserve, of which he is still a reserve officer.

MURRAY CROSMAN BINFORD, well-known architect of Portland, Maine, and descendant of an old and respected New England family, particularly of Maine, where the Crosman family has lived for many generations, was born August 21, 1893, at Saco, in this State. He is a son of Lindley Murray and Clara Brown (Crosman) Binford.

Murray Crosman Binford received his early education in the public schools of Saco, and later attended Oak Grove Seminary, graduating with the class of 1912. He attended the University of Pennsylvania, and he graduated from there with the class of 1916, after which he enlisted in the United States Navy, and secured a reserve commission. Going to the United States Naval Academy at Annapolis, Maryland, he studied for four months in the reserve officers' class, getting a regular commission, and serving on active duty from May, 1917, to June, 1919, when he returned to civil life. In 1921, Mr. Binford was associated with the firm of Miller & Reeves, of Columbus, Ohio, after which he returned to Portland, Maine, where he became identified with John Pickering Thomas, another architect of Portland, a man whose biography appears elsewhere in this work. Mr. Binford served as the treasurer of that organization, remaining as such until December, 1926, after which he resigned to follow his profession under his own name, in Portland. In this work he has made a marked success, coming to be known as one of the most able men in this type of endeavor.

Mr. Binford has been active in the civic affairs of his community, and is spoken of as a most pro-

gressive man, ready to give his assistance to any movement designed for the welfare or advancement of Portland. He is a member of the American Institute of Architects, and he holds membership in the Portland Club.

Murray Crosman Binford married, July 12, 1919, in Philadelphia, Pennsylvania, Edith Coleman Gray, daughter of Delbert B. and Olive M. (Coleman) Gray. Mr. and Mrs. Binford are the parents of two daughters: Virginia Gray, and Cynthia Alice. He and his family maintain their residence in Portland, Maine.

DANIEL H. HERRIN, of Gardiner, purchased the business of the Riverside Laundry here and established himself in that enterprise in 1906. From that moment his has grown in importance to its owner and to the community and is now one of the leading commercial establishments of the town.

Daniel H. Herrin was born in Augusta, June 1, 1865, a son of the late Daniel and Emily (Colby) Herrin. The father was a native of Smithfield, Maine, and the mother of Wiscasset, the former having been engaged in mechanical work in Augusta at the time of his death. Daniel H. Herrin is a Democrat in politics and a member of the Congregational church. He belongs to the Order of Free and Accepted Masons, York Rite; is a member of the Ancient Arabic Order Nobles of the Mystic Shrine, and of the Shriners' Club of Gardiner, and holds membership in the Benevolent and Protective Order of Elks.

Mr. Herrin married, in Gardiner, November 27, 1892, Alberta K. Weymouth, daughter of Thasker and Mary E. (Lincoln) Weymouth.

FRED W. TRIBOU—With youth and energy at his command, the indomitable spirit of conquest is likely to be fulfilled with success in the case of Fred W. Tribou, of Gardiner, whose work in the great field of automobile distribution has grown in volume from the beginning of his essay into the business.

He was born in Hampden, Maine, April 15, 1900, educated in the public schools at Rumford and graduated from the high school at Auburn. In 1918 he entered into association with the Gardiner Auto Sales Company as a salesman and for more than two years he has been manager of the Gardiner branch, which handles Ford cars and supplies. He came here from Rumford, where there is another establishment of this concern. He is a Democrat in politics and belongs to the Methodist Episcopal church. His fraternal affiliations are with the Independent Order of Odd Fellows. His parents were Charles G. and Annie (Stubbs) Tribou, both natives of Maine.

Fred W. Tribou married, in Mexico, Maine, February 18, 1923, Rita W. O'Leary, daughter of Gordon and Elizabeth O'Leary, of Green Bay, Wisconsin. Their children are: 1. Frederick W., born November 9, 1925. 2. Gladys J.

CHALMERS G. FARRELL, M. D.—Coming to Maine immediately upon receiving his degree as a Doctor of Medicine, in 1911, Chalmers G. Farrell, of Gardiner, first went to Augusta, his advent into Gardiner having been postponed until 1916. Since that day, however, his activities in his profession and in social, religious, civic and general public interests have been of such nature as to commend him most highly to his fellow-citizens and to give him a worthy

62   MAINE—A HISTORY

place among the medical practitioners of the State. Chalmers G. Farrell was born in Zanesville, Ohio, December 8, 1885, a son of the late Chalmers and Gay (Saylor) Farrell, both natives of Ohio. His father was a merchant. The son was educated in the public schools of Columbus, Ohio, was graduated from the high school there and took the medical course at the Starling (Ohio) Medical College from which he was graduated with his degree in 1911. He was called to Augusta, Maine, where he became assistant surgeon at the National Soldiers' Home, remaining in the post for four years. He then went to Dayton, Ohio, for nearly a year, at the end of which period he came to Gardiner, where he has since practiced. He is a member of the staff of the Gardiner General Hospital and has membership in the American Medical Association, the Maine State Medical Association and the Kennebec County Medical Association. He is a Republican and has been City Physician and Health Officer of Gardiner for the last two years. From September, 1918, to October 27, 1919, he served in the United States Army Medical Corps, stationed at Camp Upton, New York, and in New York City. He was mustered out of active service, with the rank of captain in the Medical Reserve Corps. He is a member of the Lodge, Free and Accepted Masons, and is vice-commander of Gardiner Post, American Legion. His church is the Protestant Episcopal.

Charles G. Farrell married, at Radnor, Pennsylvania, June 1, 1916, Gertrude R. Willson, of Augusta, Maine. They have one child, Lois Alada, born January 11, 1923.

GEORGE B. MORSE—In the commercial life of Maine, George B. Morse, of Gardiner, took an active part for many years, being a leader in the wholesale and retail tobacco business until his retirement from active affairs in 1927. Mr. Morse began his business career in Boston, Massachusetts, more than forty-five years ago, starting as a salesman for one of the leading cigar enterprises of the country and traveling steadily on the road for ten years. He was successful from the start, because of his pleasant and affable manner in meeting his customers and filling their requirements satisfactorily, thus earning a reputation for thorough dependability, both as to promptness of deliveries and quality of products. He became one of the most popular salesmen in the State and built up a large and remunerative trade, at the same time making many friendships and acquiring a complete knowledge of the tobacco industry, which were of great value to him when later he struck out for himself in this business.

Mr. Morse was born in Newport, son of John G. and Eliza A. (Emerey) Morse, both natives of Ripley, now deceased. John G. Morse was a millwright for many years, being an esteemed and respected citizen of his community, in which he took an active part, his political adherence being given to the Democratic party.

George B. Morse was educated in the public schools of Newport, and after high school, entered the Maine Central Institute at Pittsfield. After completing his formal education, he entered upon his business career and after ten years as salesman for a cigar concern of Boston, opened his own independent enterprise at Bath, in 1892, for the operation of a modern and progressive wholesale and retail tobacco business. In 1895, he moved his organization to Gardiner, where he was continually engaged for many years,

under the firm name of George Morse & Company, conducting a successful trade in tobacco products for many years until he retired. His constant and consistent progress was due to the splendid principles of quality and service to which he always adhered, never deviating from his original policy in the slightest degree. In the financial life of the town, he is a prominent factor, being a director of the Gardiner Trust Company, having held this office since the organization of this successful banking institution. Popular in fraternal circles, he is a member of the Knights of Pythias and the Benevolent and Protective Order of Elks. In politics, he is a follower of the principles of the Democratic party, and his religious affiliations are with the First Baptist Church.

HARRY M. CHURCH, D. M. D.—For more than twenty years Harry M. Church has been favorably known to residents of Gardiner, Maine, as one of the leading dentists of the town, his labors in the field having grown in usefulness as the years passed by and his practice grew. Upstanding as a citizen, known from his boyhood here, he has participated in all the activities to which he could lend a useful hand, his interest in civic, social and fraternal affairs being as lively as his professional occupation. His position in his profession is secure, his standing among his fellow-citizens unchallenged, a citizen of fine worth to the community. He was born in Gardiner, Maine, September 22, 1885, a son of James Church, native of Farmingdale, Maine, who was foreman in a machine shop there for more than forty years and served for years as an alderman, now deceased. His mother was Susan J. (Noyes) Church, a native of Gardiner, at this writing (1928) still living. Harry M. Church was educated in the public schools of Gardiner and was graduated from the high school there, after which he took a course at Tufts Dental College, being graduated from that institution in 1907 with the degree of Doctor of Dental Medicine. He established himself in practice in Gardiner in that year, working alone until 1915, when he associated himself with his brother, Carroll, in the profession, which they now conduct in partnership. He is a Republican in politics and a director in the Maine Trust and Banking Company. He belongs to the American Dental Society, the Maine Dental Society and the Kennebec Valley Dental Society. In fraternal circles he is a thirty-second degree member of the Masonic Order, affiliated with the lower grades and with the Temple, Ancient Arabic Order Nobles of the Mystic Shrine. He is a member of the Gardiner Rotary Club and the 40 Club. His church is the Methodist Episcopal.

Harry M. Church married (first), September 22, 1910, in Gardiner, Maine, Barbara Anderson, deceased November 5, 1924; he married (second), June 30, 1926, in Portland, Maine, Alice Harrison.

JOHN CLYDE ARNOLD—The entire business life of John Clyde Arnold, postmaster of Augusta, has been spent in the service of the United States Postal Department in that city. Born in Augusta, March 29, 1875, the son of John and Juliette (Richardson) Arnold, he received his early education at Cony High School. He became a clerk in the Augusta Post Office in 1893, and in 1909 was appointed superintendent of mails.

In 1915 Mr. Arnold was made postal cashier in the Augusta office and in the following year was appointed assistant postmaster. In 1922 he attained the office of postmaster, which responsible position he holds at this time (1928). He is a member of the Society of Mayflower Descendants, his ancestors having come to this country in that famous vessel. He is affiliated with the local Lodge of Free and Accepted Masons and was crowned an honorary member of the Supreme Council, Sovereign Grand Inspectors-General of the Thirty-Third and Last Degree of the Ancient Accepted Scottish Rite, at Buffalo, New York, September 21, 1926. His religious affiliations are with the Episcopal church, and in politics he is a Republican. He resides at No. 78 Green Street, Augusta.

ROBINSON COOK—Well prepared for a successful career is Robinson Cook, of Portland, who is engaged in general insurance business under his own name. His office is located in the Fidelity Building, No. 465 Congress Street, Portland, and he is taking care of a steadily increasing volume of business. Mr. Cook is a graduate of Dartmouth College.

Robinson Cook was born in Portland, Maine, January 30, 1895, son of Charles Sumner Cook, a native of Portland and a member of the legal profession, and of Annie Jefferds (Reed) Cook, who was born in Waldoboro, Maine. He received his earliest education in the public schools of Portland, continued his studies in Andover Academy, and prepared for college at the Abbott School, from which he was graduated with the class of 1914. He graduated from Dartmouth College, at Hanover, New Hampshire, in 1919, and then engaged in the insurance business in Portland. His office is located at 510 Fidelity building, No. 465 Congress Street, and he operates a general insurance business under his own name. Politically, he gives his support to the principles and the candidates of the Republican party, and he has always been interested in civic affairs. During the World War he was with the French Army as a member of the American Ambulance Corps for thirteen months, following December, 1916, and in 1918 he enlisted in the United States Navy, in which he served for about a year, receiving his discharge in 1919. He is a member of the Exchange Club, and his religious affiliation is with the Congregational church.

Robinson Cook was married, at Portland, Maine, September 27, 1922, to Eleanor Weston Cox, born in Portland, Maine, February 5, 1901, daughter of Edward W. and Lena Maude (Prince) Cox. Mr. and Mrs. Cook are the parents of two sons, both born in Portland: 1. Robinson, Jr., born September 12, 1923. 2. Charles Sumner, born December 16, 1924.

DELBERT W. ADAMS—From the beginning of his commercial career, Delbert W. Adams has been associated with the drygoods business, first as a clerk in a wholesale house when but nineteen years of age, floor salesman when twenty-two years old, and traveling salesman when a year older. He is now (1928), president and treasurer of three retail drygoods stores, one located in Augusta, one in Gardiner, both under the name of D. W. Adams Company, and another in Rumford, under the name of E. K. Day Company.

Delbert W. Adams was born in Caribou, Maine, August 31, 1868, son of David W. Adams, who was born at Rumford Point, Maine, now deceased, and of Amanda (Brown) Adams, who was born in Liver-

more, Maine. David W. Adams was one of the very early pioneers of Aroostock County, having gone there with his parents, Mr. and Mrs. David (Farnum) Adams, in 1844, when he was but nine years of age. Mr. Adams was proprietor and owner of the Adams Hotel in Caribou, which he conducted for many years. His mother, Amanda (Brown) Adams, was the daughter of Reuben Brown, who was among the early settlers of this county.

Delbert W. Adams received his education in the public schools of Caribou, and then found his first employment with R. H. White and Company, serving in the wholesale department at Boston, Massachusetts, from 1889 to 1891, and then representing the company as traveling salesman until 1894. In that year he made a change, resigning his position with White and Company, and identifying himself with Lee Tweedy and Company, of New York City, as traveling representative, covering New England. From 1894 to 1899 he continued this connection, and then spent nearly a year with Harding, Whitman & Company, of New York City, who were selling agents for the Arlington Mills of Methuen, Massachusetts. The Arlington Mills were at that time the largest dress goods manufacturing mills in the country, and in the employ of their selling agents, Harding, Whitman & Company, Mr. Adams traveled westward as far as Salt Lake City and southward as far as Louisiana, selling to the wholesale trade. In 1900, in association with Henry N. Whitman, who had been a traveling salesman in the employ of Brown, Durrell & Company, of Boston, for many years, Mr. Adams took over the old concern of Fowler and Hamlin, of Augusta, Maine, a retail drygoods store, which was located in the Meonian Block, and had been in operation for thirty-five years. The new concern was called the Whitman and Adams Company, and the business was continued under this firm name until January 1, 1913, when Mr. Adams purchased the stock of Mr. Whitman and changed the name to that of the D. W. Adams Company. In January, 1920, Mr. Adams further enlarged the scope of his interests by taking over also the entire store and merchandise of Buzzell and Weston Company, who were his largest competitors, and doing the largest drygoods business in the county at this time. He removed his original business to this location, Nos. 190-202 Water Street, Augusta, Maine, operating here also under the name of D. W. Adams Company, of which concern he is president and treasurer. Meantime, in March, 1919, Mr. Adams purchased the stock and fixtures of Bell Brothers, of Gardiner, Maine, and here too, he changed the name to that of D. W. Adams Company, of which he serves as president and treasurer. In September, 1925, he again enlarged his field by acquiring the stock and fixtures of the E. K. Day Company, of Rumford, Maine, but this business he continues to operate under the same name. Of this last-named enterprise, operating under the name of E. K. Day Company, Mr. Adams is president and treasurer, and Stanley M. Rice (q. v.), is manager and vice-president. His long association with the drygoods business, as well as his natural ability, especially his executive and administrative ability, give Mr. Adams every advantage in this line of business activity, and the last two years have brought rapid development in all of his retail drygoods enterprises. In addition to the responsibilities already mentioned, Mr. Adams is also a member of the board of trustees of the Augusta Trust Company, and a director of Edwards Manufacturing Company of Augusta. He is a Republican in his political sympathies, and is an active member of the Augusta Chamber of Commerce. He is well known in Masonic circles, being a member of all bodies and of the Consistory, in which he holds the thirty-second degree. He is a member of the Augusta Country Club and of St. Mark's Episcopal Church.

Delbert W. Adams married, in Lynn, Massachusetts, December 12, 1899, Alice Cornelia Faulkner, who was born in Charlestown, Massachusetts, daughter of Alonzo D. Faulkner, a native of Lynn, Massachusetts, and M. Anna (Sparhawk) Faulkner, of Marblehead. Mr. and Mrs. Adams are the parents of two children: 1. Marion Faulkner, who was born in Augusta, Maine, March 31, 1908. 2. Hope Sparhawk, born in Augusta, March 17, 1911.

FRANCIS E. CUMMINGS—For more than twenty years Francis E. Cummings has been identified with the post office of Portland in various capacities, ranging from substitute clerk to that of assistant postmaster, which office he now holds. He was appointed assistant postmaster, February 5, 1923, and his long association with the various departments of the post office enables him to serve with exceptional efficiency in his present position.

Francis E. Cummings was born in Westbrook, Maine, May 5, 1878, son of Francis E. Cummings, born in Portland Maine, died in 1892, and of Abbie M. (Edwards) Cummings, a native of Westbrook, Maine, whose death occurred in 1886. His father was a sea captain. He attended the public schools of Portland, graduating from Portland High School with the class of 1897. March 6, 1907, he became identified with the Portland Post Office as substitute clerk, and since that time his connection with the Portland Post Office has been continuous. He has served as foreman of carriers, as assistant superintendent of mails, and as acting superintendent of mails, and on February 5, 1923, he received his appointment to the position of assistant postmaster. Politically, Mr. Cummings gives his support to the Republican party, and has always been a public-spirited citizen. He has a most honorable military record, having served in the Spanish-American War in 1898, and later in the Philippines. He became a member of the National Guard in 1897, and a commissioned officer in 1901, and during the World War attended the Fortress Monroe Artillery School in 1918 and then became a member of the Forty-ninth Artillery Regiment in the American Expeditionary Forces, in which he served with the rank of major. He is a member and commander of Post No. 129, American Legion; a member of the Veterans of Foreign Wars, and also of the Spanish War Veterans. Fraternally, he is identified with the Blue Lodge, Free and Accepted Masons; Chapter, Scottish Rites; Mystic Shrine; and with the Knights of Pythias, and his club is the Men's Club, of Trinity Episcopal Church. He is a member of Trinity Episcopal Church, and has a host of friends in Portland.

Francis E. Cummings was married, at Woodfords, Maine, September 19, 1910, to Ethel G. Chaffey, born in Deering, Maine, daughter of Horatio and Annie (Gilbert) Chaffey. Mr. and Mrs. Cummings live in Portland.

DONALD WARD PHILBRICK—Among the younger members of the legal profession in Portland is Donald Ward Philbrick, who is a partner in the well-known legal firm of Verrill, Hale, Booth, & Ives, with offices located at No. 57 Exchange Street, Portland. Mr. Philbrick is a Bowdoin man, and received his professional training in Harvard. He is also a veteran of the World War, and was in active service overseas.

Donald Ward Philbrick was born in Skowhegan, Maine, March 16, 1896, son of Samuel W. Philbrick, a native of Skowhegan, born August 5, 1862, and of Mabel (Ward) Philbrick, also a native of Skowhegan, born August 16, 1868, died April 30, 1924. He received his earliest education in the public schools of his birthplace, graduating from Skowhegan High School in the class of 1913, and the following fall matriculated in Bowdoin College, at Brunswick, Maine, from which he was graduated in 1917, with the degree of Bachelor of Arts. After two years in military service in France, he began professional study in the Law School of Harvard University, where he completed his course with graduation in 1922, receiving at that time the degree of Bachelor of Laws. In September of the same year he was admitted to the bar of Maine, and began practice with the law firm of Verrill, Hale, Booth & Ives, at No. 57 Exchange Street, Portland. Able, energetic, and thoroughly prepared for his work he soon demonstrated the fact that he was of the calibre which commands success, and on January 1, 1925, he was admitted to partnership in the firm. He is engaged in general practice and although he has been so occupied for only about five years, he has already made for himself an assured place among his professional associates, and there is every prospect that an increasingly successful future lies before him.

Upon the entrance of the United States into the World War, Mr. Philbrick, who was just completing his course in Bowdoin College, enlisted, April, 1917, and was sent to the Officers' Training School. He was commissioned a lieutenant in the One Hundred and Sixty-seventh Infantry, Forty-second Division, known as the "Rainbow Division," of the American Expeditionary Forces, and was in active service overseas from November, 1917, to July, 1919. After the Armistice he served in the Intelligence Section at the General Headquarters of the American Expeditionary Forces. Upon his return to civilian life he entered Harvard Law School, and since the completion of his course there has been successfully engaged in general practice. He is a member of Delta Kappa Epsilon and of Phi Beta Kappa College fraternities; of the Bowdoin Club, of Portland, which he serves as secretary and treasurer; of the Portland Club; of the Portland Country Club; of the Reserve Officers' Association; and of the Military Order of the World War. He is also a member of Somerset Lodge, Free and Accepted Masons; Somerset Chapter, and De Molay Commandery, of Skowhegan, Maine; and of the Exchange Club, of which he is president. He is a member of Andrews Post of the American Legion, serving on its executive committee, and professionally is affiliated with the Cumberland County Bar Association. He is also a director of the Associated Charities in Portland. Politically, he gives his support to the Republican party, and his religious affiliation is with the State Street Congregational Church of Portland.

Donald Ward Philbrick was married, at Chipley, Florida, April 17, 1922, to Ruth Lockey, born in Chipley, daughter of William C. and Xuripha (Hutchison) Lockey, both natives of Florida. Mr. and Mrs. Philbrick are the parents of a son, Donald Lockey, born in Portland, Maine, May 3, 1923; and a daughter, Jean, born in Portland, June 3, 1927.

DAVID MURDOCK FORBES—As owner and publisher of the "Oxford County Citizen," David Murdock Forbes is at the head of a successful local publication which reaches some three thousand people. It is a weekly newspaper and before Mr. Forbes became the owner was known as the "Bethel News." The plant is located in Bethel, Maine, and the journal has been known by its present name since 1908.

David Murdock Forbes was born in Gorham, New Hampshire, August 8, 1891, son of William R. and Annie (Ross) Forbes, both born in Cape Breton, Nova Scotia, the first-mentioned a miner and a boilermaker. Mr. Forbes received his education in the public schools of Gorham, New Hampshire, and of Bethel, Maine, and finished his preparation for an active career with one year of study in Gould Academy, at Bethel, Maine. When school days were over he became identified with the "Bethel News," published by E. C. Bowler, at Bethel, beginning his connection with this paper in 1907. The following year, 1908, the name of the "Bethel News," was changed to indicate the larger scope of its interest, and was called the "Oxford County Citizen," which name it has continued to bear. In 1920 Mr. Forbes purchased the business. The publication is a weekly, filled with material of interest to the various towns and cities of Oxford County, but giving special attention to that part of the county surrounding Bethel. It is published on Thursdays, and is kept bright and newsy, progressive and modern, and is, withal, a most attractive newspaper. Mr. Forbes knows well the needs and the tastes of his subscribers, and is skillful in meeting those needs. Politically, he supports the principles of the Republican party, and he takes an active part in its local affairs. He served as tax collector of Bethel for two years, and has always been progressive in his views, generous in support of community betterment, and intelligent in his public policy. He is a member of Bethel Lodge, No. 97, Free and Accepted Masons, of Bethel, Maine; of Oxford Chapter, Royal Arch Masons, of Norway, Maine; and of Strathgloss Commandery, Knights Templar, of Rumford, Maine. He is also a member of Mount Abram Lodge, No. 31, Independent Order of Odd Fellows, and of Mollyocket Encampment, of West Paris, Maine; and of Sudbury Lodge, Knights of Pythias. He attends the Congregational church of Bethel, Maine.

David Murdock Forbes was married, August 2, 1916, in Bethel, Maine, to Emily Mae Burk, born in Bethel, December 17, 1888, daughter of Tilson B. Burk, a native of Milan, New Hampshire, and of Ida (Clark) Burk, who was born in Lynn, Massachusetts.

RALPH J. RILEY—Important in an industrial way in Livermore Falls is Ralph J. Riley, treasurer of the Record Foundry & Machine Company. He also has served Livermore Falls in several town offices, having been a selectman and a member of the

School Board. He is also active in lodge work in Livermore Falls. Mr. Riley was born in Lawrence, Massachusetts, June 7, 1882, son of Edwin and Rosa Riley. His father was born in England, and for many years has been engaged in manufacturing activity, now being president of the Record Foundry & Machine Company. Edwin Riley also is active in a fraternal way, being a member of the Free and Accepted Masons, in which order he has been through all bodies and has the thirty-second degree.

Ralph J. Riley received his education in the public schools of Livermore Falls, the Livermore Falls High School, from which he was graduated in the class of 1900; Williston Seminary, class of 1903; and the Burdett Business College, of Boston, Massachusetts. In 1905 and 1906 he worked for the Western Electric Company, in Chicago. Then he became identified with the Record Foundry & Machine Company, of Livermore Falls, manufacturing the Record line of quick-opening gate valves and Record conveyor sprockets, serving this company as treasurer. The company was organized in 1902 by his father, Edwin Riley, and others. The officers of the firm are: Edwin Riley, president; Fred Riley, manager; and Ralph J. Riley, treasurer.

Politically, Mr. Riley holds the views of the Republican party. He served his community as a selectman of Livermore Falls, and for six years was a member of the School Board of the town, 1913 to 1919. He is active in a number of lodges, being a member of the Free and Accepted Masons, in which order he is affiliated with the Blue Lodge, the Commandery, the Chapter, the Temple; and the Knights of Pythias. He belongs to the Sons of the American Revolution, the Sons of Veterans, and the Livermore Falls Automobile Association. He is a member of the Universalist church.

On November 8, 1904, in Livermore Falls, Ralph J. Riley married Myra A. Marston, born in Peru, Maine, the daughter of John and Martha Marston. Mr. and Mrs. Riley are the parents of the following children: Harley, and Rosilla, both born in Livermore Falls.

GEORGE HENRY RAND, M. D.—One of the leading physicians of Livermore Falls, Dr. George Henry Rand has been serving his community by safeguarding the public health ever since the beginning of the century. He started his medical practice in Sanford, where he remained in 1900 and 1901, but from that time onward he has been engaged in the practice of medicine in Livermore Falls.

The son of George Henry Rand, born in Canaan, Maine, and Fidelia (Stone) Rand, born in Ripley, Maine, Dr. George Henry Rand was himself born in Ripley, Maine, on October 5, 1876. He attended the public schools of Dexter, Maine, and the Dexter High School, graduating from the latter with the class of 1896. Then he went to the Boston University Medical School, from which he was graduated in the class of 1900, with the degree of Doctor of Medicine. It was in that year that he began his practice.

He has served as Health Officer in Livermore, and also as School Physician and a member of the School Board. He is a member of the Republican party and holds its political views. He belongs to the American Medical Association, the Medical Association of the State of Maine, and the Androscoggin County Medical Association, the Livermore Falls

Automobile Association, and the Free and Accepted Masons. In the Masonic Order he belongs to Oriental Star Lodge, the Commandery, Knights Templar; and the Temple, Ancient Arabic Order Nobles of the Mystic Shrine. He and his family are members of the Methodist church.

On September 27, 1906, in Livermore Falls, Dr. George H. Rand married Grace H. Ham, born in Livermore Falls, daughter of Joseph G. and Mary (Chandler) Ham, both natives of Maine. The Rands are the parents of the following children: George Henry, Mary Elizabeth, John Howard, and Bertha Louise, all born in Livermore Falls.

THOMAS WEBB WATKINS—Principal of the Kents Hill Seminary, at Kents Hill, Kennebec County, Thomas Webb Watkins has done much for the cause of education in his section of Maine, and his institution is well-known throughout New England.

Mr. Watkins was born in Boston, Massachusetts, February 23, 1885, the son of Rev. Thomas Corwin and Emma Dale (Hadley) Watkins. Following his early education in the public schools of Chelsea and Springfield, Massachusetts, Mr. Watkins graduated from the Newton, Massachusetts, High School, after which he entered Harvard University, graduating from that college in 1906 with the degree of Bachelor of Arts. Later, in 1921, Harvard conferred upon Mr. Watkins the degree of Master of Education. His first scholastic position was assumed following his graduation from Harvard, in 1906. He became principal of the high school at North Stratford, New Hampshire, holding that office until 1915, when he took up teaching at Youngstown, Ohio. He was there until 1918, when he enlisted for service in the American Army. Early in 1919 he became principal in the Northeastern Preparatory School in Boston, and in 1920 was appointed assistant headmaster of the Huntington School in Boston. In 1923 he left the Huntington School and came to Maine, since which time he has been principal of the Kents Hill Seminary. Mr. Watkins is a member of the Harvard Club, of Boston; of the Massachusetts Schoolmasters' Club; the National Education Association; the Maine Teachers' Association; the Secondary School Principals' Association, and the New England Association of Colleges and Secondary Schools. He is affiliated with the Free and Accepted Masons; the Phi Delta Kappa Fraternity; is a Methodist, and his political leaning, if any, is toward the Republican party.

On August 23, 1911, Mr. Watkins married, at Manchester, New Hampshire, M. Carlena Prescott. Mr. and Mrs. Watkins are the parents of two children: Thomas P., and Barbara.

WINFIELD F. PACKARD—Among Maine's gifted sons who, in educational matters, are equipped to lead the way in the supervision of the present day program of the public schools, Winfield F. Packard, superintendent of schools at Winthrop, Hallowell, and Manchester, has rendered to the schools, in double measure, the valued results of his training therein. As teacher, principal and superintending executive, Mr. Packard has thoroughly established his record as one who for more than a quarter of a century has been in active contact with the remarkable growth of all matters educational in the State.

Winfield F. Packard was born August 27, 1881, at Monmouth, a son of James B. Packard, native of Paris, a farmer and school teacher, and of Minnie A. (Harris) Packard, born at Green. Mr. Packard was a student in the Monmouth Public Schools, and was graduated at Monmouth Academy with the class of 1898, and at Eastern State Normal School in 1916. As a teacher, he entered upon his active career at Searsport, where he continued from 1900 to 1902, and from the latter year to 1905 he was a member of the teaching force at the Boston Agricultural School. Removing to Harpswell, Mr. Packard continued as a teacher in the public schools there from 1905 to 1907, and afterwards at Princeton from 1907 to 1915, having the superintendency of the schools there from 1911 to 1915.

Appointed as supervising principal at Augusta in 1915, Mr. Packard continued with increasing success in his work there; and in 1918, he was made superintendent of the schools at Winthrop, Hallowell, and Manchester. He is active in the Maine State Teachers' Association; and is a member of the Kennebec County Teachers' Association, and the National Education Association. Fraternally, he is affiliated with Lewys Allen Lodge, Free and Accepted Masons; Winthrop Chapter, No. 37, Royal Arch Masons; Alpha Council, No. 3, Royal and Select Masters; Trinity Commandery, Knights Templar; Order of the Eastern Star; the Consistory, Ancient Accepted Scottish Rite; and Lodge No. 87, Improved Order of Red Men. He attends the Universalist church.

Winfield F. Packard married, August 25, 1908, at Princeton, Alice Louise Kneeland, born in that township, January 5, 1892, daughter of John Alden Kneeland, who was born at Princeton, Maine, and of Stella (Simmons) Kneeland, a native of Princeton.

GUY FRANKLIN DUNTON—Important commercial and financial concerns of Portland are fortunate in being enabled to command official services of Guy Franklin Dunton, vice-president of the Chapman National Bank, treasurer of the Chase Transfer Company, and director or treasurer of nearly a dozen other concerns or associations having to do with a variety of activities in the "Pine Tree" State.

Born in South Portland, Maine, September 25, 1881, Guy Franklin Dunton is the son of James Frederick and Addie Eliza (Swett) Dunton, the former a master mariner, who followed the sea successfully for many years. He attended the public schools of Wiscasset Academy, of which he is a graduate. He supplemented his academic training with a commercial course at Shaw's Business College, Portland, from which he received its diploma on graduation.

Fully equipped to enter the world of business, for which he has always showed remarkable capacity, Mr. Dunton joined the staff of the Canadian Express Company at Portland, which he served in the capacity of clerk from 1899 to 1904. That connection furnished him with the element of practical experience that he so much desired before he should go on to a more responsible position. In the year that he left the express company, he accepted the invitation of the Chase Transfer Company, a Portland house, to become its treasurer. This position he has ever since held, having during the intervening period attained an enviable standing throughout the community for his financial acumen. Further recognition of Mr. Dunton's position of influence in the Portland community was made with his election to the board of directors of the Chapman National Bank in 1922, and to the office of active vice-president of the same institution in 1924. He also holds the offices of director and treasurer in the following companies: Preble Corporation, Eastern Extension Company, Naples Realty Company, Maine Lake-Shores, Incorporated, and the Pequawket Company; director and assistant treasurer of the Portland Nash Holding Company; director of the Maine Automobile Association, Falmouth Hotel, Maritime Bureau Chamber of Commerce, and the Preble Company.

Actively interested in philanthropies and charitable institutions, Mr. Dunton is a trustee of the Maine Eye and Ear Infirmary and a corporator of the Maine School for the Blind. He is a director of the Portland Boys' Club, and prominently identified with fraternal organizations, being affiliated with Ancient Landmark Lodge, Free and Accepted Masons; Mount Vernon Chapter, Royal Arch Masons; St. Albans Commandery, Knights Templar; the Temple, Ancient Arabic Order Nobles of the Mystic Shrine; Beacon Lodge, No. 67, Independent Order of Odd Fellows; and Portland Lodge, Benevolent and Protective Order of Elks. He is a member of the Portland Society of Arts, member and past president of the Portland Rotary Club, and a member of the Portland Club, Portland Athletic Club, Economic Club, and the Naples Country Club. He and his family have their religious affiliation with the Methodist Episcopal church.

Mr. Dunton married, October 5, 1904, at Peaks Island, Maine, Bessie May Dow, daughter of Joseph H. and Annie (Curtis) Dow. They have their residence on Coyle Street, Portland.

HAROLD G. RILEY—A man who, although still young, has attained considerable prominence in his work with the Record Foundry & Machine Company, of Livermore Falls, is Harold G. Riley. Mr. Riley started to work for this company in 1919. He is now in charge of the foundry and machine shop of the company, having been appointed superintendent in 1921. The son of Edwin Riley, he was born in Livermore Falls, December 6, 1898. He attended the public schools of Livermore Falls, the Livermore Falls High School, and later went to military school. Then he began his career with the Record Foundry and Machine Company.

When the war was on, Mr. Riley enlisted in May, 1917, and was with the American Expeditionary Forces. He also was in the Ambulance Service of the Italian Army. He was discharged from military service in May, 1919. He now belongs to the American Legion, the American Radio Relay League, Sons of Veterans, and is a member of the Republican party. He and his family attend the Universalist church.

Harold G. Riley was married, in Dover, New Hampshire, to Annie McNerney, daughter of William and Elizabeth McNerney. Mr. and Mrs. Riley are the parents of two children: 1. Patricia, born in Bar Mills, Maine. 2. Harold, Jr., born at Livermore Falls.

CHARLES ROSCOE SMITH, M. D.—A physician of wide experience and merited position is Dr. Charles Roscoe Smith. Beginning the practice of his profession at Livermore Falls, soon after he completed his medical training, he quickly won the confidence and the regard of his patients. In the years since that time, he has occupied a prominent place in the life of the community. He was born October 4, 1865, at Buxton, Maine. His father, Thomas H. Smith, also born at Buxton, was a farmer, and served as a colonel in the militia before the Civil War. His mother, Sarah (Porter) Smith, was born at Merrimac, New Hampshire.

Charles Roscoe Smith entered the public schools at Buxton, and lated attended Limerick Academy and Coburn Institute. In 1891, he was graduated from Bates College with the degree of Bachelor of Arts. He received the degree of Doctor of Medicine from Bowdoin College in 1897. Almost immediately he began the practice of general medicine at Livermore Falls, where he has remained to the present time. He is equally competent as a physician and surgeon. Politically, Dr. Smith is a member of the Republican party. He has served on the School Board for twenty-five years, and as secretary of the Board of Health for twenty years. He is affiliated with the Free and Accepted Masons, all bodies, and has taken the thirty-second degree in this order. He is also a member of the Knights of Pythias, and the Modern Woodmen of America. He is a member of his State and county bodies of the American Medical Association, and of the Livermore Falls Automobile Men's Association. He attends the Free Baptist Church of Livermore Falls.

On August 5, 1896, at Wells, Maine, Charles R. Smith married Hadassah Goodwin, daughter of Joseph A. and Adelphia Jane (Littlefield) Goodwin, both of Wells. Dr. and Mrs. Smith are the parents of two children, both of whom were born at Livermore Falls: 1. Delora Alpen, born July 1, 1900. 2. Roscoe H., born November 5, 1901.

DUGALD B. DEWAR—His broad knowledge of the general business world, and of financial opportunity and resources, both in the United States and in Canada, have opened for Dugald B. Dewar the way to his present success in his business as an investment security dealer, operating as D. B. Dewar & Company, at No. 78 Exchange Street, Portland, Maine. Whether in the capacity of salesman, textile manufacturer, or investment adviser, Mr. Dewar has readily and successfully responded to the demands of his vocation, no less than as a soldier in the ranks with his comrades at his country's call.

Dugald B. Dewar was born August 11, 1879, in New Brunswick, Canada, a son of Nevin Dewar, a farmer by occupation, and who served as a soldier in Canada, and of Barbara Ann (Sinclair) Dewar, both parents natives of Parish St. James, New Brunswick, Canada. Mr. Dewar attended the public schools in New Brunswick, and at Calais, Maine; and after leaving school, in 1892, he was first employed in a cotton mill, at Milltown, New Brunswick, and later, up to his nineteenth year, he made himself thoroughly acquainted with textile manufacturing in several mills, at Lowell, Massachusetts. Subsequent to his military service, Mr. Dewar was employed as a salesman for various concerns until 1912, in this country, and afterwards, in the course of ten years he made eighteen trips to the South American field of salesmanship, and in promotion of his own companies. Retiring from activities thus far afield, in 1922, owing to effects of war service, in April of that year, he located at Augusta, as Maine manager for Whitney, Cox & Company, investment dealers, with offices in the Chapman Building, Portland.

As an Independent voter, Mr. Dewar is active in behalf of the interests of good government. From 1899 to 1902, he was a member of the Ninth United States Infantry in the Philippine Islands and China campaigns, receiving his discharge from the service at Manila, in January, 1902.

Fraternally, Mr. Dewar is affiliated with the Benevolent and Protective Order of Elks; Free and Accepted Masons, in which he holds the thirty-second degree; and he is also a member of the Rotary Club; Portland and Augusta Country clubs; Fish and Game Association; Augusta Chamber of Commerce; Gardiner Shrine Club, and National Travel Club. His religious faith is that of the Congregational church.

Dugald B. Dewar married, June 18, 1902, at Lowell, Massachusetts, Gertrude G. Randlett, born in that city, November 3, 1881, daughter of Fred M. and Flora A. (Davis) Randlett, both born in Lowell. Their children: 1. Doris A., born in Lowell, married Robert Church Hunt, of New York City, in 1924. 2. Donald S., born in Dover, New Hampshire, now a student at University of Maine. 3. Barbara A., born in Boston, Massachusetts.

MILTON SHAW KIMBALL—The career of Milton Shaw Kimball has been identified with the banking business, and his recent appointment to the office of assistant vice-president of the Augusta Trust Company is rightfully considered as decidedly advantageous to the institution. Mr. Kimball is a graduate of Yale University, and has been identified with the Augusta Trust Company since 1924.

Milton Shaw Kimball was born in Bath, Maine, September 4, 1896, son of Frederick H. Kimball, native of Bath, Maine, engaged in the wholesale grocery business in Bath, a member of the Masonic Order, and of Mary (Shaw) Kimball, born in Greenville, Maine. Mr. Kimball attended the public schools of his birthplace, and then prepared for college in the Westminster School, at Simsbury, Connecticut. When his preparatory course was finished he entered Yale College, with the class of 1919. He began his active business career as manager of the Shaw Auto Company, of Brunswick, Maine, and continued that connection from 1919 to 1921, when he became identified with the firm of Maynard S. Bird & Company, bankers, of Portland, Maine, with whom he remained until 1924. In that year he became associated with the Augusta Trust Company, of Augusta, Maine, and this connection he has maintained to the present time (1928). In January, 1927, he was elected assistant vice-president of the Augusta Trust Company, which office he is now filling. Mr. Kimball gives his support to the Republican party. During the World War he served as a first lieutenant, balloon observation, Three Hundred and First Field Artillery, American Expeditionary Forces, and continued in service until January, 1919, when he received his discharge. He enlisted in August, 1917. Fraternally, Mr. Kimball is identified with Sola Lodge, No. 14, Free and Accepted Masons; and he is also a member of the American Leg-

ion, the Augusta Chamber of Commerce, and the Augusta Country Club. His religious membership is with the Congregational church.

Milton Shaw Kimball was married, in Omaha, Nebraska, September 20, 1919, to Helen B. Ingwersen, who was born in Chicago, Illinois, daughter of G. J. and Jessie (Brown) Ingwersen. Mr. and Mrs. Kimball have one daughter, Mary Brown Kimball, born in New York City.

WILLIS ELWOOD SWIFT, wholesale grocer in Augusta, Maine, a former mayor of that city, has been identified with many important commercial and banking enterprises in his adopted town, besides filling many State and municipal offices. Born in Sidney, Maine, September 19, 1870, where his father was a prosperous farmer, he is the son of George D. and Clara A. (Sawtelle) Swift. His early years were spent on the farm. His father was born at New Sharon, Maine, February 17, 1848, and his mother, born in Sidney, Maine, August 8, 1844, died in Sidney, August 7, 1925.

Educated in the public schools of Sidney, Willis Elwood Swift took a course in the Dirigo Business College of Augusta, Maine, and from 1890 to 1895, was bookkeeper for the hardware house of J. H. Cogan Company, of Augusta. In 1896, with H. J. Turner, he founded the firm of Swift & Turner, of Augusta, dealers in hardware and general merchandise. In 1908 the business was incorporated as the Swift & Turner Company, Incorporated, with Mr. Swift as president, and he remained with the corporation in that capacity until 1916, when he sold out his holdings. Together with Ward G. and Frank T. Holmes, he then organized the Holmes-Swift Company, of Augusta, Maine, becoming treasurer of the company, an office he still holds, with Frank T. Holmes as president. This company conducts a large wholesale grocery business at Nos. 345-347 Water Street, Augusta, Maine. In 1923, the Holmes-Swift Company purchased control of the Kennebec Grocery Company, of Waterville, Maine, and changed the name of the concern to Holmes-Swift, Incorporated. Arthur Davian was made president, and Raymond W. Swift treasurer of the new company, which has continued in business and prospered under control of the Augusta house. Its place of business is No. 5 Chaplin Street, Waterville. Mr. Swift is a director of the Waterville company, and also of the State Trust Company, of Augusta, and of the Augusta Loan & Building Association.

A Republican in politics, Mr. Swift was a member of the Augusta City Council in 1912; of the Maine House of Representatives, 1913-14; of the Maine Senate, 1915-18; of the Governor's Council, 1919-20, and again member and president of that council in 1921-22. In 1917-18 he was mayor of Augusta. He is a member of the Free and Accepted Masons, all bodies, having the thirty-second degree; of the Augusta Chamber of Commerce, the Rotary Club, the Augusta Country Club, and the Abnaki Club.

Willis Elwood Swift married Lillian Holmes, daughter of George W. and Elizabeth Holmes, in Augusta, Maine, July 22, 1894. She was born December 2, 1870, at Woodstock, New Brunswick, Canada; her father was a native of Machias, Maine. Their children are: 1. Raymond W., born April 22, 1895, in Augusta. 2. Marjorie Irene, born December 22, 1899, in Augusta.

FRANK T. HOLMES—Since December, 1921, Frank T. Holmes has been president of the wholesale grocery company known as the Holmes-Swift Company, wholesale grocers at Augusta. Mr. Holmes and his brother, Ward G. Holmes, were, with Willis E. Swift, the organizers of the concern. Frank T. Holmes was born in Jacksonville, New Brunswick, April 28, 1883, son of George W. Holmes, a shoemaker born in Machias, Maine, September 19, 1837, died in January, 1925, and of Elizabeth Holmes, born in Jacksonville, New Brunswick, August 24, 1846, died December 30, 1922.

He attended the public schools of Woodstock, New Brunswick, and of Augusta, Maine, and then found his first remunerative employment with R. F. Harmon & Company, wholesale produce dealers, with whom he remained from 1898 to 1901. His next connection was with N. T. Folsom, wholesale tobacco and confectionery dealer, with whom he remained but a short time. In 1902 he became identified with the Fuller-Holway Company, wholesale grocers, and in 1909 he was made a member of the firm, which connection was continued until 1914. In that year Mr. Holmes joined his brother, Ward G., and Willis E. Swift in the organization of the concern known as the Holmes-Swift Company, wholesale grocers, and since that time has been actively promoting the interests of this enterprise. Ward G. Holmes was the first president of the company and Frank T. Holmes was the first treasurer. Ward G. Holmes died December 22, 1921, and since that time Frank T. Holmes has been chief executive of the company. Politically, Mr. Holmes gives his support to the principles and the candidates of the Democratic party. He is a member of the Augusta Chamber of Commerce, and actively interested in its affairs. Fraternally, he is identified with the local Lodge, Free and Accepted Masons; with Cushnoc Chapter, Royal Arch Masons; and with Alpha Council, Royal and Select Masters; also with Trinity Commandery, Knights Templar. He is a member of the Rotary Club, and his religious affiliation is with the United Baptist Church.

Frank T. Holmes was married, in Augusta, Maine, June 9, 1909, to Iva B. Pierce, born in Augusta, Maine, November 25, 1883, daughter of J. Frank, a native of Windsor, Maine, who died in November, 1922, and of Emma (Hussey) Pierce, born in South Vassalboro, Maine. Mr. and Mrs. Holmes have two children: 1. Muriel E., born in Augusta, Maine, August 4, 1911. 2. Richard F., born in Augusta, Maine, December 4, 1916. Mr. and Mrs. Holmes reside at No. 112 Winthrop Street, Augusta.

STEPHEN J. HEGARTY—Twelve years of business experience preceded Stephen J. Hegarty's first connection with the Augusta Loan & Building Association, with which he has been identified since 1912, and of which he was made secretary and treasurer in 1921. In these two official positions he has been rendering valuable service, and has made himself known to his associates as a man of keen insight, clear vision, and sound judgment.

Stephen J. Hegarty was born in Hallowell, Maine, November 23, 1869, son of John H. Hegarty, a native of Ireland. He attended the public schools of his birthplace, including Hallowell High School, and then, in 1887, found his first remunerative employment with the Western Union Telegraph Company,

with whom he remained for about two years. He then became identified with the Associated Press, which connection he maintained until 1906, a period of sixteen years. His next business activity was of a different nature. He engaged in the clothing business in Augusta, Maine, in which line he continued successfully until 1912. Since that year he has been closely identified with the Augusta Loan & Building Association, and his business ability has been an important factor in the development of that enterprise. In 1921 he was made secretary and treasurer of the Augusta Loan & Building Association, and since·has continued in those official positions. He is also vice-president of the State Trust Fund and a trustee of the Kennebec Savings Bank. Politically, he gives his support to the principles and the candidates of the Democratic party. He is an active and interested member of the Augusta Chamber of Commerce, and fraternally is identified with the Knights of Columbus. His religious affiliation is with the Roman Catholic church.

Stephen J. Hegarty was married, in Augusta, Maine, June 24, 1902, to Mary B. Lynch, who was born in Augusta, Maine, December 18, 1868, daughter of Patrick and Catherine Lynch, both natives of Ireland.

WILLIAM H. NEWELL—For nearly half a century William H. Newell has been engaged in legal practice in Lewiston, Maine, and during that time he has established a professional record which places him easily among the foremost in his section of the State. In addition to his professional responsibilities Mr. Newell is also president of the Manufacturers' National Bank of Lewiston, in which official capacity he has served for the past twenty years.

William H. Newell was born in Durham, Maine, April 16, 1854, son of William B. Newell, a native of Durham, who was engaged in agricultural activities, and who was a member of the Masonic Order, and of Susanna K. Newell. He received his early education in the public schools of Durham, Maine, and then became a student in the Normal School at Farmington, Maine, after which he also studied in Kent's Hill Classical School. Like many of his professional associates, he taught school during the earliest years of his active career, using his spare time for the study of law. He read under the direction of Weston Thompson, of Brunswick, Maine, and was admitted to the Maine bar, April 25, 1878. He had been serving as principal of the school at Brunswick, Maine, while preparing for admission to the bar, and when he had passed his examinations and been admitted to the bar he continued in that position until 1882, when he came to Lewiston and opened an office. Since that time he has been successfully engaged in general practice and is widely known in this section as a keen analyst, an eloquent pleader, and a resourceful advocate. In addition to his professional responsibilities he has been a member of the board of directors of the Manufacturers' National Bank of Lewiston for thirty years, and its president for the past twenty years. Mr. Newell has always taken a very active interest in the public affairs of Lewiston and has always been ready to serve in official capacity when his professional knowledge and experience could in that way serve the community. He has served as mayor of Lewiston four different times as Auditor of Accounts, and as Solicitor, and he has been Judge of the Probate Court for the past eighteen years, and has recently been re-elected for another term of four years. He is a member of the American, State, and County Bar associations, and keeps thoroughly in touch with the progress of his profession throughout the country. He is also a member of the Lewiston Chamber of Commerce, and active in its affairs. Fraternally, he is identified with the Independent Order of Odd Fellows and with the Masonic Order, in which last he is a member of all the bodies up to and including the Consistory, in which he holds the thirty-second degree. He is a member of the American Bankers' Association, and his religious affiliation is with the Congregational church of Lewiston, Maine.

William H. Newell was married, in Lisbon, Maine, to Ida F. Plummer, of Lisbon, Maine, daughter of Edward, a native of Durham, and of Augusta (Taylor) Plummer. Mr. and Mrs. Newell are the parents of three children, all born in Lewiston: 1. Augusta P., deceased. 2. Gladys N., married Daniel T. Drummond. 3. Dorothy Q., married Roscoe E. Halliday.

RICHARD HENRY STUBBS, M. D.—For more than twenty-three years Dr. Richard Henry Stubbs has been engaged in general medical practice in Augusta, Maine, and during all that time he has been a member of the staff of the Augusta General Hospital. Dr. Stubbs has for many years been taking care of a large and important practice, and he is generally known as one of the skilled men of his profession. He is a graduate of Bowdoin College and of Harvard Medical School, and is a thirty-second degree Mason.

Philip H. Stubbs, father of Dr. Stubbs, was born in Strong, Maine, April 7, 1838, and died March 13, 1913. He was a lawyer by profession, and for many years was successfully engaged in practice in Strong, Maine. Graduating from Bowdoin College with the degree of Bachelor of Arts in 1860, and from Harvard Law School in 1863, degree of Bachelor of Laws, he passed the required examinations for admission to the bar and then devoted his energy to building up a practice in his birthplace, where he became one of the leading men of the community. He was active in local public affairs and in State affairs, served as County Attorney, and from 1883 to 1885 represented his district in the State Legislature. He married Julia Augusta Goff, who was born in Auburn, Maine, March 10, 1844, and they were the parents of Dr. Richard Henry Stubbs, of further mention.

Dr. Richard Henry Stubbs, son of Philip H. and Julia Augusta (Goff) Stubbs, was born in Strong, Maine, June 27, 1875, and received his earliest school training in a private school known as the May School, in Strong, Maine. He prepared for college in the Edward Little High School in Auburn, Maine, from which he was graduated with the class of 1894, and then matriculated in Bowdoin College, at Brunswick, Maine, where he finished his course with graduation in 1898, receiving at that time the degree of Bachelor of Arts. In college he was a member of Delta Kappa Epsilon Fraternity. He had chosen the medical profession as his future field of service and the following autumn began professional study in Harvard Medical School, from which he was graduated in 1902, with the degree of Doctor of

Medicine. After serving an internship of one year in Boston, he went to Vienna, Austria, where he did a considerable amount of post-graduate work, and upon his return to this country he also attended the Mayo clinics, and did post-graduate work in Chicago and in New York City. In 1904 he engaged in general practice in Augusta, Maine, and here he has since been engaged. In addition to the care of a large practice, Dr. Stubbs has also been a member of the surgical staff of the Augusta General Hospital since 1904, and has filled several public positions, including membership on the Maine State Board of Health, 1904-16, and he has always been actively interested in the general welfare of the city in which he lives and in which he practices his profession. He is a member of the Kennebec County Medical Society, of which he was president in 1911, and again president for the year 1928, also of the Maine State Medical Society, and of the American Medical Association. During the World War he served as a member of the Medical Advisory Board of Kennebec County, and was a supporter of all the various drives by means of which Augusta went "over the top" in her home war work. He is a member of the Augusta Chamber of Commerce. He is medical examiner for a large number of old line insurance companies. Fraternally, he is identified with the Free and Accepted Masons, holding membership in all the Scottish Rite bodies, and in the Consistory, in which he holds the thirty-second degree. His religious membership is with the Congregational church.

Dr. Richard Henry Stubbs was married, in Augusta, Maine, April 20, 1904, to Ethelyn Burleigh, who was born in Linneus, Maine, daughter of Edwin C. and Mary Jane (Bither) Burleigh, both natives of Linneus, Maine. Dr. and Mrs. Stubbs are the parents of one son, Richard H., Jr., who was born February 14, 1909.

MILTON OSWIN DEAN—The active career of Milton Oswin Dean has been closely identified with the textile industry of New England, and since 1919 he has been resident agent of the Edwards Manufacturing Company of Augusta, Maine, the largest manufacturing concern in this city. He is a descendant of John Dean who came from Chard, England, and landed in Massachusetts in 1636, and with his brother, Walter Dean, settled in Taunton, Massachusetts. He is also a direct descendant of John and Priscilla Alden of the Plymouth Colony. Mr. Dean is the son of Nathaniel Bradford and Eliza Frances (Luscomb) Dean, of Raynham and Taunton, Massachusetts. His father was for many years treasurer and general manager of Albert Field & Sons, at that time the largest manufacturers of tacks and nails in the world, having stores in many countries.

Milton Oswin Dean was born September 10, 1875, in Taunton, Massachusetts, where he attended the public schools. After finishing high school he entered the Philadelphia Textile School, receiving honors for his excellent work and being awarded the National Wool Manufacturers' medal. When his course was completed he entered the textile mills of Taunton, later going to New Bedford. In 1907 he went to work for the Dwight Manufacturing Company of Chicopee, Massachusetts, as designer and assistant superintendent. The following year he was made general superintendent of the entire plant. In 1914 he accepted a position as superintendent of the Laconia Division of the Pepperell Manufacturing Company of Biddeford, Maine. Three years later, in 1917, he went to Utica, New York, to become general superintendent of the Utica Steam & Mohawk Valley Cotton Mills. The following year he returned to the Pepperell Manufacturing Company as assistant agent, where he served until 1919. In that year he accepted his present position as resident agent of the Edwards Manufacturing Company of Augusta, Maine, in which connection he has now completed over eight years of most efficient work. He has won the confidence and the esteem of those with whom he has been associated and is known as a man of ability and integrity.

He is vice-president of the Boston Textile Club, member of the National Association of Cotton Manufacturers, member of the Associated Industries of Maine, Augusta Chamber of Commerce, trustee of the Kennebec Savings Bank of Augusta, a member of the Old Colony Historical Society, a director of the Augusta General Hospital, a director of the Augusta Young Men's Christian Association, where he formerly served as president, a member of the South Parish Congregational Church of Augusta, vice-president of the Maine Congregational Conference, and is also identified with the Free and Accepted Masons.

Milton Oswin Dean was married, in Fairhaven, Massachusetts, August 7, 1906, to Susan P. Jackson (Bachelor of Arts, Boston University, 1904), who was born in Fairhaven, Massachusetts, February 6, 1883, daughter of Albert and Elizabeth (Roe) Jackson. Mr. and Mrs. Dean are the parents of four children: 1. Priscilla Alden, born in Chicopee, Massachusetts, July 27, 1909. 2. Elenor Frances, born in Chicopee, Massachusetts, May 10, 1912. 3. Estelle Jackson, born in Saco, Maine, June 27, 1916. 4. Susan, born in Saco, Maine, February 16, 1919.

NATHANIEL BRAGDON WOODSUM, factory manager of Oakland, Maine, was born in Peru, Maine, November 6, 1869, the son of William and Harriette M. (Demeritt) Woodsum. His father, born in Sumner, Maine, January 20, 1826, died January 4, 1898, was a merchant and general storekeeper, served as justice of the peace in West Peru, and was a member of the Maine Legislature in 1876. His mother, born in Peabody, Massachusetts, June 6, 1836, died October 19, 1898.

Educated in the public schools of Peru and Dixfield, Maine, and at Kents Hill Academy, Nathaniel Bragdon Woodsum taught school in several places in Maine from 1887 to 1892, and worked for a time in the pulp mill at Livermore Falls. He then entered the service of the Portland & Rumford Falls Railroad Company and spent twelve years in general office work, which included ticket selling, and freight and express transportation. In 1905 he retired from railroad work to go into business for himself, and ever since that time he has been identified with the manufacture of toothpicks, clothes-pins and wooden novelties, and for years was manager of the wood-turning plant in Dixfield, Maine. His business connections have been with the Livermore Falls Pulp & Paper Company, and the Forster Manufacturing Company. Having managed the wood-turning plant in 1918-19, he was made manager also of the factories at Dixfield and Oakland.

Mr. Woodsum is a member and a trustee of the Methodist church. He is a Republican, but has never sought office. He is president of the Oakland Chamber of Commerce, a member of the Associated Industries of Maine, of the Maine Hardwood Association, and charter member of the Kiwanis Club. He is a member and Past Master of the Free and Accepted Masons, and holds the thirty-second degree in the Scottish Rite of that order. He is also affiliated with the Independent Order of Odd Fellows.

Nathaniel Bragdon Woodsum married (first) Bertha P. Wyman, at Peru, Maine, December 25, 1891, who was born in Peru, November 9, 1871, died July 13, 1919. He married (second) Nellie Witham Stanley, in Portland, Maine, April 16, 1921, born in Belgrade, Maine, April 10, 1876. Children of the first marriage were: Gerald R., born in Peru, February 7, 1893, and Esther M. (Grover), born in Peru, June 30, 1896.

STANLEY M. RICE—For more than twenty years Stanley M. Rice has been identified with the retail drygoods business in various cities in New England, and since 1925 he has been manager and vice-president of the E. K. Day Company, of Rumford, Maine. This concern is headed by Delbert W. Adams (q. v.), of the D. W. Adams Company, Incorporated, and is one of the leading retail drygoods concerns of Rumford.

Stanley M. Rice was born in Yarmouth, Maine, April 14, 1891, son of Oliver D. Rice, now deceased, who was engaged in the grain and flour business, and of Carrie B. (Soule) Rice, who was born in Yarmouth, Maine. After attending the public schools of Yarmouth, including the high school, he went to Portland, Maine, and entered the employ of the J. L. Libby Company, with whom he remained during the years 1907-08. He then went to Boston, Massachusetts, and associated himself with the R. H. White Company, retail drygoods merchants, and he maintained this connection for three years, 1908-1911. In 1911 he further enlarged and diversified his experience by making another change, this time identifying himself with Gilchrist and Company, engaged in the same line in Boston. Here, for a period of eight years, he gained valuable experience and rendered efficient service, but in 1919 he returned to Portland, Maine, and entered the employ of the Markson Brothers. Before the end of the year he severed that connection and identified himself with D. W. Adams, who was engaged in the retail drygoods business in Augusta, Maine, but in 1921 he associated himself with the Harvard Bazaar, of Cambridge, where he remained until 1925, when he was appointed to his present position as manager of the E. K. Day Company, at Rumford, Maine, and made vice-president of the company. This responsible position Mr. Rice is still (1928) filling. He was appointed at the time the business was taken over by Delbert W. Adams, who is president of the company.

Mr. Rice gives his support to the principles and the candidates of the Republican party. He is a member of the Rumford Business Men's Association, and is a public-spirited citizen who can be counted upon to give his support to any well conceived plan for the betterment of the community. He is a member of the Masonic Order, Lodge, Chapter, Council, and Commandery; and his clubs are the Rotary and the Oakdale Country. His religious affiliation is with the Episcopal church.

Stanley M. Rice was married, in Boston, Massachusetts, August 12, 1913, to Elizabeth Brown, who was born in Boston, Massachusetts, June 10, 1892, daughter of Charles and Amelia Brown, both natives of England. Mr. and Mrs. Rice are the parents of three children: 1. Marjorie E., born in Boston, Massachusetts, June 6, 1914. 2. Maurice E., born in Augusta, Maine, May 28, 1919. 3. Nancy Soule, born in Rumford, Maine, April 4, 1926.

THOMAS JAMES ABERNETHY—As principal of Stephens High School of Rumford, Maine, Thomas James Abernethy is rendering a distinctive service to that community. He is a Harvard man, class of 1917, and is a veteran of the World War, in which conflict he was awarded the Distinguished Service Cross and the French Croix de Guerre with the palm leaf. Mr. Abernethy was principal of the high school in Ellsworth, Maine, before coming to Rumford. He was born in Perry, Maine, September 24, 1895, son of James Abernethy, a native of the Shetland Islands, Scotland, engaged in the business of canning sardines, and of Mary Grainger (Young) Abernethy, a native of Glasgow, Scotland.

Thomas James Abernethy attended the public schools of Pembroke, Maine, graduating from Pembroke High School with the class of 1911, and prepared for college in the East Maine Conference Seminary, class of 1912. In the fall of 1913 he entered Harvard University, where he completed his course in 1917, receiving the degree of Bachelor of Arts. On July 23, 1917, he enlisted for service in the World War and was sent overseas as a member of the 147th Squadron, First Pursuit Group, of the Air Service, American Expeditionary Forces, with which he was a first lieutenant, serving with the French and American armies on the front from May 10, 1918, until November 11, 1918. For valor in service he received not only the Distinguished Service Cross of this country, but he also was awarded the French Croix de Guerre, with palm leaf. After receiving his discharge on July 12, 1919, Mr. Abernethy entered the employ of the Sunset Packing Company, of West Pembroke, Maine, with whom he remained from 1919 to 1921, as assistant manager, with his father. In 1921 he accepted a position as principal of the high school in Ellsworth, Maine, and there for a period of four years he continued to serve most successfully. In 1925 he came to Rumford as principal of Stephens High School, and here he is making his influence powerfully felt among the high school pupils. His service here is as distinctive as was his action during the World War, and though the public schools of the United States have no system of awarding distinguished service medals to notably successful teachers and administrators, still the reward of the kind of service which Mr. Abernethy is giving is one that can be seen and felt, and in the sincere coöperation of students and teachers, in the brightening faces of the high school body when their principal addresses them, and in the generally high standards and the splendid morale of the school, even an officer of the Aviation Service may well find a satisfying reward.

Mr. Abernethy is a member of the Maine State Teachers' Association; the Maine Association of Secondary School Principals; the National Association of Secondary School Principals, of which he is a member of the executive committee; the Oxford County Teachers' Association, and the Oxford County

Schoolmasters' Club. At the present time (1928) Mr. Abernethy is retaining his connection with the military service of his country as a captain in the United States Infantry Reserve. He is a member of the American Association for the Promotion of Aviation, and of the American Legion, also of the Reserve Officers' Association. Politically, he gives his support to the principles and the candidates of the Republican party, and fraternally, he is identified with Crescent Lodge, No. 78, Free and Accepted Masons; Crescent Chapter, No. 26, Royal Arch Masons; and Blanquefort Commandery, No. 10, Knights Templar. He is a member of the Rotary Club, and his religious affiliation is with the Congregational church.

Thomas James Abernethy was married, in New York City, February 25, 1918, to Edna Clarice Stoddard, who was born in Pembroke, Maine, August 24, 1896, daughter of James K. P. and Frances Afra (Rice) Stoddard, both natives of Maine. Mr. and Mrs. Abernethy have two children: 1. Thomas James, Jr., who was born in West Pembroke, Maine, June 14, 1920. 2. Mary Grainger, born in Eastport, Maine, September 7, 1925.

JAMES McDOUGALL—The long and active career of James McDougall has been devoted to the textile business, first as a mill worker, then as superintendent, and, during the greater part of his career, as agent. In the last-named capacity he has been identified with many mills in several different localities, but since December, 1911, he has been agent for the Vassalboro Mills, at North Vassalboro, Maine.

James McDougall was born in Ramsey, Ontario, Canada, September 21, 1869, son of Peter McDougall, a native of Scotland, engaged in the wool manufacturing business, and who is a captain in the Volunteer Canadian Army, and of Isabella (McEwan) McDougall. He received his earliest education in the public schools of Ramsey, Canada, and then attended the high school in Almont, Canada. When school days were over he found work in the woolen mills of Blakney, Ontario. Later, he was superintendent's assistant in the Wesson Mills at Wesson, Mississippi, and still later, for about eight months, he served as assistant superintendent of the Anderson mills at Skowhegan, Maine. His next connection was with the Kennebec Mills, at Fairfield, Maine, and there he remained for five years. At the end of that time he went to the Royalston Mills, at South Royalston, Massachusetts, as agent, for a year, and then further diversified his experience by serving as agent for the Indian Spring Mills, at Madison, Maine, for a short time. In December, 1911, he became agent for the Vassalboro Mills at North Vassalboro, Maine, and here he has remained to the present time (1928). Mr. McDougall is well known to the trade and in his present position is demonstrating both his ability and the value of a varied previous experience. He is a member of the board of directors of the Peoples' National Bank of Waterville, Maine. Fraternally, he is identified with the Masonic Order, in which he is a member of all the bodies, including the Blue Lodge, of Victoria, Province of Quebec, Canada, and of the Consistory, in which he holds the thirty-second degree. He is also a member of the Benevolent and Protective Order of Elks and of the Waterville Country Club, and his religious affiliation is with the Presbyterian church.

James McDougall was married, in Fairfield, Maine,

September 10, 1910, to Alice P. Marble, who was born in Dexter, Maine.

PHILIP F. CHAPMAN—A careful legal training has ever been regarded as a worthy asset to such members of that honored profession as enter the business world, and it is to the everlasting credit of barristers that they can hold their own in the counting room as well as at the bar. A conspicuous example of a lawyer who has attained distinction in his profession and added to his accomplishments a brilliant success as a financier is Philip Freeland Chapman, of Portland.

A consideration of Mr. Chapman's environments as well as his inherent abilities must convince one that he was predestined to success. Men who are accustomed to battle the rigorous northern winters and go regularly into the forests to blaze new trials and take the path of the hunter develop a hardihood and self-reliance that is seldom known to the peoples of warmer climates. From such forebears, who have long furnished leaders in the life of New England does Mr. Chapman spring, and he has built upon their well-laid foundation a superstructure of achievement that must·serve as his own monument in the present and constitute a beacon light to be emulated by his followers.

Philip Freeland Chapman was born November 3, 1884, at Portland; he grew to manhood in this city and has resided here among his people ever since. He entered the public schools when a boy of five, continuing through the various grades until he reached the Portland High School, from which he was graduated with a creditable record in 1902. He attended Phillips-Exeter Academy at Exeter, New Hampshire, during his senior year at High School, and was graduated from Exeter in the same year, 1902, entering Bowdoin College in the fall of 1902. In this ancient institution, the *alma mater* of so many noted men—notably lawyers like Fuller and Fessenden—he entered upon his academic duties, and four years later, in 1906, he was graduated with honors *summa cum laude*. Having fully determined that the proper exercise of his particular talents lay in the realm of law, he matriculated at the Harvard Law School; at Cambridge, Massachusetts, and by maintaining his previous high standard of scholarship was graduated with honor in 1909, with the degree of Bachelor of Laws.

A few weeks afterwards, on passing the bar examinations, he was admitted to the bar of the State of Maine, and immediately took up the practice of his profession in Portland. Practicing alone for six years, he made a splendid beginning, building up a large clientele for so young a man. In 1915 he took into partnership with him Ralph O. Brewster, a young man who had come to Portland from Dexter, Maine. This was the beginning of the well-known partnership of Chapman & Brewster. Ten years later, it is interesting to note, this same young partner, Brewster, became Governor of the State of Maine.

Mr. Chapman's native endowments and his careful training soon placed him among the leaders of his profession in Cumberland County, and also made his services and counsel indispensable in a business way. He was elected a director of the Chapman National Bank in 1911, its vice-president in 1915, its president in 1917, a position he still holds with much credit to himself and his associates and with great

satisfaction to the institution's numerous patrons. Other business institutions in which he has had an interest include the Portland & Ogdensburg Railway, of which he is a director, and of which he served as treasurer for many years; the Preble Corporation, of which he is president; T. A. Huston & Company, the Wildwood Park Association, the Portland "Evening News," the United States Trust Company, of Portland, and the Cumberland Loan and Building Association, of which two last-named institutions he served as a director for many years, and the Morris Plan Bank, of Portland, of which he is a director.

In civic affairs he is also prominent, having been identified with the affairs of the Portland Water District, serving for many years as one of its trustees. As chairman of the Board of Health of Portland for several years he rendered excellent service, with a number of innovations and reforms to his credit. As a member of the Republican party he is a close student of local, State and national affairs, and his friends assert that if he ever decides to enter broader fields involving the suffrages of his fellow-citizens, the highest honors await him.

In service, charitable and religious organizations, Mr. Chapman has always been active. He has served as a trustee of the Maine Eye & Ear Infirmary for a great many years and was for many years its secretary. He is a charter member of the Portland Kiwanis Club, was its first treasurer; a director of the Portland Boys' Club, a past director for many years of the Associated Charities of Portland, also of the Children's Protective Society, a director of the Portland Widows' Wood Society. He is an active director of the Young Men's Christian Association of Portland, having served for several years as the vice-president of this association and also a director of the Army and Navy Young Men's Christian Association. He is an active member of the Maine Historical Society, also the Portland Society of Art. In the affairs of the Williston Congregational Church he has always taken an active part, having served as one of its deacons for fourteen years.

Mr. Chapman possesses the love of an ancient Greek athlete for athletics and outdoor sports. He is an enthusiastic yachtsman and swimmer and is a skilled participant in basketball, golf and tennis, having won the State tennis championship in 1917 in singles, and a number of times in doubles. He is a loyal member and supporter of the Portland Athletic Club, having served as its vice-president for a great many years.

Mr. Chapman has always been a great lover of music and while at college was a leader of the Bowdoin Musical Club for three years and the mandola soloist of the club during that period. He is a loyal supporting member of the Portland Men's Singing Club and served for many years on the executive committee of the Western Branch of the Maine Musical Festival.

Mr. Chapman joined the Third Maine Infantry Regiment for World War duty in September, 1917, as a private. In November of that year he became a first lieutenant in Company A, and was advanced to the rank of major of the First Battalion of that command in July, 1918, later becoming its lieutenant-colonel. His command was impatiently waiting to be sent into active service when the word was received that an Armistice had been signed. He now holds the rank of lieutenant-colonel on the staff of the Governor of Maine and lieutenant-colonel in the Officers' Reserve Corps of Maine.

Mr. Chapman moves in the select social circles of Portland, and maintains membership in a number of social clubs, including the Portland Club, the Cumberland Club, the Economic Club; Portland Yacht Club; Portland Country Club; Portland Athletic Club; he is an enthusiastic member of the Bowdoin Club of Portland, and the University Club of Boston.

In fraternal circles he is a member of the Free and Accepted Order of Masons, is a Knights Templar, Portland Commandery; a Shriner, and a member of the international fraternity of Alpha Delta Phi.

Mr. Chapman has always been a very interested and loyal alumnus of his *alma mater*, Bowdoin College. He served as his class agent in connection with the Bowdoin Endowment and Alumni Funds, has always been an enthusiastic member of the Bowdoin Club of Portland, having served as its president during the year 1922, was appointed and acted as grand marshal of the Bowdoin Commencement of 1926, was elected and served two terms of three years each on the Alumni Council of Bowdoin College, being president of the Council during the year 1922.

On October 23, 1909, in Portland, Maine, Mr. Chapman married Gladys Doten, daughter of Roswell F. and Clara (Stevens) Doten, pioneer residents of Portland, and representatives of that older type of citizenship in which there are so many admirable qualities. The home life of Mr. Chapman is ideal, and in it he and Mrs. Chapman dispense a delightful hospitality. Mr. and Mrs. Chapman are the parents of three children: 1. Virginia, born September 15, 1910. 2. Marion Carter, born October 3, 1913. 3. Philip Freeland, Jr., born August 21, 1917.

In his business life Mr. Chapman puts aside all selfish interests for the benefit of the community and well lives up to the Kiwanis motto, "He profits most who serves best." He is a man of exceedingly pleasing personality and for each and every one who comes within his purview he has a kindly word of greeting and encouragement. Certainly these qualities, taken with the ones adverted to above, must commend themselves to the busines world generally in an age that has undergone such momentous changes in the last strenuous decade.

HORACE EVERITT DOUGHTY, M. D.—
Though he has been engaged in medical practice since 1909, Dr. Horace Everitt Doughty is one of the latest of his profession to open an office in Oxford, Maine. He came to Oxford, in 1927, and is building up a very satisfactory practice here. He was born in Somersworth, New Hampshire, December 24, 1873, son of Julius H. Doughty a native of Yarmouth, Maine, a mechanic by trade, a veteran of the Civil War, serving with the Thirty-seventh Maine Infantry for three years and of Fannie (Young) Doughty, born in Somersworth, New Hampshire.

Dr. Doughty attended the public schools of Farmington, New Hampshire, and after completing his course in the Farmington High School became a student in the New Hampton Literary Institute. As he had decided to enter the medical profession he matriculated at Baltimore Medical School, from which he was graduated with the class of 1909, receiving the degree of Doctor of Medicine. Upon the completion of his professional training he opened an office for general practice at Milan, New Hampshire, in 1909, and continued there until 1911, when he removed to Lisbon Falls, Maine, where he remained until 1915. In that year he again made a change, going to Andover, Maine, where he remained for twelve years. In 1927 he came to Oxford, Maine. He has already made himself known as a skilled practitioner and each month is adding to the list of his patients. Politically, Dr. Doughty gives his support to the candidates of no one political party, but casts his votes for those whom he considers personally best qualified to fill the office, regardless of party affiliations. Fraternally, he is a member of the Improved Order of Red Men; also of Searsmont Lodge, Free and Accepted Masons. His religious affiliation is with the Baptist church.

Horace Everitt Doughty was married, in Portland, Maine, and has two children, both born in Milan, New Hampshire: Edward, and Helen.

AARON P. McFARLAND—For the past fourteen years Aaron P. McFarland has been identified with banking in Boston, Massachusetts, and in Waterville, Maine. In 1926 he was made manager of the Lisbon Falls branch of the Lewiston Trust Company, and that responsible position he is efficiently filling at the present time (1928).

Aaron P. McFarland was born in Montville, Maine, August 25, 1886, son of Daniel McFarland, born in Montville, who has been proprietor of a general store there for many years, and of Josie (Atkinson) McFaralnd, also a native of Montville. After attending the public schools of his birthplace Mr. McFarland continued study in the Maine Central Institute, at Pittsfield, Maine, and then finished his training in Kent's Hill Academy. When his academic training was completed he began his business career in a general store in Montville, Maine, where he remained from 1908 to 1913. In 1913 he began his connection with the banking business by entering the employ of the Liberty Trust Company of Boston, Massachusetts. This connection he maintained until 1917, when he became identified with the Ticonic National Bank of Waterville, Maine. There he remained until 1926, when he came to Lisbon Falls, Maine, as manager of the Lisbon Falls branch of the Lewiston Trust Company, which responsible position he was filling in 1928. In his political sympathies Mr. McFarland is a Republican. He is a public-spirited citizen, always willing to give generous support to any plan which seems to him to be likely to advance the interests of the community. He is an interested member of the Waterville Chamber of Commerce and, fraternally, is identified with the Liberty Lodge, Free and Accepted Masons; with the local Chapter, Royal Arch Masons, and Dunlap Commandery, No. 5, Knights Templar, of Bath, Maine. His religious membership is with the Methodist church.

Aaron P. McFarland was married at Montville, Maine, October 14, 1911, to Nettie A. Ramsey, who was born in Montville, Maine, September 4, 1891, daughter of Oakes A. Ramsey, a native of Montville, and of Huldah (Wentworth) Ramsey, also a native of Montville. Mr. and Mrs. McFarland have one son, Edward A., born in Montville, Maine, June 28, 1912.

OLIVER MOSES (3)—As assistant treasurer and general superintendent of the Worumbo Manufacturing Company, of Lisbon Falls, Maine, Oliver Moses (3) is identified with one of the substantial manufacturing concerns of the State. Mr. Moses is a graduate of Bowdoin College and received special training in the Lowell Textile School.

Oliver Moses (3) was born April 28, 1899, son of Oliver (2), who was born in Bath, Maine, May 26, 1867, and is treasurer of the Worumbo Manufacturing Company at Bath, Maine, and of Augusta (Plummer) Moses, a native of Lisbon Falls, Maine, born February 20, 1874. Mr. Moses attended the public schools of Bath, Maine, including the high school, and then prepared for college in Phillips-Exeter Academy. When his preparatory course was completed he matriculated in Bowdoin College at Brunswick, Maine, from which he was graduated with the class of 1920, receiving the degree of Bachelor of Arts. After graduation he took a special course in the Lowell Textile School and then became identified with the Worumbo Manufacturing Company at Lisbon Falls, beginning his connection with that concern in March, 1921. He filled various positions, being promoted from one department to another, until February, 1927, when he was appointed superintendent of the concern. In March of the same year he was elected assistant treasurer, and since that time he has been filling both positions.

Mr. Moses gives his support to those local candidates whom he considers best qualified to fill the office, and classifies himself as an Independent in his political views. During the participation of the United States in the World War he was in active service in the navy. Fraternally, he is identified with Polar Star Lodge, No. 114, Free and Accepted Masons, of which he is a Past Master; Montgomery and St. Bernard Chapter, Royal Arch Masons, of which he is a High Priest; the Council, Royal and Select Masters; Dunlap Commandery, No. 5, Knights Templar, and Kora Temple, Ancient Arabic Order Nobles of the Mystic Shrine. He is a member of the Universalist church.

Oliver Moses (3) was married at Bath, Maine, December 1, 1923, to Eleanor Doyle, born in Bath, January 8, 1904, daughter of Daniel Doyle, a native of Portland, Maine. Mr. and Mrs. Moses are the parents of one son, Oliver (4), born in Bath, September 22, 1924.

FREDERICK CHARLES BAGLEY—The greater part of the active career of Frederick Charles Bagley has been identified with the paper manufacturing industry, and after sixteen years of association with the Great Northern Paper Company and some five years with the Canadian Export Company, Limited, he came to Augusta, Maine, as general manager of the Cushnoc Paper Corporation.

Frederick Charles Bagley was born in Bangor, Maine, December 10, 1877, son of Charles E., a native of Bangor, Maine, now retired, and of Ellen (Ryan) Bagley, who was born in Hampden, Maine. He attended the public schools of Bangor, including Bangor High School, and then further prepared for an active busniess career by taking a course in the Bangor Business School. When his commercial training was completed he entered the employ of the Bangor & Aroostook Railroad, which connection he maintained from 1896 to 1901. In 1901 he began his long connection with the paper manufacturing industry by entering the employ of the Great Northern Paper Company, with whom he remained for sixteen years, from 1901 to 1917, filling various positions, and gaining a thorough knowledge of the industry. In 1917 he associated himself with the Canadian Export Company, Limited, of Montreal, Canada, where he remained for four years. In 1922 he came to Augusta, Maine, and became identified with the Cushnoc Paper Corporation as general manager, and this connection he has maintained to the present time (1928). This concern manufactures news print paper, and employs about two hundred and seventy-five people. Mr. Bagley is well-known to the paper manufacturing trade, and in the various connections in which he has been employed he has gained a thorough knowledge of all branches of the industry. In his present connection he is giving valuable service and is recognized not only as a skilled technician, but also as an able administrator. He gives his support to the Republican party and, fraternally, is identified with Nollesemic Lodge, Free and Accepted Masons. He is an attendant of the Congregational church.

Frederick Charles Bagley married (first), in Waterville, Maine, April 3, 1898, Jane R. Roberts who was born in Bangor, Maine, November 17, 1876, daughter of Henry C. Roberts. He married (second), in Augusta, Maine, September 20, 1923, Bessie R. Wing, who was born in Augusta, Maine, daughter of William W. and Annette (Choate) Wing. Mr. Bagley has five children, the first two born in Bangor, Maine, the last three in Millinocket, Maine: 1. Mrs. W. H. Toppan. 2. Mrs. James W. Merrill. 3. Frederick C., Jr., 4. Lauren R. 5. Carleton W.

WILLIAM JOHN WARRELL—For more than twelve years William John Warrell has been the efficient general superintendent of the D. W. Adams Company, a retail drygoods concern of Augusta, Maine. The establishment is located at No. 190 Water Street and is one of the oldest drygoods concerns in the city, though it has been operated under its present name only since January, 1913. Mr. Warrell is a thirty-second degree Mason and is well known in club circles here.

Alexander Warrell, father of Mr. Warrell, was born in Kings County, New Brunswick, Canada, and died in 1926. He was a well-known business man of Montreal, Canada, and for many years was president of the Railway Asbestos Packing Company, of Montreal and Sherbrooke in Canada, and of Worcester, Massachusetts. He married Sarah Jane Hoey, also a native of Kings County, New Brunswick, and among their children was William John, of further mention.

William John Warrell was born in St. Johns, New Brunswick, Canada, April 12, 1881, and received his early school training in the public schools of his birthplace. Later he was a student in the Fredericton Military School. His first remunerative position was with the firm of Manchester, Robinson & Allison, wholesale and retail importers of St. Johns, New Brunswick, Canada, with whom he remained from 1902 to 1906. In the last-named year he came to the United States and located in Portland, Maine, where he entered the employ of the J. R. Libby Company as buyer and manager, remaining with them from 1906 to 1915. In 1915 he came to Augusta, Maine, as general superintendent of the retail drygoods concern known as the D. W. Adams Company, located at No. 190 Water Street in Augusta, where he has continued to the present time (1928.) Politically, Mr. Warrell gives his support to the Republican party. He is a member of the Augusta Chamber of Commerce and is well known in the local clubs, especially in the Augusta Country Club and the Rotary Club. He is also a member of all the York Rite bodies of the Masonic Order and of the Consistory, in which he holds the thirty-second degree; and of Kora Temple, Ancient Arabic Order Nobles of the Mystic Shrine. He is a member of the Abanakis Club. His religious interest is with the Congregational church, of which he is an attendant.

William John Warrell was married, in Dover-Foxcroft, Maine, September 23, 1909, to Janet E. Jack, who was born in Dover-Foxcroft, Maine, daughter of Thomas and Rachel (Dow) Jack, both natives of Scotland. Mr. and Mrs. Warrell have one daughter, Rachel Rae, born in Portland, Maine, May 29, 1910.

WINFRED HERBERT EDMINSTER—Since 1922, Norway, Maine, has been fortunate in the educational leadership of Winfred Herbert Edminster, superintendent of schools, whose liberal education and wide experience have fitted him to fill this responsible position in a progressive and constructive fashion. He is conversant with the most improved modern pedagogical ideals and methods and in touch with educational organizations and leaders throughout his State. Mr. Edminster was born in Dixmont, Maine, November 17, 1889, son of Reuben E. and Agnes V. (Garland) Edminster. His father is a prosperous farmer. The son was educated in the public schools of Dixmont, at Hampden Academy, from which he graduated with the class of 1911, and at the University of Maine, which bestowed on him the degree of Bachelor of Arts in 1916.

In 1913-14 Mr. Edminster gained his first experience as a teacher in Newburgh, Maine. The next year he taught at Enfield, and the following year, 1917-18, at Franklin, Maine. The year 1918 found him advancing in his profession to the position of principal of the high school at Lubec, Maine. In 1919 he was elected Superintendent of Schools at Lovell, Maine, serving until 1922, and since that date he has materially contributed to the intellectual progress of Norway as superintendent of schools there. He has been able to do much to further educational progress, improve the school system, and stimulate a fine ésprit de corps in his teachers. He belongs to the Maine State Teachers' Association and is president of the Oxford County Teachers' Association.

Enlisting in the United States Army during the World War, Mr. Edminster was stationed at Camp Upton from 1918 until his discharge in 1919. He is now a member of the American Legion, as well as the Kiwanis Club and the Republican party. His fraternal affiliations are with Archon Lodge, Free and Accepted Masons; Royal Arch Chapter, Royal and Select Masters; and with the Knights of Pythias. He is a member of the Congregational church.

In Nashua, New Hampshire, Winfred Herbert Edminster married Vernie B. Gould, daughter of George W. and Alice M. (Tasker) Gould, and they have a daughter, Winona Gould, born at Norway, Maine, March 31, 1925.

CLARENCE N. GOULD—For more than four years Clarence N. Gould has been the efficient principal of the Buckfield (Maine) High School. He had several years of experience before coming to Buckfield, and was well prepared for his work, being a gradfuate of Bates College, and of Leavitt Institute. Mr. Gould is also a veteran of the World War.

Clarence N. Gould was born in Leeds, Maine, April 4, 1894, son of Harry Nelson, a native of Maine, who was engaged in farming to the time of his death, and of Nellie (Roach) Gould, who was born in Leeds, Maine. After attending the public schools of Leeds and of Lewiston, he began his preparatory course in Leavitt Institute, at Turner, Maine, finishing his course there with graduation in 1914. The following fall he matriculated in Bates College, at Lewiston, Maine, from which he was graduated with the class of 1919, receiving at that time the degree of Bachelor of Science. In the fall of 1919 he began teaching in Westbrook Seminary, remaining there one year. He then accepted a position in the Hingham (Massachusetts) High School, where he continued as a teacher until 1923, when he came to Buckfield as principal of the high school, which position he has continued to fill most efficiently to the present time (1928). Mr. Gould is vitally interested in the lives of his students, and his youth and his energy, as well as his ability and his thorough preparation, have won for him the respect and the admiration of his pupils and his teaching staff. During the World War, Mr. Gould enlisted in the United States Navy, April 10, 1917, was in active service, and received his discharge March 24, 1919. Fraternally, he is identified with the Knights of Pythias, and he is a member of the Maine State Teachers' Association, and of the Maine State Principals' Association. His religious affiliation is with the Baptist church.

Clarence N. Gould was married, in Auburn, Maine, June 24, 1922, to Doris Manser, born in Lewiston, Maine, daughter of Harry Manser, a native of England, and of Gladys (Stover) Manser. Mr. and Mrs. Gould are the parents of two children: 1. Gordon Manser, born in South Weymouth, Massachusetts. 2. Jeannette, born in Buckfield, Maine.

ALLAN P. TRASK—One of the best-known and most highly esteemed citizens of Bangor, the late Allan P. Trask, whose death occurred February 16, 1928, was a leader in the commercial, social and civic life of this city, an inventor of exceptional ability and recognized success, and a public-spirited resident whose unselfish activities in behalf of his community won for him the praise and commendation of all his fellow-men. Mr. Trask occupied a position of prominence in the automobile world, particularly in the agency, sales and organization field, besides which he was nationally known throughout engineering circles for the scope of his activities, and especially achieved distinction for the product of his ingenuity, a patented device used in automotive operation. Mr. Trask was president of the S. L. Crosby Company, agents for Ford motor cars and accessories in Bangor, also president of the Trask Industries, Incorporated. In the civil life of this city, he was a popular and beloved figure in fraternal associations, while every municipal project which tended toward greater accomplishments and improvements for his city met with his unqualified and sincere support. Mr. Trask was born May 24, 1873, at Orrington, son of Edgar S. Trask, born in St. George, and Melissa (Magoon) Trask, born in Sangerville, who is now deceased. He was educated in the public schools of Orrington and at a private school in Bangor, after which he attended the Law School of the University of Maine and later took a post-graduate course in the Massachusetts Institute of Technology.

Upon completing his formal education, he entered the employ of Adolph Pfaff in the jewelry business, where he remained for six years and learned the intricacies of the watchmakers' trade. After thoroughly mastering this profession, Mr. Trask embarked on an independent business venture and opened his own jewelry establishment at Bangor in 1895, located at No. 19 Main Street. Here he conducted an enterprise of the highest type, acquiring a reputation for guaranteed products and materials which increased during the many years of its existence, in addition to which he became actively interested in the optical business, under the firm name of Otis Skinner Optical Company, continuing in half ownership of this concern until he sold out in 1922.

In 1915, Mr. Trask purchased a half interest in the S. L. Crosby Company which was at that time operating a sporting goods store at No. 150 Exchange Street; this company also being original agent for Ford products, for the State of Maine since 1907. It is an interesting fact in this connection that Henry Ford came to Bangor personally to establish this branch agency. In 1917, the Penobscot Motor Car Company was organized to conduct the agencies of the Nash, Maxwell, and Chrysler motor cars, this business being sold out in 1925 to the Utterback Gleason Company, of Bangor. In the meanwhile, 1920, the Penobscot Motor Company had erected the building at Nos. 142-150 Exchange Street, as headquarters. One of Mr. Trask's greatest ambitions was the perfection of an invention to increase the mileage of gasoline in automobile operation and he worked unceasingly on such a device, finally organizing a company known as the Trask Industries, Incorporated, of which he became president, to promote and manufacture the patented devices of his creative genius. In April, 1921, the John W. Gould Company of Oldtown was organized as a Ford Motor Car Agency and this company was also a part of Mr. Trask's widespread industrial interests. Mr. Trask was a staunch supporter of the principles of the Republican party and although he never sought political office, was an influential voice in securing for the citizens of this municipality the finest type of government. His fraternal connections were with the Free and Accepted Masons, Rising Virtue Lodge; Mt. Moriah and Royal Arch Chapters, Royal Arch Masons; St. John Commandery, Knights Templar, holding the thirty-second degree, and a member of Anah Temple, Ancient Arabic Order of Nobles of the Mystic Shrine. He was a member of the American Society of Mechanical Engineers, and the Boston Athletic Association. His religious adherence was given to the Universalist church.

Allan P. Trask married, March 11, 1896, Gertrude A. Bartlett, who was born in Brewer. Mr. Trask's father, Edgar S. Trask, during the Civil War was a sailor with the blockading fleet of the Union forces; a sea-captain, he sailed upon long foreign voyages to the time of his death.

FRANK W. RUSH—A man whose varied business experience has made him one of the leaders in the community in and near Millinocket is Frank W. Rush, who has been engaged in the retail lumber trade in this city for a number of years. Formerly active in building, Mr. Rush planned and erected many homes in Millinocket, which today stand as monuments to his skill in that line of endeavor. He also holds membership in several fraternal organizations, and is a public-spirited citizen, keenly interested in the affairs of his town, State and nation.

Mr. Rush was born on May 6, 1875, in Benedicta, Maine, the son of John Rush, native of New Jersey and a carpenter until his death, and of Katherine (Crabb) Rush, also deceased, who was a native of De Bee Junction, New Brunswick. Frank W. Rush was educated in the public schools of his native city, Benedicta, and following the completion of his schooling he worked for three years at carpentry. Then he went into the contracting and building business in Millinocket, starting a line of work which he continued for ten years. Subsequently he became engaged in the sawmill business, in which he remained for fifteen years. Then his next venture was the retail lumber trade, in which he has continued since that time. His offices in Millinocket are situated on Penobscot Avenue. He has always taken an active interest in political affairs, being affiliated with the Democratic party, and having been for several years a member of the Democratic Town Committee. His business interests, in addition to his own retail lumber establishment, include a directorship in the Millinocket Trust Company. He is a member of the local Chamber of Commerce, and also of several fraternal orders, including the Benevolent and Protective Order of Elks, in which he is affiliated with the Oldtown Lodge; the Saint Martin of Tours Council, Knights of Columbus; and the Modern Woodmen of America. When he can spare time from his business and civic activities, the favorite hobbies in which he likes to indulge are fishing and hunting. His religious affiliation is with the Saint Martin of Tours Roman Catholic Church.

In 1900 Frank W. Rush married Agnes Boynton, who was born in Sherman, Maine. They are the parents of ten children: Harold, Raymond, Agnes, Irene, Lillian, Frank, Frederick, Anna, Richard, and Bernard.

WILLIAM M. MARR—Since 1910 William M. Marr has served as superintendent of schools for Millinocket, East Millinocket, and Medway, Maine. A man of wide educational experience, extending through a quarter of a century, he has discharged the duties of his present office with a high degree of efficiency. He is otherwise active in his profession, being a member of several associations and official bodies, and he has taken a prominent part in the social and fraternal life of Millinocket. His father, James G. Marr, born in Scotland, was a contractor and engaged in this work until his death. His mother, who before her marriage was Elizabeth Middleton, born in Scotland, is also deceased.

William M. Marr was born March 18, 1872, at Westerly, Rhode Island. He attended the local public schools and Mount Hermon Academy. Later he entered Bates College, from which he was graduated in 1901 with the degree of Bachelor of Arts. He also attended a summer session at Harvard University.

When he completed his education he took a position as principal of the high school in Upton, Massachusetts, and he remained there until 1904. In that year he went to Holbrook, Massachusetts, as principal of the local high school, remaining until 1910. In 1910 he came to Millinocket, where he has since served as Superintendent of Schools for Millinocket, East Millinocket and Medway, with headquarters in the George W. Stearns School at Millinocket. Politically, Mr. Marr is a member of the Republican party. He is affiliated, fraternally, with the Free and Accepted Masons, being a member of Nollesemic Lodge. He is also a member of Mount Katahdin Chapter, Knights of Pythias. He is a member of the local Chamber of Commerce; the Masonic Club; the Maine Teachers' Association, of which he is a past president; and the National Education Society. He served for three years in the Rhode Island State Militia before the Spanish-American War. Much of his spare time he devotes to hunting and fishing. He and his family attend the local Congregationalist church.

In 1905, William M. Marr married Vilette Stillman, who was born at Westerly, Rhode Island. They are the parents of children: David S., James A., and William M., deceased.

GEORGE SETH WILLIAMS—For nearly a quarter of a century George Seth Williams has been identified with the Kennebec Light & Heat Company and with its successor, the Central Maine Light & Power Company, of which he is now (1928) vice-president and general manager. Mr. Williams is a native of Augusta, and is active in local public affairs here.

George Seth Williams was born in Augusta, Maine, September 9, 1882, son of William H. Williams, a native of Gardiner, Maine, who is engaged in the public utilities business and is also a member of the State Legislature, and of Frances E. (McMaster) Williams, a native of Augusta. He attended the public schools of his birthplace, graduating from Cony High School with the class of 1901, and then became a student in the University of Maine, where he continued study for two years. In June, 1903, he became associated with the Kennebec Light & Heat Company as lineman and wireman, and continued in that capacity until 1904, when he was made superintendent of the branch located at Gardiner, Maine. In this position he served efficiently until 1910, in which year the Kennebec Light & Power Company was purchased by the Central Maine Power & Light Company. Mr. Williams remained with the new concern as power solicitor and as superintendent for seven years, and at the end of that time, in 1917, went to Bath, Maine, as a special representative. In that same year he returned to Augusta, Maine, as general superintendent, and in August, 1925, he was made vice-president and a member of the board of directors of the Central Maine Power & Light Company. His ability and his faithfulness to the work in hand brought the confidence of his associates and also substantial reward in the form of continued promotions, and in January, 1926, he was made first vice-president and general manager of the concern. That important official and executive position he is still (1928) most efficiently filling, and he long ago demonstrated his ability to handle this part of the business. Possessed of unusual executive and administrative ability, supported by the thorough knowledge which comes from his long association with the concern, he is giving to the company and to the public the kind of service which makes for good will and harmony between the public and the utilities companies.

Politically, Mr. Williams gives his support to the principles and the candidates of the Republican party, and he is active in the public affairs of Augusta, serving as a member of the Board of Aldermen. Fraternally, he is identified with Hermon Lodge, No. 32, Free and Accepted Masons; Chapter No. 18, Royal Arch Masons; and Kora Temple, Ancient Arabic Order Nobles of the Mystic Shrine. His religious affiliation is with the Episcopal Church of Augusta, Maine.

George Seth Williams was married, in Gardiner, Maine, to Mary E. Maxcy, who was born in Gardiner, Maine, daughter of William E. and Ida M. Maxcy, both natives of Maine. Mr. and Mrs. Williams are the parents of one child: George Seth, born in Gardiner, Maine, August, 1915. The family home is in Augusta.

HARRIS S. WOODMAN—The important industry of table oil-cloth manufacture, as conducted at Winthrop by the Wadsworth & Woodman Company, of which Harris S. Woodman is treasurer, has its place of recognized leadership in this State, and the product is distributed throughout the country. Mr. Woodman has always been associated with this and related lines of manufacture; and he is today accounted one of the foremost men in his line, and a citizen of Winthrop who has a vital interest in the progress of this township and its business and civic affairs.

Harris S. Woodman was born March 11, 1881, at Auburn, son of Joseph L. Woodman, shoe manufacturer, a native of Gloucester, and Kitty M. (Spring) Woodman, who was born in Chicago, Illinois. Mr. Woodman attended the Portland Public Schools, Coburn Institute, and Colby College, at Waterville, and he was graduated at Yale College in 1903 with the degree of Bachelor of Arts. He first became identified with C. M. Bailey's Sons & Company, at Winthrop, in the manufacture of floor coverings, and he was active in the interests of that firm from 1903 to 1905, when, with Herbert E. Wadsworth, he organized the firm of Wadsworth & Woodman Company, manufacturers of table oil-cloths, with headquarters and plant at Winthrop. The president of the concern is Herbert E. Wadsworth; the treasurer, Harris S. Woodman. Mr. Woodman is also a member of the board of directors of the Augusta Trust Company; and in his political views he is affiliated with the Republican party.

During the World War, Mr. Woodman was assigned to Red Cross service in France. He is a member of the Augusta Rotary Club, Winthrop Chamber of Commerce, and Augusta Country Club. His religious faith is that of the Friends.

Harris S. Woodman married, June 30, 1910, at Rockland, Jeannette B. Healy, who was born July 14, 1882, at New Bedford, Massachusetts. They have one son, Harrison S. Woodman, born June 29, 1912, at Winthrop.

GEORGE ELLISON MACOMBER, of Augusta, Maine, banker, insurance and public official, enjoys the distinction of having built the first electric railway in the State of Maine. That was in 1890.

The Macombers are an ancient Scottish family,

descendants of Mary Chilton, the first woman who landed from the "Mayflower," she afterward married John Chilton, brother of the governor of Massachusetts. Of record in New England were John and William, who came from Inverness in 1638, it is believed, and settled in Taunton, Massachusetts. Records show that John Macomber was subject to military duty in 1643, and that he paid a seven shilling tax in 1659 on twenty-four acres of land and four head of cattle. He died between 1687 and 1690. His son, also named John, was in Queen Anne's War, 1691, and married Anna Evans, of Taunton, July 16, 1678. His son, a third John was born early enough to have participated in Queen Anne's War. He was twice married, and his will named nine children, all by his first wife, who was Elizabeth Williams. He died in Taunton, December 14, 1747. Nathaniel, eldest son of John (3) Macomber, was for many years a deacon in the Taunton Congregational Church. He married Priscilla Southworth, of Middleboro, Massachusetts, in 1773, and they had six children. Born February 9, 1709, he died November 10, 1787. George, second son of Nathaniel Macomber, was a soldier in the War of the American Revolution, and on January 27, 1767, married Susan Pauil. Born July 7, 1740, he left eleven children, and the line was carried on by his third son, also named George, born September 17, 1772, married Anna Harkness, September 17, 1801, and died January 31, 1830. Of the six children of George and Anna (Harkness) Macomber, George Washington, born September 29, 1807, at Pelham, Massachusetts, became a resident of Augusta, Maine, in early life, and was a granite cutter and general contractor, and as such was employed in the construction of the State House. He was for years a deacon in the Baptist church, and took an active part in both city and county government. He was twice married, his second wife being Hannah Kalloch, born December 10, 1820, died September 1, 1905, after a long widowhood, for George Washington Macomber died in Augusta, August 31, 1864. Of this union there were two children, George Ellison and Henry D. Macomber.

Born in Augusta, June 6, 1853, George Ellison Macomber was educated in the public schools, and subsequently entered the grocery store of Luther Mitchell, where he was a clerk for a short time. He then secured an appointment in the Augusta Post Office, where he remained six years. In partnership with his brother, Henry D. Macomber, from 1886, he developed the insurance business established by David Cargill, and which he had purchased in March, 1876, the partnership remaining unbroken until his brother's death, when Charles R. Whitten became a partner in the business, continuing until 1904. In 1908 a company consisting of E. C. Carll, Charles H. Howard and R. H. Bodwell was formed to carry on and extend the activities of this concern, now known as Macomber, Farr & Whitten.

Apart from his insurance interests, Mr. Macomber was active in many other enterprises. He was treasurer of the Augusta, Hallowell and Gardiner Electric Railway Company, built in 1890, the pioneer in this form of transportation in the State, and held that post until 1907, when the road was sold to the L. A. & W. Company. In 1892 he built and was president of the Rockland, Thomaston & Camden Street Railway, which in control of the electric and gas

lighting of Knox County, as well as the street railway. He then became treasurer of the Norway & Paris Electric Railway Company, the Austin Traction Company, of Austin, Texas, and of the Hutchinson Water, Light and Gas Company of Hutchinson, Kansas; and president of the Springfield Railway and Light Company, of Springfield, Missouri. Soon after this he became associated with the late Senator William B. McKinley of Illinois, and with Mr. Macomber serving as treasurer and joint manager they purchased and operated the Quincy (Illinois) Gas & Electric Company; the Decatur (Illinois) Street Railway; the Peoria Gas Company; the Fort Wayne & Wabash River Street Railway, in Indiana. Mr. Macomber also was treasurer and manager of the Newport and Providence Street Railway, of Newport, Rhode Island. He is also president of the Augusta Trust Company, the Kennebec Savings Bank, and of the Augusta Opera House Company; was a director of the Granite National Bank, treasurer of the Augusta Real Estate Association, and a trustee of the Maine hospitals for the insane, at Augusta and Bangor. He was one of the founders and for twenty-five years president of the Augusta General Hospital; also president of the Children's Home Society of Maine. For ten years he was president and manager of the Rapid City, Black Hills & Western Railroad, in South Dakota. Later, he built the Portsmouth, Kittery & York Street Railway; also the Dover & Portsmouth (New Hampshire) Street Railway. In 1897, acting for the Eastern bondholders, he purchased the First Street Railway in Seattle, Washington. After electrifying it and making other improvements, it was sold to Stone & Webster, who linked it with their other lines in Seattle.

As a culmination to his long career in the insurance business, he was made special agent for the following companies: Insurance Company of North America, Philadelphia Underwriters' Alliance, and the Granite State Fire Insurance Company. He is a stockholder in the Augusta Hotel Company, as well as in many other local business enterprises. After the death of ex-Governor Bodwell, Mr. Macomber became president of the Hallowell Granite Works, owning property in various parts of Maine. In 1883 he became a member of the New England Insurance Exchange, an organization controlling the rate-making for practically all of the leading fire insurance companies in New England. For the past twelve years he has been a director of the Maine Central Railroad and of the Portland Terminal Company.

Mr. Macomber's first political office was that of alderman, to which he was elected on the Republican ticket in 1884, and where he served one year. He was mayor of Augusta, 1886-1888, and was a member of the Maine House of Representatives four, and of the Maine Senate, two years. Mr. Macomber is a member of the Free and Accepted Masons, and of the Augusta Country Club. He belongs to the Baptist church, and has been liberal with his time and money in aiding many philanthropic works.

George E. Macomber married (first) Sarah V. Johnson, daughter of Hiram and Almira Johnson, in Edinboro, Pennsylvania, January 24, 1878, and after her death, married (second) Laura L. Cony, at Gardiner, Maine, June 16, 1916. Of the first marriage the children were: Alice H., married to R. H. Bodwell; and Annie J., married to Guy P. Gannett. Madeline Lord is an adopted daughter.

HON. HERBERT C. LIBBY—Whether as an educationist or as a holder of public office, Hon. Herbert C. Libby has demonstrated his possession of a wide range of abilities that, applied by his broad and thorough methods, have invariably benefited both the community, Waterville, of which he is the mayor, and Colby College, on whose faculty he is professor of public speaking and journalism. He is thus concerned with the advancement of Waterville in two of its most vital aspects; and few men are more highly regarded throughout the State, in civic life or by the student body. Professor Libby is a son of Isaac C. and Helen (Green) Libby, both natives of Maine, and both parents now deceased. Isaac C. Libby, who was a prominent Republican, was a delegate to the Harrison convention in 1888, and he also served as a member of the State Legislature; he was a cattle dealer, and a builder of electric railroads.

Herbert C. Libby was born December 28, 1878, at Burnham, and after attending the grammar and high schools at Waterville, he took the arts course at Colby College, and was graduated at Harvard College in 1904 with the degree of Bachelor of Arts. In the year, 1919, he received the honorary degree of Doctor of Letters from Colby College. Professor Libby entered upon his professional career as a newspaperman, and he was so employed at Waterville for two years. In 1908 he first became associated at Colby in his present capacity as professor and instructor of public speaking and journalism. He is a member of the board of directors of the Federal Trust Company.

A staunch Republican in the political field, Professor Libby received the popular election to the office of mayor of Waterville in March, 1926, and he continues in that position to the present. He was also superintendent of Waterville Public Schools from 1909 to 1912. He is a member of the Zeta Psi Fraternity of Colby College; has held the offices of secretary and president of the Waterville Rotary Club, and was Rotarian Governor for the district of Maine, New Hampshire, and Massachusetts, in 1924. His religious faith is that of the Congregational church.

Herbert C. Libby married, December 21, 1912, at Waterville, Mabel E. Dunn, daughter of Willard M. and Alma B. (Burbank) Dunn, of Lewiston. Their children: Willard, Carlyle, and Mark.

JOHN EDWARD NELSON, Augusta lawyer, member of Congress from the Third Maine District, was born in China, Maine, July 12, 1874, son of Edward W. and Cassandra M. (Worthing) Nelson.

After being graduated from the Waterville, Maine, High School, he entered the Friends School in Providence, Rhode Island, and passed from there to Colby College, where he was graduated in 1898. He studied law at the University of Maine, and received his degree of Bachelor of Laws from the Law School of that institution in 1904, and soon afterwards opened an office for the practice of his profession in Waterville, Maine. From 1904 to 1913 he was associated with the late Governor William T. Haines, but in the latter year he removed to Augusta, Maine, where he formed a partnership with Charles L. Andrews, the firm name being Andrews & Nelson. William T. Gardiner was subsequently admitted to the firm, thereafter known as Andrews, Nelson & Gardiner. He

was elected to the United States House of Representatives in March, 1922, to fill the term left vacant by the resignation of John A. Peters, of Ellsworth, Maine, and was reëlected to that office in September, 1922. He is a Republican.

Mr. Nelson is a member of the Zeta Psi Fraternity of North America, of the Phi Beta Kappa, and of the legal fraternity, Phi Alpha Delta. He also belongs to the Rotary, Abnaki, and Cosmos clubs, and is a member of the Free and Accepted Masons, in which he has attained the thirty-second degree. He attends (not a member) the Congregational church.

John Edward Nelson married Margaret H. Crosby, at Dexter, Maine, July 17, 1900, and their children are: Margaret W., John A., Eleanor C., Charles P., Atwood C., Edith M., Jeanette, and Faith.

CHARLES SUMNER COOK—In the legal and financial circles of Portland there is no more conspicuous or successful individual than Charles Sumner Cook. Associated with the leading industrial, financial, legal and civic activities centering in and diverging from the State metropolis, he has for more than forty years been an outstanding figure in the development of the enterprises in which he has been associated. His reputation for ability, judgment, organization and successful accomplishment, coupled with a pleasing personality and sympathy with the ambitions of his fellow-citizens, has been rewarded with many posts of importance, civic, educational, industrial and commercial. By reason of his deep knowledge of the law, his high position in the financial world and his intimate understanding of the problems of communal development that confront the people, he has won the esteem and friendship of all with whom he comes in contact. He always has been a valuable supporter of civic undertakings and a hearty coöperator in all the approved enterprises of charitable, commercial or social nature.

Charles Sumner Cook was born in Portland, November 18, 1858. His education, following preliminary in the elementary grades of the local schools, included the course at Nichols Latin School, from which he was graduated in 1877. He then entered Bates College and completed the course of four years, receiving, upon graduation, the degree of Bachelor of Arts in 1881. His active career began as principal of the Waldoboro High School, a post which he held during 1882 and 1883, then taking the examination and being admitted to the Cumberland County bar in 1886, after a study of the law for three years. In that year he became associated with the law firm of Symonds and Libby and in 1891 acquired a partnership with the Hon. J. W. Symonds. In 1892 he was a partner in the law firm of Symonds, Snow & Cook, which was enlarged to Symonds, Snow, Cook & Hutchinson in 1901. This was again changed, in 1918, to Cook, Hutchinson & Pierce, and, in 1926, to Cook, Hutchinson, Pierce & Connell.

Mr. Cook was a director in the Traders National Bank until 1906, in which year he organized the Fidelity Trust Company, which was merged with the bank named. In 1910 he negotiated the purchase of the Portland Trust Company and effected its merger with the Fidelity Trust Company. In 1926, the United States Trust Company was also merged with the Fidelity Trust Company. In the Fidelity Trust Company he was, successively, vice-president, president and chairman of the board of directors. He was elected president and director of the Brunswick Electric Light & Power Company and a director of the Sagadahoc Light & Power Company in 1910, when this organization was merged with the Brunswick concern as the Bath and Brunswick Light & Power Company, of which he became the president. This was later merged with the Central Maine Power Company. He was a director in the Boston & Maine Railroad Company, 1914-1925; president of the State Loan Company; member of the Governor's Council, 1899-1905; chairman of the council, 1901-1902; member of the board of overseers of Bates College since 1904. His membership in social organizations includes the Cumberland Club, Portland Country Club, and others. He is a member of the American Bar Association and of the American Geographical Society and wears the golden key of the Phi Beta Kappa Fraternity. In politics he is Republican.

ALBERT E. HALL, Street Commissioner of Augusta, Maine, was born May 24, 1873, at China, Maine, a son of John N. and Ida F. (Haskell) Hall, well-known members of the community.

Albert E. Hall received his education in the public schools of China, later attending the China High School. From boyhood, Mr. Hall has always taken a keen interest in local city affairs and has been very active in the service of the people. During his career he has filled with credit various positions in the administration of civic policies and he is now serving his second term as Street Commissioner of Augusta. In his political preferences he is a strong supporter of the Democratic party.

Despite the manifold duties of his work Mr. Hall has contributed freely of his time to social and fraternal activities. He is affiliated with the Modern Woodmen of the World, and is a member of the Kiwanis Club.

Albert E. Hall married, June 2, 1894, at Manchester, Maine, Louise Freeman. Mr. and Mrs. Hall are the parents of two children: Wilfred E., and Florence L. Mr. Hall and his family maintain their residence in Augusta.

BION F. JOSE—One of the prominent men in civic affairs in the State of Maine, Bion F. Jose holds the important position of Town Manager of Rumford, having entered upon the duties of this office December 15, 1927, and is giving to the citizens of Rumford a splendid administration, characterized by efficient and business-like management of municipal affairs, the improvement and extension of streets and highways and a general condition of progress and advancement in all details. Mr. Jose is a leading factor in the life of the town, while in fraternal and social organizations, he displays a deep interest. Rumford is fortunate, indeed, to have in its service a man of the splendid qualities of Mr. Jose, always concerned with the welfare of his community and satisfied only with giving his fellow-citizens the finest and most economic results of his brilliant engineering ability.

Mr. Jose was born in Cape Elizabeth, August 26, 1883, son of C. Fremont Jose, who is deceased, and Lucy (Snow) Jose. C. Fremont Jose was born in Minnesota, and for many years was engaged in the grocery business at South Portland, having a long and distinguished career in this locality, and always taking part in local affairs as an ardent Republican.

Bion F. Jose was educated in the public schools of South Portland, and after graduating from high school, engaged in highway work in the service of the State,

being thus employed for approximately twelve years. In 1924, he was induced to come to Gardiner to fulfill the duties of City Engineer and also serve as Street Commissioner. His remarkable record there speaks for itself and he was a popular and esteemed citizen of that city. He was active in the affairs of the Gardiner Trust Company, and in the affairs of politics, he follows the principles of the Republican party. On December 15, 1927, Mr. Jose was offered the position of Town Manager at Rumford, and resigned his Gardiner office to accept the managerial work. His fraternal connections are with the Free and Accepted Masons, all bodies, including the Temple, Ancient Arabic Order Nobles of the Mystic Shrine; the Knights of Pythias, the American Legion, and the Sons of Veterans. His interest and activity in civil affairs are shown by the fact that he was a member of the Gardiner Rotary Club. His religious adherence is given to the Episcopal church. During the World War, he was a soldier in the United States Army from November, 1917, until August, 1919, as a member of the Twenty-third Engineers, serving overseas for seventeen months, receiving his honorable discharge at Camp Devens, Massachusetts, and holding the esteem and acquiring the commendation of his superior officers for his distinguished and brilliant record.

Bion F. Jose married, May 3, 1921, at Fryeburg, Maine, Nellie Lord, who was born in Lovell, and they have three children: Bion L., Norman L., and Nellie L. Mr. Jose is a splendid example of a self-made man, having risen to his present position of importance by his diligent application to his ideals and his ceaseless energy coupled with rightly-directed ambition.

ORVILLE MOTT PALMER—His natural inclination and zeal to engage in a specific work of public service have served to remove all obstacles from the attainment of Orville Mott Palmer's success, his present superintendency of the Central Maine Power Company resulting from his well-recognized abilities and value as an executive. Mr. Palmer is a veteran of the World War, and is prominent in the American Legion, his service in the great conflict being on record in his contingent in its participation in some of the leading battles in France.

Orville Mott Palmer was born April 7, 1897, at Lynn, Massachusetts, a son of Manford Palmer, shoemaker, and native of Albany, New York, and of Nellie (Mott) Palmer, who died October 14, 1915. After attending the grammar schools at Norway and Oxford, he was a student for two years at Norway High School. His first industrial work was that in the employ of the B. F. Spinney Shoe Company, at Norway, just after leaving school, after which he became associated with the Norway & Paris Street Railway Company, so continuing until 1914. In April, 1925, Mr. Palmer received his present appointment as superintendent of the Central Maine Power Company, of the Norway district. In political matters, Mr. Palmer prefers the Independent way of thinking and voting.

Enlisting on May 7, 1917, in the World War, Mr. Palmer rendered the service of a loyal soldier overseas in the One Hundred and Third Regiment of Infantry, Twenty-sixth Division, at Chateau-Thierry, and in the Argonne, north of Verdun, receiving his discharge April 25, 1919. He is a member of the American Legion, and of the "Forty-and-Eight." His religious affiliation is with the Congregational church. Orville Mott Palmer married, June 18, 1919, at Norway, Pauline Proudlove. They have one son, Harry Palmer, born October 13, 1922, at Norway.

HENRY B. FOSTER—As president of the Norway National Bank and the Norway Shoe Company, makers of the famous McKay shoe for children, girls, and misses, Henry B. Foster is an outstanding figure in Norway, Maine. He is prominent in all departments of business and social life there and a leader of progress. Mr. Foster was born in Norway, August 30, 1872, son of William Frank and Almira H. (Smith) Foster, both natives of that town, where the father, a member of Oxford Lodge, Free and Accepted Masons, was a prosperous miller. The grandparents of the subject of this record were Mark P. and Jane (Tucker) Smith, and William and Calista (Wood) Foster.

After completing his education in the public and high schools of Norway and Shaw's Business College, Mr. Foster began his business career. He worked first for F. Q. Elliott in a clothing store at Norway. Through his enterprise and ability he was able to buy out this business in 1891 and operate it successfully until 1919. That year Mr. Foster was elected president of the Norway Shoe Company, which had been organized in 1915, and has so prospered that two hundred and eighty workers are now employed. This good fortune has continued under Mr. Foster's able direction. The product of the plant is known all over the United States, the market having been steadily enlarged, and the McKay shoe has come to be a very popular brand. Since 1924 Mr. Foster has also been president of the Norway National Bank, in which institution he has been a director for fifteen years. He is past president of the Norway Board of Trade, a member of the Kiwanis Club, and an Independent in politics. His fraternal affiliations are with the Free and Accepted Masons, in which order he belongs to the Chapter, Knights Templar, and the Temple, Ancient Arabic Order Nobles of the Mystic Shrine; the Independent Order of Odd Fellows; and the Knights of Pythias. He attends the Universalist church.

In Norway, Maine, January 12, 1898, Henry B. Foster married Jane M. Cole, born in Norway, Maine, daughter of George A. and Sarah E. (Allen) Cole, also natives of the town. A daughter was born to Mr. and Mrs. Foster, January 9, 1903, in Norway, to whom was given the name of Laurestine L. Foster.

FRED ELHANAN SMITH—A native son who has been identified with banking and civic activities of Norway from the beginning of his career, Fred Elhanan Smith appreciates the advantages of the home town and recognizes the opportunity centering in and about this progressive community, his civic, professional and social interests having been connected with the general advance of Norway's foremost institutions. He is a son of Howard Daniel Smith, who was born October 12, 1844, at Oxford, and Mary (Whitman) Smith, born February 28, 1846, at Woodstock. Howard Daniel Smith has been associated with the Norway National Bank for fifty years, as cashier, director and as president of the institution; he held a number of important local offices, is a Mason of the thirty-second degree in the Ancient Accepted Scottish Rite; member of the

Knights of Pythias; and of the State Grange, Patrons of Husbandry.

Fred Elhanan Smith was born February 12, 1884, at Norway, where he attended the grammar schools, and was graduated at the high school in 1902; and, taking the arts course at Bowdoin College, he was graduated there in 1906 with the degree of Bachelor of Arts. Upon graduation, Mr. Smith at once became associated with the Norway National Bank, in the capacity of teller; and being made cashier January 14, 1919, has continued to date in that service to this well-established financial institution.

Mr. Smith is an independent voter in political matters; and he has served Norway Village Corporation as assessor for two years. Fraternally, his affiliations are those of Lodge No. 18, Free and Accepted Masons, a Past Master; Oxford Chapter, No. 29, Royal Arch Masons, Past High Priest; Council No. 14, Royal and Select Masters; and he is also a member of the Norway Board of Trade. He is a charter member of the Norway Kiwanis Club, having served that body as treasurer since it was organized. He attends the Congregational church.

Fred E. Smith married, September 5, 1907, at West Paris, Blanche Penley, who was born March 20, 1885, at Greenwood, daughter of Edward W. Penley, who was born at Paris, and Abbie (Richardson) Penley, a native of Greenwood. Their children: 1. June Frances, born June 20, 1908. 2. Edwin Whitman, born April 17, 1917.

CHARLES H. HOWARD—As president and treasurer of the Charles H. Howard Company, Incorporated, Charles H. Howard is at the head of the business with which he started his career as a clerk, in South Paris, Maine. The business was formerly owned by F. A. Shurtleff, and is one of the best-known concerns of its kind in this locality.

Charles H. Howard was born in Dixfield, Maine, April 12, 1870, son of Henry F. Howard, school teacher and a member of Bethel Lodge, Free and Accepted Masons, born in Rumford, Maine, and of Clara M. (Woodbury) Howard, a native of Sweden, Maine. Mr. Howard received his earliest education in the public schools of South Paris, and then prepared for college in Hebron Academy, from which he was graduated with the class of 1889. The following autumn he entered Bowdoin College, where he completed his course with graduation, receiving the degree of Bachelor of Arts in 1893. Later, he entered the Massachusetts College of Pharmacy, from which he was graduated in 1898 with the degree of Graduate Pharmacist. After graduation he became a partner of F. A. Shurtleff & Company, of South Paris, Maine, a retail druggist, with whom he remained to the time of the death of the latter in 1909. After the death of Mr. Shurtleff the company was reorganized, under the name of the Charles H. Howard Company, Incorporated, with Mr. Howard as president and treasurer, and under this name he has continued to the present time (1928). Mr. Howard is also a member of the board of directors of the South Paris Savings Bank. Politically, he supports the principles and the candidates of the Republican party, and he is active in local public affairs, having served as treasurer of the South Paris Village Corporation from 1909 to the present time, a period of eighteen years. He is also treasurer of the town of Paris. He is a member of Paris Lodge, No. 94, Free and Accepted Masons, of which he is a Past Master; of Oxford

Chapter, No. 29, Royal Arch Masons, of Norway, Maine; Lodge No. 17, Independent Order of Odd Fellows, a Past Noble Grand. He is also a member of the Board of Trade of South Paris. His religious affiliation is with the Congregational church of South Paris, and he has been superintendent of the Sunday school since 1904.

Charles H. Howard was married (first), at South Paris, Maine, June 1, 1901, to Alice B. Green, born in Waterford, Maine, died December 29, 1918. He married (second), in South Paris, Maine, April 19, 1923, Eva E. Walker, born in Denmark, Maine, August 23, 1878, daughter of Albert W. and Jennie O. (Lord) Walker. To the first marriage three children were born: Henry G., Roland W., and Harriett, died in fifteen months. All were born in South Paris.

ARCHIBALD CHARLES ROSS—As a physician, Archibald Charles Ross has ministered for many years to the ills and the afflictions of the people of Albion, being willing at all times to give freely of his energies and talents for the benefit of those who need medical aid and advice. In addition to his medical practice, Mr. Ross conducts motion picture exhibitions in the meeting place of the Independent Order of Odd Fellows, in Albion. He was born in Avon, Maine, January 31, 1882, son of Charles Fremont Ross, a farmer, born at Phillips, Maine, in 1856, and of Martha Elva (Thompson) Ross, born at Carthage, Maine, in 1861, died at Phillips, Maine, in 1895.

Archibald Charles Ross, after having attended the public schools, was graduated from Phillips High School in the class of 1901; following which he became a student at the Bowdoin Medical School, from which he was graduated in the class of 1909 with the degree of Doctor of Medicine. Since that time he has been active in the life of Albion, not only as a physician and as an operator of motion pictures, but also as a member of different societies and fraternal orders. He is a member of the Free and Accepted Masons, in which order he is affiliated with Lodge No. 86, in Westbrook, Maine; Past Noble Grand of the Independent Order of Odd Fellows, in which he is identified with Albion Lodge, and has been through all the chairs; the Red Cross, for which organization he is director in Albion; and of different medical societies in Kennebec County. Although his activities, of a widely varying nature, keep him busy a great deal of the time, he attends whenever it is possible the Methodist Episcopal church.

In Phillips, Maine, on August 30, 1904, Mr. Ross married Florence June Webber, born in Phillips, August 6, 1886, daughter of Henry Record and Sarah Elizabeth (Wing) Webber. Henry Record Webber, who was a schoolmaster, died in Berlin, New Hampshire, in 1893; and Sarah Elizabeth (Wing) Webber, who was born in Phillips, in 1843, died in Livermore Falls, Maine, in 1912. Florence June (Webber) Ross is the great-great-granddaughter of Dr. Moses Wing, the first physician to settle in the town of Wayne, Maine, who was in active service in the War of the Revolution, and who lost a leg in that war. Mr. and Mrs. Ross are the parents of the following children: 1. Charles Fremont, born March 18, 1906; in Bowdoin College, class of 1929. 2. Carlos Cedric, born January 24, 1908, died April 18, 1913. 3. Carlswood Archibald,

born January 4, 1914. 4. Maxine Audrey, born July 4, 1916. 5. Winston McClellan, born October 22, 1922.

JAMES HENRY CROSSON—One of the successful automobile dealers of Livermore Falls, James Henry Crosson has been engaged in that line of business since 1910. In 1917 he started a Willys-Knight and Overland car agency in Livermore Falls, and at different times he has conducted different automobile agencies, such as Studebaker, Nash and Dodge. Born in Bath, New Brunswick, Canada, Mr. Crosson is the son of Elias and Rosean (Burns) Crosson. His father was born in Bath, New Brunswick, Canada, and his mother was a native of Ireland.

James Henry Crosson was educated in the public school at Houlton, Maine. After he completed his education he engaged in the automobile business. Politically, Mr. Crosson is independent of the established parties. He is a member of the Roman Catholic church, and belongs to the Knights of Columbus. He also is affiliated with the Livermore Falls Automobile Association.

On November 6, 1909, in Millinocket, Maine, James H. Crosson married Isabel May Tilley, born in Lincoln, Maine, January 9, 1891, died January 8, 1927. She was the daughter of Augustus and Annie (Bishop) Tilley, both natives of Island Falls, Maine. Mr. and Mrs. Crosson were the parents of the following children: 1. Francis Henry, born September 14, 1911. 2. Lewis Raymond, born July 22, 1916. 3. Lawrence Augustus, born January 19, 1920. 4. James Henry, born November 21, 1921. All of these children were born in Livermore Falls.

ERNEST A. FOGG—Since January, 1925, when he was appointed to the position, Ernest A. Fogg has acted as postmaster of Livermore Falls. Though previously inexperienced in this kind of work, he studied the details with his customary energy, and he has performed in a very efficient manner the duties connected with his office. His father, Benjamin A. Fogg, born at Wales, Maine, was a carpenter and builder, and engaged in this work until his death in 1924. His mother, Ida M. (Hall) Fogg, was born at Litchfield, Maine.

Ernest A. Fogg was born January 27, 1894, at Livermore, Maine. He attended the public schools of Livermore Falls and was graduated from the high school there in 1915. From 1916 to 1918, he worked for the Remington Typewriter Company, at Ilion, New York. In 1918, he became associated with the International Paper Company, at Livermore Falls, remaining with them until 1921. In that year he started a painting and paper-hanging business of his own, which he continued until 1925. On January 8, 1925, he was appointed postmaster of Livermore Falls for a term of four years. Politically, Mr. Fogg is a member of the Republican party. He is a member of the Livermore Falls Automobile Association, and of the Methodist Episcopal church.

On July 30, 1917, at Ilion, New York, Ernest A. Fogg married Mary Louise Russell. She was born at Frankfort, New York, December 12, 1892, daughter of George R. and Clara Angel Russell, of Virginia. Mr. and Mrs. Fogg are the parents of two children, both of whom were born at Livermore Falls: 1. Robert Ernest, born September 18, 1918. 2. Elizabeth Louise, born July 10, 1921.

BLAINE SPOONER VILES, forestry expert and lumberman, of Augusta, Maine, comes of a Norman-English family which settled in Boston, and furnished several soldiers to the Continental Army. The name is variously spelled in early records, sometimes as Viall, Vilas, Vyall and Villiers. The first of the Viles to settle in Maine was Joseph, who was in Milton, New Hampshire, before 1776, when he removed to Orland, Maine, being the third to make his home there. A second Joseph, son of Joseph Viles, who married Sarah, daughter of John Hancock, died at Anson, Maine, July 12, 1848, aged seventy-eight. He left a numerous family, of whom Rufus, born at Orland, July 20, 1790, married Eunice Chase, daughter of Asa and Sally (Bartlett) Merry, September 10, 1815, and died at New Portland, November 28, 1873, was the most noted. A prosperous lumberman, he was a captain in the militia, a deacon in the Congregational church. Captain Rufus Viles was twice married, his second wife being Sarah Ann Stanley, to whom he was wed, March 22, 1829, born September 11, 1811, died February 15, 1864, at New Portland. There were several children of both marriages, among those of the second being Edward Payson Viles, born May 14, 1842. He was a successful merchant, lumberman, postmaster at New Portland, twelve years, deputy sheriff six years, high sheriff of Somerset County six years, and a director in many business enterprises. In 1893 he removed to Skowegan, where he engaged in extensive lumbering operations. He was also active in many of the larger fraternal bodies, and in the affairs of the Congregational church. He married Ada A. Spooner, daughter of Lamont and Caroline (Cragin) Spooner, May 21, 1876. She was born at New England, September 22, 1847.

Son of Edward Payson and Ada A. (Spooner) Viles, Blaine Spooner Viles was born July 22, 1879, at New Portland, Maine. From the public schools of New Portland and Skowhegan, he passed to Bowdoin College, where he was graduated with the class of 1903, degree of Bachelor of Arts, and at Yale University in 1905, from which he received the degree of Master of Forestry. He then took the United States civil service examination and was appointed field assistant in the United States Forest Service. Later he went to Corbin Park, New Hampshire, as forester for the Blue Mountain Forest Association, and became manager of the park. In 1908 he engaged with John Appleton, of Bangor, in general forestry work in Maine, and soon after became associated with his father, Edward Payson Viles, in timberland developments in Skowhegan, being the third in a direct line to go into this business. His father's most important connection was as managing director of the Dead River Log Driving Company. Under the firm names of Viles and Gannett and Viles and Goodwin, the operations of Blaine Spooner Viles have been much more extensive. He is a director of the Kennebec Log Driving Company, and of the Cushnoc Paper Corporation, of Augusta; president of the Augusta Lumber Company; treasurer and manager of the Kennebec Land Company, the Northern Timberland Company, the Northeastern Land Company, the Maine Forest Products Company; president and treasurer of the Sandy Stream Log Driving Company; treasurer and manager of the Huston Brook Log Driving Company; director of the Bingham Improvement Company, and treasurer of the Augusta

Young Men's Christian Association. In 1925 he purchased the wholesale paper house of C. M. Rice Paper Company of Portland. He is also a member of the executive committee and a director of the Augusta Trust Company, and a director in the Fidelity Trust Company, of Portland. He has been a member of the Fish and Game Commission of Maine, Land Agent and Forest Commissioner of Maine, a member of the Maine Legislature, a member of the Governor's Council, and mayor of Augusta, and has served as chairman of the Republican committees for the city of Augusta and Kennebec County, and as a member of the State Republican Committee.

He is a Free and Accepted Mason of the thirty-second degree; a member of the Benevolent and Protective Order of Elks, of the Society of American Foresters, of the Delta Kappa Epsilon Fraternity, and a Shriner. He belongs to the Abnaki and Augusta Country clubs. During the World War, his civic activities were numerous. He was president of the Augusta Red Cross, industrial adviser to the Exemption Board, and secretary to the Kennebec County Committee on Public Safety.

Blaine S. Viles married A. Ethel Johnson, daughter of William C. and Annie C. Johnson, June 30, 1904, at Hallowell, Maine. Their children are E. Payson Viles, and Ada A. Viles.

WILLIAM DRUMMOND HUTCHINS, real estate operator of Augusta, Maine, was born in Bowdoin, Maine, June 8, 1869, the son of Alexander D. and Lydia J. (Brooks) Hutchins. His father, a farmer, was born in Phippsburg, Maine, February 29, 1832, and died in Bowdoinham, Maine, September 15, 1899. His mother, born in Lewiston, Maine, July 3, 1830, also has passed away.

William Drummond Hutchins was educated in the public schools of Bowdoin and the high school in Bowdoinham, Maine, and found his first employment in the grocery of H. R. Hinkley, of that town, where he began work July 18, 1887, and where he remained until 1890. For the next two years he was employed in the insurance house of S. W. Carr & Son, Bowdoinham. He then opened a store in Bowdoinham for the sale of men's furnishings, and operated it until 1902. From 1895 he was also connected with the Sagadahoc Fertilizer Company. In 1892 he entered the real estate business with the E. A. Strout Farm Agency, becoming the local manager, and later, general manager, with offices in New York City. In 1907 the W. D. Hutchins Company was incorporated in Augusta, Maine, and he has ever since devoted his time to this concern, which deals in real estate and insurance, and specializes in timberlands. He is also a director of the Augusta Trust Company, and a member of its executive committee, and treasurer of the Milo Water Company, of Milo.

Mr. Hutchins is a Methodist, and a Republican in politics. He has never, however, sought office or preferment of any kind, although he is a trustee and treasurer of the Augusta Water District. He is a member of the Knights of Pythias, and of the Chamber of Commerce, and his recreation is taken chiefly at the Augusta Country Club.

William Drummond Hutchins married Angie P. Jordan, daughter of Charles A. and Jane Mary (Springer) Jordan, November 27, 1890, at Bowdoinham. Mrs. Hutchins was born at Carmel, Maine,

September 16, 1868. Her father was a native of Gardiner, Maine, and her mother of Perkins, Maine. Their children are: 1. Leila C. (Chamberlain), born at Bowdoinham, November 15, 1892. 2. Carroll B., born July 2, 1899, at Bowdoinham.

IRVING A. FROST—The Frost Battery Service, of Rumford, Maine, is twelve years old, and during its vigorous lifetime it has grown rapidly, but healthfully, and at the present time (1928) its founder, owner, and operator, Irving A. Frost, has every reason to be content with his achievement. Mr. Frost has been identified with this line of activity since his school days, and is one of the thoroughly competent mechanicians and business men of this section of Oxford County.

Irving A. Frost was born in Rumford, Maine, May 6, 1894, and is a son of Albert Frost, born in Peru, Maine, died in 1919, and of Ida (Wing) Frost, a native of Livermore Falls. He received his education in the public schools of Rumford, and then entered the employ of John Stevens, of Rumford, who was engaged in the automobile repair and supply business. Here he remained until 1914, a period of five years, and then, being a good mechanician and having gained the experience he needed, he decided to engage in the auto supply and electrical service business for himself. In 1915 he established the Frost Battery Service, after having been engaged in the garage and repair business for himself for a year, and since that time he has maintained both a wholesale and retail electrical and battery service. He has made his establishment known for its full and excellent line of stock and for the promptness and efficiency of its service, as well as for the honesty and fairness with which its patrons are treated, and each year has brought a decided increase in the volume of the business which he carries. Politically, Mr. Frost gives his support to no one party, but casts his vote for the person most fit, regardless of party affiliation. He is a member of the Rumford Business Men's Association, and, fraternally, is identified with the Knights of Pythias. His religious membership is with the Baptist church.

Irving A. Frost was married, in Rumford, Maine, May 11, 1916, to Agnes Heath, born in Bethel, Maine, daughter of Eugene and Lura (Batchelder) Heath. Mr. and Mrs. Frost have two children: 1. Irving A., Jr., born in Rumford, Maine. 2. Albert E., also born in Rumford, Maine.

GEORGE HENRY CATES—As a general merchant, George Henry Cates has been engaged in business in East Vassalboro, Maine, since 1873, a period of more than fifty years, and he is still (1928) operating the business which for more than half a century has borne his name. Mr. Cates has been active in public affairs, served in the State Legislature in 1895, and is a member of one of the old families of this section.

George Henry Cates was born in East Vassalboro, Maine, November 17, 1852, and is a son of William H. Cates, for many years engaged in farming in Vassalboro, Maine. After attending the public schools of East Vassalboro, Mr. Cates continued his studies in Oak Grove Seminary, and in 1873, when he was twenty-one years of age, engaged in the general merchandise business in East Vassalboro. During the fifty-five years which have passed, he has con-

tinuously operated this same enterprise, and it is safe to say that practically every family in the community has, at some time, traded with Mr. Cates. No man in this section of the county is better known, and certainly no resident of the place has a larger number of friends and acquaintances. He knows the history of the place and the life histories of a large proportion of the residents of Vassalboro, and an hour or two spent with him is both valuable and entertaining. Along with his business success, Mr. Cates has found time for public and fraternal activities. He gives his support to the principles of the Republican party, in general, but he is one of the many intelligent citizens who may be classed as Independent Republicans, meaning that they give preference to personal fitness for office in casting their ballots, even though this may sometimes necessitate voting for the candidate of a party not their own. In 1895 Mr. Cates was chosen to represent his district in the State Legislature, where he served ably, giving satisfaction to his constituents and gaining credit for himself. He is a member of the local Grange, Patrons of Husbandry, and is identified with Vassalboro Lodge, Free and Accepted Masons, in which Order he holds membership in all the bodies of the York Rite, and in the Consistory, in which he holds the thirty-second degree. His religious membership is with the Friends' (Quaker) church.

George Henry Cates was married, in Liberty, Maine, June 18, 1876, to Louise Bryant, who was born in Knox, Maine, daughter of Benjamin and Nancy (Hodgman) Bryant. Mr. and Mrs. Cates have four children, all born in East Vassalboro: Lewis P., Benjamin H., Nancy C., and William K.

WILLIAM A. LORD—In North Vassalboro, William A. Lord has been catering to the needs of the residents, in the general merchandise line, for more than thirty years, and he knows well the requirements of his special patronage. Mr. Lord has served in the Legislature and is one of the best-known and most highly esteemed men of this community. The Lord family is one of the old New England families, whose members have been prominent in business, social, and political life for many generations, and he is a worthy descendant of his forebears.

William A. Lord was born, May 30, 1867, in Montville, Maine, a son of Albert W. Lord, a farmer, born in Montville, and of Sarah E. (Wentworth) Lord, also a member of a distinguished family of New England, born in Knox, Maine. He attended the public schools of Montville and of Knox, Maine, and then further prepared for an active and successful business career by taking a course in the Dirigo Business College, Augusta, Maine. After leaving school he was variously employed, part of the time in farming and trucking, and also in the general store. In 1896 he established a general store of his own in North Vassalboro, Maine, in partnership with B. K. Meservey. Nine years later, in 1905, he sold his interest in the business to his partner and purchased another store in North Vassalboro. This he has continued to operate, and during those three decades he has become very well known in North Vassalboro, where he has a host of friends, and where he is regarded as an able business man and a public-spirited citizen. He is a supporter of the Republican party, and has always been actively interested in public affairs. In 1908-09 he served in the State Legislature of Maine, and he has always been a generous supporter of all measures planned for the advancement of the general welfare of Vassalboro. He is a member and Past Commander of the Blue Lodge; Chapter, Commandery, and Shrine, Free and Accepted Masons; and of the Order of the Eastern Star, in which he is a Past Patron; also of the Independent Order of Odd Fellows. His religious affiliation is with the Baptist church.

William A. Lord was married, in Belfast, Maine, to Sadie J. Weagle, who was born in Nova Scotia, daughter of Jacob and Georgina (Firth) Weagle, natives of Nova Scotia. Mrs. Lord is a Past Matron of the Order of the Eastern Star. Mr. and Mrs. Lord are the parents of three children: 1. Carl B., born in Liberty, Maine. 2. Bernice, born in Liberty, Maine. 3. Maurice W., born in North Vassalboro, Maine.

SAMUEL CLARK CATES, M. D.—One of the younger members of the medical profession in East Vassalboro, Maine, is Dr. Samuel Clark Cates, who is unusually well prepared for his work as a physician. Dr. Cates holds degrees from four colleges and universities, including the Medical School of the University of Pennsylvania, from which he received the degree of Doctor of Medicine, and before coming to East Vassalboro, he served for two years in St. Agnes' Hospital, at Philadelphia. Dr. Cates was in the Naval Air Service during the World War.

Dr. Samuel Clark Cates was born in South China, Maine, August 26, 1890, son of David B. Cates, born in East Vassalboro, Maine, June 30, 1850, died October 15, 1923, a farmer, and of Annabelle B. Clark, born in South China, Maine, July 10, 1850, died June 4, 1921. After attending the public schools of Vassalboro, he became a student in Oak Grove Seminary, from which he was graduated with the class of 1908. The following fall he entered Colby College, at Waterville, Maine, where he finished his course with graduation in 1912, receiving at that time the degree of Bachelor of Science. The next three years he spent in the Pennsylvania State College, from which he received the degree of Master of Science in 1915. Not yet content with his academic and collegiate attainments, he studied for a year in the University of Chicago, from which he received the degree of Master of Science with the class of 1916. Some time later, he decided to enter the medical profession, but in the meantime, the United States had entered the World War, and he had promptly enlisted in the Naval Air Service, stationed at Panama Canal Zone and Cuba, doing patrol work. Soon after his return to civilian life he entered the Medical College of the University of Pennsylvania, where he completed his professional course with the class of 1924, receiving his medical degree. Always anxious to prepare himself for his work in the most thorough manner possible, Dr. Cates was not content with serving in a hospital for a single year prior to beginning practice, but served for two years, 1924-26, in St. Agnes' Hospital, Philadelphia. In 1926, he came to East Vassalboro, Maine, and opened an office. Since that time he has been building up a very satisfactory practice, and is already known as

an able physician. The thoroughness with which he prepared himself for his work is making itself evident, and Dr. Cates has, even in the short time in which he has been engaged in practice here, won the esteem of all with whom he has been associated. He is a member of Vassalboro Lodge, Free and Accepted Masons; of Dunlap Chapter, Royal Arch Masons, of China, Maine; of the Grange, Patrons of Husbandry; American Medical Association; Maine State Medical Society, and Kennebec County Medical Society; and his religious membership is with the Friends' (Quaker) church.

Dr. Samuel Clark Cates was married, in East Vassalboro, Maine, October 24, 1923, to Mae Hannah Janies, who was born in Rhonda Valley, Wales, January 9, 1899, daughter of William and Elizabeth (Meredith) Janies. Dr. and Mrs. Cates have two children: 1. David Clark, born in Philadelphia, Pennsylvania, September 4, 1924. 2. Peggy Ann, born in East Vassalboro, Maine, December 17, 1926.

WILLARD AUGUSTUS MARRINER—As proprietor of a general store in North Vassalboro, Maine, Willard Augustus Marriner has been taking care of a large patronage for the past twenty-five years. Though successful as a business man, Mr. Marriner does not devote all of his time and his energy to the management of his business. He was elected to the State Legislature, 1927-28, and has been an official of the town of Vassalboro more than twenty years.

Willard Augustus Marriner was born in Searsmont, Maine, August 1, 1872, son of Abel B. Marriner, a farmer, born in Searsmont, Maine, and of Licena A. (Luce) Marriner, who was born in Washington, Maine. After attending the public schools of Searsmont, he continued his studies in Oak Grove Seminary, and then became interested in the business of operating a general store. About 1902 he established a general store of his own at North Vassalboro, Maine, and since has continued successfully in this line of business enterprise. His store is now (1928) located on Main Street, and his business is a large one. Politically, Mr. Marriner gives his support to the principles and the candidates of the Republican party, and he has been active in public affairs in the town of Vassalboro for the past twenty years. In 1927 he was chosen by his fellow-townsmen to represent them in the Lower House of the State Legislature, to serve 1927-28. He is a member of Kennebec Lodge, No. 120, Independent Order of Odd Fellows, Past Noble Grand and member of the Encampment thereof; also a member of Vassalboro Lodge, No. 54, Free and Accepted Masons, Past Master, Blue Lodge; of the Vassalboro Grange, Patrons of Husbandry; and of the Kiwanis Club, of Waterville, Maine. He is a member of the board of trustees of the Methodist church, and as a citizen, neighbor, and friend, is highly esteemed. As a public official he is known to be a man of integrity and of unbiased judgment, and he has won in a high degree the confidence and esteem of all his associates.

Willard Augustus Marriner was married, in North Vassalboro, Maine, October 29, 1895, to Nellie E. Lawry, who was born in Searsmont, Maine, January 11, 1875, daughter of John F. Lawry, a native of Searsmont, and of Elvira B. (Ordway) Lawry, who was born in Belmont, Maine.

VINTON E. DUNN—One of the well-known contractors and builders of Augusta, Maine, is Vinton E. Dunn, who has been engaged in this line of business here since 1919. Mr. Dunn is known as an able business man and he has established a reputation for integrity which is a valuable asset. He operates under the name of V. E. Dunn, Contracting and Building.

Vinton E. Dunn was born in Belgrade, Maine, September 30, 1892, and is a son of Frank L. Dunn, a farmer, born in Belgrade, Maine, and of Mary K. (Robinson) Dunn, born in Mount Vernon, Maine. He received a good practical education in the public schools of Belgrade and then learned the carpenter's trade which he followed until 1913. In that year he engaged in the general contracting and building business for himself at Readfield, Maine, where he met with encouraging success, and continued until 1919. He then came to Augusta, Maine, and during the eight years which have passed since that time has been continuously and successfully engaged in the same line of business activity. He operates under the name of V. E. Dunn, Contracting and Building, and has erected many of the beautiful private residences of Augusta and vicinity, as well as several public buildings, and a number of business structures. Mr. Dunn is an Independent in his political views, believing that personal fitness for office is more important than party affiliations. He is a member of the Independent Order of Odd Fellows, and his religious interest is with the Baptist church, of which he is an attendant.

Vinton E. Dunn was married, in Readfield, Maine, September 30, 1913, to Inez E. Wright, daughter of L. B. and Mary (Tibbets) Wright. Mr. and Mrs. Dunn have two children: 1. Frank L., born in Readfield, Maine. 2. Patricia, born in Augusta, Maine.

WILLIAM B. WILLIAMSON, of Augusta, Maine, president of the Augusta Theatre Company, has enjoyed a varied and successful business career for so young a man. Born in Augusta, November 20, 1892, he is the son of Joseph and Vallie (Burleigh) Williamson. The elder Williamson was a lawyer, born in Belfast, Maine, a member of the Maine Legislature in 1910, and the following year county attorney of Kennebec County. He died in 1914. His wife, who survives, was born in Linneus, Maine. Joseph Williamson, grandfather of William B. Williamson, was a native of Belfast. He was an author, and among his writings was "Williamson's History of Belfast."

After a course in the public schools, and the Cony High School, in Augusta, William B. Williamson went to Phillips Andover Academy, where he was graduated in the class of 1910. He then entered Bowdoin College, where he spent two years in the class of 1911, and later studied law for two years at Boston University. Returning to Augusta, he organized the Maine Transportation Company, Incorporated, in 1911, and operated it for five years. In 1912, with William P. Gray, he founded the Augusta Theatre Company, of which he has since been president. He served on the Augusta City Council in 1913-14. In 1919, in collaboration with Blaine Viles, he produced thirty State of Maine pictures, upon scenarios written by Holman Day. He is supervisor of the Augusta district of the Maine-

New Hampshire Theatre Company; president of the Kennebec Land & Power Company; president of the Northeastern Land Company; president of the Northern Timberland Company, and a director of the Augusta Trust Company. Since 1919 he has been a director of the Maine-New Hampshire Theatre Company; is president and treasurer of the Augusta Opera House Company; vice-president of the Russell Amusement Company, and a director of the Majestic Theatre Company, the Concord Operating Company, the Capitol Theatre Company, the Capitol Realty Company, and the Concord Amusement Company. He served in the army during the World War, and is a Republican in politics, and a member of the Congregational church. He is a thirty-second degree Free and Accepted Mason, and a member of all the affiliated bodies that this rank implies, including the Shrine Club, and Kora Temple, Ancient Arabic Order Nobles of the Mystic Shrine; a member of the Knights of Pythias; the Benevolent and Protective Order of Elks; Abnaki, vice-president in 1928; past president (1922-1927) of the Augusta Country Club; a member of the University Club of Boston, and the Delta Kappa Epsilon Fraternity of Bowdoin.

William B. Williamson married Ida Gartley, daughter of Joseph and Melissa Gartley, in Augusta, August 23, 1915. She was born in Bangor, Maine, but her father, who died in 1922, and her mother were born in Canada. Their children are: 1. William B., Jr., born November 9, 1916, in Augusta. 2. Joseph, born February 11, 1918, in Augusta. 3. Richard Gartley, born August 13, 1924, in Augusta.

ROBERT M. MOORE was born January 7, 1892, at Biddeford, son of Dayton T. Moore (q. v.), and Nellie F. (Newcomb) Moore. He received his education in the grammar and high schools, and graduated from the University of Maine, at Orono, in the class of 1916, with the degree of Bachelor of Science, where he became a member of the Phi Kappa Sigma Fraternity. When his country entered the World War, he enlisted in the Signal Corps of the United States Army and served overseas. On returning home he entered the insurance firm of D. T. Moore & Son as a partner, on January 1, 1921, the concern having been established May 16, 1904, by Mr. Moore. On the death of his father, in 1921, he became president and treasurer. The concern does a general insurance business, and is one of the soundest and most reliable in this section.

In addition to having been president of the Biddeford Chamber of Commerce, Mr. Moore is a member of the local Rotary Club, the Second Congregational Church, and is a Republican in politics. He is a Mason, holding membership in Dunlap Lodge, Free and Accepted Masons, York Chapter, Maine Council, Bradford Commandery; and Kora Temple, Ancient Arabic Order Nobles of the Mystic Shrine, of Lewiston; also a member of the Independent Order of Odd Fellows, Laconia Lodge.

Robert M. Moore married, in 1917, Marcia J. Fogg, daughter of George C. and Fannie R. (Roberts) Fogg, of Biddeford, and they have two children: Thomas F., and Mary N.

DAYTON T. MOORE was born October 4, 1856, the son of Thomas M. and Asenath (Libby)

Moore, of Manchester, New Hampshire. He received a public school education and as a young man entered the employ of Simon Newcomb, one of the leading shoe manufacturers of that place, and eventually became a partner of Mr. Newcomb. Upon the latter's death the business was sold, and on May 16, 1904, at Biddeford, Mr. Moore established himself in the general insurance business, which he conducted under his own name until January 1, 1921, when he received into partnership his son, Robert M. Moore (q. v.), at which time the style was changed to D. T. Moore & Son. Mr. Moore had also been associated with the Biddeford Box Company as treasurer. During the World War he acted as local treasurer of the American Red Cross and was active in the various drives. He was president of the McArthur Library of Biddeford and a director of the Webber Hospital, his death removing a man of many affairs, whose worth to the community was such that his passing was generally and sincerely regretted.

Mr. Moore was a staunch member of the Republican party in politics, and from 1900 to 1903 he served as city clerk of Biddeford. He always took great interest in secret order work, and was a member of Dunlap Lodge, Free and Accepted Masons; York Chapter, Royal Arch Masons; and Bradford Commandery, Knights Templar. He was also a member of Laconia Lodge, Independent Order of Odd Fellows. He was a member of the Biddeford Rotary Club, and an attendant of the Second Congregational church.

Dayton T. Moore married Nellie F. Newcomb, daughter of Simon Newcomb, and they were the parents of five children: Byron N., Robert M. (q. v.), Mollie F., Carleton T., and Roger P.

WILLIAM A. FURBER—Since 1926 William A. Furber has been the owner and manager of the insurance business formerly controlled by E. S. Crosby, and he has retained the original name to the present time (1928). Mr. Furber was, prior to 1925, identified with the Bath Iron Works, of which he was treasurer, and his connection with that concern extended from the beginning of his active career to the time of the dissolution of the organization in 1925. He is treasurer of the Kennebec Bridge Association, and the Bath Water District, and is one of the enterprising and helpful citizens of the city of Bath.

William A. Furber was born in Bath, Maine, September 19, 1874, son of Charles B. Furber, who was engaged in business as a merchant and died in 1918, and of Abbie J. (Cross) Furber, who died in 1900. He received his education in the public schools and in business college, and then became identified with the Bath Iron Works in the capacity of clerk. His connection with this concern was maintained until it went out of existence in 1925, at which time Mr. Furber was holding the official position of treasurer. The Bath Iron Works, the largest industrial concern in Bath, was founded in 1884 by General Thomas W. Hyde for the purpose of manufacturing steel ships, battleships, destroyers, steamers, etc., and in peace times employed a maximum of twelve hundred people, this number being greatly increased in time of war. The official personnel at the time of the organization of the business in 1884 was as follows: President, General Thomas

W. Hyde; E. W. Hyde, treasurer. Later, E. W. Hyde became the second president, with H. H. McCarty as treasurer; the third president was John S. Hyde, who served as chief executive until 1917, when William T. Cobb was elected president and William A. Furber, treasurer, Mr. Cobb and Mr. Furber serving to the time of the dissolution of the concern in 1925.

The insurance business of which Mr. Furber is now (1928) owner and operator, was founded in 1877 by E. S. Crosby, and under the old name Mr. Furber is conducting a prosperous business. A half century of operation under the same name has brought a prestige and a following which few concerns in this line enjoy, and Mr. Furber is maintaining in every way the high standards which enabled this business to live and grow through so long a period of time. In addition to being a successful business man, Mr. Furber is helpful in the conduct of local affairs; he has served on the Board of Education for six years, three of which he has been chairman. He was a member of the City Council for three years, serving two years as councilman and one year as alderman. Fraternally, he is identified with Polar Star Lodge, Free and Accepted Masons, of which he is a Past Master and at present secretary; which the Knights Templar, of which he is Eminent Commander, and with all the other bodies of the York Rite. He is also a member of Kora Temple, Ancient Arabic Order Nobles of the Mystic Shrine. He is a member and past president of the Colonial Club, and his religious affiliation is with the Methodist church.

William A. Furber was married, in 1898, to Lucy C. Dunton, of Bath, Maine, and they are the parents of five children: Dorothy D., Helen R., Marjorie E., Esther M., and Emily G. Mr. Furber's business is located on Front Street, in Bath, and the family home is at No. 1252 Washington Street.

JOHN S. PRATT—The entire active career of John S. Pratt has been identified with the Shaw Business College at Portland, Maine, where he was engaged as an instructor after completing his own course in that school, until January, 1925, when he was made principal of the same school. Mr. Pratt is one of the faithful and able members of the faculty, and is doing splendid work here.

John S. Pratt was born in Baring, Maine, March 28, 1893, son of Fred S. Pratt, a native of Baring, Maine, who was engaged in farming to the time of his death, in 1920, and of M. A. (Scofield) Pratt, a native of Lubec, Maine, whose death occurred in 1925. Mr. Pratt attended the public schools of Lubec, and then prepared for an active business life by taking a commercial course in the Shaw Business College. Upon the completion of his course there he was offered a position as instructor in the college from which he had just graduated, and since that time he has been continuously engaged in teaching there. He is a teacher of ability and resourcefulness, and is giving excellent service to the management and first-class training to his pupils. Fraternally, he is identified with the Knights of Pythias, and his religious affiliation is with the Congregational church.

John S. Pratt was married, in 1922, to Jensine F. Christensen of Cumberland Center, Maine. Mr. and

Mrs. Pratt have one daughter, Louise Marguerite. The Shaw Business College is located on Congress Street, Portland, Maine.

CARLETON M. BAILEY—Opening a Ford and Lincoln agency in 1923, in partnership with his brother, B. D. Bailey, Carleton M. Bailey now occupies a prominent place in the business life of Livermore Falls. He is equally prominent in civic and social activities, being a veteran of the World War, a former member of the Board of Selectmen, and a member of several social organizations. His father, Dana W. Bailey, was a carriage manufacturer for thirty years, and later entered the automobile business. His mother was Esther (Young) Bailey.

Carleton M. Bailey was born July 31, 1894, at Livermore Falls, Maine. He attended the public schools of Livermore Falls and completed the high school course there in 1913. He was graduated from Colby College, in 1918, with the degree of Bachelor of Arts. During the World War he served with the 303d Field Artillery, United States Army, and saw much action near Toul, France. Returning to the United States, he became associated with his father, Dana W. Bailey, in the automobile business, and finally, in 1923, he opened his own Ford and Lincoln agency at Livermore Falls, which he has operated since.

Politically, Mr. Bailey is a member of the Republican party, and during 1920 and 1921 he served as a member of the Board of Selectmen of Livermore Falls. He is affiliated with Oriental Star Lodge, No. 21, Free and Accepted Masons, and in this order he has taken the degrees of the Chapter, Council, Commandery, and Temple, Ancient Arabic Order Nobles of the Mystic Shrine. He is also a member of the Independent Order of Odd Fellows, the American Legion, and the Livermore Falls Automobile Association. He attends the Baptist church.

On June 27, 1922, at Rumford, Maine, Carleton M. Bailey married Bertha Thorne, born at Strickland's, Maine, daughter of William S. and Ella (Burgess) Thorne. Mr. and Mrs. Bailey are the parents of a daughter, Beverly Ella, born July 2, 1927, at Livermore Falls.

WILLIAM MADISON AYER—Connected in an executive capacity with many of the leading enterprises of Oakland, Kennebec County, the late William Madison Ayer was in every sense of the word one of that community's most prominent citizens, and with his death the town and State lost a progressive and enterprising man who was ever to the fore in all projects for the advantage of the section wherein he lives.

William Madison Ayer was born in Bangor, March 22, 1856, the son of John and Olive A. (Furber) Ayer, the former a prominent railroad man and president of the Somerset Railroad Company. When less than a year old, Mr. Ayer was taken by his parents to West Waterville, Kennebec County, where he acquired his early education in the public schools of that community. Later, he attended the Maine Wesleyan Seminary, the Westbrook Seminary, and the Dean Academy at Franklin, graduating in 1876. Mr. Ayer took up the profession of civil engineering and was a member of the engineering corps employed in the survey which preceded the construction of the Somerset Railway. From January, 1876,

to December, 1879, he acted as general ticket agent for the Somerset Railway, and in the latter year was appointed manager of the Somerset Railroad Company, and superintendent and manager in 1881, which position he held until this railway was absorbed by the Maine Central Railway in 1907. He did much for the line while acting in this capacity, and was responsible for the extension of the road from Bingham to Kineo. In addition to his work with the railroad, Mr. Ayer had many outside interests. He was senior member of the firm of Ayer & Greeley, of Oakland, dealers in coal and wood; superintendent of the Dunn Edge Tool Company; manager and treasurer of the Dedlin Granite Company; president of the Oakland Woolen Company, of which concern he was one of the organizers; director of the Madison Woolen Company, and also of the Cascade Woolen Company; president of the Cascade Savings Bank, and had interests with a number of other important enterprises. He was a director of the Central Maine Power Company for many years preceding its absorption by the Insull interests. In 1902 he was appointed a member of the staff of Governor Hill, serving for four years and acquiring the rank of lieutenant-colonel. In 1891 and 1892 he was a member of the House of Representatives, and in November of the latter year was a delegate from the Third Maine Congressional District to the convention which nominated Benjamin Harrison for President. He was a member of the Maine Senate from 1904 to 1909, during his term serving as chairman of the committees on interior waters, labor, towns, and federal relations. He was also a member of the committee on military affairs during this time and served on numerous smaller committees. He was a member of Maine State Highway Commission, appointed by Governor Haines in 1913 when the commission was first established. He served ten years and was chairman for three years. He was a member of Messalonskee Lodge, Free and Accepted Masons; of Drummond Chapter, Royal Arch Masons; Mount Lebanon Council, Ancient Accepted Scottish Rite; St. Omar Commandery, Knights Templar, and Kora Temple, Ancient Arabic Order Nobles of the Mystic Shrine. He served as Grand Representative to the Grand Chapter of the Royal Arch Masons, held at Atlanta, Georgia, in 1889, and in 1904 was appointed Grand Representative of the Grand Chapter of Minnesota to the Grand Chapter of Maine.

On October 3, 1883, Mr. Ayer married Lizzie E. Otis, daughter of the late Benjamin F. and Ann (Bailey) Otis of Oakland. Mr. Ayer passed away May 10, 1926, deeply mourned and sincerely regretted by all who knew him, and who realized that their community had lost in him a man ever ready and willing to do all in his power for the good and benefit of his fellow-man.

WILSON A. CLEMENT—Fair dealing and excellence of service have characterized the business career of Wilson A. Clement, proprietor of the Belgrade Lakes Garages, since he established the first unit of his rapidly-growing business in 1918. Gaining a thorough knowledge of the automobile business, he started his career as an agent for Ford and Lincoln cars and Fordson tractors, offering expert service in general motor repairs. His trade grew so rapidly that he opened another garage at Belgrade

Lakes to take care of increasing patronage, and his reputation is established for service and materials of the highest type. Mr. Clement was born in Rome, August 7, 1884, son of Wilson and Millie (Young) Clement, both of Maine. Wilson Clement was engaged in farming all his life.

Wilson A. Clement was educated in the public schools of Rome, after which he was engaged in commercial life until 1918, when he embarked in the automobile business, independently, as mentioned previously. His two garages in Belgrade Lakes provide auto repair service and storage and accessories of the highest quality and durability, and they are both familiar stopping places for travelers in this vicinity. Mr. Clement's success is due to his thorough familiarity with all types of cars, his courteous treatment of customers and the prompt and efficient service rendered by his organization. He is a prominent member of fraternal organizations, being a member of the Order of the Eastern Star; Vernon Valley Lodge, No. 99, Free and Accepted Masons, all bodies, holding the thirty-second degree, and a member of the State Grange, Patrons of Husbandry. His religious affiliations are with the Union church.

Wilson A. Clement married, April 8, 1924, Erma Tillson of Augusta, daughter of Clyde Tillson of Sidney, and Irene (Jones) Tillson. They have one daughter, Norma, born June 12, 1926, in Augusta.

CARLETON E. YOUNG is postmaster at Winterport, Maine. He is still a young man, but has had much experience; among other things, he was in the European War, and saw service at the front. His regular business is that of engineering, and he had already been so engaged for a number of years when he enlisted in the United States Army. Mr. Young has many social and fraternal connections, and is held in much esteem in the community where he serves in his present official capacity.

Carleton E. Young was born June 11, 1895, at Winterport, Maine, son of John Henry and Mary Alice (Colson) Young, of whom the father, who was a stone mason and foreman of a highway crew, was born at Winterport, Maine, as was the mother. Mr. Young received his education in the grammar and high schools of his native town. He then followed steam engineering for four years. In 1917 he enlisted in the United States Army, becoming attached to the 101st Field Artillery, Twenty-sixth Division, serving overseas nineteen months. He was commissioned postmaster of Winterport in 1920, and still holds that office. Mr. Young is a Republican in politics. He belongs to the Blue Lodge, Free and Accepted Masons; the Independent Order of Odd Fellows, of which he is Past Grand, and he attends the Methodist church.

Carleton E. Young married, June 23, 1920, at Winterport, Maine, Grace Evelyn Coggins, daughter of Clifton and Marietta (Harriman) Coggins. There have been three children to the marriage: Mary Alice, Persis Ethel, and John Raymond.

HAROLD CHESTER FLETCHER—The automobile enterprise in all branches of its activity has in Harold Chester Fletcher an exponent who from the date that he started in business at South Paris has shown every evidence that he has kept in the lead in this part of the State. Alert and resourceful, he has sought opportunity and won merited place in his department of the business world.

Harold Chester Fletcher is a son of Herbert G. Fletcher, who was also an automobile dealer, a native of Buckfield, and who died in 1918, and of Annie M. (Doble) Fletcher, who was born in Paris. He was born August 27, 1885, at South Paris, where he attended the grammar school and was graduated from high school with the class of 1904. He was employed by N. Dayton Bolster at South Paris from June, 1904, to October, 1906, and afterwards by his father, to May, 1916. He then entered the automobile business with his father and Perley F. Ripley. Upon the death of his father in 1918, he took his partnership in the firm of Ripley and Fletcher Company, this concern having the agency for the Ford and Lincoln machines. Mr. Fletcher is a member of the board of directors of the South Paris Trust Company; and in his political activities he is an adherent of the principles of the Democratic party. In the fraternities, Mr. Fletcher is prominent and active. Besides his membership in the Maine Automobile Dealers' Association, and his office of secretary in the South Paris Board of Trade, he is affiliated with Paris Lodge, No. 94, Free and Accepted Masons, of which he is the secretary; Norway Chapter, Royal Arch Masons; Oriental Commandery, Knights Templar; Kora Temple, Ancient Arabic Order Nobles of the Mystic Shrine; the Knights of Pythias; and the Kiwanis Club. His religious faith is that of the Congregational church. Harold Chester Fletcher married, June 13, 1913, at Bethel, Lida Phillips, who was born at Livermore, daughter of Edmund F. and Florence (Brette) Phillips.

MORTON V. BOLSTER—As a retail grocer, Morton V. Bolster has been engaged in the business from the beginning of his active career, in association with E. N. Haskell, at South Paris, Maine. Mr. Bolster is a graduate of Bates College and a director of the South Paris Savings Bank.

Morton V. Bolster, born in South Paris, Maine, July 4, 1888, is a son of N. Dayton Bolster, a merchant, who was born at Rumford, Maine, died in July, 1921, and of Ada (Morton) Bolster, a native of South Paris. Mr. Bolster attended the local public schools, graduating from South Paris High School with the class of 1905, and then entered Bates College, at Lewiston, Maine, where he was graduated with the class of 1910, receiving at that time the degree of Bachelor of Arts. Upon the completion of his college course he returned to South Paris and became associated with his father and E. N. Haskell in the retail grocery business which is operated under the name of its founder, N. Dayton Bolster, father of Morton V. Bolster. The store, which is located on Market Square, South Paris, was incorporated in 1909, and takes care of a large patronage. Mr. Bolster is also a member of the board of directors of the South Paris Savings Bank, and is an active and interested member of the South Paris Board of Trade. He gives his support to the principles and the candidates of the Republican party, and, fraternally, is identified with the Independent Order of Odd Fellows. His religious affiliation is with the Congregational church of South Paris.

COLONEL CHARLES HENRY PRESCOTT—

As newspaper editor, publisher, and public-spirited citizen, Colonel Charles Henry Prescott took a prominent part in almost every phase of the life of Maine. He founded, and for forty years was publisher and the managing editor of the "Biddeford Daily Journal," of Biddeford, in which capacities he won the esteem of his fellowmen and came to be highly respected in newspaper circles. Aside from his journalistic work, Colonel Prescott's interests were by nature political, civic, business, and fraternal; he was a director or an officer in several corporations, took an active part in efforts to bring railways and other useful enterprises into Biddeford, Saco, and York County, and was candidate in 1904 on the Republican ticket for the governorship of Maine.

He was born in Barnstead, New Hampshire, August 3, 1857, a son of James Lewis and Harriet Morrill (Tripp) Prescott. His parents removed, while he was a child, to North Berwick, Maine, where his father established a manufacturing firm, which he and his sons carried on successfully for many years. As a boy, Charles Henry Prescott attended the local public schools, and went to Berwick Academy; then he became a student at Boston University, where he studied law. In 1880 he was admitted to the bar in York County, Maine; but had scarcely begun to practice his profession when, in the same year, he and his brother, William W. Prescott, purchased in Biddeford from George A. Hobbs the "Weekly Union and Journal." They published the paper jointly for about a year, at the end of which period the brother withdrew, and Charles H. Prescott became the sole owner. Three years later, in 1884, Charles H. Prescott, having acquired a thorough knowledge of the details of newspaper publication, founded the "Biddeford Daily Journal," which soon became known as one of the outstanding newspapers of the State. For forty years he continued as sole owner, publisher, and managing editor; but in the last years of his life, he was relieved of some of the duties of editorship when the business was incorporated. The "Daily Journal" twice found it necessary to seek larger quarters, going, the second time, in 1905, into the Journal Building, on Adams Street, a structure especially designed for the newspaper business, equipped with all modern conveniences and machinery.

Among his many interests in the business enterprises of Biddeford and Saco, Colonel Prescott was for many years a trustee of the York County Savings Bank, and after the death of John Berry succeeded him as president; director of the First National Bank of Biddeford, and became president of it in 1917, succeeding Charles A. Moody; and held directorships in the Union Mutual Life Insurance Company, of Portland, the North Berwick Manufacturing Company, the Biddeford Improvement Society, and other corporations or associations of an industrial nature. Active in the development of the Biddeford & Saco Railroad, he was one of the ardent supporters of this enterprise when it was first launched; and later, when it was in danger of being abandoned, was influential in reorganizing it and putting it on its feet. In the reorganized company he held the positions of president, manager, and for a long time those of secretary and treasurer, and became eventually its controlling owner. Always interested in transit and transportation facilities, he

was a director and vice-president of the Portland Street Railroad Company, which in later years was absorbed by the Cumberland County Light & Power Company.

Prominent in the councils of the Republican party, Colonel Prescott played a leading rôle in the political life of Maine. In 1883, when he was only twenty-six years old, he was elected to membership in the Maine House of Representatives and was the youngest member of that legislative body; was reëlected in 1884; and was nominated in 1885 for a third term, but declined to take the office. In 1887 he became treasurer of York County, a position which he held continuously until 1890. From 1888 until 1892 he was chairman of the Republican City Committee of Biddeford; and in 1888 was a delegate-at-large to the Republican National Convention that nominated Benjamin Harrison for the Presidency of the United States. He was a member of the Committee on Resolutions which was headed by William McKinley, then in the United States Congress, and later President. From 1893 until 1897, during the two terms of office of Governor Henry B. Cleaves, Colonel Prescott was a member of the Governor's staff; in 1895 and 1896 he was elected to the Maine State Senate from York County; and from 1901 until 1905 he was chairman of the executive council in the administration of Governor John F. Hill.

The work of charitable and educational institutions always attracted the interest of Colonel Prescott, who was a trustee of the Cornelius Sweetser estate, was instrumental in the building of the Sweetser Home for Boys in Saco, was a member of the board of managers of the Webber Hospital from this institution's inception, and was a trustee of Thornton Academy. He was a member of the Free and Accepted Masons, in which order he was affiliated with Dunlap Lodge, of Biddeford; and held memberships in the Ancient and Honorable Artillery Company of Boston, the Cumberland Club of Portland, and the Biddeford and Saco Country Club.

On January 17, 1882, he married Ellen S. Hobbs, of North Berwick, who survives him.

Colonel Prescott's death, which occurred at the family home in Saco on December 19, 1926, brought grief to the hearts of those whose privilege it was to know him as a friend and regret to many persons with whom he was less intimate but who were aware of the quality of his life's work. The business houses of Biddeford and Saco suspended operations for five minutes in honor of him; and the cars on the Biddeford & Saco Railroad, of which he was president at the time of his death, were stopped for two minutes during his funeral services as a tribute to his memory. Edward H. Drapeau, who then was mayor of Biddeford, referred to him in a published statement as "a man among men"; charitable and benevolent," and added: "So interested was he in the public benefit that he held his paper open always at the disposal of any organization."

The "Biddeford Daily Journal," in its issue of December 19, 1923, wrote of Colonel Prescott:

.... Here in the office of the newspaper to the interest of which he gave so much of his life, we knew him, first of all, as a man among men, a gentleman under any and all circumstances. Of equable temper and sanguine temperament, he had the faculty of inspiring in his employees a loyalty which endured the severest tests because it was founded on a feeling which combined the better qualities of both respect and affection. Here he was recognized as a dependable friend in time of need; a sympathizer in time of sorrow; a safe adviser in time of trouble.

To the community-at-large Charles H. Prescott was, in kind if not degree, just what he was to his co-workers in various business enterprises. His reputation for probity, conservatism and good judgment led to a demand for his services in many positions of public and private trust, and results always proved that this confidence was fully justified. Probably no other citizen ever devoted more anxious thought to the welfare, mental and moral, as well as material, of Biddeford and Saco. Here at home his passing will be greatly regretted and his presence will be sorely missed. In the broader fields of county and State, though he had gradually retired from active participation in political affairs and was slowly divesting himself of a heavy burden of business responsibilities with a view to the fuller enjoyment of a well-earned leisure, he will be missed only a little less than in his home community. For in politics and in business his advice was still sought as that of a man whose experience and judgment commanded respect and confidence.

Among men there are those who are liked on short acquaintance, but who do not wear well; and there are those who improve upon closer acquaintance and whom we like better the more we know them. Charles H. Prescott belonged to the latter class. His loyalty to his friends was proverbial. His sympathy for suffering humanity, whether in the mass or in individual cases, was acute, and the ears of his conscience were never closed to the call of distress. While the list of his open benefactions was a long one, it was exceeded by the number of cases in connection with which he did not let his left hand know what his right hand was doing.

As marking the passing of the man who for so many years was the personal embodiment of the "Biddeford Journal," who since his early manhood has been such a vital element in the development of Biddeford and Saco, who has so ably filled so many positions of responsibility, who, above all and through all, so loved his home and his home life, we believe this brief but heartfelt hail-and-farewell is amply justified.

The enviable reputation which Colonel Prescott enjoyed among newspaper men was indicated by the editorial comments which appeared in "The Portland Evening Express," the "Bangor Commercial," and other papers throughout Maine.

FORREST HARTLEY BADGER, M. D.—Of the learned professions, that of medicine seems to bring out the finest principles of a man's character, and develops his qualities of sympathy and understanding. An excellent example of how such a man will ever gain the respect and esteem of his community is furnished by Dr. Forrest Hartley Badger, one of the leading physicians of Maine, whose residence and practice is at Winthrop.

Dr. Badger was born in Rangeley, January 15, 1870, the son of James Dinsmore and Clementine Allen (Quimby) Badger. After his preliminary education in the local schools and at the Farmington Normal School, he entered Bowdoin College, graduating in 1894 with the degree of Doctor of Medicine. From 1894 to 1896 Dr. Badger occupied himself in general practice in Strong, and in the latter year removed to his birthplace, Rangeley. In 1898, however, he located in Winthrop, and remained for three years, after which he was for two years on the surgical staff of Pawtucket Hospital, Pawtucket, Rhode Island. He then returned to Winthrop, where he has remained. He has built up for himself a most remunerative practice, and has acquired to the fullest extent the confidence and trust of the community. He holds the post of physician and surgeon-in-chief at the Winthrop Hospital, and during the World War was medical examiner and member of the local draft board for Kennebec County. He is school physician for Winthrop, and former superintendent of schools for the district. He is a member of the consulting staff of Augusta General Hospital, and demonstrator of operative surgery in

Boston College of Physicians and Surgeons. He is an active member of the Kennebec Medical Society, of the Maine Medical Association, and the American Medical Association. Politically, he is a Republican, and his religious affiliations are with the Congregational church.

On February 17, 1897, at Strong, Dr. Badger married Caroline M. Gilkey. Dr. and Mrs. Badger are the parents of one child, Marcia E. Badger.

LEON A. DODGE—An eventful life has characterized the rapid rise of Leon A. Dodge, of Damariscotta to the position of one of the leaders in the world of insurance and finance. His ability and intellect, enterprise and progressive methods have led him onward until now, still a young man, he heads his own general insurance business and is cashier of the First National Bank of Damariscotta. The First National Bank of Damariscotta was organized and begun in 1864 by a group of forward-looking citizens and business men, who elected Alva A. Stetson first president, and W. M. Hitchcock first cashier, the bank being capitalized at $50,000. Its business has grown steadily and unfalteringly until today it is the oldest and largest bank in Lincoln County, and its assets at the latest recapitulation stood at $1,528,699.70. The officers in charge at the present time are Wilder W. Dodge, president; F. I. Carney, vice-president, and Leon A. Dodge, cashier.

Mr. Dodge is descended from an old and prominent family which has resided in the State of Maine continuously since Revolutionary times, having had their residence in the State of Massachusetts prior to that time.

Leon A. Dodge was born in Damariscotta, March 22, 1891, son of Wilder W. Dodge of Damariscotta, and Carrie (Richardson) Dodge of Bangor, who died in 1916. Wilder W. Dodge is a prominent figure in the mercantile life of the community, heading one of the important and successful business organizations in this town. He is also active in the realm of finance, being president of the First National Bank, and is of great aid in promoting the progress of the town in every way possible to a public-spirited citizen of the highest type.

Leon A. Dodge began his education in the local public schools, and continued his studies at Lincoln Academy, after which he entered Bowdoin College, from which he graduated in 1913 with the degree of Bachelor of Arts. Upon the completion of his college career, he entered the employ of the New England Telephone & Telegraph Company, but after a short time, withdrew to enter business with his father in the retail clothing business in Damariscotta. In 1920 he was elected cashier of the First National Bank of Damariscotta, which position he has ably filled up to the present time. In addition to his financial interests, Mr. Dodge operates independently a general insurance business which has been highly successful. Mr. Dodge is a trustee and commissioner of Lincoln Academy, a trustee of the Skidomphia Public Library, and member of the local School Board. He also serves on a number of other civic organizations. His unselfish interest in the welfare of the community has made him a popular member of all campaigns for town progress. Mr. Dodge is an ardent advocate of the principle of service to others and has the honor to be the first president of the Rotary Club of Damariscotta. He is also a believer in wholesome, athletic recreation and helped to organize the Wawenock Golf Club of which he is vice-president. In fraternal circles he is a member of the Blue Lodge, Free and Accepted Masons, and of the Delta Kappa Epsilon Fraternity. His religious affiliation is with the Congregational church, of which he is a deacon. During the World War, Mr. Dodge served in the United States Navy, receiving the rank of ensign, returning home upon his discharge from the service with the commendation of his superior officers. He is a member of Richard R. Wells Post, American Legion, and financial officer since its inception.

Leon A. Dodge married, in 1916, Christine E. Huston, of Newcastle, daughter of Joel H. and Myrtle R. (Robinson) Huston. Their children are: Joel H., born June 1, 1917, and Leon A., Jr., born May 8, 1921.

JOHN W. BRACKETT—The profession of law gives to its followers the power to be of great influence in any community, and Boothbay Harbor is particularly fortunate to have in its midst John W. Brackett, who started his career as an educator, but soon gave up that profession to enter into his chosen life-work in the legal field. Mr. Brackett is at present Probate Judge of Lincoln County, having held this position for nineteen years, justifying thoroughly the confidence that the voters have placed in him. He was born in Bristol, Maine, August 17, 1867, son of Alexander H. Brackett of Bristol, who died in 1917, and Sarah J. (McLain) Brackett of Bristol, who is still living, aged eighty-four years. Alexander H. Brackett was engaged in the merchandise trade and served the patrons of his community well and efficiently.

John W. Brackett received his education in the local public schools and after high school, entered Gorham Normal School, and finishing there, taught in the public school for a short period. Leaving the teaching profession, he entered the office of William H. Hilton, prominent lawyer of Damariscotta, where he read law. Applying himself assiduously to his work, he completed his studies and was admitted to the bar in 1895. The same year witnessed his establishment in the practice of his profession at Bristol, his native town, where he gained the respect and esteem of his fellow-townspeople during the seven years he remained there. During the period 1900 to 1904, he served as County Attorney, succeeding Emerson Hilton, and it was during this time, in 1902, that he removed to Boothbay Harbor. Shortly after making this change, he was selected as Trial Justice, which office he held until 1908, when he was appointed Probate Judge of Lincoln County. Upon the expiration of his term in 1917, Mr. Brackett was elected to the same position in which he continues to serve at the present time. He has served his town in practically all the civil offices, and at various times has been chairman of every municipal board. His exceptional record in the realm of public service has been one of unceasing effort to give to the people the finest type of judicial administration possible. While attending to the judicial and civic affairs of the community, Mr. Brackett has also been actively engaged for ten years in civil engineering and surveying work, in which profession he has given to his work his usual thorough and comprehensive attention. During the recent World War, Mr.

Brackett was prominent in Red Cross activities and participated in all the Liberty Loan drives and war work of every kind, aiding the cause greatly by his example and influence. He takes an active part in fraternal and social circles, being a member of the Blue Lodge, Free and Accepted Masons; Past Chancellor of the Knights of Pythias, and a member of the Royal Arcanum, besides his membership in various local clubs. Mr. Brackett attends the Methodist church, being on the board of trustees.

John W. Brackett married Martha M. Tibbetts, of Bristol, Maine, daughter of Thaddeus C. and Lizzie (McFarland) Tibbetts. Their children are: 1. Gail M., died 1924; married Hazel Stinson, and had one child, John D. 2. John C., married Clara Dunton, and has one child, John Cutler. 3. Max I. 4. Mabel B. 5. Dana C.

JOHN P. KELLEY—One of the most popular and best-known men in the political and business life of Lincoln County and one whose record as sheriff was so fine that the people reëlected him for the third successive term is John P. Kelley who has held all the civil offices of Boothbay Harbor, in addition to being active in the civic and business development of the town.

Mr. Kelley was born in Boothbay, July 21, 1876, son of John E. Kelley of Boothbay, who died in 1913, and Cordelia (McDougall) Kelley of Boothbay, who died in 1919. John E. Kelley served in the infantry during the Civil War and upon his return home engaged in farming and, going into politics, served the people of Lincoln County as sheriff for sixteen years. In view of his father's long and successful record, Mr. Kelley can be justly proud that the people have continued him in office for such an already exceptional period.

John P. Kelley attended the local public schools and after high school, entered Lincoln Academy. Completing his studies there, he entered the employ of the Eastern Steamship Company where his business ability and sterling qualities caused him to advance steadily, until twelve years later he was made agent at Boothbay Harbor, which position he held for fifteen years, or until June, 1926, when he went into real estate business for himself. Both in real estate brokerage and in development work, Mr. Kelley has been successful, besides helping with the civic improvement of the town. For a number of years, he has served as treasurer and collector of the Boothbay Harbor Water Company, and one of the Water Commissioners, and he also a director and treasurer of the Boothbay Harbor Cold Storage Company. In politics, Mr. Kelley is a Republican and has always been active in civil affairs, having held the offices of selectman, tax collector, overseer of the poor, Republican county chairman, deputy sheriff for six years and then elected sheriff of Lincoln County in 1923, in which office he is now serving his third term. He served in the Maine Legislature 1909-10-11-12. This record shows to what extent the people of the town and county have placed their dependence and trust in Mr. Kelley and he has shown them that they were justified. In fraternal circles, Mr. Kelley has always taken an active part, being a member of the Free and Accepted Masons, Blue Lodge and Chapter, and Past Chancellor Commander of the Knights of Pythias. He is also a member of the Sons of Veterans and of various local clubs. His religious affiliations are with the Congregational church.

John P. Kelley married, in 1898, Maggie T. Abbott, of Boothbay, daughter of Millard S. and Arvilla (Jewett) Abbott, and their children are: 1. Beulah L., married F. T. Fowle. 2. John S.

WILBUR F. ROLLINS—Wide experience in business and in banking have combined in the successful career of Wilbur F. Rollins, now manager of the York County Trust Company, of Ogunquit, Maine. Besides many years of association with his uncle, W. F. Cousens, in his store, he has also been active in general finances and in other phases of civic affairs.

Wilbur F. Rollins was born at Brockton, Massachusetts, July 19, 1889, son of Andrew M. and Clara E. (Cousens) Rollins. The father, born at Livermore Falls, Maine, died in February, 1925. The mother is a native of Kennebunkport, Maine. The father was also prominent, particularly because of his long years of association with the Century Publishing Company. After completing the public and high school course, the son began on the business career which was to place him among the leading young men of the town. He worked with his uncle, W. F. Cousens, in his large general store in Ogunquit, until 1922, when the general recognition of his efficiency and business ability brought him his present connection with the newly-formed branch there of the York County Trust Company. He has since been manager of the bank branch and active in promoting its progress. He is so well known in the vicinity and so popular that he has been able to secure for the concern much new and important business. During the World War, Mr. Rollins was a member of the Emergency Fleet Corporation and helped further patriotic drives. He belongs to the Lodge, Free and Accepted Masons; Murry Chapter, Royal Arch Masons; Maine Council, Royal and Select Masters; the Commandery, Knights Templar, and to Kora Temple, Ancient Arabic Order Nobles of the Mystic Shrine. His religious views are those of the Methodist church, on whose official board he has a place.

In 1914, Wilbur F. Rollins married Virginia Gould, daughter of George W. and Mildred M. (Stinchfield) Gould. They reside in Ogunquit, with their son, Maynard F. Rollins.

HARTLEY C. BAXTER—As head of the firm of H. C. Baxter & Brother, Hartley C. Baxter, who is a prominent figure in the industrial and business life of Brunswick, is often referred to as the dean of the canners of Maine. This company operates factories for packing corn and succotash in a number of cities and towns in Maine and Vermont, as well as in one Iowa city, and distributes its products throughout the United States and in foreign countries.

Hartley C. Baxter, the company's president, is the oldest son of James Phinney Baxter who was, with William J. Davis, a founder of the Portland Packing Company, one of the first canning firms in Maine, and who was for several terms mayor of Portland. The mother of Hartley C. Baxter was Sarah (Cone) Baxter, a native of Maine.

Born in Gorham, Maine, July 19, 1857, Hartley C. Baxter attended the public schools, and later became a student at Bowdoin College, from which he was graduated in the class of 1878 with the degree of Bachelor of Arts. After having worked with his father for a number of years in the Portland Packing Company, Mr. Baxter established, in 1886, the present company, known as H. C. Baxter & Brother, which now operates canning factories, packing corn and succotash, in the following cities and towns: St. Albans, Maine; Hartland, Maine; Fryeburg, Maine; North Fryeburg, Maine; Lovell, Maine; Conway, New Hampshire; Westminster, Vermont; Windsor, Vermont; Piermont Station, Vermont; Essex Junction, Vermont; and Wapello, Iowa. It claims the distinction of being the first canning company in Maine to pack peas on a commercial scale. The Hartland, Maine, factory is now operated on peas and stringless beans, as well as on corn. The total capacity of the factories is about one million cans per day, and last year's pack totaled about 12,000,000 cans. During the canning season the different factories employ about 750 men and women, and the annual payroll averages $150,000, but the factories are in active operation only about one month in each year. "Baxter's Finest" and "Snow Flake" are the principal brands made by the company. Officers of the company are: Hartley C. Baxter, president; J. P. Baxter, Jr., vice-president; R. H. Baxter, treasurer; John L. Baxter, assistant treasurer; and B. H. M. White, assistant treasurer. In addition to his activity with the Baxter canning companies, Hartley C. Baxter has several other business interests, being a director of different banks and corporations; a member of the Water Board of Brunswick, an office that he has held for a number of years; and having taken part in the Liberty Loan drives during the World War. He is a member of the honorary fraternity of Phi Beta Kappa, and also of Delta Kappa Epsilon. Active also in club life in Maine, he is a member of the Cumberland Club, the Portland Yacht Club, and a number of other local clubs in Maine. He and his family are Congregationalists.

Hartley C. Baxter married Mary Lincoln, the daughter of John D. and Ellen (Fessenden) Lincoln. They are the parents of the following children: 1. Sarah L., who married M. E. Langley. 2. Ellen L., who married A. E. Morrell. 3. John L., who married Constance French. 4. Emily W., who married A. B. Holmes (q. v.). John L. Baxter, who is now very active in the Baxter canning business, is one of the most promising young business men of Brunswick. He is president of the local Chamber of Commerce, and is affiliated with several other local organizations.

WESTON M. HILTON—A life of continuous application of his ideals in the practice of his profession is the record achieved by Weston M. Hilton, who has carried on the legal business founded by his father in 1865, which has since continued to be located in its original location. The Hilton law office has been familiar to several generations of the inhabitants of Damariscotta, just as it has been ever dependable and worthy of the trust and confidence reposed therein.

Weston M. Hilton was born in Damariscotta, October 1, 1870, son of William H. Hilton of Damariscotta, who died in 1912, and Mary E. (Weston) Hilton, of Bremen, who is still living. William H. Hilton was one of the best-known attorneys in Lincoln County, commencing the practice of law in Damariscotta in 1865. He was a prominent man in the affairs of the community, and while always conservative, was ever ready to adopt new ideas that agreed with his discriminating and even judgment.

Mr. Hilton received his early education in the local public schools, and after completing his course at Lincoln Academy, entered Bowdoin College from which he received his degree of Bachelor of Arts in 1891. Then he attended Harvard Medical School for two years. Deciding to enter the legal profession he commenced the study of law, being admitted to the bar in 1896. The same year, he started his professional practice in Damariscotta in partnership with his father, William H. Hilton, which he continued until 1901, when he removed to Boothbay Harbor. There he built up a successful independent practice during his short stay of four years. In 1905, Mr. Hilton returned to Damariscotta and has since continued to advance until he is now one of the leading men of his profession in the vicinity. In 1912, upon the death of his father, Mr. Hilton succeeded to the legal business founded so long before and it is now an institution in the life of the town. One of the indications of the dignity and surety of this business is the original sign which still hangs outside, bearing the name, Hilton Law Office, placed there by the senior Mr. Hilton over sixty years ago. On two different occasions, Mr. Hilton has served as County Attorney, each term being highly successful. He attends the Episcopal church. During the war, he was of great value in his work as a "four-minute" speaker, arousing the people to their duties in that time of stress, and commending them for their able assistance to their government during that period of strife. Mr. Hilton received a certificate from the government in recognition of his able work for the cause of liberty and justice. He holds membership in various local clubs.

EDGAR A. HUSSEY—"Ed. Hussey is certainly to be commended for the enterprise and courage he has shown in leading the way," is the opinion and estimate expressed by a leading business man in Augusta, when he referred to the building of the present structure that houses the Hussey Hardware Company, Bangor Street, on the east side of Augusta. That voluntary statement may well be said to voice the confidence of the entire community in Mr. Hussey as a merchant who has made a success of his ventures and has inspired others to do the same—a man, indeed, who has "led the way." He is prominent in all things that have to do with the high status of Augusta as a city of enterprise and progress, and he is esteemed for his undoubted leadership, his business sense, and probity.

Edgar A. Hussey was born November 20, 1868, at Vassalboro, son of Jeremiah M. Hussey, a farmer, also a native of Vassalboro, and Mercy M. (Merrill) Hussey, who was born at Augusta. He received his early education at Oak Grove Seminary, Cony High School, and the Dirigo Business College; and for several terms while attending school, he himself taught school. He was then employed in the store of S. S. Brooks & Company, where he obtained his fifteen years of apprenticeship in the hardware business, and laid the foundation of his successful career, both in store and in traveling salesmanship. Then, entering upon business lines of his own, he bought out the establishment in which he had been employed, and formed the Brooks Hardware Company, of which he was the treasurer and general manager.

The old headquarters of the concern stood at No. 251 Water Street, but in 1920, the concrete building at Nos. 10-12 Bangor Street was completed, and the present organization for the purposes of the Hussey Hardware Company was consummated, with these officers: President, Leroy F. Hussey; vice-president and general manager, Edgar A. Hussey; treasurer and assistant manager, Stanley E. Hussey; clerk, Albert W. Brooks; these men also forming the board of directors. The home of the corporation is the outcome of ideas that Mr. Hussey had had in mind for years. The site of the building was formerly occupied by the old John Mitchell and Chandler blacksmith shop, the work on the new stores being under way on September 1, 1921.

In political lines, Mr. Hussey gives allegiance to the Republican party; and in his fraternal affiliations he is a member of Augusta Lodge, Free and Accepted Masons, in all bodies of the Ancient Accepted Scottish Rite of the thirty-second degree, as well as of the Temple, Ancient Arabic Order Nobles of the Mystic Shrine. He is also a member of Augusta Chamber of Commerce and the Rotary Club, and his religious faith is that of the Universalist church.

Edgar A. Hussey married, in 1894, at Augusta, Lillian Parks, who was born in Hallowell. Their children, all born in Augusta: 1. Stanley E. Hussey, treasurer and assistant manager of the Hussey Hardware Company, was born December 9, 1895; graduated from the public schools, Cony High School, and Boston University. For four years he was a member of the Augusta City Council. During the World War, he was assigned for duty in the office of the Adjutant-General at the State House, and after the war, he was for three years with Brooks Hardware Company. He is a member of Alpha Kappa Psi Fraternity; Benevolent and Protective Order of Elks; Independent Order of Odd Fellows; Kiwanis Club, and Chamber of Commerce. 2. Leroy F. Hussey, president of the Hussey Hardware Company, born September 25, 1897; graduated from the public schools, Cony High School, University of Maine, and Boston University. During the World War, he was a member of the Fifty-sixth Pioneer Infantry, in service overseas. In his fraternal affiliations he is a member of the Free and Accepted Masons; the Commandery, Knights Templar; the Consistory, Ancient Accepted Scottish Rite; and the Temple, Ancient Arabic Order Nobles of the Mystic Shrine. He is also a member of Sigma Alpha Epsilon Fraternity of the University of Maine; and of the honorary fraternity, the "Skulls," of Boston University. He served two terms on the City Council of Augusta.

There are three daughters: Marjorie L. Hussey, bookkeeper of her father's company, graduate of Cony High School, La Salle College, and Chandler Fitting School; Marguerite L., graduate Cony High School, La Salle College, Simmons College, degree of Bachelor of Arts: Madeline, graduate of Cony High School, National Park Seminary of Forest Glen, Maryland, and the University of Maine.

HOWARD E. HALL—The legal profession is quite often used as a stepping stone to political power, but such was not the case with Howard E. Hall of Damariscotta, who began his studies because of his love for law and a desire to become a practicing lawyer. Despite his disinclination toward public office, his sterling qualities appealed to the citizens of this vicinity so that he was elected at various times and served the people long and satisfactorily in different high positions in the administration of public affairs. Mr. Hall was born in Newcastle, November 13, 1853, son of Elijah Hall of Nobleboro, who died in 1912, and Caroline A. (Rollins) Hall of Nobleboro, who died in 1913. Elijah Hall was engaged in shipbuilding for a long time.

Howard E. Hall attended the local public schools and Lincoln Academy, after which he entered Bowdoin College, from which he graduated in 1876 with the degree of Bachelor of Arts. His desire to study law led him to enter the office of W. H. Hilton, prominent lawyer of Damariscotta, where he diligently applied himself to his work, completed his studies, and was admitted to the bar in 1880. The same year saw him open his office as an independent practicing lawyer and such he has continued until the present time, with the exception of a short period, when, for a few years, Mr. Pierce was engaged with him in partnership. Mr. Hall's success was evident from the start and he has ever since justified the confidence and trust which his clients have placed in him. Although he shrank from political office, having no aspiration towards politics, his abilities could not be hidden with the result that he has served as County Attorney and Register of Probate for several terms. He also served as Superintendent of Schools at Newcastle. Mr. Hall is a member of both the Lincoln County and the State Bar associations. He is also a member of the Rotary Club. His religious affiliation is with the Baptist church where he holds an honored position on the board of trustees.

Howard E. Hall married, in 1890, Abbie Y. Flye, of Damariscotta, daughter of Alden and Sarah E. (Yeaton) Flye.

HERBERT W. HILDRETH—The history of the New England settlers is written in the log cabins—the first American homes—crudely and simply constructed to give protection from the elements. To the modern generation, the simplicity and beauty of these cabins have a great appeal. Realizing this, Herbert W. Hildreth, while conducting a successful business in Boothbay Harbor as contractor and builder, decided to specialize in the construction of log cabins on a scale suitable for modern use. While adapting his designs and adding all conveniences to make them suitable and comfortable for everyday occupancy, he has not lost sight of the artistic qualities of the primitive buildings, and the result is that he has to his credit some of the most beautiful as well as the most comfortable log-cabin homes in this State.

Mr. Hildreth was born in Natick, Massachusetts, October 23, 1883, son of Watson J. Hildreth of Keene, New Hampshire, who died in 1922, and Cora J. (Daniels) Hildreth of Providence, Rhode Island, who is still living. Watson J. Hildreth was engaged in the shoe industry in Massachusetts. He was also corporal of the Color Guard, Thirty-seventh Massachusetts Regiment, in the Civil War.

Herbert W. Hildreth received his education in the public schools of Natick, and after high school, learned the trade of carpenter, advancing steadily and rapidly in his work. In 1915, he came to Boothbay Harbor and engaged independently in business as a contractor and builder, acquiring for himself a reputation for safe, dependable and substantial work. Many frame houses and hotels in Boothbay Harbor and vicinity are the visible examples of his skill. Realizing the desire of many people for log-cabin homes, which would retain the artistry of the early habitations and still supply the comforts to which modern civilization has become accustomed, Mr. Hildreth decided to specialize in this type of building. Some of the cabins are constructed on a grand scale, costing from $3,000 to $15,000 and more, and with his force of more than thirty-five men, Mr. Hildreth has built within a radius of fifty miles, some of the State's finest log cabins. The structures erected by Mr. Hildreth include many lodges, tearooms, inns, and club houses, some of them costing more than $50,000. The business is growing steadily and the demand for such homes constantly increasing, which is a testimonial to Mr. Hildreth's creative ability and realization of the popular appeal of the simple and rustic quality of the first American homes. Mr. Hildreth is a member of local clubs, and is affiliated with the Baptist church. He was at one time a member of the Massachusetts State Guard, serving in Company E, of Framingham, Massachusetts.

Herbert W. Hildreth married, in 1905, Bertha S. Corkum, of Nova Scotia. Their children are: 1. Grace, married Rodney Reed. 2. Raymond. 3. Edna. 4. Herman. 5. Dorothy. 6. Ernest. 7. Marina. 8. Judson. 9. Linwood. 10. Harold. 11. Fredrick.

WILLIAM E. SAWYER—The vessels which ply through the rough waters of the North Atlantic depend greatly upon the quality and durability of the stores and supplies furnished them by their shipchandlers. Such an organization as that headed by William E. Sawyer, which can boast of a continuous record of over fifty years' service to the maritime trade, shows to what extent it has received the trust and approbation of the toilers of the sea. The business, which is the last of its type in Boothbay Harbor, was founded by Mr. Sawyer's father in 1876, and has continued to serve the needs of the community ever since. Mr. Sawyer was born in Boothbay, June 15, 1863, son of William M. Sawyer of Boothbay, who died in 1906, and Angie R. (Jack) Sawyer of Richmond, who died in 1887. William M. Sawyer was a prominent figure in the business and financial life of the community, starting his career as a merchant and then entering the shipchandlery business as mentioned above. He was active in assisting the progress of the town and served on the board of directors of several banks.

William E. Sawyer received his education in the local public schools, and upon the completion of his formal schooling, engaged in the ice business independently and continued in this industry for thirty-six years, building for himself a worthy reputation for business dependability and integrity. While thus engaged, Mr. Sawyer supplied thousands of tons of ice to the fishing fleets from Gloucester and Boston. He also entered the sail-racking business which he operated in addition to his ice business, and outfitted more than fifty of the largest type sailing vessels, besides supplying bait to fishermen. Upon the death of his father in 1906, Mr. Sawyer took over the ship-chandlery business which had been operated steadily since 1876, and has continued to run it successfully, profiting by his long experience in previous enterprises. In addition to ship supplies, he has added other lines of supplies and equipment which are to be found in the best type of general store, and the organization is a great asset to the people of Boothbay Harbor and vicinity. Mr. Sawyer takes an active part in fraternal societies, being a member of the Blue Lodge, Free and Accepted Masons; the Chapter, Royal Arch Masons; and also holds membership in the Knights of Pythias, the Loyal Order of Moose, the Royal Arcanum, and local clubs. In his religious affiliations, he is a member of the Methodist Episcopal church.

William E. Sawyer married (first), in 1896, Minnie B. Gore of Newcastle, and (second) Aldana Linekin. His children are: 1. Angie R., married Frank Williams, and they have one son and three daughters. 2. Valeria A., who is deceased, married Webb Baxter, and had one son. 3. Elmer A., who is deceased.

MERRILL A. PERKINS—From a humble beginning in business to the position of one of the leading factors in the mercantile and financial development of the town is the proud record of Merrill A. Perkins, one of the prominent business men of Boothbay Harbor, who started his business career like many other boys of the vicinity, fishing and boating along the coast. Mr. Perkins was born in Boothbay Harbor, August 12, 1863, son of Enoch Perkins of Damariscotta, who died in 1892, and Izora L. (McKown) Perkins of Boothbay Harbor, who died in 1926. Enoch Perkins, a veteran of the Civil War, was a member of Company C, Maine Volunteers, and upon his discharge from the service, engaged in the fishing trade, which he followed all his life.

Merrill A. Perkins received his education in the local public schools and after high school he engaged in the fish business in a small way at Cape Cod Point. Later he formed a partnership under the firm name of Simpson and Perkins to operate a grocery store there, which was done for one year, when the firm removed to West Boothbay where they bought out the business of A. M. Powers, which was located on the site now occupied by the Oak Grove Hotel. After two years, they sold out and removed to West Street nearer the center of town. In 1908, Mr. Perkins bought out the interest of Mr. Simpson and conducted the business in a most successful manner under his own name until 1918, when his brother, Fred D. Perkins, joined him as partner and the name of the firm was changed to its present form of Perkins Brothers. The concern is now the oldest and largest grocery firm in this town and has achieved a reputation for business dependability and integrity of which they are proud. Mr. Perkins, in addition to conducting the business which bears his name, is a leading voice in the business and financial life of the town, being a director of the First National Bank of Boothbay Harbor, president of the Boothbay Harbor Hotel Company, president of the Boothbay Harbor Cold Storage Company and associated with a number of other commercial enterprises. His value in the minds of his fellow-townsmen is attested by the fact that he is Past Master of the Free and Accepted Masons, a member of the Knights of Pythias and of prominent local clubs. During the World War he was tireless in his activities for the Liberty Loan and Red Cross drives and was prominently identified in every war-time work, giving to the cause the greatest aid possible to a

private citizen. In addition to the business and social life of the town, Mr. Perkins holds a place of esteem in religious circles, being president of the board of trustees of the Methodist Episcopal church.

Merrill A. Perkins married, in 1888, Bessie M. Simpson, of Harpswell, Maine, and their children are: 1. L. M. Lewis, married Aura Burnham. 2. Angie F., married H. A. Dodge, and they have two daughters.

H. CHANDLER REED—When men first began to travel back and forth over the world, there arose a need for habitations where they might receive food and shelter at various stopping places, and far back in history, we read of caravansaries and inns, where early travelers were entertained. These hostelries kept up with the progress of the civilized world, until today the modern hotel is the last word in comfort and convenience. Travelers or vacationists never forget a hotel in which they have been hospitably received and made comfortable, and they are ever glad to recommend to their friends a place which they know will give the greatest satisfaction. Such a hotel is the Oake Grove Hotel at West Boothbay Harbor, operated by H. Chandler Reed and his father, W. Herbert Reed. In addition to being the largest, it is the best known of all the summer hotels in this vicinity, and its register numbers the names of people of prominence in all walks of life. Mr. Reed was born at Boothbay Harbor, April 21, 1890, son of W. Herbert Reed (q. v.) and Jennie (McKown) Reed.

H. Chandler Reed received his education in the local public schools and after high school, entered Westbrook Seminary. After completing his education, he became associated with his father in his hotel operations, in which business he has since continued. Mr. Reed is known everywhere as a tireless worker in promoting the progress of the State, and is continually giving his time and energy to the advertisement of the attractive resorts and beautiful recreation spots. His work in spreading the knowledge of its advantages and resources has brought him recognition as a public-spirited citizen of great value to the commonwealth. In the development of Boothbay Harbor, he has been especially interested and is a leading figure in all campaigns for progress and advancement, with the result that this is now one of the best known resorts in Maine. In municipal affairs, he has always taken an active part, and his popularity is shown by the fact that he has held the offices of Selectman, Overseer of the Poor, and a member of the School Board. In fraternal circles, he has always been prominent, being a member of Kora Temple, Ancient Arabic Order Nobles of the Mystic Shrine, having attained the thirty-second degree in Masonry, and he is also Past Master of the Seaside Lodge, No. 144, Free and Accepted Masons; and secretary, since 1916, of Pentecost Chapter, Royal Arch Masons. He is a member of the Improved Order of Red Men, besides being interested in various local clubs. In religion, he attends the Methodist church.

H. Chandler Reed married, on September 27, 1916, Lulu Foster of this State, daughter of John and Eliza (Leighton) Foster, and they have one daughter, Constance L., born October 10, 1919.

W. HERBERT REED—An active life is that of W. Herbert Reed, who has been catering to the comfort of the traveling and vacationing public at West Boothbay Harbor since 1894, when he opened the

Oake Grove Hotel. He has since continued in the original location and now operates the hotel in connection with his son, H. Chandler Reed (q. v.). The original hotel started on a small scale and contained only five guest rooms, but its reputation for comfort and hospitality made it famous throughout the vicinity, and as its patronage increased steadily, it expanded to meet the demands made upon it. Each year witnessed some further improvement until at the present time, it has one hundred and fifty rooms and is known far and wide as a summer hotel of distinction and charm. Mr. Reed was born at Boothbay, July 16, 1854, son of Charles and Mary J. (Thorpe) Reed, of Boothbay. Charles Reed was engaged in the fishing industry and spent some time as a sea-captain.

W. Herbert Reed received his education in the local public schools and then took up the trade of sail maker, which was an important field in those days when New England clippers visited every port of the seven seas. He later entered the ship-building business, and was connected with the Boothbay Marine Railway for a time. He was also engaged in the wholesale confectionery trade on one occasion, but gave up these ventures to enter the hotel business. His success was assured from the start and his genial and courteous manner won for him many friends. After the opening of the Oake Grove Hotel as mentioned above, he soon became a prominent figure in the life of the town, aiding its advance with his progressive spirit and modern ideas. In the political life of the town, Mr. Reed was always actively interested and in his career has held many civil offices of the community. He is still prominent in political affairs, and was a member of the Board of Selectmen for many years, water commissioner, and chairman. In fraternal circles, he is a member of the Knights of Pythias, and in his religious affiliation, he attends the Methodist church, being a member of the board of trustees.

W. Herbert Reed married, on October 28, 1885, Jennie McKown, daughter of Benjamin and Anna P. (Chandler) McKown, of Boothbay. They have one son, H. Chandler Reed (q. v.).

BURNELL E. FRISBEE—In spite of his youth, the skilled and painstaking performance of special duties in accounting and participation in public affairs brought early recognition to Burnell E. Frisbee, who is town clerk of Kittery, Maine. He was born at Kittery, January 16, 1903, son of Daniel and Grace B. (Williams) Frisbee. The father was a leading grocer of Kittery, as was his father before him.

Burnell E. Frisbee was educated in public and high school, and at Bryant & Stratton's Business College, rounding out his preparation for his life's work with a special course at Bentley's. He gained experience by performing special work in bookkeeping and accounting, and was soon chosen for the responsible position of town clerk, to succeed A. O. Goodwin. In this he has proved very capable and highly acceptable to his fellow-townsmen, his thoroughness and special knowledge of accounting and office detail standing him in good stead. Mr. Frisbee belongs to the Free and Accepted Masons, to the Royal Arch Masons, and to the Royal and Select Masters. He is a communicant of the Baptist church.

FRED NEWHALL BOSTON—To the progress and the business activities of Gardiner, his native

place, Fred Newhall Boston has contributed along very important lines from the beginning of his mercantile career, his particular enterprise as a coal dealer and as proprietor of the F. N. Boston Coal Company, having become well established throughout this region. Both at Gardiner and in Waterville, he is associated in the directorship of banking institutions; and he is successfully representing his legislative district in the State House of Representatives, serving on the Committees on Prisons, and Banks and Banking.

Fred Newhall Boston was born July 27, 1886, in Gardiner, a son of Frank E. Boston, paper manufacturer, and Florence E. (Goodrich) Boston, both natives of Gardiner. Here, Mr. Boston attended the public schools, and was graduated from Rock Ridge Hall in 1908. He began his business career as a partner of A. R. Hayes, coal merchant, at Gardiner, in 1916. In 1923, he took advantage of an opportunity to purchase the entire business and has continued since as owner of the F. N. Boston Coal Company. He is a member of the board of directors of the Gardiner Trust Company, at Gardiner, and of the People's National Bank, at Waterville.

The Republican party has Mr. Boston's affiliation and active allegiance. In 1927 and 1928 he was elected to represent his district in the State Legislature. Fraternally, he is affiliated with the Benevolent and Protective Order of Elks; Free and Accepted Masons, in the Ancient Accepted Scottish Rite of the thirty-second degree; Kora Temple, Ancient Arabic Order Nobles of the Mystic Shrine; and his clubs are: Rotary, charter member and organizer; Augusta Country, and Portland Country, and Gardiner Board of Trade. His religious faith is that of the Universalist church, where he is chairman of the board of trustees.

Fred Newhall Boston married, in June, 1910, at Boston, Massachusetts, Ida M. Proctor, native of Waterville, daughter of Homer and Mary Jane Proctor. They have one son, Calvin P. Boston, born February 25, 1918, at Gardiner. Mr. Newhall finds recreation in golf and fishing.

BERNARD F. WARNER—Many boats well-known to Maine fishing circles as substantial and dependable craft which make names for themselves in that industry come from the ways of Bernard F. Warner, shipbuilder of Kennebunkport, Maine. He is regarded as one of the leaders in shipbuilding in his section, where he has conducted with success an independent enterprise for seventeen years.

Bernard F. Warner was born at Kennebunkport, November 2, 1883, son of William Warner, a shipbuilder, from Nova Scotia, and his wife, Winifred (Calvin) Warner, native of Ireland, died in 1924. Like the father, the son has been connected with shipbuilding all his life. Since he began his own yards, in 1910, he has built many substantial boats for the fishing fleets, among which may be mentioned the "Naomi Bruce," the "Phyllis A.," the "Anna C.," the "Isabel," the "Chester B. Talman," the "Charles E. Beckman," the "Alva," and the "Joseph Warner." The last-named vessel was named for his oldest son Joseph. These boats range from fifty-five to one hundred feet in length, are of excellent material, and completed at a cost of from twelve to twenty-five thousand dollars. Mr. Warner employs some fifteen men constantly in his busy yards. He is a man of sound education, acquired in the public high school, and of sturdy character and intelligence, a highly respected citizen. He is a communicant of St. Martha's Roman Catholic Church.

In 1912, Bernard F. Warner married Margaret Kelly of Philadelphia, and they have three fine children: 1. Joseph W. Warner, born November 4, 1917. 2. Robert B. Warner, born December 8, 1920. 3. Eleanor M. Warner, born December 18, 1924.

WILLIAM FOSTER—Practically the entire business career and artistic career of William Foster has been devoted to landscape gardening and horticulture. In York Harbor and along the coast of Maine his talent is known and admired. He has done more, perhaps, than any other citizen of the community for the beautification of its gardens and lawns. William Foster was born in England, April 13, 1866, son of William Foster, of England, who died in 1908, and Georgianna (Symington) Foster, of England, now (1927) living, the father having been in the hotel business.

William Foster, the son, received his education in the public schools of England, and early in youth gave apparent evidences of an interest in art. Work with pencil and brush was to him fascinating pleasure, and flowers with their variegated hues satisfied his love of color. Accordingly he specialized in studies best fitting him for the practice of landscape gardening and flower culture; and at Sherbrooke, Quebec, Dominion of Canada, he began as a young man to plot landscapes, and to apply the knowledge of the art that he had made his own. He came to York County in 1913, and has remained there since, the only one pursuing his art and craft in York Harbor, where he maintains and develops by his taste horticultural beauties for use in the designing of gardens. The greenhouses and gardens occupy three acres. Mr. Foster has created a most favorable reputation in his work. Exquisitely landscaped properties owned by the wealthier residents along the coast of Maine attest to the quality of his handiwork; sunken gardens, lawns, hedges, trees and walks have been conceived by the artist, William Foster. Like the majority of persons with a dominant sense of the esthetic, he cares little for politics or commerce, for the sake of commerce; and, while a member of the Free and Accepted Masons, Royal Arch Masons, Royal and Select Masters, Knights Templar, local societies and the Episcopal church, his chief concern is the realization and fulfillment of the artistry within him, the landscaping and beautification of premises.

William Foster married, in 1914, Genella S. Sanborn, daughter of George McClennan and Abbie (Smith) Sanborn; and of this union have been born four children: Jessamine G., William, Jr., Doris, and Richard.

ALBERT HENDERSON—Canadian by birth, Albert Henderson has been a resident of Bowdoinham, Sagadahoc County, since 1902. Numbered prominently among the public-spirited men of the community, he was appointed Sheriff of the county in 1926, by Governor Brewster of Maine, to succeed J. Horace McClure, and is now (1928) serving that office with distinction.

Albert Henderson was born in Nova Scotia, Dominion of Canada, on May 29, 1882, son of John Henderson, of Nova Scotia, and of Carrie E. (Adams)

Henderson, of New Brunswick, Canada, both of whom are deceased. John Henderson was a blacksmith. The son, Albert, attended the schools of Chelsea, Nova Scotia, and Bath, Maine, where he had come with his father at the age of ten. After completing his studies, he joined his father at the forge as a blacksmith, and worked on the battleship "Georgia" and the cruiser "Chester." During the three years that Albert Henderson worked at the trade he became a skilled blacksmith, then he engaged in the dairying business in his own name, at Bowdoinham, where he quickly established himself as a prominent figure in the community, affiliating with a number of societies and giving of his services to those public activities included in his wide field of interest. He has served the community as member of the School Board, and during the World War was useful wherever his assistance or direction was needed, on boards and committees. As Sheriff of Sagadahoc County he is greatly appreciated for his diligent application to duties involved, and in their execution has more than justified the appointment to the office. Mr. Henderson is Past Master of the Blue Lodge, of Free and Accepted Masons, holds the thirty-second degree; is Vice-Chancellor of the Knights of Pythias; Past Master of the Grange, Patrons of Husbandry; and a member of the Bath Rotary Club. He is a Methodist, and, with his wife and children, sincerely devoted to the church, a ready contributor to all worthy causes.

Albert Henderson married, in 1902, Margaret E. Reed, daughter of James B. and Rossie C. (Bishop) Reed, of Maine. Mr. and Mrs. Henderson are the parents of four children: 1. James R., born March 28, 1903. 2. Albert B., born November 1, 1908. 3. Donald B., born July 25, 1910. 4. Herbert A., born March 28, 1913.

SAMUEL JACKSON PERKINS—The present representative of a family descended from one of the first white settlers to become established in Maine, when all the western world was new, is Samuel Jackson Perkins of Ogunquit, Maine. In 1630, when Jacob Perkins dared the perils of life in the wilderness against hostile Indians and an even more hostile climate, Ogunquit was an Indian village. Later it became a stockade and later still a thriving settlement, when Jacob Perkins and the others with him who had joined in a common cause, had mastered the rudiments of pioneer life.

The present descendant, Samuel Jackson Perkins, was born October 18, 1862, in York, Maine, the son of Andrew Jackson Perkins and Martha A. (Weare) Perkins of York. He was educated in the public schools and at New Hampton Academy, New Hampshire, following which he taught school in the town of York for four years. He was a farmer and fisherman and later conducted a meat market in Ogunquit. He was proprietor and owner of the Hotel St. Aspinquid for twenty-two years. Because of illness, a few years ago, he sold the hotel and since then has spent most of his time in supervising his real estate holdings, which are extensive, here and in St. Petersburg, Florida.

He has held several town offices, such as Overseer of the Village, Tax Collector and Selectman. He is a member of the Village Improvement Society and a trustee of the Baptist church of Ogunquit. He has been associated with several clubs and fraternal organizations in Ogunquit.

He married Winifred F. Norton of York, Maine, September 27, 1888. She is the daughter of William and Miriam (Chase) Norton of York. They have two children: Helene H. Perkins, now Mrs. Philip H. King; and Dorothy M. Perkins.

CHARLES L. DOUGLAS—The business population of Brunswick, Maine, has come to regard Charles L. Douglas as one of its substantial factors. Formerly a farmer, Mr. Douglas has ventured successfully into lumber and real estate and is now concerned with many and varied interests. He was born in Brunswick, August 17, 1880, son of Isaiah Douglas of Windham and A. A. (Lunt) Douglas, of Harpswell, Maine.

Charles L. Douglas spent his boyhood on a farm, trained as many another boy of that day and age was trained in the country. He later became interested in timberlands, and ran several sawmills until 1918, when his activities began to include the development of real estate. He conducts a prosperous insurance business and a large retail and wholesale lumber business in Brunswick, in addition to his real estate offices and was instrumental in developing Douglas Park, College Park, Brunswick; Barrows Park at Newburyport, Gun Point, Harpswell and other high-class residential sections in this vicinity. Mr. Douglas is also in partnership with Stephen Litchfield in the road contracting business under the name of Litchfield and Douglas, their activities in this direction embracing the approach, on Woolwich side, to the Carleton Bridge and sections of road in various parts of the State.

Charles L. Douglas married Ruth E. Curtis of Freeport, Maine, in 1904. They have nine children, two boys and seven girls. The family home is at No. 42 Pleasant Street, Brunswick, Maine.

ALONZO B. HOLMES—One of the most promising business men of Brunswick, Maine, is Alonzo B. Holmes, identified with the insurance business since his graduation from Bowdoin College in 1921.

Mr. Holmes was born September 30, 1896, in Avon, Massachusetts, the son of Alfred W. and Clara Belle Holmes. He was educated at Thayer Academy, Braintree, Massachusetts, and later studied at Bowdoin College. He entered the insurance business immediately following his graduation and has built up a profitable clientele in all forms of insurance protection. Besides being secretary of the Brunswick Chamber of Commerce he is a member of the Brunswick Club, the Brunswick Golf Club and of the American Legion post in Brunswick. He is affiliated with the Masonic Order, in Lodge, Chapter, and Council, and with the Independent Order of Odd Fellows. While at college he was a member of the Delta Upsilon Fraternity.

Alonzo B. Holmes married Emily W. Baxter, daughter of Hartley C. and Mary L. Baxter of Brunswick (q. v.). They have one son, David Dunlap, born August 12, 1926.

WILLIAM WORSNOP—One of the most expert technicians in the textile industry of New England is William Worsnop, agent in charge of operation at the plant of the Cabot Manufacturing Company, Brunswick, Maine. While Mr. Worsnop has been in charge, this mill, one of the oldest in New England, has shown remarkable development. A new building

has been added, and equipment has been increased by twenty-five thousand spindles.

Mr. Worsnop has been in the textile line most of his life. He was born in England, November 1, 1874, son of Allan Worsnop and Ann (Saville) Worsnop. Mr. Worsnop's mother died in 1914. Mr. Worsnop came to this country as a boy and was first employed in a textile mill at Woonsocket, Rhode Island, where he remained until 1902, then went to another mill in Brattleboro, Vermont. In 1914, he left Brattleboro for Lisbon, Maine; stayed there until 1920, then came to Brunswick. With each move he had gained experience which made him invaluable at the Cabot plant. Mr. Worsnop succeeded Russell W. Eaton as agent in charge. The mill now operated by the Cabot Manufacturing Company, was founded in 1838, under the title of the Brunswick Mill. In the late "eighties," the Cabot Company assumed control for the manufacture of cotton goods, silk, rayon, twilled and dress goods. There are eight hundred and fifty workers employed in the mill, using ninety thousand spindles and two thousand eighty looms. The Cabot Mill is considered one of the largest of its kind in New England. The present executive officers are : John S. Farwell, president; Nathaniel F. Ayer, treasurer; Robert G. Vickery, assistant treasurer; and Mr. Worsnop, agent in charge of operation.

Mr. Worsnop is a member of the Rotary Club and a director of the First National Bank of Brunswick, Maine; also a thirty-second degree Mason, and a member of Kora Temple, Ancient Arabic Order of Nobles of the Mystic Shrine. Mr. Worsnop and his family are identified with the Congregational church.

William Worsnop married Margaret I. Lynch, of Slatersville, Rhode Island, daughter of Matthew and Margaret (Sullivan) Lynch. They are the parents of three children: 1. Harold R. Worsnop, born September 7, 1902; a graduate of Bowdoin College and the Harvard Business College. 2. Edna I. Worsnop, born June 4, 1910. 3. William Worsnop, Jr., born June 5, 1915.

WILLIAM B. EDWARDS had established his own business as a teamster and expressman in Brunswick, Maine, before he became head of the police and fire departments in Brunswick in 1919. Both departments have thrived under his leadership. Mr. Edwards was born in Brunswick, December 7, 1878, the son of Brice M. Edwards, of Industry, Maine, and of Susan (Tinkham) Edwards of Anson, Maine. Mr. Edwards' father was a Baptist clergyman and the family has been associated with that church in Brunswick.

William B. Edwards was educated in the public schools in Brunswick and conducted a general trucking business under his own name until 1919. His work as chief of the police and fire departments has raised these important branches of the Brunswick city service to a point of high efficiency. The paid fire department, organized at the time of Mr. Edwards' appointment in 1919, has since acquired additional apparatus and a new fire house. The present apparatus consists of a LaFrance pumper, with a capacity of six hundred gallons, an American-LaFrance Hook and Ladder truck, and a hose wagon equipped with chemical extinguishers. The fire department, under Mr. Edwards, consists of two assistant chiefs and forty call men, subject to emergency calls in Topsham, Hartwell and Brunswick. There has been no disastrous fire since Mr. Edwards became chief, probably because he has been assiduous in spreading the doctrine of fire prevention. Besides being chief of the police and fire departments, Mr. Edwards is a deputy sheriff of Cumberland County, Maine, an appointment which he has held for nine years. He also is a State detective. He is a member of the Knights of Pythias, Independent Order of Odd Fellows, and the Independent Order of Red Men.

William B. Edwards married Evelyn Blethen, daughter of Adlenzo Blethen and Elnora (Rideout) Blethen. They have a son, Ralph W. Edwards, a student at Bowdoin College.

SANFORD HILLS MATHEWS—SPENCER W. MATHEWS—Contribution to the development and prosperity of Belfast was made by two brothers: The elder, Spencer W. Mathews, who, more than three quarters of a century ago (1854), established here what became Mathews Brothers, the oldest door and sash factory in the town; and the younger, Sanford Hills Mathews, who joined with him in this enterprise. These brothers were the sons of Morrill and Rebecca W. Mathews, who lived for many years in Searsmont, Maine, and were the parents besides of six other children: Albert D., Noah M., Daniel H., Adelphus B., and a daughter, Avis H., who survived her parents and seven brothers.

The history of the Mathews firm (now owned and managed by Orlando Frost) is remarked as unusual, in these days of failures and fluctuations. As noted, it was organized in 1854, by Spencer W. Mathews and his brother, Noah M., under the style N. M. & S. W. Mathews. Sanford Hills Mathews entered the firm in 1860, and the name was then changed to Mathews & Company. The three brothers were associated thus until the death of Noah M. Mathews, in 1881, and in the fall of 1889 death again visited the company, taking Spencer W. Mathews away. That left Sanford Hills Mathews in control, and he took in with him, 1890, his son, Frank B. Mathews. In 1897 Sanford Hills Mathews followed his two brothers to the grave; and in 1898 Frank B. Mathews too was called. At that time a local newspaper commented upon the remarkable fact that the business had been more than twoscore years in one family, and continued:

No less remarkable has been its record for honorable and upright dealing. A strong proof of this lies in the fact that several of their employees, who are workmen of a high grade, remained with Mr. Mathews (Sanford Hills Mathews) from twenty to thirty years. They were deeply attached to him, and their interest was reciprocated. He manifested a kind consideration for their welfare, and his genial manner, together with a happy way of smoothing difficulties, won their esteem. This regard was not confined to local circles, but was shared by all manufacturers and others with whom he had direct dealings. A notable instance of the confidence which the firm enjoys was seen at the time of the great fire in Belfast, 1873. Their entire plant was then destroyed, lumber, machinery and buildings, and the blow was the more severe as they were just erecting a new factory. But while the embers were still glowing came letters from prominent business concerns of Boston, urging them to go on, and promising the same prices and discounts as before, with any amount of time. On the event of moving into their new factory, the firm name of Mathews Brothers was assumed.

Spencer W. Mathews, son of Morrill and Rebecca W. Mathews, was born in Searsmont, Maine, February 10, 1829. When he was twenty-one years of age, Spencer W. Mathews came to Belfast, and went to work in the sash and door business with Mr. Ames. That was in 1850. But the building belonging to Mr. Ames was burned, and Mr. Mathews sought employ-

ment elsewhere, removing to Rockland, where he pursued his employment two years, afterwards returning to Belfast. Now he had a small capital in hand, and purchased the interest of Mr. Boynton, of the firm of Boynton & Howard, sash makers. With Mr. Howard, in the old foundry, he manufactured doors, sashes and blinds. In 1854, Noah M. Mathews bought the interest of Mr. Howard, and the by now ancient firm of Mathews Brothers had begun. The progress of the works thence onward has already been indicated. This factory has been operated continuously, making for itself and directors a reputation second to none in New England's industrial chronicle. It is said of Spencer W. Mathews, that he thoroughly understood his business, and that he carefully inspected every piece of work that left the plant, during those first crucial years. Although he was requested many times, sincerely, to accept positions of public trust, Mr. Mathews consistently refused. He did engage in public-spirited works, however, and was a communicant of the Congregational church, a zealous member. He married Susan C. Heath, daughter of Simeon Heath, and she, with two daughters, survived him. Mrs. Clara A. Morison and Miss L. Belle Mathews. Mr. Mathews died September 16, 1889, of heart failure, while on a train. The feeling in Belfast was of a profound loss, the loss of a citizen whom no community could see go without sadness.

Sanford Hills Mathews, son of Morrill and Rebecca W. Mathews, and last of his brothers to survive, was born in Searsmont, Maine, May 6, 1832. When he was four years of age, his parents left Searsmont to live upon a farm, near Liberty. His native intelligence was cultivated academically at Corinth Academy, and through his life thereafter he added knowledge to his store. At nineteen he set out for himself, going to Bangor, to learn the joiner's trade. The first year he received but fifty dollars, board and room. It was early in life, in Bangor, that he became a communicant of the Baptist church. When, in 1854, he came to Belfast, he brought his letter from this church. For six years Mr. Mathews worked steadily in the summer at his trade, in winter teaching in the public schools; then, in 1860, entered into the Mathews firm, to which he subscribed the ripest years of his career. Mr. Mathews took an undeniable and possessive pride in his business. He applied himself to it early and late, and never, it is recalled, took for himself a vacation until his only son's graduation from the University of Rochester in 1885. But business did not always engross his attention. He was a model citizen, holding no municipal office, yet active in other ways on the behalf of good government. Loyal to the principles of the Republican party, he was often called into the party's councils, and his vote was often given to the side of temperance and sound morals. He gave his aid to maintenance of the highest standards in the public schools. For thirty-three years Mr. Mathews was a deacon in the Baptist Church of Belfast, and for years was superintendent of the Sunday school. He was Past Master of Phoenix Lodge, Free and Accepted Masons, and Corinthian Chapter, Royal Arch Masons. At the death of his brother Adelphus, Mr. Mathews succeeded him as director in the Masonic Temple Association; and from the time it was organized, he was director in the Belfast Building & Loan Association.

Sanford Hills Mathews married, in Belfast, May 29, 1858, Clarrie S. McDowell, of Washington, Maine, daughter of William and Eliza (Kirkpatrick) Mc-

Dowell. This union was blessed with children: 1. Frank B., graduate of the University of Rochester, 1885; in business with his father until 1898, when he died. 2. Mabel R. 3. Maude E.

The death of Mr. Mathews occurred on July 16, 1897. His was a life of simplicity, of simple obedience to duty, of earnest toil, and of ready service to those around him.

HON. PERCY N. H. LOMBARD—The State of Maine and the legal profession as a body lost one of its most prominent luminaries with the passing of the Hon. Percy N. H. Lombard, Trial Justice in Old Orchard for ten years and one of the most notable men of York County.

Judge Lombard was born at Biddeford, Maine, April 11, 1880, the second son of John F. and Clara (Taylor) Lombard. He was named for the Rev. Percy Newman Hall. Both parents are living in South Portland, with Judge Lombard's brother, Charles Russell.

While he was a child, Percy N. H. Lombard's family moved to Old Orchard, where he attended the public schools, later taking a course in the Old Orchard High School, which he followed by a term in Thornton Academy at Saco. He studied law for some time in the office of J. O. Bradbury at Saco, and then was a student at Boston University. He was, finally, graduated from the George Washington University at Washington, District of Columbia, in 1905 with the degree of Bachelor of Laws. Following his graduation he was connected with the Post Office and Treasury Departments at Washington for two years, when he was admitted to practice at the New York County bar and from that time, until his death, he followed his chosen career with offices in Portland and Old Orchard. Judge Lombard took an active interest in the affairs of his home town. He was First Selectman of Old Orchard for several terms and was representative to the State Legislature from the classified towns of Old Orchard and Kennebunkport in 1915 and 1916. It was on May 7, 1913, that he was appointed to the post of Trial Justice in Old Orchard, which office he resigned upon his election to the State Legislature. In 1917, however, at the close of his Legislative term, he was again appointed Trial Justice and, at the expiration of his seven-year term in this office he was reappointed. He exerted a strong influence in local and State political affairs and for many years represented Old Orchard on the Republican County Committee.

The interest of Judge Lombard in matters affecting his community was always active. In every movement having for its object the welfare of the residents of Old Orchard and the vicinity he was a prominent participant. It was largely due to his efforts that the town erected a very handsome elementary school building. His interest in the local Boy Scout movement was also keen and he devoted much of his time and ability to the upbuilding of that organization in Old Orchard. He was prominently indentified with Odd Fellowship, being a member of Atlantic Lodge, No. 74, Independent Order of Odd Fellows, a Past Noble Grand, and a member of the Rebekah Order. He was also affiliated with Hobah Encampment, with Canton Dearborn of Biddeford, and with the Oriental Order, H. and P. He held the office of Grand Treasurer of the United Order of the Golden Cross for the Maine District. Judge Lombard was an attendant at the Old Orchard Metho-

dist Church and was a member of the Men's Class of that edifice. He was director and treasurer of the Old Orchard Transportation Company, a member of the Old Orchard Board of Trade and the Kiwanis Clubs of Saco and Biddeford.

On January 26, 1910, Judge Lombard was married to Irma Ethel Hanson, the daughter of Edmund and Velmar A. (Tarbox) Hanson, of East Waterloo. Judge and Mrs. Lombard were the parents of two children: 1. Lorraine Hanson, born May 12, 1912. 2. Lorimer Newman, born February 6, 1914. Both are students in the local schools at this time of writing, (1927). Mrs. Lombard lives at No. 14 Westland Avenue. She is a Rebekah and Past Grand, and a member of the Old Orchard Ladies' Club.

Judge Lombard died at a private hospital at Bar Mills, October 8, 1925, at the age of forty-five years, when at the apex of his legal fame. His passing was deeply and sincerely mourned by his family, and by the vast number of his social, professional and fraternal friends. The Atlantic Lodge of Odd Fellows performed their ritual during the final ceremonies and during the services all local business concerns suspended operations for two hours as a mark of respect to their well-loved fellow-townsman. The floral tribute was the largest ever seen at a funeral service in that town, and so many wished to express their sincere sorrow at the loss of this noble character that a large number were unable to get inside the church during the obsequies. The numerous set pieces from the various organizations of which Judge Lombard was a member were magnificent in their beauty, and delegations attended from the York County Bar and from the Kiwanis clubs, of which he had been a member.

HAROLD E. LAWS—Notable among the enterprising and ambitious young men of Brunswick, Maine, is Harold E. Laws. He is the son of the late Charles H. Laws, of Boston, Massachusetts, who was a veteran of the Civil War with an interesting military experience. Serving in the Thirty-eighth Massachusetts Infantry, he was wounded at the battle of Chancellorsville; he was a member of the Veterans of the Civil War. His son is a member of the Sons of Veterans, to which inherited distinction he has added his own personal military service during the World War. Harold E. Laws' mother was Elizabeth (Tupper) Laws, a native of Nova Scotia. His father died in 1924.

Harold E. Laws was born at Cambridgeport, Massachusetts, December 18, 1894. He was educated in the public school and high school and later in the Boston Embalming College. During the World War he enlisted in the Ordnance Department and was with the American Expeditionary Forces overseas with the rank of sergeant. After the overseas service, at the close of the war, he came to Brunswick, Maine, where he has been engaged in the business of funeral directing, since 1920. He has brought his business up to a state of high efficiency, and by his courtesy, sympathetic manner and modern equipment, he has enlarged his field of activity to cover a territory with a radius of more than ten miles. Mr. Laws is a member of the Blue Lodge, Free and Accepted Masons, the Knights of Pythias, the Sons of Veterans, the Brunswick Club, the Brunswick Golf Club, the Rotary Club, and is Past Commander of the American Legion. He is a member of the Episcopal church.

In 1917, Harold E. Laws married Amy G. Gould,

daughter of Wallace O. and Edith A. (Goddard) Gould of Lisbon Center, Maine. They have two children: 1. Edythe A. 2. Natalie R.

ELLIS LEEDS ALDRICH—Bringing to Maine an experience of law practice in the State of New York, Ellis Leeds Aldrich is now one of the leading attorneys in this State. He is the son of Charles H. Aldrich and Josephine (McDonald) Aldrich of Riverhead, Long Island, New York. His father died in 1899.

Ellis Leeds Aldrich was born in Brooklyn, New York, on June 12, 1874. He attended public school and then matriculated in Cornell University, where he received the degree of Bachelor of Arts, in 1897. Two years later, from the same institution, he received the degree of Bachelor of Laws. That was in 1899. He was admitted to the bar in New York City in 1900 and commenced the practice of law with the firm of Baldwin and Slater, where he remained until 1903. He then opened an office of his own, practicing under his own name until 1923, when he came to Maine and entered the practice of law at Brunswick, where he has been since. Mr. Aldrich is a man of energetic public spirit and while conducting his law practice in New York City, he was a member of the Board of Education at Montclair, New Jersey, where he was also active in various Liberty Loan campaigns. Since his residence in Maine, he has continued his public service by being a member of the State Legislature and having appointments on committees in that body. He is a Maine enthusiast and a valuable addition to its list of patriotic citizens. His social and fraternal affiliations are the Brunswick Club, the Brunswick Golf Club, the Rotary Club, Blue Lodge, Free and Accepted Masons, and he is a member of the Congregational church.

In 1901, Ellis Leeds Aldrich married Jane E. Norton, daughter of Thomas Norton. They have two children: 1. Janet N. 2. Sherwood, a student at Bowdoin College.

HOWARD H. BOODY—Born and raised in North Windham, Maine, Howard H. Boody, now (1928) conducts one of the largest general stores in the State. Moreover, as one of the best versed men in Maine in economic and political affairs, and as an extensive property and real estate owner in North Windham, he has had an important part to play in local matters. He was born at North Windham on December 16, 1862, the son of Henry H. Boody, of Limington, Maine, who died in 1877, and of Eliza L. (Lombard) Boody, who died in 1902, his father having been a merchant as well as interested in the lumber industry.

After attending the public schools in North Windham, Howard H. Boody entered business directly. When only twenty years of age he became a merchant. Since then his record has been one of earnest endeavor and integrity, and his rewards have been numerous, commercially and politically. For the last twenty-five years, under changing administrations, he has been postmaster at North Windham. In 1924 he was elected representative to the State Legislature, and he has held at one time or another virtually all of the public offices within the power of the town to give him. He is president of the Windham Mutual Fire Insurance Company, and holds a large amount of stock and a place on the board of directors in several of the largest businesses in the State. It is perhaps

singular that a man so strong in commerce and so favored in politics should belong to no fraternal orders of local clubs; but such is the case with Mr. Boody. He and his family are members of the Union church.

In 1888 Mr. Boody married Mary C. Westcott, of Standish, Maine, daughter of William Westcott and Caroline (Bolton) Westcott.

ARTHUR H. SHOWALTER—Deservedly proud of his accomplishments in business during his career in New England, Arthur H. Showalter, at thirty-nine years of age, is vice-president of the extensive Androscoggin Pulp Company, at the South Windham, Maine, plant. The organization is international in its distribution and is the largest manufacturer of paper matches in the world. Arthur H. Showalter, as vice-president and operating manager has an opportunity to demonstrate further his already proved ability as a leader of men, organizer of companies and mechanical engineer. He holds the degree of Mechanical Engineer from Purdue University, where he graduated in 1910, and during the World War he was in charge of the construction of long-range guns for the United States at the Baldwin Locomotive Works, Philadelphia, Pennsylvania.

Arthur H. Showalter was born at Angola, New York, March 29, 1888, the son of Aquilla C. Showalter and Mary E. (MacConel) Showalter, of Ohio, his father having been general superintendent of the Nickle Plate Railroad. Following his public school education and graduation from Purdue, Mr. Showalter organized the Rand Plastogen Wall Board Company, at North Tonawanda, New York, and continued in this business until the United States entered the war, in 1917, when he disposed of his holdings to enter the army as an enlisted man. He was assigned to the Army Transport Service and in that division reached the rank of captain. It was after this that he was put in charge of gun construction in Philadelphia. Mr. Showalter also made the rank of lieutenant of senior grade, which title was held in reserve until 1921, when he returned to civilian life, becoming assistant treasurer of the Androscoggin Company. From this office he raised himself to the highest active position the organization affords. The history of the Androscoggin Pulp Company dates back many years, as the first pulp wood mill ever to be constructed in Maine was on the site now occupied by the South Windham plant; and in addition, the company operated a plant at Steep Falls, Maine, until, in 1927, approximately four hundred men were employed at the manufacture of articles for domestic and export trade. In addition to paper matches, the company specializes in the production of several items, such as a locking combination used by manufacturers of ginger ale and other manufacturers. The pulp company controls its own stock in timberlands, its growth has been steady and with such men as Arthur H. Showalter in high executive positions, its future is believed to be guaranteed. Mr. Showalter is a member of the Boston City Club, the Willendale Country Club and a number of other organizations. His interests are so widely distributed that attention to them all might appear difficult, yet Mr. Showalter has time for them in detail and to spare. One of his interests, or hobbies, is invention; he has invented several devices for which he is well known. Indeed, to many persons, he is better known as an inventor than as an executive of the pulp company. He is a member of the Baptist church. Arthur H. Showalter married, in 1921, Marguerite B. Dickinson, of Lockport, New York. Mr. and Mrs. Showalter are the parents of two children: 1. Sarah Elizabeth, born July 13, 1922. 2. Arthur H., born February 5, 1926.

GEORGE R. CONNOR—Connected with the textile industry all of his business career, having learned his trade at Shipley, England, George R. Connor succeeded Bertram Spencer as superintendent of the Limerick Mills in 1919, and since that time has been in charge of about five hundred men, at Limerick, Maine.

George R. Connor was born October 27, 1886, at Shipley, England, the son of Edward Connor, contractor and builder, and Esther (Osborne) Connor, who died in 1887. After attending public school in the place of his birth, Mr. Connor decided without loss of time that textiles, for him, would be an interesting lifework, and he at once enrolled in a leading textile school. His studies there concluded, he served a seven years' apprenticeship. Mr. Connor's imagination and vision of the future in his chosen craft turned to the United States, and he came to this country in 1910, first locating in the village of Greystone, Rhode Island, where he remained for two years, when he joined the staff of the Limerick Mills. During the eight years that followed he amply demonstrated his understanding of textile manufacture. He had the ability to work with the men he directed; he was one of them. And, as superintendent since 1919, this ability has not grown less with his rise in authority. Skilled craftsman and leader, whose popularity has grown steadily stronger amid the people of Limerick, Mr. Connor answered the call across the sea, enlisting in the Twentieth Engineers' Corps. With the American Expeditionary Forces he was in service eighteen months, and won the rating of sergeant. He is affiliated with the Free and Accepted Masons, Past Master of Limerick Blue Lodge; the Benevolent and Protective Order of Elks, of Sanford; and the Limerick Town Club. He serves on the School Board, and is a member of the Baptist church.

George R. Connor married Emily Atkinson, of Shipley, England, in 1907, she being the daughter of George Atkinson and Elizabeth Atkinson, of England. Mr. Connor finds recreation out-of-doors, especially with baseball and fishing.

JOHN H. SMITH—Identified with the textile industry all of his life, both in the woolen centers of England, where he was born, and in Limerick, Maine, where he has lived since 1906, John H. Smith is now (1928) general manager of the Limerick Mills, his position having attached to it considerable weight, as the Limerick Mills are the largest manufacturers of yarns in New England.

John H. Smith was born at Bradford, England, November 16, 1871, son of John Smith, of Bradford, who died in 1871 after a lifetime in the textile industry, and of Sophia (Richardson) Smith, who died in 1889. Living in the heart of the milling district of England, it was not unnatural that John, Jr., should follow in his father's trade, after completing his education in the Bradford public schools. He learned the business before coming to the United States and effecting his connection with the Limerick Mills. After serving in several capacities, proving his worth to

the organization, he at last reached the position of highest executive. Although his duties are complicated and vast in tending to the affairs of the greatest yarn manufacturing and marketing concern in New England, Mr. Smith still finds time for things outside. During the war he was actively engaged in Red Cross work. He is Past Master and member of the Blue Lodge, Chapter, and Council of the Free and Accepted Masons, and a member of the Benevolent and Protective Order of Elks of Sanford, and of the Limerick Town Club. He is serving his second term as a member of the Limerick Town School Board. Mr. Smith and his family are members of the Episcopal church. His recreations are cricket, football, and fishing.

John H. Smith married Edna Lightowlers, of England, in 1902, his wife being the daughter of Thomas and Elizabeth (Yewdall) Lightowlers, of Bradford. They have one child, Thelma K. Smith, a student at the Wheaton College at Norton, Massachusetts.

ELLEN H. (LIBBY) EASTMAN—Said to be the first woman certified public accountant in Maine, Ellen H. Eastman, née Libby, has been called one of the outstanding business women in the State, and accorded many distinctions in club life and as a writer of brochures on accountancy. She now (1928) occupies the office of town auditor at Sanford.

Ellen H. (Libby) Eastman was born at Porter, Maine, October 30, 1891, the daughter of Walter J. Libby, of Porter, and Arvilla (Walker) Libby, of Brownsfield, Maine. Ellen H. Eastman secured her early education in the public schools of Porter, then spent one and one-half years in Bates College, at Lewiston, Maine. She taught school for two years, entered the office of Sokokis Lumber Company for five years and while there applied her time in reading law in the office of the late J. Merrill Lord, attorney, and at the same period did several assignments at public accounting. Through conscientious application to problems of accountancy, reaching a complete understanding of all its ramifications, she became the first of her sex ever to be a certified public accountant in the State, in 1918, and has since devoted the greater part of her active time to this profession. Ellen H. Eastman is the president and one of the founders of the Federation of Business and Professional Women's Clubs of Maine, also past president of the Business Women's League of Sanford, Maine. She is prominent in many other social organizations. She is a recognized authority on subjects concerned with accountancy and income taxation and is enrolled to practice as agent before the Treasury Department and the United States Board of Tax Appeals. She was elected representative of the American Society of Public Certified Accountants, the first woman in America ever accorded that honor. Ellen H. Eastman is one of the best-known and most popular women in the State. She has the creative imagination and ability to launch new ventures and the calm ability to make them function after being launched. In a recent nation-wide contest conducted by the National Federation of Business and Professional Women's Clubs she was adjudged by the Maine Committee the "Pre-eminent Business Woman of Maine."

Ellen H. Libby was married, in 1922, to Harland H. Eastman, of Springvale, Maine, son of Herbert P. and Sadie E. (Witham) Eastman, of Springvale.

ELIAS SMITH—The legal profession in Limerick, Maine, is well represented by Elias Smith, who has the distinction of being the only lawyer in that community. Born August 31, 1857, at Stow, Oxford County, Maine, Mr. Smith is a son of Aaron and Mary W. (Cole) Smith, both of whom are now deceased. Aaron Smith, the father, who was a native of Cornish, Maine, was engaged in farming until the time of his death in 1902. The mother, Mary W. (Cole) Smith, who was also a native of Cornish, died in 1922, at the age of ninety-five.

Elias Smith received his education in the public schools of the community in which he was born, later graduating from Comer's Commercial College, Boston, Massachusetts. For some time he studied law under the competent preceptorship of the late J. Merrill Lord, and he was admitted to the bar in 1900. He began the practice of his profession in Limington, Maine. Later he returned to Limerick, where he established his office and has remained. So well has he managed the legal affairs of his fellow-citizens that the town of Limerick has been well satisfied to have Mr. Smith as its only lawyer. A country gentleman of the old school, he has won the deep regard and affection of all who know him.

Mr. Smith has also taken an active interest in civic affairs and during his residence in Limington, he served for one year as treasurer of that town. He has also served as Superintendent of Schools for the town of Limerick. Among those organizations which pertain to his profession in which he holds membership are the Maine State Bar Association and the York County Bar Association. He is affiliated with the Independent Order of Odd Fellows.

Elias Smith married, in 1926, Lavina W. Smith, a daughter of Major and Sarah Elizabeth Smith of York County. Mr. and Mrs. Smith attend the Baptist church. Mrs. Smith is a member of the Patrons of Husbandry and has taken degrees therein. Her father, a Civil War veteran, served three years in Company K, Twelfth Maine Infantry.

RAYMON A. QUINT—Having spent the greater part of his business career in the interests of the Western Maine Power Company, which distributes light and power to seventeen municipalities and controls some half-dozen subsidiaries within a radius of fifty miles of Limerick, Raymon A. Quint, now (1928) division superintendent of the organization, with principal offices in Limerick, is one of the best-known men in the western portion of the State. He is also identified with the Limerick Mills, as vice-president, and is officially connected with other large businesses. Raymon A. Quint was born in North Berwick, Maine, May 6, 1884, son of Anson, who is chairman of the Board of Selectmen of Sanford Maine, and Olive C. Quint, who died in 1900.

Mr. Quint received his early education in the public schools of Sanford, after which he matriculated in the State University, whence he graduated in 1907 with the degree of Bachelor of Science, and a record of three years on the college eleven and four years on the baseball team. Recognition which he at first received on gridiron and diamond was carried over to the world of business soon after graduation, when he entered the employ of the Western Maine Power Company. With that organization he has served in many capacities, through the force of his talent and strength occupying the office of general manager, until at present (1928) he is division superintendent. Muni-

cipalities served with light and power by the company include Limerick, Newfield, Limington, Steep Falls, Baldwin, East Baldwin, East and North Sebago, Hiram, Denmark, Bridgton, Harrison, Otisfield, Naples, Casco, Raymond, Fryeburg. Among the electrical and power companies subsidiary to the larger one are the Conway Electric Light & Power Company, Ossipee Water and Electric Company, Swans Falls Company and the Fryeburg Electric Light & Power Company, with the main office at Limerick and branch offices at Bridgton, Conway, and Fryeburg. The growth of the Western Maine Power Company has been rapid, and through the period of development Mr. Quint has demonstrated his great business ability, giving his every energy to its expansion, until the benefits derived by outlying territory never theretofore served by power and electricity for lighting, cannot be estimated, and have won for him wide friendship. Mr. Quint's sound judgment was quickly recognized by his business associates, both within and without the company. He was made vice-president of the Limerick Mills and a director and agent of the Maine Land & Lumber Company, together with officerships in other concerns of importance. His interests include many civic affairs. He has been chairman of the Board of Selectmen of Limerick for the past seven years, a town committeeman for nine years, member of the School Board for eight years, and holds other local directorates. In politics Mr. Quint is Republican. He is a member of the Free and Accepted Masons, Blue Lodge, of which he is Past Master; the Chapter; the Council; the Grange, Patrons of Husbandry; and of Sanford Lodge of Elks. He was a member of the original Registration Board during the World War. Mr. Quint is a lover of the out-of-doors, and finds recreation in hunting and fishing. He attends the Baptist church.

Raymon A. Quint was married, in 1907, to Minnie M. Roberts, of North Berwick, and is the father of one child, Zelma Elaine, born January 18, 1916.

EDWARD R. BACHELDER—One of the prominent citizens of Kezar Falls, Maine, a farmer and business man who has found time to serve the community in numerous public posts, is Edward R. Bachelder, who now combines the management of a large farm with the presidency of the Sokokis Lumber Company.

Born December 9, 1860, at Baldwin, Maine, son of Edward F. and Elizabeth E. (Guptill) Bachelder, of that town, where his father was a farmer, he received his education in the public schools, and a grounding in the manifold duties of the farmer on the home place, and his first insight into the possibilities of the lumber business by working at spare times in the sawmills near his home. His first permanent position was in the shop of the T. L. Eastman Cannery Company, where he stayed for two years, and then passed to the establishment of F. T. Flint, where he remained thirteen years, and was in charge of their cannery plant. He then went into business for himself, opening a hardware store in his own name. After having successfully operated this business for fourteen years, he sold it, and has since confined himself to his farm and lumber interests.

He has served the town in the various public capacities of Surveyor of Lumber, Sealer of Weights and Measures, as a member of the Board of Health, town treasurer, and in other local offices, and is now town auditor. He is a member of the Free and Accepted Masons, of the Knights of Pythias, and of the Business Men's Club. With his family, he attends the Methodist Episcopal church.

In 1884, Edward R. Bachelder married Maria A. Lovejoy, daughter of Henry and Mary (Smith) Lovejoy, of Denmark, Maine, and their children are: 1. Franklin L., a graduate of the Parsonsfield Seminary. 2. William O., who was the first graduate of Porter High, and through whom Mr. Bachelder has six grandchildren. 3. Rita C.

MYRON H. RIDLON—As the proprietor of a well-equipped and up-to-date pharmacy, the only one in Kezar Falls, Mr. Ridlon is well known as an important business man of that community. Born August 14, 1883, at Porter, Maine, Mr. Ridlon is a son of Herbert L. and Ella R. (Davis) Ridlon, both natives of Porter. Herbert L. Ridlon is engaged in farming.

Myron H. Ridlon received his preparatory education in the public and high schools of the community in which he was born. He entered the University of Maine and graduated with the class of 1908, when he received the degree of Bachelor of Pharmacy. After becoming a registered pharmacist, Mr. Ridlon remained for two years in Portland in order to gain practical experience in his work. At the end of that time he removed to Kezar Falls, where he established a modern and well-equipped pharmacy. He has been so successful in this enterprise that he has met with no competition and at the present time he is the only pharmacist in Kezar Falls. Mr. Ridlon has a splendid store, of which he is justly proud.

Although the building up of his business has demanded a great deal of his time and attention, Mr. Ridlon has taken a keen interest in many outside activities. During the World War, he served as president of the Red Cross, both in Porter and Kezar Falls. He is fraternally affiliated with the Blue Lodge, Free and Accepted Masons; and the' Chapter, Royal Arch Masons; the Knights of Pythias, and the Improved Order of Red Men. He is also a member of the Business Men's Club of Kezar Falls.

Myron H. Ridlon married, in 1906, Grace E. Davis, a daughter of George E. and Ida E. (Berry) Davis of Parsonsfield, Maine. Mr. and Mrs. Ridlon are the parents of a son and a daughter: 1. Myron G., born May 27, 1907. 2. Eleanor I., born October 27, 1910. Mr. Ridlon and his family attend the Methodist church, of which Mr. Ridlon is a member of the official board.

WILLIAM B. RANDALL—A well-known attorney of Cornish, Maine, Mr. Randall is also the owner and manager of one of the finest modern farms in that vicinity. Born March 17, 1868, in Cornish, Mr. Randall is a son of John W. and Dorcas M. (Barker) Randall, both of whom are now deceased. John W. Randall, the father, who was a native of Parsonsfield, was engaged in the insurance business and also as a merchant until the time of his death in 1921. The mother, Dorcas M. (Barker) Randall, who was a native of Cornish, died in 1875.

William B. Randall received his preparatory education in the public school of Cornish, later graduating from the Fryeburg Academy. He then attended Bowdoin College for a short time and left that institution to complete his law studies under the

competent preceptorship of George F. Clifford of Cornish, Maine. Mr. Randall was admitted to the bar in 1892, and immediately after established his practice in Cornish. Since then he has built up a reputation for integrity and sound judgment and he is now considered one of the foremost citizens of that town. Mr. Randall also manages a two hundred and fifty acre farm on Towle Hill, which he has brought to a high state of cultivation. This farm has been in the Barker family for one hundred and seventy years and Mr. Randall takes a great pride in making it one of the finest in the vicinity.

Civic affairs have been of great interest to Mr. Randall and he has at various times held many of the town offices of Cornish. During the World War he served as a member of the Draft Board. He is affiliated with Blue Lodge, Free and Accepted Masons, and he is also a member of the Grange, Patrons of Husbandry.

William B. Randall married, in 1894, Blanche Thompson, a daughter of Oscar and Jennie (Ingraham) Thompson of Cornish, Mrs. Randall's father, Oscar Thompson, is a veteran of the Civil War. Mr. and Mrs. Randall are the parents of a son, Robert T. Randall, who graduated from Burdett Business College and who married Jennie Evans of Parsonsfield, Maine. Mr. Randall and his family attend the Congregational church.

ORMAN L. STANLEY—Well known as one of the most enterprising men in the State of Maine, is Orman L. Stanley of Kezar Falls. One seldom meets a man whose vision of the needs and possibilities of his community have been brought into actuality as have the progressive movements inaugurated by Mr. Stanley. To him is credited the founding of the Kezar Falls National Bank, of which he has been an officer since it opened its doors for business. And, seeing the possibilities for land development, he organized the Oxford Land Company, promoting its activity. He is the son of Preston J. Stanley and Naomi (Stacey) Stanley of Porter, Maine. His father died in 1902.

Orman L. Stanley was born at Porter, Maine, December 14, 1876. He received his education at public schools and the Parsonsfield Seminary. He taught school for two years and was then appointed postmaster of Kezar Falls by President William McKinley. He served as postmaster for sixteen years. It was during his incumbency of this office that he opened a small drygoods store. But no business under the guidance of such an enterprising man could remain small, and this concern has expanded into a general merchandize store of large size. In 1910, Mr. Stanley saw the need for a bank at Kezar Falls and set about to organize one. He was the prime mover in the establishment of the bank which has grown from an original capital of $25,000 to a capital and surplus amounting to $125,000 and total resources of $1,000,000. Mr. Stanley is a vice-president of this institution and has been cashier since it started business. He is also president of the Oxford Land Company. Although a man occupied with big business activity, Mr. Stanley has found time to serve in the State Legislature. He was a member of that body from 1909 to 1911, and a member of the State Senate from 1917 to 1919. During the World War, he was chairman of all Liberty Loan drives and received a certificate for his efficient service in this work. He is a member of the Order of Free and Accepted Masons, having attained to the thirty-second degree in that fraternity; a Past Chancellor and member of the Grand Lodge, Knights of Pythias; and of many local clubs. In politics he is a Republican and in religion he is a Methodist, being a member of the official board of the Methodist church. In 1900 Orman L. Stanley married Elizabeth M. Ridlon, daughter of Walter R. and Carrie (Wakefield) Ridlon of Kezar Falls, Maine. They have four children: 1. Doris E., a graduate of Bates College, degree of Bachelor of Arts. 2. Mildred S., a graduate of Bates College, degree of Bachelor of Arts. 3. Carolyn M., a graduate of Bates College, in 1928, degree of Bachelor of Arts. 4. J. Malcolm.

WALTER L. WEBB—When a man has had the satisfaction of seeing his business grow from a small beginning to be one of the foremost of its kind in the State, he may be said to have had a full life. Such is the good fortune of Walter L. Webb of Cornish, Maine, whose beautiful printing establishment, now known as the Webb-Smith Printing Company, turns out some of the most beautiful work done by the printing craft. His father, Jason L. Webb, was a granite and marble man of New Hampshire, and his mother was Ann D. (Copp) Webb, of Maine. His parents are both deceased.

Walter L. Webb was born at Hiram, Maine, September 23, 1876. He was educated in public and high school and Shaw Business College. His first work was in the employ of several different wholesale houses in Portland, Maine, then in 1899, he started a printing business at Cornish, Maine. Beginning with a small hand press, doing job and commercial printing, his business grew steadily until in 1912 it was incorporated under the name of the Webb-Smith Printing Company. This organization does one of the largest catalogue printing businesses in the State and also an extensive business in printing tax bills, which is not confined to the one State but ramifies all the New England district. He is a member of the Methodist church.

In 1898, Walter L. Webb married Laura E. Weeks of Parsonsfield, Maine, daughter of Noah and Amanda (Hastey) Weeks. They have one child, a daughter, Doris G., who is a member of the faculty at Bridgton Academy, where she has full charge of all music for the Academy and stands very high in music circles in New England.

FRANK H. HARGRAVES—Outstanding as a citizen and business man is Frank H. Hargraves, of West Buxton, Maine. He is the son of Edward Hargraves, a native of England who was engaged in the manufacture of woolens at Shapleigh, Maine. His mother was Elizabeth P. (Leavitt) Hargraves of Effingham, New Hampshire. Both parents are now deceased.

Frank H. Hargraves was born at Effingham, New Hampshire, May 13, 1854. He attended public school and Farmington Little Blue school and afterwards graduated from Bowdoin College, in the class of 1877, with a degree of Bachelor of Arts. His first business experience was in association with his father in manufacturing woolens as Shapleigh, Maine. Later he came to West Buxton, where, in 1894, he established the Saco River Woolen Company. He was instrumental in the organizing of the York County Mutual Fire Insurance Company and has been its president ever since it was founded. This insurance company

is one of the oldest in the county and its steady growth from a small beginning to its present large size has been due to a great degree to the efficient business methods inculcated and practiced by its most able president. He was also president of the Hollis and Buxton Bank until that organization was taken over by the Casco Mercantile Trust Company. He has served in the State Legislature and was a member of the State Senate for two terms. He was a member of the Governor's staff during the administration of Governor Cobb, and was chairman of all Liberty Loan drives in Hollis and West Buxton. He is Past Master of the Order of Free and Accepted Masons, and a member of the board of trustees of the Baptist church.

In 1892, Frank H. Hargraves married Nellie M. Lord, daughter of Albion K. P. and Sarah J. (Dunn) Lord of West Buxton, Maine. They have two children: 1. Hobart L., a graduate of Bowdoin College, who served as second lieutenant of Infantry during the World War. 2. Gordon S., a graduate of Bowdoin College, who served as second lieutenant of Artillery during the World War.

FRED W. SMALL—Since 1914, when he was admitted to the Maine State bar, Fred W. Small has been prominent in his profession. Though he spent the war years in the service of his country, he has built up a very successful practice at Steep Falls, and he takes an active part in the civic affairs and fraternal life of the community. His father, Samuel N. Small, of Steep Falls, Maine, died in 1927. His mother, Mary A. (Allen) Small, also of Steep Falls, is still living.

Fred W. Small was born June 8, 1892, at Limington, Maine. He entered the local public schools and later attended the University of Maine, from which he was graduated in 1914 with the degree of Bachelor of Laws. Soon afterwards he was admitted to the bar, and began the practice of his profession at Westbrook, Maine. He remained there for about two years during which he served as City Solicitor, and at the end of that time he came to Steep Falls, where he has since been located.

During the World War, Mr. Small enlisted as a member of the Twelfth Company, Coast Artillery Corps. He was later transferred to the Quartermaster Corps and commissioned a second lieutenant. He saw several months service with the American Expeditionary Forces in France. Mr. Small is now a first lieutenant in the Officers' Reserve Corps. Fraternally, he is affiliated with the Free and Accepted Masons, having taken the degrees of the Chapter, Council and Commandery in this organization. He is also a member of the Knights of Pythias, of which he is Commander, of Crescent Lodge, No. 20. Mr. Small is a member of the Board of Selectmen of the town of Standish. In the fall of 1927, Mr. Small removed to, and opened an office in Gorham, Maine, but still maintains his office in Steep Falls. He and his family attend the Baptist church.

In 1923, Fred W. Small married Laura A. Bragdon of Westbrook Maine. She is the daughter of William B. Bragdon, former mayor of Westbrook, and of Mary L. (Hodgkins) Bragdon. Mr. and Mrs. Small are the parents of one child, Natalie L., who was born November 27, 1924.

FREDERICK M. COLE, M. D.—After following his profession in Gardiner for more than twenty years,

Dr. Frederick M. Cole has a substantial position in the medical circles of the community, his services being in demand by a large number of patients, whose faith in his ability is warranted by his success. Being a native of the town, his friends are of all ages and ranks, while the trust of his townsmen has been shown by his election to public office of trust.

Frederick (Fred) M. Cole was born in West Gardiner, April 6, 1879, son of Arthur S. and Margaret (McKinnon) Cole, the father, a native of the State, was a carpenter and, in politics, a staunch Republican. The son received his early education in the public schools of Gardiner; at the Nichol's Latin School in Lewiston, from which he was graduated in 1898; in Baltimore Medical School, which he attended for three years, and at the Boston College of Physicians and Surgeons, from which he was graduated, with the degree of Doctor of Medicine, in 1908. He served as an interne in the Boston Hospital for a year, returning to Gardiner in 1908, where he established himself in general practice. He is a member of the staff of the Gardiner General Hospital; is an alderman and has been City Health Officer. In politics he is a Republican; in religion, a Baptist. In fraternal circles he is affiliated with the Free and Accepted Masons, in which he holds the thirty-second degree; also a member of the Independent Order of Odd Fellows; of the Maine and Kennebec County Medical societies, and the Rotary International.

Dr. Frederick M. Cole married, September 18, 1906, Margaret B. Grant. They have one child: Archie R., a student at Bates College, class of 1929.

EDWIN W. ELLIS—Adaptation for a manufacturing business has been illustrated clearly in the case of Edwin W. Ellis, of Gardiner, who for more than twenty years has shown an ever-growing activity in the conversion of lumber into finished doors, sashes and blinds. His deep interest in the affairs of local and State government has appealed to his fellow-citizens, while his financial acumen has brought to him the reward of accurate judgment of values. His worthiness as a citizen has been attested by the respect and devotion of the community in which he has lived for the greater part of his life.

Edwin W. Ellis was born in Athol, Massachusetts, July 7, 1866, a son of Edwin and Lois L. (Wood) Ellis, both natives of Orange, Massachusetts, who are deceased. He was educated in the public schools of Athol and at the Byrant & Stratton Business College, Boston. His first work was in a sash and door factory in Athol, where he remained for several years, then coming to Gardiner, where he became associated with James Walker & Son Company. Four years after his engagement with this manufacturing house he was made its manager, a post he still administers. He is first vice-president of the Gardiner Trust Company, a member of its executive board, and a director. A Republican in politics, he served in the State Legislature two years, 1915 to 1917, and for two years was president of the Gardiner Board of Trade. He has the thirty-second degree in the Masonic Order, being a member of all bodies of that fraternity, and of the various departments of the Independent Order of Odd Fellows. His religion is that of the Protestant Episcopal church.

Edwin W. Ellis married, at Gardiner, July 3, 1909, Clara E. Walker, a native of Gardiner, daughter of Captain James and Julia (Douglas) Walker, the father having been a captain in the Fifteenth Maine Regiment during the Civil War. Their only child is William Roland, born June 16, 1916.

SIDNEY R. BATCHELDER—With a growing practice and enjoying the confidence of a large community, in which he is held with the highest esteem, Sidney R. Batchelder, attorney-at-law, of Kezar Falls, Maine, has attained a prominence that might be the envy of many. He is a native of the State, the son of Timothy S. Batchelder and Ida S. (Stevens) Batchelder of Waterboro, Maine, and learned his law by application and apprenticeship in the office of an established firm, Cleaves, Waterhouse & Emery of Biddeford, Maine.

Sidney R. Batchelder was born at Kennebunk, Maine, April 10, 1895. His early schooling was in public school and he graduated from high school. Then, desiring to learn and practice law, he entered the office of Cleaves, Waterhouse & Emery at Biddeford, and read law in that office until he passed his bar examination in 1917, after which he began the practice of his profession at Kezar Falls, Maine, where he continues to make his residence. He was in military service during the World War, 1917-1919, enlisting June 1, 1917, first in the Thirteenth Coast Artillery National Guards, from which he was transferred to the Fifty-fourth Coast Artillery Corps; was in service overseas; later transferred to the Sixty-fifth Coast Artillery Corps which saw service at the front. He was discharged from military service on February 19, 1919. He then continued his practice of law which has built for him the clientele that he enjoys today. He is a member of the York County Bar Association and the State Bar Association of Maine. He is a member of the Blue Lodge, Free and Accepted Masons; and of the Chapter, Royal Arch Masons; the Knights of Pythias; the Improved Order of Red Men; the American Legion, adjutant of his local and one of the organizers; and Kezar Falls Club, of which he is secretary. He served as member of the School Board, for five years, and has been a selectman of the town of Parsonsfield for three years of which he at present is chairman. In religion, he is a member of the Methodist church.

Sidney R. Batchelder married Elizabeth L. Stevens of Biddeford, Maine, in 1920. They have two children: Robert S., and Marjorie E.

CHARLES ROBERT COOMBS—An outstanding and substantially successful member of the community of Belfast, Maine, is Charles Robert Coombs, who has been engaged professionally in Belfast for a number of years as funeral director, has held public office, and has constantly expended his personal forces for the furtherance of communal welfare. Mr. Coombs comes of an old Maine family; he is a grandson of Robert Coombs, Jr., who was a native of Islesboro, where he was born, January 25, 1799.

Robert Coombs, Jr., was a sea captain, having gone to sea as a boy; later he retired from it, however, and in 1830 removed to Belfast, where he purchased a farm and settled upon it for the remainder of his life. His death occurred July 9, 1862. He had married, on Christmas Day, 1823, Jane Gilkey, like himself a native of Islesboro, born April 9, 1807; and they were the parents of fourteen children, among them Robert Coombs, third member of the family by the name of Robert.

Robert Coombs (3) was born at Islesboro, July 3, 1828, and as his father had done, went to sea at an early age. At the age of nine years he worked as cook's helper in a galley, and at sixteen was master of the fishing schooner "Jane," of Belfast. He commanded many vessels during his career, among which are many schooners well remembered off the coast: "Dime," "Eri," "Royal Welcome," "Tippecanoe," "Pensacola," "Fred Dyer," "Lydia Brooks;" and brig "Russian," the barks "P. R. Hazeltine" and "Diana," and the ships "Live-Oak" and "Cora." The last was named after his daughter, Cora. In the Civil War, Captain Robert Coombs sailed in the "Diana," under the Hanoverian flag, from America to the United Kingdom and India. On the "Cora" he sailed around the world, most of the voyages being in the Pacific when in this vessel. For twenty years his craft was away from American waters, and its log recorded many adventures. Captain Coombs married, June 11, 1850, Harriet E. Pendleton, of Belfast, daughter of Jared Pendleton of Belfast, where she was born April 13, 1831; she died June 7, 1894. They were the parents of four children: 1. Walter H., in the antique furniture business in Belfast. 2. Charles Robert, of whom follows. 3. Cora J., born September 18, 1852; wife of Alexander Leith, banker, of Scotch birth, since deceased. 4. A child, who died in infancy.

Charles Robert Coombs, son of Robert Coombs, (3) and his wife, Harriet E. (Pendleton) Coombs, was born March 20, 1862, in Belfast, three months before the death of his grandfather, also in Belfast. Charles Robert Coombs attended the public schools of his birthplace. Between the age of nine and eleven, however, he went to England with his mother, as, at the time, his father was at sea. While in England he continued his schooling in the public schools, and upon returning to the United States concluded his academic education in Belfast. As he had a bent for things commercial he entered the already famed Bryant & Stratton's Business College, in Boston; and in the month of February, 1882, returned to Belfast to take charge of the furniture and undertaking business that his father had purchased. When his father died, November 7, 1897, Mr. Coombs disposed of the furniture lines and devoted his direction exclusively to the mortuary endeavor. This he has continued to do through the succeeding years up to the present time (1928), and the business has grown to large proportions. It is one of the few modernly appointed· funeral homes in this neighborhood, and, in the forty-odd years of his management has supplied services for more than five thousand people.

A Republican, as were his father and grandfather before him, Mr. Coombs is loyal to the principles of government upheld by the party, and in Belfast is possessed of a considerable influence politically, which he exerts without fanfare, quietly, and always to the best interest of the community. He has held a number of public offices, including the office of mayor; and both in and out of office has devoted time and intelligence to the problems of Belfast. For several years he was president of the Belfast Board of Trade, and is a figure in the social and fraternal life of the town. He is particularly prominent in the Masonic Order, and is a member of Phoenix Lodge, No. 24, of which he is Past Master; member and Past High Priest of Corinthian Chapter, No. 7, Royal Arch Masons; member of King Solomon's Council, No. 1, Royal and Select Masters; and Palestine Command-

ery, No. 14, Knights Templar, of which he is Past Commander. He is a charter member of Primrose Chapter of the Order of the Eastern Star, of Belfast, a member of the Knights of Pythias, and the Independent Order of Odd Fellows. In the last-named organization he has held all local chairs. During the World War, although too advanced in years for service overseas, Mr. Coombs did serve tirelessly on various boards and committees in charge of the prosecution of war work from within this country, and was instrumental in the subscription of funds to the several Liberty Loan campaigns. In religious belief he is a Unitarian, attends the church of that denomination in Belfast, and is devout in its work. A temperate man, kindly, he is of large heart; his contributions to charitable and to kindred causes of a worthy character are generous in proportion and ready in the giving, regardless of race or creed by whom the appeal is sponsored. Of him it is said by those who know him best, that he is an honorable man, a patriot, and a valuable citizen of his country, State and community.

Mr. Coombs was united in marriage on September 3, 1902, in Belfast, to Helena C. Matthews, of Belfast. Mrs. Coombs was born in Cambridge, Massachusetts, January 11, 1872, a daughter of J. M. and Carrie M. (Couillard) Matthews, later of Belfast. J. M. Matthews was born at Warren, Maine, and was a soldier in the Civil War. He was engaged in the printing business and died at an early age. His wife was a school teacher, and followed that vocation for a number of years. Mr. and Mrs. Coombs have two children: 1. Horace M., born August 20, 1910. 2. Alice, born January 6, 1912.

ADELBERT MILLETT, M. D.—One of the leaders of his profession of surgery in this State, a man of splendid intellect, engaging manners and broad experience in and out of his special field, Dr. Adelbert Millett followed his career in Belfast and its neighborhood for thirty-two years prior to his death, November 17, 1910. He possessed hosts of friends, was active in fraternal organizations and in church work and had served in the Seventy-seventh Session of the State Legislature.

Dr. Millett was born in Auburn, March 7, 1858, son of Israel and Martha M. (Perkins) Millett. His education began in the public schools of Auburn, after which he attended Hebron and Bridgton academies. This preliminary work was followed by a course at Bates College, from which he was graduated and later received the degree of Master of Arts, and at Dartmouth, from which last-named institution he was graduated in 1888 with the degree of Doctor of Medicine. His post-graduate work was done at the New York Medical School and Hospital, in New York City. He established himself first in practice at Searsmont, March 22, 1888, removing to Belfast in May, 1911. There he became a member of the surgical staff of the Waldo County Hospital. From 1893 until his death he was a member of the United States Board of Surgeons for the Board of Pensions. He was a Democrat and on the Belfast School Board, in which work he took a deep interest. He was also a member of the American Medical Association and of the Waldo County Medical Society. His fraternal affiliations included membership in the Phoenix Lodge, thirty-second degree, Free and Accepted Masons; General Knox Chapter, Royal Arch Masons; Council, Royal and Select Masters; and

Commandery, Knights Templar; the Consistory, Accepted Scottish Rite Masons. He was also a member of the Order of the Eastern Star and a patron of Primrose Chapter. A member of the Belfast Congregational church, he was clerk of the parish and a deacon.

Dr. Adelbert Millett married, May 1, 1910, Mrs. Estelle K. (Banks) Haley, a widow, daughter of Joseph W. and Elsie (Brown) Banks, of Belfast. Mrs. Millett is the mother of two children by her first husband.

THOMAS J. FROTHINGHAM—One of the largest and best-known laundries in the State of Maine is that founded by Thomas J. Frothingham in 1889, which was incorporataed in 1920, under the name of the Globe Laundry. Mr. Frothingham was born in Brooklyn, New York, July 1, 1861, and is a son of Thomas Frothingham, a native of New York City, a mechanic by trade, who died in 1917, and of Abigail E. (Carter) Frothingham, also a native of New York City, who died in 1875.

Thomas J. Frothingham received his education in the local public schools and then entered the employ of the A. and S. E. Spring Company, importers, of Portland, Maine, with whom he remained for eleven years. In 1880 he decided to engage in business for himself and chose the laundry business as his line of enterprise. He established on Temple Street, in Portland, the Globe Laundry, and by 1920 the business had reached proportions which warranted its incorporation. At that time Mr. Frothingham took as partners his two sons, W. A. and T. W. Frothingham, both of whom have remained in the business to the present time (1928). The Globe Laundry is one of the oldest and largest in the State of Maine, employing one hundred and ten hands, and it operates in the States of Maine, New Hampshire, and Vermont. The plant has twenty-four thousand square feet of floor space and the company maintains a large fleet of gas and electric equipment, and is known as one of the finest equipped concerns of its kind in the State. So successful has this enterprise been that the Globe Laundry and its owners are well known among many of the big business men of Portland.

Mr. Frothingham is a member of the board of directors and a member of the executive board of the Casco Mercantile Trust Company. Fraternally, he is identified with Ancient Landmark Lodge, Free and Accepted Masons, in which order he is also a member of all the York Rite bodies, and of the Consistory, in which he holds the thirty-second degree. He is also a member of the Knights of Pythias. He is a member of the Portland Club and of the Economic Club, and his religious affiliation is with the Universalist church.

Thomas J. Frothingham was married, in 1885, to Angie B. Pennell, of Portland, daughter of Thomas and Lettice (Barstow) Pennell. Mr. and Mrs. Frothingham have six children: 1. William A., who is a graduate of the Lowell Textile School, now associated with his father in the Globe Laundry business. 2. Ethel M., who married Robert R. Drummond. 3. Thomas W., a graduate of the University of Maine, now associated with his father in the Globe Laundry business. 4. Arthur P., a graduate of Dartmouth College. 5. Robert H., a graduate of Hebron Academy. 6. Elizabeth A. The Frothingham home is located at No. 276 Bradford Street, in Portland.

NOAH E. RANKIN—One of the most successful commercial schools of the State of Maine is Gray's Business College, of Portland, which shows on its roster the names of many of the most prominent men of the State. The success of this college is due to the untiring efforts of those founders and those who have carried on the work in later years. To no single individual is the present standing of the college more indebted than to Noah E. Rankin, who has been identified with its work through practically the entire period of his business career, of more than forty years. Beginning as an instructor, he was made head master, which position he filled until 1926, since which time he has been half owner and principal of the institution.

Noah E. Rankin was born in Hiram, Maine, December 15, 1866, son of Thomas W. Rankin, a native of Hiram, Maine, engaged in business here as a merchant to the time of his death in 1870, and of Elizabeth (Bedell) Rankin, of Parsonsfield, Maine, who died in 1915. Mr. Rankin received his education in the public schools of his birthplace, including the high school, and then became associated with Gray's Business College. Here his interest, his energy, and his ability have been centered for more than four decades, and his entire active career has been built into the success of the college. As headmaster he served for several years with the greatest efficiency and faithfulness and continued in this position until the death of Frank L. Gray, in 1926, when he became half-owner of the school. Throughout the State of Maine there are prominent men whose success bears witness to the thoroughness of the training received in Gray's Business College at Portland. Though others have aided in building the working system and the successful organization of the college, no one person has contributed so much as has Mr. Rankin. The college is located on Congress Street, in Portland. Mr. Rankin's religious affiliation is with the Universalist Church, All Souls, which he serves as chairman of the board of trustees.

Noah E. Rankin was married, in 1891, to Emma Flint, of Hiram, Maine, and they are the parents of four children: 1. Eleanor, who married Donald M. Foss. 2. Doris. 3. Amy. 4. Barbara. The family home is located at No. 414 Stevens Avenue, in Portland.

FRED H. THORNE—There are many beautifully designed buildings in the city of Portland which owe their graceful lines and fine proportions to the skill and ability of Fred H. Thorne, who has been engaged in architectural design since 1905. Mr. Thorne has his office on State Street.

Fred H. Thorne was born in St. Johns, New Brunswick, Canada, November 18, 1878, son of John F., a native of England, who was a marine engineer and who died in 1911, and of Isabella (Bissett) Thorne, a native of St. Johns, New Brunswick. He received a good education in the public schools, and after completing his high school course, worked at various vocations before he took up the study of architecture in the offices of Frederick A. Tompson. He remained with Mr. Tompson until 1916, later engaging in similar work until the war intervened making a total period of seventeen years, before engaging in business for himself, opening an office on State Street here in Portland. Mr. Thorne operates under his own name and has designed many buildings and some of the finer type of residences in this city and in the territory surrounding the city. He is known as a skillful architect and a man of reliability in his business methods, and he has already built up a very prosperous business. Politically, he gives his support to the candidates and principles of the Republican party, and he is a member of the Woodfords Club.

Fred H. Thorne was married, in 1910, to Winifred G. Pelton, of Portland, Maine, daughter of John F. and Abbie (Buck) Pelton. Mr. and Mrs. Thorne have four children: 1. Evelyn. 2. Gordon. 3. Jeannette. 4. John H. The family home is located at No. 29 Devonshire Street, in Portland.

CARROLL H. WENTWORTH—A treasurer of the Gorham Savings Bank, Carroll H. Wentworth has won the esteem and support of his fellow-townsmen. A son of Herbert E. and Isa G. (Woodbury) Wentworth, he was born at Waldo, Waldo County, March 27, 1895. He received his education in the public schools and the Higgins Classical Institute, and had his first banking experience with the Forest City Trust Company of Portland. This position he resigned to enter the United States Navy. Enlisting in 1918, he served in training camps about a year. After his discharge he came to Gorham where he was made assistant treasurer of the Gorham Savings Bank, in April, 1921, and in 1922 he was appointed treasurer, a position he still holds. It is due largely to his energy and farsightedness that this bank, founded nearly sixty years ago, has more than doubled its earnings in the last six years, and now takes position in the million dollar class in the State. In addition to his local position in the banking world, Mr. Wentworth is treasurer of the Maine Savings Bank Association, a position which gives him a wide acquaintance and influence in banking circles.

In his fraternal affiliations, Mr. Wentworth is a member of the Free and Accepted Masons, Chapter and Council; and Order of the Eastern Star; a member of the Grange, Patrons of Husbandry; and of the American Legion. His club is the Kiwanis, and he finds recreation in fishing.

Carroll H. Wentworth married, in 1917, Mildred H. Sanborn, daughter of Fred E. and Cora H. Sanborn of Portland. Mrs. Wentworth is a member of the Eastern Star, the Grange, and of the Auxiliary, American Legion.

CLARENCE E. CARLL—Closely identified with every activity that works for the growth and development of Gorham, stands Clarence E. Carll, whose interests from childhood have been those of his native town. He is a son of Van W. and Lizzie E. (Sawyer) Carll, and was born April 26, 1885. He was educated in the local public and high schools and started his business career immediately after leaving high school, entering the insurance office of E. C. Carll, the oldest insurance agency in the town of Gorham. In 1921, Mr. Carll bought out the agency and now conducts it under his own name. While he has always been identified with the insurance business, he has also found time for other ventures, and in 1917 the Carll Canning Company was organized with C. E. Carll as president, and E. C. Carll as treasurer. Recently these two gentlemen reversed their positions and C. E. Carll is acting as

treasurer to this rapidly expanding interest. Started on a small scale this business has had a phenomenal growth and is now operating a plant consisting of factories in Gorham and Buxton, with private railroad sidings by which goods are shipped all over the United States and Canada. Outside of his connection with the Gorham Savings Bank, of which he is a trustee, Mr. Carll has no official touch with any town interests, but his personality and influence are felt in many quarters. Any movement for the advancement of Gorham is sure of his active support, and as a Rotarian he thoroughly exemplifies all that name carries. In his fraternal affiliations he is a member of the Blue Lodge, No. 38, Free and Accepted Masons, while his religious fellowship is with the Congregational church.

Clarence E. Carll married, in 1909, Lillian Richardson, also of Gorham, and they are the parents of two children, Sarah E., and Eleanor.

WALTER E. RUSSELL—A deep interest in educational affairs from early boyhood has brought Walter E. Russell to the position he occupies today as principal of the Gorham State Normal School, and the classification of one of the important educators of the State.

Walter E. Russell, son of Charles Russell, M. D., of Waterford, and Asenath (Willis) Russell, of Hanover, was born August 6, 1869, at Fayette. Dr. Russell was a graduate of the College of Physicians and Surgeons, Baltimore, Maryland, and a practicing physician until his death in 1888.

Taking his degree of Bachelor of Arts at Wesleyan in the class of 1893, after preparing at Kents Hill Seminary, Mr. Russell taught for one year in the State Normal School at New Britain, Connecticut, coming in 1894 as an instructor to the Gorham State Normal School. After eleven years as a teacher he was appointed principal, a position he still holds (1928). During his many years in this position he has advanced this institution to its place among the foremost educational interests of the State. Incorporated in 1879 as a Vocational School, the one building has developed into seven, all standing in a beautiful campus of thirteen acres. One of the buildings is used as a practice school. All these schools are operating under a staff of twenty-four teachers. During these fifty-eight years since its incorporation, this school has had but two principals, the first appointed in 1879, William J. Corthell, and the present incumbent. Over five thousand pupils have become prominent citizens of the country, and many of them gladly acknowledge that they owe much to the kindly interest and helpful direction of Mr. Russell.

Whether national, State or civic, Mr. Russell has confined his activities largely to things educational and has held executive positions in such associations both national and State. One exception is the Gorham Savings Bank, of which he is a director, and where his knowledge of human nature is much appreciated. He is a member of the Lions International of Portland, and the Grange, Patrons of Husbandry. During the World War he devoted many hours to work for his country and received a certificate of appreciation from the United States Government. A Methodist in religious affiliations, he is a member of the official board of his church.

In 1896, Walter E. Russell married Winifred S. Stone, daughter of Cyrus and Celia (Cleaves) Stone, both of this State. Mr. and Mrs. Russell have five children: 1. Earle S., graduate of Normal School, and of Columbia University with the degree of Bachelor of Science; and at Harvard with the degree of Master of Arts. 2. Willis C., a graduate of Wesleyan University; and of American University with the degree of Master of Arts. 3. Helen G., a graduate of Wellesley College, Bachelor of Arts; and of Columbia University with the degree of Master of Arts. 4. Robert E., a graduate of Wesleyan College. 5. Celia, a student at Wellesley College.

RAY P. HANSCOM—Deeply concerned in the growth and welfare of Ogunquit, York County, is Ray P. Hanscom, attorney-at-law, resident in the community since 1903 and, because of his constructive ideas and practices in the public work which he undertakes as a citizen, is numbered among those outstanding in the community. Mr. Hanscom may be classed as self-made, for during his school years he was almost entirely self-supporting and all his higher education was financed by himself. He had a sign writing studio in Ogunquit, Maine, from 1906 to 1916. He had studied Art under good masters and he has painted extensively in oil for commercial and pleasure purposes. He is still interested in this and later photography, in which he may be classed as a good amateur. While he was secretary of the Ogunquit publicity he showed many local movie views made by himself. He has been complimented by many for his photography.

Ray P. Hanscom was born on October 20, 1886, at Kennebunk, Maine, son of William Hanscom, of Kennebunk, and Carrie A. (Cole) Hanscom, of York, Maine. Mr. Hanscom attended the public schools of Kennebunk, and read law in the offices of O. F. Fairfield, at Somersworth, New Hampshire, and had three years' study with La Salle Extension University of Chicago, Illinois. He was admitted to the Maine bar in 1916, and later the United States District Court, and during his career in Ogunquit has enjoyed a remunerative practice. He is a member of the York County bar, and the Maine State bar. Commercially he is interested in a hotel, as half owner and joint proprietor of the Passaconaway Inn, located in the York Cliffs, one of the most charming taverns on the coast of Maine. During the World War, Mr. Hanscom served on a number of boards and committees, oftentimes as chairman, assisting in war work. He belongs to several local social clubs, and is a member of the Blue Lodge of the Free and Accepted Masons; the Improved Order of Red Men, and Past Sachem thereof.

Ray P. Hanscom married, in 1906, Cora M. Perkins, of Ogunquit, daughter of Moses and Hannah (Ramsdell) Perkins; and they are the parents of two children: 1. Carolyn C., born February 28, 1917. 2. Kathryn M., born September 24, 1921.

PHILIP DANA—From the beginning of his active career, Philip Dana has been identified with the Dana Warp Mills, and with the Haskell Silk Mills since 1922, and at the present time (1928) he is treasurer of the first mentioned concern and also of the Haskell Silk Mills. In addition to these responsibilities he is president of the Westbrook Trust Company and is officially identified with several other important business organizations. He is a graduate of Bowdoin College, from which he holds two degrees, and he is treasurer of the college. Mr. Dana is well known throughout the New England section of the country, and is one of the helpful and public-spirited citizens of Westbrook. He was a director of the National Association of Cotton Manufacturers in 1914-20 and 1922-28.

Philip Dana was born in Portland, Maine, August 3, 1874, son of Woodbury K. and Mary Little (Hale) Dana. His father, Woodbury K. Dana, was the founder of the Dana Warp Mills and a business man of marked ability (q. v.). Philip Dana attended the public schools of Westbrook and then became a student in Bowdoin College at Brunswick, Maine, from which he was graduated with the class of 1896, receiving at that time the degree of Bachelor of Laws. Later, he received from his alma mater the honorary degree of Master of Arts. When his college course was completed, he further prepared for an active career as a manufacturer by taking a course in the Philadelphia Textile School, and then became associated with the Dana Warp Mills of Westbrook, and in 1922, with the Haskell Silk Mills. In 1911 he was made president of the Dana Warp Mills, and he retained that office until 1924, when, after the death of his father, his brother, Luther, was elected president and he was made treasurer, which office he is still filling. The Dana Warp Mills is one of the old concerns of this section, dating back to 1866, when the business was founded in a modest way by Mr. Dana's father, Woodbury K. Dana, under the name of Dana and McEwan, for the purpose of manufacturing cotton warps. W. K. Dana soon purchased the interest of his partner, and in 1892 the business was incorporated with Lyman M. Cousens as president and W. K. Dana as treasurer. Upon the death of Mr. Cousens in 1911, Philip Dana was made president, his father remaining as treasurer, and in 1924, after the death of the father, Luther Dana was elected president and Philip Dana, treasurer. At the present time the plant of the Dana Warp Mills is equipped with fifty-two thousand spinning spindles and sixteen thousand twister spindles, with a floor space of three hundred thousand square feet, and the corporation has a capital stock of one and a half million dollars. Lyman A. Cousens is vice-president, and Kenneth G. Stone is superintendent. Though Mr. Dana has taken so active a part in the conduct and the success of the Dana Warp Mills, his time and his attention have not been limited to this business. He is treasurer of the Haskell Silk Mills; president of the Westbrook Trust Company; a member of the board of directors of the First National Bank of Portland, and a director of the Cumberland County Power and Light Company, of Portland, Maine. Fraternally, he is identified with Temple Lodge, Free and Accepted Masons, and he is also a member of the Chapter, Royal Arch Masons.

Philip Dana married Florence Hinkley, daughter of Rufus and Louise (Prindle) Hinkley, and they are the parents of four children: Philip, Jr., Woodbury K., Howard T., and Frances.

WOODBURY KIDDER DANA—One of the successful manufacturers of this State, who has left behind him a substantial monument to his skill and his business acumen, is the late Woodbury Kidder Dana, founder of the Dana Warp Mills, of Westbrook, Maine. Mr. Dana was a native of Portland, Maine, but his father was born in Massachusetts, and Mr.

MAINE—A HISTORY 113

Dana early found employment in the mills of Lewiston, Maine. After the close of the Civil War he engaged in the manufacture of cotton warps, under his own name, and the enterprise which he then established has developed into the well-known Dana Warp Mills, with a capital stock of one and a half millions.

Woodbury Kidder Dana was born in Portland, Maine, June 7, 1840, son of Luther Dana, who was born in Natick, Massachusetts, in 1792, and died in Portland, Maine, in 1870, and of Louise (Kidder) Dana. He received his education in the public schools of Portland and in Lewiston Falls Academy, and when his course in the Academy was completed secured employment in the mills at Lewiston. With the exception of the period during which he served in the Civil War, his connection with the textile manufacturing industry was continued throughout his life. On August 12, 1863, he enlisted for a three-year term, at Lewiston, Maine, and was mustered into the service of the United States at Augusta, Maine, November 13, 1863, as a private in Company K, Twenty-ninth Regiment, Maine Volunteers. His regiment left for the front January 31, 1864, arriving at Portland the same day, and on the second day of February sailed for New Orleans, where he was promoted to the rank of corporal. He continued in service until the close of the war, and then returned to his native State. In 1866, in association with Mr. McEwan, he established a business of his own, under the name of Dana and McEwan, for the purpose of manufacturing cotton warps, and the first plant was a small two-story wooden building located at the upper falls of Saccarappa, in the town of Westbrook. Mr. McEwan never took an active part in the business and soon sold his interest to Mr. Dana. The name was then changed to W. K. Dana & Company, and in 1892 the business was incorporated under the present name of the Dana Warp Mills, with Lyman Cousens as the first president and W. K. Dana as treasurer, which official position Mr. Dana held to the time of his death, May 1, 1924. By this time the concern had grown from a small concern containing six hundred spindles to a plant with a capital stock of one hundred and thirty thousand dollars. Between 1900 and 1903 the number of spindles was increased from eight thousand to forty thousand, and by 1908 the size of the mill had been doubled. Upon the death of Lyman M. Cousens in 1911, Philip Dana was made president, and his father continued as treasurer to the time of his death. At that time the plant was equipped with fifty-two thousand spindles for spinning and sixteen thousand for twisting and with a well-appointed dye plant having a capacity of one hundred thousand pounds per week, and the capital stock of the concern at the present time (1928) is $1,500,000. Upon the death of Mr. Dana, Luther Dana, the younger son, was made president and Lyman A. Cousens was elected vice-president.

A man of pronounced ability, able, energetic, and resourceful, he was one of the reliable men who could be counted upon to contribute his full share to whatever project he allied himself with, and he was greatly respected among his associates. Politically, he gave his support to the Republican party, being one of its staunch adherents, and he was a member of the Masonic Order, identified with the Blue Lodge, the Chapter, and the Commandery. Woodbury Kidder Dana was married, August 2,

1869, to Mary Little Hale, daughter of Samuel T. Pickard, of Auburn, Maine, and they became the parents of the following children: 1. Louise W. 2. Hannah L., who married F. H. Swan, of Providence, Rhode Island. 3. Philip (q. v.). 4. Luther (q. v.). 5. Ethel May. 6. Helen P. 7. Mary Hale, who married E. Farrington Abbott, of Auburn, Maine.

LUTHER DANA—As president of the Dana Warp Mills of Westbrook, Maine, Luther Dana is at the head of one of the oldest established manufacturing concerns in this section of the State. He has been identified with the business from the beginning of his active career, and has been president since 1924. Mr. Dana is a Bowdoin College man and is now (1928) one of the overseers of the college, and active in the work of its athletic committee.

Luther Dana was born in Westbrook, Maine, November 21, 1880, and after completing his course in the local high school matriculated in Bowdoin College, from which he was graduated in 1903, with the degree of Bachelor of Arts. After graduation he immediately became associated with the Dana Warp Mills, of Westbrook, and this connection has been maintained continuously to the present time (1928). Since 1924 he has been president of the concern. The business was established in 1866 by W. K. Dana, in association with Mr. McEwan, under the firm name of Dana and McEwan, for the purpose of manufacturing cotton warps. The first plant was a small, two-story brick building located at the upper falls at Saccarappa, in the town of Westbrook. The original mill contained six hundred spindles, and turned out a goodly amount of warp, but Mr. McEwan never took an active part in the business, and within a few years sold his interest to W. K. Dana, his partner. Lyman M. Cousens, the first president of the newly incorporated concern, incorporated in 1892, died in 1911, and Philip Dana was made president, with W. K. Dana as treasurer and Luther Dana, superintendent. The business had been incorporated under the name of the Dana Warp Mills, with a capital stock of $130,000, and from the time of its incorporation on the growth was even more remarkable than in the early years of its existence. Between 1900 and 1903 the number of spindles was increased from eight thousand to forty thousand, and by 1908 the business had so grown that the size of the mill was doubled. At the present time (1927) the plant is equipped with fifty-two thousand spinning spindles and sixteen thousand twister spindles, there is also a well equipped dye plant which has a capacity of one hundred thousand pounds per week, and the capital stock of the corporation is $1,500,000. Until 1924 Philip Dana was president and W. K. Dana was treasurer, and Luther Dana superintendent, but W. K. Dana died May 1, 1924, and since that time Luther Dana has been president; Lyman A. Cousens, vice-president; Philip Dana, treasurer; and Kenneth G. Stone, superintendent. The concern employs about six hundred hands, and its plant now totals a floor space of three hundred thousand square feet.

Mr. Dana is well known in this section as a business man of ability and of integrity, and in addition to his responsibilities as president of the Dana Warp Mills he is also a member of the board of directors of the Westbrook Trust Company. He has served as a member of the School Board of Westbrook, and during the period of the World War was food ad-

Maine—8

ministrator for the city of Westbrook. Fraternally, he is identified with Temple Lodge, Free and Accepted Masons; St. Albans Commandery, Knights Templar; and he is also a member of Kora Temple. Ancient Arabic Order Nobles of the Mystic Shrine, He is a member of many of the local clubs, and his religious affiliation is with the Congregational church. Mr. Dana has never lost his interest in and his close touch with Bowdoin College, and he is now (1928) a member of its board of overseers and prominent on its athletic committee. He is a son of Woodbury K. and Mary Little (Hale) Dana, an account of whose life appears in this work in connection with the sketch of Philip Dana, older brother of Mr. Dana.

Luther Dana was married to Mary W. Decrow, and they are the parents of two children: 1. Louise D., who is a student in Simmons College. 2. Mary W., who is also a student.

FRANK D. FENDERSON—The legal career of Frank D. Fenderson covers a period of nearly twenty-eight years and all but five years of that period have been passed in Parsonsfield and Limerick, Maine. Mr. Fenderson has been clerk of the courts for York County since 1913. He has been active in public affairs and served in the State Legislature in 1911. He was born in Parsonsfield, Maine, June 15, 1878, son of Nathan W., a farmer who was born in South Malden, Massachusetts, and died December 20, 1917, and of Abbie F. (Brackett) Fenderson, who was born in Parsonsfield, Maine, and died November 24, 1906.

Frank D. Fenderson prepared for college at Limerick Academy and then entered the University of Maine, from which he was graduated with the class of 1899, receiving the degree of Bachelor of Laws. He was admitted to the bar September 30 of that year and at once opened an office for practice in Limerick, Maine. There he continued until June 1, 1904, when he entered the employ of the New England Telephone & Telegraph Company, which connection he maintained until 1908. He then returned to Limerick as a member of the law firm of Lord and Fenderson, the senior member being the late J. Merrill Lord, this connection continuing until December, 1912, when Mr. Fenderson retired from the firm to become clerk of the courts for York County. In addition to his responsibilities as clerk of the courts, Mr. Fenderson is interested in several business enterprises. He is director of the Limerick National Bank and treasurer of the Sokokis Lumber Company at Kezar Falls and he is identified with several other corporations and is president of the Limerick Mills. Throughout his career, Mr. Fenderson has been active in public affairs. He served as a member of the School Board at Parsonsfield, Maine, was a member of the Board of Selectmen at Limerick, Maine, and in 1911 was elected to represent his district in the State Legislature. He gives his support to the Republican party and takes a very active part in its affairs. He was a member of the Republican State Committee for York County from 1918 to 1924. During the period of the World War he was a member of the original draft board. Fraternally, he is identified with Freedom Lodge, Free and Accepted Masons, and also with all of the York Rite bodies of that order and with the Consistory, in which he holds the thirty-second degree. He is an interested member of the Alfred Grange, Patrons of Husbandry, and also of the Portland Club, the Sanford Town Club, the Sons of the American Revolution, and the Maine Historical Society. His religious affiliation is with the Congregational church of Limerick, Maine.

Frank D. Fenderson was married, July 11, 1905, to Laura A. Jose, of Newport, Maine, daughter of Orin R. and Laura A. (Hight) Jose. Mr. and Mrs. Fenderson are the parents of one son: Jose Webster Fenderson, who was born March 30, 1914. The family home is in Parsonsfield, Maine.

FREDERICK L. ANDREWS—Several years on the oceans of the world as a seaman, followed by a few years as worker in a machine shop, gave Frederick L. Andrews a combination of practical experiences which were of inestimable value to him when he entered the employment of the Hyde Windlass Company, the largest firm in the world manufacturing those most necessary pieces of ship's furnishings, in which concern he holds a high executive position. He was born at Bridgewater, Massachusetts, May 26, 1868, the son of Thomas F. L. and Arvilla L. (Robinson) Andrews, the prominent lumber dealer, who died in Bridgewater in 1903. His wife passed away in 1920, after she had seen her son rise to a prominent position in the career he had chosen.

Frederick L. Andrews was educated in the public schools of his native city and then, at an early age, went to sea. After some years of this employment he decided to settle down ashore and in 1890 he took a position in a machine shop in Bridgewater. In 1903 he became a part of the force of men employed by the Hyde Windlass Company at Bath, and quickly rose to the position of superintendent of the plant. He was later advanced to the position he now holds —that of vice-president and general manager.

A member of the Colonial Club, the Sagadahoc Club and the Engineers' Club of New York, Mr. Andrews is also affiliated with the Free and Accepted Masons. He is a member of his local Blue Lodge and of the Consistory, and is also a member of Kora Temple, Ancient Arabic Order Nobles of the Mystic Shrine.

In 1896, Frederick L. Andrews was married to Julia F. Litchfield, the daughter of George E. and Sarah A. (Reed) Litchfield. Mr. and Mrs. Andrews are the parents of two children: 1. Edwin R., was for two years at Annapolis; married to Helen E. Palmer; one child, Frederick P. 2. Charles R., a graduate of Dummer Academy, South Byfield, Massachusetts, and of Hebron Academy, Hebron, Maine; married to Winifred Lobdell.

RODNEY E. ROSS—A graduate of Harvard College Law School and holding the degree of Bachelor of Laws, Rodney E. Ross no longer applies his talents to the legal profession. After a few years of practice he took the office of treasurer of the Hyde Windlass Company, at Bath, later succeeding J. R. Andrews in the post of president, which he now holds. The Hyde Windlass Company was established in 1833 by General T. W. Hyde, with the object of manufacturing ship and marine hardware and, in 1897, was associated with the Bath Iron Works. J. R. Andrews bought the property where the factory is now located and when the concern was incorporated, General Hyde was made president. He was succeeded in this office by J. R. Andrews; Rodney E. Ross was the next president, taking the post in 1924, with F. L. Andrews as vice-president, and general manager. The Hyde Windlass Company is the largest concern of its kind in the world, its machinery being found on ships flying every flag in the world.

Rodney E. Ross was born at Kennebunk on April 9, 1889, the son of Frank M. and Louisa Dane (Morton) Ross, the former one of the leading practicing physicians of the town. The early education of Mr. Ross was obtained in the public and high schools of his native town, following which he attended Bowdoin College, at Brunswick, graduating with the degree of Bachelor of Arts in 1910. He then took a course in the Law School of Harvard College and was granted his degree as Bachelor of Laws in 1913. As has been stated, after a few years of practice, he took the treasurership of the Hyde Windlass Company and in 1924 was made president of the concern. In addition to his interests with the Hyde Windlass Company, Mr. Ross is vice-president of the Bath Trust Company. He is also a director of the Bath City Hospital, and director of the Old Folks' Home in the same city. He is very active in all community affairs and takes a deep interest in all projects for the advancement of Bath. He is a member of the Colonial Club and other local social organizations, and of the Engineers' Club of New York City. He is also affiliated with the Free and Accepted Masons, is a member of the Consistory, and of Kora Temple, Ancient Arabic Order Nobles of the Mystic Shrine. His religious faith is Episcopal.

Mr. Ross was married to Lina Andrews, who was the mother of his two children: 1. Barbara, born 1915. 2. Rodney E., Jr., born 1917. The second wife of Mr. Ross was Gladys C. McLellan.

CLINTON DONNELLY WILSON—A leader of educational circles in the State of Maine, Clinton Donnelly Wilson, of Bath, is superintendent of the schools of this city, which influential position he has held since his appointment in 1923. Mr. Wilson ranks high as an educator of great ability and energy, and having been engaged in scholastic work since 1915, and ever a believer in modern methods of teaching, he has advanced with the times, giving to the pupils in his charge, the advantages of the most efficient and complete education possible to obtain. Although still a young man, he has already acquired a splendid reputation for maintaining such a high average standard of intelligence in the schools under his supervision. Mr. Wilson was born in South Hartford, New York, February 7, 1890, son of Clinton W. and Mary D. Wilson. Clinton W. Wilson was a clergyman who was beloved and respected by all, being a minister of the Congregational church.

Clinton Donnelly Wilson was educated in the public schools, graduating from the Plymouth, New Hampshire, High School, with the class of 1909. He then entered Bates College, from which he was graduated in 1913, and he took further studies at the Harvard University Summer School. After his graduation from college, he embarked on a literary career, being attracted by the work of the press, and he served as foreman of a newspaper office until 1915. He then gave up this vocation, and accepted a position as teacher and coach at Lawrence Academy, Groton, Massachusetts, remaining at that institution of learning for one year. He was then

elected instructor and coach at the Danielson, Connecticut, High School, and he filled the duties of these offices to the satisfaction of all concerned until 1919, when he came to Bath to act in the same capacity. His excellence as an instructor of superior ability and his popularity and inspiring qualities as athletic coach, being responsible for so much enthusiasm and victorious energy, soon brought him deserved recognition, with the result that he was elected principal of the Morse High School to which he originally came as instructor, and from 1920 to 1923, he efficiently administered the affairs of this splendid high school, advancing its standing to first rank among similar institutions. In 1923, he was appointed to his present office as Superintendent of Schools of Bath, and his régime has met with the coöperation and eager support of the entire city, which recognizes the value of Mr. Wilson in municipal educational affairs.

Mr. Wilson is a popular member of the Rotary Club and the Colonial Club, and in fraternal circles, is prominently identified with Polar Star Lodge, Free and Accepted Masons, of Bath. In politics, he is a staunch supporter of the Republican party, although he has never sought public office, and his religious adherence is given to the Congregational church.

Clinton Donnelly Wilson married, July 8, 1915, at Plymouth, New Hampshire, Ruth Beal, daughter of Frank J. and Elizabeth L. Beal.

JOHN J. KEEGAN—In Bath, Maine, the name of John J. Keegan is one which commands not only respect and confidence but sincere affection in the hearts of a large portion of the residents of the city. He has been engaged in general legal practice here since 1910, but the building up of a successful legal career is only a part of the record of his activities. He has been untiring in his effort to maintain the standing and the prestige which the city has held for so many years, and he has spared no effort to secure its advancement along all desirable lines. He is Judge of the Municipal Court, and is very prominent in the affairs of the Knights of Columbus. Mr. Keegan was born in Trescott, Washington County, Maine, June 5, 1885, son of Thomas F. Keegan, a native of Lubec, Maine, who was for many years a teacher, and during the later period of his life was engaged in business as a packer of sardines, and Catherine (Andrews) Keegan, who was born in Lubec, Maine, and died in 1915.

After attending the local public schools, John J. Keegan became a student in the University of Maine, at Orono, from which he was graduated with the class of 1907, receiving the degree of Bachelor of Laws. He was admitted to the bar that same year, and began practice at Van Buren, Maine. Later he located at Lubec, Maine, where he remained until 1910. In that year he came to Bath, and here he has since been successfully engaged in general practice. He is taking care of a large and important general practice, and has made for himself a name and a place in his profession and in the hearts of his fellow townsmen. He succeeded A. J. Dunton as Judge of the Municipal Court, and during the period of the World War served as chairman of the draft board, for which service he holds a certificate. He is one of the public-spirited citizens who is always ready to serve, either in private or in public capacity, if by so doing he can further the best interests of the city. He is very active in the Knights of Columbus, being a fourth degree member, and a Past Grand Knight, also State Advocate and State Deputy, and otherwise prominent in the general affairs of the order. He is a member of the Colonial Club and his religious affiliation is with the St. Mary's Roman Catholic Church.

John J. Keegan was married, in 1913, to Margaret L. Lundrigan, of Bath, Maine, and they are the parents of one son, John J., Jr., who was born April 19, 1920. Mr. Keegan has his offices at No. 72 Front Street, in Bath, Maine.

JOHN W. CUMMINGS—One of the leading authorities on feldspar in this country is John W. Cummings, president and treasurer of the J. W. Cummings Feldspar Company, of Bath, Maine. Mr. Cummings has had a lifelong experience in this field, and since 1915 has been mining, grinding, pulverizing and distributing feldspar for all commercial purposes.

Born in Pottsville, Pennsylvania, August 12, 1859, John W. Cummings is a son of Thomas Cummings and of Margaret (White) Cummings, both natives of Pottsville, the first-mentioned of whom was a mining engineer, and died in 1897, and the last-mentioned of whom died in 1926. Mr. Cummings received his education in the public schools, including the high school, and then was engaged in drilling for coal, at Pottsville for a few years. He then became interested in the feldspar business in Connecticut, and in Trenton, New Jersey, continuing in those fields until 1915, when he came to Bath, Maine, and organized the J. W. Cummings Feldspar Company. Mr. Cummings has been president and treasurer of the concern since its organization, and has developed a prosperous and substantial business, which has in its main plant about thirty employees. They have a private railroad siding with a capacity of ten cars, and during the years which have passed since the concern was established, it has experienced a steady and healthy growth. The products are distributed throughout this continent and in several foreign countries. The plant is located on Washington Street, in Bath. Fraternally, Mr. Cummings is identified with the Benevolent and Protective Order of Elks. His religious affiliation is with St. Mary's Roman Catholic Church.

John W. Cummings was married (first) to Mary McGurl; (second) to Mary A. Lemond. To the first marriage three children were born: Francis M., Thomas J., and Margaret C. To the second marriage five children were born: M. Rita, John W., Jr., Richard, Robert, and Edward. The family home is at No. 149 Oak Street, in Bath.

JOHN C. STEWART—Having held practically every public office in the town, John C. Stewart, attorney, now (1928) in his seventy-ninth year, is loved and respected by everyone in York Village, Maine. Though he studied medicine at Dartmouth and took his degree of Doctor of Medicine there, he turned to the law, studying in the office of the late Judge Burbank, of Saco, and at the age of forty-five opened practice in York Village.

John C. Stewart was born June 19, 1850, at Ryegate, Vermont, the son of Duncan Stewart of Ryegate, born in 1826, died in 1882, and of Margaret

(Ritchie) Stewart of Scotland, born in 1830, died in 1905, his father having been a farmer in Vermont. Following his preparatory education in the public schools of Ryegate, Mr. Stewart matriculated at Dartmouth, where he took two degrees, that of Bachelor of Arts in 1873, and that of Doctor of Medicine in 1877. Then he turned to the law, and was admitted to the bar in Maine in 1895, a member of both the State and County Bar associations. Once begun in the legal and public field, Attorney Stewart held office after office, until he had served in every capacity save that of assessor of the town. For six years, from 1882 until 1888, he was deputy sheriff, and in 1891 he was elected to the State Senate. In addition to the practice of law and the duties involved in exercising public office, Attorney Stewart finds time for setting on the board of the York County Trust Company, and for participation in the activities of five fraternal associations.

He is Past Master of the Blue Lodge of the Free and Accepted Masons; a member of the Junior Order United American Mechanics; the Ancient Order of United Workmen; the Royal Arcanum; and the Golden Cross, of which organization he has been Supreme Medical Director for twenty-five years. He was one of the founders of the York Village Improvement Society, the operations of which always have interested him deeply. Always he has had the welfare of the village and the just treatment of official privileges extended to him at heart, and has never abused a trust bestowed upon him. Attorney Stewart is known as "a grand old man." He is a bachelor.

ROGER ASHURST PUTNAM—Native of York, York County, Maine, Roger Ashurst Putnam was born June 26, 1890, son of Joseph Perley and Sophia (Marshall) Putnam, both of whom are deceased, his father having been prominent in affairs of York Village for a number of years, and highly respected in the community, there in business as auctioneer and operator in real estate.

Roger Ashurst Putnam received his elementary and high school education in the public schools of York Village, and then entered upon courses of study at St. Johnsbury Academy, St. Johnsbury, Vermont. Following this preparatory work he matriculated in Bowdoin College, Brunswick, Maine, but transferred at the end of a year to Colby College, at Waterville, Maine. At Colby he distinguished himself in oratory and debate, and when he graduated, in 1915, was chosen class orator. For some time he had considered the law as a profession, and upon the urging of close friends and through his own preference, having considered the profession carefully, he was ready, on graduation from Colby, to prepare for a career as solicitor. Accordingly he entered the Boston University Law School, at Boston, Massachusetts, and applied himself diligently and intelligently to lectures and courses, winning commendation alike from professors and classmates. When he returned to York to set out upon an active career he brought to the law a fine preparation, and, with his natural and cultivated talent at public speaking, soon proved the wisdom of his choice in profession. A Republican, Mr. Putnam began at once to take part in the political matters of York Village and York County, staunch in his loyalty to the principles of the party, but supporting candidates outside the party pale when he believed them to be most properly suited to the office sought. Though not a member of the denomination, Mr. Putnam regularly attended the Congregational church; his donations to causes of charity, whether or no they came to his attention through the church, were always substantial, and bestowed in a spirit of sympathy and kindness. He was a member of the Benevolent and Protective Order of Elks, and of the Blue Lodge of the Free and Accepted Masons. Popular and respected fraternally and politically, and having demonstrated ably his ability in the law and in matters of public policy, Mr. Putnam was elected, on March 8, 1920, to the office of town clerk, and for five years thereafter he served most devotedly to this charge of trust, until his death, on June 15, 1925, eleven days prior, had he but lived, to his thirty-fifth birthday. His loss was felt keenly by his many friends in York Village and elsewhere, in whose hearts he had long occupied a place of affection.

Only seven months before his death Roger Ashurst Putnam married, November 8, 1924, at York Village, Eleanor Louise Hennessey, daughter of Patrick Joseph and Ellen (Kiley) Hennessey; and was the father of a child, born to the widow, Mrs. Putnam, on October 20, 1925, Roger Ashurst, Jr.

WILLIAM R. CAMPBELL—As State Agent of the Employers' Liability Assurance Corporation, William R. Campbell has supervision over about one hundred agencies in the State of Maine. He is well known among insurance men in this State, and has made an enviable record in raising the Employers' Liability Assurance Corporation to its present rating in Maine.

William R. Campbell was born in Bath, Maine, a son of Scott C. Campbell, of West Bath, Maine, contractor and builder, who died in 1927, and of Susan E. (Hutchins) Campbell, of this State, who died in April, 1918. He attended the public schools of Phippsburg and Gray's Business College of Portland, and then secured employment, at the early age of sixteen, in the First National Bank of Bath as a clerk, continuing in this connection for about three years. At the end of that time he left the bank and was engaged in various enterprises for a few years, after which he purchased the insurance business of Charles S. Pettingill, which he continued under his own name until 1897. In that year he was made Deputy Collector of Customs, filling this office for six years. In 1903 he went to Waterville, Maine, as special agent for the Employers' Liability and Assurance Corporation, and later also became associated with the firm of L. T. Boothby & Sons Company, insurance, and W. A. R. Boothby, State Agent of the Employers' Liability Assurance Corporation, continuing until 1918, when he went to Portland as State Agent for the Employers' Liability Assurance Corporation, under the title of Campbell, Payson & Noyes, which position he is still (1928) most efficiently filling. Mr. Campbell supervises about one hundred agencies in the State of Maine, and is known all over the State as one of the most active and progressive, and also one of the real builders of the Employers' Liability Assurance Corporation in this State. After coming to Portland, Mr. Campbell also became associated with the firm of Morse, Payson, and Noyes. H. S. Payson died in 1920, and his son, H. M. Payson, became a member of the firm.

Mr. Wadsworth Noyes died in April, 1926. It is interesting to note that W. A. R. Boothby was the first man to write a liability policy in the State of Maine, and the second in the United States to write that kind of a policy. In addition to the interests and responsibilities already mentioned Mr. Campbell is a member of the board of directors of the Falmouth Building and Loan Association. He is a member of the Portland Club, of the Cumberland Club, the Waterville Country Club, Vesper Country Club, Portland Country Club, on which he serves as a member of the board of governors, and of several other organizations, including the Maine Historical Society. He attends the Congregational church.

William R. Campbell was married, in 1900, to Mary L. Lincoln, of Bath, Maine, daughter of George M. and Frances L. (Berry) Lincoln. Mr. and Mrs. Campbell make their home at No. 13 West Street, in Portland.

CHARLES A. HALLEN—For more than twenty-four years, Charles A. Hallen has been engaged in building up the New England Cabinet Company, of which he is the founder and of which, since 1918, he has been president and treasurer and owner of a controlling interest. Though the fortunes and the names of this concern have been varied since its foundation in 1903, Mr. Hallen has always been one of the important factors in its development, even when others where holding the important offices and when others owned a controlling share in its stock. Now he has regained actual control, and is developing the business along the lanes which have always seemed to him the natural line of progress for this enterprise. The concern manufactures all kinds of store fixtures and furniture, and is located on Holyoke Wharf, Commercial Street, Portland.

Charles A. Hallen, son of Anders and Maria (Nillson) Hallen, both natives of Sweden, the first-mentioned of whom was engaged in farming, was born in Sweden, January 17, 1866, and received his education in his native land, attending the local schools through those which parallel our high schools, and then continuing in an industrial school. In 1889, when he was twenty-three years of age, he left the land of his nativity and came to this country, settling in the city of Boston, where he became an instructor in manual training. He remained in that connection until late in 1890, when he came to Portland, Maine, and entered the employ of W. A. Allen. For eight years he maintained this connection and then made a change, accepting a position as designer in the employ of the Williams Manufacturing Company, with whom he remained until 1903. In that year he engaged in business, in partnership with others, under the name of the Johnson-Hallen Company, locating at No. 62 Union Street, and manufacturing store fixtures and furniture. In 1909 the name was changed to that of the Berry-Clark Company, Incorporated, with W. B. Berry as president; Scott Clark, as treasurer; and Mr. Hallen a member of the board of directors. The following year, 1910, the name was again changed, this time to its present title, the New England Cabinet Works, with J. S. Maxey as president; and R. S. F. Maxey as treasurer. In 1918 Mr. Hallen purchased a controlling interest in the concern, and became president and treasurer of the enterprise, offices he has continued to hold to the present time (1928). This concern is one of the oldest in Portland engaged in the manufacture of store fixtures, and has about twenty-five employees.

Politically, Mr. Hallen gives his support to the principles and the candidates of the Republican party. Fraternally, he is identified with Deering Lodge, Free and Accepted Masons; Greenleaf Chapter, Royal Arch Masons; St. Albans Commandery, Knights Templar; also with Kora Temple, Ancient Arabic Order Nobles of the Mystic Shrine, and he is a member of the Scandinavian Association.

Charles A. Hallen was married, in 1893, to Mattie Fredin, of Brownsville, Maine, and they are the parents of two children: 1. Charlotte P., who married H. Falconi, and has two daughters. 2. Pearl E., who married Mr. Easton, and also has two daughters. He married (second), in 1908, Sophia F. Hendrickson.

JOSEPH M. McCARTY—Justifiedly proud of the business which he has built for himself, Joseph M. McCarty, of Sanford, operates a company which bottles and distributes carbonated beverages, the largest firm of its kind in York County. The name of the company which he established in 1920, is the Sanford Spring Water Company. Mr. McCarty is the son of John J. McCarty, of Dover, New Hampshire, who died in 1926, and of Harriet (Curtin) McCarty, of Somersworth, New Hampshire, who died in 1883. His father was engaged for the greater part of his life in the ice business.

Joseph M. McCarty was born in Dover, New Hampshire, September 12, 1880, and as a boy attended the public and high school. His first business venture was in the meat business, in which he was engaged for many years. Starting in this line of work with Mr. McIntyre, he worked subsequently with J. P. Vallery, then with H. A. Roberts, with whom he was employed until 1913, when he opened a market of his own in Sanford. He continued to operate this meat market until 1920, when he established his present business under the name of the Sanford Spring Water Company. This business, which is owned solely by Mr. McCarty and which is up-to-date in every way, being equipped with motorized machines, has a large distribution for its product, operating in a radius of twenty-five miles from Sanford. Mr. McCarty is active in club, association, and fraternal life in Sanford, as well as an active Rotarian and a member of the Benevolent and Protective Order of Elks. He and his family are members of the Church of Notre Dame, Springvale, Maine.

In 1908, Joseph M. McCarty married Alice M. Broggi, of Sanford, the daughter of Frank and Pasquina Broggi. They are the parents of one child, Adele H.

CARL T. PLUMMER—After devoting eighteen years to the hotel business in Bridgton, Cumberland County, Carl T. Plummer decided that the field of finance offered greater opportunities for his abilities and he took the post of treasurer in the Bridgton Savings Bank, an institution of which his father, Mellin Plummer, was one of the principal founders.

The first president of this institution, which was one of the leading financial concerns of Bridgton, was W. W. Cross. He was succeeded in office by Rufus Gibbs, he in turn by Judge A. H. Walker, and the last president, before the bank was absorbed by the Casco Mercantile Trust Company of Portland, in 1926, was Walter Davis. The Bridgton National Bank, with which Mr. Plummer was interested, was established in 1908, with W. N. Staples as first president, succeeded by Dr. E. S. Abbott as second president, when it was, in turn, absorbed by the Casco Mercantile Trust Company of Portland. Mellin Plummer was treasurer of the Savings Bank from 1887 to 1924 and the total assets of the two institutions when they were absorbed amounted to $1,-563,848.27.

Carl T. Plummer was born at Bridgton, October 20, 1884, the son of Mellin and Clara A. (Murphey) Plummer, the former a leader in the financial circles of Bridgton, following which he went to Bowdoin College for two years. As has been stated, he was in the hotel business for eighteen years, when he decided to take up banking. He is now (1928) assistant treasurer and a director of the Casco Mercantile Trust Company. He was a member of the State Legislature in 1924 and 1925 and has always been to the fore in any matters of community interest and benefit. During the World War Mr. Plummer was chairman of all the Liberty Loan drives and in many ways did his share in that great struggle. He is affiliated with the Free and Accepted Masons, of which he is a Past Master; holds the thirty-second degree, Ancient Accepted Scottish Rite; and is a past officer of Kora Temple, Ancient Arabic Order Nobles of the Mystic Shrine. His college fraternity is Theta Delta Chi. He is one of the organizers and an active member of the Lions International Club and a member of the board of trustees of the local Congregational church.

In 1905, Carl T. Plummer married J. Winifred Burnham, of Bridgton.

JOSEPH BENNETT PIKE—One of the successful members of the legal profession in Bridgton is Joseph Bennett Pike, who has been engaged in general practice here since 1904. Mr. Pike completed a special course in the law school of Boston University, and is now serving his third term as Judge of the Municipal Court of North Cumberland County. He was born in Otisfield, Maine, May 24, 1877, son of Freeman H., a native of Otisfield, who was engaged in business as a merchant to the time of his death in 1900, and of Olevia (Bennett) Pike, who was born in Naples, Maine, and died in 1925, at the age of eighty-six years.

Joseph Bennett Pike received his early education in the public schools of his birthplace and then prepared for college in Hebron Academy. As he had early decided upon the legal profession as his future field of activity he then entered Boston University, where he pursued a special course. After completing his special course in Boston University he continued his legal studies in the office of James S. Wright, of South Paris, Maine. In 1902 he successfully passed the required examinations for admission to the bar and in that same year began general practice at Harrison, Maine. Two years later, in 1904, he came to Bridgton, Maine, and here he has been engaged in general practice since, a period of more than twenty-three years. In addition to the responsibilities in connection with his large private practice, Mr. Pike is also Judge of the Municipal Court of North Cumberland County, in which office he is now (1928) serving his third term. He was also a member of the board of directors of the

Bridgton National Bank, and its attorney until it was absorbed by the Casço Mercantile Trust Company of Portland, Maine. In local public affairs he has always been interested and helpful. He served as a member of the Board of Selectmen of Bridgton for three years and has been town clerk since 1917. During the World War he served as a member and later chairman of the legal advisory board and was active in helping the city of Bridgton to achieve its home war work. Fraternally, he is identified with the Independent Order of Odd Fellows, in which order he has passed through all the chairs and is a member of the Encampment. He is also a member of Crooked River Lodge, Free and Accepted Masons; of the Royal Arch Masons and of the Knights Templar. He is one of the active and interested members of the Bridgton Chamber of Commerce, and is a member of the Lions International Club. Judge Pike is not only one of the leading men of the town of Bridgton but he is well known throughout the southern part of the State of Maine. His religious affiliation is with the Methodist church, which he serves as a member of the official board.

Joseph Bennett Pike was married, in 1904, to Lotta I. Moody, who was born in New York City, daughter of Thomas B. and Ida (Hudson) Moody. Mr. and Mrs. Pike have three children: 1. Joseph B., Jr., born May 15, 1905, and who is doing graduate work at Yale University. 2. Sarah M., born April 25, 1908. 3. Barbara F., born June 5, 1911. Mr. and Mrs. Pike make their home at No. 59 High Street. in Bridgton.

REVEREND P. E. DESJARDINS—Until the latter part of the third quarter of the nineteenth century is was necessary for communicants in the Roman Catholic church residing in Westbrook, Maine, to go to Portland for religious services; but in 1872 members of the faith established in Westbrook a small mission. Here, in this humble structure, but their own and in their own community, communicants were led in service by a priest, from Biddleford, who came to Westbrook periodically to officiate. Thus was the beginning. In 1877, five years after erection of the little mission house, ground was broken for the present church, St. Hyacinth's Roman Catholic Church, which was completed in 1879. At this time the parish consisted of one hundred and seventy-five families, and was under the charge of Rev. Father A. de Celle, who officiated until 1901, and who, a most devout man of God, sincere, tireless in the speaking of His word, wrought a considerable growth of communicants. In 1901 when he turned over the parish to Rev. Alex Dugré, St Hyacinth's was indeed well established. Rev. Dugré carried on the charge for ten years, and was succeeded in 1911 by Rev. A. A. Hamel, and he in turn, in 1916, ceded the responsibility to Rev. Father P. E. Desjardins who has since that date been at the head of the parish. Meanwhile the number of families within the ministry of the church had increased to seven hundred and fifty; in 1893 a fine parochial school had been constructed to meet the demands of parishioners for suitable and religiously directed education. This school is continued, and offers instruction up to and including the eighth grade. The mental standards are high, and are attended to by a staff of sixteen teachers. In 1916, when Rev. Father Desjardins assumed charge of St. Hyacinth's, the

church, school and parish, a second parish was established, St. Mary's being set off from St. Hyacinth's. So that at the present time (1928) there are two flourishing parishes in Westbrook, where prior to 1872 there have been none. In charge of the second parish is Rev. M. Culbert; and it is hoped that within a dozen years, perhaps, St. Mary's may equal in number of communicant families St. Hyacinth's, which, under Rev. Father Desjardins has continued to expand.

It is difficult here to present anything of a biographical character pertaining to Rev. Father Desjardins, for the reason that in his self-effacing office as a man of God he is most reluctant to speak of himself, and indeed refuses to do so. The surname Desjardins is, of course, of French origin. Rev. Father Desjardins was born at Waterville, Maine, a son of Samuel and Mary (Mercier) Desjardins. But it is only of the Rev. Father's works, together with recognition in some small manner of the respect, love and even reverence in which he is held by his parishioners, that we who write these lines are able to discuss. For upwards of a decade his heart, soul and effort have been with his charges; he knows them every one, and looks upon them not with censure, but with kindness and an unfailing spirit to help. Is there a birth, Rev. Father Desjardins must be called; is there a death, so too; and if there is a marriage, then too he must be there. Thus tied securely and completely to his parish, by his love and duty as a pastor, he is most intimately concerned in the welfare of his flock, his children all. Fraternity? Politics? Commercial enterprise? They are not for the Rev. Father. His solely and entirely the needs of the parish spiritually, and yes, materially too; for if he knew for a moment that a parishioner was in need of shelter, heat or sustenance, he would provide. Small wonder then that parishioners have warmness in their hearts for him, and it is to their credit.

WILLIAM W. EDELSTONE—One of the leading industries of Westbrook, Cumberland County, is the cord tire fabric and twin manufacturing business operated by the Edelstone Brothers Fabric Mill, Incorporated, of which concern William W. Edelstone is president, with his brother, Harry Edelstone, as treasurer. This first has risen from a small concern which manufactured only cord tire fabric to a large factory with over twenty thousand feet of floor space, distributing its products nationally.

William W. Edelstone was born at Troy, New York, September 25, 1890, the son of Ezekiel and Dora I. (Simon) Edelstone, the former a prominent merchant of that city, now retired from active business. Following his early education in the public schools of his community, Mr. Edelstone entered Lowell (Massachusetts) Textile School, where he took a general course in the manufacture of cotton goods and their by-products. He began his career in the cord tire fabric business in 1916 and in 1922, with his brother Harry (of whom further), started operations in Westbrook under the firm name of William W. Edelstone Fabric Company. The business flourished and they commenced the manufacture of cords, both flat and square, for tire fabrics. They also manufactured a line of novelty fabrics. In 1924 the name of the firm was incorporated and the name changed to the Edelstone Brothers Fabric Mills, Incorporated, with, as stated, William W. Edelstone as president of the concern and his brother as treasurer. The twine manufactured by the company is one of the by-products of their fabric business and is sold throughout the country in the five and ten-cent stores. The firm employs upwards of thirty persons in its factory and the products have a national reputation for excellence of quality.

Mr. Edelstone is very prominent in Jewish circles throughout the State of Maine, as well as in Portland. He is one of the trustees of the Hebrew School at Portland, trustee of the Hebrew United Charities and many other similar organizations, a member and treasurer of the Young Men's Hebrew Association of Portland, treasurer of the Veritans, director of the Fairview Country Club, and is actively affiliated with the B'nai B'rith. He is also a member of Boston Lodge, of the Benevolent and Protective Order of Elks.

Mr. Edelstone married, in 1916, Gertrude B. Bloomberg, a native of Poland. Mr. and Mrs. Edelstone are the parents of two children: Sumner A. and Phyllis, who reside with their parents in a very attractive residence at No. 379 Deering Avenue, Portland.

Harry Edelstone, the brother of William W. Edelstone, is, as stated, treasurer of the Fabric Mills. He was born at Troy, New York, October 15, 1882, and after his early education in the public schools took a course in one of the local business colleges. He is a member of B'nai B'rith and president of the Veritans, being also affiliated with a number of other fraternal and social organizations. In 1912, Harry Edelstone married Sophie Grass, and they are residents of Portland.

WILLIAM P. F. ROBIE—One of the very well-known citizens of the State of Maine is William P. F. Robie, son of former Governor Frederick Robie. Mr. Robie was engaged in farming until a few years ago, and since his retirement he has been devoting his time and his energy to the establishment of a bird sanctuary. He has striven to make Gorham, Maine, a safe place for birds and with this end in view has secured helpful legislation. He has also prepared the way for the acquisition of about four thousand acres of field and woodland for the preservation of wild bird and animal life.

William P. F. Robie was born in Dorchester, Massachusetts, November 5, 1863, son of Frederick Robie, formerly governor of the State of Maine, who died in 1912, and of Mary O. (Priest) Robie, a native of Biddeford, Maine, who died November 5, 1898. He attended the local public schools and then prepared for college in Fryeburg Academy. When his preparatory course was completed he matriculated in Bowdoin College, from which he was graduated with the class of 1889, receiving at that time the degree of Bachelor of Arts. When his college training was over he chose the occupation which has been followed by his forebears for several generations and engaged in farming. This calling was entirely to his liking and he continued in agricultural activities to the time of his retirement a few years ago. Mr. Robie is a man of sound business ability, and has been officially identified with several institutions of the town of Gorham. Some time ago he resigned all of these responsibilities, except his affiliation with the Baxter Memorial Library of which he continues as a mem-

ber of the board of trustees and vice-president. Since that time he has devoted himself to a work which has long been in mind, and so successfully has he made his plans and carried them out that there is every prospect that the Narragansett Bird and Game Sanctuary in Gorham will in time become a haven and a sanctuary for wild bird and animal life. He has secured the signed agreement of adjoining land-owners making it possible to acquire about four thousand acres of field and woodland for the preservation of wild life, and has also secured State legislation in aid of his project. Mr. Robie is one of the very highly esteemed men of the State, and has always been helpfully interested in the development of educational and other interests of Gorham. During the period of the participation of the United States in the World War Mr. Robie served as fuel and food administrator for the town of Gorham, and holds the usual certificates. Fraternally, he is identified with Alpha Delta Phi College Fraternity, and with Lodge No. 38, Free and Accepted Masons, of which he is a Past Master. He is a member of the local Grange, Patrons of Husbandry; of the Fish and Game Association, the Audubon Society, of Maine and of Massachusetts, the Maine Historical Society, and the Loyal Legion, and his religious membership is with the Congregational church.

William P. F. Robie was married, in 1891, to Flora Barton, of Maine, daughter of Alonzo Drisco and Mary A. (Pineo) Barton. Mr. and Mrs. Robie are the parents of five children: 1. Mary F., a graduate of the University of Maine, Bachelor of Science degree. 2. Frederick, a graduate of the University of Maine, Bachelor of Science degree. 3. John W., a graduate of Bowdoin College, Bachelor of Arts degree. 4. Catherine, a graduate of the State Normal School and of the Sargent School of Physical Culture. 5. Elizabeth, a graduate nurse of the Children's Hospital, of Portland, Maine. Mr. and Mrs. Robie make their home in Gorham.

EUGENE I. CUMMINGS—One of the citizens of the town of Westbrook who has been prominently identified with its public affairs for a long time is Mayor Eugene I. Cummings, who, after serving in various local offices was elected mayor in 1925 and is still serving in that capacity (1928). Mayor Cummings has carried out a very excellent program in the exercise of his office as head of the town affairs, and he is well liked and highly approved by his fellow-townsmen. He was born in Gray, Maine, August 29, 1867, son of Samuel P. Cummings, a native of Gray, Maine, who was a blacksmith by trade and who was a veteran of the Civil War, serving in the infantry and ranking from sergeant to major, and of Ruth (Foster) Cummings, who was born in Gray, Maine, and died in 1916, having survived her husband seventeen years.

Eugene I. Cummings received his education in the local public schools, including the high school, and then entered the employ of the S. D. Warren Company, manufacturers of book paper, at the Cumberland Mills. He began his connection with this concern in 1890, and since that time has maintained his association with it. For more than twenty-three years he has been employed in the sheet metal department of the Cumberland Mills, and he is an expert in this field. For several years Mr. Cummings has been active in the affairs of the town of Westbrook, and he has never been one to shirk the responsibilities of local public office. He has served as a member of the Board of Aldermen, as a member of the Board of Registration, and as deputy sheriff, and in 1925 he was elected to fill the important office of mayor of the town. He also has been a member of the School Board. He has been a most efficient and faithful executive, is giving entire satisfaction to the intelligent and public-spirited portion of the community, and adhering steadily to the policy of maintaining and promoting the best good of the community. He was at one time a member of the Maine National Guard, Company M, First Regiment, with the rank of first lieutenant, and he is a veteran of the Spanish-American War, of 1898, in which conflict he served as sergeant. Fraternally, he is identified with Warren Phillip Lodge, Free and Accepted Masons, and with the Knights of Pythias, of which he is a Past Chancellor. He is a member of the United Spanish War Veterans' Association, and Past Commander of the Portland, Maine, body of that organization. His religious membership is with the Congregational church.

Eugene I. Cummings was married, in 1892, to Mabel Herrick, of East Corinth, Maine, daughter of Chester Herrick. Mr. and Mrs. Cummings have three children: 1. Hazel E., who married George F. Conklin, and has one child. 2. Chester H., who married Bertha Lord, and has two children. 3. Ethel R. The family home is at No. 142 Forest Street, in Westbrook.

RUFUS K. JORDAN—In his early manhood Rufus K. Jordan learned the profession of civil engineer and, as such, was associated with S. L. Stevenson in Westbrook, Cumberland County, for about six years. In 1889 he purchased the foundry business of G. H. Raymond, since which time he has conducted it under his own name. This foundry dates back to about 1878, when it was first operated by Samuel Lisk, who sold it to Mr. Raymond, who in turn found a ready purchaser in Mr. Jordan. The foundry enjoys a fine reputation, which is by no means confined to its locality, for grey iron castings and, in fact, is well and favorably known throughout New England. It employs a force of upwards of thirty men and has a large plant, with a floor space of several thousands of square feet.

Mr. Jordan was born in Westbrook, November 28, 1863, the son of George D. and Caroline E. (Bixby) Jordan. The former was a carpenter and builder, born in Gray, Cumberland County, in 1805; died in Westbrook in 1882. Following his preliminary education in the public schools of Westbrook, Mr. Jordan entered the employment of S. L. Stevenson, where he studied the profession of civil engineering, quickly acquiring the knowledge he sought. As stated, he was with Mr. Stevenson for about six years, when he decided to take over the foundry business of G. H. Raymond. He is still engaged in this business and during the years he has been conducting it, he has established himself as one of the prominent men of his community. He has been very active in the political affairs of Westbrook; was alderman, city of Westbrook, Maine, two terms; mayor, city of Westbrook, Maine, two terms; treasurer, city of Westbrook, Maine, five years; in Legislature, State of Maine, two terms. Always to the fore in any project for the advancement of Westbrook and its citizens, Mr. Jordan has gained the respect and esteem of his community by his public spirit and his energetic enthusiasm for all that tends to the benefit of his town.

He is affiliated with Temple Lodge, No. 86, Free and Accepted Masons, and is Past Sachem of the local Lodge, Improved Order of Red Men. In addition to his foundry interests Mr. Jordan is a director of the Westbrook Trust Company. He is a member of the Monjoy Club of Portland, and of the Rotary Club, and the Chamber of Commerce of Westbrook.

On November 28, 1885, Mr. Jordan was married to Iva Barker Quimby, of North Windham, Cumberland County, the daughter of George and Mary (Barker) Quimby. Mr. and Mrs. Jordan are the parents of five children, as follows: 1. George K. 2. Caroline, married Paul Smith; mother of one child. 3. William R., served in the United States Navy during the World War. 4. Rufus N. 5. Leonard B.

HENRY C. REED—One of the best-known men in Maine insurance and fraternal work, Henry C. Reed has been connected with every movement that has been designed for the progress and uplift of Richmond, and is one of the outstanding figures of the town. He is the son of Levi Reed, who died in 1888, and of Diana (Bickford) Reed, who died in 1909, both parents having been of Richmond. His father was a farmer.

Henry C. Reed was born in Richmond, February 2, 1853. He attended the public schools and high school, and also received a business training. For seventeen years he was engaged in the retail grocery business in Richmond under his own name. January 1, 1906, he organized the Fraternities Health and Accident Association of Richmond, Maine, of which he is secretary and manager. He is secretary-treasurer of the Richmond Loan and Building Association. He has held several public municipal offices, being town auditor and a selectman. He is a member of several local clubs and fraternities. He belongs to Richmond Lodge, Free and Accepted Masons, in which order he holds the thirty-second degree, and is a member of Kora Temple; of Independent Order of Odd Fellows, in which order he has been through all the chairs, and is a member of the Grand Lodge and Grand Encampment. He is secretary of the Insurance Federation of Maine.

Henry C. Reed married (first) Angie Finch, and (second) Mary P. Hodges.

HENRY R. DREW—In point of service, Henry R. Drew is one of the oldest attorneys in Sagadahoc County, Maine, having been engaged in the practice of law in Richmond ever since he was admitted to the bar in 1881. He has contributed to Richmond through these years the service made possible by his legal training, both to his clients and to the general populace of Richmond. He has served as town clerk of Richmond. His parents were Albin P. Drew, of Richmond, Maine, who died in 1889; and Mary M. Shaw, of Bowdoinham, Maine, who died in 1905. His father was a ship carpenter by trade.

Henry R. Drew was born in Richmond, October 7, 1854, and was educated through public school, high school and academy training. After studying law in the office of the late Judge Hall, of Richmond, he was admitted to the bar in 1881. Since that time he has continued a general law practice under his own name. He is a member of the Sagadahoc County Bar Association and the Maine State Bar Association. At the time of the World War, he was a member of the Legal Advisory Board, and participated in the Liberty Loan campaigns. For years he was a member of the County Republican Committee for the town of Richmond, and chairman of the Republican Town Committee. At times Mr. Drew has had competitors, but is now the only attorney in Richmond. He has an extensive acquaintance among prominent men of the State, past and present.

In 1906, Henry R. Drew married Etta F. Gordon, of Bangor.

BENJAMIN E. KELLEY—One of Boothbay Harbor's most important and prominent citizens is Benjamin E. Kelley, owner, editor and publisher of the "Boothbay Register," one of the leading weekly journals of the State. The pressroom is equipped with the most modern machinery for the production of an up-to-date paper and, in addition, Mr. Kelley has a first-class plant for job and commercial printing. Mr. Kelley was born June 20, 1879, at Boothbay Harbor, the son of John E. and Cordelia (McDougall) Kelley, the former a prominent public official, having officiated as sheriff of Lincoln County for eighteen years and as deputy sheriff for a considerable period. He was a prominent farmer and actively interested in politics in Lincoln County. He died in 1913; his wife, the mother of Mr. Kelley, died in 1920.

The early education of Benjamin E. Kelley was obtained in the public schools of his community, after which he attended Lincoln Academy. He graduated from Bowdoin College in the class of 1902, with the degree of Bachelor of Arts. For three years Mr. Kelley was a teacher in the public schools of Greenwich, Connecticut, after which he took up newspaper work, being connected with a number of metropolitan dailies until 1914, when he purchased the interests of C. E. Kendrick in the "Boothbay Register." After taking over this paper he changed it from a four-page, eight-column publication, to an eight-page, six-column weekly, greatly improving its appearance. In a very short time he established it as one of the vital forces of Lincoln County in political and community affairs. He has given freely of his services to his fellow-citizens, having served as clerk and treasurer, at Greenwich, Connecticut, and as a member of the School Board of Boothbay Harbor. In connection with the latter office it is worthy of note that after his term as a member of the School Board Mr. Kelley was instrumental in making the additions to the high school completed. During the World War Mr. Kelley was energetic in the work of Liberty Loan drives and other war work, and was either chairman or secretary of several of the bodies concerned in this work in Boothbay Harbor. Fraternally, Mr. Kelley is affiliated with the Benevolent and Protective Order of Elks and the Knights of Pythias. For a number of years he was secretary of the Chamber of Commerce. His religious affiliations are with the Congregational church.

In 1912, Benjamin E. Kelley married Irene A. Russell, daughter of Charles and Lillie (Green) Russell, the former a prominent citizen of Greenwich, Connecticut.

HARVEY D. GRANVILLE—A prominent lumberman of Maine, Mr. Granville is one of the organizers of the Sokokis Lumber Company, of Kezar Falls, and he is well-known throughout the State for his activity in promoting good roads. Born January 7, 1874, at Parsonsfield, Maine, Mr. Granville is a son of Rufus M. and Carrie A. (Pentz) Granville,

both of whom are now deceased. Joseph J. Granville, the great-grandfather of Harvey D. Granville, came to Maine in 1782, where he was one of the seventeen original incorporators of Parsonsfield. He was a captain in the State Militia, and fought in the Revolutionary War. His son, George, the father of Rufus, was born in Parsonsfield and later took up a farm where the old homestead now is. Rufus M. Granville was a native of Parsonsfield, and followed the trade of carpenter until the time of his death, in 1893. Carrie A. (Pentz) Granville, who was a native of Boston, Massachusetts, died in 1892. The Pentz family is an old-established one of Long Island. The pioneer members thereof were Tories, and provided the British troops with supplies, during the Revolution.

Harvey D. Granville received his preparatory education in the public schools of the community in which he was born, later graduating from Parsonsfield Seminary. After completing his education, Mr. Granville became a teacher in the public schools, a vocation which he followed for fifteen years. In 1908, he helped organize the Sokokis Lumber Company at Kezar Falls, and was the first president of the concern. He was succeeded in this office by William H. Burgess, and at the present time, E. R. Bachelder is president. The products are distributed throughout the Eastern States. The company owns more than five thousand acres of timberland, where they practice a system of reforestation, to replace the cut timber.

The construction of good roads in the State of Maine has been a matter of interest to Mr. Granville and he has given much time and energy to their promotion. He has held many town offices and for some time he was Road Commissioner for Parsonsfield. During 1920, 1921, and 1923, he served as representative to the State Legislature, and he is now a member of the State Senate. Mr. Granville is called the "Father of the Good Roads Bill," a measure which was passed in both the House and the Senate. During the World War, he was chairman of the Liberty Loan Drives in that section. He is, fraternally, affiliated with the Masonic Order up to and including the thirty-second degree; Knights Templar; Past Master of Blue Lodge; and a member of the Knights of Pythias. He is also a member of many local clubs.

Harvey D. Granville married, in 1903, Alice E. Fogg, a daughter of David S. and Elizabeth (Staples) Fogg. Mr. and Mrs. Granville are the parents of one child, Harry F., born June 3, 1904. Mr. Granville and his family attend the Methodist church.

HERMAN HARTUNG—From a comparatively small coal and wood business to the largest concern in Boothbay Harbor, Lincoln County, dealing extensively in lumber, with a complete mill equipment, and employing upwards of twenty men, is the record made by the firm headed by Herman Hartung, and it is generally admitted that it is to hard work, business efficiency and financial acumen of Mr. Hartung that this wonderful progress is mainly due.

Mr. Hartung was born at Manchester, Kennebec County, March 13, 1853, the son of Christian and Marguerite (Kerber) Hartung, the former a native of Germany who was born in that country in 1828. Mr. Hartung's father came to this country when but a boy and after a four-year course in the public schools in New York City came to Manchester, where he acquired a splendid reputation as an upright business man and foremost citizen. After passing through the public schools of Manchester, Mr. Hartung took a position with the Cumberland Superphosphates Company at Boothbay Harbor, with which concern he became superintendent. In 1901, he formed a partnership with P. G. Pierce, under the name of Pierce and Hartung, for the purpose of carrying on a coal and wood business, handling also lumber, paint, roofing, hardware, etc. The concern has its own wharf, lighters, planing mill, and garage buildings. The business progressed very rapidly and in a few years it became one of the most important firms in the building and contracting line in Maine.

Mr. Hartung takes a leading part in all community affairs in Boothbay Harbor. He is affiliated with the Free and Accepted Masons, and is a member of the Chapter, Royal Arch Masons. He is also a member of the local Lodge of the Knights of Pythias, and holds office in the auxiliary branch of that order, the Pythian Sisters. He is a member of the Sagadahoc Club and is affiliated with the Congregational church.

Herman Hartung married Amelia Torrence of Manchester, daughter of William and Clementine (Hoxie) Torrence. Mr. and Mrs. Hartung are the parents of three children: 1. Mattie E., married to Victor Gott; they have two children: Harvey, and Gerald. 2. Ernest C., married to Ida Greenleaf; children: Harold, died at age of twelve, and Evelyn. 3. Nora B., married to C. C. Mathews; two children: Ina, and Louise.

FRANCIS B. GREENE—Under the name of F. B. Greene & Son, Francis B. Greene has been engaged in business as a wholesale merchant in Boothbay Harbor, Maine, for a number of years, but though he is prominent and respected as a business man, he is more widely known as the author of a very excellent history of Boothbay Harbor. This work, published in 1906, received favorable notice and comment from all over the United States, and carried the name of the author into many libraries. Mr. Greene was at one time assistant secretary of the Senate of the State of Maine, and he has also served as Superintendent of Schools.

Francis B. Greene was born in Augusta, Maine, June 16, 1857, son of Abiathar, a native of Farmington, Maine, who was a manufacturer of axes and carriages, and who died January 26, 1906, and of Myra H. (Winans) Greene, a native of Milton, Ohio, who died January 22, 1906. Mr. Greene attended the local public schools, and then continued his studies in the Maine Central Institute, later completing his preparation for an active business career by taking a commercial course in the Dirigo Business School. He had decided to enter the practice of law and with that end in view entered and read law in the office of E. F. Pillsbury, continuing his studies until he was admitted to the bar in 1880. He had attained his goal but, after being admitted to the bar, he became interested in an entirely different line of business activity and accepted a position as traveling salesman. He was notably successful in this line and after a time established his present business, as a wholesale merchant, under the name of F. B. Greene and Son. This enterprise he has continued to conduct until the present time (1928). He is very well-known in this section of the State, is universally liked and respected by all with whom he comes in contact, and is one of the energetic and public-spirited citizens of

this locality. He was formerly assistant secretary of the Senate of the State of Maine, and locally, he has been especially interested in educational affairs, serving as superintendent of Boothbay Harbor schools for four years. Along with his business success and his public activities Mr. Greene is also well known in this section as a writer of history, having compiled a history of Boothbay Harbor which was published in 1906, and which received favorable comments from all over the country. Mr. Greene's history is quoted as an authority on matters pertaining to the Boothbay district, and he is ranked among the better grade of historians.

Fraternally, he is identified with Seaside Lodge, Free and Accepted Masons; also with the Royal Arch Masons; and with the Order of the Eastern Star. He is a member of the Sons of the American Revolution, the Maine Historical Society, and the New England Historical and Genealogical Society. His religious affiliation is with the Congregational church.

Francis B. Greene was married (first), in 1880, to Cora E. Murray, of Windsor, Maine, daughter of John O., and Elizabeth (Wight) Murray. She died, and he married (second) Nettie F. Woodward, daughter of Samuel and Octavia (Masters) Woodward. To the first marriage one daughter was born, Maude W., who married P. R. McAusland. To the second marriage two children were born: 2. Grace M., who married E. S. Dunton. 3. Francis B., Jr., who married Bertha E. Saunders.

F. BURTON HAGGETT—The oldest hardware concern in Wiscasset, Lincoln County, is the establishment owned by F. Burton Haggett, who has developed the business from a single small store, operated by himself and his late brother, to a large plant consisting of four extensive places, handling hardware, auto supplies, and general merchandise. In addition, Mr. Haggett started the first garage to be opened in Wiscasset. He was born at Edgecomb, Lincoln County, December 14, 1869, the son of Arnold B. and Sarah (Clifford) Haggett, both of Edgecomb. Mr. Haggett's father was a farmer, to which he added the profession of school teacher. He died in 1921, aged eighty-nine years, his wife having predeceased him in 1911.

After completing his courses in the public schools of Edgecomb, F. Burton Haggett remained on his father's farm for a few years and then learned the trade of tinsmith, which he followed until 1898, when he went into business for himself in Wiscasset. The business prospered from the start and Mr. Haggett took in his brother, Henry W. Haggett, as partner, using the firm name of Haggett Brothers. As has been stated, the business grew until it is now the largest and oldest in its line in Wiscasset. Henry W. Haggett died a few years ago, and since then Mr. Haggett has operated the business alone. He is an active member of the Knights of Pythias and is affiliated with a number of the local social organizations.

In 1896, F. Burton Haggett maried Luella G. Evans, daughter of William and Sarah Evans of Walpole, Massachusetts. They are the parents of two children: 1. Lawrence B., married Helen Reed; they have two children: Jeanette, and Henry B. 2. Fred B., a student at Moody Theological College.

FRED F. PENDLETON—From time to time, anywhere along the Atlantic coast may be seen a first-class, excellently built boat which bears witness to the skill of Fred F. Pendleton. The fame of Mr. Pendleton as a boat builder is known up and down the coast, and many an owner in towns far removed from Wiscasset, Maine, is grateful for the craftsmanship and for the high qualtiy of material which went into the making of his vessel.

Fred F. Pendleton was born in Camden, Maine, March 29, 1873, son of Henry D., a native of Camden, Maine, who was engaged in business as a carriage manufacturer, and died in 1919, and of Abbie (Blagdon) Pendleton, who was born in Wiscasset, Maine, and died in 1916. Mr. Pendleton received a good, practical education in the local public schools and then followed his dominating interest, which was boat building. He learned the trade at a very early age and for two years was employed with the Herreshoff Company at Bristol, Rhode Island. He continued in the employ of others until 1901, when, at the age of twenty-eight, he engaged in business for himself at Wiscasset, Maine. Beginning in a small shop, his skill gradually brought him more and more patronage and as the years have passed his business has steadily grown. He soon out-grew the first small shop, and at the present time (1928) is the owner of a boat-building business which requires the services of about twenty men. Mr. Pendleton builds pleasure boats, from fifty-foot size up, and some of the finest types of pleasure boats on the Atlantic coast are the products of his skill. He is the sole owner of the business and his reputation as a builder of the best type of boats is known all along the Atlantic coast. Mr. Pendleton is a member of all the Scottish Rite bodies of the Free and Accepted Masons, and of the Consistory, in which he holds the thirty-second degree; ;he is also a member of the Improved Order of Red Men, of which he is a Past Sachem. He is an active member of the Wiscasset Chamber of Commerce and is a public-spirited citizen, though he prefers to serve the community as a private citizen rather than in an official capacity. His religious affiliation is with the Methodist church.

Fred F. Pendleton was married, in 1896, to Myrtie L. Hall, of Jefferson, Maine, and they are the parents of one son, Chester H., who is a resident of Wiscasset, Maine, and who married Carolyn Haggett. Mr. and Mrs. Pendleton make their home in Wiscasset.

FRED E. GIGNOUX—The most important steamship line in the State of Maine is the intercoastal steamship line represented by Fred E. Gignoux. The service was founded in 1920, but since 1924 has been operated by Mr. Gignoux. He has a fleet of sixty-seven boats and is also agent for practically every steamship line which touches at this port. In addition to these business responsibilities Mr. Gignoux is active in several military organizations, is a veteran of the Spanish-American War, Philippine Insurrection, and World War, and at the present time (1928) is colonel of the 303d Field Artillery.

Fred E. Gignoux was born in New Jersey, June 20, 1876, and is a son of Julis Ernest, a native of Staten Island, New York, who was a successful mining engineer to the time of his death in 1914, and of Margaret E. (Mayer) Gignoux, also a native of Staten Island, New York, who died in 1885. Mr. Gignoux received his education in the public schools of his native district and in the University of Nevada, spent

several years in the military service, and then became identified with the J. G. White Company, with whom he remained for a number of years. Upon the outbreak of the Spanish-American War, in 1898, he enlisted and was soon commissioned a first lieutenant. He served throughout the period of the conflict, and has always retained his interest in military affairs. In 1902 he came to Portland, Maine, and in 1920 became the leader of a group of business men who established an intercoastal steamship line. Four years later the company was disbanded and since that time Mr. Gignoux has carried on the business alone under his own name. He represented a fleet of sixty-seven boats, the largest American fleet afloat. He is a member of the board of directors of the Fidelity Trust Company and his sound judgment and his business acumen have long been recognized by his associates who bring to him many of their difficult problems. As has been stated, Mr. Gignoux has always retained his interest in military affairs. He is Past President of the Maine State Reserve Officers' Association; Past Commander of the Millitary Order of the World War, of Maine, and at the present time (1928) is colonel of the 303d Field· Artillery. He is prominent in practically all of the military affairs of the State, and is also identified with a number of other organizations, including the Purprodick Club, of which he is president, the Public Health Association, the American Legion, the Maine Historical Society, the Portland Club, the Portland Country Club, and the Rotary Club. He is also a member of the Cape Shore Country Club and of many other local organizations. Mr. Gignoux is affiliated with the Ancient Order of the Caribou.

Fred E. Gignoux married (first) Sophie Matthiessen; (second) Katherine Denison. To the first marriage two children were born: 1. Marie. 2. Fred E. Jr., who is a sophomore in Yale College. To the second marriage three children were born: 3. Edward T. 4. Margaret. 5. Natalie A.

PERCY L. NICKERSON—One of the oldest grain establishments in Bath, Maine, is that owned and operated by Percy L. Nickerson and his brother, A. E. Nickerson. The business was founded in June, 1910, and in 1915 was removed to its present well-equipped building on Commercial Street.

Alfred E. Nickerson, father of Mr. Nickerson, was born in Waldo County, Maine, and was one of the prominent and public-spirited men of that county, serving in various public offices and in both houses of the State Legislature. He was also a soldier in the Civil War and was wounded at Spottsylvania Court House. He married Augusta Strout, a native of Belfast, Maine, who died in 1897.

Percy L. Nickerson was born in Waldo County, Maine, September 23, 1875, and received his early education in the public schools of his birthplace. He prepared for college in Westbrook Seminary, and then matriculated in the University of Maine, but did not complete his course there. He had been reared on the farm, and from boyhood had been accustomed to agricultural activities. Upon leaving college he engaged in farming and continued in that line until June 2, 1910, when he and his brother, A. E. Nickerson, organized the Bath Grain Company, and located at Bath, Maine, for the purpose of establishing a grain, hay, and straw business. They were originally located in the old Blacking building, but in 1915 they erected a new building to meet the needs of their business, on Commercial Street. There they have since been building up a large and important business enterprise. They have a private railroad siding and are one of the oldest concerns of their kind in Bath. The business has grown until at the present time (1928) their patronage is drawn from the territory included within a radius of fifteen miles surrounding their place of business. Mr. Nickerson is a member of the Bath Chamber of Commerce and the Rotary Club. His religious affiliation is with the Universalist church.

Percy L. Nickerson was married, in 1901, to Josephine M. Strout, of Harrington, Maine, who died in September, 1926, daughter of Alexander and Ida (Walls) Strout. Mr. and Mrs. Nickerson are the parents of one daughter, Pauline A., who was born November 7, 1905; she married J. T. Smith, April 16, 1927.

READ NICHOLS COMPANY—The story of this concern is a most interesting one and it is closely associated with the history of Sagadahoc County. In 1876, Read Nichols founded the business under his name for the purpose of dealing in masons' materials and supplies, handling considerable contracting work, as well. The business was incorporated in 1899, with Mr. Nichols as president and D. E. Pierce as treasurer, the latter of whom passed away in 1900. Mr. Nichols passed away in 1923, at the advanced age of one hundred and one years. The firm has since abandoned the contracting trade, applying itself exclusively to the manufacture of brick and the supplying of general building materials.

Charles H. Hooper, who is now the president and treasurer of the concern, became associated with Read Nichols Company well over a quarter of a century ago. He had been timekeeper for the old Goss Iron Works, at Bath, for some years after which he had become interested in various enterprises until, in 1900, he entered the employ of the Read Nichols Company. In 1911, he was made treasurer of the firm and in 1922 was appointed to his present, executive office of president and treasurer. Charles L. Nichols, son of Read Nichols, was president of the company in 1919, 1920, and 1921. Frank M. Harnden was treasurer from 1900 to 1911.

MARK W. SEWALL—The largest and oldest concern in Bath, Sagadahoc County, dealing in coal, wood, ice and petroleum, is the firm operated by Mark W. Sewall, under the firm name of M. W. Sewall & Company. The firm employs more than a score of hands and has a capacity of over 78,000 tons of coal in its bins and motor trucks.

Mark W. Sewall is a native of Bath. He was born in that city, January 26, 1867, the son of Edward and Sarah Elizabeth (Swanton) Sewall, the former a prominent shipbuilder and one of Bath's leading and progressive citizens. Following his early education in the public schools of his native city, Mr. Sewall took a short course in a business college, after which he entered the employ of the Maine Central Railroad as a clerk in the cost department. After a short experience as a clerk, Mr. Sewall journeyed to the West and for two years worked on a cattle ranch. He returned to Bath in 1887 and bought out the coal business of J. F. Hayden, which he has carried on up to the present day under the firm name of M. W. Sewall & Company. Mr. Sewall is the sole

owner of this extensive and flourishing business, to which he ever gives his personal attention. He is a member of the Colonial Club.

In 1890, Mark W. Sewall married Rachel F. Thompson, daughter of Joseph A. Thompson, of Bath. Mr. and Mrs. Sewall are the parents of three children: 1. Donald C., a graduate of Bowdoin College; married Marguerite Mongo; they have one child, a boy. 2. Edward, graduate of Yale University; married Millicent Clifford; has two children, a boy and a girl. 3. Joseph T.; entered Annapolis, but did not graduate; married Gara Dunton. All three of Mr. Sewall's sons served with distinction in the World War.

OWEN J. LEDYARD was born in Bath, Maine, March 6, 1872, a son of James C. and Mary J. (Owen) Ledyard. He was educated in Bath public schools, and entered Bowdoin College with the class of 1895, although he did not graduate.

He entered the clothing business with his brother, James P. Ledyard, in 1894, remaining in the same business until the death of their father, James C. Ledyard, September 26, 1907, when the clothing business was disposed of. He then obtained the agencies for several fire insurance companies, and established an insurance office at No. 93 Front Street, Bath, Maine, at which business he still remains. The holding of the Ledyards in real estate are among the most valuable in the business district in Bath; Owen J. Ledyard being agent for the others.

Always an active sportsman, he is interested particularly in yachting, fishing, gunning, baseball, and polo. He is successful above the average especially in yachting, having won an even one hundred first prize flags for the class in which his yacht, "Swift," was racing, for the most part on the Kennebec River in front of the city of Bath.

Mr. Ledyard served in both branches of city government: Assessor of Taxes, and Recorder of the Lower Court. He is a Knight Templar; a member of the prudential committee of the Central Congregational Church; vice-president of the Old Ladies' Home Association of Bath, Maine, incorporator of the public library and the Bath Savings Institution; vice-president of Bath Rotary Club, and a member of the Men's Club of the Central Church. He is treasurer of the Republican City Committee.

Owen J. Ledyard married Rena Estelle Franks, in 1908, daughter of Alendal and Sophronia (Snowman) Franks.

WILLIAM A. GARNER—One of the leading citizens of Kezar Falls, Maine, is William A. Garner, who, following the illustrious example of his father, has continued as an officer in the Kezar Falls Woolen Company, where he began his business career in association with his father, who was treasurer and agent for the Kezar Falls Woolen Manufacturing Company from the time of its organization, in 1881, until the time of his death, in 1925. It is one of the large textile mills of the State and makes fabrics for women's garments which are sold throughout the nation. One of the characteristics of the organization is the encouragement of athletics among the employees, which has developed a ball team of considerable merit.

William A. Garner was born at Lewiston, Maine, June 9, 1876. He was the son of the late Allen Garner and Mary E. (Jordan) Garner. He was educated in public school, Parsonsfield Seminary and technical

126   MAINE—A HISTORY

schools in Philadelphia, Pennsylvania. His chief business interest has been the manufacture of woolen goods and in this he has held the position of treasurer of one of the large woolen mills in the State, the Kezar Falls Woolen Manufacturing Company. But his interests have by no means been confined to one business, for he is president of the Kezar Falls National Bank; treasurer and manager of the Kezar Falls Water Company; treasurer and manager of the Kezar Falls Light & Power Company, and a director of the A. Huston Company of Portland, Maine. He is a member of the Order of Free and Accepted Masons, the Knights of Pythias, the Kezar Falls Business Men's Association, and of the official board of the Methodist church.

In 1901, William A. Garner married Bertha M. Ridlon of Porter, Maine, daughter of William Ridlon and Ruth (Taylor) Ridlon. They have three children: 1. Ruth E., graduate of Bates College with a Bachelor of Arts degree, and of Katherine Gibbs School. 2. Allen F., student at Hebron Academy. 3. John W., student of Kezar Falls High School.

JOSEPH W. RANDLETTE—In his life in the town of Richmond, Joseph W. Randlette has proven himself not only a business success, but a success in his community life as well. He has always had the best interests of his town at heart and to him are due many of its modern improvements. He begrudges neither time nor effort given in its interest and has been the means of inspiring and guiding the efforts of other citizens in its projects. Born March 9, 1874, in Richmond, he is the son of George B. and Laura J. (Spaulding) Randlette. The father, born in China, Maine, moved to Richmond in 1850, and was for years a well-known clothing merchant of Richmond, later serving as superintendent of the Richmond Water Works. He died in 1908. The mother died in 1923.

Joseph W. Randlette was educated in the public and high schools of Richmond, afterward going to University of Maine, where he graduated in 1896, receiving the degree of Mechanical Engineer in electricity. He began the practice of his profession with the New England Telephone & Telegraph Company, continuing with them until 1908 when, at his father's death, he succeeded him as superintendent and treasurer of the Richmond Water Works. He retains his position there up to the present day, and is also resident agent of the Aetna Life Insurance Company.

The Richmond Water Works was founded in 1886 as a part of the Lewis and Maxey System of water works. In 1900 a reorganization took place and the name of the present executive officers are: B. A. Close, president; John A. Waterman, clerk and auditor; and Joseph W. Randlette, superintendent and treasurer. The company has about twelve miles of mains supplying 1,800 people. In 1915 the plant changed from steam to electricity; in 1918 a purification plant was installed, and in 1921 a new filter system was installed. Much of the success of this company has been due to Mr. Randlette, who has been at the head of many of its most progressive movements.

Mr. Randlette is affiliated with the Free and Accepted Masons, and is a Past Master of Richmond Lodge; and with the Independent Order of Odd Fellows, in all branches of the order, he has passed

through the chairs. He and his family are affiliated with the Universalist church.

In 1900, Joseph W. Randlette married Alice M. Hamilton, daughter of Charles G. and Antoinette (Lewis) Hamilton of Orono, Maine. There is one child, Howard H., born February 18, 1901, who is a commercial engineer with the New England Telephone and Telegraph Company of Boston, Massachusetts.

W. WALLACE GARDNER—Having been for most of his business life connected with the shoe manufacturing industry, W. Wallace Gardner, through his business in Richmond, Maine, has made an outstanding reputation for himself, and, through his fine business ability, has made this business one of international scope. He was born in Boston, Massachusetts, September 13, 1874, the son of W. A. and Ruth S. Gardner. The mother, before her marriage, lived in Eastport, Maine; she died in 1925. The father, W. A. Gardner, of New Jersey, was a veteran of the Civil War, having given signal service in the infantry.

After completing his education in the public schools, W. Wallace Gardner became interested in the shoe industry. He soon established his own business in Beverly, Massachusetts, and encouraged by its rapid growth, moved to Richmond, Maine, where he established his present business in 1912. This business, under the name of the Richmond Shoe Company, of which Mr. Gardner is the president, and C. W. Bell the treasurer, occupies a floor space of 22,000 square feet and employs one hundred men. In the manufacture of ladies' and men's shoes their products are widely known for their quality and style, and the business has had a steady growth, which is a compliment to the ideals and ability of the management. Mr. Gardner gives much credit for the success of the firm to H. V. Patch, one of the founders.

While a resident of Beverly, Mr. Gardner was a member of the Common Council and of the Board of Aldermen. He is a member of the Lodge, Free and Accepted Masons, and has held all the chairs in the Independent Order of Odd Fellows of Richmond. He is a charter member of the Richmond Chamber of Commerce, which he served as secretary for a number of years. Mr. Gardner attends the Methodist church and has given loyal support to its movements.

W. Wallace Gardner married Gertrude Rice, of Salem, Massachusetts, and to their union have been born four children: 1. Leighton E., who married Inza Soule. 2. Marian S., married John Young, and has one child, Florence. 3. Leslie R. 4. Hazel G.

LESLIE F. ROBERTS—Prominently identified with the development of the town of Richmond, Sagadahoc County, Leslie F. Roberts has ever been to the fore in all projects for the advancement of his community. Head of the firm which is operated under his own name, he is the only funeral director in Richmond, and has an imposing suite of funeral parlors and the only motor ambulance service of the section.

Leslie F. Roberts was born in Brockton, Massachusetts, December 9, 1882, the son of Frank H. and Eva M. (Ladd) Roberts, the former a prominent agriculturalist of that section. The father of Mr. Roberts was a native of Wayne, Maine, who died in

1907. His mother was of Abbot, Maine, and died in 1893. Following his preliminary education in the public schools of his community, Mr. Roberts took a course in the high school and then engaged in various occupations until 1920. At that time he acquired the business in Richmond of C. Flagg & Son, manufacturers of coffins and operators of a high-class furniture store. In that business he has continued, with increasing success and well-sustained popularity. The firm's area is eighty by one hundred and ten feet, mostly covered by improvements. Mr. Roberts was one of the founders of the Richmond Chamber of Commerce and has officiated as president and secretary of that body. He is a director of the Richmond Building & Loan Association, of which he is one of the founders. He is a member of the Congregational church, and is affiliated with Richmond Lodge, No. 63, Free and Accepted Masons; the Commandery, Knights Templar; Kora Temple, Ancient Arabic Order Nobles of the Mystic Shrine. He is also a member of the Lodge and Encampment, Independent Order of Odd Fellows.

In 1905, Leslie F. Roberts was married to Winnifred C. Foster, daughter of Arthur and Estella (Griffith) Foster. Mr. and Mrs. Roberts are the parents of two children: 1. Carl F., born November 5, 1906. 2. Sherman F., born November 10, 1910. Mrs. Roberts is a member of the Order of the Eastern Star, of which Mr. Roberts is Past Patron.

VICTOR R. E. CAREY, D. D. S.—President of the Kennebec Valley Dental Association, a member of the Bath Dental Association, and of the Maine State Dental Association, Dr. Victor R. E. Carey occupies a leading position in his profession, not only of his community but also throughout the State. He is recognized among his fellow-practitioners as a most competent exponent of the science of dentistry, and is also a leading figure in community affairs. He was born in Hallowell, June 12, 1891, the son of Philip H. and Elizabeth J. (McDavitt) Carey, the former a native of Ireland, and the latter of Rockland, Knox County. Philip H. Carey, who was in the granite business, died in 1900.

Victor R. E. Carey had his early instruction in the public schools of his community, and then took a course at Hallowell High School. Upon his graduation he entered Fordham College, graduating in 1914, with the degree of Bachelor of Science. He taught school for a time to help finance his education. He then attended the Dental College of Baltimore, Maryland, from which he received the degree of Doctor of Dental Surgery in 1919. In the meantime the United States had entered the World War, and Dr. Carey was assigned to duty with the Dental Corps. As soon as he received his degree of Dental Surgeon Dr. Carey located at Bath, where he commenced the practice of his chosen profession. In 1922, he removed to Richmond, where he rapidly acquired a substantial and ever-increasing practice. He is, of course, active in the local Post of the American Legion, and in 1927, was elected a member of Sagadahoc County Committee, American Legion. He is a member of the Richmond Chamber of Commerce. He is of the Alumni of Fordham College and, in religion is of the Roman Catholic faith, being a member of St. Ambrose Roman Catholic Church.

In 1918, Dr. Carey was married to Mary H. Gray, the daughter of John and Augusta (Ferbach) Gray. Dr. and Mrs. Carey are the parents of one son, John R., born January 10, 1922. Dr. Carey was a football and baseball coach during his college days.

JAMES H. GALLAGHER—One of Richmond's substantial business men and a leader in the community is James H. Gallagher, who has been identified with the business of monument-making practically all of his life. Ever to the fore in all projects for the advancement of his town and its inhabitants, Mr. Gallagher is recognized as one of Richmond's foremost figures and progressive citizens. He was born in Boston, Massachusetts, December 21, 1861, son of Edward and Anne (Fisher) Gallagher, the former a ship-rigger who came from his native town in County Donegal, Ireland, when a young man, meeting and wedding his wife in her native town of Boston. The father was a Civil War veteran, having served with the Ninth Maine Regiment, 1861-1865. Edward Gallagher died in 1886 and his wife in the following year, 1887.

The early education of James H. Gallagher was obtained in the public schools of Boston, after which he started in the monument business with A. W. Wentworth and Company, of that city. With Mr. Wentworth he acquired a thorough knowledge of the business and during his term of employment with him taught several pupils the art of lettering on stone. Wishing to acquire an experience in the cutting of the stone used for monuments, Mr. Gallagher went to Vermont, where he worked for a time in the quarries of that State. In 1898, he started in business for himself at Waterboro, York County. He moved to Richmond in 1916, since which time he has built for himself a very substantial business. He is president of the Richmond Cemetery Association, and president of the Maine State Memorial Craftsmen Association, which office he has held since 1924. He is a charter member of, and active in, the Richmond Chamber of Commerce. Fraternally, he is affiliated with Richmond Lodge, No. 63, Free and Accepted Masons, and of the Consistory. He is also a member of the Independent Order of Odd Fellows, has been through all the chairs of that order and is one of the Grand Lodge of his State. Another fraternity of which he is an active member is the Knights of Pythias. He has never taken any active part in local or State politics.

In 1883, James H. Gallagher was married to Minnie B. White, of Augusta, the daughter of Harry B. and Clarinda F. (Littlefield) White, the former a very well-known bridge-builder, and the latter a descendant of the first white settlers to locate in the town of Belgrade, Kennebec County. Mr. and Mrs. Gallagher are the parents of a daughter, Mabel, married to H. J. Anderson, and mother of two children: 1. Bernard J. 2 Eula, married Mr. Pierce.

HENRY E. HOUDLETTE—Instrumental in the organization of several business groups and associations, Henry E. Houdlette is one of the most valuable members of the community of Richmond. He organized and is past president of the local Chamber of Commerce, and the Loan & Building Association. He also has been prominent in other work and in local club and fraternal life, and is regarded as one of the foremost men of Richmond.

He is the son of Philip Waterman Houdlette, of Dresden, Maine, who died in 1912, and of Mary Elizabeth Houdlette, also of Dresden, who died in 1917. His father was a farmer.

Born in Dresden, Maine, April 8, 1862, Henry E. Houdlette was educated in the public schools and high school. His first venture for himself was in the retail grocery business in Dresden. In 1904 he moved to Richmond, where he conducted a similar business, which he sold in 1910 to Thurlow and Williams. Since that time he has been engaged in the general insurance business in Richmond, and also does an extensive real estate business, and specializes in the care of estates. He organized the Chamber of Commerce and the Loan & Building Association in Richmond. He was the first president of the Chamber of Commerce, and is now secretary of the Richmond Realty Corporation. He is also a director of the Richmond Loan & Building Association. In the way of political office, he has held the town treasurership of Richmond for years. In January, 1906, he was one of the incorporators of Fraternities Health and Accident Association, and has been director and treasurer since the company was founded.

Fraternally, he is associated with the Richmond Lodge, No. 63, Free and Accepted Masons; a member of Kora Temple, Ancient Arabic Order Nobles of the Mystic Shrine; treasurer of both the Blue Lodge and the Chapter; the Independent Order of Odd Fellows, a Past Noble Grand and Past Chief Patriarch, and all the chairs; and of the Knights of Pythias, of which he is a Past Chancellor. He also is a member of the Gardiner Shrine Club and other local clubs, and is an attendant of the Congregational church.

In 1885, Henry E. Houdlette married Julia E. Simpson, of Dresden.

FRANK LESLIE FERREN, M. D.—Among the members of the medical profession in this section of Maine who have established important practice, and who have made for themselves an assured place in their chosen field of service, is Dr. Frank Leslie Ferren, of Westbrook, whose offices are located at No. 741 Main Street. Dr. Ferren is a graduate of the Medical School of Bowdoin College, and is a member of the staff of the Maine General Hospital.

Dr. Frank Leslie Ferren was born in Levant, Maine, October 18, 1874, son of Luther Selwin Ferren, a native of Alton Bay, New Hampshire, who was a farmer and who died in 1913, and of Elmira (Millett) Ferren, a native of Maine, whose death occurred in 1922. Dr. Ferren attended the local public schools, and then became a student in the Eastern States Normal School, Castine, Maine. Later, he became a student in the Medical School at Bowdoin College, from which he was graduated with the class of 1906, receiving at that time the degree of Doctor of Medicine. For a year he was resident physician of Eastern Maine General Hospital. In 1907 he began practice as a physician and surgeon at Westbrook, Maine, and during the twenty years which have passed since that time he has been successfully engaged in general practice here. He is a member of the courtesy staff of the Maine General Hospital, and he is also identified with the Cumberland County Medical Society, the Maine State Medical Society,

the American Medical Association, and Portland Medical Society. His thorough knowledge and his faithfulness have won him the confidence and the sincere regard of his many patients, and he is well known in this section of Cumberland County.

Fraternally, Dr. Ferren is identified with Lodge No. 137, Free and Accepted Masons, in which order he also belongs to the Chapter, Royal Arch Masons; the Council, Royal and Select Masters; St. Albans Commandery, Knights Templar; Kora Temple, Ancient Arabic Order Nobles of the Mystic Shrine. He is also a member of Alpha Kappa Kappa College Fraternity. He is a member of the Portland Medical Club, the Kiwanis Club, and the Portland Country Club, and his religious affiliation is with the Congregational church.

Dr. Frank Leslie Ferren married, May 6, 1907, Susan E. Smart, a native of Hermon, Maine, daughter of A. N. Smart, who was born in New Hampshire, and of Clara (Overlock) Smart, of Hermon, Maine, whose death occurred February 12, 1907. Dr. and Mrs. Ferren have two children: Vinal L., and Doris L. The family home is located at No. 741 Main Street, and Dr. Ferren's offices are in his home.

ALEXANDER G. WILSON—Although born in the Far East, Alexander G. Wilson has given to the country of his adoption a loyal fidelity that has made him a valued citizen. Coming to Westbrook forty years ago he has faithfully served the town in various capacities and made himself most valued in larger circles. He was born April 16, 1860, in East India, a son of William and Julia (Nyhen) Wilson. William Wilson was an officer in the British Army and was in service in the Far East when he died in 1867.

Coming to America as a lad, Alexander G. Wilson was educated in the public schools, finishing with a course at Gray's Business College, Portland. He came to Westbrook in 1887 and became identified with the Warren Paper Mills, which connection was maintained for twenty-three years, and severed only to enable him to become city clerk, in 1910. Mr. Wilson's civic life has been most interesting and valuable. For many years he was a member of the School Board, serving two years as chairman. He was also a member of the Board of Aldermen, and is a past president of that influential body. After serving as city clerk eleven continuous years, Mr. Wilson resigned to carry on the insurance business which he purchased in 1921, and which has rapidly developed under his direction. During these long years of service, Mr. Wilson has held the warm regard and good will of his fellow-citizens to an unusual degree. His splendid executive work during the World War added much to Westbrook's war record.

Mr. Wilson is a member of St. Mary's Roman Catholic Church, and a most loyal fourth-degree Knight of Columbus. Since 1923 he has held the position of State of Maine Secretary in this organization, which speaks eloquently of his ability and interest. He is also a past State Secretary of the Foresters of America.

Alexander G. Wilson married, in 1900, Elizabeth A. Sullivan, of Winchendon, Massachusetts, daughter of Mortimer and Anne (Cassidy) Sullivan. Mr. and Mrs. Wilson are the parents of three children:

1. Georgia M., now Mrs. McLean Adams, and the mother of two daughters. 2. William H., a graduate of the Westbrook High School. 3. Francis A.

HORACE H. TOWLE—Since February, 1917, Horace H. Towle has been engaged in legal practice in Westbrook, Maine, where he has established a reputation for sound knowledge and for skill in dealing with difficult situations. He has been Recorder of the Court at Westbrook since 1920, and has also served as city solicitor. In addition to his professional and public activities, Mr. Towle has been very active in the Kiwanis Club, of which he was one of the organizers, and he is a veteran of the World War. He was born in Portland, Maine, November 20, 1890, and is a son of Horace H., a native of Portland, who was identified with the railroad industry and who died in 1918, and of Amelia H. (Homsted) Towle, a native of Skowhegan, Maine.

Horace H. Towle received his early education in the local public schools and prepared for college in Yarmouth Academy. When his preparatory course was completed he matriculated in the University of Maine, at Orono, from which he was graduated with the class of 1916, receiving the degree of Bachelor of Laws. He was admitted to the bar, and came to Westbrook in March, 1917, where he opened an office for practice. Upon the entrance of the United States into the World War, in April of that year, Mr. Towle promptly assisted in organizing a battery at Westbrook, a company known as Battery B, First Maine Heavy Field Artillery, but he was later transferred to the Fifty-sixth Pioneer Infantry of the American Expeditionary Forces, and was commissioned first lieutenant. Upon his return to civilian life after the close of the war, Mr. Towle returned to Westbrook, where he has since been successfully engaged in practice under his own name. Mr. Towle is a member of the Cumberland County Bar Association, and has made for himself an assured place in his profession. Along with the care of his private practice, Mr. Towle has served as city solicitor, and he has been Recorder of the Westbrook Court since 1920. He is a member and past secretary of the Westbrook Chamber of Commerce, and fraternally, he is identified with the Independent Order of Odd Fellows, and with Temple Lodge, Free and Accepted Masons. Mr. Towle has been a member of the Kiwanis Club since its organization, has served for two years as secretary, and has been one of the most active members in forwarding the interests of the club. He is also a member of the local post of the American Legion, Past Commander of Stephen W. Manchester Post No. 62, and a member of the Officers' Reserve Corps. His religious interest is with the Congregational church, of which he is a member.

Horace H. Towle married, in 1917, Edith Joy, of Hancock, Maine, daughter of Greenleaf and Grace (Wooster) Joy. Mr. Towle has his office at No. 820 Main Street, in Westbrook, and his home is located at No. 66 Strandwater Street, Westbrook.

WADE L. BRIDGHAM—Much service has been given to his community by Wade L. Bridgham, a prominent attorney of Westbrook, Cumberland County. He has served the city of Westbrook as city clerk, city solicitor, and as alderman from Ward Three. Ever to the fore in all plans for the material

Maine—9

advancement of his community, Mr. Bridgham has well merited the respect and esteem accorded him by his fellow-citizens. He was born in Harrison, Cumberland County, August 8, 1889, the son of William C. and Frances (Smith) Bridgham, the former a native of Poland, Androscoggin County, and the latter of Phillips, Franklin County. William C. Bridgham was a prominent citizen of Bridgton, and a veteran of the Civil War, in which conflict he fought with the Twelfth Maine Regiment.

Wade L. Bridgham received his early and preliminary education in the public and high schools of Bridgton. He taught school for five years, two years in the public schools and three in private institutions, after which he entered the University of Maine, graduating in 1917 with the degree of Bachelor of Laws. He was admitted to practice at the bar in 1919, and immediately opened offices at Westbrook. He is a member of the Bar Association of Cumberland County, and is affiliated with Temple Lodge, Free and Accepted Masons; also with the Chapter and Council of that order. He is a member of Phi Alpha Delta Fraternity. He took a course at the Officers' Training School at Plattsburg, but was unable to get overseas into active service. He is secretary of Westbrook Rotary Club, a member of the Willowdale County Club, and of the American Legion. In religion he is a Congregationalist.

On October 18, 1921, Wade L. Bridgham was married to Ruth D. Blake. Mr. and Mrs. Bridgham are the parents of one son, Wade L., Jr., born November 4, 1922.

MARSHALL G. SANBORN—As treasurer of the company founded and carried on by his father until the time of his death in 1913, Marshall G. Sanborn of Steep Falls, Maine, has proven his ability as one of the most progressive business men in this section of the State. His father started a business in 1870 under the name of A. F. Sanborn & Company for the purpose of manufacturing lumber and boxes. As his sons became associated with him in the business and were taking active part in its promotion, in 1902, the business was incorporated as A. F. Sanborn & Sons Company, with A. F. Sanborn as president and Marshall G. Sanborn as treasurer. Upon the death of A. F. Sanborn in 1913, Levi F. Sanborn was made president of the company; Marshall G. Sanborn retained as treasurer, and C. H. Sanborn was made secretary.

Marshall G. Sanborn was born at Limington, Maine, January 28, 1871. His father was Andrew F. Sanborn of Scituate, and his mother was Annie M. (Marshall) Sanborn of Steep Falls, Maine. After receiving a public school education, he went into business with his father and has given all of his time to the interest of promoting the growth of this business. In the beginning, the business was for the purpose of manufacturing lumber and boxes, but as opportunity for other output presented itself, the company began to manufacture barrel heads, staves, and cooperage supplies, and has continued to carry on this business. This department is now the major portion of their operations and the distribution of the product covers the vast territory of the Eastern States. Marshall G. Sanborn is treasurer and member of the Board of trustees of the Steep Falls Public Library; a member of the Blue Lodge, Free and Accepted Masons; of the Knights of Pythias; of the Portland Club;

and of the Baptist church. During the World War he was active in all Liberty Loan drives.

In 1893, Marshall G. Sanborn married Nellie E. Ridlon, of Limington, Maine. Mrs. Sanborn's father was Isaac Ridlon, a native of Hollis, Maine, and her mother was Hannah J. (Hobson) Ridlon of Steep Falls, Maine.

HARRY P. BRIDGE—The largest department store in Bath is also the oldest, having been in existence for a period of seventy-five years. From 1852 to 1923 it was operated under the name of its founder, D. T. Percy, and later D. T. Percy & Sons. Since it was purchased by Mr. Bridge and his partner, Mr. Merrill, it has been conducted under the firm style of the Bridge-Merrill Company, Incorporated, with Mr. Merrill as president and Mr. Bridge as treasurer.

Harry P. Bridge was born in Hampden, Maine, August 1, 1890, son of C. E. and Nellie (Silver) Bridge, both natives of this State. He received his education in the local public schools, including the high school, and at Bowdoin College. He became interested in mercantile business, especially in the management of department stores. He learned the business in the employ of various concerns, and in 1923, in association with J. A. Merrill, purchased the old and reliable business of D. T. Percy & Sons, Incorporated. The name was changed to Bridge-Merrill Company, Incorporated, of which J. A. Merrill is president and Harry P. Bridge treasurer. This department store has been in operation for three-quarters of a century, and is the best-known concern of its kind in the city. It was established by David T. Percy in 1852 and operated under his name until his sons were admitted to partnership, when the name was changed to D. T. Percy & Sons. The business was incorporated in 1906 and continued to be a leader in its field during the years intervening between that date and the time of its purchase by its present owners. The store is located on Front Street in Bath, and it draws its patronage from all parts of the city and from a wide area surrounding. Fraternally, Mr. Bridge is identified with the Benevolent and Protective Order of Elks; with Polar Star Lodge, Free and Accepted Masons; Zeta Psi Fraternity, and his club is the Colonial. He is a member of the Universalist church.

Harry P. Bridge was married, in 1927, to Martha Barker, a native of this city. Mr. and Mrs. Bridge make their home at No. 21 Linden Street, in Bath.

JOHN P. CAREY, Jr., is one of the rising attorneys of Bath, Sagadahoc County, and is recognized among his associates in the legal profession as one of the younger generation of lawyers who will make their mark in the legal annals of the State. He was born in Bath, May 29, 1900, the son of John P. and Mary J. (Kane) Carey, the latter a native of Glasgow, Scotland, who came to the United States at an early age. His father is a landscape gardener. Following his preliminary education in the local schools, John P. Carey, Jr., went to Boston University for a year, and then entered Suffolk Law College, from which he was graduated with the degree of Bachelor of Laws in 1924. He financed his own education, was admitted to the bar in 1923, and commenced the practice of his chosen profession in Boston, in association with the well-known legal firm of Ropes, Gray, Boyden & Perkins. He came to Bath in 1926, since which time he has carried on an independent practice of the law. He is a member of the Massachusetts Bar Association and of the Sagadahoc County Bar Association. Fraternally, he is a member of the local lodge, Benevolent and Protective Order of Elks, and is affiliated with St. Mary's Roman Catholic Church.

E. MOTLEY FULLER, M. D.—There are few physicians in the State of Maine who have attained the prominence which is accorded Dr. E. Motley Fuller, of Bath, Sagadahoc County, whose standing, professionally, fraternally, and socially, is of the highest. Dr. Fuller is past president of his County Medical Association, and an associate member of the New England Association of Roentgenologists. He is also examining physician for the United States Pension Board, is is very prominent in Masonic circles. Dr. Fuller was born in Bath, March 10, 1880, the son of Dr. E. Motley and Elizabeth E. (Gross) Fuller, the former a prominent physician who held the rank of major under the administration of Governor Plaisted. The elder Dr. Fuller and his wife both died in 1913.

Following his early education in the public and high schools of Bath, Dr. E. Motley Fuller took a course at Bowdoin College, from which institution he graduated in 1901 with the degree of Bachelor of Arts. He then attended the Medical School of Maine, from which he received the degree of Doctor of Medicine in 1904. From July, 1904, to July, 1905, he served as interne in the Maine General Hospital, and from September, 1905, to September, 1906, in a similar capacity at the Kensington Hospital for Women. During the World War, Dr. Fuller was a member of the Medical Advisory Board of Sagadahoc County. Past president of the Bath Rotary Club, he is also a member of the Colonial Club and the Bath Medical Club. He ranks high in the Masonic fraternity, being a Past Master of Polar Star Lodge, Free and Accepted Masons; Past Commander of Dunlap Commandery, Knights Templar; a member of St. Bernard Chapter, Royal Arch Masons; Mount Vernon Council, Royal and Select Masters; Maine Consistory, Ancient Accepted Scottish Rite; Kora Temple, Ancient Arabic Order Nobles of the Mystic Shrine, and the Order of the Eastern Star. Dr. Fuller is a valued member of the surgical staff of the Bath City Hospital.

On June 13, 1908, Dr. Fuller was married to Dassie C. Hubbard, of Brunswick, Cumberland County. Dr. and Mrs. Fuller are the parents of two children: 1. E. Motley, Jr., born August 2, 1910. 2. Elizabeth E., born November 11, 1917.

WILLIAM C. CHADBOURNE—Son of the pioneer funeral director in Bath, Sagadahoc County, William C. Chadbourne is, in point of service, the oldest in that line of business in the city. He has been connected with the undertaking business all his life, having started when nineteen years of age with John M. Clark, remaining with him until the latter's death in 1907. Mr. Chadbourne then carried on the business for Mr Clark's estate until 1918, when he obtained control of all other interests and continued it under his own name. His establishment is modern in every respect, equipped with a motor ambulance service and funeral parlors.

William C. Chadbourne was born in Bath, February 11, 1854, the son of William S. and Hannah M. (Dunham) Chadbourne, the former, as stated, the pioneer funeral director of Bath, having taken up that business after some years as a ship's carpenter. Following his early education in the public and high schools of Bath, Mr. Chadbourne entered the business in which he has continued up to the present. In 1888 William C. Chadbourne was married to Ella A. Winslow, the daughter of Thomas and Mary (Berry) Winslow; Mrs. Chadbourne, like her husband, is a native of Bath. Mr. and Mrs. Chadbourne are the parents of one child, Arthur R. Chadbourne, who married Alice Rullman, and they have one child, Arthur R., Jr. Mr. Chadbourne's place of business is at No. 32 Broad Street, Bath, and he has a very charming residence at No. 352 Front Street.

ARTHUR J. DUNTON—Since his admission to the bar in 1898, Arthur J. Dunton has been engaged in general legal practice in Bath, Maine, where his offices are located at No. 72 Front Street. Mr. Dunton has served as mayor of Bath, and in 1927 was serving his third term as County Attorney. He is a graduate of the Law School of Boston University, a director of the First National Bank of Bath, and is identified with several business concerns as a director.

Born in Bath, Maine, July 9, 1871, Arthur J. Dunton is a son of James E. Dunton, of Bath, who was engaged in business as a wholesale and retail grocer, and who died in 1897, and of Angeline (White) Dunton, a native of Bowdoin, Maine, whose death occurred in 1925. Mr. Dunton received his earliest school training in the public schools and then prepared for college in Hebron Academy, from which he was graduated with the class of 1892. After taking a special course in Colby College, he matriculated in the Law School of Boston University, where he finished his course with graduation in 1898, receiving the degree of Bachelor of Laws. He was admitted to the bar that same year, and since has continued in legal practice under his own name. He is a member of the Sagadahoc County Bar Association, the Maine State Bar Association, and the American Bar Association, and stands high in the esteem of his associates. In addition to the cares of his private practice, Mr. Dunton is identified with several financial and business concerns, being a director of the First National Bank of Bath, a director and former president of the Bath Box Company, and a director of other local concerns. He is also active in local public affairs, having served as mayor of Bath, was Judge of the Municipal Court from 1908 to 1912, and in 1927 was serving his third term as County Attorney. During the period of the participation of the United States in the World War he was government Appeal Agent at Bath, and assisted with practically all of the war work in that city. He is well known in fraternal circles, being a member of the Independent Order of Odd Fellows, Knights of Pythias, Delta Kappa Epsilon, and Phi Delta Phi fraternities, and he is also a member of the Colonial Club. His religious affiliation is with the First Baptist Church, which he serves as a member of the board of trustees.

Arthur J. Dunton was married, in 1913, to Madelyn P. Clifford, daughter of Charles W. and Addie (Strout) Clifford, and they have one daughter, Madelyn, who was born March 7, 1919. They make their home at No. 823 High Street, in Bath.

FREDERICK J. HINCKLEY—From boyhood "Captain" Frederick J. Hinckley has been associated with the sea. His first sea voyage was taken when he was fourteen years of age, accompanying his father, who was master of a sailing vessel, and at eighteen he was master of his own vessel. Since his retirement from a sea-faring life in 1897 he has been engaged in the ship brokerage and insurance business, and for more than twenty-four years he has been treasurer of the Popham Beach Steamboat Company, of which he was one of the organizers.

Frederick J. Hinckley was born in Georgetown, Maine, November 25, 1854, and is a son of Ephraim O. Hinckley, who died in 1918, and of Maria (Oliver) Hinckley, both natives of Georgetown, the first-mentioned of whom was a mariner, and one of the best-known captains on the Maine coast, and the last-mentioned of whom died in 1892. Captain Hinckley, as he is generally called in Bath, received his education in the local public schools, and when he was fourteen years of age, went to sea with his father. That first trip was made just at the close of the Civil War, and Captain Hinckley continued to follow the sea for nearly thirty years. He was master of his own vessel at the early age of eighteen years and he has made many long voyages during his time. After his retirement from a sea-faring life, in 1897, he engaged in the ship brokerage business, but gradually turned to the insurance business, in which he is still engaged, carrying fire, marine, liability, and casualty risks. Captain Hinckley has been engaged in this profession under his own name, for a longer period of time than has any other individual in Bath, and he is one of the best-known insurance men in the county and a general favorite. In addition to his activities and interests as an insurance man Captain Hinckley is also one of the organizers and treasurer of the Popham Beach Steamboat Company, which was organized by a group of Maine men in 1903 for the purpose of operating a steamboat to carry the United States mail, freight, and passengers. Of this concern George E. Thompson is president and Captain Frederick J. Hinckley is treasurer. Captain Hinckley is a member of several local organizations, and his religious affiliation is with the Congregational church.

Frederick J. Hinckley was married to Mary E. Holbrook, and they were the parents of one daughter, Blanche E., who married S. H. Rowland, and has two children; Cecil B., and Frederick F. Mrs. Hinckley died in 1925. Captain Hinckley makes his home at No. 47 Lincoln Street, in Bath.

N. GRATZ JACKSON—For nearly twenty years N. Gratz Jackson has been engaged in the embalming and funeral directing business in Bath, where his establishment is located on Front Street. His is the longest established concern of its kind in the city, and he is known as one of the most proficient in his field. Mr. Jackson is also a public-spirited citizen who has done much for the promotion of the interests of Bath, one of his most notable achievements being the organization of the Kennebec Bridge Association, which was instrumental in the building of the bridge across the Kennebec River, at Bath.

As president of that association he has been individually responsible for much of its success.

N. Gratz Jackson was born at Wiscasset, Maine, October 20, 1872, a son of Silas Y. Jackson, a native of Wiscasset, Maine, who was a ship carpenter, and who was connected with the Quartermaster's Department in the Army of the Potomac during the Civil War, whose death occurred in 1915, and of Lucy (Shaw) Jackson, a native of Etna, Maine, who died in 1916. Mr. Jackson attended the local public schools, and then became a student in Bowdoin College. After continuing his studies there for a time, teaching school while obtaining his education, he left college and continued teaching for one year. He then was employed and continued as a salesman until 1908, when he learned the embalming and funeral directing business, in which he has since been engaged. In length of service he is the oldest mortician in Bath, and he is taking care of a very large patronage, drawn from a large section of Sagadahoc County surrounding Bath. In 1912 he was appointed coroner of Sagadahoc County, to succeed J. W. Ballou, and has continued in that office to the present time (1928). He was one of the organizers and a founder of the Kennebec Bridge Association, and as president of this organization was individually responsible for the successful building of the bridge across the Kennebec at Bath. He is still president of that association and in that capacity is doing much for the welfare of the community. During the World War he was county chairman of the "four-minute" speakers and holds his certificate. Fraternally, he is a member of Polar Star Lodge, Free and Accepted Masons, of which he is a Past Master; and he is a Past Eminent Commander of the local Commandery, Knights Templar. He is a past president of the Board of Trade and of the Chamber of Commerce, and is one of those energetic and steadily loyal citizens who can be depended upon to give generous aid to any reasonable project for the promotion of the general welfare. He is especially interested in the development of Bath, and has done much for this community.

N. Gratz Jackson was married, in 1896, to Elizabeth Farnham, of Boston, Massachusetts, daughter of Oscar and Elizabeth (Karcher) Farnham. They are the parents of four children: 1. H. Laton, a graduate of the University of Maine, with the degree of Electrical Engineer; served as a second lieutenant in the World War. 2. Karcher S., a student. 3. Mark A., a student. 4. James M., a student. The family home is located at No. 1 Shaw Street, in Bath.

HENRY W. OWEN, Jr.—For more than six years, Henry W. Owen, Jr., has been serving as postmaster of Bath, Maine, his term in that office having begun soon after his discharge from the United States Army, in November, 1920. At the present time (1928) Mr. Owen is lieutenant-colonel of the Two Hundred and Fortieth Maine National Guard.

Henry W. Owen, Jr., was born in Bath, Maine, April 3, 1875, son of Henry W. and Mary Elizabeth (Brown) Owen, both natives of Bath, and both of whom died in 1924, the first-mentioned having been for many years engaged in the retail grocery business under the name of Owen Brothers, but during the later years of his life engaged as a sign painter. Mr. Owen attended the local public schools, and then

matriculated in Bowdoin College, from which he was graduated with the class of 1896, receiving the degree of Bachelor of Arts. In June, 1897, he became associated with the Bath "Daily Times," and soon became editor of that publication, which position he filled until 1917, when the entrance of the United States into the World War changed his plans. As captain of the Fourth Company, Maine Coast Artillery, in which unit he was commissioned in 1912, he responded to the President's call and served until November 30, 1920, when he was discharged. Upon his return to civilian life he was appointed by President Harding to fill the position of postmaster of Bath, succeeding F. W. Hartnett, and this office he has efficiently filled to the present time (1928). The first postmaster of Bath, under the Federal Government, appointed in 1791, was Dummer Sewall, and Mr. Owen is proving himself a worthy successor of that first incumbent. Since his return from service in the World War, Mr. Owen has re-joined the Two Hundred and Fortieth Coast Artillery, Maine National Guard, his old regiment, in which he ranks as lieutenant-colonel. Fraternally, he is identified with Polar Star Lodge, Free and Accepted Masons, a Past Master; and with the American Legion. His clubs are the Rotary and the Colonial. He attends the Church of the New Jerusalem. Mr. Owen is very familiar with the history of shipbuilding in Bath, and is one of the well-known and highly esteemed citizens of this community.

Henry W. Owen, Jr., was married, in 1914, to Ruth W. Turner, of Bath, Maine, daughter of Edward H. and Carolyn (Ridley) Turner. Mr. and Mrs. Owen are the parents of three children: 1. Edward H., born March 17, 1917. 2. William W., born July 9, 1919. 3. Maurice M., born May 15, 1921. The family home is at No. 35 Park Street, in Bath.

FREDERICK E. DRAKE—One of the oldest insurance concerns in the State of Maine is that of James B. Drake & Sons, established in 1858, of which Frederick E. Drake has been treasurer since the incorporation of the concern in 1912. The offices are located at No. 72 Front Street, Bath. The firm formerly owned a fleet of sailing vessels, but this has been discontinued. Mr. Drake has been prominently identified with various civic organizations, and is known as one of the public-spirited citizens of Bath. His father, James B. Drake, was an able and energetic business man, versatile, and capable of successfully giving attention to more than one line of business enterprise at the same time. In 1858 he established, in Bath, an insurance business under his own name. In 1905 he admitted his two sons, J. Edward, and Frederick E., to partnership, and at this time the name of the concern became James B. Drake & Sons, which name it still retains. Mr. Drake also owned a fleet of sailing vessels, mostly four-masted boats, but this department of his interests was discontinued some years ago. James B. Drake died June 18, 1906, and the business is continued by his sons. He married a Miss Lincoln, of Bath, Maine.

Frederick E. Drake was born in Bath, Maine, December 14, 1874, and after attending the local public schools, became a student at Bowdoin College, from which he was graduated with the class of 1898, receiving the degree of Bachelor of Arts. When his college course was completed he entered his father's business, marine and fire insurance, and in 1905 he and his brother were admitted to partnership under the name of James B. Drake & Sons, under which title the business still continues. In 1912 the concern was incorporated with J. Edward Drake as president, and Frederick E. Drake as treasurer, and the brothers have continued to fill these respective offices to the present time (1928). Mr. Drake is a member of the board of directors of the First National Bank of Bath, and he is active in civic affairs. During the period of the participation of the United States in the World War he served as chairman of the Red Cross organization, and was county director of the War Savings campaign. Fraternally, he is identified with Psi Upsilon College Fraternity, and is well known in club circles, being a member of the Portland Country Club, Brunswick Country Club, and the Colonial Club. He is a member of the Episcopal church, which he serves as warden, and he has many friends in Bath and vicinity.

Frederick E. Drake was married, in 1905, to Henrietta B. Plummer, of Philadelphia, and they are the parents of three children: 1. James B., an undergraduate of Bowdoin College. 2. Frederick E., Jr., student at Holderness, New Hampshire. 3. William P., a student. The family home is at No. 1002 Washington Street, in Bath.

EDWARD W. BRIDGHAM—Since 1911 Edward W. Bridgham has been engaged in general law practice in Bath, Maine. His offices are at No. 53 Front Street, and he has achieved an assured place in his profession. He was born in Bridgton, Maine, October 15, 1881, son of William C. Bridgham, a native of Poland, Maine, formerly engaged in the retail grocery business, but now retired, and a veteran of the Civil War, who served with the Twelfth Regiment Infantry, and of Frances S. (Smith) Bridgham, of Phillips, Maine.

Edward W. Bridgham attended the local public schools, and then prepared for college in Bridgton High School, later matriculating in the University of Maine, at Orono, where he graduated with the class of 1909, receiving at that time the degree of Bachelor of Laws. He continued his studies for another year and, in 1910, received the degree of Master of Laws. He was admitted to the bar, February 17, 1911, and immediately opened offices for general practice. With the exception of five years as a law partner of Judge Keegan, he has been engaged in general practice under his own name to the present time (1928). He is a member of the Sagadahoc County Bar Association, the Maine State Bar Association, and the American Bar Association, and he is highly esteemed among his professional associates. He served as County Attorney of Sagadahoc County, for six years, succeeding Arthur Stetson, and also served as City Solicitor. During the World War he was one of the "four-minute speakers," and was active in all of the home war work of the community. He is a member of Phi Alpha Delta College Fraternity, and is one of the active members of the Rotary Club, being one of the organizers of the local club, which he has served as president.

Edward W. Bridgham was married, in 1911, to Isabel J. Cook, of Jamacia Plain, Massachusetts, and they are the parents of two children: 1. Edward W., Jr., born July 3, 1913. 2. Janet, born April 9, 1919. Mr. and Mrs. Bridgham reside at No. 1074 Washington Street, Bath.

WILBUR F. COUSENS—Having been in turn a salesman, teacher, merchant, legislator, and one of the most public-spirited citizens of Ogunquit, since 1879, Wilbur F. Cousens retired from active participation in business in 1921. He is a director of a trust company, and a devout member of the Methodist church, finding time to sit in session with the church board and to act as its treasurer; moreover, during his life he has written a considerable number of articles on historical subjects, and in this occupation he continues to contribute his thought and research. Mr. Cousens is one of the most universally loved and respected citizens of Wells and York County, and is now (1928) in his eighty-first year.

Wilbur F. Cousens was born July 31, 1848, at Kennebunkport, Maine, son of Enoch Cousens, of Kennebunkport, born in 1818, died in 1904, and of Betsy B. (Lowe) Cousens, of Lyman, Maine, who died in 1861. Enoch Cousens was prominent in all circles, political, commercial and educational in Kennebunkport. During his long and interesting life he served the community as merchant, postmaster, one of the leading men of the locality, for several terms as a member of the Maine State Legislature, and also served as collector of customs, weigher, gauger and inspector of customs.

Wilbur F. Cousens received his preliminary education in the public schools of Kennebunkport, later attending the Seminary at Kents Hill, Maine. He then matriculated at Wesleyan University, Middletown, Connecticut, where he studied for four years with the class of 1872, and was one of six members of this class who attended the fifty-fifth anniversary in 1927. Mr. Cousens' first entrance into the business world was in connection with the boot and shoe trade in Boston, Massachusetts, and after a number of years' experience he became a traveling salesman for the firm of D. C. Griswold and Company, of this city, with whom he remained for some time. After severing his connection with this firm he became associated as traveling salesman with the house of Locke, Twitchell & Company of Portland, Maine. For one year he was principal of and an instructor in the Columbia Falls High School; then, in 1879, Mr. Cousens came to Ogunquit, and established himself in business, dealing in goods at retail, expanding the items handled until the business became that of a general store. After more than forty years as store proprietor, he sold out.

In the course of his residence in Wells he has held all save a few of the public offices in the town, and has distinguished himself through the adroitness with which he has handled affairs as Supervisor of Schools, town treasurer, and also treasurer of the Village of Ogunquit Corporation for several years until by his request a successor was chosen, and on the various boards and committees created to deal with the exigencies of the World War, on which he was a conscientious member, serving, despite the advancing years, in a manner to evoke praise from his associates. Like his father a Democrat, and a hearty subscriber to the principles for which the party stands, Mr. Cousens was sent to the Maine State Legislature when the Australian ballot was adopted by the State, he being a strong supporter of this method of voting. He was also instrumental in getting a bill passed by the Legislature to incorporate the Village of Ogunquit, and in making satisfactory arrangements with

134 MAINE—A HISTORY

the town of Wells concerning the amount of money to be retained by Ogunquit for schools, roads, and other village improvements. Mr. Cousens has filled all of his offices ably and faithfully, earning a reputation for prudence, foresight, and business acumen. In his fraternal affiliations, Mr. Cousens is a member of the Free and Accepted Masons, a member of the Royal Arch Masons, and of Kora Temple, Ancient Arabic Order Nobles of the Mystic Shrine, also of the Independent Order of Odd Fellows, and Grange, Patrons of Husbandry. His religious fellowship is with the Methodist church.

Wilbur F. Cousens married (first) Clarette S. Godine, now deceased; he married (second) Amanda M. Thompson, also deceased; and (third) Mary M. Maxwell.

PHILIP I. JONES—For more than three decades Philip I. Jones has been identified with the insurance business in Portland, and since 1896 he has been a member of E. C. Jones & Company, Incorporated, which has its offices on Exchange Street in Portland. Mr. Jones is well known among insurance men in this State, and has served as president of the Maine Association of Insurance Agents, and of the Cumberland County Board of Fire Underwriters.

Philip I. Jones was born in Portland, Maine, June 3, 1858, son of Benjamin W. and Cordelia (Ingraham) Jones, both natives of Maine, and both deceased, the first-mentioned of whom was a sea captain for many years, but in later life was port warden. Mr. Jones received his education in the public schools and then became associated with Hayes & Douglass, crockery merchants, with whom he remained for twenty-one years. At the end of that time he engaged in business for himself under the name of the Westwood Paper Company, but two years later he sold out and became associated with his brother, E. C. Jones, in the insurance business. The brothers were co-partners, the concern having been established in 1896 by E. C. Jones as a general insurance business operated under his own name. In 1898 Philip I. Jones entered the business, and the name was then changed to that of E. C. Jones & Company, and so has continued. In January, 1925, the concern was incorporated, with Philip I. Jones as president and treasurer; R. M. Pennell, vice-president; and Lawrence C. Jones, assistant secretary. This concern is one of the older insurance companies of Portland, and is one of the best known and most progressive. Mr. Jones has always been active in the general insurance organizations, such as the Maine Association of Insurance Agents, which he has served as president; and the Cumberland County Board of Fire Underwriters, of which also he has been chief executive. He is a member of the Benevolent and Protective Order of Elks, a member of the Society of governors of the Society of Colonial Wars, and a member of the Sons of the American Revolution. He is also a member of the Portland Yacht Club; Portland Athletic Association; the Bramhall League, of which he was president; and the Maine Historical Society. His religious membership is with the Episcopal church, and he is treasurer of the Cathedral Chapter of St. Luke.

Philip I. Jones was married, in 1879, to Mabel Churchill, of Portland, Maine, daughter of James M. and Harriet (Hoole) Churchill. Mr. Jones died in 1907. Mr. and Mrs. Jones had two children: Law-

rence C., and Helen Creighton. The family home is located at No. 216 Vaughan Street, in Portland.

ELMER H. HOBBS—A business man of considerable ability, who is widely known throughout Maine, is Elmer H. Hobbs. He is the owner of a monument business which is located at Sanford, and of an automobile service station at Waterboro, where he lives. Mr. Hobbs has held local office several times, and has taken an active part in the social life of his community. He is the son of Dr. Frank H. Hobbs, and of Elizabeth R. (Hamilton) Hobbs, both of Waterboro. Dr. Hobbs was a physician, graduated from Bowdoin College in 1900 with the degree of Doctor of Medicine, who practiced his profession at Waterboro until his death in 1914. He held town offices on several occasions, and was one of the most important and most respected men of Waterboro. Mrs. Hobbs is the president of the York County Young Women's Christian Association, and very prominent in Maine society.

Elmer H. Hobbs was born on September 28, 1891, at Waterboro, Maine. He attended the local public schools and later entered Westbrook High School. In 1910 he was graduated from Bowdoin College with the degree of Bachelor of Arts. When he completed his education he entered the monument business at Sanford in association with James H. Gallagher, and this arrangement continued until 1916 when the partnership was dissolved. Since that time Mr. Hobbs has continued the business under his own name. In 1923 he established an automobile service station at Waterboro, with a storage capacity of twenty cars, and under his personal direction, this venture has also proved very successful.

Mr. Hobbs has served as treasurer and tax collector for the town of Waterboro. He is a director of the York County Farmers' Union. He is affiliated, fraternally, with the Free and Accepted Masons, and is also a member of the Grange, Patrons of Husbandry, of which he is Past Master. He attends the local Baptist church, and is a member of the board of trustees of that institution.

In 1912, Elmer H. Hobbs married Natalie N. Knight, of Maine, the daughter of Levi and Alice (Clough) Knight. Mr. and Mrs. Hobbs are the parents of several children: 1. Elizabeth R., born October 13, 1913. 2. Frank H., born April 15, 1916. 3. Priscilla N., born June 6, 1922. 4. Rebecca A., born September 18, 1926.

EDWIN A. PALMER—Having gone into the insurance business in Bar Mills in 1890 and having continued since that time in the same line of business, Edwin A. Palmer is the oldest man in point of service in the insurance business in Bar Mills. Before he engaged in the insurance business, he was in the lumber industry, as was his father before him.

The son of Benjamin J. Palmer, of Buxton, Maine, who died in 1879, and of Mary A. (Goodwin) Palmer, of Buxton, who died in 1905, Edwin A. Palmer has lived practically all his life in the ancestral homestead which has been occupied by several generations of his ancestors. He was born in Buxton, Maine, on July 28, 1859, and attended the public schools and Westbrook Academy. For some time after he completed his education he was engaged in the lumber business, but since 1890 has been identified continuously with the insurance business. During the

World War he was a member of the Draft Board. Active in the affairs of the Improved Order of Red Men, he is a Past Sachem and a Past District Deputy of that order. He belongs to the Congregational church.

THOMAS J. DENENCOUR—With an unwearying application which is of signal value to any career and an ideal of service which has won for him the loyal patronage of his customers, Thomas J. Denencour has made for himself a place in the business world of Saco, Maine, which is proof of a fine ability. He has not faltered under disappointment but has, rather, felt it an incentive to further effort. Born April 27, 1885, at Westville, New Hampshire, he is a son of Gregoire and Marie (Labrie) Denencour of the Province of Quebec. His father passed way in 1924 and the mother in 1908. The father worked at various trades.

Educated in the public and high schools of Exeter, New Hampshire, Thomas J. Denencour entered a shoe factory and was engaged in the cutting of shoes at Haverhill, Massachusetts, and other places until 1917, at which time he bought the laundry business of M. R. Hinckley of Saco, Maine. After carrying on the business, himself, for a few years, he took as a partner, H. A. Mondor. The firm having been originally founded by Mr. Herbert Dame, who conducted it for many years, they continued the business under the name of the Dame's Laundry. They now employ upward of fifteen people and their operations cover a radius of fifteen miles. The most modern machinery is used and the most up-to-date methods including a motor truck delivery. In addition to their regular laundry business, they also do rug cleaning. During his ten years in the laundry business, Mr. Denencour has brought his firm to a very creditable standard of success and proven himself one of the substantial business men of the town. Mr. Denencour is affiliated with the Knights of Columbus and is a member of the local club of Saco. He and his family are members of the Most Holy Trinity Roman Catholic Church.

In 1918, Thomas J. Denencour married Jennie Bienvenue, of Haverhill, Massachusetts. Of this union there was one child, Paul J.

PHILLIPS ABBOTT, having practiced his profession in the city of New York for upwards of fifty-three years, retired therefrom in 1923 and established himself in the village of Yarmouth, Maine, but such men seldom sever all ties with their old associations. Mr. Abbott still retains an interest in business life, and has financial interests in certain directions.

Born October 20, 1849, at Norwich, Connecticut, he is the grandson of Jacob Abbott and the son of Charles E. and Mary Elizabeth (Spaulding) Abbott. His father, a native of Maine, was a clergyman, who however, later in life retired from the ministry and carried on a successful school for the teaching of classical subjects. His mother, the daughter of Dr. Spaulding, a missionary, was born in the Island of Ceylon, India.

Educated by private tutors, Mr. Abbott took up the study of law and was for fifty-three years a patent and trademark attorney in the city of New York. He made of his profession an outstanding success, retiring from active work in 1923. He then went to Yarmouth, Maine, to a beautiful home which

he owns there, and where he has passed his time ever since.

Mr. Abbott is one of the principal stockholders of the Sportoccassin Shoe Manufacturing Company, now the Abbott Shoe Comany, specialists in the manufacture of sporting and athletic footwear.

In 1868, Phillips Abbott married Jennie L. Beardsley of Clinton, New York, the daughter of Dr. Henry L. and Susan (Ladd) Beardsley; of this marriage there is one child, Donald B., a graduate of Amherst, who is married to Dorothy C. Smith of Berkley, Maryland.

WILLIAM H. ROWE—One of the leading figures in the business life of Yarmouth, William H. Rowe, who has been a druggist in this town ever since he left Colby College, has held from time to time many important public offices, and in the course of his public duties he has rendered valuable services to Yarmouth and the community upon more than one occasion. There is scarcely any branch of public activity or work in which Mr. Rowe is not interested, as he has taken part at different periods of his career in library and educational work. He has written two books, entitled "Shipbuilding Days in Yarmouth," and "Yarmouth Personages," and is now preparing a third, an historical work, "Ancient North Yarmouth and Yarmouth—A History—1635-1928." He is especially interested in historical and genealogical matters.

Mr. Rowe was born in Yarmouth, March 6, 1882, the son of a farmer, Charles C. Rowe, of New Gloucester, Maine, and of Mary J. (Hutchinson) Rowe, of Brunswick, Maine. As a boy he attended the public schools and the high school of Yarmouth, then studied at Colby College. When he left college, he engaged almost immediately in the drug business, and he has the distinction of being not only a careful druggist but the oldest in his line in Yarmouth. Always having been a public-spirited man, he has held many offices, having been a member of the School Board for thirteen years; chairman of the School Board, eight years; town clerk, ten years; and a member of the Maine House of Representatives for two terms, 1917-1918 and 1919-1920. During his service in the Legislature he was chairman of the library and insane hospital committees and secretary of the Cumberland County delegation. Active in political matters, he is affiliated with the Republican party and a member of the Town and County Republican committees. He is president of the board of trustees of the Merrill Memorial Library, and is a trustee and president of North Yarmouth Academy. He is a member of the standing committee of the Maine Historical Society and a member of the New England Historic-Genealogical Society, and is especially interested in the history of Yarmouth and the vicinity. He is a member of the Baptist church, in which he is a deacon During the World War he was local chairman of the "four-minute" speakers, and was chairman of the Registration Board. He is kept busy much of the time by his work with fraternal organizations, being a member of the Free and Accepted Masons, in which order he holds the thirty-second degree and is a Past Master and Past High Priest. In college he was a member of the Phi Delta Phi Fraternity.

In 1908, William H. Rowe married Anna M. Dubois, of Nashua, New Hampshire, the daughter of Charles B. and Mary A. (MacLauchlan) Dubois.

FELIX T. SHELTRA—One of the most progressive business men of Biddeford, Maine, and a man who is active in the affairs of the city, is Felix T. Sheltra, who conducts a real estate business under his own name. Although the real estate business was for him a gradual development, there is no doubt that he has transferred more property than any other man in Biddeford and Saco. His interest in civic matters is demonstrated by the fact that he has been several times councilman representing the Fifth Ward. Born in Gorham, Maine, on September 20, 1885, the son of Uldrick Sheltra, of New York City, New York, who died in 1908, and Elisa Plourde, of New Jersey, who is still living, Felix T. Sheltra was educated in the public schools and high school. His father was an electrical engineer. Mr. Sheltra conducted a barber shop in Biddeford, Maine, until 1919, although ever since 1910 he had been devoting increasing activity to the real estate business. As the latter business grew, he spent more and more time in it, until he finally sold his barber shop, in 1919. At the present time he is doing development, loans, and brokerage work, and both he and his community are justly proud of his achievement. In addition to his activity in municipal affairs and his other accomplishments, Mr. Sheltra is a director of the local Kiwanis Club. He is a charter member of the Chamber of Commerce and on its Steering Committee, and one of the guarantors. He enjoys hunting and fishing. He and his family are communicants in Saint Joseph's Church.

Felix T. Sheltra was married, in 1906, to Aurore Tourville, of Hancock, Michigan. His wife is the daughter of Thomas Tourville and Lea (Pruno) Tourville. Mr. and Mrs. Sheltra are the parents of three children: 1. Royal N., born December 10, 1910. 2. Paul E., born September 7, 1919. 3. Carl F., born May 31, 1922.

ANTON HAHN—The first man in Maine to distribute sausage, both wholesale and retail, in a large way, is Anton Hahn, who learned his trade in Germany, from which country he came to the United states in 1911. He has made a careful study of his business, much to the satisfaction of all those who deal with him, with the result that his is the largest private concern of its kind in Saco and the State of Maine. He is the son of Conrad Hahn, who died in 1912, and of Lissette (Keller) Hahn, who died in 1908, both of Germany. His father was engaged practically all his life in farming. Anton Hahn attended the schools of Germany, and spent three years there in university study. He was born on January 10, 1884. When he first came to the United States, in 1911, he settled in Portland, where he was employed in 1912 at the trade which he had learned in Germany—sausage manufacturing. Later in that year he started in business for himself in Saco, where he has continued since under his own name. His activities, aside from his attention to his business, are indicated by his membership in the Knights of Columbus, fourth degree; the Kiwanis Club; and the Saco Business Men's Association. He belongs to Most Holy Trinity Roman Catholic Church.

In 1912, Anton Hahn married Sarah Burns, of England. By this marriage there are two children: 1. Florence L., born October 30, 1914. 2. Barbara M., born May 7, 1917.

SAMUEL OSHER—Devoted to the business which by his own energy and resourcefulness he has built up, Samuel Osher is head of a hardware company which is beyond a doubt the largest firm of its kind, not only in Biddeford, but in York County, Maine. He is earning the reward of service which he has given to his community, and is very proud of the business which he has developed. He was born in Russia, the son of Elisha Osher and Ida (Ginserg) Osher. His father, a builder and contractor, died in 1902.

Samuel Osher went to the public schools, both in Russia and in the United States, leaving the country of his birth in 1907 to settle in the city of Biddeford. He was eighteen years old when he came to the United States, having been born on March 10, 1889. For his first few years in the United States he was employed in the Saco-Lowell shops, at Biddeford, where he remained until 1912. In that year he engaged in business for himself at No. 13 Alfred Street, doing a small hardware business. Later he bought out the business of George A. Anton, and erected his present place of business exactly opposite his original location. In addition to hardware, Mr. Osher handles paints, oils, plumbing and many other items. His business quarters occupy five thousand square feet of space. He is rated as one of the largest taxpayers in Biddeford. A real estate operator for eight years, he is owner of many properties on Main Street, in Biddeford; also in Portland, on prominent streets.

Samuel Osher participates in the social life of the community, being a member of clubs and fraternal orders. He is affiliated with the Independent Order of Odd Fellows and with the Fraternal Order of Eagles. His religious association is with the Jewish synagogue.

In 1917, Samuel Osher married Leah Lazarowitch, also a Russian, daughter of Mendell and Gertrude Lazarowitch. He is the father of three children: 1. Elisha, born August 2, 1918. 2. William, born September 20, 1921. 3. Hyman, born January 11, 1924.

JOSEPH A. CORDEAU—One of the most public-spirited men of his community and president of a shoe manufacturing company which is the sole representative of that industry in Saco, Maine, is Joseph A. Cordeau. Although he has been identified with the shoe industry practically all his life, he is known as well in Saco for his activities in the affairs of the city as for the product which he manufactures and distributes nationally. Mr. Cordeau, who is president of the Trail Moc Shoe Company, was born July 29, 1878, at Marlborough, Massachusetts, the son of Peter and Edith (Gandreau) Cordeau, both of the Province of Quebec. His father who was connected with the shoe industry, died in 1891, and his mother died three years later.

After Joseph A. Cordeau attended the public schools, he became engaged in the shoe industry, with which he has been identified throughout his business career. He was vice-president of the Saco Shoe Manufacturing Company before the organization of the Trail Moc Shoe Company in 1923, since which time he has been president of the latter firm. The Trail Moc Shoe Company established for the purpose of manufacturing various types of shoes and moccasins, employs one hundred and twenty-five persons in the output of a product which is sold in all parts of the country. This company, the only one of its kind in Saco, utilizes 12,000 square feet of floor space, and its capacity production is 1,200 pairs of shoes per day. Mr. Cordeau is president of the firm; E. N. Richardson, treasurer; and George W. Blin, assistant treasurer.

Mr. Cordeau's interest in public affairs is shown by the fact that he is past chairman of the board of directors of the Biddeford-Saco Kiwanis Club, and a member of the Chamber of Commerce. Not only is he active in both of these organizations, but he is a supporter of whatever is designed to promote civic development. He is a Past Chancellor of the Knights of Pythias. Religiously he is identified with the Congregational church, of which he is a member. He has served in various branches of the Army.

In 1895, Joseph A. Cordeau married Ellen Connor, and they had one child, Pearl G. Cordeau, who became the wife of George T. Woodward; by that marriage there was born a child, Patricia L.

WILLIAM T. POWELL—Soldier and journalist, William T. Powell went into the theatrical business as manager of the Bath Opera House, at Bath; and through his efficiency has increased the patronage of the cinema to a degree never before recorded in its history. Native of Canada, Mr. Powell has given practically the whole of his business and professional career to the United States, and in Bath, Rumford Falls, Maine; Burlington, Vermont, and Keeseville, New York, enjoys many cordial friendships. In Bath he is rapidly becoming a prominent figure.

William T. Powell was born March 16, 1898, at Prescott, Prescott County, Province of Ontario, Canada, son of William E. Powell, of Prescott, and Elizabeth (Mills) Powell, of Ogdensburg, New York, who died in 1922. William E. Powell was an officer in the Governor-General's Foot Guards of Canada, and was engaged in railroading, but William T. Powell, having completed his early education in the public schools and a number of the requirements for a bachelor's degree in the University of Vermont, developed an intense interest in newspaper work. His first journalistic connection was with the Burlington, Vermont, "Free Press," where he learned, as a "cub," the manner in which news copy is written. Following this introduction to the newspaper profession he went to Keeseville, New York, as editor of a weekly; then to the editorial direction of a paper at Rumford Falls, Maine. Thus in 1926, when he became manager of the Opera House, at Bath, he was able, through his long experience at judging human interest in print, to attract large audiences to see his selections on the silver screen. Whether or not Mr. Powell has discovered that the human interest attached to the screen is similar to that of the public prints, or he has adapted the one to the other most skillfully, the fact remains that the Opera House cinema has enjoyed a considerable popularity. The showhouse was erected in 1913, with Hiram Abrams as proprietor, and has, since the founding date, been under the control of the Bath Theaters Corporation. Only the best of available first-run pictures are shown, and the seating capacity, approximately 1,000, is often insufficient to meet the demands of patrons. In 1924, fire destroyed the building, but its reconstruction, with additional features of more modern invention, was effected without loss of time. After the war broke out in 1914, Mr. Powell enlisted in the

Second Canadian Heavy Battery, in the service of the Canadian Expeditionary Forces, and was subsequently transferred to the Royal Flying Corps. When he was discharged, in July, 1921, he held the rank of first lieutenant. Mr. Powell professes no political adherence. He is a member of the Rotary Club, and of the Episcopal church.

William T. Powell married, in 1921, Mary M. Best, of Vermont; and to this union have been born three children: Phyllis, Beth, William T., Jr.

ARTHUR L. CORRIVEAU—As an optometrist, Arthur L. Corriveau has contributed a valuable service to Biddeford and the surrounding community. He began his practice in 1922 and has continued with it since. He is the son of Joseph and Aglae (Rancourt) Corriveau, both natives of the Province of Quebec, who came to the United States when young, and were married at Waterville, Maine.

Arthur L. Corriveau was born June 20, 1889, at Waterville, Maine. He attended the Skowhegan public schools, and later went to the Rochester School of Optometry, from which he was graduated in the class of 1922. Immediately after he had finished his professional school work he began his practice as an optometrist in Biddeford, Maine.

He is a member of the Knights of Columbus and of the Fraternal Order of Eagles, and of several French clubs, including Saint Jean de Baptiste. He and his family are members of St. Joseph's Roman Catholic Church.

In 1925, Arthur L. Corriveau married Agnes Doyle, of Biddeford, the daughter of John and Isabelle (Haswell) Doyle. He has built up a fine practice, and already is known as a man whose services have redounded to the benefit of the community.

WALTER S. MITCHELL—A man who has taken at all times an active interest in the civic affairs of Saco is Walter S. Mitchell, who is sole owner of one of the oldest insurance companies in York County. His business ability was a considerable aid to the city when, although he had never sought political office, he was chosen as city treasurer of Saco, and handled the city's funds for a number of years. He was born in Saco on December 23, 1864, the son of Stephen S. Mitchell, of Kennebunk, Maine, who died in 1897, and of Sarah Kimball, of Waterford, Maine, who died in 1916. His father was a druggist.

In his early life Walter S. Mitchell attended the public schools and high school. At the beginning of his business career he became associated with the mills of the Pepperell Manufacturing Company. He became superintendent of the mills. Later he went to Massachusetts, where he became agent for one of the textile mills in 1924. Then he bought out the G. A. Carter Insurance Company, which at that time was owned by Harry S. Sawyer, and since then has continued in the insurance business, retaining the name of the G. A. Carter Insurance Company, one of the oldest insurance companies in York County.

In addition to his activity in the business and civic life of Saco, Mr. Mitchell is president of the local Kiwanis Club, and a director of Webber Hospital. At the time of the war he was local food administrator and a member of various boards. He holds the thirty-second degree in the Masonic Order, and he is active in the Unitarian church, of whose executive committee he is a member.

Walter S. Mitchell married, in 1901, Lottie A.

Mitchell, and by this marriage is the father of three children: 1. Persis E., born July 10, 1902; graduated from Pratt Institute, and married John Q. Craigin, by which marriage there was one child, Jean E. Craigin. 2. Nelson P., born February 21, 1904; is a graduate of Carnegie Institute of Technology. 3. Alfred B., born August 9, 1905, a graduate of the University of Maine.

CHARLES KENNARD FENDERSON—One of his city's best-known automobile dealers and a man who is active in the business life of Biddeford is Charles Kennard Fenderson, manager of the York County Motor Company, which distributes the Nash car. He is also identified with banking interests. He was born in Saco, on February 13, 1886, the son of J. H. and Ada (Kennard) Fenderson, both of Saco. His father died in 1920.

After he had attended the Saco public schools and Thornton Academy, Charles K. Fenderson became associated in business with his father, who was a jeweler in Saco. After he had followed this business for a number of years, he moved to the Middle West, where he lived for a time. Returning East, he became a director of the Portland Nash Company, of Portland, then helped to organize the York County Motor Company in October, 1926. The motor company of which he has been manager since its organization, was originally located in Saco, but later moved to No. 269 Main Street, Biddeford, where it is now located. The officers of this company are: E. E. Chadburn, president; F. E. Barnfield, vice-president; and L. B. Fenderson, treasurer.

Charles Kennard Fenderson is a member of the Portland Club, the Willowdale Country Club and several other clubs. Fraternally, he is a member of the Saco Lodge, Free and Accepted Masons; and Kora Temple, Ancient Arabic Order Nobles of the Mystic Shrine. When the war was raging, he did work with the Young Men's Christian Association in France.

Mr. Fenderson married, in 1912, Bertha King, of Portland. He is the father of one child, Charles Warren Fenderson.

FREDERIC E. BANFIELD—Practically the entire career of Frederic E. Banfield has been identified with the concern known as the Saco-Lowell Shops, of which he is now (1928) agent of the Biddeford plant, located in Biddeford, Maine. Mr. Banfield is a graduate of Brown University, from which institution he holds two degrees, and he is officially connected with two other important and prosperous business concerns.

Frederic E. Banfield was born in Newton, Massachusetts, June 21, 1885, son of Frederic E. Banfield, a native of Middlesex County, Massachusetts, a prominent Boston dentist, who died in 1925, and of Gertrude E. (Danforth) Banfield. He received his early and preparatory education in the public schools of his birthplace, and then matriculated in Brown University, from which he was graduated with the class of 1906, receiving at that time the degree of Bachelor of Philosophy. Later, he did post-graduate work in Brown University and received the degree of Mechanical Engineer. Upon the completion of his post-graduate course he became identified with the Saco-Lowell Shops, and his connection with that concern has been continuous to the present time. He was promoted through various positions to that of assistant agent, and then, in 1923, was made agent of

the Biddeford plant, succeeding E. E. Blake. The Saco-Lowell Shops manufacture textile machinery, and is the largest concern of its kind in the United States. Mr. Banfield is filling his position as agent of the Biddeford plant in a manner which leaves nothing to be desired. He is one of the able and conscientious men who add to natural ability the faculty of making the responsibilities of a position in the employ of others as fully theirs as if they were the owners of the entire plant, but yet are adept in the art of working successfully with other people. He is a member of the board of directors of the N. L. Birge Company, of Bristol, Connecticut, and vice-president of the York County Motor Corporation, of which he was one of the organizers. His sound judgment and his keen insight make him a very desirable member of any group planning to found a "going concern," and his opinion is often sought by those of his associates who have recognized his special ability. He is a member of the American Society of Mechanical Engineers and the Biddeford Chamber of Commerce, and is one of the public-spirited men of the town, although he makes his home in Saco. Fraternally, he is identified with the Phi Sigma Kappa College Fraternity and the honorary Sigma Xi Scientific Society, and he is a member of the Rotary Club and of the Biddeford and Saco Country Club. His religious membership is with the Congregational church. Mr. Banfield is an ex-president of the Brown Alumni Association of the State of Maine.

Frederic E. Banfield was married (first) to Marguerite Birge of Bristol, Connecticut; (second) to Alberta Hoefman of Worcester, Massachusetts. To the first marriage one child was born, Richard W.

DR. ARTHUR LEON JONES, since the beginning of his practice as a physician, has won for himself a signal place in the professional life of Old Orchard Beach and the surrounding country. The son of Amory H. Jones and Clara A. (Young) Jones, Dr. Jones was born at Farmington, New Hampshire, June 19, 1875. His mother was a native of Rochester, New Hampshire.

Arthur Leon Jones is a graduate of Dartmouth, of the class of 1896, at that time receiving the degree of Bachelor of Arts. In 1908 he received the degree of Doctor of Medicine, from the Maine Medical School, at Brunswick, Maine. He then began his practice in Old Orchard, where the years have brought him substantial success. He is a member of the York County and Maine State Medical societies, and the American Medical Association. He was secretary of the York County Medical Society for twelve years and is a past president. His fraternal affiliations are with the Free and Accepted Masons, in the Lodge and Chapter; the Independent Order of Odd Fellows, a Past Grand; and with the Improved Order of Red Men, of which he is Keeper of Wampum.

In a public capacity Dr. Jones has been Superintendent of Public Schools, trustee of the Public Library, selectman, assessor, and treasurer. He was president of the Board of Trade for six years and has always been very active in the progressive work being done in Old Orchard. He has been town treasurer for seven years. He and his family attend the Methodist church of which he is a trustee.

He is an examiner for the Prudential, Travellers, and Mutual Life Insurance companies. During the World War he was on the Medical Advisory Board.

He is also a director of the Old Orchard (Maine) Publicity Bureau. In 1913, Dr. Jones married Cora L. Milliken of Old Orchard, Maine, daughter of B. Frank and Mary (Jameson) Milliken. Children of this union: 1. Leon F., born March 30, 1915. 2. Roger M., born August 30, 1916.

FRED I. LUCE—Beginning his career as a merchant, Fred I. Luce has of recent years given all of his time to the political affairs of Old Orchard Beach. He is considered the best versed man in public affairs in this part of the country and has been signally honored in his public life. The son of Rev. Israel and Alice E. (Ostrim) Luce, he was born November 29, 1863. The father passed away in 1908 while the mother survives at the age of eighty-eight years. Both were residents of New York State. Rev. Israel Luce was a prominent Methodist Episcopal minister of the Maine Conference. He was one of the founders of the Orchard Beach Camp Meeting Association, and was serving as president when he died, at which time he was succeeded in that office by his son, Fred. I. Luce.

Mr. Luce began his business career at the age of sixteen, after a grade school education. His first duties were as clerk in the post office and general store, after which he was employed as a merchant of drygoods and men's furnishings and continued in this enterprise for fifteen years. He then entered the retail grocery business in which he continued for seven years. Since that time he has devoted all of his energies and talents to the many public offices which he has held. These include selectman, of which body he has been chairman; town treasurer; tax collector; deputy sheriff; treasurer of the County of York, for six years; and, at the present time town clerk; and executive secretary of the Board of Trade. He is affiliated with the Knights of Pythias, of which he is Past Chancellor and Keeper of the Records and Seals, and is president of the board of trustees of the Methodist church.

Fred I. Luce married, in 1885, Katie L. Ramsdell of Lunenburg, Vermont, daughter of Alanson K. Ramsdell. There are two children: 1. Edith E., married George E. Kirkpatrick; mother of Alan F. Kirkpatrick. 2. Israel Gilbert, a student at the University of Maine.

HAROLD W. BISHOP—The active career of Harold W. Bishop has been identified with the insurance business, and he is the owner of one of the longest established general insurance concerns in Boothbay Harbor. He has held nearly all the offices in the gift of the town, served in the State Legislature in 1922, and at the present time (1928) is serving his second term as representative. His work in the building of the Public Library was a valuable contribution to the life of the town of Boothbay Harbor, and his fellow-townsmen fully appreciate the energy and devotion with which he served in the office of treasurer and as a member of the board of trustees of the Library Association.

Harold W. Bishop was born in Eastport, Maine, September 24, 1884, son of Willard F., who was engaged in business as a sardine packer throughout his active career, but is now retired, and of Mary E. (Glenham) Bishop, a native of Digby, Nova Scotia, both of

whom are living (1928). Mr. Bishop received a good education in the public schools of Eastport and Boothbay Harbor, including the high school, and then became identified with the insurance business. Practically his entire career has been associated with that line of business in Boothbay Harbor. His concern is one of the oldest in the community, and under his own name he is taking care of a large general line of insurance. He is a member of the board of trustees of the Boothbay Savings Bank, and he is one of the most active in local public affairs. He has served as a member of the Board of Selectmen, as town treasurer, and as chairman of the Water Board for the past twelve years. In fact, there are very few local offices which he has not filled, and he has extended his activity to the affairs of the State. He was elected a representative to the State Legislature in 1922, and at the present time (1928) he is serving his second term in the Legislature. One of the most important of Mr. Bishop's contributions to the community was the work which he did in securing the building of the Boothbay Harbor Public Library. He served as treasurer of the Library Association and as a member of the board of trustees, and was indefatigable in his labors in this connection. His fellow-townsmen recognize the fact that he was one of the most important factors in putting through this project. During the period of the participation of the United States in the World War, Mr. Bishop served as a member of the legal advisory board for this district and he holds a certificate. He is a member of the Boothbay Harbor Chamber of Commerce, which he helped to organize, and he is also its treasurer. Fraternally, he is identified with Seaside Lodge, Free and Accepted Masons; also with the Royal Arch Masons; and with the Royal and Select Masters. He is also a member of the Knights of Pythias, of which he is a Past Chancellor. His religious affiliation is with the Congregational church.

Harold W. Bishop was married, in 1907, to Vesta Hodgdon, of Boothbay Harbor, Maine, daughter of Roscoe and Elisa L. (Tibbetts) Hodgdon.

GEORGE WALTER WEEKS, M. D.—For almost forty years Dr. George Walter Weeks has carried on the practice of medicine in the town of Cornish, Maine. His familiar figure is well known to many who have grown to manhood and womanhood in this vicinity and to them it is not unusual to see the "Doctor" going forth with fishing outfit to spend some hours of recreation in this restful, silent sport which has been the chief play of many philosophers, poets and statesmen. He is much beloved by the families where for years he has responded to their calls, night or day, to give relief from pain. He is the son of Ivory B. Weeks of Cornish, Maine, and Mary A. (Moulton) Weeks of Parsonsfield, Maine. Both parents are deceased.

George Walter Weeks was born on a farm at Cornish, Maine, September 1, 1861. He was educated in public schools, Limerick Academy, and Maine Medical College, where he graduated with the degree of Doctor of Medicine in the class of 1888. His whole life has been spent in his profession and while he has done much general practice, he has a specialty of the treatment of rheumatism. For three years he was Superintendent of Schools at Limington, Maine. In politics he is a Democrat. He is a member of the Free and Accepted Masons. On January 1, 1889, George Walter Weeks married Estelle F. Libby of Limington, Maine, who died in 1895. They had two children: 1. DeForest, who is a practicing physician of Portland, Maine; married Addie Wagner of Portland, and has three children. 2. Marguerite, a graduate of Brewster Free Academy; also a graduate of the School of Nurses of the Maine General Hospital; she is a registered nurse, and makes her home with her father.

ELLSWORTH W. SAWYER—Since 1918, Ellsworth W. Sawyer has served as postmaster of Kezar Falls, Maine. Mr. Sawyer is an energetic and capable man of considerable experience, and he has discharged the duties connected with his position very efficiently. He has been active in the social and fraternal life of the town. His father, Freeman W. Sawyer, of Porter, Maine, is a farmer and a member of the Three-Quarter Century Club. His mother, who was Sarah Towle, also of Porter, is now deceased. Ellsworth W. Sawyer was born August 5, 1877, at Porter, Maine. He entered the local public schools and later attended Parsonsfield Seminary. When he completed his education he taught school for six years, and at the end of that time went into the mercantile business at Lynn, Massachusetts. Returning to Porter, he was employed for seven years as overseer of finishing in the local woolen mills. The next three years he spent as a traveling salesman, and in 1918 he was appointed postmaster of Kezar Falls, a position which he has held since. Politically, Mr. Sawyer is a member of the Republican party, and he served for ten years as town clerk, and for fifteen years as a member of the local school committee. He is affiliated, fraternally, with the Free and Accepted Masons, having taken the degrees of the Chapter in this organization. He is also a member of the Knights of Pythias, and the Modern Woodmen of America. He and his family attend the Methodist Episcopal church. On January 3, 1898, Ellsworth W. Sawyer married Mabel S. Stanley, of Porter, the daughter of Samuel and Julia Stanley. Mr. and Mrs. Sawyer are the parents of seven children: 1. Clarence, who married Harriet Bibber, of South Harpswell. 2. Beatrice, married Roy S. Pierce, of Gray. 3. Frances, married Russell Cutting, of Porter. 4. Allison. 5. Robert. 6. Evelyn. 7. Samuel. The last three of these children attend the local schools. Mr. and Mrs. Pierce are the parents of four children: Evelyn, Elaine, Lawrence, and Robert.

SAMUEL GUY SAWYER, M. D.—In 1900, Dr. Samuel Guy Sawyer began the practice of medicine at Cornish, Maine. Pleasant, energetic and obviously capable, he quickly won the confidence of the community where he has since remained. Apart from his very successful practice, Dr. Sawyer is a partner in a local garage firm, and for several years he served as Superintendent of Schools for Cornish. He has taken an active part in the fraternal life of the town. His father, William H. Sawyer, is a farmer of Lim-

ington, Maine, who has held numerous town offices and represented his community in the State Legislature. His mother, who was Ida T. Bragdon, was also born at Limington. Samuel Guy Sawyer was born December 1, 1871, at Limington, Maine. He entered the local public schools and later attended Limington Academy. In 1900 he was graduated from Bowdoin College with the degree of Doctor of Medicine. Soon afterwards he settled in Cornish to begin a general practice and he has remained there since. About 1918 he became a member of a local garage firm, associated with Mr. Jameson and Mr. Foss, a partnership which has proved to be very successful. Politically, Dr. Sawyer is a member of the Republican party, and for several years he served as Superintendent of Schools in Cornish. He is affiliated, fraternally, with Greenleaf Lodge, No. 117, Free and Accepted Masons, in which organization he has taken the degrees of the Chapter, Council and Commandery. He is a member of the Kora Temple, Ancient Arabic Order Nobles of the Mystic Shrine. He is also a member of the American Medical Association, York County Medical Association, and the Maine Medical Association. He attends the local Congregational church. On November 30, 1905, Samuel Guy Sawyer married Ellen Louise Pierce of Boston. They are the parents of children: 1. Kendrick B., now attending Hebron Academy. 2. Norman P., also at Hebron Academy. 3. Donald G., who attends the local high school. 4. S. Phillip, now in grade school.

SAUL S. HAYES—In the days when famous actors and actresses toured the country presenting the best dramas of the day, before the centralization of the drama in a few important cities, Saul S. Hayes traveled over the entire world as a member of the Hallen and Hayes vaudeville team, appearing with national and international celebrities on the variety stage. The advent of the motion picture as an important force in everyday life caused him to retire from the legitimate stage to enter the motion picture business where his experience gained in the theatre would assist him in giving the people of Boothbay Harbor the very best attractions to be obtained. Mr. Hayes was born in Russia, September 15, 1884, son of Jacob Soroker, who died in 1908, and Anna Soroker, who is living. Jacob Soroker was a merchant in Russia, and from him his son inherits the business ability which has contributed to his successful ventures in theatrical enterprises. Having used the name Hayes in his profession, Saul Hayes later adopted this cognomen legally, and since has been known as Saul S. Hayes. He received his education in the public schools of Boston, Massachusetts, and upon the completion of his formal education entered theatrical work, continuing in that profession until 1914, when he took advantage of the opportunity to become manager of the Opera House at Boothbay Harbor, which position he has held up to the present time. He also organized the Hayes Amusement Corporation in 1927, becoming treasurer, and building the New Strand Theatre seating 1200 people, and to operate during the summer with high-class pictures with proper presentations. This new theatre is one of the most modern along the coast.

The Opera House has a seating capacity of six hundred and fifty, and these two theatres owe their financial and artistic success to Mr. Hayes' courteous and efficient management and his sincere efforts to give the people the best entertainment possible. During the World War, Mr. Hayes took an active part in all patriotic work and assisted the various drives by giving them publicity through his theatre. Mr. Hayes is popular in fraternal circles, being a member of five Masonic bodies, among them the Blue Lodge, Free and Accepted Masons, and Kora Temple, Ancient Arabic Order Nobles of the Mystic Shrine. He is also a member of the Knights of Pythias. In religion, he is affiliated with the Jewish faith.

Saul S. Hayes married, in 1913, Lucy Asher, and their children are: 1. Alfred, born April 5, 1915. 2. Louise, born May 18, 1919.

HARRY P. JAMESON—Well known as a business man of Cornish, Harry P. Jameson is equally prominent in social and civic affairs. For many years he was a dealer in general merchandise, very successfully directing the business which he owned. More recently he has been a partner is a local garage firm, and he also serves as postmaster of Cornish. He has always taken an active part in the social and fraternal life of the town. He is the son of John F. Jameson, a merchant, prominent in the public affairs of Cornish, and of Eliza (Bryan) Jameson, both now deceased.

Harry P. Jameson was born March 19, 1865, at Cornish, Maine. He entered the local public schools and later attended the New Hampton Institute in New Hampshire. In 1883 he began work for his father in the latter's store in Cornish, and this arrangement continued until his father's death in 1902. At that time Mr. Jameson took over the business and continued alone until 1918, when he sold out to the Cornish Farmer's Union. Soon afterward he joined Mr. Foss and Dr. Sawyer in establishing a garage at Cornish, in which he has since retained an interest. With the exception of one period of about six years, Mr. Jameson has been postmaster of Cornish since 1902.

By political inclination Mr. Jameson is a member of the Republican party. He was a member of the Board of Selectmen of Cornish for three years. He is affiliated, fraternally, with the Free and Accepted Masons, having taken the degrees of the Chapter, Council and Commandery, in this organization. He and his family attend the local Congregational church.

On October 25, 1892, at Cornish, Harry P. Jameson married Rose Wedgewood, born at Limington, the daughter of Dr. John T. Wedgewood, of Cornish, and Ruth (Topliff) Wedgewood, of Freedom, New Hampshire. Mrs. Jameson, who is a very talented musician, is the organist of the Congregational church, and is very prominent in local social circles. Mr. and Mrs. Jameson are the parents of two children: 1. Ruth, married Harry D. Watson, a professor at the University of Maine. 2. Fannie O. B., who lives with her parents.

WILLIAM ROY COPP—For many years William Roy Copp has been prominent in the life and affairs of Cornish, Maine. He has been treasurer and manager of the mercantile firm of I. N. Brackett Company, Incorporated, since 1900, and is also the owner of a clothing manufacturing company under his own name, W. R. Copp, which business he directs. Mr. Copp has held local offices several times, has represented his community in the Maine State Legislature, and has served with distinction on many boards and associations, both civic and benevolent in nature. He takes an active part in the fraternal life of Cornish. His father, Daniel P. Copp, of Jackson, New Hampshire, was a carpenter and mill man. His mother, who before her marriage was Sarah Ann Davis, was born in Pennsylvania.

William Roy Copp was born at Richmond, Indiana County, Pennsylvania. Moving to Maine with his family he attended the local public schools at Cornish, working evenings and Saturdays in the mercantile store of J. F. Jameson. When he had completed his education, he found employment as a clerk in the store of Preston Durgin, where he remained for more than ten years. During this period he served as town clerk and treasurer for about seven years. In 1892 he went into the store of his father-in-law, I. N. Brackett, as a clerk, and this arrangement continued until the death of Mr. Brackett. At this time the firm was incorporated under the name of I. N. Brackett Company, Incorporated, with Mr. Copp, his wife, and the son of Mr. Brackett serving as officers. At a later time Mr. Copp bought out Mr. Brackett's stock, but continued the business under the same firm name. Finally, about 1918, Mr. Copp's son, Lincoln B. Copp, came into the firm, and soon afterwards became president, a position he now holds. About 1915 Mr. Copp took over the business formerly known as the Cornish Clothing Company, which he now personally owns and conducts. In this business he employs thirty-five people and manufactures pants exclusively for the J. B. Pearson Company, of Boston. Mr. Copp is also treasurer and one of the organizers of the Cornish Water Company. He is treasurer of the local Cemetery Association, and president of the Cornish Agricultural Association.

Politically, Mr. Copp is a member of the Republican party. In 1905 he was a member of the State Legislature, serving on the Educational Committee. During the World War he served as president of the Liberty Loan Drives for the Cornish district. He was also a "four-minute" speaker, and acted as treasurer of the local branch of the American Red Cross, a position which he still holds. For many years he was active as a member of the Cornish School Board. He is affiliated, fraternally, with the Free and Accepted Masons, having been Master of the Blue Lodge for several terms, and in this organization he is a Knight Templar and a Royal Arch Mason, holding the thirty-second degree. He was the first Patron of the Eastern Star in Cornish. Mr. Copp is also a member of the Independent Order of Odd Fellows, and he and his family attend the Congregational church of Cornish, of which he is treasurer and a trustee.

In 1891, at Cornish, William R. Copp married Sadie Brackett, the daughter of Isaac N. and Eliza (Stone) Brackett, of Cornish. Mrs. Copp is a Past President of the "99" Literary Club, and a Past Matron in the Order of the Eastern Star. Mr. and Mrs. William Roy Copp are the parents of one child, Lincoln B., born April 22, 1895. He attended the local public and high schools, and later entered the University of Maine where he was graduated in 1917 with the degree of Bachelor of Arts. During the World War, Lincoln B. Copp served as a second lieutenant in the Three Hundred and Fourth Infantry, United States Army. Since 1922 he has been president of the I. N. Brackett Company, Incorporated. He is affiliated with the Free and Accepted Masons, and is a Past Master of his Blue Lodge, also a thirty-second degree Mason. His political preference is with the Republican party, and he is a member of the Sigma Nu Fraternity, while his religious affiliation is with the Congregational church. On December 6, 1917, Lincoln B. Copp married Irva Farnham, of Sheridan, Wyoming, and they are the parents of two children: Alice Brackett, and Virginia Farnham.

FRANK L. STROUT—Since 1915, Frank L. Strout has been treasurer and general manager of the Strout Company, Incorporated, general merchants of Steep Falls, Maine. He is a man of considerable ability and wide merchandising experience, and under his direction this firm has become one of the most successful in its section of the State. He is the son of Thomas Strout, a minister of Raymond, Maine, and of Rachel (Hicks) Strout, who was born at Gorham, Maine. Both of his parents are now deceased.

Frank L. Strout was born October 1, 1867, at Gorham, Maine. He attended the public schools of Gorham and after completing his education began work in a clothing store. He remained there for only a short time, and then for three years he sold nursery stock. In 1895 he became a clerk in the store of Cousins and Tucker, general merchants of Steep Falls, and he has been connected with this store since that time. In 1915 he bought out his former employers, and formed the Strout Company, Incorporated, in association with A. E. Nickerson of Portland, who is president of the company, and R. L. Stevens, also of Portland, who acts as secretary. Mr. Strout is treasurer and manager. This company, besides handling all kinds of general merchandise, is the only firm dealing in grain between Standish and Cornish, in which latter town they have recently opened a branch store. Mr. Strout also conducts a small insurance business.

By political inclination he is a member of the Republican party. He is a former member of the local Board of Selectmen and also acts as a Justice of the Peace. He is affiliated, fraternally, with the Knights of Pythias, a Past Chancellor therein; and is a member of the Portland Club. He is a member of the local Baptist church.

On October 14, 1886, Frank L. Strout married Stella M. Lombard of Baldwin, Maine. Mr. and Mrs. Strout are the parents of six children: 1. Roy M., married Lillian Jose. 2. Iza B., married Ralph Harrington. 3. Mary P., married William M. Burnell. 4. Raymond, married Lena Stanley. 5. Rachel, married Simon W. Moulton. 6. Arthur Gordon, died December, 1925, in his sixteenth year. Raymond and Rachel are twins.

WILLIS E. SANBORN, who was born April 17, 1860, and who died April 23, 1925, was one of the most prominent and most respected men of Springvale, Maine. For over forty years he was actively engaged in business there, and at the time of his death was senior partner in the very successful insurance firm of W. E. Sanborn and Son, and a director of many other local companies. Though Mr. Sanborn's position in the business world was high, it was no higher than his place in the esteem and affection of his fellow-townsmen. He took an active part in all phases of the community life, and was actively interested in its welfare. His father, Ephraim Sanborn, born in Baldwin, Maine, was a farmer and a mill owner, and engaged in these occupations until his death. His mother, who was Sarah Walker, is also deceased.

Willis E. Sanborn was born at Denmark, Maine. He entered the public schools of North Bridgton, and later attended Gray's Business College at Portland. In 1882 he came to Springvale in company with his father and they established a lumber plant at the "Province Mill," now the location of a Sears-Roebuck Shoe Company factory, which they ran for a number of years. In 1897 Mr. Sanborn was elected a member of the Maine House of Representatives, where he served on the committee of Mercantile Affairs and Insurance. On the expiration of his term he acted for five years as postmaster of Springvale, after which he entered the insurance and real estate business, at first alone and later in partnership with his son, Kenneth S. Sanborn, under the firm name of W. E. Sanborn & Son. After the conflagration which swept the village in 1905, Mr. Sanborn adjusted over two hundred separate claims for fire losses without delay and to the entire satisfaction of both the claimants and his companies.

Mr. Sanborn was an incorporator of the Bridgton Water Company, and a director of the Bridgton Water and Light Company. At the time of his death he was a director and treasurer of the Springvale Shoe Shop Company, a director of the Springvale Realty Company, a trustee of the Nasson Institute, and for many years had been a member of the Town Committee. He was affiliated, fraternally, with Springvale Lodge, Free and Accepted Masons; White Rose Chapter, Royal Arch Masons, of Sanford; the Commandery, Knights Templar; and Kora Temple, Ancient Arabic Order Nobles of the Mystic Shrine, of Lewiston. He was also a member of the Springvale Camp of the Modern Woodmen of America. He attended the Free Baptist Church of Springvale.

On August 8, 1888, Willis E. Sanborn married Lizzie A. Shaw, of Sanford, the daughter of Joseph Shaw, who was a farmer, and of Sarah (Hurd) Shaw, both of Sanford. Mr. and Mrs. Sanborn became the parents of two children: 1. Kenneth, who married Mildred Littlefield. 2. Helen, who married Harland S. Rowe. Mr. and Mrs. Kenneth Sanborn are the parents of two children, Joyce and Glenna. Mr. and Mrs. Rowe have one child, Richard S. Mrs. Sanborn is president of the Springvale Woman's Club, and a member of the Order of the Eastern Star.

FRED A. TARBOX—The name and the attainments of Fred A. Tarbox have received their due recognition throughout this State and in other States of the Union, in most important lines of police investigation and allied matters in relation to detective agency work, both under his own supervision at Biddeford, and as general and special investigator in Maine, and in Washington. Faithfully and successfully, Mr. Tarbox devoted his talents and energies to such matters having specifically to do with the safety of the public, and his keen and vigorous intellect, his quick perceptions, and his basic understanding of the law, as well, combined to secure for him his foremost place among the investigators of his generation.

Fred A. Tarbox was born May 7, 1861, at Biddeford, a son of Abijah and Sophronia (Pitcher) Tarbox, of Biddeford, Abijah Tarbox having been a city marshal of that city, and deputy sheriff of York County. After he had attended the public schools in Biddeford, Mr. Tarbox studied law in the office of Benjamin Hamilton, in that city, but before he had completed his studies he accepted the opportunity then offered him to enter upon those lines of duty that were to develop into his life-work, in 1888 receiving his appointment as chief of the police department of Biddeford. In 1892 he removed to Fitchburg, Massachusetts, where he accepted a similar appointment, where he continued as police chief to 1896; and from that date to 1904 he was chief of the department at Newton, Massachusetts.

In 1904, Mr. Tarbox accepted a position with the Pinkerton Agency, and he was sent to Scotland Yard, England, to make a study of the finger-print system of identification. After three years with this famous detective headquarters, he returned to Biddeford, and opened his own office in this city, where he organized the Tarbox Detective Agency, which he conducted with success to 1917, when he received his appointment as special investigator for the State of Maine, with his headquarters in the office of the State Attorney-General, in Augusta, so continuing to the time of his death, in 1922. The following tribute was from the pen of a friend of Mr. Tarbox:

Along the line of duty, the lives of most people are looked upon as matter of fact careers. This is not gainsaying that the late Fred A. Tarbox, long in public life and a well remembered figure in this community for many years, did not live also a matter of fact existence, but it was punctuated, by reason of the nature of his profession, with some adventure, not wholly unmixed with danger.

Mr. Tarbox made many friends in central Maine while maintaining his official office at the State Capitol. It can further be said that unlike many others occupying a similar position, he even made friends among the criminal classes. By the adoption of conservative methods, he did not develop among this element such antagonism as might be expected.

Mr. Tarbox, in his several police administrative positions, both in Maine and Massachusetts, came in contact with offenders of all kinds, and came to know, in a way the psychology of criminology. Mr. Tarbox was a United States Deputy Marshal, as was his father, Abijah Tarbox.

Mr. Tarbox has also acted as Senate Police, in Washington, District of Columbia, under Senator Frye; and for several years he was fish and game warden of York County. A Free and Accepted Ma-

son, and associated with all the intermediate bodies of Masonry, he had attained the thirty-second degree in the Ancient Accepted Scottish Rite. Fred A. Tarbox married (first) Mrs. George Hardy, of Biddeford, who died in July, 1898. He married (second), in 1899, Alice Butler, of Newton, Massachusetts; divorced. Mr. Tarbox married (third), September 11, 1911, Cora E. Whitten, of Biddeford.

JESSE A. RANDALL, M. D.—As the oldest practicing physician in Old Orchard Beach and as one who has always held to the best progressive ideals of his profession, Dr. Jesse A. Randall is an outstanding figure in the life of that town. He was born at Limington, Maine, the son of Noah and Susan (Huntress) Randall. The father was an enterprising farmer who died in 1904. The mother was a resident of Hiram, Maine, and passed away in 1887.

Jesse A. Randall took his degree as Doctor of Medicine at Bowdoin College in 1888, later going to Boston for post-graduate work in the Boston City Hospital. His many years of fine achievement have shown the wisdom of his choice of a profession, for he has proven himself one of the ablest practitioners in that part of the country. He is a member of the York County and Maine State Medical societies and of the American Medical Association. Beginning his practice in West Newfield, Maine, in 1888, he later went to Waterboro, in 1901, and thence to his present home in Old Orchard Beach, in 1893. Dr. Randall is affiliated with the Knights of Pythias and is Past Chancellor of that organization. He is also a member of the Independent Order of Odd Fellows.

In 1892, Jesse A. Randall married Lillian M. (Libby) Small, daughter of Butler and Sarah E. Libby of East Cambridge, Massachusetts, but from a Maine family. Mr. Libby was a Civil War veteran, having held the rank of captain. He died in 1917. Mrs. Libby was Sarah E. Brooks of New Hampshire, who came to Maine when an infant. Mr. and Mrs. Randall have one son: Horace B. Randall, born July 12, 1897; married Bertha Trefry, and is the father of Robert R.

JOHN HALEY—A descendant of one of Maine's first settlers, the late John Haley was an authority on the history of his State and country, a writer of considerable literary ability and at the time of his death, in 1921, was one of the most admired and respected residents of the city of Saco. His long career as a public-spirited and patriotic citizen was enhanced by his upright character and great strength of principle, and he acquired the esteem of all by his perseverance and fortitude under adverse conditions. He was practically self-educated, being an avid reader and informing himself in the various branches of knowledge, being particularly attracted to history, and so well versed was he in Civil War history that former officers at times referred questions to him for his decision. Mr. Haley was a typical example of that fine type of American of humble birth who made his life a record of dignity and honor.

Mr. Haley was born in Biddeford, March 3, 1840, son of Nathan Gilpatric Haley and Mehitable Barnes (Lee) Haley. The first family ancestor in this country was Thomas Haley, who was here in 1653. The direct Colonial ancestors were among the founders of Biddeford, and several of them served in the Colonial wars and held office in the earlier period of the city's history. Nathan Gilpatric Haley was engaged in the trade of ship carpenter for many years, and his father, John Haley, participated in the War of 1812 serving in the United States Navy, and in one of his many engagements, was captured and sent as a prisoner to Dartmoor. William Haley, father of John Haley, was a soldier in the Revolutionary War, serving two enlistments, in 1778 and in 1780.

John Haley was educated in local public schools, and for a short time attended high school. As a boy, he worked in the York Mills at Saco, from 1854 to 1862. Filled with patriotism and a desire to serve his country, he enlisted in Company I, Seventeenth Maine Volunteers on August 18, 1862, as a private, later being promoted to the rank of corporal. He saw active service in twenty-six battles as follows: Fredericksburg, Chancellorsville, Gettysburg, Wapping Heights, Auburn Mills, Kelly's Ford, Locust Grove, Mine Run, Wilderness, Spottsylvania, Po River, Fredericksburg Turnpike, North Anna, Cold Harbor, Totopotomy Creek, Hare House, Hatcher's Run (2), Deep Bottom (2), and Peeble's Farm. He served all through the siege of Petersburg; he never had a furlough; never was wounded, although he suffered from sunstroke and other disabilities; but was at the front at all times despite sickness, never being made prisoner. Mustered out of service in the summer of 1865, he received letters of praise and commendation from various officers for his distinguished record. Returning to his home, he worked in the machine shop in Biddeford until 1866, when he was appointed station agent at Saco for the Boston & Maine Railroad, Eastern division. In this capacity he was successfully occupied until 1876, when he resigned to become bookkeeper and paymaster for the Saco & Biddeford Gas Company at Biddeford. He filled the duties of this responsible position satisfactorily until 1890, acquiring a splendid reputation for his efficiency and thorough attention to details, and then for a short period of time, was a reporter for the Biddeford "Daily Times" of Biddeford. From 1892, until the time of his death, April 7, 1921, he capably filled the post of librarian at the Dyer Library of Saco, an office which required intellectual ability and literary experience. Always interested in the advancement of community welfare and progress, he took an active part in civic affairs, and served for three years on the School Board of this city, was city historian for the last four years of his life and was selected as a member of the committee to choose the soldiers' monument which was a gift to the city. In fraternal organizations he did not take an active part, having belonged to the Golden Cross from which he later resigned, and it was not until late in life that he became a member of the Grand Army of

the Republic. Always modest regarding his liabilities, he preferred the recreation afforded by his literary pursuits, and consequently belonged to few clubs, although he was, in his early years, prominent in the Maine Library Association, and at one time was a member of the Maine Historical Society. During his career, he wrote much for publication, on political subjects earlier in life, and later on Civil War and local history. He was possessed of a keen, analytical mind, and unusual musical and artistic talents which, however, the circumstances of his life prevented his furthering. He printed by hand three copies of a book of some 400,000 words, based on his war diaries and letters, written clearly and simply, and at times, reaching considerable emotional intensity and beauty.

John Haley married, December 16, 1874, in Saco, Abbie A. Batchelder, daughter of Captain Stephen Prescott and Hannah (Dearing) Batchelder, and to this union were born two children: 1. Adelaide, born October 16, 1875. 2. George Edwin, born July 27, 1877. In his early life, Mr. Haley was a member of the Baptist church, which was the religion of his wife and his mother, but later in life he became a Universalist.

JUDGE REUEL ROBINSON—In the death of Judge Reuel Robinson, on Sunday, June 19, 1927, the State of Maine lost one of its most distinguished and versatile citizens, a jurist, orator, educator, and author, whose place is secure in the esteem and affection of the citizens of Camden, the city of his adoption, and of which he was then serving his second term as postmaster.

Born in Palmyra, Maine, September 25, 1858, son of Daniel and Susan (Bruce) Robinson, Reuel Robinson entered the Maine Central Institute, and while preparing for college there, began teaching at the age of seventeen. In 1877 he was graduated from the Pittsfield Institute, and four years later received his Bachelor of Arts degree from Bates College, where he was class orator, and in 1884, was awarded the degree of Master of Arts. Called to Camden as principal of the High School, his life thereafter was bound up in the civic and industrial development of the community. The law appealed to him more strongly than the teaching profession, and he began his studies in the office of the late Thaddeus R. Simonton. He was admitted to the bar in 1888, but his immediate election as Judge of Probate prevented him from practicing for the next four years. In 1892 he opened an office and until his appointment as postmaster in 1922, devoted himself to his profession. His leadership was valued in the Republican party, and in 1916 he was delegate to the Chicago convention that nominated Charles E. Hughes for the presidency, and he was regularly a delegate to the county, district and State conventions before the primary law made these unnecessary. He was a director and assistant treasurer of the Camden Woolen Company, and for many years was its president and treasurer. He was one of the organizers of the Penobscot Woolen Company, of which he was a director and treasurer. He served several years as president of the Camden Yacht

Building and Railway Company, and was always one of its directors. He was greatly in demand as a public speaker, and in 1907 delivered the centennial address in his native town, and spoke on a similar occasion at Newport, in 1914. For three years he was editor of the Camden "Herald," and was a prolific contributor to its columns after his retirement. He was a member of the Maine Historical Society. The "History of Camden and Rockport," and the "History of Amity Lodge" are works of his pen, of permanent value.

In 1884, Judge Robinson was admitted to Amity Lodge, Free and Accepted Masons; he served as Secretary of Keystone Chapter and as High Priest. He was Eminent Commander of Camden Commandery, Knights Templar, a member of Hiram Council, Royal and Select Masters, and belonged to Kora Temple, Ancient Arabic Order Nobles of the Mystic Shrine. He was also a member of the Independent Order of Odd Fellows, was Grand Master of the Grand Lodge of Maine, 1893-94, and for the two years following, a representative to the Sovereign Grand Lodge. He was also a member of the Camden Business Men's Association, a trustee of the Public Library, a member of the Megunticook Golf Club and Camden Yacht Club.

On December 22, 1885, Judge Robinson married Blanche G. Atkins, of Camden, who survives him.

No more sympathetic estimate of Judge Robinson is on record than that of General Herbert M. Lord, director of the United States Bureau of the Budget, who said: "When I entered Bates College, Judge Robinson was a student there. He was very highly regarded in the college for his high character and ability. I learned then to have a high respect for him, and years after, his coming to Camden enabled me to renew our college acquaintance. I knew him intimately and had a most affectionate regard for him. His life was always characterized by high ideals, and he was in every way a good citizen. He was a steadfast friend, and whenever he served in an official capacity, he has given to the duties the best that was in him, which was a great deal."

ROBERT EVERETT OWEN—One of the young men in the educational circles of Maine, who truly expresses the qualities of the born educator, is Robert Everett Owen, of Vassalboro, who has been principal of Oak Grove Seminary for a number of years.

Mr. Owen was born in Gardiner, May 19, 1892, son of Charles E. and Nellie E. (Nason) Owen. He was educated at Coburn Classical Institute and Colby College, from which he received his degree of Bachelor of Science, after which he attended Harvard University, acquiring the degree of Master of Education. From 1914 to 1918, Mr. Owen served as principal of Erskine Academy, winning the confidence and respect of his pupils, and establishing a reputation for himself as a principal of great executive ability, with a sincere interest in the welfare of his students. In 1918, he was elected to his present position, and he has ever continued to work diligently for the advancement of his school. Mr. Owen is a member of Zeta Psi Fraternity, of Colby College, and in his religious affiliations, is a member of

the Society of Friends. He is also a member of the Rotary Club, of Waterville. In political views, he follows the principles of the Republican party.

Robert Everett Owen married, June 24, 1914, at Clinton, Eva I. Pratt.

PERLEY F. RIPLEY — An active member of that progressive group of men who represent Paris and its business and civic interests in a most substantial way, Perley F. Ripley stands for all things that relate to the improvement and betterment of the community. He is a foremost factor in local government matters, is a constructive official and adviser in financial activities, and is known throughout the State for his enterprise and leadership in the automobile business. Perley F. Ripley was born September 3, 1875, at Paris, a son of James O. Ripley and Ellen F. (Hammond) Ripley, both parents also natives of Paris. James O. Ripley, who is now deceased, was a chair manufacturer at West Paris; a Civil War veteran, he served three years in a Massachusetts regiment, and received wounds in battle.

After attending the public schools and Paris Hill Academy, Perley F. Ripley conducted a general store until 1909, and in 1910, he began his successful career in the automobile business at South Paris, with his agency for Ford cars, and a general service station, and with branches at both Bridgton and Portland. In 1917, Mr. Ripley first became associated with the Paris Trust Company as its president, and he holds that office today, as well as that of director of the company. A Republican in his political views, he is active in all town matters, and particularly as a member of the Republican Town Committee. In motor matters, too, he is very prominent, as treasurer of the Maine Automobile Association at Portland; and he is also an executive of the Maine Publicity Bureau, and president of its budget committee.

Fraternally, Mr. Ripley is affiliated with all bodies of Free and Accepted Masonry; with the Knights of Pythias, and the local Grange, Patrons of Husbandry; as well as with the Kiwanis Club, and the Portland Club. His religious faith is that of the Universalist church.

WILLIAM W. QUINTON—One of the prominent men in the industrial and financial life of Maine is William W. Quinton, authority on textiles and one of the incorporators of the Waterville Savings Bank at Waterville. Mr. Quinton has had many years of experience in the textile industry throughout New England and came to Waterville in 1923, as agent for the Lockwood Company, and at once became a popular figure in community affairs as well as a leading factor in the business development of the town.

Mr. Quinton was born in Gloucester, Massachusetts, July 14, 1882, son of William M. Quinton of Saint Stephen, New Brunswick, and Agnes S. (Deane) Quinton of Deer Island, New Brunswick, both of whom are deceased. William M. Quinton was for many years engaged in the fishing industry in Gloucester, but later in life removed to Saint Stephen, where he occupied himself in farming.

William W. Quinton received his early education

in the public schools of Saint Stephen, including the high school. After finishing his studies, he became connected with the St. Croix Mills at Milltown, New Brunswick, where he remained from 1898 until 1905, learning the textile business. He then accepted a position with the Cocheco Manufacturing Company at Dover, New Hampshire, as assistant designer, remaining there until 1907, when he went to Woonsocket, Rhode Island, as overseer of weaving for the Clinton Manufacturing Company, filling this position until 1913, when he was transferred to the company's plant at Pontiac, Rhode Island, where he was engaged for one year. In 1914, he became associated with the Whitin Brothers at Linwood, Massachusetts, in the same capacity, holding this position until 1917. Mr. Quinton was then engaged by the Nashua Manufacturing Company of Nashua, New Hampshire, as manufacturing superintendent, and continued successfully until 1921, when he was appointed agent for the Hansahoe Manufacturing Company at Valley Falls, Rhode Island. In 1923, he became agent for the Lockwood Company at Waterville, and he continues to serve the best interests of his company as well as aiding local progress. Mr. Quinton was a member of the Seventy-first Regiment of Infantry, Maine Militia, and is a member of the Associated Industries of Maine and of the National Association of Cotton Manufacturers. In fraternal circles, he is a popular member of Free and Accepted Masons, Blue Lodge and Chapter, and an enthusiastic member and director of the Rotary Club, and the Waterville Chamber of Commerce, of which he is also a director (1928). In his religious affiliations, he is a member of the Methodist Episcopal church.

William W. Quinton married, on November 8, 1905, at Saint Stephen, New Brunswick, Florence A. Hall, born December 28, 1884, at Saint Stephen, daughter of Ambrose and Mary C. (Cunningham) Hall, both of Saint Stephen. Their children are: Edith Mae, born October 26, 1906, in Woonsocket, Rhode Island; and Deane Reginald, born August 28, 1908, also of Woonsocket.

FREDERICK THAYER HILL, M. D.—Native of Waterville, Kennebec County, physician specializing in otology and laryngology in this community, having practiced here during the greater number of years which he has spent actively in his profession, Frederick Thayer Hill, M. D., enjoys a most distinguished reputation in diagnosis and treatment of diseases of the ear and throat, and is known widely in medical and scientific circles of the United States for research in the field of oto-laryngology. During the years, 1925-26-27, Dr. Hill was chairman of the staff of the Sisters' Hospital. While the interest closest to him is his profession, Dr. Hill participates whole-heartedly in projects for the betterment of the community, and is here accounted prominent among the public-spirited citizens.

Frederick Thayer Hill was born June 14, 1889, a son of James F. and Angie (Foster) Hill. He received his elementary and high school education in Waterville, and early gave evidence of possessing a

mind of more than average ability, though he had not, prior to graduation from high school, given particular manifestation of a leaning toward medicine unless it be the facility with which he handled formulæ in chemistry. In college his interest in science came into fuller flower, and in 1910, the year he attained his majority of years, he graduated from Colby with the degree of Bachelor of Science. In Colby College, an institution of which Waterville is justly proud for its history (it was founded in 1820), he took advantage of the excellent scientific media there maintained, and by the time he was graduated had firmly resolved to continue along this course as it developed into the medico-scientific. Accordingly, he matriculated in the Medical School of Harvard University, at Boston, Massachusetts, and for four years diligently and intelligently pursued a curriculum culminating in the degree of Doctor of Medicine, conferred upon him in 1914. Immediately, he was appointed to the Aural staff of the Massachusetts Eye and Ear Infirmary, as house surgeon. In this year he was certified by the Maine State Board of Registration. In 1916 he retired from the staff of the Eye and Ear Hospital to give his time to independent practice, which he continued until shortly after America's entrance into the World War, April 6, 1917. He enlisted in his country's causes, giving of his medical knowledge as military surgeon, and was mustered out with an honorable record in 1919. It was during this year that he began permanent residence and practice in Waterville, and during succeeding years has shown himself a valuable worker for the public good.

In the field of medico-scientific literature, Dr. Hill has become widely known, as noted, through authorship of several articles on diseases of the ear, published in "Annals of Otology," "The Military Surgeon," and his papers on allied subjects appearing in the "Laryngoscope" and the journal of the Maine Medical Society. As scientist and master of science as applied in treatment of the ear and throat, Dr. Hill is holder of unquestioned rank; moreover, as a writer his manuscripts give evidence of talent carefully developed. Though scientific writings must be most precise, still, he has displayed a singularly easy style when such a style has been proper. He was certified by the Massachusetts State Board of Medicine in 1919. He is a member of the Maine State Medical Society, the American Medical Association, the New England Otological Society, and the American College of Surgeons. He is a past-president of the Kennebec County Medical Society, and a Fellow of the American Otological Society, the American Laryngological, Rhinological, and Otological Society, and an Associate Fellow of the American Laryngological Association. In all of these professional organizations Dr. Hill is active, and is, furthermore, member of the Maine Historical Society; the Free and Accepted Masons; the American Legion, serving as Commandant of George Bourque Post in 1921; the Rotary Club, of Waterville; Harvard Club, of Boston, and the Ancient and Honorable Artillery Company of Boston. He is a member of two college fraternities, Zeta Psi and Alpha Kappa, and a communicant of the Universalist church, generous in contributions to charitable and kindred worthy causes, no matter by what race or creed sponsored, giving in a spirit truly humanitarian. A Republican, he is loyal to the principles of government upheld by that party, and is possessed of a considerable influence in local political movements.

Frederick Thayer Hill married, June 16, 1924, Ruby Choate, of Waterville, and they are the parents of a daughter, Virginia, born April 30, 1926.

HOMER EUGENE ROBINSON is president of the National Bank of Rockland, Maine, and probably one of the youngest men in the State holding such a position. He was born in Rockland, received his education there, and has there pursued his business career. His interests have been diversified, and when he left school he engaged in the coal dealing field. Then as success came, the profession of banking won him, and his progress in that field has been constant. Responsibility came to him as he showed himself ready and able to shoulder it, and beginning in the banking profession as a clerk he went from one responsibility to another until he became head of the bank in which he was principally interested. Mr. Robinson has numerous connections of various kinds, social, fraternal, and commercial, and is an influential figure in many ways, though a business man first of all.

Homer Eugene Robinson was born at Rockland, Maine, July 14, 1884, son of Levi G. and Clara (Simmons) Robinson. The father was a blacksmith, born at Warren, Maine, December, 1859, and the mother was born at Tennant's Harbor, St. George. He attended the Rockland Public School, the St. George High School, and Rockland Commercial College. After leaving school he started with John I. Snow, coal dealer, at Rockland, and continued with that firm for four years, from 1902 to 1906. He then left the coal business and went into banking, becoming connected with the Rockland National Bank, where he took a position as bookkeeper. In 1911 he became cashier of the same bank, and served in that capacity until 1925, in which year he was elected president. Mr. Robinson is both director and president of the Rockland National Bank. Among the associations and clubs of which he is a member are: the Chamber of Commerce, charter member and treasurer since organization; the Rotary Club; Knights of Pythias, of which he is Past Chancellor; Free and Accepted Masons, Aurora Lodge, No. 50, being also a thirty-second degree Mason and a live member of Kora Temple, Ancient Arabic Order Nobles of the Mystic Shrine; the Commandery, Knights Templar; the American Bankers' Association, and the Rockland Country Club. He is a Republican in politics, and attends the Congregational church.

Homer E. Robinson married, at Rockland, Maine, January 24, 1906, Leah Clark, born at Jonesport, Maine, December 4, 1883, daughter of William N. and Elizabeth (McDonald) Clark, both natives of Jonesport.

HAROLD PERKINS BLODGETT is superintendent of the Rockland district for one of the large light and power companies of Maine. He has been in the service of light and power companies for over a quarter of a century, but he has had other business experience besides and has engaged in other kinds of work. As a youth he worked for a time at farming. He has been engaged in the manufacture of bricks, and he has tried his hand at the curing of fish. He has been an official in one of the great telephone companies. It will thus be seen that he has been in more than one line of endeavor, and that, although engaged in work that is highly technical and calling for much concentration and a more than the usual intelligence, he is a good business man.

Harold Perkins Blodgett was born at Penobscot, Maine, November 14, 1877, son of Leroy and Anna (Wilson) Blodgett. The father, who was a sailor, was born at Brooksville, Maine, and the mother was born at Penobscot, Maine. Mr. Blodgett attended the public schools at Penobscot, Maine, and also completed courses with the International Correspondence Schools. After leaving school he worked on a farm with an uncle at Penobscot, Maine. Then he was employed with the firm of F. P. Gross, engaged in the manufacture of bricks and the curing of fish at Orland, Maine, remaining there two years. Then he was with the Waterville & Fairfield Light & Power Company, at Waterville, and remained with that company from 1900 to 1903. Then he went with the New England Telephone Company, and remained with that concern from 1903 to 1906. He then was with the Kennebec Light & Heat Company, at Gardiner, Maine. In 1910 the Central Maine Power Company took over the Kennebec Light & Heat Company, and Mr. Blodgett went with it. He has been with the Central Maine Power Company from that time to the present. He was superintendent of the district at Gardiner, Maine, in 1917, and superintendent of the Belfast district in 1919. He was appointed superintendent of the Rockland district in 1920 and continues so to the present time. Mr. Blodgett is an Independent in politics. He belongs to the Belfast Masonic Club; is a member of the Free and Accepted Masons, holding the thirty-second degree; and is a member of the Rockland Rotary Club, of which he is past vice-president; the Chamber of Commerce; the Knox County Fish & Game Association, and the Camden Business Men's Association. He attends the Universalist church.

Harold P. Blodgett married, at Rockland, Maine, October 6, 1924, Maude E. Duncklee, born in Georgia.

THOMAS JENNESS FRENCH—Since he was nineteen years of age, Thomas J. French has been with the Camden National Bank, progressing from the rank of teller to that of cashier. He was born at Lincolnville Beach, Maine, November 12, 1874, son of Thomas Drinkwater French, born at Lincolnville, died in June, 1911, and of Isadora (McCobb) French, born at Lincolnville, died in October, 1913, his father having been a sea captain.

Thomas J. French attended the common schools in Camden, with three years in high school, and after a year in other work, he entered the Camden National Bank, and is now (1928) one of its directors and its cashier. He has taken a liberal interest in public affairs, and has held office on the Camden Board of Selectmen and as town treasurer. He is known to have the welfare of Camden at heart and to have worked for civic progress whenever occasion demanded. He is a member of Amity Lodge, Free and Accepted Masons; the Decemvir Club; the Camden Business Men's Association, and the Rotary Club.

Thomas Jenness French married (first), at Camden, Maine, October 15, 1903, Leila M. Bucklin, daughter of Charles A. Bucklin and Viola (Knowlton) Bucklin. He married (second), October 16, 1923, Alice H. Knowlton, daughter of E. Frank Knowlton and Nellie (Holt) Knowlton. By his second marriage he is the father of one child, Jennice Knowlton French, born June 2, 1925.

CHARLES CLARK WOOD is president and director of the Camden National Bank, Camden, Maine. His entry into the banking business was by way of steady progress in outside business of various kinds, and he has also been prominent in public affairs, having been a member of the Maine Legislature in 1899. He is also director of the Knox Woolen Company, manufacturers of paper-machine felts, at Camden, Maine. It can be seen that Mr. Wood has a diversified business experience behind him, and his numerous social connections show that he leads a busy life.

Charles Clark Wood was born at Camden, Maine, February 16, 1869, son of Ephraim M. and Sarah E. (Cleveland) Wood, both of whom were natives of Camden, Maine. He attended the public schools of Camden and the Camden High School, graduating from this latter institution in 1885. After leaving high school he attended Eastman's Business College at Poughkeepsie, New York. When he left school and went to work he engaged at first in the drygoods business and was for a number of years a member of the firm of Follansbee & Wood at Camden, Maine. In 1922 he became an officer of the Knox Woolen Company, at Camden. Mr. Wood has been connected with the Camden National Bank since 1907, and has served as its president since 1910. He served, as has been noted, as a member of the Maine Legislature in 1899. He belongs to the Odd Fellows; Masonic bodies, including the Knights Templar, and the thirty-second degree, Scottish Rite; the Rotary Club, and the Camden Board of Trade.

Charles C. Wood married, at Camden, Maine, September 15, 1910, Miss Inez C. Munroe, born at Lincolnville, Maine.

WILLIAM A. COBB—A power engineer of great ability and wide experience is William A. Cobb. Entering this profession soon after he completed his education, he has advanced through two companies. Now he is superintendent of the Belfast district for the Central Maine Power Company. His father, William A. Cobb, a merchant, was born in Danville,

Maine. His mother, Mary (Peables) Cobb, was also born in Danville.

William A. Cobb, the son, was born in Auburn, Maine, on March 22, 1885. He entered the public schools at Auburn, and in 1904 was graduated from the Edward Little High School in that town. He attended the University of Maine, and in 1908, was graduated with the degree of Bachelor of Science. In the same year, he became associated with the Union Water Power Company as an engineer, and he remained with this company until 1920. In 1920, he transferred his services to the Central Maine Power Company, and in March, 1925, he was made superintendent, for that company, of the Belfast district. He has continued in this position since that time.

Politically, Mr. Cobb is a member of the Republican party. He is affiliated with the Free and Accepted Masons, and he is a member of the local chapter of the Rotary Club. He attends the First Church of Belfast.

On June 16, 1909, William A. Cobb married Bell N. Harris, at Sherman Mills, Maine. She was born July 21, 1884, at Colebrook, New Hampshire, the daughter of Freeman C. and Grace Cawlwell Harris. Mr. and Mrs. Cobb are the parents of two children: 1. Mary Elizabeth, born at Wilsons Mills, Maine, July 30, 1910. 2. Lucy Margaret, born at Wilsons Mills, July 28, 1917.

HON. CARLETON DOAK—Since 1910, when he was admitted to the bar, Judge Carleton Doak has been prominent in Maine legal and civic circles. He is a lawyer of ability, and his record is one of distinguished service to the State and to his community. His father, George R. Doak, was born at Searsport, Maine. His mother, Abbie (Carleton) Doak, was born at Camden, Maine. George R. Doak was a jeweler at Belfast, and a member of the Moses Webster Lodge of the Free and Accepted Masons, in which order he had taken the thirty-second degree.

Judge Carleton Doak was born at Vinalhaven, Knox County, Maine. He attended the public schools of Vinalhaven and Belfast, and was graduated from the Belfast High School in 1904. He entered the University of Maine and, in 1910, received the degree of Bachelor of Laws from that institution. On February 11, 1910, he was admitted to the Maine State bar, at Bangor, and soon afterwards he began the practice of his profession at Belfast. He has continued the general practice of law there since that time, with offices in the Odd Fellows' Building.

Politically, Judge Doak is a member of the Republican party, and for six years he served as chairman of the Republican City Committee of Belfast. For two years, he acted as city clerk of the city of Belfast, and for another period of two years, he was city solicitor. He was chairman of the Board of Tax Assessors of Belfast for three years, and he also served as chairman of the Board of Registration of Voters. In August, 1923, he was appointed Judge of the Belfast Municipal Court for a term of four years, and was reappointed in August, 1927.

Judge Doak is a member of Phoenix Lodge, Free

and Accepted Masons, and he is a Knight Templar. He is also a member of the Phi Delta Phi Fraternity, and of the Maine State and Waldo County Bar associations. He attends the Unitarian church.

On May 17, 1916, at Belfast, Carleton Doak married Nellie Brown, who was born at Belfast, January 4, 1896. She is the daughter of the late Edgar Brown, of Belfast. Judge and Mrs. Doak are the parents of several children, all of whom were born at Belfast: Carleton, Jr., Camilla, George R., James, Norman, and Nellie B.

EDWARD EVERETT RODERICK—It is due to such men as Edward Everett Roderick that the State of Maine holds such a high position in the field of educational endeavor. Mr. Roderick is school superintendent of the Belfast-Searsport District, and it is the general opinion that he has in every way justified his selection for that important office.

Mr. Roderick was born in Waterville, July 5, 1889, the son of Joseph Samuel and Elizabeth (Bishop) Roderick. Following his graduation from the Winslow High School in 1907, he entered Colby College, but later was graduated from Oskaloosa College, Oskaloosa, Iowa, with the degree of Bachelor of Arts, in 1912, and Master of Arts the following year. His first employment was as timekeeper and paymaster for the Johnston & Mitchell Construction Company in the summer of 1911. After receiving his degrees and leaving college, Mr. Roderick officiated as teacher in the schools at Winslow, Howland, Winthrop, and East Maine Conference Seminary, at Bucksport, and was District Superintendent of the Orrington, Eddington and Holden School District up to 1918. He was then appointed District Superintendent of the Belfast-Searsport District, which position he still holds. Doing graduate work in Psychology during summer sessions he is just completing the requirements for a Master's degree, with a major in Psychology, at the University of Maine. Mr. Roderick is a trustee of the Belfast Public Library, holds the office of president, Maine Teachers' Association, a director of the local Rotary Club. Appointed by Governor Brewster as a member of Advisory Commission for Investigation of Higher Education in Maine, a member of Legislative Commission of National Education Association, and a member of the Code of Ethics Committee of the National Education Association. He is a member of the local Lodge, Free and Accepted Masons. His residence is at No. 4 Grove Street, and his office is in the Crosby High School Building, at Belfast. In addition to his scholastic activities, Mr. Roderick is president of the Correct Posture Seating Company, Incorporated, of Belfast, having given much time and study to the perfection of school seating methods, and was granted patent papers as co-inventor of the Correct Posture Chair Desk.

On September 2, 1911, Mr. Roderick married Eurydice B. Houston, at East Bradford. Mr. and Mrs. Roderick are the parents of two children, a daughter, Drusilla M. Roderick, and a son, Burleigh H. Roderick.

SELWYN THOMPSON—In business and civic circles, Selwyn Thompson, manufacturer, of Belfast,

Maine, is one of the most versatile and active citizens in this community. He is the son of Ithama B. and Dorcas (Clement) Thompson. His father, a farmer, also served in the State Legislature and as County Commissioner. Mr. Thompson did not follow his father's vocation of farming, but very early in life began a business career which he has carried on in Massachusetts and in his native State.

Selwyn Thompson was born July 4, 1856. He was educated in the public schools of Montville and spent one year at Freedom Academy. At the age of twenty years, he went to Massachusetts, where he was connected with the penal institution of the city of Boston for seven years. He then owned and conducted a store in Boston until 1887, when he returned to Maine, settled at Belfast, and founded the Selwyn Thompson Company. In 1889 the Thompson Foster Company was inaugurated and in 1892, the Thompson Manufacturing Company was begun by Mr. Thompson for the purpose of manufacturing working men's clothes. Since 1902, Mr. Thompson has been president and treasurer of this company. He was an alderman of Belfast for one term and from 1913 to 1922 he was president of the Belfast & Moosehead Railroad. He is a director of the City National Bank of Belfast; chairman of the board of trustees of the Belfast Public Library; a member of the Free and Accepted Masons, a Knight Templar, and a member of the Independent Order of Odd Fellows. He is also a member of the Chamber of Commerce and Associated Industries of Maine. He is a Democrat in politics and a member of the Universalist church.

Selwyn Thompson married three times: first in Boston, Massachusetts, to Lutie May Vickery, who died in 1884. His second marriage took place in Appleton, Maine, on January 5, 1888, to Abbie M. Burkett of that city; she died in 1922; they had one child, Lynwood B. (q. v.). He married (third), in 1924, Mary Elizabeth Blakeley.

LYNWOOD BURKETT THOMPSON, manager and assistant treasurer of the Thompson Manufacturing Company, of Belfast, Maine, is an illustrious son of an illustrious father, and is associated with his father in carrying on the business established by the senior Mr. Thompson. Lynwood Burkett Thompson, as his father, has been not only active in business affairs, but in civic and social organizations that in their history record many deeds of these two notable citizens of Belfast.

Lynwood Burkett Thompson was born at Belfast, Maine, August 21, 1889. He was educated in the public schools of Belfast, Maine, and at the University of Maine, from which institution he graduated in 1912. He began work with the Munson-Whitaker Company before he finished college, in 1911, and remained with this organization for a year. In 1913, he went into business with his father's firm, the Thompson Manufacturing Company, makers of working men's clothing. He has held a number of prominent public positions and offices in different clubs. From 1917 to 1921, he was a Councilman of Belfast; in 1924, 1925, and 1926, he was a member of the Sea and Shore Fisheries Commission of the State of Maine; in 1926 and 1927, he was a member of the City Park Commission. He is prominent in the Free and Accepted Masons; a Knight Templar, having passed through all the chairs in all the York Rite Masonic Orders; he is a Scottish Rite Mason of the thirty-second degree; and a member of Divan Anah Temple, Ancient Arabic Order Nobles of the Mystic Shrine; he is a member of the Lambda Chi Fraternity of the University of Maine. He was the first president of the Rotary Club of Belfast, of which he is a member, and also first president of the Belfast Masonic Club. He is an attendant of the Universalist church.

On October 18, 1913, Lynwood Burkett Thompson married Leila Myrtle Howard, daughter of Fred and Mary (Vose) Howard of Belfast. They have two children: Howard Selwyn, and Elizabeth Burkett.

GEORGE LEACH ST. CLAIR—Having the interests of his city and State always in mind, George Leach St. Clair, of Rockland, has served his fellow-citizens in various public offices and is at present representing this district as a member of the State Legislature for the term of 1927-28. In addition to his political activities, Mr. St. Clair is one of the foremost business men of this vicinity in his position as secretary and treasurer of the St. Clair & Allen Corporation, leaders in the wholesale confectionery industry of Maine. In his position of prominence in commonwealth affairs, he has ever conscientiously and successfully served the best interests of his constituency, having the welfare and progress of the State and its people as his ideal, to which he has concentrated all his energy and influence.

Mr. St. Clair was born in South Hope, November 25, 1874, son of Asa Payson and Ervilla Emma (Leach) St. Clair. Asa Payson St. Clair was postmaster at South Hope for a number of years, also operating a large grocery business there. He later entered the wholesale confectionery business at Rockland. His political activity has no doubt been inherited by his son, as the elder Mr. St. Clair was selectman of South Hope, served as alderman of Rockland, and was elected to the Legislature of Maine to serve the term, 1915-16.

George Leach St. Clair was educated in the public schools of South Hope and Rockland, and after high school, entered the business organization of his father. He familiarized himself thoroughly with the organization and the operation of the industry and, due to his remarkable qualities and splendid executive ability, advanced steadily until he was elected to his present position of secretary and treasurer. In the public affairs of Rockland, Mr. St. Clair has been consistently active, having served as member of the Common Council of this city, while in its industrial and material advancement, he has always been a leader. Prominent in financial circles, he is a director of the Rockland Bank. Although his success in industrial matters attests to his thorough attention to business, he has always found time to devote to his fraternal interests and organizations of that nature, in which his popularity is evidenced by the fact that he is one of the foremost members of Aurora Lodge, Free and Accepted Masons; King Solomon's Temple Chapter, Royal Arch Masons; King Hiram's Council, Royal and Select Masters;

Claremont Commandery, Knights Templar; Aram Temple, Ancient Arabic Order Nobles of the Mystic Shrine; Order of the Eastern Star, in which he is Past Patron, having occupied the chairs in the Chapter and Commandery. His social contacts and associations are extensive, and he is one of the most active members in the Country Club and the local Rotary Club. He attends the Universalist church, although not a formal member of this body.

George Leach St. Clair married, July 28, 1922, at Rockland, Katharyn F. Ulmer, daughter of Orris E. and Inez L. (Kent) Ulmer. Mr. St. Clair has a son by a former marriage, Frank Adams St. Clair, a graduate of Bowdoin College, now with the New York Telephone Company; he lives at Newark, New Jersey.

NATHAN HOUSTON SMALL—A native of Belfast, Maine, with experience in many lines of business, travel and study, Nathan Houston Small brings to the editorial chair of the "Republican Journal" of Belfast, a wide appreciation of men and events which makes him well qualified to take an intelligent view of the many subjects to be valued by the editorial eye of an up-to-date publication. He is the son of Alfred A. and Ella A. (White) Small.

Nathan Houston Small was born at Belfast, Maine, March 21, 1891. He is a graduate of the Belfast High School, the University of Maine, where he obtained a degree of Bachelor of Arts, and of Harvard University, Cambridge, Massachusetts, where he was awarded a degree of Master of Business Administration. After finishing his work at the University of Maine, in 1913, he took a position as teller in the City National Bank of Belfast, where he remained until 1916, when he went to Harvard University Graduate School of Business Administration. He finished his studies at Harvard in 1918 and enlisted in the United States Navy, where he held the rank of chief yeoman. From 1919 to 1920, he was stationed in Washington, District of Columbia, and Bangor, Maine, as an auditor with the United States Department of Internal Revenue, Income Tax Division. From 1920 to 1921, he was executive secretary of the Maine sardine section of the National Canners' Association; from 1921 to 1923, he was engaged in the business of auditing and accounting and in 1924, he became manager and editor of the "Republican Journal" of Belfast, which position he continues to hold. He is a member of the Free and Accepted Masons. He is a Republican in politics and attends the Congregational church.

Nathan Houston Small married Edna J. Dyer of Bangor, Maine, December 9, 1914.

FRANK J. HAM—As collector of internal revenue, Frank J. Ham, a resident of Augusta, has maintained the creditable standards that he established in the previous public offices that he held in Augusta and in other cities of Maine. A native and a lifelong resident of Maine, for many years he has taken an active part in the political life of the State, both as an influential member of the Republican party and as the holder of different public positions, such as sheriff of Kennebec County and warden of the Maine State Prison. He has also been an important figure as a business man in the State. He was born in Canaan, Maine, May 30, 1865, the son of John and Narcissia (Austin) Ham. His father, a farmer and a native of Mercer, Maine, was active in the Civil War, in which he fought in a number of engagements; his mother was born in Belgrade, Maine. Frank J. Ham, as a boy, attended the public schools of Belgrade, and later went to the Belgrade High School. After he left school, he worked for L. A. Bartlett, who conducted a general store in Belgrade, in which he was employed from 1896 to 1901. At the same time he was a deputy sheriff of Kennebec County. He left the Bartlett store in 1901, when he was elected High Sheriff of Kennebec County, an office which he held for two terms, or four years, from 1901 to 1905. From 1905 to 1911 he operated a sporting goods store in Belgrade Lakes, and at the same time was probation officer and deputy sheriff of the county. In 1912 he was chairman of the Republican County Committee, and in 1913 he was appointed warden of the Maine State Prison, a position which he continued to hold for two years. In 1913 he became chairman of the Republican committee, and remained as such until 1921. In 1916 he again was appointed warden of the State Prison. He continued as warden until 1921, when he was appointed Collector of Internal Revenue at Augusta, a position which he has held until the present time. Not only is he actively engaged in the work of the Republican Club, but he participates freely in the fraternal life of the community, being a member of the Free and Accepted Masons, in which order he has gone through all the bodies and holds the thirty-second degree. He and his family are members of the Universalist church.

In Belgrade, on January 1, 1898, Frank J. Ham married Jennie E. Damren, of Belgrade, the daughter of John Damren, also a native of Belgrade. Frank J. and Jennie E. (Damren) Ham are the parents of the following children: 1. Miles F., born in Belgrade, December 15, 1899. 2. Doris Lee, born in Belgrade, May 27, 1901.

JAMES W. HANSON—Having spent the greater part of his life in service in his country's military forces, James W. Hanson has been an Adjutant General of the State of Maine since November 1, 1922. He has served in three conflicts—the Spanish-American War, the Philippine Insurrection, and the World War. He is the son of John F. Hanson, born in Mount Vernon, Maine, in April, 1859, died in 1926; and of Julia E. (Scates) Hanson, born in Augusta, Maine, in 1860. His father was a farmer. James W. Hanson was born in Belgrade, Maine, August 31, 1879. He attended the public schools of Belgrade, later going to Kents Hill Academy and the Shaw Business College. He was graduated from Shaw Business College in the class of 1896.

In 1898, he enlisted in Company F, First Maine Infantry, National Guard, at Augusta, Maine, and gave active service during the Spanish-American War with this organization. Then, on April 25, 1899, he enlisted in the Nineteenth Infantry of the United States Army; on April 24, 1902, he completed service in the Philippine Islands, whither his work with the

Nineteenth Infantry had taken him. From July, 1902, until 1916, he served in the First Maine Infantry and the Second Maine Infantry. He went, in 1917 and 1918, with the Second Maine Infantry and the One Hundred and Third Infantry in the American Expeditionary Forces as captain, and later as major. From November, 1918, until September, 1919, he was lieutenant-colonel on the camp staff of the Seventeenth United States Infantry, at Camp Meade, Maryland. From December, 1920, until May, 1922, he was major in the Ordnance Department; and from May until November 1, 1922, major in the One Hundred and Fifty-second Field Artillery. Since November 1, 1922, he has been Adjutant-General in the State of Maine. Mr. Hanson is a member of the American Legion, the Free and Accepted Masons, and the Grange, Patrons of Husbandry. Politically, he holds the views of the Republican party. He is a member of the Congregational church.

On June 2, 1909, James W. Hanson married Zana B. Bickford, of Somersworth, New Hampshire, who was born September 4, 1885, the daughter of Jonathan Bickford, born in Somersworth, New Hampshire, and of Fannie M. Bickford. The marriage took place in Dover, New Hampshire. Mr. and Mrs. Hanson are the parents of one child: Phyllis L., born in Mount Vernon, Maine, September 1, 1914.

DANIEL STEWART YOUNG—As a hardware merchant, Daniel Stewart Young, president of the Brooks Hardware Company, of Augusta, is one of the leading business men of the city. A native and a lifelong resident of Augusta, he is thoroughly conversant with local conditions and is acquainted with most of the older inhabitants.

He was born in Augusta, June 4, 1884, the son of Daniel S. and Elizabeth G. (Batson) Young, both natives of Maine, his mother having been born in New Castle, Maine. His father was a stone-cutter by occupation. As a boy, Daniel Stewart Young attended the public schools of Augusta, and later went to Cony High School. When he left school he worked for several local firms until, in 1903, he became identified with the Brooks Hardware Company, Incorporated. In 1923 he became a member of this firm, of which he is now the president. Mr. Young is actively interested in the political life of the town, and professes the opinions and the doctrines of the Republican party. Aside from his own business, he participates freely in the general industrial life of Augusta, being an active member of the local Chamber of Commerce; and in fraternal affairs through his membership in the Free and Accepted Masons, in which order he is affiliated with the Augusta Lodge. He and his family are members of the Methodist Episcopal church.

In Augusta, Daniel S. Young married Maude F. Spaulding, and they are the parents of one child, Ida Muriel, born in Augusta, October 10, 1904.

HARVEY JAMES DeFOREST—One of the unique industries of Maine is the manufacture of "hooked" rugs, the invention of Harvey James DeForest, of Turner, Androscoggin County, who has made that town famous as the center of the manufacture of this product.

Mr. DeForest was born in Dennysville, Washington County, November 28, 1886, the son of James Henry and Amelia Jones (Reynolds) DeForest, the latter a descendant on both sides of her family from John and Priscilla Alden. The Reynolds family can also trace its descent directly to one of the name appearing in English records of 1520.

The father of Mr. DeForest was a well-known builder of Dennysville, but structural work did not appeal to the son and he took up the trade of shoemaker. He started in one of the large New England shoe factories and showed such mechanical ability that in a very short time, at the age of twenty years, he was made foreman. He had left school at the age of fourteen, two years of which were in the Stetson High School at Randolph, Massachusetts. He was afflicted with deafness, and this, barring him to a certain extent from many of the lighter pleasures of life, caused him to devote much of his time to constructive work. He became proprietor of a small machine shop where he perfected many inventions, the leading one being a process for making hooked rugs. The value of his invention was soon apparent and he had little difficulty in obtaining the necessary capital and establishing at Turner the De-Forest Associates, Incorporated, manufacturers of the now well-known "Priscilla Turner" hooked rugs.

Mr. DeForest married, February 26, 1910, at Montello, Brockton, Massachusetts, Carrie Annis, daughter of William and Susan (Patrequin) Annis. Mr. and Mrs. DeForest are the parents of three children: 1. Howard Emerson, born December 4, 1910. 2. Ruth Elva, born November 4, 1912. 3. Lorraine, born August 17, 1914.

LEROY H. SMITH, M. D.—Before settling in Winterport, Maine, where he has been practicing medicine and surgery since 1919, Dr. Leroy H. Smith enjoyed a more varied experience than usually falls to the lot of a young physician, including service in the Medical Corps of the United States Army during the World War.

Born in Winterport, Maine, November 14, 1892, he was the son of Mandel C. and Lura Loud (Downes) Smith. His father, who was born in Winterport, April 19, 1866, was a farmer; and his mother, also a native of Winterport, was born July 25, 1873. Leroy H. Smith received his early education in the schools of Winterport, and was graduated from the High School in the class of 1910, and then entered the University of Maryland, where he received his degree of Doctor of Medicine in 1917.

From July 1, 1917, until February 1, 1918, Dr. Smith was in the service of the Rockefeller Foundation, New York City, and did work in the rural districts of South Carolina. On March 1 of that year he entered the service of the Army, was commissioned first lieutenant in the Medical Corps, being assigned to United States General Hospital No. 14, at Fort Oglethorpe, Georgia. While Dr. Smith was in the service he was on the staff of the Post-Graduate School of Medicine, where he was an instructor

for eight months, and for the next eight months, chief of the department of laboratories, receiving his honorable discharge from the service on July 3, 1919.

Dr. Smith is a member of the Free and Accepted Masons, Winterport Blue Lodge, and also a member of the Independent Order of Odd Fellows. He belongs to the Maine State Medical Society, the Penobscot County Medical Society, and the American Medical Association. He attends the Methodist Episcopal church.

Leroy H. Smith married, February 12, 1918, Frances Lougee, at Shortville, New York, who was born in Winterport, February 15, 1894, daughter of Caleb R. and Anna Hardy (Scott) Lougee, who were born, respectively, in Dover and Winterport, Maine. Dr. and Mrs. Smith are the parents of: 1. Basil Lougee, born December 24, 1919, in Bangor, Maine. 2. Earle Stuart, born February 11, 1921, in Bangor.

ALBERT FOSTER DRUMMOND—Devoting his life-work to finance, with a beginning as a clerk, following a substantial education and with college degree, Albert Foster Drummond, of Waterville, has reached an enviable place in the business affairs of his community and won the esteem and confidence of his fellow-citizens. His reward for duties well performed, for a deep interest in all that is of importance to Waterville and its neighborhood, has been noteworthy. His career has been one of constant progress toward a high goal and marked by the ever-widening circle of his friends in business enterprise, in fraternal circles and in civic activities.

Albert Foster Drummond was born in Waterville, May 26, 1866, a son of Everett Richard and Aubigne (Bean) Drummond. He was educated in Coburn Institute and received the degree of Bachelor of Arts from Colby College in the class of 1888. In that same year he became a clerk in the Waterville Savings Bank, from which he rose, successively, to assistant treasurer and then to treasurer, in 1912. Since 1920 he has been a trustee of the Waterville Savings Bank; has filled the office of City Councilman and Alderman; treasurer and trustee of the Waterville Public Library; and from 1920 to 1925 occupied the position of treasurer of the Waterville Historical Society. Mr. Drummond was a trustee of Colby College from 1918 to 1923, and is serving for the term from 1925 to 1930. In his fraternal affiliations, he is a member of the Free and Accepted Masons and Delta Kappa Epsilon College Fraternity, while his club is the Waterville Rotary, in which he takes an active interest.

Albert Foster Drummond married, September 25, 1889, at Buckfield, Josephine L. Prince, daughter of Hon. Charles H. and Emma (Atwood) Prince. Mr. and Mrs. Drummond are the parents of the following children: 1. Louise M., married George L. Beach, and they have three children: Hugh, Prince D., and George L., Jr. 2. Prince A., married Elizabeth Macomber, and they have one child, Frederick M. 3. Katherine, married Errol L. Taylor, and they are the parents of three children: Errol L., Jr., Walter G. and Richard Drummond. 4. Clark, married Grace Van Benthuyson, and they have one daughter, Audrie L. 5. Everett Richard.

IRVING R. FOSSETT—The Central Maine Power Company serves a large number of people in this section of the State most efficiently and satisfactorily. Since January 26, 1925, Mr. Fossett has been assistant treasurer of the concern, but his association with the Central Maine Power Company extends back to 1918. Irving R. Fossett was born in Pittston, Maine, May 13, 1891, son of Roy A. Fossett, a native of Whitefield, Maine, who for nineteen years has been in charge of the mason work at Togus, Maine, and who is a member of all the York Rite bodies of the Free and Accepted Masons, in Gardiner, Maine, and of Carrie E. (Dunton) Fossett, also a native of Whitefield, and who, previous to her marriage was a school teacher. He attended the public schools of Pittston, of Randolph, and of Gardiner, Maine, completing his studies in Gardiner High School, and then prepared for an active business career by taking both courses in the Shaw Business College, where he completed his courses in 1909. He found his first employment with Uncle Sam at the National Soldiers' Home in Maine, in the office of the quartermaster and the governor, and later was identified with various concerns, including the Kennebec Box Company, and the Hubbard Lumber Company, at Randolph, Maine, which last-named connection he maintained from September 1, 1916, to December, 1918. At that time he became identified with the Central Maine Power Company of Gardiner, Maine, as cashier of the Gardiner office, and here he gave entire satisfaction, rendering service of a quality which commanded recognition. In June, 1922, he was promoted to the position of general cashier for the company, and on January 26, 1925, he was again promoted, this time being made assistant treasurer of the Central Maine Power Company. Politically, Mr. Fossett supports the principles and the candidates of the Republican party, having been a previous member of the Gardiner Republican Committee, as well as treasurer of the Randolph Town Committee. He was a member of Company M, Second Maine Infantry, and was discharged for disability in 1911. He is actively interested in and a member of the Augusta Chamber of Commerce, the Augusta Young Men's Christian Association, and holds a certificate in first aid to the injured in the American National Red Cross, Augusta Chapter. He is well known in the Masonic Order, being a member of all the York Rite bodies and of the Consistory, in which he holds the thirty-second degree, and is Past High Priest of Gardiner Chapter, Royal Arch Masons; and Past Commander of Maine Commandery, No. 1, Knights Templar. He is an attendant of the Methodist church. Mr. Fossett has many friends in Augusta and in Gardiner, and is known as a business man of sound judgment and initiative, and as a public-spirited citizen who prefers to serve as a private citizen and as a successful business man, rather than as a public official. His hobby is baseball, he having played at the National Soldiers' Home, besides playing football and basketball while in school.

Irving R. Fossett was married, in Augusta, Maine, March 27, 1914, to Cecile I. Rice, who was born in Gouldsboro, Maine, December 9, 1889, daughter of Elmer E. and Bessie E. (Bickford) Rice, the first-mentioned of whom was born in Gouldsboro, and the last-mentioned of whom is a native of Winter Harbor, Maine. Mr. and Mrs. Fossett are the parents of three children: 1. Norman R., who was born in Gardiner, January 31, 1918. 2. Edgar M., born in Gardiner, May 3, 1919. 3. Athleen E., born in Gardiner, January 26, 1925.

HON. ELVINGTON PALMER SPINNEY, of North Berwick, Maine, was born in Georgetown, Maine, June 30, 1868, son of Palmer Oliver Spinney and Mary Jane (Todd) Spinney. His parents were sturdy New England stock and natives of Georgetown. His father in early life was a sea captain; later he engaged in trade in Lewiston, Maine, and in 1875 the family moved from Lewiston to Brunswick, Maine, where they made their home until their deaths, the father at the age of eighty-two years; the mother at the age of eighty-four years. Most of the Spinney ancestors were sea-faring people. One, for his bravery on the high seas, in defense of his native land, during the War of the Roses, received knighthood at the hands of an English king. The Spinney crest hangs in Westminster Abbey.

Elvington P. Spinney received his early education in the public schools of Lewiston and Brunswick. He graduated from Bowdoin College, with a Bachelor of Arts degree, in the class of 1890. After leaving college he devoted his energies to teaching for three years: one year as science teacher in Hillside Seminary in Wisconsin; one year as principal of Paris Hill Academy, Paris, Maine; and one year as principal of Alfred Academy, Alfred, Maine. During his teaching he employed all his spare moments in studying law. He read law in the offices of Barrett Potter of Brunswick, and with Samuel M. Come of Alfred. He was admitted to the York County bar in 1895, and to the United States Courts in 1898. As soon as he was admitted to practice law, in 1895, he opened an office in North Berwick, where he is still in active practice. His practice is widely extended, often to remote parts of the State of Maine, as well as in New Hampshire and in Massachusetts. Besides his general law practice, he is counsel for banks, industrial corporations, four towns and two village corporations. From 1911 to 1919, two terms, he was judge of the Yorkshire Municipal Court.

Judge Spinney is a member of the York County Bar Association, the Maine State Bar Association, and the American Bar Association. He is a member of and Past Noble Grand of Eagle Lodge, Independent Order of Odd Fellows; member of and Past Chief Patriarch of Columbian Encampment; a member of and Past Sachem of Negutaquit Lodge of Improved Order of Red Men; he is a member of the Canton, the Grange, the Rebekah Lodge, of the Pocahontas; he is a member of the Bauneg Beg Country Club; of the Sanford Town Club; is a Congregationalist, and chairman of the board of trustees of the Congregational church; and a member of the Alpha Delta Phi Fraternity. During the World War he was a member of the Legal Advisory Board, the Draft Board, and the "Four-Minute Men." Being an Independent in politics, he never sought public office, but he has served his town for several years as selectman, and has held other town offices. He is interested in all civic, educational and philanthropic movements in his home town.

On October 30, 1895, Judge Spinney married Grace E. Burbank of Alfred, Maine. They have two children: 1. Dorothy S. Gillette, of Los Angeles, California; a graduate of Wellesley College in 1923; married, in 1923, Waldo A. Gillette, a graduate of Harvard in 1922. 2. Leon L. Spinney, of North Berwick; a graduate of Bowdoin College in 1926, and now a student in the Boston University Law School.

FRED WILSON BURRILL—A long and successful experience as teacher, principal, and supervisor, preceded the unusually fine service which Fred Wilson Burrill has been rendering as superintendent of schools at Augusta, Maine, since 1923. Mr. Burrill is a Bates College man, and has behind him a long record of efficient service. He is active and prominent in the National Education Association, of which he is a State director, and he has won in a high degree the respect and esteem of his associates in Augusta.

Fred Wilson Burrill was born in Corinna, Maine, September 14, 1872, son of Wesley Burrill, a farmer, who was born in Corinna, Maine, August 29, 1849, and died in March, 1925, and of Rebecca (Simpson) Burrill, a native of Dixmont, Penobscot County, Maine, whose death occurred in 1905. He attended the public schools of his birthplace, and then prepared for college in the Maine Central Institute, from which he was graduated with the class of 1893. The following autumn he matriculated in Bates College, at Lewiston, Maine, where he completed his course with graduation in 1897, receiving at that time the degree of Bachelor of Arts. He at once began teaching, accepting a position as principal of the high school in Gorham, New Hampshire, where he remained for two years, 1897-99. He then went to Houlton, Maine, as first principal of the Houlton High School, which position he held until 1904, a period of five years. His next connection was as principal of the high school in Franklin, New Hampshire, where he remained for one year only, 1904-05, leaving to accept a position as Superintendent of Schools in his home town, Corinna, Maine, where he remained from 1905 to 1908. In 1908 he was appointed Superintendent of Schools at Island Falls, Maine, where he served from 1908 to 1913. His next position was at Brewer, Maine, as Superintendent of Schools, in which capacity he served from 1913 to 1923, a period of ten years. At the end of that time he came to Augusta, as Superintendent of Schools, and here he has been rendering most efficient service to the present time (1928). Mr. Burrill is an educator of tried and proved worth, a man of broad culture and of large administrative ability. As a director of the educational activities of the young people of this city he is exerting a most wholesome and vitalizing influence, and has won the commendation and the esteem of associates and of fellow-citizens alike. Politically, Mr. Burrill gives his support to the Republican party. He is a member of the executive committee of the Maine Teachers' As-

sociation, a State director of the National Education Association, also State director of the New England Association of School Superintendents, and influential in the affairs of those organizations. He is a member of the Augusta Chamber of Commerce, and fraternally is identified with Parian Lodge, No 160, Free and Accepted Masons, and with the Knights of Pythias. He is a member of the Rotary Club, and his religious affiliation is with the Congregational church.

Fred Wilson Burrill was married, in Richmond, Maine, August 30, 1899, to Carrie Louise Odiorne, who was born in Richmond, Maine, August 4, 1876, daughter of Joseph and Louise (Price) Odiorne, both natives of Maine. Mr. and Mrs. Burrill are the parents of two children, both of whom are graduates of Bates College: 1. Richard O., who was born in Houlton, Maine, June 17, 1900, and who served in the World War as a member of the Three Hundred and Seventeenth Field Signal Battalion. 2. Meredith F., who was born in Houlton, Maine, December 23, 1902, and is an instructor in Lehigh University. The family home is at No. 6 Crooker Street, Augusta.

FRANCIS HAMILTON FARNUM—Born in Norristown, Pennsylvania, September 28, 1881, Francis Hamilton Farnum, now one of the executives of the Central Maine Power Company, with offices at Augusta, spent most of his life, up to 1923, in military pursuits, from the time of his graduation at West Point in 1903 until he was appointed chief-of-staff of the Fortieth Division in France during the World War.

Mr. Farnum was the son of Francis D. and Mary H. (Chain) Farnum. Following his education at the public and high schools of Norristown, he entered the United States Military Academy at West Point, New York, in 1899, graduating as a second-lieutenant in 1903. He served in the Philippines in 1903 and 1904, in Cuba 1906, in the Philippines 1911 to 1914; and in 1907 was appointed instructor in tactics at the United States Military Academy, at West Point. He was inspector and instructor of the Second Maine Infantry in 1917, and was in charge of mobilization, and chief-of-staff of the Fortieth Division in France in 1919. Mr. Farnum is affiliated with the Free and Accepted Masons and is an active worker in the local post of the American Legion. He is a member of the Episcopal church, and in politics is a Republican. He has a very charming home at No. 114 Western Avenue, Augusta, and, as stated, his office is with the Central Maine Power Company.

On September 28, 1916, Mr. Farnum married, at Augusta, Florence L. Gannett. Mr. and Mrs. Farnum are the parents of three children: Henrietta G., Francis H., Jr., and Mary H.

HAROLD D. JENNINGS—Since 1907 Harold D. Jennings has been identified with the business of providing light and heat for the public, first as an employee of the Kennebec Light & Heat Company, and later as an official of the Central Maine Power Company, of which he is now (1928) treasurer. Mr. Jennings is a resident of Augusta, Maine, and takes an active part in the public affairs of that city, serving at the present time as president of the Common Council.

Harold D. Jennings was born in Cornville, Maine, June 9, 1883, son of the late Robert D. Jennings, who was born in Salem, Maine, and of Abbie (Chapman) Jennings, who is a native of Athens, Maine. He attended the public schools of Fairfield, Maine, graduating from Goodwill High School with the class of 1903, and then continued his studies for two years in Dartmouth College. After finishing his two years in college he made a change and became a student in Shaw's Business College, from which he was graduated with the class of 1907. He began his active career in the employ of the Kennebec Light & Heat Company, serving first as clerk, and later as cashier and auditor. Possessed of sound business judgment and willing to work long and hard, he early attained a high place in the confidence of his business associates, and in 1920 he was made assistant treasurer of the Central Maine Power Company. On January 1, 1924, he was promoted to the official position of treasurer of this big concern, and this position he was filling in 1928. Mr. Jennings is a Republican in his political affiliations and is an active worker in the affairs of the party. He is a Councilman from Ward Six of Augusta, and president of the Common Council, and has always been one of the public-spirited citizens who could be counted upon to contribute a full share toward the advancement of the general welfare. He is an interested member of the Augusta Chamber of Commerce. Fraternally, he is identified with Augusta Lodge, No. 141, Free and Accepted Masons, in which he is a member of all the York Rite bodies and of the Consistory, in which he holds the thirty-second degree. He is a member of Augusta Country Club, and of the Kiwanis Club, and his religious affiliation is with the Universalist Church of Augusta, Maine.

Harold D. Jennings was married, in Clinton, Maine, in 1908, to Etta B. Ricker, who was born in Clinton, Maine, March 18, 1885, daughter of Alfred, a native of Clinton, and of Edith Ricker, who was born in Fairfield, Maine. Mr. and Mrs. Jennings make their home in Augusta, Maine.

EVERETT H. MAXCY, lawyer of Augusta, Maine, and the present general counsel for the New England Public Service Company, was born September 8, 1888, at Gardiner, Maine. He is a son of William E. and Ida J. (Heseltine) Maxcy, of Gardiner. William E. Maxcy, the father, is a well-known insurance broker of Gardiner.

Everett H. Maxcy received his early education in the public schools of the community in which he was born, and he later attended the Gardiner High School, graduating in 1906. He pursued his academic training at the University of Maine, and graduated from there with the class of 1911, when he received the degree of Bachelor of Arts. He received his legal training at Harvard Law School, and graduated from there with the class of 1914, when he received his degree as Bachelor of Laws. Returning to his home at Gardiner immediately afterwards, he there began a general practice of his profession, continuing thus from 1914 till March, 1918. After the war

period, Mr. Maxcy returned to Gardiner and carried on his practice until August, 1920, at which time he became identified with the Central Maine Power Company, at Augusta. He is at present general counsel for the New England Public Service Company.

During the period of the emergency created by the entry of the United States into the World War, Mr. Maxcy served as a second lieutenant, United States Coast Artillery, and he remained in this branch of the service until after the close of hostilities. Since his return to civilian life he has taken an increasingly keen interest in the civic affairs of his community. In his political preferences he is Republican. He holds membership in several professional organizations, among the more important being the American Bar Association and the Maine State Bar Association. He is also a member of the local Kiwanis Club, the Augusta Country Club, and he is fraternally affiliated with Hermon Lodge, Free and Accepted Masons, of Gardiner.

Everett H. Maxcy married, December 28, 1914, at Gardiner, Maine, Ethel M. Blair, who was born at Bowdoinham, Maine, a daughter of La Forest and Katherine C. (Gamble) Blair. Mr. and Mrs. Maxcy maintain their residence in Augusta.

HON. RAYMOND FELLOWS—The worthy son of an eminent father, Hon. Raymond Fellows, prominent member of the bar at Bangor, Maine, eventually attained the zenith of official recognition in legal affairs of the State in 1925, when elected as Attorney-General for the Commonwealth of Maine.

Oscar F. Fellows, father of the Attorney-General, was born at Bristol, New Hampshire, September 10, 1857, son of Milo and Susan D. (Locke) Fellows. He was a student at the New Hampton (New Hampshire) Literary Institute, and was admitted to the practice of law in 1881. He was a member of the Maine House of Representatives from 1901 until 1903, having been its Speaker in the latter year; was Collector of Customs for the Port of Bucksport, Maine, for a period of four years; was County Attorney for Hancock County, Maine, for four years; and was appointed by President Roosevelt as counsel for the United States Government on the International-St. John River Commission. He was a member of the Methodist Church and a Republican in political affiliation. He married, May 24, 1883, Eva M. Fling, daughter of the Hon. L. W. Fling, of Bristol. Oscar F. Fellows passed from this life in 1921.

Raymond Fellows, son of Hon. Oscar F. and Eva M. (Fling) Fellows, was born at Bucksport, Maine, October 17, 1885. He acquired his earlier education in the public schools of his native town, was a student at the East Maine Conference Seminary, matriculated at the University of Maine, and was graduated from that institution as a member of the class of 1908, with Bachelor of Arts degree, subsequently studying in the law department of the same university.

After completing his collegiate studies, Mr. Fellows became associated with the law offices of his father, under whose able preceptorship he studied, and was duly admitted to the bar of Maine in 1909, following which he became a law partner of his father, and thus continued, with offices at Bangor, until the death of Oscar F. Fellows in 1921, being now in partnership with his brother, Frank Fellows, in the offices originally occupied by himself and father.

A staunch advocate of the principles of the Republican party, Mr. Fellows has been most prominent in the councils of that organization for a number of years. In 1910, he was appointed a member of the board of trustees of the State Hospitals by the then Governor Fernald; he was elected Attorney-General of the State of Maine in the month of January, 1925.

Mr. Fellows is a member of the American Bar Association, the Maine Bar Association, the Penobscot County Bar Association, member of the bars of the Supreme Court of the United States, the District Court of the United States, and the Circuit Court of Appeals. He is also affiliated with the Maine Historical Society, the Bangor Historical Society, the Tarratine Club, and the Unitarian church, at Bangor.

On February 11, 1909, at Bucksport, Maine, Raymond Fellows was united in marriage to Miss Madge Gilmore, a native of Dedham, Maine, daughter of former State Treasurer Pascal P. and Alma M. (Hart) Gilmore, the latter a native of Holden, Maine. To this union have come the following children: 1. Margaret, born at Bangor, Maine, November 22, 1909. 2. Rosalie, born at Bangor, May 10, 1913. 3. Frank, born at Bangor, November 26, 1914. The official address of Mr. Fellows is the State House, Augusta, Maine.

PLINY A. CROCKETT—Prominent in educational and business circles in West Buxton, Maine, is Pliny A. Crockett, branch manager and assistant treasurer of the Casco Mercantile Trust Company. It is rare to find one who has been actively interested in educational work for a number of years, as active and efficient in modern business as is Mr. Crockett, who has shown the happy faculty of finding time to serve in civic affairs while engaged in commercial banking. He is the son of Willis Crockett of Hollis, Maine, who was born in Limington, Maine, and of Esther A. (Haley) Crockett, a native of Hollis. Both parents are now deceased.

Pliny A. Crockett was born November 16, 1873, at Hollis, Maine. He was educated in the public schools and Nichols Latin School. On the completion of his education, he taught in the public schools for two years, then he was engaged in farming for a number of years and at the same time was agent for the Mutual Life Insurance Company. He continued in this line of work until 1920 when he was made treasurer of the Buxton and Hollis Savings Bank, an institution which was established in 1878. When this bank was taken over by the Casco Mercantile Trust Company of Portland, Maine, Mr. Crockett was retained as branch manager and assistant treasurer, which position he continues to hold. In his public service, Mr. Crockett was a member of the Hollis Board of Selectmen for four years; Superintendent of Schools for six years, and a member of the school

committee for six more years. He was also a member of the State Legislature in 1925 and 1927, where he has served on the Education Committee, being House chairman in 1927, was House chairman of the Library Committee, and on the State Banking Committee. He is Past Master of Buxton Lodge, Free and Accepted Masons, and Past Worthy Patron of Pleasant River Chapter, Order of the Eastern Star. He is a member of the Portland Farmers' Club and a deacon in the Baptist church. In his public and business activities, Mr. Crockett is well known throughout the State.

Pliny A. Crockett married, in 1900, Lucy M. Smith, daughter of Ether Smith and Anne M. (Weymouth) Smith of Hollis, Maine. They have one child, a daughter, Pauline, who is a student at Mount Holyoke College.

HENRY MILTON CHAPMAN, M. D.—Among those noble men whose skill, kindness and high integrity in the medical profession have endeared them to all who come in contact with them, none stands higher in the esteem of his fellowmen than stood Henry Milton Chapman of Bangor, Maine. He was the son of the late Milton Chapman, a prominent farmer in the Newburg section, and was given the best opportunity for a higher education in different institutions of learning, both in this country and abroad. Taking advantage of his opportunities and endowed with talent and appreciation of his privileges, he equipped himself for the great humanitarian work which he carried on so unselfishly to the benefit of so many suffering and needy persons.

Henry Milton Chapman was born at Newburg, Maine, August 22, 1871, the son of Milton and Rosina (Kenney) Chapman. His early life was spent at his father's farm and attending school until he was fourteen years of age when he entered the academy at Newburg, then known as the Hampden Academy. After finishing his academic work in that school, he matriculated in New York University from which institution he was graduated in 1895, and began to practice medicine at Ashland, Maine, where he soon had a large number of devoted patients in all parts of Aroostook County. In this country practice, Dr. Chapman gave to his work the most sincere and diligent attention, never finding any too hard, or any person too humble to serve as only a man of the highest honor can serve as family friend and physician. Days and nights were alike to him in his work, for at all hours, he was on duty carrying cheer and comfort where it was most needed and setting an example to those who would besmirch the profession with work for selfish ends. He continued in this section until 1904 when he was married and, taking his young bride, he went to Europe for further study, returning to his native State and making his residence in Bangor where he continued to make friends of all who knew him or had the blessing of his help in times of sickness. For twenty-one years, Dr. Chapman enjoyed a constantly growing practice in Bangor where he also took part in many social activities, for his genial disposition made him a welcome associate in health as well as in sickness. He was a member of the Order of Free and Accepted Masons, the Ancient Arabic Order Nobles of the Mystic Shrine, the Tarratine Club and both country clubs of Bangor, and also of the Rotary Club. When this country went into the World War, Dr. Chapman volunteered his services and enlisted in the Medical Department, where he attained the rank of major in work he did overesas, where he was held in the highest regard by army officials of high rank. After his war work, he returned to Bangor and resumed his practice here which he kept up with the same vigor and unselfish attention until his sudden illness which terminated in his death on August 24, 1925. He is survived by his widow and son.

On September 21, 1904, at Houlton, Maine, Henry Milton Chapman married Deborah Dunn, daughter of a well-known lumberman, George Bancroft Dunn and his wife, Lucinda Rich (Cushing) Dunn. Dr. and Mrs. Chapman had one child: 1. George Dunn, now (1928) a student at Williams College.

CHARLES H. CAHILL—In the matter of feeding the public, Charles H. Cahill has become an expert, for he has been engaged in this business now for nearly thirty years, as proprietor of the Colonial Café at Bath, and of the New Meadows Inn, at West Bath. Mr. Cahill is also one of the leading citizens of Bath, and has been four times elected mayor, the last time in 1926. He has given the city of Bath the most efficient service in this official capacity, and his business ability and his civic devotion are greatly appreciated by the community.

Charles H. Cahill was born in Bath, Maine, July 6, 1870, son of Andrew R. Cahill, a native of Nova Scotia, who died in 1894, and who during his active life was engaged as a blacksmith, and of Mary E. (Staples) Cahill, a native of Bowdoinham, Maine, who died in 1915. Mr. Cahill received his education in the local public schools, including the high school, and then secured employment in a pharmacy, continuing there for nine years, from 1889 to 1898. In 1898, he engaged in the restaurant business for himself, opening the Colonial Café, at Bath, and later opening the New Meadows Inn, at West Bath. He has been very successful in both of these places, and has made both places known for their good food and excellent service. Mr. Cahill caters to a very large crowd of summer people each season, and also has a substantial all-the-year-round trade. Though so successful in his business activities, however, these do not absorb all of Mr. Cahill's energies. He finds time for a very large amount of public service, is trustee of the public library, a member of the board of directors of several concerns, and has rendered especially valuable service as a public official. He was a member of the Common Council for some time, later served as a member of the Board of Aldermen, and in 1920 was elected mayor of Bath. In 1921 he was reëlected, and in 1925 was again elected, and reëlected in 1926, making four terms in all. Each time he was elected on the Democratic and Citizens' ticket, and during each term he rendered the kind of service which made adherents of all parties his supporters. Fraternally, Mr. Cahill is a member of the Benevolent and Protective Order of Elks, Knights of Pythias, and Fraternal Order of Eagles, and he is also a member of the Colonial Club and the Sagadahoc Club. His religious membership is with the Episcopal church.

Charles H. Cahill was married, in 1912, to Grace E. Woodbury, of Auburn, Maine, daughter of Nathan F. Woodbury. Mr. and Mrs. Cahill are the parents of two children: 1. Charles H., Jr., born March 31, 1913. 2. Martha W., born July 3, 1916. The family home is at No. 781 High Street, in Bath.

HON. HARRY MANSER—One of the most useful and important members of the bar, not only to a large circle of clients, but to his fellow-citizens in general, whom he has served in important offices, is Judge Harry Manser, of Auburn, Maine, who is also widely known throughout the Masonic fraternity.

Judge Manser's father, William Manser, was a landscape gardener, born in England, December 5, 1832, and was married there to Eliza Canham, born May 27, 1839, also in England. Their children were: 1. Annie E., wife of George W. Snow, of Somerville, Massachusetts, now deceased. 2. Hattie, married John E. Booth, of Lewiston, Maine. 3. Harry, born April 20, 1874, in Hever, County of Kent, England. The elder Mr. Manser died in London at the age of sixty-two, and his widow died at Somerville, Massachusetts, in December, 1918.

Coming to the United States at the age of thirteen with his mother and two sisters, they settled in Lewiston, Maine, where Harry Manser attended the public schools, earning his own livelihood at the same time. On being graduated, Mr. Manser studied stenography, and later found employment in the law offices of White and Carter, where he put in his spare time studying law. On September 19, 1896, he was admitted to the Maine bar, and at once began the practice of his profession in association with White and Carter, with whom he remained until 1903. His interest in politics was always keen and he allied himself with the Republican party in early manhood. In 1902 Mr. Manser removed to Auburn, Maine. He had served one year as city solicitor in Lewiston, and in 1903, he was appointed Municipal Judge of Auburn, holding this office for eight years. On his retirement in 1911, Judge Manser was made city solicitor of Auburn, and held that office one year. In 1918 he was reappointed Municipal Judge, serving until 1926, when he declined a reappointment. Since this time he has devoted himself to his private practice, acquiring a large and increasing clientele. A substantial recognition of his standing in the profession was the appointment of Judge Manser in 1914 as one of the State Board of Bar Examiners.

In his fraternal affiliations, Judge Manser is a member of the Free and Accepted Masons, and of the Knights of Pythias. He served as Grand Warden of Maine in the New England Order of Protection from 1903 to 1905, and from 1905 to 1907, served as Supreme Warden of the entire jurisdiction. In his religious faith he is a member of the High Street Methodist Episcopal Church.

Harry Manser married, June 24, 1898, in Lewiston, Maine, Gladys M. Stover, daughter of James T. and Ella (Hunt) Stover, both natives of Maine. Mrs. Stover is now dead, and Mr. Stover lives in California. Three children were born to Judge and Mrs. Manser: 1. Doris E., born March 2, 1900; graduated from Bates College in the class of 1922. 2. Marjorie S., born May 18, 1902, graduate of Bates College, class of 1924. 3. Harriet, born August 9, 1909, now (1928) a student.

MRS. FLORA M. GILMAN—Throughout her life an educator, and one whose specific training and experience have highly qualified her as the leader and director of the business school in Bangor that bears her name, Mrs. Flora M. Gilman is both a teacher of attainments and a school principal of painstaking discrimination and executive ability. The Gilman Commercial School is acknowledged to be one of the foremost institutions of its practical and thorough aims in the State.

Mrs. Gilman was born Flora M. Crowell, in Exeter, Maine, daughter of William E. Crowell, of Exeter, where she was graduated at the grammar and high schools, afterwards receiving special tutoring in commercial courses. When she was fifteen years old, she began to teach in the public schools, so continuing for about twenty years, about fifteen years of that period in the schools of Bangor. In 1913, Mrs. Gilman founded the Gilman Commercial School, its first location being at No. 47 Main Street, Bangor, where it occupied one large and two small rooms. Presently, with the continued growth of the institution, larger quarters were sought, and in 1915, the school was removed to No. 4 Broad Street, to occupy an entire floor. At first there were but six pupils; the number is now one hundred, and the courses taught are: Shorthand, normal training, accountancy, and civil service, the school ranking as high as any commercial school in the State, and the graduates being secured positions throughout Maine.

Mrs. Gilman is a member of the Bangor Chamber of Commerce, Business and Professional Women's Club, Eastern Commercial Teachers' Association, and her religious faith is that of the Universalist church.

Flora M. Crowell married Walter H. Gilman, who was born in Bangor, and is now deceased. Their son, Carl W. Gilman, an optician, served in the United States Navy, in the World War, from July 2, 1918, to September, 1921, with the rank of seaman.

WILBER H. KNOWLES—As president of the Knowles and Dow Company, and treasurer of the C. M. Conant Company, Wilber H. Knowles is identified with two of the enterprising and prosperous farm implement and automobile sales concerns of Bangor. The first-mentioned concern was organized in 1906, and the partners, Mr. Dow and Mr. Knowles, purchased the business of C. M. Conant & Company in 1918.

Christopher Columbus Knowles, father of Mr. Knowles was born in Corinna, Maine, where he received his education, and where he was engaged as a farmer throughout his active life. He was a veteran of the Civil War, serving with the Forty-third Maine Volunteer Regiment, and was a member of the Grand Army of the Republic, in which he took a deep interest to the time of his death in 1919. He married Lucy Smith, who was born in St. Albans, Maine, and who died in 1876.

Wilber H. Knowles, son of Christopher Columbus and Lucy (Smith) Knowles, was born in Corinna, Maine, March 17, 1869, and received his earliest school training in the public schools of his birthplace. Later he attended Corinna Academy, and then completed his preparation for an active life in Coburn Institute, at Waterville, Maine. Upon the completion of his education, he engaged in farming, and continued in that line of activity for seven years. He then came to Bangor and entered the employ of the C. M. Conant Company, with whom he remained until 1906. In that year he formed a partnership with John Dow, and

under the firm name of Knowles and Dow, engaged in business for himself, handling a complete line of farm implements. In 1913 Knowles and Dow took over the agency for Buick automobiles, adding this to their established line of farm implements, and five years later, in 1918, they purchased the interests of the C. M. Conant Company, with which Mr. Knowles was employed when he first came to Bangor. Since that time they have operated both concerns most successfully. Mr. Knowles is president of the Knowles and Dow Company, and treasurer of the C. M. Conant Company, and is known as one of the very able business men of this city. Politically, he gives his support to the principles and the candidates of the Republican party. He is a member of the Bangor Chamber of Commerce, and fraternally, is affiliated with the Independent Order of Odd Fellows, and with the United Commercial Travelers. He is a member of the Luzerne Country Club, and finds his favorite recreation in automobiling and fishing. His religious interest is with the Baptist church, of which he is an attendant.

Wilber H. Knowles was married, in 1892, to Lizzie J. Young, who was born in Corinna, Maine, and they are the parents of five children: 1. Eleanor G., a graduate of Bates College, class of 1916. 2. Marie M., a graduate of Smith College, class of 1917. 3. Lucy M., graduate of Boston School of Oratory, class of 1919. 4. Lillian M., graduate of Boston Art Museum. 5. Gertrude M.

LESTER WARREN CARPENTER, M. D.—Seventeen successful years as a general practitioner and also as a specialist in diseases of the throat and nose have made Dr. Lester Warren Carpenter, of Limerick, Maine, an expert in his field, and have won for him an assured place among his professional associates. Dr. Carpenter is a graduate of the medical department of Bowdoin College, and during the World War served in the United States Army Medical Corps, ranking as captain at the time of his discharge. He is now (1928) a captain in the Army Medical Reserve Corps. Since 1924 he has been engaged in general and special practice in Limerick, Maine.

Dr. Lester Warren Carpenter was born in Waterboro, Maine, November 23, 1883, son of Nathaniel Warren Carpenter, who for forty-six years was engaged in business as proprietor of a general store, but is now engaged in farming, and of Mary A. (Chase) Carpenter, both residents of Waterboro. As a boy he attended the local public schools and when his high school course was completed he entered Bowdoin College, from which he was graduated in 1910, receiving at that time the degree of Doctor of Medicine. After serving his internship in the Maine General Hospital, Dr. Carpenter began practice at Goodwin's Mills, York County, Maine, in 1910. The following year, 1911, he came to Limerick, where he was engaged in general practice until the time of his enlistment for service in the World War, in 1918. In that year he enlisted in the Medical Corps of the United States Army, in which connection he was stationed at various hospitals and also served for one year as transport surgeon. Faithfulness and ability brought promotion from the rank of first lieutenant to that of captain, and when the war was over he was retained in the service of the United States War Department and assigned to the Marine Army Hospital, at Portland, where he rendered valuable service for three years. Upon his return to civilian life, in 1921, Dr. Carpenter engaged in general practice at Sanford, Maine, but his health was not robust, and it became necessary that he remove to the country. Accordingly, in 1924, he returned to Limerick, where he has since been successfully ministering to the needs of. the residents of this locality. He takes care of a general practice and also specializes in diseases of the nose and throat, and the people of this neighborhood find in him a faithful and skilled physician and a valued friend. Dr. Carpenter is a member of the York County Medical Society and of the American Medical Association. Fraternally, he is identified with Freedom Lodge, No. 42, Free and Accepted Masons, of Limerick, of which he is a Past Master; with Cornish Chapter, Royal Arch Masons; and with Old Orchard Council, Royal and Select Masters. He is also a Past Patron of Eastern Star Lodge, No. 132, of Limerick; and is a member of the Benevolent and Protective Order of Elks. Politically, he gives his support to the principles and the candidates of the Republican party, and he is active and helpful in local public affairs, willing to bear his share of the burdens of public office and giving generous support to well-planned projects for the general good. He has served several times as a member of the school committee and also as a member of the Board of Health, and to the duties of these offices he has given careful and able attention. While living in Sanford, Dr. Carpenter was a member of the Sanford Town Club, the Sanford Men's Singing Club, and the Sanford Kiwanis Club. He is now a member of the Limerick Town Club, and an attendant of the Congregational church, which he serves as a member of the choir.

Dr. Lester Warren Carpenter was married, at Waterboro, Maine, December 25, 1905, to Mabelle E. Walker, daughter of Eugene W. and Mary L. (Movrill) Walker, of Waterboro, both of whom are still living (1928), residents of Gorham, Maine. Mr. and Mrs. Carpenter are the parents of two children: 1. Forrest Walker, attended Bates College. 2. Morris Warren. Mrs. Carpenter is a Past Matron of Eastern Star Lodge, No. 132, of Limerick, and a member of the Research Club, of Limerick. She and her sons are. members of the Congregational Church of Limerick, and Mrs. Carpenter and her husband both are members of the church choir.

HOLMAN A. HOLBROOK—Though still a young man, Holman A. Holbrook is unusually well prepared for the work in which he is engaged, as manager of the General Ice Cream Corporation, of Lewiston, Maine, a concern which manufactures ice cream and deals in dairy products. He is a graduate of the University of New Hampshire, and at one time was assistant instructor in the Connecticut State College, assisting in the department of dairying and the manufacture of dairy products. He has also served as government inspector, and has had experience in the manufacture of ice cream, and in the supervision and management of creameries. Altogether he has been most thoroughly prepared for success in his present position, and is giving to the General Ice Cream Corporation, a most vigorous and efficient management.

Holman A. Holbrook was born in Lemington,

Vermont, February 14, 1894, son of Charles R., a native of Lemington, Vermont, now deceased, who was a successful farmer and who served as a member of the Vermont Legislature, and of Agnes E. (Limes) Holbrook, also a native of Lemington, Vermont. The father was a member of the Knights of Pythias, and was a man highly respected among his associates. Holman A. Holbrook, the son, attended the public schools of Lemington, Vermont, and then became a student in Colebrook Academy, at Colebrook, New Hampshire, where he completed his course with graduation in 1911. Later, he matriculated in the University of New Hampshire, from which he was graduated with the class of 1917. For three years, 1917-1920, Mr. Holbrook served as assistant instructor in the Connecticut State College, in the department of dairying and the manufacturing of dairy products. During this time he also served as government inspector in the United States Dairy Division, making butter for the United States Navy. In 1920 he engaged in the ice cream business, with B. C. Hallock as a partner, under the firm name of Hallock and Holbrook, operating at Willimantic, Connecticut, but in 1921 he was made superintendent of the creamery owned by the Dixville Notch Corporation, at Dixville Notch, New Hampshire, and there he remained until 1922. In that year he still further widened his experience by accepting a position with the Pittsfield Milk Exchange, at Pittsfield, Massachusetts. In 1923 he was made manager of the Kent Ice Cream Company, at Burlington, Vermont, where he remained until 1926, when he accepted his present position as manager of the General Ice Cream Corporation, at Lewiston, Maine. Here he is giving to the concern with which he is connected the benefit of his early preparation and of his widely varied experience and there is every indication that he will bring to the concern a steadily increasing success. Mr. Holbrook is one of the many business men of these times who give their allegiance to no one political party, but class themselves as Independents, giving support to those candidates whom they consider best fitted for the offices to which they aspire, regardless of party affiliations. He is a member of the Lewiston Chamber of Commerce, and of the United Commercial Travelers, and fraternally, is identified with the Blue Lodge, Free and Accepted Masons; and with Alpha Tau Alpha College Fraternity. His religious membership is with the Congregational Church of Lewiston, Maine. Mr. Holbrook has many friends in all of the many communities in which he has lived, and is well-known here in Lewiston as a good business man, a public-spirited citizen, and a cultured gentleman, whom his friends trust and respect, and in whose companionship they find pleasure.

Holman A. Holbrook was married, in Tripoli, Iowa, October 7, 1920, to Dorothy Marie Pockels, who was born in Tripoli, Iowa, daughter of Theodore, born in Waverly, Iowa, and of Lucia (Cunningham) Pockels. Mr. and Mrs. Holbrook have three children: 1. Marion, born in Pittsfield, Massachusetts. 2-3. Kent and Kathryn, twins, born in Burlington, Vermont, April 5, 1926. The family make their home in Lewiston.

CHESTER C. FOWLES—Since September 9, 1927, Chester C. Fowles has been serving as treasurer of Kennebec County, Maine, and he will be candidate, to succeed himself, in the June primaries, 1928. Mr.

Fowles has had a varied experience, and for two years held a position in the Maine State Department of Agriculture. He is a member of the Kennebec Farm Bureau, and has served as deputy collector in the Internal Revenue Department.

Chester C. Fowles was born in Whitefield, Maine, November 18, 1887, son of Miles H., a farmer and a Democrat, who was born in Whitefield, Maine, and of Martha H. (Temple) Fowles, a native of Bangor, Maine. His early education was received in the public schools, and his special preparation for a business career was received in Shaw Business College, of Augusta, Maine. After finishing his commercial training, he secured a position as clerk in the National Soldiers' Home, in Augusta, Maine, where he remained for two years, 1909-1910. He then went with the Vickery and Hill Publishing Company, of Augusta, and from 1910 to 1915 continued that connection, serving first as correspondent and later as clerk and assistant foreman of the mailing department. This experience was of value to him, and his next employment was as deputy collector in the Internal Revenue Department, where he remained for a period of two years. During the period of the World War he served as farm labor specialist in the Department of Agriculture, taking office in June, 1917, but later he served as corporal in Battery E, Coast Artillery, at Fort McKinley. Upon the death of Honorable Bert P. Stuart, of Belgrade, Maine, Mr. Fowles was appointed treasurer of Kennebec County, and took office September 9, 1927, his term to run until January 1, 1929. He was a candidate to succeed himself in the June primary, 1928. Politically, Mr. Fowles gives his support to the principles and the candidates of the Republican party, though his father was a Democrat, and as has already been stated he has held several public offices, including that of Deputy Collector of Internal Revenue, farm labor specialist, and now treasurer. Fraternally, he is identified with Bethlehem Lodge, Free and Accepted Masons; Cushnoc Chapter, Royal Arch Masons; and Trinity Commandery, Knights Templar. He is also a member of Gardiner Lodge, Independent Order of Odd Fellows; American Legion and of Kennebec Farm Bureau. He is a Protestant and an attendant of the Congregational church.

Chester C. Fowles was married, in Rockland, Maine, September, 1920, to Mary Hopkins, of Port Clyde, Maine, daughter of Frank, who was born in Port Clyde, Maine, and of Lectie (Hart) Hopkins, a native of St. George, Maine. Mr. and Mrs. Fowles have no children. Mr. Fowles has his office in the County Court House, Augusta, and he and Mrs. Fowles make their home in Augusta.

HAROLD H. BOURNE—A summary of the activities of Harold H. Bourne during his seventeen years in the practice of the law reveals his continuous and effective public service. After thirteen years as trial justice of Kennebec, Maine, he took up the duties of Judge of the Municipal Court, which he has for four years administered with unfailing wisdom and justice. He has borne his share, also, of civic responsibilities and has generously answered the call of his country for its war needs.

Harold H. Bourne was born in the old town of Kennebunk, Maine, May 16, 1886, son of a well-known attorney, Herbert E. Bourne, also a native of the town, and his wife, Marcia (Jordon) Bourne,

now deceased. The son was educated in public and high school and began on a college course at Boston University, which circumstances prevented his completing. Instead, he rounded his law course in his father's office and received sound instruction in both the principles and the ethics of his profession from that astute and high-minded lawyer. Admitted to the bar in 1910, Mr. Bourne began a general law practice in Kennebunk, in which has so prospered as to give him high professional rank throughout his section. He is a member of the York County and Maine State Bar associations, and of the finance committee of the last-named organization.

In 1910 Judge Bourne assumed the office of trial justice of Kennebunk, in which he continued until 1923. This long experience fitted him for the more complicated duties of the higher office of Judge of the Municipal Court in 1923, when the court was established, and enabled him to prove the able encumbent who has won the respect and esteem of his constituency, and led to his reappointment in 1927. He was chairman of the Board of Selectmen for two terms, and during the World War served on the Legal Advisory Board and the Speakers' Bureau, winning a certificate as a "four-minute" speaker of eloquence and force. He belongs to York Lodge, Free and Accepted Masons; Murray Chapter, Royal Arch Masons; the Commandery, Knights Templar; Maine Consistory, Ancient Accepted Scottish Rite. He is a past president of the Rotary Club, a member of the Sons of the American Revolution, and the Sons of Colonial Wars. For many years he has been clerk of the Unitarian church.

In 1912, Harold H. Bourne married Sally B. Goodwin, of Kennebunk, daughter of Fred R. and Cedelia (Gooch) Goodwin, and they have children: Dorothy R., Marcia, Sally, and John.

ERNEST SAUNDERS—Actively engaged in the florist business for more than forty years, Ernest Saunders is one of Lewiston's foremost business men, while in the civic and social affairs of this city, he has been prominently active, being deeply interested in philanthropic and welfare work throughout this section, while in fraternal circles, he is a popular and appreciated member. Mr. Saunders opened his florist and market-gardening business here in 1887, at No. 578 Main Street, where it has become an institution in the commercial life of the city. He is prominent in financial circles and is actively concerned with everything that tends towards the expansion and development of this municipality and the progress and well-being of its people.

Mr. Saunders was born in Auburn, October 22, 1871, son of Samuel W. and Fanny (Haskell) Saunders. He was educated in the public schools of this State, and as aforementioned, engaged in the florist business independently while a youth. In 1890, he gave up the market-gardening business and devoted all his efforts to the establishment of a superior florist trade, advancing steadily in his chosen field by his diligence and constant striving for nothing but the best. Through the high quality of his products and the courtesy and attention given to all customers, Mr. Saunders achieved an enviable reputation which he has retained throughout his long business career. For a while he dealt in real estate in which he was successful, while in the financial affairs of the city, he is active as a director of the Manufacturers' Bank, being elected to this position in 1912, and he is also a trustee of the People's Saving Bank, being appointed to this post, 1910. He was elected treasurer of Mt. Auburn Cemetery, 1914, and a director of the Central Maine General Hospital, 1925. In politics, he is a staunch supporter of the Republican party and served as alderman in this city for several years, his political career being characterized by a sincere and devoted interest in the cause of municipal advancement. In his fraternal connections, Mr. Saunders is identified with the Free and Accepted Masons, the Independent Order of Odd Fellows, the Knights of Pythias, and the Benevolent and Protective Order of Elks.

Ernest Saunders married, June 25, 1905, at Lewiston, Mary Crawshaw, and to this union have been born three children: Fannie E., Mary E., and Ernest J.

FORREST CLARK TYSON, M. D.—Dr. Tyson was born in Madison, Lenawee County, Michigan, February 2, 1881, the son of Charles and Arabella (Ball) Tyson, the former a prominent business man of that city. Forrest Clark Tyson graduated from the high school at Adrian, Michigan, in 1900, after which he took a year's study in the State Normal College at Ypsilanti, Michigan. He then went to Boston, where he entered Tufts College, graduating in 1905 with his degree of Doctor of Medicine. For the next eighteen months he was medical house officer at the Massachusetts State Infirmary at Tewkesbury, and from May 24, 1906, to January 21, 1914, served as assistant superintendent of the State Hospital at Bangor, Maine. On the latter date he accepted the appointment of superintendent of the Augusta State Hospital, which post he has since held.

Dr. Tyson is a member of the American Medical Association and the American Psychiatric Association and the New England Society of Psychiatry and Neurology. He is affiliated with the Free and Accepted Masons, and is a member of the Ancient Accepted Scottish Rite Masons, thirty-second degree. Dr. Tyson is a member of the National Committee for Mental Hygiene. His social affiliations include the Augusta Rotary Club, the Abnaki Club of Augusta, and the Augusta Country Club, and he is a member of the First Congregational Church of Augusta.

On May 13, 1905, Dr. Tyson married Margaret M. Matheson, daughter of Alexander and Mary (Sherieff) Matheson. Dr. and Mrs. Tyson are the parents of three children, as follows: 1. Forrest Clark, Jr., born June 29, 1908. 2. Charles Matheson, born June 17, 1910. 3. Dudley Ball, born December 31, 1918.

STUART BROWN COPELAND—One of the most interesting and important of Maine's industrial institutions is the Eastern Manufacturing Company at Bangor, of which Stuart Brown Copeland is vice-president, also officiating as resident manager in charge of mill operations at South Brewer and Lincoln and of the subsidiary corporation, the Lincoln Pulpwood Company, which manages the timberlands owned by the concern and secures the necessary supplies of pulpwood for the mills.

Mr. Copeland was born in Davenport, Iowa, December 17, 1889, the son of George Edward and Eliza Mae (Brown) Copeland, the former at one time superintendent of agencies for the Northwestern Mu-

tual Life Insurance Company of Milwaukee, who retired from active business November 1, 1925, and died February 27, 1927. The early education of Stuart Brown Copeland was obtained in the public schools of Milwaukee, from which he was graduated in 1903. He then took a course in the Eastern Division High School of the same city and, on his graduation in 1907, entered the Massachusetts Institute of Technology, at Boston, from which he received his degree of Bachelor of Science in 1911. In May, 1912, Mr. Copeland entered the employ of the Katahdin Pulp and Paper Company, at Lincoln, Maine, as plant engineer, and the following year was appointed mechanical superintendent. In 1914, he was given the post of assistant general manager and, upon the absorption of the Katahdin Company by the Eastern Manufacturing Company, continued at Lincoln as resident manager. Two years later, in January, 1916, Mr. Copeland removed to Bangor, where he took the post of engineer in charge of construction and general assistant to the president of the Eastern Manufacturing Company, with headquarters at the mill located in South Brewer. While at this post Mr. Copeland still continued to supervise operations of the plant at Lincoln. Since 1919, Mr. Copeland has occupied the post of vice-president of the Eastern Manufacturing Company and its subsidiary corporations, and has also acted as resident manager in charge of mill operations at South Brewer and Lincoln, together with the Lincoln Pulpwood Company. Mr. Copeland is very active in all community organizations. He is a past president of the Rotary Club and the Tarratine Club, of Bangor, and a member of the Penobscot Valley Country Club of the same city, also of the New University Club of Boston, Massachusetts. His fraternities are Gamma Delta Phi of the Eastern Division High School, of Milwaukee, Wisconsin, and Delta Tau Delta of the Massachusetts Institute of Technology. He is also affiliated with the "Osiris" and the Round Table of the same school. In addition to his work with the Eastern Manufacturing Company, Mr. Copeland is a director of the Merrill Trust Company of Bangor. He is an active member of the Bangor Chamber of Commerce, the Boston Chamber of Commerce, the Marine Traffic Association, and the American Society of Mechanical Engineers.

Stuart Brown Copeland married, October 12, 1912, at Brookline, Massachusetts, Madeline Herbert Draper. Mrs. Copeland died January 23, 1920, leaving two children, as follows: 1. Barbara, born in Lincoln, August 31, 1914. 2. George Edward (2), born in Bangor, December 20, 1916.

The Eastern Manufacturing Company of Maine was incorporated in 1899, at which time it commenced the manufacture of unbleached sulphite pulp in a newly constructed mill, which was the beginning of the present pulp mill at South Brewer, Maine. The original pulp mill was built adjacent to a large sawmill, and for the purpose of converting into pulp the waste slabs developed in the sawing of spruce lumber and dimension. At that time the Penobscot region was world famous for its lumber output, and this particular sawmill was one of the pioneer tidewater mills in the State. It had come into the control of the then owners—the Ayers —about 1884, and it was they who built the pulp mill and organized the Eastern Manufacturing Company.

The sawmill, which eventually developed into one of the largest in the East, was operated for some time as a separate company, but was ultimately transferred to the Eastern Manufacturing Company and operated by them until 1916. It was abandoned and razed in 1917.

Through the years the pulp mill at South Brewer was enlarged and modernized. It gradually grew away from the use of waste slab wood, which, as the principal raw material, was replaced by the use of the full log and latterly by so-called "round pulpwood." The quality of the product was improved by this shift in raw material, and later a system was added for bleaching the pulp. For the past twelve years or more the mill has been producing nothing but the highest grade of bleached sulphite pulp, and for the last ten years has successfully produced considerable annual tonnages of spruce cellulose for use in the manufacture of Rayon.

In 1896 the company entered the paper manufacturing field—with the building of the start of the present paper mill at South Brewer—by the installation of one paper machine and auxiliary equipment. Manilas and other coarse papers were manufactured. In 1901 two more paper machines and auxiliary equipment were added and the paper business increased. A few years later the manufacture began to shift from coarse papers to fine papers and the dry lofts and rag pulp mill were added in 1905. A box shop was also added in this same year for the manufacture of the wooden packing cases in which it is customary to ship fine papers. Other auxiliary finishing departments followed shortly, and the mill finally discontinued the manufacture of coarse papers entirely and has for nearly twenty years produced only fine papers and white paper specialties. Papetries and writing papers have long comprised a very considerable proportion of the output, and in the past few years the mill-brand lines of bond, ledger and other standard papers have been developed.

In the latter part of 1914 the company took over the Katahdin Pulp & Paper Company of Lincoln, Maine, and the corporate merger was accomplished in 1915. The latter company, which at that time was owned almost entirely by George E. Keith had a bleached sulphite pulp mill and a one-machine paper mill, part of the production of which was on white papers. The entire production was immediately swung over into white papers. The Katahdin Pulp & Paper Company was incorporated in 1889. It commenced operations by the remodeling of an existing soda pulp mill and the production of unbleached sulphite pulp for sale in the market. The one-machine papermill was added in 1910 and manilas and coarse papers produced. In 1913 a bleaching department was added to the pulp mill, and the production of white papers commenced. The Katahdin Pulp & Paper Company was not an outgrowth of a sawed lumber business, but it did for a few years unsuccessfully embark in this business in addition to the pulp business. This company also owned timberlands which ultimately came over to the Eastern Manufacturing Company.

In connection with the absorption of the Katahdin Pulp & Paper Company, the timberlands of the latter company were transferred to a newly organized corporation, the Lincoln Pulpwood Company, which later became—and is today—a subsidiary of the Eastern Manufacturing Company. The Lincoln Pulpwood Company was, shortly after its organization, charged with the handling of the Eastern's timberlands, as well as its own, and given the task of handling the procurement of the pulpwood supply for the company's pulp mills, which function it still performs. When retirement of the outstanding mortgage of the Lincoln Pulpwood Company was completed in 1926, its lands were transferred to the Eastern Manufacturing Company (Massachusetts), under terms and conditions of the latter company's mortgage indenture of December 1, 1921.

Up until the latter part of 1918 or early 1919, the headquarters of the company were located at Bangor (South Brewer) Maine. About that time, however, the company opened an office in Boston, and established executive headquarters there. Early in 1923 the treasury department was moved from Bangor to Boston, and later the sales organization was also established there, so that for the past four years or more the principal office of the company has been in Boston.

The pulp produced in the company's own mills has always formed the principal raw material of its paper mills. It has always controlled its principal raw material for pulp manufacture, pulpwood, through the ownership of timberlands.

Until the year 1919 the capital stock of the company was closely held and the control was in the hands of the Ayer family, although the Old Colony Trust Company—trustee under a then mortgage indenture—did in 1919 take a hand in the management. Mr. Stuart W. Webb of their organization represented the bank and later became treasurer, chairman of the board and latterly president of the Eastern Manufacturing Company.

In 1919 the company was changed to a Massachusetts corporation, and its capitalization increased. One hundred and forty thousand shares of a new common stock of five dollars par value were issued. Of this issue approximately ninety thousand shares were given to holders of the former $100 par value common on an eight for one basis, and approximately fifty thousand shares were sold to an underwriting syndicate. At the same time the existing issue of ten thousand shares of preferred stock ($100 par value), was converted into a second preferred stock, and a new first preferred stock, 32,500 shares of $100 par value, was issued and sold to an underwriting syndicate. In 1921 an issue of $3,000,000 of first mortgage sinking fund gold bonds was authorized by the preferred stockholders, and bonds to the extent of $2,500,000 were sold through an underwriting syndicate.

Through the course of the years, the plants of the company have been rebuilt and enlarged, and are today fitted with equipment of modern type for the manufacture of the irrespective products. The two paper mills together produce approximately 28,000 tons per year of fine white papers, comprising bonds, ledgers, writings, papetries, mimeographs, cover and off-set papers, etc., which is nationally distributed through paper convertors and paper merchants. The two pulp mills have a combined production of 40,000 tons of high-grade bleached sulphite pulp per year. Of this amount some 23,000 tons is consumed in the company's own paper mills, and about seven thousand tons is being sold in the form of spruce cellulose for Rayon manufacture. The balance is sold to other paper mills making the higher grades of fine papers.

The plants of the company are well electrified and most of the equipment is motor driven. Electric power is obtained from the Bangor Hydo-Electric Company and steam requirements are supplied by good boiler plants, which are oil fired. Each mill has an ample supply of pure process water by virtue of a well developed chain of lakes. Both mills are also well equipped with automatic sprinkler systems and adequate fire protection systems. Satisfactory systems are in use for the economical handling of pulpwood, and the mills have excellent sidetrack facilities for the receiving of raw materials and shipping of their finished products. The principal mill—at South Brewer —is located on tidewater, which is of decided advantage in taking in fuel oil, pulpwood and boxboards.

The main plant at South Brewer is unique in that it is the only pulp and paper mill in New England, and one of the few on the Atlantic seaboard, which is located directly on tidewater. This fact plays an important part in permitting transportation direct to the mill by steamer of pulpwood from along the coast of Maine and from the Maritime Provinces. The company itself, through a subsidiary, owns some sixteen thousand acres of very good spruce lands in Nova Scotia, and brings to its docks in tank steamers the fuel oil used in firing its boilers.

Early in 1928 there occurred an executive re-organization of the company, at which time Frank D. True of Portland, Maine, was elected chairman of the board, and Edward M. Graham, president of the Bangor Hydro-Electric Company of Bangor, Maine, was elected president. Stuart B. Copeland, vice-president, is head of all of the operations of the company, and the sales are in charge of Fred A. Leahy, vice-president, who is located in New York City. Albert D. Pomeroy is treasurer of the new company, and its general offices have again been concentrated at the main plant at South Brewer, Maine.

WALTER WHITMORE CHADBOURNE—A native and lifelong resident of Maine, Mr. Chadbourne, a product of his native State's educational system, has been a member of the faculty of the University of Maine, ever since he had concluded his own education in 1922. Having specialized during his college years in the study of economics, he is teaching this subject now. Though one of the younger members of the faculty, he has made for himself already a well-established reputation for thorough scholarship and he has also succeeded in making himself well liked amongst the student body.

Walter Whitmore Chadbourne was born at Danforth, Washington County, September 5, 1899, a son of James H. and Lizzie A. Chadbourne. His father is the proprietor of the Hotel Vendome at Danforth and is well and favorably known in the hotel industry in Maine. Professor Chadbourne received his preliminary education in the public schools of Danforth, graduating from Danforth High School in 1916. He then became a student at the University of Maine, Orono, from which he was graduated with a degree of Bachelor of Arts in 1920. The next two years he spent in graduate studies at the Harvard University Graduate School of Business Administration, from which he received the degree of Master of Business Administration in 1922. In the same year he received an appointment as instructor in economics at the University of Maine. In 1925 he was promoted to Assistant Professor, which position he still holds.

Professor Chadbourne is especially interested in the history of banking in Maine, on which subject he has made exhaustive researches, the results of which he expects to publish before long in the form of a doctor's thesis. During the World War he served as a private in the Central Officers' Training School, being stationed at Plattsburg, New York, and at Camp Lee, Virginia. He is a member of the Masonic Order and of the University of Maine Chapter of Sigma Chi Fraternity. For many years he has been very much interested in collecting old coins and paper money, especially those issued by the United States and by the early State banks, of which he has assembled a very interesting collection. This interest also finds expression in his membership in the American Numismatic Association.

Professor Chadbourne was married at Danforth, July 31, 1924, to Belle Springer, a daughter of Herbert F. and Eliza Springer. His family home is located at No. 51 College Avenue, Orono.

HARRIE BADGER COE—A member of an old and prominent Maine family, Mr. Coe himself was born in Maine and has lived there throughout his life with the exception of two years, spent overseas during the World War as a captain in the American Red Cross. After having been connected for more than a quarter of a century with the Maine Central Railroad Company, he engaged for almost ten years in the advertising and printing business. Since the end of the World War he has devoted himself to social service and to publicity work and since 1924 he has been connected in an executive capacity with the State of Maine Publicity Bureau. A man of great executive ability and of a very pleasing personality, he enjoys the confidence of an unusually large number of prominent men and women in all parts of Maine, being especially widely known amongst hotel owners, many of whom have been greatly benefited by his publicity work. He is also prominently active in the religious and social life of his native city, Portland, where he has made his home for practically all of his life.

Harrie Badger Coe was born in Portland, March 11, 1866, a son of the late Henry Hersey and Frances Ellen (Todd) Coe. His father was for many years connected with the Burnham & Morrill Company of Portland, one of the largest canning houses in Maine, of which he was bookkeeper and cashier at the time of his death in 1879. Mr. Coe was educated in the public schools of Portland. At the end of his first year at Portland High School his father's untimely death made it necessary for him to cut short his pursuit of education and at the age of fourteen years, in 1880, he entered the employ of the Maine Central Railroad Company as an office boy in the passenger traffic department. Receiving frequent promotions to different positions of ever-increasing responsibility and importance, he eventually was made chief clerk of this department. From this position he resigned in 1908 after twenty-eight years' service to form the Printwell Company, of which he became manager. This company did a large advertising and printing business and under Mr. Coe's very able direction enjoyed a very high reputation. He resigned as its manager in 1917 to accept service with the American Red Cross in France and Italy. After the end of the World War he returned to Maine from abroad. His health having broken down as the result of his war , work, he accepted, in 1920, a position with the Great Northern Paper Company and engaged in social service work among this company's lumber camps in the north woods. He continued in this work for some eighteen months, after which, having regained his health, he returned to Portland and accepted the position of Publicity and Retail Secretary of the Portland Chamber of Commerce. In 1924 he resigned this position, accepting that of General Secretary of the State of Maine Publicity Bureau, of which he has been manager since 1926. He is also secretary of the Maine Hotel Association. In these two offices he has done exceptionally able and valuable work in connection with giving publicity to the many great advantages possessed by Maine as a recreation center. He is widely known throughout the State and has also made many friends for himself and for his native State amongst the thousands of visitors who come to Maine every summer, many of them visiting the State as the result of the work of his Bureau and frequently relying on its services during their stay. The headquarters of the Bureau, located on Longfellow Square, Portland, have become known throughout the country as one of the most efficiently conducted offices of this type, a reputation largely resulting from Mr. Coe's work. In 1927 he accepted an invitation extended to him by the publishers of this work to become its editor-in-chief, a position for which he was admirably fitted by his unusually extensive knowledge of the history, development and present conditions of all phases of life in Maine. Mr. Coe's service as a captain with the American Red Cross was very important and offered him still another opportunity to prove his unusual executive ability. He was stationed in France and later in Italy, being placed in charge of the shipping department and of thirty-two warehouses in Italy and Sicily. He is a member of the Portland Club, of the Board of Governors of which he has been a member for several years; the Portland Kiwanis Club; the Round Table; the State Street Parish Club; the Cumberland County Fish & Game Association; the Maine Sportsman's Fish & Game Association; the National Aeronautic Association; the Maine Automobile Association; and the Veterans of Foreign Wars. In politics he is a supporter of the Republican party, while his religious affiliations are with the Congregational church, and more particularly with the State Street Congregational Church of Portland.

Mr. Coe was married (first), at Portland, September 10, 1895, to Gertrude Libby Kilborn, a daughter of William T. and Lucietta (Libby) Kilborn. Mrs. Coe died in May, 1918. He was married (second), at Portland, May 24, 1924, to Abba Harris, a daughter of Newton Whitman and Tilly (Huston) Harris. Mrs. Abba (Harris) Coe for many years has been prominently active in religious and club circles and prior to her marriage was also widely known in business circles as a member of the firm of Harris & Jackson with headquarters at No. 51½ Exchange Street, Portland, one of the most successful direct mail service organizations in Maine. By his first marriage Mr. Coe is the father of two sons: Philip Kilborn Coe, born at Portland, September 26, 1897, now manufacturers' sales manager for the Goodyear Tire & Rubber Company of California with headquarters at Los Angeles, California, and Kilborn Bray Coe, born at Portland, March 25, 1899, now vice-president and manager of the Forest City Motor Company of Port-

land. Mr. and Mrs. Coe make their home at No. 1563 Forest Avenue, Portland.

MILTON B. HILLS is in the lumber business, having establishments at Belfast, Maine, and Lincolnville, Maine. His business career has had lumber for its chief interest, although as he developed he dealt also in various side lines. After learning the business he struck out for himself and has won much prosperity. He has not been content with merely handling lumber, buying and selling it, he cuts his own timber, and deals in hardware and other kinds of supplies. His firm carries his own name, and his staff of employees run to thirty.

Milton B. Hills was born at Northport, Maine, August 4, 1887, son of Melville E. and Lizzie (Prescott) Hills. The father, who was a farmer, was born at Lincolnville, Maine, November 11, 1850, and the mother was born at Northport, Maine. He attended the public schools at Northport, Maine, and Bucksport Seminary. When he left school he engaged in the lumber business and has remained so occupied to the present time. His first job was at Lincolnville, but in 1909 he started in for himself, and later opened the same business at Belfast, Maine. This business he has continued to operate to the present time, having greatly developed it, but he has also kept his office at Lincolnville. Mr. Hills operates under his own name—Milton B. Hills—and has in his employ an average of from twenty-five to thirty people. He cuts his own timber, deals in hardware supplies, and all kinds of building materials and masons' supplies. He owns 8,000 acres of farm and timberlands, and more than four hundred sheep. Mr. Hills is a Republican in politics. He belongs to the Maine Lumber Dealers' Association; the Chamber of Commerce; Free and Accepted Masons, Blue Lodge; Maine Sheep and Wool Growers' Association; and the American Sheep and Wool Growers' Association. He attends the Methodist church at Belfast.

Milton B. Hills married, at Camden, Maine, June 10, 1914, Grace F. Fuller, born at Appleton, Maine, March 21, 1885, daughter of Will and Alice (Barnes) Fuller, both natives of Appleton.

HENRY F. MERRILL—Many and varied are the business connections of Henry F. Merrill, treasurer and general manager of the Randall & McAllister Coal Company of Portland, the largest and oldest concern in the State of Maine which is engaged in the wholesale and retail handling of coal. The offices are located at No. 84 Commercial Street, and the business is of a scope which requires the services of two hundred men, distributing coal to all the New England States and to the Maritime Provinces. Mr. Merrill is president of the Federal Loan & Building Association, and is also identified with eleven other business organizations as a director. Moreover, he is chairman of the Maine Division of the New England Council, is teacher of the largest Bible class in the State of Maine, and is a member of thirty-one clubs.

Henry F. Merrill was born in Portland, Maine, February 15, 1864, son of Samuel N., a native of Falmouth, Maine, who was an engineer in the Custom House in Portland, and who died in 1874, and of Elizabeth N. (Foster) Merrill, a native of Falmouth, Maine, whose death occurred in 1872. Mr.

Merrill received his education in the public schools, and then engaged in active business life, but he has always been a student and a reader and has continued self-directed study throughout his career. In 1924 he received from Colby College the degree of Master of Arts. After completing his school training Mr. Merrill learned the trade of bookbinder, and remained with his first employer for a period of six years. At the end of that time he became identified with the Randall & McAllister Coal Company, which connection has been maintained to the present time (1928). He served in various capacities until 1898, when he was made treasurer, and in 1923 made manager, which position he is now filling, rounding out now a period of nearly thirty years in those offices, and forty-seven years of continuous connection with the Randall & McAllister Coal Company. Success in this business connection, however, represents but a part of the achievements of Mr. Merrill. The business is an old one, dating back to 1858, when a co-partnership was formed by a Mr. Sawyer and Mr. Randall under the firm name of Sawyer and Randall, the original location of the business being on Commercial Street, not far from the present location of the business. Sawyer and Randall were dealers in fuel, most of which was wood in those days. In 1873 H. F. McAllister became a member of the firm and the name was changed to its present title of Randall & McAllister. In 1893 the business was incorporated, with John F. Randall as first president of the corporation, and in 1898 he was succeeded by his son, E. A. Randall, who is still president of the concern (1928). As treasurer and general manager, however, Mr. Merrill takes a burden of the responsibilities of the actual management of the business and so effectively is he attending to this end of the business that the two hundred employees of the Randall & McAllister Coal Company are kept busy to capacity. In addition to the interests of this connection, Mr. Merrill is president of the Federal Loan and Building Association, a member of the board of directors of the Chapman National Bank, and of the Morris Plan Bank, and is a director of nine other corporations. He is chairman of the Maine Council division and of the New England Council, and is actively interested in the Young Men's Christian Association, being president of the Maine State organization, and vice-president of the Portland Young Men's Christian Association. During the World War he served as chairman of all Maine Young Men's Christian Association work in providing War Young Men's Christian Association secretaries, and was chairman of the Cumberland County "drives." Mr. Merrill is also president of the board of directors of the Port of Portland, who have built the Maine State Pier, a State institution which is proving a great success both financially and from the point of view of developing Maine's industries.

Though so busily engaged with business and civic and ethical activities, Mr. Merrill also finds time for the enjoyment of music. He was the first president of the Portland Men's Singing Club, and was the first chairman of the Music Committee of the City of Portland, continuing in that office for nine years. He is very well known in general club circles, being a member of thirty-one clubs, including clubs in Boston and other places, and he is the only one in Portland who holds membership in both the Rotary Club and the Lions Club. He is also affiliated with Portland Free and Accepted Masons; Mount Vernon Chapter, Royal Arch Masons; Portland Council, Royal and Select Masters; Portland Commandery, No. 2, Knights Templar; Maine Consistory, Sublime Princes of the Royal Secret, thirty-second degree; Kora Temple, Ancient Arabic Order Nobles of the Mystic Shrine. His religious affiliation is with the St. Lawrence Congregational Church, which he serves as a member of the standing committee, and in the Sunday school, of which he teaches the largest Bible class in the State of Maine, a class of more than two hundred members.

Henry F. Merrill was married, in 1889, to Mabel A. Randall, of Portland, Maine, daughter of John F. and Elvira S. (Sargent) Randall. Mr. and Mrs. Merrill are the parents of one daughter, Ruth E., who married George E. McGowan. The family home is at No. 5 Eastern Promenade, Portland.

ZELMA MERWIN DWINAL—Among members of the legal fraternity of Camden, Maine, is found Zelma Merwin Dwinal, who was admitted to the Maine State bar in 1918, after having spent his earlier career in other activities which prepared him to undertake the work of an attorney with a broad knowledge of men and conditions in many parts of the country. He is the son of Fred E. and Luetta (Briggs) Dwinal.

Zelma Merwin Dwinal was born at Mechanic Falls, Maine, on March 12, 1884. He received a high school education, followed by college and university work, at Bates College and Georgetown University. He was principal of Richmond High School from 1906 to 1909, and of Livermore Falls High School from 1909 to 1910. He was doorkeeper of the United States Senate from 1910 to 1912, when he returned to school work and was principal of the Camden High School from 1912 to 1917. He was admitted to the bar in 1918. He has practiced law in Camden since 1918, and since 1919 has been manager and owner of the Talbot Insurance Agency. From 1921 to 1925 he was County Attorney for Knox County; he was a member of the House in the Eighty-second Maine Legislature, and of the Maine Senate in the Eighty-third. He is a past chairman of the Board of Selectmen, a member of the Free and Accepted Masons, the Rotary Club, the Camden Business Men's Association, and the Rockland Country Club. He is a Republican in politics and a member of the Congregational church. Zelma Merwin Dwinal married Harriette M. Newall at Richmond, on December 18, 1907. They have three children: Charles F., Barbara N., and Lucille N.

WILLIAM CASE BIRD—During practically the whole of his business career, William Case Bird, of Rockland, Maine, has been connected with the production of building materials, or their sale, and until recently was vice-president in charge of production for the Rockland & Rockport Lime Corporation, manufacturers of a wide variety of lime products. On January 1, 1928, Mr. Bird severed his connections with the Rockland & Rockport Lime Corporation and located in New York City, where he is associated with Bird & Goodwin, Incorporated, Bankers, at No. 31 Pine Street.

Born in Rockland, Maine, July 1, 1888, he was the

son of Hanson Gregory and Jennie (Willey) Bird. His father, a native, of Rockland, who survived until 1900, was a limeburner. His mother was born in St. George, Maine. Educated in the public schools in the class of 1907, and at Phillips-Exeter Academy, where he was graduated in 1908, he entered the Massachusetts Institute of Technology, and received his degree of Bachelor of Science in 1912. His first professional employment was with the Port Credit Brick Company, of Port Credit, Ontario, Canada, where he was engaged in 1912-13, going from there to the Dierks Lumber & Coal Company, of Kansas City, Missouri, where he remained from 1913 until 1916. Returning East, he joined the staff of the Rockland, Thomaston & Camden Street Railway Company, and was its general manager until 1920. He then became general superintendent of the Rockland & Rockport Lime Company and was vice-president in charge of operation from 1926 to 1928. Mr. Bird is past-president of the Chamber of Commerce, and before his departure from Rockland was a valued member of the Rotary Club, and of the Forty Club. He was also a director of the Rockland Community Chest, the Rockland Loan & Building Association, and of the Rockland Country Club. He is a member of the Free and Accepted Masons, belonging to the Blue Lodge and Scottish Rite organizations of that order. He is a Republican, and attends the Universalist church.

On October 17, 1917, William C. Bird married Ruth C. Gurdy, of Rockland, Maine, daughter of Harry O. and Julia (Smith) Gurdy, both natives of Rockland.

ELKANAH E, BOYNTON—His training and experience have pointed to his present success in the career of Elkanah E. Boynton, one of the foremost pharmacists in that section of the State of which Camden is a flourishing center, his interest in his profession being accompanied with the elements of enterprise and skill that have been the means of keeping his establishment in the front rank with the best drugstores in Maine. One of Camden's leading citizens, as well, Mr. Boynton's services to the activities of the business, the civic, and the social life of the community are such as to require his direction of the responsibilities of important office in the advancement of Camden.

Elkanah E. Boynton was born April 6, 1870, in New York City, a son of Alvah E. and Hattie A. (Spear) Boynton, both natives of Rockland. There Mr. Boynton attended the public schools of Rockland and was graduated at the Massachusetts College of Pharmacy, in Boston, Massachusetts. He started in the general retail drug business in 1890, at Camden, and he has continued in that city in the same line to the present. In 1924, he purchased a drug and medicine manufacturing plant, now known as the Pendleton Company.

A Democrat in the political field, Mr. Boynton is chairman of the Camden Board of Selectmen; and he is also a member of the Camden Board of Trade. Fraternally, he is affiliated with the Free and Accepted Masons in all its branches, including the Ancient Accepted Scottish Rite of the thirty-second degree; with the Independent Order of Odd Fellows; and he is also a member of the Camden Rotary Club, of which he is president, and of the Camden Yacht Club. His religious faith is that of the Congregational church.

Elkanah E. Boynton married, April 12, 1892, at Rockland, Jennie Ingraham, who was born at Rockland, daughter of Henry B. Ingraham.

WILLIAM H. BROADHEAD—Possessed of an experience in the woolen trades dating from his youth in 1894, William H. Broadhead is now (1928) considered by mill men of New England to be one of the most capable managers and executives that the industry contains. In 1920 he became agent and superintendent of the Camden (Maine) Woolen Company, in which capacities he has since continued, also being agent of the Penobscot Woolen Company, of Camden. His father also was in the woolen industry, having served as designer of fabric and as mill superintendent. Mr. Broadhead was born in England, January 6, 1876, the son of Benjamin and Mary (Hollingsworth) Broadhead, both of whom were born in England. Benjamin spent his life in the English mills, entering them as a young man and familiarizing himself thoroughly with all the ramifications making the manufacture of cloth the specialized craft it is. As he was gifted with a fine sense of the artistic, he was made a designer; and his talent for handling workers, by whom he was held in favor, carried him higher in the trade, to the office of superintendent.

His son, William H. Broadhead, therefore, was born into the trade, coming to Providence when a child and getting his first instruction in the Providence, Rhode Island, grade and high schools, after which, with the firmly-rooted liking already taking growth into serious consideration of the textile industry as a career, he studied one year in the Philadelphia Textile School, at Philadelphia, Pennsylvania. William H. Broadhead came to the United States from England in 1886, when he was ten years old, and a scant eight years later he entered the employ of the National and Providence Mills, at Providence. Here he learned in practice what he had taken up in theory at Philadelphia, and after ten years, in 1904, he was a master of the textile industry, both woolen and worsted. At this time he was made superintendent of the Hampden Woolen Mills, at Hampden, Massachusetts, which position he retained until 1906, when he went with the Plainfield Woolen Company as superintendent of its plant at Central Village, Connecticut, and there he remained until 1916. During the World War he was superintendent of the Cleveland Woolen Mills at Cleveland, Tennessee, and in 1920 became agent and superintendent of the Camden and the Penobscot Woolen companies, at Camden. He is now (1928) a director of the Penobscot Woolen Company and has a number of other business and fraternal affiliations, including membership in the Tamy Shanter Club, the Camden Board of Trade, the Rotary Club, Camden Yacht Club, the Business Men's Club, Camden Yacht Club, the Business Men's Club, and the Blue Lodge of the Free and Accepted Masons. In local politics he is Independent, and in national politics a Republican.

William H. Broadhead married, at Springfield, Massachusetts, Frances P. Connell, born at Springfield, daughter of Eugene and Maria Connell. Mr. and Mrs. Broadhead are the parents of one child, Walter F., born at Central Village, Connecticut, April 16, 1909.

MARK RODGERS is a prominent business man of Camden, Maine. Though born in England he came to this country at an early age and had the advantage of an education here. His father had been in the textile business, and this determined the line of his own career for after completing his education he, too, engaged in the textile business and has remained in it. He now holds a responsible position in an important woolen company.

Mark Rodgers was born in England on March 22, 1888, son of Fenton and Eva Rodgers, both of whom were natives of Great Britain. Having been brought to this country, he attended the public schools at Maynard, Massachusetts, and in course of time was employed with the Camden Woolen Company at Camden, Maine, becoming boss weaver. In 1919 he was made superintendent of the Penobscot Woolen Company, and has continued to hold that position to the present time. Mr. Rodgers is a Republican in politics. He belongs to the Board of Trade, the Free and Accepted Masons, County Lodge, and the Improved Order of Red Men. He attends the Episcopal church.

Mark Rodgers married, at Worcester, Massachusetts, Anna Kennedy, daughter of James J. and Nellie Kennedy, of Worcester, Massachusetts. Children: 1. Joseph Henry, born at Worcester, Massachusetts, June 19, 1914. 2. Wilfrid Claymore, born at Camden, Maine.

WILLIAM E. HATCH—The career of William Ellis Hatch, who is now (1928) in his sixty-third year, resident at Camden, Maine, has been varied. When a young man he went to sea, becoming an able seaman during the eight years he spent upon it, his father before him having been master of a ship out of Islesboro, Maine; then, after eight years of seafaring life, deciding that greater opportunity was in store for him on land, learning the trade of carpenter, in which he has been occupied, first as an artisan, and in later years as builder and contractor, since the last of the nineteenth century. He has constructed a number of fine homes in Camden.

Mr. Hatch was born at Islesboro, Maine, December 13, 1866, son of Amasa Hatch, sea captain throughout his life, who was born at Islesboro, and Mary (Johnson) Hatch, born at St. Andrews, Canada. Directly after leaving public school at Islesboro Mr. Hatch went to sea. Soon after his marriage, however, he decided that a business on land would be preferable. Accordingly he went into the trade of carpentry at Islesboro, and in 1900 established himself in the general contracting and building business at Camden, where he has founded a reputation much in favor as a builder of houses. He has also constructed school buildings, and in 1928 built the new Camden Public Library Building. Mr. Hatch is well liked in the community, his long residence there having been replete with warm social contacts. He is known as a man of unimpeachable character, who constantly has allied his influence with local forces tending toward public progress and improvement. He is affiliated with the Camden Board of Trade, and fraternally, with the Blue Lodge, Free and Accepted Masons.

William E. Hatch married, at Islesboro, December 25, 1892, Lena Farnsworth, born at Islesboro, in August, 1866, daughter of William and Lucy (Ames) Farnsworth, both natives of Islesboro. Mr. and Mrs. Hatch are the parents of four children, a fifth, the second child, having died in 1917: Arthur C.; Amasa

P., deceased; Ellis J.; Muriel and Theodore, all of whom were born at Islesboro.

OSCAR H. EMERY—In Camden, where he has spent practically the whole of his professional career, having located here in 1911, one year after he began practice, Oscar H. Emery, attorney-at-law and now (1928) member of the Town Board of Selectmen, is an interested participant in all phases of the progressive life of the community. Aside from his general practice of law he is affiliated with several social and fraternal organizations, having to do not alone with his profession but with the business affairs of Camden. A Democrat, he has had a close connection with local politics since 1916.

Mr. Emery was born at Bar Harbor, Maine, October 26, 1887, the son of Herbert F. Emery, born at Bar Harbor, died in November, 1924, and of Nancy (Peach) Emery, also born at Bar Harbor. Herbert F. Emery loved the soil, and during his life was a farmer and builder of roads. Well and favorably known in Bar Harbor and vicinity, he took part in civic affairs and always had in his heart a desire to help those with whom he was in contact. He was a member of the Bar Harbor Lodge of the Free and Accepted Masons, and was respected sincerely throughout his career.

Oscar H. Emery received his early education in the public schools of Bar Harbor, and graduated from Hebron Academy in 1906. Having worked to pay for his education, he taught school for a year after graduating. When nineteen, he entered the University of Maine, from which he graduated in 1910 with the degree of Bachelor of Laws and on October 11 of that year was admitted to Maine State Bar Association. Mr. Emery started to practice law at Southwest Harbor, Maine, immediately after being admitted to the bar; but after a year he removed to Camden, which has since been his residence. In 1916 he was made Judge of the Probate Court of Knox County, and this office he held for four years. Aside from membership in the State Bar Association, Mr. Emery is affiliated with the Knox County Bar Association, and, like his father having a deep interest in the soil, is a member of the Grange, Patrons of Husbandry. He is also a member of the Blue Lodge, Free and Accepted Masons; Royal Arch Masons, Royal and Select Masters, Knights Templar; Phi Alpha Delta Fraternity, University of Maine; president (1925-26 and 1927-28) Camden Parent-Teachers' Association; the Camden Board of Trade, and the Business Men's Club. Both Mr. Emery and his wife attend the Congregational church.

Oscar H. Emery married, at South Thomaston, Maine, November 30, 1911, Helen Bartlett, born April 19, 1887, at South Thomaston, daughter of James Merrill Bartlett, who was born at South Thomaston, and Agnes (Deane) Bartlett, born in Dundee, County of Forfar, Scotland. Mr. and Mrs. Emery are the parents of two children: 1. Barbara B., born at Camden, July 26, 1914. 2. Oscar H., Jr., born at Camden, May 1, 1918.

HENRY G. HUTCHINSON—Biddeford's business builders, the city's civic leaders, and its citizenship in general, delighted to pay honor to Henry Gilbert Hutchinson while he was alive, and an active factor in all the progressive life of the community, and upon his death, they, and all his hosts of friends in this part of the State, mourned the passing of a man who in a score of ways proved himself a friend and co-worker in all effort made for Biddeford's betterment and expansion among the cities of Maine. Mr. Hutchinson's association with numerous institutions and organizations was proof of their vitality and substantialness; his friends were legion in every civic institution; and his life was one of the greatest usefulness.

Henry Gilbert Hutchinson was born December 28, 1850, in Buxton Center, a son of Leonard and Phoebe (Sanborn) Hutchinson, and he attended the schools there, and was graduated at Gorham and Limerick academies. Mr. Hutchinson came to Biddeford in 1872, and employment was found as a clerk in the James S. Dudley drugstore, in the Crystal Block, where he later became a registered pharmacist. In 1873, he purchased the drugstore at the corner of Main and Jefferson streets, where the Morin Drug Company store now is, and he continued in that business until 1881. In the latter year, Mr. Hutchinson entered the employ of the W. A. Wood Company as a traveling salesman, covering the Maine and New Hampshire territory; and in 1889 he took over the Gove Insurance Company and formed partnership with George A. Carter of Saco, under the firm name of H. G. Hutchinson and Company. This company, representing fifty insurance agencies, was considered the most extensive insurance house in Maine; it was conducted several years under the firm name, and upon its dissolution, Mr. Carter took the Saco business, and Mr. Hutchinson that of Biddeford, so continuing to the time of his death, which took place February 13, 1927.

The interests of the civic life of Biddeford were of prime importance to Mr. Hutchinson, who had served as a member of the Board of Aldermen for two years; was appointed in 1903 as a member of the Police Commission, and later as chairman of the board; and had served as tax collector for a term.

For ten years, Mr. Hutchinson was secretary and treasurer of the York Loan & Building Association; and he was also secretary and treasurer of the Greenwood Cemetery Association. Fraternally, he was affiliated with Dunlap Lodge, Free and Accepted Masons; York Chapter, Royal Arch Masons; Bradford Commandery, Knights Templar; Maine Council, Royal and Select Masters; and the Ancient Arabic Order Nobles of the Mystic Shrine. He was also a member of Mavoshen Lodge, Knights of Pythias, and Portland Lodge, Benevolent and Protective Order of Elks. He was an active member of the Second Congregational Church, and served for several years as treasurer of the church society.

Henry G. Hutchinson married, September 14, 1875, Sophie Jordan, daughter of Richworth and Sophie (Lunt) Jordan, whose ancestors were among the pioneer settlers of Biddeford. Their daughter, Josephine, married, August 6, 1902, Alfred S. Bradford, and they have one son: Alfred S. Bradford, who has had the management of the H. G. Hutchinson Insurance Corporation since the death of his grandfather, and whose other officers are: Mrs. Josephine Bradford, president, and Mrs. H. G. Hutchinson, clerk. Mr. Bradford, who is a graduate of Allen Military School, and of Northeastern University, is a member of the York County Fish and Game Association.

ALFRED S. BRADFORD—Taking up the reins of the management of the H. G. Hutchinson Insurance Corporation where they were laid aside by his grandfather, Henry Gilbert Hutchinson, at the time of his death in 1927, Alfred S. Bradford is continuing, with a laudable degree of success, the plan and purpose of that business concern, one of the most extensive and inclusive of insurance companies in Maine. Mr. Bradford is an expert in all insurance interests, and a very able and thorough exponent of their entire field of application.

Alfred S. Bradford was born July 7, 1904, in Biddeford, Maine, a son of Alfred S. Bradford, who was in the service of the United States Government at Portland, and died in 1904, and Josephine (Hutchinson) Bradford, who survives her husband. After attending the public schools in Biddeford, Mr. Bradford was graduated at Allen Military School, and then in the commercial course at Northeastern University. He has been associated with the insurance business from the time of his graduation from college, when he at once entered the office of his grandfather, H. G. Hutchinson; and he has been the manager of the corporation since his grandfather's death, in 1927.

The story of this well-known insurance concern dates from 1889, when Henry Gilbert Hutchinson purchased the insurance business of E. Gove; and later, forming partnership with George A. Carter, of Saco, they became one of the largest and strongest insurance concerns in this part of the State. The original location was at Pool Street, whence the firm removed in 1902 to the present offices in the Masonic Building. The business was incorporated, June 8, 1917, with H. G. Hutchinson as president and treasurer, and with Harry B. Ayer and George C. Fogg as the other members of the corporation. Upon the death of Mr. Hutchinson, reorganization was effected; Mrs. Josephine Bradford was made president and treasurer, and Mrs. H. G. Hutchinson, clerk. This is one of the oldest insurance companies in Southern Maine.

Mr. Bradford is a Republican in his political views; and with his vote and influence he supports the principles of his party, though he has not sought public office. He is a member of the York County Fish and Game Commission, and his religious fellowship is with the Second Congregational church.

MARCUS P. CHANDLER—Succeeding his father, who until his death in 1926, had been a druggist in Camden, Maine, for thirty-five years and who had enjoyed the distinction of the presidency of the Maine State Board of Pharmacy for three consecutive terms, an honor seldom conferred, Marcus P. Chandler has been a druggist in Camden since 1918. He was born at Camden on January 13, 1901, son of Luie M. Chandler, who was born at Northport, Maine, and Eleanor (Wardwell) Chandler, born at Stockton Springs, his father having been a well-known citizen of Camden, a charter member of the local Rotary Club and of Amity Lodge, No. 6, Free and Accepted Masons, of which he is Past Master, also all other bodies including Maine Consistory, and a pharmacist respected by druggists throughout the State of Maine.

Marcus P. Chandler attended the public schools of Camden, and before graduating from high school began the association with his father in the drugstore, when he was seventeen years old. This early contact with the dispensing of drugs proved to Mr. Chandler that he would like pharmacy as a career, and after he graduated from high school, with the class of 1919, he matriculated in Bowdoin College, at Brunswick, Maine, in the class of 1923. Later he passed the State Board examination, after which he rejoined his father in the business at Camden. Luie M. Chandler died three years later, on January 16, and Marcus P. Chandler became sole proprietor. Though he is now (1928) only twenty-seven years of age, Mr. Chandler is firmly established in the commercial and fraternal life of the community. He is a member of the Blue Lodge, Free and Accepted Masons; the Rotary Club; the Camden Board of Trade, and the Rockland Country Club. He is a Democrat, and both he and his wife are members of the Congregational church.

Marcus P. Chandler married, at Rockland, Maine, on September 16, 1925, Elizabeth McDougall, who was born at Rockland on February 22, 1901, daughter of H. N. McDougall, born at Prince Edward Island, Canada, and of Caro (Billings) McDougall. Mr. and Mrs. Chandler are the parents of a daughter, Eleanor Caro, born at Portland, Maine.

M. ALTON FRENCH—Identified as general manager and member of the Carleton-French Company of Camden since 1915, M. Alton French is one of the prominent merchants of the community, where he has been in business with the same organization since 1899. When he first formed his association with the company it was known as the Carleton-Pascal Company, dealers in general groceries, meats, crockery and woodenware, which items are now (1928) its principal lines of trade.

M. Alton French was born at Lincolnville in Waldo County, Maine, on January 7, 1881, the son of Fred E. and Ida Lock (Munroe) French, both of whom were born in Lincolnville. Mr. French's father was a grocer and shoe manufacturer, and the boy decided early in high school days that he would enter some similar business; so, after attending the public schools of Lincolnville he enrolled in the Childs Business College, at New Haven, Connecticut. When barely nineteen years old he started work with the Carleton-Pascal establishment at Camden, making himself more important to that enterprise from that time until, in 1915, he entered the firm, and the name was changed to include his own. It is located at No. 1 Elm Street. Mr. French is a member of the board of directors of the Penobscot Woolen Company, and among his numerous fraternal and social connections are the Camden Board of Trade, the Camden Business Men's Club, and the Rotary Club. He is affiliated with the Masonic Club, and a member of the Free and Accepted Masons, Blue Lodge, in which he has gone through all bodies and holds the thirty-second degree; he is also a member of the Camden Yacht Club.

M. Alton French married, at Camden, in October, 1902, Clara Haskell, born at Union, Maine, daughter of George and Lucey (Jones) Haskell.

ALEXANDER M. WEATHERBEE—Originally in the banking business, following the completion of his education, Alexander M. Weatherbee, of Wiscasset, for a time studied law in the office of his father, Artemus Weatherbee, at Lincoln, Maine, then returned to financial association. Since 1924 he has

been manager of the Wiscasset branch of the Augusta Trust Company.

He was born in Phillips, Maine, May 22, 1895, and received his education in the public schools at Lincoln, spending one year in Bangor at the Theological Seminary. Following these he took several home study courses, among them one in law and one in banking from Columbia University. He began his active life in the banking business with the Lincoln Trust Company, of Lincoln, Maine, in 1920, remaining there for three years, then going to the office of his father, for the further study of the law. His present post he accepted in 1924. He is a Republican in politics and past president of the Wiscasset Chamber of Commerce. His church is the Congregational. His father was born in Lincoln and his mother, Mary (Matthews) Weatherbee, in New Brunswick, Canada. The elder Weatherbee had been a member of the Maine Legislature. He was a thirty-second degree member of the Order of Free and Accepted Masons, belonging to all bodies of that organization, to the Independent Order of Odd Fellows, and to the Ancient Order of United Workmen.

EDMOND CYR—The town of Waterville is fortunate to have as one of its foremost civic leaders, Edmond Cyr, one of the most prominent men in the progressive development of this city, who heads the important firm of Edmond Cyr & Company, with offices located at No. 105 Main Street, conducting an extensive building and contracting business of the highest type. Mr. Cyr is a prominent factor in the financial life of the city in the interests of which he has given so much of his time and energy in the various public offices which he has held, and assuredly, he is an adopted son of whom this city may well be proud. Mr. Cyr was born in Maria, Province of Quebec, Canada, May 12, 1878, son of Salmon and Angelique (Audette) Cyr, both natives of Maria, Quebec. Salmon Cyr was actively engaged in the farming industry and was an esteemed member of his community.

Edmond Cyr was educated in the public schools of Maria, and came to the United States at the age of seventeen. After being connected with the building trade for a number of years, he engaged in an independent contracting business in this city, in 1907, which he has continued successfully since. His company operates in this city and vicinity, conducting a general contracting business which has met with favor and acclaim by all on account of the superior methods of construction used in all their erections, and the quality and durability of all materials. Many beautiful and artistic structures stand as monuments to the intelligent and careful work of the builders under Mr. Cyr's direction, and in this way, he has done much to forward the progress and favorably impress visitors to this city. In politics, he displays an active interest, having served two years in the City Council here, 1912-13; also two years as Alderman from Ward Seven, 1914-15, while in 1925-27, he served as a member of the Maine State Legislature as the representative elected by the citizens of this district, this being an honored recognition by this section of his services and enthusiastic work in behalf of the public good. While at the State Capitol, Mr. Cyr gained an enviable reputation for his keen and expert knowledge of the important affairs of state and his zeal in furthering the interests of his commonwealth and its people. He is a director of the Federal Trust Company, of this city, and is an active member of the Chamber of Commerce, and the Kiwanis Club. In fraternal circles, he is identified with the Knights of Columbus, fourth degree, and the Benevolent and Protective Order of Elks. His religious adherence is given to the Roman Catholic Church of Notre Dame. He is a Democrat in politics.

Edmond Cyr married, February 9, 1903, at Maria, Quebec, Laura Guites, who was born in Maria, May 31, 1886, daughter of Henry Guites, a native of Maria, and Leonie (Duchane) Guites, a native of St. Rock, Province of Quebec. They have two children: Odilon J., born at Maria, October 22, 1904, and Henry Moses, an adopted son, born at New Richmond, Province of Quebec.

WILLIAM HENRY COOK—A leading figure in the active life of Waterville, William Henry Cook renders incalculable aid to the progress and development of this city in his position as general manager and part owner of the Elmwood Hotel, creating through the attention and service accorded to all guests a feeling of good will and pleasure that goes far toward establishing a reputation for this city of hospitality and modern advancement. Mr. Cook, in partnership with N. H. Barrows, owns this splendid hostelry, having become associated with its operation in 1912, and he has managed its affairs since that time. The Elmwood Hotel is one of the most beautiful buildings, from an architectural standpoint, in this city, containing one hundred and fifty spacious and well-appointed rooms, and employing more than sixty persons to care for the requirements of its guests. Mr. Cook was born in Chelsea, Massachusetts, March 23, 1878, son of Charles E. Cook, a native of St. Albans, Vermont, and Mary Cook.

William H. Cook was educated in the public schools of Chelsea, graduating from Chelsea High School, in in 1896, after which he entered Dartmouth College, where he received his degree of Bachelor of Letters with the class of 1900. After practicing his profession for some time, he became interested in the hotel business, and as aforementioned, in 1912, became associated with Mr. Barrows in his present hotel enterprise. His success has been due to his unwavering policy of quality service and superior accommodations, and travelers and visitors to this city depend with absolute certainty upon the Elmwood Hotel as a place where they receive a warm and hospitable welcome and courteous treatment amidst the most comfortable and homelike surroundings in an atmosphere of cordial sincerity scarcely equaled in any other inn. Mr. Cook is active in local civic affairs, being an ardent supporter of all causes which tend to promote the well-being of this city and its people, and although in politics, he is an Independent, still he takes a constructive interest in all affairs of a municipal nature. He is a member of the New England and Maine State Hotel Men's associations, the local Chamber of Commerce, the Rotary Club, and the Waterville Country Club. His fraternal connections are with the Free and Accepted Masons, in which he has attained the thirty-second degree in all bodies of that order, the Masonic Club; Theta Delta Chi, and the Sphinx fraternities. His religious adherence is given to the Congregational church.

William Henry Cook married, November 4, 1912,

at Waterville, Mabel Ferris, born at South Norwalk, Connecticut, a daughter of Charles and Mary Ferris.

LINWOOD B. DUNHAM—One of Maine's most loyal and prominent sons, Linwood B. Dunham, of Monmouth, spent many years amid the vast farming regions of the Far West, successfully engaging in agriculture in that section of this glorious country, after which he returned to his native State and has since been a valuable asset to the commonwealth in the knowledge he gained in his many years' experience in Western farming. Mr. Dunham is farm foreman at the Maine Agricultural Experiment Station, with which he has been identified since 1924, shortly after his return to the East, and by his modern and improved methods, coupled with an enthusiasm and energy which is seen in everything he does, he has made a remarkable record for efficiency in his department of this station. His advice and ideas are eagerly sought by the farmers of the entire State who appreciate the advantages and the knowledge disseminated by this splendid service, which supports and aids the agricultural industry of the State to such a great degree. Mr. Dunham was born in North Penobscot, August 3, 1891, son of Ezra K. and Amelia C. (Marks) Dunham, both of whom were born at North Penobscot. Ezra K. Dunham was active in farming circles, also prominent and active as a carpenter and builder of great ability and success.

Linwood B. Dunham was educated in the public schools of Penobscot; then entered Wesleyan University where he studied for one year. In 1907 he left his native State to seek success in the Far West, and took up a homestead grant in Montana, operating a farm of three hundred and twenty acres, raising wheat with great success until 1920, when he accepted a position in Helena, Montana, as foreman of a large cattle ranch, where he gained much valuable experience which has been highly advantageous in his present position. Mr. Dunham remained in this position for two years, after which he was engaged as foreman of the South Pondero Sheep Ranch for about a year and a half. Then operating his own farm in Montana until 1924, he accepted his present position in the service of the State as foreman of the farm of four hundred acres. In politics, he is an active supporter of the principles of the Republican party, while his religious affiliations are with the Methodist church. Mr. Dunham is deeply concerned with the prosperous future of the agricultural industry in this progressive State, and all his influence and abilities are concentrated on that ideal and the State is surely fortunate to have the services of one who has the interests of his commonwealth and his fellow-citizens so thoroughly at heart.

GEORGE S. BURGESS—Active in promoting agricultural progress in the State of Maine, George S. Burgess has been identified with the splendid work being conducted by the Maine Agricultural Experiment Station, at Monmouth, since 1921. This branch of the station, known as Highmoor Farm, has done much to assist the farmers of the entire commonwealth by solving various problems, giving advice on the efficient and economic management of farms, and introducing new methods and varieties of agriculture. Mr. Burgess supervises the department devoted to cattle on this farm, having charge of a herd of one hundred experimental cattle, and by careful observations and practical demonstrations has aided the farmer materially.

Mr. Burgess was born in Union, November 10, 1896, son of Frederick and Sarah (Ware) Burgess, both natives of Union. Frederick Burgess was actively engaged in agricultural work and was a prominent and respected member of his community. George S. Burgess was educated in the public schools of Union, and after high school, entered the University of Maine, graduating from the College of Agriculture with the class of 1921, and accepting his present position immediately after his graduation. His careful and efficient management of the dairy department at Highmoor Farm has brought him the acclaim and admiration of all who have witnessed the results obtained. Mr. Burgess holds the title of herdsman of the station and is constantly engaged in formulating ideas and methods which will further the progress of the men who depend on agriculture and dairying for their living, to give them the opportunity to obtain the maximum of profits with the minimum of cost and effort. He is popular in fraternal affairs being a member of Union Lodge, No. 31, Free and Accepted Masons. In Grange No. 176, of Union, he is an energetic and enthusiastic worker, in Politics, he follows the principles of the Republican party, while his religious adherence is given to the Methodist church.

George S. Burgess married, June 22, 1925, at North Yarmouth, Iva Merchant, born February 13, 1900, at Litchfield, daughter of William Merchant, born at North Yarmouth, and Sarah (Woodman) Merchant, a native of Raymond.

VALMORE E. BOLDUC, M. D., who is noted as one of the rising young physicians of York County, Maine, and well-known surgeon of Sanford, Maine, was born May 6, 1897, at Somersworth, New Hampshire, a son of Ovide and Mary Louise (Paul) Bolduc, both natives of the Province of Quebec, Canada.

Valmore E. Bolduc received his preliminary education in the public schools of the community in which he was born. Upon the completion of these courses of study he entered the University of Vermont, and he graduated from there with the degree of Bachelor of Arts. He then began his medical studies at the same university, from which he graduated with the class of 1921, when he received his degree as Doctor of Medicine. For a time, Dr. Bolduc served as interne at St. Luke's Hospital at New Bedford, Massachusetts, and United States Veterans' Hospital, No. 24 (Parkers Hill Hospital), Boston. In 1921, he removed to Sanford, Maine, where he began the practice of his profession. He has carried on a general medical and surgical practice since that time, meeting with eminent success, and looked upon as a physician who is destined to become one of the foremost members of his profession in York County, Maine. He is also a member of the staff of the Maine General Hospital, the Eye and Ear Hospital, and the Webber Hospital, at Biddeford, Maine. During the World War, Dr. Bolduc, being too young to be in active service, was nevertheless, enlisted in the United States Navy Department at the University of Vermont.

Despite the manifold duties which his profession entails, Dr. Bolduc has found time in which to participate in many activities. Among the learned organizations which pertain to his profession, in which

he holds membership are, the American Medical Association, the Maine State Medical Society, and the York County Medical Society. He is fraternally affiliated with the Benevolent and Protective Order of Elks, and the Knights of Columbus. He is also a member of the Sanford Town Club, and several other local clubs.

Dr. Valmore E. Bolduc was married, in 1924, to Blanche A. Drohan, who was born in West Quincy, Massachusetts. Dr. and Mrs. Bolduc are the parents of one child, Arthur V., born December 14, 1925. Dr. and Mrs. Bolduc attend St. Ignatius Roman Catholic Church.

PERCY SHEPHERD MERRILL, M. D.—With a general medical practice in Waterville, Percy Shepherd Merrill, Doctor of Medicine, has proven himself to be a physician of ability and skill in the years since 1901, when he began his practice in this town. Before that time he had practiced for a year in Gardiner, Maine. The people in Waterville have found in Dr. Merrill an unusually faithful medical man, one who is willing and ready to devote his time and energy tirelessly to those whom he advises and treats professionally, and who is ever eager to acquire new knowledge in the fields of medicine and surgery and to acquaint himself with the latest developments and discoveries in these fields. He has participated freely in relief work in his profession, having been a member of the relief expedition to Halifax in 1915, and has always taken an active interest in public affairs and in the civic and social life of the community.

Dr. Merrill was born in Bangor, Maine, November 2, 1872, a son of Albert F. Merrill, who was born in Corinth, Maine, and of Harriet (Thomas) Merrill, who was born in Milo, Maine. The father was a grain merchant by occupation. As a boy, Dr. Merrill attended the public schools in Bangor and Waterville, and later went to the high school in Waterville, from which he was graduated in the class of 1890. He became a student at Colby College, from which institution he was graduated in the class of 1894; and at New York University and the Bellevue Hospital Medical College, from which he was graduated in the class of 1899 with the degree of Doctor of Medicine. He served an internship of one year at the hospital in Bridgeport, Connecticut, after which he became engaged in a general medical practice in Gardiner, Maine, in 1900. He continued to practice in Gardiner in 1900 and 1901, and then, in the latter year, he became engaged in a general medical practice in Waterville, which he has maintained until the present time. He is active in the work of the various medical associations, being affiliated with the American Medical Association, the Maine State Medical Association, and the Kennebec County Medical Association. His religious affiliation is with the Congregational church, of Waterville.

In New York City, on May 11, 1905, Dr. Merrill married Mina Miller, a native of Syracuse, New York.

WILLARD BAILEY ARNOLD—As president of the W. B. Arnold Company, of Waterville, Maine. Willard Bailey Arnold is one of the prominent and valued citizens of his community, satisfying with his store a real need in the town and being one of Waterville's industrial leaders. His experience has been varied and even unusual; for early in life he acquired an interest in aeronautics, which he maintained by studying the subject in school and later becoming an instructor in flying in Waco, Texas. He was one of the men who, when the United States entered the World War, were able to offer efficient service in one of the newer branches of the science of warfare—that of fighting in the air.

Mr. Arnold was born in Waterville, on February 1, 1897, a son of Fred J. and Aileen (Foster) Arnold. As a boy, he attended the public schools in Waterville; then the Coburn Classical Institute; the Phillips-Exeter Academy; and finally Colby College, at which for two years he was a student. On November 12, 1917, he left college and enlisted in the Air Service of the United States Army. At Cornell University, he attended the School of Military Aeronautics, where he became conversant with every detail of the airplane and air warfare and expert in the art of flying. Subsequently he was instructor in flying at Rich Field, in Waco, Texas. In 1918 he was commissioned a second lieutenant in the air service of his country, and was stationed in Texas as instructor in stunt flying. He was discharged from the Army Air Service in March, 1919, at which time he came to New York and engaged in the bond business in Wall Street. After he had continued in this work for two years, from 1919 to 1921, he became interested in the hardware business. Now he operates the hardware establishment known as the W. B. Arnold Company, one of the leading companies of its kind in Waterville. Mr. Arnold is active in the fraternal life of his community, being a member of the Free and Accepted Masons, in which order he is affiliated with the Blue Lodge; and holds memberships in several important organizations in the town, such as the Rotary Club, the Chamber of Commerce, and the Waterville Country Club. Maintaining his interest in aeronautics, he is a member of the Aero Club of America. Deeply interested in political matters, he is a Republican, and supports the principles and candidates of the Republican party. His religious affiliation is with the Unitarian church.

On January 5, 1925, in Waterville, Maine, Mr. Arnold married Bertha L. Terry, and they have one son, Willard B. (3), born April 20, 1927.

HOWARD FOSTER HILL, M. D.—One of the younger practicing physicians of Waterville, Kennebec County, specialist in treatment of diseases of the eye, is Howard Foster Hill, Doctor of Medicine, who was born here, August 22, 1895, a son of Dr. James F. and Angie (Foster) Hill, and brother of Frederick Thayer Hill, specialist in diseases of the ear and throat, born in 1889, also practicing in Waterville, president of the staff of Sisters' Hospital since 1925. Dr. Frederick Thayer Hill is widely known as a specialist in the oto-laryngological field. Dr. James F. Hill was for many years in practice in Waterville, and enjoyed the highest of reputations in the profession.

Howard Foster Hill received his early education in the elementary schools and high school of Waterville, and entered Coburn Classical Institute. Upon completion of courses in the institute he matriculated in Colby College, Waterville, and graduated after a distinguished scholastic record, with the degree of Bachelor of Arts, in 1917. He next attended summer classes in Harvard University, and became interested in medicine. This interest had been developing for some time, through contact with his father and also through the influence of his brother, who had graduated from Colby in 1910, and in 1917 was launched on his medical career. Accordingly, Mr. Hill entered the School of Medicine, Harvard University, and graduated thence in 1923, after a thorough preparation in general medicine with special attention to ophthalmology. Finding his inclinations and talent notably suited to this field, Dr. Hill, in the year of his graduation from Harvard, undertook more intensive work, in the Massachusetts Eye and Ear Infirmary, and served as interne in Chestnut Hill Hospital, Philadelphia, Pennsylvania, where he was able further to carry on research in ophthalmology. Next he became one of the staff of surgeons, as resident member, in the Wills Eye Hospital, Philadelphia, and there continued in special post-graduate investigation pertaining to his specialty, terminating it in the latter part of 1925 to begin actual practice in Waterville. Dr. Hill was granted the certificate of the National Ophthalmological Board in 1927, and in the same year was elected president of the Maine Eye and Ear Association, in which office he has functioned to the benefit of the body as a whole, thereby adding to his rapidly growing professional prestige. Dr. Hill is associated with a number of professional organizations, principal among them the American Medical Association, both the State and County Medical societies, the New England Ophthalmological Society, and the Academy of Ophthalmology. Fraternally, in the non-professional direction, he is active in the Free and Accepted Masons, in which he holds the thirty-second degree; and he is a member of the Officers' Reserve Association, the Waterville Country Club, the Masonic Club, the Harvard Club of Boston, and the two college fraternities, Zeta Psi and Alpha Kappa Kappa, the former a national social organization and the latter restricted in membership to students of medicine.

Barely one month after the United States declared the existence of a state of warfare with Germany, Mr. Hill enlisted in the regular army. He was put into the motor transport service, supply train of the First Division, and in 1918 was attached to the artillery. Overseas he fought valiantly, engaging in several principal battles, of which stand out the Toul Sector defensive, in January, 1918, lasting until May, 1918; the Cantigny Sector, April 25 to June 8, the Montidier-Noyon defensive, from June 9 to June 13; the Cantigny defensive, June 14 to July 9, and the St. Mihiel Drive, September 12 to 14. When mustered out of the service in 1919, Dr. Hill held the rank of sergeant.

Dr. Hill is known as one of the public-spirited men of Waterville, and is constantly associated with progressive movements here. He is a Republican, loyal to the party's principles, and possessor of a considerable influence in political matters, which he prefers to exercise quietly and to good effect, in the interests of the community-at-large. He is a Rotarian and a communicant of the Methodist church. Toward charitable and similar appeals of a worthy character he is ever sympathetic, giving generously in a spirit humanitarian.

Howard Foster Hill married, February 18, 1928, Elizabeth Meeker of Stamford, Connecticut, and soon thereafter departed for Europe with his bride.

FRED WALLACE ELWELL—One of the foremost business men of Camden, Maine, is Fred Wallace Elwell, who since 1922 has been the sole owner and proprietor of the firm which for decades has been known as Follanbee and Wood, and which deals in a general line of drygoods of all sorts. Mr. Elwell was employed in this business for many years before he finally bought it, and is, as a result of his many years of experience in this store and his lifelong acquaintance with people and conditions in Maine, thoroughly suited to the work which he has chosen, and is in a position to build up his stock on the basis of what his community desires and needs. In the few years in which he has been operating this business, therefore, it has become an unusually valuable enterprise from the viewpoint of the public. Mr. Elwell at all times has taken an active interest in political and civic matters, and has shown himself willing to support those causes which he has believed would improve conditions in his town.

Mr. Elwell was born June 9, 1878, in Tennant's Harbor, Maine, a son of William A. Elwell, born in 1843, and of Carrie (Hodgman) Elwell, a native of Camden, Maine. His father's occupation was that of sailmaker. As a boy, Fred Wallace Elwell attended the public schools of Camden; then attended the high school in Waterville, Maine; and finally went to the Thomaston High School, from which he was graduated in the class of 1896. In that year, he started to work for the firm of Follanbee and Wood, which was engaged in the drygoods business in an extensive way in Camden, having become associated with this company on July 20, 1896. Then, after he had worked for many years with this company, and had learned every detail of the business, he purchased it, in June, 1922, since which time he has operated it on his own account. Keenly interested in political matters, Mr. Elwell is aligned in his convictions with the Republican party, in whose principles he is a firm believer and for whose candidates he votes. He has strong fraternal affiliations, being a member of the Free and Accepted Masons, in which Order he is identified with Amity Lodge, No. 6; the Chapter, Royal Arch Masons; the Commandery, Knights Templar; and the Council, Royal and Select Masters. An active Rotarian, he is a member of the local organization of the Rotary Club in Camden. His religious affiliation is with the Congregational church.

In Camden, on June 21, 1905, Fred W. Elwell married Jessie H. Start, who was born in Camden, December 3, 1879, a daughter of Franklin L. and Annie S. (Horton) Start.

MAINE HILLS—One of the outstanding business men of Belfast, is Maine Hills, who has been engaged continuously in the drug business in that town since 1914, under the firm name of Read and Hills. This firm handles a general line of pharmaceutical preparations, does a large prescription business, and deals extensively in candies and confections. Mr. Hills has as his partner in this enterprise Norman A. Read, who is an active business man in this section of Maine. Their store is situated in Post Office Square, in Belfast, and is one of the most up-to-date that can be found in this vicinity. Mr. Hills always has been deeply interested in public affairs, and in all civic and social problems of his community, in which matters he participates freely, showing himself to be ready and willing at all times to support whatever

causes or movements he believes will be beneficial to his town.

Mr. Hills was born in Belfast, Maine, October 30, 1883, a son of Isaac and Catherine J. Hills. His father, who was a dentist by profession, was born in Northport, Maine; while his mother was born in Canada. As a boy, Maine Hills attended the public schools of Belfast, Maine, his native town; but left school at an early age to start to work. As time went on, he became interested in the drug business, and then in 1914 he became engaged with Mr. Read in the partnership which now holds such a prominent place in the life of the community in and near Belfast—that of Read and Hills. Although this store started in a small way, it has grown and developed with the passing years, so that its position now is a healthy one, and it is respected as one of the really essential business enterprises of this section. Mr. Hills has won the deserved reputation of exercising the greatest care in the preparation of his prescriptions and of dealing ever fairly with his customers. He is actively interested in political matters, his affiliation in this way being with the Democratic party, of whose principles and candidates he is a staunch supporter. His fraternal affiliations are strong. He is a member of the Free and Accepted Masons, in which order he has taken all the degrees of the York Rite, and is identified with the Temple, Ancient Arabic Order Nobles of the Mystic Shrine. In his religious convictions, he holds to the faith of the First Unitarian Church.

Mr. Hills, in Belfast, Maine, on September 22, 1913, married Geneva Heal, who was born in Lincolnville, Maine, a daughter of Amasa Heal, who also is a native of Lincolnville. Maine and Geneva (Heal) Hills are the parents of two children: 1. Maine, Jr., who was born in Belfast, September 22, 1917. 2. Stetson Parker, who was born in Belfast, March 29, 1921.

ELMER MARSHALL BABB—One of the younger and most progressive of inhabitants of Belfast, Maine, is Elmer Marshall Babb, who, as secretary, treasurer and general manager, has operated the Windsor Hotel, controlled by the Windsor Hotel, Incorporated, under the corporate laws of the State, since 1925. Mr. Babb was born at Cumberland Mills, Maine, August 14, 1895, son of Harry M. and Lucy G. Babb. Harry M. Babb was born at Portland, Maine, and is now (1928) there employed as superintendent of the Thomas Laughlin Company; Lucy G. Babb was born at Newhall, Maine.

Elmer Marshall Babb received his early education in the public schools of Portland, and upon graduation from high school matriculated in Boston University Business College, at Boston, Massachusetts, where he undertook to master those principles and practices of commercial life that have since served him so beneficially in the hotel business. When, in the month of April, 1917, the United States declared a state of war with Germany, Mr. Babb enlisted immediately, in the cause of his country. For two years, until April, 1919, when he was mustered out of service, he was with the United States Navy, and distinguished himself honorably in naval aviation. There followed a period of a few years when Mr. Babb acted in various commercial capacities, and his first undertaking of an independent character, and incidentally the largest that he had erstwhile ap-

174   MAINE—A HISTORY

proached, was the management of the Windsor Hotel, in Belfast.

Belfast was settled in 1770, and by its first inhabitants, who for the greater number were from Ireland, named after Belfast of their native land. During the Revolution it was the scene of fighting with the British, and, it is said, treasures antedating the Revolution were hidden up the Passagassawaukag River by Indians and traveling bands of whites. Indian warfare was fierce and frequent, and from time to time relics of these battles have been uncovered. Previous to settlement by the pioneers, Belfast and surrounding territory was overrun by the most dreaded of all Indian tribes, from which Penobscot Bay derived its name. Belfast is sixty miles from Bar Harbor and a hundred and ten miles from Portland. Boats make daily trips from Boston. All these things Mr. Babb considered before assuming management of the hostelry, and when he was convinced that such a picturesque and historic locality, with the hotel overlooking the bay and the Islesboro Colony, could not fail to attract visitors, then he went ahead boldly, nor has his judgment been wrong, but otherwise. The hotel itself may be called historic, for it was first constructed in 1806, thirty-six years after the founding of the town. It has been remodeled frequently, and has eighty rooms, up-to-date in all respects, with a renowned cuisine. Near it is the Northport Golf Club, considered one of the sportiest courses in the State; and there are facilities for tennis, boating, bathing and mountain-climbing in summer, and for skiing and skating in winter. As proprietor of this house Mr. Babb has been successful, employing most modern methods of hotel management and business. Moreover, as proprietor of the hotel he is responsible to a large number of visitors for their impressions of Belfast, and in the making of a good impression through his hotel does thereby assist the community in favor, to the final benefit of Belfast and its people.

Mr. Babb is a charter member of the Rotary Club, which holds its weekly luncheon meetings in the Windsor Hotel. He is a member of the Blue Lodge, Free and Accepted Masons; and of the Boston Masonic Club; the Knights of Pythias; American Legion, and Veterans of Foreign Wars. He belongs to the Northport Golf Club; and in all of these organizations he is active. He attends the United Church, and is known for the generosity with which he responds to charitable and kindred worthy appeals no matter the race or creed by whom the causes are sponsored.

DANIEL A. HURD, president of the North Berwick National Bank, and treasurer of the North Berwick Company, is one of the ablest and finest citizens that the town of North Berwick, Maine, has ever had, a man whole-heartedly devoted to the welfare of his community. Born November 4, 1840, at North Berwick, Mr. Hurd is a son of Isaiah and Mary S. (Smith) Hurd, both of whom were natives of North Berwick. Isaiah Hurd, who was a descendant of one of the first families to settle in North Berwick, was a farmer, and died in 1848. Mary S. (Smith) Hurd died in 1884.

Daniel A. Hurd received his preliminary education in the public schools of North Berwick, and entered Lebanon Academy. For many years after this he managed the home farm with marked success.

At the age of forty-two he was appointed postmaster of North Berwick by President Benjamin Harrison, an office in which he served for one term. At the end of that time he became identified with the North Berwick Company, and the North Berwick National Bank. The latter institution, a State bank, was the first bank to be established in North Berwick. William Hill, who was one of the greatest of North Berwick's sons, was the prime mover in the founding of this bank, which was incorporated as a National bank in 1865. The first president was William Hill, the second was Frank O. Snow, and Mr. Hurd is its third president. The cashiers were: P. Hussey, C. W. Greenleaf, Theodore Gould, Nathaniel S. Austin, and at the present time, Wesley M. Johnson. The capitalization of this bank is fifty thousand dollars, and its total assets are $859,808.92. The present vice-president is George W. Perkins. The North Berwick Company is one of the oldest textile manufactories in Maine. In 1832, William Hill, together with Isaac Barney and John B. Lang, bought a small machine shop on a part of the ground now occupied by the present plant. This was turned into a woolen mill and operated as a partnership until 1837, when it was incorporated under the present name. It was successful, and expansion was rapid under Mr. Hill's energetic and capable management. In 1859, Mr. Hill bought the entire control and it has never left the family. In the meantime Mr. Hill had become one of the outstanding figures in Maine. Prominent both financially and socially, he died in 1882. Mrs. Mary Hurd, wife of Daniel A. Hurd, and the daughter of William Hill, has been the president and acting head of this company for a number of years. The plant consists of two mills, employing over a hundred men, and at present they are engaged in the manufacture of ladies' dress goods. Their products are distributed all over the United States. Mr. Hurd has never been too deeply engrossed in business affairs to give a deep and loving regard to his native town. Among the gifts which he has bestowed, perhaps the finest is the beautiful modern Public Library which has just been completed.

Despite the manifold duties which his business career has entailed, Mr. Hurd has devoted a great deal of his time to civic affairs. He has held many local offices, including those of deputy sheriff, collector, treasurer, and selectman. He was elected and served as Representative to the Maine State Legislature, and twice as State Senator. Mr. Hurd was a delegate to the National Republican Convention which nominated William McKinley for President. During the World War, Mr. Hurd served on many boards and committees. In addition to the various local clubs of which he is a member, he is also fraternally affiliated with the Yorkshire Lodge, Free and Accepted Masons, the Chapter and Commandery. He is also affiliated with the Independent Order of Odd Fellows, of which he is a Past Noble Grand, and the Encampment.

Daniel A. Hurd married, in 1893, at North Berwick, Mary R. (Hill) Hobbs, widow of William Hobbs, and daughter of William Hill. Mrs. Hurd has been deeply interested in the welfare of her community, devoting much of her time to its service. She has also made many large and substantial gifts of money and buildings to North Berwick. Mr. and Mrs. Hurd attend the Congregational church, and are most liberal in its support. Mrs. Hurd, in 1926, gave to the town of North Berwick a complete fire engine equipment, and in 1927 she gave a fine brick fire building for the department.

LEONARD A. DAVIS—Farmer, manufacturer and public official, Leonard A. Davis, of Benton, Maine, has been among the most useful citizens of his community, and has been especially active as a member of fraternal organizations. Born March 6, 1865, at Burnham, Maine, the son of Edward and Vesta (Brown) Davis, he comes of pioneer Maine stock. His father, who was a farmer and stone-mason, was born in Burnham, and his mother in Benton, Maine.

Educated in the public schools of Burnham, and at Maine Central Institute, his first employment was with the Kennebec Fibre Company of Benton, Maine, where he remained from 1889 to 1903, and for the succeeding five years he became associated with the Andre Cushing Company, of St. Johns, New Brunswick, and left their employ in 1908 to take up farming. He spent several years in farming, and then operated a general store in Benton, Maine, until October, 1925, when he purchased the factory of the Maine Chair Company, at Burnham, Maine, which he has since conducted under his own name, manufacturing chiefly restaurant furniture, and employing twenty operatives.

Mr. Davis was chairman of the Board of Selectmen of the town of Benton from 1908 to 1910; is a member of the School Board, and has been town auditor for the past sixteen years. He was a member of the Maine Legislature in 1905, representing the towns of Benton, Clinton, Windsor and China. He is a member of the Blue Lodge, Free and Accepted Masons; is Past Grand of the Independent Order of Odd Fellows; a member of the Associated Industries of Maine; of the Modern Woodmen, and Past Council of the State Grange, a sixth degree Patron of Husbandry, and Past Master of the Local Grange. He attends the Congregational Church at Benton Falls, Maine, of which he is a trustee. He is chairman of the Town Republican Committee and member of the Kennebec County Republican Committee.

Leonard A. Davis married (first), January 1, 1890, at Pittsfield, Maine, Augusta Barnes, a native of Newport, Maine, daughter of John B. and Rosina (Haskell) Barnes. She died in September, 1918, at Camp Devens, and he married (second) Isabel Seavey, native of Fairfield, Maine, daughter of Charles B. and Rhoda (Spencer) Seavey. Mr. Davis is the father of two children, born in Pittsfield: Herbert W., who served in the army during the World War, and Elenor I.

JOSEPH C. GRANT—In his dual capacity as owner and director of a canning factory and operator of a sawmill in Clinton, Joseph C. Grant is one of the eminently successful business men of his community. With a yearly output of about a half a million cans, the firm has on its payroll, during the busy summer season, nearly a hundred employees. During the winter months only about a tenth of that number is required. He was born at Canterbury, New Brunswick, March 26, 1863, son of Samuel Lawrence and Victoria Grant, born in Woodstock, New Brunswick. Samuel L. Grant was born in South Hampton, New

Brunswick, and was a farmer and manufacturer all of his life.

The early education of Joseph C. Grant was obtained in the public schools of Houlton, Maine. He joined the Canadian Army, where he remained for three years, during which time he took a three months' special course in the handling of big guns at Quebec, Canada. After his discharge from the army he was engaged in various lines of endeavor, and in 1908 established a canning factory at Unity Plantation, Maine. In 1919 he opened a canning factory at Clinton, Maine, under the firm name of J. C. Grant & Son, and here he has remained to the present time. He has proved himself an honorable business man and is highly esteemed by his community. In his political affiliations he is a Republican, and in his fraternal relationship is a member of the Free and Accepted Masons, having attained the twenty-eighth degree; a member of the Independent Order of Odd Fellows and of the State Grange, Patrons of Husbandry. Mr. Grant and his family attend the Baptist Church of Clinton.

Joseph C. Grant married, at Bar Harbor, Maine, Mamie O. Decker, of Unity Plantation, daughter of Cyrus N. Decker, born at Jefferson, Maine. Mr. and Mrs. Grant are the parents of seven children: Mamie, Hazel, Genevieve, Mark, Theodore, Vera, and John.

FLOYD R. BESSE is head of a tannery business at Clinton, Maine, and the tannery has been a heritage handed down in the family, for his father and grandfather were tanners before him. The firm, in connection with the business, also operates a wholesale and retail store at Boston, Massachusetts. Mr. Besse is a bank director besides having many social and fraternal connections. He was born February 1, 1890, at Albion, Maine, son of Everitt B. and Jessie (Rowe) Besse. The father, a tanner, was born at Albion, Maine, and the mother at Palermo, Maine.

Floyd R. Besse attended the public schools at Albion, Maine, and Hebron Academy, graduating in the class of 1911. When he left school he joined his father and uncle in the tanning business. In 1891, Frank L. Besse, uncle of Floyd R. Besse, started a tannery at Clinton, Maine, and continued operating it until 1925, at which time Floyd R. Besse took over the business, and when another brother joined it became known as Besse Brothers. Mr. Besse's brother, Carol E. Besse, operates the firm's store at Boston, Massachusetts, which bears the name of Besse, Osborne & Odell, and does a wholesale and retail business at No. 51 South Street. The firm at Clinton specializes in sheepskin russets, imitations and the like. Mr. Besse is a director of the Peoples National Bank, at Waterville, Maine. He is a Republican in politics. He belongs to the Benevolent and Protective Order of Elks, Independent Order of Odd Fellows, Free and Accepted Masons, Lodge No. 146; Chapter, Commandery, and Temple, and the Rotary Club at Waterville, Maine. He attends the Baptist church.

Floyd R. Besse married, at Albion, Maine, Charline Abbott, daughter of Charles W. and Cordelia (Libby) Abbott, both of whom were born at Albion, Maine. Children: 1. Belden A., born at Clinton, Maine, December 24, 1918. 2. Boyle A., born at Clinton, Maine, July 18, 1925.

DREW THOMPSON HARTHORN—In educational circles of the State, Drew Thompson Harthorn holds a prominent position, being principal of Coburn Classical Institute and a popular and convincing lecturer on topics of education. He is prominent in the civic affairs of Waterville and is actively interested in community progress, particularly in all school projects.

Mr. Harthorn was born in North Livermore, June 1, 1871, son of William M. and Martha E. (Wyman) Harthorn. He received his education in the public schools, and after high school, entered Colby College, from which he received his degree of Bachelor of Arts in 1894; degree of Master of Arts in 1897, degree of Doctor of Literature in 1926. He served as principal of Wilton Academy from 1894 to 1905, where he established a reputation for ability of the highest character. From 1905 until 1907, he was principal of Rumford Falls High School, when he returned to Wilton Academy, remaining there for five years. In 1912, he was appointed to his present position as principal of Coburn Classical Institute, and has ever continued to be an energetic worker in advancing the interests of this school. Mr. Harthorn is an active member of the New England Association of Colleges and Preparatory Schools, National Education Association, and Maine Teachers' Association. In politics, he is a member of the Republican party, and in fraternal circles is a popular member of the Free and Accepted Masons, Delta Kappa Epsilon Fraternity and the Rotary Club. In his religious affiliations, he is a member of the Baptist church. During the recent World War, Mr. Harthorn was a member of the Legal Advisory Committee and also was of great assistance as a "four-minute" speaker.

Drew Thompson Harthorn married, July 7, 1897, at Wilton, Edith S. Vaughan.

LOUIS O. LOMBARD—In these days of modern agricultural development, Louis O. Lombard takes an active part in supplying the farmers and producers with the latest and improved types of tractors and trucks. Mr. Lombard is past vice-president of the Lombard Traction & Engine Company, the name of which was changed in 1927 to the Lombard Tractor & Truck Corporation, in which organization he is one of the important factors. He was born in North Lincoln, September 15, 1890 son of Samuel W. Lombard of Springfield, and Ella (Snow) Lombard of North Lincoln. Samuel W. Lombard was engaged in the manufacturing business all his life.

Louis O. Lombard received his early education in the public schools of Waterville, and after high school, attended Morgan's Business College. After the completion of his studies, he became associated with the Lombard Traction & Engine Company, which was founded by his uncle, Alvin O Lombard, in 1900, and in this organization, he advanced steadily until he was appointed vice-president. When the company was reorganized and the name changed in 1927, Mr. Lombard assumed charge of the assembly of tractors and continues to fill this responsible position. He is one of the leaders in the business life of the community and takes an active part in all civic affairs. In politics, he is an adherent of the principles of the Republican party. In his fraternal connections, he is a member of Waterville Lodge, No. 33, Free and Accepted Masons. His religious affiliations are with the United Baptist Church.

Louis O. Lombard married, on June 6, 1915, at North Belgrade, Grace Damren of Belgrade, daughter of John and A. (Bickford) Damren.

GREENLEAF KENNETH BARTLETT—One of the young men of prominence in the commercial life of Maine, is Greenleaf Kenneth Bartlett of Belgrade, who has been associated with his father in the general merchandise business since 1924, and operates an independent and prosperous real estate and insurance business. Mr. Bartlett has already acquired a notable reputation for his modern efficient methods and courteous treatment in all his business transactions and is an important factor in the business life of the town.

Mr. Bartlett was born in Belgrade, November 8, 1903, son of L. A. and Mary S. Bartlett, both of Belgrade Lakes. L. A. Bartlett is a prominent figure in the State Grange organization and has been active in the mercantile trade for many years, founding his present business about 1902. Mrs. Bartlett is the present obliging postmistress at Belgrade Lakes.

Greenleaf Kenneth Bartlett received his early education in the public schools of Belgrade, and after high school, entered Bates College, where he studied two years, and then continued his course at the Massachusetts Institute of Technology for two more years. After the completion of his college career, he entered his father's business and also organized his present realty and insurance agency. Mr. Bartlett is actively interested in all campaigns for community development and is an ardent supporter of all projects to aid the welfare of its citizens. In politics, he is a member of the Independent party. In fraternal connections, he is a member of the Vernon Valley Lodge, Free and Accepted Masons and of the Delta Upsilon Fraternity. He attends the Union Church.

PEARL GLOVER WILLEY—Principal owner and general manager of P. G. Willey & Company, dealing in coal, lumber and building supplies at Camden, Pearl Glover Willey has devoted his attention to business since he became clerk in the retail store of F. A. Peterson, at Rockland, Maine, at the age of seventeen years. Now (1928) at the age of fifty-three, after experience in retail trade in a number of the New England cities, he is firmly established as one of the leading merchants in Camden.

Pearl Glover Willey was born at Rockland, Maine, February 28, 1875, son of Matthew K. Willey, born at Friendship, Maine, and Melissa A. (Hall) Willey, born at St. George, Maine, his father having been master of a ship. After attending the public schools and the Commercial College at Rockland, Mr. Willey, in 1892, became clerk in the Peterson store, dealing in shoes and men's furnishings, remaining there until 1894, when he entered the employ of Mr. Wentworth in his general merchandise store. Here he stayed two years, and during the two years that followed was associated with Fuller and Cobb; then, in 1897, he went to Boston, to the Shepard-Norwell Company, returning to Rockland July 1, 1899, to become identified with A. J. Bird and Company, immediately taking charge of the concern's business at Camden under the firm name of Bird Brothers & Willey, coal and building supplies. In March, 1912, Mr. Willey purchased the stock belonging to two of the Bird brothers, thereby gaining control of the firm and changing its name to P. G. Willey and Company. It is located at No. 9 Bayview Street. Mr. Willey is known in Camden for his ability in merchandising and more widely for the soundness of his views and readiness of support in worthwhile civic enterprises. He has numerous fraternal connections, among which are membership in the Camden Yacht Club; the Business Men's Club; the Camden Board of Trade; Amity Lodge, No. 6, Free and Accepted Masons; Keystone Chapter, No. 24, Royal Arch Masons; King Hiram Council, Royal and Select Masters; Camden Commandery, No. 23, Knights Templar; Kora Temple, Ancient Arabic Order Nobles of the Mystic Shrine; the Masonic Club, and the Rockland Country Club. Mr. Willey is a Republican in political allegiance, and a member of the Episcopal church.

Pearl Glover Willey married at Hudson, Massachusetts, Caroline Hicks Thorndike, of Hudson, daughter of Captain Lane Thorndike, born at South Thomaston, Maine, and Ada (Hicks) Thorndike, born at Rockland, Maine. Mr. and Mrs. Willey are the parents of two children, both born at Camden: 1. Nerita, born in September, 1899. 2. Matthew K., born in September, 1902.

CHARLES W. BABB, director and treasurer of an important textile company at Camden, Maine, has been many years in the textile business, and over forty with the textile company of which he is, and has long been, one of the heads. He worked in different fields, however, before he entered the textile industry. As a youth he was a machinist, employed in different lines of manufacture. He was for a time in a locomotive works, and spent a few years in various machine shops. But finally the woolen business claimed him and that has been his chief occupation since. He was born at South Thomaston, Maine, January 16, 1863, son of Harrison P. and Harriett A. (Newhall) Babb. The father, a ship carpenter and farmer, was born at Somerville, Maine, and the mother at Washington, Maine.

Charles W. Babb attended the public school at South Thomaston; the South Thomaston High School, and Rockland Commercial College. His first job was doing machine work for D. Knowlton & Company, at Camden, he having been employed by this firm for two years, from 1880 to 1882. He was with the Manchester Locomotive Works, at Manchester, New Hampshire, one year, and then was two years in the machine shop of C. M. Barstow, at Camden, Maine. Subsequently, he was a year with Brown & Sharp Machine Company, of Providence, Rhode Island, and after that was identified with the Knox Woolen Company, of Camden, Maine, as overseer of the weaving department. This was in 1886. In 1890 he was made superintendent and director of the company; was elected treasurer on November 11, 1901, and has remained treasurer and director up to the present time. Mr. Babb is a Republican in politics. He belongs to the Blue Lodge, Free and Accepted Masons; the Chapter, Royal Arch Masons; the Council, Royal and Select Masters; the Commandery, Knights Templar; the Temple, Ancient Arabic Order Nobles of the Mystic Shrine; and the Rotary Club, the Board of Trade, the Camden Yacht Club, and the Business Men's Association. He attends the Episcopal church.

Charles W. Babb married, at Camden, Maine, October 10, 1893, Theresa Parker, born at Camden, January 23, 1868, daughter of Moses L. and Mary F.

(Cleveland) Parker, both natives of Camden. Children: 1. Elizabeth M., born at Camden, September 21, 1901. 2. Charles W., Jr., born at Camden, May 1, 1906.

JOHN K. FARRAR—The historic old office of High Sheriff of Penobscot County, Maine, has in John K. Farrar an incumbent ideally suited to the combined dignity and power requisite for the effective discharge of the complicated and important duties. Seven years of intensive training acquainted him with both the administrative and judicial phases of the work when he was deputy sheriff under his capable predecessors. His varied business experiences give him an insight into men and affairs, and his personality, a combination of graciousness, geniality, and loyalty to the ideals of community welfare, brings him the popularity which has made his two years of office so highly successful.

John K. Farrar was born in Charlestown, Maine, September 2, 1885, son of a prosperous farmer, Josiah Farrar, of Charlestown, Maine, and his wife, Melissa (Trim) Farrar, also a native of Charlestown. The son completed his education in the public and high schools of his birthplace. For two years after graduation, he worked for the Boston Elevated Railroad. On his return to Maine, he worked for several years in the lumber industry and gained a wide insight into men and methods. His experience was capitalized in 1909, when Mr. Farrar entered into the business world on his own account, establishing a general store at Corinth, Maine, which prospered for nearly a decade under his vigorous management. In 1918 came his appointment as deputy sheriff of Penobscot County, by Arthur L. Thayer, high sheriff. So well did he fit into his new office that in 1919 he was reappointed by Ormand B. Fernandez, the next incumbent of the high sheriff's office, with the additional duties of turnkey of the Penobscot County Jail. Six years of whole-hearted devotion to his responsible duties proved Sheriff Farrar a dependable and capable public servant, and in 1925 brought his election to the office of High Sheriff, which he has since continued to fill. Meantime, he has served his fellowmen in various political offices. A Republican, he was for three years a member of the Board of Selectmen of Corinth, and for a year treasurer and tax collector for the town. He belongs to Olive Branch Lodge, No. 124, Free and Accepted Masons, and other bodies of the Order, including the Ancient Arabic Order Nobles of the Mystic Shrine. He is a member of Corinthian Lodge, Independent Order of Odd Fellows, and the Bangor City Club. In connection with his profession, he is a member and director of the Sheriff and Police Association of America. He attends the Universalist church. His favorite forms of recreation are hunting and fishing.

December 8, 1909, John K. Farrar married Blanche Colby Keniston, born in Peabody, Massachusetts, and they have a son, John K. Farrar, Jr.

JAMES GILBERT HUTCHINS, M. D.—Physician and a veteran of the World War, James Gilbert Hutchins has practiced medicine in Camden, Knox County, Maine, since 1916, and is respected alike by members of the profession and lay citizenry for the record he has made. Dr. Hutchins is a native of Maine. He was born at Orland on August 27,

Maine—12

1876, the son of Ashur B. Hutchins, who was born at Penobscot, Maine, and of Clara Mary (Snowman) Hutchins, also born at Penobscot, his father having been engaged in the manufacture of brick.

Dr. Hutchins' early education was taken in the place of his birth, in the public schools, after which he matriculated in the East Maine Conference School at Bucksport, Maine, and graduated with the class of 1898. In 1901 he took the degree of Doctor of Medicine from the Maine Medical School, and joined the staff of the Silsby Hospital, at Rockland, Maine, to serve out his period as interne. This accomplished, he began practice at Stonington, Maine, in 1902, where he stayed until 1916, when he removed to Camden. Dr. Hutchins was accorded several honors, and among them an appointment of four years as examiner for the criminal insane of Knox County. The appointment was made by the Governor of Maine and carried with it prestige and growing distinction for Dr. Hutchins. He has been medical examiner for the New York Life Insurance Company, the New England Mutual Insurance Company, and the Metropolitan Life Insurance Company. At present (1928) he is serving as Health Officer of Camden, and Examiner of the Blind. During the World War Dr. Hutchins was with the Sixtieth Field Artillery at Camp Jackson, South Carolina, as first lieutenant in the Medical Corps. He held a captain's commission in the Medical Corps, Maine National Guard, in 1922. While a civilian, as when he was a soldier, his primary interest is in the practice of medicine, and he is a member of the medical associations of Knox County, the State of Maine, and the American Medical Association. Dr. Hutchins gives his active support to various civic enterprises which he believes are for the welfare of the townspeople, and is a member of the Camden Board of Trade and the Camden Business Men's Club. Fraternally, he is affiliated with the Blue Lodge, Free and Accepted Masons; the Chapter, Royal Arch Masons, and the Council, Royal and Select Masters. He is a member of the Baptist church.

Dr. Hutchins married, at Belfast, Maine, on February 3, 1900, Isabel M. Sawyer, of Deer Isle, Maine, born October 24, 1877, daughter of Admiral G. Sawyer, who was born at Deer Isle, and Lucy (Pickering) Sawyer also born at Deer Isle. Dr. and Mrs. Hutchins are the parents of one child, Florence Clara, born at Stonington, Maine, on April 5, 1909.

GEORGE MIXER, a prominent merchant and manufacturer of Camden, Maine, has never departed very far or very long from the neighborhood of the locality in which he was born, but he has, nevertheless, had a varied experience in the business world. He has worked in a quarry and excelled as a stonecutter in various parts of Maine. He has been engaged in banking, has tried his hand at other lines of business and has taken a prominent part in public affairs. At the present time he is head of a valuable candy business and is director of a national bank.

George Mixer was born at Penobscot, Maine, June 14, 1857, son of Horace and Lucy (Grindell) Mixer. The father, a farmer, was born at South Paris, Maine, and the mother at Penobscot, Maine. Mr. Mixer received the usual education in the public schools of Penobscot, and then started working for the Hall Quarry, at Mount Desert Island, in which occupa-

tion he continued for a period of five years. As he continued at the quarry business he learned the art of stone cutting and followed this arduous but interesting craft for fifteen years. This work carried him to Belfast, Augusta, and other points in Maine, and it was in these places in the main that this work was carried on. Mr. Mixer decided to take up a business of his own, and eventually chose one far removed from the art of stone sculpturing. He started in the confectionery business in Camden, in 1893, and has continued in that business to the present time. His firm is known as the Mixer Candy Kitchen. Mr. Mixer is a director of the Camden National Bank. He is a Democrat in politics. He is a member of the Board of Trade, the Knights of Pythias, and the Improved Order of Red Men. He attends the Baptist church.

George Mixer married, at Belfast, Maine, Anna Coombs, born at Vinalhaven, Maine, daughter of William and Mary Ann Coombs; her father was born at Vinalhaven, and her mother at Isle au Haut, Maine.

ORLANDO E. FROST—One of the most prominent manufacturers of Belfast, Maine, is Orlando E. Frost, son of Jacob L. and Sarah (Doe) Frost. He has been interested in manufacturing ever since he began his business career, but while devoting the best part of his time to his business, Mr. Frost has also found time to give to civic affairs and taken a prominent part therein.

Orlando E. Frost was born at Saint Albans, Maine, December 14, 1864. He began work with the Rice & Griffin Manufacturing Company of Worcester, where he remained for fourteen years; for two years he was superintendent. His next business connection was with the Selden Cypress Door Company, Palatka, Florida, for two years, as superintendent. From Palatka he came to Mathew Brothers as manager, and he remained in that capacity until 1898. He afterwards became owner of the business and still operates it. In 1923 he was elected mayor of Belfast and held that position until 1926, and he represented his district in the State Legislature in 1925. He is a Republican in politics and a member of the Federated Church. He is a member of the Free and Accepted Masons, and holds the thirty-second degree of the Scottish Rite.

On August 26, 1895, Orlando E. Frost married Annie Tucker of Boston. They have two children: Myrtle E., and Kathleen E.

FRANK A. PETRICH—To the business of the direction of a number of the most important civic departments of Belfast, Frank A. Petrich has applied his capabilities as a public official of sterling worth, and standing with that foremost group of Belfast men who plan and work for the best interests of city and community, and he has the esteem and confidence of his associates in office, and of his constituency. In city treasurership or clerkship, or in whatsoever other civic employ, Mr. Petrich has been placed, he has performed his duties with efficiency, faithfulness and thoroughness.

Frank A. Petrich was born August 27, 1890, in Wisconsin, a son of Robert Petrich, a building contractor, and Pauline (Summercorn) Petrich, both natives of Wisconsin. Attending the public schools of Eau Claire, Wisconsin, Mr. Petrich was graduated from the high school in that city with the class of 1902; and he began his business career in Minneapolis, Minnesota. Becoming identified with the theatre business as theatrical manager, Mr. Petrich continued in that line until 1923, and for ten years he was associated with the Loews, Incorporated, in New York City.

Coming to Belfast, Mr. Petrich's business abilities received recognition in his appointment to office and in the manner in which he has conducted the affairs of city departments. He has received election three times as city treasurer, clerk in 1924, and reëlected, and tax collector, reëlected; having been elected first as treasurer in 1924 for a one-year term. Elected treasurer of the Belfast Water District in 1925, and reëlected, he has continued in these positions to the present. He is also a member of the Belfast Chamber of Commerce, and attends the First Federated Church.

Frank A. Petrich married, in 1908, at Minneapolis, Minnesota, Elsie Elizabeth Groebch, who was born June 16, 1887, in New York City, daughter of Otto and Elizabeth Groebch, and they have two children: Adelane, born in Minnesota, November 28, 1909; and Doris, born August 7, 1912.

CHARLES SUMNER TAYLOR is a prominent lawyer of Belfast, Maine. In professional experience he has been strictly a lawyer, though he was in the army during the World War. He has, among his other experiences, been city solicitor for two terms. He does a general law practice and has been a conspicuous figure in his adopted city for more than a decade.

Charles S. Taylor was born at Hodgdon, Maine, May 10, 1892, son of Edgar C. and Charlotte E. (Woodworth) Taylor. The father, who was a decorator, was born at Biddeford, Maine, and the mother was born at Linneus, Maine. He attended the public schools at Hodgdon, Maine, and at Deer Isle, Maine, and also the high school at Deer Isle, from which he graduated in the class of 1912. He then went to the University of Maine, from which he graduated in 1916, with the degree of Bachelor of Laws. He was in the United States Army from 1914 to 1917, Maine National Guard, Company G, One Hundred and Third Infantry. He was admitted to the Maine bar in 1917. He started practicing in Belfast, Maine, in that year, and has continued so doing to date, engaging in general law practice. He has been twice city solicitor of Belfast.

Mr. Taylor is a Republican in politics. He belongs to the Free and Accepted Masons, Blue Lodge and Chapter, and is a member of the Maine State and County Bar associations. He attends the Baptist church.

Mr. Taylor married, at Augusta, Maine, June 28, 1916, Lida M. Stinson, born October 20, 1895, at Deer Isle, Maine, daughter of Jack and Flora O. (Gray) Stinson, both natives of Deer Isle. There has been one child to the marriage, Charles Evans, born August 7, 1917, at Deer Isle.

CLYDE RAYMOND CHAPMAN—County Attorney of Waldo County, Maine, since 1925 Clyde Raymond Chapman, lawyer, began practice at Belfast in 1920, and has firmly established himself in the legal profession there. He has many fraternal connections and is quite widely known in the State as

clerk of the House of Representatives, which office he held from 1919 until 1925, for three terms.

Clyde Raymond Chapman was born at Fairfield, Maine, July 28, 1889, son of George M. and Laura E. (Keene) Chapman. Following his early education in the public schools of Fairfield he undertook courses in the Coburn Classical Institute; matriculated at Bowdoin College, graduating in 1912 with the degree of Bachelor of Arts; later enrolling in the Maine Law School, from which he graduated in 1917 with the degree of Bachelor of Laws. Mr. Chapman was admitted to the State Bar Association the following year and immediately became associated with the law firm of Williamson, Burleigh & McLean, leaving them in 1919, when he was made clerk of the State House of Representatives. The next year, while clerk of the Lower House, he began practice for himself in Belfast, and during the first year was appointed Judge of the Municipal Court, a position which he held until 1924. In 1923 he was city solicitor, and two years later assumed the post of county attorney. As his record testifies, Mr. Chapman has been busily engaged in political affairs since the commencement of his law practice, and constantly he has had the best interests of Belfast as his own concern, with the greatest good to the citizens of Waldo County as his goal of effort. He is highly respected by the legal fraternity for his ability and character. Mr. Chapman has many connections, and among them membership in the Zeta Psi Fraternity, the Phi Alpha Delta Fraternity the Free and Accepted Masons, thirty-second degree, Commandery and Shrine. His residence is at the corner of Cottage and Condon streets, and he maintains offices in the Odd Fellows' Block, at Belfast.

Mr. Chapman married, at Augusta, Maine, February 14, 1919, E. May Humphrey, and is the father of one child, Gordon C.

FRED E. ELLIS—Chief of Police in Belfast since 1923, Fred E. Ellis has performed in a very efficient manner the duties connected with his office. He has served as a police officer in Belfast for more than thirty years. His present position shows the high merit of his services. His father, Elisha W. Ellis, born in Monroe, Maine, was a farmer. His mother, Mary A. (Robbins) Ellis, was born in Swansville, Maine. Elisha W. Ellis served through the American Civil War as a first lieutenant in Company B, of the Nineteenth Maine Infantry. He saw much active service and was wounded at the battle of Gettysburg. He also served ten months and eight days in Libby Prison, Richmond, Virginia.

Fred E. Ellis was born at Belfast, Maine, on February 4, 1867. He entered the public schools at Belfast, and later attended a business college in Augusta. After completing his education, he took up carpentering, and he engaged in this work for a number of years. Afterwards he became a dealer in antiques, and remained in this business for fifteen years, at Belfast. About the beginning of the twentieth century he became a member of the police force of the town of Belfast. He has maintained this connection since that time, serving as constable and deputy sheriff. In 1923, he was appointed Chief of Police, which office he still retains, having been reappointed three times.

Politically, Mr. Ellis is a member of the Republican party. He is affiliated with the Free and Accepted Masons, Scottish Rite, and has taken the degree of Knights Templar in this Order. He is also a member of the Unitarian church. On June 13, 1900, at Belfast, Fred E. Ellis married Vesta Stearns, daughter of John Y. Stearns, born at Belfast. They are the parents of two children: 1. Louise M., born at Belfast, April 14, 1902. 2. Elmer H., also born at Belfast, in September, 1904.

DANIEL I. GOULD—Sixteen years of successful general legal practice in Bangor, Maine, have made Daniel I. Gould well known in this section of Penobscot County. Mr. Gould is a Bowdoin College man and a graduate of the Law School of the University of Maine, and has made for himself an assured place among his professional colleagues in Maine. He is well known in fraternal circles, and has a host of friends in Bangor and vicinity.

Daniel I. Gould was born in Harborville, Nova Scotia, November 21, 1875, son of John Rufus, a native of Boston, Massachusetts, who followed the sea and was a sea captain for more than twenty years, now retired, and of Susan (Haggerty) Gould, who was born at Black Rock, Nova Scotia, and is also living (1928). Mr. Gould received his earliest school training in the public schools of New Hampshire, and then continued study in Proctor Academy, at Andover, New Hampshire, after which he prepared for college in Colby Academy, at New London, New Hampshire. When his preparatory course was completed he matriculated in Bowdoin College, with the class of 1903, in the Bachelor of Arts course. He then entered the Law School of the University of Maine, from which he was graduated with the class of 1911, receiving at that time the degree of Bachelor of Laws. Meantime, from 1903 to 1907, he had been engaged in teaching, financing in that way his professional training, and entering the University of Maine in the fall of 1908. Since 1911 he has been engaged in general legal practice in Bangor, where he has built up an enviable reputation as a skilled lawyer. He has his offices at No. 31 Central Street, and is taking care of a large and important clientele. He is a member of the Penobscot Bar Association, and stands high in the esteem of his professional associates. Politically, he gives his support to the principles of the Democratic party in general, but he is one of the many independent voters of 'these times, who reserve for themselves the right to cast their ballot for the candidate whom they deem best fitted for the office, without too close regard for party affiliations. In 1906 Mr. Gould enlisted in the Maine National Guards, as a private, but in 1908 he was commissioned a second lieutenant, in 1910 a first lieutenant, and in 1914 he was commissioned a captain. He received his discharge in March, 1918, holding at that time the rank of captain of Company G, Maine National Guard, with which company he served on the Mexican border. During the period of the participation of the United States in the World War, Mr. Gould served as captain of G Company, and trained that company for overseas service. After the training and mobilization of the Twenty-sixth Division, he was taken, with several other captains, from the Fifty-second Brigade and assigned to duty in the Quartermaster's Department, where he served until March, 1918, when he received his honorable discharge. He is well known in fraternal circles,

being identified with Kenduskeag Lodge, Knights of Pythias, of which he is a Past Chancellor, and also of the Grand Lodge of that same order; of the local Grange, Patrons of Husbandry; Independent Order of Odd Fellows; Bangor Lodge, Loyal Order of Moose; New England Order of Protection; and of the college fraternities, Alpha Delta Phi and Phi Alpha Delta, being the organizer of the Maine chapter of the last-named fraternity, the Maine chapter being known as Hannibal Hammond Chapter. Mr. Gould finds his favorite recreation in hunting, fishing and rifle shooting, and in the last-named art he is an expert. He was national rifle champion, small bore rifle, in 1913, and national champion, three hundred yards rapid-fire shooting in 1911, 1912, and 1913. For a period of four years he served as assistant coach of the State Rifle Team. His religious affiliation is as a Free Thinker.

WILLIAM J. O'CONNOR, M. D.—Engaged in the practice of industrial surgery and general surgical work, William J. O'Connor, who has been a physician in Augusta since he finished his professional training at Bowdoin Medical College in 1915, is regarded as one of the most competent and careful men practicing medicine in this community. Dr. O'Connor has his offices at No. 341 Water Street. He was born in Bangor, on October 2, 1884, the son of Frank and Isabel (McCarthy) O'Connor, both natives of Bangor. The father, who was a prominent wholesale junk dealer in Bangor, died in 1910.

Dr. O'Connor was educated in the public schools of Bangor; in the Bangor High School, from which he was graduated in the class of 1902; and at the Bowdoin Medical College, from which he was graduated in the class of 1915, with the degree of Doctor of Medicine. After he completed his education, he started his general medical practice in Augusta, and since that time has devoted most of his attention to industrial surgery and surgical work. For two years he was senior surgeon at Augusta General Hospital. Other institutions in which he has served are the General Hospital, Portland, Maine, (two years); Massachusetts General Hospital, where he was house physician for a year; Post-Graduate Hospital, New York City, and the Mayo Clinic. He is a member of the Maine State Medical Association, the Kennebec County Medical Association, and the American Medical Association. During the World War he served in the medical department of the Third Infantry of the Maine National Guard, and was engaged in the United States Public Health Service. He is a fourth degree member of the Knights of Columbus. In his political views he is independent of the recognized parties. He and his family are members of St. Mary's Catholic Church, of Augusta.

In Portland, on June 7, 1916, Dr. O'Connor married Marguerite Quailey, who was born in Portland, Maine, on October 13, 1890, the daughter of James E. and Mary (McCarthy) Quailey, both natives of Portland. Dr. William J. and Marguerite (Quailey) O'Connor are the parents of two children: 1. William Robert, born in Augusta, September 27, 1918. 2. Mary Elizabeth, born September 7, 1924.

JOHN D. NEWMAN—Since 1890, when he completed his education, John D. Newman has been connected with the hardware trade. His experience in this business has been wide, and his energy and acumen have brought him to his present successful position. He is treasurer and general manager of the Brooks Hardware Company, Wholesalers, of Augusta, Maine. His father, Chester Newman, was a farmer and millman. His mother, before her marriage was Cornelia Eaton.

John D. Newman was born December 25, 1875, at East Otto, Cattaraugus County, New York. He was educated at Springville Academy, Erie County, New York, and on August 7, 1890, he became associated with A. D. Ward, a hardware merchant of Augusta, Maine. He remained there for five years. In 1895, he entered the employ of S. S. Brooks & Company, hardware wholesalers of Augusta. On January 1, 1899, this company was incorporated, and Mr. Newman became one of the original incorporators, and its president in August, 1899. He filled this position from that time until a later reorganization, when Daniel S. Young became president of the company, and Mr. Newman took over the duties of treasurer and manager.

Fraternally, Mr. Newman is affiliated with the Free and Accepted Masons having taken the degrees of the Chapter, Council, Commandery, and Temple. He is a member of the local Chamber of Commerce and the Augusta Country Club. From 1906 to 1908 he served as councilman of the city of Augusta, representing the First Ward.

On February 20, 1901, at Augusta, Maine, John D. Newman married Ethel I. Hussey, who was born at Augusta, October 12, 1877. She is the daughter of J. M. Hussey, born at Vassalboro, Maine, and of Mercy Merril Hussey, who was also born in Maine.

CHARLES E. HOXIE, general contractor, of Augusta, Maine, was born in Sidney, Maine, October 21, 1855, son of Silas and Eliza (Sherman) Hoxie. His father was a farmer, carpenter and mason, a native of Maine, and his ancestors of Cape Cod, Massachusetts, while his mother was a native of Nantucket Island.

Educated in the Sidney public schools, and at Towle Academy, of Winthrop, Maine, Charles E. Hoxie started in the general building and contracting business on his own account in 1875, at Augusta, Maine, and has continued in business there ever since. Many of the most notable buildings in that city are proof of his enterprise and skill. Mr. Hoxie is a member of the Univeralist church, and a Republican. He is a member of the Free and Accepted Masons, and a Knight Templar. He is also a member of the Independent Order of Odd Fellows, and of the Ancient Order of United Workmen. He belongs to the Augusta Chamber of Commerce, and to the Abnaki Club.

Charles E. Hoxie married Lottie P. Severance, of Augusta, in June, 1879. Their children were: Marion Willcox, Beulah (deceased), and Ethel, all born in Augusta, Maine.

FREDERICK H. OWEN, clothier, of Augusta, Maine, was born in that city, May 9, 1891, son of Frederick Howard, and Lizzie E. (Barker) Owen. His father was a writer and journalist, and high in the councils of the Free and Accepted Masons. He was born in Augusta, and his wife was a native of Bangor, Maine.

Frederick H. Owen attended the public schools of Augusta, attended Cony High School, then studied at the Dummer Academy, and went from there to the Concord School, where he was graduated in the class of 1910. He also spent some time in Cornell University. Returning to Augusta, he was employed, first by C. E. Hoxie & Company, general contractors, and then became associated with Charles Biladeau, the Augusta clothier, where he was a member of the firm for nine years. He is now manager for the firm of E. E. Davis & Company, dealers in men's and boys' clothing at No. 210 Water Street, Augusta.

Mr. Owen saw service on the Mexican border in 1916 as a member of the National Guard, and he is now a first lieutenant in Company F, One Hundred and Third Infantry, Maine National Guard. He is a member of the Blue Lodge, Free and Accepted Masons, and of the Benevolent and Protective Order of Elks. He also belongs to the Augusta Chamber of Commerce, and the Augusta Country Club. He is a member of the Episcopal church, and a Republican.

Frederick H. Owen married Josephine C. MacLellan, daughter of Caius and Margaret (McLeod) MacLellan, in Augusta, Maine, June 28, 1914. Mrs. Owen's father was a native of New Castle, New Brunswick, Canada. Their children were: William Robert, Margaret Elizabeth, Joseph M., and Frederick Howard Owen, Jr., all born in Augusta.

WALLACE DIPLOCK, who has been in the furniture business in Augusta, Maine, for thirty-four years, the latter part of that time on his own account, was born in that city, December 10, 1881. His father was George Diplock, carpenter and builder, and a veteran of the Civil War, while his mother was Mary (Smith) Diplock; both were natives of Readfield, Maine.

Educated in the public schools of Augusta, Wallace Diplock found his first business opportunity in the furniture store of A. A. Soule, in Augusta, and there he remained for twenty-eight years, starting in business on his own in 1921. Since then, he has built up an extensive connection through personal effort, modern methods and general efficiency. He is a member of the Chamber of Commerce, and finds relaxation in his associations in the Benevolent and Protective Order of Elks. Mr. Diplock is a communicant of St. Mark's Episcopal Church, and in politics he is an Independent.

Wallace Diplock married Pearl R. Shaw, daughter of Charlie and Mattie Shaw, who like her parents, was born in Augusta. Mr and Mrs. Diplock are the parents of two children: John Wallace, and Serneia, both born in Augusta.

ROYAL HENRY BODWELL, insurance man of Augusta, Maine, who died July 8, 1918, was an excellent type of the Bowdoin graduate who gives his life to business and the duties of citizenship. Born in Keene, New Hampshire, January 2, 1879, he was the son of Edward S. and Ada M. (Porter) Bodwell. The father, a merchant, was a native of Brunswick, Maine, and survived until December, 1925.

After the customary schooling in Brunswick, where he was graduated from the high school in 1897, Royal Henry Bodwell entered Bowdoin College and was graduated with the degree of Bachelor of Arts with the class of 1901. He then became identified with the Massachusetts Thread Company, remaining with that corporation until 1905, in the Boston offices. Going next to Augusta, where he had formed numerous friendships, he was made a member of the firm of Macomber Farr & Whitten, insurance agents, and retained that connection for the remainder of his life. In politics a Republican, he served as a member of the Common Council, and was deeply interested in various fraternal organizations. A member of the Lodge, Free and Accepted Masons, and the Commandery, Knights Templar, he was also a charter member of the local Lodge, Benevolent and Protective Order of Elks, a charter member of the Rotary Club, and of the Augusta Country Club. His religious affiliation was with the Christian Scientists.

Royal Henry Bodwell married Alice Macomber, daughter of George S. and Sarah (Johnson) Macomber, October 4, 1906, in Augusta. She was born March 17, 1878. Their children were: Howard, born November 3, 1907; graduate of Bowdoin, Bachelor of Arts, 1929; and Anne Porter, born July 22, 1912.

During his residence in Augusta, Mr. Bodwell had made a large and widening circle of friends and business acquaintances, and he is remembered there as a good friend and neighbor, and a business man with high ethical ideals, from which he never deviated.

SAMUEL LANCASTER HUNTINGTON—In the list of men who have substantially aided the industrial and commercial interests of their State, the name of Samuel Lancaster Huntington stands out prominently as a public-spirited citizen of the highest type who has always by his example and influence, furthered the progress of this great commonwealth. Mr. Huntington is a descendant of Simon and Margaret (Baret) Huntington, who came to this country from England in 1633, and were the ancestors of a family which has resided for generations at Old Hallowell, on the Kennebec River. Among his other ancestors is the Reverend John Mayo, who came here from England in 1639 and became the first pastor of the Old North Church, now known as the Second Church, of Boston. Through his mother, Mr. Huntington is descended from Governor Thomas Prence, Elder William Brewster, of "Mayflower" fame, and from other important members of the Plymouth Colony.

Mr. Huntington was born in Hallowell, October 22, 1843, son of Samuel Whitmore Huntington and Sally Ann (Mayo) Huntington. Samuel Whitmore Huntington was a prominent merchant and manufacturer of Hallowell and was always a leader in progressive affairs.

Samuel Lancaster Huntington received his early education in the Hallowell public schools and later attended Hallowell Academy. Upon the completion of his course, being then eighteen years of age, he entered the business of his father, who was engaged in manufacturing clothing and uniforms for the soldiers of the Union Army. The Civil War had only recently commenced and Mr. Huntington had eagerly offered his services but was unable to pass the rigid physical tests. He continued his association with his father until two years after the close of the war, when, desiring to learn the wholesale drygoods business, he entered the employ of the firm of Storer and Cutler, of Portland, Maine. He was later clothing salesman for his father and uncle, Samuel W. and Benjamin Huntington, of Augusta, and later became a member of the firm of Huntington, Nason and Company, wholesale and retail clothiers of Augusta. After this business was dissolved, Mr. Huntington continued in

business independently, and in 1901, began selling clothing specialties to the wholesale trade. In this work, he originated several models of warm coats for men's wear, and they were so favorably received that he was given, by the manufacturers, the exclusive right to sell them in the United States. In addition to his wholesale and retail clothing business, in 1925, Mr. Huntington took on as a side line, plumbing and heating at Damariscotta. This venture was most successful from the start, and today he is doing a wholesale and retail business, having the largest and best-equipped pipe shop in Lincoln County. In the entire State there is probably no man who can equal his record for continuous service in the clothing trade.

In the general life of the community Mr. Huntington has always been an active figure and has always supported all campaigns for modern and progressive methods. Prominent in fraternal circles, Mr. Huntington was admitted to Augusta Lodge, Free and Accepted Masons, in 1869, and shortly afterwards to Jerusalem Chapter, Royal Arch Masons, of Hallowell. He is one of the oldest Knights Templar in the State, having been a member of Trinity Commandery, Augusta, since 1871. In 1892 he became a member of the Ancient Order of United Workmen. Although not a member of the Sons of the American Revolution, he possesses all the necessary qualifications, being eligible through his mother's grandfather and great-grandfather, Ebenezer and Thomas Mayo, both of whom took active part in the War for American Independence. In politics, Mr. Huntington has always been an Independent, casting his first vote for Abraham Lincoln in 1864, and since then has not allied himself with any party excepting the Progressive, preferring complete independence in his choice of candidates and in judging the issues they advance.

Samuel Lancaster Huntington married, at Boston, Massachusetts, November 7, 1877, Nellie A. Yeaton, who died in 1917, daughter of John and Abbie (Rollins) Yeaton, of Chelsea, Maine. Their daughter, Mary Wentworth, resides with her father at "Fairview," their beautiful home at Damariscotta.

ALFRED LANTAGNE—Entering the business world when he was a very young man, Alfred Lantagne has been identified with important industrial enterprises during his active career, and has directed his efforts and energies with marked distinction and success. He is a descendant of the sturdy and rugged French Colonists who early settled in the New World and possesses the heritages and traditions of those early republic-builders to whom this country owes so much of its progress and advancement. Mr. Lantagne has been influentially and prominently active in the civic and social affairs of Biddeford, Maine, and enjoying the confidence, esteem and respect of his fellows, has been elected to various offices of community importance. In his official capacity he has contributed many beneficial and significant developments and administrative policies designed to promote the welfare of his city, and has performed the functions of his office to the marked satisfaction of his host of friends and supporters and with reflected honor and reputation to himself. He is the son of Philias and Delia (Honde) Lantagne, both of whom were natives of the Province of Quebec, Canada, but who are now deceased. The father, during his life, was engaged in mill work, first in his native community, and thereafter in

Biddeford, Maine, whence he had come in the latter part of the nineteenth century.

Alfred Lantagne was born at Biddeford, Maine, September 10, 1888, and received an excellent primary school education in the parochial schools of Biddeford. Upon the completion of his scholastic training he entered the industrial field, and was employed by the Pepperell Manufacturing Company of Biddeford. He devoted himself with whole-hearted application and diligence to the mastering the details and methods of his business, and rose with rapid gradation through the various positions open by promotion to him. His faithful service, together with his natural ability and business acumen, gained for him the approbation, admiration, and confidence of his superiors, and he soon became what is known as the second hand in the department in which he was employed. He continued for many years in this capacity, winning friends and well-wishers who were deeply impressed by his sincere purpose and inviting personality. In 1925, the voters of Biddeford selected him as a member of the Common Council of the city. Thereafter he was appointed to the post of city clerk, succeeding Arthur H. Hevey, and he resigned from his position on the Common Council. At the expiration of that term, Mr. Lantagne was reëlected to the office of city clerk, in 1927, and is continuing in his official capacity in the city government at this time (1928).

He is at the same time one of the leaders of the active French colony in Biddeford, and has been chosen on various occasions to represent them in the numerous civic enterprises carried on by that group. He was one of the organizers and founders of the Fremont Club in Biddeford, and his is the distinction of serving as its first president, and to him belongs substantially a great amount of credit for the influence and strength of that organization in the district. Mr. Lantagne is also a member of the Union of St. John, and having completed a term of three and one-half years as president of the body, was reëlected to that office in 1927. He is likewise a member of the board of directors and executive officer of the National Association of the Union of St. John; and also a member of Portland Lodge, Benevolent and Protective Order of Elks. In politics, he is a Republican, and is closely and intimately associated with the activities and policies of his party. His religious affiliation is with the Roman Catholics, and with his family he is a communicant of the St. Joseph Church in Biddeford.

In 1909, Alfred Lantagne married Josephine Babineau of the Province of Quebec, Canada, a daughter of Dominick and Octavie (Patry) Babineau. Mr. and Mrs. Lantagne are the parents of Armand C., who was born November 3, 1911, and is now a student of the Sacred Heart College.

DOLORE B. DUMONT—A career in the making often affords those who are observant an opportunity to foretell future accomplishment. The enthusiasm and unwearying energy with which Dolore B. Dumont has approached his profession show to the initiated a future success which will be a credit to the town he has chosen as the scene of his efforts.

Born October 29, 1900, at Skowhegan, Maine, he is the son of John T. and Lucy (Breton) Dumont. The father, a carpenter, the merit of whose work is widely known in his district, is a native of Skowhegan, and

the mother comes from the Province of Quebec. Educated in the public schools of Skowhegan and at the Massachusetts College of Optometry, where he graduated in the class of 1925, Mr. Dumont began the practice of his profession at Biddeford in that year. He took over the business of the Littlefield Optical Company and has continued under that name up to the present time as an optometrist and optician. He is a young man of promise and has already laid a substantial foundation for an excellent success. He is a member of the local club of Biddeford and is affiliated with St. Matthew's Roman Catholic Church.

ALPHEUS C. HANSCOM, D. D. S.—The oldest dentist in Sanford, in point of service, Alpheus C. Hanscom, Doctor of Dental Surgery, began dental practice here in 1902, and has since continuously followed his calling in this community. Born at Lebanon, Maine, March 13, 1874, he is the son of Edwin and Olivia (Libby) Hanscom. His father, a farmer and blacksmith, died October 15, 1916, at the age of eighty-seven, and his mother, who was a native of North Berwick, died December 10, 1899.

Dr. Hanscom obtained his early education in the public schools and then entered Bates College, Lewiston, Maine, where he received the degree of Bachelor of Arts in 1897. His professional training was received in the Dental School of the University of Pennsylvania, where he was graduated with the degree of Doctor of Dental Surgery in the class of 1902. Returning to Maine, he began the professional activity that has won him high rank among his colleagues and a gratifying degree of public favor. He is a member of the York County and Maine State Dental associations, and of the National Dental Association.

While Dr. Hanscom's interests have naturally centered in his profession, he has given generously of his time and thought in civic affairs and the public service. He has been a member of the local School Board since 1914, serving as chairman of the board, and during the World War was appointed by Governor Milliken to the Medical Advisory Board. Another local institution with which he has been identified is the Sanford National Bank, of which he was a director until 1927. He is a member of Preble Lodge, Free and Accepted Masons, and fraternizes also with Chapter, Council and Commandery, having held the office of High Priest. He is a member also of the Baptist church, of which he has been a trustee.

In 1906, Dr. Hanscom married Etta M. Pierce, of Lebanon, Maine, daughter of Fred L. and Ellen A. (Brackett) Pierce. Their children are: 1. Fred E., born July 3, 1908. 2. Oscar E., born June 30, 1912. 3. Caroline born May 26, 1916. 4. Ward T., born October 24, 1919.

WELLINGTON A. MOORE—A prominent figure in the lumber industry in Bath, Maine, is Wellington A. Moore, treasurer of the Bath Box Company, a substantial and prosperous concern of that city. Long experience in this industry and the general business ability of Mr. Moore have been contributory factors to the success enjoyed by the Bath Box Company.

Wellington A. Moore was born at New Brunswick, May 19, 1875, son of Harris E. and Sarah (Dunn) Moore. The father has also been interested in lumber throughout his business career and was treasurer of the Bath Box Company in 1912, at the time of its incorporation. Both parents were natives of New

Brunswick. The son attended the public schools and early began to learn of the lumber business. The company whose growth he has done so much to further was established in 1911 as the successor to the N. G. Shaw Lumber Company and was incorporated a year later, in 1912. F. J. Derry was elected president, and H. E. Moore, treasurer. A year later, the former was replaced by A. J. Dunton, who in turn gave place to James A. Gillies in 1914. Mr. Gillies has since remained president of the Bath Box Company, of which F. W. Coniser is vice-president, and the subject of this record treasurer. The company was organized to manufacture wholesale and retail lumber and shooks. One hundred and fifty workers are constantly employed, and their products are distributed throughout New England, with an exclusive market in Bath, where there is no other concern of this type. The plant occupies several acres and makes use of a private railroad siding, its size and widespread market being the product of a steady and wholesome growth. To his business Mr. Moore gives most of his time and attention, for he is keenly interested in all its details of operation and expansion. He is a member of the Free and Accepted Masons, Solar Lodge, of the Royal Arch Masons, the Royal and Select Masters, and the Knights Templar. His club is the Colonial, his church, the First Congregational.

Wellington A. Moore married (first) Alca S. Fuller, now deceased; and (second) Ruth M. Adams. The children of the first marriage are: Madison A. F. Moore, who served four years in the United States Navy, and Madeline I. Moore; while the child of the second marriage is Shirley L. Moore.

RALPH S. NORTON—A leading factor in the insurance activities of Portland and a considerable section of the State of which this city is the flourishing center, Ralph S. Norton has been associated with this important business as long as most of the veterans in insurance in Maine who have made a success in their line. He is known throughout the State and beyond its borders for his painstaking and thoroughgoing methods in the general interests of insurance, and no one is better informed as to every vital matter in all forms of insurance, and few have developed a wider range of territory.

Ralph S. Norton was born April 19, 1866, at Falmouth, a son of B. R. Norton, who died in 1872, and Vivian (Branscomb) Norton, who died in 1890. After attending public schools and graduating from a business college, Mr. Norton immediately became identified with the insurance activities, and he has continued therein practically throughout his career. The firm of Norton and Hall was established in 1897, and was incorporated in 1900, with Mr. Norton as the president, and A. E. Hall as treasurer, and J. E. Shearman as clerk, the purpose of the firm having been, as it has always continued to be, to deal in all forms of insurance. Later, Charles S. Webster was admitted to the firm, and the firm title became as at present, Norton, Hall & Webster.

A Republican in his political views, Mr. Norton with his vote and influence supports the principles of that party. Fraternally, he is affiliated with the Independent Order of Odd Fellows. He is a vestryman of St. Mary the Virgin Protestant Episcopal Church.

Ralph S. Norton married Alice G. Randall, of Portland, and they have two children: Ruth, and Robert B.

CHARLES L. VEAZIE—Efficiency and devotion to the best interests of the community as a holder of various public offices have established as one of the progressive and popular citizens of Rockport, Maine, Charles L. Veazie, for the past decade town clerk of that city. Mr. Veazie is also an electrician and interested in the electrical supply business.

Charles L. Veazie was born at Rockport, Maine, July 4, 1883, son of Charles B. and Alice (Carey) Veazie, both natives of Rockport. The father, now deceased, long conducted a meat market there and as a Republican held various town offices. The son attended the public and high schools in Rockport. His business career began by five years of association with the New England Telephone Company. He was then United States Deputy Shipping Commissioner at Rockport for three years, passing from that occupation to the insurance profession which he for three years followed with much success. He was salesman for the National Biscuit Company for two years, after which he returned to the type of work which is most congenial to him because it offers him a share in managing municipal affairs. He was town treasurer of Rockport for five years and then was elected to the position he has held for the past ten years and continues to occupy, that of town clerk of Rockport. Meantime, his electrical business also prospers. In politics he is a Republican, and in September, 1926, he was elected for four years as Register of Probate for the county. He is a member of the Baptist Men's League of Rockland.

February 15, 1913, at Rockport, Charles L. Veazie married Effie L. Ingraham, a native of the same town, daughter of Enos and Marion (Upham) Ingraham. Mr. and Mrs. Veazie have a daughter, Mary Veazie, born June 5, 1916.

FREDERICK P. ABBOTT—The two outstanding phases of the career of Frederick P. Abbott have been those of his long and successful business activities and his most interesting years devoted to travel, in company with his talented wife, who is now deceased. While engaged in the business of the purchase and sale of real estate in Biddeford, Mr. Abbott held a place second to no other in the development of valuable property and as a general realtor. Then came the well-won privilege of the prolonged vacation, and the broader acquaintanceship with cities at home and the lands overseas.

Frederick P. Abbott was born April 25, 1863, at Biddeford, a son of Erastus Abbott, a native of Portland, and Bertha Abbott, of Waldermall. After attending the public schools, Mr. Abbott established himself in the real estate business at Biddeford, and he continued therein for many years, and with great success, as he was recognized as the leading realtor throughout this section, up to the date of his retirement. Mr. Abbott then, with Mrs. Abbott, spent a number of years in travel, these, doubtless among their happiest years, being passed in visiting many parts of the United States, as well as in touring the countries of the Old World.

In the political field, Mr. Abbott has always been affiliated with the Democratic party, although he has never sought public office. He is very active in the order of the Free and Accepted Masons, with his membership in all bodies of the Ancient Accepted Scottish Rite to the thirty-second degree.

Frederick P. Abbott married, August 6, 1902, Sarah Rideout, daughter of Rev. William and Ruth Rebecca Rideout, a review of whose life follows.

SARAH (RIDEOUT) ABBOTT—The notable sphere of usefulness to which Mrs. Sarah (Rideout) Abbott devoted her life was the gainer in varied humanitarian matters, her work in behalf of women's organized interests, child welfare, and national defense, the latter during the World War, receiving the merited recognition that is the fruit of nobly directed effort such as was hers throughout her career of charitableness and beneficence.

Sarah Rideout was born in the Province of New Brunswick, Canada, daughter of Rev. William Rideout, a clergyman of the Baptist church, at Callas, New Brunswick, and Ruth Rebecca (Bradford) Rideout. After attending school in New Brunswick, she taught in the Callas schools for several years, and afterwards was a member of the teaching force in the schools of other sections, notably at the Mitchell Military Academy, in Massachusetts, where she remained seven years; at the New Haven (Connecticut) High School, and, for a short time, at the Middletown (Connecticut) High School.

Sarah Rideout married, August 6, 1902, Frederick P. Abbott, who then engaged in the real estate business at Biddeford, and a review of whose career appears in the preceding sketch. Mr. Abbott purchased a beautiful home about three miles from Saco, on the Saco River, and there they resided for many years.

Mrs. Abbott, now deceased, was a woman of great ability, and had at all times interested herself in work for women and their organized effort, and she had become very prominent among the club women of Maine. At the time of the World War, the national government, with the sanction of the Governor of her native State, appointed Mrs. Abbott as head of women's organizations of the Council of Defence. For her untiring efforts therein, as well as for her interests in the Child Welfare movement, Mrs. Abbott was awarded the Congressional Medal.

NAPOLEON SPENARD—Active in the automobile business and in the civic affairs of Biddeford, Maine, Napoleon Spenard has come to be one of the best liked men of the city. Before 1922, he was identified with the textile industry, having perfected and patented a method of manufacturing shuttle eyelets, a business which he carried on until that year.

He was born June 28, 1884, in the Province of Quebec, Canada, the son of Ernest Spenard, of the Province of Quebec, who died in 1926, and of Julia (Senville) Spenard, also of Quebec, who is still living. His father was identified with the mill industry. The boy was brought to the United States when five years old.

Napoleon Spenard, after he had attended the public and parochial schools, became associated with the Pepperell Manufacturing Company, with which company he was employed for twenty-six years. For twenty-one years of that time he was a foreman in this textile manufacturing company's plants, until 1923. In 1917 he perfected the shuttle eyelet, and,

still with the company, he traveled extensively throughout the country introducing this device. He was always mechanically inclined.

While still with the Pepperell Company, and making his patented shuttle eyelet, he took an agency for automobiles, in 1922, starting in business in a small one-room establishment at No. 19 Grove Street. The business gradually increased, and in the spring of 1924 ground was broken for Mr. Spenard's present building, which was completed in November, 1924. It is one of the largest garages and automobiles sales agencies in southern Maine, having a capacity of one hundred and twenty-five cars. In June, 1922, the business was incorporated under the name of N. Spenard and Company, of which Mr. Spenard, since that time, has been president and treasurer. The company handles Chandler, Oakland and Pontiac cars in York County.

He has taken a considerable interest in the political life of the city, having served as a member of the Board of Aldermen from the Fourth Ward and having been a candidate for the State Legislature. He is a member of the Rotary Club, and is affiliated fraternally, with the Benevolent and Protective Order of Elks; the Foresters of America, and the Catholic Order of Foresters, and St. John's Club; he is a charter member of the Chamber of Commerce. He is a Roman Catholic, being a member of St. Andrew's Church.

Napoleon Spenard married, in 1904, Jean Lambert, of the Province of Quebec, the daughter of Albert Lambert. There are two children: Eva J., born June 17, 1905, who is organist at St. Andrew's Church; and Germaine, born May 10, 1908.

JAMES ALEXANDER DUNNING, who was born in Bangor, November 16, 1865, and who died in Havana, Cuba, October 7, 1925, was a prominent business man of Maine and one of the best-known and most beloved men of the community in and about Bangor. He was president and treasurer of the R. B. Dunning Company, a large wholesale house handling all kinds of agricultural implements, woodenware, dairy supplies, seeds, and plumbing and heating supplies, a business which had been conducted by different members of the Dunning family since its inception in 1835. His death was a profound personal loss to many in this section, for he was a man of fine character, generous and genial, and one who was active in every charitable enterprise and every movement for the betterment of Bangor.

He was born in the house in which his widow, Mrs. Marian A. Dunning, now lives, at No. 744 Union Street, Bangor, on November 16, 1865, the son of Robert B. Dunning, who conducted the R. B. Dunning Company before him, and of Frances (Garland) Dunning, who died in February, 1910. The Dunning ancestry in America has been traced back to three brothers who came from England, one of whom settled in New York State, one in New Brunswick, and one in Maine. As a boy, James Alexander Dunning attended the public schools of Bangor, devoting his summers to tutoring, and later he studied for two years at the University of Maine. When he completed his academic work, he taught for a time in the country schools of Maine, then worked for his uncle in a general store in Munson. At the age of twenty-one years he went to California, where he spent strenuous days in different sorts of employment, having been a helper in a hotel restaurant and a steward in the Stockton Insane Asylum. He continued to work in California until he was called home because of his father's illness. After his father's death in February, 1896, he became interested in the R. B. Dunning Company, in Bangor, the firm which had been established and conducted by his forefathers.

The Dunning company is one of Bangor's oldest and largest wholesale houses, dealing in seeds and farming implements of all kinds. It was established in 1835, at No. 52 Broad Street, Bangor, by James Dunning, whose brother, Alexander Dunning, became interested in the firm in the early "forties," so that the company then was known as J. and A. Dunning. Late in the "forties" Alexander Dunning sold his share of the business; after which Robert B. Dunning, another brother, became a member of the firm, which then came to be known as J. and R. B. Dunning. It was late in the "fifties" when James Dunning sold his share of the business and Robert B. Dunning continued the firm under the name of R. B. Dunning & Company. In 1894, two years before Robert B. Dunning's death, there were three brothers in the company, which was a co-partnership. In 1897 the business was incorporated. On February 16, 1923, John Garland Dunning, senior member of the firm, having been in the company since 1873, when he became associated in the management with his father, Robert B. Dunning, met his death; and not long afterward George W. Dunning, one of the brothers and former president of the corporation, retired from the firm, of which James Alexander Dunning was president and treasurer.

In addition to his activity in the R. B. Dunning Company, James Alexander Dunning was a director of the Merrill Trust Company, a member of the Rotary Club, the Chamber of Commerce, the Penobscot Valley Country Club, and the Tarratine Club; a member of the Free and Accepted Masons, in which order he is affiliated with the Royal Arch Chapter, St. John's Commandery; the Eastern Star Lodge of Perfection, the Palestine Council of the Princes of Jerusalem, the Bangor Chapter of the Rose Croix, the Tamerlane Conclave of the Red Cross of Constantine, Past Illustrious Potentate of Kora Temple in Lewiston and of Anah Temple in Bangor, of the Ancient Arabic Order Nobles of the Mystic Shrine. In addition to being an organizer of Anah Temple, he became on June 15, 1920, a Potentate, an office in which he served twice, each time in a different temple, having been the only man, with the exception of one other, in the world to receive this honor. He also was a member of the Ancient and Honorable Artillery Company of Boston, with which organization he was touring Havana, the Cuban capital, at the time of his death. In his political opinions he was a Republican, although no office seeker, having refused several times a request to be a candidate for the mayoralty. Active at all times in charitable work, he earned the reputation of having headed every charity list in Bangor. He also participated in all movements which he thought would be effective in the improvement of the industrial, civic and social life of the city.

In Brooklyn, New York, on October 22, 1900, James A. Dunning married Marian A. Tyler, the daughter of George F. and Almira B. (Dunning) Tyler. Her father, who was engaged in the wholesale provisions business in Boston, is at the time of

writing (1928) eighty-four years old, and living with Mrs. Dunning in Bangor. Mrs. Dunning proved to be a constant source of inspiration to her husband, whose home she graced with love and affection and with tender care for the five children.

The five children of James Alexander and Marian A. (Tyler) Dunning, all of whom are at home with their mother, are: James A., Jr., Ruth S., Phyllis, John G. (2), and Hope.

FRANK EDWARD MALIAR—Stereotyping is hard work, hot and muscle-developing, a labor that was followed for five years by Frank Edward Maliar, of Lewiston, before he engaged in the long distance motor-trucking business here that has brought success to him and his brother, William H. Aside from his business activities he has been recognized by his fellow-citizens for his value and rewarded with public office of trust and honor. He has an enviable military record during a period when his country needed men of his calibre and is an upstanding citizen and a successful business man, with a host of friends who have a deep appreciation of his worth.

Mr. Maliar was born in Lewiston, Maine, June 23, 1897, a son of John Robert Maliar, one of the best-known and respected citizens of this community for many years. He was born in Bath, Maine, in 1859, and was deputy sheriff of Androscoggin for two years and a captain in the fire department for thirty-one years. He served in Lewiston as alderman and as councilman and was for twelve years a member of the police department, retiring from that work with the rank of deputy marshal. His wife, the mother of Frank Edward, was Sarah A. (Osborne) Maliar, a native of New Brunswick, Dominion of Canada. Frank Edward was educated in the public schools of Lewiston and began his life's work in the plant of the Lewiston "Journal," where he was engaged in the stereotyping department from 1912 until 1917. He then engaged in the general trucking business here, making long distance moving his specialty. Associated with his brother, William H., the business grew into one of the largest and most prosperous in the State, with an efficient number of motor trucks of the latest construction and operated under the firm name of Maliar Brothers, at No. 90 Middle Street, Lewiston. William H. Maliar is president of the company, while Frank Edward is secretary and treasurer. He is a Democrat in political affiliation and by that party was elected to a seat on the Board of Aldermen for a term of two years. During the participation of the United States in the World War he served, by enlistment, from February 12, 1917, until March, 1918, when he was discharged. Prior to that he had served on the Mexican border with the Eighth United States Cavalry. He is a member of the American Legion and of the Fraternal Order of Eagles and the Benevolent and Protective Order of Elks. His church is St. Joseph's Roman Catholic, of Lewiston.

Frank Edward Maliar married, in Lewiston, Maine, August 6, 1925, Mildred Smith, of Winthrop, Massachusetts, daughter of William and Eleanor (Monahan) Smith. They have one child: Frank Edward, Jr., born in Lewiston, August 26, 1926.

JOHN P. BREEN—Buying and selling real estate, privately and by auction, throughout the State of Maine, has brought into broad prominence John P.

Breen, who makes his home and headquarters in Lewiston. In active business here for twenty years, he has established a reputation for fair dealing and keen business ability. For his civic interests he has been rewarded by selection for public office of honor and trust, a certain indication of wide popularity. He is in the very prime of life, with opportunities for a wider sphere of action and still greater success, which his friends hope, in the event of a decision, will not remove him from the scene of his successful activities in this district.

Mr. Breen was born in Lewiston, Maine, July 9, 1880, a son of Thomas F., a native of Toronto, Ontario, Dominion of Canada, now an employee of the Maine Central Railroad, and of Mary (Coughlin) Breen, who was born in County Cork, Ireland. John P. was educated in the public schools of Lewiston and at Nichols Latin School. He entered the real estate business at Lewiston in 1908 and has since conducted it here, enlarging his work as time passed, until he is now a familiar figure in all sections of the State. He is a director in the Home Agency, was a member of the State Legislature in 1927 and an alderman from Ward One, Lewiston, for three years. He is a member of the Grange and of the Fraternal Order of Eagles. He is a communicant of St. Joseph's Roman Catholic Church.

John P. Breen married, in Lewiston, Maine, in October, 1902, Edith G. Curran, of this city, daughter of John and Margaret (Connor) Curran, born in Lewiston, October 10, 1880. They have three children: 1. Mary Edith, born in Lewiston, deceased. 2. John Joseph, born in Lewiston, deceased. 3. Madeleine U., born in Boston, Massachusetts.

ALOUISIUS F. MARTIN—One of the youngest members of the bar now in practice in Lewiston is Alouisius F. Martin, who has been established here since the autumn of 1927, following a year and some months in Portland. Selecting a comparatively small community for his professional labors, rather than essaying competition in great centers with multitudes of practitioners having years of experience, this young lawyer has taken a wise course. He will find here many able lawyers whose services are in constant demand, yet he will also discover that the competition is not so bitterly selfish as in those larger fields and that his own chances of attaining a place at the top of the ladder of fame are entirely within his personal abilities. He has been welcomed to the professional ranks and his career will be watched with unselfish interest by every experienced member of the bar here, their combined good will being extended to him in his every effort.

Mr. Martin was born in Webster, Massachusetts, May 31, 1902, a son of Frank S., a native of Essen, Germany, who emigrated to America and became a manufacturer of clothing in Worcester, Massachusetts, and of Patricia (Viecorek) Martin, native of Warsaw, Poland. Their son acquired his education in the public schools of Webster, was graduated from high school and attended the Bartlett Preparatory School. This was followed by a course at Columbia University, New York City, at Holy Cross and, finally, at the Boston University Law School, from which he was graduated in the class of 1924 with the degree of Bachelor of Laws. Admitted to the bar of the State of Maine in 1925, he began a general practice in Portland, but later came to Lewiston, where he is

now established at No. 215 Lisbon Street. He is Independent in politics and a member of the Roman Catholic church.

CARL MILLETT GOWELL—Steadfast regard for duty, industrious perseverance in learning his business and honest devotion to his employers' interests have brought their reward in the shape of promotion to high position of Carl Millett Gowell, treasurer of the sash manufacturing establishment of the W. C. Dain Company, of Lewiston.

Carl Millett Gowell was born in Auburn, Maine, June 12, 1892, a son of Wallace I., and Rose E. Gowell, his father being a letter carrier of that city. His education was acquired in the elementary and high schools of Auburn, from which he was graduated in 1909. In that year he went to work for the company with which he is still associated, receiving promotion from time to time, until he was made treasurer, which he at present holds.

Mr. Gowell married, October 18, 1914, in Livermore Falls, Maine, Edith Alden. The couple has five children: 1. George W. 2. Rose. 3. Elsie F. 4. Carl Millett, Jr. 5. Edward D.

HERMENEGILDE JOHN COTE—During his long service in association with the sash manufacturing establishment of the W. C. Dain Company, of Lewiston, Hermenegilde John Cote has firmly cemented the ties that bind together men of business and personal integrity and has made for himself a name in the community for industry and citizenship of the highest quality. With no other assistance save a determination to achieve success and an industrious nature that could not be gainsaid, he has mounted to the top of the industrial ladder in his chosen field, being now the president of the establishment with which he has been long identified.

Mr. Cote was born in St. Arsene, Province of Quebec, Dominion of Canada, August 30, 1870, and came to Maine shortly after a rudimentary education in the primary schools, where he became associated with the company which he now heads. He is a communicant of SS. Peter and Paul's Roman Catholic Church and a member of the Jacques Cartier Club.

Hermenegilde John Cote married, in Lewiston, Maine, January 16, 1906, Lucy Thibault, daughter of Joseph and Justine Thibault. The children are: 1. Albert J., born January 11, 1907. 2. Alice L., born January 19, 1909. 3. Marguerite R., born January 31, 1911. 4. H. Paul, born July 16, 1917.

DANIEL JOHN McGILLICUDDY — Distinguished in the legal profession and in the national legislative halls, a champion of fairness to all, with a keen mind and a comprehensive grasp of the details of the law, Daniel John McGilicuddy, of Lewiston, is one of the representative citizens of Maine. Having practiced his profession here for almost half a century his fame is more than local, for he not only has been selected by the electorate to represent his district in the State Legislature but has been three times elected to the National House of Representatives. He is a man of most attractive personality, of deep convictions and is possessed of a faculty of influencing others in public movements which he has studied and believes to be for the good of the body politic as a whole. His sturdy citizenship is unbiased although he has been a staunch Democrat and supporter of that political party. He is known and respected as a fair and just man and an able representative of the people who select him for office of honor and distinction.

Daniel John McGillicuddy was born in Lewiston, Maine, August 27, 1859, a son of John M. and Ellen (Byrnes) McGillicuddy. He was educated in the public schools and attended Bowdoin College, from which he was graduated in 1881. He was admitted to the bar of Maine in 1883 and began the practice of law in Lewiston as McGillicuddy & Morey. His first public service was as a member of the School Board of Lewiston, after which he was elected to the State Legislature and served from 1884 until 1885. He was elected mayor of Lewiston in 1887 for one term and in 1890 for one term, and in 1902 for one term. His election from the Second Maine District to Congress followed and he was appointed a member of the Judiciary Committee, one of the most important committees of the National House. He was reëlected to the Sixty-third Congress and reappointed to the same committee, and again received the approval of his constituents by a third election, this time being assigned to membership on the Ways and Means Committee. He drafted the first Workmen's Compensation Act, which was signed by President Wilson, and was a member of the sub-committee that drew up the revenue bill of 1916. He is a member of the Democratic National Committee, of the Knights of Columbus and of the Benevolent and Protective Order of Elks. His religious affiliation is with the Roman Catholic church.

Mr. McGillicuddy married, at Lewiston, Maine, July 5, 1898, Minnie M. Sprague, of this city.

LEON LEIGHTON, Jr., was born in Lewiston, Maine, June 27, 1897, a son of Leon, a native of Auburn, where he was born, September 4, 1874, and Margaret (Booth) Leighton, who was born in Lewiston, April 20, 1874. His father is proprietor of a hotel at Thomaston, Maine, and a member of all Masonic bodies and other fraternal organizations. Leon, Jr., was educated in the Lewiston public and high schools and was graduated from the Milton Academy in the class of 1915. He then went to Bowdoin, from which institution he was graduated in the class of 1919 with the degree of Bachelor of Science. During the participation of the United States in the World War he served from May 16, 1918, until August 28, 1919, when he was honorably mustered out with the rank of second lieutenant of Infantry. In 1920 he became associated with the stock and bond-brokerage house of Timberlake & Company, of Portland, Maine, where he continued until 1923, when he purchased the business of the Chadwick Heel Company, at Lewiston, changed the name to the Leighton Heel Company, Incorporated, and has since continued to operate it as such, with himself as president and treasurer. The concern manufactures leather board and combination heels and employs an average of forty-five hands. Mr. Leighton is a Republican in politics, member of all Masonic bodies and Ancient Arabic Order Nobles of the Mystic Shrine, and an attendant of the Protestant Episcopal Church of St. Michael's. He is a member of the Martindale Country Club, the Rotary Club and the Lewiston Chamber of Commerce. His college fraternity is Psi Upsilon. In the commercial field he is a member of the Maine Associated Industries.

Mr. Leighton married, in Auburn, Maine, May 31, 1922, Lucia Alford, born in Hyde Park, Massachusetts, January 11, 1898, daughter of Abbott and Lena (Barker) Alford, both natives of Oldtown, Maine. They have one child. Nathalie Margaret, born in Lewiston, Maine, August 1, 1923.

NARCISSE PRUDENT RENOUF—One of the best-known insurance men of Biddeford, Maine, is Narcisse Prudent Renouf, president of the Biddeford Agency, Incorporated, Insurance. Mr. Renouf has been identified with the insurance business for more than thirty years, and is an expert in this field. He carries a general line of every kind of insurance and bonds, and is identified with the county, State and national insurance organizations. Mr. Renouf had had an active and varied business career before engaging in the insurance business, and the experience gained in these various enterprises is proving to be of distinctive value in his present line of activity.

Narcisse Prudent Renouf was born at Trois-Pistoles, Temiscouata County, Province of Quebec, April 7, 1865, son of Philippe and Luce Roy (Desjardine) Renouf; and grandson of Philippe Renouf, a ship owner and navigator, who came from the island of Jersey, England, and settled here about the first decade of the nineteenth century. At the age of seventeen years, Mr. Renouf graduated from the local normal school, and in May, 1882, he removed to Troy, New York, to make a new home. For eight years he followed various occupations, including bookkeeping, store clerk, textile-weaving, and whaling, going on a whaling expedition for eighteen months along the Gulf Stream, the West Indies, the Canaries, and the Azores. He next apprenticed himself to a photographer, and when his apprenticeship was completed, opened a studio in a building adjoining the present Lewis Polakewich & Sons Department Store. That was in April, 1890. In June, 1896, he began his long connection with the insurance business by securing the agency for two fire insurance companies, and his connection with this business has been continuous to the present time (1928). In the spring of 1909, he admitted to partnership Joseph Lachance, and early in 1910, when the Standard Fire Insurance Company of Connecticut was organized, the agency served this company, and Mr. Renouf was its first special agent for Maine. At the close of the World War, Mr. Renouf and Mr. Lachance added the real estate business to their general insurance line and for some five years were very actively engaged in this new department of their business. On January 2, 1925, their insurance business was incorporated under the name of the Biddeford Agency, Incorporated, Insurance, with Narcisse Prudent Renouf as president; Joseph Lachance, treasurer, and Juliette H. Nadeau, as clerk. The concern represents twenty-four fire insurance and three miscellaneous companies, and its offices are located at No. 138 Main Street, Biddeford, Maine. Mr. Renouf is a member of the Official State of Maine Agents' Association, the Insurance Federation of Maine, the National Association of Insurance Agents, and of the York County Board of Fire Underwriters. Politically, he gives his support to the Republican party, and for a period of twenty years, beginning 1892, gave much time to public affairs. He was a member of the Board of

Health for three years and secretary one year, and was a generous supporter of all well-planned public measures. Fraternally, he is identified with the Sociétié of St. Jean Baptiste of Biddeford, of which he has been a member since 1890; of the Sociétié des Artisans, of which he has been a member since 1896; and of the Canado-Americain, of which he has been a member since 1924. His religious affiliation is with St. Joseph's Roman Catholic Church of Biddeford.

Narcisse Prudent Renouf was married, at St. Joseph's Church, September 7, 1891, to Heloise Painchaud, of Biddeford, eldest daughter of Professor Painchaud, founder of Painchaud's Band. Mr. and Mrs. Renouf are the parents of two children: 1. P. J. Albert, who is with his father in the insurance agency. 2. Myrabelle, who is associated with her mother at home in the musical profession. The family home is at No. 256 South Street, Biddeford, Maine.

Mrs. Renouf is an accomplished musician. On Sunday mornings she is soloist at First Parish Congregational Church, Saco, Maine; Sunday evenings is director of the Mixed Choir at United Baptist Church, Saco, Maine. She is local director for South Berwick, Biddeford, Saco, and Kennebunk, Maine, in connection with the "Maine Festival," given in Portland each year, and she has not missed one during the last thirty years.

EDWIN P. WEBSTER—For years identified commercially, and as a citizen, with Lewiston, Edwin P. Webster is one of the prominent figures of the community, active in its every phase of general progress, but particularly so as this progress concerns commerce. Respected by all who know him, his position is both honored and substantial. As an incorporator and official of the Haskell Implement & Seed Company, Incorporated, he assists in the control of a business whose size has increased materially within the span of several years, and whose presence in Lewiston is felt as a large unit in the community's economic composition. The company's offices, ware and storage houses and yards are at Nos. 20-22-24 Chapel Street. While no contemporary history of the State of Maine may properly be presented without full attention to the chronicle of Lewiston, it is equally true that this chronicle of Lewiston would indeed be incomplete without the record of one whose prominence locally compares with that of Mr. Webster.

Mr. Webster was born in Medway, Maine, May 16, 1870, son of Daniel and Alice Elizabeth (Parker) Webster. Daniel Webster was a farmer, industrious, highly esteemed by his neighbors. He was a native of Bangor, Maine. Alice Elizabeth (Parker) Webster was a native of Coaticook, Province of Quebec, Canada. It was they who gave to their son the right principles of conduct and thought which have assisted him to considerable success in his career. To them, his recollection turns constantly, in gratitude, and in tender affection.

Mr. Webster attended the public and high schools of Bangor, Maine. On completion of his education in 1891, he entered the post office in Bangor, Maine, working through various departments rising to superintendent of Money Order Department. He continued this position until March 1, 1903, when he became identified with the George B. Haskell Company,

Incorporated, of Lewiston. His position was that of salesman, handling the concern's agricultural implements, hardware, grain and grass seeds. As such he continued for about twelve months, then became invoice clerk, and in 1910 general manager. As manager he retained office until January 1, 1923, when, joined in association with Daniel W. Webster, he bought control of the company. They filed articles of incorporation at the State House, and in the new charter Edwin P. Webster was named vice-president and treasurer, while his partner was named president. The company's name style was altered to the present style, Haskell Implement & Seed Company, Incorporated, and Mr. Webster continues to act as general manager, much to the firm's well-being.

Mr. Webster is a supporter of the Republican principles of party government, and locally wields a considerable influence politically, for the greatest good to the greatest number of people. He has served the community as alderman from the Second Ward, but has been in no sense an office seeker. Fraternally, he is affiliated with the Free and Accepted Masons, in which order he is a member of the Blue Lodge. He is a member, and an active one, of the Lewiston and Auburn Chamber of Commerce. He was one time president of the Lewiston Rotary Club, and is past president of the New England Dealers' Implement Association. He is a member of the Martindale Country Club, and attends the Universalist church. During the period of America's participation in the World War, Mr. Webster acted with much benefit to his country on several boards and committees charged with war work, and was of material assistance in the several campaigns of the Liberty Loan.

On November 28, 1908, in Auburn, Mr. Webster was united in marriage with Wilhelmina J. Atwood, who was born in Auburn, daughter of Tascus and Helen (Jameson) Atwood, the former a native of Auburn, and the latter of Lincoln, Maine. To this union have been born children: 1. Priscilla A., November 17, 1909. 2. Edwin P., Jr., January 8, 1913. The family residence is at No. 318 Court Street, Auburn.

CHENEY C. BROWN—One of the prominent citizens of Lewiston, respected and sincerely esteemed by all who know him, successful in business and large contributor to the public welfare, is Cheney C. Brown, president and treasurer of Carman Thompson Company, Incorporated, dealers in steam, mill and plumbing supplies, with offices and warehouse at Nos. 12-14 Lincoln Street. For more than forty years Mr. Brown has resided in Lewiston, and has witnessed its devolopment along the sound lines which have caused it to become the substantial community that it is today. He has worked zealously not alone for the progress of his own special business, but for the rounded development of Lewiston as a valuable unit in the composition of State and nation. His efforts have been rewarded, appreciated for their force and constancy, by the people of the town, who hold him in warm regard.

Mr. Brown was born in Lisbon, New Hampshire, April 6, 1860, son of Silas Solomon and Kate (Howie) Brown, of whom the former was a native of Bristol, New Hampshire, and the latter of Keith, in Scotland. Silas Solomon Brown was a contractor, storekeeper, and a man of affairs; upright, dominant of personality, genial withal, and beloved of many. He served his community well, notably as county commissioner and as non-official worker for the public weal. In Lisbon, New Hampshire, his standing as man and citizen was of the highest.

In the public schools of his native community, Lisbon, Cheney C. Brown secured his elementary and secondary academic education, then entered New Hampton, New Hampshire, Literary Institute, whence he graduated with the class of 1880, well up toward the forefront in scholastic markings. There followed eight years of varied experience in several lines of endeavor, and in 1888 was begun Mr. Brown's connection with the organization which, in its present form, he has come to control. His first position with the Carman Thompson Company, of Lewiston, was as bookkeeper, at which he continued for twenty years, until 1908. He then purchased the company, and operated it successfully, independently of associates, until 1920. In 1920 a reorganization was effected; the company was incorporated with all the advantages incumbent upon corporate management; and Mr. Brown remained at its head with the two most important offices, of president and treasurer. Frank L. Tracy who has been associated with the company for a number of years is a director, Stanley S. Brown, son of C. C. Brown, is secretary. He is a Republican, loyal in support of the party's principles of government. Fraternally, he is affiliated with the Free and Accepted Masons, and belongs to the Auburn and Lewiston Chamber of Commerce, and Lewiston Rotary Club, in all of which he is active. He is a communicant of the Court Street Baptist Church, of Auburn.

On March 18, 1890, in Portsmouth, New Hampshire, Mr. Brown was united in marriage with Annie G. Sides, who was born July 9, 1854, in Portsmouth, daughter of Charles H. Sides, also a native of Portsmouth. Mr. and Mrs. Brown are the parents of one child, Stanley Sides, born November 4, 1893, in Auburn, Maine. They make their home at No. 250 Summer Street, Auburn.

NATHANIEL W. BLANCHARD—Coming of a family which had made the name of Blanchard famous by the building of sea craft which held first place among the ships of the time, it is not surprising that Nathaniel W. Blanchard should follow the lure of the sea. Beginning at the bottom of the ladder, as all true sailors of merit do, he won laurels all along the way he had chosen to travel and achieved his ambition comparatively early in life. Born, April 29, 1852, at Yarmouth, Maine, he is the son of Perez N. and Cynthia E. Blanchard. Mrs. Blanchard's maiden name was also Blanchard though the two families are not related. She passed away in 1895 and Mr. Blanchard died in 1883. The father was famous as a builder of boats at Yarmouth, Maine.

Nathaniel W. Blanchard was educated at North Yarmouth Academy and Eastman Business College, after which he went to sea, serving as mate on several vessels. He was made a captain of the "P. N. Blanchard," and commanded this boat for fifteen years, during which time he sailed around the world. Retiring from active service in 1900 he has since lived at Yarmouth, his native town.

His fraternal affiliation is with the Free and Accepted Masons in the Blue Lodge and Chapter, and he is also a member of the Portland, Maine, Society.

Mr. Blanchard has been a trustee of North Yarmouth Academy since 1883, replacing his father in this office when the latter passed away. He is the oldest living member now. He also served on the Library Board for seventeen years. He and his family are members of the Congregational church.

In 1883, Nathaniel W. Blanchard married Grace S. Greenleaf of Yarmouth, daughter of Henry C. and Susan (Harvey) Greenleaf. The father passed away in 1876, the mother in 1891. Of this marriage there were born three children: 1. Lelia. 2. Nathaniel, Both died at Hong Kong in infancy. 3. Rena May, a graduate of Boston University; now with Standard Oil Company of Boston.

WILLARD O. CHASE, Superintendent of Schools for Oldtown and Orono, Maine, was born November 10, 1872, in Brownville, Maine, the son of Orrin O. and Martia (Paine) Chase, both now deceased. Orrin O. Chase was born in Bowerbank, Maine, was a veteran of the Civil War, having served with the Fifteenth Regiment, Maine Volunteers, and was engaged in farming until the time of his death. The mother, Martia (Paine) Chase, was born in Atkinson, Maine.

Willard O. Chase received his preparatory education in the public and high schools of Dover, Maine. He then entered the Farmington Normal School, later attending the Aroostook Normal School. Upon his graduation from the latter institution he took special courses at the University of Maine and later he undertook extension courses at the University of Chicago. After completing his education, in 1894, he accepted a position as teacher in the schools in Dover, Maine, for a short time. He then went to Macwahoc and Kingman, Maine, where he taught for three years. He resigned from this position to accept the principalship of the Limestone High School in Limestone, Maine, an office which he held for four years. The following three years he served as Superintendent of Schools for Limestone. Mr. Chase also taught at Island Falls, Maine. For some eight years he gave up his school work and engaged in retail selling. In 1911 he became Superintendent of Schoos for Presque Isle, a position which he held until 1918, when he removed to Oldtown, Maine, to become Superintendent of Schools for Oldtown and Orono, Maine. Mr. Chase has continued to hold this office during successive years, an indication of the respect and esteem in which he is held by his fellow-citizens.

In his political preferences, Mr. Chase is a strong supporter of the Republican party and he has served for one term on the Board of Selectmen of Presque Isle and also as delegate to the Republican State Convention. Among the organizations which pertain to his profession in which he holds membership are: the National Education Association, the Department of Superintendents of the New England Association, the Maine Teachers' Association, of which he has served on the executive board, and the Penobscot County Teachers' Association, of which he is past president. He is fraternally affiliated with the Star of the East Lodge, Free and Accepted Masons; General Custer Lodge, Knights of Pythias, of Presque Isle, of which he is Past Chancellor; Modern Woodmen of America; the Royal Arcanum, of which he is Past Regent; Oldtown Lodge, Benevolent and Protective Order of Elks, and the Grange, Patrons of Husbandry.

Willard O. Chase married, in 1896, Ina Penney, who was born in Holden, Maine. Mr. and Mrs. Chase are the parents of two children: 1. W. Linwood, who served during the World War as personnel officer at Fort Meggs, Washington, District of Columbia, with the rank of second lieutenant. 2. Marion I. Mr. Chase and his family are members of the Universalist church, of which Mr. Chase is a trustee. The two children of Mr. Chase are engaged in educational work. Lieutenant W. Linwood Chase was until recently a teacher in the Horace Mann School of Columbia University, but is now devoting his entire time to study, with a view to securing his Master's degree. The daughter, Marion I., is teaching her second year in the Junior High School, at Port Jervis, New York.

HOWARD R. HOUSTON—Since 1922, Howard R. Houston has performed in a very efficient manner the duties connected with his position of Superintendent of Schools of the city of Brewer. Mr. Houston has successfully avoided the depressing influence of mere routine, and under his administration the keen and vital contact, that is so important in the relation between teacher and child, has been consistently maintained. His father, Joseph E. Houston, born at Bucksport, Maine, was a farmer and engaged in this work until his death in 1919. He was a veteran of the Civil War, having served with the Twelfth Maine Volunteers, and was a member of the Walter Parker Post, Grand Army of the Republic. Mr. Houston's mother was Susan (Jameson) Houston, born at Rockland, Maine.

Howard R. Houston was born at Bucksport, Maine, on August 7, 1888. He entered the public schools there and later graduated from Hebron Academy and Castine Normal School. In 1913 he was graduated from Bates College with the degree of Bachelor of Arts. He decided to enter the teaching profession and in 1917 received the degree of Master of Arts at the Teachers' Professional College, Washington, District of Columbia. He also took special courses at Harvard University and University of Maine. During this time he taught for one year at Bridgewater Academy, Bridgewater, Maine. In 1914 he became Superintendent of Schools at Mattawamkeag Union, Maine. He remained there until 1916. From 1916 to 1919 he was Superintendent of Schools at Bucksport Union and from 1919 to 1922, Superintendent of Schools at Wilton Union. In 1922 he came to Brewer and has been Superintendent of Schools there from that time.

Politically, Mr. Houston is associated with the Republican party. He is affiliated with Wilton Lodge, No. 156, Free and Accepted Masons; Franklin Chapter, Royal Arch Masons; St. John Commandary, No. 3, Knights Templar, and Anah Temple, Ancient Arabic Order Nobles of the Mystic Shrine. He is a member of the Maine Teachers' Association; the Franklin County Teachers' Association, of which he is a past president; the Maine Association of School Superintendents; the National Association of School Superintendents; the National Education Association; and the Penobscot County Teachers' Association, of which he is president.

In 1915, Howard R. Houston married Ethel Rollins, who was born at Calais, Maine. They are the parents of the following children: 1. Priscilla, age ten. 2. Joseph R., age eight. 3. John J., age six.

HENRY F. DRUMMOND—As principal owner and treasurer of the Bangor Box Company, of Brewer, Maine, Henry F. Drummond is at the head of the largest and oldest paper-box manufacturing concern in Penobscot County, and one of the largest in the State of Maine. He has been identified with the business since 1906, and is an expert in his field. Mr. Drummond is also a talented musician and has been a member of the board of directors of the Bangor Symphony Orchestra for several years.

Frank H. Drummond, father of Henry F. Drummond, was born in Winslow, Maine, and was engaged in the lumber industry to the time of his death in 1916. He was also agent for the Willimantic Thread Company, Willimantic, Connecticut, for several years. In 1906 he purchased the concern now known as the Bangor Box Company. The concern was established in 1888 by Charles D. Pressey, located on French Street, in Brewer, and there Mr. Pressy continued the business until 1906, when it was purchased by Frank H. Drummond. The business was then incorporated under the name of the Bangor Box Company, and Mr. Drummond's son, Henry F. Drummond, was made manager. Upon the death of Frank H. Drummond, in 1916, the son became the principal owner. Frank H. Drummond was married to Charlotte Chalmers, who was born in Bangor, Maine, and who survives her husband.

Henry F. Drummond, son of Frank H. and Charlotte (Chalmers) Drummond, was born in Bangor, Maine, October 10, 1879, and received his early education in the public schools of his birthplace. He then matriculated in the University of Maine at Orono, Maine, from which he was graduated with the class of 1900 as electrical engineer. He followed the profession of electrical engineer in the employ of the General Electric Company of Schenectady, New York, for five years, and then, in 1906, gave up his position in order to become manager of the Bangor Box Company of Bangor, Maine, which his father had just purchased. Upon the death of his father, in 1916, he became the principal owner of the concern, and has since continued as treasurer and manager. The Bangor Box Company is the largest and longest established box concern in Penobscot County, and is one of the largest in the State of Maine at the present time (1928). When the business was established, in 1888, most of the work was done by hand, and paper shoe-boxes were the only product. At the present time the Bangor Box Company employs about thirty hands and all its work is done by machinery. It manufactures a complete line of paper boxes and folding cartons and also does commercial printing.

Politically, Mr. Drummond gives his support to the Republican party. He is well known in club circles, being a member of the Rotary Club, the Tarratine Club, the Penobscot Valley Club, the Conduskeag Canoe and Country Club, and of other local organizations. He is an accomplished musician, and for many years has been a member of the Bangor Symphony Orchestra. Fraternally, he is identified with the Knights of Pythias, of which he is a Past Chancellor, and with the Kappa Sigma College Fraternity. Mr. Drummond finds his chief recreation in music, and his religious affiliation is with All Souls' Congregational Church.

Henry F. Drummond was married, in 1904, to Ida Nieman, who was born in Albany, New York, and they are the parents of two children: Charlotte C., and Ruth O.

CHARLES E. SMITH—A varied business career has been that of Charles E. Smith, who since 1925 has been president of the Newport Trust Company, of Newport, Maine. Mr. Smith has been in the marble and granite business, in the hotel business, in the creamery business, and he has also been interested in building operations in Newport. He is also one of the active and public-spirited citizens of the city, has served in numerous local public offices, and has served in both houses of the State Legislature. Charles E. Smith was born in Skowhegan, Maine, November 10, 1856, son of Cyrus S., who was born in Monmouth, Maine, and was engaged in the granite and marble business to the time of his death in 1909, having completed a period of fifty-six years in the business, and of Louina (Soule) Smith, who was born in Skowhegan, Maine, now deceased.

Mr. Smith received his education in the public schools of his birthplace and in Newport High School, and upon the completion of his high school course engaged in the marble and granite business, which he followed for ten years. During the greater portion of this time he was in business for himself, but after ten years of association with this line of business activity he made a change and for four years was engaged in the hotel business in Madison, Maine. Being a man of versatile abilities and of enterprising spirit he next engaged in the creamery business, which he successfully managed for another decade. During this time he built the electric light plant for the town of Newport, Maine, and made himself generally useful in various public offices. In 1919 he was appointed a member of the board of trustees of the Maine State Hospital, on which he has continued to serve to the present time (1928). In 1925 he was elected president of the Newport Trust Company of Newport, Maine, which responsible executive position he is filling with marked ability. Along with his various business responsibilities Mr. Smith has found time to serve in many public offices. He was chairman of the School Board of the town of Newport for seven years and chairman of the Board of Selectmen for two years, and has also served as a member of the board of trustees of the Public Library Association. In 1911 he was elected to represent his district in the Lower House of the State Legislature, where he served one term, 1911-12; and the following year he was elected to serve in the State Senate, 1913-14. Mr. Smith is a member of Meridian Splendor Lodge, Free and Accepted Masons, of which he is a Past Master; of Stephen's Chapter, Royal Arch Masons, of which he is a Past High Priest; of Skowhegan Commandery, Knights Templar, and of Anah Temple, Ancient Arabic Order Nobles of the Mystic Shrine. He is also a member of Nakomis Chapter, Order of Eastern Star; of Old Hickory Lodge, Independent Order of Odd Fellows; and of Victoria Lodge of the Order of Rebekahs. Mr. Smith is identified with Sebasticoke Grange, Patrons of Husbandry, of which he is a Past Master. He has been a member of the

Board of Trade for several years, and has served as president of the board. During the World War Mr. Smith was chairman of the Liberty Loan drives for Newport; chairman of the Newport Chapter, American Red Cross; chairman of the "four-minute" speakers of Newport, and chairman of the Food Commission. He is deeply interested in the advancement of the general welfare of the community in which he lives, and his hobby is civic work. His religious affiliation is with the Christian church, which he serves as secretary of the church corporation.

Charles E. Smith was married, in 1888, to Ada V. Mussey, who was born in Unity, Maine, and died in January, 1927.

WILLIAM F. GOODWIN—One of Biddeford's prominent business men, whose character and achievements have won for him the esteem of the citizens of the community, is William F. Goodwin, who has been identified for many years with the automobile industry. He is also active in banking circles, and has been prominent in club and fraternal orders. He is president of the Rotary Club. Born in Biddeford, Maine, February 25, 1879, he is the son of George F. Goodwin and Hannah A. Baldwin, both of Biddeford. His father, who was engaged in the real estate business, died in 1898, and his mother died in 1913.

William F. Goodwin attended the public schools of Biddeford, and later pursued courses of study at the University of Maine, and the Massachusetts Institute of Technology. For four years he was employed by the Saco-Lowell Company, of Biddeford, as draftsman. Then he went into the electrical business with L. O. Bullock, in 1907, under the name of Bullock and Goodwin. These two men took over the Ford agency in Biddeford in the following year, and incorporated the business under the name of the Biddeford Motor Mart. Mr. Bullock was president of this company, and Mr. Goodwin was treasurer.

In 1909 Joseph E. Etchelds was made president of this company, while Mr. Goodwin continued as treasurer. At the present time, his wife, Rose (Deering) Goodwin, of Saco, Maine, whom he married in 1903, is president of the Biddeford Motor Mart, while he remains as treasurer. The business originally was located at No. 401 Main Street until the great fire took place in 1911. Then the company moved to No. 398 Main Street, and later to No. 397 Main Street, where it remained until Mr. Goodwin erected his present building at Elm and Main streets in 1918. In addition to this building the company has, near the railroad, two assembly plants, one with a capacity of one hundred cars and the other with a capacity of forty cars. It is the oldest company of its kind in Biddeford, and also the largest.

Mr. Goodwin's business activity is not limited to the automobile business, however, for he is a director of the York National Bank.

As charter member and first president of the Rotary Club he is active in many ways in the life of the city. He is also a past president of the Biddeford-Saco Country Club, and a member of several other clubs. He is a charter memer of the Chamber of Commerce, and director of the Masonic Band. For recreation, he plays golf. He is a member of the Lodge, Free and Accepted Masons; the Chapter,

Royal Arch Masons; Council, Knights Templar; Kora Temple, Ancient Arabic Order Nobles of the Mystic Shrine; also a member of the Mystic Shrine; also a member of the Benevolent and Protective Order of Elks. He and his family are members of the Congregational church.

By his marriage to Rose Deering, of Saco, Maine, in 1903, William F. Goodwin is the father of one daughter, Dorothy A. Goodwin, who is a graduate of Thornton Academy; at Kendall Hall, well-known private school, in 1927.

JUDGE FREDERICK E. DOYLE—A prominent member of the Penobscot bar, and with his offices from the beginning of his activities in Millinocket, Frederick E. Doyle has secured his excellent repute and high standing in his profession through his studious interest in all branches of the law, and his well-recognized abilities as a pleader and a thoroughgoing counselor. As judge of the Millinocket Municipal Court, he is known as a prudent and painstaking official, and as one who has a most complete understanding of the usages and requirements of bench and bar in this section.

Frederick E. Doyle was born January 14, 1881, at Ellsworth, a son of Daniel Doyle, also a native of Ellsworth, and for more than forty years, to the time of his death in 1917, caretaker of Senator Hale's estate in that town, and Margaret (Whitby) Doyle, a native of Bangor, and who died in 1918. After attending the grammar and high schools at Ellsworth, Judge Doyle was matriculated at Holy Cross College, Worcester, Massachusetts, where he was graduated in 1901, with the degree of Bachelor of Arts; and preparing for his profession at the Law School of the University of Maine, he was graduated there in 1906, with the degree of Bachelor of Laws. Admitted to all courts of the State, as well as of the Federal courts, he has continued to practice his profession at Millinocket since 1906, with his offices on Penobscot Avenue. In his affiliation with the Republican party, Judge Doyle has served for ten years as chairman of the Republican Town Committee, and for a similar period as a member of the Republican County Committee. In 1911-12, he represented his District in the Maine State Legislature; and from 1908 to 1915, he served as a member of the Millinocket Board of Selectmen. In 1913, he received his present appointment as Judge of the Millinocket Municipal Court. He is a member of the Penobscot Bar Association.

During the World War, Judge Doyle was a member of the Legal Advisory Board for Penobscot County, and he was also chairman of the "four-minute" speakers for this district. Fraternally, he is a member of St. Martin of Tours Council, Knights of Columbus, of which order he is a Past Grand Knight, and member of its fourth degree, and has also served as State Deputy for Maine. He was elected the first Exalted Ruler of the Millinocket Lodge, Benevolent and Protective Order of Elks; and is a member of Sigma Beta Pi College Fraternity, and of the Millinocket Chamber of Commerce, of which he is a vice-president; and his hobbies are camping, hunting, and fishing. He is a communicant of St. Martin of Tours Roman Catholic Church.

Judge Frederick E. Doyle married, in 1910, Elizabeth M. Lahey, who was born at Patten.

CHARLES SAWYER BRYANT, M. D.—A prominent and esteemed physician of Millinocket, Maine, is Dr. Charles Sawyer Bryant, who is the son of George S. Bryant, a native of Plainfield, New Hampshire and Amy L. (Sawyer) Bryant, a native of Milford, New Hampshire. His father conducted a photographic supply business. Both parents are now deceased.

Charles Sawyer Bryant was born at Boston, Massachusetts, December 28, 1873. He was educated in the public and high schools near Boston, and then attended Harvard College, from where he was graduated in the class of 1896 with the degree of Bachelor of Arts. He entered the Harvard Medical School and attained the degree of Doctor of Medicine, in the class of 1900. He served an internship at the Boston Children's Hospital. In 1901, he came to Millinocket, Maine, where he began a private practice of general medicine and surgery, and has continued to make this his home. He is the oldest practicing physician, in point of service, in Millinocket. In 1920, he opened a small private hospital with seven beds and completely equipped operating room, where surgical and obstetrical cases are taken care of. Dr. Bryant is a member of the Penobscot County Medical Society; the Maine State Medical Society; the Donald V. Henry Post of the American Legion; and of this Post he has been the only Commander He has been Esteemed Leading Knight of Millinocket Lodge, Benevolent and Protective Order of Elks; a member of Nollesemic Lodge, Free and Accepted Masons; Mount Katahdin Chapter, Royal Arch Masons, of which he is Past High Priest; Saint John's Commandery, Knights Templar; Anah Temple, Ancient Arabic Order Nobles of the Mystic Shrine; Millinocket Lodge, Independent Order of Odd Fellows; Northern Lodge, Knights of Pythias, of which he is a Past Chancellor; Modern Woodmen of America; and a member of the Chamber of Commerce. He is a director in the Millinocket Trust Company. He is a Republican in politics and has served two years as chairman of the School Board, and for three years was Health Officer of the town of Millinocket and for eight years was chairman of the Board of Health. He was commissioned captain in the United States Army, Medical Corps, in 1917, with the Fifth Sanitary Train, Fifth Division, and served one year in France with the American Expeditionary Forces, taking part in the battles of St. Mihiel and Meuse-Argonne. He was discharged in 1919 with the rank of major and in 1924, he was commissioned major in the United States Army Medical Reserve Corps. He is a member of the Congregational church, in which he holds the position of deacon.

WILLIAM H. O'CONNELL—Not only is William H. O'Connell to be congratulated for successfully directing the interests of the J. F. Kimball Trading Company, at Millinocket, to their present well-known status in the mercantile world in this part of the State, but he is fully as well known and appreciated in Millinocket for his public-spirited interest in whatsoever pertains to the betterment of the community, the upbuilding of its utilities and the establishment of institutions for the public welfare and enjoyment.

William H. O'Connell was born at Milford, a son of Michael O'Connell, a carpenter, native of Douglasfield, New Brunswick, and now deceased, and of Katherine (Fitzgerald) O'Connell, native of Vermont, also deceased. Mr. O'Connell attended the public schools in Milford, and he was graduated at the Eastman Business College, at Poughkeepsie, New York, after which he worked in the lumber business for three years as a bookkeeper. In 1907, Mr. O'Connell first became associated with the J. F. Kimball Trading Company, at Millinocket, and he has continued since with the same firm, rising to its chief official position; as well as its treasurership. This company was established in 1899, under the name of J. F. Kimball; and when Mr. Kimball disposed of the business in 1907, the title was changed to the J F. Kimball Trading Company. The business is that of general department store, the most complete establishment of the kind north of Bangor, carrying all sorts of goods that are to be had in general department emporiums; and added to this, it is the oldest of the business houses in Millinocket. Prominent in all civic affairs, Mr. O'Connell is chairman of the committee on swimming pool for the children of Millinocket; he was a member of the budget and plans committee of the Stearns High School; he is a member of the committee that erected the municipal skating rink and also chairman of Millinocket to the Mattawamkeag Road Committee. Mr. O'Connell is an adherent to the principles of the Republican party, and a member of the board of directors of Millinocket Chamber of Commerce. Automobiling is his hobby. William H. O'Connell married, in 1909, Minnie L. Ray, born at Sangerville. Their children: Madeline R., Arthur W., and Herschel E.

THOMAS J. CORRIGAN—Heading the only company of its kind in Millinocket, Thomas J. Corrigan, as president of the Millinocket Foundry and Machine Company, is one of the leaders among business men in this part of the State. The company, which was established in 1906 by him and his brother, J. W. Corrigan, and which has continued under this leadership since that time, was originally a brass and bronze foundry, conducted solely by the two brothers. Then, in 1907, the business was converted into an iron castings company, and it continued as an iron foundry until 1914, when a machine shop was added. Making a complete line of iron castings, as well as machines and tools, it is now the only machine and foundry shop in Millinocket. It employs about forty hands, and does considerable work for the Bangor & Aroostook Railroad, the Great Northern Paper Company, and many other large corporations in Maine. The establishment is situated opposite the Bangor & Aroostook Railroad station, in Millinocket.

Thomas J. Corrigan, the president of this firm, was born in Island Brook, Province of Quebec, Canada, on March 4, 1874, the son of John Corrigan, a native of Saint Agatha, Province of Quebec, who was a farmer until his death, and of Mary (Gaughan) Corrigan, a native of Saint Sylvester, Province of Quebec, who is still living. Thomas J. Corrigan was educated in the public schools in Island Brook, his Canadian birthplace, and after he had completed his schooling he spent six years in the sawmill business. Then he quit this work, and became engaged in the foundry business, in which he remained until

1906. In that year he and his brother, J. W. Corrigan, started the Millinocket Foundry and Machine Company, of which he is now president. In his political convictions Thomas J. Corrigan is independent of the existing parties, preferring to cast his votes for the men whose work he believes will make for sound government, regardless of their partisan affiliations. He is a member of the Commercial Club, in Millinocket, and his religious affiliation is with the St. Martin of Tours Roman Catholic Church. When he is not busy with his foundry and machine establishment and with his other activities, he takes pleasure in his favorite hobbies, which are fishing and hunting.

Thomas J. Corrigan married, in 1920, Annie E. Crozier, who was born in Saint Agatha, Province of Quebec, Canada, and they are the parents of two children: Charles Joseph, and Helen Jean.

THOMAS FOSS BURRILL—Prominent in the ranks of business men in Corinna and in the State of Maine stands Thomas Foss Burrill, who is president of the Kenwood Woolen Mills and has been actively interested in that company since 1909. The mill itself is one of the oldest in this section, and the oldest in Corinna, having been established in 1870. The products that it manufactures include a complete line of woolen shirtings and suitings. It is operated by water power, steam, and electricity, and provides employment for one hundred and fifty persons. The mill is situated on Spring Street, at Kenwood Avenue. On the premises there is a general store, which is conducted for employees only. Thomas Foss Burrill, president of this company, was born in Corinna and has spent most of his life here. His father was Stephen S. Burrill, who, also a native of Corinna, was a farmer by occupation until his death, and a veteran of the Civil War, having served with Company G of the Ninth Maine Regiment. He was a member of the Grand Army of the Republic. The mother, who also is deceased, was Harriet (Foss) Burrill, a native of St. Albans, Maine.

Thomas Foss Burrill was born on July 6, 1855, and was educated in the public schools and the high school of his native town, Corinna. When he completed his education, he conducted a planing mill in Corinna for eighteen years. Then he became engaged in the lumber business until 1909, when he became associated with Elwin R. Clark and they purchased what is now known as the Kenwood Woolen Mills. This company was established in 1870, under the name of Charles A. Dorman, who ran a mill for two years in Corinna. Then Charles Greenwood took over the mill, whereupon the name of it became the Greenwood Mill, and continued as such until 1909, when Mr. Burrill and Mr. Clark purchased it. For nine years it was known as Burrill and Clark, until in 1918 the business was incorporated under its present name, Kenwood Woolen Mills, Incorporated. The officers of the company are: Thomas F. Burrill, president; Elwin R. Clark, treasurer; E. B. Clark, secretary.

Mr. Burrill, who is actively interested in political matters, is a Republican in his convictions, and for several years served as chairman of the Republican Committee. His business interests are not entirely confined to the woolen mills, since he also is president of the Corinna Trust Company and the West

Penobscot County Telephone Company. Before the Spanish-American War he enlisted in the Maine State Militia. Participating freely in the fraternal life of the town, Mr. Burrill is a member of the Free and Accepted Masons, in which order he is affiliated with the Parian Lodge, No. 160, of which he is a Past Master; Saint John's Chapter, Royal Arch Masons; De Molay Commandery Knights Templar; Kora Temple, Ancient Order Nobles of the Mystic Shrine; and all Scottish bodies, including the Consistory, Ancient Accepted Scottish Rite. He is a member also of the Independent Order of Odd Fellows, of which he is Past Grand in the Stone Ezel Lodge. In the Masonic Lodge he is affiliated with the Order of the Eastern Star, in which he is a Past Patron. He also is a member of the Rebekahs. He is very fond of traveling, a hobby in which he indulges when his business and organizational duties permit him some time for relaxation. His religious affiliation is with the Methodist Episcopal church.

In 1883, Thomas Foss Burrill married Hattie L. Dearborn, who was born in Corinna. They are the parents of two children: Ethel B., and Norman F.

ELWIN R. CLARK—Outstanding among the business men and textile manufacturers of Corinna, Maine, is Elwin R. Clark. He is the son of Alverada M. and Lilla H. (Greenwood) Clark. His mother was born in England. His father was born in Corinna, Maine, and has been for years a loom fixer, first in the Greenwood Mills and later in the Kenwood Mills.

Elwin R. Clark was born in Corinna, Maine, June 5, 1882. His education carried him through the local public schools, the Dexter High School and the School of Mechanic Arts of Boston, Massachusetts. After completing his technical education, he returned here and began work with the Greenwood Mills. In 1909, he became associated with Thomas F. Burrill and bought out the Greenwood Mills and changed the name to Burrill and Clark. In 1918 the name was again changed to the Kenwood Mills and Mr. Clark has been treasurer of this company since that time. He is a member of Parian Lodge, Free and Accepted Masons; Saint John's Chapter, Royal Arch Masons; De Molay Commandery, Knights Templar; Kora Temple, Ancient Arabic Order Nobles of the Mystic Shrine. He is a director of the Corinna Trust Company and director and part owner of the Corinna Manufacturing Company. He is a Republican in politics and attends the Methodist church. His hobby is yachting.

In 1905, Elwin R. Clark married Ethel B. Burrill, of Corinna, Maine. They have two children: Gerald B., and Mary Elizabeth.

WILLIAM J. HIBBERT—In financial circles of the State, the name of William J. Hibbert is well known as that of a man, who has risen by his own earnest efforts to his present position as one of the leading factors in the business affairs of Lewiston. Mr. Hibbert is the genial cashier of the First National Bank of Lewiston, having the distinct honor to be elected in 1925 to that position in the bank which he entered as messenger in 1893. In the civil and political life of the town, he has always been active and participates in all projects for community

advancement. Mr. Hibbert was born in Cavendish, Vermont, August 17, 1871, son of Samuel Hibbert of Flowery Field, England, who died in 1914, and Anne (Lockwood) Hibbert of Cavendish, who died in 1904. Samuel Hibbert was engaged in the restaurant business for the greater part of his life, conducting the Hibbert Restaurant in Lewiston, which was famous throughout the State and a favorite attraction for travelers.

William J. Hibbert received his early education in the public schools of Cavendish and Lewiston, after which he entered Graham Business College. After the completion of his course, he entered the employ of the Androscoggin Savings Bank in 1891, remaining there until 1893, when he became a messenger with the First National Bank of Lewiston. His courtesy and thorough dependability caused him to advance steadily, and in 1902, he was appointed assistant cashier, filling this position successfully until 1925, when he was elected cashier as aforementioned. In politics, Mr. Hibbert is a member of the Democratic party, and served three years as Auditor of the city of Lewiston, and also three years on the Board of Control of the city. He is an enthusiastic supporter of all campaigns for the improvement and progress of the city, and is a prominent member of the Chamber of Commerce. He holds active membership in the Lewiston Lodge, Benevolent and Protective Order of Elks, and in the Calumet Social Club, and is a graduate of the American Bankers' Institute. He finds recreation in golf and billiards. William J. Hibbert married Mary E. Kelly of Lewiston, who died in 1913.

JAMES P. RUNDLE—After having engaged for some years in other business, J. P. Rundle recognized the new possibilities opening for theatrical enterprises, and through his connection with it, has made himself one of the outstanding and successful men of Biddeford, Maine. Born April 18, 1872, in England, he is a son of Richard Rundle who died in 1897.

Receiving his education in the public schools, and, later, at business college, James P. Rundle was engaged in the printing business at Saco, Maine, until 1909. After this he devoted all of his time to theatrical enterprises, at first as a partner to Frederick Yates in the management of the Biddeford Opera House. After the death of Mr. Yates, in 1910, he continued the business which he conducts at the present time. The history of this theatre dates back many years. It was first operated by Kenneth Sutherland, after which the management was taken over by a Dr. Purcell. In the early days this theater housed some of the best road shows in America and many of the noted stars of another generation have appeared on its boards. In 1911, due to the dearth of good road companies and to the beginning of the popularity of motion pictures, the policy of the house was changed and since that time first-run pictures and vaudeville have been shown. The seating capacity is 1,044. He is also president of the White Way Amusement Company, of Old Orchard, Maine. Very active in his public life, Mr. Rundle is a member of various boards and committees in Biddeford. He is also a member of the Rotary Club, charter member of the Chamber of Commerce of Biddeford, the Biddeford and Saco Country Club, a member of the board of directors; and of several theatrical associations. He and his family are members of the Most Holy Trinity Roman Catholic Church.

In 1915, James P. Rundle married Marion L. Sands, of Saco, Maine.

THOMAS C. WHITE—As sole owner of the general insurance and investment business which operates under the name of White and Whittum, in Lewiston, Thomas C. White is at the head of the oldest investment and insurance concern in Androscoggin County. He is a graduate of Bowdoin College and has been engaged in the insurance business since 1909.

Thomas C. White was born in Lewiston, Maine, September 8, 1881, son of Wallace H. White, who was born in Livermore, Maine, a successful lawyer to the time of his death in 1920, and of Helen (Frye) White, who was born in Rockland, Maine, died in 1926. He received his early education in the public schools of Lewiston and then prepared for college in Nichols Latin School. He was graduated from Bowdoin College, at Brunswick, Maine, with the class of 1903, receiving the degree of Bachelor of Arts, and after graduation entered the employ of the Maine Central Railroad Company, in the engineering department, where he remained for three years. He then became associated with the Haskell Implement & Seed Company, which connection he maintained for another three years. In 1909 he began his long connection with the insurance business by purchasing a half interest in the H. C. Little & Son Insurance Agency. In 1910 the name of the company was changed to Benson and White, and the partnership was continued until 1920, when Mr. White purchased Mr. Benson's interest and admitted William H. Whittum as a partner under the name of White and Whittum. At this time the investment business of C. C. Benson & Company was consolidated with the insurance business under the name of White and Whittum, and the partnership with Mr. Whittum was continued until 1926, when Mr. White purchased Mr. Whittum's interest, thus becoming sole owner of the concern. He does a general insurance and investment business, and his concern ranks as the oldest of its kind in the county. The business is located at No. 163 Main Street, where a very large amount of business is transacted each year.

Mr. White is a member of Alpha Delta Phi College Fraternity, and is identified with numerous local organizations, including the Lewiston Chamber of Commerce, and the Martindale Country Club. He is a member of the Maine Association of Insurance Agents, and of the National Association of Insurance Agents. Politically, he supports the Republican party. He takes an active interest in local civic affairs and is one of the many public-spirited citizens of the city who are always ready to contribute generously of their time and ability for the advancement of the general welfare. He served for two years as a member of the Board of Councilmen of the city of Lewiston, and is as ready to serve as a private citizen. Mr. White served as a second lieutenant of the Ninth Company, Maine National Guard, in 1910. He finds his chief recreational activity in golf, and while he is a member of the Prudential

Committee of the Congregational church, he also is interested in the general work of the church.

Thomas C. White was married, June 10, 1908, to Martha H. Pratt, a native of Lewiston, Maine, and they are the parents of two sons: Thomas C., Jr., and William F.

WALTER L. EMERSON—In the civic and business life of Lewiston, Walter L. Emerson is known as an advocate of progress and an earnest supporter of all projects for the further development and advancement of his community. Mr. Emerson is a leading figure in the real estate and insurance field, having been associated with his father until the latter's death in 1927, since which time he has continued the business alone.

Mr. Emerson was born in Litchfield, March 15, 1888, son of George A. Emerson of Litchfield, who died in 1927, and Augusta J. (Frost) Emerson of Lisbon, who died in 1922. George A. Emerson was born in Litchfield, May 2, 1852, and his early life was spent in farming. He later served as assistant-postmaster in Lewiston for several years, filling this position with great success. He then entered the newspaper business and was engaged on the Lewiston "Journal" for some time. In 1908, he organized a real estate and insurance business, which he continued to operate prosperously until his death. Always active in local civic affairs, he was elected to the Maine State Legislature and served during 1917 and 1918.

Walter L. Emerson received his education in the public schools of Lewiston, and after high school, entered the University of Maine, from which he received his degree in 1909, as Bachelor of Science in Civil Engineering. He then became associated with the civil engineering firm of Sawyer and Moulton, of Portland, spending a year and a half with this concern where he gained much valuable experience. In 1910, Mr. Emerson became a partner with his father in the real estate and insurance business and the firm name was changed to that of George A. Emerson and Company. This is now one of the leading enterprises of its kind in this city, specializing particularly in insurance, representing a large number of insurance companies, and Mr. Emerson is special agent for Maine, of the Middlesex Mutual Fire Insurance Company. He is also a director of the Central Maine Building and Loan Association. In all affairs for civic progress, he takes an active part, being a member of the Kiwanis Club, of which he is past president, the Chamber of Commerce and the Insurance Federation of the State of Maine. He holds membership in the Martindale Country Club, and in fraternal circles, is a popular member of Rabboni Lodge, Free and Accepted Masons, in which he is Past Master, and he is Past High Priest in the King Hiram Chapter, Royal Arch Masons; member of Lewiston Commandery, Knights Templar; and Past Potentate of Kora Temple, Ancient Arabic Order Nobles of the Mystic Shrine; also a member of Beta Theta Pi Fraternity. In politics, he follows the principles of an Independent, and in religious affiliations, is a member of the Episcopal church. For recreation, he finds great enjoyment in golf and outdoor life.

Walter L. Emerson married, in 1910, Jessie M. Crowley of Lewiston, and they have one son, Walter L., Jr.

CARROL J. TRICKEY—ELWIN ROWE TRICKEY—One of the chief industries of Corinna, Maine, is the Corinna Manufacturing Company, which specializes in cotton warp suitings, and has its place of business on Main Street, where about seventy operatives are employed. Its history is that of the Trickey famly, its founders and proprietors.

Born in Exeter, Maine, May 6, 1859, Carrol J. Trickey was educated in the public and high schools of Corinna, and on being graduated from the high school, engaged in farming, but in 1904 became associated with the Borden Condensed Milk Company, remaining with that concern until 1918. In 1912, however, he started the Corinna Manufacturing Company, in partnership with J. H. Winchester and B. H. Smith, and the business was continued by them until 1920, when Mr. Trickey bought out his partners, and incorporated the business, assuming the presidency, and placing his son, Elwin Rowe Trickey, in the responsible post of treasurer. The family has been long settled in Maine, and Benjamin Trickey, who married Mary C. Jewell, of Exeter, Maine, and was the father of Carrol J. Trickey, was born in Wolfeboro, New Hampshire, and as a young man removed to Maine, settling in Exeter and was a farmer there until his death.

Carrol J. Trickey is a member of Parian Lodge, Free and Accepted Masons, and of Ezel Lodge, Independent Order of Odd Fellows. He is a Republican, and has served for years on the Republican Town Committee, and was sent to the Maine Legislature as a representative in 1908; has served for many years as a member of the Board of Selectmen of Corinna, of which he has been chairman. His relaxations are hunting and fishing. Mr. Trickey is a member of the Methodist Episcopal church.

In 1884 he married (first) Nellie I. Rowe, of St. Albans, Maine, their children being: Elwin Rowe, of further mention, and Eveline M. Mrs. Trickey died in 1922. Mr. Trickey married (second) Lou Wood, of Corinna, by whom he has one child, Robert R.

Born in Corinna, Maine, August 11, 1891, son of Carrol J. and Nellie I. (Rowe) Trickey, Elwin Rowe Trickey was educated in the public schools of Corinna, and at Maine Central Institute. He worked at farming until 1922, when he became associated with his father in the Corinna Manufacturing Company, of which he has been treasurer since 1924. He is a member of Parian Lodge, Free and Accepted Masons; of St. John's Chapter, Royal Arch Masons; De Molay Commandery, Knights Templar; Anah Temple, Ancient Arabic Order Nobles of the Mystic Shrine; and of all Scottish Rite bodies, including Maine Consistory. He also belongs to Stone Ezel Lodge, Independent Order of Odd Fellows. Like his father, he is a Republican, and enjoys hunting and fishing. He attends the Methodist Episcopal church.

In 1918, Elwin Rowe Trickey married Sarah Buzzell, of Bangor, Maine.

FRED CLIFFORD—A successful business man of Millinocket, Maine, but withal a keen sportsman, knowing the woods and streams and lakes of his native State as only a native can, Fred Clifford some seven years ago started what is known as Kidney Pond Camp, on the lake of that name in Piscataquis

County, providing accommodations for fifty people, with fifteen guides in attendance. The place is only seven miles from Mt. Katahdin, a region famous to the sportsmen who hunt or fish in Maine, and it has become so popular that its proprietor is more widely known outside his home town than any business man in it. It is more than probable that Mr. Clifford would maintain the camp, whether it proved a source of profit or not, but there is every reason to assume that it affords a handsome revenue.

Son of Benjamin Augustus Clifford, and Jane (Lancaster) Clifford, his acquaintance with the woods began at early age, for his father was a lumberman, and, incidentally, the first white boy to be born in Lee, Maine, back in 1822. The elder Clifford had been a sharpshooter with the Maine Volunteers during the Civil War, was active in the Grand Army of the Republic, and became a successful farmer toward the close of a long and useful life.

Educated in the public schools of Lincoln, Maine, and in Mattenawcook Academy, Fred Clifford settled in Millinocket in early manhood. For two years he was the proprietor of a boarding house, and for the next ten years he ran a dairy farm, but in 1911 became associated with Forrest G. Fogg (q. v.), as Fogg & Clifford. The partners purchased the hardware business which had been founded in 1889 by F. M. Peasley, to which had later been added a furniture business. The store is on Penobscot Avenue and Central Street, and is today the largest business of its kind in Millinocket.

Mr. Clifford is a member of Nollesemic Lodge, Free and Accepted Masons, and of Mt. Katahdin Chapter, Royal Arch Masons. He is also a member of the Chamber of Commerce. He is active in Republican politics, and has served for many years on the Republican Town Committee, of which he has been chairman. He attends the Baptist church. If he can be said to have a hobby other than those represented at his camps, it is baseball.

In 1900, Fred Clifford married Ada Day, a native of Hartland, New Brunswick, Canada.

FORREST G. FOGG—From 1907, having completed a thorough business training, supplemented by a year's actual experience in retail salesmanship, Forrest G. Fogg has been engaged in the hardware and furniture business in Millinocket, Maine, and is senior member of the firm of Fogg & Clifford, the largest store devoted to these wares in the region.

Son of William Henry and Lucy (Page) Fogg, he was born in Burlington, Maine, August 13, 1885. His father was in the lumber business until his recent retirement, and both parents were natives of Burlington. Mrs. Fogg died in 1921. Educated in the public schools of Burlington, and at Shaw's Business College, in Bangor, Maine, Forrest G. Fogg then spent a year in the grocery business, and in 1907 became associated with F. M. Peasley, who had established a hardware and furniture store some years before. In 1907 he went into partnership with Fred Clifford (q. v.), and the firm of Fogg & Clifford purchased Mr. Peasley's business, and has since enlarged and improved it.

Mr. Fogg is a member of Nollesemie Lodge, Free and Accepted Masons, and is a trustee of the Millinocket Lodge, Benevolent and Protective Order of Elks. He is also a member of the Chamber of Commerce. He attends the Congregational church, and is identified with the Republican party. His recreations are fishing, hunting, motor-boating and automobiling.

In 1906, Forrest G. Fogg married Katherine Carrol, who was born in Limestone, Maine. Their children are: Kenneth R., and Lucile Fogg.

GILBERT BURTON MORAN—One of the leading business men of Millinocket, Maine, Mr. Moran is the proprietor of one of the oldest and largest merchandising establishments in that community. Born June 14, 1872, at Forest City, New Brunswick, Canada, Mr. Moran is a son of Peter and Sarah Moran. Peter Moran, who was born at Prince Edward Island, Canada, was engaged in the lumber business until the time of his death. Sarah Moran is a native of New Brunswick, Canada.

Gilbert Burton Moran received his education in the public schools of Kingman, Maine. Upon the completion of these courses of study, he entered the clothing business. In 1892, he removed to Island Falls, Maine, where he was engaged in the clothing business for two years. In 1900, he removed to Millinocket where he established a clothing business for himself. The store is located on Penobscot Avenue, where Mr. Moran carries a complete supply of men's equipment. He has been eminently successful in this enterprise and the business now ranks as one of the oldest and largest merchandising establishments in Millinocket. Mr. Moran is also vice-president of the Millinocket Trust Company.

Although the management of a large business of this type demands a great deal of time and attention, Mr. Moran has taken an active interest in the business and social life of his community. In his political preferences he is a supporter of the Republican party. He is affiliated with Nollesemic Lodge, Free and Accepted Masons; Mount Katahdin Chapter, Royal Arch Masons; the Council, Royal and Select Masters; the Consistory, Ancient Accepted Scottish Rite; St. John's Commandery, Knights Templar; and Anah Temple, Ancient Arabic Order Nobles of the Mystic Shrine; the Knights of Pythias; and Millinocket Lodge, Benevolent and Protective Order of Elks. He is also a member of the Millinocket Chamber of Commerce, of which he is past president, the Masonic Club; the Tarratine Club, and the Penobscot Valley Country Club.

Gilbert Burton Moran married, in 1898, Elsie (Sherban) Sawin, who was born in Caribou, Maine. Mr. and Mrs. Moran are the parents of one daughter and three sons: Phyllis, Gilbert Burton, Jr., Lester Dwinal, and Charles Clinton. Mr. Moran and his family attend the Congregational church.

EUGENE J. RUSH—For many years Eugene J. Rush has been prominent in the business life of Millinocket, Maine. Moving there in 1901, he became associated with the firm of Rush Brothers, dealers in ladies', girls', and children's ready-to-wear clothing, in which business he has since engaged. In 1923 he became sole owner of the firm, continuing it under the name of Eugene J. Rush. Mr. Rush is a man of value to his community where he has many friends. His father, John Rush, born in New Jersey, was a carpenter and engaged in this work until his death. His mother, Katherine (Crabb) Rush, born at Debec Junction, Province of New Brunswick, Canada, is also deceased.

Eugene J. Rush was born August 21, 1881, at Benedicta, Maine. He entered the public schools there, and when he completed his education became connected with the firm of Rush Brothers at Millinocket, Maine. This was in 1901. For over twenty years he remained with this firm, which handled ready-to-wear clothing for ladies and girls, and finally in 1924 he bought out the business, which he has since continued for himself. The store is located at No. 102 Penobscot Avenue.

By political inclination Mr. Rush is a member of the Democratic party. He is affiliated, fraternally, with the Modern Woodmen of America, and is also a member of the local Chamber of Commerce. He and his family attend the Roman Catholic Church of St. Martin of Tours. For diversions Mr. Rush is fond of baseball and football.

In 1909, Eugene J. Rush married Maud B. Bishop, who was born at Winn, Maine. Mr. and Mrs. Rush are the parents of children: Eugene, Charles, Mary, Pearl, and Jane.

CHARLES J. RUSH—Since 1910 Charles J. Rush has been engaged in the building and contracting business at Millinocket, Maine. He has been very successful in this field, doing a considerable proportion of all the building work in the vicinity, and in addition he is the owner of a large hardware store which is the oldest in Millinocket today. Mr. Rush is prominent in the civic and fraternal life of his community. His father, John Rush, born in New Jersey, was a carpenter and engaged in this work until his death. His mother, Katherine (Crabb) Rush, born at Debec Junction, Province of New Brunswick, Canada, is also deceased.

Charles J. Rush was born October 2, 1872, at Benedicta, Maine. He attended the local public schools and when he completed his education he began work as a river driver in the Maine woods. After four years, in 1891, he went to Rumford, Maine, where he served for a year and a half on the police force, and for two years acted as foreman in the Sulphite Mills there. For a year he engaged in a sawmill, and for about four years he engaged in carpentry work. Finally, in 1900, he came to Millinocket and established the building and contracting business which he has continued since that time. In 1907 he opened his hardware store, and in the same year established the Millinocket Opera House, the only theater in the town, of which he is the sole proprietor.

Politically, he is a member of the Democratic party. He is affiliated, fraternally, with the Benevolent and Protective Order of Elks, and the Knights of Columbus. He is a director of the Millinocket Trust Company, and a member of the local Chamber of Commerce, the Winchester Association, and the Master Plumbers' Association of the State of Maine. Mr. Rush and his family attend the Roman Catholic Church of St. Martin of Tours.

In 1900, Charles J. Rush married Delia R. Bishop, who was born at Winn, Maine. They are the parents of one child, Helen M.

BYRON G. PRIDE—For over forty years Byron G. Pride has been in the coal, wood and ice business in Westbrook, Cumberland County, under his own name, during which time he has developed from a small concern with but one horse and a single wagon, to an enterprise employing over fifteen persons, with there motorized trucks, aiding eight horses and wagons to deliver his staples within a radius of eighteen miles. In point of service, Mr. Pride is the oldest man in his business in the community and he has good reason to be proud of the record he has made in his community in little more than twoscore years. He was born in Westbrook, March 23, 1847, the son of David P. and Abbie (Hall) Pride, the former a prominent farmer. Both Mr. Pride's father and mother were born in Westbrook, descendants of old pioneer stock. The elder Pride died in 1884, his wife having passed away the preceding year.

Following his early education in the public schools of Westbrook, Byron G. Pride entered Westbrook Seminary. Upon finishing his scholastic career, Mr. Pride took up several lines of endeavor and it was not until 1887 that he went into business for himself as a purveyor of coal, wood and ice. He started in a modest way, with one horse and wagon, but he soon increased this by the addition of men and vehicles, as soon as his fellow-townsmen realized that he was dependable and upright in all his business dealings. Today, Mr. Pride is rated as one of Westbrook's important citizens and of its foremost and progressive business men. For many years he has been a member of the official board of the local Methodist church. He is affiliated with the Independent Order of Odd Fellows and with the Encampment, and is also a member of the Knights of Pythias.

On October 27, 1874, Byron G. Pride was married to Mary J. Smith, the daughter of William and Sarah (Libby) Smith, of Gorham, Cumberland County. Mr. and Mrs. Pride have had two children: 1. Maud Estella, died April 9, 1926. 2. Merritt G., married Inez E. Palmer; they have two children: Mary Eunice, born January 17, 1917; Byron G., born November 1, 1917.

FRANK C. BOWLER—Since 1911 Frank C. Bowler has been chief engineer of the Great Northern Paper Company, at Millinocket, Maine. A man of considerable energy and ability, he is widely experienced in engineering and technical work, and has discharged the duties connected with his present position very efficiently. Mr. Bowler is also active in the social and fraternal life of Millinocket. He was born on May 27, 1874, at Westbrook, Maine, son of Stephen L. and Augusta (Colburn) Bowler. His father was a Congregationalist clergyman, and during the American Civil War, he was connected with the United States Christian Commission. at Washington, District of Columbia. He died in 1914, and his wife, who was born at Orono, Maine, also died in that year.

Frank C. Bowler attended the public schools of Bethel, and the high school of Berlin, New Hampshire. Later he entered the University of Maine, from which he was graduated in 1894 with the degree of Bachelor of Mechanical Engineering. When he completed his education, he began work with the New England Sulphite Digester Company, with whom he remained for one year. For two years he was employed at Bangor in the office of the City Engineer, and for a short time he did survey work on the Washington County Railroad. From 1897 until 1911, he worked as a civil engineer and draftsman for Hardy S. Ferguson. At the end of that time he

became associated with the Great Northern Paper Company as chief engineer, and in this position he has since remained.

Politically, Mr. Bowler is a member of the Republican party. He is affiliated, fraternally, with the Free and Accepted Masons, being a member of Nolesemic Lodge, of which he is also Past Master. In the Masonic organization he is a member of the Mount Horeb Chapter, St. John's Commandery, and Anah Temple of the Shrine, and all bodies of the Scottish Rite, including the Consistory. He is also a member of the Alpha Tau Omega Fraternity, and Millinocket Lodge, Benevolent and Protective Order of Elks. He is a member of the Tarratine Club, the Penobscot Valley Country Club, the Millinocket Chamber of Commerce, the American Society of Civil Engineers, and the Maine Motorists' Association. Much of his spare time he devotes to automobiling. He and his family attend the local Congregational church.

In 1921, Frank C. Bowler married Dawn Fernald, who was born in Berlin, New Hampshire. They are the parents of one child, Dorothy.

ROBERT MARSHALL HUME—With the exception of a few years, practically all of Robert Marshall Hume's professional career has been devoted to the interests of the Great Northern Paper Company, at Millinocket, where, as chemist and in the superintendency departments of that noted plant, he has proven himself a valued ally in the present-day development of the plans of the company. All of Millinocket's civic and social welfare, and the advance of its institutions and its citizenship, have Mr. Hume's consistent support, and he is highly regarded by his associates and his many friends.

Robert Marshall Hume was born May 17, 1893, at New Haven, Connecticut, a son of John Hume, a native of Ayton, Scotland, and Annie (Marshall) Hume, who was born to Edinboro, Scotland, and who is now deceased. John Hume, a cabinetmaker, is a member of the firm of Gerrish and Hume, at New Haven. In that city, Robert Marshall Hume attended the public schools, and was graduated at the Sheffield Scientific School, of Yale University, with the degree of Bachelor of Philosophy in 1913. After graduation, he worked for six months for the Winchester Repeating Arms Company, in New Haven. In February, 1914, he first became associated with the Great Northern Paper Company, at Millinocket, in the capacity of chemist. In 1916, Mr. Hume was made foreman of the sulphite mill of this establishment, and in 1917, he was appointed assistant superintendent of the Millinocket Mill, and in 1919, night superintendent. Today, he is superintendent at the plant.

Mr. Hume, though much interested in civic matters, and a Republican in his political views, has not sought public office further than his capable service for three years as a member of the Millinocket School Board. He enlisted in the United States Army, in May, 1918, Ordnance Department, was stationed at Muscle Shoals, in Alabama, and received his discharge in January, 1919, then returning to Millinocket. Fraternally, he is affiliated with Nolesemic Lodge, Free and Accepted Masons, of which he is a Past Master; Somerset Chapter, Royal Arch Masons; De Molay Commandery, Knights Templar; Maine Consistory, Ancient Accepted Scottish Rite,

Anah Temple, Ancient Arabic Order Nobles of the Mystic Shrine; and the Knights of Pythias. He is a member of the Masonic Club; American Legion; Millinocket Chamber of Commerce; and his hobby is fishing. He attends the Congregational church.

Robert Marshall Hume married, in 1920, Blanche Towne, who was born in East Dover; and they have two sons, Robert M., Jr., and William T.

HERBERT E. PREBLE—A factor of progress and enterprise in the mercantile activities of Millinocket, Herbert E. Preble is one of the foremost coal and wood dealers in this section, rendering his service to the community and the general public with satisfactory results to his increasing business constituency. He has an interest in all matters that pertain to the advancement of Millinocket, and he possesses the regard of all with whom his business deals.

Herbert E. Preble was born September 19, 1878, in Oldtown, a son of Charles E. Preble, now deceased, who was a farmer, born in Bradford, and of Edna (Smart) Preble, a native of Oldtown, who survives her husband. After attending and graduating at the common and high schools at Oldtown, Mr. Preble was engaged as a surveyor of lumber for seventeen years. In 1922, he established his present coal and wood business at Millinocket, with his office in Doctor's Block, and his yards on Grant Street, where he is meeting with merited success. Politically, Mr. Preble is a Republican, and with his vote and influence he supports the principles and candidates of that party. Fraternally, he is affiliated with Nollesemic Lodge, Free and Accepted Masons; Mount Katahdin Chapter, Royal Arch Masons; St. Aldemar Commandery, Knights Templar; Anah Temple, Ancient Arabic Order Nobles of the Mystic Shrine; with Tarratine Lodge, Independent Order of Odd Fellows; and the Oldtown Lodge, Benevolent and Protective Order of Elks. He is also a member of the Masonic Lodge; and the Millinocket Chamber of Commerce; and his hobbies are hunting and fishing. He attends the Methodist Episcopal church.

Herbert E. Preble married, in 1904, Elizabeth Woods, of Ellsworth; and they have two children: Wesley E., and Carl W.

CARL VICTOR STOCKWELL—As sole proprietor of the Whalen Drug Company, in Millinocket, Carl Victor Stockwell has proved himself, in the few years in which he has owned this store, a careful druggist and a successful business man. Before he acquired this company in 1923, he was engaged in banking. Having spent the greater part of his life in Maine, Mr. Stockwell is thoroughly conversant with conditions in Millinocket and with the people of the town. This knowledge of his community, together with his own native business talents, places him in an excellent position to become one of the leaders in the town.

Mr. Stockwell was born on August 28, 1893, in Bangor, the son of Edward D. Stockwell, a native of Bangor, who is engaged as a commercial traveler, and of Fannie (Wiley) Stockwell, native of North Bangor. Carl Victor Stockwell attended the public schools and the high school in Bangor, and then became associated with the Millinocket Trust Company when he started his business career. His first posi-

tion with this company, which he obtained in 1913, was that of bookkeeper. In 1918 he was made assistant treasurer, in which capacity he remained until 1923. In that year he went into the drug business for himself, buying what is known as the Whalen Drug Company, which he continued to operate under that name. He is sole proprietor of this store, and in addition to it Mr. Stockwell has the agencies for the Victor and Edison phonographs. The company is one of the most up-to-date and progressive in Millinocket. Interested in all political matters of the town, he is affiliated with the Republican party. He is a member of the Chamber of Commerce, as well as of certain fraternal organizations, including the Free and Accepted Masons, in which he is identified with the Nollesemic Lodge, the Mount Katahin Chapter, and the St. Aldemar Commandery; and the Benevolent and Protective Order of Elks, in which he belongs to the Millinocket Lodge. His religious affiliation is with the Congregational church. Fishing and hunting are his favorite hobbies.

In 1917, Carl V. Stockwell married Freda Curren, who was born in Patten, Maine, and they are the parents of one child, Carl V., Jr.

FRANK H. SPEED—In the real estate and insurance business Frank H. Speed is a prominent figure in Millinocket, where he holds the position of president and manager of the Millinocket Insurance Agency. He has been engaged in this type of work since 1910, before which he was employed by the Bangor & Aroostook Railroad. He was born in Maine and has spent most of his life in this State, with the result that he is thoroughly familiar with industrial conditions here and with the people themselves. He was regarded so highly in business circles in the town that he was made the first president of the Millinocket Chamber of Commerce. A public-spirited citizen, keenly interested in the affairs of his town, he is especially active in fraternal and organizational work in his community.

Mr. Speed was born in La Grange, Maine, on July 26, 1887, the son of Perley E. Speed, a native of Bradford, Maine, who was a merchant until his death in 1926, and of Alice M. (Carey) Speed, also a native of La Grange, who is living. Frank H. Speed attended the public schools of La Grange, and then became a student of Doe's Business College, in Bangor. When he completed his education, he went to work as a river driver for four years, between the ages of thirteen and seventeen years. Then he was employed by the Bangor & Aroostook Railroad, for which company he spent three years firing a locomotive. In 1910 he came to Millinocket, where he went into the real estate and insurance business for himself, a line of work which he has continued since that time, as president and manager of the Millinocket Insurance Company. He was first president of the local Chamber of Commerce, and is a director and a trustee of the Millinocket Masonic Association. He belongs to several fraternal orders, including the Free and Accepted Masons, in which he is affiliated with the Nollesemic Lodge, the Mount Katahdin Chapter, all bodies of the Scottish Rite, including the Maine Consistory, Anah Temple of the Shrine; and the Benevolent and Protective Order of Elks, in which he holds a membership in Millinocket Lodge; and the Independent Order of Odd Fellows, in which he is affiliated with the Millinocket Lodge.

He also is a member of the Order of Eastern Star in the Masonic Order. In his political opinions he is a Republican, and served as secretary of the Republican Town Committee. His favorite hobbies are fishing and gardening. He is a member of the Baptist church of Millinocket, of which he is treasurer and chairman of the board of trustees.

In 1914, Frank H. Speed married Lena Comstock, a native of Argyle, Maine, and they are the parents of Robert Edward Comstock Speed.

GEORGE W. MacKAY, D. D. S.—Outstanding among the dental surgeons of this vicinity is Dr. George W. MacKay of Millinocket, Maine. He is the son of the late Rev. Kenneth and Margaret (Grant) MacKay of Pictou, Nova Scotia. His father was a minister in the Presbyterian church.

George W. MacKay was born in Richmond, New Brunswick, March 9, 1876. He was educated in the public schools of Houlton, Maine, and in the Ricker Classical Institute. After finishing school, he entered the department of dentistry in the Baltimore Medical College and graduated from there in the class of 1900 with a degree of Doctor of Dental Surgery. In 1907, he took a post-graduate course at the Harvard Dental College. After passing the State Board examination, he opened an office in Millinocket, Maine, where he has continued in the practice of general dentistry. He is a member of the Maine State Dental Society and was at one time president of this organization. He is a member of the New England Dental Society. In 1924 he was elected secretary of the Maine State Examining Board, and is the present incumbent of this office. He is a member of the American Dental Association and the Penobscot Valley Dental Society. His college fraternity is the Psi Omega. He is a member of the Order of Free and Accepted Masons; Mount Katahdin Chapter, Royal Arch Masons; St. Aldemar Commandery, Knights Templar; Anah Temple, Ancient Arabic Order Nobles of the Mystic Shrine; and the Scottish Rite bodies, including the Maine Consistory; Northern Lodge, Knights of Pythias, being a past Chancellor, and a member of the Modern Woodmen of America. He belongs to the Masonic Club and to the Chamber of Commerce. In addition to busy professional life and the business of his duties as officer in different societies, he is agent for one of the popular automobile companies and carries on this business with the same degree of enterprise as he puts into all that he undertakes. During 1895 to 1897 he was a member of the Maine State Militia. During the World War, he served on the Medical Advisory Board of Penobscot County and was a member of the Preparedness League of American Dentists.

In 1906, George W. MacKay married Annie R. Jones, of Houlton, Maine. They have one child: Robert Grant.

NAZAIRE J. GENDRON—A small furniture business started in Sanford, Maine, in 1906, speedily outgrew its quarters on High Street, and in 1910 was removed to No. 190 Main Street. It continued to grow, and was incorporated in 1920, with Nazaire J. Gendron, its founder, as president, and L. DeLisle as secretary. That year a new venture was added to the activities of the furniture company, which began dealing in retail lumber and cabinet making, serving its patrons within a ten-mile radius by means of motor trucks.

Back of both enterprises is the energy, intelligence and obliging disposition of Mr. Gendron, who had enjoyed a somewhat varied career in business before starting on his own account. Born in the Province of Quebec, Canada, June 13, 1878, son of Vital and Celina (Vadnais) Gendron, he was educated in the Canadian public schools. His father is still living (1927), aged eighty-three, but his mother died in 1914. Coming to the United States as a youngster, he found his first employment with the Metropolitan Life Insurance Company, at Biddeford, Maine, and later was associated with the Garland Manufacturing Company, at Saco, Maine. For two years prior to his venture in Sanford, he was connected with the Commercial Tea Company, and the knowledge of men and business methods obtained in these distinctive lines was the foundation on which he has built success.

In 1914, Mr. Gendron was selectman of Sanford, but is not keenly interested in politics. The family attends St. Ignatius Roman Catholic Church, and is identified with its many charities. He is a member of the Knights of Columbus, of the Catholic Order of Foresters, and of the Benevolent and Protective Order of Elks.

Nazaire J. Gendron married Suzanne Langlois, of the Province of Quebec, daughter of Joseph and Celina (Martineau) Langlois, in 1905. Their children are: Armand, Paul, Mary, Henry, Regina, Albert, Romeo, and Julianna Gendron.

ERNEST T. YOUNG, M. D.—One of the successful practicing physicians in Millinocket is Ernest T. Young, who has had his offices in this town since 1925, when he removed from East Millinocket. In the few years in which he has been practicing, he has acquired a large following of residents of the town who come to him regularly for medical advice and treatment. His skill and care and his willingness to devote his time and talents freely to the work of curing the ill have won for him the confidence and the regard of the community.

He was born on April 11, 1892, in Wiscasset, Maine, the son of John F. Young, also a native of Wiscasset, who was a farmer until his death in 1913, and of Isabella (Hamm) Young, who was born in Brunswick, Maine, and who died in 1923. As a boy, Ernest T. Young attended the public schools in Wiscasset; then went to the Wiscasset Academy; the Northeastern Preparatory School; the Tufts Pre-Medical School; and the Tufts Medical School, from which he was graduated in the class of 1921, with the degree of Doctor of Medicine. Then he spent a year as an interne at the Eastern Maine General Hospital, where he obtained further experience for the practice of his profession. In 1922 he took up the practice of medicine and surgery in East Millinocket, where he remained until 1925, in which year he removed to Millinocket, where he has practiced since that time. His offices are situated in the Stearns and Gonya block on Penobscot Avenue. Dr. Young is active in the ranks of his professional colleagues, holding memberships in several organizations, including the American Medical Association, the Maine State Medical Society, and the Penobscot County Medical Association. Keenly interested in political matters, he is a Republican. He is a member of the

Millinocket Chamber of Commerce and of the Lucerne in Maine Country Club. He also is a member of the Free and Accepted Masons, in which order he is affiliated with the Nollesemic Club. During the World War, Dr. Young served his country as a member of the Naval Reserve Corps.

In 1924, Ernest T. Young married Doris E. Nickerson, who was born in Hampden Highlands, Maine. They are the parents of one child, John Thomas.

CLARENCE W. HARRIGAN, D. D. S.—As a dentist in Millinocket, Clarence W. Harrigan, who began his practice here in 1918, has built a large clientele of men, women and children, who come regularly to him for dental advice and treatment. His care and skill in the exercise of his profession have won for him the esteem and the confidence of those members of the community who are his patients. Keenly interested in the public affairs of his town and vicinity, he is regarded by his fellow-townsmen as a leading citizen. He was born on August 30, 1894, in Houlton, the son of Wilfred Harrigan, a native of Houlton, who was a farmer until his death in 1924, and of Generia A. (Hogan)) Harrigan, also a native of Houlton, who died in 1927. Clarence W. Harrigan attended the public school in Houlton, his birthplace; and subsequently went to the St. Francis Xavier Preparatory School, in Antigonish, Nova Scotia, Canada, and to the Tufts Dental College, from which he was graduated in the class of 1917 with the degree of Doctor of Dental Surgery. In 1918 he took up his practice of dentistry in Millinocket, which has occupied his attention since that time. His offices are situated on Penobscot Avenue. Active in the ranks of his professional colleagues, he holds memberships in the American Dental Association and the Maine State Dental Association. His fraternities are the Psi Omega and the Knights of Columbus, in the St. Martin of Tours Council. He is a member of the local Chamber of Commerce. During the World War he served his country, having been commissioned on August 27, 1917, as a first lieutenant in the United States Army Dental Corps. He continued to serve until May, 1919, when he was discharged with the rank of first lieutenant. In his political opinions he is a Republican. When he is not busy with his practice and with his other activities, he takes time to indulge in his favorite hobbies, hunting and fishing. His religious affiliation is with the St. Martin of Tours Roman Catholic Church.

In 1921, Clarence W. Harrigan married Hazel M. St. John, a native of Millinocket, Maine. They are the parents of one child, Patricia Ann.

HARRY J. GONYA—Since 1920, Harry J. Gonya has been the proprietor of the drugstore located at the corner of Penobscot Avenue and Central Street, Millinocket, Maine. He is a man of wide experience in his profession, and his energy, ability, and thorough training have brought him considerable success. He owns one of the finest drugstores in the State of Maine today. Mr. Gonya takes a prominent part in the civic and fraternal life of his community. His father, Jerome A. Gonya, born at Island Pond, Vermont, is engaged in the automobile and clothing business. His mother, who before her

marriage was Louey White, was also born at Island Pond.

Harry J. Gonya was born on February 3, 1892, at Tupper Lake, New York. He attended the public and high schools of Millinocket, Maine, and later entered the Philadelphia College of Pharmacy, where he was graduated in 1914 with the degree of Doctor of Pharmacy. When he completed his education he began work for his uncle, who owned a drugstore at Bar Harbor, Maine, and he remained in this position until 1920. In that year he returned to Millinocket and opened his own drugstore at the corner of Penobscot Avenue and Central Street. He has continued this business very successfully since that time, employing at present four clerks, two of whom are registered men.

Politically, Mr. Gonya is a member of the Democratic party. He is affiliated, fraternally, with Millinocket Lodge, Benevolent and Protective Order of Elks. He is also a member of the local Chamber of Commerce and the Maine Pharmaceutical Association. He is greatly interested in baseball and football. He and his family attend the Roman Catholic Church of St. Martin of Tours.

In 1914, Harry J. Gonya married Alice Connelly, who was born in Philadelphia. They are the parents of two children: Helen Elizabeth and Yvonne Marie.

GARFIELD JOHN JONES—Outstanding among the most enterprising and progressive men of Millinocket, Maine, is Garfield John Jones of the firm of Jones Brothers, Insurance Agents. He is the son of John T. and Cassie M. (Callahan) Jones, of New Brunswick, Canada, where his father has been engaged in farming and conducting a livery stable.

Garfield John Jones was born at Hartland, New Brunswick, Canada, on December 12, 1883. He was educated in the public schools of Old Town and Bangor, Maine, and Shaw's Business College of Bangor. On completing his education he came to Millinocket and, in association with his brother, William Jones, started a fruit and confectionery business. They carried on this line for fifteen years when they sold out and ran a grocery business, a moving picture theatre, and a billiard hall. They continued thus until 1922, when they sold their holdings and entered the real estate and insurance business under the name of Jones Brothers, Insurance Agents, and have continued in this line. Mr. Jones is a member of Millinocket Lodge, Benevolent and Protective Order of Elks; Modern Woodmen of America; St. Martin of Tours Council, Knights of Columbus, of which organization he is Past Grand Knight and is now financial secretary. He is a member of the Chamber of Commerce and has served a number of years on the Democratic Town Committee. He is a member of St. Martin of Tours Catholic Church. His recreation is in the enjoyment of basketball and baseball.

In 1917, Garfield John Jones married Gertrude Lenehan, a native of New Brunswick, Canada.

JOHN F. STEVENS, M. D.—As one who is deeply interested in the civic and educational progress of Millinocket, Dr. John F. Stevens holds a place of great esteem among the citizens of Millinocket, where he has practiced medicine for a long period, and is well known as a physician and surgeon of repute. Dr. Stevens is an acknowledged leader in matters concerning public health, and is also identified with all advanced interests of the medical world.

John F. Stevens was born May 6, 1870, at Castine, a son of Samuel B. Stevens, a sea captain to the time of his death, in 1871, and Helen (Bridgham) Stevens, now deceased; both parents also natives of Castine. After attending a private school, Dr. Stevens prepared for his profession at the Medical School of Dartmouth College, where he was graduated in 1899, with the degree of Doctor of Medicine, and then took a post-graduate course at Harvard University Medical School. In 1900 he came to Millinocket, where, with his offices on Penobscot Avenue, he has continued to practice his profession. In the political field a Republican, Dr. Stevens served for several years as a member of the Republican Town Committee; and he has also served as town physician, and as a member of the School Board. He is also the head of the Millinocket Library, and member of its board. In his professional affiliations, Dr. Stevens belongs to the Maine State Medical Society, Penobscot County Medical Association, American Medical Association, American Public Health Association; and he is also a member of Nollesemic Lodge, Free and Accepted Masons; Alpha Kappa Kappa College Fraternity; and the Masonic Club; and his hobby is literature. He attends the Unitarian church.

HAROLD C. GATES—Since 1924, Harold C. Gates has served as postmaster of Millinocket, Maine. He is a man of considerable experience in official position, having served as a member of the police force of Millinocket and acted as deputy sheriff, and in both of these positions, as well as in his present place as postmaster, he has performed his duties very efficiently and to the complete satisfaction of his community. Mr. Gates is also assistant chief of the local fire department. His father, Fred M. Gates, born in Old Town, has been chief of police at Millinocket for the last twenty-five years. His mother, Hattie (Hook) Gates, was born at Lee, Maine.

Harold C. Gates was born January 1, 1891, at Old Town, Maine. He attended the public schools and the high school of Millinocket, and when he completed his education began work for the Bangor & Aroostook Railroad, where he remained four years. At the end of that time he became a member of the Millinocket police force, serving for seven years, and for two years he acted as deputy sheriff. In 1920 he became assistant paymaster for the Great Northern Paper Company, remaining until 1924, when he became postmaster of Millinocket. He has continued in this office since that time.

Politically, Mr. Gates is a member of the Republican party. He is affiliated, fraternally, with the Nollesemic Lodge, No. 205, Free and Accepted Masons; a member of the Benevolent and Protective Order of Elks; and is also a member of the National Postmasters' Association. For twenty-two years he has been a member of the local fire department and has served as assistant chief of this organization since 1923. He is also a member of the Millinocket band. He and his family attend the local Congregational church. In his spare time Mr. Gates is usually to be found hunting, fishing or motoring.

In 1908, Harold C. Gates married Mary E. McGowan, who was born at New Castle, New Brunswick. They are the parents of: Harold F., Dorothy M., M. Ellen, Eveline M., and Mary E.

MARTIN E. GRUMLEY, M. D.—The steadily increasing practice of Dr. Martin E. Grumley in Millinocket and that part of the State of which Millinocket is a flourishing center, has been secured by him through those abilities that have been readily recognized by the general public, as well as by his colleagues and associates in the medical profession. He is a thorough, skillful and efficient doctor and surgeon, and has an established place in the esteem of his large medical parish.

Dr. Martin E. Grumley was born February 11, 1892, at Halifax, Nova Scotia, a son of Thomas Grumley, a lumberman, native of Halifax, who died in 1911, and Mary (Brennan) Grumley, who was born in Windsor, Nova Scotia, and survives her husband. Dr. Grumley attended the grammar and high schools at Halifax, and was graduated at St. Mary's College in 1912 with the Bachelor of Arts degree. He entered upon his professional career as a laboratory worker in Boston, Massachusetts, where he continued for three years, and then took the course at Tufts Medical College, Medford, Massachusetts, where he was graduated in 1921, with the degree of Doctor of Medicine. His internship was at the Eastern Maine General Hospital, where he remained for a year, and at Bangor State Hospital, where he continued for six months, his preparatory work for his professional activities thus including at least seven years of continuous study in all branches. In 1923, Dr. Grumley came to Millinocket, where, with his offices on Penobscot Avenue, he has continued to practice general medicine and surgery. He is a member of the American Medical Society, Penobscot County Medical Society, and the Maine State Medical Association.

During the World War, Dr. Grumley served in the United States Army Medical Reserve Corps. He is a Democrat in his political views; a member of the Millinocket Chamber of Commerce; and his hobby is fishing. He is a communicant of St. Martin of Tours Roman Catholic Church.

Dr. Martin E. Grumley married, September 26, 1925, Georgia Fassett, who was born in Abbot Village. They have one son, Robert Fassett Grumley.

JAMES H. DOWNS—As an example to those who would limit the years of initiative and strenuous activity in the business world, James H. Downs of Cornish, Maine, is an outstanding personality. Taking his years of experience as an asset to his business, at the age of fifty when many others would have contemplated retiring, he established a business of his own, which he has continued to operate and see grow to such proportions that he has been obliged to increase facilities in order to meet the demand for his goods. He is the son of Ivory Downs and Merinda (Grant) Downs of Lyman, Maine. Both parents are now deceased.

James H. Downs was born at Lyman, Maine, May 15, 1850. After receiving a common school education, at the age of nineteen years, he began working at home by making pants for Boston concerns. After working in this fashion for two years he became a contractor for these houses and remained in that capacity for twenty-nine years when he conceived the idea of making and selling his own goods. In order to put this plan into execution, he started a small factory where he manufactured pants, and went on the road to sell his own goods. It was not long before the excellent quality of his goods created a demand for his output and his business began to grow with that steadiness that comes to any business conducted as Mr. Downs has carried on his, good goods and fair dealing to all customers. The expansion was such that it became necessary to have another factory and he now owns and operates two plants, keeps three men on the road all the time and employs over sixty people in his factories. He is the oldest man in the State in this line of business, and in supplying the needs of the trade throughout all New England he makes all grades of goods from khaki work pants to the finest flannels. He is still very active in business. In politics, Mr. Downs is a Republican. He served as town clerk of Waterboro for four years. He is a member of the Free and Accepted Masons and of the Congregational church.

James H. Downs married Gussie F. Parker, at Waterboro, in 1893. Mrs. Downs died in 1923. They had two children: 1. Florence, who married Lester Landes of Pasadena, California. 2. Ida, who married Ormond C. Hartford, of Cornish, Maine, and with whom Mr. Downs makes his home.

FREDERICK M. GATES—Chief both of the police and the fire departments of Millinocket, Frederick M. Gates for the larger portion of his active career has guarded the public interests here and in Old Town with a high standard of faithful service, that has won for him the lasting regard of two generations in these communities. Chief Gates has demonstrated his efficiency in public life in other departments of civic activity, besides; and as deputy sheriff for Penobscot County, also, he possesses the esteem of his constituency in this section of the State.

Chief Frederick M. Gates was born May 13, 1861, at Old Town, a son of Joel M. Gates, who was born in Ware, Massachusetts, and Clara (Moody) Gates, born in Bradley, Maine, now deceased; Joel M. Gates, who was a bridge-builder by occupation, died while in service in the Civil War, as a member of the Thirteenth Maine Volunteer Infantry. Frederick M. Gates attended the grammar and high schools at Old Town, and then worked for a year in sawmill business, and afterwards, consecutively, for five years at the cooper's trade, a year for the Bangor & Piscataquis Railroad, two years for the Maine Central Railroad, and for various departments of public works.

Chief Gates began his present line of activity as a constable for the city of Old Town, and continued in that official capacity for about twenty years. He also served as Old Town's first city marshal at two different periods for twelve years. Resigning that position, he removed to Millinocket in 1900, where he served for a year as chief of police; and afterwards returning to Old Town, he served as a member of the police department until 1902. In that year, he accepted the office of chief of police at Millinocket, and since has continued in the duties of that office, having also received the appointment of chief of the fire department in 1906. Since 1906, also, he has held

the office of sheriff for Penobscot County. In the political field, Chief Gates gives his allegiance to the Republican party, and he has served several years as a member of the Millinocket Republican Town Committee. He was chairman of the Board of Health for ten years; and for eight years he held the office of Superintendent of Streets.

Fraternally, Chief Gates is affiliated with Star of the East Lodge, Free and Accepted Masons; Katahdin Chapter, Royal Arch Masons; Millinocket Lodge, Independent Order of Odd Fellows; Knights of Pythias; Millinocket Lodge, Benevolent and Protective Order of Elks; Modern Woodmen of America; and the Millinocket Chamber of Commerce. He attends the Congregational church.

Frederick M. Gates married, in 1890, Harriet Hook, who was born in Lee, Maine. Their children: Harold C.; Fred M., who served as a member of the Maine National Guard during the World War; Maud; Florence; and William.

HENRY WHITING BALL, M. D.—His interest in his profession and its value to his community has brought Dr. Henry Whiting Ball into a deserved prominence in his practice, owing to the fact that he has made himself expert in surgery, as well as in a specialty of the eye and ear, and in general medicine. He is highly regarded both in his professional associations and by the district in Lincoln and its neighborhood, where he has been in practice from the beginning of his career.

Dr. Henry Whiting Ball was born January 30, 1883, in Fall River, Massachusetts, son of Henry A. Ball, native of Franklin, Maine, a farmer, and for seventeen years customs officer at the Mt. Desert Ferry, died in 1920; and of Mary Bell (Patrequin) Ball, who was born in Taunton, Massachusetts, and survives her husband. Dr. Ball attended the public schools at Hancock Point, in Maine, and Higgins Classical Institute; and preparing for his profession at the Medical School of Bowdoin College, was graduated there in 1909 with the degree of Doctor of Medicine. A year of internship at the Maine Eye and Ear Infirmary at Portland, further advanced him in his plans for his career; and in 1912, Dr. Ball came to Lincoln, where he has been in practice to the present, with his offices on Main Street.

In the political field, Dr. Ball is affiliated with the Republican party; and since 1914, he has been a member of the United States Pension Board. He is a member of the Penobscot County Medical Society, and of the Phi Chi College Fraternity; and his hobbies are hunting and fishing. He is a communicant of the Roman Catholic church.

Dr. Henry Whiting Ball married, in 1920, Caroline E. Gonyer, who was born at Orono.

ROBERT O. LOVELY—The pharmacy conducted by Robert O. Lovely at Lincoln, and well known throughout this section of the State as the Lincoln Drug Company, fully meets the demands of the modern drugstore, its proprietor, Mr. Lovely, having by his own valued experience and foresight established his well-equipped and regulated store in a community of appreciative patrons. Mr. Lovely has the repute of a skilled and conscientious pharmacist, and in his citizenship, as well, he is associated with Lincoln's most progressive activities.

Robert O. Lovely was born December 27, 1887, at

MAINE—A HISTORY 205

Grand Lake Stream, a son of Henry A. Lovely, a farmer, who was born in Crouseville, and Almeda (Sprague) Lovely, a native of Grand Lake Stream. Mr. Lovely attended the schools of that township, and Ricker Classical Institute, and he received his degree in Pharmacy at the University of Maine, in the class of 1915. He entered upon his profession at Old Town, where he was employed until 1917, when he removed to Lincoln, and here started in business on his own account, and as proprietor of the Lincoln Drug Company, with his store on Main Street.

A Republican in his political inclination, Mr. Lovely supports the principles and candidates of that party. During the World War, he was active in all matters pertaining to the drives and the requirements of the hour; and previous to the war, he served four years as a member of Company L, Maine National Guard. Fraternally, he is affiliated with the Free and Accepted Masons, and all bodies of the York Rite, as well as Anah Temple, Ancient Arabic Order Nobles of the Mystic Shrine; Order of the Eastern Star; Independent Order of Odd Fellows; and Lambda Chi Alpha College Fraternity. He is also a member of the Maine Pharmaceutical Association and the Rexall Club; and his diversions are hunting and fishing. He attends the Congregational church.

Robert O. Lovely married, in 1916, Eveline C. Hillman, who was born in Houlton, and they have one daughter, Priscilla.

WILLIAM A. BROWN—His business as a jeweler brings William A. Brown into prominence as one of the leading merchants of Lincoln, where he established his present business in 1904, his training and experience in Waltham, Massachusetts, great center of watch-making, having secured for him his recognized place as an expert. As a town official, too, he has rendered such civic service as to be accounted a citizen of leading worth in town government affairs.

William A. Brown was born October 15, 1881, at Lincoln Center, the son of Charles Alfred Brown, a native of Carroll, and a farmer to the time of his death, which occurred in 1924, and Marietta J. (Weatherbee) Brown, who was born in Springfield, and survives her husband. Mr. Brown attended the Lincoln schools, and was graduated at Mattanawcook Academy, after which he was employed for two years in the hardware business in the firm of E. A. Weatherbee Company. He then removed to Waltham, Massachusetts, where he attended Waltham Horological School for some six months; and returning to Lincoln, he here established himself in his present successful business as a jeweler on Main Street. He is a registered optometrist, and a member of the Maine Association of Opticians. Mr. Brown entered the automobile business in 1910, and in 1913 obtained the agency for Overland and Willys-Knight machines, for the Lincoln district.

In political matters, Mr. Brown is a Republican, and he served for a year as town treasurer. He is a member of the board of trustees of Mattanawcook Academy. His hobbies are hunting and fishing, and he attends the Congregational church.

William A. Brown married, in 1906, Margery E. Weatherbee, who was born in Lincoln; and they have one son, Alfred Gardiner Brown.

WILLIAM H. SMITH—Having spent most of his life on and about farms, William H. Smith finds himself well qualified for his present work. He has established a real estate business in Newport, specializing in the sale of farms. In addition he holds the agency for the International Harvester Company in the Newport district. His father, Howard A. Smith, born in Harmony, Maine, was a farmer and engaged in this work until his death in 1927. His mother, who was Martha Lord, born in Lebanon, Maine, is still living (1928).

William H. Smith was born December 9, 1887, at Palmyra, Maine. He attended the public schools there and later entered the Maine Central Institute. After completing his education, graduating in 1906, he worked as a farmer until 1920. In that year he became agent for the Strout Farm Agency, and he continued with this company until 1926 when he went into business for himself, with offices in the Bank Block, Newport. Besides his own real estate business and the agency for the International Harvester Company, Mr. Smith is sole owner of a farm of seven hundred and fifty acres, located near Newport. Politically, he is a Republican. He is affiliated with the Meridian Splendor Lodge, Free and Accepted Masons; Stevens Chapter, Royal Arch Masons; Skowhegan Council, Royal and Select Masters; and Old Hickory Lodge, Independent Order of Odd Fellows. He is also a member of the Newport Rod and Gun Club.

In 1919, William H. Smith married Edna Brackett, who was born in Palmyra, Maine. She died in 1920. In 1925 he married Annette Frazier, who was born in Presque Isle. By his first marriage he was the father of a child, Elmer Vincent.

EUGENE H. RUSSELL—The entire active career of Eugene H. Russell has been identified with the garage and service station business in Newport, Maine. At the present time he is the owner and manager of Russell's Garage, and in addition to general repair and storage work he is agent for the Nash motor cars, and Newport representative of the American League of Automotive Service. He carries a complete line of automobile accessories and his garage is located on Main Street, in Newport. Nelson Russell, his father, was born in Penobscot County, Maine. He received his education in the local public schools, and for several years has been in the employ of the Boston Elevated Railroad Company. He is also engaged in business as a general merchant. He married Etta M. Sanborn, who was born in Etna, Maine, and died in 1916.

Eugene H. Russell, son of Nelson and Etta M. (Sanborn) Russell, was born in Etna, Maine, July 25, 1896, and received his education in the public schools of his birthplace, and in Wentworth Institute, of Boston, attending the last-named institution for two years. When his education was completed he found employment in the automobile business, in various connections, continuing in this line until the entrance of the United States into the World War. He then enlisted for service, becoming a member of the heavy artillery, stationed at Fortress Monroe, Virginia, as instructor in the automobile school there. He continued there until after the signing of the Armistice, when he was discharged with the rank of waggoner. Upon his return to civilian life he entered the employ of Friend and Friend, Ford agents of Newport, Maine, with whom he remained as foreman for three and one-half years. At the end of that time he severed his connections with Friend and Friend and identified himself with Fernald's Garage, as foreman. In this capacity he continued to serve until 1925, when he purchased the business and changed the name to its present style of Russell's Garage. In addition to repair and storage work, Mr. Russell is agent for Nash motor cars and is Newport representative of the American League of Automotive Service. He carries a complete line of automobile accessories and supplies, and his garage, which is located on Main Street, is very well patronized. Politically, Mr. Russell supports the principles and candidates of the Republican party. He is a member of Meridian Splendor Lodge, Free and Accepted Masons; and of Stevens Chapter, Royal Arch Masons. He is also an interested member of the Newport Rod and Gun Club, and finds his favorite recreation in hunting and fishing. His religious interest is with the Christian Church of Newport, of which he is an attendant.

Eugene H. Russell was married, in 1923, to Bertha Rich, who was born in Waterville, Maine.

SYDNEY B. RING—After a wide experience in merchandising, which included several years as a traveling salesman for wholesale houses in the women's ready-to-wear trade, Sydney B. Ring has established himself in business in Newport, Maine, where his store is now one of the largest and most complete catering to women to be found anywhere in the State.

Born in Bath, Maine, December 1, 1872, the son of Elbridge G. and Mary A. (Shaw) Ring, he is of New England descent on both sides. His father, who was born in Palmyra, Maine, was employed as carriagemaker until he died. He had been a veteran of the Civil War, and as such, prominent in the affairs of the Grand Army of the Republic, a member of Libby Post, and its past commander. He served with the Massachusetts Volunteer Infantry, and was wounded in action. His widow, who was born in Augusta, Maine, is still living (1928).

Educated in the public schools of Newport, Maine, and of Amesbury, Massachusetts, Sydney B. Ring found his first employment as clerk in a men's furnishing store, where he remained for fifteen years. He then became a traveling salesman, and spent twenty years on the road, selling women's ready-to-wear garments, and acquiring a thorough knowledge of what in those years developed into the most important of the garment industries. In 1924 he opened his own store in Newport, Maine, doing a general drygoods business, and naturally specializing in the field he had studied from the wholesaler's angle for so many years. Today he is the largest dealer in women's ready-to-wear garments in Newport. His place of business is one of the most up-to-date in Maine, and a millinery department has proved especially popular. He belongs to the Newport Rod and Gun Club, and is a member of Meridian Splendor Lodge, Free and Accepted Masons, and of Stevens Chapter, Royal Arch Masons.

In 1911, Sydney B. Ring married Leona H. Weymouth, who was born in York, Maine.

ZEB L. MERCHANT—A well-known citizen of Norway, Maine, engaged in the drygoods business, is Zeb L. Merchant, whose store carries a complete

line of drygoods and wearing apparel. He became sole owner of this establishment in 1916, which employs about seven people and is a leading institution of its kind in the community. Mr. Merchant was born in South Royalton, Vermont, September 9, 1866, the son of Zeb L. and Camille (Faneuf) Merchant, both deceased. The father was engaged for the greater part of his life in agricultural pursuits in Quechee, Vermont, and at the time of the Civil War was a member of the Vermont Volunteers, while his mother was a native of Canada.

Zeb L. Merchant, Jr., received his education in the public schools of Quechee. At the age of sixteen he began working in a general store, and ever since that time has followed this line of activity. In 1911 he formed a partnership with E. A. Sargent and purchased the Prince Sisters' store in Norway, Maine, this association continuing for the following five years. In 1916 this partnership was dissolved, and up to the present (1928), Mr. Merchant has been alone in business, handling drygoods, wearing apparel for women, misses, children, and infants' wear. Some men are born with a merchandising instinct, and in this category belongs Mr. Merchant, under whose able supervision and management the business is each year enjoying an increased volume of trade. He is active in the civic affairs of the town, participates in the work of the Merchants' Association and of the Board of Trade, being a member of both of these organizations. His political preference is with the Republican party. Mr. Merchant is a member of Joshua L. Chamberlain Sons of Veterans Camp, and life associate member of William Henry Stone Post, American Legion, of Norway, and is a communicant of St. Catherine's Church of Norway and South Paris.

THOMAS STUART CLEMENT, D. D. S.—In Newport, Maine, Dr. Thomas Stuart Clement has been engaged in general dental practice since 1922. He has his offices in the Bank Block, and is taking care of a large and important practice. Dr. Clement is well known in fraternal circles, and has many friends in Newport.

Thomas Stuart Clement was born in Orland, Maine, October 15, 1899, son of George Melvin Clement, who is engaged as a quarryman in North Jay, and of Mary (Davis) Clement, a native of Oak Hill, Maine. Dr. Clement attended the public schools of Frankfort, Maine, and after completing his course in Frankfort High School matriculated in Baltimore College, taking the course in dental surgery. He was graduated with the class of 1922, receiving the degree of Doctor of Dental Surgery, and then opened his office in North Jay, Maine, where he was successfully engaged in practice until 1923. In that year he came to Newport, Maine, where he has since been practicing. During the World War he served with the Student Army Training Corps. Fraternally, he is a member of Xi Psi Phi College Fraternity, also of Theta Nu Epsilon. He is a member of Meridian Splendor Lodge, Free and Accepted Masons; of Victory Lodge, Knights of Pythias; and of Old Hickory Lodge, Independent Order of Odd Fellows. Politically, he gives his support to the principles and the candidates of the Republican party. He finds his favorite form of recreation in fishing, and his religious affiliation is with the Methodist church.

Dr. Thomas Stuart Clement was married, in

1926, to Laura Harriet Munson, Maine, and they are the parents of one daughter, Phylis Lorraine.

CLYDE L. PINGREE—One of the successful business men of Newport, Maine, is Clyde L. Pingree, of the firm which operates under the name of Hanson and Pingree, hardware, plumbing, and heating. The firm also carries on a wholesale business in paint supplies. Both of the partners are able business men, and have established a reputation for prompt and courteous service and for fair dealing. Mr. Pingree takes an active part in the affairs of the Republican party and is active in local public affairs. Ireson I. Pingree, father of Clyde L. Pingree, was born in Parkman, Maine, and was engaged as a stationary engineer to the time of his death, in 1924. He married Addie M. Severance, who was born in Maine, and is now deceased. This branch of the Pingree family descends from Samuel Pingree, great-grandfather of Clyde L. Pingree, who was one of the first to settle in the town of Parkman, Maine, the records showing that he was the second of the pioneers to settle upon the site of that town.

Clyde L. Pingree, son of Ireson I. and Addie M. (Severance) Pingree, was born in Parkman, Maine, April 16, 1887, and received his education in the public schools of Sangerville, Maine. After completing his school training he worked for a year and a half in the grocery business, and then entered the employ of the Wood and Bishop Company, of Bangor, Maine, serving as salesman. That connection he maintained for a period of seven years and then, in 1912, came to Newport, Maine, where he became associated with A. G. Hanson, as a partner, under the name of Hanson and Pingree Company. During the years which have passed since that time the Hanson and Pingree Company has conducted a prosperous business in hardware, plumbing, heating, and wholesale paint supplies, and has become one of the thoroughly well established concerns of this city. Mr. Pingree is a member of the New England Hardware Dealers' Association and is well known to the trade. Fraternally, he is identified with Meridian Splendor Lodge, Free and Accepted Masons, of which he is a Past Master; of Stevens Chapter, Royal Arch Masons; and of Skowhegan Council, Royal and Select Masters. He is also a member of the Newport Rod and Gun Club and of the Winchester Club of New England. Politically, he is an ardent supporter of the tenets of the Republican party and he takes a very active part in its affairs. He has served for three terms as chairman of the Republican Town Committee, two terms on the Republican County Committee, and while on the county committee he served as a member of the finance committee. Mr. Pingree takes his rest and recreation during his vacation period in camping and is an enthusiastic devotee of this particular form of out-of-door recreation. His religious membership is with the Methodist church.

Clyde L. Pingree was married, in 1911, to Oena Grey Vining, who was born in Wilton, Maine, and they are the parents of one son, Reginald Sewall.

NORRIS H. FRIEND—The senior partner of Friend and Friend, the largest automobile dealers and garage firm in Newport, Norris H. Friend owes his position to his own ability. Discovering that the surest way to quantity business is quality service, he has tried to meet the needs of motorists and the

modern motor car in every way. His business shows that he has been very successful in this field.

Mr. Friend was born in Etna, Maine, on December 16, 1894. His father, Harry A. Friend, also born in Etna, was an apple buyer until 1917, when he entered the garage business, continuing with Friend and Friend at Newport until his death in 1924. He served two years as deputy sheriff. Mr. Friend's mother, who was Lue Miller, born in Austin, Nevada, is still living.

Entering the public schools at Etna, Norris H. Friend completed his education at the Maine Central Institute and shortly afterwards became a salesman for the American Tobacco Company. He left this position in 1917 to enter the United States Army. After his enlistment, on May 17, he was assigned to the First Division Motor Truck Train, with the rank of first sergeant, and went to France. He served eighteen months in all with the American Expeditionary Forces. Returning to America he received his discharge on May 25, 1919, and soon afterwards became associated with his father in the firm of Friend and Friend with offices on Main Street, Newport. This firm was the first recognized Ford Sales and Supply Agency in Newport. In addition to the Ford business they do general repair work and handle supplies for all other makes of cars. In 1923 a branch office was opened at Pittsfield, Maine, operating on the same general policy. After the death of Harry A. Friend, in 1924, Norris H. Friend became the senior member of the firm and Earle E. Friend was admitted to junior membership. This reorganization has continued effective to the present time.

Politically, Mr. Friend is a member of the Republican party. He is affiliated with the Old Hickory Lodge, Independent Order of Odd Fellows, and is a member of Meridian Splendor Lodge, Free and Accepted Masons; Stevens Chapter, Royal Arch Masons; St. John's Commandery, Knights Templar; and Anah Temple, Ancient Arabic Order Nobles of the Mystic Shrine. He is also a member of Corinna Post of the American Legion, and Veterans of Foreign Wars. Mr. Friend attends the Universalist church and is fond of fishing and traveling.

In 1923, Norris H. Friend married Isabel Cooper, who was born in Belfast, Maine. Their son, Peter Cooper Friend, was born November 24, 1925.

J. ALBERT LETHIECQ, M. D.—For many years Dr. J. Albert Lethiecq has been a prominent figure in the professional and civic life of Brewer. The spirit of service to humanity, manifested in his choice of a career, has made him invaluable to his community, in the larger aspect of civic service as well as in his less spectacular, but hardly less important, capacity of physician and friend. Dr. Lethiecq was born in Beaucaucourt, Province of Quebec, Canada, on October 16, 1865, the son of Gustavus Lethiecq and Eleanor Lemay, both of Beaucaucourt. His father was a carpenter and engaged in this work until his death. His mother is still living.

Joseph A. (J. Albert) Lethiecq attended the public schools of Beaucaucourt, and this training was supplemented with special tutoring. In 1889 he was graduated from Levalle University with the degree of Doctor of Veterinary Surgery. For four years he practiced as a veterinary surgeon until, in 1892, he began the course at Jefferson Medical College leading to the degree of Doctor of Medicine. This degree he received in 1894. Since that time he has actively practiced his profession, specializing in surgery. He took special work in surgery at Jefferson College, and a special course in anatomy at Philadelphia Polyclinic. He has visited at Mayo Hospital and several other clinics for work in his field of specialization. He is on the staff of the Eastern Maine General Hospital.

Politically, he is affiliated with the Republican party. For several years he served as chairman of the City of Brewer Board of Health, and for several years he was a member of the School Board of that city. He has also served at various times as City Physician and School Physician. He is a director of the Brewer Savings Bank. A member of St. Joseph's Roman Catholic Church, he is also associated with two fraternal organizations, the Knights of Pythias, and the Modern Woodmen of America. He is connected with a number of associations, among them, the American Medical Association; the Penobscot County Medical Society, of which he is past president; and the Maine State Medical Society. In the little time which is his for recreation, he may usually be found hunting, fishing, or in his garden.

In 1898, J. Albert Lethiecq married Madelle C. Somes, who was born at Mount Desert, Maine. They are the parents of four children: Arline M. (deceased), Aris S., Dorothy S., and Margaret Eleanor.

JOHN E. LITTLEFIELD—One of the prominent business men of Brewer, who is active in club and fraternal life of the city, is John E. Littlefield, treasurer of the Brooks Brick Company. He has been associated at different periods in several trades and businesses. Mr. Littlefield was born in Stockton Springs, Maine, on May 10, 1868, the son of John Littlefield, born in Prospect, Maine, and of Julia A. Pattee, born in Monroe, Maine. Both of his parents are now deceased. His father was a ship builder until the time of his death, and the son worked for a number of years with his father in the ship frame business.

John E. Littlefield attended the public schools and the high school of Brewer, as well as the University of Maine. When he completed his education, he worked for four years for Fred T. Hall, of Bangor, in the grocery business. At the age of twenty-two he became associated with his father in the firm of John Littlefield & Sons Company, of Brewer, in the ship frame business. Upon the death of his father he continued the business alone until 1913, when he took his son, John Littlefield, into the company as a partner. A short time later he took in Waldmar B. Littlefield, and continued this partnership until 1922. In that year the business was discontinued, and all of Mr. Littlefield's time was devoted to the Brooks Brick Company, of which he has been treasurer since 1906. John Littlefield, Jr., is assistant treasurer of the same firm, and Waldmar B. Littlefield is manager of the mud yard. In his political affiliations he is a Republican. He is a member of St. Andrew's Masonic Lodge; all bodies of the York and Scottish Rites, including Anah Temple, Ancient Arabic Order Nobles of the Mystic Shrine; and of the Knights of Pythias. He is affiliated with a number of clubs and associations: the Tarratine Club, the Penobscot Valley Country Club, the Conduskeag Canoe

and Country Club, the Chamber of Commerce of Bangor, and the Common Brick Manufacturers' Association of America. When he is not busy with the activities of the brick company and his other interests, he finds recreation in archery, fishing and hunting.

In 1890, John E. Littlefield married Sarah A. Bunker, who was born near Brewer. They are the parents of children: John, Waldmar B., Theodore, Julia A., and Fred E.

JOSEPH E. HUGGARD—One of the most modern and scientifically equipped embalming and funeral directing establishments in the State of Maine is the one owned and operated by Joseph E. Huggard of Brewer. Mr. Huggard has been engaged in the undertaking business since 1896, and has been operating under his own name since 1908. His establishment is located at No. 255 North Main Street, and his is the only modern morgue in the county.

Joseph E. Huggard was born in Queens County, New Brunswick, Canada, February 1, 1874, son of Joseph, who was born in the North of Ireland, and came to Canada as a boy and lived in Queens County where he was engaged as a farmer to the time of his death in 1883, and Eliza J. (O'Neil) Huggard, who was born in New Brunswick, Canada, and is still living (1928). He attended the public schools of his native district, and upon the completion of his school training worked in various positions until 1892. In that year he entered the employ of the Bangor Foundry & Machine Company, where he learned the trade of the moulder. Here he remained for three years, and then, in 1895, went to Bath, Maine, where he followed the trade of moulder for one year. In 1896 he became associated with E. E. Hussey in the undertaking business and this connection was maintained until 1908 when, upon the death of Mr. Hussey, Mr. Huggard took over the business. From then until 1918, Mr. Huggard operated under the name of Wood & Huggard, but in that year he purchased Mr. Wood's interest of the heirs and since he has operated under his own name. His office is located at No. 255 North Main Street, in Brewer, and at the present time (1928) Mr. Huggard has as fine equipment as can be found anywhere in the State of Maine. He has the only De Luxe hearse in the county and he has long ago made a reputation for prompt, courteous, and efficient service. He has the only modern morgue in the county, and is known as one of the most skillful embalmers in this part of the State.

Fraternally, Mr. Huggard is identified with St. Andrew's Lodge, Free and Accepted Masons; with all the bodies of the York and Scottish Rites; also with Anah Temple, Ancient Arabic Order Nobles of the Mystic Shrine. He is a member of Wildey Lodge, Independent Order of Odd Fellows; and of the Encampment; also of the Rebekahs. He also holds membership in Colonel Brewer Lodge, Knights of Pythias; and James G. Blaine Court, Independent Order of Foresters. He is a member of the Bangor Chamber of Commerce, and professionally, is identified with the Maine Funeral Directors' Association, and the National Funeral Directors' Association. His clubs are the Kiwanis and the Canadian. Politically, Mr. Huggard gives his support to the principles and the candidates of the Republican party. He finds healthful recreation in fishing and hunting, also traveling, and his religious affiliation is with the Methodist church, in the work of which he takes an active part, serving as president of the Epworth League.

Joseph E. Huggard was married, in 1897, to Maude B. Kenney, a native of Brewer, Maine, and they are the parents of two children: Frederick K., and Marion B.

J. FRED O'CONNELL—A man of prominence in the political and business life of Maine is J. Fred O'Connell. He has shown great executive ability in building up his own real estate and insurance business, though much of his time has been given to the many official and semi-official positions he has been called upon to fill. His eloquence has made him much in demand as a public speaker. Mr. O'Connell was born at Milford, Maine, April 30, 1874. His father, Michael C. O'Connell, was born at Chatham, New Brunswick, Canada, and was engaged as a carpenter until his death. His mother, Catherine (Fitzgerald) O'Connell, born at Island Pond, Vermont, is also deceased.

One of a family of fifteen children, J. Fred O'Connell attended the public schools of Milford. Completing his education there he took up surveying and found employment as a lumber surveyor until 1905. In that year he entered the real estate and insurance business in Old Town, Maine, continuing there until 1913, when he moved his headquarters to Bangor. He has remained in Bangor since that date. By political inclination, Mr. O'Connell is a Republican and he has a remarkable record of public service with that party. For eight years he served on the School Board of Milford. During that time he was for one year a member of the Board of Selectmen of the same town and for several years a member of the Milford Republican Town Committtee. In 1912 he was elected to the State Legislature and in 1913 was appointed High Sheriff of Penobscot County by Governor Haynes. He remained in this office until 1915. In 1920 he was elected a member of the Republican State Committtee, serving until 1926, and for two years of this period he was in charge of the headquarters for Eastern Maine. For several years he has been a delegate to the Republican State Convention.

Mr. O'Connell is affiliated with the Old Town Lodge, Benevolent and Protective Order of Elks. He is also a member of the United Commercial Travelers' Association and of the Penobscot Valley Country Club. During the World War he served as chairman of the Town of Milford Liberty Loan Drives and was a "four-minute" speaker for Penobscot County. Mr. O'Connell devotes much of his spare time to public speaking.

In 1921, J. Fred O'Connell married Melissa Henderson, who was born at Algash, Aroostook County, Maine.

MAGNUS G. RIDLON, M. D.—One of the careful physicians of Porter, Maine, Magnus G. Ridlon, M. D., engages extensively in public health work, being Health Officer for Kezar Falls, Porter, and Parsonsfield. He has conducted a general practice in Porter ever since he left school in 1908.

He is the son of Walter H. and Caroline (Wakefield) Ridlon. His father, who in his early life was engaged in the lumber business, died in 1926, at the

age of seventy-eight years; and his mother, who came from Eaton, New Hampshire, is also deceased. Magnus G. Ridlon was born in Freedom, New Hampshire, December 13, 1880. He received his education in the public schools and high school; Bridgton Academy, from which he was graduated in 1902; Bowdoin Medical College, from which he was graduated with the degree of Doctor of Medicine in 1907. While acquiring his education, Dr. Ridlon was employed at various times. He was at first a clerk in a store, and later did work for the United States Government, in order to put himself through college. For a year he served as an interne at the Maine Eye and Ear Infirmary, Portland, Maine; then, in 1908, commenced his own practice in Porter. During the World War, he served on the Medical Advisory Board of Oxford County. He is a member of the Knights of Pythias and of the Improved Order of Red Men. His religious affiliation is with the Methodist church.

In Fryeburg, Maine, October 15, 1908, Magnus G. Ridlon married Odelia Turner, of Waterville, Nova Scotia. They have one child, Edythe Mae.

EVERETT S. HURD, president and manager of the Dakin Sporting Goods Company, one of the best-known concerns of its kind in New England, was born July 5, 1895, in Liberty, Maine, a son of William Watson and Maude Ellen (Taylor) Hurd, both members of old Maine families. William Watson Hurd was born at Liberty, Maine, was engaged in the tannery business until his death in 1915. Maude Ellen (Taylor) Hurd, who is still living, was born in Freedom, Maine.

Everett S. Hurd received his preparatory education in the public schools of Pittsfield, Maine, later attending the Maine Central Institute. He entered the University of Maine, where he was captain of the tennis team, and graduated with the class of 1917, when he received the degrees of Bachelor of Science and Electrical Engineer. After his graduation, he began his career as an electrical engineer for the Westinghouse Electric Company of Pittsburgh, Pennsylvania, where he remained for a year. He removed from there to Newark, New Jersey, where he was associated with the Electric Arc Cutting & Welding Company for a year and a half. He then went to Detroit to work for four years with the Gibb Instrument Company. At the end of this time he returned to Bangor, Maine, and bought the Dakin Sporting Goods Company, of which he is now president and manager. The Dakin Sporting Goods Company was founded in 1900 under the name of Holt and Kendall and at that time its chief business was repairing guns and bicycles and manufacturing sinkers for fishing tackle. In 1906 Mr. Holt sold out his interest to Cyrus S. Winch and the name was changed to Kendall and Winch. This partnership continued until 1913, when the business was incorporated under the name Kendall and Winch. In that year a department for the sale of sporting goods was added to the business, also the agency for Harley-Davidson motorcycles, which represents the first and only agency for this machine in Bangor. In 1920 the business was purchased by Eugene H. Dakin and the name was changed to Dakin Sporting Goods Company. In 1924 Mr. Hurd bought out Mr. Dakin's interest and he has conducted the business since, under the old name. This company is the largest sporting goods store in Northeastern Maine, carrying a complete equipment of sporting goods and game requisites. The company now supplies over two hundred and fifty schools in the State of Maine, also many colleges, with athletic equipment. In his political preferences, Mr. Hurd is an Independent. During the World War, he was commissioned (July 12, 1918) a second lieutenant in the United States Army, Engineering Corps. He was honorably discharged December 14, 1918. He is affiliated with the Knights of Pythias and the college fraternities Phi Kappa Sigma and Tau Beta Pi. He is also a member of the Bangor Chamber of Commerce and the American Welding Society, of which he is a charter member.

Everett S. Hurd married, in 1919, Marguerite Littlefield, who was born in Fryeburg, Maine. Mr. and Mrs. Hurd are the parents of a daughter, Ellen R. Mr. Hurd and his family attend the Baptist church.

FRANCIS M. BEASLEY, of Old Town, Maine, designer of textile fabrics, and mill agent, was born in Millville, Massachusetts, April 27, 1884, the son of Frank R. and Isabella (Edmonds) Beasley. The elder Beasley, a native of Waterloo, Vermont, was a mechanic, who remained at work until his death. His widow, who was born in Scotland, is still living.

After attending the public schools in Blackstone, Massachusetts, Francis M. Beasley entered the Philadelphia Textile School, where he spent a year, and on completing his studies there in 1902, found employment with the American Woolen Company, in their Manton mills, Manton, Rhode Island. He worked there for some time, and then went to the Weybossett mills, of Providence, Rhode Island, seeking always to improve his craftsmanship. His next employment was in the Saranac mills, Blackstone, Massachusetts, and after a time there, he returned to the Manton mills as a designer's assistant. His next step upward was a post as superintendent and designer with the Niantic Manufacturing Company, of East Lyme, Connecticut. In 1913 he was made superintendent and designer for the Ounegan mills of the American Woolen Company at Old Town, Maine, and in 1915 he was made agent for this establishment, a post he still holds.

Mr. Beasley is a Free and Accepted Mason, a member of all bodies of the York Rite, including Knights Templar, and is a Past Master of Star of the East Lodge, and a member of the Masonic Club. He attends the Methodist church, of which he is trustee and steward, and his one hobby is baseball. He is a Republican.

Francis M. Beasley married Ethel G. Wales, of North Smithfield, Rhode Island, in 1906. Their children are Doris L., Helen W., and Gertrude W.

MOSES L. JORDAN, Jr.—One of the important lumber men of Maine who, although young in years, has attained a prominent position in the industry in this State, is Moses L. Jordan, Jr., president of the well-known Jordan Lumber Company of Old Town. He is the son of one of the most respected and valued citizens of Old Town, whose passing left a vacancy which his son is gradually filling with credit to himself and his community.

Moses L. Jordan, Jr., was born July 7, 1883, in Old Town, the son of Moses L. and Clara L. (Day) Jordan (q. v.). He received his education in the public grammar and high schools of Old Town, later attending and graduating from Shaw's Business College in Bangor, Penobscot County. In 1900 he became associated with his father in the Jordan Lumber Company, acting in the capacity of manager of the sawmill and the driving of logs on the East Branch water. The Jordan Lumber Company was established in 1888, by Moses L. Jordan, Sr., who began operating a box-mill on Water Street and the same year began work with a sawmill and a stave mill in Milford. In the spring of that year the elder Jordan sold a half interest to the late Harry D. Stewart and for many years the business was known as Jordan and Stewart. After Mr. Stewart's retirement, in 1893, the business was incorporated under the name of the Jordan Lumber Company. Later the Milford site was taken over by the Bodwell Water-power Company and the Jordan concern built its double-band sawmill farther up the river, in Milford, the entire product being used to supply the box-shook industry in Old Town. The heavier lumber was produced by a single-band sawmill on another site in Milford, commonly known as the Lower Mill. Since that time the Jordan Lumber Company has grown steadily until it has become the only extensive lumber manufacturing corporation remaining in the city. Some years later the company bought the casket manufacturing business of Charles L. Ratcliffe, and its output now includes long and short lumber, boxboards, box-shooks, house-finish, mouldings, hardwood flooring and casket-making. On several occasions fires have crippled various portions of the business but in each case Mr. Jordan, senior, replaced the burned buildings with a fine brick plant. Upon the death of his father, Moses L. Jordan, Jr., became president and manager of the Jordan Lumber Company, exemplifying in his own person the high personal and professional standards inaugurated by his father. In his political preferences he is a strong supporter of the Republican party. He is fraternally affiliated with the Star of the East Lodge, Free and Accepted Masons; is a member of the local Chapter, Royal Arch Masons; of the Council, Royal and Select Masters; of the York Consistory, Ancient Accepted Scottish Rite, and of the Commandery, Knights Templar. He is also affiliated with the Independent Order of Odd Fellows, and Oldtown Lodge, Benevolent and Protective Order of Elks.

Moses L. Jordan, Jr., married Jennie A. O'Keefe, who was born in Old Town, Maine. Mr. and Mrs. Jordan attend the Episcopal church, of which Mr. Jordan is a vestryman.

MOSES L. JORDAN—For almost forty years Moses L. Jordan was a prominent figure in the business and social life of Old Town, Penobscot County, to which community he gave much of his time and ability. His time and his money had ever been given for everything pertaining to the best interests of the city and no worthy cause failed to receive his assistance. Monuments to his industry, energy and ability are to be found in Old Town and the vicinity in the shape of homes, mills and business blocks, all of which owe their inception to him. His death, at the age of seventy-eight years, came as a distinct shock to the community in which he had lived for so many years. He was a loving and devoted husband and father, a good neighbor, and a splendid example of the finest type of American citizen. His name will ever occupy a conspicuous place in the historic annals of Old Town.

Moses L. Jordan was born in Mariaville, Maine, one of a family of four brothers and three sisters. In early manhood he located in Veazie, Penobscot County, where he became interested in lumbering and in the operating of lumber mills, his first contract being the sawing of many thousands of shingles for a local firm. After a few years in Veazie he removed to Old Town, where he built up an extensive business in the manufacturing of lumber, both long and short products coming from his several mills. One important branch of his plant was the mill on South Water Street, where he manufactured box shooks. It is said that boxes from this plant have encircled the globe with the products they were constructed to protect.

Facing all but insurmountable difficulties from time to time, Mr. Jordan was a man of great vision, industrially. He looked ahead and prepared for future conditions with a judgment which was rarely at fault, the result being the present solid foundation of the Jordan Lumber Company's extensive manufacturing and land-holding interests, of which he was for so many years the active head and principal holder. His first plant in Old Town was a small place on Water Street, the predecessor of what is now a substantial box mill. It was in 1888 that he began operations in this plant and in the same year he started a sawmill on the present site of the Hydro-Electric Company's power station in Milford. About the same time he started a stave mill in Milford, where the company's shingle and band sawmill is now located. In May, 1888, he sold a half interest in the business to Harry D. Stewart and for several years the two were associated in the management of the exensive and rapidly growing business as Jordan and Stewart. When Mr. Stewart retired from active business the firm was incorporated as the Jordan Lumber Company. One of the members of the new concern was Virgil E. Tucker, who had joined the organization in 1891, and the other incorporators were John Cassidy of Bangor, Joseph W. Bodwell and J. L. S. Hincks.

When the Bodwell Water Power Company took over the site of the Jordan corporation at Milford, that concern built its double-band sawmill, which is now used to supply the mills at Old Town with material for box shooks. The heavier lumber product of spruce dimensions is produced by a single band sawmill on another site in Milford, known as "the lower mill." By the purchase of the business of Charles L. Ratcliffe, casket manufacturer, Mr. Jordan added another branch to his increasing industry and in a very short time his organization became the leading manufacturing corporation of Old Town and the vicinity. The company was engaged in the production of long and short lumber, box-boards, box-shooks, house finish, mouldings, hardwood floorings, and casket-making. To every branch of these manifold industries Mr. Jordan gave his personal attention, and inculcated in his employees a spirit of loyalty and devotion to his business which still remains as a monument to his memory. Fires crippled the mills from time to time, but Mr. Jordan persevered in the face of all obstacles. When the wooden structure on Water Street was destroyed in 1909, Mr. Jordan replaced it with the present building

of solid brick, and in 1912 he erected the present suite of offices adjoining the plant.

With all his manifold business interests Mr. Jordan found time for fraternal affiliations. He was active in the Star of the East Lodge, Free and Accepted Masons, and in Tarratine Lodge, Independent Order of Odd Fellows. He also belonged to Old Town Lodge, Benevolent and Patriotic Order of Elks, and was a member of the local Methodist church.

Moses L. Jordan married Clara L. Day. Mr. and Mrs. Jordan were the parents of four children, two of whom are deceased; the two surviving children are: Moses L., Jr. (q. v.), and Edith L., married to Leslie R. Lord, of Old Town.

Mr. Jordan died November 15, 1926, at his home in Old Town. The leading citizens of Old Town and the vicinity attended the funeral services and his casket was smothered in a wealth of floral tributes, tendered by those who realized that the community had lost a man of unswerving devotion to his ideals and a citizen who ever placed the benefit of his community ahead of any possibility of personal gain.

J. EDWARD GOODIN, proprietor of the Star Printing Company, one of the oldest printing concerns in Old Town, Maine, was born October 13, 1887, in New Brunswick, Canada. Mr. Goodin is a son of Camille and Philomine (Commeau) Goodin, both of whom were natives of New Brunswick. Camille Goodin was a shoemaker until the time of his death, and is survived by Philomine (Commeau) Goodin.

J. Edward Goodin received his education in the public schools of Old Town, Maine, afterwards learning the printing trade, which he followed from 1903 until 1918, when he bought the Star Printing Company of which he is now proprietor. The Star Printing Company was founded in 1895 by Orman Fernandez, who conducted the concern until 1915, when he sold it to A. W. Hall. Mr. Hall sold the business in 1918 to Mr. Goodin. The Star Printing Company is equipped to handle book, poster, and job-printing.

In his political preferences Mr. Goodin is a staunch supporter of the Democratic party. He is fraternally affiliated with the Old Town Lodge, Benevolent and Protective Order of Elks; the Knights of Columbus; and the Catholic Foresters of America.

J. Edward Goodin married, in 1918, Elizabeth O'Brien, who was born in Houlton, Maine. Mr. and Mrs. Goodin are the parents of two daughters; Barbara M., and Gertrude P. Mr. Goodin and his family attend St. Joseph's Roman Catholic Church.

HARRY W. CHAPMAN—As president of the old and well-known firm of T. M. Chapman & Sons Company, Harry W. Chapman has for many years been associated with one of the most interesting industries in Old Town, Maine. Born on October 24, 1879, in Old Town, Mr. Chapman is a son of Thomas M. and Mandana (Wallace) Chapman, both of whom are now deceased. Thomas M. Chapman, who was born in Newburgh, Maine, was the founder and head of T. M. Chapman Company, until his death in 1888. Mandana (Wallace) Chapman, was a native of Old Town.

Harry W. Chapman received his education in the

public and high schools of Old Town, later taking some courses of study from the Milwaukee Correspondence School. When his education was completed, in 1882, he became associated with the T. M. Chapman Company. His first work was learning the trade of machinist. He continued in the various phases of the business, and filling different positions, until the firm was incorporated in 1900, when he was made treasurer of the company. He held this office until the death of his brother in 1907 when he became president of the company.

The history of the T. M. Chapman & Sons Company is essentially the history of the Chapman family. Founded in 1851 by Thomas M. Chapman, the company employed only three men, and was engaged in the manufacture of a machine for filing. The business was located on Main Street, occupying one floor, and all the work was done by foot power. Gradually other wood-working machinery was added to the output. They have carried on this line of work since that time. In 1882 Thomas M. Chapman took his son, Fred M. Chapman, into the business as a partner, and the firm name was changed to T. M. Chapman & Son. Thomas M. Chapman died in 1888, and his son, Fred M. Chapman, carried on the business. In 1900, it was incorporated under the name of T. M. Chapman & Sons Company. The officers then were: Fred M. Chapman, president; Harry W. Chapman, treasurer; and Ralph W. Chapman, secretary. Upon the death of Fred M. Chapman, in 1907, Harry W. Chapman became president and Ralph W. Chapman was made treasurer. In 1924, F. Kenneth Chapman was made a member of the firm, holding the office of production engineer. At the present time the company is working on a machine for the manufacture of paper plates. They now employ some sixty men and are engaged, as well, in general machine repair and foundry work for other companies.

The younger brother, Ralph W. Chapman, was born May 28, 1872, in Old Town, Maine. He received his education in the public and high schools of Old Town, later studying under a private tutor. Upon the completion of his studies, in 1890, he also became associated with the T. M. Chapman & Sons Company, learning the trade of machinist and draftsman. At the time of the incorporation of the business, in 1900, he became secretary, and later, in 1907, he became treasurer. In 1917 the firm began the manufacture of electrical equipment, particularly of the type used by physicians, the Morse Wave Generator, used in therapy, the Auditor, which is used for the deaf, and the G-X-Galvanic-Faradic Plate. Ralph W. Chapman is the inventor of many of the various machines now manufactured by the company. A member of the Republican party, he served for five terms as city electrician for Old Town. He is fraternally affiliated with the Royal Arcanum. Ralph W. Chapman married, in 1901, Nellie C. Dorr, who was born in Brewer, Maine.

Harry W. Chapman married, in 1924, Sadie Fitzgerald, who was born in Dexter, Maine. Mr. and Mrs. Chapman are the parents of one daughter, Geraldine F. Mr. Chapman and his family attend the Universalist church.

ORMAN B. FERNANDEZ—When the ultimate history of the State of Maine, its leading communities and men who have been of greatest and most last-

ing significance in the progress of these communities is written, the name of Orman B. Fernandez will appear in its connection with Old Town. Of the theatrical and advertising firm of McPhee & Fernandez, his interests, commercially and artistically, are extensive, comprising ventures in centers other than Old Town. But it is in Old Town that he makes his residence; here are his chief offices, and here he has unwound the major portion of the thread of his career. His position is that of a dominant, conscientious figure, whose ends have been the worthiest possible, whose methods have been unfailingly honorable in accord with his character, and for whom the respect of his associates has come about naturally.

Born in Dover-Foxcroft, November 24, 1870, Mr. Fernandez is a son of Fernando and Franca C. (Gilman) Fernandez. Fernando Fernandez was a native of Northern Spain, and he gave his active years to employment as farmer and mechanic. Franca (Gilman) Fernandez was a native of Maine, born in Sangerville, the youngest of a family of eleven children. Five of her brothers saw active service under Union colors in the Civil War. Both Fernando and Franca C. (Gilman) Fernandez are dead.

As his father maintained a farm until the time of his demise, Orman B. Fernandez was reared upon the soil, and took from it the simplicity, honesty and directness that have molded his life through manhood. Upon completion of his academic training in the public schools of Sangerville and Dexter, he served a three years' apprenticeship at the printer's trade under the firm of Day & Bunker, of the Dexter "Gazette." During this period also he acquired a knowledge of poster advertising, which was to stand him in good stead. For a number of years he worked "at the cases" in several Maine towns as practical compositor and printer, and in 1897, at the age of twenty-six years, founded the Star Printing Company, of Old Town. This he conducted until 1915, when he disposed of it and joined with William E. McPhee in amusement enterprises. As early as 1913 he had taken a personal interest in the theater, and had promoted several out-of-door attractions, successfully; so that he did not enter into the new partnership of McPhee & Fernandez without practical knowledge of this aspect of the firm's undertakings. The firm acquired and operated the Strand and New Central theatres, both of Old Town, the Lincoln Theater, of Lincoln, and bought holdings in theaters of Bangor as well. Hand in hand with the theatrical venture, the firm expanded in the enterprise of poster advertising. This too has taken on extensive proportions, and is today most profitable, largely because of the ability instilled into the combination of endeavors by Mr. Fernandez.

While he has thus been busily engaged in furtherance of his proper work, Mr. Fernandez has been no less active in general affairs. From 1905 until 1907 he was call chief of the Old Town Fire Department; from 1908 until 1913, and again in 1917, he served as city marshal; and from 1919 until 1925 he was sheriff of Penobscot County, three terms. It is perhaps as county sheriff that he is best called to mind in official memory of the town. Never in the history of Penobscot County, it is said, was that important office more ably or dutifully filled and administered than under Mr. Fernandez. A Republican, nominated and elected sheriff on the party's ticket, yet, it is noted, he had the support of hundreds of voters outside the party. He has been chairman of the Republican city and county committees. During the World War he was attached to the office of the adjutant-general of the State of Maine, as a special investigator. Fraternally, Mr. Fernandez is affiliated with the Free and Accepted Masons, in which order he is a member of all bodies; with the Benevolent and Protective Order of Elks, in which he is a member of Old Town Lodge; the Knights of Pythias, and the Modern Woodmen. He is a member of the Masonic Club of Old Town, the Masonic Club of Bangor, the Penobscot Valley Country Club, and the Old Town Firemen's Relief Association. In religious adherence he is a communicant of the Universalist church.

In 1912, Orman B. Fernandez was united in marriage with Ethel A. Mann, of Old Town, and they are the parents of three children: Alice G., Ramon F., and Orman B., Jr.

Citizens of Old Town pay the tribute of friendship, well founded and sincere, to Mr. Fernandez. His ability, individuality, and knowledge of the duty which he owes to humanity, together with his steadfast effort to fulfill this obligation in the fullest measure of conscience—these have made him of inestimable value to community, State and Nation.

FOSTER CHARLES SMALL, M. D., physician and surgeon and at present mayor of Belfast, Maine, and coroner of Waldo County is a leader in his profession in Waldo County and a prominent factor in the business and social life of his community. He has been extremely successful since beginning a general practice in Belfast fifteen years ago, and is now considered one of the most competent physicians in the State. He is a well-known member of the staff of Waldo County General Hospital.

Dr. Small was born in Swanville, Maine, December 4, 1885, the son of Charles Edwin and Hattie E. (Morin) Small. His mother was a native of Prospect, Maine, and his father, a painter, was born in Belfast, Maine. Dr. Small was educated in the public schools of Swanville, Maine, and later went to the high schools in Searsport and Brooks, Maine. His interest in medicine began about the time of his graduation from high school and he determined to make it his life-work. With this career in view, he entered the Medical School of the University of Vermont, from which he was graduated in the class of 1912, with the degree of Doctor of Medicine. The customary training as an interne he had obtained while in medical school, so that he was qualified to begin general practice immediately upon graduation, which he did in Swanville, continuing there for a few months before removing to Belfast, where he has lived ever since.

During the World War, Dr. Small served as a member of the Medical Advisory Board for Waldo County, examining recruits who had been drafted into service. He has been president of the Waldo County Medical Society for two years and is a member of the Maine State Medical Association, the Rotary Club, the Knights of Pythias, the Order of the Eastern Star, various Masonic and other fraternal organizations. Despite the arduous duties of his profession, he has found time to interest himself in Republican politics, to such an extent that he was

elected mayor in 1926 and reëlected in 1927 on the Citizens' ticket; was president of the Belfast Common Council for two years and served a year as alderman, from 1925 to 1926. Ever since he came to Belfast he has been active in the affairs of the Universalist church, which he serves at present as president of the board of trustees.

JOHN THOMAS QUINN—One of the younger members of the legal profession in Bangor, Maine, is John Thomas Quinn, who since 1925 has been engaged in general legal practice here, with offices at No. 16 Broad Street. Mr. Quinn is a graduate of Georgetown Law School, of Washington, District of Columbia, and since 1925 has been coaching in football at the University of Maine, as freshman coach in 1925 and as assistant 'varsity coach since 1926, his contract running until 1929. He is also a member of the City Council of Bangor.

John Thomas Quinn was born in Bangor, Maine, February 20, 1898, son of Michael, a native of Bangor, engaged in the lumber business here, and of Mary (Gaffney) Quinn, native of County Clare, Ireland. He received his early education in the public schools of Bangor, and after completing his course in Bangor High School attended the University of Maine for two years. He then began professional study in the Law School of Georgetown University, in Washington, District of Columbia, where he completed his course with graduation in 1923, receiving at that time the degree of Bachelor of Laws. Continuing study there one year longer, he received, in 1924, the degree of Master of Laws and then returned to Bangor, where he opened an office at No. 16 Broad Street and engaged in general practice. He has been admitted to all the courts of the State and to the Federal courts. During his college days Mr. Quinn was greatly interested in football, and since coming to Bangor as a professional man, he has retained his interest in that sport and has continuously been engaged as a coach, first, in 1924, as coach of the Brewer High School, at Brewer, Maine, and in 1925 as coach of the freshman team in the University of Maine. In 1926 he signed a contract for three years as assistant coach of the 'varsity team of the University of Maine. He is a member of the Penobscot County Bar Association. During the period of the participation of the United States in the World War he served in the Officers' Training School at Fortress Monroe, Virginia, where he was stationed for two months. In his political faith he is a Republican, and he is one of the actively interested and public-spirited citizens of Bangor. In 1926-27 he was serving as a member of the City Council, and he is one of the generous supporters of every progressive movement for the advancement of the interests of the city of Bangor. Fraternally, he is identified with Phi Kappa Epsilon; with Delta Nu Chapter of Sigma Nu Fraternity; Iota Chapter of Gamma Eta Gamma Fraternity; and with Pio Nono Council, No. 114, of the Knights of Columbus. He is also a member of the American Legion, of which he is acting Judge-Advocate; and he is a member of the Bangor Chamber of Commerce. He is fond of all out-of-door sports, and especially interested in motoring and fishing, and his religious affiliation is with St. John's Roman Catholic Church.

John Thomas Quinn was married, in 1924, to Ethel Marie Bielaski, who was born in Washington, District of Columbia, and they are the parents of one son, John T., Jr.

JUDGE EDWARD I. GLESZER—One of the very well-known men of the legal profession in Bangor is Judge Edward I. Gleszer, who opened an office for general practice here in 1914, and who is now Judge of the Municipal Court of Bangor, appointed in 1926 for a term of four years. Judge Gleszer is very active in local public and civic affairs and keeps in close touch with all the service clubs and organizations of the city. He is an effective speaker, and has kept the city thoroughly well informed concerning the work of the municipal court.

Edward I. Gleszer was born in Hartford, Connecticut, September 17, 1892, son of Samuel Gleszer, a native of Poland, engaged in the real estate business in Hartford, and of Rebecca (Taiz) Gleszer, native of Poland, who died in 1921. He received his early education in the public schools of Hartford, and then attended Trinity College for one year. He had determined to enter the legal profession, and after one year in Trinity College began the study of law in the Law School of New York University, in New York City. A year later, however, he made a change and completed his course in the Law School of the University of Maine, from which he was graduated with the class of 1914, receiving at that time the degree of Bachelor of Laws. He was admitted to the bar that same year and at once opened an office in Bangor, where he has since been engaged in general practice. In 1926 he was appointed by Governor Brewster, as Judge of the Municipal Court, for a four-year term, and to the duties of this office he is giving more than the usual amount of time and attention. He is the first judge of this court who has brought before the citizens of Bangor the need of keeping in touch with their municipal court and knowing not only its legitimate functions but the general character of its work in this city, and following one of the objectives of the Federation of Women's Clubs, he has made speeches along this line, speaking to every service club in the city of Bangor, and to many other service organizations in this and other States. The Bangor Municipal Court takes care of cases coming under civil jurisdiction involving a value of three hundred dollars or less, and of criminal cases concurrent to the jurisdiction of the Supreme Court, except in cases of felony, and Judge Gleszer has met the responsibilities of his judicial office with great wisdom and discretion. He is a member of the Penobscot County Bar Association, and of the American Bar Association, and politically, he gives his support to the Republican party. He takes an active part in local public affairs and has served as a member of the board of registration, from 1922 to 1926 was recorder of the Municipal Court, and has served as delegate to various Republican conventions. Fraternally, he is identified with Bangor Lodge, No. 244, Benevolent and Protective Order of Elks; and with Phi Delta Phi College Fraternity, Reed Chapter. He is a member of the Kiwanis Club, the Bangor Welfare Society, and the Bangor Humane Society. During the World War he was a member of the Legal Advisory Board of Penobscot County, and he has, since his residence here, been an active supporter of all well-planned community enterprises. He finds

his chief recreation in motoring with his family, and his religious affiliation is with the Hebrew Temple. Edward I. Gleszer was married, in 1914, to Ada M. Cohen, who was born in Bangor, Maine, and they are the parents of one son, Roland M.

IRVING W. SMALL—The position of Superintendent of Schools in any city of size in the United States presupposes a considerable amount of learning and ability, as well as tact and patience, where boards of education try to keep a middle-of-the-road course in the matter of what subjects teachers shall teach, and just how far. The trials and joys of the leader of a school system are well known to Irving W. Small, Superintendent of Schools at Bangor, whose career has been ripened with an experience covering twenty years, in which he has had ample opportunity to study methods, pupils and men. Mr. Small is regarded as an exceptionally able teacher and executive, and his stay in several communities has been very fortunate for the crusade of learning, when conservative spirits have put their feet down upon anything new in teaching. Mr. Small's father, John A. Small, was born at New Castle, Maine, and engaged in lumbering until his death. His mother, Sophia A. (Farnsworth) Small, now deceased, was a native of Beddington, Maine. He is a direct descendant of Hannah Weston, of Jonesboro, Maine, who in turn was a descendant of Hannah Dustin. Irving W. Small was born April 2, 1879, at South Beddington, Maine. He attended the Beddington public schools, Bridgton Academy of North Bridgton; Bryant & Stratton's Business College at Boston, and the State Normal School at Farmington, Maine, from which institution he graduated in the class of 1906. Not satisfied with these liberal advantages, he attended for three summers the University of Maine Summer School; Columbia University Teachers' College at New York City, one summer; and finally one extension course at the University of Maine. On completing these extensive courses he taught school in North Waterford, Maine, for one term, then one term at Beddington. He then served one year as principal of the Boothbay Centre High School. Then he accepted a position with the Mitchell Military Boys' School at Billerica, Massachusetts, where he taught for two and one-half years. After this he was made supervisor of grade schools and teacher in the high school at Bar Harbor, Maine. This place proved most congenial and he welcomed it as a happy home. He had so well prepared himself for this post that the duties of it fell naturally into place and he discharged them with a becoming ease and grace. For fourteen and a half years he toiled with his pupils giving some of the best years of his life and, happily, getting results that were beyond his expectations. At the end of this long period of service he accepted, in 1924, the position of general supervisor of grade schools, in Bangor, Maine. This position he filled creditably until 1927, when he was advanced to the position of Superintendent of Schools of this city.

To revert a moment to ancestry, the name Small is associated with some of the most noteworthy accomplishments in American history. Although the members of it have not been as prolific as some families, what it has lacked in quantity has been made up in quality, and we find the Smalls writing their names high and large wherever they are located. To mention only a few of the members and also a very limited number of avocations, the name occurs prominently in the works of the Small, Maynard & Company, Boston publishers, while in the South it is borne by the Rev. Samuel W. Small, Baptist preacher, orator and historian, while his son, Sam W. Small, Jr., is a much-quoted news correspondent at Washington, District of Columbia, as well as expert political commentator.

Outside of his professional duties Mr. Small finds time to engage in various activities. He is a leading and valued member of Island Lodge, No. 120, Independent Order of Odd Fellows of Bar Harbor. He belongs to the Maine State Teachers' Association, of which he was chairman of the kindergarten and primary section; the Penobscot County Teachers' Association; the National Education Association, of Washington, which has been such a power in the passing of enabling legislation, and is now strenuously engaged in the fight for a Department of Education headed by a member of the President's Cabinet; and the International Kindergarten Union. Although Mr. Small is not active in politics, he is strongly committed to the tenets and principles of the Republican party, and makes a study of political problems as they affect the life of the people of the United States. He is quite an outdoor person and his hobbies are fishing, hunting and camping, whenever he can find the time to go. He is a member and attendant of the Methodist Episcopal church.

Irving W. Small married, in 1911, Geneva May Turner, native of Millbridge, Maine, and representative of an old-established family. Their union has been blessed with four children: Donald I., Gerald T., Harland F., and Lawrence F.

WARREN E. CRAIG—After twenty-five years of teaching and some twelve years of successful experience as a real estate and insurance man, Warren E. Craig became Register of Deeds for Penobscot County, which official position he has filled since 1919, a period of eight years. Mr. Craig was Superintendent of Schools in Dixmont, Maine, for six years.

Warren E. Craig was born in Dixmont, Maine, October 8, 1869, son of Luke B., a native of Dixmont, who was engaged as a farmer there to the time of his death, and of Hannah A. (Reed) Craig, also a native of Dixmont, and also deceased. He received his education in the public schools of his birthplace and in Hampden Academy, and then became a teacher in the Dixmont public schools. After a few years of experience in his native town, he left Dixmont and taught in other places in Maine, continuing in the teaching profession until he had completed fifty-three terms in all. At the end of that time he gave up teaching and engaged in the real estate and insurance business for himself in Bangor, Maine. In this enterprise, he was successful, and he continued as a realtor and as an insurance man until 1919, when he accepted the position of Register of Deeds for Penobscot County, which official position he is still (1928) efficiently filling. He is the tenth incumbent of this office, and is giving entire satisfaction to those whom he serves. Politically, Mr. Craig gives his support to the principles and the candidates of the Republican party, and he has always taken an active interest in local public affairs. He served as a member of the Board of Selectmen of Dixmont, Maine, for five years, and was Superin-

tendent of Schools there for six years. Fraternally, he is identified with Archon Lodge, Free and Accepted Masons; with the Knights of Pythias; and with North Star Grange, No. 47, Patrons of Husbandry. He is one of the highly esteemed citizens of Bangor, and one of the very efficient members of the official personnel of the capital city. His religious interest and that of his family is with the Universalist church, of which they are attendants. Mr. Craig is a very well-read man, and finds his favorite recreation in his reading, which covers a wide range of subjects.

Warren E. Craig was married, May 12, 1909, to Hattie W. Humphrey, who was born in Bangor, Maine, and they are the parents of two daughters: Ruth H., and Marjorie R.

J. FRED SHEEHAN—To make a satisfactory sheriff or deputy sheriff in these days of accelerated transportation and multiplicity and complexity of laws, taken with rapidly changing public sentiment, requires a combination of human virtues and attributes. Such a combination is possessed by J. Fred Sheehan, deputy at Bangor, who not only performs his duties to the satisfaction of the administration and equitable considerations but preserves his popularity in the neighborhood as well.

J. Fred Sheehan was born at Bangor, February 21, 1875, and his success thus becomes a matter of considerable local pride. His father, Jeremiah Sheehan, also a native of Bangor, engaged in the trade of stone mason until his death, and thus carved out of the materials of nature many enduring structures which stand as his monuments today. His mother, Louise (Russell) Sheehan, a woman of strong attributes of character, and a native of New Hampshire, is still living to enjoy the fruits of her son's gratifying success.

Mr. Sheehan received his education in the grammar and high schools of Bangor, on the completion of which he obtained a position in a sash and door factory at Bangor, in 1897, with which concern he worked hard and efficiently, part of the time continuing his studies, for fifteen years. In 1912, Sheriff J. Fred O'Connell, sheriff of Penobscot County, appointed Mr. Sheehan deputy, and he served until 1914, when he accepted a position with the Priest Drug Company in this city and was assigned to duty as a traveling salesman, which position he filled capably until 1919, when he was appointed to his old post as deputy, by Sheriff Arthur Thayer. Sheriff Thayer's term expired in six months, and Mr. Sheehan returned to Priest's Drug Store as salesman, where he remained until 1921, when Sheriff Orman B. Fernandez (q. v.) appointed him to his old job as deputy. He has filled this office acceptably ever since, having been reappointed by Sheriff John Farrar in 1925.

Mr. Sheehan is a member of the United Commercial Travelers' Association. In political affairs he is a supporter of the principles of the Republican party, and in a quiet way makes his influence felt in the various elections. He is a member and attendant of the St. John's Roman Catholic Church. His hobbies are hunting and fishing, when he can find the time from his official duties.

JAMES D. MAXWELL—Engaging in the general practice of law at Bangor, as senior partner in the firm of Maxwell and Conquest, James D. Maxwell is prominent throughout the State as an attorney of well-proven abilities and established qualifications in his profession, an honored member of the Maine bar. He is interested in every phase of civic progress and of good government, and is popular in both his professional and social life. He is a son of Charles T. Maxwell, who was born in Amsterdam, New York, and is a manufacturer of woolen goods in Philadelphia, Pennsylvania, and Elizabeth (Peck) Maxwell, also a native of Amsterdam.

James D. Maxwell was born March 30, 1883, in Amsterdam, New York, and after attending the public and high schools in Bangor, he was graduated at Tufts College, Somerville, Massachusetts, in 1903, with the degree of Bachelor of Science. Mr. Maxwell then took the course in the Law School of the University of Maine, and was graduated there in 1908 with the degree of Bachelor of Laws, meantime reading law in the office of State Judge Charles A. Bailey, of Bangor, for two years. From 1908 to 1914, Mr. Maxwell was in the practice of his profession at Island Falls, in Aroostook County, and coming to Bangor he continued to practice in his own name until 1921, when he became associated with Edward J. Conquest, and formed the present partnership of Maxwell and Conquest, with offices at No. 16 Postoffice Square. He is a member of the Penobscot County Bar Association, and the Maine State Bar Association.

Politically, Mr. Maxwell's views are those of the Republican party; and from 1916 to 1920, he held the office of Recorder of the Bangor Municipal Court. During the World War, he was active in all the drives of the time, and he also served as a member of the Legal Advisory Board of Penobscot County. Fraternally, Mr. Maxwell is affiliated with Island Falls Lodge, Free and Accepted Masons; the Royal Arch Masons; Knights of Pythias; and Zeta Psi Fraternity. He attends All Souls' Congregational Church, and his hobby being music, he is a member of the Bangor Symphony Orchestra, and is a well-known violoncello player.

James D. Maxwell married, in 1908, Clara G. Grout, who was born in the Province of New Brunswick, Canada, and they have children: Elizabeth, and Margaret.

WALTER B. REED—Since 1891, Walter B. Reed has been business manager of the Bangor "Daily News." Mr. Reed is a graduate of Eastman Business College of Poughkeepsie, New York, and is known as one of the able business men of the city of Bangor. The publishing offices are located at No. 170 Exchange Street, in Bangor. Mr. Reed is active in local public affairs and is also a director of the Bangor Publishing Company.

Walter B. Reed was born in New York City, April 4, 1867, son of Captain Joseph B. Reed, who was born in Bucksport, Maine, in 1831, and who followed the sea, engaged in foreign trade, until 1884, when he was lost at sea after thirty-nine years, and of Maria A. (Bartlett) Reed, who was born in Orrington, Maine, is now deceased. He attended the public schools of Orrington, and then continued study in Hampden Academy, after which he completed his training in Eastman Business College at Poughkeepsie, New York. Upon the completion of his commercial training he entered the employ of the H. W. Smith Lum-

ber Company of Bangor, Maine, and there he remained for four years, from 1887 to 1891. In the last-named year he became associated with the Bangor "Daily News" as business manager, and during the thirty-six years which have passed since that time he has continued in that position. He is a member of the board of directors of the Bangor Publishing Company, and is known in the city as an expert in his own particular field. Politically, Mr. Reed supports the principles of the Republican party, and he has served for one term in the Bangor City Council. He is a member of St. Andrew's Lodge, No. 83, Free and Accepted Masons; member of Maine Consistory, Ancient Accepted Scottish Rite; and Anah Temple, Ancient Arabic Order Nobles of the Mystic Shrine; also a member of the Bangor Masonic Club. He finds recreation and pleasant companionship through membership in the Conduskeag Canoe Club and his religious affiliation is with All Souls' Congregational Church, which he serves as a member of the board of trustees.

Walter B. Reed was married, in 1893, to Josephine B. Gage, who was born in Addison, Maine, and they are the parents of two children: 1. Gladys G. 2. Helen P.

WALLACE N. PRICE, M. D.—The splendid professional service which Dr. Wallace N. Price has been rendering in Gardiner, Maine, since 1921, is based upon careful preparation and upon an experience of twenty-seven years in Richmond, Maine, before coming to Gardiner. Dr. Price is engaged in general practice of medicine and surgery and is taking care of the needs of a large number of patients. He is also mayor of Gardiner.

Wallace N. Price was born in Calais, Maine, October 29, 1871, son of Charles W. Price, a native of Boston, Massachusetts, born August 28, 1844, died April 25, 1913, a veteran of the Civil War who served in both the Army and the Navy, and while serving with the Seventh Regiment Infantry of Maine, was wounded in action, and of Albina (Colbath) Price, who was born May 1, 1844. He received his early and preparatory education in the public schools of Richmond, Maine, and after the completion of his course in Richmond High School began professional study in the Medical School of Maine, from which he was graduated with the class of 1894, receiving at that time the degree of Doctor of Medicine. Upon the completion of his professional training he opened an office and engaged in general medical and surgical practice in Richmond, Maine. There he built up a practice which steadily grew and to which he gave the devoted and skilful service which won the commendation and genuine gratitude of many of his patients. For twenty-seven years, 1894 to 1921, Dr. Price continued to minister to the needs of his large practice in Richmond. At the end of that time he came to Gardiner, where since 1921 he has been successfully engaged in general and surgical practice In addition to the responsibilities of his profession Dr. Price is a member of the board of directors of the Gardiner Trust Company, and he takes an active interest in local public affairs. He gives his support to the principles and the candidates of the Democratic party, and in 1926 was elected mayor of Gardiner, to serve for the term of 1926-27. In 1913 he was elected to represent his district in the State House of Representatives, and in 1915 he was elected to serve in the State Senate. During the World War he served as a member of the Twentieth District Medical Advisory Board. He is a member of the Gardiner Board of Trade, and vice-president of the Rotary Club, and fraternally, he is identified with the Masonic Order, in which he holds the thirty-second degree. He has been Past Master of Richmond Lodge for five years, is Past Grand High Priest of the Grand Chapter, Royal Arch Masons and Past Commander of the Knights Templar, of Bath, Maine. He is also a Past Chancellor of the Knights of Pythias; and a member of the Benevolent and Protective Order of Elks, of Gardiner. Professionally he is identified with the Kennebec County Medical Association, the Maine Medical Society, and the American Medical Association. Dr. Price has a host of friends, both in Richmond and vicinity and in Gardiner, and is known as a public-spirited citizen of the community.

Dr. Wallace N. Price was married, in East Pittston, Maine, September 20, 1893, to Mary B. Moores, who was born in Concord, New Hampshire, March 28, 1872, daughter of ——— G. and Nellie (Danforth) Moores.

ARTEMUS WEATHERBEE—One of the prominent attorneys of Penobscot County, Maine, is Artemus Weatherbee, of the firm of Butterfield and Weatherbee, whose offices are located at No. 31 Central Street in Bangor, and at Lincoln. Mr. Weatherbee has been engaged in legal practice for nearly thirty years, and is known as one of the able and resourceful attorneys of Penobscot County.

Artemus Weatherbee was born in Lincoln, Maine, November 26, 1869, son of Albert W., a native of Springfield, Maine, who was engaged in legal practice to the time of his death in 1903, and of Lucinda E. (Butterfield) Weatherbee, who was born in Springfield, Maine, and died in 1902. Mr. Weatherbee received his early education in the public schools of Lincoln, and then continued study in Mattanawcook Academy. He had early determined to enter the legal profession, and upon the completion of his academic course he began reading law in the office of his father, Albert W. Weatherbee, in Lincoln. He was admitted to the bar in 1898, and since that time has been successfully engaged in general legal practice in Lincoln. In 1926 he became associated with Wilfred I. Butterfield under the name of Butterfield and Weatherbee, and at the present time (1927) the firm is taking care of a large and important clientele. Mr. Weatherbee is a member of the Penobscot Bar Association, and is known in this locality as a man of sound legal knowledge and of marked ability.

Politically, Mr. Weatherbee supports the principles of the Republican party, and he takes an active part in its affairs. He has served for four years as District Attorney for Penobscot County and has served in the State Legislature for eight years, from 1901 to 1903, and in 1905 and 1919. In 1903 he was a member of the committee appointed to revise the State statutes, and during all of his long term in the State Legislature he served with credit to himself and satisfaction to his constituents. Locally, he has served as a member of the Board of Selectmen for two years, and as Superintendent of the Schools of Lincoln for a period of seventeen years. Along with his private legal practice and his public responsibilities Mr. Weatherbee has also found time for financial responsibilities. He is president of the Lincoln Trust Company and a member of the board of trustees of the Bangor Savings Bank. Fraternally, Mr. Weatherbee is identified with Horeb Lodge, Free and Accepted Masons; Fellowship Lodge, Independent Order of Odd Fellows; and with the Ancient Order of United Workmen, in which organization he has served as Grand Master of the Grand Lodge for two terms. During the period of the participation of the United States in the World War he served as a member of the Legal Advisory Board of Penobscot County. Mr. Weatherbee finds relief from the cares of his professional activities in fishing. His religious affiliation is with the Congregational church.

Artemus Weatherbee was married (first), in 1890, to Mary J. Matthews, who was born in New Brunswick, Canada, and died in 1902. He married (second), in 1905, Helen L. Adams, who was born in Lincoln, Maine. To the first marriage four children were born: 1. Ruth L. 2. Alexander M. 3. Albert A., who served in France with the American Expeditionary Forces during the World War, and was gassed twice. 4. Mary E. To the second marriage one son has been born, Randolph A.

ALBERT H. SARGENT—His present successful and efficient management of the business of the Bangor Gas Light Company is a result of Albert H. Sargent's continuous experience throughout his career along the same and similar lines both in this State and in Massachusetts, the excellent standard of the Bangor Company having been attained through Mr. Sargent's expert attention to its local and its present-day requirements. Mr. Sargent is a son of George A. Sargent, who was born in Haverhill, Massachusetts, and was a shoe manufacturer until his death, which occurred in 1900, and Abbie (Ayer) Sargent, also a native of Haverhill, who died in 1882.

Albert H. Sargent was born April 30, 1873, at Haverhill, Massachusetts, where he was a student in the public and high schools. In 1894, he started to learn the business that has become his life-work, at first as a meter-reader for the Haverhill Gas Light Company, and when he relinquished his duties with that company in 1908, it was as assistant treasurer. For a time, Mr. Sargent engaged in business on his own account, and up to 1918, he was proprietor of a general store at Atkinson, Maine. He removed to Bangor, that year, where he was given the position of chief clerk of the Bangor Gas Light Company; and in 1926 he was appointed to his present office, that of manager of the company.

Mr. Sargent is a Republican in the political field, and he served for two terms as a member of the New England Gas Association, and the American Gas Association; and he is a member of the Tarratine Club, Penobscot Valley Country Club, Kiwanis Club, and Bangor Chamber of Commerce; and his hobbies are fishing and hunting. His religious faith is that of the Congregational church.

Albert H. Sargent married, in February, 1896, Emily Wentworth, who was born in Orrington, Maine.

EUGENE TREAT SAVAGE, treasurer of the T. R. Savage Company, wholesale grocers of Bangor, has attained his important position through the aid of a good education and the application during nearly thirty years of those units of economic production which political economists hold are necessary to success in any line. He has followed the business to the point where it enjoys the reputation of being the largest of its kind in Bangor; he won the rank of lieutenant-colonel of the United States Army overseas in the World War and in other ways has shown a versatility that makes him a highly useful citizen in this community.

Mr. Savage was born in Bangor, April 14, 1879, son of Thomas R. Savage, a prominent and useful man in his day. He was educated in the local public schools, the Hotchkiss Preparatory School at Lakeville, Connecticut, and Yale University, New Haven, which institution he finished in the class of 1900. On completing his education he accepted a position with the T. R. Savage Company, which had been established some years before by his father. In 1902, when the business was incorporated, he was made secretary and a director in recognition of his hard work, and in 1915 he was elected treasurer, a post he has held with conspicuous ability ever since.

In addition to this activity Mr. Savage has found time for others. He is a director, vice-president and a member of the executve board of the Merrill Trust Company of Bangor; and a director of the Union Iron Works, and the Maine & Real Estate Title Company. He is a Maine member of the New England Council; on the executive board of the New England Shippers' Advisory Board; and vice-president of the Maine Traffic Association.

In political affairs Mr. Savage is a member of the Republican party, in whose contests he has offered several times for office and very successfully. He served two years in the Bangor City Council, the last year of which his colleagues elected him president, and he then served a year on the Board of Aldermen. He entered the United States Army in 1917, for World War service, and in January, 1918, was commissioned major in the Ordnance Corps, and became camp ordnance officer at Camp Hancock, Georgia. Later he was advanced to the post of chief ordnance officer of the Machine Gun Training Center at the same place, after which he went to France as division ordnance officer of the Second Division, which distinguished itself in some of the fiercest fighting of the war. In June, 1919, he was discharged with the rank of lieutenant-colonel, United States Army. He is an active member of the American Legion, and a commander in the Bangor Post of the Military Order of the World War. The fraternal orders in which Mr. Savage holds membership include the following: St. Andrew's Lodge, Free and Accepted Masons; all bodies, York and Scottish Rites, including Anah Temple, Ancient Arabic Order Nobles of the Mystic Shrine. He attends the Congregational church. His clubs include the Delta Psi Fraternity; University of Washington, District of Columbia; Yale of Boston; Belmont Spring Country; Tarratine, in which he is a director; Penobscot Valley Country, in which he is one of the board of governors; Conduskeag Canoe and Country; and the Northport Country. He has been vice-president of the Chamber of Commerce; a director of the Maine State Chamber of Commerce; president for three years of the New England Wholesale Grocers' Association; and a director of the National Wholesale Grocers' Association. His hobby is golf.

Eugene Treat Savage married, in 1901, Anne Curtis Boutelle, of Bangor, and their union has been blessed with three children: Suzanne B., Boutelle and Patricia.

ROBERT B. DUNNING—Throughout his business career, Robert B. Dunning has had a vital interest in the increasing activities of the firm of R. B. Dunning Company, and as a member of that firm and clerk of its corporation, he is a decided factor in its advancement among the foremost of the business concerns in Bangor. A veteran of the World War, Mr. Dunning holds a high place in the esteem of his associates and his fellow-citizens. He is a son of George W. Dunning, who was president of the R. B. Dunning Company until his retirement in 1923, and Hattie M. (Dunbar) Dunning, who is now deceased, both parents natives of Bangor.

Robert B. Dunning was born October 1, 1895, in Bangor, where he attended the public and high schools. He took the academic course in the University of Maine, then became associated with the R. B. Dunning Company as a salesman. In 1923, he was made a member of the firm, and he holds the office of clerk of the corporation. Mr. Dunning is a Republican in his political views, and supports the interests of his party, though he has not sought political office. At the call of the World War, Mr. Dunning enlisted in, June, 1917, in the Ambulance Corps, and he was attached to the French Army Ambulance Corps; he served overseas fourteen months, and was discharged in 1919, with the rank of sergeant of the first class. Fraternally, he is affiliated with St. Andrew's Lodge, Free and Accepted Masons, and with the Ancient Accepted Scottish Rite, as well as with Anah Temple, Ancient Arabic Order Nobles of the Mystic Shrine. He is also a member of Phi Gamma Delta Fraternity, and the Tarratine Club; and his hobbies are tennis and boating. His religious faith is that of the Universalist church.

Robert B. Dunning married, in 1926, Frances Kilgoure, who was born in Millbridge.

RALPH S. CROWELL—The honor of the presidency of one of the oldest and most successful of hardware firm in the United States, that of the Rice and Miller Company, at Bangor, belongs to Ralph S. Crowell, whose executive direction of the firm's affairs throughout the more recent and important years of its history, has been signalized with numerous features of progress and expansion. Mr. Crowell is a son of Fred Crowell, who was born in Dexter, and was associated with wholesale produce interests, and Annie (Savage) Crowell, a native of Corinth, and who survives her husband.

Ralph S. Crowell was born September 2, 1887, at Bangor, and after attending the public and high schools here, was graduated from Bowdoin College in the class of 1910, with the degree of Bachelor of Arts. He then entered upon the activities of salesmanship, and was employed in banking concerns, and with the Eastern Steamship Company. In 1913, Mr. Crowell first became associated with the Rice and Miller Company, and he is now the president of this concern that has a remarkable history in the business world. An excerpt from its long and valued record is as follows: About the year 1817, Lewis and Levi Cram started their business of hardware in the locality that was the nucleus of the present Rice and Miller establishment, then an old wooden block, where the owners dealt in drugs and medicines, as well as hardware. The old block was replaced in 1836 by a brick building; and with the retirement of Lewis Cram, his brother Levi continued, with Benjamin Plummer as a partner. With the disposal of Levi's interests to David Mosman the firm name became Plummer and Mosman, until John Wooderson, a clerk in the store, bought out Mr. Plummer, when the title became David Mosman & Company. Again, in 1851, John Winn purchased the Mosman interests, and with his son, John A. Winn, and John W. Fiske, as partners, the firm name was Wooderson, Winn & Fiske. Upon the retirement of Winn and Fiske, two years later, Mr. Wooderson continued alone until 1856, when he sold out to Henry A. and James H. Butler, the new firm of Butler & Company continuing until 1860, when Henry Butler retired. The new partnership of Fogg and Bridges was formed in 1861 by Edmund H. Fogg and Humphrey A. Bridges, this firm meeting with the first serious disaster, when on January 1, 1869, they lost heavily in the great $250,000 fire. In 1869, G. Irving Rice became a clerk in the store of which he afterwards became proprietor. The firm 'of Fogg and Bridges were the victims of another fire in 1872, and two years afterwards, Mr. Bridges retired, Mr. Fogg remaining sole proprietor until his death in 1877. The business was then sold to G. Irving Rice and Charles C. Skinner, Rice and Skinner continuing their partnership until 1883, when, with the admission of W. L. Miller, the firm name was changed to Rice, Skinner & Company. In 1885, Mr. Skinner's interests were purchased by his partners, and the firm name became Rice and Miller, so continuing until 1908, when the firm was incorporated as Rice & Miller Company.

The wholesale department of the firm grew so rapidly that in January, 1917, the retail department was discontinued; new quarters were acquired at No. 34 Broad Street for the automotive equipment and radio departments; the sporting goods department was installed on the second floor of the building, No. 30 Broad Street; and for warehouse space the Morse Building, No. 210 Broad Street, and the French Building, Nos. 175-179 Broad Street, were leased, and the Neally Building, No. 104 Broad Street, purchased. It is understood that there are but four other firms in hardware in the United States with a business record that exceeds that of the present Rice & Miller Company. The officers of the company are: Ralph S. Crowell, president; E. E. Patten, treasurer; and Roscoe L. Crockett is manager of the sporting goods department; Louis F. Larsen, of the automotive equipment department; Guy P. Clement, of the radio department.

In political matters, Mr. Crowell is a Republican, and with his vote and influence he supports the principles of that party. He is a member of the Bangor Chamber of Commerce, and of the Penobscot Valley Country Club. His religious faith is that of the Unitarian church.

Ralph S. Crowell married, June 17, 1911, Helen Miller, who was born in Bangor. Their children: Joan Crowell; and William Miller Crowell.

TERENCE B. TOWLE was born at Bangor, Maine, October 26, 1875, where he attended the grammar and high schools of the city of Bangor. Preparing for his practice, he entered Boston University School of Law, in October, 1895, and was graduated from there in June, 1898, receiving from Boston University the degree of Bachelor of Laws.

In August, 1898, in Bangor, county of Penobscot, State of Maine, he was admitted to practice as a member of the bar for the State of Maine. For a few years after his admission to the bar, he was associated in practice with Hon. P. H. Gillin of Bangor, and later opened his own offices at No. 7 Hammond Street, Bangor, where he has continued to practice and is now located.

He has been admitted to the State, Federal, and United States Supreme courts, and is a member of the Penobscot Bar Association, Maine State Bar Association, and American Bar Association.

Mr. Towle was Reporter of Decisions of the Supreme Court of the State of Maine for a term of four years, having been appointed thereto by Hon. Oakley C. Curtis, then Governor of the State of Maine. During the World War he was a member of the Legal Advisory Board. Fraternally, he is affiliated with the local Council of the Knights of Columbus, and is a communicant of St. John's Roman Catholic Church.

Terence B. Towle was married, in 1906, to Frances C. Hinckley, of Blue Hill, Maine.

EDWARD C. TRACY—As manager of one of the largest districts on the books of the Metropolitan Life Insurance Company of |New York City, Edward C. Tracy has his offices at Bangor, Maine, where he has been located since 1920. Mr. Tracy's district includes five counties, and his is the largest life insurance agency in Bangor.

Edward C. Tracy was born in Canton, Maine, June 18, 1880, son of Charles A. Tracy, a native of Norway, Maine, who is engaged in business as a builder and contractor, and of Ida L. (Wittemore) Tracy, a native of Dixfield, Maine, whose death occurred in 1918. The paternal grandfather, Daniel E. Tracy, was born in Durham, Maine, and was a graduate of Bowdoin Medical College. He served as a surgeon during the Civil War, and died as the result of a fever contracted while in service.

Edward C. Tracy attended the public schools of Livermore Falls, Maine, including the high school, and when his school training was completed secured a position as a specialty salesman, in which line he continued from 1898 to 1903. In 1903 he associated himself with the Metropolitan Life Insurance Company as an agent, working for the Providence, Rhode Island, office, and in 1904 he was transferred to Lewiston, Maine, still as an agent. In 1905 he was again transferred, this time to Augusta, then as assistant manager of the Augusta district, which position he filled until 1911. In that year he was made assistant manager of the Portland district, where he remained for a period of seven years. In 1918 he was promoted to the position of manager of the district which had its headquarters at Meriden, Connecticut, and two years later he was again transferred, this time coming to Bangor, Maine, as manager of the largest district, in extent of territory, which the Metropolitan Life Insurance Company carries. The district includes Washington, Waldo, Penobscot, Hancock, and Aroostook counties, all large counties, though some of these are not very thickly populated, and Mr. Tracy is now (1928) completing his eighth year as manager of the district. He is known as a skilled and highly efficient insurance man and as an able manager of the men in his district, and his standing with his company is very high. In his political sympathies Mr. Tracy is a Republican. He is well known in Masonic circles, being a member of Rising Virtue Lodge, Free and Accepted Masons; and of all the bodies of both York and Scottish Rites; and of Anah Temple, Ancient Arabic Order Nobles of the Mystic Shrine, of Bangor; also of the Masonic Club. He is a life-member of the Benevolent and Protective Order of Elks, and is identified with several community organizations, including the Maine Public Health Association, is a councilor of the Boy Scouts of America, a member of the Young Men's Christian Association, of the Bangor Chamber of Commerce, of the Lions Club, and of the Metropolitan $100,000 Club. He is fond of fishing, boating, and hunting, and his religious affiliation is with the Universalist church.

Edward C. Tracy was married, May 5, 1906, to Elsie L. Hill, who was born in Providence, Rhode Island, and they are the parents of three children: Donald E., Lillian E., and Marion L.

JOHN H. DENNIS—With the exception of the two years during which he was deputy sheriff of Oxford County, John H. Dennis has been chief of the police department of Rumford, Maine, since 1916. He has been identified with the department since 1911, and is well qualified for his present position as chief.

John H. Dennis was born in Portland, Maine, December 29, 1871, son of John Dennis, who was born in Ireland, but came to this country and settled in Portland, where he was a longshoreman, and of Margaret Dennis. After attending the public schools of Portland, Maine, Mr. Dennis learned the trade of the mason, which he followed until 1911, when he became identified with the police department of Rumford, Maine, as a patrolman. Five years later, in 1916, he was promoted to the responsible position of chief of the department, and in this capacity he rendered service of a quality which attracted the attention of his associates and won him a more responsible position as deputy sheriff of Oxford County, Maine. Resigning his position as chief of police of the Rumford department, in 1923, he served as deputy sheriff until 1925, when he resumed his position as chief of police of Rumford, which office he has continued to fill to the present time (1928). Mr. Dennis is one of the many citizens who reserve for themselves the right to cast the ballot for the best candidate, regardless of partisanship. He classes himself as an Independent, and votes accordingly. He was a member of Maine National Guard, Company E, five years. Fraternally, he is identified with Rumford Lodge, No. 862, Benevolent and Protective Order of Elks; with the Knights of Columbus; and with the Loyal Order of Moose, and his religious affiliation is with the Roman Catholic church.

John H. Dennis was married, in Rumford, Maine, October 30, 1899, to Margaret Hickey, who was born in Boisetown, New Brunswick, daughter of Robert Hickey. Mr. and Mrs. Dennis have three children, all born in Rumford: 1. Nellie M., now Mrs. Dyer. 2. Sarah P. 3. Weston R.

CHARLES H. REID, Jr.—The professional knowledge and training of Charles H. Reid, Jr., is being freely placed at the service of the city and of the State in which he was born and in which he has spent his life. As a successful attorney he is taking care of a large general practice, with offices at No. 7 Hammond Street. As a public official he has served in several local offices, also as a United States Commissioner, and as a delegate to all the Republican State conventions for the past twenty years. He is now (1928) a member of the Board of Aldermen of the city of Bangor.

Charles Henry Reid, father of Mr. Reid, born in Bangor, was engaged in the hotel and restaurant business for many years. During the Civil War he served with Company B, Twenty-second Maine Regiment, Volunteer Infantry. He was a member of B. H. Beal Post, Grand Army of the Republic. He married Kate M. Hickson, who was born in Bangor, Maine; both are now deceased.

Charles H. Reid, Jr., son of Charles Henry and Kate M. (Hickson) Reid, was born in Bangor, Maine, April 10, 1879, and received his early and preparatory education in the public schools of his birthplace. When his preparatory work was completed he entered the Law School of the University of Maine, where he completed his course with graduation in 1903, receiving at that time the degree of Bachelor of Laws. He at once opened an office for general practice, at No. 7 Hammond Street, in Bangor, where he has since been located. He has been admitted to practice in all the courts of the State, the Federal courts, and the Supreme Court of the United States, at Washington, District of Columbia, and has made for himself an assured place in his profession. He is a member of the Penobscot County Bar Association, and is well known among his professional associates as an able and resourceful attorney whose knowledge of the law is sound and extensive, and whose ability to grasp quickly and clearly the essential facts of a case is one of his professional assets.

In addition to the care of his private practice, Mr. Reid finds time for much public service. He served as Recorder of the Municipal Court of Bangor from 1907 to 1911, has been United States Commissioner for the District of Maine since 1911, and in 1927 was elected a member of the Board of Aldermen of the city of Bangor. For the past twenty years he has served as a delegate to every Republican State convention, and he is an important factor in the affairs of the Republican party in this section of the State. Fraternally, also, he is well known. Twice he has served as Exalted Ruler of Bangor Lodge, Benevolent and Protective Order of Elks. He is a member of Daniel Chaplin Post, No. 5, Sons of Veterans, and has served as Judge Advocate-General for the Division of Maine; and he is a member of the Gamma Eta Gamma Fraternity, of which he is High Chandler Emeritus. During the period of the World War he served as a member of the Legal Advisory Board, and he is actively interested in all that pertains to the welfare of the city of Bangor. Mr. Reid finds relief from the strain of his professional and other

MAINE—A HISTORY 221

activities by active, out-of-door recreation, and is especially fond of the woods and of camping. His religious affiliation is with the Roman Catholic church, being a member of St. Mary's parish, in Bangor.

Charles H. Reid, Jr., was married, January 10, 1910, to Mary C. Gayton, who was born in Bangor, Maine, and who has served as president of the Ladies' Auxiliary to the Sons of Veterans and is a member of the board of directors of the Sons of Veterans for the State of Maine. Mr. and Mrs. Reid have one son, Henry.

FREDERICK B. DODD—In the city of Bangor, Maine, Frederick B. Dodd has been engaged in general legal practice since 1913. His offices are located at No. 49 Hammond Street, and he is one of the well-established members of the legal profession in this city. He is a graduate of the Law School of the University of Maine.

Frederick B. Dodd was born in Cherry Valley, Prince Edward Island, May 22, 1886, son of John A. Dodd, a native of Cherry Valley, Prince Edward Island, who has been engaged as a fisherman for many years, and of Mary E. (Jenkins) Dodd, also a native of Cherry Valley. He attended the public schools of his birthplace, and then, having chosen the legal profession as the field of activity to which he would devote his energies, he became a student in the Law School of the University of Maine, at Orono. In 1913 he successfully passed the examinations for admission to the bar of the State of Maine, and since that time he has been successfully engaged in general practice. He has been admitted to practice in all the courts of the State and in the Federal courts, and he has specialized in commercial law. He is a member of the Penobscot Bar Association, and of the Maine State Bar Association, also of the Commercial Law League of America. During the participation of the United States in the World War Mr. Dodd served for three months in the Officers' Training Camp, at Plattsburg, New York, and he is one of the many public-spirited citizens who prefer to serve their community as a private citizen, rather than in public office. Politically, he gives his support to the principles and candidates of the Republican party. He is a member of Rising Virtue Lodge, Free and Accepted Masons, of Bangor; of all the bodies of the Scottish Rite; and of the Maine Consistory; and he is also a member of the Knights of Pythias. Mr. Dodd is one of the many professional men who delight in the quiet and the relaxation of a fishing trip, and when the cares of his profession press heavily or his energies begin to run low because of long continued and strenuous work, he slips away for a season of rest and for communion with nature. With a rod in his hand, and fisherman's luck to lure him to adventure, his mind lays down its load and regains its buoyancy and its elasticity, as his invigorated body recuperates and becomes ready again to give its support and its aid to the work in hand. In his religious affiliation Mr. Dodd is an Episcopalian.

Frederick B. Dodd was married, in 1922, to Eva H. Hillman, who was born in Bangor, Maine, and they are the parents of two sons: Herbert Day, and Thomas A.

GERARD P. COLLINS—One of the younger men of the legal profession in Bangor, Maine, is Gerard P. Collins, who, though he is one of the Georgetown Law School, class of 1924, has already firmly established himself in general practice in Bangor, and who is also serving as city solicitor, in which capacity he is at the present time (1928) serving his second term.

Gerard P. Collins was born in Bangor, Maine, May 27, 1902, son of Dr. Michael J. Collins, a native of Bangor who was engaged as a dentist there to the time of his death in 1919, and of Elizabeth M. (Gillis) Collins, also a native of Bangor, who survives her husband. He received his early and preparatory education in the public schools of his birthplace, and then, having decided to enter the legal profession, began professional study in the law school of Georgetown, from which he was graduated with the class of 1924, receiving at that time the degree of Bachelor of Laws. After graduation he returned to Bangor and opened an office at No. 16 Broad Street, where he has since been successfully engaged in practice. In 1926, two years after engaging in practice here, he was elected city solicitor for Bangor, and when his term expired in 1927 he was re-elected.

Mr. Collins is a member of the Bangor Chamber of Commerce, and is very active and able in representing legally the interests of the city. He is a member of the Penobscot County Bar Association, a trustee of the Knights of Columbus Association, a director of the Bangor Knights of Columbus Home Association; and fraternally, is identified with Gamma Eta Gamma College Fraternity, and with Pio Nono Council, No. 114, Knights of Columbus. He is a Republican in his political allegiance, and is a generous supporter of all projects planned for the advancement of the general welfare of Bangor. His favorite recreation is golf, but he is fond of all out-of-door sports, and is popular among the young folks as well as among the older men of Bangor. His religous affiliation is with St. Mary's Roman Catholic Church.

ELMER E. McFARLAND—The entire active career of Elmer E. McFarland has been identified with the banking business, first with the Eastern Trust & Banking Company of Bangor, and later with the Merchants National Bank of Bangor, of which last mentioned he is now (1928) cashier, having filled that responsible position since 1926. Mr. McFarland has served on the City Council of Bangor, and has always been interested in the general welfare of the city. He is a member of the Masonic Order and a Shriner, and is well and favorably known in this city.

Elmer E. McFarland was born in Trenton, Maine, October 9, 1886, and received his early education in the public schools of his birthplace, later becoming a student in Bangor High School. Upon completing his studies he entered the employ of the Eastern Trust & Banking Company of Bangor, in 1907, beginning as a messenger boy. He worked his way up steadily and eleven years after coming into the bank as a messenger boy he was made, in 1918, assistant treasurer of the bank. That position he held until 1924, when he left the Eastern Trust and Banking Company and associated himself with the Merchants

National Bank of Bangor, as assistant cashier. In 1926 he was promoted to the position of cashier, which office he is still filling (1928). He is a member of the Bangor Chamber of Commerce. In his political faith he is a Republican, and he has served two terms as a member of the Bangor City Council. Fraternally, he is identified with Rising Virtue Lodge, No. 10, Free and Accepted Masons, being a member of all the Scottish Rite bodies and of the Shrine. He is a member and president of the Kiwanis Club, and a member of the Penobscot Valley Country Club. His favorite forms of recreation are golf and fishing, Mr. McFarland; is a son of Charles L. McFarland, who was born in Ellsworth, Maine, and is engaged as a lumberman and merchant, and of Orissa (Garland) McFarland, also a native of Ellsworth, Maine.

Elmer E. McFarland was married, in 1910, to Sarah F. McGrath, who was born in Bangor, Maine. They make their home at No. 16 Hayward Street, in Bangor.

ALFRED I. BABB—A varied career has been that of Alfred I. Babb, who has spent many years in the printing and publishing business, has been a seaman for seven years, has been in government employ in the revenue service, and at the present time (1928) is assistant business manager of the Bangor "Commercial." He is also a member of the board of directors of the J. P. Bass Publishing Company, of Bangor, publishers of the Bangor "Commercial."

Zebulon G. Babb, father of Mr. Babb, was born in Boothbay, Maine, and at an early age began to "follow the sea." He was a sea captain to the time of his death, and during the Civil War was one of the blockade runners who transported munitions and supplies to the Union armies in the South. He married Harriet F. Cates, who was born in Machiasport, Maine, and who is deceased, and among their children was Alfred I., of further mention.

Alfred I. Babb, son of Zebulon G. and Harriet F. (Cates) Babb, was born in Rockland, Maine, November 16, 1871, and received his early education in the public schools of his birthplace, later taking a course in Rockland Business College, and taking extension courses in LaSalle University. When his education was completed he entered the office of the Rockland "Free Press" as a "printer's devil," served his apprenticeship in the printing business here, and then remained for a period of six years. His next connection was with the Providence "Telegram," of Providence, Rhode Island, where he was in charge of the advertising department for one year, but at the end of that time he went to sea, and for seven years served in different capacities in sailing vessels. Having considerably widened his experience by seven years on the sea, he then further extended his general knowledge of the country by working as a printer in various cities throughout the Eastern United States, continuing to change his connections and his location for several years. Finally he returned to Rockland and entered the employment of the Rockland "Daily Star," as foreman, and later accepted a position as foreman of the composing room of the "Evening Reporter," at Woonsocket, Rhode Island, where he was also evening reporter, and editor of one page of the paper. After five years in this connection he went to Machias, Maine, and purchased a weekly paper known as the Machias "Republican,"

of which he was editor and publisher until 1921. In that year he sold out and entered government employ in the Internal Revenue Department, where he served for two years. At the end of that time, in 1924, he became associated with the Bangor "Commercial," as manager of the job department. Later he took charge of the composing room, and since 1925 he has been assistant business manager of the publication. He is also a member of the board of directors of the Bass Publishing Company, of Bangor, publishers of the Bangor "Commercial." He is a member of the Bangor Chamber of Commerce, in his political beliefs he is a Republican, and his favorite forms of recreation are billiards, bowling, and boating.

Alfred I. Babb was married, in 1900, to Clara Boardman, who was born in Thomaston, Maine, and they are the parents of two children: 1. J. Donald, 2. Frances F.

LEONARD HARRIS FORD, M. D.—For more than eight years Leonard Harris Ford has been engaged in general medical practice in Bangor, Maine, where he has offices at No. 217 State Street. Dr. Ford is a graduate of the University of Maine, class of 1899, and prior to his service in the World War was engaged in practice in East Eddington and in Brewer, Maine. He was in active service overseas during the World War, with rank of captain, and is now (1928) a major in the Reserve Corps, United States Army.

Dr. Leonard Harris Ford was born in East Eddington, Maine, July 27, 1878, a son of Charles H. W. Ford, a native of East Eddington, engaged as a farmer and a lumberman to the time of his death in 1921, and of Nettie M. (Bridgham) Ford, who was born in Charleston, Maine, and who survives her husband (1928). Dr. Ford received his early and preparatory education in the public schools of East Eddington and then entered the University of Maine, at Orono, from which he was graduated with the degree of Bachelor of Science in 1899. Later, he decided to enter the medical profession and became a student in the Medical School of Maine, where he completed his course with graduation, receiving the degree of Doctor of Medicine in 1906. After an interneship of one year in the Eastern Maine Central Hospital, he opened an office for general practice in East Eddington, where he continued until 1916, when he removed to Brewer, Maine. There he practiced until the entrance of the United States into the World War, when, on July 12, 1917, he enlisted, as a member of the Medical Corps of the Maine National Guard, in which he was commissioned a first lieutenant. He was assigned to the First Maine Heavy Field Artillery, as acting regimental surgeon, and was later transferred to the 102nd Machine Gun Battalion of the Twenty-sixth Division. On September 18, 1918, he was commissioned captain. He went overseas with the Twenty-sixth Division and took part in all of the battles in which that division was engaged. Returning to this country he received his discharge at Camp Devens, Massachusetts, April 30, 1919. In 1920 he was commissioned a captain in the Maine National Guard and was assigned to the 103rd Infantry, Medical Detachment. In 1921 he was commissioned a major and made regimental surgeon, and in 1925 he was discharged with the rank of major and placed in the Reserve Corps of the United States Army, with the rank of major. Meantime, upon receiving his discharge from the American Expeditionary Forces in 1919, Dr. Ford came to Bangor and since that time he has been engaged in general practice here, with offices at No. 217 State Street. Dr. Ford is known as a skilled physician, and stands high among his professional colleagues. He is visiting physician for the Eastern Maine General Hospital, and since 1923 has been acting assistant surgeon in the United States Public Health Service, for Bangor.

He is a member of the Penobscot County Medical Society, the Maine State Medical Society, and the American Medical Association, and is one of the most able and progressive men of his profession in this city. Fraternally, he is identified with the Alpha Kappa Kappa College Fraternity and with the Masonic Order, being a member of St. Andrew's Lodge, No. 83, Free and Accepted Masons; Mount Horiah Chapter, No. 6, Royal Arch Masons; Bangor Council, Royal and Select Masters; St. John's Commandery, No. 3, Knights Templar; Tamerlane Conclave, No. 4, Knights of the Red Cross of Constantine. He is also a member of Wildey Lodge, Independent Order of Odd Fellows; and of James W. Williams Post, No. 12, American Legion, of which he is Past Commander. Politically, Dr. Ford gives his support to the principles and the candidates of the Democratic party, and he has taken an active part in local public affairs. In 1922 he served as a member of the Common Council of the city of Bangor, and from 1922 to 1924 he was a member of the Board of Aldermen of Bangor. Since 1922 he has been secretary of the United States Pension Board for Penobscot County, and he is one of the public-spirited citizens who is always ready to aid in furthering the interests of the community in which he lives. Dr. Ford finds healthful recreation in fishing, and is interested in baseball and football. He attends the Universalist church, of which he is a member of the parish committee.

Dr. Leonard Harris Ford was married, in 1909, to Cora A. Phillips, who was born in Holden, Maine, and they are the parents of three children: Leonard Harris, Jr., Alvah Phillips, and Paul Greenwood.

HARRY J. CHAPMAN—One of the outstanding citizens of Maine who has won laurels in the legal profession and who is also a successful author, is Harry J. Chapman, of Bangor, who has his offices at No. 31 Central Street, where he has been engaged in general practice since his admission to the bar in 1883. He is the author of "Lords of Acadia," a story of Colonial Maine, and as a writer and as a lawyer, he has fully demonstrated his ability.

Charles D. Chapman, father of Mr. Chapman, was born in Newburgh, Maine, and was engaged in business for many years as a merchant lumberman. He was active in public affairs, serving as high sheriff of Penobscot County for several years, and in 1882 was elected to the Maine House of Representatives. He was a veteran of the Civil War, in which conflict he served as sergeant in Company M, Second Regiment, Maine Cavalry, and was wounded in action. He was a member of B. H. Beals Post, Grand Army of the Republic, and continued active in its affairs to the time of his death, which occurred

April 1, 1887. He married Hannah L. Haynes, who was born in Passadumkeag, Maine, and died July 7, 1914.

Mr. Chapman was born in Passadumkeag, Maine, April 12, 1856, and received his early education in the public schools of his birthplace. He then prepared for college in the East Maine Conference Seminary, at Bucksport, Maine, and when his preparatory course was completed, he matriculated in the University of Wisconsin from which he was graduated with the class of 1882, receiving at that time the degree of Bachelor of Laws. He was admitted to the bar of Wisconsin that same year, and the following year was admitted to the bar of the State of Maine. Since that time, 1883, he has been continuously and successfully engaged in general legal practice in Bangor, where he has his offices at No. 31 Central Street. Mr. Chapman is a member of the Penobscot County Bar Association, and is active in local public affairs. He served for a period of two years as a member of the Bangor City Council, and was Judge of the Bangor Municipal Court for four years. During the period of the participation of the United States in the World War he served as a member of the Legal Advisory Board of the city of Bangor, and he is one of the public-spirited citizens who is always ready to aid in advancing the general welfare of the community. In addition to the responsibilities and activities connected with the care of a large and important legal practice, Mr. Chapman has also found time for a large amount of literary work. He is generally well liked in Bangor and has a host of friends in this city.

Harry J. Chapman was married, May 27, 1891, to Clara L. Clarke, who was born in Winterport, Maine, and they are the parents of one child, Elizabeth H., wife of George Earle Miucher, and has two sons.

ALTON C. WHEELER—As a successful attorney Alton C. Wheeler has been engaged in general practice in South Paris, Maine, since 1904. He has made for himself an assured place among his professional associates, and is known as an able and resourceful practitioner. Mr. Wheeler has served in the State Legislature and as a presidential elector. He is a trustee of the University of Maine, and has served as an overseer of Bates College.

Pierce E. Wheeler, his father, was born in Mason, Maine, and was a mechanic in South Paris, Maine, for many years. He took an active part in the conduct of local political and civic affairs, served as assessor of South Paris Village for a number of years, and gave his support to the Republican party. He married Lucy E. Chapman, who was born in Bethel, Maine; both are now deceased.

Alton C. Wheeler, son of Pierce E. and Lucy E. (Chapman) Wheeler, was born in Bethel, Maine, December 29, 1877, and received his early education in the public schools of South Paris, Maine. When his preparatory course was completed he became a student in Bates College, of Lewiston, Maine, where he finished his course with graduation in 1899, receiving the degree of Bachelor of Arts. For three years after graduation he was engaged in teaching in high schools in Maine and in Massachusetts, but in the meantime he was studying law and was planning to enter that profession. He was admitted to the bar in 1904, and from 1904 to 1910 was a member of the law firm of Wright and Wheeler, engaged in general

224 MAINE—A HISTORY

practice. During the seventeen years which have passed since that time he has been engaged in general practice alone. He is a member of the Oxford County Bar Association, of the Maine State Bar Association, and of the American Bar Association, and is known as an able and resourceful lawyer. In addition to the responsibilities of his practice, he is one of the incorporators of the South Paris Savings Bank, and he was formerly a member of the board of directors of the Paris Trust Company. Mr. Wheeler has always been active in public affairs, giving his support to the principles and the candidates of the Republican party, and his associates have entrusted him with important offices. He served in the State Legislature from 1911 to 1913, was presidential elector in 1920, and has always been one of the most active in forwarding any movement planned for the advancement of the general welfare. He was a member of the board of overseers of Bates College from 1920 to 1924, and is a member of the board of trustees of the University of Maine. Fraternally, he is identified with the Masonic Order, being a member of the Blue Lodge, the Chapter, and the Commandery; of Mount Mica Lodge, No. 17, Independent Order of Odd Fellows; and of Hamlin Lodge, No. 34, Knights of Pythias. He is a member and past president of Bates College Club, and is one of the active members of the South Paris Congregational Church, and he serves as moderator of the church association.

Alton C. Wheeler was married, in Auburn, Maine, April 18, 1905, to Edith Ham Hayes, who was born in Auburn, Maine, daughter of William B., deceased, and of Anna W. (Ham) Hayes, who survives her husband (1927). Mr. and Mrs. Wheeler are the parents of one daughter, Miriam, who was born October 18, 1912.

CHARLES H. BARTLETT—For a period of forty-four years Charles H. Bartlett has been successfully engaged in legal practice in Bangor, where he has his office in Room 310, No. 6 State Street. Mr. Bartlett is a Harvard man, and long ago established his reputation as an able and resourceful member of his profession. He is the son of a lawyer, and the father of a lawyer, as his son, Charles D., is also a practicing attorney in Bangor.

Ichabod D. Bartlett, father of Mr. Bartlett, was born in Dover, New Hampshire, and very early chose the legal profession as his future field of service. After completing his professional preparation and successfully passing the examinations for admission to the bar of Maine, he engaged in practice in Bangor, as a member of the firm of Rowe and Bartlett, and this connection he maintained to the time of his death, which occurred in 1861. He married Elizabeth F. Hammatt, who was born in Bath, Maine, and who died in 1909.

Charles H. Bartlett, son of Ichabod D. and Elizabeth F. (Hammatt) Bartlett, was born in Bangor, Maine, December 4, 1858, and received his earliest education in the public schools of his birthplace. He prepared for college in Phillips-Exeter Preparatory School, from which he was graduated with the class of 1878. In the autumn of 1879 he entered Harvard University, at Cambridge, Massachusetts. At the beginning of his junior year, however, he left college and entered the offices of Wilson and Woodard, in Bangor, where he studied law; he gained his degree

later when he returned to the Law School of Harvard University for another year's study. Again he entered the office of Wilson and Woodard, and so effectively did he pursue his reading and study that in 1883 he was admitted to the bar of the State of Maine. He began practice in Bangor that same year, and since that time he has been continuously and successfully in practice here. He is known as one of the very able and successful men of his profession, and his office is at No. 6 State Street, where his many clients know and respect him as a man of integrity as well as a skilled lawyer. His inherited ability, together with association and careful preparation, have given him an unusually thorough knowledge of the practical aspects of the profession, and his sincerity and honesty have made for him many friends both among his professional associates and among those with whom he has been brought in contact through other fields of interest. He is a member of the Penobscot Bar Association, and keeps thoroughly in touch with the general activities of his profession in this section of the State. Politically, he gives his support to the principles and the candidates of the Republican party, and he has served for a period of three years as a member of the Board of Public Works. In addition to the cares of his private practice, Mr. Bartlett is president of the Bangor Savings Bank, and a member of the board of directors of the First National Bank. He is a director of the Maine Central Railroad. Fraternally, he is identified with Delta Kappa Epsilon College Fraternity, and he is also a member of the Hasty Pudding Club. He is a past president of the Rotary Club, a member of the Penobscot Valley Country Club, and of the Kebo Club, and he is also a member of the Bangor Chamber of Commerce. During the World War he served as a labor member of the Legal Advisory Board of the city of Bangor, and he was active in the various drives by means of which the city accomplished its allotted portion of the home war work. Mr. Bartlett finds healthful recreation on the golf links, and he attends the Unitarian church. He is a direct descendant of Francis LeBaron, tracing his descent through the maternal side, and is one of the highly esteemed citizens of the city of Bangor.

Charles H. Bartlett was married, in 1885, to Virginia D. Hight, who was born in Bangor, and died in 1890, leaving one son, Charles D. Bartlett, who served in Texas with the Aviation Corps during the World War, and who is now (1928) a practicing attorney in the city of Bangor, Maine.

CHARLES R. BOND—For a quarter of a century Charles R. Bond has been treasurer of the Eastern Grain Company, of Bangor, Maine, a concern with which he has been associated since he completed his high school course in 1895. Mr. Bond is an able business man, and a public-spirited citizen of repute.

Charles R. Bond was born in Stetson, Maine, August 9, 1874, son of George M., who was born in Jefferson, Maine, and was engaged in the harness and general store business to the time of his death, and of Ella (Marden) Bond, who was born in Belfast, Maine, and who survives her husband (1928). Mr. Bond received his education in the public schools of Stetson, and after leaving high school, in 1895, entered the employ of the C. R. Ireland and Company, of Bangor, as bookkeeper. Seven years later, in 1902, he formed the Eastern Grain Company, being made treasurer of this company, and this official position he has continued to fill to the present time (1928). He is a director of the Merchants' National Bank. He is a member of Pacific Lodge, Free and Accepted Masons; of the Knights of Pythias; and of the Bangor Lodge, Benevolent and Protective Order of Elks; also of the United Commercial Travelers. He is a member of the Rotary Club and of the Tarratine Club, and politically, he supports the principles of the Republican party. His favorite forms of recreation are horse racing and football, and his religious interest is with the Universalist church, of which he is an attendant.

Charles R. Bond was married, in 1896, to Mary A. McCard, who was born in Exeter, Maine, and they are the parents of two children: Granville M., and Charles R., Jr.

W. MERRITT EMERSON, M. D.—One of the best-known men of the medical profession in Bangor is Dr. W. Merritt Emerson, who has been engaged in medical and surgical practice here since 1918. Dr. Emerson's offices are located at No. 131 State Street, and he specializes in thyroid work. He is a graduate of the University of Vermont, and is so well known in Masonic circles.

Dr. W. Merritt Emerson was born in Carmel, Maine, October 12, 1890, son of Justus S. Emerson, who was born in Maine and is engaged in business as a contractor and builder, and of Susie (Hartley) Emerson, who was born in Philadelphia, Pennsylvania. Dr. Emerson attended the public schools of Bangor, Maine, and then matriculated in the University of Maine, at Orono, Maine, where he continued his studies for one year. He then made a change and continued his studies in Temple University for one year, after which he entered the University of Vermont, from which he was graduated with the class of 1917, receiving the degree of Doctor of Medicine. For one year he served as an interne in the New York City Lying-In Hospital, and then, in 1918, came to Bangor, Maine, where he has since been engaged in medical and surgical practice. Along with a large general practice, Dr. Emerson makes a specialty of thyroid work, and he is widely known as an expert in diseases which result from trouble with the thyroid glands. He is a member of the Penobscot Medical Society, of the Maine State Medical Society, of the American Medical Association, and also of the American Association for the Study and Prevention of Goitre. He is an associate of the American College of Physicians.

Politically, Dr. Emerson supports the principles and the candidates of the Republican party, and he has served for one year as school physician. Fraternally, he is identified with Washington Lodge, No. 3, Free and Accepted Masons; Burlington Chapter, No. 3, Royal Arch Masons; St. John's Commandery, Knights Templar; and Anah Temple, Ancient Arabic Order Nobles of the Mystic Shrine. He is also a member of Phi Chi College Fraternity, and of Cap and Skull Fraternity. He belongs to the Lions Club, and he is an attendant of the Episcopal church. He finds his chief recreation in automobiling, and in his special study of thyroid diseases.

Dr. W. Merritt Emerson was married, in 1918, to

Helen Hanlon, who was born in Burlington, Vermont, and they are the parents of one son, W. Merritt Emerson, Jr.

CALDWELL SWEET—It is doubtful if, throughout the State at the present time, a mercantile and professional experience, that of druggist, can quite duplicate that of Caldwell Sweet, veteran druggist with the record of a half century of continuance in that business in Bangor, and a man known and respected throughout the State, whether by druggists or physicians for the excellent standards that he has maintained in the changes that have come to him, to his business, and to the city within that period. One of the old-time "apothecaries," he is yet, today, one of the present-day pharmacists, skilled and adept in his vocation, vigorous and alert, and a citizen highly esteemed for his many enduring qualities of proven community service and friendship.

Caldwell Sweet was born May 11, 1850, at Bangor, in the same house where he now resides, a son of Abel Sylvester Sweet, a house painter, and Abigail (Bailey) Sweet. While attending the Bangor public schools, Mr. Sweet started in the drug business as a clerk in a store owned by B. F. Bradbury, located at the corner of Hammond and Central streets, and where the Buckley drugstore stood before the widening of Central Street. Later, Mr. Sweet entered upon clerical duties in a store that stood on the corner of State and Park streets on the site now occupied by the Park Theatre, this store having been purchased by Mr. Bradbury from Ambrose Warren. After conducting the store for four years, Mr. Bradbury sold it to J. F. Patten, and Mr. Sweet was then given charge of the store at the corner of Hammond and Central streets; and a year afterwards he joined in partnership with N. S. Harlow under the firm name Harlow and Sweet, in the store adjoining the Bradbury store. After a partnership of nearly two years, Mr. Sweet, in 1874, sold out his interest to Mr. Harlow, and in March of the same year he engaged in business with Isaiah Emery in the Harriman House Block, on the site now occupied by the Woolworth Five and Ten Cent Store. This entire block was destroyed by fire in December, 1874, and Mr. Sweet then severed his partnership with Mr. Emery.

On January 19, 1875, Mr. Sweet leased the present corner property, the prescription desk and stock room being contained in the one front room, the back part then being rented to Titcomb and Ellis, jewelers. A few years later a lease was taken of the block in the rear formerly occupied by the wholesale department of the business, the store on the ground floor being rented to others. It was then that the wholesale drug department was started on Central Street in the Danforth Block, since now occupied by the Central Market. A soda-water business was started and was developed until 1925. Then it was destroyed by fire, and this branch of the business was moved from there to its present location, No. 104 Broad Street.

Mr. Sweet is the dean of the business men of the street, and he has witnessed the many radical changes that share in the building and progress of the city. Among those who have worked long and faithfully for him are: Walter Barker, of the wholesale department, who has been with the business for twenty-five years; Walter Tate, formerly in charge of the shipping and stock rooms, and served with the firm for twenty-three years; William Mountaine, chemist in the wholesale department, who has completed twenty-two years. A Republican in his political convictions, Mr. Sweet votes for the ticket of that party, but he has never held public office. He was formerly a member of the Tarrantine and the Conduskeag Canoe clubs; and his religious faith is that of the Congregational church.

Caldwell Sweet married (first) Julia Prescott, who died March 30, 1885. To this marriage was born: Julia Prescott, who died in infancy, and Helen M., now living at home. Mr. Sweet married (second), May, 10, 1893, at Northampton, Massachusetts, Nellie K. Warner, daughter of Sheldon and Bathsheba (Ford) Warner; and they are the parents of one child: Caldwell, Jr., of further mention.

Caldwell Sweet, Jr., was born July 27, 1896, at Bangor, where he attended the public and high schools. He then took a year's course at Columbia University, after which he became associated with the firm of Caldwell Sweet Company, of Bangor, wholesale druggists. In 1922, he was made a member of the firm, and has continued to the present as vice-president and general manager of the company. In political matters he is a Republican.

Mr. Sweet enlisted in the United States Army in June, 1917, with the Fifty-sixth Pioneer Infantry, and served for a year in France with the American Expeditionary Forces, receiving his discharge in June, 1919, with the rank of corporal. Fraternally, he is affiliated with Rising Virtue Lodge, Free and Accepted Masons; American Legion; Penobscot Valley Country Club, and Bangor Chamber of Commerce; and his hobbies are all out-of-door sports. He attends All Souls' Congregational Church.

JOSEPH W. HAMLIN—After many years of teaching experience, Joseph W. Hamlin has become the leader and the administrator, in the Beal College of Commerce, in Bangor. He has been president of the college since 1925, and under his able leadership Beal College is taking its place among the best commercial schools in the country. The college occupies the whole of the top floor of the Stetson Building in Bangor, and is the largest of its kind in Bangor and one of the largest in the State of Maine.

Joseph W. Hamlin was born at Bethel, Maine, June 15, 1885, son of Joseph W., a native of Ottawa, Canada, who was engaged in business as a merchant to the time of his death, and of Ella (Estes) Hamlin, a native of Woodstock, Maine, who survives her husband. He received his early education in the public schools of Bethel, Maine, and then prepared for college at Kent's Hill Seminary. When his preparatory course was completed he matriculated at the University of Maine, at Orono, Maine, from which he was graduated with the class of 1908, receiving at that time the degree of Bachelor of Science. After graduation he taught school at Rumford, Maine, for a period of two years, after which he taught at Harpswell, Maine, for three years. His next teaching position was at Stockton Springs, where he remained for five years, going from there to Kezar Falls, Maine, where he taught for three years. At Milo, Maine, he held a teaching position for one year, and then, for three years, he held a position in Hampden Academy. His next position was as superintendent of schools for Vassalboro and Winslow, Maine,

and here he remained giving notably efficient service until 1925, when he was made president of Beal College of Commerce, in Bangor, Maine.

Beal College of Commerce was founded in 1891 by Mary E. Beal, who operated the school under the name of Beal Business College, continuing the school until 1922, a period of thirty-one years. In 1922 the business was sold, and at this time it was incorporated under the name of Beal College of Commerce, with Michael Kane, president; and Edward M. Cassiley as clerk. The school was continued under this leadership until 1925, when Joseph W. Hamlin was elected president, and Golda G. Hamlin was elected clerk. Under this last-named leadership the school has continued to the present time (1928), and so efficient has been the administration that the Beal College of Commerce is not only the largest of its kind in Bangor, but is also one of the largest in the State. The college is located on the top floor of the Stetson Building, No. 23 Hammond Street, Bangor, Maine, and in addition to teaching all commercial courses, auditing and accounting, and secretarial science, also specializes in Normal training for high school commercial teachers. Mr. Hamlin's long experience as a teacher and as a school administrator enables him to make this department of his college an especially efficient and interesting one, and students who have received their training here are giving marked satisfaction in the various positions which they are filling. The college helps graduates to secure positions, and furnishes commercial teachers, bookkeepers, secretaries, stenographers, and clerks. Thoroughness, and practical application of the subjects taught are the outstanding features of the instruction given here, and the reports which come in from the firms and schools employing graduates of Beal College indicate that the training given here is of the best. The present enrollment of the college is about one hundred and twenty, and this is the only business school in the State of Maine which has fraternities and other societies. This feature of the college gives to its students some of the touch of general interest found in colleges that are not commercial, and greatly develops the school spirit and the spirit of coöperation among students and instructors.

Mr. Hamlin is a Republican in his political sympathies. Fraternally, he is identified with the Masonic Order, in which he holds membership in Lodge and Chapter; with the Knights of Pythias; and with Kappa Sigma College Fraternity. Professionally, he is identified with the Eastern Commercial Teachers' Association, the Maine State Teachers' Association, and the National Education Association. His favorite form of recreational activity is motoring, and his religious interest is with the Universalist church.

Joseph W. Hamlin was married, in 1914, to Golda G. Gushee, who was born at Damariscotta, Maine, and they are the parents of one child, Althea M.

FREDERICK A. PATTERSON—One of the best-known architects in Bangor is Frederick A. Patterson, who has been engaged in this line of activity here for a quarter of a century, and who specializes in public buildings of all kinds, schools, libraries, business blocks, banks, etc. His offices are located at No. 16 Central Street. Mr. Patterson is well known in fraternal circles here, and has a host of friends in this city.

Frederick A. Patterson was born in Belfast, Maine,

June 8, 1867, son of Amasa T. Patterson, a native of Belfast, Maine, who was engaged as a farmer to the time of his death in 1882, and who served in the Aroostook War, and of Ann G. Stevens, now deceased, who was a native of Dixmont, Maine. Amasa T. Patterson was a descendant of Robert and James Patterson, founders of the town of Belfast, Maine, being the first to settle on the site of this town. Frederick A. Patterson received his education in the public schools of his birthplace, and then served an apprenticeship of seven years at the woodworking trade. At the end of seven years he went to Boston, where he followed his trade for one year. At the end of that time he returned to Belfast for one year, still following his trade, and then came to Bangor, where for about six years he worked at his trade in the employ of others. In the meantime he had made a study of architecture, and in 1902, he engaged in business for himself as an architect and since that time he has been continuously and successfully following that profession. He is one of the longest established members of his profession in the city of Bangor, and he also is one of the busiest of his line in this city. He specializes in school work, business blocks, libraries, banks, and other public buildings, and the greater part of his work is done in the State of Maine. At No. 16 Central Street, in Bangor, he may always be consulted by those who are planning to build.

Mr. Patterson is a Democrat in his political sympathies, and fraternally, he is identified with Rising Virtue Lodge, Free and Accepted Masons, in which order he is a member of all the bodies of both the York and Scottish Rites; also of Anah Temple, Ancient Arabic Order Nobles of the Mystic Shrine. He is a member of Waldo Lodge, No. 12, Independent Order of Odd Fellows, and of Penobscot Encampment, No. 25; also of Canton Pallas, No. 4. He is a member of the Masonic Club and of the Bangor Chamber of Commerce, and his favorite forms of recreation are hunting and fishing.

Frederick A. Patterson married Florence I. Gilmore, who was born in Searsport, Maine.

JAMES M. GILLIN—For the past fourteen years James M. Gillin has been engaged in general legal practice in Bangor, Maine, where he has his office at No. 15 Columbia Street. Mr. Gillin has been active in public affairs in Bangor, holding several local offices, and he has also served as a member of Governor Baxter's staff for a period of four years, with the rank of colonel.

James M. Gillin was born in Bangor, Maine, March 9, 1891, son of Patrick H., a native of Houlton, Maine, who is engaged as an attorney there, and of Mary A. (McKinnon) Gillin, who was born in Antigonish, Nova Scotia. He attended the public schools of Bangor, and then entered Bowdoin College, at Brunswick, Maine. Later, he became a student in the Law School of the University of Maine, in Orono, Maine, from which he was graduated with the class of 1913, receiving at that time the degree of Bachelor of Laws. He was admitted to the bar that same year, and since that time has been engaged in general legal practice in Bangor. He is a member of the Penobscot Bar Association, of the Maine State Bar Association, and of the American Bar Association, and is known among his associates as an able and resourceful attorney. In his political sympathies and beliefs he is

a Republican, and he is one of the progressive and public-spirited citizens who is always ready to serve the best interests of the city in which he lives. He served as a member of the City Council of Bangor for one term, as a city solicitor for two terms, and for a term of four years he was a member of the staff of Governor Baxter, serving with the rank of colonel. At the time of the entrance of the United States into the World War he enlisted in the United States Army and was commissioned a first lieutenant, in August, 1917. He was first assigned to the Infantry, but later was transferred to the Air Service, where he remained until he received his discharge, in January, 1919, with the rank of first lieutenant. Mr. Gillin is a member of Alpha Delta Phi College Fraternity, also of Phi Alpha Delta College Fraternity, and he is well known in local club circles, holding membership in the Tarratine Club, Boston City Club, Penobscot Country Club, Lucerne in Maine Country Club, and in the American Legion. He is fond of golf and tennis, and has a host of friends in this city. In addition to the responsibilities already mentioned above, Mr. Gillin is also head of the Lucerne in Maine legal department. His religious affiliation is with St. John's Roman Catholic Church. Mr. Gillin has his office at No. 15 Columbia Street, in Bangor.

James M. Gillin was married, in 1917, to Hazelle Delano, who was born in Bangor, Maine, and they are the parents of three children: 1. James M., Jr. 2. John Marshall. 3. Hazelle D.

HON. H. E. WADSWORTH—One of the principal figures of Winthrop, Maine, is the Hon. H. E. Wadsworth, who has served his community long and well, in varied important capacities, directly and indirectly: directly in the public offices that he has held with signal dignity and distinction, and notably in this connection as a representative in both houses of the Maine State Legislature; and indirectly through semi-public and philanthropic organizations. Further, he has assisted in the community's progress as a manufacturer, and employer of labor; for in this wise he has attracted capital to the town, and has, through payment of good wages to his workmen, enabled them to live well and to raise their families as good citizens. He is a director of the State Young Men's Christian Association. His acquaintanceship throughout the State of Maine is considerable. He numbers among his intimates men whose names signify position and wealth. Himself endowed liberally with those qualities of character and bearing which tend to attract and retain friendship, in friendship he is indeed wealthy. By his associates he is regarded with respect and affection in equal share.

Mr. Wadsworth was born in East Livermore, Maine, October 25, 1868, son of Elijah and Ruth (Record) Wadsworth. Elijah Wadsworth was born in East Livermore, March 5, 1825, and there died, in December, 1897, after a long, industrious and useful career given to farming. Ruth (Record) Wadsworth, too, was born in East Livermore, June 24, 1840, and died there in February, 1914. Both parents gave to their son the best of trainings in the home, and early inculcated in him right principles of thought and conduct, which have remained with him through manhood, and have assisted him mightily. In the public schools of East Livermore, Maine, Mr. Wadsworth secured his basic academic instruction, then, for a brief period, studied in Hebron

Academy, completing his preparation for college in Coburn Classical Institute, from which he graduated in 1888. Without delay he matriculated in Colby College, at Waterville, Maine, and from it, in 1892, received the degree of Bachelor of Arts. During thirteen years that followed he was variously employed, but in 1905 he joined in association with a Mr. Woodman, and organized the firm of Wadsworth & Woodman, for the manufacture of table oilcloth. The firm prospered, and in 1907 the partners filed articles of incorporation, under the firm style of Wadsworth & Woodman Company. The business has continued to grow, expanding soundly along all lines, until, at the present time (1928), the services of thirty-five employees are required. Mr. Wadsworth is president of the corporation; Mr. Woodman is its treasurer. Their organization produces in one average day some eleven hundred pieces of the table oilcloth, each piece twelve yards in length; and Wadsworth & Woodman quality is known to dealers who handle the product throughout New England and in certain centers elsewhere. This enterprise is one of the most substantial and reliable in Winthrop.

Mr. Wadsworth is active in all civic affairs in which the most conscientious of citizens interest themselves. In politics he wields a wide influence, always for the good of the people at large rather than for the aggrandizement of party or self. While in the Senate and State House of Representatives he assisted in the adoption and administration of many reforms and measures of benefit to his constituency. He is a member of the board of directors of the Federal Trust Company, of Waterville, Maine; a director of the Port of Portland, Associated Industries of Maine, and the Maine Automobile Association. Also, he is a member of the board of managers of Oak Grove Seminary, and chairman of the board of trustees of Colby College. In the Winthrop Chamber of Commerce he is active, and belongs to the Rotary Club of Augusta, Maine. He is a communicant of the Quaker Church, of Winthrop Center, Maine.

WINGATE F. CRAM—From the beginning of his active career Wingate F. Cram has been associated with the Bangor & Aroostook Railroad Company, and since 1917 he has been clerk and treasurer of the company. Mr. Cram is a native of Bangor, and with the exception of the years during which he was in preparatory school and in college, he has always been in Bangor. He is a Harvard man, has many friends in this locality, and is one of the progressive citizens of the city.

Wingate F. Cram was born in Bangor, Maine, December 4, 1877, son of Franklin Webster Cram. He attended private schools in Bangor, and then prepared for college in Phillips Andover Academy. When his preparatory course was completed he matriculated in Harvard College, from which he was graduated with the class of 1900, receiving the degree of Bachelor of Arts. Upon the completion of his college course he became associated with the Bangor & Aroostook Railroad Company, and in 1909 he was made assistant to the president. Eight years later, in 1917, he was made clerk and treasurer of the company, and these two positions he has continued to fill to the present time (1928).

Mr. Cram is a Republican in his political sympathies, and he is well known in club circles here,

being a member of the Tarratine Club, Conduskeag Canoe and Country Club; Harvard Club, of New York City; Penobscot Valley Country Club, and of other local organizations. He is a member of the Bangor Chamber of Commerce, and active in its affairs.

Wingate F. Cram was married, in 1905, to Anna Sabin, who was born in Jackson, Michigan, and they are the parents of two children: Cynthia, and Sibyl.

JAMES M. McNULTY—After a long experience in the various phases of the lumber business, James M. McNulty became identified with the Barker Lumber Box Company as president, and still retains that executive office (1928). Mr. McNulty has been engaged in the lumber business for himself, in various connections, since 1883, a period of more than forty-four years. He was born in Stillwater, Maine, June 29, 1861, son of Charles, who was born in Ireland, and who was engaged as a laborer to the time of his death, and of Katherine (McCue) McNulty, who was born in St. Sylvestine, Province of Quebec, Canada, now deceased.

James M. McNulty received his education in the public schools of Stillwater, and when school days were over worked in various positions, mostly connected with the lumber trade, until 1883, when he engaged in business with William Engel, rafting, and running logs on the river, under the name of William Engel and Company, of Bangor. He continued as a member of this firm until 1904, a period of twenty-one years, and then, upon the retirement of Mr. Engel took over the management of the business, continuing it alone until 1913, when the enterprise was purchased by the firm of McNulty, Pierce, and Townsend. In 1916, Mr. McNulty sold his interest in this business, and went to California, where he remained for two years. At the end of that time he returned to Maine, and formed a partnership with Mr. Whittier, under the firm name of McNulty and Whittier, and engaged in a general lumber business. After a time, however, Mr. McNulty associated himself with the Barker Lumber Box Company, of Bangor, of which he was made president, and he is still holding that office (1928). Mr. McNulty is a Republican in his political affiliation and he is active in public affairs. He served on the Deep Water Commission of the State of Maine for a period of three years, and he has always been one of the public-spirited citizens who could be depended upon to contribute a generous share in forwarding the general welfare of the community. Mr. McNulty is a past president of the East and West Branch Penobscot Lumbermen's Association, and a member of the board of directors of the Midamwamkee Lumbermen's Association. He is a member of the Tarratine Club and of the Penobscot Country Club, and his religious affiliation is with the Roman Catholic church.

James M. McNulty was married, in 1900, to Winifred Lynch, a native of Bangor, Maine, now deceased.

DONALD S. HIGGINS—There has been no portion of the successful career of Donald S. Higgins in which he has not been associated with the insurance field, and his entire experience in that business has been developed under the auspices of the one great organization, the Travelers' Insurance Company, of Hartford, Connecticut. Representing that company today as its Eastern Maine general agent, Mr. Higgins has expanded its interests and steadily increased its value in this section of New England, his place of leadership receiving recognition in the insurance world, and by general business and professional organizations. He is a son of Leon Forrest Higgins, a native of Ellsworth, who for more than twenty years, and to the time of his death, which took place July 28, 1923, was general agent for Eastern Maine of the Travelers' Insurance Company, and Josephine Helen (Shackley) Higgins, who was born in Brewer, and survives her husband.

Donald S. Higgins was born January 6, 1897, at Brewer, where he attended the public and high schools. He was then graduated at Bowdoin College, Brunswick, with his degree of Bachelor of Arts, in the class of 1919, and he was elected life secretary of his class. Mr. Higgins at once became associated with the Travelers Insurance Company, and in 1919, he worked in the head office at Hartford for a year where he took their valued training course. In 1921 Mr. Higgins came to Bangor, in the employ of the company, and in 1923 he was made general agent for Eastern Maine, and has so continued to the present, with his offices at No. 27 State Street, in Bangor. In political matters, he is a staunch Republican, though he has not at any time sought public office. In 1917 Mr. Higgins served as the Officers' Training School, at Plattsburg, New York; in September of that year he enlisted in the United States Navy, and serving during the war as ensign, received his discharge in April, 1919.

Fraternally, Mr. Higgins is affiliated with St. Andrew's Lodge, No. 83, Free and Accepted Masons, of which he is a Past Master; and with all bodies of the Ancient Accepted York and Scottish Rites, as well as with Anah Temple, Ancient Arabic Order Nobles of the Mystic Shrine; Conduskeag Lodge, Knights of Pythias; and Wildey Lodge, Independent Order of Odd Fellows. His clubs are: Bowdoin of Penobscot Valley, of which he is a past president; Penobscot Valley Country; University; Rotary; Bangor Chamber of Commerce, of which he is a member of the board of directors; Maine Association of Insurance Agents; Insurance Federation of America, and Maine Automobile Association. His hobby is Masonic work. Mr. Higgins' religious faith is that of the Methodist Episcopal church, and he is a member of the board of trustees of the First Methodist Episcopal Church at Brewer.

Donald S. Higgins married, October 21, 1922, Marion P. Harvey, a native of Richford, Vermont. Their children: Leon Forrest (2), Elizabeth Harvey, and Donald S., Jr.

HAROLD M. GOODWIN, M. D.—Since 1921 Harold M. Goodwin has been engaged in medical and surgical practice in Bangor, with offices at No. 3 Third Street, where he has been taking care of a large and steadily growing practice. He is a graduate of Harvard Medical School and is a veteran of the World War, having served overseas with the British Army from 1915 to 1916, and with the American Expeditionary Forces from 1917 to 1919.

Dr. Harold M. Goodwin was born in Danforth, Maine, March 11, 1886, son of Herbert, a native of Clinton, Maine, who was engaged in the lumber business during the early years of his active career, and later was in the grocery business to the time of his death, in 1918, and of Ella M. (Powell) Goodwin, who was born in Topsfield, Maine, and survives her husband. Dr. Goodwin attended the public schools of Lincoln, Maine, and then prepared for college in Mattanawocock Academy. Later, he became a student in Bates College, from which he was graduated with the class of 1908, receiving the degree of Bachelor of Arts. He then began professional study in the Harvard Medical School, where he finished his course with graduation in 1913, receiving the degree of Doctor of Medicine. From the beginning, Dr. Goodwin had determined to fit himself as fully as possible for the responsibilities of the profession which he had chosen as his future field of service, and after receiving his medical degree he further prepared himself by a surgical internship in the Boston City Hospital, where he finished with the class of 1915. In 1916 he served in the Providence Lying-In Hospital, and then, from 1919 to 1921, he served as chief surgeon for the Employer's Liability Insurance Company, of Boston. Since 1921 he has been engaged in medical and surgical practice in Bangor, with offices at No. 3 Third Street. In 1915, Dr. Goodwin went overseas with the First Harvard Medical Unit and served with the British Medical Corps, located at General Hospital No. 2, of the Royal Army Medical Corps, commissioned a first lieutenant. In November, 1915, the Harvard Medical Unit took over the American Red Cross Hospital at Paignton, England, and in August, 1916, Dr. Goodwin was discharged from the British service and came back to this country. Here he took a course in the Lying-In-Hospital, at Providence, Rhode Island, as stated above, and in 1917 he went to Lincoln, Maine, where he was engaged in practice until September, when he was commissioned a first lieutenant in the United States Army, Medical Corps. In 1919 he was promoted to the rank of captain in the United States Army Medical Corps, and he served overseas, at Base hospitals Nos. 7 and 20, for a period of fourteen months, receiving his discharge in August, 1919, ranking at the time as captain. In 1922 he was commissioned a captain in the Medical Corps of the Maine State National Guard, and in 1924 he was commissioned a major. At the present time (1928) he is regimental surgeon of the One Hundred and Third Infantry. He is a Mason, and a member of the American Legion. Professionally, he is identified with the Penobscot Medical Society, the Maine State Medical Society, and the American Medical Association, and is a member of the surgical staff of the Eastern Maine General Hospital. Dr. Goodwin finds his recreation in golf and fishing, and his religious affiliation is with the First Universalist Church of Bangor.

Dr. Harold M. Goodwin was married, in 1923, to Gladys R. Colby, who was born in Bangor, Maine, and they are the parents of two children, twins: Carolyn Colby, and Eleanor Powell.

HARVEY W. BOWLES—Under his supervision, the interests of the general agency of the Massachusetts Mutual Life Insurance Company have continued to prosper and to increase in territory and popularity. Mr. Bowles, in general charge for the county and section, is widely known, a business man of long established repute, and has a host of friends in his specialty of life insurance in Maine.

Harvey W. Bowles was born February 8, 1874, at

Columbia Falls, in Washington County, a son of George H. Bowles, a native of Machias, who engaged in the lumber business to the time of his death in 1883, and Leona R. (Wass) Bowles, a native of Addison, who died in 1926. Mr. Bowles attended the grammar school and the Columbia Falls High School and Shaw's Business College. Entering upon his business life, Mr. Bowles, for nineteen years, was associated with the drygoods activities in Bangor. In 1910, he first became interested in insurance matters, when he accepted a position as special agent in the employ of the New England Mutual Insurance Company, and he continued with that company for three years. In 1913, Mr. Bowles became associated with Massachusetts Mutual Life Insurance Company as general agent, and he has remained as such to the present, with his offices at No. 6 State Street, Bangor. In politics, he is an adherent to the principles of the Republican party. Faternally, he is affiliated with the Knights of Pythias; and he is also a member of Tarratine Club; Penobscot Valley Country Club; Conduskeag Canoe and Country Club; Insurance Federation of the State of Maine; Life Underwriters' Association of the State of Maine; and his hobbies are fishing and out-of-door sports. He attends the Universalist church.

Harvey W. Bowles married, in 1900, Belle A. Merrill, who was born in Bangor; and they have two children: Doris A., and Merrill H.

L. RAY THURSTON—The active career of L. Ray Thurston has been identified from the beginning with the First National Bank of Bangor, of which he is now (1928) cashier. Mr. Thurston began as a messenger in 1914, and by ability, application, and faithfulness, has made for himself an assured place in the work and policy of the bank, and is one of the important factors in its present success.

Nelson T. Thurston, father of Mr. Thurston, was born on Mount Desert Island, Maine, received his education in the local public schools, and during the early years of his career was a sea-faring man. Later, he engaged in the insurance business, in which he is still actively employed (1928). He married Sarah M. Thayer, who was born in Hampden, Maine.

L. Ray Thurston, son of Nelson T. and Sarah M. (Thayer) Thurston, was born in Hampden, Maine, June 15, 1894, and received his early education in the public schools of Bangor, Maine. After finishing his course in Bangor High School, he became a student in the Portland School of Accounting, and also took extension courses in Columbia University. When his school days were over, he became identified with the First National Bank of Bangor, and his connection with this financial institution has been continuous to the present time. Beginning as messenger, he worked his way up, giving most faithful and efficient service, and in 1920 he was made assistant cashier. In 1926, he was made cashier of the bank, and this responsible position he is efficiently filling at the present time (1928). He is a member of the Bangor Chamber of Commerce, and politically gives his support to the principles and the candidates of the Republican party. In July, 1918, Mr. Thurston enlisted in the United States Army, and was assigned to the 151st Depot Brigade, Fifty-fourth Company, with which he served as a first-class private until he received his discharge in December, 1918. Mr. Thurston finds recreational activity and interest in raising

police dogs and in boating, and his religous interest is with the Christian Science church, of which he is an attendant.

L. Ray Thurston was married, in 1919, to Teresa E. Tuck, a native of Bangor, and they are the parents of two children: Paul Thayer, and Terese M.

ARTHUR P. LATNO, Doctor of Medicine, a promising young surgeon of Old Town, Maine, was born June 1, 1894, at Bradley, Maine, a son of Alex and Josephine (Paradise) Latno, both now deceased. Alex Latno, the father, who was born at Three Rivers, Canada, was engaged in farming until his death. Josephine (Paradise) Latno, was born at Van Buren, Maine.

Arthur P. Latno, received his preparatory education in the public schools of Bradley, Maine, later graduating from the Old Town High School. Upon the completion of these courses of study, he entered Boston University where he remained for one year. He then transferred to the University of Vermont Medical School, and he graduated from there with the class of 1919, when he received his degree at Doctor of Medicine. Immediately thereafter he gained his practical training as an interne in the Fannie Allen Hospital at Winooski, Vermont. He removed to Old Town, Maine, where he began the practice of his profession. Dr. Latno has remained there since, carrying on a general practice of medicine and surgery, and building up a fine reputation as a physician. During the World War, Dr. Latno, who was studying at the time, served in the Medical Reserve Corps at the University of Vermont.

Despite the manifold duties which his profession entails, Dr. Latno has participated generously in civic affairs. In his political preferences he is independent, and he served for one year as city physician for Old Town. Among the learned organizations which pertain to his profession, of which he is a member, are the American Medical Association, the Maine State Medical Society, and the Penobscot County Medical Society. He is fraternally, affiliated with the Old Town Lodge, Benevolent and Protective Order of Elks, the Knights of Columbus, and the college fraternities, Phi Chi and Alpha Sigma. He is also a member of the Penobscot Valley Country Club and the Old Town High School Alumni Association, of which he has been president since 1920. He is a member of the Old Town Rotary Club and a member of the American Legion.

Dr. Arthur P. Latno married, in 1923, Florence M. Marcotte, who was born at Winooski, Vermont. Dr. and Mrs. Latno attend St. Joseph's Roman Catholic Church.

DR. ARTHUR A. SHAW—Thirty-six years of faithful and efficient medical practice in Clinton, Maine, have made Dr. Arthur A. Shaw well known and very highly esteemed in the territory surrounding Clinton. He is a graduate of Bowdoin College, and has been active in public affairs for many years, serving in local and State offices. He has served in both houses of the State Legislature, and is still interested in the civic affairs of Clinton, serving on the Board of Health and as vice-president of the Library Association.

Arthur A. Shaw was born in Etna, Maine, April 7, 1864. His father, Benjamin F. Shaw, a native of

Etna, Maine, was employed in the mill business in Lowell, Massachusetts, for seven years. The outbreak of the Civil War changed the course of his life, and after serving as a corporal in the Sixth Massachusetts Regiment until the close of the war, he returned to Etna, Maine, where he was engaged in farming during the remainder of his active life, giving his support to the Republican party. The mother of Dr. Shaw, Cornelia (Harmon) Shaw, was born in Madison, New Hampshire. Both are now deceased. Dr. Shaw attended the local public schools and then prepared for college in the Maine Central Institute, at Pittsfield, Maine, where he completed his course with graduation in 1887. The following fall he matriculated in Bowdoin College, at Brunswick, Maine, from which he was graduated with the class of 1891, receiving the degree of Doctor of Medicine. In August of that year he opened an office in Clinton, Maine, and during the more than thirty-six years which have passed, he has been successfully engaged in general medical practice here. He is a member of the Kennebec County Medical Association, of the Maine Medical Society, and is well known as a skillful and faithful family physician. Along with his professional duties Dr. Shaw has found time for much public service. He is a member of the board of directors of the Waterville Savings Bank, and is deeply interested in local and State affairs. He gives his support to the principles and candidates of the Republican party, has served on numerous boards and is (1928) a member of the Board of Health of Clinton; chairman of the School Library Association, which he serves as vice-president; and he was formerly a member of the School Board. In 1905 he was elected on the Republican ticket to serve as a representative in the State Legislature, and in 1909 he was elected to serve in the State Senate. Fraternally, he is identified with the Masonic Order, holding membership in the Lodge, Chapter, and Commandery; and he is also a member of the Independent Order of Odd Fellows. His religious membership is with the Methodist church, which he serves as a member of its board of trustees.

Dr. Arthur A. Shaw married, August 8, 1894, Ethel Foster of Clinton, daughter of William G. and Lidia (Berry) Foster. To this marriage have been born three children: 1. Winifred C., born August 6, 1896; graduated from Colby College in 1918, with the degree of Bachelor of Arts. 2. Donald A., born August 7, 1900; graduate of Colby College in 1921, with the degree of Bachelor of Arts; graduated from Harvard Law School in 1928, with the degree of Bachelor of Laws. 3. Kenneth E., born December 18, 1903; graduate of Colby College in 1925, with the degree of Bachelor of Arts; Boston University Law School, class of 1929.

ALBERT G. AVERILL, lawyer, war worker, and Judge of the Old Town (Maine) Municipal Court, was born in Crawford, Washington County, Maine, and with the exception of two years, 1907 to 1909, when he was engaged in the practice of law in St. Paul, Minnesota, has been a resident of Maine all his life. His father, Frank S. Averill, born also in Crawford, Maine, was in the lumber business. He was a Civil War veteran, having served in the Sixth Regiment of Maine Volunteer Infantry, and was twice wounded in action at Fredericksburg, and was active in the affairs of the Calais (Maine) Post, Grand Army of

the Republic. He married Maria A. Wormwood, deceased, who was born in Washington County, Maine, and attained the unusual distinction of honorary membership in the Sixth Maine Regiment.

Educated in the public schools of Calais, Maine, where he was born October 11, 1874, Albert G. Averill, after being graduated from the high school, entered Colby College, and received his degree of Bachelor of Arts, in the class of 1898. He read law in the offices of several Calais attorneys, and was admitted to the bar of the State of Maine in 1902. From 1898 to 1907, he taught school, and then, after two years in Minnesota, opened his own office in Old Town, where he has been in active practice ever since, at No. 80 North Main Street. He is a member of both the Washington, and the Penobscot County Bar associations, is a Republican, and has served continuously as Judge of the Old Town Municipal Court since 1919.

During the World War he served as chairman of the local Legal Advisory Board, was one of the "four-minute" men, and took an active part in the Liberty Loan and other patriotic "drives." He is a member of Star of the East Lodge, Free and Accepted Masons, and of all bodies of the York Rite, including St. John's Commandery, Knights Templar; of Old Town Lodge, Benevolent and Protective Order of Elks; of the Independent Order of Odd Fellows, and of the Knights of Pythias. He attends the Baptist church, is a member of the Tarrantine Club, and finds his chief recreations in automobiling and fishing.

Judge Averill married Louise Pierce, of Old Town, in 1908. She was graduated from Wellesley College in the class of 1900. The children are Caroline M., Roswell P., and Louise H.

FRANKLIN E. BRAGG—The present-day activities of the hardware firm of N. H. Bragg and Sons, of Bangor, are due in a very large measure to the executive qualifications of the head of the concern, Franklin E. Bragg, who has devoted his entire business career and interests to the firm and its advancement in the distribution of its iron and steel specialties, throughout this State and beyond its borders. Mr. Bragg is both one of the foremost of the hardware dealers in Maine, and a prominent Bangor citizen whose association with its varied financial and benevolent institutions and social organizations is surety of his public-spirited interests in city and community. He has been identified with the Orono Pulp and Paper Company, as a member of the board of directors, since 1913, and in 1923, was elected president of the firm.

Franklin E. Bragg, a son of Charles F. Bragg, a native of Maine, who died in 1921, and was senior partner in the firm of N. H. Bragg Company, and Florence (Wingate) Bragg, a native of Bangor, was born November 14, 1874, at Bangor, where he attended the grammar and high schools. He was graduated at Massachusetts Institute of Technology with the class of 1897, and immediately became associated with the firm of N. H. Bragg and Sons, of which he is now the president.

The present firm of N. H. Bragg and Sons was established in 1854, by Norris H. Bragg, who continued the business alone until 1864, when his son, N. E. Bragg, was received as partner. The partnership continued thus until 1874, when C. F. Bragg became a member of the firm, the business being incorporated in 1905 under the name of N. H. Bragg & Sons as at present, and with the following-named officers: C. F. Bragg, president; F. E. Bragg, treasurer; R. E. Bragg, clerk. In 1921, upon the death of C. F. Bragg, Franklin E. Bragg was made president of the firm and Roland E. Bragg treasurer and clerk. The founder of the firm having been a blacksmith at Dixmont, he conceived the idea of coming to Bangor for the purpose of starting a supply house for other blacksmiths, so that originally the business was that of a supply house for the blacksmith trade. At present the firm employs twenty-four people, and occupying the building No. 74 to 86 Broad Street, they are the largest jobbers of iron, steel, and heavy hardware in Bangor.

In his political views Mr. Bragg is a Republican, and though he has not sought civic office, with his vote and influence he supports the principles of that party. He is a member of the board of directors of the Merchants National Bank; president of the Home for Aged Women; vice-president of the Home for Aged Men; trustee of the Good Samaritan Home and member of its board of management; and director of the Eastern Maine General Hospital. Fraternally, he is affiliated with the Knights of Pythias; and he is a member of the board of directors of the New England Iron and Hardware Association; member of the Bangor Rotary Club, of which he is a past president; member of the Bangor Chamber of Commerce; member of the board of governors of the Penobscot Valley Country Club; and member of the Conduskeag Canoe and Country Club, and the Tarratine Club. He attends All Souls' Congregational Church.

Franklin E. Bragg married, in April, 1900, Grace B. Woodbury, who was born at Brewer. To this union have been born three children: 1. Frances W., wife of D. J. Eames; graduate of Smith College. 2. Eleanor W., graduate of Pine Manor School. 3. Charles F. (2), student at Exeter Academy.

HARVEY E. KNOWLES—Since 1924, Harvey E. Knowles has been one of the owners of the only wholesale boot and shoe concern in the city of Bangor, the J. M. Arnold Shoe Company, of which Earle J. Homestead (q. v.) is president. Mr. Knowles began his connection with this concern as a bookkeeper about twenty years ago, and has been a member of the firm since 1908. He was born in Corinna, Penobscot County, Maine, October 27, 1876, son of Charles Knowles, a native of Corinna, who was a veteran of the Civil War, having served with the Eleventh Regiment, Maine Volunteers, and who was engaged in farming to the time of his death in 1908, and of Almina (Bigelow) Knowles, who was born in Corinna, and died in 1926.

Harvey E. Knowles attended the public schools of Corinna, and Dexter High School, and then took a course in a business college in Bangor. When his commercial training was finished he secured a position as bookkeeper with the Sawyer Boot and Shoe Company, of Bangor, with whom he remained for five years. In 1904 he became associated with the J. M. Arnold Shoe Company of Bangor, as bookkeeper, and in 1908 he was made a member of the firm. This business was founded in 1868, under the name of Arnold and Sawyer. The partnership was continued until 1889, when the partnership was dis-

solved. In 1868, when the concern was started it was a small retail shoe business with a small store on Main Street in Bangor. After the partnership of Mr. Arnold and Mr. Sawyer was dissolved, Mr. Arnold continued the business under the name of the J. M. Arnold Shoe Company, organizing the new company in 1889, and locating at No. 170 Exchange Street, Bangor, and moved to No. 115 Franklin Street, in 1912. Of this new concern Jesse M. Arnold was proprietor until April 5, 1893, when he died, and the business passed to his two sons. In January, 1908, one of the sons died, and Mr. Knowles became a member of the firm. On January 6, 1924, the remaining son of Mr. Arnold, the founder of the business, died, and it was then that Mr. Knowles and Mr. Homstead, the last-mentioned of whom had been associated with the company as salesman for some seventeen years, took over the business, which had been developed into a wholesale boot and shoe concern, with Mr. Homstead as president. This concern is the only one of its kind in Bangor, and all its shoes bear the name of "The Arnold Shoe." The J. M. Arnold Shoe Company is also distributor for the United States Rubber Company products. They occupy a five-floor building, aggregating about 15,000 square feet of floor space, and employ about twenty people. Mr. Knowles is a Republican in his political sympathies and for three years he served as a member of the City Council of Bangor. He is a member of St. Andrew's Lodge, Free and Accepted Masons, of which he is a Past Master; and he is a member of all the bodies of the Scottish and York Rites; and of Anah Temple, Ancient Arabic Order Nobles of the Mystic Shrine. He is also a member of the Knights of Pythias, of which he is a Past Chancellor. He is a member of the Bangor Chamber of Commerce, of the Masonic Club, and of the Kiwanis Club, and finds his favorite forms of recreation in wood-working and in hunting. His religious affiliation is with the Methodist church.

Harvey E. Knowles was married, in 1902, to Ollie Morrissey, who was born in Danforth, Maine.

EARLE J. HOMSTEAD, president of the J. M. Arnold Shoe Company, was born in Brewer, Maine, January 11, 1890, son of George E. Homstead, a native of Palmyra, Maine, who is engaged in business as a retail shoe merchant, and of Mary Louise (Howard) Homstead, who was born in Guilford, Maine, and died in 1903. He received his education in the public schools of Brewer, and after the completion of his studies in the high school became associated with the J. M. Arnold Shoe Company as errand boy, beginning his service in that capacity in 1905. Two years later, in 1907, he was made a salesman in the employ of the same company, and in that capacity he continued until after the death of the second of Mr. Arnold's sons in 1924, when he and Harvey E. Knowles (q. v.) took over the business, Mr. Homstead becoming president of the company. Since that time he has efficiently discharged the duties of his office, and the J. M. Arnold Shoe Company is not only maintaining its high standing, but is steadily growing. Mr. Homstead gives his support to the principles and the candidates of the Republican party. He is a member of St. Andrew's Lodge, Free and Accepted Masons, and of all the bodies of both the York and Scottish Rites; also of Anah Temple, Ancient Arabic Order Nobles of the Mystic

Shrine. He is a member of the Bangor Chamber of Commerce and of the United Commercial Travelers, and of the Conduskeag Canoe Club, the Country Club, and the Tarratine Club. He is fond of fishing.

Earle J. Homstead was married, in 1913, to Hildred Kendall, who was born in Brewer, Maine.

H. CLIFTON EYE—The experience of a lifetime, and in association with long-established concerns engaged in the business of funeral directing, has secured for H. Clifton Eye his deserved repute of leadership in Bangor, as well as elsewhere in this State and in Massachusetts, as one whose business has become a profession, in which he has attained the highest grade of usefulness in his calling. Mr. Eye is the proprietor of the oldest of the undertaking establishments in this part of the State, and he is also a representative citizen of Bangor, and advocate of every movement for civic progress.

H. Clifton Eye was born February 19, 1866, at Calais, a son of George W. Eye, a native of Maine, was engaged in the business of undertaker to the time of his death, and Elizabeth (Cook) Eye, a native of Red Beach, also now deceased. Mr. Eye attended the public schools of Calais, and was graduated at the high school and Calais Academy; and in 1884 he first entered upon the business of funeral directing, in the employ of J. S. Waterman & Sons, one of the most prominent undertakers in Boston, Massachusetts. He continued with this firm for fifteen years. In 1899, he removed to Calais, where he became associated with his father, George W. Eye, in the same line of business. In 1904, Mr. Eye came to Bangor, where he purchased the undertaking business of Major William Z. Clayton, continuing therein until 1925, at which time his son, Ralph W. Eye, became associated with the business. Major Clayton had established the firm in 1869, and it is therefore the oldest, as well as the most extensive under the present management, with its location at No. 117 State Street.

In the political field, Mr. Eye is a member of the Republican party, and is a member of the Board of Aldermen of Bangor (1928). Fraternally, he is affiliated with St. Andrew's Lodge, Free and Accepted Masons, and in all the bodies of both York and Scottish Rites; and the Ancient Arabic Order Nobles of the Mystic Shrine. He is also a member of the Knights of Pythias, of which he is a Past Chancellor. He is a member of the Maine Funeral Directors' Association; Tarratine Club; Conduskeag Canoe and Country Club; Masonic Club; and Penobscot Valley Country Club; and his hobbies are baseball and horses. His religious faith is that of the Congregational church.

H. Clifton Eye married, in 1890, Julia Gertrude Farnham, a native of Milltown, New Brunswick; and they have one son, Ralph F. W. (q. v.)

RALPH F. W. EYE—Both his specific training for his vocation, and his general business and collegiate preparation, have combined to secure the success that has come to Ralph F. W. Eye in his profession as a funeral director. In association with his father, H. Clifton Eye, at Bangor, he is conducting a business that is of no secondary importance regarding its centralized plant, its present-day equipment, and its superior professional qualifications.

Ralph F. W. Eye was born May 11, 1902, in New Brunswick, Canada, a son of H. Clifton Eye, a well-known undertaker (q. v.), and of Julia Gertrude (Farnham) Eye. He attended the Bangor public and high schools, St. John's Military School, at Manlius, New York, and the Little Hall private school, at Cambridge, Massachusetts; and after a year at Harvard College, he took courses in business administration at Boston University and at Maine University Summer School. He then became associated with his father, H. Clifton Eye, in the business of funeral director, at Bangor, in which he continues to the present. This business was established at Bangor by Major William Z. Clayton in 1869, and was purchased by H. Clifton Eye in 1904, and is known as the oldest and most extensive in this section of the State.

Mr. Eye, in politics, is an adherent to the policies of the Republican party. Fraternally, he is affiliated with St. Andrew's Lodge, Free and Accepted Masons; and with the College Fraternity, Lambda Chi Alpha; he is a member of the Penobscot Valley Country Club; and his hobbies are golf and swimming. He attends All Souls' Congregational Church.

Ralph F. W. Eye married, August 27, 1924, Muriel Goodere, who was born in Brownville.

FRANCIS H. BATE—One of the younger members of the legal profession in Winthrop, Maine, is Francis H. Bate, who began the study of law in 1922, and who opened his offices in Winthrop in 1927, directly after his admission to the bar in March of that year. Mr. Bate is also engaged in the insurance business and he is secretary and treasurer of the Winthrop Chamber of Commerce, in which capacity he has served since March, 1926. He is a veteran of the World War and Past Commander of the local Post, American Legion, and is very active in the State organization.

Francis H. Bate was born in Ticonderoga, New York, July 27, 1886, son of William Bate, who was a native of England, where he was a miner, but later came to this country and was a miner in New York State, and of Annie (Seymore) Bate, who survives her husband. He attended the public schools of Ticonderoga, and after finishing his preparatory course in Ticonderoga High School, began study in Bowdoin College, at Brunswick, Maine, where he completed his course with graduation in 1916, receiving at that time the degree of Bachelor of Arts. He had early decided upon the legal profession as his future field of achievement, and in the fall of 1922 he began professional study in Harvard Law School. After one year spent in study there he entered the Law School of Boston University, where he studied for another year, and then successfully passed the examinations for admission to the Maine bar. Meantime, however, he had followed the method of raising funds for his education which has been followed by innumerable professional men in New England. After his graduation from Bowdoin College he engaged in teaching and during the year of 1921-22 he was superintendent of schools in Canton, Maine. It was the following fall that he began the study of law in Harvard Law School, 1922, and he was admitted to the bar March 1, 1927. He is now (1928) laying the foundations of what promises to be a successful legal career, but he is not depending wholly upon the well-known slow growth of legal practice. He had already engaged in the insurance business and he is continuing that line of activity while he builds up his legal practice. During the period of the participation of the United States in the World War, Mr. Bate enlisted in the Navy and served on transport duty from October, 1917, to February, 1918, when he was discharged with the rank of lieutenant of the junior grade. He is a member of the Kennebec County and Maine State Bar associations. He has been secretary and treasurer of the Winthrop Chamber of Commerce since March, 1926, and he is actively interested in local public affairs in Winthrop. He was the first Commander and organizer of Winthrop Post, No. 40, American Legion; he is also Past Vice-State Commander of the American Legion. He attended the National Convention of the American Legion held in Paris in 1927. Fraternally, he is identified with all the York Rite bodies of the Masonic Order and with Kora Temple, Ancient Arabic Order Nobles of the Mystic Shrine; and he is also a member of the Independent Order of Odd Fellows. He is identified with one of the fraternities of Bowdoin College, and his religious affiliation is with the Congregational church.

Francis H. Bate was married, in Portland, Maine, in June, 1922, to Nellie L. Sullivan, who was born in Portland, Maine, daughter of John C. Sullivan. Mr. and Mrs. Bate make their home in Winthrop.

FRED PAUL RAY—Few successes among the younger generation of business men have exceeded that of Fred P. Ray, head of the Ray Motor Company, No. 28 Postoffice Square, Bangor. Mr. Ray began his career in the clothing line, but after a few years, in view of the tremendous expansion of the automobile industry in this country, he obtained the agency for the high-class Chandler car and the Selden motor truck, and has been pushing these products vigorously and with gratifying results ever since. He is a leader as well in civic activities and has won a commendable place in the community.

Fred Paul Ray was born at Mount Lebanon, Syria, April 15, 1892, and in the shadow of this sanctuary received his first religious instruction and divine inspirations. He received his education in the public schools of his native land and of Bangor, on the completion of which he entered the ladies' garment and clothing business. He continued in this line for himself until 1917, when he became associated with Frank S. Sawyer in the firm of the Sawyer & Ray Motor Company, Bangor agents for Mitchell automobiles, and Chase trucks. A short time later he took over the agency for the Grant six-cylinder motor cars. In 1918 Mr. Ray bought Mr. Sawyer's interest in the business, and the firm was continued under the original name until 1919, when it was changed to the Ray Motor Company. In 1921 he took over the Chandler agency, and became distributor for that car for the eastern half of Maine, which connection has continued ever since. Mr. Ray is president of the company, while his brother, Joseph A. Ray, is treasurer, and for a good many years has been an associate.

Mr. Ray moved to Bangor from Bar Harbor in 1917, at which time he was selling the Chase truck and the Harley-Davidson motorcycle. He first took the motorcycle as a side line, and while in the clothing business also handled the sale of the Chase trucks. Their service department has grown in ten years

from two to nineteen men. This is located on Howard Lane behind the showrooms, and contains accommodations for fifty cars, while at their other place at No. 54 Cumberland Street they have space for sixty additional.

Mr. Ray is a popular member of the St. Andrew's Lodge of Free and Accepted Masons, and all bodies of the Scottish Rite, including Anah Temple, Ancient Arabic Order Nobles of the Mystic Shrine. He is a member of the American Legion by virtue of having served as a supply sergeant in the United States Army during the World War. He is a member of the National Automobile Dealers' Association and of the Bangor Automobile Dealers' Association, of which organization he was formerly secretary. Mr. Ray's clubs include the Tarratine, Masonic and others to which he gives such time as he can spare from his regular duties. He is a member and attendant of the Protestant Episcopal church, and his hobby is fishing and hunting.

LOUIS KIRSTEIN—Because of the remarkable activities that were inaugurated in land development under his far-sighted supervision in that part of the State of which Bangor is a flourishing center, Louis Kirstein is destined to be remembered as the pioneer realtor upon a very extensive scale, as well as a director of insurance matters whose successful ventures became of State-wide importance. Coming to Maine without funds or influence, Mr. Kirstein evolved his own business plans, and soon established a realty institution that which comparatively a few years has directly benefited a host of homeseekers and business people.

Louis Kirstein was born in Soldau, Germany, March 10, 1848, and died in Bangor, January 3, 1924. Coming to the United States in his early years, he at once took up his residence in Bangor, and remained here to the close of his useful career, with the exception of a few years of travel in the north part of the State, and his management of a general store in Houlton for a short period. In 1891, Mr. Kirstein established a men's clothing store on Exchange Street, in Bangor, which he disposed of for reasons of ill health, when he began to engage in the real estate and insurance business, opening his offices at No. 36 Main Street.

In 1894, Mr. Kirstein embarked in fire insurance and real estate, with his offices in the Merrill Trust Building, and he so continued to the date of his death. In 1908, he formed the corporation of Louis Kirstein and Sons, in association with Abram L. Kirstein, who is now actively engaged in the firm's business, and Bernhard M. Kirstein, who is now vice-president of the firm of S. W. Straus and Company, in New York City.

During the World War, Mr. Kirstein served as treasurer of the Jewish Relief organization. He was instrumental in establishing the Home for Aged Men, on State Street; and he was a member of all branches of Odd Fellowship.

Louis Kirstein married, November 17, 1872, Sophia Prinz, also a native of Soldau, in Germany; and on the occasion of their fiftieth wedding anniversary, November 17, 1922, Mr. Kirstein dispensed a very large amount of money to the poor and needy of the city of Bangor, much of it through the organizations established for relief work. He has at various times contributed other money for such purposes, without making his actions public.

The Louis Kirstein & Sons Company, the largest real estate agency in Maine, employing some fifteen people in the Bangor office, does a business amounting to $2,000,000, annually, dealing largely in timberland and farms, in addition to its local realty and insurance interests. One of this company's developments is known as the "Little City in Itself," and is located at the terminus of Center Street in Bangor, this being the largest successful event of the kind in this section. It was started in 1908; and in 1912, another development was inaugurated, known as the Fairmount Development, with the organization of the Fairmount Realty Company, and upon an even larger scale than the former property. Meantime, also, the city of Bangor was given a park in the center of the Fairmount location, and to be known as Fairmount Park, the surrounding district being disposed of for high-class residences, solely. In 1920, the company instituted another land development, known as "The Highlands," and in 1925, Fairmount Addition was started, eighty-four per cent of the lots being sold during the first two weeks of the opening.

The corporation has been instrumental in much building operations, both for firms and individuals, and they are the owners of the Kirstein Block, on Central Street, in Bangor. They are Eastern and Northern Maine agents for S. W. Straus & Company, New York City, in first mortgage and real estate bonds, and an extensive business is done in arranging for first mortgages. The present personnel of the company follows: Abram L. Kirstein, president and treasurer; Bernhard M. Kerstein, vice-president; Simon O'Leary, Jr., director.

Abram Louis Kirstein, president of Louis Kirstein & Sons, was born March 10, 1882, in Bangor, where he was graduated at the high school. He is also treasurer and director of the Fairmount Realty Association, the One Hundred Associates of Bangor, and the United Investment Company; director of the Merchants' National Bank; former member of the School Board; member of the Tarratine Club; the Conduskeag Canoe and Country Club; Independent Order of Odd Fellows; Knights of Pythias; Benevolent and Protective Order of Elks; Rotary Club; Chamber of Commerce; Bangor Historical Society; National Economic League, and Portland Real Estate Board. He is a Republican in his political views.

WILFRED I. BUTTERFIELD—His general law practice at Bangor has brought Wilfred I. Butterfield into contact with legal matters of vital importance in his profession, and he has won a repute both as an attorney and as a judge of sterling worth, clear and comprehensive in plea and ruling. He has held office both in Kingman and Bangor, and has upon all occasions served his constituency and the public in general with pronounced ability and intelligence. He is a son of Jerome Butterfield, who was born in Springfield, and is associated with real estate and timberland business, and Adra Anna (Robinson) Butterfield, a native of Sydney, who died in 1898.

Wilfred I. Butterfield was born April 10, 1883, in Kingman, and he attended the public schools there, and attended Springfield High School, and Phillips Academy, Exeter, New Hampshire. Graduating in

the liberal arts course at Harvard College, he received his degree of Bachelor of Arts in the class of 1909, and preparing for his profession at the Law School of Harvard University, he was graduated there in 1912, with the degree of Bachelor of Laws. For a while, Mr. Butterfield joined his father in the country store and potato business at Kingman, and from 1916 to 1919, he practiced law in Kingman, when he removed to Bangor. Here, in 1926, was formed the present law firm of Butterfield and Weatherbee, with offices at No. 44 Central Street. Mr. Butterfield is a member of the Penobscot County Bar Association.

Mr. Butterfield is a Republican in his political views. In 1920, he received the appointment of clerk of the Bangor Municipal Court, serving thus until 1922, when he was appointed judge of that court, in which office he continued until 1926. In 1916-19, inclusive, he was town clerk and tax collector for the town of Kingman.

During the period of the World War, Mr. Butterfield was active in many ways for the cause of the hour. He was a "four-minute" speaker; he served as a member of the Legal Advisory Board of Penobscot County, and he was an assistant fuel administrator. Fraternally, he is affiliated with Rising Virtue Lodge, No. 10, Free and Accepted Masons; Mount Moriah Chapter, No. 6, Royal Arch Masons; Anah Temple, Ancient Arabic Order Nobles of the Mystic Shrine; the Order of the Eastern Star; and Sigma Alpha Epsilon Fraternity. His clubs are: Kiwanis, Tarratine, Masonic, and his hobby is camping. His religious faith is that of the Universalist church.

Wilfred I. Butterfield married, May 10, 1916, Margaret Ayer, who was born in Lincoln. Their children: Wilfred I., Jr, Ruth E., Jerome A., deceased.

WILLIAM S. MASON—The demands of the steadily increasing activities of the Bangor Fire Department have, in Fire Chief William S. Mason, an official whose response is as alert and ready in the matter of adequate equipment as for meeting the exigencies of fires and the best and surest means of subduing that element. Chief Mason, by consecutive reappointment, has demonstrated that he is a man well fitted for this most important office, and that his practical plan and work were instrumental in placing the department on its present excellent firefighting basis. His father, who was chief of the Bangor Fire Department for ten years, was John Mason, a native of Belfast, Ireland, and for fifty years was a carriage builder and blacksmith; he married Ellen C. Coleman, also born in Belfast, Ireland, died in 1925.

William S. Mason was born March 24, 1864, in Bangor, Maine, where he attended the public and high schools. He then followed the same trade as his father, that of blacksmith and carriage builder, and in which he continued for thirty years. For sixteen years he engaged in business in his father's name, John Mason and Sons; and in 1907, he received his first appointment as fire chief, so continuing seven years, or until 1914, when he went on the road for a year as a saleman for department supplies. In 1915, Mr. Mason was reappointed chief, and he served until 1918, when he left to resume carriage building and blacksmithing, under the name of W.

S. Mason. In January, 1927, Chief Mason received his present appointment as head of the Bangor Fire Department.

In political matters, Mr. Mason is a Republican, and he served six years as a member of Bangor City Council. Fraternally, he is affiliated with Oriental Lodge, Independent Order of Odd Fellows; and he is a member of the International Fire Chiefs' Association, and of the Massachusetts Fire Chiefs' Club. He is a communicant and vestryman of St. John's Protestant Episcopal Church. His hobbies are fishing and hunting.

William S. Mason married, June 25, 1885, Eveline S. McGreevey, who was born in Bangor. Their children: 1. Frank W. 2. Annie M. 3. Edwin S., served in the United States Army during the World War, as first sergeant; was located at Newport News, Virginia, as instructor in the Air Force.

CHARLES H. BUSSELL is postmaster at Pittsfield, Maine. He has also been a successful lumberman, and has had much experience also in the woolen business. He takes a keen interest in public affairs and has occupied official posts in connection with the water works and School Board. He is generally recognized as a good all-round business man and official, who can always be counted on to do his part when the public interest is at stake.

Charles H. Bussell was born at Milford, Maine, October 6, 1878, son of Isaiah W. and Helen M. (Coffin) Bussell; the father, who is still living, was a lumber man, and was born at Argyle, Maine, and the mother, who died in April, 1925, was born at Burlington, Maine. Mr. Bussell attended the public schools at Milford, Maine, and the Maine Central Institute, at Pittsfield, Maine, and then the Bangor Business College. He was then employed in the lumber and log driving business for a period of seven years. He was employed for ten years in the woolen business, then in the lumber business under the name of I. W. Bussell Company at Milford, Maine, five years. He was appointed postmaster in March, 1922, and reappointed in 1926. As indicated he takes an active part in civic affairs also, and has been on the School Board and has been one of the trustees of the Water Works Board. Mr. Bussell is a Republican in politics. He belongs to the Free and Accepted Masons. He is a member of the Universalist Men's Club, and he and his family attend the Universalist church.

Charles H. Bussell married, April 29, 1897, at Pittsfield, Maine, Abbie Hutchins, daughter of James E. and Lucy (Shaw) Hutchins. Children: 1. Linwood C., who married Gladys Harrington, of Rockland, Maine. 2. Arline H., who married Mr. Kenneth G. Smith, of Everett, Massachusetts, now deceased. 3. Norris H., now with Swift and Company. 4. Esther S., who is now a teacher.

CHARLES G. MOULTON—The surname Moulton and the corporate name Limerick Mills have become well known in the textile industry throughout New England. The one is synonymous with the other and the story of the mills and the man are almost inseparable, touched liberally with the romance of industry. At the present time (1928) we find the Limerick Mills capitalized at half a million dollars, with Mr. Moulton owning all the capitalization excepting the qualifying shares of the directors;

and we find the plant in process of enlargement and reconstruction which, upon completion, will result in one of the largest manufacturing establishments of its kind in Maine and all New England. This great industrial success has been wrought in fewer than thirty years, largely through the individual effort and foresight of Mr. Moulton, who is accounted a business man of eminence, a leader in industry.

Mr. Moulton was born May 30, 1864, at Alfred, Maine, son of George D. and Nancy Frost (Young) Moulton, both of whom are deceased. George D. Moulton was born in February, 1824, engaged in farming all his life, and died in January, 1907. Nancy Frost (Young) Moulton was born in 1828, and died in 1909.

Charles G. Moulton received his academic training in the public schools of Alfred. He graduated from high school in 1882, at the age of eighteen years, having worked, during the last two years of study, in the office of the Register of Deeds for York County. The early years of his business life followed the relatively uneventful course usual to that period between graduation and the beginning of one's actual career; but in that period of diversified contacts Mr. Moulton secured experience equally diversified. In 1889, he went to Limerick, to take the place for six weeks of the cashier, William W. Mason, of the Limerick National Bank, and has been identified with the bank since that time, filling the office of cashier for many years and later the presidency, which office he still holds. When he was nearly thirty-four years of age he became associated with four men, Charles H. Adams, S. O. Clark, Allen Garner, and J. Merrill Lord, in the planning of a mill company. It was on May 20, 1899, that they secured charter for Limerick Mills, whose then modest capitalization was thirty thousand dollars. Officials as named in those original articles were: Mr. Adams, president; Mr. Lord, clerk; and Mr. Moulton, treasurer. The company took over the old Holland Mill, known as the Holland Blanket Mill, reputed to have been the oldest textile plant in Maine, or one of the oldest, and without doubt the oldest in York County. The mill was in financial difficulties; its machines were antiquated, in many instances useless, causing the incorporators of Limerick Mills to believe that certain pieces must have been on the site one hundred and fifty years before, when the first plant was founded there. Trouble after trouble developed to annoy and vex Mr. Moulton and his associates; and in those early struggles one quality belonging to Mr. Moulton assisted greatly toward the subsequent success: his faculty for recognizing in men their special aptitudes, enabling him to place them in the most advantageous positions. Two such men were J. Henry Smith, general manager, and George R. Connor, superintendent, both of whom through loyalty and capability, have assisted Mr. Moulton in the building up of the enterprise, and to whom he holds himself greatly indebted for its success. One of the troubles most serious to the five associates during the infancy of the corporation was the problem of power. The small waterpower available to the mill, also some of the tenements in connection with the plant, were rendered useless from a washout which occurred in the spring freshets of 1901. This necessitated the reconstruction of the dam, which was accomplished in a substantial manner with granite from a local quarry. It soon became necessary to obtain additional power. This resulted in the organization of a power company; the purchase of a power site on the Little Ossipee River, on which was erected a hydro-electric generating station, known as the Ledgemere Power Station. This power unit incidentally became the Western Maine Power Company, serving a substantial territory in Southwestern Maine and in New Hampshire, and has since been purchased and consolidated into the Central Maine Power Company. But that is incidental to the story of Limerick Mills. In 1901, Mr. Clark succeeded Mr. Adams to the presidency; in 1903, Mr. Garner succeeded Mr. Clark; and in 1904, Mr. Moore (John F. Moore, who was not one of the original incorporators of the company) became president. In 1905, the capital stock was increased to one hundred thousand dollars; in 1909 it was raised to three hundred thousand. Throughout all this time Mr. Moulton continued in the important office of treasurer. In 1920, Mr. Moore went out as president, and was succeeded by Frank D. Fenderson, with Raymon A. Quint as vice-president and Mr. Moulton in the double rôle of treasurer and agent. In fact, Mr. Moulton, since 1899, and the plant's foundation, has been the steady, reliable, guiding spirit, as treasurer. In 1926, the capitalization was increased to five hundred thousand dollars, and it is thought likely that within a few years it will again be increased, perhaps to an even million. Limerick Mills covers several acres, and in this spacious manufactory are twenty-six thousand spindles for worsted goods, twelve thousand twist spindles and ten sets of drawing. As a spinning mill it is equipped to produce the finest of worsted and mohair yarns, which go into the best of mohair plushes, for automobiles, etc. For a number of years almost the entire output of Limerick Mills was sold to the Sanford Mills, Sanford, Maine. This industry, by reason of sound management, has not only survived the textile depression of post-war over-production, but has, as made manifest, increased in magnitude. Mr. Moulton is also president of the Limerick National Bank, and obviously, a dominant citizen in his community, Limerick. He has never been too engrossed in the complexities of commerce and industry to participate in the welfare work of this community. For years he was a trustee of Limerick Academy, and is now a trustee of Parsonsfield Seminary. His many philanthropies have done much to build up the town. During the World War he served on boards and committees in charge of the prosecution of the conflict, and was active in the several campaigns of the Liberty Loan. Fraternally, he is affiliated with the Free and Accepted Masons, and is a member of the Home Market Club of Boston, the Limerick Town Club, and is a trustee of Parsonsfield Seminary.

Charles G. Moulton married (first), in 1900, Frances E. Mason, daughter of Jeremiah M. and Martha E. (Woodman) Mason; and to this union was born a daughter: Olga F., who married Bernard A. Libby and is the mother of two children, Dorothy and Charles. Frances E. (Mason) Moulton was a lady of fine intelligence, and one of the first, if not the first, of women to become president of a National bank in the State of Maine. She served as president of the Limerick National Bank from 1897 until the time of her death in 1919. Mr. Moulton married (second) Mrs. Fannie M. Pease, daughter of James

Hart Brown. Mr. Moulton and his wife attend the Baptist church.

Endowed liberally with those attributes of character that endear one to his friends, as well as he is possessed of marked commercial direction, Mr. Moulton retains the sincere affection and esteem of all who know him. He is of impressive presence, forceful, firm in opinion but ready at once to alter an opinion when confronted by evidence in point; he is kindly, genial, and energetic of mind and body; and in every consideration he is valuable to community, State and Nation.

ABRAHAM M. RUDMAN—The ability of Russians and their descendants to make comfortable places for themselves in the cosmology of American affairs has been strikingly illustrated in the careers of Lewis Rudman and his son, Abraham M. Rudman, of Bangor, who are engaged in the furniture business and the practice of the law, respectively. Lewis Rudman, a native of Russia, has made a success of his business for many years, and is rated as one of Bangor's most respected citizens. His son maintains law offices at No. 44 Central Street, having practiced law since the World War and having made gratifying progress, more so with each succeeding year.

Abraham M. Rudman was born at Bangor July 1, 1896, his mother, still living to participate in his triumphs, having also, been a native of Russia. He attended the grammar and high schools of Bangor, where he made very satisfactory records, and at the end of which courses he decided that his opportunities lay in the realm of the law. He accordingly entered the Law School of the University of Maine, and graduated in the class of 1917, with the degree of Bachelor of Laws. The World War having broken out just before his graduation, he proved his allegiance to his native land by entering the United States Navy, in which he rendered effective service and after the Armistice was discharged. He took up his practice at Bangor, has been here ever since, and has made a most gratifying record, and looks forward enthusiastically to the promises of a rosy future. He was admitted to practice in all the Maine courts and the Federal Court.

Mr. Rudman is a valued member of the Penobscot County Bar Association and the Maine Bar Association. In politics he adheres to the principles of the Republican party. His fraternal associations include the Phi Delta Phi Legal Fraternity; Bangor Lodge, Benevolent and Protective Order of Elks, and the Knights of Pythias. Mr. Rudman is fond of outdoor life, and his hobby, which he gratifies often, is fishing.

In 1923, Abraham M. Rudman married Irene E. Epstein, a native of Boston, Massachusetts, and a son, Robert S. Rudman, has been born as a blessing to their union.

JOHN S. DOW—As an enterprising and forward-looking business man, John S. Dow has few superiors in Bangor. Mr. Dow has demonstrated the value of intensive salesmanship when applied to industry and commerce, for he has made a notable success out of a farm implement business and also out of an automobile agency. Mr. Dow is essentially a self-made man, having had little financial backing at the start, and having been thrown upon his own

238 MAINE—A HISTORY

resources to make his way. It is out of such experiences, when they do not snap the cord, that the best American manhood proceeds. While it is true that success in a business way is no longer the tedious, lifelong process that once it was, several fundamental rules still govern human performances, and must inevitably be applied if the individual would reach a competence and receive the applause of his fellowmen. Such principles are well understood by Mr. Dow as he handles his agricultural machinery and Buick automobiles.

John S. Dow was born at Newport, Maine, on November 21, 1880, the son of Edgar R. Dow, native of Plymouth, this State, and Augusta M. (Dudley) Dow, born in St. Albans, Maine, and still living to see her son's gratifying success. His father engaged as postmaster and sheriff of Newport, but in the latter part of his life was in the condensed milk business, which also attracted the son.

John S. Dow received his education in the grammar and high schools of Newport and the Doe Business College at Bangor, at the completion of which he obtained a position with the Borden Milk Company at Newport, with which concern he did satisfactory work for four years. He then answered a call, to the service of a condensed milk concern, at West Liberty, Iowa, where he remained two years. In 1906, Mr. Dow returned to Bangor and was warmly welcomed by his friends, to whom he imparted the information that he had become associated with Wilbur H. Knowles in handling farm implements under the firm name of Knowles & Dow Company. In 1912, in addition to continuing this business, they took over the Buick Motor Car agency, and continued both businesses until 1919, when they bought out the ·C. M. Conant Implement Company, which they have operated successfully ever since. The Buick agency has been continued under the name of the Knowles & Dow Company, with offices and showrooms at Nos. 52 and 54 Postoffice Square, and with a service station in the rear. This agency is probably the oldest in Bangor today, and its friends are legion.

In fraternal order circles, Mr. Dow is a member of Meridian Splendor Lodge of the Free and Accepted Masons; the Chapter, Royal Arch Masons; the Independent Order of Odd Fellows; the Bangor Lodge of Elks; the Knights of Pythias; and the United Commercial Travelers' Association; a member of the Chamber of Commerce, and of the Tarrantine Club. In politics Mr. Dow's affiliations are with the Republican party.

ELLIS Y. ELDRIDGE—One of the largest automobile dealers in Bangor, Maine, at the present time (1928) is Ellis Y. Eldridge, founder and principal owner of the E. Y. Eldridge Company, distributors for Studebaker cars for three counties, for Cadillac cars for five counties, and for LaSalle and Erskine cars for Bangor. The business is located at No. 84 Summer Street, where service for all these cars is provided.

Ellis Y. Eldridge was born in Surry, Hancock County, Maine, April 4, 1881, son of Henry Eldridge, a native of Surry, who is engaged in the painting and contracting business, and of Laura (Philips) Eldridge, also a native of Surry, Maine, who died in 1900. Mr. Eldridge attended the public schools of Gardiner, Maine, and after completing his studies in

Gardiner High School took a commercial course in Shaw's Business College in Augusta. Upon the completion of his commercial training he took a position as bookkeeper in the employ of Armour and Company, with whom he remained for a period of two years. In 1901 he came to Bangor and entered the employ of the American Railway Express Company, a connection which he maintained continuously for seven years. In 1908 he again changed his occupation, as well as his connection, by entering the Second National Bank of Bangor, where he remained until 1912. In that year he became associated with the Bangor Motor Company, as manager, and here he found the interest and the line of business which appeals most to his tastes and to his special abilities. In 1925 he organized the E. Y. Eldridge Company and engaged in the automobile sales business for himself, locating at No. 40 Summer Street, in Bangor. The company holds the agency for the Studebaker cars for Penobscot, Hancock, and Piscataquis counties; the agency for the Cadillac cars for Penobscot, Piscataquis, Hancock, Aroostook, and Washington counties; and the agency for the LaSalle cars for Bangor. They give service as well as sell Studebaker and Cadillac cars, and their concern is the largest of its kind in Bangor. The volume of business has developed to proportions which require the services of twenty-five employees, and Mr. Eldridge has established a reputation for sound business methods and for personal integrity which is, in itself, a valuable asset. Politically, Mr. Eldridge supports the principles of the Republican party. During the Spanish-American War, in 1898, he served in the Second Regiment Maine State Militia. Fraternally, he is identified with Rising Virtue Lodge, Free and Accepted Masons; and he is also a member of all the York Rite bodies and all the Scottish Rite bodies of that Order, also a member of Anah Temple, Ancient Arabic Order Nobles of the Mystic Shrine. He is a member of the board of directors of the Bangor Chamber of Commerce, and past president of the Bangor Auto Dealers' Association, and is well known in club circles, being a member of the Tarrantine Club, Penobscot Valley Country Club, and of the Conduskeag Canoe and Country Club, of which last he was purser for several years. He is fond of hunting, fishing, canoeing, and motor-boating, and has a host of friends in Bangor and vicinity. His family attends the Christian Science church.

Ellis Y. Eldridge was married, in 1915, to Celia Merrill, who was born in Newport, Maine, and they are the parents of one son, Merrill.

H. ROY BARD—As manager of the Bangor branch of the Henley-Kimball Company, of Boston, distributor for Hudson and Essex automobiles, H. Roy Bard has been located in Bangor since 1919, his establishment being located at the corner of May and Summer streets. He is a valued member of the Bangor Chamber of Commerce.

H. Roy Bard was born in Limestone, Maine, January 14, 1888, and received his education in the public schools of Fort Fairfield, Maine. When his school training was completed he found his first employment in the telegraphic department of the Bangor & Aroostook Railroad Company, but in 1908 he engaged in the automobile business, in which line he has continued to the present time (1928). In 1915 he became associated with the Henley-Kimball Company, of Boston, distributor for Hudson and Essex automobiles, and this connection has been maintained to the present time. From 1915 to 1919 he was connected with the Portland branch of this company, handling the wholesale end for the State of Maine, but in 1919 he came to Bangor and established The Henley-Kimball Company branch for the distribution of cars in this territory. The establishment on the corner of May and Summer streets, in Bangor, is well known and very well patronized, and Mr. Bard is one of the leading personalities among the men of the trade in Bangor. He has served as treasurer and subsequently as president of the Bangor Auto Dealers' Association, and as a member of the board of directors of the Bangor Chamber of Commerce he is influential in the business life of the city. Politically, he gives his support to the principles and the candidates of the Republican party, and fraternally he is identified with Rising Virtue Lodge, No. 10, Free and Accepted Masons; and with the Knights of Pythias. He is a member of the Tarratine Club, of the Penobscot Valley Country Club, of the Conduskeag Canoe and Country Club, of the Lucerne in Maine Country Club, and of the Lions Club, and has a host of friends here. His favorite forms of recreation are fishing and hunting, and his religious interest is with the Universalist church, of which he is an attendant. Mr. Bard is a son of Charles N. Bard, who was born in Lisbon Falls, Maine, and was engaged as a contractor and builder and as a farmer to the time of his death, in 1907, and of Hattie F. (Leighton) Bard, who was born in Corinna, Maine, and survives her husband.

H. Roy Bard was married, in 1918, to Eleanor W. Dennis, a native of Portland, Maine, and they are the parents of two children: Eleanor D., and Charles N.

GEORGE W. FLETCHER—GILBERT F. FLETCHER—FRANK G. ERICKSON—FLETCHER AND BUTTERFIELD COMPANY—The Fletcher and Butterfield Company, wholesale and retail monument dealers at No. 85 Central Street, Bangor, is one of the oldest and most substantial concerns of its line in this section, and the association with it of such dependable business men as George W. Fletcher, Gilbert F. Fletcher, and Frank G. Erickson, has given it a standing of the highest kind.

The firm was first established in 1830 under the name of the S. B. Bradbury Company, and continued under this style until 1867, when it was purchased by George M. Fletcher, who continued in the business alone for a short time, when he admitted as a partner Benjamin F. Butterfield and changed the name to Fletcher and Butterfield. The firm continued in this style until 1890, when Mr. Butterfield died. Mr. Fletcher continued the business until 1913, when he died. It was then incorporated, and George W. Fletcher, Gilbert F. Fletcher (sons of George M. Fletcher), and Frank G. Erickson became officers; they have remained under this leadership ever since. The company has a quarry at Marshfield, Maine, and quarries the celebrated Marshfield pink granite, which has found such vogue and sale throughout the country. The entire output of this quarry is shipped to a Western concern for distribution, and its products make it the largest concern in the State of Maine today. The manufacturing plant is located at Brew-

er, Maine. The company is equipped to cut and manufacture any design of stone desired, also granite.

As for the partners, we begin with George W. Fletcher, who was born at Bangor, August 23, 1881, son of George M. and Ella A. (Butterfield) Fletcher. George M. Fletcher, native of Wilton, Maine, was the original founder of the Fletcher and Butterfield Company, and engaged in the granite business until his death in 1913. During the Civil War he served in the Union Army as a member of Company K, Eighth Regiment of Maine Volunteers, with the rank of assistant hospital steward, and in later years was active in the B. H. Beal Post of the Grand Army of the Republic. His wife, also a native of Wilton, died in 1910, closing a life of great usefulness, characterized by her womanly graciousness and charitable acts.

Mr. Fletcher received his education at the grammar and high schools of Bangor, at the completion of which he engaged in the jewelry business, and followed it twelve years. In 1912 he became associated with the Fletcher and Butterfield Company, of which concern he is now the capable president. Mr. Fletcher is an excellent business man, who enjoys the confidence and admiration of his associates and contemporaries, and he has taken such an active interest in civic affairs as to win the name of splendid citizen. He is a member of St. Andrew's Lodge, Free and Accepted Masons; the Royal Arch Masons and the Knights of Pythias. In politics he is allied with the Republicans. He is a member of the Universalist church. His hobby is his family and home life.

George W. Fletcher married, in 1919, Grace Lowe, born at Deer Island, Maine, and they have three children: Stanley, Ruth and Barbara.

Gilbert F. Fletcher, partner in the Fletcher and Butterfield Company, was born at Bangor, December 20, 1878, the son of George M. and Ella A. (Butterfield) Fletcher, and brother of George W. Fletcher. He received his education in the public schools of Bangor, and at the completion of his courses learned the steamfitting and installation of automatic sprinklers. He followed these lines thirteen years, a decade of this time being with the R. I. Supply and Sprinkler Company. In 1910 he came to Bangor from the field and became associated with the Fletcher and Butterfield Company. Since 1913 he has been treasurer of the concern, and the success of the firm has been largely due to his financial programs.

Mr. Fletcher is a member of the Spanish-American War Veterans, having served in the Spanish-American War as a private in the First Regiment of Maine Infantry, United States Army. He belongs to the Knights of Pythias, and St. Andrew's Lodge, Free and Accepted Masons. He is active in the local Kiwanis Club and in the campaigns of the Republican party. His religious affiliation is with the Universalist church. He is fond of the great outdoors, and enjoys hunting and fishing.

Gilbert F. Fletcher married, in 1904, Eunice E. Ellison, a native of Boston.

Frank G. Erickson, who was born at Providence, Rhode Island, June 6, 1884, the son of Andrew O. native of Gothenberg, Sweden, and Olivia (Jacobson) Erickson, born at Gothenberg, died in 1887; his father was a sea-faring man for thirty years, but the latter part of his life was spent in the furniture business. Mr. Erickson was educated in the Providence public schools, the Technological High School of the same city and the Boston Business College. On the completion of his education he worked ten years in the parquetry and hardwood floor business at Boston, then entered the stove business at Malden. In 1913 he removed to Bangor as a partner in the Fletcher and Butterfield Company, and has continued successfully with this firm ever since.

Mr. Erickson is a member of St. Andrew's Lodge, Free and Accepted Masons, both York and Scottish Rite bodies, including Anah Temple, Ancient Arabic Order Nobles of the Mystic Shrine. In political affairs he is an adherent of the Republican party. He is a member of the Universalist church. His hobbies are boating and automobiling. He is fond of the sea and water, having inherited the fondness from his honored father, who, by the way, served as mate under Captain Sigsbee, commander of the deep water United States boat "Blake"; Sigsbee, it will be remembered, commanded the Battleship "Maine" when she was the subject of an explosion in the harbor at Havana, Cuba, in 1898, which mysterious affair was the cause of a declaration of war against Spain by the United States. Mr. Erickson served with Sigsbee before the sinking of the "Maine."

VERNER E. GILPATRICK—The position of city solicitor is one carrying with it considerable responsibilities, and the proper fulfillment of its duties presupposes more than ordinary ability. Verner E. Gilpatrick, now a successful practicing attorney at Bangor, acted as City Solicitor of Brewer for three years. He took further interest in Republican politics, notably as chairman two years of the Republican City Committee, one year as a member of the Penobscot County Committee, and one year as second selectman in the town of Orono.

Mr. Gilpatrick was born at Orient, Maine, July 21, 1894, son of Elmer E. Gilpatrick, retired lumberman, and Sarah A. (Logue) Gilpatrick, native of Medway, Maine, who is also still living. His father, born at Danforth, this State, engaged successfully in the lumber business until his retirement, and became a stockholder in the Summit Lumber Company. He is recognized as one of the best business men of this section, and enjoys the reputation of a good citizen.

Mr. Gilpatrick attended the grammar and high schools of Island Falls, Maine, and graduated from the University of Maine in the class of 1917, with the degree of Bachelor of Arts, after which he took a short course in the Law School of the University of Maine. Desiring to avail himself of all the practical instruments possible, he read law in the office of Donald Snow, of Bangor, and in 1923 was admitted to the bar. He has practiced here ever since, with offices in Suite 2, No. 77 Central Street. He has been admitted to practice in all the State courts and the Federal Court.

Mr. Gilpatrick enlisted in March, 1917, for service in the World War, as a private in the One Hundred and Sixty-Fifth Battalion of the Canadian Expeditionary Forces, and was discharged at London, in July, 1918, whereupon, on July 15 following, he enlisted in the American Army with the Four Hundred and Fifty-sixth Motor Transport Corps, stationed at Base Section No. 3, London, England. He returned to this country and was discharged in July, 1919.

Mr. Gilpatrick is a member and attendant upon the services of the Congregational church. He is a member of the Penobscot County Bar Association; the Phi Alpha Delta Law Fraternity; Mechanics' Lodge of the Free and Accepted Masons; all Masonic bodies including the Scottish Rite, and Anah Temple, Ancient Arabic Order Nobles of the Mystic Shrine; and the Bangor Lodge, Benevolent and Protective Order of Elks. He belongs to the Hannah Dustin Society of Haverhill. His hobby is hunting and fishing.

WILLIAM WIDGERY THOMAS—This State of Maine has given many men to public life, and of them all the late William Widgery Thomas stands in the foremost rank. As a diplomat he served his country loyally and well, and he received the well-deserved guerdon of a wonderful career when, on his retirement from official duties in 1905, the then Secretary of State Hay wrote to him a letter of thanks for his great work for his country and for the world, in which the representative of the United States Government said: "You have had the longest, the most distinguished, the most useful term of service that any American has ever had." As United States Bearer of Despatches he carried the treaty to Turkey which this country had made with the Ottoman Empire; he was vice-consul general at Constantinople in 1862 and 1863; was war consul from 1863 to 1866 and acting consul at Galatz, Sweden, during those turbulent years, and was Minister to Sweden and Norway from 1883 to 1885, from 1889 to 1894, and from 1897 to 1905. He was the first Minister to hoist the American flag at Stockholm, Sweden, and on three different occasions it was his diplomacy that settled controversies between the United States, Great Britain and Germany.

Mr. Thomas was born in Portland, in this State, the son of Peter and Elizabeth White (Goddard) Thomas. The family is of Welsh origin, the first of the name coming to this country about 1650, and settling in Massachusetts. The earliest of the family to arrive in Maine came here in 1769, where he married Harriet Cox, descendant of George Cleve, one of the men who founded and settled Portland in 1632. Elizabeth White Goddard, the mother of William Widgery Thomas, of this record, was the daughter of Henry Goddard, a native of Portland, prominent there in the hardware and shipping business.

Mr. Thomas acquired his early education in the public schools of Portland, after which he entered Bowdoin College, at Brunswick, from which institution he graduated in 1860 with the degree of Bachelor of Arts. He then took a course in Harvard Law School, and was admitted to the Maine bar in 1861, practicing law in Portland from 1863 to 1869, during the intervals of his diplomatic missions. From Bethany College, Lindsborg, Kansas, Mr. Thomas received the degree of Doctor of Laws in 1901, and the same degree was conferred upon him by Bowdoin College in 1913. He was a member of the Maine Historical Society and the Swedish Geographical Society. He was also a member of the Royal Shooting Club of Sweden and the Royal Swedish Association of Literature, History and Antiquities. He was very fond of yachting and was founder of the Portland Yachting Club.

Politics, naturally, had much of an attraction for Mr. Thomas. He was commissioner of Public Lands

MAINE—A HISTORY   241

and Immigration from 1870 to 1873. During 1873, 1874 and 1875, he was an active member of the State Legislature and was Speaker of the House during the two latter years. He was appointed president of the State Republican Convention, and was State Senator in 1879. He was deeply interested in the colony of New Sweden, which he founded in this State in 1870, and upon which he spent much of his time and money. He was notable as an author and orator, and among his best-known literary works are the following: "Sweden and the Swedes," published in 1891; "The Story of New Sweden," and a translation from the Swedish language of "The Last Athenian."

On October 11, 1887, Mr. Thomas married (first), in Stockholm, Sweden, Dagmar Elizabeth Tornebladh, daughter of Henrik Ragnar Tornebladh, of that city. He was a Latin scholar, author and orator, and a director of the Bank of Sweden. Mrs. Thomas passed away in 1912. Mr. and Mrs. Thomas were the parents of two children: William Widgery, who died in infancy, and Oscar Percival, who resides in Portland. On June 2, 1915, Mr. Thomas married (second) his deceased wife's sister, Mrs. Aina Christina (Tornebladh). Mr. Thomas adopted the son of Mrs. Thomas by her first marriage, Wolfgang Ragnar Thomas, and the latter is at this time of writing (1928), a student at Bowdoin College, Brunswick, Maine.

It was on February 25, 1927, that Mr. Thomas died at his home in Portland. Political and social circles throughout the country were greatly shocked to hear of the death of a man who had played such a leading part in the late historic annals of the nation, and his widow and family received many sincere messages of sympathy and sorrow when the news of his passing was made public. With Mr. Thomas, indeed, there passed a man of brilliant mind, ever alert to serve his country and to cast the mantle of peace over the world.

FRANK FELLOWS—Well known as an attorney of Bangor, Frank Fellows has been equally prominent in the civic and social life of his community. It was due in a considerable degree to his efforts that the local chapter of the Kiwanis Club was organized.

His father, Oscar F. Fellows, a very successful New England lawyer, was born in Bristol, New Hampshire, September 10, 1857, the son of Milo and Susan (Locke) Fellows. Oscar Fellows was educated at the New Hampton (New Hampshire) Literary Institute, and admitted to the bar in 1881. On May 24, 1883, he married Eva M. Fling, daughter of the Hon. L. W. Fling of Bristol. He was a member of the Maine House of Representatives from 1901 to 1903, and Speaker of the House during 1903. He served for four years as Collector of Customs for the Port of Bucksport, and as counsel for the United States on the International St. John River Commission.

Frank Fellows was born at Bucksport, Maine, November 7, 1889. He attended the public schools there and the East Maine Conference Seminary. Later he entered the University of Maine, a member of the class of 1912, and he studied for two years in the University of Maine Law School. During this period he read law in the office of his father, Oscar F. Fellows. In 1911 he was admitted to the bar and

Maine—16

began the practice of his profession in Portland, Maine. In 1915 he was appointed deputy clerk in the United States District Court, and in 1917 he became clerk, serving in this capacity until 1920. In the fall of that year he moved to Bangor and became a member of the law firm of Fellows and Fellows, remaining with them, after the death of his father on December 28, 1921, until the present time.

Politically, Mr. Fellows is associated with the Republican party, and he is a member of the Phi Gamma Delta and Phi Delta Phi fraternities. He is affiliated with the Kiwanis Club, helping in the organization of the local branch and acting as its first secretary, and of the Tarrantine Club. He is also a member of the Penobscot Bar Association and the State of Maine Bar Association. He attends the Unitarian church, and is fond of automobiling, motor-boating, fishing and reading.

In 1910, Frank Fellows married Georgie E. Maling, who was born at Brewer, Maine. They are the parents of children: Elizabeth, Oscar, Joan, Raymond, and William A.

JAMES ALBERT CAHNERS—A man prominent in many fields is James Albert Cahners. Though educated to the law and maintaining his legal connections, he has built up a successful furniture company. His membership in many benevolent and civic organizations shows the variety of his sympathies and interests. His father, Samuel Cahners, born in Odessa, Russia, engaged in the furniture business until his death in 1911. His mother, who was Celia Kopit, also born in Russia, is still living.

James Albert Cahners was born in Cambridge, Massachusetts, on September 5, 1888. He attended the public and high schools of Stoughton, Massachusetts, and the Burdett Business College of Boston. In 1911 he was graduated from the University of Maine with the Bachelor of Laws degree. Having completed his education he took up the practice of law in Bangor and in Boston until, in 1916, he became associated with Adolph B. Friedman and started what is now known as the Eastern Furniture Company stores, in several Maine cities with headquarters in Bangor. He has been president and general manager of this company since that time.

Politically, Mr. Cahners is a Republican and he served for several years as Bail Commissioner in Bangor. He is a member of several fraternal organizations: The Modern Woodman of America; the Foresters; B'nai B'rith, and the Knights of Pythias. He is also a member of the Penobscot Bar Association, and the Maine State Bar Association. He is a member of the Maine Supreme Judicial Court, the Supreme Court of Massachusetts, and a member of the United States Court. He is a past president of the Veritans Service Club, a member of the Chamber of Commerce, vice-president of the Bangor Chapter of the American Red Cross Society, a director of the Bangor Welfare Society, and president of the Zionist Society of Bangor. He is also a member of the State of Maine Firemen's Association.

In 1911, James A. Cahners married Katherine L. Epstein, who was born in Bangor. They are the parents of: Charlotte R., Norman L., Fulton T., and Walter.

VICTOR BRETT—An unusual record is that of Victor Brett, who has served as city clerk in Bangor,

Maine, for fifty years. He was admitted to the bar in 1875, and from that time to the present (1928) has been located in Bangor. Mr. Brett is one of the best-known men in this city, and has held the office of which he is now an incumbent longer than any other official in the municipal service.

Victor Brett was born in Old Town, Maine, October 17, 1851, son of Ezra Carey Brett, attorney-at-law, a native of Poland, Maine, and of Jane (Norton) Brett, who was born in Livermore, Maine. Both are now deceased. As a young lad Mr. Brett attended the public schools of Old Town, and then prepared for college in Westbrook Seminary. When his preparatory course was completed he became a student in Tufts College, with the class of 1872. As he had decided upon the legal profession as his field of future service, he attended and was graduated from the Albany Law School and admitted to practice in the State of New York. In 1875 he was admitted to the bar of the State of Maine, and began legal practice in the office of General Mitchell, of Bangor, with whom he continued until 1876. In that year he was elected clerk of the city of Bangor, and the efficiency with which he has served, as well as the hold which he has upon the esteem of his associates, is indicated by the fact that for fifty years he has served in that capacity. Few men in this State, or in any other State in the Union, can parallel this record, and Mr. Brett has, so far as the people of Bangor are concerned, become a part of the office in which he serves. His familiar figure is one of the best-known about the City Hall, and his long familiarity with the records enables him to render exceptionally valuable service there. Mr. Brett is a member of the Knights of Pythias, of which he is a Past Chancellor; of the Order of the Maccabees; and of Bangor Lodge, Benevolent and Protective Order of Elks. He is a member of the Penobscot County Bar Association, and of the Tarrantine Club. Politically, he gives his support to the Republican party, as do a majority of the inhabitants of the State of Maine. He has served for eight years as a member of the Maine State Militia, serving for two years of that time as adjutant of the Second Maine Regiment, and for six years as its colonel. His religious interest is with the Universalist church.

Victor Brett was married (first), December 29, 1875, to Abbie Lillian Ames, who was born in Bangor, Maine, and died in 1919. He married (second) Mary A. Canty, a native of Veazie, Maine. To the first marriage one child was born, Howard Brett.

STEPHEN S. BUNKER—A long and varied experience as engineer and in railroad construction work in many sections of this country, and in South America, preceded the entrance of Stephen S. Bunker into State employ in Maine, and after nine years in that connection he became city engineer of Bangor, which position he has filled from 1922 to the present time (1928). Mr. Bunker is a veteran of the World War, having served in France for twenty months during that conflict.

Stephen S. Bunker was born in Bar Harbor, Maine, August 20, 1876, son of David A. Bunker, a native of Trenton, Maine, and who for many years engaged as a contractor and builder, and who was a veteran of the Civil War, New York Volunteer

Cavalry, and a member of the Grand Army of the Republic, and of Jeannette (Higgins) Bunker, also a native of Bar Harbor, Maine. After attending the public schools of Bar Harbor and completing his course in the high school, Mr. Bunker matriculated in the University of Maine, from which he was graduated with the class of 1897, receiving at that time the degree of Bachelor of Science. Upon the completion of his college course he found his first employment with the Washington County Railroad Company, with which he remained for one year. He then entered the employ of the Seaboard Airline Railroad Company, and later of the Louisville & Nashville Railroad; afterward he was associated with other railroads in the South, and also did construction work. In 1902 he was connected with the Jersey City Water Works for a short time, and then went to Oklahoma, where he was in the employ of various independent railroad companies. In 1904 he went to Bolivia, South America, where he was engaged in railroad construction work, and after a year of experience in this section of the world he returned to the United States, locating in Florida, where he associated himself with the Appalachicola Railroad Company for a year. His next field was in the Middle West, working on sewerage jobs and on street railway work in Ohio and Michigan. In 1908 he went back to South America and went up the Amazon River, working on the Madeira and Mamora Railroad for four years. In 1913, after the long and varied experience recorded above, he entered the employ of the State of Maine as engineer in the Highway Department, where he remained until 1922, when he accepted his present position as engineer for the city of Bangor. He is rendering most effective service in that office, and during the five years of his incumbency has made some very desirable improvements in certain phases of the city's municipal housekeeping.

Mr. Bunker is a Republican in his political principles. Upon the entrance of the United States into the World War, in 1917, he went to Plattsburg Training Camp, having enlisted in May, and in July of the same year he was commissioned a captain of Engineers, in the United States Army, and went overseas with the American Expeditionary Forces. For twenty months he served in France, at Montoir, near Nazaire, in the building yard, and in 1919 was discharged with the rank of captain. In 1922, he was commissioned a major in the Reserve Corps. While in France he served first with the Seventy-third Engineers, but later was transferred to the Seventy-second Engineers. He is a member of the American Society of Civil Engineers; president of the Reserve Officers' Association, and a member of the Military Order of the World War, being actively interested in all these organizations. He is also a member of the Bangor Chamber of Commerce and of the Kiwanis Club. He finds his favorite recreation in fishing, and his religious affiliation and that of his family is with the Congregational church.

Stephen S. Bunker was married, in 1903, to Emma Sanford, who was born in Bath, Maine, and they are the parents of three children: 1. Jeanette Mary, a linotype operator. 2. Paul S., attended the University of Maine, and is (1928), a civil engineer in the County Engineer's office, at Defiance, Ohio. 3. Ruth Elizabeth, a student of Earlham College, in Indiana.

ROSS ST. GERMAIN—His active practice of his profession in both State and Federal courts, has brought Ross St. Germain into the front rank with Bangor attorneys-at-law who ably and creditably serve the highest interests of the bar. Mr. St. Germain is well known both in business and law circles, is a veteran United States Army cavalryman, and has the esteem and good will of his associates and his increasing clientele.

Ross St. Germain was born December 9, 1880, in Machias, Maine, a son of Joseph St. Germain, who was born in Rochester, New York, and Hannah (Gratto) St. Germain, a native of Machias, Maine, both parents now deceased. Joseph St. Germain, who was a contractor and builder, was a veteran of the Civil War, and member of Machias Post, Grand Army of the Republic. Serving with Company ·C, of the Sixth Regiment, Maine Volunteer Infantry, he was wounded in action, receiving the Distinguished Service Cross from the United States Government for bravery; and he was also a prisoner at Andersonville Prison.

Ross St. Germain attended the grammar and high schools at Greenville, and studied at Foxcroft Academy. He then read law in the office of H. L. Smith, of Greenville, and in 1910 was admitted to the bar, practicing law in Greenville for five years. During the succeeding years, relinquishing his practice for that period, Mr. St. Germain entered the employ of the Great Northern Paper Company. In 1922, he again took up his profession and entered upon his present successful practice at Bangor, with offices at No. 10 Columbia Building. He is a member of the Maine State Bar and the Piscataqua Bar associations, and has been admitted to practice in all the State and Federal courts.

From 1901 to 1904, Mr. St. Germain served with Troop M, Thirteenth Regiment, United States Cavalry, in the Philippine Islands, receiving his discharge with the rank of sergeant. He is a member of Columbia Lodge, No. 200, Free and Accepted Masons, of Greenville; and his hobby is fishing.

Ross St. Germain married, October 25, 1906, Mildred G. Edgerly, who was born in Dover, Maine. Their children: Glenn, Wayne, Faith, Jeanne, Ross, Jr., and Albert E.

CHARLES E. WOODWARD—The Lyford-Woodward Company, of Bangor, Penobscot County, has a display of merchandise and a clientele equal to any of the better Fifth Avenue shops, and of this high-class concern Charles E. Woodward is president and treasurer, which office he has held since 1909. For forty years this concern has been dealing in furs of the highest grade and other merchandise. A branch store has been established at Bar Harbor in order to take care of the summer trade and this store carries a stock of exclusive merchandise, which appeals strongly to the colony gathered there for the summer season.

Charles E. Woodward was born in Ellsworth, Hancock County, September 13, 1860. He received his early education in the public schools of his birthplace, and when school days were over learned the trade of the printer, in which he continued for six years. He then changed his line of work and found employment in a general store. He soon decided that this was the field in which he could achieve a substantial success, but he waited until he had made

himself familiar with all the departments of the business with which he was connected before venturing to engage in business for himself. In 1887, in association with Thornton Lyford, he became a partner in an enterprise which operated under the name of T. Lyford and Company, but in 1890 the name was changed to that of the Lyford-Woodward Company, under which name the firm now operates. The concern has from the beginning dealt in only the highest grade of goods, and now carries a complete line of furs and hats. The Lyford-Woodward Company is the largest dealer in furs in the State of Maine, and is also one of the best-known firms in America, catering to the society trade and including among its patrons many of the wealthiest and most exclusive families in the United States. Mr. Woodward has become an expert in the selection of goods for the exclusive trade to which the concern caters, and in order to keep his concern up to date he journeys to the markets of Paris and other European cities in order to keep in touch with the very newest merchandise in the market. Since 1909, Mr. Woodward has been president and treasurer of the company, and under his able management the reputation of the Lyford-Woodward Company has permanently established itself as one of the leading firms in the country. The branch store at Bar Harbor, Maine, is a busy place during the summer season, and many of the summer residents there plan during the year to make extensive purchases when they arrive in this State. From their homes in New York and in other cities, they keep in touch with the Lyford-Woodward concern, and thus continue their patronage throughout the year. In addition to his responsibilities as president and treasurer of this well-known concern, Mr. Woodward is also interested in several local financial institutions, being a trustee of the Penobscot Savings Bank, and a director of the Bangor Building and Loan Company. He is a member of the Penobscot Country Club, and is fond of traveling. His religious affiliation is with All Souls' Congregational church, with which organization he serves as a member of the board of trustees.

Mr. Woodward is married and has two daughters.

RALPH A. DYER—Few of the younger men in the State have made so thorough and successful a canvass of the insurance field as has Ralph A. Dyer, representative of a large number of the standard insurance companies, and very able exponent of the benefits of insurance. With his offices at No. 15 State Street, Bangor, Mr. Dyer has met with well-·merited success and has a host of friends throughout his territory of activity.

Ralph A. Dyer was born October 31, 1884, at Cherryfield, Maine, a son of Andrew Dyer, who was born in Washington County, and Carrie E. (Davis) Dyer, deceased, a native of Cherryfield. Mr. Dyer attended the grammar schools, and was graduated at· the Eddington High School, as well as at Shaw's Business College, after which he was employed by the firm of Henry Lord & Company, of Bangor. He was also in the employ of John Ross & Son, Bangor, for twelve years, and for a period he was manager of the H. F. Ross ·Coal Company, which· was controlled by John Ross & Son.

In 1914, Mr. Dyer entered upon the real estate and insurance business on his own account, and the next year, 1915, he received the appointment of spe-·

244   MAINE—A HISTORY

cial agent of the New York Life Insurance Company for the State of Maine; and again, in 1920, he was appointed general agent of the Columbia Casualty Company of New York for Eastern Maine. Since 1920, Mr. Dyer has devoted his entire time to the interests of insurance, and as representative of twelve other companies, he writes insurance of all kinds, with his offices at No. 15 State Street. He is a member of Tarratine and Penobscot Valley Country clubs; New York Life $200,000 Club; Insurance Federation of the United States, and the Bangor Chamber of Commerce.

Ralph A. Dyer married, at Ellsworth, in 1907, Elizabeth Donovan, who was born in Cherryfield. Their children are: Ralph A., Jr., John R., and Barbara F.

DONALD S. McNAUGHTON—In business at Gardiner, Kennebec County, since 1905, when he opened a shoe store, Donald S. McNaughton, now in the insurance business, and accounted among the prominent men of the community, was born at Black River, New Brunswick, Canada, August 14, 1874, son of John McNaughton, born at Black River, died in 1897, and of Margaret (Ward) McNaughton, who died in 1924. The father was a lumberman and farmer, active in Black River politics, and a Liberal. Donald S. McNaughton attended the public schools of Black River, left Canada, settled in Gardiner, and went into business for himself at the age of thirty years. He conducted the shoe store fourteen years, until 1919; meanwhile, in 1915, opening a furniture and undertaking business, in partnership with H. N. Wakefield, which business he now (1928) continues. In April, 1920, Mr. McNaughton purchased the insurance business owned by Augustus Bailey, who had conducted it fifty-five years. Besides the insurance, Mr. McNaughton has developed a general real estate business which extends to many points over the State. In addition to his commercial interests in Gardiner, Mr. McNaughton is a public figure of considerable importance and popularity, enjoying the favor of all major parties, though himself a Republican. This confidence was manifest in 1924, when he was elected mayor of Gardiner, for one year. His record in office was decidedly favorable, and the conscientious efforts by him put forth in the interests of the community have been appreciated. Mr. McNaughton has constantly had the support of the civic leaders, and during the year as mayor found that needed measures in local administration were readily enacted and enforced through their coöperation. He is affiliated with a number of fraternal organizations, including the Blue Lodge, Free and Accepted Masons, of which he is Past Master; the Chapter, Royal Arch Masons; the Council, Royal and Select Masters; the Commandery, Knights Templar; Maine Consistory, Ancient Accepted Scottish Rite; Kora Temple, Ancient Arabic Order Nobles of the Mystic Shrine; Past Patron of the Order of the Eastern Star; member of the Knights of Pythias, and of the Independent Order of Odd Fellows. He is a director of the Gardiner Board of Trade; member of the Shrine Club, and charter member of the Rotary Club. Mr. McNaughton is active in the Methodist church, both as member and as treasurer of the board of trustees, and as custodian. His influence for good upon the young people and men and women

with whom he comes in contact has often been remarked.

Donald S. McNaughton married, June 1, 1903, at Gardiner, Louella G. Wakefield, daughter of Hollowell Wakefield, born at West Gardiner, and Mary (Wakefield) Wakefield, also born at West Gardiner.

ROLAND E. LANCASTER, FORREST G. LANCASTER—As there has been no portion of his business career in which Roland E. Lancaster has not been associated in one way or another with the automobile interests, whether from chauffeur and repairer to the ownership of his present well-known automobile distributing establishment at Bangor, he is one of the most experienced men now engaged in that line in the State. President and general manager of the Morris-Lancaster Company, of Bangor, of which his brother, Forrest G. Lancaster, is the treasurer, he is a merchant of distinctive enterprise and abilities in his chosen field. He is a son of Harry E. Lancaster, a cooper, who was born in Hudson, and Mattie F. (Spencer) Lancaster, a native of Veazie.

Roland E. Lancaster was born January 31, 1893, in Veazie, and after attending the schools there, he was graduated at Bangor High School. In 1909, he first entered the automobile business, continuing with the Palm Street Garage until 1911, when he took a position as chauffeur. In 1913, he resigned his position and for a year he was employed in Boston, Massachusetts, in the repairing business. Then, removing to Orono, he became associated with A. L. Weed, and with him bought out the Orono Motor Company. Purchasing Mr. Weed's interest in that partnership in 1915, Mr. Lancaster continued this agency for the Paige Motor cars until 1917, when he sold out and enlisted in the United States Army. In 1918, he joined the interests of the Packard Company of Bangor, so continuing until 1919, when he and his brother, Forrest G. Lancaster, opened what was known as Lancaster's Garage, of Orono, with the Paige Motor agency, this business continuing until 1923, when the Morris-Lancaster Company, of Bangor, was organized, for the distribution of Paige and Jewett cars for four counties—Hancock, Washington, Piscataquis, and Penobscot. The garage in Orono was used as a service station, and in 1924, this station was removed to Salem Court, in Bangor. Mr. Lancaster is president and general manager of his company, and Forrest G. Lancaster is treasurer, their concern also having a branch in Dexter, which was organized in 1927. In political matters, Mr. Lancaster is an Independent voter.

Enlisting in the Air Service of the United States Army, in 1917, Mr. Lancaster was stationed at Petersburg, Virginia; at Kelley Field, Texas, and at Morrison, Virginia, where he was an instructor in mechanics. He received his discharge in 1918 with rank of sergeant. Fraternally, he is affiliated with the Knights of Pythias, and Bangor Lodge, Benevolent and Protective Order of Elks. He is a member of the Bangor Automobile Dealers' Association, and a director of the Maine State Automobile Dealers' Association. His religious faith is that of the Congregational church.

Forrest G. Lancaster, brother of Roland E. Lancaster, was born October 8, 1888, at Veazie, and after attending the public schools there, he was graduated at Bangor High School. For two and a half years he was employed in the office of the Great Northern Paper Company, at Bangor, and during the following eight and a half years, he was in the employ of the I. N. Pierce Lumber Company. In 1919, Mr. Lancaster began to engage in business in his own name in the direction of the business of a public garage, at Orono, as well as agent for Paige and Jewett cars. Then, with his brother, he brought about the organization of the Morris-Lancaster Company, of Bangor, now one of the largest of the Bangor automobile agencies, as distributors for the above-named cars, in Hancock, Washington, Piscataquis, and Penobscot counties; and maintaining a service station at No. 16 Salem Street, Bangor. Roland E. Lancaster is the president and general manager, and Forrest G. Lancaster treasurer of the concern.

In political matters, Mr. Lancaster is a Republican, and with vote and influence he supports the principles of that party. Enlisting in the United States Army in June, 1918, he was overseas for nine months with the American Expeditionary Forces, and saw active service in France in the Meuse-Argonne offensive, with the Third Corps of Artillery, attached to the First Army. He received his honorable discharge with the rank of sergeant. Fraternally, Mr. Lancaster is affiliated with Mechanics Lodge, Free and Accepted Masons, at Orono; Old Town Chapter, Royal Arch Masons; Bangor Council, Royal and Select Masters; St. John's Commandery, Knights Templar, and he is also a member of the Masonic Club, and Bangor Automobile Dealers' Association. His hobbies are baseball, hunting, and fishing. He attends the Universalist church.

Forrest G. Lancaster married, September 11, 1917, Adelaide E. Ranney, who was born at Winn, Maine; and they have one son, Robert T. Lancaster.

ALBERT J. COLE—One of the most widely known and popular men now engaging in the automobile business in the State, Albert J. Cole, general manager of the Darling Automobile Company, of Bangor, has won a host of friends for his successful efforts to please the patrons of the general agency that he ably represents, and for his unfailing geniality, enterprise and tact in salesmanship and in the management of the affairs of his concern. He was born December 27, 1893, in Lowell, Maine, a son of Sydney Cole, a horse trainer, who was born in Exeter, New Hampshire, and died in 1900, and Roxie (Spencer) Cole, a native of Lowell, who died in 1913. After Mr. Cole had graduated from grammar and high schools, he was employed as a baggage man at the Maine Central station in Enfield, and when he left there it was in the capacity of alternate freight agent for the company. Afterwards, taking over the mail route from Enfield to Burlington, he was engaged in operating that route for eight years, in conjunction with which he also worked a large farm and ran a general store at Enfield. At about that time, also, he established the present Cole's Express business.

In 1925, Mr. Cole purchased an interest in the Ludovic P. Swett Company's agency for the Reo Motor cars, which interest he disposed of in 1926, when he took over the agency for the Reo Motor cars for Hancock and Washington counties, continuing therein until January, 1927, when he became associated with the Darling Automobile Company,

of Bangor; and as partner and general manager, he has the distribution of Reo Motor cars for ten counties throughout the State. In his political views, he is a Republican, though he has never sought public office. Fraternally, Mr. Cole is affiliated with Horeb Lodge, Free and Accepted Masons, and with all bodies of the Ancient Accepted Scottish Rite, including the Maine Consistory. He is a member of the Bangor Chamber of Commerce; and he attends the Universalist church.

Albert J. Cole married, July 10, 1912, Amy A. Stone, who was born in Enfield. Their children: Gerald A., Chester R., Winona A., Dorothy M., and Galen L.

WILMOT I. BROOKINGS—Since 1923, Wilmot I. Brookings has been associated with the embalming and funeral directing business, and since 1925, he has been associated with Irving C. Trufant in the ownership and management of the undertaking business formerly owned by the Galen S. Pond Company, of Bangor, Maine. Mr. Brookings is a native of this State and saw active service during the World War.

Wilmot I. Brookings was born in Gardiner, Maine, November 14, 1897, son of Wilmot H., regarded as a paper manufacturer and farmer, and of Estelle (Sherman) Brookings, a native of Pepperell, Massachusetts, now deceased. He attended the public schools of Gardiner, and then continued his studies in Kent Hill Academy, after which he enlisted in the United States Navy. When his term in the Navy expired he engaged in the wholesale leather business, in which he continued for a year and a half. At the end of that time he entered the employ of the Thomas G. Plant Company, of Boston, in which connection he worked as a shipping clerk for a short time. His next connection was with the Doutee Casket Company, of Boston, with whom he remained for two years. In 1923, he went to Houlton, Maine, and entered the employ of the Dunn Furniture Company, working in their undertaking department for one year. In 1924, he went with the Boston Burial Case Company for a short time, and in 1925, he associated himself with Irving C. Trufant (q. v.), purchasing the undertaking business of Galen S. Pond. This is one of the old established concerns of the city, founded in 1849, and Mr. Brookings and Mr. Trufant are operating it under the name of Galen S. Pond Company. The young men are making a decided success of the enterprise, and the long period of time during which it has been in operation is a decided business asset. Both of the partners are able and enterprising men, and they are maintaining the high standards already established by the concern which they took over. Mr. Brookings is a Republican in his political affiliations. He is a member of Rising Virtue Lodge, Free and Accepted Masons; and of the American Legion, and he is fond of baseball and football. His religious affiliation is with the Methodist church.

Wilmot I. Brookings was married, in 1921, to Heloise Lovejoy, a native of Augusta, Maine, and they have two children: John Wilmot, and Mary E.

IRVING C. TRUFANT—For more than a quarter of a century Irving C. Trufant has been identified with the embalming and undertaking business, first in the employ of others, and then in partnership, continuing to change from time to time until he had mastered the business and had made himself thoroughly familiar with conditions in various localities. Since 1925, he has, in partnership with Wilmot I. Brookings, been the owner of the undertaking establishment in Bangor known as the Galen S. Pond Company.

Irving C. Trufant was born in Harpswell, Maine, November 23, 1879, son of Charles E., a native of Harpswell, who was a sailor during the early years of his active career, but has been engaged in farming during his later life, and of Marietta (Doughty) Trufant, also a native of Harpswell, both of whom are living (1928). Irving C. Trufant attended the public schools of his birthplace, and then took a course in Bliss Business College. Later, he entered the Massachusetts College of Embalming. In 1901, he engaged in the undertaking business in Bath, Maine, as a partner of Fred Curtis, and this connection was maintained until 1911, when Mr. Trufant withdrew and went to Skowhegan, Maine, where he entered the employ of Lord and Caswell, undertakers, with whom he remained for eight years. In 1919, he made another change, this time going to Portland, Maine, where he was associated with the H. L. Berry Casket Manufacturing Company until 1921. In that year he went to Webster, Massachusetts, as superintendent of the Middlesex Casket Company, with whom he remained until 1923, when he entered the employ of the Boston Burial Case Company in Boston Massachusetts, where he remained until September, 1925, when he came to Bangor. Here he purchased the undertaking business of Galen S. Pond, an old concern which was established in 1849, by Enoch Tibbets. The business was continued by Mr. Tibbets until 1869, and then was taken over by Abel Hunt, who conducted it forty-two years. In 1911, it was taken over by Galen S. Pond, and in 1925, Mr. Trufant and Mr. Brookings purchased the business of Mr. Pond. They are both able and progressive men, and the long established custom of the concern has been retained by the new owners, who are operating under the name of the Galen S. Pond Company. They are maintaining the high standards of service and of business integrity set by the founder and continued by succeeding proprietors, and there is every evidence that the young men will achieve increasing success as the years pass.

Mr. Trufant is a Republican in his political sympathies. He is well known in Masonic circles, being a member of Polar Star Lodge, Free and Accepted Masons, of Bath, Maine, of which he is a Past Master; of Montgomery and St. Bernard chapters, Royal Arch Masons; and of Dunlap Commandery, No. 5, Knights Templar. He is also a member of Lincoln Lodge, No. 10, Independent Order of Odd Fellows, of which he is a Past Grand. Mr. Trufant is a member of the Tarrantine Club, and his favorite recreational activity is fishing. His religious interest is with the Congregational church, of which he is an attendant.

Irving C. Trufant was married, in 1905, to Olive Weeks, who was born in Bath, Maine, and they are the parents of one daughter, Catherine Delight.

CHESTER EDWARD NORRIS—With the exception of some years spent as a builder and contractor, Chester Edward Norris has directed the affairs of his steadily increasing automobile interests both in this State and in New Hampshire, and today, as partner and sales manager with the J. M. Norris Company in Bangor, his popularity as well as his thoroughgoing business efficiency are established. He is an active citizen too, in all that pertains to the well-being of the community and the progress of city and State.

Chester Edward Norris, a son of George Edward Norris, a contractor and builder, native of Trenton, now deceased, and Rose (Milliken) Norris, deceased, who was a native of Hancock, was born February 28, 1881, in Hancock, Maine. After attending the public schools there, he was graduated at Ellsworth High School, and he then entered upon a few years in contracting and building. In 1919, Mr. Norris first became engaged in the automobile line, when he was made manager of the Packard Company at Manchester, New Hampshire; and in 1921, he removed to Bangor where he was given the agency of the Packard automobile. In 1922, this agency became consolidated with the J. M. Norris Motor Company, in which Mr. Norris was made a partner, and in which he has continued to the present as clerk and sales manager. In his political convictions, he is a Republican, though he has not sought political preferment.

Fraternally, Mr. Norris is affiliated with Lygonia Lodge, Free and Accepted Masons, of which he is a Past Master; Acadia Chapter, No. 31, Royal Arch Masons; Blanquefort Commandery, No. 13, Knights Templar, of which he is a Past Commander; and the Ancient Accepted Scottish Rite, including the Maine Consistory; and Kora Temple, Ancient Arabic Order Nobles of the Mystic Shrine. He is also a member of Bangor Lodge, Benevolent and Protective Order of Elks; and the Order of the Eastern Star; and his clubs are: Tarrantine and Penobscot Valley Country; Bangor Chamber of Commerce; and Bangor Automobile Dealers' Association; also the Masonic Club; and the Derryfield Club, of Manchester, New Hampshire. His religious faith is that of the Universalist church, and his hobbies are hunting and fishing.

Chester Edward Norris married, in 1925, Pauline Morse, who was born in Bangor, and they have two sons, John Morse, and Chester Edward.

EDWARD M. CASSILY—The interests of funeral directing in its various branches have no more thoroughgoing factor in Bangor than Edward M. Cassily, who has made this the business of his career, and he is rightly accounted one of the best equipped and capable of the undertakers in this part of the State. Mr. Cassily is a veteran of the World War, and he is active in all matters that pertain to the advancement of Bangor and its institutions.

Edward M. Cassily was born July 26, 1890, in Dover, New Hampshire, a son of Thomas J. Cassily, a native of Providence, Rhode Island, removed to Dover, New Hampshire, where he was engaged in business until his death, and of Elizabeth (Daley) Cassily, a native of Ireland, who survives her husband. Mr. Cassily attended the public and high schools at Dover, and had private tutorship for four years. He then entered upon the business of funeral director, at first in Dover, where he continued up to the time of his World War service; and in 1919, he became associated with Ralph White, of Bangor, for six months, when, with Michael Kane as a partner, the firm of Cassily and Kane was established, so continuing to the present, with headquarters at No. 115 York Street.

On April 17, 1917, Mr. Cassily enlisted in the Coast Artillery Corps, and was stationed with his contingent at Fortress Monroe, Virginia; he received his discharge January 27, 1919, with the rank of second lieutenant. In politics, he is a Republican. Besides his membership with the Maine Funeral Directors' Association, and the National Association of Funeral Directors, Mr. Cassily's affiliations are with the Knights of Columbus, and the Ancient Order of United Workman. He is also member of the American Legion, and his hobbies are fishing and hunting. He is a communicant of St. Mary's Roman Catholic Church.

Edward M. Cassily married, in 1910, Minnie E. Butler, born in Dover, New Hampshire; and they have one son, Charles F. Cassily.

JOSEPH R. PAQUIN—Biddeford is fortunate in her long list of men of the legal profession. One of the self-made men and lawyers of this town who is very prominent among the French people of this section is Joseph R. Paquin, who has been engaged in practice here since 1909, and whose offices are located in the Paquin Building, in Biddeford. Mr. Paquin is of French parentage, his parents being natives of Canada, both born in the Province of Quebec.

Joseph R. Paquin was born in Saco, Maine, July 30, 1880, son of David Paquin, a machinist, who died in 1894, and of Malvina (Chenevert) Paquin, who survives her husband. He attended the local parochial school, and then became a student in Montreal College in Montreal, affiliated with Laval University, from which he was graduated with the class of 1900, receiving at that time the degree of Bachelor of Arts. He then studied theology in the Grand Seminary of Montreal for three years, then studied law in the offices of Cleaves, Waterhouse & Emery, at Biddeford, and successfully passed the examinations for admission to the bar in March, 1909. From that time to 1918 he was engaged in general legal practice under his own name, but in 1918 he became associated with the law firm of Emery and Waterhouse, and that connection he maintained until 1922, when he opened an office of his own and engaged in practice under his own name. He is well known among his professional associates, being a member of the York County Bar Association, the Androscoggin Bar Association, the Maine Bar Association, and the American Bar Association. In addition to the responsibilities of his large general practice, Mr. Paquin is also a member of the board of directors of the First National Bank of Biddeford. He also takes an active part in local public affairs, was a member of the Common Council in 1909, and has also served as chairman of the Board of Registration. He is a member of the Catholic Order of Foresters, and a member and past president of the Union St. Jean Baptiste, also a member of several French societies. His religious affiliation is with St. Joseph's Roman Catholic Church.

Joseph R. Paquin was married, in 1910, to Marie R. Poirier, of Biddeford, Maine, daughter of Joseph and Julie (Larose) Poirier. Mr. and Mrs. Paquin are the parents of one daughter, Dorothy E. M., who was born January 28, 1919. Both Mr. and Mrs. Paquin are well known and well liked in Biddeford,

and are held in especially high esteem among the numerous French families of this part of York County. Their home is at No. 223 South Street.

BERTRAM LEWIS BRYANT, M. D.—A frequent contributor to medical journals, long associated with the more important public institutions of the State of Maine in a professional capacity, Dr. Bertram Lewis Bryant is one of the most distinguished of New England physicians.

The family has been long settled in Maine, and Abraham Bryant, one of the pioneers of Bethel, Maine, where he was a farmer, served in the War of 1812. His son, Benjamin R. Bryant, was also a farmer, and served in the Civil War with the Thirty-eighth Regiment of Massachusetts Volunteers, and in later life was active in the affairs of the Grand Army of the Republic. He married Ellen F. Davis, a niece of Dr. Gilman, of Portland, Maine, organizer of the Maine General Hospital, and a member of its staff for many years.

Bertram Lewis Bryant was born in Bethel, Maine, May 28, 1872, and after being graduated from Gould's Academy, entered Bowdoin College, where he received the degree of Bachelor of Arts in 1895, and the degree of Master of Arts in 1897, and the degree of Medical Doctor in 1898. From 1895 to 1898, he was assistant in chemistry at Bowdoin College. From 1899 to 1905 he was pathologist of the Emergency Hospital. In 1905, he was appointed visiting physician to the Eastern Maine General Hospital, and afterwards was made consulting physician to the Bangor State Hospital, and the Waldo County Hospital. During the World War he served on the Committee of Defense. He has been president of the Maine Anti-Tuberculosis Association, and vice-president of the Maine Public Health Association. He is a member of the Theta Delta Chi and the Phi Beta Kappa Fraternities, of the Penobscot County Medical Association, the American Medical Association, secretary of the Maine Medical Society, and their delegate to the American Medical Association. He is also a member of the Tarrantine Club, the Conduskeag Canoe Club, and the Penobscot Valley Country Club. Dr. Bryant is a Republican, and a member of the Congregational church.

Dr. Bertram L. Bryant married Lillian True, of Bethel, Maine, August 3, 1899. They have one daughter, Katharine.

G. WALTER HURD, first permanent chief of the Old Town, Maine, Fire Department, was born in that city, January 2, 1876, and educated there in the public schools. After being graduated from the high school, he found work in a general store, where he was a clerk for some time, and then entered the employ of the Old Town Woolen Company, remaining with that organization for four years.

He then went into business for himself, starting what is known now as the G. Walter Hurd Transfer Company of Old Town, Maine, and retaining the control thereafter. His father, Edward K. Hurd, proprietor of a sawmill, and active in the civic life of the community, was born at Exeter, Maine, and survived until 1900. He married Clara C. Mitchell, who was born in Old Town, and outlived him, dying in 1911. They were Methodists, and G. Walter Hurd still attends the Methodist church. And, like his father, he is a Democrat.

His interest in the local fire department began in 1893, when he was made call man. Elected chief of the fire department in 1910, he served until 1913. He was elected call chief in 1917-18, reëlected in 1921 and 1923, and again in 1926. He became the first permanent chief of the Old Town Fire Department in 1927.

Mr. Hurd's favorite hobby is baseball, but he has long been associated with the more important fraternal bodies, and is Past Exalted Ruler of Old Town Lodge, Benevolent and Protective Order of Elks, and is a member of the Grand Lodge of that order, and is also a member of the Knights of Pythias, of the Maine Association of Fire Chiefs, and of the New England Association of Fire Chiefs.

G. Walter Hurd married, in 1911, Emma Hooper, who was born in Hamilton, Bermuda.

JAMES A. McNAUGHTAN, a well-known carpenter and contractor of Old Town, Maine, and a man who has devoted much of his time to the service of his city, was born March 9, 1863, in Macadam Junction, New Brunswick, Canada. Mr. McNaughtan is a son of James A. and Catherine (Harrington) McNaughtan, both of whom are now deceased. James A. McNaughtan, who was born in Glasgow, Scotland, was engaged in farming until the time of his death. The mother, Catherine (Harrington) McNaughtan, was born in England.

James A. McNaughtan received his education in the public schools of Old Town, Maine. Upon the completion of these courses of study, he learned the carpenter's trade. He has followed this line of work since that time, later establishing a business for himself as contractor. In this he has met with eminent success, having been engaged in the construction of many of the finest buildings in Old Town. Mr. McNaughtan has never been too engrossed in his business affairs to take an interest in the welfare of his community. A staunch supporter of the Democratic party, he was appointed city marshal of Old Town in 1907, and he served in this capacity for five terms. He also served for five and a half years as deputy sheriff for Penobscot County and he has served several terms on the City Commission.

Despite the manifold duties which his work entailed, Mr. McNaughtan has found time to take an interest in other activities. He is fraternally affiliated with the Star of the East Lodge, Free and Accepted Masons, the Chapter, Royal Arch Masons, the Council, Royal and Select Masters, the Consistory, Ancient Accepted Scottish Rite; the Commandery, Knights Templar; Anah Temple, Ancient Arabic Order Nobles of the Mystic Shrine; and the Independent Order of Odd Fellows. He is also a member of the Odd Fellows Club and the National Association of City Marshals.

James A. McNaughtan married, in 1888, Sadie I. Hussey, who was born in Carmel, Maine. Mr. and Mrs. McNaughtan attend the Methodist church, of which Mr. McNaughtan is a trustee.

RICHARD D. CROWE—Adept in all branches of the business of the funeral director, Richard D. Crowe has been long established in his vocation at Bangor, where he has always resided, and in all of whose civic and municipal progress he has a practical interest of one who believes in the advancement of his native city. His undertaking headquarters are

first-class in location, equipment and all matters necessary to secure the highest degree of repute in this important calling.

Richard D. Crowe was born November 7, 1875, in Bangor, a son of John Crowe, a native of Benedicta, where he was lumberman, and Catherine Shea, born in County Cary, Ireland, died in 1919. Mr. Crowe attended the public schools, and upon graduation became associated with the undertaking business of the firm of Finnegan Brothers, remaining with them until 1918, when he bought out the business, still continuing, however, under the old firm name, and with the place of business at Nos. 171 and 175 Park Street.

In his political views, Mr. Crowe is a Democrat, and with his vote and influence he supports the principles of that party. Fraternally, he is affiliated with Bangor Lodge, Benevolent and Protective Order of Elks; Knights of Columbus; New England Order of Protection; Ancient Order of Hibernians; and Order of United Workmen; and he is a member of the Maine Funeral Directors' Association, and the National Association of Funeral Directors. His hobbies are baseball and football. He is a communicant of St. John's Roman Catholic Church.

Richard D. Crowe married, in 1914, Mary I. Fahey, also a native of Bangor; and they have two sons, Richard D., Jr., and John Branden.

JOHN M. NORRIS—His long-continued and extensive association with the motor car business in Bangor and throughout the State, has given John M. Norris a foremost place among the practical, enterprising and successful men now engaged in the vast business of automobile distribution. The John M. Norris Motor Car Company, Bangor, holds no secondary place in agency activities and general car service, and Mr. Norris, whose business life was founded upon the lines of contractor and builder, has thoroughgoing ideas concerning the construction and the durability features of the ever-increasing motor interests.

John M. Norris was born January 1, 1885, at Hancock, a son of George Edward Norris, deceased, who was born in Trenton, and was a contractor and builder, and Rose (Milliken) Norris, deceased, who was born in Hancock. Mr. Norris attended the Hancock public schools, and he was graduated at Bar Harbor High School and Beal's Business College, and he then entered upon the business of contractor and builder. In 1913, he first began his present activities in the motor car interests, when he established the John M. Norris Motor Car Company, then under the name of Used Cars Sales Company. This enterprise was thus continued until 1919, when the title was changed to Bangor Stutz Company, Maine State distributors for the Stutz cars; and it was in 1922 that the name was changed to J. M. Norris Motor Company, when Packard cars were added for Eastern Maine distribution. In 1925, the Rolls Royce cars were added for State distribution, and the firm has continued to the present, carrying these three leading cars, one of the oldest agencies in Bangor, and with the Crymbals Garage as their service station. Mr. Norris is president and treasurer of the company.

Mr. Norris has never held public office, though in all matters he is a public-spirited citizen; and his political views are those of the Republican party.

MAINE—A HISTORY 249

Fraternally, he is affiliated with Lygonia Lodge, Free and Accepted Masons, Acadia Chapter, No. 31, Royal Arch Masons; Blanquefort Commandery, No. 13, Knights Templar; and with Anah Temple, Ancient Arabic Order Nobles of the Mystic Shrine. He is a member of Tarrantine Club, Penobscot Valley Country Club, Bangor Chamber of Commerce, and Bangor Auto Dealers' Association. His hobbies are hunting and fishing.

John M. Norris married, in 1911, Bertha Olive Haney, who was born in Bangor.

JOHN T. KELLEHER—To the present-day demands of the business of the funeral director, John T. Kelleher has brought the valued experience and the personal qualifications of one who for more than a quarter of a century has had the high regard of the community as a considerate and conscientious undertaker and embalmer, and whose equipment has received merited commendation for its thoroughly modern methods. Mr. Kelleher is active in the civic interests of Bangor, and he has held public office to the satisfaction of his constituency and the general public.

John T. Kelleher was born October 6, 1873, in Bangor, a son of James Kelleher, a farmer, now deceased, who was born in County Cork, Ireland, and Bridget (Foley) Kelleher, who is now deceased, and was born in Galway, Ireland. After attending the public schools in Bangor, Mr. Kelleher entered upon the livery stable business in which he successfully continued, gradually taking over the vocation of funeral undertaker, in which he first established himself in 1900. Under the firm name of J. T. Kelleher and Sons, Mr. Kelleher has his funeral headquarters at No. 155 Hammond Street, Bangor. In his political convictions a Republican, Mr. Kelleher has served for one year as a member of the Bangor City Council, and for six years he was a member of the Board of Selectmen, and a member of the Board of Overseers of the Poor.

Fraternally, Mr. Kelleher is affiliated with the local Council of the Knights of Columbus; Ancient Order of Hibernians; Bangor Lodge, Benevolent and Protective Order of Elks; Order of Maccabees; and Woodmen of America; and he is also a member of the Maine Undertakers' Association. His hobbies are hunting and fishing. He is a communicant of St. Mary's Roman Catholic Church.

John T. Kelleher married, in 1898, Agnes Jordan, who was born in Bangor. Their children: James F., Mary, John L., Dorothy, Harold, Edward, and Eleanor.

WILLIAM HAINES STONE—Few men of the legal profession in Biddeford, Maine, are better known than is William Haines Stone, who has been engaged in general legal practice here since 1911. Mr. Stone is a graduate of Bowdoin College and of Harvard Law School, and is now (1928) representing the city of Biddeford in the State Legislature. He has been active in local public affairs, and is held in high esteem both by his professional associates and by his fellow-townsmen.

William Haines Stone was born in Minneapolis, Minnesota, January 21, 1885, son of Edwin Stone, a prominent attorney of Biddeford, Maine, who died June 8, 1922, and of Nellie (Haines) Stone, daughter of William P. Haines, one of the most prominent

men of the State of Maine. He attended the public schools of the city of Biddeford and after graduation from high school matriculated in Bowdoin College, where he completed his course with graduation in 1906, receiving the degree of Bachelor of Arts. After engaging in business, he entered Harvard Law School and received the degree of Bachelor of Laws in 1911. He was admitted to the Maine bar that same year, having passed the examinations for admission to the Massachusetts bar in 1910, and in 1911, he associated himself with a law firm in Boston, with which he remained for a period of four years. In 1915, he formed a partnership with his father, Edwin Stone, under the name of Stone and Stone, at Biddeford, Maine, and that association was continued to the time of the death of the father in 1922, since which time Mr. Stone has been engaged in practice alone. He is a member of the York County Bar Association, and has made for himself an assured place among his professional associates. In addition to the care of a large and important practice, Mr. Stone has found time for a large amount of public service, and in public capacity he gives the same careful and devoted attention that he gives to his private practice. He is a Democrat in his political allegiance, and has always been an active participant in the conduct of public affairs, both local and State. He has served as a member of the Common Council, was city solicitor in 1917, 1918, and 1919, has served as a member of the Board of Education, and is now a member of the State Legislature, representing the city of Biddeford (1927-1928). During the World War he did meritorious work as chairman of the Fifth Liberty Loan Drive, and as "four-minute" speaker, and he gives his support to all plans for the advancement of the general welfare of the city. Fraternally, he is identified with Dunlap Lodge, Free and Accepted Masons, in which Order he is a Past Master; also with York Chapter, Maine Council and Bradford Commandery. He is a member of Biddeford and Saco Country clubs, and his religious interest is with the Congregational church.

William Haines Stone was married to Gertrude L. Irving, of North Kennebunkport, Maine, daughter of Frank M. and Sadie (Smith) Irving. Mr. and Mrs. Stone are the parents of one daughter, Dorothy H., who was born May 3, 1918. The family home is at No. 24 Orchard Street in Biddeford.

REV. JOSEPH A. LAFLAMME—In Biddeford, Maine, and vicinity Father Joseph A. Laflamme is one of the most revered and loved of men, among the French residents of this section. He is revered because of the qualities of character which he has displayed during the many years of his pastorate at St. Joseph's Roman Catholic Church, and because of the valuable service which he has rendered. Father Laflamme was ordained in 1899, and from 1899 to 1920 served in Bangor and in Rumford, Maine. Rev. Joseph A. Laflamme was born in the Province of Quebec, Canada, May 27, 1874, son of David Laflamme, a farmer of the Province of Quebec, who died in 1916, and of Marceline (Audet) Laflamme, also a native of the Province of Quebec, who survived her husband ten years, her death occurring in 1926. Father Laflamme received a careful and early preparatory course of training and then became a student in Van Buren College, from which he was graduated with the class of 1895, receiving the degree of Bachelor of Arts. He then continued study in the College of Montreal and in Grand Seminary, and was ordained in 1899. His first charge was as curate at St. Mary's Church, in Bangor, Maine. Two years later he was made assistant at St. André, where he served 1900-01, leaving to take charge of the Church of St. Jean de Baptiste, at Rumford, Maine. Here he remained for eighteen years, watching over the place as it grew from a wilderness village into one of the most prosperous towns of Maine, and rendering there the kind of service which cannot be overestimated. In 1920 he was made pastor of St. Joseph's Church in Biddeford, and since that time he has won the hearts of the French residents of this section most completely. He is a true "Father" to his congregation and is revered among his parishioners, whom he serves with a devotion which takes him out of his study and away from his church into the homes and into the fields where his people work and where they have the problems of life to meet.

The history of St. Joseph's Church of Biddeford, goes back to 1870, when it was founded as the first French church in Biddeford, with Father F. A. Pomsardin as its first pastor. Father Pomsardin remained until 1877, when he was succeeded by Father Dupont, whose pastorate covered thirty-eight years, closing in 1915, when he was succeeded by Father Arthur Hamel, who served from 1916 to 1919. In 1920 Father Laflamme was appointed pastor and since that time he has been rendering a service which has greatly benefited the parish, financially and spiritually. During the period of the existence of St. Joseph's as a separate parish it has greatly increased. There were only fifteen hundred French residents in Biddeford and Saco who were communicants when the parish was organized in 1870. Now St. Joseph's Church has five thousand members, and the parish worships in the church which was built in 1870, the baesment of the present church having been built in that year and used for services until the growing congregation made advisable the building of the present church edifice, the interior decoration and the windows of which are among the finest in New England. Father Laflamme is a true shepherd of his flock and he has the reward which cannot be reckoned in dollars and cents, the great reward of the love and reverence of those whom he serves.

LOUIS B. LAUSIER—In political affairs in Biddeford, Maine, Louis B. Lausier is always a factor to be reckoned with. From the beginning of his legal career he has been active in local public affairs, has served as alderman and city solicitor, and twice he has been elected to represent his district in the State Legislature. He has been successfully engaged in general legal practice in Biddeford since 1906, and his offices are located at No. 148 Main Street.

Born in Biddeford, Maine, November 17, 1879, Louis B. Lausier is a son of Antoine Lausier, a native of Athabaska, Canada, who died in 1892, and of Laura (Cartier) Lausier, also a native of Athabaska, who survives her husband. He received his early and preparatory education in the parochial schools, and then became a student in St. Anne de La Pacatiere College, from which he was graduated with the class of 1898. He had determined to enter the legal profession, and after graduation from college began the

study of law in the offices of the late Judge Haley, with whom he continued until he was admitted to the bar in 1906. In that same year he began legal practice in his own name, and has successfully continued to the present time (1928), building up a large and important practice. In addition to the care of the cases of his many clients, Mr. Lausier is attorney and a member of the board of directors of the Pepperell Trust Company, of Biddeford, Maine, and he is also very active in local public affairs. He gives his allegiance to the Democratic party, and has filled several local public offices, as well as serving in the State Legislature. He has served as alderman of Biddeford, elected from the Fourth Ward, as city auditor, as city solicitor, and is chairman of the Democratic City Committee. In 1919 he was elected to represent his fellow-citizens of his district in the State Legislature, and in 1925, he was again honored with election to that body. During the period of the participation of the United States in the World War, Mr. Lausier was a member of the Legal Advisory Board, and in all that pertains to the public welfare he is an active and very able worker. Fraternally, he is identified with the Benevolent and Protective Order of Elks, the Catholic Order of Foresters, and the Modern Woodmen of America, and he is also a member of the Artisans Club. His religious affiliation is with St. Joseph's Roman Catholic Church.

FILLMORE P. HARRIS—The legal profession is well represented in Biddeford, both by the older men of the profession and by the younger men who are just beginning their careers. Among those who have been successfully engaged in general practice for more than fifteen years is Fillmore P. Harris, whose offices are located on Adams Street. Mr. Harris is also Judge of the Municipal Court of Biddeford.

Fillmore P. Harris was born in Portland, Maine, January 11, 1882, son of Walter Harris, connected with the Maine Central Steamship Company, who died in 1886, and of Laura E. (Higgins) Harris, who died in 1889, both natives of Maine. He received his education in the public schools of Machias, including the high school, and then studied law in the offices of Cleaves, Waterhouse and Emery. He proved to be able and energetic, as well as persevering, and in 1912 he successfully passed the examinations for admission to the bar of the State of Maine. In 1912 he engaged in practice in Biddeford, and since that time he has been continuously engaged in practice here. Mr. Harris has, from the beginning of his active career, taken a sincere interest in civic affairs in Biddeford, and has contributed the benefits of his professional knowledge and experience to the duties of public office, serving for thirteen years as recorder in the Municipal Court, and at the present time (1928) is serving as Judge of the Municipal Court of Biddeford. He has also aided in many unofficial projects, and during the World War was very active in all the various drives, serving as chairman for York County, during the Salvation Army drive, also as chairman for the Young Men's Christian Association drive. He was chairman of the "four-minute" speakers, with the usual certificate, and in all the home war work was an important factor in carrying Biddeford "over the top." Fraternally, Mr. Harris is identified with the Knights of Pythias; Loyal

Order of Moose, of which he was Dictator for four years; and of S. S. Andrew's Camp, No. 51, Sons of Veterans, which he served as Commander. His club is the Kiwanis, and his religious affiliation is with the Congregational church.

Fillmore P. Harris was married, in 1909, to Helen M. Brown, of Barre, Vermont, daughter of Patrick and Mary A. (Leonard) Brown. Mr. and Mrs. Harris make their home at No. 12 Beacon Avenue, in Biddeford.

REV. ARTHUR M. DECARY—For more than twenty-eight years Father Arthur M. Decary has served as assistant pastor of churches in Brunswick, Augusta, and pastor at Fort Kent and Biddeford, Maine. Since 1919 he has been the efficient and able pastor of the Roman Catholic Church of St. Andre, in Biddeford, where he long ago won the confidence and the esteem of his fellow-townsmen. Father Decary is a graduate of the College of Montreal, and pursued his theological studies in Grand Seminary. He was ordained in 1899 and has been continuously in service since that time, developing both the financial condition and the spiritual life of the churches in which he has served. In Biddeford he has continued the work of Father Bergeron, whom he succeeded, and he is carrying forward all branches of the work in a manner highly satisfactory to the church authorities who placed him here and also in a manner which has the approval of his parishioners.

Father Arthur M. Decary was born in Montreal, Province of Quebec, October 12, 1872, son of Charles, a farmer, and Helene (Volois) Decary, both of whom are living (1928), the father eighty-nine years of age, and the mother eighty-four. After completing his early and preparatory education he became a student in the College of Montreal, from which he was graduated in 1894, with the degree of Bachelor. He then pursued his theological course in Grand Seminary, and in 1899 was ordained. His first charge was as assistant pastor in Brunswick, Maine, but later he was sent to a Roman Catholic church in Augusta, as assistant pastor, where he remained until 1904, when he was made pastor at Fort Kent, serving there until 1909, when he came to Biddeford as pastor of the Church of St. Andre, succeeding Father Bergeron. The Church of St. Andre in Biddeford was organized November 30, 1899, when the basement of the present church building was laid. The basement was used as a place of worship until the main structure was completed in 1907, which work was completed during the pastorate of Father Bergeron, who served from 1899 to the time of his death in 1919. Father Decary was then appointed pastor and during the eight years which have passed since he took charge here as pastor he has accomplished a very praiseworthy work. The church numbers more than 5,700 souls, and has a parochial school which has an enrollment of twelve hundred pupils, who are organized into twenty-four classes, taught by twenty-eight teachers. Father Decary is one of those much-loved pastors who enter into the lives of their parishioners, and whose practical influence is felt throughout the parish. The spiritual life of the church he seeks in every way to lift and develop, but he does not overlook the practical everyday services by means of which his object can best be accomplished. The people of Biddeford in general, as well as the members of his own church, recognize the sterling qualities of character and the devotion which Father Decary brings to his work, and they esteem him accordingly, giving to him that love and reverence which is very dear to those who devote their lives to the service of others.

HON. HARRY BENNETT AYER—One of the foremost jurists of his day in the State of Maine is Hon. Harry Bennett Ayer, Judge of the Probate Court of York County, which judicial position he has held for the past ten years. He is also president of the York County Bar Association, and is recognized all over the State as one of the leading men of his profession. He is well known in Masonic circles, and has long ago proven himself a man of unusual ability and of wide and deep legal knowledge.

Judge Harry Bennett Ayer was born in Cornish, Maine, April 14, 1871, son of James C. Ayer, a farmer of Cornish, and of Mary A. Bennett, of Parsonsfield, Maine, whose death occurred in 1910. He attended the public schools of his native district, including Cornish High School, and then studied law in the office of the late George F. Clifford. He successfully passed the necessary examinations for admission to the Maine bar, in June, 1895, and immediately opened an office for general practice, under his own name, in Westbrook, Maine, where he remained for one year. One year later he removed to South Berwick, Maine, and formed a partnership with Abner Oakes, under the firm name of Oakes and Ayer. Five years later, in 1901, this partnership was dissolved, and Mr. Ayer was elected Register of Probate, succeeding Frank Wilson. He retained that position until 1917, when he was elevated to the bench as Judge of Probate for York County, and that judicial position he has continuously held since that time. During his term of office he has displayed in a high degree those judicial qualities which are indispensable on the bench, clear grasp of the essential facts of a case, keen discernment of the motives actuating his associates, wide knowledge of the law, and a fearless love of justice which insists upon being satisfied at all costs. He is a member of the York County Bar Association, of the Maine State Bar Association, and at the present time (1928) is serving as president of the York County Bar Association. He has for several years been recognized as one of the leading men of the bench in the State of Maine, and he has commanded in a very high degree the respect and esteem of his professional associates. In addition to the care of his professional responsibilities Mr. Ayer is a member of the board of directors of the First National Bank of Biddeford, and he is one of the leading public-spirited citizens of the community. During the World War he served on various boards and committees and contributed a valuable share to the task of carrying Biddeford "over the top" in its home war work, and he has always been a willing supporter of any project which seemed to him to be well planned for the advancement of the general welfare. Fraternally, he is identified with Greenleaf Lodge, No. 117, Free and Accepted Masons, of Cornish, Maine; Aurora Chapter, Royal Arch Masons; Maine Council, Royal and Select Masters; Bradford Commandery, Knights Templar; and Kora Temple, Ancient Arabic Order Nobles of the Mystic Shrine. He is a Past Master of his lodge, and is very well known in Masonic circles. He is also a member of the Benevolent and Protective Order of Elks. He is identified with the Kiwanis Club, of which he is a past president; with the Sons of the American Revolution; with the Maine Historical Society; and with numerous other clubs and organizations to the number of about a dozen.

Judge Harry Bennett Ayer was married, April 5, 1899, to Susan Elizabeth Bacon. Mr. and Mrs. Ayer make their home in Saco, Maine.

REV. MICHAEL F. DRAIN—Among those who are rendering valuable service in the town of Biddeford, Maine, is Rev. Father Michael F. Drain, pastor of St. Mary's Roman Catholic Church, succeeding Father O'Brien. Father Drain is a graduate of St. Mary's College, and was ordained by Bishop Healy. He has held pastorates in Portland, Maine, and in several other communities of this State, and since 1926 has been pastor of St. Mary's in Biddeford.

Father Michael F. Drain was born in Ireland, February 5, 1870, son of Samuel and Jane (Savage) Drain, both natives of County Down, Ireland. After completing his early and preparatory education he became a student in St. Mary's College, from which he was graduated with the degree of Bachelor of Arts, and later he completed his theological courses and was ordained by Bishop Healy. His first pastoral work was in the Cathedral of Portland, Maine, and later he served in Yarmouth, in Pittsfield, in Lisbon, in South Berwick, and in Lewiston, all in the State of Maine. In 1926 he came to Biddeford as pastor of St. Mary's Church, and here he is still (1928) rendering most efficient and valuable service.

The history of St. Mary's of the Assumption, in Biddeford, goes back to about 1855, but the actual beginnings of what was later to become the parish of St. Mary's is identified with the diocese of Boston, which in 1825 was presided over by Right Rev. Benedict J. Fenwick, of Boston, and which at that time included the present diocese of Portland. It is a matter of record that in 1825, Bishop Fenwick journeyed through Maine and visited Saco, where on August 15, 1825, he celebrated mass at the home of Dr. Green on Upper Main Street, opposite the present Frank G. Deering residence. This, so far as is known, was the first mass celebrated in this section of the State of Maine. By 1850 Irish settlers had become so numerous in the vicinity of Saco that religious services were held as often as once a month and were conducted by a priest from Portland, and later by a priest from Portsmouth, New Hampshire, Father McCallum. Later mass was celebrated regularly in the hall over the present counting room of the Pepperell Manufacturing Company, in the building now standing on Main Street above Crystal Arcade, and still later it was celebrated every Sunday in the hall of the original city building, where the parishioners continued to worship until they went into the new church on the corner of St. Mary's and Hazel streets. In 1855 the diocese of Portland was separated from the diocese of Boston, with the Right Rev. David W. Bacon as first Bishop of Portland, and soon afterward a new parish was established in Biddeford under the name of "St. Mary's of the Assumption," with Rev. Thomas Kenney as first pastor. Father Kenney erected the original St. Mary's Church, but he died in 1857 and was succeeded by Rev. Patrick Bacon who came from Ireland, and

was rector of St. Mary's from 1857 to 1859, when, because of ill health, he returned to Ireland. In 1860 Rev. Eugene Vetromile came as rector of St. Mary's. He was a native of Italy, and during his pastorate the present parochial school lots and other valuable property were secured. He was especially interested in the children, and continued as pastor until 1868, when he died and was succeeded by a French priest who came as rector, Father Picard, who remained but a short time and returned to France because of ill health. In 1868 Rev. Eugene Müller, of German extraction, became rector, but his pastorate closed the following year, 1869. Father Bartley was the next incumbent, with Father Ponsardin as assistant and really as acting rector for the French portion of the parish in Biddeford. About April, 1870, Rev. John Brady, who had been pastor for many years at Houlton, Maine, was appointed pastor, and in April of that year the French parishioners were separated from St. Mary's parish and formed into a new parish, with Father Ponsardin as pastor, the new parish being the present parish of St. Joseph's. The French Catholics had purchased an old Protestant church standing at the southeastern corner of Alfred and Bacon streets (the present Central Theatre Building) in which they worshipped until the completion of their splendid new church on Elm Street. In 1886, Father Brady erected the present rectory of St. Mary's and removed from the old rectory at the southwestern corner of St. Mary's and Elm streets. The young curate, Rev. Francis Finn, who assisted Father Brady for a time, died after a year or so, and in later years Father Brady had associated with him as acting rector, Rev. John Harrington, later pastor of the Catholic church at Orono, Maine. On August 18, 1890, Father Harrington was succeeded, as acting rector, while Father Brady was still nominal rector, by Rev. Timothy Patrick Linehan, who had served as rector of the Cathedral of the Immaculate Conception, in Portland, for twelve years. When Father Brady finally withdrew, Father Linehan was appointed rector by Bishop Healy, and within two years after his arrival in Biddeford he had built the present parochial school at the corner of Elm and St. Mary's streets. In that year, 1892, Father Linehan brought to the parish the first group of Sisters of Mercy to teach in the parochial school, and he also, shortly after the school was completed, thoroughly renovated the church building. The Sisters of Mercy at first occupied the old rectory as a convent, but as soon as the debt on the school building was entirely cancelled, Father Linehan began the erection of the beautiful convent which now stands on the northern side of St. Mary's Street, between the rectory and the parochial school building, forming a part of the group of fine church buildings on St. Mary's Street, extending from Elm Street to Hazel Street.

About 1897, Father Linehan erected St. Margaret's-by-the-Sea, at Old Orchard, naming the church after the patron saint of his revered mother, Margaret Foley Linehan, and twice during his pastorate he found it necessary to build an addition to St. Margaret's to accommodate the worshippers there. In 1916 he erected St. Brendan's Church at Biddeford Pool, and he continued to minister to all three churches until 1921, when, to lessen his burdens in his advancing years, the Bishop relieved him of the care of St. Margaret's-by-the-Sea. Meantime, in

1915, Father Linehan had purchased for the church the historic Woodman property on Main Street, Saco, and soon afterward a new parish was formed in Saco. He also purchased enough additional acreage alongside of St. Mary's Cemetery to raise the total acreage of the cemetery to forty acres. On August 18, 1915, the twenty-fifth anniversary of the beginning of Father Linehan's pastorate, at St. Mary's, an honor jubilee was held in Biddeford, in recognition of the great service he had rendered. His pastorate of thirty-two years ended with his death, which occurred in February, 1922. Rev. C. J. Enright, Father Linehan's curate, was made acting rector and served until May, 1922, when Rev. Denis J. O'Brien of South Berwick, was appointed permanent rector of St. Mary's by Bishop Walsh. In October, 1924, Father Ballou was sent to assist Father O'Brien.

In accordance with the wishes of Bishop Walsh Father O'Brien was almost immediately burdened with the task of demolishing the old church, which had been pronounced unsafe and beyond reasonable repair, and building a new church edifice. The cornerstone of the new building was laid in October, 1923, after much labor and hard work on the part of Father O'Brien, who also renovated St. Mary's rectory and greatly improved the cemetery. In February, 1924, Father O'Brien succeeded in establishing the envelope system of church contribution, thus easing some of his financial worries in connection with the work of the church, and two months later, in April, 1924, he passed to his reward. Father Ballou was then made administrator of St. Mary's, also of the affairs of St. Brendan's Church at Biddeford Pool, and he served until 1926, when Rev. Michael F. Drain was made pastor.

Father Drain is carrying on the splendid work achieved by those who served before him at St. Mary's, and has already won the confidence and esteem of the community-at-large, as well as of his many parishioners. The new St. Mary's Church is a Gothic structure, 171 feet long by 66 feet wide, with a seating capacity of one thousand people on the main floor and space for one hundred more in the gallery. It was designed by O'Connell and Shaw, of Boston, Massachusetts.

J. SIGISMOND GUERIN—Among the interests which have claimed the time and attention of the leading business men of Biddeford, Maine, in the banking enterprise, and one who has gained substantial and distinguished success and prominence in this field is Mr. Guerin. He is one of the well-known and highly respected citizens of the section and fills an important rôle in the civic and community life of Biddeford. Mr. Guerin has been active in the social, political and religious activities of his community and is a leader in the various movements devoted to the advancement and progress of his city. He is the son of Narcisse and Marie R. (Ste. Marie) Guerin, both of whom were natives of the Province of Quebec, Canada, but are now deceased.

J. Sigismond Guerin was born October 1, 1880, at Biddeford, Maine. He went to the parochial schools of the city, and for many years after leaving school was engaged in newspaper work on the "Biddeford Journal." He remained with that enterprise for thirteen years and had risen during that time to the position of business manager. At the end of that long period, after having won the popularity and good will

of his associates and all those with whom he came in contact, he severed his relations with the "Biddeford Journal" and entered the employ of the First National Bank of Biddeford, in the capacity of clerk. He did not long remain in the position, for his wholehearted application to his tasks and his skillful and able discharge of his duties soon brought him promotion. In 1919, he was made assistant cashier of the institution, and in 1924 when a vacancy occurred in the office of cashier, he was advanced to that position, succeeding J. E. Etchells, which he now holds (1928). In 1921, Mr. Guerin was city auditor for Biddeford. He is a member of the board of directors of the York Loan & Building Association and a member of the board of directors of the Webber Hospital. Mr. Guerin is affiliated with many of the local clubs of Biddeford, and is a prominent and influential member of those bodies. He is likewise a member of the Union of St. Jean Baptiste of America. In religious creed, he is a member of the St. Andre Roman Catholic Church, and is active in the philanthropic work of the parish.

In 1916, Mr. Guerin married Bertha Auger of the Province of Quebec, Canada, a daughter of Emery and Melina (Mercier) Auger, and they are the parents of the following children: Charles A., Robert G., Paulette H., George H., and Madeline T.

LAURENCE C. ALLEN—One of the younger lawyers of Sanford who is thoroughly devoted to all the interests of his profession is Laurence C. Allen, who, although he opened his own offices as recently as 1926, is rapidly establishing himself in his general practice. His inherent abilities, so carefully directed and encouraged in the early days of his life by his father, the late Hon. Fred J. Allen, himself a distinguished lawyer, are such as to indicate a brilliant future for him in his professional career.

He was born August 5, 1899, in Sanford, the younger of the two sons of Fred J. Allen, a prominent attorney-at-law, who died in 1917, and of Ida S. (Leavitt) Allen, both of them natives of Alfred. His late father, the Hon. Fred J. Allen, studied law in the office of Samuel M. Came, in Alfred; was admitted to the Maine State bar in 1893; was in partnership in Sanford with Natt T. Abbott until the death of Mr. Abbott; and from 1910 to 1917 was the senior member of the firm of Allen and Willard. He was organizer and counsel for many corporations, was active in the Sanford National Bank, and was one of the organizers and directors of the Fidelity Trust Company, of Portland. From 1901 to 1905 he was a member of the Maine House of Representatives; from 1905 to 1909 a member of the State Senate; and in his second term was president of the Senate. He served as superintendent of the Sanford schools, and gave the town the site for the new high school building. Prominent in fraternal circles, he was a member of the Free and Accepted Masons and of other orders. On June 8, 1892, he married Ida S. Leavitt. They had two sons: Frederic A. Allen, manager of the Sanford Pharmacy; and Laurence C. Allen, Sanford attorney. A review of the life of the Hon. Fred J. Allen appears on following page.

Laurence C. Allen attended the public schools of Sanford, and later became a student at Bowdoin College, from which he was graduated in the class of 1923, with the degree of Bachelor of Arts. Then he took courses of one year each at the Harvard Law School and at Cornell University, in which he prepared himself for practicing the legal profession. His third year of law study he spent in the offices of Willard and Ford, in Sanford. In September, 1926, he was admitted to the Maine bar, and on October 1 of the same year began his practice. One of his special hobbies always has been the breeding of poultry, an activity in which he has been so keenly interested that he has become the proprietor of the Beau-Site Farms. In connection with his poultry business, which he conducts from the offices in which he practices law, he handles eggs for hatching and stock for sale. He advertises the Dirigo strain of Partridge Plymouth Rocks, the "beauty-utility breed," prize winners in New York, Boston, and other cities. Mr. Allen began the poultry business some years ago with his father, who also was a chicken fancier, and he is now an an expert on poultry and the contributor of articles to trade papers and magazines. For the last few years he has specialized in Partridge Plymouth Rocks.

Mr. Allen, active in both legal and poultry organizations, holds memberships in the Maine Bar Association; the York County Bar Association; the Sanford Town Club; the Psi Upsilon Fraternity of Bowdoin College; the Hudson Law Club of Harvard University; the Maine State Poultry Association, in which he is a member of the executive committee; the International Partridge Plymouth Rock Club; and he is a life-member of the American Poultry Association. Fraternally, he is a member of the Free and Accepted Masons, in which order he is affiliated with the Preble Lodge and with the Royal Arch Chapter. His religious affiliation is with the Unitarian church.

On November 17, 1925, Laurence C. Allen married Dorothy L. Grant, of Hartford, Connecticut (formerly of East Brookfield and Allston, Massachusetts), who died February 22, 1927. She was the daughter of Harry E. and Mary P. (Warren) Grant. By this marriage Mr. Allen is the father of one son, Frank Leavitt Allen, who was born February 21, 1927.

THE HON. FRED J. ALLEN—A dominant figure in the history of Sanford, who for the town's welfare gave abundantly of his influence and means, the Hon. Fred J. Allen, who was born in Alfred, July 27, 1865, and died in Sanford, February 2, 1917, was one of the foremost attorneys and legal advisers in this part of the State. Also a legislator and an industrialist, he was distinguished for his activity in matters pertaining to the development of the community. He was the son of John and Caroline P. (Hill) Allen.

Born in Alfred, Fred J. Allen attended the public and high schools in that town, and later attended the Nichols Latin School, in Lewiston, from which he was graduated in 1886. By teaching school and clerking in hotels he worked his way through Bowdoin College, from which he was graduated in 1890 with the degree of Bachelor of Arts. He prepared for his professional career by studying in the law office of Samuel M. Came, of Alfred, and was admitted to the bar in Maine in 1893. He opened an office in Sanford in that year, and afterward formed a partnership with Natt T. Abbott, in which he

remained until Mr. Abbott's death. In 1910 the law firm of Allen and Willard was formed, and it continued until Mr. Allen's death.

For twenty years Mr. Allen was prominent in the ranks of the Republican party. A member of the Maine House of Representatives for two terms, from 1901 until 1905, he was active on important committees and in securing legislation toward abolition of the fee system in many of the State departments. Then, from 1905 to 1909, he served two terms in the State Senate, of which he was president in his second term. He was in line for the governorship of Maine, but because of ill health he did not permit his name to be used as a candidate. His public service also included his superintendency of the public schools of Sanford in 1897 and 1898. In 1914 he presented to the town a large and valuable site for its high school building. His interest in local history prompted him to buy, at his own expense, the original document of the Purchase of the Town from the Indians (Sanford then was known as Phillipstown); then he bound this document, gave it to the Maine Historical Society, and donated engrossed copies of it to Sanford and Kennebunk.

Mr. Allen organized and served as attorney for many corporations, including the Goodall Worsted Company, the Maine Alpaca Company, the Goodall Netting Company, the Sanford Mills, and several railways, later known as the Atlantic Shore Railway. He was one of the organizers of the Fidelity Trust Company, of Portland, and was a member of the board of directors of that company; and he was active in the affairs of the Sanford National Bank, both as director and counsel. It was largely through his efforts that the new home of the Sanford National Bank was erected.

Mr. Allen's broad fraternal interests included membership in the Free and Accepted Masons, in which order he was affiliated with the Preble Lodge; the White Rose Chapter, Royal Arch Masons, of Sanford; St. Amand Commandery, Knights Templar, of Kennebunk; the Ancient Accepted Scottish Rite of the thirty-second degree; and Kora Temple of the Ancient Arabic Order Nobles of the Mystic Shrine. He also was a member of the Improved Order of Red Men, in which he was affiliated with the Sagamore Tribe; the Cumberland Club, of Portland; the Psi Upsilon Fraternity at Bowdoin College; the York County Bar Association; the Maine State Bar Association, of which he was president in 1916, and the American Bar Association. He was a member of the First Parish Unitarian church.

The Hon. Fred J. Allen married, June 8, 1892, Ida S. Leavitt. Their children are: 1. Frederic A., manager of the Sanford Pharmacy. 2. Laurence C, attorney-at-law in Sanford, concerning whom a review appears in preceding biography.

CHESTER A. WEED, Superintendent of Schools of Biddeford, Maine, was born May 15, 1883, in Suffolk County, New York, a son of William H. and Susie E. (Baldwin) Weed, both of whom are natives of Suffolk County. William H. Weed spent thirty-four years in the service of the United States Government, and he is now (1928) retired.

Chester A. Weed received his preparatory education in the public schools of the community in which he was born. He later graduated from the Jamaica Normal School, Jamaica, Long Island. Upon the completion of these courses of study he began his professional career as a teacher in the public schools of Lawrence, New York. He remained there for four years, and after teaching in various schools, in 1917 he removed to Biddeford, Maine, to take the position of principal of the Emery School. His work in this position was so excellent that in 1920 he was made Superintendent of Schools in Biddeford, an office which he is filling at the present time.

Despite the manifold duties of the work in which he is engaged Mr. Weed has nevertheless found time to take a keen interest in many activities. In his political preferences he is a strong supporter of the Republican party. He is fraternally affiliated with Bethlehem Lodge, Free and Accepted Masons. He is also a member of the York County Fish and Game Association, and the Biddeford and Saco Rotary Club.

Chester A. Weed married, in 1906, Hazel P. Banta, a daughter of Edwin C. and Emma (Polhemus) Banta. Mr. and Mrs. Weed are the parents of four sons and a daughter: Delphine V., Albert W., Kenneth M., Emmerson G., and Chester A., Jr. Mr. Weed and his family attend the Episcopal church.

EDWARD S. TITCOMB—Actively concerned with a large proportion of the legal interests of town and county, former County Attorney Edward S. Titcomb has the well-earned repute of an adviser and pleader of leading rank in his profession, and one whose success is based upon abilities of a high order, a comprehensive understanding of general law, and a broad and thorough training and experience, whether in probate or attorneyship.

Edward S. Titcomb, a son of William Titcomb, who has been a conductor on the Boston & Maine Railroad for forty-four years, and Maria S. (Stone) Titcomb, both parents natives of Kennebunk, was born January 21, 1890, at Kennebunk, where he was a student in the public schools. He prepared for his profession in the Law School of Boston University, where he was graduated in 1913 with the degree of Bachelor of Laws. Admitted to the bar in October of that year, Mr. Titcomb established himself in general practice at Sanford, so continuing to the present, with the exception of a period when he was associated with S. M. Came, at Alfred. He is a member of the York County, Maine State, and American Bar associations. He is a member of the board of directors of the Sanford Trust Company.

Offices of public trust held by Mr. Titcomb in the course of his legal career, were those of Register of Probate, from 1916 to 1920; and county attorney, from 1920 to 1924. Fraternally, he is affiliated with York Lodge, Free and Accepted Masons; and he is also a member of the Sanford Town Club; Bauneg Beg Country Club; Sanford and Springvale Rotary Club; and is president of the Fish and Game Club. His religious faith is that of the Congregational church.

Edward S. Titcomb married, September 30, 1916, Margaret N. Hewey, daughter of James E. and Adelaide M. (Roberts) Hewey.

JAMES A. HAMLIN—To intelligent people the gauge of community stability and progress is the public school system. The town which has an up-to-date program of school-building and operation in the hands of a superintendent who has vision and force is likely to be sought as a favorable residential center by desirable and constructive citizens. Of this type is Sanford, Maine. James A. Hamlin has for the past five years been Superintendent of School there. He has coöperated ably with the School Board, with his fellow-townmen, and with his teachers, and has performed a large public service in his quality of educational leadership. The fine new high school, complete in every detail, operating with a liberal and well-rounded program which offers excellent educational opportunities to all types of students, an institution of which the town is proud, is in large part the result of Mr. Hamlin's vision and efforts.

James A. Hamlin was born in Oxford County, Maine, July 26, 1879, son of a lumber dealer, Charles B. Hamlin, of Oxford County, and his wife, Etta M. (Sylvester) Hamlin, of Dover, Maine. The son graduated from Bowdoin College in 1900 with the degree of Bachelor of Arts and pursued his postgraduate studies at the University of Maine. He was principal of New Gloucester High School; later principal at Madison for three years. Then for ten years he was principal of the Old Town High School, and for five years filled the office of Superintendent of Dexter Schools, thus gaining an insight into the needs of a community along the line of secondary educational opportunities which has served him in good stead in his present position. In 1922 he was chosen Superintendent of Schools at Sanford, succeeding Bertram E. Packard. The whole community realizes the value of his accomplishments in Sanford and responds to his attractive and forceful personality.

In other respects, also, Mr. Hamlin has entered heartily into community progress. A member of the Rotary and Sanford Town clubs, he served the latter as president for a time. During the World War he was a "four-minute" speaker, receiving the customary certificate in recognition of his services. His fraternal affiliations are with the Free and Accepted Masons, the Royal Arch Masons, and the Royal and Select Masters; with the Independent Order of Odd Fellows; the Benevolent and Protective Order of Elks, of which he is Past Exalted Ruler; with the Knights of Pythias, of which he is Past Chancellor; and with Rotary International. He attends the Baptist church.

In 1911, James A. Hamlin married Mabel P. Grant, of Maine, daughter of Franklin P. and Helen (Herrick) Grant. Children: Helen E., Franklin P., Donald J., and Margaret F.

JUDGE GEORGE A. GOODWIN—A lawyer whose personality and achievements have been significant in upholding the high traditions of the Maine bar, George A. Goodwin has also for the past six years added to his renown by his wisdom and integrity as Municipal Judge of Sanford, Maine. He resides in Springvale, nearby, where his law office is situated. His interest in public affairs extends not only to educational and civic affairs in his own town, but to those of Sanford, and to public welfare in general.

Judge Goodwin was born at North Berwick, Maine, December 15, 1862, son of Samuel and Sarah A. (Johnson) Goodwin, and descended from a family long native to that section of the country. The father was a prosperous farmer, who gave his son a good education in the public schools, at Coburn Academy, and at Bates College, from which he graduated in 1885 with the degree of Bachelor of Arts. Upon this foundation it was easy for the ambitious young man to build a successful legal career. He read law in the offices of the well-known firm of Savage and Oakes, winning admission to the bar in 1889. That same year he set up an office of his own which became the center of important affairs for Springvale and vicinity and which offered a high quality of legal assistance to an ever-enlarging clientele. In 1925, thirty-six years after Judge Goodwin began to practice, he took into partnership his son, Linwood J. Goodwin, and the firm continues as Goodwin and Goodwin to occupy a place of leadership in the community.

Throughout this long professional career, Judge Goodwin has been active in public affairs. In 1905-1907 he was elected to the State Legislature and served on the Judiciary Committee the second term. He served his town as Superintendent of Schools and as member of the School Board. In 1921 came his elevation to the bench as Judge of the Municipal Court of Sanford, a town more than a hundred and fifty years old, with a large and substantial population and important business developments. The judge is now serving his second four-year term. He is also president of Nasson Institute of Sanford. He belongs to the York County and Maine State Bar associations and the Springvale Town Club, as well as the Springvale Lodge, Free and Accepted Masons, and the Independent Order of Odd Fellows. He is a communicant of the Free Baptist Church.

In 1893, George A. Goodwin married Etta L. Gile of Waterboro, Maine, daughter of Nathaniel and Olive H. (Johnson) Gile. Children: 1. Charles G. Goodwin, who served his country during the World War as a member of the American Expeditionary Forces in France. 2. Linwood J. Goodwin, graduate of Boston University with the degree of Bachelor of Laws, his father's partner in the law firm of Goodwin and Goodwin, and now a member of the State Legislature.

DR. GEORGE C. PRECOURT began the practice of his profession as a physician and surgeon at Biddeford in 1909, and has successfully continued a general medical practice ever since. His ability and popularity have been amply attested by the fact that in 1926 he was elected mayor of Biddeford, and made such a good record at the start that he was reëlected overwhelmingly in 1927 as the representative of the Republican Progressive ticket. Dr. Precourt brings to his profession an equipment born of an experience in the Bowdoin College Medical School and the New York City Hospital. He is one of the few men of French parentage to be so signally honored by his fellow-citizens of all nationalities as to be elected mayor of Biddeford on two occasions.

Dr. George C. Precourt was born at Saco, Maine, December 24, 1883, son of Joseph J. and Lucy (Parent) Precourt; his father, a man of outstanding qualities, of the Province of Quebec, Canada, died in 1907, while his mother, a woman of great personality and character, also a native of that province, is still living (in 1928) at the age of seventy-nine. Dr. Precourt attended the grammar and high schools, after which he matriculated at Bowdoin College at Bruns-

wick, from which institution's Medical Department he graduated in the class of 1908, with the degree of Doctor of Medicine. He took post-graduate work at the New York City Hospital, and presently settled at Biddeford in 1909, and has carried on his practice here ever since. He is a member of the American Medical Association, the Maine Medical Association, and the York County Medical Association, of which latter organization he is secretary. In addition to his regular practice he finds time to serve on the surgical staff of the Webber Hospital. Dr. Precourt has exhibited considerable interest in military affairs, and during the World War was commissioned a first lieutenant attached to the One Hundred and Third United States Artillery; and he holds this rank now in the status of a reserve officer. He is a member of the Société de St. Jean Baptiste; member of the Knights of Columbus, fourth degree, and of St. Andrew's Roman Catholic Church.

Dr. Precourt married, in 1913, Hilda Precourt, of the same surname as himself, a daughter of Octave and Elise (Martel) Precourt, members of high-esteemed families on both sides of the house.

PERLEY H. FORD—From many directions, professional, civic, military, social, have come to Attorney Perley H. Ford numerous demands for his valued service, whether as State Commissioner, county attorney or colonel on the staff of Governor Baxter, or comrade and officer in the World War; and his response has invariably been ready, efficient, and constructive. Prominent in legal activities, as a member of the firm of Willard and Ford, at Sanford, Mr. Ford has participated as a pleader in the courts of the county, and has forwarded the plan and work of important civic committees by his coöperation and counsel.

Perley H. Ford, a son of John H. Ford, a blacksmith, and Elizabeth (Harvey) Ford, both parents natives of Aroostook County, was born June 21, 1887, in Aroostook County, Maine, and he attended the public schools of Kennebunk, Maine. He took a two years' course at Bates College, at Lewiston. In 1909-11, Mr. Ford was principal of Woodstock, Bryant Pond (Maine) High School, and principal of Mechanic Falls (Maine) High School in 1911-1914. Preparing for his profession at the University of Maine, he was graduated from its Law School in 1917, with the degree of Bachelor of Laws, and a member of Phi Kappa Phi Honor Fraternity. Mr. Ford was admitted to the bar in the same year, and establishing himself in general practice at Sanford, joined in partnership with Hiram Willard, as Willard and Ford. He is a member of the York County and the Maine State Bar associations. His directorship of the Sanford National Bank, and of the Nelson-Clarke Company has benefited the expanding interests of those concerns; he has held the office of County Attorney of York County since 1924; has served on committees for many vital projects of civic welfare, and was one of the Commissioners on the War Memorial at Kittery, Maine.

Enlisting in the World War, Mr. Ford was at first assigned to Fort McKinley with the Fifty-fourth Regiment of Artillery, and served with the American Expeditionary Forces as a second lieutenant of the Forty-third Railroad Artillery. He received his discharge at Camp Devens with second lieutenant ranking; and is a reserve officer with

MAINE—A HISTORY 257

captain's rank, in the judge-advocate department. Fraternally, he is affiliated with Jefferson Lodge, Free and Accepted Masons; the Chapter, Royal Arch Masons; the Benevolent and Protective Order of Elks; the Kiwanis Club, of which he was one of the organizers, and was president for two years; T. W. Cole Post, American Legion, of which he is a Past Commander; Sanford Town Club; Bauneg Beg Country Club; and he was Maine State Commander of the American Legion in 1922-1923. His religious faith is that of the Baptist church.

Perley H. Ford married, August 23, 1911, Eva M. Wood, of Livermore Falls, daughter of Samuel S. and Clara (Hibbard) Wood.

HIRAM WILLARD—In this section, the name of Hiram Willard, of Sanford, is synonymous with achievement in the annals of the law, and Mr. Willard bears his honors with ease and grace, for he is distinctly an outstanding figure, and known far beyond the local borders. Hiram Willard was born November 9, 1878, at Aroostook, Maine, son of Samuel Willard, a native of that county, who died in 1884, after a useful career as a merchant, and Elizabeth (Harvey) Willard, of Van Buren, this State, who has been spared to see and enjoy the conspicuous success of her able son.

Mr. Willard attended the grammar and high schools of his native neighborhood, where he made a very satisfactory record, after which he matriculated at Bridgton Academy. At the end of this latter course, where he profited greatly, he entered Boston University Law School at Boston, Massachusetts, having determined to become a lawyer; and in 1906 his labors were rewarded with the bestowal of a diploma conveying the degree of Bachelor of Laws, *cum laude*. He taught school at various times, to assist in paying his way through college. He was first admitted to the Massachusetts bar, in July, 1906, since he intended to practice in that State; but on reconsideration, he decided his best opportunities lay in Maine, and in February of the following year, 1907, he was settled at Sanford and standing the examinations for the bar of Maine. He passed the examinations and was forthwith admitted to practice before the Maine courts. Mr. Willard has practiced here ever since with great success and satisfaction to himself, and his keen interest in the affairs of the city and of his neighbors has brought him a deserved popularity and caused him to be called upon for assistance in any number of local campaigns. He has been a liberal giver to charity, and a constant supporter to the works and programs of the Baptist church.

Mr. Willard served four years—from 1912 to 1916—as county attorney of York County, in which activity he added greatly to an equipment already abundant, and during the World War he acted as a member of the Legal Advisory Board, whose services were requited with warm thanks of a grateful government. His financial and business standing in the community have been recognized in the fact that he was made a director in the Sanford National Bank.

Mr. Willard is a leading and valued member of the Chapter, Council and Commandery of the Free and Accepted Masons; the Improved Order of Red Men; and the Benevolent and Protective Order of Elks, of the Sanford Lodge of which he served as

the first Exalted Ruler. He finds recreation in the atmosphere of the Sanford Town Club, the Bauneg Beg Country Club and other social organizations, while his civic activities find expression in the programs of the Kiwanis Club. Professionally, he is a member of the York County, Maine State and American Bar associations.

Hiram Willard married, in 1902, Christine M. Pitts, of Maine, and they are the parents of four children: 1. Lester H., graduate of Dartmouth College, Hanover, New Hampshire, in the class of 1924, with the degree of Bachelor of Arts; graduated from Harvard Law School, Cambridge, Massachusetts, class of 1927, with degree of Bachelor of Laws; often received straight "A" grades. 2. George S., a student at Bowdoin College, Brunswick. 3. Elizabeth A. 4. Frances C. The two last-named children are (1928) high school students.

EUGENE C. SMITH—As treasurer of the Smith and Rumery Company, of Portland, Maine, Eugene C. Smith is an important factor in the noteworthy success of one of the leading concerns engaged in the production of architectural wood work in the State of Maine. For the past quarter of a century the name of this concern has been symbolic of superior interior and exterior woodwork, and their craftsmen make artistry of design and superiority of workmanship paramount in every bit of work that comes from their plant. A shop-drawing department (a subsidiary unit in the Smith & Rumery Company organization), fundamentally designed to assist the architect, the contractor, and the layman, is known as Sarco Service, and this name is applied also to the products of the plant, which are frequently spoken of as Sarco products. The business is located at Nos. 1 to 55 Center Street, in Portland.

Eugene C. Smith was born in Portland, Maine, and received his education in the public schools of his birthplace. When school days were over he became identified with the Smith & Rumery Company, and this connection has been continuously maintained to the present time (1928). Smith & Rumery Company was incorporated in 1898, with A. D. Smith as president, Frank A. Rumery as treasurer, and Eugene C. Smith, clerk, the object of the concern being construction work and the retail handling of lumber. In 1901, A. D. Smith died, and his son, Eugene C. Smith, came into the firm as treasurer. Mr. Rumery withdrew in 1912, and John S. Pierce was made president; Eugene C. Smith, treasurer and general manager; Alfred N. Plummer, vice-president, and Vernon F. West, clerk. At this time, 1912, construction work was discontinued, and the whole attention of the concern was devoted to architectural woodwork. In this field the concern has achieved an enviable success, and its name long ago came to be a guarantee for superior material, artistic workmanship, and sound business methods. Their shop-drawing department is a boon to contractors and architects as well as to customers who are without technical training, for this department furnishes reproductions of original detail drawings for all architectural woodwork produced at this plant. Experienced draughtsmen trained in versatility and in the importance of adaptability have made this department an indispensable unit to many buyers of architectural woodwork—and Sarco service is free to customers of the Smith and Rum-

Maine—17

ery Company. The following short list will serve to show the spread of this concern's business which covers New England, New Jersey, and New York: the Arlington First Baptist Church, of Arlington, Massachusetts; the additions and alterations of Cushing Academy; Sigma Nu Fraternity House, of Dartmouth College, Hanover, New Hampshire; the Lake Street School, in Auburn, Maine; the Memorial Chapel of Middlesex School, in Concord, Massachusetts; the Press Herald Building, Federal Street, Portland; the residence of Governor Roland H. Spaulding, Rochester, New Hampshire, and the Wellesley Falls School, at Wellesley, Massachusetts. It is now furnishing the woodwork for the residence and garage for Hon. Dwight W. Morrow, at Englewood, New Jersey.

During the period of the World War, Mr. Smith was chairman of the Expediting Committee in Portland, and was active in all the home war work of the city. Fraternally, he is identified with the Independent Order of Odd Fellows, of which he has been District Deputy Grand Master for the State of Maine. He is also a member of the Ancient Landmark Lodge, a Past High Priest of Mt. Vernon Chapter and a member of Portland Commandery, Free and Accepted Masons. He is a member of the Kiwanis Club, and a past president; past president of the Portland Athletic Club; a member of the board of governors of the Portland Club, a member of the Willowdale Country Club, and identified with several other clubs. His religious membership is with the Congregational church.

Eugene C. Smith was married, in 1901, to Clara K. Davis. Mr. and Mrs. Smith make their home at No. 58 Neal Street, in Portland. Mr. Smith is a son of Augustine D. Smith, and of Elmira (Macomber) Smith. His father, Augustine D. Smith, was born in West Buxton, Maine, and was for forty years a contractor and builder in Portland.

FIRST CONGREGATIONAL CHURCH (Rev. Alex. Sloan, Pastor)—An outstanding leader in the spiritual and educational advancement of South Berwick, for two hundred and twenty-five years has been the First Congregational Church, of which the Rev. Alex. Sloan has been pastor since 1922. The picturesque old building now in use has served the congregation since 1825, a period of a full century. The church was organized in 1702, with Rev. John Wade as the first pastor during a brief period which ended with his death a few months after he took over the charge. His successor, Rev. Jeremiah Wise, began a half century of service in 1707. During this period and through the influence of the church and members transferred from it several other churches were established. Mr. Wise exerted wide and beneficent influence throughout all the district. The next pastor, Rev. Jacob Foster, soon, in 1777, gave up his charge in order to become chaplain of one of the patriotic regiments under General Washington. Rev. John Thompson came to South Berwick in 1783 and had a successful pastorate of forty-four years. In 1829, Rev. Mr. Keeler began on what proved to be a seven-year period of fruitful service at the head of the church. Then folowed: Rev. Andrew Rankin, 1837 to 1840; Rev. William B. Homer, 1840 to 1841, when he died; Rev. B. R. Allen, 1842 to 1854; Rev. Mr. Emerson, in South Berwick for a year and later in charge of a

much larger Massachusetts church; Rev. E. W. Allen, 1858 to 1865; Rev. Sylvanus Hayward, 1866 to 1873; Rev. George Lewis, Doctor of Divinity, who served until his death thirty-seven years later. This good and learned man was succeeded by Rev. Mr. Haskell, for three years, who in turn gave place to Rev. Paris E. Miller, there for eight years. The church has had three edifices in its long history, the present built in 1825.

WALLACE N. FLANDERS—The entire active career of Wallace N. Flanders, to the present time (1928), has been identified with the banking business, and he has been continuously associated with the same institution, though under different names. He is now assistant treasurer and manager of the South Berwick branch of the Casco Mercantile Trust Company of Portland. This was formerly known as the South Berwick Savings and Trust Company, but was taken over by the Casco Mercantile Trust Company in 1925.

Wallace N. Flanders was born in Reading, Massachusetts, October 18, 1895, son of Benjamin F. Flanders, a native of East Clarendon, who was associated with the Boston & Maine Railroad Company and who died in 1915, and of Martha (Mears) Flanders, of South Berwick. He attended the public schools of Reading, and then became a student in Berwick Academy, from which he was graduated with the class of 1915. When his school training was completed he secured a position as clerk in the employ of the South Berwick Savings & Trust Company, and after a time was made assistant treasurer. In this official capacity, he, with the treasurer, Mr. Wentworth, became important factors in the growth and development of the institution. When Charles H. Wentworth died, Mr. Flanders was made treasurer. Meantime the general movement toward concentration of interests and amalgamation of separate financial institutions was making itself felt throughout the country and the South Berwick Savings & Trust Company, which was really a product of that movement, was soon to be further affected by this concentrating movement. The original bank of South Berwick was established in 1823, as a State bank, and the Savings Bank of South Berwick was established in 1866. In 1917, there was an amalgamation of the two banks under the name of the South Berwick Savings & Trust Company, and in 1925, further grouping of interests took place when the Casco Mercantile Trust Company of Portland took over the South Berwick Savings & Trust Company as a branch. George C. Yeaton had been president of the Savings Bank until his death in 1918, when he was succeeded by Edwin A. Stevens, who continued in office until the South Berwick Savings & Trust Company became a branch of the Casco Mercantile Trust Company, in 1925. The last-mentioned bank has total assets of more than a million and a half, and much of the credit of the notable success of the Berwick institution is due to Charles H. Wentworth and to Mr. Flanders. When the Casco Mercantile Trust Company took over the South Berwick Savings & Trust Company as a branch, Mr. Flanders was retained as assistant treasurer and manager, both of which positions he is still (1928) efficiently filling. Mr. Wentworth had been treasurer of the bank for a period of thirty years, and Mr. Flanders is proving himself a worthy successor of one of the most active and effective officials the bank ever retained. Mr. Flanders is a public-spirited citizen, but he is not one who desires the honors and the emoluments of public office. He prefers to serve community, State and Nation in the more quiet and unobtrusive ways in which a successful business man may serve as a private citizen, and he does so most effectively. During the period of the World War he was active in all the various drives, and he is always a willing supporter of plans instituted for the advancement of the general welfare of the community. Fraternally, Mr. Flanders is identified with St. John Lodge, Free and Accepted Masons, and with all the bodies of the York Rite of that order, and he is a Past High Priest and a Senior Warden. He belongs to several other local organizations, and is one of the active and well-liked leaders in South Berwick. His religious affiliation is with the Free Baptist church.

Wallace N. Flanders was married (first) to Eva Turner, daughter of Dr. Henry H. Turner; (second) to Mildred M. Maddox, of South Berwick, Maine, daughter of Albert S. Maddox. Mr. and Mrs. Flanders are the parents of one daughter, Louise T., who was born July 20, 1918.

As treasurer of Berwick Academy, succeeding Charles H. Wentworth, Mr. Flanders is contributing to the improvement of the educational advantages of the community, and is also demonstrating the quality of his loyalty to the community in which he lives and in which his business interests are located.

GEORGE L. EMERY—One of the best-known men of the legal profession in the State of Maine is George L. Emery, of Biddeford, senior member of the law firm of Emery and Waterhouse. Mr. Emery has been identified with some of the biggest legal cases in the State of Maine, and is recognized as one of Maine's greatest jurists.

George L. Emery was born in Biddeford, Maine, June 5, 1876, son of Lewis W. Emery, a native of Kennebunkport, Maine, who was engaged as a machinist to the time of his death in 1894, and of Susan A. (Hamilton) Emery, of Waterboro, Maine, whose death occurred in 1894. He received his education in the local public schools, including the high school, and then studied law and was admitted to the bar in 1897, after studying in the offices of Mr. Marshall at West Buxton, and of Charles W. Ross, of Biddeford, Maine. After his admission to the bar, in 1897, he engaged in general practice in West Buxton, under his own name, but in 1898, he came to Biddeford. He was made a recorder in the local court in 1899, and became a member of the law firm of Cleaves, Waterhouse & Emery, which association was continued until 1914, when Mr. Cleaves withdrew from the firm to become chairman of the Public Utility Commission of Maine. The firm then became Emery and Waterhouse, and so continues to the present time. Mr. Emery is a member of the York County Bar Association, of the Maine State Bar Association, and of the American Bar Association, and he has attained a very high place among his professional colleagues. He is known as one of the most able attorneys in this section of the State, and has handled some of the most important legal cases in the State of Maine.

He served as County Attorney, 1902-1904, was made Judge of the Municipal Court, at Biddeford, in 1914, and served two terms; and was chairman of the Maine State Republican Committee in 1924. During the World War he was chairman of the Legal Advisory Board and was very active in all of the various "drives" by means of which Biddeford went "over the top" in meeting her share of the allotted home war work. Mr. Emery is a member of the board of directors of the York County Mutual Fire Insurance Company, and he is also one of the actively public-spirited citizens of the community. In club circles, too, he is active and always a welcome member. He was the first president of the Biddeford Kiwanis Club, is a member of the Portland Club, of the Farmers' Club, and of the Izaak Walton Club, the last-mentioned of which he has served as president. His religious membership is with the First Parish Church.

George L. Emery was married, December 21, 1899, to Mabel A. Moulton, of Hollis, Maine, daughter of William S. and Mary D. (Coffin) Moulton, and they are the parents of one daughter, Rebecca J., who is a graduate of Thornton Academy. The family home is at No. 208 South Street, in Biddeford.

CHARLES H. AUTHIER—The foremost interests of the York County Bar Association have, in Charles H. Authier, an exponent of the various branches of the law, and, with an extensive practice, a man who holds an honored place in his profession. The town of Sanford has recognized Mr. Authier's qualifications. His fraternal affiliations are those wherein he has received merited office, and, a veteran of the World War. Mr. Authier served with that high degree of loyalty that has characterized all his life-work. He is a son of Henry Authier, a native of Oxford, Massachusetts, who died March 3, 1923, and was for many years an accountant with the Bradley Car Company, and of Parmelia (Ledoux) Authier, a native of the Province of Quebec, Canada, who died January 17, 1911.

Charles H. Authier was born March 12, 1894, at Webster, Massachusetts; and he was graduated, successively, at Assumption College in the class of 1914, and at Saint Mary's College, Baltimore, Maryland, in 1916, with the degree of Bachelor of Arts. Mr. Authier then took a two-year course at Boston University, after which, preparing himself for his profession, he was graduated at the Law School of Yale University in 1921, with the degree of Bachelor of Laws. Admitted to the bar in October, 1922, Mr. Authier began the practice of his profession the same year at Sanford, where he has successfully continued to the present. He is a member of the York County Bar Association. During the World War, he shared the soldiers' experiences overseas as a member of the Seventy-sixth Division, and received his discharge from the service at Camp Lee, January 14, 1919.

Fraternally, Mr. Authier is affiliated with Sanford Lodge, Benevolent and Protective Order of Elks, of which Lodge he is a Past Exalted Ruler; Father McGinnis Council, Knights of Columbus, in which he has held the office of Grand Knight; St. Jean de Baptiste Society; Franco-American Foresters d'Amerique; Kiwanis Club; Sons of Veterans; Thomas W. Cole Post of the American Legion, of which he is Commander. He is a communicant of Saint Ignatius Roman Catholic Church.

Charles H. Authier married, October 6, 1924, Clara Bouffard, of Sanford, Maine, daughter of Claude and Emma (Talbot) Bouffard. Their children: Charles H., Jr., born July 18, 1925, and Estelle N., born September 8, 1926.

WILLIS LESTER WATSON—A newspaper editor or publisher always occupies the position of teacher to the readers of his paper, and in this category comes a man who has added much to the community life of Kennebunk, namely, Willis Lester Watson, treasurer and manager of the Star Print, of which Willis E. Watson is president; Perley L. Watson, vice-president, Roy A. Evans, clerk, and Carl E. Watson is a director.

Willis Lester Watson was born March 23, 1855, at Biddeford, Maine, son of Marcus and Mary A. (Smith) Watson. His father, a native of Dayton, this State, died in 1915, and his mother, of Kennebunkport, died in 1882. Marcus Watson was also a publisher and prominent man of his day, while Mrs. Watson exercised a charitable and Christian influence in this community.

Mr. Watson attended the public schools, but early entered newspaper work, and is one of the oldest men still in business in Kennebunk. The genesis of his paper was the year 1876, when it was established as a daily by Marcus Watson & Son at Biddeford. On August 27, 1877, it was purchased by, the present owner and on September 4 of that year the name was changed to the "Eastern Star." Mr. Watson soon removed the paper to Kennebunk, and changed the edition to a weekly. In 1921, the name was changed to the "Kennebunk Star," and in 1924, the business was incorporated as the "Star Print," to accommodate book and job printing as well. At this time the previously listed officers were installed. The paper has a representative Maine circulation and covers quite a radius in influence. To its upbuild Mr. Watson has added perhaps more than any other man, and he has made a fine place for himself in this community. He is a thirty-second degree Mason and a member of York Lodge, Free and Accepted Masons; is Past Chancellor and Past District Deputy of the Knights of Pythias; and charter member and an organizer of Maple Lodge, No. 19; member of the Independent Order of Odd Fellows and the Encampment of that order. He belongs to the Lafayette Club. In religious circles he is a member of the Congregational church, and was formerly a standing committeeman.

Willis L. Watson married, in 1878, Ida M. Morrill, of Bangor, daughter of Levi H. Morrill, a veteran of the Civil War, and Emily A. (Ferry) Morrill, and their union has been blessed with four children: 1. Willis E., married Florence Cook, and they have two sons and two daughters. 2. Carl E., married Goldie E. Russell, and they have a son. 3. Perley L., married Louise Lombard, and they have a son and a daughter. 4. Edna M., now deceased; married Roy Evans.

JOSEPH DANE—The name Dane, as told within itself, is of extremely ancient origin, and applies to the sturdy natives of Denmark, who have played an important part in Nordic affairs since the days of mythology. Danes under the command of the ancient conquerors of England settled in the then known West, and not only preserved their name, by which they were called by the English, but gave their name to many others not of Denmark.

Gradually, representatives of this family settled in America and found their proper place in everyday affairs. In more recent days we find Joseph Dane, of Kennebunk, worthily living up to the reputation of the line as a constructive citizen and treasurer of the Kennebunk Savings Bank. Mr. Dane was born March 16, 1864, at Kennebunk, son of Nathan and Caroline L. (Goodwin) Dane, of the same city. His father was a leading farmer and later became treasurer of a savings bank, a course that made him not only independent but highly respected for his scholarly attainments. His grandfather, a typical product of New England soil, was also a prominent man, having been treasurer of the State of Maine during the Civil War.

Mr. Dane attended the public schools, and on completing his studies there followed in his father's footsteps on the farm. He farmed until 1903, when he accepted a position with the Kennebunk Savings Bank. He soon learned the various details of the banking business, and won a commendable place among his superior officers. It was an interesting circumstance that Joseph Dane, his great-uncle, became the first president of this institution, having joined a group of business men in its establishment in 1872. Mr. Dane was succeeded by Robert W. Lord. Later Nathan Dane, the father, became treasurer, and he was succeeded by his son, the incumbent. Its recent statements show assets in excess of $2,000,000.

Mr. Dane served as town treasurer fifteen years and superintendent of Hope Cemetery for twenty-five years. He is a member of the York Lodge, Free and Accepted Masons, and is likewise a member of the Independent Order of Odd Fellows.

Mr. Dane married, in 1893, Loucinda L. Bragdon, of Kennebunk, and their union has been blessed with a son, Joseph Dane, Jr.

WILLIAM P. FERGUSON—Of all the officers on the roster of a bank, the man who is of the most importance in the eyes of the public (like the front line soldier) is the man who actually handles the money. The position of cashier is charged with great responsibility, and gives the holder an unusual opportunity for public service, in that he must make contact with hundreds if not thousands of people, and in this duty with the Springvale National Bank, of Springvale, William P. Ferguson has shown his ability.

Mr. Ferguson was born September 8, 1887, at North Berwick, Maine, son of W. Proctor Ferguson, of Shapleigh, this State, and Hattie E. (Earle) Ferguson, both of whom represented families of culture and accomplishment in this section, his father having been a teacher, and later a member of the United States Civil Service, and is now retired, having been spared to share in the success of his worthy son.

Mr. Ferguson has been in the banking business practically the entire time of his career, and has never worked at any other bank than the Springvale, with which he obtained a position soon after he had left high school. This bank was organized Octo-

MAINE—A HISTORY 261

ber 16, 1905, with a capital of $25,000, by a group of business men. George W. Hanson was made the first president, and he was succeeded on the occasion of his death, by the incumbent, Roy N. Stiles. The original home of the bank was in the Fogg Block. In 1913, due to greatly enlarged business, the bank built a new structure, and in 1920 the capital stock was increased to $50,000. The latest statement of the bank shows assets in excess of $2,500,000 and a generally prosperous condition. This represents a growth from $2,219,639.71 as of the statement of December 1, 1926. The other executive of the bank is D. H. Johnson, vice-president.

Mr. Ferguson is also a director of the Springvale Shoe Company, to which he has devoted that same accuracy, painstaking effort and pleasant address, to the extent that a director can, in his relations with the concern's constituents. He is a leading and valued member of the Springvale Lodge, Free and Accepted Masons. He belongs to the Sanford Town Club, the Bauneg Beg Country Club, the Fish and Game Club, and the American Legion, of which he is past secretary. Mr. Ferguson's interest in literary affairs and education in general is evidenced by the fact he is secretary of the Springvale Public Library.

EVERARD JORDAN GOVE—For nearly five years Everard Jordan Gove has been serving in Uncle Sam's employ as postmaster of Biddeford. Previous to receiving his appointment as postmaster Mr. Gove had a varied business experience as florist, and as newspaper man. He is secretary of the Fish and Game Association of York County, and is very well known in this section of the State. Born in Biddeford, Maine, November 21, 1870, Everard Jordan Gove is a son of Edward H. Gove, an attorney of Biddeford, and of Elizabeth (Jordan) Gove, also of Biddeford, who died in 1910. He attended the local public schools, including the high school, and when his school training was completed, engaged in the florist business in Biddeford, under the name of Gove Brothers, continuing in that line until 1903. In that year he became associated with the Biddeford "Journal," as news editor, and that connection he maintained until 1922, when he was appointed by President Warren G. Harding to succeed Joseph E. Brooks as postmaster of Biddeford. During the nearly five years which have passed since that time he has continued to fill that office, giving entire satisfaction to the people of Biddeford and vicinity. In his political sympathies Mr. Gove is a Republican, and at one time he served as a member of the Board of Education. He has been identified with the Red Cross organization for a number of years, and he has always been a generous supporter of all projects wisely planned for the advancement of the general good. He is a member of the Kiwanis Club, and his religious membership is with the Second Congregational Church.

Everard Jordan Gove was married, in 1893, to Edith G. Hussey, of Biddeford, Maine, daughter of Dr. Charles E. and Elizabeth (Hutchinson) Hussey. Mr. and Mrs. Gove are the parents of two children: 1. Ruth Elizabeth, who married P. W. Monohon, and has two children, Paul Jordan, and Stephen Everard. 2. Burtin J., a graduate of Harvard University, from which he received the degree of Doctor of Medical Dentistry. Mr. and Mrs. Gove

make their home at No. 95 Graham Street, in Biddeford.

HENRY C. HAMEL—Under the firm name of Hamel and Hamel, Henry C. Hamel and his wife, Helen Cashman Hamel, are engaged in legal practice in Biddeford, Maine. Mr. Hamel has established a reputation as a skilled practitioner and an able and resourceful advocate, and Mrs. Hamel, who was admitted to the Massachusetts bar in 1917, and to the Maine bar in 1922, is the first woman to engage in legal practice in Biddeford.

Henry C. Hamel was born in Quincy, Massachusetts, July 30, 1882, a son of Thomas Hamel, of Maine, who for many years was identified with the granite industry at Quincy, but is now retired, and of Emily (Rouleau) Hamel, of Warwick, Maine, whose death occurred June 11, 1925. He received his early education in the local public schools, and then prepared for college in Adams Academy. When his preparatory course was completed he matriculated in Van Buren College, from which he was graduated with the class of 1905, receiving at that time the degree of Bachelor of Arts. He studied law in the Law School of Boston University, and successfully passed the examinations for admission to the bar in 1912. From 1912 to 1919, he was engaged in United States Consulate work in the Province of Quebec, but in the last-named year he came to Biddeford and engaged in general practice. He is now a member of the law firm of Hamel and Hamel, his wife being the other partner in the firm. He is a member of the York County Bar Association, the Maine Bar Association, and the American Bar Association, and is well known in this section of the State. In 1920-21 he first served as solicitor of the city of Biddeford, and again in 1923-24, 1925-26 and 1927, and 1928, in which capacity he rendered excellent professional service. He is identified with the Benevolent and Protective Order of Elks, and with several local clubs, and his religious affiliation is with St. Joseph's Roman Catholic Church.

Henry C. Hamel was married, in 1921, to Helen Cashman, of Quincy, Massachusetts. Mrs. Hamel is a native of Quincy, Massachusetts, and was admitted to legal practice in Massachusetts, in 1917, and to the Maine bar in 1922. She is the pioneer in the legal field in Biddeford, so far as women are concerned, and since 1922 she has been engaged in general practice in partnership with her husband, under the firm name of Hamel and Hamel. Both are known as able and resourceful practitioners, and have made for themselves and for the firm a reputation which is a valuable business asset. Mr. and Mrs. Hamel make their home at No. 17 West Myrtle Street, in Biddeford, and their office is located in the Paquin Building.

RICHARD HARDING ARMSTRONG—In association with William P. Donahue, Richard Harding Armstrong has opened an office for general legal practice on Washington Street, in Biddeford, Maine. Mr. Armstrong was associated with his partner in the compilation, editing, and publishing of a work entitled "Florida Chancery Jurisprudence," which is recognized as authority in its field, and when that work was completed both young men came to Biddeford and prepared for general practice by opening their office on Washington Street. They are building up a practice and there is every indication that a successful future lies before them.

Richard Harding Armstrong was born in Biddeford, Maine, March 26, 1903, son of John Henry and Abbie (Moore) Armstrong, and descendants of old families of Biddeford. He attended the public schools and then attended Suffolk Law School, later matriculating in the Mercer University at Macon, Georgia, from which he was graduated in 1924, with the degree of Bachelor of Laws. He was admitted to the bar of the State of Georgia, in June, 1924, and then engaged in practice for a time, and edited the "Georgia Code of 1926." In 1925 he became associated with William P. Donahue in the compilation of the work entitled "Florida Chancery Jurisprudence," and the two young men completed and published that work in January, 1927. When the work was finished, the two opened an office in Biddeford, where they are now (1928) laying the foundations of a general legal practice. Fraternally, Mr. Armstrong is identified with Dunlop Lodge, Free and Accepted Masons; and with the Benevolent and Protective Order of Elks, of Charlottesville, Virginia. He is a member of Psi Chi College Fraternity, and of the Adana Society, and his religious convictions are those of the Episcopal church, although he is not a member.

Richard Harding Armstrong was married, in 1927, to Irma M. Dawson, of Charlottesville, Virginia, daughter of Henry and Nancy (Patterson) Dawson.

WILLIAM PHILLIP DONAHUE—Among the younger members of the legal profession who are engaged in practice in Biddeford, Maine, is William Phillip Donahue, whose offices are located on Washington Street. Mr. Donahue was admitted to the bar in 1925, but was engaged in editorial work until 1927, when, having completed in collaboration with Mr. Armstrong, the work entitled "Florida Chancery Jurisprudence," he returned to Biddeford and engaged in general legal practice. He is laying the foundations of what promises to be a successful legal career.

William Phillip Donahue was born in Biddeford, Maine, January 3, 1901, son of William H. Donahue, of Three Rivers, Canada, and of Margaret (Maxwell) Donahue, of Biddeford, Maine. He attended the public schools of Biddeford, and after completing his high school course became a student in the Law School of Boston University, from which he was graduated with the class of 1925, receiving at that time the degree of Bachelor of Laws. He was admitted to the Maine bar in the same year, but did not immediately engage in practice. Instead, in association with Mr. Armstrong, he began the compiling and editing of a work which was published under the title of "Florida Chancery Jurisprudence." This work is recognized as an authority in its field, and has had a wide sale. When this bit of work was completed Mr. Donahue returned to Biddeford, in January, 1927, and opened an office on Washington Street, where he is building up a general practice. He is a member of the York County Bar Association, and his political principles are those of the Republican party.

DR. JOSEPH RAOUL LAROCHELLE—Of the many native Canadians who have moved across the border and settled in Maine, few have been more

welcome or made a more comfortable position for themselves than Dr. Joseph Raoul Larochelle, of Biddeford, who is the capable president of the York County Medical Association.

Dr. Larochelle was born March 14, 1881, in the Province of Quebec, Canada, son of Herode Larochelle, a Quebec farmer, who died in 1915, and Claire Jean Larochelle, who is still living to enjoy her son's gratifying success. He brings to his profession an unusual equipment in the fact that he has been extensively educated in this country and abroad. In 1901 he graduated from St. Anne de la Pasatiere College with the degree of Bachelor of Arts. Deciding to be a physician, he entered Laval University of Quebec, from which institution he was graduated in 1907 with the degree of Doctor of Medicine. He took post-graduate work at Harvard University, at Cambridge, Massachusetts, and at the New York Hospital, in 1913, then went to France for additional studies in the Necaire Hospital and at St. Vincent's; in 1925 he returned to St. Vincent's for extra courses. He then settled at Biddeford, and has done well from the start. This was in 1907, and he has engaged in general practice. He is a member of the American Medical Association, the Maine Medical Association; and is a member of the surgical staff and chief obstetrician of Webber Hospital. During the World War he was chairman of the Medical Advisory Board, and received a certificate from the government for his good work at Biddeford. For fifteen years he has been physician to the Fraternal Order of Eagles; and he holds membership in the Benevolent and Protective Order of Elks and the Society of St. Jean de Baptiste. He is a member of the St. André Roman Catholic Church, and of the Biddeford-Saco Country Club.

Dr. Larochelle married twice, his wives having been sisters. His first wife, Jeannette Roussin, daughter of William E. and Elda (Cordeau) Roussin, deceased, bore him two children: J. Raoul, born in September, 1919, and J. Guy, born in May, 1921. He married (second) Adrianne Roussin.

Dr. Larochelle enjoys one of the largest practices in Biddeford and is one of the town's most wide-awake citizens.

ALBERT R. GOODWIN—One of the late residents of Biddeford who was closely identified with the financial development of the place was Albert R. Goodwin, cashier of the Biddeford National Bank to the time of his death, which occurred in 1924, and also one of the founders of the Pepperell Trust Company of Biddeford, its first treasurer, and later its vice-president and secretary. He was also a director of the Biddeford-Saco Coal Company.

Albert R. Goodwin was born in Biddeford, Maine, February 29, 1864, son of Joseph P. and Mary Ann (Hayford) Goodwin. He received his education in the public schools of his birthplace, including the high school, and then learned the trade of the carpenter in the Laconia Mills. Later he was placed in the cloth hall of the mill, in charge of the stamping department, and there he continued until 1880, when he made a radical change in the nature of his employment, by entering the Biddeford National Bank as a clerk, under his brother, Charles E. Goodwin, who was then cashier and later became assistant cashier. In 1915, Albert R. Goodwin succeeded his brother as cashier, and that official position he filled with efficiency to the time of his death, which occurred February 13, 1924. In addition to his responsibilities in connection with the Biddeford National Bank, Mr. Goodwin was also one of the founders of the Pepperell Trust Company, which was organized in 1907, in association with a group of business men of this section. Charles E. Goodwin, brother of Mr. Goodwin, was its first president, Albert R. Goodwin was its first treasurer, and Ernest A. Goodwin, son of Albert R., was its first assistant treasurer. The bank was originally organized as the Goodwin Trust Company, but in 1915 its name was changed to its present style of the Pepperell Trust Company of Biddeford. In 1927, the officers were: Ernest L. Morrill, president; Jere G. Shaw, vice-president; and Ernest A. Goodwin, treasurer and secretary. The bank has made substantial and steady progress until at the present time its resources amount to $1,308,684, which amount is steadily increasing. Mr. Goodwin was also a member of the board of directors of the Biddeford National Bank, and of the Biddeford-Saco Coal Company. Politically, he gave his support to the principles and the candidates of the Democratic party, and he was always interested in the civic affairs of Biddeford. He was a member of the Knights of Pythias and of the Biddeford-Saco Country Club, and his religious affiliation was with the Second Congregational church.

Albert R. Goodwin was married to Edith L. Sawyer, and they became the parents of Ernest A. Goodwin, an account of whose life follows this record. Albert R. Goodwin died February 13, 1924, mourned by a host of friends who knew and loved him because of his sterling qualities of character, and because of his attractive personality.

ERNEST A. GOODWIN—No official of the Pepperell Trust Company of Biddeford has served in office so long or been more active in the forwarding of its interests than has Ernest A. Goodwin, who has been secretary and treasurer since the resignation of his father in 1912. Mr. Goodwin is widely known in this locality as a financier of ability and resourcefulness. To the efficient manner in which he has guided the affairs of the bank the greater part of its prosperity and high standing are due.

Ernest A. Goodwin was born in Biddeford, Maine, May 1, 1887, son of Albert R. Goodwin, a banker, whose record precedes this, and of Edith L. (Sawyer) Goodwin of Buxton. He attended the local public schools and then prepared for college in Phillips-Exeter Academy, at Exeter, New Hampshire, after which he matriculated in Harvard University. He continued his study there for some time, but finally left before graduation in order that he might accept the position of secretary and assistant treasurer of the Pepperell Trust Company, of Biddeford, of which his father was one of the founders. In 1912, he succeeded his father as treasurer of the bank, and that official position he has continued to fill to the present time (1928). The Pepperell Trust Company was organized in 1907, by Albert R. Goodwin, father of Ernest A. Goodwin, in association with a group of business men of this section, with Charles E. Goodwin as its first president; Albert R. Goodwin, treasurer, and Ernest A. Goodwin, assistant treasurer. In 1912, Ernest A. Goodwin succeeded his

father as treasurer, and that official position he has retained to the present time (1928). At the time of its organization the bank was incorporated as the Goodwin Trust Company, but in 1915, its name was changed to the present style of the Pepperell Trust Company. At this time Ernest L. Morrill was made president; Jere G. Shaw, vice-president, and Ernest A. Goodwin continued as treasurer and secretary. All these officials still remain in office (1928). The bank has grown steadily and has made for itself a high place in the confidence and esteem of those whom it serves. Its total resources now amount to $1,308,684, and are steadily increasing and the number of its depositors has grown constantly since the organization of the bank. Mr. Goodwin is the one most important factor in the management of the bank at the present time, and to his ability and sound judgment much of the high standing of the bank is due.

In addition to his responsibilities in connection with the Pepperell Trust Company, Mr. Goodwin is also a director of the Biddeford & Saco Coal Company. He has been actively interested in civic affairs in Biddeford, and for a term of three years served as city treasurer. Fraternally, he is identified with Dunlap Lodge, Free and Accepted Masons, also with the Chapter and Council of that Order; and he finds healthful recreation and agreeable social contacts as a member of the Biddeford and Saco Country clubs. His religious affiliation is with the Second Congregational Church.

Ernest A. Goodwin was married, in 1909, to Hortense Leavitt, of Scarborough, Maine. Mr. and Mrs. Goodwin are the parents of two children: 1. Patricia L., who was born August 28, 1918. 2. Joan, born March 21, 1921. The family home is at No. 260 Elm Street, in Biddeford.

JOSEPH EDMOND HARVEY—One of the members of the legal profession in Biddeford who is influential in the affairs of the Republican party is Joseph Edmond Harvey, who is also a veteran of the World War, having served overseas with the Twenty-sixth Division, and having taken part in most of the engagements in which the American Expeditionary Forces participated, including Soissons, Toul Sector, Chateau-Thierry, Aisne-Marne, St. Mihiel, and Verdun. His offices are located at No. 124 Main Street, where he has been successfully engaged in general practice for more than eleven years.

Joseph Edmond Harvey was born in Saco, Maine, November 2, 1895, son of Joseph Harvey, a native of the Province of Quebec, who was engaged as an iron moulder, and whose death occurred in 1920, and of Victorine (Chicoine) Harvey, who is still living. He attended the public schools at Saco, Maine, Thornton Academy, and then became a student in the University of Maine, at Orono, Maine, from which he was graduated with the class of 1916, receiving at that time the degree of Bachelor of Laws. He successfully passed the examination for admission to the bar that same year, and at once opened an office in Biddeford, where he has since been successfully engaged in general practice. Mr. Harvey is a member of the York County Bar Association and of the Maine Bar Association, and is well known among his professional associates. In addition to the responsibilities of his practice he is very active in the affairs of the Republican party, has served as chairman of the city committee of the city of Biddeford, Maine, and was city solicitor in 1921-22 of Saco, Maine. Upon the entrance of the United States into the World War Mr. Harvey enlisted for service and was sent overseas with the 103d Field Artillery of the Twenty-sixth Division, with which unit he served for nearly two years, taking part in the offensive at Soissons, in the Toule Sector, Chateau-Thierry, Aisne-Marne, St. Mihiel, and Verdun, and receiving his discharge July 8, 1919, with the rank of ordnance sergeant, senior grade. While in France, Mr. Harvey pursued a course of study at the Université de Rennes, Rennes, France, for a period of seven months. He is one of the organizers of the American Legion, in Saco, and is a member of the Veterans of Foreign Wars. Mr. Harvey is well known and much liked in this section of the county, and is closely allied with various civic organizations. He is always ready and willing to aid in any project which promises advancement for the town of Biddeford, and he is known as the kind of public-spirited citizen who has the highest good of the community at heart. He has a host of friends here, who value him not only because of his skill and his professional knowledge, but because of those qualities of character which win and hold the esteem of others.

Joseph Edmond Harvey was married, November 15, 1922, to Anne B. McCormick, of Lewiston, Maine, daughter of James A. and Sarah (Boland) McCormick. Mr. and Mrs. Harvey are the parents of one daughter, Justine Celeste, who was born November 25, 1925. The family home is at No. 51 Nott Street, Saco, Maine.

CHARLES S. NEAL—A varied career during his long and eventful life during which time he attained the respect and esteem of his host of friends and associates, Charles S. Neal has been recognized for many years as a leading citizen of Biddeford, Maine. For more than the past decade, he has been identified prominently in the direction and management of a funeral parlor, first in Portland, Maine, and later in Biddeford, where he is a partner of W. I. Dennett in the leading establishment of its kind in the community. The accoutrements of his parlor and the standard of his offices and services are designed for the comfort and convenience of his clients to such a successful and efficient degree that the firm caters to nearly all of the better class in the section. His reputation and ability are widespread, and the long experience which is his has contributed materially and substantially to the general good will which is accorded him by all. In addition to these commercial interests, Mr. Neal has likewise been active in social, fraternal and civic affairs of his community and holds distinguished rôles in the various organizations with which he is or has been affiliated.

Charles S. Neal was born November 28, 1868, at West Gardiner, Maine, a son of Henry M. and Bernice (Densmore) Neal, both of whom were natives of West Gardiner, Maine. He attended the local public and high schools of West Gardiner, and upon the completion of his scholastic career, early entered the business world. For a number of years after leaving school, Mr. Neal engaged in the calling of photographer and gained substantial success in this

particular field as a result of his artistry and sense of rhythm and perspective. Thereafter he became associated with the State Hospital at Danvers, Maine; was supervisor in which capacity he remained for nine years, devoting himself with untiring energy and application to the performance of his duties. At the end of that period, Mr. Neal made one further change and removed to Portland, Maine, where became identified with the business in which he has continued since. He joined forces with John S. Cushman of Portland as a funeral director. He soon mastered the essential methods and principles of the business, and remained until May, 1918, in Portland. On May 1 of that year, he came to Biddeford as an assistant to W. I. Dennett in the funeral parlor establishment, and during the ensuing years proved such an enthusiastic, capable and loyal lieutenant to his superior that in April, 1926, Mr. Dennett and he formed a partnership under the firm style, Dennett and Neal, funeral directors. The consideration which is afforded all those who seek the offices and assistance of this establishment has gained for the firm high prestige and appreciation of their host of friends and neighbors, and by setting the standard of service and quality of performance the firm has gained the general recognition as the foremost funeral parlor establishment.

Mr. Neal has always been active in the fraternal organizations of the community, and is a prominent member of Dunlap Lodge, Free and Accepted Masons; Bradford Commandery, No. 4, Knights Templar; Kora Temple, Ancient Arabic Order Nobles of the Mystic Shrine; and Improved Order of Red Men. He also belongs to Pomona Grange, Patrons of Husbandry, and several other local organizations, including the Society of Sons of Veterans. He is a member of the Fish and Game Association, and has been a hard and active worker in the interests and promotion of the welfare of the body. His favorite sport and hobby is hunting and fishing, and his is the distinction of being one of the best sportsmen in the section. For many years he was also a member of the Second Regiment, Maine Volunteer Militia, attached to Company D. In politics he is a staunch and ardent Republican and supports his party and its civic advancement policies loyally and actively. He has never sought public office, preferring to contribute his services in this behalf as a private citizen. With his family he is a communicant of the Congregational church, and attends the church of that denomination in his community. He is active in the affairs of the parish and gives equal support to its enterprises that he gives to all of his other activities either business or personal.

Charles S. Neal married Zulah M. Norcross, a daughter of Millard F. and Mary Ella (Boyd) Norcross, and they are the parents of the following children: 1. C. Millard. 2. Anna Mae, married to Gerard Joy. 3. Ralph N. 4. Elwood A. 5. Robert D.

DR. STEPHEN A. COBB, of Sanford, well-known physician and surgeon, has built up a most gratifying practice and taken high rank as a citizen of his community. Dr. Cobb was born December 9, 1887, at Gardiner, this State, son of Stephen A. Cobb, for many years a steamboatman, and Harriet F. (Chadwick) Cobb, of Maine, who died in 1925. The father's activities centered around Chelsea, where he was a familiar figure among a group of transportation men whose type has largely been crowded out by the modern march of invention.

Dr. Cobb attended grammar and high schools, and graduated from Bates College in the class of 1909, with the degree of Bachelor of Arts. He then matriculated at the Harvard Medical College, Cambridge, Massachusetts, from which institution he graduated in the class of 1914, with the degree of Doctor of Medicine. He further added to a generous equipment with an interneship at the Peter Bent Brigham Hospital, Boston, and the Boston City Hospital. His advance in his profession is evidenced by the fact that Governors Milliken and Brewster honored him with the position of medical examiner for York County. He started the practice of his profession at Sanford, where he has ever since carried on a general practice, and industrial surgery. He is a prominent and valued member of the York County and Maine State Medical societies, and the American Medical Association. During the World War he joined the Medical Corps of the United States Army and was assigned to Camp Jackson. Later, he transferred to Base Hospital No. 54 of the American Expeditionary Forces, where he attained the rank of first lieutenant. He has maintained his interest in military affairs and now holds the title of captain in the Medical Reserve Corps. He is the author of several articles which have appeared in various medical journals. Aside from his regular surgical duties, he has given considerable attention to meningitis, which modern science treats much more intelligently and effectively than was the custom in earlier days.

Dr. Cobb is a popular member of the Hermon Lodge, Free and Accepted Masons; the Benevolent and Protective Order of Elks, Exalted Ruler, 1928; the Improved Order of Red Men; and the Knights of Pythias. He belongs to the Bauneg Beg Country Club, of which he is vice-president; the Rotary Club; the Sanford Town Club, of which he is past president; the Veterans of Foreign Wars; the American Legion; and the French World War Society of Huit Hommes-Quarante Chevaux. His religious affiliation is with the Unitarian church.

Dr. Cobb was married, in 1915, to Ruby V. Wood, of Boston, Massachusetts, daughter of William A. and Margaret (Varnum) Wood, and they have a daughter, Helen Elizabeth Cobb.

WALTER I. DENNETT—For many years Walter I. Dennett has been one of the leading citizens of Biddeford; popular in business, club, church and fraternal order circles, and withal a thoroughly constructive citizen, he enjoys an exceedingly high standing. As a young man he was employed in the furniture business, but in 1885 entered upon his present occupation, in which he has continued since with considerable success, to the extent of having created what is, perhaps, the largest concern of its kind in the city. For a considerable part of this time he also acceptably filled the office of Coroner of York County.

Walter I. Dennett was born October 6, 1854, at Saco, Maine, son of Alvin D. and Phoebe (Hill) Dennett; his father, a well-known farmer of Saco, died in 1897; his mother, who was identified with Buxton, passed away in 1907. Mr. Dennett attended the grammar and high schools of his native

city, and presently accepted a position with the J. S. Stevens Furniture Company. He made gratifying progress with this concern until 1885, when he removed to Biddeford and entered the undertaking business for himself under his own name. He continued alone to April 1, 1926, when he took in as partner Mr. Neal, and the firm name was changed to Dennett & Neal. Mr. Dennett was the first man here to make use of a motor ambulance and hearse, and is the oldest in point of service in York County. Their concern is ranked as a leader, and carries a large and complete stock, part of which makes the sample room very attractive.

Mr. Dennett is quite prominent in local club and secret order work. His fraternal order affiliations include membership in Dunlap Lodge, No. 7, Free and Accepted Masons; Kora Temple, Ancient Arabic Order Nobles of the Mystic Shrine; York Chapter, No. 5, Royal Arch Masons; Maine Council, No. 7, Royal and Select Masters; Bradford Commandery, No. 4, Knights Templar; Independent Order of Odd Fellows, including the Encampment; and the Knights of Pythias of Canton. He is a devout member of the Methodist Episcopal church and a liberal supporter of its charities. He is one of the best liked men in Biddeford.

Mr. Dennett married, at Saco, in 1881, Mary Nichols, of Nova Scotia, who represents an old-established family of this Canadian Province. She died April 26, 1927.

EUGENE T. RICKER—As one of the youngest fire chiefs in New England, Eugene T. Ricker, of Biddeford, enjoys a splendid reputation as a fire fighter and capable public officer. He has no interest which comes ahead of the prevention and suppression of fire, and it is the elevation of this constant ideal that keeps him alert night and day, watching after the interests of property holders with a zealous eye.

Eugene T. Ricker was born at Biddeford, December 30, 1899, and consequently was not twenty-seven years of age when chosen chief of the local fire department. His father, Edward Ricker, of Biddeford, Maine, a restaurant proprietor, died in 1905; while his mother, Catherine (Barry) Ricker, of Biddeford, passed away in 1900. Mr. Ricker received his education at the grammar and high schools, after which he formed a connection with the Saco-Lowell Works at Biddeford, as timekeeper and bookkeeper. He started this work in 1917, and served until 1926, when he was elected chief, succeeding Albert Veilleux.

The story of the Biddeford Fire Department dates back to its organization in 1855, when a group of citizens met in the City Hall and organized the department with Nason A. Kendall as the first chief. In 1868 the first steamer was bought and named the Richard Vines, in honor of the first white man to settle in what is now Biddeford. Chief Kendall was succeeded by the following men: William Thompson; Thomas Quimby; Eben Simpson; George H. Munroe; Eben Simpson; Joseph W. Brooks, two years; Moses Harriman, one year; Charles Brown, one year; James Hunt, Jr., one year; George W. Bryant, one year; Charles H. Blood, one year; Millard C. Hallett, one year; William Boston, ten years (died in the service); Charles Hoyt, one year; John Leonard, two years; C. M. Watson, two

years; Benjamin Goodier, four years; D. L. Mulca-
hey, three years; Ed J. Sullivan, five years; Charles
H. Bonser, four years; Frank Cantra, two years;
E. J. Sullivan, one year; James O. Smith, two
years; Joseph Hotte, one year; Charles Johnson,
one year; James O. Smith, two years; Albert
Veilleux, one year; then Eugene T. Ricker, in 1926.
The department has grown from a very small affair
with a handful of men and a hand-reel to fifty-four
men, eleven permanent and forty-three call men;
one chief, and two assistant chiefs. The apparatus
consists of two steam engines, one motor pump;
two of the most modern types of ladder trucks, and
two horsedrawn hose carriages. The present structure on Washington Street was erected in 1907, and
conforms in every way to the needs of the department.

Mr. Ricker is a member of the International Association of Fire Chiefs, the New England Association of Fire Chiefs, and the Massachusetts Fire
Chiefs' Club. He is a member of St. Mary's Roman
Catholic Church.

Eugene T. Ricker married, in 1924, Marie A. Lambert, of Biddeford, daughter of Alfred J. and Marie
(Vennette) Lambert. A daughter, Catharine A.,
born January 6, 1925, has blessed their union.

EDWARD E. HUSSEY—Authority over three
thousand employees is a heavy responsibility, and
one requiring a high order of business ability and integrity, such as is possessed by Edward E. Hussey,
vice-president and general manager of the Sanford
Mills, manufacturer of mohair plush, at Sanford.
Mr. Hussey has exhibited such a rare order of ability in this enterprise that he is rated as one of the
most important men in the city, and enjoys highest
place among his associates and contemporaries.

Edward E. Hussey was born, March 27, 1861, at
Boston, Massachusetts, on the eve of the outbreak
of the Civil War between the North and the South.
His father, Burleigh S. Hussey, a leading merchant
of Rochester, Maine, died in 1872, while his mother,
Lavinia T. (Miller) Hussey, who nursed him through
the, four dread years of war, died in 1896. Mr. Hussey attended the grammar and high schools of his
native city, after which he entered business with the
Sanford Mills, which concern was organized in 1867,
by Thomas Goodall, under his own name, to manufacture horse blankets and robes. In 1877, the name
was changed to its present title and incorporated
with Thomas Goodall as president and Henry Chase
treasurer. The second president was Ernest Goodall, and John Hopewell was second treasurer; they
were succeeded by the incumbent officers, George
B. Goodall, president; Edward E. Hussey, vice-
president and general manager; and Frank B. Hopewell, treasurer. In the line of mohair plushes the
concern is the oldest and the largest in the United
States, and perhaps also of the world. An idea of
the growth of the firm may be had from the statement that from crowded quarters at the start it has
grown to a plant whose buildings cover twenty-
eight acres and whose employees' payroll numbers
more than three thousand souls.

In addition to this important connection Mr. Hussey is vice-president of the Sanford Trust Company
and president of the Sanford Water Company. Possessed of cool reasoning powers, great patience and
perfect poise, he makes the ideal executive. With

the employees in the capacity of general manager
he is kind and at the same time firm; he has done
much for the employees in the way of modern recreational improvements which were unknown to the
industries of earlier days, and he enjoys a real measure of popularity among them.

Mr. Hussey is a contributor to the work of the
Unitarian church, while his social activities center
in the Bauneg Beg Country Club, the Sanford Town
Club and other local organizations.

Mr. Hussey married, in 1882, Abbie J. Bodwell of
Sanford, daughter of William and Eliza (Bennett)
Bodwell, members of families of prominence and
accomplishment in this section.

ARTHUR J. LESIEUR—It is unusual to find a
man so versatile that he can operate a law office
and an insurance business at the same time, yet
that is the rôle essayed by Arthur J. Lesieur, of
Sanford, Maine, and with gratifying success, too.
Mr. Lesieur inherits from his father before him, an
energetic and popular insurance man, a leaning toward that line, while native ability suggested his
connection with the law, in which he enjoys high
place. He handles fire and casualty insurance, and
engages in the general practice of the law.

Arthur J. Lesieur was born January 21, 1894, at
Salem, Massachusetts, son of Albert Lesieur, now
retired, a native of the Province of Quebec, Canada,
and Alvina (Deschamps) Lesieur, a woman of rare
personality and character, who passed away in 1910.
Mr. Lesieur graduated from St. Joseph's Seminary with the degree of Bachelor of Letters, and was
duly admitted to the bar in 1920, after having stood
the requisite examinations for admission, and also
at the end of a period of study of great value from
practical considerations in the law office of Leroy
Haley at Biddeford. Thereupon he entered upon
the practice of his profession at Sanford, under his
own firm name, and continued general practice ever
since. During the World War, before his admission
to the bar, Mr. Lesieur enlisted for service, and
served with the Twelfth Division, after which he was
discharged and returned to Sanford. He has done
well alike at the law and in the insurance business.

Mr. Lesieur is a member of the Board of Selectmen of Sanford, the Benevolent and Protective Order of Elks; the St. Jean Baptiste Society; and
fourth degree member of the Knights of Columbus.
His religious affiliation is with the St. Ignatius
Roman Catholic Church.

Mr. Lesieur married, in 1922, Germanie A. Beaulieu, of Biddeford, daughter of Thomas and Al-
phonsine (Ledoux) Beaulieu, and their union has
been blessed with a daughter, Suzanne E, born November 28, 1925.

ROBERT A. ALEXANDER—Since 1922, Robert
A. Alexander has been continuously in Uncle Sam's
service as postmaster of Saco, Maine, and during the
five years which have passed since that time he has
very efficiently attended to the duties of that office.
He takes an active part in the conduct of the town
affairs, and has served as chairman of the Saco
Republican Committee.

Robert A. Alexander was born in Saco, Maine,
January 30, 1890, son of Robert Alexander, of Glasgow, Scotland, who was identified with the mill
industry and who died in 1911, and of Marion L.

(Arbuckle) Alexander, also a native of Scotland, who survives her husband. After attending the local public schools he completed his education in Thornton Academy, and then entered the employ of the York Manufacturing Company, of Saco, in clerical capacity. For fourteen years he continued in that connection, and then, on March 27, 1922, he was appointed, by President Warran G. Harding, as postmaster of Saco, succeeding Rufus L. Doe. Since that time he has served the people of Saco and vicinity most efficiently. Politically, Mr. Alexander gives his allegiance to the Republican party, in the affairs of which he takes an active part, having served as chairman of the Republican Committee of Saco, and consistently supporting its principles and its candidates. He served as city auditor for a period of four years, and has always been a progressive and public-spirited citizen, ready to forward in every possible way the best interests of the community in which he lives. During the World War he served as chairman of several of the Red Cross drives and was an important factor in the attainment of the goals set for Saco in the home work of the war. Fraternally, he is identified with Saco Lodge, Free and Accepted Masons, in which Order he holds membership in all the York Rite bodies and in the Consistory, in which he holds the thirty-second degree, and he is also a Past High Priest. He is a member of the Independent Order of Odd Fellows, in which he has been through all the chairs, and he is also a member of the Encampment. His religious affiliation is with the United Baptist Church.

Robert A. Alexander was married (first) to M. E. Bugbee, of Danielson, Connecticut. She died, and he married (second) Mary E. Bennett, a native of New Hampshire State. To the first marriage one daughter was born, Helen A., who was born July 10, 1920. Mr. and Mrs. Alexander make their home at No. 41 Spring Street, in Saco.

ADDISON G. PULSIFER—One of the best-known and most successful architects in Maine is Addison G. Pulsifer, of the firm of Pulsifer and Eye, Incorporated, of Lewiston. Mr. Pulsifer has an experience of more than thirty years to his credit in this profession, and has designed a large number of public buildings, as well as many of the larger and finer type of dwelling houses. The offices of the firm are located at No. 163 Main Street, in Lewiston.

Addison G. Pulsifer was born in Auburn, Maine, December 11, 1874, son of Haley A. Pulsifer, a native of Poland, Maine, engaged as a shoemaker at the time of his death in 1925, and of Lenora A. (Perno) Pulsifer, who was born in New Hampshire, and is still living (1928). He attended the public schools of his birthplace, and after leaving Auburn High School entered the employ of Coombs, Gibbs, & Wilkenson, architects of Lewiston. That was in 1896, and for ten years he remained with this firm. At the end of that time he went to Worcester, Massachusetts, where he became associated with the firm of Frost, Briggs, & Chamberlain. Two years later he made another change, this time going to the Norcross Brothers Company, of Worcester, but in 1910 he returned to Lewiston, Maine, and associated himself with Eugene J. Gibbs, under the firm name of Gibbs and Pulsifer, architects. This partnership was continued until 1927, when it was dissolved and Pulsifer and Eye, Incorporated, was organized. Mr.

Pulsifer is president of the concern, which has its offices at No. 163 Main Street, in Lewiston, and the firm has made for itself a reputation which is one of its most valuable business assets. Among the many important buildings designed by this well-known concern may be mentioned two buildings at the Tuberculosis Sanitarium in Northern Maine, the dormitory at the Normal School, at Machias, Maine; the school buildings at Lubec and at Eastport, Maine; and the Central Maine General Hospital. Numerous hotels and beautiful residences of the finest type of building also have been designed by this firm, which today ranks as one of the best in the State, and also as one of the largest concerns of its kind.

Fraternally, Mr. Pulsifer is identified with Ancient Brothers Lodge, Free and Accepted Masons, Auburn; and with the Grotto, Mystic Order Veiled Prophets of the Enchanted Realm, Worcester. He is also a member of Abou Ben Adhem Lodge, Independent Order of Odd Fellows of Auburn. He is a member of the Chamber of Commerce of Auburn, also of the Sprague Club and of the Martindale Country Club, and is fond of all kinds of sports, taking a special interest in hunting and fishing. His religious affiliation is with the Universalist church. Politically, he supports the principles of the Republican party.

Addison G. Pulsifer was married, in 1901, to Mildred M. Lyceth, a native of Auburn, Maine, and they are the parents of one son, Walter L.

GEORGE A. NUTTER—To merge an entire life with that of a single company, to grow with it, guide its destinies and watch it develop with the years into a sound and respected institution, is an achievement highly regarded by the business world of any city. Such an achievement is that of George A. Nutter and the Mutual Fire Insurance Company of Saco, Maine.

Ever since his school days, Mr. Nutter has been identified with the affairs of the Mutual Fire Insurance Company, which has recently celebrated its one hundredth anniversary. He was born in Saco, Maine, February 16, 1890, the son of Frank W. and Lucinda (Leslie) Nutter. He attended the grammar school in Saco and was graduated from Thornton Academy and immediately entered the employ of the Mutual Fire Insurance Company, rising step by step until he reached the position he now holds, that of treasurer and general manager.

Mr. Nutter has always been vitally interested in the development and growth of his native town, and is associated with several business and fraternal organizations. He is a member of the Kiwanis Club and is active in the congregation of the Unitarian church.

George A. Nutter married Reba H. Hobson, daughter of William A. Hobson, and they have a daughter, Dorothy F. Nutter, born October 4, 1922. Mr. Nutter's offices are at No. 268 Main Street, Saco, and he and his family occupy one of the attractive homes in the city.

EDWARD E. CHADBOURNE—The entire active career of Edward E. Chadbourne has been identified with the York Manufacturing Company, of Saco, Maine, of which concern he is now (1928) agent. His connection with the company began when he was fifteen years of age, and he has held various positions, rising through successive promotions to the responsible position which he now holds, that of agent for all manufactures of the company. The York Manufacturing Company is engaged in the manufacture of colored cloths, and is one of the oldest and largest concerns of its kind in the country. Edward E. Chadbourne was born in Saco, Maine, August 15, 1868, son of J. F. Chadbourne, of Kennebunkport, Maine, who died in 1912, and of Annie B. (Smith)) Chadbourne, also a native of Maine, who died in 1910. He attended the local public schools until he was fifteen years of age, and then began his long connection with the York Manufacturing Company. Able, faithful, and thoroughly interested in his work, he was promoted from one position to another and as the years passed gained the experience which has made him of especial value to the firm. Finally he was made agent for all manufactures of the company, and that position he is still filling. The York Manufacturing Company was founded in 1831, its incorporators being Charles Bradbury, Charles Cartwright, James Johnson, Ether Shepley, Jonathan King, George Fletcher, and Josiah Calef. Charles Bradbury was its first president and Samuel Batchelder its first agent. Mr. Batchelder was succeeded by Samuel J. Wetherell, as agent, then Amos H. Boyd served in the same capacity, Harrison Temple, Ira H. Foss, and Elmer E. Page being his successors, and finally Edward E. Chadbourne. The company was formed for the purpose of manufacturing colored cloths, and since its organization in 1889 it has steadily grown until at the present time (1928) it is one of the largest concerns of its kind in the United States, with 2,100 employees, occupying 1,350,000 square feet of floor space, and sending its products to all parts of the country. In addition to his responsibility as agent of the York Manufacturing Company, Mr. Chadbourne is a member of the board of directors of the York National Bank, and of the Saco National Bank, and a member of the board of trustees of the Saco and Biddeford Savings Bank. He was at one time a member of the Common Council of Biddeford, and is known as a public-spirited citizen as well as an able business man. He is a member of the Rotary Club, and has a host of friends in York County. Edward E. Chadbourne was married, in 1889, to Elizabeth Bonser, of Biddeford, Maine, and they are the parents of two children: Helen C., and Paul C.

HERBERT R. JORDAN—Among the men who have been closely identified with the growth and expansion of particular communities in the State of Maine, Herbert R. Jordan stands out in bold relief as one of the influential and substantial citizens of Saco, Maine. He is a prominent member of society and an outstanding figure in the commercial and industrial circles of the district. His contributions to the welfare and development of Saco, his native town, have been marked with sincere public spirit and strict integrity and probity and his support and patronage to the various philanthropic and altruistic movements have been unstinted and generous. To him belongs much distinction and a large part of the credit for the position and importance of the town. His family have been residents of the State of Maine from early Colonial periods, through the pioneer days and its admission to the Union as a State, and during all of this time have added to the

roll of honor of the community many names of those who bear the name Jordan. He is the son of Rishworth and Mary E. (Hill) Jordan, both of whom are now deceased. The father for many years was engaged in the retail grocery business, in which the son was likewise associated, and later entered the real estate business to which he devoted himself with success and admiration of his fellows until his death in 1903.

Herbert R. Jordan was born in Saco, Maine, June 28, 1857, and attended the local public and high schools of the town. Upon the completion of his formal scholastic career, he entered the business world, and joined his father in the retail grocery business. Possessed of keen business ability and ever alert to opportunities, he helped build one of the largest grocery establishments in the town. The town of Saco was still a small community when Mr. Jordan began his career, but he saw the vast possibilities lying in wait for those who would grasp them, and he started purchasing large tracts of land in the neighborhood, which he parcelled out and sold as residential communities and business sites. He soon began to devote all of his time and efforts to the promotion of his real estate interests. With foresight and business acumen he made attractive advancements to various large business and manufacturing enterprises to locate in Saco, and at the present time because of the untiring efforts of Mr. Jordan together with the natural advantages offered by the town in the shape of waterpower and and communication, this section is recognized as one of the most important manufacturing districts in the State. In addition to these interests, he has been active in civic affairs and has been influential in the administration of the policies of his party in the government of the town, although he has never sought public office. He is a member of the local lodge, Independent Order of Odd Fellows and also the Encampment of the body. He belongs to Cumberland Club, of Portland. He is actively affiliated with the First Parish Church of Saco. Mr. Jordan is associated in business with the firm of McPherson and Nicoll at No. 100 Broadway, New York City. He enjoys the high esteem and good will of all with whom he comes in contact. He has carried his family traditions and heritages to further honor and has earned the right to have his name included among those who have been responsible for the advancement of the community.

Herbert R. Jordan married (first) Caroline Hooper of Saco, Maine, a daughter of Gideon Hooper, and he married (second) Annie E. Leavitt, a daughter of Francis and Sarah A. (Grant) Leavitt of Saco. His children are: 1. Rishworth O., a graduate of Harvard University with the degree of Bachelor of Arts. 2. Elizabeth H., who is married to R. W. Shartel.

HON. WILLIS T. EMMONS—One of the very prominent and highly esteemed citizens of Saco, Maine, is Judge Willis T. Emmons, who has been engaged in general legal practice here for more than forty years. He has been very active in public affairs in Saco, serving in various public offices, including that of Judge of the Municipal Court, mayor, and Collector of Customs for the District of Maine and New Hampshire. His fellow-citizens have honored him with all confidence and esteem and have chosen him to fill offices of trust and responsibility, knowing full well the duties of these offices would be discharged with efficiency and faithfulness, and he has never betrayed the trust placed in him.

Willis T. Emmons was born in Biddeford, Maine, December 27, 1858, son of Leonard, a contractor and builder of Biddeford, who died in December, 1885, and of Sophia (Tripp) Emmons, a native of Newry, Maine, whose death occurred in 1923. He attended the Saco public schools, and then continued study in Thornton Academy. He early decided to enter the legal profession and studied law in the offices of Burbank & Derby, where he prepared for his legal studies in Harvard Law School. He was admitted to the bar in 1879, and opened an office for general practice that same year in Saco, since which time he has been continuously and successfully engaged in the practice of his profession. He is a member and former president of the York County Bar Association, a member of the Maine State Bar Association, the American Bar Association, and has achieved a high place among his professional associates. In addition to the conduct of a large and important practice, Mr. Emmons has also served in many positions of honor and trust, giving to the discharge of the duties of his full positions the full benefit of his legal knowledge and experience. In connection with his professional career it is interesting to note that he has, perhaps, held more elective and appointive offices than any other man in York County. He served as a Judge of the Municipal Court of Saco from 1882 to 1890; was mayor of Saco from 1887 to 1889, inclusive; County Attorney from 1895 to 1899; clerk of the courts from 1900 to 1912; and was Collector of Customs for the Maine and New Hampshire districts, with office in Portland. In March, 1928, forty-one years after his first election as mayor, he was again elected to that office and is now serving in that capacity (1928). He is known as a man of wide and accurate legal knowledge, as an effective advocate, and as a man of genuine ability in judicial practice. Fraternally, he is identified with Saco Lodge, Free and Accepted Masons; York Chapter, Royal Arch Masons; and Maine Council, No. 7, being a Past Commander of Bradford Commandery. He is also a member and Past Noble Grand of the Independent Order of Odd Fellows; Past Chief Patriarch of the Encampment; and a member and Past Chancellor of the Knights of Pythias. Mr. Emmons is identified with several local clubs, and his religious affiliation is with the Unitarian church.

Willis T. Emmons was married (first), in 1878, to Anna V. Leavitt. She died and he married (second), Lillian M. Tarbox. To the first marriage was born one son, Harold L., who is a graduate of Harvard University, with the degree of Doctor of Dental Medicine. Mr. Emmons resides at No. 62 Spring Street, Saco.

FRED B. WHEATON, D. M. D.—Both a professional and business man, holding leadership both in dentistry and as a factor in civic progress, Dr. Fred B. Wheaton is rightly accounted as one who has kept pace with every movement launched for the advancement of Biddeford and its institutions. One of the foremost dentists in this section of the State, and representing in his practice the best ideals of his profession, Dr. Wheaton is likewise highly esteemed in his financial associations and in varied municipal activities.

Fred B. Wheaton, a son of Calvin Wheaton, who died in 1908, and Josephine (Hoar) Wheaton, who survives her husband, both parents natives of New Brunswick, Canada, was born January 8, 1884, in New Brunswick, where he attended the public, high, and business schools. Preparing for his profession at the Dental School of Tufts College, in Boston, Massachusetts, he was graduated there in 1909 with the degree of Doctor of Medical Dentistry, and he began the practice of his profession at Portland in that year. In 1910, he removed to Biddeford, where he has continued in general dentistry to the present.

Prominent in banking matters, Dr. Wheaton holds the office of vice-president of the York County Savings Bank; and he is a member of the board of directors of the First National Bank of Biddeford. During the World War, he rendered the service of loyal citizenship at all times, and he was a member of various boards and committees. Fraternally, Dr. Wheaton is affiliated with Dunlap Lodge, Free and Accepted Masons; the Consistory, Ancient Accepted Scottish Rite; and Kora Temple, Ancient Arabic Order Nobles of the Mystic Shrine. His clubs are: Kiwanis, Biddeford and Saco Country Club, and he is a member of the York Fish and Game Commission. His religious faith is that of the Universalist church.

Dr. Fred B. Wheaton married, in 1909, Grace C. Emery, of Biddeford, also a graduate of Tufts College Dental School, with the degree of Doctor of Mechanical Dentistry, a daughter of Caleb J. and Llewellor (Bassett) Emery.

DR. SULLIVAN LANE ANDREWS—A recognized specialist in the medical profession is Dr. Sullivan Lane Andrews, who came to Lewiston in 1914 and has since continued to minister to the medical needs of his fellow-citizens. Dr. Andrews specializes in the treatment of eye, ear, nose and throat affections and has established for himself a reputation for great ability and skill. He was born in Paris, August 7, 1877, son of Alfred P. Andrews of Paris, who died in 1881, and Ada M. (Lane) Andrews of Sumner, who died in 1901. Alfred P. Andrews conducted a successful horse, cattle and grain business until his death.

Sullivan Lane Andrews received his early education in the public schools of Paris, after which he entered Westbrook Seminary, graduating from that institution in 1896. He then entered Maine Medical College and received his degree of Doctor of Medicine with the class of 1901. He has also taken post-graduate work at the New York Post-Graduate School, besides other special courses in eye, ear, nose and throat work. In 1901, he began his career, starting as general practitioner in Clinton, where he practiced successfully until 1910. For three years, from 1911 to 1914, Dr. Andrews was engaged in special work at Rumford, after which, he removed to Lewiston and commenced his special practice. He has ever continued to acquire the respect and admiration of the townspeople as well as to receive the plaudits of his fellow-physicians of the vicinity, who consult him regarding many cases. He is a leading member of many important medical organizations including the Maine State Medical Society, American Medical So-

270   MAINE—A HISTORY

ciety and is past president of the Androscoggin Medical Society. Also, past president of the Maine State
Eye and Ear Association, and a Fellow of the American College of Surgeons. Since 1915, Dr. Andrews
has been a member of the staff of the Central Maine
General Hospital. In the civic life of the town, he
takes a great interest, always with the idea of service to others, as evidenced by his being past president
and now District Governor of the Thirty-eighth Rotary District for the Rotary Club and an active member of the Chamber of Commerce. In fraternal circles, he has always been popular, being a member of
Sebasticook Lodge, Free and Accepted Masons, in
which organization he is Past Master; Dunlop Royal
Arch Chapter; Lewiston Commandery, Knights
Templar; Kora Temple, Ancient Arabic Order Nobles of the Mystic Shrine, and member of all bodies
of the Ancient and Accepted Scottish Rite. He was
Junior Grand Warden of Maine Lodge in 1910; and
he is a member of the Phi Chi Medical Fraternity.
He is a director of the Lewiston Chapter, American
Red Cross Society, and in politics, is a member of the
Democratic party. In his religious affiliations, he is
a member of the Universalist church, where he serves
as a trustee. During the World War, Dr. Andrews
took an active part in all patriotic work, and served
officially as an efficient member of the Medical Advisory Board. He finds great recreation and relaxation from his professional duties in fishing and outdoor life.
     Sullivan Lane Andrews married, September 9,
1902, Ida L. Cain of Lenox, Iowa, and their children
are: Alfred C., and Paul S.

     ARTHUR F. MAXWELL—A native of Bidde-
ford, Maine, and recognized as one of the most progressive of the younger generation in the community, Arthur F. Maxwell, after a number of
years of experience in one of the large manufacturing enterprises of the city, has been associated
in several responsible and trustworthy positions
with the First National Bank of Biddeford. He
has risen with rapid gradation from the office of
teller in that financial institution to that of assistant cashier, in which capacity he has been serving for the past three years, and at the same time,
he has devoted marked interest and activity in the
promotion of civic welfare and advancement. Already he has become an outstanding community and
public figure in Biddeford, and is filling the office of
city treasurer with substantial and distinguished success.
     Arthur F. Maxwell was born at Biddeford, Maine,
June 19, 1899, a son of Archie V. and Ina F.
(Welch) Maxwell, of whom the father who was
born in Wales, Maine, was engaged for many years
in mill work. Mr. Maxwell received a liberal education at the public and high schools of Biddeford,
and at the completion of his scholastic training early
entered the business world. At first he was employed in the office of the Pepperell Manufacturing
Company of Biddeford, where he applied himself
with such wholehearted energy and application that
he won the esteem and confidence of his superiors
and of all with whom he came in contact. Thereafter he became a teller in the First National Bank
of his native city and within a few years was advanced to the position of assistant cashier and since
1924, he has continued to fill that position. He is

also a trustee of York County Savings Bank. He
has contributed materially to the growth of the bank
and to the prosperity which it enjoys in the community. His pleasing and inviting personality, his
considerate and willing manner, together with his
natural ability and comprehensive knowledge of the
business methods and details, have won for him the
respect and general good will of those with whom he
does business, and he is considered by all a representative, progressive and popular member of the
community, commercially, socially, and politically.
Mr. Maxwell is city treasurer of Biddeford and his
administration of his office is marked with the same
efficient and diligent supervision which he gives to
his private enterprises and pursuits. In fraternal circles, he is affiliated with Dunlap Lodge, Free and Accepted Masons, of which he is a Past Master; and
he is also a prominent member of the local Chapter and Council of the Order. He is likewise a member of the local Lodge, Independent Order of Odd
Fellows, and the Encampment. With his family he
is a communicant of the Methodist faith, and attends the church of that denomination in Biddeford.
He is also active in the work of this church, and is
a member of the official board.
     In 1922, Arthur F. Maxwell, married Rena B.
Chappell of Kennebunkport, Maine, a daughter of
Willis W. and Alice (Berton) Chappell. Mr. and
Mrs. Maxwell are the parents of two children: 1.
Archie A., born December 22, 1924. 2. Richard A.,
born May 22, 1926.

     ERNEST H. ROBBINS—A native of Biddeford,
Maine, Ernest H. Robbins possesses a deep sense of
loyalty and love for his community, and has directed his every activity and able efforts to the promotion of the welfare and advancement of his community. For the past five years he has been city
marshal of Biddeford, and under his supervision and
direction of the police force of the city, his department has functioned with highest efficiency and
benefit to the residents of the section. He is familiar with all the problems confronting the dispatch of his office, for he rose by his natural ability from the rank of patrolman to that capacity
which he now fills, and to him belongs substantial
and distinguished recognition and credit for the law-
abiding atmosphere and the safety of property and
persons in Biddeford. He is a fearless administrator
of the law and has achieved the respect of every one
and the confidence of his subordinates as well as his
superiors. He is likewise active in the various civic,
patriotic and social movements of the city and has
contributed generously and wholeheartedly to every
campaign designed for the progress and prosperity
of Biddeford.
     Ernest H. Robbins was born October 23, 1876,
at Biddeford, Maine, a son of James H. and Ruannah
(Davis) Robbins, both of whom are now deceased.
He attended the local public schools of his native
district, and then became associated with his father
in the management and conduct of the latter's farm.
After the father's death, in 1908, Mr. Robbins continued in his agricultural pursuits until 1911, at
which time he disposed of his holdings and joined
the police force of Biddeford as a patrolman. His
sincere and earnest devotion to duty soon won promotion for him and he was made captain of the police force after a few years. In 1921, he was elected

city marshal and chief of police, to succeed Thomas Stone, and has continued in that capacity since. Chief Robbins has created an excellent police force in the city of Biddeford with eight regular policemen, two captains and an assistant chief of police. During the summer months this force is supplemented by many special officers to protect the summer visitors who come to Biddeford. Chief Robbins can be duly proud of his accomplishments in directing the police force, and his activities meet with general approbation from all sides. For many years prior to his accepting his present office, he was a member of the street commission, and with characteristic energy and civic loyalty, contributed to the upbuilding of the community and he was influential in bringing valuable improvements for the residents of the city. Throughout his whole life, he has been illustriously patriotic and has offered his services in all the national and local enterprises. Chief Robbins is a veteran of the Spanish War, having served in the Maine contingent during the conflict, receiving the rank of sergeant. He is a member of the local Lodge, Independent Order of Odd Fellows, and the Knights of Pythias, and is also a member of the Society of Spanish War Veterans. His religious affiliation is with the Methodist Church of Biddeford.

In 1910, Ernest H. Robbins married Blanche Norwood of Biddeford, Maine, a daughter of George and Elizabeth (Dodge) Norwood, and they are the parents of the following children: Emma E., Elva E., Marjorie M., and Ruannah D.

CECIL J. SIDDALL—Popular and able in the practice of the law, a leader in civic and secret order work, Cecil J. Siddall, of Sanford, has made an enviable place for himself in the estimation of his fellow-townsmen. His offices are at No. 6 Washington Street, while his residence is at No. 30 Jackson Street, this city.

Mr. Siddall was born March 2, 1894, at Sanford, the son of Thomas Siddall, of the milling industry, native of England, and Lillie (Sutcliffe) Siddall, born in Franklin, New Hampshire, both of whom are living (1928) to enjoy their son's gratifying success. The name Siddall is prominent in the annals of England, and a worthy bearer of it on this side was the late John M. Siddall, editor of the "American Magazine," of New York City.

Mr. Siddall attended the grammar and high schools, where he made a splendid record, and after which he matriculated at the University of Maine, from which institution he was graduated in the class of 1917, with the degree of Bachelor of Laws. During the World War he entered the service and was assigned to United States Ordnance Depot No. 120, Thirty-fourth Division, United States Army. Before entering the military service he had been admitted to the bar in 1916 by a special course of study. He accordingly took up the practice of law, which was halted, as intimated, by the world conflagration. His original firm name was Siddall & Eaton, but after two years this partnership was dissolved and he went it independently.

For three years Mr. Siddall was a member of the Board of Selectmen, in which his knowledge of the law proved valuable, and from which he took valuable experiences as an assistance to him in the prosecution of the law. He served as a Representa-

tive in the State Legislature during the year 1923, and still further added to an equipment already sufficiently ample to serve his numerous clients. At the present time he is Register of Probate for York County. He has done unusually well and looks forward to greater triumphs.

Mr. Siddall is a valued and prominent member of Preble Lodge of the Free and Accepted Masons, also is affiliated with the Chapter and Commandery; he is Past Exalted Ruler of the Benevolent and Protective Order of Elks; and is a member of the Improved Order of Red Men, and of the Knights of Pythias. He is a member of the York County and Maine State Bar associations. His social and civic activities center largely in the Kiwanis Club, the Sanford Town Club and the Bauneg Beg Country Club. In religious affairs he is an attendant of the Baptist church.

FRANK A. RUMERY—Perhaps no single individual has been more active in the development of the new residential sections of Portland than has Frank A. Rumery, building contractor and dealer in lumber, one of the best-known building contractors in the State. Mr. Rumery is also very prominent in the activities of the Young Men's Christian Association, both State and local, and is a member of the board of directors of both organizations. Mr. Rumery was born in Hollis, York County, Maine, May 7, 1867, son of Charles F. Rumery, a native of Hollis, who was engaged in the lumber industry there, and who died in 1912, and of Lovisa M. (Sawyer) Rumery, a native of Buxton, Maine, who survives her husband (1928).

Frank A. Rumery received his education in the public schools, and then secured employment in a grocery store, where he remained for about two years. He then entered the employ of A. D. Smith, a building contractor, with whom, in 1898 he formed a partnership under the name of Smith and Rumery, dealing in lumber and also conducting a contracting business. This association was continued until 1911, when Mr. Rumery sold his interest. During the sixteen years which have passed since that time Mr. Rumery has conducted an extensive contracting business under the name of Frank A. Rumery & Company, and has erected many private dwelling houses and also some of the finest public buildings in Portland, some of the more notable of these being the Masonic Temple, in Portland, the department store of Porteous, Mitchell & Braun, Hebron Sanatorium, one of the finest and most modern of school buildings, at Berlin, New Hampshire, the new Young Men's Christian Association building at Portland, and many others of similar importance and excellence of construction. In addition to his activities as a contractor, Mr. Rumery has been one of the most active in the development of some of Portland's fine residential districts, the most noteworthy of these developments of his being the old Ricker Estate, later known as the Rollins Estate, considered one of Portland's very finest suburban residential sections. Mr. Rumery is a man of ability and of varied interests, and though he is so notably successful in his business, these interests do not absorb all of his time and attention. He finds time to render very able and efficient service in the activities of the Young Men's Christian Association, and as a member of the board of directors of both the State and local organizations places his business ability and his skill and knowledge as a builder and contractor at the service of the organization. His interest in the Young Men's Christian Association dates back to the early years of his career, and has been continuously maintained throughout his life to th epresent time, much to the advantage of that worthy and helpful organization. Mr. Rumery is also a member of the board of directors of the Forest City Trust Company, in which capacity his knowledge of real estate values is of material value. Fraternally, he is identified with Portland Lodge, Free and Accepted Masons; and he is also a member of the Woodfords Club, the Economics Club, and the Portland Chamber of Commerce, of which last he is a member of the board of managers. His religious interest is with the Congregational church, of which he is a member and which he serves as a member of the standing committee.

Frank A. Rumery was married, in 1890, to Ida M. Hamblen, and they are the parents of five children: 1. Harriet C., a graduate of Mount Holyoke College, who married R. H. Bryant. 2. Gladys M., graduate of a business college, married Clinton Eason. 3. Earle H., attended the University of Maine, University of Pennsylvania, and Massachusetts Institute of Technology; married Helen Caldwell. 4. Dwight C., graduate of Yale College. 5. Hope W., graduate of a business college, married Roger Stone. Mr. Rumery has his offices on Congress Street. The family home is at No. 326 Stevens Avenue, in Portland.

CONVERS E. LEACH—In Portland, Maine, there is no more skilled and well-informed insurance man than Convers E. Leach, who has been a partner in the firm of Anderson, Adams & Company since 1900, and who, with Leon W. Helson, is now one of the two owners of this long established insurance agency. The offices are located at No. 38 Exchange Street, in Portland, where the partners are taking care of a large and growing business. Mr. Leach has been identified with this line of business from the beginning of his active career, and is an expert in his field.

Convers E. Leach was born in Portland, Maine, June 4, 1866, son of Convers O. Leach, who was a native of Portland, and was in government service to the time of his death in 1908, and of Harriet E. (Curtis) Leach, who was born in Newburyport, Massachusetts, and died in 1918. He attended the public schools of Portland, including the high school, and then became associated with the insurance business in the employ of W. D. Little & Company. In 1900, when he was thirty-four years of age, he was made a partner in the concern, and some years later, in association with Leon W. Helson, he purchased the interests of the other owners, and he and Mr. Helson became the owners of this long established and well-known insurance business.

The original firm was established in 1843, under the name of W. D. Little & Company. Twenty-four years later, in 1867, Captain Thomas J. Little, on his return from service in the Civil War, with his brother, William F. Little, sons of W. D. Little, became the owners of the interests of W. D. Little & Company. The following year the firm of Rollins and Adams was established, and shortly afterward the firm of Palmer, Anderson & Company was or-

ganized by J. S. Palmer, who later was postmaster of Portland, and by Horace Anderson, who was the son of ex-Governor Anderson, of Maine. In 1895 a combination of the three concerns was effected under the firm name of Anderson, Adams & Company, which name has been retained to the present time (1928). Charles C. Adams of this firm, whose father was a member of the firm of Rollins and Adams Agency mentioned above, is the last survivor whose name was included in any of the three original firms, and he is now retired. In his long business career he survived the passing of all the business associates with whom he was originally associated. Convers E. Leach has been president of the Cumberland County Board of Fire Underwriters, and is widely known among insurance men in this section of the State. Politically, he gives his support to the principles and the candidates of the Republican party, and fraternally, he is identified with the Free and Accepted Masons, in which Order he has the distinguished honor of holding the thirty-third degree. He is a member of the Portland Congregational Club, of the Woodfords Club, and of several local clubs, and his religious membership is with the Congregational church, which he serves as a member of the standing committee. Leon W. Helson, Mr. Leach's partner, was in the office of the Insurance Department of Maine for a period of five years, serving during the latter part of that term as acting commissioner.

Convers E. Leach was married, in 1889, to Gertrude E. Lang, of Portland, daughter of Caleb N. and Ellen N. (Cummings) Lang, who died January 5, 1925.

LEWIS ORRIN BARROWS—As a member of the firm of Barrows and Barrows, Lewis Orrin Barrows is part owner of the only drugstore in Newport. Mr. Barrows is not only an able and successful business man but he is also an efficient public official, and at the present time (1928) is serving as a member of the executive council of the Republican State Committee.

George M. Barrows, father of Lewis O. Barrows, was born in Hampden, September 3, 1863, son of Lewis, who was born in West Hampden, Maine, and was engaged in the wholesale potato business and as a proprietor of a general store to the time of his death. He received his early education in the public schools in Hampden Academy. Later he was a student in Bucksport Seminary for one year, after which he was enrolled in the Pittsfield (Maine) Central Institute for four years. When his course there was completed he entered the Massachusetts College of Pharmacy, where he studied for one year. He then became associated with J. S. Towne, of Brunswick, Maine, as a partner in the retail drug business. This connection was maintained until 1893, when Mr. Barrows sold his interest and came to Newport, Maine, where he established a retail drug business of his own. The business was continued under the name of George M. Barrows until 1917, when Mr. Barrows admitted his son as a partner, and changed the name of the business to that of Barrows and Barrows, under which firm name the business is still operated. Mr. Barrows is a Republican in his political sympathies, and he is active in the affairs of his party. He served for one term in the Lower House of the State Legislature and for one term in the State Senate. He has been active in local affairs, serving as a member of the Board of Selectmen for six years and as town treasurer for four years. Along with his responsibilities as the owner and manager of a successful retail drug business, Mr. Barrows is also a member of the board of directors of the Newport Trust Company, which he formerly served as vice-president. George M. Barrows was married, in 1892, to Theo L. Jose, who was born in Newport, Maine.

Lewis Orrin Barrows, son of George M. and Theo L. (Jose) Barrows, was born in Newport, Maine, June 7, 1893, and received his earliest school training in the public schools of Newport. He prepared for college in Hebron Academy, being class president in his junior year, and then entered the University of Maine, from which he was graduated with the class of 1916, receiving at that time the degrees of Bachelor of Science and Graduate Pharmacist. Upon the completion of his college course, in 1917, he became associated with his father, George M. Barrows, in the retail drug business, and at this time the name of the business was changed to the firm name of Barrows and Barrows under which style it has been operated to the present time. The drugstore of Barrows and Barrows is the only one in Newport, and father and son are conducting a most prosperous enterprise. Like his father, Mr. Barrows is an earnest advocate of the principles of the Republican party. He has been treasurer of the town of Newport since 1920, and he is active in the affairs of his party, serving at the present time as a member of the Republican State Committee, being the youngest member of that committee. In January, 1927, he was made a member of the executive council, and there is every prospect that he will be an unusually valuable member of that council. It is interesting to note that Mr. Barrows began his association with State political affairs at the early age of fourteen years, when he served as page in the Maine State Senate. Fraternally, Mr. Barrows is a member of Beta Theta Pi College Fraternity, and he is well known in Masonic circles, being a member of Meridian Splendor Lodge, Free and Accepted Masons, of which he is treasurer; Stevens Chapter, Royal Arch Masons, of which he is a Past High Priest; St. Omar Commandery, No. 12, Knights Templar; and Anah Temple, Ancient Arabic Order Nobles of the Mystic Shrine. He is also a member of Anah Temple Band. His club is the Maine Rexall Club, of which he is a past president. He is third vice-president of the Maine Pharmaceutical Association, oldest organization of its kind in the United States. In 1916, Mr. Barrows served on the Mexican border with the Second Regiment, Maine Infantry, and was a member of the band. He finds his favorite form of recreation in motoring and in music, as a member of the band. His religious affiliation is with the Christian church.

Lewis Orrin Barrows was married, in 1917, to Pauline M. Pomeroy, who was born in Holyoke, Maine. Mr. and Mrs. Barrows are the parents of three children: 1. Robert Waldo. 2. Edward Pomeroy. 3. Wallace Hight.

BEN A. MATHES—A native of South Berwick, always associated with every movement for the development of the township, Ben A. Mathes, secretary and treasurer of the shoe manufacturing firm of Roberts and Marshall, both in his business and civic life is representative of the interests of good

citizenship and of community welfare. In shoe salesmanship and in the direction of the duties of office, he has always stood for the best ideals in business, and has won merited success throughout his career.

Ben A. Mathes was born October 26, 1892, at South Berwick, a son of George A. and Nettie M. (Reynard) Mathes, and he was graduated at the public schools and at Berwick Academy. Until 1921, he engaged in salesmanship, and he then became a member of the firm of Roberts and Marshall, shoe manufacturers at South Berwick. This concern was established in 1920 by George R. Roberts and Samuel P. Marshall, for shoe manufacturing; and in 1921, Mr. Mathes bought out the interest of Mr. Roberts, and the business was incorporated, with Samuel P. Marshall as president, William G. Wentworth as vice-president, and Ben A. Mathes as secretary and treasurer. They employ about twenty people, the scope of the product of the factory is national, and the plant consists of the entire building, with about 10,000 feet of floor space. The growth of the firm's activities has been gradual and sure. Mr. Mathes has also been identified with various newspapers as correspondent.

Mr. Mathes has served as selectman of the town of South Berwick and in other minor offices; and during the World War, he was active as a member of boards and committees. Fraternally, he is affiliated with St. John Lodge, Free and Accepted Masons; Unity Chapter, Royal Arch Masons; and St. Amand Commandery, Knights Templar; and with Kora Temple, Ancient Arabic Order Nobles of the Mystic Shrine. He is secretary of the South Berwick Board of Trade, and his religious faith is that of the Baptist church.

Ben A. Mathes married, January 7, 1922, Marian E. Pike.

SAMUEL P. MARSHALL, president of the shoe manufacturing firm of Roberts and Marshall, was born February 7, 1893, at Rollinsford, New Hampshire, son of Samuel Marshall, of Vermont, and Celia (Degnan) Marshall, of Canada. After attending the public schools, he became identified with the shoe manufacturing business, and has so continued throughout his career. He is a member of St. John Lodge, Free and Accepted Masons, and of the Council of Royal and Select Masters; and his religious faith is that of the Baptist church.

Samuel P. Marshall married Gertrude Clay, and they have three children: Ruth, Philip, and Alberta.

WILLIAM G. WENTWORTH, vice-president of the shoe manufacturing firm of Roberts and Marshall at South Berwick, was born September 12, 1882, at South Berwick, son of Charles Wentworth, of Rollinsford, New Hampshire, and Delia (Chaney) Wentworth. He attended the public schools, and Berwick Academy, and then began to engage in shoe manufacturing, as vice-president of the firm of Roberts and Marshall. Fraternally, he is affiliated with St. John Lodge, Free and Accepted Masons; with the Independent Order of Odd Fellows, and Odd Fellows Encampment. His religious faith is that of the Baptist church.

William G. Wentworth married, August 19, 1903, Nellie Marshall, and they have one daughter, Doris M. Wentworth.

Maine—18

JOE P. DAVIS—To the steadily increasing interests of the post office at South Berwick, Postmaster Joe P. Davis has rendered that high standard of service that has secured for him the esteem of all who coöperate for the general advancement of this, one of the most enterprising townships in this section of the State. Mr. Davis is a public servant of intelligence and reliability, and in the discharge of his official duties he has received the approval of all with whom he is associated.

Joe P. Davis was born March 18, 1893, at South Berwick, son of Richard M. Davis, a tailor, and Elizabeth J. (Dodge) Davis, both of South Berwick, the family having resided here for generations. Mr. Davis attended the public schools, and was graduated at Berwick Academy in the class of 1912, and he was then engaged for seven years in boat building at Kittery. In 1922, Mr. Davis received his first appointment from President Harding as postmaster at South Berwick, succeeding David N. Chaney, and he received his second appointment to office from President Coolidge, in 1926.

Fraternally, Mr. Davis is affiliated with St. John Lodge, Free and Accepted Masons; with the Independent Order of Odd Fellows; with Odd Fellowship Encampment, and with the Rebekah degree of that Order. His religious faith is that of the Methodist Episcopal church.

Joe P. Davis married, August 4, 1919, Beatrice S. MacIntyre, of New Brunswick, daughter of Samuel L. and Mary J. (Shannon) MacIntyre. Their children: 1. Beatrice Evelyn, born February 25, 1921. 2. Richard S., born February 23, 1922. 3. Joe P., Jr., born July 20, 1923. 4. Carl V., born March 29, 1925.

EDWARD K. ALLEN—Few men engaged in any line of business in York County have a more extensive acquaintanceship and friendship with the general public than has Edward K. Allen, who through his very efficient management of the Hotel Sanford, at Sanford, has been the means of bringing that hostelry into the front rank of hotels in the county and demonstrating his qualifications in very capable and pleasing hotel management. He is besides public-spirited in all matters that have to do with the betterment and general advancement of the community, and a reliable factor in the business and the social interests of Kennebunk.

Edward K. Allen was born October 17, 1881, at Sanford, a son of Alfred Allen, engaged in the mill industry at Sanford, and Clara E. (Jacobs) Allen, who died October 14, 1926. Mr. Allen attended the public and high schools, and for a few years he was employed as a foreman in the Sanford Woolen Mills. He then became associated with the business of the Sanford Hotel, at first as clerk, and since 1924 as the manager of that hostelry, succeeding W. H. Bennett in that position. This hotel is known as the oldest and most substantial in Sanford, where many notable people have stopped, and whose efficient management has given it a very fine repute throughout southern Maine.

During the World War, Mr. Allen was active in all the movements of this community in behalf of the World War. Fraternally, he is affiliated with Preble Lodge, Free and Accepted Masons; Bethany Commandery, Knights Templar; and with Kora Temple, Ancient Arabic Order Nobles of the Mystic Shrine. He is a Past Sachem of the Improved Order of Red Men. Among his clubs is the Bauneg Beg Country Club; and his religious faith is that of the Unitarian church. His family on the maternal side is of the early settlers of Sanford.

Edward K. Allen married, June 1, 1909, Annie L. Stilphen, of Westport, daughter of George M. and Vesta (Cram) Stilphen.

FRANKLIN R. CHESLEY—As an able member of the legal profession and a business man whose sound judgment and resourcefulness can be counted upon, Franklin R. Chesley is well known. He is a member of the executive committee of the Maine State Savings Banks Association, and is a very prominent man in Saco.

Franklin R. Chesley was born in Pittsfield, Massachusetts, December 1, 1888, son of Israel S. Chesley, a native of Amesbury, Massachusetts, and of Bertha M. (Russell) Chesley, who was born in Pittsfield, Massachusetts, and died October 25, 1903, Mr. Chesley received his early education in the public schools and from private tutors, and then completed his preparation for college by studying for one year at Amherst. He then entered the University of Maine, at Orono, taking the law course, which he completed with graduation in 1911, receiving the degree of Bachelor of Laws. He was admitted to the bar that same year, and at once opened an office for general practice in Saco, where he has since continued. In addition to the care of his general practice Mr. Chesley is active in local public affairs and in financial affairs in this locality. He is vice-president and a member of the board of trustees of the Saco-Biddeford Savings Bank, and a member of the executive committee of the Maine State Savings Banks Association, and his counsel is much sought in financial affairs. He was solicitor for the city of Saco, 1912-14, inclusive, was County Attorney, succeeding Hiram Willard, for two terms; and was appointed Judge of the Municipal Court of Saco, 1920-24, and reappointed, 1924-28. He is also vice-president of the Wardwell Home, and a trustee of Thornton Academy, to both of which responsibilities he gives careful attention. During the World War Mr. Chesley was attached to the Naval Aviation Department, and since 1920 he has served as president of the Red Cross organization of York County. Fraternally, he is identified with Saco Lodge, Free and Accepted Masons; and with Delta Kappa Epsilon College Fraternity. He is also a member of the Biddeford-Saco Country Club, and of other local clubs. His religious membership is with the Congregational church.

Franklin R. Chesley was married, October 31, 1911, to Annie S. Lowell, of Saco, Maine, daughter of Enoch and Mary (Gilpatrick) Lowell. Mr. and Mrs. Chesley are the parents of one son, Franklin R., Jr., who was born March 14, 1914.

ELLIOT ROGERS—One of the very well-known men of the State of Maine is Elliot Rogers, who has been identified with the manufacture of leatheroid and its products during practically all of his business career, and who is now (1928) president of the Rogers Fibre Company, of Kennebunk. Homer Rogers, father of Elliot Rogers, was born in South Sudbury, Massachusetts, and was at one time proprietor of the famous Wayside Inn, which Henry

Ford has purchased and is preserving as nearly as possible in its original condition, in honor of the poet, Longfellow. He served as a member of the Infantry, as sergeant, during the Civil War, and was one of the organizers of the Leatheroid Manufacturing Company, which was later consolidated with two other concerns under the name of the Rogers Fibre Company. He married Ellen E. Perry, of South Sudbury, whose death occurred in 1921.

Elliot Rogers, son of Homer and Ellen E. (Perry) Rogers, was born in South Sudbury, Massachusetts, February 10, 1872, and received his early school training in the local public schools. Later he continued his studies in the Boston Latin School, and then entered the Massachusetts Agricultural College, from which he was graduated with the degree of Bachelor of Science. Later he matriculated in Boston University, where he also received the degree of Bachelor of Science. When school days were over, he became associated with the business which his father had helped to organize, and which was then operating under the name of the Leatheroid Manufacturing Company.

In 1876 a group of business men consisting of Emery Andrews, Stephen Moore, Homer Rogers, and C. W. Goodnow, and others, were the controlling group in the National Leather Board Company, which in 1886, was operating factories and mills in various parts of the country. These men founded the Leatheroid Manufacturing Company, with Emery Andrews as president. This organization continued until 1918, when the National Leather Board Company, the Leatheroid Manufacturing Company, and another concern engaged in the same line of production were consolidated under the name of the Rogers Fibre Company, under which name it is still operating (1928). They employ a maximum of two hundred and twenty-five hands, and the plant at Kennebunk provides 300,000 square feet of floor space. As they are the only manufacturers of insulated fibre in the world, their products are of international interest, and in addition to their leatheroid products some of their manufactures are used as mill supplies. As president of the Rogers Fibre Company, Mr. Rogers has fully demonstrated his administrative and executive ability, and each year is bringing a marked increase in the prosperity and efficiency of the concern. Mr. Rogers is well known in the Masonic Order, being a member of York Lodge, and of all the bodies of the York Rite, also of the Consistory, in which he holds the thirty-second degree; and of Kora Temple, Ancient Arabic Order Nobles of the Mystic Shrine. He is also a member of Phi Sigma Kappa College Fraternity. In club circles, too, he is well known, holding membership in the University Club, of Boston; the Portland Club; the Farmers' Club, of Portland; and in several country clubs. His religious affiliation is with the Unitarian church.

Elliot Rogers was married, in 1896, to Mary H. Thompson, of Kennebunk, Maine, and they are the parents of two children: 1. Natalie T., who is a graduate of Smith College. 2. John, a graduate of Williams College.

LOUIS ROGERS—As vice-president of the Rogers Fibre Company, of Kennebunk, Maine, and a forceful contributor to its rapid expansion, Louis Rogers is widely prominent in business. This con-

cern is one of the largest in the world manufacturing insulated fibre and enjoys a world market. Mr. Rogers is in charge of the plant at Bar Mills, Maine, and resides in Portland.

Louis Rogers was born in Boston, Massachusetts, November 30, 1880, son of Homer Rogers, now deceased, a manufacturer of Sudbury, and his wife, Ellen E. (Perry) Rogers, of Natick, also deceased. The father was at one time proprietor of the famous Wayside Inn, now the property of Henry Ford. He was an Infantry sergeant during the Civil War. He organized the Leatheroid Manufacturing Company, later consolidated with two other concerns to form the Rogers Fibre Company. From 1876 to the present day, a period of over half a century, this important industry has continued.

The son of Homer Rogers, Louis Rogers was early destined for the fibre board industry. After completing his education in the public and high schools and rounding it off with a course at Burdett Business College, he entered the fibreboard industry. He came to Bar Mills in 1910 and has since been in charge of the mill there which is the property of the Rogers Fibre Company, which owns a number of mills. It was in 1918 that the National Fibre Board Company, with which Homer Rogers was associated, combined with the Leatheroid Manufacturing Company under the name of the Rogers Fibre Company. Some two hundred and twenty-five workers are employed, of whom eighty are at Bar Mills. By an addition to the latter in 1916, the capacity was more than doubled, this increase in space and volume of business being an eloquent testimonial to the ability of Mr. Rogers, who has for seventeen years directed its activities. He is also vice-president of the company, which supplies a world market with leatheroid products and produces mills supplies. Mr. Rogers is also a director of the George H. Priggen Steel Company.

Aside from business, Mr. Rogers has many social and civic interests. He is a member of Deering Lodge, Free and Accepted Masons, and of several clubs, including Willowdale Country Club. He attends the Congregational church.

In 1907, Louis Rogers married Edith E. Allen, daughter of Henry Allen, and they are the parents of three children: 1. Berta, a student at Mt. Holyoke College. 2. Allen, a student at Bowdoin College. 3. Joseph Rogers.

EDOUARD DELORGE—For the past twenty-eight years Edouard Delorge has been successfully engaged in the baking business in Biddeford, Maine, where he was born, and where he has lived all his life. Mr. Delorge is well known as an expert in his special field.

Edouard Delorge was born in Biddeford, Maine, October 16, 1873, son of Alexandre Delorge, a lumber surveyor, and Celina (Charbonneau) Delorge. He began to earn his living at an early age, and the greater part of his education was secured in the evening schools of Biddeford. He early learned the trade of the baker, and his entire active career to the present time (1928) has been devoted to his baking business, which now has about sixty employees, and the product of which is distributed over the counties of York and Cumberland. The plant has a floor space of 44,000 square feet. Ability and industry have brought substantial success, and in addition to his interest in the bakery business, Mr. Delorge is a member of the board of directors of the Pepperell Trust Company. He is very well known and is held in high esteem among his associates in Biddeford and vicinity. His clubs are the Kiwanis and Fremont, and his religious affiliation is with St. Joseph's Roman Catholic Church.

Edouard Delorge was married, in Biddeford, Maine, January 3, 1898, to Clairina Morin, daughter of Louis and Emerence (Cote) Morin. Mr. and Mrs. Delorge are the parents of six children: 1. A. B. Alice, who was born May 6, 1901. 2. Jeannette, born August 27, 1903. 3. Florence, born February 13, 1905. 4. Roland, born November 23, 1910. 5. Cecile, born January 25, 1913. 6. Paul, born December 23, 1915. The family home is at No. 20 Bacon Avenue, in Biddeford.

CHARLES H. COLE—In all matters that pertain to the progress of Kennebunk, a constructive personality, Charles H. Cole, one of the foremost real estate and insurance men in this part of the State, is recognized and highly honored as a factor in the maintenance of Kennebunk's institutions, its business life and projects, and the welfare of the community. He has not only held public office in the general satisfaction, but his own business activities are of the most exemplary kind in method and use.

Charles H. Cole was born October 21, 1856, at Kennebunk, son of Horace Cole, of Wells, who died in 1894, and Emmeline E. (Simpson) Cole, of Kennebunkport, who died in 1888. Mr. Cole attended the grammar and high schools of his native town, and he was afterwards for four years employed by a large leather concern in Boston, Massachusetts. Returning to Kennebunk, he was for a time employed in a local shoe factory, and in 1881 he entered into business on his own account as a retail grocer, so continuing to 1888.

Mr. Cole first established himself in the insurance business in his own name in 1888, and in 1915 he received into partnership one of his sons, Joseph T. Cole, and in 1924 another son, Walter R. Cole, when the title of the firm was changed to C. H. Cole & Sons, insurance and real estate dealers, Mr. Cole himself being the oldest engaging in this line in Kennebunk. He is a member of the board of trustees of the Kennebunk Savings Bank; and he served as town clerk of Kennebunk for ten years. He was treasurer of the Free Library Association for sixteen years.

Fraternally, Mr. Cole is affiliated with York Lodge, Free and Accepted Masons, a Past Master; with the Murray Chapter, Royal Arch Masons, a Past High Priest; a charter member of his Consistory of the Ancient Accepted Scottish Rite. He is also a Past Chancellor of the Knights of Pythias; and is a member of the Kennebunk Chamber of Commerce. His religious faith is that of the Congregational church, and he is a member of the board of trustees of that church in Kennebunk.

Charles H. Cole married, March 5, 1884, Agnes Titcomb, also of Kennebunk, daughter of Joseph and Mary (Wise) Titcomb. Their children: 1. Robert T. Cole, a graduate of Worcester Polytechnic Institute. 2. William A. Cole, a graduate of Harvard College with the degree of Bachelor of Arts, and of the Law School of Harvard University with the degree of Bachelor of Laws. 3. Joseph T. Cole, attended University of Maine, married and has two children. 4. Walter R., attended Phillips-Exeter Academy and Brown University; enlisted in the National Guards; served with Company M, Coast Artillery Corps; stationed at Fort McKinley; went overseas with American Expeditionary Forces as a lieutenant in Battery F, 146th Field Artillery; served overseas eighteen months. 5. Mary E. Cole, married A. W. Day, and they are the parents of one son.

RALPH ANDREWS—As an attorney Ralph Andrews has been engaged in practice in Kennebunk, Maine, since 1922. He is a graduate of Bowdoin College, and was admitted to the bar in 1922. Mr. Andrews has many friends in York County, and is active in local public affairs, serving at the present time (1928) as recorder of the local court and as a member of the budget committee of the town.

Ralph Andrews was born in Kennebunk, Maine, January 7, 1881, son of Emery Andrews, a manufacturer, who was born in Ware, Massachusetts, and who died in 1903, and of Ellen S. (Chamberlain) Andrews, who died in 1886. His brother, Henry E. Andrews, is a member of the faculty at Bowdoin College. Mr. Andrews attended the public schools of his birthplace and then prepared for college in Thornton Academy, and one year at Phillips-Exeter Academy, after which he became a student in Bowdoin College, from which he was graduated with the class of 1903, receiving the degree of Bachelor of Arts. After graduation he was identified for a number of years with the Leatheroid Manufacturing Company, of which his father was one of the organizers, but later he decided to study law. He was admitted to the bar in 1922, and in the same year he opened an office for general practice in his native town of Kennebunk. Here he has continued to the present time. He is a member of the York County Bar Association, the Maine State Bar Association, and the American Bar Association, and has the respect and esteem of his professional associates. In addition to the responsibilities of his private practice, Mr. Andrews is active in the town government. He served as town treasurer for two years, has been recorder in the local court since its organization, in 1927 being reappointed for another term, and is now a member of the budget committee of the town. He is a member of York Lodge, Free and Accepted Masons, in which Order he holds membership in all the York Rite bodies, is Past Master of York Lodge, No. 22, and Past Commander of St. Amand Commandery, No. 20, and a member of the Maine Consistory, in which he holds the thirty-second degree. He is also a member of Psi Upsilon College Fraternity, and a member of the Kennebunk Chamber of Commerce. His religious interest is with the Congregational church, of which he is a member.

Ralph Andrews was married, in 1906, to Mary Agnes Little, of Dorchester, Massachusetts, daughter of George W. and Annie (Burgees) Little. Mr. and Mrs. Andrews are the parents of one daughter, Catherine, who was born November 28, 1921. The family home is on Summer Street in Kennebunk.

DR. JAMES H. MACDONALD—One of the younger members of the medical profession in Kennebunk, Maine, is James H. Macdonald, physician and surgeon, who has his office on Main Street. Dr.

Macdonald was for five years an associate of Dr. Pitt in the management of Pine Tree Sanitarium, at Wells, Maine, and he is still (1928) an associate physician there.

Dr. James H. Macdonald was born in Toronto, Canada, August 5, 1892, son of James Macdonald, a native of the Province of Quebec, Canada, who was a railroad contractor, and whose death occurred in 1925, and of Margaret (Jackson) Macdonald, a native of Williamsford, Canada. As a boy he attended the public schools, and then continued his studies in the high school at Smith Falls, Canada. When his preparatory course was finished, he matriculated in the University of Toronto, from which he was graduated in 1917, with the degree of Bachelor of Medicine. After serving his internship he enlisted in the Canadian Medical Corps, and was commissioned a captain. He served two years overseas in the Canadian Medical Corps, in England, France and Belgium, in various units, ending up with the Eighth Canadian Field Ambulance. He was discharged from the active army on September 30, 1919. In 1919, he was made superintendent of the D. S. C. R. Hospital, at Fredericton, New Brunswick, where he remained until 1921, when he came to Wells, Maine, as a partner of Dr. Pitt in the institution known as the Pine Tree Sanitarium. This connection he maintained until June, 1926, when he opened an office on Main Street in Kennebunk, Maine, where he has since been engaged in general practice. He is a member of the York County Medical Association, and of the College of Physicians and Surgeons, in Toronto, Canada, and is known as a skilled practitioner. Fraternally, he is identified with the Blue Lodge, Free and Accepted Masons, at Fredericton, New Brunswick; and with the Knights of Pythias in Kennebunk, Maine. His religious affiliation is with the Episcopal church.

PARKER D. SEARLE—The feat of doubling a newspaper circulation in a restricted community has long been the ambition of newspaper editors in various sections, but in the case of Parker D. Searle, owner and proprietor of the weekly "Sanford Herald," it has been done, in fact, Mr. Searle has more than doubled it, and in four years, too. Mr. Searle has accomplished this result in the four years since he obtained control of the paper on April 10, 1923, as owner and publisher. In addition, he has built up a nice job printing business, is active in civic affairs and enjoys a popularity that is unusual even for the occupant of an editorial perch.

Mr. Searle was born September 19, 1889, at Orwell, Vermont, son of Fayette D. Searle, a highly respected farmer, and Lillian (Parker) Searle, both of Cornwall, Vermont. He attended grammar and high schools, and became identified with the newspaper and job-printing business at various times, with several concerns.

Mr. Searle enlisted for the World War as a member of Company F, First Regiment, New Hampshire National Guard, serving as company clerk until his transfer to Base Headquarters at Bordeaux, France, when he was promoted to sergeant-major. He was very popular with the members of this organization, as he is with his lodge brothers of the Knights of Pythias, and the Junior Order of the United American Mechanics; his interest in military affairs is also expressed in his association with the

American Legion, whose fires of patriotism he has assisted in perpetuating.

Parker D. Searle married Lucy Mae Cushman, and their children are Philip D., and Parker C.

FRED L. DOWNS—The newspaper business has always been regarded as an inadequately paid venture which becomes a splendid stepping-stone on occasion to something else whose rewards are more commensurate with the effort expended; business managers, publishers and advertising managers have not yet seen fit to invent a scale of division of profits which will make editorial writers and reporters and desk men want to spend their lives in it for the sake of fascination and excitement. Consequently, the "game" loses thousands of men yearly who have dependents to support or more attractive paths to tread. Now and then a man like Fred L. Downs is versatile enough to develop a side-line, which, with what he can extract from "space," or salary, or both, enables him to make out very well. Mr. Downs went through the lean days of newspaper corresponding for more than a decade, at the end of which he established a real estate agency, and that proved the turning point in his career, because he began to make real money, until he now enjoys an admirable standing in the community, and is beginning to realize that a good part of the joy in life consists in possessing a well-filled purse and loyal friends to entertain.

Fred L. Downs was born August 20, 1887, at Sanford, son of George A. Downs, of the textile industry of North Berwick, and Sarah Elizabeth (Sherburne) Downs of this city. He received a common school education, and tried several occupations until the year 1909, when he drifted into the newspaper business and decided to try his hand at writing. He sent things of interest into the offices of quite a number of metropolitan papers, and by dint of perseverance and the merit of his items worked up a clientele with such papers as the Portland "Express," and the Boston "Globe." These associations have continued to the present time, and his scope has been enlarged to cover ten towns in this particular section, which he reports with ability and a fine degree of industry. All of Mr. Downs' time was not consumed in this occupation, so in 1920 he opened up a real estate agency under his own name, the Fred L. Downs Real Estate Agency, which has for its purpose the purchase and selling of land and improved properties. He found that the combination worked out well, for often while selling or inspecting real estate he would pick up an item of news, and quite as often while searching out an item of news he would stumble into a real estate deal, in the course of his travels about the territory embracing his ten towns. He is the sole owner of his real estate business, which he has put on a firm foundation.

Mr. Downs' commercial and literary activities were interrupted by the World War, and he was given the duty of taking charge of the pictorial records of this section, which he kept and augmented with an efficiency which evoked favorable comment everywhere. Mr. Downs is a valued and prominent member of the Sanford Kiwanis Club, and represents this organization as the representative of his particular industries. His social life centers in the Sanford Town Club, while his religious affiliation is with the Unitarian church, which he attends regularly unless called out of town.

Fred L. Downs married, in 1914, Marion A. Clark, of Vermont, a daughter of Joshua and Susan (Saunders) Clark, members of an old-established family in this section.

JOHN H. HICKEY, the present mayor of Old Town and one of its most prominent citizens, well known in real estate and insurance circles, and for many years active in civic affairs, was born in Bradley, Maine, on January 11, 1884. He was the son of James and Mary A. (Sherry) Hickey, both of whom are now deceased. The father, James Hickey was born in Frampton, Province of Quebec, and came to Maine as a young man, and was employed in the lumber industry up to his death in 1913. The mother, Mary A. (Sherry) Hickey, was a native of Bangor, Maine. Her death occurred in 1922.

The family moved from Bradley to Old Town when John H. was a boy of six years. It was here he received his early education, attending the Old Town public schools, later graduating from the Bangor Business College. Thus equipped he began the serious problem of a business career.

His first position was in the minor capacity of shipping clerk for T. R. Savage & Company, wholesale grocers, of Bangor. Subsequently he served under Walter E. Hellenbrand, agent for the American Express Company's office in Old Town for four years, at the expiration of which time he succeeded Mr. Hellenbrand as agent of the Old Town office. Later he was offered and accepted the position of paymaster for the Nekonegan Paper Company, in the Old Town office, in which capacity he served for twelve years. In 1917, he found himself, and decided to work for John H. Hickey, establishing at this time the real estate and insurance business in which he has been so signally successful.

There is more than the financial returns of his business for Mr. Hickey to be proud of. He has the human spark in his make-up. He has established a reputation for integrity that is more precious than gold. His success has not been a wholly selfish one, as is too often the case. He has been almost as active in his service to the city as he has been in the conduct of his business, giving unstintedly of his time. He has served three terms as mayor of Old Town. He also served one term as collector of taxes, one term as a member of the Board of Aldermen, one and a half years as city treasurer of Old Town, member of the School Board for one term, and in 1915-16 served as treasurer of Penobscot County. Mr. Hickey is an Independent Democrat. In 1915 he was the youngest man ever elected to the mayoralty chair and in February, 1928, he was unanimously chosen by his party to represent them in the coming campaign for the same office for the fourth term.

However, his manifold duties in business and civic life do not preclude Mr. Hickey from social and fraternal activities. He is a member and trustee of Old Town Lodge, No. 1287, Benevolent and Protective Order of Elks, of which he is Past Exalted Ruler and has the distinction of being the first man to hold this office in the Old Town Lodge; and he is a member of the Grand Lodge of Elks of which he was District Deputy for Maine East. He is president of the Old Town Rotary Club, chairman of the local branch of the Red Cross, secretary of the Victory Athletic Field Assoication, member of the Tarratine Club of Bangor, of the Old Town Grange, Patrons of Husbandry, and of the Father Drullette Council, Knights of Columbus. He is a member of the Insurance Federation of the State of Maine, and of the Maine Association of Insurance Agents, and of the Penobscot Valley Country Club. Taking it all in all, Mr. Hickey is a pretty busy man, and the greatest tribute the writer can pay to him is that he is a man and human.

Mr. Hickey married, in 1913, Alice K. Murphy, a native of Old Town and the daughter of Cornelius and Mary Ann (McClellan) Murphy, the former born in Derby, New Brunswick, March 21, 1840; the latter a native of Bangor, Maine, born December 25, 1840; both of whom are now deceased. Cornelius Murphy was one of the pioneer lumbermen of Maine, and for many years one of Old Town's most prominent citizens. To Mr. and Mrs. Hickey have been born three children: Frederick H., William E., and Mary Louise. The family are members of St. Mary's Roman Catholic Church.

J. WILL LEAVITT—An outstanding figure in the business and civic life of Sanford, Maine, is that of J. Will Leavitt, general insurance representative, prominent in social and fraternal circles. Of like community significance is his wife, Mrs. J. Will Leavitt, who practices law independently and has the distinction of being the first and only woman attorney in Sanford.

J. Will Leavitt was born February 16, 1872, son of Alonzo Leavitt, proprietor of a general store at Alfred, and of his wife, Susan C. (Nason) Leavitt, also of Alfred. The father died in 1922. The son attended grammar and high school, and Shaw's Business College. His first business years were devoted to work with the railroad, in the course of which he became auditor and learned much about conditions in Maine and the economic status of localities and citizens. In 1917 he purchased the insurance agency of George P. Chase, which had been established nearly three decades earlier, in 1890. This highly respected enterprise has become a power throughout the section in the energetic and capable hands of the new owner. Mr. Leavitt has introduced new methods and new lines of business and has greatly extended the scope of his organization, which now ranks among the foremost general insurance offices in Maine. Besides conducting this office, Mr. Leavitt is a director of the Sanford National Bank, and the York Utilities Company. He is a member of the Lodge, Free and Accepted Masons, and of Kora Temple, Ancient Arabic Order Nobles of the Mystic Shrine. He belongs also to the Benevolent and Protective Order of Elks. His clubs are the Sanford Town, the Rotary, and the Bauneg Beg Country clubs. He is a member of the Unitarian church.

In 1901, J. Will Leavitt married Belle Ashton, of Colorado, daughter of Thomas G. and Mary A. (Kernon) Ashton, natives of England. The daughter was educated in the public schools and business college and studied law in the office of the late Fred J. Allen. Admitted to the bar, June 2, 1900, she began her practice in association with Mr. Allen. At his death she began the independent practice she has since continued. She is gifted with a fine fund of common sense, combined with keen business ability, qualities which have insured her rapid professional advancement. She is secretary and attorney for the Sanford Building and Loan Association, one of the flourishing institutions of its kind in the State, of which the president is Seth Sugden. Mrs. Leavitt's manner of handling the legal affairs of this concern has been so intelligent as to win for her generous praise from all her colleagues. During the World War, she took a prominent part in all Red Cross work and in the various patriotic drives, and since the Armistice she has given aid to all philanthropic movements. She is a member of the Order of the Eastern Star and Past Matron, and of the Searchlight Club, the Bauneg Beg Country Club, and the Business and Professional Women's Club.

HORACE EMERSON EATON, an attorney whose offices are in the Sanford Trust Company Building, Rooms Nos. 309 and 310, has resided in Sanford since January, 1917. He was born in Calais, Maine, in 1882, son of Albion H. and Annie (Whidden) Eaton. After attending the Calais public schools he entered Colgate Academy, Hamilton, New York, where, after taking the four-year course, he was graduated in 1901. Going to the Cambridge, Massachusetts, Latin School that fall for special science courses, he completed one year there and entered Harvard in 1902, remaining at the Cambridge University for one year. After engaging in newspaper work with the Portland "Advertiser," Portland "Press," Bangor "Commercial," and Bangor "News," during which period he was staff correspondent at Bar Harbor for the "Commercial" during four summer seasons, he entered the University of Maine Law School in 1910, receiving his Bachelor of Laws degree in 1913.

Before moving to Sanford, Mr. Eaton studied and practiced law with Hinckley & Hinckley, in Portland. While there he became a member, in 1916, of the Second Company Coast Artillery, Maine National Guard, and in January, 1917, he transferred to the Sixth Company, in Sanford. With this company he entered the United States service when the National Guard was called out in the fall of 1917. He served as corporal and sergeant at Fort Levett, Portland, and at Camp Devens, Massachusetts, on guard duty, and the United States Arsenal at Watertown, Massachusetts, on guard duty, until January 1, 1918, when he was assigned to attend the Third Officers' Training Camp at Fort Oglethorpe, Georgia. After three months at Fort Oglethorpe he was sent to Saumur, France, where he remained for three months in attendance at the United States Army School of Artillery Fire, and at the end of this time he was commissioned a second lieutenant, Field Artillery, United States Army.

Thereafter, until January, 1919, he was attached to United States Army Headquarters at Brest, France (Base Section No. 5), as trial judge advocate of Special and General Courts, and during this period he visited Cherbourg, St. Male, Dinart, Le-Mans, Tours, and other cities, in the United States Rents, Requisitions and Claims Service. He was discharged at Camp Meade, Maryland, February 19, 1919.

In the fall of 1920, he recruited a coast artillery company in Sanford for the reorganized Maine National Guard. Of this company he was commanding officer, with rank of captain, for three years. On May 12, 1923, he was promoted, with commission as

major, and he commanded the first battalion of the Maine Coast Artillery until his resignation and transfer to the Reserve, with rank of major, a year later.

Mr. Eaton was largely instrumental in organizing the Thomas W. Cole Post, American Legion, in Sanford, and he was the first Post Commander. In politics he has always been a Republican, and for several years he served as a member of the Republican Town Committee. His hobby is newspaper work, in which he is still actively interested. At the present time he is associate editor of the Sanford "Tribune-Advocate,"' and is correspondent for various daily papers.

LUCIUS B. SWETT—The legal fraternity of Sanford is agreed on the ability of Lucius B. Swett, of this city, who has been practicing law here with great success since 1906, and who has filled important appointive and elective offices, including on one occasion that of judge.

Mr. Swett was born February 25, 1880, at Hollis, Maine, son of Frank A. Swett, of Hollis, a highly respected farmer who died in 1905, and Maria A. (Whitehouse) Swett, of Waterboro, Maine, a woman of many lovable traits of character, who departed this life in 1922. He attended the public schools and Fryeburg Academy, at both of which institutions he made a commendable record and took advantage of his several opportunities. Thereupon, having decided that the paths of success are best reached through the practice of the law, he matriculated in the Law School of the University of Maine, and graduated with the degree of Bachelor of Laws in the class of 1906. Although he was admitted to the bar in 1906, he did not immediately practice, but added to his generous equipment by teaching school three years. In 1909, Mr. Swett formed a law partnership with Mr. Burnham under the firm name of Burnham and Swett, for the general practice of the law at Kittery, Maine. In 1911, Mr. Swett was appointed to fill the unexpired term of Willis T. Emmons, as clerk of the York County Court, and he satisfactorily discharged the duties of this office until 1913, when he returned to the general practice of the law. In 1916, he was appointed to fill out the unexpired term of Judge Hobbs of North Berwick, and at the conclusion of this duty he went back to his practice, at which he has continued most successfully ever since, having been transferred to Sanford.

Mr. Swett is a member of the York County and Maine State Bar associations. In religious affairs he adheres to the Baptist church, and in politics he is a Democrat. During the World War he rendered effective service as a member of the Legal Advisory Board, for which he received the thanks of a grateful government.

Mr. Swett has been married twice. His first wife, Captola E. Dodge, whom he married in 1907, is deceased. His second wife, wed in 1919, was Margaret A. Harrison. By Captola E. (Dodge) Swett he had a daughter, Ruth V. Swett.

GEORGE W. HESELTON, a well-known attorney-at-law, and a resident of prominence at Gardiner, Maine, was born in that community on November 2, 1856, a son of Reuben, Jr., and Sarah G. Heselton, of Maine. Reuben Heselton, Jr., was for a great many years a carpenter and contractor in his native State.

George W. Heselton received his early education in the public schools of the community in which he was born, and later attended Amherst College. He was formally admitted to practice law before the bar of the Supreme Court of Maine, at Augusta, Maine, in October, 1881. On December 12, 1906, he was admitted to practice before the United States Supreme Court. On April 6, 1910, he was admitted to practice in the Circuit Court of the United States, since which time he has carried on a general practice of his profession in Maine. He has also been active in the public and general affairs of both his county and his State. In his political views Mr. Heselton is a staunch supporter of the Republican party; he served six years as County Attorney of Kennebec County. He has also been a member of the Maine State Senate. Mr. Heselton has taken an interest in strictly commercial pursuits as well, and he is now a director of the Gardiner Trust Company, and an officer of the Gardiner Building & Loan Association. He is affiliated, fraternally, with the Lodge, Free and Accepted Masons; the Chapter, Royal Arch Masons; the Council, Royal and Select Masters; the Commandery, Knights Templar, and Kora Temple, Ancient Arabic Order Nobles of the Mystic Shrine. He is also a member of the Knights of Pythias, in which organization he holds the rank of Grand Chancellor and Supreme Representative; he is a member of the Gardiner Shrine Club, and of the Boston (Massachusetts) City Club.

George W. Heselton married, June 14, 1899, at Hallowell, Maine, Mary Eleanor Stafford, a daughter of Edward and Catherine Stafford. Mr. and Mrs. Heselton are the parents of three children: 1. John, born March 17, 1900. 2. Henry, born April 16, 1901. 3. Mary, born May 27, 1915. Mr. Heselton is a member of the Congregational church, while his wife and family attend the Catholic church in Gardiner, Maine.

REVEREND PATRICK H. REARDON, the well-known and beloved pastor of St. Joseph's Church in Gardiner, Maine, was born March 4, 1859, at Bangor, Maine. Father Reardon is a son of Jeremiah and Rosanna (Agnew) Reardon, both of whom were born in Ireland. Jeremiah Reardon, the father, was engaged as a marble cutter in Bangor, Maine, an occupation that he followed all his life.

Patrick H. Reardon received his preliminary education in the public schools of Bangor, Maine, after which he voyaged to Ireland, where he began his classical studies at Mount Mellary Seminary in Ireland. Returning to this continent, he pursued his theological education in Laval University at Quebec, Canada. He was ordained June 13, 1886.. Returning to Maine, he was appointed assistant to Father Conlon, Calais, October 3, 1887. He was transferred to Portland, Maine, as an assistant to the Very Rev. J. W. Amsphy at St. Dominick's Church, where he served for three years. In 1890, he was transferred to Bangor, Maine, as assistant to the Very Rev. M. C. O'Brien, V. G., at St. Mary's Church, where he stayed until October 3, 1893. Then he was transferred to Benedicta, Maine, where was pastor for almost eight years. This parish was a large one, about one hundred and fifty miles north to south, and seventy miles east to west, and more

than ten thousand square miles in area. Father Reardon rode and walked to all points in his domain, at least once a year. On November 3, 1900, he went to Gardiner, Maine, as pastor of St. Joseph's Church. He went to work there with his usual energy. In 1928, he had increased the church property in value more than ten times the amount it was when he became the pastor. He has built a fine granite church that seats nine hundred on the main floor. He has acquired and modernized a large Parish House and a beautiful cemtery, all unencumbered.

Always devoting himself with unselfish interest to the welfare of his people, Father Reardon has played an active part in the life of his community. In his political preferences he is inclined towards the Republican party. He is fraternally affiliated with the Knights of Columbus, and is a fourth degree member. He is also a member of the Rotary Club of Gardiner, Maine.

J. FRANKLIN ANDERSON—When the financial leaders of Gardiner, Maine, looked about for an executive to whom might be entrusted the responsible duties of treasurer of the Gardiner Trust Company, they selected J. Franklin Anderson, a young but thoroughly experienced baker. Force and energy are his, as well as careful training and a wide knowledge of finance in general, and the trust field in particular.

J. Franklin Anderson was born in New Brunswick, Maine, September 7, 1890, son of J. Franklin and Olive (Tranter) Anderson, both natives of New Brunswick, and both now deceased. The father was a lumberman of prominence in that vicinity. The son was educated in the public and high schools of Calais, Maine. His banking career began in that town, when he had a position with the International Trust Banking Company. He was alert and ready to learn, winning advancement for himself during his sixteen-year connection with this institution. Then came a wider opportunity with the Maine Trust Company, in Gardiner, with which he was associated for two years. Since May, 1927, Mr. Anderson has been treasurer of the rapidly growing Gardiner Trust Company. His political alignment is with the Republican party and his interest in affairs of local significance is great. He was for six years alderman on the Town Board of Calais. He is a member of the Free and Accepted Masons; of the Knights Templar; of Kora Temple, Ancient Arabic Order Nobles of the Mystic Shrine; and is treasurer of the Rotary and the Forty clubs of Gardiner, Maine. His religious affiliation is with the Episcopal church.

DR. ALLEN McDONALD SMALL—Foremost among those whose names have brought honor to Deer Isle is Dr. Allen M. Small, who has been following the merciful profession of medicine since 1895. Since he graduated from Bowdoin Medical School, where he achieved an excellent record as an earnest and keen student, Dr. Small has been engaged in general practice, obtaining especial prominence as a surgeon of great merit. He was born in Deer Isle, October 12, 1872, son of Edward S. Small and Clara J. (Powers) Small, both of Deer Isle. Edward S. Small was engaged as a carpenter and builder and carried on a successful career in these trades.

Dr. Small received his early education in the public schools of Deer Isle, after which he attended Kents Hill Seminary, where he was a member of the Literary Club. Completing his course there, he entered Bowdoin Medical School, from which he received his degree as Doctor of Medicine in 1894, beginning his practice the next year at Freedom, acquiring a reputation as a physician of thorough knowledge and great skill, ever ready to minister to the sick and suffering of the vicinity. Dr. Small is a prominent member of both the State and County Medical associations and is active in fraternal circles, being a member of Unity Lodge, No. 91, Free and Accepted Masons, having attained his thirty-second degree in all bodies of both the Scottish and York Rites; Anah Temple, Ancient Arabic Order Nobles of the Mystic Shrine; of the Knights of Pythias, and of the local Grange, Patrons of Husbandry. In politics, he is a member of the Republican party and greatly interested in civil affairs, being County Commissioner of Waldo County, and also County Medical Examiner. He is a member of the Congregational church. At one time he was a member of the staff of Waldo County Hospital.

Dr. Small married (first), on November 4, 1895, Luella F. Small, daughter of Amos T. Small of Deer Isle. They had three children: Vivian Sullivan, Florian E., and Marian. Dr. Small married (second), Edith Williams, born at Bangor, December 4, 1879, daughter of Rev. P. T. Williams of Wales, and of Ruth Williams, of Pennsylvania.

FREDERIC A. DANFORTH—An experienced accountant and auditor, well known through his connection with important concerns and significant enterprises, Frederic A. Danforth is now successfully busy as third vice-president of the Gardiner Trust Company. He is interested in several other concerns, and is secretary of the Building & Loan Association, of Gardiner, Maine. He was born in Gardiner, September 30, 1872, son of Eugene L. and Ada E. (Libby) Danforth. The father, born in Gardiner, was a sawmill proprietor there and a leader in Republican affairs. He is now deceased, but his wife, born in Avon, Maine, resides in Gardiner.

Frederic A. Danforth was educated in the local public and high schools, graduating 1890. He began his banking career as a clerk in the Merchants' National Bank in Gardiner, maintaining this connection for ten years, and being elected a director of the institution. He was also director of the Maine Trust and Banking Company. For a time thereafter, Mr. Danforth served as clerk of the Kennebec Light and Heat Company, from which he advanced to public accounting. His present position as a vice-president of the Gardiner Trust Company is the outgrowth of this wide experience. Since 1894, Mr. Danforth has been secretary of the Building & Loan Association, and he was city auditor for ten years. He is a Republican in politics and a member of all bodies of both branches of the Free and Accepted Masons.

ELLERY BOWDEN, Judge of the Probate Court of Waldo County, Maine, since 1917, lawyer

and former City Attorney of Belfast, was born in Penobscot, Maine, March 3, 1870, the son of Elisha R. and Clara (Grindle) Bowden. His father, who came originally from Surrey, Maine, was afterwards a merchant and manufacturer of lumber and bricks in Penobscot and served in the Engineering Corps throughout the Civil War.

Ellery Bowden was educated in the public grammar and high schools in Penobscot and entered the East Maine State Normal School, from which he was graduated, to enter the East Maine Conference Seminary at Bucksport, Maine. He showed a great interest in law and finally left the seminary to study law under the Hon. Oscar F. Fellows in Bucksport, and remained in his office for the next three years, during which he taught school a part of the time. He was admitted to the bar in Belfast, in January, 1894, and began to practice his profession in Winterport, Maine, where he has continued ever since, dividing his time between Winterport and an equally exacting practice in Belfast.

He became a powerful factor in Republican politics in his part of the State, and nominated for City Attorney in Belfast in June, 1894, and was elected to that office the following September, the same year of his admittance to the bar. He continued as City Attorney of Belfast until January 1, 1901. He was appointed Register of Deeds by Governor Cobb in 1908, and served one term. Governor Milliken appointed Mr. Bowden Judge of the Probate Court in 1917, and he was reëlected in 1918, 1922, and in 1926, holding this office at present.

Mr. Bowden is moderator of the Town Meeting, an office he has held since 1895, in Winterport, and he served as a member of the School Board there for ten years; also on the budget committee of the town. He is a trustee of the Winterport Public Library. Mr. Bowden is a Royal Arch Mason, an Odd Fellow and was Grand Master of the Grand Lodge of Maine, in the latter order; also a member of the Maine State Bar Association, and is active in the affairs of the town of Winterport.

ARTHUR S. BAKER—The North National Bank of Rockland, Maine, recently elected a new president, and in this election the directors conferred a signal honor upon a man whose perseverance in the business world, ever since his graduation from high school, has earned him the fullest measure of success in his community.

The president of the North National Bank, Arthur S. Baker, was born in Rockland, June 8, 1880, the son of the Rev. J. R. Baker and Ellen J. (Cochran) Baker. He was graduated from the Rockland High School in 1900, and Rockland has been his home ever since. The year after leaving high school he entered the employ of Cochran, Baker & Frost, one of the oldest insurance concerns in this section of the State, and was admitted to partnership in 1911. In the years that have followed he has seen the business expand two and one-half times. It is an interesting coincidence that this concern was established in 1853, only one year before the charter was granted to the North National Bank, with which his time and efforts are now so closely divided.

The North National Bank first saw the light of day in the small office in Crockett Block, directly above the store now occupied by J. A. Jameson Company. This was in 1854, when the north end

282   MAINE—A HISTORY

of Rockland gave promise of becoming the center of commercial activity; the trading of the community having followed the business line around what is now "The Meadows," thence to Blackington's Corner and finally to that section of the Shore Village, as Rockland was termed in the early days.

From its location it derived its name and having been founded by shrewd business men and conducted upon sound principles of management in due course assumed a place of prominence among the newly incorporated banks of this section of Maine. The first president of the North National Bank was John Bird, who served from 1854 to 1868; the paternal grandfather of Elmer S. Bird. He was succeeded by A. J. Bird, who served from 1868 until 1892, and he in turn by Sidney M. Bird, who occupied the office from 1892 until 1907. In the interim, the bank has been housed at various times in rooms over the present savings bank, in the quarters now occupied by the Western Union Telegraph Company and finally in its present location at the foot of Lime Rock Street. Nathan T. Farwell was president from 1908 until 1910, and Elmer S. Bird was president from 1910 until Mr. Baker assumed office, in January, 1926.

Mr. Baker was elected a director of the bank in 1918, and three years later was made vice-president and has been closely associated with President Bird in the details of security purchases and discounts, and he entered upon his administration as president fortified by this valuable special training and with a clear conception of all its duties.

He is affiliated with Aurora Lodge, Free and Accepted Masons; King Solomon's Temple Chapter, Royal Arch Masons; King Hiram Council, Royal and Select Masters; Claremont Commandery, Knights Templar; and Rockland Lodge, Benevolent and Protective Order of Elks, of which he has served as trustee.

JOSHUA N. SOUTHARD—Among the leading citizens of Rockland, Maine, who has spent most of his life there and has risen by his own efforts, is Joshua N. Southard, vice-president of the North National Bank and a former councilman and alderman of Rockland. He has been employed by the bank since 1902, and was elected a vice-president in January, 1926, marking another epoch in the career for which he has proved so well adapted. In 1927, he was elected director of the Rockland Chamber of Commerce, for a three-year term.

Mr. Southard was born in Rockport, Maine, July 11, 1880, the son of Edgar J. and Julia B. (Clark) Southard. His father had been a shipbuilder for fifty years in Rockport, but Joshua N. Southard showed early evidence of his desire to enter the world of finance and business. Until he was twenty years old, he remained in Rockport, receiving his education in the town schools and later studying bookkeeping and other phases of commerce and business at the Rockland Commercial College. With this preparation he went to Boston, to enter the employ of Hallowell, Donald & Company, dealers in wool, as a bookkeeper. His health was not rugged and because of this fact he returned to Rockland as agent for the Bluehill Steamship Company, which operated the steamers "Catherine," "Juliette," and "Rockland." A year with this company and three years as bookkeeper in the coal office of John I.

Snow, was followed by a desire to learn the banking business.

Mr. Southard was first employed by the North National Bank in 1902, as a bookkeeper, and a few years later he was promoted to the office of assistant cashier and again as vice-president. Despite his devotion to business, Mr. Southard has served the city government of Rockland for five years, four as Councilman and one as Alderman, and has been a member of the School Committee for the past two years. He is active in the First Baptist Church of Rockland, being chairman of its finance committee and was president of the Baptist Men's League for two years.

Mr. Southard is a trustee of Knox Lodge, Independent Order of Odd Fellows, a member of the Encampment and a Past Captain of Canton Lafayette; he is a thirty-second degree Mason and member of the Ancient Arabic Order Nobles of the Mystic Shrine; a member of the house committee of Rockland Lodge, Benevolent and Protective Order of Elks, and treasurer of Pioneer Council, Boy Scouts of America.

JUDGE EDWARD K. GOULD—Success in his practice of the law over a long period, and an almost equally noteworthy performance for many years as a public official, entrusted with responsible and varied duties, have brought into wide prominence Edward K. Gould, of Rockland, Maine. He is Judge of the Probate Courts of Knox County.

Edward K. Gould was born in Rockland, Maine, September 28, 1865, son of John L. Kallach, a native of Rockland, who was adopted by Stephen Gould of Freedom, but lived in Rockland most of his life. The father, a seaman, served two years in the Civil War, a corporal of Company B, Fourth Maine Regiment, and his adopted father was a merchant of Rockland. The mother, Rosetta J. Gould, a native of Rockland, died in 1917, while the father died in 1869. Edward K. Gould was educated in the public and high schools of Rockland and rounded out his preparation for a career by a course in the Rockland Commercial College. He studied law under Hon. True P. Pierce, of Rockland, for a three-year period, and with such zeal and intelligence that he was, in September, 1888, admitted to the Maine bar.

That year, Judge Gould began the practice which has since prospered in Rockland, although he has given much time to public affairs. He was City Solicitor of Rockland for four years: 1889-90; 1909-10; 1912-13; and 1915-16. In the interim he served as Register of Probate for Knox County, 1892 to 1900, as treasurer of the county under appointment by Governor Haynes, in 1914, and as mayor of Rockland in 1901-02. For more than twenty years Judge Gould has been trustee of the Rockland Public Library and for five years was a member of the School Board. In 1923, he was elected to his present position of Judge of Probate, Knox County. In political alignment he is a Republican. He is attorney for the Rockland Building & Loan Association, vice-president of the Knox County Bar Association, and a member of the Maine State Bar Association. Judge Gould served in the Maine Militia for five years, and Gould's Light Battery, providing one hundred and sixty soldiers for the United States in the Spanish-American War. He is past State President of the Maine Society, Sons of the American Revolution, and Past Division Commander of the Sons of Union Veterans, and he belongs to the Maine Historical Society. His fraternal affiliations are with the Free and Accepted Masons, in which he holds the thirty-second degree, and the post of Grand Commander of the Knights Templar. He is also a member of the Patrons of Husbandry.

MILTON M. GRIFFIN—A decade of experience in cost accounting and in various business developments preceded the election of Milton M. Griffin to his present office of County Clerk of Courts, Rockland, Maine, and equipped him with singular fitness for this responsible post. He was born in Lincolnville, Maine, May 30, 1890, son of Llewellyn E. and Alfreda (Monroe) Griffin, both natives of Lincolnville. The father, a steamfitter in Rockland, is a warm supporter of the Republican party.

Milton M. Griffin was educated in the Rockland grammar and high schools and rounded out his preparation for a business career by a course in commercial college, that of Bryant & Stratton, in Boston, from which he graduated in 1910. For ten years he was employed in cost accounting. After the World War, in which he served, he entered the delivery business in Rockland and remained thus employed until 1921. Then came his election to his present office of County Clerk, in which he has proved so capable and so devoted to the interests of the public that he has won universal approval and reëlection.

When his country's call came to arms, Mr. Griffin enlisted in the Signal Corps, at Springfield, Massachusetts, and was later transferred to the Aviation Corps. He was overseas from February, 1918, to March, 1919, was a sergeant, and was discharged at Garden City, Long Island, in April, 1919. He is a member of the Independent Order of Odd Fellows, the American Legion, and the Free and Accepted Masons, Blue Lodge. He belongs also to the Baptist Men's League. His political alignment is with the Republican party.

In Rockland, Maine, February 14, 1920, Milton M. Griffin married Sarah (Pettee) Pettee, daughter of Alfred H. and Clara (Barter) Pettee. Mr. and Mrs. Griffin have a daughter, Barbara Griffin, born January 29, 1921.

BYRON BOYD, who has developed an important lumber business in Augusta, Maine, and was Secretary of State of Maine for ten years, is a native of Canada. Born at Victoria Corner, Carleton County, New Brunswick, August 31, 1864, he received his early education in the schools of Linneus, Maine; coming to the United States with his parents when four years of age, and completing his education at Houlton Academy and at Colby, where he was graduated in 1886, with the degree of Bachelor of Arts.

He then taught school in Bar Harbor for a year, and for the next two years engaged in the real estate business in Bar Harbor. In 1889 he became a clerk in the office of the Secretary of State, and was promoted to deputy. In 1895, he was elected Secretary of State, and held that office continuously until 1905. From 1903 to 1910, he was chairman of the Republican State Committee. On his retirement from office, he undertook the development of

cedar lumber products, and has manufactured railroad ties, telegraph poles and roofing shingles of this material.

Mr. Boyd's father, Dr. Robert Boyd, and his mother, who was Eliza J. Savage, were both born in New Brunswick, Canada, but Dr. Boyd, who had received his degree of Doctor of Medicine, from the Harvard Medical School, practiced in Linneus, Maine.

In January, 1895, Byron Boyd married Lucy E. Burleigh, daughter of Governor Edwin Chick and Mary J. (Bither) Burleigh. Their children, all born in Augusta, are: 1. Dorothy (Brown). 2. Richard, married Lucille Purinton. 3. Mary (Hawkins). 4. Burleigh Boyd.

JAMES F. CARVER—A substantial and progressive business man, James F. Carver, mayor of Rockland, Maine, is a political leader of vision and civic ambition, who has already accomplished much for the welfare of his city. He was born in Rockland, July 21, 1873, son of Altheus O. and Harriet (Thompson) Carver, the father a native of Rockport, and a seaman. The mother was a native of Rockland.

In his native town James F. Carver grew up, acquiring a good education in the local public and high schools and rounding out his schooling with a course at the Rockland Commercial College. He has long pursued two lines of business, operating a restaurant and a book and stationery shop in Rockland. In his dual activities he has prospered, attaining a position of leadership. A Republican in politics, he was for two years president of the City Council, of which he was a member for years. For ten years he was on the Board of Registration. His election to the office of mayor of Rockland came January 1, 1925, and he fulfilled the high expectations of his ability and strength in this office, being reëlected December 6, 1927. Mayor Carver has served his State for fourteen years in military capacity. He was a member of the Maine National Guard and, with the First Maine Volunteers, participated in the Spanish-American War. During his later years he held the rank of captain. He is enrolled in the Free and Accepted Masons, in which he has the thirty-second degree. His club is the Rockland Country.

FRANK F. HARDING—The official position which was so ably filled by Frank F. Harding, of Rockland, Maine, as city marshal, and his successful business record combine to give him wide local prominence. He is known as a man of courage and resourcefulness, loyal to the best interests of his town and unusually public-spirited.

Frank F. Harding was born in Rockland, January 6, 1869, son of William P. and Vesta (Ford) Harding, both now deceased. The former, born in Hope, Maine, was a Republican in politics and successfully engaged in the teaming business in Rockland. The mother was born in Albion, Maine. Their son, Frank F. Harding, received a good education in the public and high schools of Rockland. For a decade after he reached maturity, Mr. Harding followed the grocery business in his native town, prospering in an enterprise which became one of the substantial enterprises of the town. He served the city as marshal, then was an officer in State Prison, Thomaston, Maine, two years, and then in the commissary of that institution for seven years. His election to the office of Sheriff, in September, 1926, is eloquent testimony to his ability in public office. Since January, 1927, he has held this responsible post.

In politics, Mr. Harding is a Republican. He was on the Common Council of Rockland for three years and on the Board of Aldermen for a year. He is a member of the Blue Lodge, Free and Accepted Masons, the Royal Arch Masons, and the Royal and Select Masters, as well as all branches of the Independent Order of Odd Fellows, and Past Noble Grand and past officer in all subordinate lodges. His religious adherence is given to the Episcopal church in Rockland.

CHARLES H. MOREY—Since March, 1924,
Charles H. Morey has been the able and efficient city treasurer of Rockland, Maine. Mr. Morey is a Republican and has been active in local public affairs here in Rockland for a number of years. He was born in Rockland, Maine, November 9, 1876, son of Charles B. Morey, who was engaged in trucking and who was active in the Republican party, a native of Deer Isle, Maine, and of Susan (Duncan) Morey, a native of Burntcoat, Maine, both now deceased.

Charles H. Morey received his education in the public schools of Rockland, including the high school, and then secured a position as clerk with the Art & Wall Paper Company. In 1903, he went to work for the Bodwell Granite Company as bookkeeper, remaining with them until they closed their offices in 1918. Later he engaged in the retail shoe business for himself in this town, in which he continued for a period of four years. In 1924, he was elected city treasurer and that public office he is still filling (1928), being reëlected in 1926. Mr. Morey is a Republican in his political affiliations and has for many years been active in promoting the welfare of Rockland. He has been a member of the Common Council and clerk of that body for a number of years, and is one of the public-spirited citizens who can always be depended upon to give generous support to any well planned project for the advance of the general good. Fraternally, he is a member of the Blue Lodge, Free and Accepted Masons; and his religious affiliation is with the First Baptist Church of Rockland, which he serves as a deacon and as Sunday school superintendent.

Charles H. Morey was married, in Rockland, Maine, September 10, 1913, to Susie B. Sherer, who was born in Rockland, Maine, daughter of Charles E. and Louise C. Sherer. Mr. and Mrs. Morey are the parents of two children: Cleveland D., and Eleanor E.

ALBERT WINSLOW—Citizens of Rockland,
Maine, point with pride to one of their number who by his own efforts has risen to a position of considerable importance, Albert Winslow, former Street Commissioner, State Road Inspector, alderman and at present Register of Deeds. From a position of obscurity as clerk in the office of an express company in Rockland, he has mounted the ladder of success until he is now regarded as a political power in his community.

Mr. Winslow was born in Rockland on September 12, 1869, the son of David and Sarah F. (Benner)

Winslow. His father, native of Waldoboro, Maine, was a contractor and afterwards a road commissioner in Rockland and his mother, the former Sarah Benner, was born in Rockland. He was educated in the public schools of Rockland and was graduated from the Rockland High School. At first Mr. Winslow decided on a business career and entered the office of a Rockland steamship company as a clerk, where he remained for two years, then became employed by an express company in a similar capacity for ten years more. Politics occupied much of his time, and he became involved more and more in the affairs of the Republican party in Rockland. He served in the Common Council for two years, then gave up business altogether upon his appointment as Street Commissioner of Rockland. When his term of office ended, he was elected to the Board of Aldermen, where he served for two years. He was elected Register of Deeds on January 1, 1927, and has occupied this office with distinction ever since.

Mr. Winslow served as a first sergeant of the Rockland Light Infantry for two years; is a member of Blue Lodge, Free and Accepted Masons, and a communicant of the Universalist church in Rockland. He married Jennie Rouse, daughter of Dr. James A. and Mary (Pratt) Rouse, both deceased, in Rockland, on May 24, 1891.

FREDERICK O. BARTLETT, M. D., the city
physician of Rockland, Maine, has filled that position there for eight years, and for eighteen years before that was a member of the Board of Health in St. George, Maine. Dr. Bartlett is one of the best-known physicians in this part of the State and has acquired an enviable reputation in his profession. He was born in Hope, Maine, January 20, 1856, the son of Daniel and Eliza (Fletcher) Bartlett, both deceased. Both of Dr. Bartlett's parents had come of farming stock, and his father operated a large farm in Hope, Maine, at the time of Dr. Bartlett's birth.

Dr. Bartlett was educated in the public school at Hope, and later attended the high school in Camden, Maine. At first he had some idea of becoming a teacher, and entered the West Brook Seminary, a normal school, where he remained for a year. He withdrew, however, to enter the Medical School of the University of Vermont, from which he was graduated in 1887 with the degree of Doctor of Medicine. He began practice in Waldoboro, Maine, and continued there for two years, removing to Washington, Maine, where he practiced medicine for one year. Then he moved to St. George, Maine, and lived there for eighteen years, building up a profitable practice and attaining a reputation as a competent physician and surgeon. Since 1909, Dr. Bartlett has been engaged in general practice at Rockland, Maine, and has been city physician for the past eight years, the last two of which he has served under Mayor Carver.

He is a member of the Knox County Medical Society and the Maine State Medical Association, is a Royal Arch Mason, and a member of the Odd Fellows. He has always been an ardent Democrat, and served in the State Legislature, representing Hope, Appleton and Washington, in 1881-2, and has been a member of the State Pension Board for sixteen years. Before coming to Rockland, Dr. Bartlett served as Superintendent of Schools in St. George,

Maine, for twelve years and had served in a similar capacity in Waldoboro, Maine, for two years. Since coming to Rockland, Dr. Bartlett has become active in the affairs of the Universalist church.

Dr. Bartlett married Stella M. Wright, daughter of Calvin D. and Esther (Humes) Wright, in Washington, Maine, on December 17, 1890. They have two children: 1. Russell E., a farmer. 2. Fred O. Bartlett, an osteopath, in Plainfield, New Jersey.

RICHARD O. ELLIOT—Of the ships that went down to the sea, back in those days of wind and sail and clipper races, some of the staunchest vessels to carry the American flag into strange harbors and foreign ports were fashioned in the yards of Richard O. Elliot, in Thomaston, Maine. For more than thirty years, Mr. Elliot has built ships of various designs and for various purposes, mostly coastwise schooners. He is now a partner in the shipping firm of Dunn and Elliot. Mr. Elliot was born in Thomaston, Maine, on February 6, 1873, the son of George and Mary Ella (Libby) Elliot. The family on his father's side had followed the sea for generations and George Elliot, also a shipbuilder, taught his son to carry on his calling.

Richard O. Elliot went to the public school in Thomaston and at the end of the customary course, determined to follow in the footsteps of his father, carrying on the family trade of shipbuilding. He entered the Massachusetts Institute of Technology, for the necessary technical training and was graduated from that institution in 1896. He devoted himself to shipbuilding, learning all he could about the business, under the guidance of his father and various shipbuilding firms for whom he worked. After forming a partnership with Richard E. Dunn, under the name of Dunn and Elliot, shipbuilders, Mr. Elliot expanded his activities to include banking and finance. In 1910 he became a director and vice-president of Georges' National Bank, Thomaston, Maine, and was appointed president of that bank in 1919, a position which he occupies at present. He is also a trustee of the Thomaston Savings Bank, and has been selectman, moderator, and town auditor of Thomaston. Mr. Elliot is a member of the Royal Arch Masons, and of the Ancient Arabic Order Nobles of the Mystic Shrine, also of the Knights of Pythias, of which he is Past Chancellor Commander.

Richard O. Elliot married Lavinia Grant, daughter of James and Georgia (Hall) Grant, on June 21, 1898, in Thomaston, two years after his graduation from the Massachusetts Institute of Technology. They have one child, Madeline Elliot, who married Warren Bulkeley, and is the mother of Warrener, Peter, and Elizabeth; she lives in Marblehead, Massachusetts.

PAUL ARTHUR CYR, D. D. S.—In 1919, Paul Arthur Cyr began the practice of dentistry at Augusta, Maine. Skilled in his profession he quickly won the confidence of those who consulted him, and in a few years has built up a very successful practice. Dr. Cyr served in the United States Army during the World War, and he takes an active part in the civic and fraternal life of Augusta. His father, Arthur Cyr, born at Grand Isle, Maine, is a farmer. His mother, who was Marie Violette, was also born at Grand Isle. The family members trace their ancestry to the Acadians.

Paul Arthur Cyr was born June 30, 1895, at Grand Isle, Maine. He entered the local public schools and later attended St. Mary's College at Van Buren, Maine, and the Baltimore College of Dental Surgery, from which he was graduated in 1918, with the degree of Doctor of Dental Surgery, and where he was a member of Psi Omega Dental Fraternity, Alpha Chapter. On December 19, 1917, he enlisted in the United States Army, serving as a first lieutenant of the Reserve Corps until his discharge on March 5, 1919. Soon afterwards, on May 1, 1919, he began the practice of general dentistry at No. 341 Water Street, Augusta, Maine, where he has remained since.

Politically, Dr. Cyr is a member of the Republican party. He is affiliated, fraternally, with the Knights of Columbus, the Benevolent and Protective Order of Elks, and the American Legion. He is also a member of the Augusta Chamber of Commerce, the Calumet Club, and the American, Maine State, and Kennebec County Dental associations. He and his family attend the local Roman Catholic church.

On June 15, 1920, at Augusta, Maine, Dr. Paul A. Cyr married Ida Marie Lacombe who was born at Augusta on October 22, 1899. She is the daughter of Joseph and Lucy (Belanger) Lacombe, the both natives of Canada. Dr. and Mrs. Cyr are the parents of several children, all born at Augusta: Paul A., Jr., Raymond L., Jeanette Ida, and Pauline. Dr. Cyr and his family reside on Riverside Drive, Augusta.

H. CLAIR MILLER—On three evenings each week H. Clair Miller provides for the residents of Winthrop, Maine, and for those who dwell in the rural district surrounding Winthrop, diversion and recreation in the form of plays and moving pictures. He purchased an old church building, which he completely remodeled, and since engaging in the theatrical and motion picture business he has been uniformly successful. Mr. Miller is a graduate of Bates College, and is active in local public affairs, serving at the present time (1928) as vice-president of the Winthrop Chamber of Commerce.

H. Clair Miller was born in Readfield, Maine, July 24, 1887, son of Henry P. Miller, who was born in Halifax, Nova Scotia, and who has been engaged in the marble and granite business in Readfield and Winthrop for fifty years, and of Juliana (McCarty) Miller, a native of Auburn, Maine. He received his earliest school training in the public schools of Readfield, and then continued his studies in Winthrop High School, from which he was graduated. He then entered Bates College, completing his course there with graduation in 1909, receiving the degree of Bachelor of Arts. For two years after his graduation from college he was engaged in teaching in the high school at Boothbay, Maine, he secured a position as clerk in the office of the Secretary of State, which position he held for another two years. He then became an employee of Uncle Sam as postmaster of Winthrop, Maine, and for nearly nine years he received and distributed the incoming and outgoing mails for the people of Winthrop, filling the position with an efficiency and faithfulness which won for him the warm commendation of those whom he served. He then engaged in the theatrical and motion picture business. He purchased an old church building, completely remodeled it, and began entertaining the people of Winthrop three evenings a week. He has shown discretion and sound judgment in controlling the character of entertainment presented and has met with very gratifying success. In addition to his theatrical and motion picture business, Mr. Miller is also associated with his father in the granite and marble business, in Winthrop. Along with his other interests, Mr. Miller takes an active part in civic affairs, and since 1926 has been vice-president of the Winthrop Chamber of Commerce. Politically, he gives his support to the principles and the candidates of the Democratic party. He is well known in Masonic circles, being a member of the local Lodge, of which he is a Past Master; Past High Priest of the Chapter, Royal Arch Masons; and Past Noble Grand of Crystal Lodge, Independent Order of Odd Fellows. He is also a Past Dictator of the Loyal Order of Moose. He is a member of the Kora Temple, Ancient Arabic Order Nobles of the Mystic Shrine, of Lewiston, Maine; and of Alpha Council, Royal and Select Masons; Trinity Commandery, Knights Templar, and is a member of Winthrop Grange, Patrons of Husbandry. His religious affiliation is with the Congregational church.

CHARLES E. GLOVER, Superintendent of Schools at Waterville, Maine, is a teacher of unusually wide experience in this section and Rhode Island, and one who finds time from his official duties to give liberally of himself to civic affairs. He is the son of George H. Glover, Boston merchant, a native of Dorchester, Massachusetts, and Eliza C. (Bancroft) Glover, both of whom represented leading families of this section, and are now deceased.

Charles E. Glover is a native of Boston, Massachusetts, where he attended the public schools. Having determined to become a teacher, he matriculated at the Bridgewater Normal School, from which institution he was graduated in the class of 1891. For two years he took courses in pedagogy in Brown University at Providence, Rhode Island, after which he taught at that city for six years. For six years he filled the office of Superintendent of Schools at Warwick, Rhode Island. He then withdrew for the time from the teaching field and traveled for five years for a Boston publishing house, returning to the teaching field as Superintendent of Schools at Fort Fairfield, Maine. Next, in June, 1924, he came to Waterville as superintendent of the school system. It will be seen that Mr. Glover has thus been in the harness of instructor for approximately thirty years, during which time he has indelibly impressed his character and personality upon the lives of thousands of pupils.

Mr. Glover is thorough and accurate in his methods; he is progressive but at the same time not overly so, suiting the needs of the pupils to modern conditions but retaining the best in the old. He takes no active interest in politics, but is an adherent of the tenets of the Republican party. He has been recognized by his elevation to some of the highest offices among his associates and contemporaries, including president of the Kennebec County Teachers' Association and the Maine State Teachers' Association. He is a valued member of the National Education Association, the National Association of School Superintendents, and the Northeastern Association of School Superintendents. He

is a director in the Waterville Rotary Club and a leading member of the Chamber of Commerce. He has been through the Blue Lodge, Free and Accepted Masons, and is active in the membership of the Independent Order of Odd Fellows. His religious affiliation is with the St. Mark's Protestant Episcopal Church of Waterville.

JOHN LEWIS THOMAS—Himself an accountant of long established repute, both in Maine and Connecticut, John Lewis Thomas is equipped by long experience as a business teacher, director and executive, as the proprietor of the first-class business school that bears his name, the Thomas Business College, in Watervile, to give the mind of youth in preparation for careers in general business. As an accountant and as a business manager, Mr. Thomas possesses the distinguished regard of business firms and of civic institutions, in both of which he has rendered the service of expert accountant. He is a son of William Thomas, a native of Birmingham, England, a coppersmith at Peterborough, New Hampshire, and Mary A. (Jones) Thomas, who was born in Dudley, England.

John Lewis Thomas was born January 25, 1888, at Cliftondale, Massachusetts, and he attended the public and high schools at Peterborough, New Hampshire. He took the accounting course at the Connecticut Business University, New Haven, Connecticut, where he was graduated in 1909. After a brief period of employment with the New York, New Haven & Hartford Railroad, he began to teach in the Connecticut Business University, so continuing until 1911, when he removed to Waterville, where he bought out the plant that has been successfully developed as Thomas Business College, and where he is also widely known as a public accountant.

The Republican party claims Mr. Thomas' political activities, and during 1916-1918, he held the office of city auditor of Waterville. He is first lieutenant in the Officers' Reserve, Quartermaster's Corps, United States Army. Fraternally, Mr. Thomas is affiliated with the Free and Accepted Masons, in the Ancient Accepted Scottish Rite; and the Knights of Pythias, Past Chancellor Commander, and now (1928) District Deputy, both at Waterville; also Peterborough, New Hampshire, Grange, No. 35, Patrons of Husbandry, and he is a communicant of the Protestant Episcopal church.

John Lewis Thomas married, February 19, 1912, at New Haven, Connecticut, Helen A. Hecht, daughter of Samuel and Catherine (McGarty) Hecht, and they are the parents of two children: Briley M., and John L., Jr.

ELISHA PRATT—One of the well-known bankers of Rumford, Maine, is Elisha Pratt, president of the Rumford Falls Trust Company, who has been identified with this well-known financial institution since 1895, and has been its president since 1926. Mr. Pratt was formerly engaged in teaching, and was Superintendent of Schools in Turner, Maine. He has also served in the State Legislature.

Elisha Pratt was born in Turner, Maine, October 23, 1856, son of Timothy and Betsy (Jones) Pratt. He received his education in Coburn Classical Institute, Maine, and then was engaged in teaching for several years. Later, in 1895, he was made treasurer of the Rumford Falls Trust Company, and his connection with this financial institution has been continuous since that time. He continued as treasurer until 1926, when he was made president, which official position he is still (1928) filling. Mr. Pratt gives his support to the principles and the candidates of the Republican party, and has always been interested in civic affairs. He was Superintendent of Schools at Turner, Maine, for some time, and was also chosen by his associates to represent them in the State Legislature. He is a member of the local Lodge, Free and Accepted Masons; of the Independent Order of Odd Fellows; of the Knights of Pythias, and of the Rotary Club. His religious affiliation is with the Universalist church.

Elisha Pratt was married, at Turner, Maine, May 1, 1884, to Ada M. Berry.

LEWIS M. IRISH—For nearly three decades Lewis M. Irish has been identified with the business life of Rumford, Maine, and during all that period he has been associated with the Rumford Falls Trust Company, of which he is now (1928) treasurer and secretary.

Lewis M. Irish was born in Hartford, Maine, May 27, 1879, son of Horace A. Irish, a native of Hartford, Maine, who was engaged in the die block manufacturing business in Buckfield, Maine, was a Republican in his political principles, and died December 31, 1905, and of Virginia A. (Mason) Irish, who was born in Frederick, Maryland, and who survives her husband. He attended the public schools of Buckfield, and after completing his high school course entered Gray's Business College, in Portland, Maine. In 1899 he became associated with the Rumford Falls Trust Company, as clerk, and since that time his connection with this bank has been continuous. In 1902 he was promoted to the position of assistant treasurer, in 1927 he was made treasurer and secretary. During the more than a quarter of a century which has passed since he became connected with the bank, he has given able and faithful attention to the duties of these official positions, and has been one of the important factors in the maintenance and development of the bank. In addition to his connection with the bank he is also interested in the Ellingwood Novelty Company, of Buckfield, Maine, a concern engaged in the manufacture of brush and dye blocks. He is a Republican in his political sympathies, and is a member of the Free and Accepted Masons; also of the Royal Arch Masons. Mr. Irish is one of the well-known citizens of Rumford, is a member of the Rotary Club, and has many friends in this community and in Buckfield.

Lewis M. Irish was married, in Rumford, Maine, June 6, 1906, to Julia A. Jones, daughter of Benjamin and Clara M. (Berry) Jones, and they have three children: Benjamin J., Horace M., and Maynard M.

ELISHA L. STETSON—Some twenty-three years ago Elisha L. Stetson entered the employ of the Rumford Falls Trust Company, as clerk. Since 1911 he has been cashier in the Dixfield, Maine, branch of that bank, and he has also engaged in the insurance business in Dixfield for some years.

Elisha L. Stetson was born in Hartford, Maine, March 7, 1883, and is a son of Lewis Stetson, a

farmer and a supporter of the Republican political party, and of Martha (Alley) Stetson, both natives of Hartford, Maine, the last-mentioned of whom died in June, 1912. Mr. Stetson attended the public schools of Hartford, and then became a student in Leavitt Institute, at Turner, Maine, from which he was graduated with the class of 1903. The following year he became associated with the Rumford Falls Trust Company, as clerk, and since that time his connection with the Rumford Falls Trust Company has been continuous. In 1911 he was made cashier of the Dixfield branch of the bank, and that responsible position he is still most acceptably filling (1928). He is also engaged in the insurance business in Dixfield, and is active in its affairs. Like the majority of the residents of the State of Maine, he is a supporter of the Republican party. He served as a member of the School Board for a period of ten years, and for two years was town treasurer. Fraternally, he is identified with Lodge No. 57, Free and Accepted Masons, of which he is a Past Master, and his religious membership is with the Congregational church, which he serves as a member of the board of trustees.

Elisha L. Stetson was married, in Rumford, Maine, June 23, 1908, to Lucy L. Jones, who was born in Turner, Maine, daughter of Benjamin, deceased, and of Clara (Berry) Jones, who is living (1928). Mr. and Mrs. Stetson have two children: 1. Clara M., born July 13, 1909. 2. Robert L., born June 3, 1914.

WARREN BIGELOW SANBORN, M. D.—A specialist in pediatrics, Warren Bigelow Sanborn ministers especially in his medical practice in Augusta to the children of the community who are ill or injured. Dr. Sanborn has been conducting a general practice as a physician in Augusta since 1922, when he came to this city from Winthrop, Maine, where he had had his offices for the ten preceding years. In addition to his general practice here he is very active in medical circles, especially in this section of Maine, where he has held public office and has participated in the work of the associations existing in his profession.

He was born in Augusta, on February 3, 1878, the son of Bigelow T. Sanborn, a native of Standish, Maine, who for forty-two years was superintendent of the Maine Insane Hospital, and of Emma (Martin) Sanborn, who was born in Augusta. Dr. Sanborn, when a boy, attended the public schools of Augusta; went to Cony High School, Augusta, from which he was graduated in the class of 1898; then to Brown University, from which he was graduated in the class of 1902; and finally to the Atlantic Medical College, in Baltimore, Maryland, from which he was graduated in the class of 1908. He first practiced as a physician in Winthrop, Maine, where he remained from 1912 until 1922; then he came to Augusta, where he took up a general practice, specializing in a subject that always had interested him especially, diseases of children. Active in medical circles, he is a trustee of the Maine State Hospital; Medical Examiner of Kennebec County; past chairman of the Augusta Red Cross Chapter; director of the Young Men's Christian Association of Augusta, and State medical director of the State Young Men's Christian Association; a member of the American Medical Association, the Maine State

Medical Association, and the Kennebec County Medical Association; and a member of the staff of the Augusta General Hospital. September 1, 1927, he accepted the position of Superintendent of Augusta General Hospital. He also is affiliated with the Augusta Country Club and with the Augusta Chamber of Commerce. Politically, he is identified with the Republican party. He and his family are members of the Congregational church.

In Winthrop, on April 12, 1912, Warren B. Sanborn married Helen Gale, who was born in Winthrop, on August 2, 1888, the daughter of Harry and Winifred (Noyes) Gale, both natives of Winthrop. Dr. Warren Bigelow and Helen (Gale) Sanborn are the parents of one child, Jane, who was born in Winthrop, on June 16, 1919.

LEROY E. WILLIAMS—Nineteen years of continuous service in the cause of education as Superintendent of Schools and the presidency for a time of the Maine Teachers' Association, have brought into State-wide prominence Leroy E. Williams, Superintendent of Schools at Rumford, Maine. He is a man of learning and ability and a pedagogue and school administrator of wide experience.

Mr. Williams was born in Bowdoinham, Maine, April 26, 1878, and educated at the public and high school there. He attended Bates College, graduating in 1901 with the degree of Bachelor of Arts, and he subsequently continued to take up courses in line with his work, acquiring the degree of Master of Arts from Bates in 1927. He first taught school at Lisbon Falls, and for five years was principal of the high school. From this post, in which he proved his fitness for further responsibility, he was advanced to the position of superintendent of the Lisbon Falls district and held office for three years. From Lisbon Falls he went to Mt. Desert as superintendent for five years. It was in 1916 that he came to Rumford, where he has since been Superintendent of Schools, thus rounding out nineteen years in that administrative capacity and attaining the unique distinction of being the oldest district superintendent in point of tenure of office in the State of Maine. Mr. Williams is a member of the National Education Association and of the Department of Superintendents of the national body.

ARTHUR E. FORBES—As treasurer and manager of the Arthur E. Forbes Company, Incorporated, Arthur E. Forbes is at the head of one of the well-known publishing concerns of Oxford County, and is editor and publisher of the Oxford "Democrat," one of the most progressive local news sheets of this section of the State of Maine.

Arthur E. Forbes was born in Paris, Maine, May 30, 1862, and is a son of Elbridge Forbes, a farmer, who was born in Massachusetts, but lived all but his early years in Paris, and Angeline (Thayer) Forbes, who also lived in Paris nearly all her life.

After attending the public schools of Paris, Mr. Forbes, in 1878, entered the office of the Oxford "Democrat" as a printer's apprentice, and worked three years in that capacity. He then entered St. Lawrence University at Canton, New York, from which he was graduated with the class of 1885. After graduation he again went to work in the office of the Oxford "Democrat" as a printer, and in

the fall of 1885 he, in company with George M. Atwood, purchased the business. The plant was then located at Paris Hill, but in 1895 it was removed to South Paris, where it has since remained.

The business was conducted by the partnership of Atwood & Forbes from 1885 until January 1, 1926, when Mr. Atwood sold his interest to Fred W. Sanborn of Norway. A little later the business was incorporated under the name of Arthur E. Forbes Company, of which Mr. Forbes is treasurer and manager.

Mr. Forbes has always been actively interested in the welfare of Paris, served on the School Board at one time, and he has also served two terms in the State Legislature, 1919-20, and 1921-22. He is a member of the Masonic Order, Blue Lodge, and Chapter; and of the Order of the Eastern Star, and he is the oldest living member of the Maine Press Association. His religious interest is with the Universalist church.

WALTER L. GRAY—For nearly three decades Walter L. Gray has been successfully engaged in general legal practice in Paris, Maine. He is a graduate of Colby College, Waterville, where he took both the Bachelor's and the Master's degrees, and he was admitted to the bar in 1899. In addition to his legal activities, Mr. Gray is also general manager of the Mason Manufacturing Company, of Paris, a concern which is engaged in the manufacture of toy furniture.

William L. Gray, father of Mr. Gray, was born in Paris, Maine, received his education here, and then became a painter. He gave his support to the Republican party, and upon the outbreak of the Civil War enlisted in the Twenty-third Maine Regiment, later being transferred to the Thirty-second Regiment, serving altogether for more than two years. He was wounded at Gettysburg. He married Matilda J. Morse, who was born in Dixmont, Maine, and both are now deceased.

Walter L. Gray, son of William L. and Matilda J. (Morse) Gray, was born in Paris, Maine, January 24, 1870, and received his earliest school training in the public schools of Paris. He prepared for college in Hebron Academy, from which he was graduated, and then entered Colby College, at Waterville, Maine, where he graduated with the class of 1895, receiving at that time the degree of Bachelor of Arts. The degree of Master of Arts was conferred on him at the Commencement in 1926. Like so many of the legal profession in Maine, especially those who have long been engaged in practice, Mr. Gray began his active career as a teacher, continuing to teach for three years, but giving all his spare time to the study of law. On February 18, 1899, he was admitted to the bar, and he at once opened an office for general practice in Paris, where he has since been continuously engaged. For some seven years he was a partner of Judge Wilson, but Judge Wilson died March 4, 1906, and since that time Mr. Gray has practiced alone. He is a trustee of Hebron Academy, and as general manager of the Mason Manufacturing Company, of Paris, Maine, has demonstrated his business ability. He has been vice-president of the Paris Trust Company since 1925, and vice-president of the Norway National Bank, 1917. He is a member of the board of directors of both banks and is well known in financial circles in this part of the State.

In his political convictions he is a Republican, and in 1905 he was chosen to represent his district in the State Legislature. He is referee in bankruptcy, and during the period of the participation of the United States in the World War he served as chairman of the local board. Mr. Gray is a member of the Oxford County Bar Association, the Maine State Bar Association, and the American Bar Association. Fraternally, he is identified with the Masonic Order, holding membership in Blue Lodge, Chapter, Commandery, and Shrine; and with the Knights of Pythias. He is a member and was first president of the Kiwanis Club, and his religious affiliation is with the Congregational church. Mr. Gray, in addition to the various business responsibilities mentioned above, is also secretary of the Building and Loan Association.

Walter L. Gray was married, in Paris, Maine, June 14, 1899, to Madge S. Wilson, who was born in Paris, Maine, daughter of Judge George A. and Annie (Blake) Wilson, both of whom are deceased.

IRVING O. BARROWS—Possessing the good will of his fellow-citizens, and the high regard and confidence of his associates in the financial world, Irving O. Barrows holds those positions of leadership in the banking institutions of Paris and South Paris that have been secured solely through his life-long application to the various branches of banking, and his well-proven abilities to carry on the important duties of finance. Mr. Barrows has also held with distinction a number of civic positions, therein, too, meeting the requirements of his constituency, and substantially aiding township and community in their progress.

Irving O. Barrows was born March 13, 1892, at South Paris, a son of Oscar E. Barrows, who has retired from the lumber industry and is a Republican in his political views, and Eunice (Porter) Barrows, both parents natives of Paris, and both residing in that township. Mr. Barrows received his education in the public and high schools of South Paris, and in 1910, he first became associated with banking matters as clerk of the Paris Trust Company. During a brief period, however, for about six months in 1916, Mr. Barrows turned his attention to the lumbering interests, but in June of the following year, 1917, he received his appointment to his present treasurership with the Trust Company. He is also a member of the board of trustees of the South Paris Savings Bank, having been connected with the duties of that position since 1925. Mr. Barrows has always been affiliated with the Republican party; and for a year he held the office of tax collector of Paris. He was also secretary of the Board of Trade for three years.

In Masonic matters, Mr. Barrows is an active factor: he is a member of the local Lodge of the Free and Accepted Masons; the Royal Arch Chapter; the Commandery, Knights Templar; the Consistory, Ancient Accepted York Rite; and the Temple, Ancient Arabic Order Nobles of the Mystic Shrine. He is also a member of the Knights of Pythias; and of the Kiwanis Club, and the Paris Hill Country Club. His religious faith is that of the Congregational church, and in all the departments of the work of that church he is active and prominent.

Irving O. Barrows married, August 11, 1915, at South Paris, Ada Turner, daughter of Frank A. and Bertha (Keene) Turner.

ALDEN B. HAYES—As Superintendent of the Public Schools of South Paris and Woodstock, Maine, Alden B. Hayes has been rendering most efficient service since 1922, a period of five years. Mr. Hayes is a graduate of the University of Maine, and had been engaged in teaching some six years prior to his appointment as Superintendent of the Schools of Paris and Woodstock.

Frederick F. Hayes, father of Mr. Hayes, was born in Sebec, Maine, and during the early years of his active career was Superintendent of Schools at Dover-Foxcroft and Sebec. Later he entered government employ as a railroad mill clerk, and continued in that position for twenty-seven years. He was a supporter of the Democratic party, and his death occurred May 5, 1919. He married Nellie Burgess, who was born in Sebec, Maine, and who survives him.

Alden B. Hayes, son of Frederick F. and Nellie (Burgess) Hayes, was born in Sebec, Maine, August 19, 1891, and received his earliest school training in the public schools of Bangor, Maine. When his course in the Bangor High School was completed, he matriculated in the University of Maine, from which he was graduated with the class of 1914, receiving at that time the degree of Bachelor of Science. For two years after the completion of his college course he served as an engineer in the employ of the Draper Corporation of Hopedale, Massachusetts, and then returned to Bangor and accepted a position as assistant in the Mechanic Arts department of the public schools of Bangor. Two years later he was made head of the department in that same school, and that position he filled for four years, until 1922. In that year he came to South Paris as Superintendent of the Schools of Paris and of Woodstock, Maine, and here he has since then located. Mr. Hayes has won in a high degree the confidence and esteem of those with whom he has been associated, and in the leadership which he has established among his students he is rendering a valuable service to the community. Politically, he gives his support to the principles and the candidates of the Republican party. He is a member of St. Andrew's Lodge, Free and Accepted Masons, of Bangor; of Mount Moriah Chapter, Royal Arch Masons, of Bangor; and of St. John Commandery, Knights Templar, of Bangor. He is a Past Patron of Tuscan Chapter, Order of the Eastern Star, of Bangor. Professionally, he is identified with the National Education Society, with the Oxford County Teachers' Association, and with the Oxford County Schoolmasters' Association, of which he is president; also with the Maine State Teachers' Association. His religious affiliation is with the Universalist Church of Bangor, Maine.

Alden B. Hayes was married, at Bangor, Maine, September 21, 1915, to Mildred Williams, who was born in Millbridge, Maine, daughter of J. Tilden, a carpenter, who was born in Great Pond, Maine, and of Carrie (Sprague) Williams, a native of Millbridge, Maine, both of whom are deceased.

GEORGE M. ATWOOD—To men of the energies and abilities of George M. Atwood is rightly accredited Paris' place and progress among the long-established townships of present-day enterprise in this State, for, through his active contact with law matters, finance, civics and journalism, he has fully met with the requirements of a high standard of citizenship, his personal attainments in both business and professional matters being utilized for community welfare.

George M. Atwood was born October 6, 1860, at Buckfield, a son of William H. Atwood, a native of Calais, and a merchant at Buckfield for fifty years, and Helen M. (Atwood) Atwood, who was born in Buckfield. Mr. Atwood attended the public schools of his native town, and taking the preparatory course at Hebron Academy, he matriculated at Columbia University Law School, where he was graduated in 1885 with the degree of Bachelor of Laws. As half owner of the Oxford "Democrat," Mr. Atwood was associated with Arthur E. Forbes for forty years, at South Paris; and entering the field of finance in 1900 actively as treasurer of the Savings Bank, of which he had been a member of the board of directors for forty years, he continues in that treasurership to the present. A Republican in political matters, Mr. Atwood has always maintained that party's interests. He has been a member of the South Paris School Board for seventeen years; and he served with a well-recognized efficiency as Oxford County treasurer from 1889 to 1927. He is a member of the board of directors and the executive committee of the Paris Trust Company at Manavista, Florida; has served as a member of the board of trustees of Hebron Academy; and since 1885 he has been a member of the Oxford County Bar Association. He is treasurer of the Paris Hill Country Club.

George M. Atwood married, April 5, 1886, at Portland, Anna Harlow, of Dixfield, daughter of Elbridge G. and Roselle (Stanley) Harlow; and they have children: 1. William E. 2. Raymond L., who was a first lieutenant in the Naval Aviation Corps, during the World War.

IRVILL HARRY CHENEY—In fostering and aiding the agricultural industry within its borders, the State of Maine has made important advances within recent years with the able assistance of men thoroughly trained in this work, men who have the best interests of their commonwealth ever in mind. One of the most prominent men in this work, Irvill Harry Cheney, is superintendent of the Maine Agricultural Experiment Station, located at Monmouth, having been appointed to this responible position in 1926, and ever since continuing to conduct the affairs of this model organization with increasing success. The establishment which Mr. Cheney manages covers four hundred acres of land and is continually engaged in experimenting in all varieties of farm problems. By its researches and discoveries, it has materially aided the progress of agriculture in this State. Mr. Cheney was born in Auburn, March 1, 1894, son of Harry and Florence Cheney. Harry Cheney was active in the affairs of his community for many years and is now living retired.

Irvill Harry Cheney was educated in the public schools of Auburn, and attended the Edward Little High School in that city, graduating from the Brunswick High School with the class of 1912. He entered the employ of the Pepperell Manufacturing

Company, at Biddeford, in 1914, to learn the textile business and he remained with this concern until 1917, when he enlisted in the United States military forces. After the war, Mr. Cheney returned to this company and remained for approximately eight weeks. Part of the time of his enlistment was spent at Harvard University, and after leaving the realm of commerce, he later entered Maine State College, from which he was graduated with the class of 1926, receiving his degree of Bachelor of Science. Immediately upon graduating, he accepted his present post with the State and by the results which he has achieved, has justified the wisdom of his superiors in their choice. Actively identified with fraternal affairs, he is a prominent member of Bangor Lodge, Free and Accepted Masons, having attained to the thirty-second degree in that organization, and holding membership in Anah Temple, Ancient Arabic Order Nobles of the Mystic Shrine. He is a member of George T. Files Post, No. 20, American Legion, and in politics, is a staunch supporter of the Republican party. During the World War, he enlisted in the Navy, September 5, 1917, and saw much active service as a radio operator during those troublous times, distinguishing himself by efficient performance of the duties entrusted to him. He received his discharge September 21, 1919.

Irvill Harry Cheney married, May 4, 1914, at Brunswick, Gladys Umberhind, of Bath, daughter of George and Margaret Umberhind, both natives of Richmond. To this union have been born two children: James, born at Saco, and Margaret, born at Biddeford.

HARRY M. SHAW—The prosperity and the general civic advancement of South Paris are due in no small measure to the lifelong interest that has been taken in its institutions, and its business and professional status by its native sons. Both township and county have benefited from the activities of Harry M. Shaw who, in a distinctly public-spirited way, has aided the general progress of this community in his professional associations as an attorney-at-law, and in those of local office. He is a son of Calvin W. Shaw, a farmer, who was a Republican in politics, and whose death occurred October 29, 1925, and Achsa (Durrell) Shaw, who died September 18, 1920, both parents natives of Paris.

Harry M. Shaw was born January 17, 1885, at Paris, and after receiving the benefits of the public and high schools there, he prepared for his profession at the Law School of the University of Maine, where he was graduated in 1915. He was admitted to the bar in 1917, and after practicing for two years at South Paris in the office of J. S. Wright, he established himself in his own name in 1919. He is now counsel for the South Paris Savings Bank. A staunch Republican in his political views, Mr. Shaw has aided his party interests both in office and by his vote and influence; and he performed the duties of tax collector for South Paris during 1917-1925, inclusive. His county attorneyship in 1921-1923 gave added honors to the traditions of that office; and his fellow-citizens are sure of his very capable administration of the affairs of the Oxford County treasurership, an office he now holds.

Mr. Shaw is a member of the Oxford County Bar Association, and the Maine State Bar Association. His fraternal affiliations are with the Free and Accepted Masons; the Royal Arch Chapter of Masons; Old Fellowship and its Encampment; and the Knights of Pythias; and he is also a member of the Paris Hill Country Club. He is treasurer and chairman of the board of trustees of the Universalist church.

Harry M. Shaw married, June 23, 1917, at Buckfield, Maine, Alice E. Allen, who was born in that town, a daughter of Charles Vernon and Edna (Holland) Allen. They have one son, Carl Vernon Shaw, born May 18, 1924.

DR. DELBERT M. STEWART—Twenty-two years of faithful and successful medical practice have placed Dr. Delbert M. Stewart high in the esteem of the people of South Paris, Maine, where he has been ministering to a large patronage since the beginning of his professional career. Dr. Stewart has ushered into the world, kept in the world, and eased and cured the ills of three generations of some of the families of South Paris, and his patients, both old and young, are numbered among his personal friends. He is Town Health Officer and has served as a member of the School Board.

Dr. Delbert M. Stewart was born in Wales, Maine, September 13, 1875, son of Joseph L. Stewart, a farmer of Wales, and an Independent Republican, who was born in Lewiston, Maine, and of Mary E. (Murch) Stewart. Mr. Stewart received his early education in Monmouth Academy and in Nichols Latin School, and then entered Bates College, at Lewiston, Maine, from which he was graduated in 1899, with the degree of Bachelor of Arts. In order to pay his educational expenses, Mr. Stewart worked in a shoe store. He taught night school for a time and was a reader for the Glee Club. From 1899-1901, he was principal of the Kittery High School. Having decided upon the medical profession as his future field of service, he began professional study in the Medical School of the University of Maine, from which he was graduated in 1904 with the degree of Doctor of Medicine. For a year and a half following his graduation he was assistant surgeon in the National Home for Disabled Volunteer Soldiers, at Togus, Maine. He then opened an office in South Paris, Maine, and since that time has been continuously and successfully engaged in general practice here. Dr. Stewart is one of the skilled and faithful family physicians who give to their patients the best they have, and who never spare themselves in the service of their fellows. He is known and esteemed in South Paris and in a wide section surrounding this community, and during the nearly a quarter of a century of his practice here he has made and kept many friends. Dr. Stewart is a member of the State Medical Association, of the Oxford County Medical Association, and of the American Medical Association, and is highly regarded by his professional associates. In addition to his professional activities, he is also a member of the board of directors of the Paris Trust Company, of which he is also secretary and a member of the executive board. He is a Republican in his political convictions, and for the last three years has served as Health Officer of South Paris. He has also served as a member of the School Board. During the period of the participation of the United States in the World War, Dr. Stewart served as a captain in the Medical Corps. He was stationed at Camp Fort

McKinley for a year and at Camp Custer, Michigan, for another year. He received his discharge in 1919, and at once returned to his practice at South Paris. Fraternally, Dr. Stewart is affiliated with the Knights of Pythias, the Free and Accepted Masons, in which Order he is also identified with the Shrine; and he is a member of the local Grange, Patrons of Husbandry. He was formerly a member of the board of directors of the Building & Loan Association, and he is now (1928) president of the library board. He is a member of the Kiwanis Club, and of the Paris Hill Country Club, and his religious affiliation is with the Congregational church.

HENRY H. HASTINGS—Since his admission to the bar, in 1899, Henry H. Hastings has been engaged in general legal practice in Bethel, Maine, where he is known for his sound knowledge, his discernment, and his resourcefulness in handling cases. He is a member of the board of directors of the Paris Trust Company, and has for years been active in promoting the interests of education in this district.

Henry H. Hastings was born in Bethel, Maine, March 25, 1865, son of St. John Hastings, a native of Bethel, who was engaged in farming here to the time of his death, and who was a zealous Republican, and of Elizabeth (Atherton) Hastings. Mr. Hastings received his early school training in the public schools of Bethel, and then prepared for college in Gould Academy, after which he entered Bowdoin College, at Brunswick, Maine, from which he was graduated with the class of 1890, receiving the degree of Bachelor of Arts. After completing his college course he began the study of law, but taught school to pay his way, and continued in both the teaching and the legal study until October, 1899, when he was admitted to the bar. He at once engaged in practice in Bethel, and has continued to the present time (1928). During the twenty-eight years in which he has been continuously engaged in practice, Mr. Hastings has built up a very large clientele, and has made himself known not only as an able attorney but also as a shrewd business man and a public-spirited citizen. He served in the State Legislature in 1903-05, and was State Senator in 1907-09. He is president of the Bethel Water Company and a member of the board of directors of the Paris Trust Company, in which capacity his legal knowledge and his keen sense of values have been valuable. Mr. Hastings has also found time for a large amount of public service. He was appointed by Governor Baxter as chairman of the Board of Prison Commissioners and at present is chairman of that board. He was a member of Governor Baxter's Council, 1921-22; served as a member of the Town Committee for many years, and has been a member of the State Republican Committee for several years. He has served as Probate Judge since 1925. In local affairs he is active, and is especially interested in education. For thirteen years he served as Superintendent of Schools. Professionally, Mr. Hastings keeps closely in touch with the various legal organizations. He is a member of the Oxford County Bar Association and Maine State Bar Association, and among his colleagues is highly esteemed. His religious affiliation is with the Congregational church, and he is a member of the board.

Henry H. Hastings married, February 16, 1916,

Ethel M. Richardson, and they have one child: Henry H., Jr., born October 13, 1918.

CARL B. LORD—An admirable record in scholarship, excellent patriotic service during the World War, and an engaging personality, have combined to place Carl B. Lord, of North Vassalboro, in the foremost ranks of the educational workers of the State of Maine, despite his comparative youth.

Born in Liberty, Maine, May 13, 1894, the son of William A. and Sadie J. (Weagle) Lord, he received his early education in the schools of Vassalboro. His father, who is still living, was a grocer there for many years, and active in the affairs of the Republican Town Committee. He was born in Montville, Maine. On being graduated from the local schools, Carl B. Lord continued his studies at Oak Grove Academy, and received its diploma in 1911. He enrolled for the scientific course at Colby College, and was graduated with the degree of Bachelor of Science, in 1915. He next took a special course in the Graduate School, and at the beginning of the World War, underwent an intensive course of training at Annapolis. He was commissioned as ensign in the United States Naval Reserve Corps, and assigned to the Pay Corps of the Navy, where he served until peace was restored. Returning to New England, he taught school for a year in Massachusetts, and was then offered and accepted the post of principal of the public school at Winslow, Maine, and four years lated was Superintendent of the Public Schools of Winslow, Vassalboro and China, Maine. A Republican, like his father, he has never held office, but retains his commission in the United States Naval Reserve Corps.

Mr. Lord is a member of the Free and Accepted Masons, and Senior Warden of the Blue Lodge; a member of the Alpha Tau Omega Fraternity of Colby College, and of the American Legion. He is also one of the trustees of the Baptist church at Vassalboro.

Carl B. Lord married, June 10, 1919, Bessie Clarke, of Washington, District of Columbia, and their children are: Bernice M., and John W.

FRANK L. ELLIOTT—As manager of the Oakland branch of the Augusta Trust Company, Frank L. Elliott is one of the most prominent citizens of Oakland. He was born May 8, 1894, in Portland, Maine, a son of John and Anna C. (Peterson) Elliott, both of whom are now deceased. John Elliott was born in Kings Court, New Brunswick, and followed the blacksmith trade in Portland until his death in 1900.

Frank L. Elliott received his education in the public schools of Portland, and after school days were over, became associated with the banking business, whih he has followed ever since. His first position was with the Fidelity Trust Company of Portland, where he remained until 1916. In that year he resigned from this position to enter the employ of the Casco Mercantile Trust Company of Portland, serving as assistant credit manager until September, 1920. In July, 1917, the Casco Mercantile Trust Company granted him a leave of absence when he was called into active service. He later removed to Houlton, Maine, to become assistant cashier of the Farmers' National Bank, remaining there until 1921, when he resigned his position and

removed to Oakland, Maine, accepting the post of cashier in the Messalonskee National Bank. His deep sense of integrity, probity and conscientiousness have placed him high in the estimation of his fellows and when the Messalonskee National Bank was purchased, in 1924, by the Augusta Trust Company, Mr. Elliott was retained as manager, a position which he holds at the present time.

During the period of the World War, Mr. Elliott was granted a leave of absence from the Casco Mercantile Trust Company of Portland to enlist in the Coast Artillery Corps, Maine National Guard, March, 1917. In March, 1917, he enlisted in the Eleventh Company, Coast Artillery Corps, Maine National Guard, which was called into active service in July, 1917, and spent eight months in training at Fort McKinley. He was sent overseas in 1918 with the Fifty-fourth Artillery Corps as waggoner, but was transferred to the Sixtieth Coast Artillery Corps, Battery C, with which outfit he took active part in the St. Mihiel Offensive and the battles of the Meuse-Argonne. Mr. Elliott received his honorable discharge in February, 1919.

Despite the many duties which his work has entailed, Mr. Elliott has nevertheless found time in which to take a keen and active interest in other affairs. He is a member of the Chamber of Commerce and has served this organization as its secretary and a director. He has coached the Williams High School Basket Ball Team with great success for the past three years. In his political preference he is a member of the Republican party, and in his fraternal affiliations is a member of all the Masonic bodies up to the Consistory, Scottish Rite, and the Chapter and Council in the York Rite; he also is enrolled with the American Legion. In 1920, Mr. Elliott was finance officer of the American Legion Post of Portland. He was also Vice-Commander of the Harry Decker Post, No. 51, American Legion, at Oakland, and in 1925 was made Commander, a position he held for one term; also other service since 1922. In 1926 he became Grand Correspondent for the Société 40 Hommes et 8 Chevaux. He served the Legion as county committeeman for Aroostook County in 1921, and in 1926 served in the same capacity for Kennebec County.

Frank L. Elliott married, July 6, 1917, at Portland, Maine, Helen O. Stuart, who was born in Machiasport, Maine, a daughter of Isaac N. and Ina Stuart. Mr. and Mrs. Elliott are attendants of the Universalist Church of Oakland.

WILL CLOUGH ATKINS—Probably no man has been more active in many of the phases of public life of Gardiner than Will Clough Atkins, who has been practicing law here since he was admitted to the bar in Kennebec County in 1894, and who now holds the office of Judge in the Gardiner Municipal Court. Not only is he active in the public life of his community, but also holds directorship in local banks and financial institutions and membership in a number of fraternal orders.

The son of Edwin H. and Mary E. (Clough) Atkins, he was born in Hallowell on August 25, 1873. He received his education in the public schools of Gardiner; at Yale University, from which he received the degree of Bachelor of Laws in 1896; and at Bates College, which awarded him the degree of Master of Arts in 1915. Professing the political views of the Republican party, he was elected to several local offices on the Republican ticket. He was city solicitor; president of the Common Council of Gardiner; president of the Board of Aldermen; and mayor of Gardiner in 1907-1908. He has been recorder of the Gardiner Municipal Court and judge in that court since 1910, and is a past president of the Gardiner Board of Trade. He is a director of the Gardiner Trust Company, the People's National Bank, and of the Gardiner Building & Loan Association. He holds memberships in the Benevolent and Protective Order of Elks; the Free and Accepted Masons, the Knights of Pythias, and the Rotary Club. His religious affiliation is with the Universalist church. He is secretary-treasurer of Kennebec Bar Association; Kennebec Law Library Association, and Association of Municipal Court Judges.

In Farmingdale, Maine, on May 15, 1901, Will C. Atkins married Alice M. Tasker.

CHARLES H. NEWCOMB, M. D., a prominent physician and surgeon at Clinton, Maine, more than seventeen years, has done a general practice and surgery there, and has occupied a number of responsible positions. He also has been connected with one of the big railroads as surgeon, and saw active service in the Medical Corps, United States Army, at the front in the World War.

Charles Howard Newcomb was born at Newburg, Maine, September 8, 1880, son of Augustus and Elizabeth (Nealey) Newcomb. The father, a farmer and Civil War veteran, who saw active service with Company A of the Twenty-first Maine Infantry, was born at Newburg, Maine, where the mother also was born. Dr. Newcomb attended the public schools, and Hammond Academy, Castine Normal School, from which he graduated in the class of 1899, and Bowdoin Medical School, from which he graduated as Doctor of Medicine in the class of 1907. He started as Medical Doctor and assistant surgeon with the Canadian Pacific Railway, with which he was connected from 1907 to 1909. From 1910, to the present time he has engaged in general practice and surgery at Clinton, Maine. He is also on the staff of the Sisters' Hospital at Waterville, Maine. During the World War he was with the American Expeditionary Forces, Medical Corps. He enlisted June 21, 1918, and was discharged June 21, 1919. He was first lieutenant and saw active service near St. Mihiel. Dr. Newcomb is a Democrat in politics, and belongs to the Free and Accepted Masons, the Independent Order of Odd Fellows, and the American, State and County Medical associations. He attends the Baptist church.

Charles H. Newcomb married, July 24, 1912, at Dexter, Maine, Elizabeth L. Moore, born at Dexter, daughter of Frank E. and Emeline L. (Ellis) Moore. Her father was born at Dexter, her mother at Levant, Maine.

SAMUEL D. SOULE, superintendent of the Water District, and one of the foremost citizens of Gardiner, Maine, was born October 20, 1868, at Woolwich, Maine, a son of Silas M. and Anna E. (Dodge) Soule, both now deceased. Silas M. Soule, the father, who was born in Woolwich, was for many years a well-known sea captain. The mother, Anna E. (Dodge) Soule, was a native of Edgecomb, Maine.

Samuel D. Soule received his early education in the public schools of Woolwich, later attending the American Business School. Upon the completion of these courses of study, he journeyed to Boston, Massachusetts, where he was employed as a baker for four years. Becoming interested in electricity, for in those days electric lighting was still a new invention, he gave up this work to go to Bar Harbor, Maine, where he started an electric light business, which he conducted successfully for four years. At the end of that time, in 1886, he went to Augusta, Maine, to take a position with the electric company there. In 1889, he removed to Gardiner, Maine, where he conducted an eelctric light business with eminent success for a number of years. In 1906, Mr. Soule was appointed superintendent of the Water District for Gardiner, a position which he has filled since with credit to himself and satisfaction to the community. He maintains his offices at No. 141 Water Street, Gardiner.

Despite the many exacting duties of the work in which he has been engaged, Mr. Soule has found time in which to serve the people of his community in other than a private capacity. For six years he was chief engineer of Gardiner. In his political preferences he is a strong adherent of the Republican party. He has been active in club and social life and affiliated with all bodies of the Masonic Order, up to and including the Shrine, and is also a member of the Shrine Club. He has been treasurer of Evergreen Encampment, Independent Order of Odd Fellows, for twenty years; is a member of the Benevolent and Protective Order of Elks, and the Modern Woodmen of America. He is also a member of the Gardiner Library Association, of which he is president and treasurer.

Samuel D. Soule married, December 22, 1895, at Gardiner, Maine, Alice W. Morrison, who was born in Greene, Maine, a daughter of Moses B. and Mary E. (Wentworth) Morrison. Mr. and Mrs. Soule are the parents of a daughter, Florence M., born September 24, 1896, and is now Mrs. Russ. Mr. and Mrs. Soule maintain their residence at No. 191 Central Avenue, Gardiner, in which community they attend the Baptist church.

CHARLES F. WALKER—Native of Gardiner, Maine, where he occupies a distinguished position in public and commercial life, Charles F. Walker was born September 19, 1872, son of James Walker, born at Litchfield, Massachusetts, deceased, and Julia (Douglas) Walker, born at Gardiner, deceased, his father having been a man of considerable importance and courage. James Walker was engaged in the manufacturing business in Gardiner, and was active in local politics, forever during his career an interested worker for the welfare of the citizenry. A Republican, he was twice elected mayor of the community; and his record of office was of the highest. He was a veteran of the Civil War, in which he fought under the Union colors for four years and nine months, leaving the service with the rank of captain, attached to the Fifteenth Maine Regiment.

Charles F. Walker received his early education in the city of his birth, and after his graduation from high school enrolled in the Dirigo Business College, at Augusta, Maine, where he acquired a comprehensive knowledge of the world of commerce. When he left business college he went into the factory owned by his father, then engaged in the manufacture of boxes; in 1902, the character of the business was altered, to the manufacture of door sashes and frames. At the present time (1928), Charles F. Walker is president and principal owner of the factory, and, as such, together with his wide connections in all phases of local affairs, is among the most enterprising men of the community. He is a Republican, and is now (1928) a member of the Board of Aldermen of Gardiner. He is a director of the Gardiner Trust Company, and affiliated with a number of fraternal organizations, including the Modern Woodmen of America; the Lodge, Free and Accepted Masons; the Temple, Ancient Arabic Order Nobles of the Mystic Shrine; Order of the Eastern Star; the Shrine Club; the Independent Order of Odd Fellows; the Benevolent and Protective Order of Elks; and the Sons of Veterans. He is a member of the Methodist church.

Charles F. Walker married, at Gardiner, October 12, 1892, Gertrude M. Hamilton, born at Pittston, Maine, daughter of Charles H. Hamilton, born in Waldo County, Maine, and Mattie (Kimball) Hamilton, born at Augusta, Maine. Mr. and Mrs. Walker are the parents of three children, the fourth, James Lee Walker, having met his death in 1912, at the age of twenty years: Madeline H., Helen D., and Dorothy.

EDWARD R. VEAZIE—The outstanding success in the great and humanitarian profession of insurance which has come to Edward R. Veazie, of Rockland, Maine, within the brief period of four years is eloquent testimony to his business ability, and his interest in his community and its citizens. He is a member of the firm of Roberts and Veazie, Incorporated. In municipal affairs he is active and constructive, holding the office of county treasurer and supporting every forward-looking movement.

Edward R. Veazie was born in Waterville, Maine, September 12, 1888, son of Edward and Mary (Fuller) Veazie. The father, born at Simonton Corner, Maine, was a prominent drygoods merchant in Waterville; the mother is a native of Rockland. The son was educated in the public and high schools of Rockland. His first position was with the wholesale grocery establishment of Francis Cobb Company, in Rockland, and lasted for eight years, during which he proved his business ability and his loyalty to the interests of employer and customers. After his honorable discharge from naval service during the World War, Mr. Veazie was for two years in the automobile business. It was in 1923 that the firm of Roberts and Veazie was estabished to care for the insurance needs of Rockland, and for four years Mr. Veazie has enjoyed remarkable success. The original firm was George Roberts Company, established in 1916. In 1922, he became an agent for this firm—in 1923 he became a partner—in 1926 the name was changed to Roberts and Veazie, Incorporated.

A Republican in politics, he was city clerk during 1915-16. So capable did he prove that in 1923 he was appointed county treasurer and filled that office with such energy and efficiency that he was elected to it in 1924, and has since continued in office. Mr. Veazie was an ensign in the United States Naval Reserve during the World War, stationed at the Boston Navy Yard, and received his discharge in July, 1919. He entered the National Guard of Maine in 1921 as second lieutenant and was transferred to the State Reserve in 1924 as first lieutenant, a rank he continues to hold.

A member of the Free and Accepted Masons, with the thirty-second degree, he belongs to all the bodies of that Order except the Ancient Arabic Order Nobles of the Mystic Shrine, and is Past Commander, Claremont Commandery, Knights Templar; and he has served as Grand Warden of the Grand Commandery of Maine. His clubs are the Fort and the Country of Rockland. He is a charter member of Winslow-Holbrook No. 1 Post of Maine. He attends the Universalist church.

On April 29, 1914, Edward R. Veazie married, at Thomaston, Maine, Katherine C. (Feehan) Andrews, daughter of John H. and Sarah (Marr) Feehan. Mrs. Veazie had a son by her former marriage, John T. Andrews, and there is a daughter born of the second union: Louise Roberts Veazie.

EDWIN R. KEENE—Varied indeed has been the career of Edwin R. Keene, who, since 1921, has been city clerk of Rockland, Maine. Mr. Keene was born at Appleton, Maine, February 25, 1870, son of Edwin S., himself a native of Appleton, and Martha E. (Wentworth) Keene, born at Camden, Maine, both deceased, his father having been by occupation a farmer and in political fealty a Republican.

Edwin R. Keene attended the public schools of Appleton, where he received his early education, and later attended the Rockland Commercial College. For a number of years following graduation from the commercial school he did clerical work, for which his training had fitted him excellently. His next employment was on a railroad; his next on a newspaper; then, in Appleton, he engaged in business with a sawmill; and finally, after having studied civil engineering, he pursued that scientific profession, in Rockland, for twenty years. From 1910 until 1918 he was connected with the State Highway Department, on construction work, and for five years was city engineer of Rockland. Mr. Keene has, since his first years of residence in Rockland, been a participant in public affairs. A Democrat, he is well acquainted with members of that party throughout the Rockland neighborhood, where he has many warm friends and admirers. In his work on the State highways, as city engineer, and as city clerk, he has won praise from those versed in the duties of the respective offices. He is one of the outstanding men of the community, a member of the Blue Lodge, Free and Accepted Masons; the Chapter, Royal Arch Masons; the Council, Royal and Select Masters, and of the Spiritualist church.

Edwin R. Keene married, at Appleton, November 18, 1893, Bessie C. Dunton, daughter of George C. and Rosetta (Arnold) Dunton. Mrs. Keene died January 10, 1910, survived by her husband, and three children: 1. Harold B., living in Nebraska. 2. Chauncey M., of Rockland. 3. A. Bertrand, of New York City, New York.

RICHARD E. DUNN—For thirty-one years has Richard E. Dunn, with his partner, Richard O. Elliot, built ships which roamed the seven seas, carrying all manner of cargoes into ports throughout the world. Perhaps no other citizen of Thomaston,

Maine, has attained so unique a place in the growth of this seafaring town, for Mr. Dunn has seen the sails he once made to carry his own and other gallant ships give way to the unromantic efficiency of steam, and the horses he once drove ashore step aside for the automobile. Yet Mr. Dunn has kept pace with these developments, for he still makes ships, some of them propelled by steam, and he owns the largest garage in Thomaston.

He was born in Thomaston, Maine, July 31, 1863, the son of Thomas W. and Eliza A. (Childs) Dunn, educated in the grammar and high school of Thomaston, and as a youth learned the trade of sailmaking. He continued this occupation for various firms in and near Thomaston, also acquiring the rudiments of shipbuilding, so that when he and Richard O. Elliot formed the partnership of Dunn and Elliot, sailmakers and shipbuilders, Mr. Dunn brought to the firm a practical knowledge of the business they were about to pursue.

Mr. Dunn, like his partner, has become interested in the financial development of Thomaston. Since 1915, he has been a director of Georges' National Bank, Thomaston, and for the past eight years he has been a vice-president of that bank. He has been a trustee of the Thomaston Savings Bank for more than three years, and is associated with many other business and financial institutions in Thomaston. He was a Democratic selectman in Thomaston for three years and served one term in the Legislature from Thomaston, being elected in 1917. Mr. Dunn is a member of the Knights of Pythias, a Past Chancellor Commander, and is actively associated with the affairs of the Congregational church in Thomaston.

Richard E. Dunn married Ella W. Watts, daughter of Alfred F. Watts, in Thomaston, October 14, 1888.

HOLLIS H. GILCHREST—Success in the granite industry for four decades and ability in the discharge of his duties as State Representative have brought into prominence as a constructive citizen Hollis H. Gilchrest, of Thomaston, Maine. He was born in St. George, in that State, June 14, 1875, son of Ira W. and Catherine (Wall) Gilchrest, both now deceased. Both were natives of St. George, and the father was a sea captain during most of his life.

After completing the course in the public schools at St. George, Mr. Gilchrest began his long association with the granite industry. This he thoroughly mastered, beginning in South Thomaston, Maine, in 1887. Since 1920, he has been a prominent factor in the monument business in Thomaston. He is likewise an outstanding political leader, for he was on the Board of Assessors for a time, and has served two terms in the State Legislature. His political alignment is with the Republican party. He belongs to the Knights of Pythias.

At Rockland, Maine, Hollis H. Gilchrest married Maud Shea, born in South Thomaston, daughter of Alden G. and Bertha (Coombs) Shea. Children: Harriet and Catherine.

CHARLES AULT—Since his advent into Maine, where he long has been established in manufacturing of shoes on a large and successful scale, Charles Ault has constantly grown in the esteem of his fellow-citizens. A man of broad vision, keen business mind, high civic interests and industrious na-

ture, he has been a valuable addition to the commercial activities of Auburn, in which city he maintains his headquarters and his home. Nor has he neglected association with matters unconnected with his mercantile operations, but rather has been a considerable factor in the growth of charitable and social organizations, while his religious affiliations have been of commanding importance.

He was born in Hagerstown, Indiana, December 19, 1882, a son of Lee and Mary E. (Bowen) Ault. Coming to Maine, he became engaged in shoe manufacturing, eventually establishing the Ault-Williamson Shoe Manufacturing Company, at Auburn, of which he is president and treasurer. He is also past president of Associated Industries and president of the Auburn Savings Bank; vice-president New England Shoe and Leather Association; director National Boot and Shoe Manufacturing Association; member of the New England Council and Maine Development Commission, and a trustee of Bates College. He is a member of the Scottish Rite and Shrine of the Masonic Order, and is a member of the Augusta Golf Club, the Auburn Golf Club, and the Mid Pines Country Club, Pinehurst, North Carolina. His politics is Republican, his church the Congregational. His residence at No. 14 Cushman Place, Auburn.

Charles Ault married (first), June 24, 1907, Lucretia Leakey, at Newcastle, Indiana. He married (second) Ruth Dobson, on September 20, 1922. His children are: Mary M., Jane B., John L., Robert D., and Richard W.

LEVI SEAVEY—Native of Maine and, since 1872, a resident in Thomaston, Maine, Levi Seavey is president and one of the board of directors of the Thomaston Savings Bank, and owner and proprietor of one of the most modern retail shops dealing in clothing and shoes in this section of the State. He was born at Cushing, July 23, 1855, son of Levi Seavey, native of Cushing, died in 1857, and Margaret U. (Wiley) Seavey, also born at Cushing, also deceased; the father having followed the sea.

Levi Seavey, the son, was educated in the public schools of Cushing, and engaged in various experiences in the world of business before he came to Thomaston. At the age of thirty-four years he purchased the retail establishment which he now (1928), controls, and devoted the succeeding years to a careful study of merchandising and the upbuilding of the business. He was one of the first merchants in Thomaston to appreciate the scientific methods of store management that appeared early in the twentieth century, and always has kept in close contact with new developments in metropolitan areas, converting such ideas as seemed fitted to use in Thomaston. While merchandising has been an absorbing study and career, Mr. Seavey has been actively concerned in public affairs. He is a Democrat, but is supported by leaders of all parties when he takes part in local matters, as he often does, for the welfare of Thomaston. He has been a member of the Board of Selectmen, treasurer of the town, and is at present (1928) serving as town auditor. During his early business life in Thomaston Mr. Seavey was known as a merchant, but when he formed his association with the Thomaston Savings Bank, of which he has long been president, he became better known as a banker; and in recent years, since he has held and is holding public office, he is known first as a banker, second as town auditor, and third as a merchant, one of the outstanding men in the community whose interests are diversified, to the benefit of the public. Mr. Seavey is a member of the Knights of Pythias, of the Free and Accepted Masons, thirty-second degree, Ancient Arabic Order Nobles of the Mystic Shrine, and of the Methodist church.

Levi Seavey married, at Thomaston, June 21, 1883, Effie J. Simmons, daughter of Luther M. Simmons; and they are the parents of one child: Margaret, who married H. C. Moody.

SAMUEL WATTS—Among all that hardy company of seamen and builders of ships who made the name of Maine famous throughout the maritime world, there is no name more revered for his works or for his sturdy Americanism than that of the late Samuel Watts, of St. George and Thomaston. From boyhood a follower of the sea, he was one of those heroic figures from whom the colorful story of Rudyard Kipling's "Captains Courageous" was inspired. It was the sea that inspired in him an intensive religious faith, yet which begot in him no creed, for he was of that mental calibre that brooked no schisms, but held that one God and one faith were sufficient for all men. His was a broad nature, a kindly nature, his character above question, his sincerity in all things a thing of beauty. Such men are rapidly passing into the Beyond. They were the pioneers of American civilization, the men who spread the wings of their own ships and sailed into the ports of every sea on earth, carrying the Flag in triumph until the inroads of steam put an end to the clipper ship of American invention. Samuel Watts represented this class of manhood, the passing of which is mourned throughout the land. They were real Americans.

Mr. Watts was born in St. George, Maine, October 3, 1812, a son of Joseph and Sarah (Stone) Watts. His father was a farmer and became financially interested in a number of vessels. Samuel Watts acquired such education as the limited facilities of the town then afforded, and at the age of thirteen years went to sea. When he was scarcely a man in years he had become a captain, in which capacity he followed the sea for many years. Upon retirement he built, owned and managed many vessels, remaining in that occupation until the business began to fall off, when he interested himself in other lines. Having acquired a competence, he maintained a winter residence in Boston and spent his summers in Thomaston, where his long experience at sea and in the construction of ships made him an authority whose advice was eagerly sought and followed by the younger generation. At the time of his death, March 1, 1900, he was financially interested in several banks in Thomaston and in Boston. In politics he was a Democrat and represented Thomaston during one session of the State Legislature. He also served once as a delegate to the Democratic National Convention. He was not a member of any religious organization but contributed largely to the support of the Baptist and Methodist Episcopal churches in Thomaston, and to the Baptist church in St. George, where he was born.

Samuel Watts married, at St. George, Maine, in October, 1837, Clarissa B. Mills, daughter of James and Mary (Hathorn) Mills. There were nine children, six of whom died in infancy. Those living to maturity were: 1. Mary J., born July 15, 1838. 2. Sarah, born June 10, 1840. 3. Emma, born June 2, 1849. Sarah and Emma are deceased. Mary J. Watts is still living in the Thomaston home, nearly ninety years of age.

BENJAMIN KELLEY, Jr.—Born January 4, 1834, in Belfast, Benjamin Kelley, Jr., was a son of Benjamin Kelley, and a grandson of Benjamin Kelley. The family is one of the oldest and most honored in Belfast. Benjamin Kelley, the grandfather, was born in Boothbay, Maine, there attended public school, engaged in farming and trade, and died, most highly respected. In Boothbay was born the second Benjamin Kelley, late in the year 1800; there he received his education, and learned the craft of tool-making. He became skilled in the manufacture of edged tools, and in 1820, when less than twenty years of age, organized the tool factory that has been for many years a principal industry of Belfast, under the style of B. Kelley & Company. Here he spent the remainder of his life, and all of his career as manufacturer. He was keenly alive to methods for the advancement of the community. A Republican, he was loyal to the principles of the party and a power in local political circles. He held a number of public offices in the town, and was accounted one of its substantial men. He married Catherine Campbell, and they were the parents of children, among whom was Benjamin the third, Benjamin, Jr.

Benjamin Kelley, Jr., was educated in a private academy, and when a young man began to learn tool-making, under his father's supervision. He was an apt apprentice, and soon was able to take charge of various branches of the manufactory. He became a member of the organization, and after the death of his father continued it with ever-increasing success, particularly in the production of axes, for which the company is perhaps most noted, though its edged tools of all characters are in demand. Like his father, Benjamin Kelley, Jr., was constantly interested in public affairs, and more than did his part in community development. Much that is good in Belfast today owes its origin in full or in large measure to the foresight and tireless activity of Benjamin Kelley, Jr., in this direction. Just as he took pride in his business, so did he take pride in Belfast. A Republican and staunch in support of its principles, Mr. Kelley was frequently urged to become candidate for public office, and occasionally he assented to such pleas. As member of the Board of Aldermen, his record was exemplary of adherence to the trust of the people, which never was betrayed. In the fraternal orders he was a moving spirit; a member of the Free and Accepted Masons, and holder of high office in that organization. He was affiliated with the Independent Order of Odd Fellows, Chief Patriarch, Encampment and Canton of Pallas, No. 4. In church work he was devoted, a member of the Universalist denomination, for a number of years church treasurer. Toward charity Mr. Kelley was ever of large heart. He contributed generously to all causes of worth, regardless of race or creed, giving in a spirit truly humanitarian.

Mr. Kelley married (first), in 1860, Laura Rankin,

MAINE—A HISTORY   297

of Winterport, Maine, who died in 1863. He married (second), in 1865, Mary E. Rankin, of Richmond, Virginia, cousin of his first wife and a daughter of Captain Richard Rankin, an intrepid mariner of renown. To this union were born three children: 1. Walter B. 2. Edward H., journalist, newspaer editor, of Bangor, Maine. 3. Elizabeth A. When Mr. Kelley died, almost the whole population of Belfast grieved. He was beloved of rich and poor, weak and strong, and is remembered for his many noble qualities of character, and for his goodness.

LLOYD A. HARMON, postmaster at Clinton, Maine, followed the woodenware business with success for many years. and is recognized as a very capable business man. He has always taken an active interest in public affairs. He was born January 12, 1889, at Skowhegan, Maine, son of Henry and Annie (Weymouth) Harmon. The father, a farmer, was born at Canaan, Maine; the mother, who is still living, was born at Clinton, Maine.

Lloyd A. Harmon attended the public schools at Clinton, Maine, including the high school, and then went to Shaw's Business College at Portland, Maine. He followed the woodenware manufacturing business with his stepfather in Clinton for approximately ten years. In August, 1922, he was made postmaster under the Harding administration, and has been postmaster since. He was president of the Postmasters' Association of Maine for two years. He is a Republican in politics, and was town clerk of Clinton for number of years. He is a Past Master of the Free and Accepted Masons, and member of the Chapter and Commandery in that Order. He attends the Methodist church at Clinton, Maine.

Lloyd A. Harmon married, November 1, 1918, at Benton, Maine, Jennie Warren, who was born at Benton, Maine, daughter of James W. and Ellen (Gifford) Warren. Her father was a farmer, now deceased; her mother is living (1928). There has been one child to the marriage: Priscilla Jane, born November 17, 1926.

THOMAS J. SOUTHARD, shipbuilder and insurance man, has, through an innate business talent, made himself one of the leading men of affairs in Richmond, Maine. Mr. Southard was born September 28, 1869, in Richmond, the son of Charles H. T. J. Southard, who died in 1912 and Olive S. (Foster) Southard of Winthrop, born at The Forks, Maine. The mother died in 1900. Mr. Southard, Sr., was a shipbuilder and banker of Richmond and one of the outstanding business men of the place.

After completing his education in the public schools in Richmond and at Phillips-Exeter Academy, at Exeter, New Hampshire, Mr. Southard was associated with the shipbuilding business of his father until it was discontinued in 1899, after which he entered the insurance field. Here he has made a substantial success which carries out the high traditions of the family. He has also held the controlling stock in the First National Bank of Richmond, which he sold to the Augusta Trust Company in 1916.

He is a member of the Free and Accepted Masons, holding the thirty-second degree; Knights Templar, and Kora Temple, Ancient Arabic Order Nobles of the

Mystic Shrine. He has held all the chairs in the Independent Order of Odd Fellows and is a member of the Benevolent and Protective Order of Elks. He is also a member of the Richmond Chamber of Commerce. During the World War, Mr. Southard was secretary of publicity for Richmond and carried on this work in a most efficient manner.

Thomas J. Southard married (first) Ruth M. Maxwell; he married (second) Grace E. Fairclough.

LEON C. ROBERTS—Since he was a lad of eighteen years, Leon C. Roberts has been identified with the embalming and funeral directing business, and since he was twenty-one years old he has been engaged in that line of business under his own name. He came to Winthrop in 1923, and since that time has, in addition to his undertaking business, carried a complete line of house furnishings, and has also been agent for the "Maytag" washers. He is on the executive board of the Chamber of Commerce.

Leon C. Roberts was born in Wayne, Maine, October 28, 1886, son of Nathan Roberts, who was engaged in farming, and of Inez (Graves) Roberts, both natives of Wayne, Maine, and both now deceased. Mr. Roberts received a practical education in the public schools of Auburn, and then for two years was employed in a shoe factory at Brockton, Massachusetts. When he was eighteen years of age, he returned to Canton, Maine, and became associated with his uncle, W. L. Roberts, who was engaged in the undertaking business there. After three years spent with his uncle, during which time he made himself thoroughly familiar with every detail of the business, he went to Readfield and established an undertaking and furniture business of his own. There he continued until 1923, when he came to Winthrop and established the business which he has since conducted under his own name. In addition to the regular embalming and funeral directing work, he carries a complete line of house furnishings, and undertakers' supplies, and he also has the agency for this district for the "Maytag" washing machine. He has built up a very successful and prosperous enterprise. Mr. Roberts has always taken an intelligent and a helpful interest in local public affairs, has served as a member of the Board of Selectmen of Readfield, and is a member of the executive board of the Winthrop Chamber of Commerce. Fraternally, he is Past Master of Lafayette Lodge, Free and Accepted Masons, of Readfield; a member of Winthrop Chapter, Royal Arch Masons, and of all the York Rite bodies, also of the Consistory, in which he holds the thirty-second degree. He is also a member of the Independent Order of Odd Fellows, and his religious affiliation is with the Congregational church. Mr. Roberts has a host of friends in Winthrop and he is known as one of the public-spirited citizens of the place. As a business man his ability and his sound judgment are well recognized, and as a citizen he is held in the highest esteem.

Leon C. Roberts was married, in Auburn, Maine, October 19, 1908, to Madeline E. Douglas, who was born in Canton, Maine, daughter of Harry and Lottie (Ellis) Douglas, both of whom are living (1928). Mr. and Mrs. Roberts are the parents of two children: 1. Carleton, born September 29, 1911. 2. Douglas, born March 5, 1914.

WILLIAM H. HARRIS, M. D.—One whose practice of the profession of medicine in Augusta has brought to him the confidence and esteem of the community-at-large is William H. Harris, who, in addition to his general professional conduct as physician and surgeon, is attendant surgeon to the Augusta General Hospital, which position he has held since the foundation of that institution, in March, 1898. At various times he has filled important offices having to do with public affairs and medical organizations. Throughout his residence in Augusta he has contributed liberally of money and personal effort to worthy programs of civic and social development, and is widely known for loyalty of citizenship.

Dr. Harris was born in Appalachicola, Florida, August 7, 1861, the son of Charles Miller and Isabella (Jewett) Harris. Charles Miller Harris was a native of South Carolina, a lumberman of considerable position. Isabella (Jewett) Harris was a native of Maine, born at Bangor. Her father was the late A. G. Jewett of Belfast, a noted lawyer of Maine who was appointed Foreign Minister to Peru in 1844.

In the public schools of Belfast, Maine, Dr. Harris secured his elementary and secondary education, graduating from high school with marks of high standing. After having taken his diploma from high school, in 1880, when but nineteen years of age, he went to California, and there worked in the fruit business, remaining on the West Coast four years, from 1880 to 1884. Meanwhile, he had searched his preferences rigidly in quest of a proper career, and, decided upon medicine, returned to the East in 1884, to become a student in Dartmouth College, and in July, 1888, took the degree of Doctor of Medicine from the University of Vermont. Thus, at nearly twenty-seven years of age, he found himself on the threshold of a career that was to become of signal distinction.

Dr. Harris opened his first offices for the practice of medicine at Dixfield, Maine, in the fall of 1888; continued in Dixfield until 1890, and in 1891 came to Augusta. Here his prestige has augmented in progression through the years until the present time (1928), and his clientele is among the largest in this part of the State. Since 1904, he has devoted the chief course of his work to surgery, being possessed of an admirable reputation therein. Honors accorded to him have been many. He is past president of the Augusta Medical Association, past president of the Kennebec County Medical Association, a member of the Maine State Medical Association, the American Medical Association, for eighteen years was Medical Examiner of Kennebec County, and for twelve years a member of the State Board of Registration, Medicine and Surgery. For eight years he has been attending surgeon at the National Soldiers' Home. He is now consulting surgeon at the Gardiner General Hospital and the Augusta State Hospital; is president of the United States Pension Examining Board of Kennebec County, a member of the Abnaki Club, Augusta Country Club, and the Free and Accepted Masons, in which Order he has proceeded through all bodies and holds the thirty-second degree. A Republican, he owns an influence in political matters, particularly as they concern Augusta and the county. In religious adherence he is a communicant of the Episcopal church.

The Augusta General Hospital belongs to the list of those local public institutions that are called indispensable, just as are Augusta's fire department, police department, schools and churches. And here it is interesting to note that thirty years ago the city had no hospital. Private homes were the only places in which could be treated cases of sickness and accident. To a group of medical men and thoughtful citizens the situation was impossible. As has been recounted, Dr. Harris came to Augusta in 1891. In that year the late Dr. L. J. Crooker of Augusta secured from State Legislature a charter for the erection of a hospital; but the rights of this charter were never by him exercised. Public-spirited citizens joined with the medical fraternity in their determination to have a city hospital, and opened their purses to the extent of seven thousand dollars, by subscription. In April, 1898, the hospital opened its doors. During the month preceding, Dr. Harris, in association with Drs. O. C. S. Davies and J. E. Tuell, was instrumental in perfecting the general hospital's organization, and in leading public opinion to the fulfillment of a civic need. The organization first had the style, under State charter, of the City Hospital Corporation, but after several years this was changed to the Augusta General Hospital. It has grown progressively, efficiently, and today stands well forward among the finer hospitals of Maine, largely through the efforts of Dr. Harris and his associates. From the very beginning he has been attendant surgeon to the hospital, which, hardly after it had opened its doors, was confronted with a great emergency—the Spanish-American War had ended. Soldiers were coming home from Chickamauga Park, stricken with typhoid and malaria. Tent hospitals on the muster field were quickly filled, and military authorities appealed to the city for help. For nine months the city hospital fought for the lives of Augusta's young veterans. Another emergency was met with like expediency after the World War, and in all movements of this great humanitarian institution Dr. Harris has been a leader. Dr. Harris served during the World War as Examining Surgeon of Division No. 1 of the Local Exemption Board for Kennebec County.

Dr. Harris married, in Augusta, September 15, 1887, Martha Jewett North, who was born in this city, September 15, 1866, daughter of Dr. James W. and Virginia (Freer) North. Of this union were born six children, of whom five died in infancy and one survives: Charles Miller Harris, born in Augusta, January 25, 1905, graduate of the University of Maine, 1928, degree of Bachelor of Arts.

HENRY W. BUTLER—Both in industry and in city government, Henry W. Butler has carried along the traditions of native worth and practical ability that have been qualities of excellence in his family for generations. Following a considerable period during which Mr. Butler had engaged in both the grocery and the carpentry business, he was appointed to his present overseer of the poor clerkship. He is a son of Moses and Zoe (Darveau) Butler, both natives of Canada. Moses Butler, an active Republican, was a member of the first city government of Waterville, and for forty-five years he was a blacksmith in the employ of the Maine Central Railroad.

Henry W. Butler was born January 6, 1870, at Waterville, whose public schools he attended. For some twenty years he engaged in the grocery business, and at thirty-five years of age he became a carpenter, continuing in that line for seventeen years. On March 25, 1925, Mr. Butler received his appointment as clerk of the Overseers of the Poor at Waterville, a position that he continues to fill to the satisfaction of his constituency. Mr. Butler is affiliated with Local No. 348, Carpenters and Joiners of America; and he is a communicant of the Roman Catholic church.

Henry W. Butler married, October 16, 1889, at Waterville, Elizabeth Laliberte, of Canada. They have two children: Alfred H., and Lena.

VIRGIL A. LINNELL—Rumford's postmaster has long been a merchant and business man in this section of the State. His capable and systematic usages in business are well known, and his popularity and thoroughness in his present office are established features of his administration. He is prominent in all civic and community matters, and has very ably held local office in other departments of public service.

Virgil A. Linnell was born September 24, 1869, at Levant, a son of Eugene Linnell, a native of this State, who engaged in mining in the West, and was a Republican in his political views, and Sarah L. (Osgood) Linnell, a native of Exeter; both parents now deceased. Mr. Linnell attended the schools of his birthplace, and learning the carpenter's trade, he continued therein for twenty years, in Rumford since 1892 and until 1915, when he became a dealer in builders' supplies, so continuing until 1924, when he became temporary postmaster, in August of that year. He received his postmaster's commission on January 8, 1925, an office he now holds. A Republican in his political views, he has always been active in the interests of that party, and has held the office of assessor. Fraternally, Postmaster Linnell is affiliated with the Lodge, Free and Accepted Masons; with the local Commandery, Knights Templar, and he is a member of the Shrine Club. His religious faith is that of the Universalist church.

Virgil A. Linnell married, February 22, 1892, at Hartland, Eva A. Norton, a native of Levant, daughter of George and Mary (French) Norton. Their children: Dorothy, Eldora, and Norton.

CHARLES A. MIXER, C. E.—The industrial and community interests of Rumford are of great advantage as a result of the constructive work in public utility that has been performed by chief engineer of the Rumford Falls Power Company, Charles A. Mixer, in the development of his plans of vast range for the conservation of power, as well as those consummated for street system, canals and bridges. Mr. Mixer's earlier work in his profession is evident throughout the West, as well as in New England, and he has received a very wide recognition as one of the most accomplished men in his profession.

Charles A. Mixer was born June 9, 1859, in Hamilton, Ohio, a son of Alfred A. Mixer, also a native of Hamilton, where he was a machinist throughout his life, and where he served in the Home Guard during the Civil War, and Martha J. (Hinkle) Mixer, who was born in Hamilton. Mr. Mixer attended the grammar and high schools at Hamilton, where he was also a student in engineering, and held the offices of deputy surveyor and assistant city engineer.

He then added a wider activity in his profession, in his association with engineering enterprises in Michigan; at Denver, Colorado, at Cincinnati, Ohio, at Buffalo, New York, and in Providence, Rhode Island. In 1892, Mr. Mixer first came to Rumford, at the invitation of the Rumford Falls Power Company, in order to work out and put in operation a modern plant for that company, as resident engineer. Today, as chief engineer of the company, he has been the means of laying out an adequate street system, canals, and bridges, together with a power station; and he has also performed a task of gigantic proportions in the building of the dams at Rumford.

Mr. Mixer is active in all matters that have to do with the general progress and prosperity of Rumford. A Republican in his political views, he has served as a member of the school committee; as a trustee of the public library; and as a member of the Rumford Park Commission. His professional affiliations are many and leading, inclusive of his past presidency of the Maine Association of Engineers; his membership with the Illuminating Engineers' Society; with the American Society of Civil Engineers; American Institute of Electrical Engineers; American Association for the Advancement of Science; and he is also a member of the Cosmos Club, of Rumford. Mr. Mixer is a very active factor in the work of the Baptist church at Rumford, where he is a member of the board of deacons, and of the board of trustees; and he was a member of the organizing committee of 1896.

Charles A. Mixer married, February 5, 1885, at Buffalo, New York, Nellie M. Norton, a native of Buffalo, and daughter of Increase and Phoebe Norton. Their children: 1. Charles Norton. 2. Alfred L., married Florence Sandbergh. 3. Martha L. 4. Alice R., married Richard Rouillard.

ALBERT BELIVEAU—His abilities and activities as an attorney-at-law have secured for Albert Beliveau his merited success and attainments in his field of general practice at Rumford and through the State. Both as county attorney, and in his association with the Judge-Advocate office in the World War, as well as in his broad interests in his profession before and since the war, Mr. Beliveau has demonstrated his value as a member of the bar and of the many legal associations of which he is a prominent member.

Albert Beliveau was born March 27, 1887, at Lewiston, a son of Severin Beliveau, a native of Canada, and now retired at Rumford, and Cedulie (Roberge) Beliveau, a native of Canada, who died in August, 1923. He attended the public schools at Lewiston and at Livermore Falls, and preparing for his profession at the Law School of the University of Maine, he was graduated there with his degree of Bachelor of Laws in 1911. Admitted to the bar in that year, he has since engaged in general practice, with his present offices at Congress Street, in Rumford. He is a member of the State Bar Association, and the American Bar Association.

In his political views a Democrat, Mr. Beliveau supports his party principles with his vote and influence; and during 1915-16, he held the office of county attorney. During the World War, he served as a second lieutenant in the Judge-Advocate's office in the American Expeditionary Forces; was overseas one year, and received his discharge at

Camp Dix, New Jersey. Fraternally, he is affiliated with the Benevolent and Protective Order of Elks, and the Knights of Columbus, at Rumford; with Société St. Jean Baptiste; with the American Legion, of which he was Department Commander in 1923; and Oakdale Country Club. He is a communicant of St. John the Baptist Roman Catholic Church, at Rumford.

WILLIAM J. FLANAGAN—County Attorney William J. Flanagan has well certified as to his qualifications as an attorney-at-law in general practice since the date of his admission to the Maine bar, his activities in the extensive field that he has developed being inclusive of a wide range of legal business, and his election to his present office demonstrating the confidence of his constituency in his abilities. A veteran of the World War, also, he served with his comrades in France, winning the honors of promotion and the esteem of his associates then and throughout his professional career. William J. Flanagan was born January 1, 1893, at Melrose, Massachusetts, a son of Patrick F. Flanagan, shipbuilder and stockbroker, who was born in Cambridge, Massachusetts, and Margaret (Cahill) Flanagan, also a native of Cambridge, both parents now deceased. Mr. Flanagan, after attending the Melrose public schools, was graduated at Boston College in 1912, with the degree of Bachelor of Arts; and preparing for his profession at the Law School of the University of Maine, he was graduated there in 1917 with the degree of Bachelor of Laws. After the World War, he entered upon general practice, and was admitted to the bar in 1921, establishing himself at Rumford. He is a member of the American Bar Association; Maine State Bar Association; and Oxford County Bar Association. In his political views, he is a Republican, and he is at present (1928) county attorney for Oxford County. Enlisting in the World War, Mr. Flanagan joined the First Maine Field Artillery, in June, 1917, and served overseas ten months, successively as sergeant-major and as second lieutenant; receiving his discharge at Camp Devens in July, 1919. He is now a second lieutenant in the Officers' Reserve Corps. Fraternally, Mr. Flanagan is affiliated with the local Council, Knights of Columbus, and he is a member of the Rumford Rotary Club. He is a communicant of St. Athanasius Roman Catholic Church.

JOHN A. BABB—As farmer and postmaster, John A. Babb has been one of the residents of Dixfield, Maine, during the greater part of his active career. He is serving his second term as postmaster, and is known as a skilled agriculturist. John A. Babb was born in Dixfield, Maine, December 29, 1875, son of Ira O., who was born in Mexico, Maine, March 14, 1850, and died April 5, 1926, a farmer, lumber man, and stone mason, who gave his support to the Republican party, and of Francelia A. (Hutchins) Babb, born in Dixfield, Maine, April 6, 1849. Mr. Babb received a good practical education in the public schools of Dixfield, and then engaged in farming, following also lumbering and construction. For four years he was engaged in road construction in a number of Southern and Western States, but later he returned to New England, and served as deputy sheriff for six years when, on December 19, 1922, he was appointed postmaster of Dixfield. On February 16, 1927, he was reappointed to the postmastership, and he is now beginning his second term in that official capacity. He still continues his farming, and he is active in local public affairs. Like his father, he supports the Republican party, and he is active in its affairs. He served for six years as deputy sheriff under Harry D. Cole, of Oxford County, and he has always been generous in his support of any project which seemed to him to be wisely planned for the advancement of the general welfare of the community. He is a member of the Lodge, Free and Accepted Masons; the Chapter, Royal Arch Masons; also of the Independent Order of Odd Fellows; and he is an interested member of the Dixfield Board of Trade. His religious affiliation is with the Presbyterian church. John A. Babb was married, in South Greenfield, Missouri, December 25, 1904, to Edith A. Cox, daughter of Samuel and Fannie J. (Mitchell) Cox. Mr. and Mrs. Babb have one son, Richard E., who was born April 8, 1906.

JOHN WESLEY WOOD—Specializing in the manufacture of infants' shoes, John Wesley Wood, of Auburn, is today the head of the most extensive plant of that character in the United States. Although of foreign birth, he is a citizen of the highest reputation and unswerving Americanism, a man of upright character and unblemished reputation. Although never seeking office, he is affiliated with the Republican party in politics and has ever shown an intense interest in the civic affairs of the community and of the Nation. He is a busy man, yet he has found time and inclination to become affiliated with fraternal and commercial organizations and to mingle with his fellow-citizens in all of their various activities, these attributes bringing to him the high regard of all with whom he has become associated. He was born in Malton, Ontario, Canada, December 4, 1876, both his parents being of English nativity. His father was John Wood, a farmer, now deceased; his mother, Mary (Cushman) Wood. He acquired his education in the grammar and high schools of Freeport, Maine. When he was sixteen years of age he entered the employ of A. W. Shaw Company, of Freeport, manufacturer of shoes, remaining there until 1912, when he went to the Dingley-Foss Shoe Company, of Auburn, as salesman. He remained in that occupation for about five years. In 1917, he went to Norway, Maine, as general manager and president of the Norway Shoe Compay, a corporation manufacturing infants' shoes. In 1919, he sold his interest in this company and coming to Auburn he associated himself with Guy L. Smith, organizing the shoe-manufacturing house of Wood & Smith, Incorporated, in Auburn. This concern was established to make infants' shoes exclusively and today is said to make more than any other factory in the country, employing some three hundred people. Mr. Wood is a thirty-second degree Mason and holds membership in all grades of that organization, including the Temple, Ancient Arabic Order Nobles of the Mystic Shrine. He belongs to the Martindale Country Club, the Home Market Club of Boston, the Shrine Club, the Maine Associated Industries, Auburn Chamber of Commerce and the Rotary clubs of Lewiston and Auburn. His church is the Universalist. He is president and general manager of the Wood & Smith Company, while Guy L. Smith is treasurer. Mr. Wood married, in Auburn, Maine, December 22, 1921, Eula Bicknell, of Norway, Maine, daughter of William A. and Sarah Bicknell.

FREDERICK W. SMITH—During the larger portion of his business career engaged in manufacturing, both in New York State and in Maine, Frederick W. Smith, manager for the Berst, Forster, Dixfield Company, at Dixfield, is a factor in the increasing success of the concern that he thus represents, and a man of broad business enterprise. He is a veteran of the World War, and is active in all activities that have to do with the progress and prosperity of the community.

Frederick W. Smith was born January 16, 1875, in Brooklyn, New York, a son of Andrew A. Smith, who was born in Berlin, Connecticut, was a broker and shoe manufacturer in New York, and served as a member of the Brooklyn Park Commission, and Anna S. (Wilhelm) Smith, a native of Philadelphia, both parents now deceased. After attending the Brooklyn public schools in Brooklyn, Mr. Smith took the course at the Brooklyn Latin School, and was graduated at Nazareth Hall, Pennsylvania, in the class of 1892. He then established himself in New York City, in the brokerage business, continuing therein five years; and for two years he was engaged in the manufacture of tin cans in his own name, in Brooklyn, removing to Maine in 1901.

In 1920, Mr. Smith became associated with the firm of Berst, Forster, Dixfield Company, at Dixfield, as assistant manager, this firm conducting six plants for the manufacture of toothpicks, clothespins and various articles made from wood, and he has held the position of manager at Dixfield since 1921. In political matters, he is a Republican, and with vote and influence he supports the principles of that party.

In the World War, Mr. Smith was active gratuitously in Young Men's Christian Association work, overseas for eight months. Fraternally, he is affiliated with the Free and Accepted Masons; Royal Arch Chapter; Knights Templar Commandery, at Lewiston; and the Temple, Ancient Arabic Order Nobles of the Mystic Shrine. He is a member of the Shrine Club; the Country Club, at Oakdale; and the Sons of the American Revolution; and a life-member of St. David Society. His religious faith is that of the Congregational church.

Frederick W. Smith married, February 17, 1901, in New York City, Wynifred Staples, born in Carthage, daughter of Eugene Hale and Eva (Sanborn) Staples. They have one daughter, Lydia, born January 18, 1903, married William Jordan.

FRANK E. IRISH—After a varied experience in several different lines of business activity, Frank E. Irish purchased a grocery store in Dixfield, Maine, and here he has been successfully engaged since 1924. Lorenzo Irish, father of Mr. Irish, was born in Peru, Maine, and in addition to his agricultural activities was interested in mercantile business. He is now (1928) proprietor of a grocery store in Canton, Maine, where he supports the principles of the Republican party, and where he has many friends. He married Mary Kidder, who was born in Peru,

Maine, and is now deceased, and among their children was Frank E., of further mention.

Frank E. Irish was born in Peru, Maine, June 11, 1897, and received his early school training in the public schools of his birthplace. Later he continued study in the high school at Canton, Maine, for two years, and when that course was completed he engaged in the grocery business in Peru, continuing there for three years. He then went to Rumford, Maine, where for three years he was employed in a creamery. His next job was in a grocery store in Rumford, but after spending one year in that connection he purchased the grocery business of George Heffron, in Dixfield, in 1924, and since that time has been successfully conducting that enterprise. Mr. Irish is a Republican and an earnest supporter of the policies of that party, and he is also a public-spirited citizen, who is anxious to advance the interests of the town of Dixfield. He is a member of Tuscan Lodge, No. 22, Independent Order of Odd Fellows; and of Peru Grange, Patrons of Husbandry; and his religious interest is with the Methodist church of Rumford, Maine.

Frank E. Irish was married, in Vermont, June 29, 1916, to Ruby Mahar, who was born in Pembroke, Maine, daughter of Joseph and Annie (Clark) Mahar. Mr. and Mrs. Irish have two children: 1. Joseph, born October 29, 1918. 2. Robert, born January 3, 1923.

ARCH. L. COBURN—The greater part of the active career of Arch. L. Coburn, to the present time, has been identified with the lumber business, in which he is still (1928) actively engaged. Mr. Coburn is active in local public affairs, and is one of the able and progressive citizens of Dixfield, Maine.

Arch. L. Coburn was born in Carthage, Maine, April 21, 1880, and is a son of John Gardner and Osca (Newman) Coburn, the last-mentioned of whom was born in Carthage, Maine, and died in 1913. John Gardner Coburn, the father, was engaged in farming and in milling, in Carthage, and is still active. At the time of the outbreak of the Civil War he enlisted in the Twelfth Maine Regiment, and served throughout the period of that conflict. He is a Republican in his political beliefs, and in his younger years was active in local public affairs.

Arch. L. Coburn, then, attended the public schools of Carthage and Jordan High School, in Lewiston, Maine, and then continued his studies in Wilton Academy, at Wilton, Maine. When his academic course was completed he engaged in farming for a time and then began buying and selling lumber. He had a mill of his own, and as time passed he increased both his milling business and his timber acreage. He cuts his own lumber, and now (1928) has a large mill at Dixfield, Maine, where he is taking care of a large and growing business. Mr. Coburn is well known to the trade in this section, and both as a business man and as a citizen has the respect and esteem of his associates. He is independent in his political convictions, giving his support to those candidates who seem to him to be best fitted for the offices to which they aspire, regardless of party affiliations. He is active in local affairs, and can always be counted upon to give generous support to any project which seems to him to be well planned for the advancement of the general welfare of the community. He is a member of the Independent Order of Odd Fellows; also of the Free and Accepted Masons, in which last he holds membership in the Blue Lodge, and in Chapter, Commandery, and Temple. Mr. Coburn has a large number of loyal friends in Dixfield.

Arch. L. Coburn was married, in Dixfield, Maine, March 2, 1903, to Della Hildreth, who was born in Oxford County, Maine, daughter of Weston and Mary Ann (Searles) Hildreth, both of whom are deceased. Mr. and Mrs. Coburn have one son, Robert, born February 18, 1914.

ALBERT E. SMALL—Established in the building supplies and real estate business throughout his career, Albert E. Small is rightly accounted one of the leading men in these interests in Mexico and a large section of the State of which Mexico is a prosperous center. Mr. Small is an expert contractor, a builder of acknowledged skill, and a real estate dealer than whom no one is better informed with regard to realty values in this section. He is a son of Kingsbury Small, who was born at Bowdoin, was for years a master mechanic, and is president of a coöperative grocery business with his headquarters at Lisbon Falls, and Leonora (Hatch) Small.

Albert E. Small was born October 5, 1872, at Chelsea, Massachusetts, and he attended the public schools at Lisbon Falls, in Maine. He then entered upon his vocation as a building contractor, and for twenty-eight years he has been actively associated with many of the building enterprises in this part of the State, as well as with the real estate matters in which he has partnership with Albert Beliveau, of Rumford. His hardware and builders' supplies headquarters were established at Mexico in 1907, under the firm name of A. E. Small & Son, Incorporated, his son, Clifford O. Small, a well-known business man, being his partner.

In political matters, Mr. Small is a Republican, in he has been continuously active in civic affairs, and is a member of the School Board. Fraternally, Mr. Small is affiliated with the Independent Order of Odd Fellows; the Knights of Pythias and the local Grange, Patrons of Husbandry. His religious faith is that of the Congregational church.

Albert E. Small married Lena O. Park, daughter of Henry W. Park, who was postmaster and conducted a store at Mexico, and Emma L. (Gleason) Park, who survives her husband. Their children: Clifford O., Lucy A., and Albert E., Jr.

DAVID D. NEEDELMAN—As proprietor and operator of "Davies Drug Store" in Mexico, Maine, David D. Needelman is making good use of his premedical training. After three years of study in the pre-medical department of Bowdoin College he is well prepared to render unusually effective service in his present calling, and his patrons have learned to appreciate his knowledge and training.

David D. Needelman was born in New York City, December 25, 1898, son of Max Needelman, who was born in Russia, but came to this country and settled in New York City, where he is a designer of ladies' garments, and of Anna (Beckelman) Needelman, also a native of Russia, who is living in New York City. Mr. Needelman attended the public schools of New York City, where his parents first settled after their arrival in this country, but later he attended the grammar school in Portland, Maine. Leaving Portland High School, he entered the medical department of Bowdoin College, where he continued study for three years. Meantime, he had been employed in the credit department of a garment manufactory in New York City for one year, but after leaving Bowdoin College he purchased the retail drug business of Charles W. Smith, proprietor of one of the old establishments of Mexico, Maine, and since that time he has conducted the business under the name of Davies Drug Store. Since taking over the business Mr. Needelman has added much to his equipment and his stock and has greatly increased the volume of business. Politically, he gives his support to the Democratic party. During the World War he was for three months a member of the Student Army Training Corps, of the University of Maine. Fraternally, Mr. Needelman is identified with the Knights of Pythias, at Mexico, Maine, and with Phi Epsilon Pi College Fraternity of the University of Maine, and he is a member of the Oakdale Country Club. His religious affiliation is with the Hebrew Synagogue of Rumford, Maine.

David D. Needelman was married, at Old Orchard, Maine, September 7, 1924, to Jennie M. Cohen, who was born in Rumford, Maine, daughter of Mr. and Mrs. Louis Cohen, the former of whom is engaged in the bottling business in Rumford. Mr. and Mrs. Needelman have one daughter, Barbara Lee, born July 17, 1926.

DR. HENRY M. HOWARD—For the past three years Dr. Henry M. Howard has been engaged in general medical practice in Rumford, Maine. He has his offices on Congress Street, and is taking care of a large patronage. Dr. Howard is a graduate of the Medical School of Bowdoin College, and was engaged in public health work before coming to Rumford in 1924.

Dr. Henry M. Howard was born in Andover, Maine, September 5, 1896, and is a son of Marshall, a farmer, who was born in Maine, and of Mary (Glover) Howard, a native of Rumford, Maine, both of whom are living (1928). After attending the public schools of Andover, Maine, Dr. Howard prepared for college in the Kent's Hill High School, and then entered Bowdoin College, where he graduated from the medical department in 1921, with the degree of Doctor of Medicine. For two years following his graduation he was engaged in public health work in Rumford, Maine, and in 1924 he opened an office and engaged in general practice here. He is building up a very substantial clientele, which is steadily growing and has made for himself an assured place in the esteem and confidence of his associates. Politically, Dr. Howard gives his support to no one political party, but casts his ballot for those candidates whom he considers to be personally best fitted for the offices to which they aspire. During the World War he enlisted in the United States Navy and served in Hospital No. 55. He is now (1928) a first lieutenant in the Medical Reserve Corps. He is a member of the Maine Public Health Association, of the Oxford County Medical Association, the Maine State Medical Society, and the American Medical Association. Dr. Howard is fond of out-of-door sports, and is a member of the Oakdale Country Club, also of Alpha Kappa Kappa, the medical fraternity of Bowdoin College. His religious affiliation is with the Congregational church. Dr. Henry M. Howard was married, in Portland, Maine, April 28, 1921, to Theresa Marie Sloane, who was born in Boston, Massachusetts, daughter of Thomas and Kathryn (O'Neil) Sloane. Dr. and Mrs. Howard are the parents of two children: 1. Marshall, born September 4, 1922. 2. Ann, born August 10, 1925.

JOHN M. GOOGIN—In the active business life of Lewiston and Auburn, John M. Googin, who makes his residence there, is a leading figure, being president of the old-established and well-known Googin Fuel Company, Incorporated, an organization which had its inception fifty years ago, in 1878. Mr. Googin, whose successful achievements attest to his remarkable business ability and unremitting energy, has, nevertheless, always found time to devote to the interests of his community and its people, and his zealous efforts in behalf of education, his constant work in the promotion of civic welfare and his activities in the realm of fraternal organizations have won for him the esteem and commendation of all h's fellow-citizens. The coal business which Mr. Coogin heads has achieved a distinguished record during its long period of service to the public in both these cities, having always maintained the same high principles on which it was founded, these being quality and service at all times. In addition, the concern operates a complete blacksmith shop which has been in continual service for more than fifty years and is almost an institution in the commercial life of this locality.

Mr. Googin was born in Lewiston, April 2, 1883, son of Melvin J. Googin, who died, 1924, and of Carrie E. (Holland) Googin, who was born in Lewiston. Melvin J. Googin was born in Old Orchard and, in 1878, in connection with John Harper, founded the present coal business which bears his name. He also opened the blacksmith shop which still fulfills its usefulness, and in real estate development of these cities took a foremost part.

John M. Googin was educated in the public schools of Lewiston and after graduating from Lewiston High School became associated with his father in the latter's business, continuing ever since to give his attention to the coal trade, familiarizing himself thoroughly with the various details of the work, and exhibiting from the first the qualities of efficiency and excellent managerial ability which brought him to the presidency of the firm when it was incorporated and given the name of the Googin Fuel Company, Incorporated. This firm is one of the largest in the State, with a reputation for thorough dependability and general excellence of the various commodities which it dispenses, having two coal offices, one located at No. 67 Elm Street, Auburn, and the other at No. 114 Bates Street, Lewiston, from which it serves both communities with the highest degree of satisfaction.

Mr. Googin takes an important part in educational affairs, having been a member of the Lewiston School Board. In politics, he is a staunch supporter of the principles of the Democratic party and in this connection, served as a member of the State Senate for the term, 1917-1919, and while at the State Capitol gave his best efforts to further the interests of his constituency; at the same time, receiving the highest praise for his splendid accomplishments in the affairs of the commonwealth. His fraternal affiliations are with the Free and Accepted Masons, in which he is Past Master of Rabboni Lodge; he belongs to the Commandery, Knights Templar, and the Temple, Ancient Arabic Order Nobles of the Mystic Shrine; in addition to which he is Past Exalted Ruler of the Benevolent and Protective Order of Elks. In his religious adherence, Mr. Googin is prominently identified with the Episcopal church of Auburn. During the World War, Mr. Googin rendered great service to the cause in his capacity as chairman of the Lewiston Exemption Board, and in all patriotic activities he assisted in a most substantial manner by his influence and support, being active in all Red Cross and Liberty Loan drives.

John M. Googin married, June 10, 1920, in Auburn, Helen M. Hilton, who was born in Lewiston, daughter of Dr. John and Lucy (Jones) Hilton, both natives of Lewiston, and to this union have been born three children: Melvin Jerome, John M., Jr., and Helen H.

GUY L. MEADER—Associated throughout his career with all the interests that have to do with funeral directing, embalming, and with monumental work, Guy L. Meader is senior partner of the oldest and most up-to-date undertaking establishment at Rumford and this part of the county, and through his complete training and experience he has won a repute of importance in the supervision of the care of the dead, of entombment, and the most desirable memorial work. He is a son of Edwin Meader, Doctor of Dental Surgery, who was born in Lewiston, and died in 1902, was a dentist in Lisbon for many years, and was a Republican in politics, and Vesta Jane (Crowley) Meader, who was born in South Lewiston, and survives her husband.

Guy L. Meader was born October 18, 1880, in Lewiston, and he was graduated at the Lisbon grammar and high schools. Taking the course in embalming at the New England Institute of Anatomy in Boston, Massachusetts, he was graduated there November 25, 1911, and having already registered as a funeral director he continued in the profession with undertakers in Auburn, and was a member of the firm of Dillingham and Meader there for one year. Removing to Rumford in 1911, Mr. Meader was in the employ of E. W. Howe Company, funeral directors, until 1917, when he purchased the business in partnership with Henry P. Perry, both carrying on very successfully and satisfactorily this old-established concern. This firm are also known throughout this county for the excellence of the granite work, memorial monuments, and the like, which has a large share of the activities of the business.

A Republican in his political views, Mr. Meader held the office of county coroner for five years. Besides his prominence as a member of the Maine Undertakers' Association, his fraternal affiliations are with the Free and Accepted Masons, inclusive of all bodies of Masonry; Swift River Grange, Patrons of Husbandry; Loyal Order of Moose; and he is a member of the Oakdale Country Club. His religious faith is that of the Baptist church.

Guy L. Meader married, June 14, 1914, Amy Lillian Lovejoy, who was born in Waltham, Massachusetts, daughter of Levi Frank Lovejoy, who is engaged in the jewelry business at Rumford, and Lillian (Uran) Lovejoy. They have one son, Gerald W. Meader, born July 26, 1915.

DONALD B. PARTRIDGE—One of the well-known members of the legal profession in South Paris and in Norway, Maine, is Donald B. Partridge, clerk of the courts, attorney, and town clerk of Norway, who has been engaged in legal practice in Norway since 1924. Mr. Partridge is a graduate of Bates College, and is actively interested in local public affairs. His father, Winfield Scott Partridge, was born in Norway, Maine, and was a merchant here for thirty years. He was well known in this locality, and was active in local politics, giving his support to the Republican party. At the time of the Civil War he was a member of the Coast Guard. His death occurred November 19, 1912. He married Frances Barrows, who was born in Norway, Maine, and died October 14, 1916.

Donald B. Partridge, son of Winfield Scott and Frances (Barrows) Partridge, was born in Norway, Maine, June 7, 1891, and received his preparatory education in the public schools of his birthplace. When his high school course was completed he entered Bates College, at Lewiston, Maine, from which he was graduated with the class of 1914, receiving at that time the degree of Bachelor of Science. For a period of three years after his graduation, Mr. Partridge engaged in the teaching profession as principal of the Canton, Maine, High School. At the end of that time he became interested in the legal profession, and in 1919 he was elected clerk of the courts, in which office he served so effectively that he was reëlected in 1922 and again in 1926. He is now (1928) serving his third term. Meantime, Mr. Partridge had been studying law, and in 1924 he was admitted to the bar. Since that time he has been engaged in general legal practice in Norway, and has built up a very satisfactory patronage. Mr. Partridge is an effective speaker and during the past ten years has addressed audiences all over the State of Maine. He is a member of the board of directors of the Paris Trust Company, and both as a business and professional man has fully demonstrated his ability. He gives his support to the principles and the candidates of the Republican party, and is active in its affairs. For six years he served as chairman of the town committee, and he was chairman of the county committee for three years. He served as chairman of the Norway School Board for three years, and since 1926 has served as town clerk of Norway. Fraternally, Mr. Partridge is affiliated with the Masonic Order, being a member and Past Master of the Blue Lodge, of the Royal Arch Masons, of the Royal and Select Masters, and of the Knights Templar. He is a member of the Oxford County Bar Association, and of the Maine State Bar Association, and is identified with the Knights of Pythias, of which he is Past Chancellor Commander. He is also a member of the Sons of Veterans, and of the Kiwanis Club, Norway, of Paris, Maine, ex-president and secretary three years. He attends the Universalist church.

Donald B. Partridge was married, in Norway, Maine, December 30, 1914, to Geneva Sturtevant, who was born in Stoneham, Massachusetts, daughter of Alvin Partridge, deceased, and of Bertha (Whitman) Sturtevant. Mr. and Mrs. Partridge are

the parents of three sons: 1. Donald B., Jr., born January 17, 1917. 2. Charles S., born January 16, 1923. 3. Jerry C., born August 20, 1925.

EARLE R. CLIFFORD—Following a period of teaching in the public schools, and soon after the close of his World War service, Earle R. Clifford entered upon his duties in the postmastership of South Paris, where he has continued to the present, a popular and efficient public official. He has a vital interest in whatsoever pertains to the advancement of civic and community matters, and is a factor in local education.

Earle R. Clifford was born October 13, 1893, at South Paris, a son of Wallace K. Clifford, an implement dealer, and in politics a Republican, and Apphia (Parsons) Clifford, both parents natives of South Paris, and both now deceased. Mr. Clifford secured his education in the grammar and high schools at South Paris, and he was graduated at Bates College in 1915, with the degree Bachelor of Arts. He taught school at Brewer for two years, and at Turner's Falls for a short time, and then enlisted for service in the World War. On October 1, 1923, Mr. Clifford received his appointment to the postmastership at South Paris, and he continues in that position to the present.

In the political field, Mr. Clifford is an adherent of the Republican party, and he holds the office of chairman of the South Paris School Board. When the World War started, he enlisted in the Quartermaster's Corps of the United States Army, and was engaged in the service for eighteen months, receiving his discharge as a second lieutenant at Washington, District of Columbia. He is an active member of the American Legion, and has held the office of adjutant and served with committees on the local post. Also, he is affiliated with the Independent Order of Odd Fellows, and the Knights of Pythias; his religious faith is that of the Congregational church.

Earle R. Clifford married, October 13, 1920, at Old Orchard, Marion L. Cleaves, daughter of Thomas L. and Berea S. (Sylvester) Cleaves; and their children are: Thomas L., Helen L., and Earle R., Jr.

EDWIN N. HASKELL—To the business men of long tenure of mercantile interests is largely due the present-day enterprise of South Paris, that township having for nearly a half century having recognized, year by year, the steadfast and always dependable worth of Edwin N. Haskell, member of the N. Dayton Bolster Company, a drygoods and general store with which he has been connected from the beginning of his successful business career. A native son, Mr. Haskell has proven his loyalty and public spirit in his quarter of a century in office as the South Paris Village Corporation Clerk.

Edwin N. Haskell was born July 25, 1862, at South Paris, a son of Ezekiel W. Haskell, who engaged in agriculture, and was an adherent to the Republican party, and Harriet L. (Rideout) Haskell, both parents natives of New Gloucester, and both now deceased. He attended the schools of South Paris, and in April, 1879, he first began as clerk in the store with which he has continued until the present. Until 1893 he was a clerk in the N. D.

Bolster drygoods and general store, and he then took a partnership in the business, and in 1909 became an officer in the corporation. He now has nearly a half century of active service in the one establishment.

Mr. Haskell's political activities have at all times staunchly favored the Republican party; in public office he is an efficient incumbent, and since 1903 he has fulfilled the duties of corporation clerk. In his fraternal affiliations, Mr. Haskell is a member of the Independent Order of Odd Fellows, and the Knights of Pythias; and he is a member of the Board of Trade, and has held the position of president of the Merchants' Association. His religious faith is that of the Congregational church; he is active in the work of the local church, and is its treasurer.

Edwin N. Haskell married, January 19, 1909, Florence M. Jewett, a native of Denmark, in this State, daughter of Algernon S. and Maria Jewett. Their children: Nelson J., and Eleanor L.

BURTON W. GOODWIN—Public service, whether in civic life or in a large business field of activity, has met with a wholehearted response on the part of Burton W. Goodwin, from whose ancestors, long connected with important industries in Maine, he has inherited a wealth of capable endeavor and of earnest and thorough workmanship, whose fruits are evident in township and State office, and in the management of his foundry business at Rumford.

Burton W. Goodwin was born December 31, 1879, at Carthage, a son of William Woodbury Goodwin, a native of Kennebunk, who engaged in the lumber business at Carthage, and who died June 5, 1926, and Ella A. (Berry) Goodwin, a native of Carthage, who survives her husband. The Carthage Public Schools and Wilton Academy were the sources of Mr. Goodwin's early education, and he then matriculated at the University of Maine, where he was graduated in 1903, with the degree Bachelor of Science. He was thus prepared to modernize the business of plumbing and steam-fitting in the most practical and thorough way, and starting out in that business at Mexico, in 1904, he has continued therein to the present, where he is also president and superintendent of the Mexico Water Company. In 1915, he became manager of the Clarke Foundry Company, at Rumford, and he has held the position of treasurer of that company since 1922.

To the Democratic party, Mr. Goodwin has always devoted his political interests; and he has held the office of selectman in Mexico for thirteen years, and he is also a member of the School Board in that town. From 1913 to 1915, also, he served his district in the State Legislature. Fraternally, Mr. Goodwin is affiliated with Blazing Star Lodge, Free and Accepted Masons, at Rumford; Walton Lodge, No. 132, Knights of Pythias, at Mexico; and Lodge No. 86, Benevolent and Protective Order of Elks, at Rumford.

Burton W. Goodwin married, in June, 1907, at Kennebunk, Ora I. Edgecomb, a native of Limington, in York County, daughter of Loring and Etta (Rich) Edgecomb. Their children: Dorothy Etta, William Burton, and Wilson.

HENRY G. PERRY—The larger portion of his business career has found Henry G. Perry one of the

Maine—20

most prominent of the undertaking fraternity of Rumford and this section of the State, where he has won the confidence and esteem of appreciative neighborhoods for the specific abilities that he is widely acknowledged to possess in his calling. He directs all the branches of the funeral profession with thorough understanding and consideration, and his headquarters and equipment are of the most approved present-day order. He is a son of Peter Perry, a mill-worker and lumberman, who was born in Paris, France, and became active in the Republican party in Maine, and of Lucy (Lessard) Perry, a native of Canada; both parents are now deceased.

Henry G. Perry was born April 5, 1877, at Fairfield, and he attended and was graduated at the grammar and high schools there. He entered upon his business career in the employ of furniture dealers at Rumford, where he continued a few years, and for a period of ten years he was associated with hotel work in the Rangeley Lakes region. Then, turning his attention to his present vocation, he was for some time in the employ of the undertaking firm of Gauthier, Vater Company, in Rumford. In 1917, Mr. Perry joined in partnership with Mr. Meader, and under the firm name of Meader and Perry, the present first-class funeral directing concern of that name is one of the established firms in the county, they having added a monumental and memorial department to their business in 1922.

The Democratic party has always found Mr. Perry a faithful adherent; and he has held the office of treasurer of the town committee for several years. Fraternally, he is affiliated with the Knights of Columbus, having held the office of financial secretary in the local Council; with Lodge No. 862, Benevolent and Protective Order of Elks, at Rumford; Independent Order of Odd Fellows; Société St. Jean Baptiste, and Ancient Order United Workmen. He is a communicant of St. John's Catholic Church.

Henry G. Perry married, October 12, 1912, Margaret Carroll, who was born in Lewiston, daughter of Patrick and Mary Carroll. They have one daughter, Elizabeth Barbara Perry, who was born December 9, 1921.

HORATIO GATES FOSS—The name of Foss has been recognized in Maine for generations, for leadership and traditional Americanism, and the heritage of accomplishment received from his forebears has been ably upheld by Horatio Gates Foss, of Auburn, who was born in Wayne, Maine, February 22, 1846, a son of Jeremiah and Elizabeth N. (Hankerson) Foss, the father a shoemaker.

Horatio Gates Foss, after finishing his educational work in the public schools of Wayne, helped his parent in his work. In the year 1875 he came to Auburn, where he became associated with the shoe manufacturing firm of Dingley, Strout & Company. In the following year he became a partner in the concern, without change of its title until 1887, when the retirement of Mr. Strout caused a change of name to Dingley, Foss & Company, with Mr. Foss as general manager. He was later made vice-president, an office which he still holds. The concern employs from five hundred to six hundred people and manufactures men's, youths' and boys' leather shoes, and canvas shoes for women, misses and children. Mr. Foss also is interested in a number of other enterprises, being a stockholder and director in the

First National Bank of Auburn and in the Auburn Trust Company. He is a Unitarian in religion and holds membership in many fraternal organizations, among them being the Benevolent and Protective Order of Elks and the Masons. In the last-named he holds the thirty-second degree and is a member of Asylum Lodge, of Wayne, Free and Accepted Masons; Bradford Chapter, Royal Arch Masons, of Auburn; Lewiston Commandery, Knights Templar; Maine Consistory, Sublime Princes of the Royal Secret; and Kora Temple, Ancient Arabic Order Nobles of the Mystic Shrine. He has held public office of honor and responsibility, having represented the city of Auburn in the State Senate in 1913. Although he is what the world is pleased to call a self-made man, he has done so well with his native talents that he stands out conspicuously as a man of exceptional culture and broad knowledge.

Mr. Foss married, in 1878, at Lewiston, Ella M. Fletcher, of Solon, Maine, daughter of Ezra and Mary Fletcher.

HERBERT C. ROWE—One of the oldest merchants in Bethel, Maine, in point of service to the public, for he entered his father's store while still in his "teens," is Herbert C. Rowe, whose drygoods establishment is among the most important of those in the community devoted to retail business.

Born in Bethel, October 26, 1877, the son of Ceylen and Mary (Grover) Rowe, he received the usual training of the Bethel public schools, and then attended the sessions of Chauncey Hall, in Boston, Massachusetts. On returning to Bethel, he became a regular employee in his father's drygoods store, and aided in the expansion of the business to which he eventually succeeded. Father and son were Republicans, Congregationalists, and ever ready to assist in any forward movement undertaken by the community. Neither, however, was an office seeker, although Herbert C. Rowe is treasurer of the village.

Mr. Rowe is vice-president of, and very active in the development of, the Bethel Water Company, which possesses over 4,000 acres of watersheds, and which distributes as fine a water supply as can be found in the State of Maine. He is also active in the fraternal orders, being a member of the Free and Accepted Masons, Past Master of the Lodge and now District Deputy; member of the Chapter, Royal Arch Masons; the Council, Royal and Select Masters; the Commandery, Knights Templar, and Kora Temple, Ancient Arabic Order Nobles of the Mystic Shrine; also a member of the Knights of Pythias, serving (1928) as Chancellor Commander, and enrolled with the Patrons of Husbandry.

Mr. Rowe married Alice M. Russell, at Bethel, Maine, July 3, 1907. Their children are: Herbert R., and Rosalind M.

LEVI C. BARKER—One of the veterans of the United States postal service is Levi C. Barker, of East Vassalboro, Maine, who has been continuously in office since 1889, a record not likely to be surpassed in many parts of the United States. He has, however, never relinquished a carriage and wagon business, which has grown into the largest of its class in Kennebec County, and he is keenly interested

in farming, although perhaps more for pleasure than for profit.

Born in Waldoboro, Maine, July 28, 1864, the son of Lorenzo and Kate (Cudworth) Barker, he spent his boyhood in that town, where his father was in business as a harness maker. Both parents were born in Maine, the father at Waldoboro, the mother at Thomaston. After being graduated from the public schools of East Vassalboro, Levi C. Barker took the course at the Business College of Augusta, Maine, and completed his education at Oak Grove Seminary, Vassalboro. On April 1, 1882, he was employed by G. H. Cates, as clerk in a general store at East Vassalboro, and he is still in this employ. After the automobiles came and wagons were not in demand, he went into the lumber business. A Republican, Mr. Barker's advice has always been welcomed by the leaders of that party. He is a member of the Second Methodist Church of Vassalboro. He belongs also to the Independent Order of Odd Fellows, and to the local Grange, Patrons of Husbandry.

Mr. Barker married (first) Sweetie Bragg, September 27, 1885, who died November 27, 1910; he married (second) Nancy Cates, September 17, 1919. Of the first union, Charles L. Barker, born June 14, 1889, married Gertrude Richardson, of Vassalboro, and their two children are Kenneth R., and Thomas L.

JAMES L. SIMPSON—Practically the whole of the mature life of James L. Simpson, now postmaster of North Vassalboro, Maine, an office he has held since 1921, has been devoted to the postal service, interrupted only by the time he gave to his country, either as a State Guardsman, or in the Regular Army. His readiness to respond to the call to colors was perhaps a matter of inheritance, for his father, a Maine farmer, served in the Civil War from 1861 to 1865, as sergeant in Company E, Seventeenth Regiment, Maine Volunteer Infantry.

Born in Winslow, Maine, March 14, 1884, son of John H. Simpson and Ruth T. (Starkey) Simpson, both natives of that place, and now deceased, James L. Simpson was educated in the public schools, and entered the postal service in Vassalboro, Maine, immediately upon being graduated, rising through various grades until his appointment as postmaster. In 1899, he had joined the Maine State Guard, and after two years' service, entered the United States Army in 1903, was assigned to the Twenty-eighth United States Infantry, and served four years. In June, 1916, he joined the Second Maine Volunteer Infantry as a bugler, and saw service on the Mexican border. During the World War he enlisted in the 103d Regiment of United States Infantry, which was part of the Twenty-sixth Division, as a mechanic, and spent eight months at Camp Bartlett. He was discharged at Westfield, Massachusetts. He is a member of the American Legion, of the Free and Accepted Masons, and of the Independent Order of Odd Fellows. With his family, he attends the Methodist church.

James L. Simpson's marriage to Ola M. Kittredge, daughter of Andrew Kittredge, of Winslow, Maine, took place in that city, September 30, 1908.

WALTER W. HENDEE, M. D.—After a distinguished career in the service of the United States

Government, and with the Medical Corps of the United States Army during the World War, Dr. Walter W. Hendee returned to his native State of Maine in 1918, and opened an office in North Vassalboro for the general practice of medicine.

Born in Augusta, Maine, the son of Edwin Carleton and Florence Emily Abbott (Whitman) Hendee, his boyhood was spent in Augusta, where both parents still live, and where his father for thirty-five years was a valued employee of the post office, and a leader in Republican politics. After completing the course in the public schools and the Cony High School of Augusta, he spent three years in the Medical School of Bowdoin College, and completed his medical training at the College of Physicians and Surgeons in Boston, Massachusetts, where he received his degree of Doctor of Medicine in 1914. Soon afterwards he was appointed assistant surgeon to the National Solders' Home at Togus, Maine, where he served three years, and was then transferred to the National Soldiers' Home at Dayton, Ohio, where he remained another year. In 1918, he entered the medical service of the United States Army, and was sent to Camp Greenleaf, in Georgia, where he spent three months, receiving his discharge at the close of the war. He then settled in North Vassalboro, which had been his mother's home town. He has served there on the School Board for three years, and also has taken part in various patriotic and philanthropic enterprises. He is charter member and Commander of the Vassalboro Camp of the American Legion, and now serving his fourth term; a member of the Kennebec County Medical Association, the Medical Society of the State of Maine, and of the American Medical Association. He is also chairman of the Cemetery Association of Vassalboro. He is a member of the Free and Accepted Masons, including Chapter and Commandery, and of the Protestant Episcopal church.

Walter W. Hendee married, September 10, 1924, Charlotte Smith, of Vassalboro.

ALTON F. HUSSEY—Varied activities are by no means unusual in America, but those of Alton F. Hussey, of East Vassalboro, Maine, are partly due to inheritance, and partly to opportunity, for he is the owner of the business of A. F. Hussey & Company, morticians, in which his father was senior partner, and is also the local representative of the most important of American life insurance companies. Of late years he has undertaken a realty development on the shore of Webber Lake, called "Pleasant Point Cottages," in partnership with C. A. Lacroix, of Portland.

Born in East Vassalboro, Maine, May 14, 1883, son of Frank O. and Selina (Bragg) Hussey, both natives of that place, Alton F. Hussey was educated in the public schools of East Vassalboro, and then took a special course of training at Erskine Academy, South China, Maine. From that institution he went to the Massachusetts College of Embalming, and upon being graduated, returned to East Vassalboro, and went into business with his father. This partnership was terminated in 1923, by the death of the elder Hussey, whose widow, however, is still living.

Mr. Hussey has long been identified with all progressive movements of his town. He is a member of the Grange, Patrons of Husbandry; of the Ki-

wanis Club of Waterville, Maine; of the Maine Undertakers' Association, and of the Maine Life Underwriters' Association. He is a Republican, and attends the Methodist church with his family. His fraternal affiliations include the Independent Order of Odd Fellows, in which he holds high rank, being Past Captain of Uniform Rank; the Free and Accepted Masons, Past Master, Vassalboro Lodge; the Chapter, Royal Arch Masons, and the Commandery, Knights Templar.

Alton F. Hussey married Jennie Fletcher, daughter of William and Emma (Washburn) Fletcher, of China, Maine, and they have one daughter: Ina Fletcher.

FREMONT A. HUNTON—The government official who qualifies for his post by years of experience in business, and in minor positions of public trust, is apt to be the most popular, especially with the business men of the community he serves, a statement wholly true of Fremont A. Hunton, postmaster at Readfield, Maine, and known to practically every resident there.

Son of Samuel and Betsy (White) Hunton, both natives of Readfield, and now deceased, Fremont A. Hunton was born there, May 31, 1859. His father was a farmer, descended from the earliest settlers of Kennebec County, and a veteran of the Civil War. Educated in the public schools, the future postmaster went to Boston to seek employment, became a clerk in a retail establishment, and after ten years returned to Maine, where he was made superintendent of the N. T. Gordon grain mill in Readfield, where he remained fourteen years. In 1921, President Harding appointed him postmaster of Readfield, an office to which he was reappointed by President Coolidge. A Republican by inheritance, Mr. Hunton had previously served as town clerk for two years, and had been a member of the School Board for seven years. A member of the Free and Accepted Masons, and of the Independent Order of Odd Fellows, and of the Foresters, Mr. Hunton has been a life-long attendant of the Methodist church.

Fremont A. Hunton was married, in Readfield, Maine, in 1883, to Esther A. Farrington, who died April 27, 1926, and like her husband, was a native of Readfield, and descended from pioneer stock.

DR. FRANK M. ROSS—The name Ross is interminably connected with Scotland, where its members have yielded nothing of valor, learning or piety to any other clan. The members of this great family in America likewise have carried their banners high, while keeping their feet planted upon the ground of practical affairs. In this category comes Dr. Frank M. Ross, of Kennebunk, whose achievements in his profession once resulted in his elevation to the vice-presidency of the Jefferson Medical College at Philadelphia, which today ranks with Johns Hopkins in institutions of this kind and is one of the most important parts of the University of Pennsylvania. Reverting to the Scotch Rosses, it is worthy of mention in passing that certain men of this name established themselves early in the nineteenth century in the Cherokee Nation of Indians in the Southeast, and that one of their descendants, John Ross, became principal chief of this tribe and took place with some of the leading American statesmen. Dr. Ross, who practiced for fifty years, is the fourth generation of his line to practice medicine, his great-grandfather, grandfather and father having followed the profession.

Dr. Ross was born January 4, 1851, at Kennebunk, son of Orrin S. Ross, a graduate of Bowdoin College, Brunswick, and a doctor, and of Elizabeth H. (Holden) Ross, of Sweden, Maine, who died in 1922. Dr. Orrin S. Ross died in 1917, a highly respected and much beloved citizen, and one who left indelibly upon the life of this community the impress of his unusual personality. Undoubtedly the qualities transmitted to the son have resulted in a large success in the profession and as well eminence in the business world, for Dr. Ross is a prominent banker and builder.

Frank M. Ross attended the public schools of Kennebunk and graduated from Bowdoin College in the class of 1877, with the degree of Doctor of Medicine. He began the practice of his profession in 1878 at Kennebunk, and has carried on a general practice ever since, for half a century, which is longer than any contemporary. As dean of the Kennebunk medical profession he is deeply revered and respected, while in the business world he enjoys the confidence and admiration of all who have ever dealt with him. He is a member of the York County and Maine State Medical societies and the American Medical Association. His business connections include the presidency of the Ocean National Bank and the presidency of the Kennebunk Building & Loan Association for twenty-one years. He is also a trustee of the Kennebunk Savings Bank. His sagacity in these connections give denial, in so far as he is concerned, to the oft-repeated statement that doctors make poor business men.

Dr. Ross is a member of York Lodge, Free and Accepted Masons, in which Order he has taken thirty-two degrees. He has been honored by his lodge brothers with the positions of Past Master, District Deputy and Illustrious Commander, which last-named post he has filled with great credit to himself and his brethren three times; also he was treasurer of St. Armand's Lodge, twenty-four years.

Dr. Ross married Louisa D. M. Morton, of Kennebunk, daughter of Edward W. Morton, former president of the Ocean National Bank, and of Olive Morton, who also came from a prominent family. Their children are: Annie D. M., Florabel L., and Rodney M. Ross, a graduate of Maine College and now president of the Hyde Windlass Company. Dr. and Mrs. Morton are much interested in antique furniture, glass and china, and many fine specimens thereof adorn their home in Kennebunk. Their summer home is pleasantly situated on the road to Kennebunkport.

HENRY L. HUNTON, a well-known attorney of Oakland, Maine, and member of an old New England family, was born February 21, 1865, at Readfield, Maine, the son of George C. and Annie E. (Wood) Hunton, both of whom are now deceased. The Hunton family is of old "Mayflower" stock, the first member having come from the Isle of Jersey, England, landing at New Hampshire in 1664. George C. Hunton, who was born on September 2, 1837, at Readfield, Maine, and who died April 11, 1902, was a well-known farmer of Maine. Annie E. (Wood) Hunton was born July 20, 1838, in Maine, and died October 28, 1908.

Henry L. Hunton received his preliminary education in the public school at Readfield, Maine, later attending Maine Wesleyan Seminary, Kents Hill, Maine. Upon the completion of these courses of study, he read law for three years under the competent preceptorship of Judge Emory Beane of Readfield. On March 12, 1889, he was admitted to the bar and then began the practice of his profession in Oakland, Maine. Since that time Mr. Hunton has become one of the most prominent attorneys in that town, a man noted for the excellence of his attainments. Always interested in the welfare of his community, he has been very active in the service of the people. He was a member of the building committee for the Public Library and is now a member of the board of trustees. He was also a member of the building committee for the high school. He served as Superintendent of Schools of Oakland in 1901 and 1902. In 1921, Mr. Hunton was elected to the State Legislature, where he served one term. At the present time (1928), he is attorney for the Oakland branch of the Augusta Trust Company.

Mr. Hunton has ever found time to take a part in other affairs. Among the professional organizations of which he is a member are the Maine State Bar Association and the Kennebec County Bar Association. He is affiliated with all bodies of the Masonic Order up to and including the Council, Royal and Select Masters, and is a past officer of these bodies. He is also a member of the Knights of Pythias, of which he is a past presiding officer. An avocation in which he is deeply interested is the raising of fancy poultry and he received five first prizes for his birds at the St. Louis World's Fair. At one time he served as president of the Maine State Poultry Association.

Henry L. Hunton married, September 18, 1889, at Lewiston, Maine, Harriet P. Peabody, born in Leeds, Maine, a daughter of Frank S. and Almina (Sumner) Peabody. Mr. and Mrs. Hunton are the parents of a daughter, Alice Almina, who was born February 4, 1891, in Oakland; she is a graduate of Colby College, and instructor of English in Jordan High School, Lewiston. Mr. Hunton and his family attend the Baptist church, where he is president of the Bible class.

DEAN E. WHEELER—Tact, sympathy, and an understanding of human nature are prerequisites to the profession of the mortician, of which Dean E. Wheeler, of Oakland, Maine, is an admirable exponent, representing a second generation of service in the community.

Born in Oakland, Maine, December 25, 1882, son of William Harrison and Eliza Florence (Winslow) Wheeler, he was educated in the public schools, and became one of his father's assistants at an early age. The elder Wheeler, who was a native of Waterville, Maine, born September 16, 1842, died September 8, 1925, had been a cabinetmaker in his youth, and was employed in the Maine Central car shops, where he also learned painting and glazing. This skill in craftsmanship proved valuable when he embarked in the retail furniture business, and probably was a factor in the partnership organized in 1884, with H. W. Wells, in which a furniture and an undertaking business were combined. In 1885, Mr. Wheeler bought out Mr. Wells, and removed to Church Street, into a building erected by the partners in 1884. Meantime, Dean E. Wheeler had passed through the public schools, had taken a special course of training in the Massachusetts College of Embalming, and in 1906, he was admitted to partnership, the firm doing business as W. H. Wheeler & Son. This association continued until the death of W. H. Wheeler, in September, 1925, when his widow assumed his place as senior partner. Mrs. Wheeler, whose family dates back to the early Colonial period of American history, was born in what is now Oakland, Maine, June 8, 1845.

Like his father, Dean E. Wheeler is a member of the Universalist church, and a Republican. His father was one of the charter members of the local Lodge, Free and Accepted Masons, Council and Chapter, and of St. Omar Commandery, Waterville, Knights Templar, of Maine. Dean E. Wheeler is also a member of the Free and Accepted Masons, including Blue Lodge, Chapter and Council. He is a member of the Independent Order of Odd Fellows, of the Kiwanis Club, the Grange, and the Chamber of Commerce.

OSCAR C. S. DAVIES, M. D.—Devotion of his talents and skill to the well-being of his fellow-men marked the career of the late Dr. Oscar C. S. Davies, one of Augusta's foremost physicians. There was never an occasion when his science was needed for the alleviation of suffering that he did not respond and his death was deeply and sincerely mourned by the many he had soothed in their hours of pain.

Dr. Davies was born at Sidney, Kennebec County, October 8, 1855, the son of Alonzo and Julia A. (Sargent) Davies. His early education was obtained in the public schools of his community, following which he took a course at the Coburn Classical Institute, Waterville, Kennebec County. He then entered Colby College, transferring later to Bowdoin College, from which he graduated in 1879 with the degree of Bachelor of Arts. He then attended Maine Medical School and in 1883 obtained from that institution his degree of Doctor of Medicine, then practiced and studied in New York City for five years. Then he was assistant physician at Augusta State Hospital until 1890. This was followed by a trip to Austria, where he took post-graduate studies in the University of Vienna. Upon his return from Austria he began a general practice of his profession in Augusta, where he officiated as a general practitioner. He did not confine his work to his private practice alone, but filled many important positions as well. He served as a member of the surgical staff of the Augusta General Hospital from 1898 to 1924, and was also chairman of the staff of the Augusta General Hospital from 1898 to 1900, and from 1922 to 1924. In the latter year he was appointed Surgeon Emeritus. He also served as City Physician for Augusta, and as County Examiner for insane criminals from 1905 to 1925; as chairman of the Augusta Board of Health; and as the attending specialist of the United States Veterans' Bureau from 1921 to 1924. Dr. Davies was prominent in Augusta General Hospital, having been one of the originators and founders. In his political preferences Dr. Davies was a Republican. Despite the manifold duties which his profession entailed, Dr. Davies found time to take a keen interest in many organizations. He was a member of his State and County Medical associations, and was fraternally affiliated with the Masonic Order, being Past Master of his Blue Lodge and a member of the Commandery.

On December 4, 1890, Dr. Davies married Mary B. Harlow, a daughter of Henry M. and Louisa Stone (Brooks) Harlow of Augusta. Mrs. Davies' father, Henry M. Harlow, a native of Vermont, was superintendent of the Augusta State Hospital for forty years. Her mother, Louisa Stone (Brooks) Harlow, was a native of Augusta. Dr. and Mrs. Davies were the parents of four children, one son and three daughters, as follows: 1. Louise; Bachelor of Arts degree, Wellesley College. 2. Henry H. Bachelor of Arts, Bowdoin College, 3. Julia S., attended Wellesley College; married Ralph G. Johnson, August 14, 1926; lives in San Gabriel, California. 4. Mary B., Bachelor of Arts degree, Wellesley College, 1928.

Dr. Davies passed away February 18, 1927. His death was the occasion of many sincere tributes of sorrow from those he had attended and from his brethren of the fraternal societies of which he was a member. Unsparing to himself when occasion arose for his professional services, he was a loss to the community in which he resided and for many years Dr. Davies will be remembered in Augusta as one who was ever ready to answer the call of duty, and who freely gave of his skill and ability to all in need of his service.

WILLIAM O. FROTHINGHAM—The entire business career of William O. Frothingham of South Paris, Maine, has been identified with the shoe trade in South Paris, and the same was true of his father before him, he having organized the concern now conducted by Mr. Frothingham. During the thirty years that he has been a resident of South Paris he has been closely connected with city and county affairs, and has taken a lively interest in civic improvements, in the general direction of commerce, and in the administration of office. Members of Oxford County fully appreciate the efforts of Mr. Frothingham as secretary and treasurer of the County Agricultural Society, a post he has retained for twenty years.

William O. Frothingham was born at South Paris on November 13, 1863, the son of William A. Frothingham, born at Portsmouth, New Hampshire, and Helen J. (Everett) Frothingham, born at Norway, Maine, both now dead. William A. Frothingham left a record of civic service to be remembered long and with gratitude in South Paris. He founded the shoe business inherited by William O. Frothingham and conducted by him in partnership with his brother for a time, after which the brother retired; he was postmaster for two terms, acted on the County Board of Commissioners, and a Democrat, served a term on the State Legislature, 1874-1875. William O. Frothingham has followed his father's example of helpful citizenship, supporting movements which he believes are in the right and for the greatest good to the greatest number, and opposing all others as stubbornly as he can. For four terms he was county sheriff; he is a director on the board of the South Paris Building & Loan Association, a member of the Free and Accepted Masons, and of both the

Norway and South Paris Kiwanis clubs. He belongs to the Congregational church.

William O. Frothingham married, at South Paris, in July, 1891, Jennie Leighton, who died November 10, 1918, the union resulting in the birth of one child: William L.

CHARLES W. ABBOTT—As postmaster of Albion, Maine, Charles W. Abbott exercises his duties in an efficient and creditable manner, being now thoroughly familiar with the work, which he began in 1914. Before that time he had been a blacksmith for forty-one years, a trade which he had learned early in life from his father, who had practiced it before him.

The son of Benjamin F. and Sarah J. (Drake) Abbott, both of whom were natives of Albion, Charles W. Abbott was born in East Benton, near Albion, on June 4, 1866. After he had attended the public schools, he became a blacksmith in his native town, where his father, an active Democrat, had been a blacksmith all his life. For forty-one years he continued as a blacksmith, until, in 1914, he left this work to become postmaster. Since that time he has been postmaster of Albion. The postmastership is not the first public office which he has held. For about seven years he was town clerk in Albion, having been elected to this office on an independent ticket, since he never affiliated himself with any of the existing political parties. Active in the fraternal life of his community, Mr. Abbott is a member of the Grange, Patrons of Husbandry; of the Free and Accepted Masons, in which Order he is affiliated with the Chapter, Royal Arch Masons, and is now District Deputy for District No. 7; and of the Independent Order of Odd Fellows. In religious matters he is identified with the Christian Church of Albion.

On November 27, 1890, in Albion, Charles W. Abbott married Cordelia P. Libby, a native of Albion, the daughter of Ebenezer and Mary (Pratt) Libby, both of whom are now deceased. Charles W. and Cordelia P. (Libby) Abbott are the parents of the following children: 1. Voyle, who is married. 2. Charline, also married. 3. Floyd, a teacher in the public schools. 4. Katherine.

CAPTAIN JOHN R. ANDREWS—With the distinction which few men can truthfully claim—that of having served his country in the Civil War and in the World War—the late Captain John R. Andrews certainly deserved the commendations which were so freely bestowed upon him. Although in the World War he was not able to enter into the activities of the campaign overseas, he performed most important work in one of the Government shipyards, where he was in charge of designing and construction.

Captain Andrews was born in Scarboro, Cumberland County, September 25, 1841, the son of James and Maria (Chase) Andrews. His early education he obtained in the public schools of Saco and Biddeford and he later attended the academy at Limington, York County, from which he graduated. He taught school in Cumberland Mills for a time and then took a position with the firm of Chadwick & York at "King's Corners," Biddeford. At the end of a year with this concern he became associated with Louis O. Cowan, then editor of the Biddeford "Journal." When the Civil War broke out the State of Maine was called upon for a regiment of cavalry and Captain Andrews hastened to enlist in the troop. He was mustered into the regiment on September 20, 1861, and into the service of the United States Government on October 31, of the same year. On September 1, 1862, he was commissioned second lieutenant, and he quickly rose to first lieutenant and then to the rank of captain. He fought all through the war and was honorably discharged in 1865. He returned to Saco for a short time and then moved to Iowa, where he became interested in farm lands. In 1866, he was appointed an officer in the Pension Department and for four years resided in Washington. Returning to Saco at the close of his term in the Pension Department, Captain Andrews was appointed postmaster of that town, which office he held for twelve years. He then went to Ohio and engaged in business as a railroad contractor. After four years of this work he was for some time in the various gold fields of the West as superintendent of mines for a New York syndicate. In this capacity he was also engaged at different times in the graphite mines of New Jersey and in the iron mines at Gouverneur, New York. In 1906, he returned to Saco and established a boat-building plant on the bank of the Saco River. After three years in Saco, Captain Andrews closed his plant and moved to Seattle, Washington, where he opened a similiar establishment. He remained in Seattle until 1915, when he returned to Maine with the intention of retiring from active business. Two years later the United States was drawn into the World War and Captain Andrews, although seventy-six years old, at once volunteered his services to the Government. He was placed in charge of designing and made superintendent of construction in the Atlantic Ship Yards at Portsmouth, New Hampshire, where he remained until the close of hostilities.

As an example of Captain Andrews' skill in the designing of yachts, it may be mentioned that in this line of work his name is known in every port where yachts are built. It is recalled that in 1917 the "Rudder Magazine" announced a contest which was open to nautical draftsmen throughout the world. This was the designing of a yacht for "Barney" Barnatto, the well-known South African diamond millionaire. After many designs had been carefully examined, Captain Andrews was announced to be the winner of the contest. His many contributions to the various nautical magazines were always very interesting to all yachtsmen.

On November 16, 1865, following his honorable discharge from the United States Army, and upon his return to Saco, Captain Andrews was married to Elizabeth J. Milliken, the daughter of Joseph and Nancy (Waterhouse) Milliken, the latter a prominent carpenter of that town. Captain and Mrs. Andrews were the parents of five children: 1. Mary A., married J. F. Beckwith, of Malta, Ohio; she now resides in Saco. 2. Anna W., married Henry W. Putnam, of Carthage, Missouri. 3. Kate, married Oliver P. Throgmorton, of Indianapolis, Indiana. 4. Charles J., now a resident of Detroit, Michigan. 5. Edwin S., in business at Detroit.

On February 14, 1925, the active career of Captain Andrews was ended by his death. His loss was most deeply mourned by his devoted family and by the true, firm and loyal friends he had made in Saco and in his many journeyings throughout the country.

He will be long remembered as a splendid example of a loyal citizen of his country, State and community, and as a man who ever gave the best that was in him to whatever line of endeavor in which he entered.

DELBERT F. COUSENS—Starting his business career as carpenter, Delbert F. Cousens, of Limerick, Maine, has become a building constructor on a large scale. Among the more important structural erections by which he is known are the State Prison, at Thomaston; the Bates Mill, at Lewiston; the Normal School at Castleton, Vermont; the house of the president of Dartmouth College, Hanover, New Hampshire; and the Limerick plant of the Limerick Mills, which is the largest manufactory of yarns in New England. In addition to his business affairs Mr. Cousens serves the town in an advisory capacity from time to time, devoting his technical knowledge to the welfare of the community when questions of community planning of streets and buildings came under consideration. He is a popular figure among the people of Limerick.

Delbert F. Cousens was born April 14, 1876, at Limington, Maine, son of Marshall Cousens, of Hiram, Maine, and Ida E. (Elwell) Cousens, of Buxton, Maine, his father having been a veteran of the Civil War. Mr. Cousens received his education in the public schools and went immediately into business, where for a period he undertook various connections, but soon decided to enter the field of building construction. In order to ground himself in the essentials of the work he began with hammer, saw and square, then with the principles of building mastered went into business independently. His success brought new contracts, and each contract brought other contracts, until his reputation as a builder of good buildings became fixed. Mr. Cousens is the type of man who takes pride in his work, and when undertaking a new structure he demands of his workmen that it be faultless in detail, whether or not the detail is visible. He, as a master artisan, is something of an artist; and with the pride he takes in creating new and beautiful buildings for homes, for education, for commerce, and for industry he has achieved artistic grace along with financial benefits, and has accumulated a sizeable fortune. He is a member of Standish Lodge, No. 70, Free and Accepted Masons; and of Limerick Town Club.

Delbert F. Cousens married, at the age of thirty, on April 9, 1907, Althea F. Young, of Biddeford Pool, York County, Maine, daughter of Abram and Mary Young. Of this union one child, Barbara Louise, was born, on October 15, 1917.

FERNE B. TREADWELL—His years of application to the specialty in which he excels, the automobile business, has been the means of bringing Ferne B. Treadwell to the fore in Lincoln and this part of the State, both in the Ford and Fordson agencies, and the general garage and repair interests. Mr. Treadwell, a veteran of the World War, is interested in all matters that pertain to the welfare of Lincoln, his business life, and civic improvement.

Ferne B. Treadwell was born January 14, 1895, at Prentiss, a son of R. G. Treadwell, a blacksmith, also a native of Prentiss, and of Allera G. (Coffin)

Treadwell, who was born in Lowell, Maine. After attending the public grammar and high schools at Lee, Mr. Treadwell worked for seven years in the automobile repair business. In 1926, he became associated with A. E. Webber, and they took over the Casino Motor Company, of Lincoln, with its location on Main Street, where they are popular agents for Fordson and Ford cars. Mr. Treadwell also buys and sells horses.

In the political field, Mr. Treadwell is a Republican, and though he has not sought public office, he is interested in the progress of the community. In July, 1918, he enlisted in the Ninth Ammunition Train of the United States Army, receiving his discharge in 1919, as a corporal. Fraternally, Mr. Treadwell is affiliated with Basker Higgins Lodge, Free and Accepted Masons; Mount Horeb Chapter, Royal Arch Masons; St. John's Commandery, Knights Templar; and Anah Temple, Ancient Arabic Order Nobles of the Mystic Shrine; also Kingman Lodge, Independent Order of Odd Fellows; Knights of Pythias; and the American Legion; and his hobbies are fishing and hunting. His religious faith is that of the Congregational church.

Ferne B. Treadwell married, in 1922, Josephine O'Roak, who was born in Macwahoc. Their children: Helen Ruth, and George Donald.

HAROLD E. TAYLOR—For more than eight years Harold E. Taylor has been filling the position of bookkeeper in the Ticonic National Bank of Waterville, Maine, where he has been employed since his return from service in the World War. Mr. Taylor was born in New York City, but he has spent the greater part of his life in New England. He is well known and well liked in Waterville and vicinity, and he has many warm personal friends here.

Harold E. Taylor was born in New York City, New York, April 21, 1895, son of John Taylor, a native of New York City, who was a sea captain during nearly all of his active career, and of Nellie (Withington) Taylor, who was born in Springfield, Massachusetts, both of whom are deceased. He attended the public schools of Winterport, Maine, including the high school, and then entered the Normal School at Castine, Maine. Later he attended business college. Upon the entrance of the United States into the World War he enlisted as a member of the Fifty-sixth Pioneers, with which he served overseas, as bugler, for one year, receiving his discharge July 16, 1919. Upon his return to civilian life he secured a position as clerk with the Gulf Refining Company, with whom he remained for one year, and then, late in 1919, obtained a position as clerk in the Ticonic National Bank, where he is now (1928) bookkeeper. In his political faith Mr. Taylor is a Republican. He is a member of the local Grange, Patrons of Husbandry; of the Independent Order of Odd Fellows; the American Legion, and the Veterans of Foreign Wars. His religious affiliation is with the Baptist church of Waterville, Maine. Mr. Taylor is one of the representative citizens of the community and is public spirited in the sense of the private citizen who is always ready to lend a hand in the promotion of plans made for the general welfare.

Harold E. Taylor was married, in April, 1917, at Augusta, Maine, to Flossie Baker, who was born in Belgrade, Maine, and they are the parents of two

children: Luella H., and Edward H., both of whom
are attending school. The family home is in Waterville.

EVERETT W. HODGKINS, M. D.—For a decade
one of the leading physicians of Thomaston, Maine,
who is at the same time prominent in professional
circles throughout the State, is Dr. Everett W. Hodgkins. He had careful theoretical preparation for his
profession, followed by wide practical experience.
His native ability in this line; his grave, yet courteous demeanor; his unwearying patience and sympathy, all serve to bring him popularity and success.
    Everett W. Hodgkins was born in Jefferson, Maine,
May 6, 1883, son of Winfield and Caroline (Hall)
Hodgkins, both now deceased, who were born in
Jefferson, Maine, where the father was a teacher.
The son was educated in the grammar schools of
New Castle, Maine, and the high school in the same
town. He then received the degree in pharmacy from
the Boston College of Pharmacy, after which he
studied medicine in the Medical College of the University of Vermont, graduating in 1916, with the
degree of Doctor of Medicine. Dr. Hodgkins then
continued his studies in the form of post-graduate
work in various Chicago hospitals, where he worked
and studied for a year and a half. At the end of this
careful preparatory period, he came to Thomaston
and set up the practice which has since grown to
such gratifying proportions. The skill and sincerity
of Dr. Hodgkins are beyond question, and his professional results are encouraging to all who suffer
the many general ailments which attack the human
body.
    In politics he is a Republican. He was on the
Examining Board of ·the Coast Artillery during the
World War and the National Guard Reserve. His
college fraternity was the Chi Chi, and his fraternal
affiliations are now with the Free and Accepted Masons, and the Knights of Pythias. He is a communicant of the Baptist church.
    On December 24, 1906, in Bristol, Maine, Everett
W. Hodgkins married Emma Sproul, daughter of
Gifford Sproul, now deceased, and of Nettie (Fossett)
Sproul.

MARCELLUS CAIN—For nearly a quarter of a
century Marcellus Cain has been engaged in business in Clinton, Maine, as an embalmer and funeral
director, also as a dealer in furniture. He is one of
the best-known and most successful in his profession
in this part of the State, and is also one of the prominent Republicans of this section. At the present time
(1928) he is serving as a representative in the State
Legislature.
    Marcellus Cain was born in Clinton, Maine, Au-
gust 9, 1873, son of Daniel Cain, a native of Kennebec
County, a farmer, who was a Republican and who
served in the State Legislature, and of Betsy (Chase)
Cain, born at Blanchard, Maine, both now deceased.
After attending the public schools of Clinton, Mr.
Cain took a commercial course in Shaw's Business
College, in Portland, Maine, and then, after being
variously employed for a time, learned the embalming and funeral directing business. For the
past twenty-four years he has been engaged in the
undertaking and furniture business in Clinton, and
there is no mortician in the county who is accounted
more skillful and more successful than is he. Along

with the successful management of his business, Mr.
Cain finds time for active service in local public
affairs and for the larger duties of State service. He
served as chairman of the Board· of Selectmen of
Clinton for a period of three years; was a member
of the School Board for three years, has served on
the Republican County Committee, and in 1927 was
elected to represent his district in the State Legislature, acquitting himself honorably and to the entire satisfaction of his constituents. Fraternally, Mr.
Cain is identified with Sebasticook Lodge, Free and
Accepted Masons, of which he is a Past Master;
also with Pine Tree Lodge; and he is a member of
St. Omar Commandery, Knights Templar, of Waterville, Maine. He is a member of the local Grange,
Patrons of Husbandry; and professionally is identified with the Maine Funeral Directors' Association,
which he is now (1928) serving as president. He is
also a member of Greenlawn Rest Association. His
religious affiliation is with Brown Memorial Church,
which he serves as a member of the board of trustees.

JAMES LOUIS BOYLE—Though a native of
New Brunswick, Canada, Mr. Boyle has been a resident of Maine, ever since he reached manhood. Engaged in the practice of law at Waterville, Kennebec
County, he is one of the most widely known of the
younger members of the Maine bar. His ties to the
State of his adoption have also been greatly strengthened by some two years' overseas service with the
Twenty-sixth Division during the World War. He
is particularly well-known amongst ex-service men
as the Adjutant of the Maine Department of the
American Legion, which office he has held ever since
this organization was formed and in which capacity
he has rendered very valuable, effective and unselfish service.
    James Louis Boyle was born at Chance Harbor,
New Brunswick, Canada, August 25, 1886, a son of
Peter and Alice (Doone) Boyle. He received his
preliminary education in the public schools, after
which he became a student at the University of
St. Joseph, St. Joseph, New Brunswick, graduating
in 1906, with a degree of Bachelor of Arts. Later
he took up the study of law, for which purposes he
attended the University of Maine, Orono, where
he received the degree of Bachelor of Laws in 1912,
and that of Master of Laws, in 1913. He then
engaged in the practice of law, interrupting, however, a successfully started career soon after the
United States had entered the World War on the
side of the Allies in April, 1917. Enlisting as a
private in the Maine National Guard in June, 1917,
he went overseas with the 101st Sanitary Train,
Twenty-sixth Division, in which he served during
1917-19. Receiving his honorable discharge with the
rank of sergeant, April 29, 1919, he returned to
Maine and resumed the practice of law at Waterville, Kennebec County. Since then he has continued his professional career with great success,
maintaining offices at No. 108 Main Street, Waterville. Mr. Boyle is, perhaps, most widely known in
Maine in his capacity as adjutant of the Maine Department of the American Legion. He has been
actively connected with this organization since its
earliest days and, indeed, he was, together with General Albert Greenlaw of Eastport, one of the Maine
representatives to the meeting held in the winter of

1919 at the old Cercle Theatre in Paris, France, at which the American Legion was formed. After his return to the United States he also attended the St. Louis Caucus in May, 1919, being one of eight representative Maine ex-service men invited by Governor Carl E. Milliken to represent the State of Maine. Immediately after the St. Louis Caucus had adjourned, the Maine delegates voted to form a temporary organization and Mr. Boyle was elected its secretary. On him devolved most of the work of arousing interest in the American Legion amongst Maine ex-service men and it was through him that official membership application blanks were sent out in large numbers. Before long twenty-five Posts had been formed, after which a State meeting was called by Chairman Greenlaw and Secretary Boyle. At that time Mr. Boyle was a resident of Augusta and it was Augusta Post which he represented at this meeting, held in Augusta. He was also one of the Maine Delegates to the National Convention of the American Legion held at Minneapolis in November, 1919, during which he served as a member of the Committees on Credentials and Convention Rules. Ever since 1919, he has served as secretary or adjutant of the Department of Maine, his very effective and active work in this office bringing him recognition in the form of reëlection at each annual State Convention. He devotes a great deal of time and effort to this work, traveling extensively throughout the State and frequently visiting and addressing some of the one hundred and thirty-eight local Posts of the American Legion located in all parts of Maine. Much of the great success of the Legion in Maine is due to his devotion to this cause, and he is the only department executive officer who has held office continuously since the Maine Department was first formed. He is also a member of the Waterville Rotary Club, while his religious affiliations are with the Roman Catholic church.

Mr. Boyle married, at Augusta, October 2, 1922, Ethel M. Parlin, a daughter of Herbert and Ellen M. Parlin. Mr. and Mrs. Boyle are the parents of one daughter, Patricia Doone Boyle, born August 18, 1923. They make their home at Waterville.

EZRA W. BOSWORTH was born in Southampton, Massachusetts, January 19, 1867, son of Reuben E. Bosworth and Sarah A. (Wright) Bosworth, both of whom were natives of Montgomery, Massachusetts, and who are now deceased.

Ezra W. Bosworth was educated in the public schools of Southampton, Massachusetts, after which he attended business college in Brooklyn, New York, and the following eight years did stenographic work in manufacturing and railroad offices. In 1895 he entered the grain business in Hiram, Maine, which was continued successfully for fifteen years.

In November, 1910, Mr. Bosworth purchased an interest in the Fryeburg Lumber Company and became treasurer of this concern, carrying on a very successful business until 1922, when the plant was sold to the Conway Box Company. During this time he was connected with the Electric Lighting companies in this vicinity, holding the position of treasurer of the Fryeburg Electric Light Company and the Conway (New Hampshire) Electric Light &

Power Company. He has continued his connection with the lumber industry, acquiring tracts of timberland.

In 1925 he organized the Fryeburg Motor Company, erecting a steel, fireproof garage on Main Street, carrying a general line of automobile supplies and accessories and providing an efficient and expert repair department, conducting the business on a policy of service and satisfaction to all customers. In his capacity as head of the Fryeburg Motor Company, he catered to a steadily increasing trade, which recognized the thorough dependability of this organization. He sold this business in 1928.

In civic affairs of the town Mr. Bosworth takes an active part and lends his assistance to all movements for progress and expansion. His fraternal connections are with Pythagorean Lodge, Free and Accepted Masons, of which organization he is also a member of the Chapter and Commandery. In politics he is a supporter of the Republican party, and his religious affiliations are centered in the Universalist church.

Ezra W. Bosworth married (first), October 17, 1892, at Denmark, Maine, Jennie Bean, born at Denmark, who died in 1898, daughter of George R. and Sarah (Jordan) Bean. To this union was born one daughter, Bethesda, born at Lyndonville, Vermont, December 13, 1893. Mr. Bosworth married (second), April 21, 1904, at Denmark, Mary Berry, born at Portland, Maine, May 8, 1880, daughter of Albert F. Berry, a native of Jefferson, New Hampshire, and Maria (Hobbs) Berry, a native of Norway, Maine, and they have one son, Delbert B., born April 17, 1908, at Hiram, Maine.

THOMAS J. PARK—In the manufacture of woolen goods, few men are more adept and experienced than is Thomas J. Park, president and treasurer of Park Mills, Incorporated, of Sabattus, Maine. For forty years he has been identified with the textile industries, and as a manufacturer of wool suitings he is thoroughly familiar with every phase of that department of the woolen manufacturing business. He is a director of the Manufacturers' National Bank, of Lewiston, and is a member of the Maine Associated Industries.

Mr. Park is of Scotch parentage, his father, the late William Park, having been a native of Galashields, Scotland, born in November, 1834, died in May, 1914; was engaged in the woolen manufacturing industry in Scotland, but later came to this country, where he continued to manufacture woolen goods. Catherine (Campbell) Park, mother of Mr. Park, was born in Galashields, Scotland, and died in June, 1900.

Thomas J. Park was born in Pittsfield, Maine, July 26, 1873, but received his education in Canada, attending the public schools of Sherbrooke, Canada, and then continuing his studies in Sherbrooke Academy. From earliest years he was identified with the woolen manufacturing industry, and as president and treasurer of the Park Mills, Incorporated, of Sabattus, Maine, he has for many years been well known to the trade. Forty years of continuous experience in this field have made him truly an expert and his business ability is well known. Asso-

314 MAINE—A HISTORY

ciated with him, in official capacity, are his two sons, Gordon R. Park, vice-president; and Ralph T. Park, secretary. As a member of the board of directors of the Manufacturers' National Bank, of Lewiston, Mr. Park is contributing his well-tested ability to the success of that institution, and he is an interested member of the Maine Associated Industries, also of the Auburn Chamber of Commerce. His religious affiliation is with the Methodist church.

Thomas J. Park was married, in East Lyme, Connecticut, November 25, 1896, to Nora A. Beckwith, who was born in East Lyme, April 23, 1872, daughter of Robert and Phoebe (Maynard) Beckwith, both natives of East Lyme. Mr. and Mrs. Park have two sons: 1. Gordon R., born in East Lyme, August 6, 1898, who is associated with his father in the woolen manufacturing business as vice-president of the Park Mills, Incorporated, of Sabattus. 2. Ralph T., born in East Lyme, June 8, 1900; now secretary of the Park Mills, Incorporated, of Sabattus. Father and sons are able and congenial business associates, and all three have many friends in this section of the State. The elder son, Gordon R., served overseas during the World War, enlisting in April, 1918, and serving actively in the defensive sector with the American Expeditionary Forces until the signing of the Armistice, receiving his discharge August 13, 1919. The family home is located at No. 294 Minot Street, Auburn.

DON CARLOS HUBBARD—As vice-president of the Webster Rubber Company, of Sabattus, Maine, manufacturers of rubber moulded goods, such as rubber heels, rubber soles, sheet stock, and rubber door mats, Don Carlos Hubbard is identified with the only industry of its kind in the State of Maine. In 1927, was added a department for the reclaiming of tires and tubes. The concern turns out about two hundred thousand rubber heels per week, and employs, on an average, seventy people. Mr. Hubbard is a thirty-second degree Mason, and is an active and interested member of the Auburn Chamber of Commerce.

Born in New Gloucester, Maine, December 6, 1881, Don Carlos Hubbard is a son of Philip H. Hubbard, a lumber dealer and farmer, who was born in Palmyra, Maine, and of Kate M. (Hurd) Hubbard, a native of New Jersey. He received his education in the public schools his birthplace, including the high school, and then, when his high school course had been completed he went to Rumford Falls with Stanley Bisbee, where he learned the trade of steamfitter, remained about three years. In 1908-1909, he was engineer at Poland Spring with Hiram Ricker & Sons, then to J. H. Stetson Company in Lewiston for about one year, when in 1911 he entered the employ of the Cushman Hollis Company, of Auburn, Maine, as master mechanic. The concern was engaged in making shoes, and Mr. Hubbard remained with this firm until September 28, 1924, when he was elected vice-president and general manager of the Webster Rubber Company, of Sabattus, Maine, which official and executive positions he is still (1928) filling. The Webster Rubber Company manufactures a variety of moulded rubber goods, but specializes in rubber heels, of which, as has already been stated, they produce more than two hundred thousand per week. In addition to this

staple product, the concern also manufactures sheet stock and rubber door mats, and the volume of its output has increased to proportions which require the services of about seventy employees. Mr. Hubbard is a business man of ability, and skilled in his special field, and is rendering most valuable service to the company. In his political sympathies he is a Republican. From 1909 to 1911 he was a member of the Coast Artillery, National Guard, and he has always been interested in civic affairs. He is one of the active members of the Auburn Chamber of Commerce, and is well known in the Masonic Order, being a member of Cumberland Lodge, No. 12, Free and Accepted Masons, and of all the York Rite bodies, up to and including the Consistory, and the Temple, Ancient Arabic Order Nobles of the Mystic Shrine. Mr. Hubbard has many loyal friends in Auburn and vicinity, who esteem him for his solid worth as a man and as a citizen, as well as for his ability as a business man. He is a member of the Congregational church, of Auburn, Maine.

Don Carlos Hubbard was married, in Poland, Maine, January 1, 1908, to Marie Shackford, who was born in Poland, Maine, daughter of Flavius B. Shackford, who has served in the State Legislature of Maine, and of Josie (Cobb) Shackford, both natives of Poland, Maine. The Shackford family is one of the very old families of New England, and includes among its members many who have achieved distinction. Mr. and Mrs. Hubbard have four children: 1. Flavius B., born in Poland Spring, Maine. 2. Doris J., born in Lewiston, Maine. 3. Donald H., born in Lewiston, Maine. 4. Esther M., born in Auburn, Maine. The family make their home at No. 12 Josslyn Street, Auburn, Maine.

EVERETT PHOENIX SMITH, B. S.—In the field of education, Everett Phoenix Smith is rendering splendid service as principal of Leavitt Institute, at Turner, Maine. Mr. Smith is a graduate of Colby College, and had served as an administrator in various schools and academies in this State for a period of eight years prior to his coming to Turner, in 1924. He has been very successful in his work here, and has made a warm place in the hearts of those with whom he is associated, exerting a vital influence among his students and teachers, and greatly improving the general efficiency of the Institute. During 1920 and 1921 Mr. Smith was a member of the firm of Smith and Smith, grocers, of Augusta.

Everett Phoenix Smith was born in Waterboro, March 1, 1889, son of Frank Smith, who is engaged in farming, and of Addie Augusta Smith. He attended the elementary schools of Waterboro, and then prepared for college in Kent's Hill Seminary, at Kent's Hill, completing his course there with graduation in 1912. In the fall of 1912 he entered Colby College, at Waterville and in 1916, he received from that institution of learning the degree of Bachelor of Science. He had chosen to become an educator, and his first appointment after receiving his degree was to the position of principal of the high school at Mattawamkeag. The following year he served as sub-master of the high school at Bar Harbor, and in the fall of 1917, he was installed as principal of Potter Academy, at Sebago, where he continued to serve until the close of the spring term in 1924. Since that time he has been located in

Turner, as principal of Leavitt Institute, where he has already established a reputation for scholarship, for administrative ability, and for vital interest in all that pertains to the welfare of the youth of the place. Young enough to still be closely in touch with the interests and aspirations of youth, well prepared for his work, enthusiastic, and devoted to his profession, Mr. Smith is steadily adding to the prestige of Leavitt Institute, and his wholesome influence is an important factor in the community. In addition to his work at Colby College, Mr. Smith has also added to his professional preparation by study in the Harvard summer session of 1923, and he is steadily increasing his equipment for his work, by reading and study. He was a member and president of the Literati Society of Kent's Hill, while he was a student there, and he is also a member of Colby Chapter, of the Delta Upsilon College Fraternity; of the Masonic Order, and of the Patrons of Husbandry. His religious membership is with the Baptist church.

Everett Phoenix Smith was married, in Augusta, June 21, 1917, to Susie May Smith, daughter of Freeborn Bartlett and Loreda (Withee) Smith. They have four children: 1. Stanley Bartlett, born March 29, 1920. 2. Elaine Wilma, born December 31, 1921. 3. Alden Everett, born July 5, 1923. 4. Lawrence Conrad, born July 21, 1926. The family home is at Turner Center.

CLARK B. RANKIN, M. D.—Practicing the medical profession in Maine for almost half a century, for the last thirty-three years in Mechanic Falls, Clark B. Rankin stands high among the professional members of the community. A man of sterling character, sound ethics, amiable disposition and having a friendly attitude toward all that make for the improvement of the general welfare, he is reckoned one of the outstanding citizens of his town and the State of Maine.

He was born in Hiram, Maine, September 7, 1858, a son of Charles Rankin, also born in Hiram, and of Octavia (Colby) Rankin, born in Denmark, Maine. His father was a lumberman and served the State in the Senate in 1879. Clark B. Rankin received his early education in the public schools of Hiram and then attended Nichol's Latin School, of Lewiston, from which he was graduated in the class of 1876. He then went to Bates College and was graduated from that institution in 1880 with the degree of Bachelor of Arts. This was followed by the course at Bowdoin Medical College, which graduated him with the class of 1883, awarding him the degree of Doctor of Medicine. He began his general practice in that year, establishing himself in Bryant's Pond, where he remained until 1894, when he decided to transfer his practice to Mechanic Falls, where he has since been located. In politics he is a Democrat, in religion he is affiliated with the Federated Church. Also, he has been Pension Examiner for Norway, Maine. In fraternal organizations he is a thirty-second degree member of the Free and Accepted Masons, belonging to all bodies, also holding membership in the Knights of Pythias and in the local Chamber of Commerce.

Mr. Rankin married, at Bryant's Pond, Maine, Lydia L. Stephens, daughter of Ezra and Laura (Andrews) Stephens, all natives of Paris, Maine. The couple have the following children: 1. Charles

S., born in Woodstock, Maine, in 1892. 2. Clark C., born in Woodstock, in 1894.

ROBERT JEAN DYER—An honorable record of service for his country in its hour of need, when he enlisted in the army and rose in rank to become second lieutenant, marks a part of the career of Robert Jean Dyer, now postmaster of Turner, appointed by President Coolidge for a term of four years from December 10, 1926. Mr. Dyer began his work with a college education that stood him in good stead, and brought him into contact with his fellow-citizens where they could observe his labors and make judgment of his abilities. That these were found more than satisfactory was proven when the opportunity came to show their appreciation by his recommendation for public office of honor and trust. He has shown himself to be a man of high character and worth to the community, giving full value for all trusts reposed in him.

He was born in Turner, June 8, 1895, a son of Aubrey Jean, a liveryman and taxicab driver, and of Anna (Snell) Dyer. His education was acquired in the public schools of his native town and at Leavitt Institute, Turner Center, where he spent four years, then attending Bates College, in Lewiston, where he remained for three years, leaving it to enlist in the army, on October 3, 1917. He was attached to the 303d Field Artillery as sergeant of Company A, later transferred to Company B, Seventieth Field Artillery, when he was commissioned second lieutenant. He was honorably discharged March 10, 1919, and at once became associated with the Union Water Power Company, of Lewiston, working with the survey outfits and as general repair man until June 1, 1922. He then entered the employ of the W. B. Bradford Estate, where he worked as a clerk until his appointment as postmaster of Turner, on December 10, 1926. He is independent in politics and this is his first office. He is a member of Industry Lodge, No. 74, Knights of Pythias, of Lewiston, and attends the Baptist church of Turner.

Robert Jean Dyer married, in Ayer, Massachusetts, December 8, 1917, Louise Hall, daughter of Mandeville and Marcia (Varney) Hall. They are the parents of three children: 1. Robert Hall, born June 16, 1918. 2. Marshall Humphrey, born May 20, 1920. 3. Richard Paul, born August 14, 1922.

HAROLD T. BRIGGS—Entering business soon after his education had taken him through a partial course at college, Harold T. Briggs, of Mechanic Falls, Maine, became associated with a financial institution, since which time he has given that branch of activity his sole attention. The result has been a continuous advance, with a proportionate advantage to the public which he and his business serve, since he has shown a constant tendency to promote the general welfare of the community while he is advancing his own cause. His has been a case of application of the Golden Rule, a position which has won for him the recognition of every good citizen as a man of exceptional worth to the body politic.

He was born in South Paris, Maine, January 25, 1885, a son of Fred C. Briggs, who was manager for the Paul Manufacturing Company of Boston, and of Lila (Stone) Briggs. Attaining his early education in the public schools of South Paris, where he was graduated from high school with the class of

1902, he took a course of one year at Colby College, then entering business. He became associated with the Paris Trust Company and remained with that institution during 1917 and 1918 when he was made assistant treasurer of the Wilton Trust & Banking Company, a position he retained until January, 1919. He was then offered and accepted the position of assistant cashier of the People's National Bank, at Waterville, Maine, where he remained until 1923. He then went to the Lewiston Trust Company, as manager of its branch at Mechanic Falls, where he still presides in that post. During his residence in Waterville he was auditor of the Kennebec Water District and treasurer of the Waterville Country Club. He is a Republican in politics and has been president of the Mechanic Falls Chamber of Commerce. His college fraternity is Zeta Phi, and he attends the Universalist church.

Mr. Briggs married, in South Paris, August 28, 1906, Maude Marion Lunt, born in Farmington, daughter of Oscar and Lila (Locke) Lunt, both natives of Farmington. They have two children: 1. Mary Burnham, born in South Paris. 2. Ruth Marjorie, born in South Paris.

EDWIN B. MILLIKEN—For fifty years Edwin B. Milliken, of Auburn, has been identified with the shoe business of this State, beginning as a boy and rising to the post of general superintendent of one of the most prominent houses in this section of New England.

He was born in Minot, March 25, 1863, and attended the public schools there until he was fifteen years of age, when he began his life-work. His father was Benjamin Milliken, a native of Scarborough, and a carpenter by profession; his mother, Martha Milliken, a native of Hartford, Maine.

Edwin B. Milliken began his career at Mechanic Falls, later becoming foreman of the Pray-Small Company, where he remained for five years. He then entered the service, in Auburn, of the Howard, Briggs & Pray Company, where he continued from 1901 until 1912, when he transferred his talents to the Ault-Williamson Shoe Company, of Auburn, rising to the superintendency in 1925 and still occupying that post. He is a Republican in politics and holds membership in the Independent Order of Odd Fellows, the Auburn Chamber of Commerce and the Young Men's Christian Association. His church is the People's Methodist Episcopal.

Mr. Milliken married, in Auburn, Annie Drake, daughter of Henry and Ellen (Dillingham) Drake.

JOHN HOWARD RANDALL—One of the owners of the successful coal dealing firm of Randall & McAllister, of Portland, Maine, as well as sole owner of a beautiful farm of four hundred acres at Harrison, John Howard Randall is one of the substantial citizens of the community, where he has lived for many years.

He was born in Portland, June 12, 1867, a son of John F. Randall, of Freeport, Maine, and of Elvira S. (Sargent) Randall, of Portland, the first-named also having been a coal dealer. John H. Randall was educated in the public schools of Portland and at Gray's Business College there. Since young manhood he has been engaged in the coal business and has owned his present farm for about twenty years.

In politics he is a Republican and in religion a Congregationalist.

He married, at Harrison, Maine, December 8, 1896, Lida A. Trafton, born in Naples, Maine, March 30, 1876, daughter of Frank Trafton, of Harrison, who died May 10, 1918, and of Clara L. (Chaplin) Trafton, who was born in Naples and died January 24, 1926.

LESTER B. SHACKFORD—From a beginning as a clerk in a shoe manufacturing house, Lester B. Shackford of Auburn, rose to be sales manager of a branch of the establishment and in a total of six years to the vice-presidency of the company. This record is one that graphically portrays the business ability, as well as the personality of the man, for without both in coöperation there is little hope for such rapid elevation. Still in his youth, he is bound to reach even greater heights in the commercial world.

He was born in Poland, Maine, May 7, 1893, a son of Flavius B. Shackford, who was born in Poland, Maine, January 6, 1861, and died January 6, 1919, and of Josephine E. (Cobb) Shackford, also born in Poland, August 30, 1866. His father was a farmer and had been a member of the State Legislature. He was a member of the Free and Accepted Masons, being affiliated with Cumberland Lodge, and was a Knight Templar.

Lester B. Shackford was educated in the public schools of Poland and at Hebron Academy, afterward attending Bowdoin College and being graduated therefrom in the class of 1913, with the degree of Bachelor of Arts. His first work was with the International Banking Corporation of New York and later with the Poland Spring Company of New York up to the opening of the World War. After the war he entered the employ of the Ault-Williamson Shoe Company of Auburn, Maine, and later was made sales manager, in the planning department. In 1923, at the opening of the St. Louis branch of this company he was transferred to St. Louis as Western sales manager. Two years later he was elected vice-president of the company, which manufactures comfort and semi-dress shoes for women.

His military record began with his enlistment June 15, 1917, after the entrance of the United States into the World War, when he was attached to the Medical Corps and station at Camp Upton, New York. He served until May, 1919, when he was honorably discharged. He is a Mason, belonging to all York Rite bodies, and is a member of the Kiwanis Club, the Martindale Country Club and the Chamber of Commerce of Auburn. He is a Republican in politics and an attendant of the Congregational church.

Mr. Shackford married, April 5, 1923, in Auburn, Anna E. Reichert, born in Providence, Rhode Island, daughter of Carl E. Reichert, a native of Germany, and of Anna E. Reichert, of Providence. They have two children: Anna E., born in St. Louis, Missouri, March 13, 1925, and Lester B., Jr., born in Auburn, April 20, 1928.

WILLIS ALLEN TRAFTON—Forced to go to work to support his widowed mother when he was but twelve years of age, Willis Allen Trafton instantly gave evidence of the mettle of which he was made and, never faltering during the years, rose to a position of commanding importance in the industrial world of Maine. He is today one of its most respected and influential citizens, as well as one of the most capable business men of Auburn.

Willis Allen Trafton was born in Alfred, Maine, February 11, 1876, a son of Freeman E. and Ruth Annie (Knight) Trafton, his father also a native of Alfred and a meat dealer there until his death at the early age of thirty-six years. There were three sons in the family, two younger than Willis. The last-named attended the public schools of Alfred until he was nine years of age, when his mother and family removed to Auburn. Here he again went to school, but after three years of study he was compelled to look for employment, in order to assist his mother, whose lot was serious after the death of her husband, seven years earlier. His first occupation was as errand boy in the Barker Mill, where he worked for three years, then becoming payroll clerk at the age of sixteen years in another establishment. Again he made a change, this time to become associated with the First National Bank of Auburn in a clerkship. He was advanced to be a bookkeeper and then to teller, in which occupation he remained for seventeen years, accepting the post of treasurer of the Dingley-Foss Shoe Company in 1909, continuing until 1923, when he took over control of the company and became president and general manager. He is, in politics, a Republican, and in religion a member of the High Street Congregational Church, which he assists by liberal and frequent benefactions. His political affiliations with the Republican party extend only to national questions; in local affairs he is liberal in that degree that makes the perfect citizen, looking only toward the improvement of conditions that affect his fellow-citizens and the prosperity of the community. He is a member of the board of directors of the Central Maine General Hospital, and board of fellows of Bates College. He is a thirty-second degree member of the Masonic Order, holding membership in Tranquil Lodge, No. 49, Free and Accepted Masons; Bradford Chapter, No. 38, Royal Arch Masons; Dunlap Council, No. 8, Royal and Select Masters; Lewiston Commandery, No. 6, Knights Templar; and Kora Temple, Ancient Arabic Order Nobles of the Mystic Shrine, of Lewiston.

Mr. Trafton married, in Auburn, November 15, 1905, H. Frances Dain, daughter of William C. and Helen (Wiggin) Dain, of Auburn. Four children have resulted from this marriage: 1. Stephen Dain, born May 13, 1907, who graduated from Bowdoin College, class of 1928. 2. Helen Ruth, born December 26, 1909; student at Mount Holyoke College, class of 1931. 3. Mary Frances, born August 24, 1917. 4. Willis Allen, born November 13, 1918.

HARRY H. COCHRANE—Critics have found the ecclesiastical and mural art work of Harry H. Cochrane of singular beauty, and the demand for it has spread throughout New England and across the United States. But Maine is his native State; Monmouth is his home; and to him, whatever things of beauty he may accomplish elsewhere, his love for town and commonwealth comes uppermost. Although Monmouth is not the place of his birth, it is the one of his earliest remembrance, for it was while still a small child that he came here with his father

from his birthplace in Augusta to dwell in the small community which he has chosen ever since to call his own.

It happened one day while Mr. Cochrane was a student in the schools of Monmouth that a fresco artist came to town. The boy was fascinated, as he stood watching the artist decorate the church upon which he was working. It was his first glimpse into the sphere of mural art which was to become his later *metier*. From that moment, Mr. Cochrane has observed, he had no peace of mind until he had completed mural work on his first church. He had displayed a ready talent at drawing while in the grade school, inherited from his father who in his early days was a portrait artist and, later, a government architect. By the time he was sixteen years of age he knew that the choice of a career, for himself, rested in art alone, and he wrote to his father, then employed in architectural work with headquarters in Washington, District of Columbia, asking to be sent to an art school in New York City. But the elder Mr. Cochrane replied that his son was too young, for him to wait. He did not, it is to be noted, attempt to discourage the boy's artistic ambitions; for in that, father and son were as one. It was a disappointed boy who received the news, however, and there followed a period during which he groped rather blindly toward progress, unassisted by instructors, whom he had never had, but whom he now needed in order to advance properly. He followed his father's counsel, and waited.

Opportunity came to Mr. Cochrane in due time. He went to New York City, and straightforth to St. John Harper, head of the school which had served the great Sargent, with the request that he be allowed to enroll in the life class. But no! Such a thing was unheard of. One needed preparation first in the lower classes. Talk of rules ensued. Finally Mr. Cochrane proposed this: That he submit certain works which he had done, and then abide by the decision of the trustees as to entrance. He waited, as patiently as could be imagined—then came the word. He was admitted. Not only that, but he might take his choice of either of the two upper classes in the school. This was only the beginning. Eventually he studied in the Chicago Art Institute, after employment by a portrait company in Massachusetts. It so happened that in some work he was doing for this company, an architectural background was needed, and Mr. Cochrane designed it. A German artist in the company, regarding the work, suggested that he take up fresco as a medium, and the commendation of the old and experience painter found fruit; Mr. Cochrane studied fresco, and turned his energies earnestly to ecclesiastical art. His works in churches have become of great renown, until at the present time (1928), his record includes decorations for some one hundred and fifty such institutions in Maine alone, and his handiwork appears in every State in New England save one, in churches and public buildings. His panel entitled "The Vision of Rotary," has attracted attention and deep appreciation. This is an interpretation of the thought of the order, beautifully executed, and a splendid tribute to the teachings of the Rotary code. At the left of the picture stands the Temple of Peace. In the center two figures with square and compass direct the advance of Rotary's well-known Wheel of Progress, up from which lower dark clouds typifying the Sea of Greed and Malice in age-long conflict.

The work which many critics consider the finest Mr. Cochrane has produced is that executed for Kora Temple, Lewiston, Maine. Mr. Cochrane himself, incidentally, is a Noble in the Ancient Arabic Order Nobles of the Mystic Shrine. Although completed some time ago and known generally by members of the Order in New England, the collection was not put before the public until 1928. This work is impressive. One of the panels, that representing the conquest of Jerusalem or the Crusader Knights, is sixty-one feet in length. It contains a richness of coloring that is remarkable, presenting a fine conception of these characters from the Age of Chivalry, in which Mr. Cochrane delights. Even at close view, the figures stand out clearly from a background which gives great depth, and the approving comment of one who spent years of his life in Jerusalem has borne out the exactitude with which details are included. On the right appears a kneeling figure in full Templar costume, representing Hugh de Payen, founder and first head of the Knights Templar. The representation of a man on horse to the left is that of Godfrey de Bouillon, in the dress of a Knight of the twelfth century. In the foreground appears the hero, Tancred, to whom is ascribed the feat of having repulsed an army of Saracens, unassisted. Here he is shown at the head of his forces in a moment of triumph. Behind the action of the scene stretches a quiet valley showing Jerusalem, the Mosque of Omar, and that of Elaska of Templar fame. The Temple collection includes other works of lesser size and magnificence, all of which do honor to the artist. Of his single canvasses two may be remarked upon here: "The Man on Horseback," which work brought Mr. Cochrane to the front as a painter of other than classical themes, and "Joan of Arc," at the moment when she faces martyrdom, a masterpiece of character portrayal.

Perhaps it is unusual to the degree of uniqueness, to find a person so gifted in so many different directions as Mr. Cochrane. He is very well known as musician and writer. He has composed a musical drama, "The First Crusade," which was staged some years ago with great success in all of the larger cities of Maine, and has recently been in demand by some of the most prominent cities of the West.

Not only is Mr. Cochrane an artist of wide reputation, but one who meets the most exacting tests, and after years of work continues in his own country to be a prophet. The visitor to Monmouth hears many a story of the artist, illustrating that with him both money and fame are secondary considerations. It has been said of him, aptly:

A true artist, not only in skill of hand, but at heart, to whom satisfaction in his art and service through his talent is first.

FREDERICK WILLIAM FORD, Jr., city manager of Auburn, Maine, attained that important position before his thirty-fifth year. He had already filled other posts of importance elsewhere. Technically educated for public works, he came to Maine, equipped for the career he had set for himself.

He was born in Somerville, Massachusetts, February 13, 1892, a son of Frederick William Ford, of Somerville, and of Esther (Harvey) Ford, of New York City. His father is a journalist, being news editor of the Boston "Transcript." He was a member of the Medford City Council. The son was educated in the public schools of Medford, graduating from the high school there in the class of 1910. He then attended Tufts College and was graduated therefrom with the class of 1914, and the degree of Bachelor of Science. In 1916, he was commissioned in the Engineers, Officers' Reserve Corps, was called to active service, May, 1917, with the American Expeditionary Forces, and was assigned to the Thirty-fifth Engineers, later being made master mechanic of the railroad assembling plant of the American Army at La Rochelle, France. He was promoted to a first lieutenancy and served overseas for eighteen months, being honorably mustered out of the service, June 26, 1919. In that year he became associated with Lockwood, Greene & Company, Engineers, of Boston, as resident engineer on plant construction, retaining that position until 1922, when he was appointed superintendent of streets of Methuen, Massachusetts, later becoming superintendent of public works. In 1926, he was called to Auburn, to assume the position of city manager, which post he still retains. He is a Republican in politics and belongs to the Universalist church. His organization memberships include the American Legion, the Chamber of Commerce and the Rotary Club, in which he is a director. He is a thirty-second degree member of the Free and Accepted Masons, affiliated with all lower orders and with the Temple, Ancient Arabic Order Nobles of the Mystic Shrine. His Blue Lodge is the John Hancock.

Mr. Ford married, in New Britain, Connecticut, October 7, 1922, Ellen Horsfall, born in New Britain, September 14, 1891, daughter of Frederick Horsfall, born in England, and of Jane (Harris) Horsfall, a native of Meriden, Connecticut. They have two children: 1. John Horsfall, born in Methuen, Massachusetts, August 2, 1923. 2. Marjorie Mae, born in Auburn, Maine, May 29, 1926.

GEORGE H. ESTES is assistant agent of Continental Mills, Lewiston, and resident of Auburn. Continental Mills manufactures cotton textiles, has been in operation for sixty years (1928), employs some six hundred hands on the average from year to year, and maintains selling offices at No. 71 Worth Street, New York City, and at No. 31 Bedford Street, Boston. It is known the world over for the reliability of its product, and this product includes plain and fancy pongees, broadcloths, rayon stripes, smooth and twill-face filling sateens, plain and fancy lawns, twills for pocketings and linings, pillow tubings, narrow sheetings, and poplins. Just as Continental Mills is a dominant industrial enterprise of Lewiston and among the foremost in New England, so is Mr. Estes' position one of great importance, for upon the agent and assistant agent of a great mill rests responsibility of equal greatness.

Mr. Estes was born in New Bedford, Massachusetts, April 4, 1888, son of Henry B. and Effie (Bolles) Estes. Henry B. Estes was born in Lawrence, Massachusetts, and has long been engaged in textile manufacturing. Effie (Bolles) Estes was born in Manchester, New Hampshire. Both parents gave to their son a judicious home training, inculcating in him right principles of thought and conduct which have remained with him through manhood, and have assisted him in the pursuit of his career.

In Auburn, where he has continued to make his home since boyhood, Mr. Estes acquired his first academic instruction in the public schools. He graduated from Edward Little High School, Auburn, with the class of 1905, then entered Phillips-Exeter Academy, studied there for two years, and graduated well prepared for higher studies in 1907. Thereafter he matriculated in the Massachusetts Institute of Technology, in 1911, aged twenty-three years, taking the degree of Bachelor of Science. Thus prepared, he became identified during the year of his graduation with Continental Mills, and has remained with this organization continuously. Five years after the commencement of the connection, in 1916, he was made superintendent. In 1923, he became assistant agent, and as such has performed much good for the company's prosperity. Mr. Estes is a supporter of the Republican party, and is influential in its workings, in Lewiston and Auburn, to some fair degree, though he does not concern himself as "seeker after office," but rather finds course for his constructive forces through participation in various movements for the general welfare. He is affiliated, fraternally, with the Free and Accepted Masons, in which he is a member of all bodies and holder of the thirty-second degree. He belongs to the Rotary Club, Martindale Country Club, and is a communicant of the High Street Congregational Church of Auburn.

In Dubuque, Iowa, April 3, 1915, Mr. Estes was united in marriage with Dorothy Plaister, who was born in Dubuque, July 16, 1892, daughter of Joseph D. Plaister, native of England, and of Winona (Morrill) Plaister, native of Lowell, Massachusetts. They are the parents of one child, Marion, born December 9, 1922, in Auburn. The family residence, in Auburn, is at No. 82 Gamage Avenue.

FRED BACON GREENLEAF—One who has contributed liberally to the advancement of Auburn as a community is Fred Bacon Greenleaf, member of the contracting and engineering firm of J. A. Greenleaf Sons Company, with offices at No. 20 Washington Street. Here he has spent the greater share of his career to the present time (1928), and is accounted prominent among leading and representative citizens.

Mr. Greenleaf was born in Auburn, Maine, August 15, 1883, the son of John A. Greenleaf, the father's name now being perpetuated in the style of J. A. Greenleaf Sons Company. He has an elder brother, William Andrew Greenleaf (q. v.), who is president and chief directing head of the company.

In the elementary schools of his native community, Mr. Greenleaf secured his basic academic instruction, and graduated from Edward Little High School, class of 1902. In 1907, he took the degree of Bachelor of Science from Dartmouth College, and in 1908, that of Civil Engineer, from the Thayer School of Engineering. Thus well prepared for a career at science and engineering he returned directly after graduation to Auburn, here to form his first connection with the Greenleaf corporation, which even then specialized in mill contracts, hydraulic developments, and heavy construction, with particular attention to pulp and paper mills. He left the com-

pany, however, after a comparatively brief period, to become resident engineer for the International Paper Company, and this connection continued until 1913, when he severed it to become superintending engineer for H. P. Cunningham Construction Company. In 1914, he returned to the Greenleaf organization, and has continued with it, in important capacity, through the years succeeding. He is now treasurer and member of its board of directors, and, in association with his brother, has caused the business to expand considerably.

While he has been busily engaged in the furtherance of his actual career. Mr. Greenleaf has not failed to act the part of a good citizen, nor to entertain diversified interests. A Republican, he is active in matters of a political character, and for three terms served the district as representative to the State Legislature, where his record was productive of legislation favoring Auburn and vicinity. He is a member of the American Society of Civil Engineers, Thayer Society of Engineers, the Phi Kappa Psi Fraternity, and the Benevolent and Protective Order of Elks. He is a communicant of the Episcopal church.

On June 10, 1914, at Victoria, Texas, Mr. Greenleaf was united in marriage with Mary M. Jones, and they have one child, Laurie J. Greenleaf. Mr. and Mrs. Greenleaf make their home at No. 72 Hillcrest Avenue, Auburn.

WILLIAM ANDREW GREENLEAF—Prominent among the leading figures of Auburn is William Andrew Greenleaf, president of the contracting and engineering firm of J. A. Greenleaf Sons Company, with office at No. 20 Washington Street. This well known and prosperous organization undertakes mill contracts, hydraulic developments, heavy constructions, with special attention to pulp and paper mills. Not alone as a man of business, but also as citizen of loyal public spirit, Mr. Greenleaf occupies himself. He has watched the development of Auburn from his earliest days, has witnessed its progressive changes for the better, and in nearly all of them, since his maturity, has played an important part.

Mr. Greenleaf was born in Auburn, October 22, 1880, son of John A. Greenleaf, whose name Mr. Greenleaf's company bears, as noted. He has two younger brothers, Fred Bacon Greenleaf (q. v.), who is treasurer and member of the board of directors of J. A. Greenleaf Sons Company, and Frank Farnham Greenleaf, also a member and director of the firm. Mr. Greenleaf received his earliest academic instruction in the elementary schools of Auburn, graduated from Edward Little High School, and matriculated at Dartmouth College, in 1901. He has made his career with the Greenleaf corporation, and maintains in addition to principal direction of its undertakings several important connections in commerce and finance. These include membership on the boards of directors of the Auburn Loan & Building Association, and the Auburn Savings Bank. A Republican, he is staunch in support of the party's principles of government, and possesses a goodly influence in local politics, which he exercises with discretion, always to the benefit of the community as first consideration, rather than to the strength of the party. Fraternally, Mr. Greenleaf is affiliated with the Free and Accepted Masons. His religious adherence is with the Congregational church. In June, 1914, Mr. Greenleaf was united in marriage with Grace P. Pulsifer. The ceremony was performed in Auburn, where Mr. and Mrs. Greenleaf have made their home continuously through the succeeding years, at No. 28 Holley Street. They are the parents of children: 1. John A. 2. Jane F. 3. Helen L. 4. Claire.

LOUIS MALO—Prominently identified with the general contracting business in Lewiston since 1908, Louis Malo is held to be one of the most valuable citizens of this district, his works adding to the importance of the community in their quiet story of commercial progress. In later years his two sons have shared this reputation of their father, with whom they have been associated. Thus has a man of natural force and industry given to the city which he selected for his creative works a total of three strong links in the chain of commercial enterprise. His reward for work well done, under a code of business ethics that has met the wholesome approbation of a large clientele, is the appreciation of the community-at-large for the acquisition of this busy man of foreign blood who has chosen to become a part of the industrial forces of the Union.

Louis Malo was born in St. Damas, Dominion of Canada, August 7, 1871, a son of Louie and Celinde (Darsigny) Malo, both natives of Canada, the father later having been a carpenter and contractor of Lewiston, Maine. The son acquired his education in the public schools of Lewiston and afterward engaged in various works, establishing himself in the contracting business in Lewiston in 1908, with headquarters at No. 51 East Avenue. The present officers of this company, titled L. Malo & Sons, are: Louis Malo, president; Alfred Malo, treasurer; Maurice Malo, secretary and manager. They employ an average of twenty people. The head of the concern is independent in politics and attends the Roman Catholic church. He belongs to the Catholic Order of Foresters and to the Order of St. John the Baptist.

Mr. Malo married, August 10, 1891, at Lewiston, Caroline Turcott, a native of Canada and a daughter of Zoel and Caroline (Campagna) Turcott, also natives of Canada. They are the parents of the following children: Felix, Alfred, Maurice, Emile, Lucien, Philibert, and Eva, all born in Lewiston.

HERBERT WILLIAM GETCHELL—When he was seventeen years of age Herbert William Getchell, now of Auburn, Maine, began work with the drug firm of Smith and Cook, of this city. In that business he has remained, learning from the bottom to the top and rising step by step to the proprietorship of his own drug establishment, which he has successfully conducted here since 1913, independent of others. He is one of the highly respected citizens of the community, interested alike in civic, fraternal, religious and social affairs, a man with a multitude of friends and a valuable clientele in his business.

He was born in Lewiston, Maine, May 13, 1875, a son of Ezra E. Getchell, born in North New Portland, Maine, a veteran of the Union Army in the Civil War, in which he served in the cavalry. In his after years he was a boss weaver in a cotton mill.

Herbert's mother was Melissa L. (Barnes) Getchell, a native of Lincoln, Maine. Herbert W. Getchell was educated in the public schools of Auburn and graduated from the high school here. He began work with Smith and Cook in 1892 and continued with that house until 1895, when he went with Otis J. Cook in the same business, remaining there for eight years, when he formed a partnership with Harry Bumpus, with whom he conducted a drugstore in Auburn for ten years. He then severed his connection with this house and, in 1913, established himself independently, thus continuing until 1928 when he sold the business. For six years he was a member of the School Board. He is a member of the Masonic Order, being affiliated with the lower bodies and with the Temple, Ancient Arabic Order Nobles of the Mystic Shrine. He belongs to the Auburn Chamber of Commerce and attends the High Street Methodist Episcopal Church.

Mr. Getchell married, in Auburn, Maine, in 1897, Amy Hatch, daughter of Willis and Josephine (Wright) Hatch. They have two children: 1. Wellington Clyde, born in Auburn, Maine, May 14, 1898. 2. Glendan Herbert, born in Auburn, Maine, May 21, 1906.

JOSEPH WESTON ALBISTON was born in South Manchester, Connecticut, June 13, 1895, a son of James H. and Genevieve (Chapman) Albiston, and was educated in the public schools of Connecticut, graduating from the New Britain High School. He then studied mechanical engineering at Rensselaer Polytechnic Institute, Troy, New York. During the World War he served overseas as an officer in the Coast Artillery Corps, of the United States Army, being honorably discharged in 1919 with the rank of first lieutenant. In 1919, he entered the employ of the Russell and Erwin Manufacturing Company, then going to the Chalmers Lumber Company as manager of the hardware department, from 1921 until 1924. In March of that year he became president of the Albiston-Chalmers Company, a position which he still administers. His college fraternity is Chi Phi, and he is a member of Tranquil Lodge, Free and Accepted Masons, Kiwanis Club and the Congregational church. He is a Republican in politics and maintains his residence at No. 7 Field Avenue, Auburn, Maine.

Mr. Albiston married, February 10, 1922, at Malden, Massachusetts, Dorothy R. Bush. They are the parents of two children, James Huggin and Weston Bush.

RALPH AUGUSTUS GOODWIN, M. D., born in Danforth, Maine, December 13, 1884, a son of Herbert and Ella May (Powell) Goodwin, received his early education in the public schools and at Mattanowcook Academy, Lincoln, Maine, where he was graduated. He then went to Bates College and from that institution was graduated with the degree of Bachelor of Arts in 1908. This was followed by the course at the Harvard University Medical School, from which he was graduated and received the degree of Doctor of Medicine in the class of 1913. He came to Auburn and established himself in practice, where he has since remained. He is a member of the staff of the Central Maine General Hospital at Lewiston, specializing in surgery. From

1922, up to the present time he has been physician for Bates College, and from 1919 to 1924 was visiting physician for Oxford Spring Sanitarium for wounded veterans of the World War. In 1926, he was president of the Lewiston-Auburn Kiwanis Club and in 1924 and 1925 was president of the Androscoggin County Medical Society. He was president of the Bates Club in 1923, and is now a member of the Free and Accepted Masons, of the American Medical Association, and of the Bates Round Table Club.

Mr. Goodwin married, in Auburn, Maine, April 20, 1916, Helen F. Pulsifer, and they have three children: Ralph A., Marguerite F., and Jeannette L.

GARD WILSON TWADDLE, M. D.—In the ranks of the medical profession of Maine recruits of worth are constantly taking their places, to carry on when their elders shall have passed. Education for these places in this exacting calling demands of the individual a vast amount of labor and patient study, both of which have been given it by Gard Wilson Twaddle, of Auburn. Among the very young physicians and surgeons in his community, Dr. Twaddle in a few years has established an enviable reputation as an operator and diagnostician, commanding the faith of his patients and winning the respect of his fellow-practitioners by his conscientious work and detailed knowledge of his craft. Accepting the Democratic faith as his political belief, he has not given politics further thought than what is demanded of the good citizen, in which he cannot be criticized. His professional work is his sole concern, in which the community which he so well serves is to be congratulated.

Gard Wilson Twaddle was born in Bethel, Maine, January 31, 1890, a son of John Adam Twaddle, a physician of Bethel and a native of Weld, Maine, and of Harriett (Bown) Twaddle, born in Bethel. He acquired his early education in the public schools of Bethel and at Hebron Academy, from which he was graduated in the class of 1911. He then took the course at the Medical School of Bowdoin College and was graduated from that institution with the degree of Doctor of Medicine in the class of 1916. He established himself in practice at No. 57 Goff Street, Auburn, where he has since remained. He is a member of the State and County Medical associations and is on the staff of the Central Maine General Hospital. He is a member of the Congregational church, and is affiliated with the Free and Accepted Masons, in which he holds the thirty-second degree, and is a member of the Temple, Ancient Arabic Order Nobles of the Mystic Shrine.

Dr. Twaddle married, in Falmouth, Maine, May 1, 1918, Jessie L. Farley born in The Forks, Maine, a daughter of Andrew E. and Rilla (Hannwell) Farley, both natives of Maine. The couple have one child: Gard, Jr., born in Auburn, July 30, 1921.

ARTHUR HOWARD COOPER—For many years the shoe-manufacturing house of Wise and Cooper has been a familiar industry to residents of Auburn, Maine, who join in appreciation of the value of this establishment to the commercial activities of their center. Nor is this appreciation confined to the enterprise itself since, without the careful administration of the officers, of whom Arthur Howard Cooper is treasurer, there must have been

Maine—21

less of success achieved for the work that has been done. In addition to his work in manufacturing, he has been a busy man in other fields associated, as well as having been a citizen of the most pronounced type in his high regard for the interests of his fellows and the promotion of all things that appear for the improvement of the general welfare.

Arthur Howard Cooper was born in Bowdoinham, Maine, March 2, 1857, a son of Hiram and Margaret (Cate) Cooper. He was educated in the schools of that town and at Richmond Academy. Upon entering business he engaged in shoe manufacturing, firm name of Wise & Cooper. This continued until 1906, when the incorporation was effected, with John B. Wise, president, and Arthur Howard Cooper, treasurer. Mr. Cooper is also a director of the Manufacturers' Box Company and auditor of the Auburn Home for Aged Women. He is president of the First Auburn Trust Company and a director therein. In politics he is a Democrat, and is an attendant of the Congregational church. He holds membership in the Young Men's Christian Association, the Kiwanis Club and the Martindale Country Club.

Mr. Cooper married, in Belfast, Maine, December 3, 1889, Henrietta R. Forbes. There are two children: Harold, and Lawrence A. Cooper.

PERRY W. HAYDEN—Considerable success has followed Perry W. Hayden in his career. To the citizens of Auburn, who know him as directing head of Norris, Hayden Laundry Corporation, he hardly needs an introduction. The laundry is located at No. 14 Mechanics Row, and in its work twenty-two men and women are employed steadily from year to year. Although Mr. Hayden has lived in Auburn for a time comparatively brief, he has impressed himself well on the consciousness of the community, and has assisted in the shaping of its course of development along substantial lines. He is known as one of the most prominent, loyally public-spirited and progressive figures of Auburn.

Mr. Hayden was born in Schaghticoke, New York, April 1, 1873, son of Joel Babcock and Fannie (Van Gordan) Hayden, of whom the former was a native of Massachusetts, and the latter of the province of Ontario, Canada. Joel Babcock Hayden was for many years in business as dealer in coal, and upright in commerce as he was in his personal affairs, a man of character and force of value to the community he served so conscientiously. He took an active part in all matters pertaining to the welfare of Schaghticoke, New York. He was a member of the Independent Order of Odd Fellows, and, genial, was popular in all circles which he frequented.

In the public schools of Long Island, New York, Perry W. Hayden acquired his academic education, and forthwith set out upon his many experiences in the world of commerce. They were varied and extensive, and it was not until the month of June, 1919, that he came to the laundry business in Auburn. Here he became identified with Sherwood B. Norris, who at the time was conducting a general laundering enterprise with fair profit. The firm then took the style of Norris, Hayden Laundry Corporation, which style has been preserved. In 1927, Mr. Hayden purchased Mr. Norris's share of the business, and under the reorganization effected thereupon remained as president and treasurer, while his son, Perry Davenport Hayden, holds the office of vice-president. Mr. Hayden votes independently of either of the major parties in political questions, exercising the privilege of franchise to the greatest good to the greatest number of people, without regard for party machinations. He is a member of several organizations of commercial and social character, including the Laundry Owners' National Association, the Chamber of Commerce, Kiwanis Club, and Young Men's Christian Association, in each of which he is an active worker. He is a communicant of the High Street Congregational Church of Auburn.

On November 23, 1903, in Reading, Pennsylvania, Mr. Hayden was united in marriage with Sarah S. Shunk, who was born in Reading, daughter of William O. Shunk, also a native of Reading. They are the parents of children: 1. Perry Davenport, born in Reading, October 7, 1904, now associated with his father in the laundry business, as noted. 2. Louise, born in Reading, June 15, 1906. The family residence is at No. 81 Winter Street, Auburn.

FREEMAN GEORGE DAVIS—Conspicuous among the business men of Maine for a combination of unusual ability, civic virtue, honesty of purpose and integrity of action, Freeman George Davis, of Lewiston, for nearly thirty-six years of active life in the community was respected and honored by a legion of friends and acquaintances. He made friends because of his personality and held them because of his uprightness of character and his wholesome vitality and his beneficence of thought and deed. He possessed an altruistic mentality that made him popular in all circles wherein he found himself drawn, or to which he was called by the voice of the electorate as its representative, serving the people with unswerving fidelity, a citizen of the highest value to the commonwealth of which he was a potent member.

He was born in Sangerville, Maine, July 17, 1864, a son of George W. and Philena (Carle) Davis, both of that town, and was educated in the public schools there, graduating from high school and then attending Lewiston Business College. In 1892, he engaged in the wholesale grocery business in Lewiston under the firm name of Curtis, Davis & Record, later purchasing his partners' interests in the business, which he conducted independently for many years. In the early days of the concern the business was small, but Mr. Davis built it up until it became a power in the commercial field, with heavy assets and solid credits, a distinct force in the section of the State and favorably known throughout the country. He was a natural trader and believed in turning profits back into the business, thus ever enlarging where the demand for his wares merited the action. His stock came from all parts of the United States and his customers were almost equally widespread. He was frugal and far seeing, upright in his dealings, social, kindly, shrewd, industrious and efficient. One of his most enjoyable business relations was as a director and vice-president of the First Auburn Trust Company, with which he was for many years associated. As a bank director he was very efficient, constant in attendance at the meetings of the board, willing to do any sort of service for the institution and seeking no reward for his work. In

the exercise of his talents he actively participated in the functioning of the High Street Congregational Church. He was a member of the parish committee, was active in raising money, did committee work on building, repairing and other essentials and gave these an attention not less than he used in his mercantile business.

In politics he was a Republican and had served the people of Auburn, through his election to the offices of alderman and councilman. He was a member of the Young Men's Christian Association and of the Auburn Chamber of Commerce. In Masonry he held the thirty-second degree, affiliated with Tranquil Lodge, Free and Accepted Masons, and with other bodies of that organization. He also belonged to the Kiwanis Club, to the Independent Order of Odd Fellows and the Benevolent and Protective Order of Elks.

In January, 1928, Mr. Davis left Lewiston for a trip to the Pacific coast, going by way of New Orleans and pausing in other Southern cities. The journey was made largely for the purpose of visiting his source of supplies for the establishment in Lewiston, which he bought in large quantities, many of the commodities coming from California. He was accompanied by his wife. A severe cold, from which he was suffering when he left home, resulted in mastoiditis by the time he reached California and he was compelled to undergo a surgical operation, which was performed in the Lutheran Hospital, in Los Angeles. Complications resulted and were followed by his death, February 26, 1928, in his sixty-fourth year.

Freeman George Davis married (first); in Auburn, Maine, Mary A. Stanchfield, of Auburn; he married (second) Etta L. Crooker, of Auburn. He was the father of two children by the first marriage: 1. Lena A., who married J. Harry Dailey, of Auburn. 2. Frank C., deceased in 1922.

FRED S. CURTIS—For more than twenty-seven years Fred S. Curtis has been engaged in business as an embalmer and funeral director in Bath, Maine, and though he is the longest established in his line, under his own name, in Bath, he is also the most progressive of his profession in this city. He is likewise the only undertaker in Bath who has equipped his establishment with modern and convenient funeral parlors. He has been active in the affairs of the town, serving in various public offices and is a thirty-second degree Mason. Mr. Curtis was born in Bath, Maine, April 18, 1869, son of Edward B., native of Harpswell, Maine, a blacksmith, and a veteran of the Civil War who served as a member of Company K, Nineteenth Regiment, born 1844, died December 30, 1921, and of Emma Frances (Williams) Curtis, a native of New York, who died in November, 1900.

Fred S. Curtis received a good education in the local public schools, then learned the trade of iron moulder. He was employed at the Bath Iron Works until 1898, and in 1900 he started his own business enterprise as an embalmer and funeral director. In that line of business activity he has since continued, and during the many years in which he has been conducting a modern and progressive undertaking business he has been the leading mortician of the city. He has kept thoroughly abreast of the most modern and scientific methods in his profession, and has given his patrons the benefit of the best to be had in this special field of service. He is the longest established undertaker in Bath, and through the years he has been keeping pace with the progress of the times. He was the first to place at the service of the people of Bath a completely modern horse-drawn hearse, and when the motor superseded the horse he was the first to procure and place in operation a motor hearse. He has also purchased a motor ambulance, and this comparatively new department of service is appreciated by the residents of Bath. Another respect in which Mr. Curtis has been in advance of his competitors is in the furnishing of modern and well furnished funeral parlors, and his were the only ones in the city in 1927.

For many years Mr. Curtis has been intelligently and helpfully interested in the conduct of local affairs. He has served as a member of the City Council, and also as a member of the School Board, and has been active in supporting many movements for betterment in the community. During the period of the participation of the United States in the World War he took care of many returned bodies of soldiers, and helped in the various drives by means of which the city accomplished its home war work. Fraternally, he is identified with Polar Star Lodge, Free and Accepted Masons; also with all the bodies of the York Rite and with the Consistory, in which he holds the thirty-second degree; and with Kora Temple, Ancient Arabic Order Nobles of the Mystic Shrine. He is also a member of the Independent Order of Odd Fellows, and of the Knights of Pythias. His religious affiliation is with the Congregational church. Mr. Curtis is interested in music, and has been a member of the choir of the Congregational church for many years. For fifteen years he was coroner of Sagadahoc County. His business is located at No. 105 Center Street, in Bath, and he makes his home at No. 38 Pleasant Street, in Bath.

Fred S. Curtis was married, March 6, 1895, to Mary S. Trufant, of Harpswell, Maine, daughter of Charles E. and Marietta (Doughty) Trufant. Mr. and Mrs. Curtis are the parents of two children: 1. Mildred T., who married Carl S. Albee, and has one child, Curtis S. 2. Christine C.

HERBERT ARTHUR GIVEN—A record of steady and consistent progress in the world of commerce has been that of Herbert Arthur Given, of Auburn, one of the outstanding younger men of this city, who occupies the responsible position of manager for Armour & Company in their Lewiston branch, distributing their products throughout Lewiston, Auburn and the surrounding territory. Mr. Given was appointed to his present post in February, 1926, which is a remarkable advance in view of the fact that he first became associated with this great industrial organization in 1919, but by his sincere and earnest attention to the interests of his firm and his energetic business methods he attracted much favorable attention and his value was consequently recognized and appreciated.

Mr. Given was born in Bowdoinham, September 2, 1890, son of William S. Given, born in Bowdoinham, and of Stella (Norton) Given, born in Wiscasset, his father being prominent as a broker in hay and farm produce at Bowdoinham.

Herbert Arthur Given was educated in the public schools of Bowdoinham and after high school, en-

tered Kent's Hill Academy, from which he was graduated with the class of 1909, and became associated with his father until 1913. From 1913 to 1919, he served in the employ of the United States Government in the Railway Mail Service, and after relinquishing this occupation, became associated with Armour & Company at Lewiston as salesman, continuing in this work and building up much new and profitable business until 1921, when he was promoted to the office of assistant manager, filling the duties of this office until 1926, when he became manager in charge of the Lewiston branch, directing the operations of this great meat-packing company in this territory, having added considerably to the already substantial patronage by his courteous and considerate treatment of all customers. In civil life, he takes a deep and active interest in all affairs of his community, and is popular in fraternal organizations, being prominently identified with the Free and Accepted Masons, in which he is a member of the Blue Lodge, while he is also a member of the Commercial Travelers' Association. In politics, he follows the principles of the Republican party and his religious affiliation is with the High Street Methodist Church. In military activities, he is a member of the Civilian Officers' Training Corps.

Herbert Arthur Given married (first), March 19, 1915, at Portland, Lucinda E. Seigars, born in Damariscotta, and to this union were born four children: 1. Herbert Clifton, born in Portland, January 10, 1916. 2. Russell Glenwood, born in Portland, July 10, 1919. 3. Robert Harlan, born in Lewiston, June 24, 1920. 4. Nathalie Louise, born in Lewiston, January 27, 1923. Mr. Given married (second), November 2, 1924, at Auburn, Emma E. Marston, born in Biddeford.

SAMUEL STEWART—A prominent figure in the textile industry in Maine, Samuel Stewart of Lewiston is one of this town's distinguished sons who holds a high place in the commercial affairs of this community in his position as agent of the Bates Manufacturing Company. Mr. Stewart was engaged in several industrial enterprises outside this city and State since entering upon his career in the realm of textile manufacture, but in 1919, he returned to his native city to fill the duties of his present position. He is active in financial circles of the city and is identified with all civic activities, being especially interested in public improvements and in promoting good-fellowship among his fellow-citizens.

Mr. Stewart was born in Lewiston, October 25, 1876, son of Albert and Sarah (Kemp) Stewart. He was educated in the public schools of Lewiston, and after finishing high school, entered the Lowell Textile School, from which he was graduated with the class of 1898. After a few years spent in gaining practical experience to supplement his thorough knowledge of the technical side of the industry, he accepted a position with the Boston Huck Company in the capacity of superintendent, and he remained with this concern until 1909, and as agent from 1909 to 1913, distinguishing himself by his efficient and progressive management of the plant and showing great care and consideration for his employees, whose hearty coöperation greatly increased the output of the mills. From 1913 to 1919, Mr. Stewart acted as agent for the Edwards Manufacturing Company, at Augusta, after which he came to Lewiston as aforementioned. Under his expert care and keen supervision the affairs of the Bates Manufacturing Company have progressed consistently and his régime has been characterized by continued prosperity and satisfaction to both employees and officials. He is a director of the Manufacturers' National Bank of Lewiston and of the Maine Central Railroad. He is president of the Central Maine General Hospital and a trustee of the Augusta Trust Company. His political principles are those of the Republican party, while his fraternal connections are with the Free and Accepted Masons. His popularity in local affairs is attested by membership in the local Rotary Club, and his religious affiliations are with the Episcopal church.

Samuel Stewart married, September 19, 1900, at Auburn, Georgia M. Penley, and to this union have been born two daughters: Evelyn E., and Ruth F.

ALBERT H. CONANT—For nearly eighty years the finished lumber supply house of Conant has been one of the leading commercial enterprises of Auburn, where it was founded by Benjamin Conant in 1850. Carried on by his sons, it is one of the units of progress that mark this community, its operators men of the highest standing in the business and social world. Conducted today under the sole direction of Albert H. Conant, it is a business of value to both its owner and the community, being an employer of labor in mass and distributor of standard material for building operations throughout a large district of New England. Mr. Conant is a citizen of the most engaging character, industrious, virile, wholesome and of unimpeachable integrity.

He was born in North Auburn, Maine, January 6, 1868, a son of Benjamin Conant, of Turner, Maine, and of Lucy (Bonney) Conant. His father was a lumber dealer and founder of the house, a member of the city government of Auburn and of the Independent Order of Odd Fellows.

Albert H. Conant was educated in the public schools of Auburn and was graduated from its high school. Upon leaving school he became identified in the lumber business with his brother, who had been in the mill under his father at the time of the death of the last-named in 1884. The elder brother died in 1908 and the business was incorporated in the following year, with Albert H. in control. The mill manufactures all sorts of boxes, doors, sash and blinds and employs between seventy-five and one hundred men. Mr. Conant is a Republican in politics and a member of the First Church of Christ, Scientist. He is a member of the School Board and of the City Council of Auburn and belongs to the Rotary Club, the Chamber of Commerce and the Maine Associated Industries.

Mr. Conant married Grace L. Wyman, of Auburn, Maine, daughter of Edward C. and Mary (Leavitt) Wyman.

ARTHUR EDWARD WILSON—In the commercial history of New England, the shoe industry has played an important part, and in the State of Maine, one of the outstanding men in the leather and shoe trade is Arthur Edward Wilson of Auburn, founder and president of the A. E. Wilson Company, Incorporated, wholesale distributor of shoe-manufacturing supplies. Mr. Wilson has been identified

with this great industry for the entire period of his business career, and it was in 1919, that he formed the organization which bears his name, and is now one of the leaders in the field. Under his capable direction, this concern has grown steadily and consistently and is now one of Auburn's most substantial and progressive industrial enterprises, adding materially to the prosperity of the community. This city is indeed proud to claim Mr. Wilson as one of its most esteemed adopted citizens and he evidences his deep attachment and interest in its advance by his participation in everything pertaining to municipal welfare and the well-being of his fellow-citizens, being particularly active in affairs of a fraternal nature.

Mr. Wilson was born in Lynn, Massachusetts, February 14, 1884, son of Emory Centre Wilson, born at Topsham, Maine, and of Adeline Frances (Fawcett) Wilson, born in Danvers Port, Massachusetts. Emory Centre Wilson has been active for many years in the retail butcher business.

Arthur Edward Wilson was educated in the public schools of Lynn, and after high school, attended the Salem Commercial School, at Salem, Massachusetts, and immediately afterwards struck out upon his commercial career. He first became identified with the United Shoe Machinery Corporation and remained with this firm from 1903 to 1919, at first learning the various details of the organization and acquainting himself thoroughly with all the processes and operations of the industry, advancing rapidly by reason of his sincere interest in his work and his ability in executing the various duties entrusted to him with skill and despatch. After numerous promotions, he was appointed special representative for the company and traveled out of Boston in the interests of the firm, winning the commendations of his superiors for the large volume of business regularly secured on his commercial trips. In 1919, Mr. Wilson decided to establish an independent concern, and accordingly, he selected Auburn as the site for his modern enterorise of which he became president, and George W. Webber, secretary, with offices located at No. 7 Minot Avenue. The business of the company has progressed with splendid success, due particularly to the splendid reputation the firm enjoys for quality products and prompt, efficient service, supplying some of the largest and most important shoe manufacturers of the country with necessary equipment for the proper operation of their plants.

In the life of the city, apart from its commercial aspects, Mr. Wilson occupies a prominent position, being actively interested in the great fraternal organizations, the Free and Accepted Masons, of which he is a member to the thirty-second degree. He also is a member of the Knights of Pythias, and the Benevolent and Protective Order of Elks. His social activities are confined to the Martindale Country Club. In politics, he is a staunch advocate of the principles of the Republican party, and although he has never sought public office, lends his support and influence to all civic campaigns which have for their ultimate aim the advancement and improvement of the municipality and the welfare of the people. His religious adherence is given to the High Street Congregational Church.

Arthur E. Wilson married, April 3, 1909, at Dorchester, Massachusetts, Edith Molly Wallace, who was born in East Boston, Massachusetts, September 13, 1888, daughter of George W. Wallace, born in South Boston, Massachusetts, and of Dorothy (Martin) Wallace, born on Prince Edward Island, Canada. To this union there is one daughter, Jeannette Elizabeth, born in Dorchester, May 23, 1911.

CLARENCE E. DARLING—One of the well-known, representative and public-spirited citizens of Auburn, in this community Clarence E. Darling has spent the whole of his career to the present time (1928). Born here on December 28, 1891, he is a son of John L. and Lillian (Davis) Darling, his father having been a shoemaker for many years, in Auburn, born in Bowdoin, Maine.

In the public schools of his native community, Clarence E. Darling obtained his academic education, and in 1906, at the age of fifteen years, became identified with the Darling Automobile Company. This association has endured through the years succeeding, and Mr. Darling is manager of the car department, as well as a director in the company's organization. This company handles Reo passenger machines and "Speed-Wagons." It maintains, in addition to headquarters in Auburn, branch offices in Augusta and Bangor, and all kinds of automotive equipment are handled by the combined units, which accomplish a large sales volume annually.

While he has thus been busily occupied with the course of his career, Mr. Darling has not failed to take an active part in general affairs of the town. Independent in politics, he seeks rather for the common good of the greatest number of people than for party supremacy. Fraternally, he is affiliated with the Free and Accepted Masons, in which he holds the thirty-second degree, and is a member of all bodies, including the Temple, Ancient Arabic Order Nobles of the Mystic Shrine. He is a member also of the Auburn Chamber of Commerce, and the Rotary Club, in the workings of both of which he is prominent. He attends the Congregational church.

On July 19, 1911, in Auburn, Mr. Darling was united in marriage with Grace Caroline Hersey, who was born in Auburn, daughter of Stillman and Susan (McIntyre) Hersey, of whom the latter was born in Peru, Maine. To this union were born four children, all in Auburn: 1. Owen. 2. Blaine. 3. Beverly. 4. Virginia.

OTTO H. OLFENE—In the commercial development and progress of Auburn, there is no more active citizen then Otto H. Olfene, president and treasurer of the well-known business concern, the Olfene Public Market Company, Incorporated. Mr. Olfene has been connected with the marketing and produce business in this city since 1889 and is thoroughly familiar with the operation of this branch of industry, having risen to his present high position by his steady application of the principles of honesty and quality goods, never deviating from his splendid standards during the long course of his active career.

Mr. Olfene was born in Hanover, Germany, April 26, 1866, son of William H. and Louise (Hapy) Olfene, both natives of Germany. William H. Olfene brought his family to Lewiston in 1871, where he engaged in the woolen business and was active as a mill man for many years.

Otto H. Olfene was educated in the public schools of Lewiston, and after high school, entered Portland Business College. In 1889, at Auburn, he formed a partnership with O. F. Holmes for the operation of a grocery and meat enterprise which opened for business on January 22, 1889, under the firm name of Olfene & Holmes, and continued as such until January 6, 1908, when the partnership was dissolved. Mr. Olfene acquired a splendid reputation as a business man of the highest character and was successful from the start. After conducting an independent business for some years, in 1916, he formed the present organization known as the Olfene Public Market Company, Incorporated, of which he is president and treasurer, and his son, Ralph D. Olfene, is manager and vice-president, conducting a general market and employing on the average of twenty-three assistants. This enterprise is located at Nos. 176-180 Court Street, Auburn, and is an establishment on which the citizens of this city and vicinity can depend with absolute certainty, being assured of courteous, efficient service and goods of the most superior quality. Although his success is commercial affairs attests to his thorough attention to business, still Mr. Olfene is never too busy to devote some of his time to public affairs and the welfare and advancement of his city and its people. He is prominently active in the affairs of the Free and Accepted Masons, and has attained the thirty-second degree in that splendid Order. He takes an important part in civic progress and improvement as an influential member of the Chamber of Commerce. His religious adherence is given to the Congregational church.

Otto H. Olfene married, in Lewiston, Mabel Louise Williams, born in Gardiner, September 4, 1868, daughter of John and Louise Williams, who were natives of Gardiner, and to this union have been born two children: 1. Ralph D., born in Auburn, September 8, 1890. 2. Winifred O., born January 16, 1892, in Auburn, married Bancroft H. Wallingford.

FRANK X. EMOND—In Biddeford, the name of Frank X. Emond has long been associated with superior service as a funeral director, especially among the French residents of this section of the county. Mr. Emond conducted his father's business from 1919 to 1922, but since 1922 has been engaged in the embalming and funeral directing business under his own name. His establishment is thoroughly modern, with attractive funeral parlor and motor ambulance, and he is a skilled mortician, a graduate of the Boston Institute of Anatomy.

Frank X. Emond was born in Biddeford, Maine, August 23, 1887, son of Jean, a native of St. Lawrence Isle, Province of Quebec, Canada, who was engaged as a merchant and funeral director to the time of his death in 1919, and of Anastasia (Loisselle) Emond, a native of Biddeford. After attending the parochial school of his birthplace, he continued his studies in the public high school, and then was associated with his father in the furniture business for a number of years. Meantime, he had taken the course and received his diploma in the Boston Institute of Anatomy in 1912, after which he returned to Biddeford, and was associated with his father in both the furniture and the embalming and funeral-directing business. After the death of his father in 1919, he conducted the business for his mother until July 20, 1922, since which time he has conducted the undertaking business under his own name, at No. 32 Pool Street, in Biddeford. His modern and well-equipped establishment enables him to skillfully and adequately minister to the needs of his patrons, and his well-furnished and convenient funeral parlor is an accommodation to many. A motor ambulance adds greatly to the efficiency and to the up-to-dateness of his service, and he is taking care of a clientele drawn not only from Biddeford, but from a large area surrounding this community. Mr. Emond is a member of the Improved Order of Red Men, the Catholic Order of Foresters, and the Union of St. Jean de Baptiste, and he is also a member of the Fremont Club and of several French clubs. His religious membership is with the Roman Catholic Church of St. André.

Frank X. Emond was married, in 1913, to Marie L. Fournier, of Biddeford, Maine, daughter of Philemont and Arthenia (Belanger) Fournier. Mr. and Mrs. Emond are the parents of seven children: Isabelle, Theresa, John P., Gertrude, Cecile, Claire, and Bernadette. The family home is at No. 32 Pool Street, where Mr. Emond's business also is located.

ELMER ROAK DARLING—Treasurer and member of the board of directors of the Darling Automobile Company of Auburn, Elmer Roak Darling is accounted to be one of the most progressive of younger men in this community. The success which has met his efforts in commercial direction has been the reward of a talent that is genuine.

Elmer Roak Darling is a native of Auburn. He was born May 27, 1903, and is the eldest child and son of Veranus S. and Florence (Roak) Darling. His brothers, younger than himself, are Frank and Richard Darling. His father, Veranus S. Darling, was a pioneer in the automobile business in the State of Maine, and a son of Veranus S., Sr., and Martha (Bickford) Darling, born November 14, 1876, in West Bowdoin, Maine. After a public school education he came to Auburn and found employment in the local factories. Those were the days of the old-fashioned bicycle, and as the new-style machine with sprocket and chain drive began to come into popularity Mr. Darling opened a bicycle repair shop. He was a natural mechanic, and when still greater opportunity offered itself in the automobile, he was ready for it. In point of service, he was the second oldest automobile distributor in the State. He organized the company which still bears his name, and became State agent for the Reo machine. He was a director of the Maine Auto Dealers' Association, and a member of the Androscoggin Automotive Dealers' Association. At one time he was president of the Auburn Chamber of Commerce, while fraternally, he was affiliated with the Free and Accepted Masons, in which Order he held the thirty-second degree; and Lewiston Lodge, Benevolent and Protective Order of Elks. He was a member of the Auburn Kiwanis Club, the Lake View Grange, and attended the High Street Congregational Church. He was a director of the First Auburn Trust Company, and the last time he attended a meeting of that board he expressed his desire that Auburn grow, and told of his willingness, accordingly, to support the then newly-proposed hotel, the Lenox. He put money into this project, and in this and

scores of other mediums was of service to the community's advantage. Death came to Veranus S. Darling at his home in Auburn, January 9, 1924. For his character, the works by him accomplished in a full life of endeavor, and for the natural affection with which he was ever regarded, he will be recalled warmly to the hearts of those who knew him.

From his father, Elmer Roak Darling inherited a certain business and mechanical ability that has already been demonstrated. He attended the public schools of his native Auburn, graduated with high scholastic standing from Edward Little High School, Auburn, and matriculated in Boston University, Boston, Massachusetts, whence he graduated in 1927, aged twenty-four years, with the degree of Bachelor of Arts. Without delay thereafter he became identified with the Darling Automobile Company, as director and assistant treasurer, which executive position he retains to the present time (1928). In political inclination he is of independent choice, and supports those movements which he knows will be of benefit to the people at large, regardless of party interests. He is a member of the Auburn Chamber of Commerce, of the Kiwanis Club, and attends the Congregational church.

GEORGE RICHARD HUNNEWELL—A leader in the industrial life of Maine for more than fifty years, George Richard Hunnewell is one of Auburn's most distinguished sons, who has achieved a position of prominence in the commercial world and at the same time has always used his energy and influence to increase the prestige of his community and promote its progress and development. Mr. Hunnewell is president and treasurer of the G. R. Hunnewell Fur Company and also president of the Darling Auto Company, both of which figure among the outstanding business enterprises of this city and contribute in a large measure to civic prosperity.

Mr. Hunnewell was born in Auburn, March 23, 1853, son of George W. and Rachel (Sawyer) Hunnewell. He was educated in the district public schools and upon the completion of his formal education, entered the realm of commerce, becoming connected with the fur-buying and sporting goods business, in which branch of endeavor he has since continued. During his long and active career he has established a record for handling only the finest type of sporting goods and the most dependable pelts and furs. Some years ago, Mr. Hunnewell became president of the Darling Automobile Company and directs the management of this successful concern, which handles some of the most exclusive makes of motor cars and supplies this city and vicinity with expert motor service and accessories. He is dean of Auburn's business men and is respected and esteemed by all, while in civic activities, he has given generously of his time and material aid to everything that tended to further the best interests of his fellow-citizens and their city. He is a staunch supporter of the principles of the Republican party.

George Richard Hunnewell married (first) Hattie S. Waterhouse, in Auburn, February 22, 1886, and he married (second) Grace A. Johnson in Auburn, June 3, 1913. His children are: Mabel W., Leona W., Florence M., and Elwood J. Mr. Hunnewell resides on his country place outside this city, and his offices are located at No. 27 Turner Street.

WILLIAM H. CUMMINGS—One of the prominent citizens of Auburn, is William H. Cummings, general manager and treasurer of the Auburn Motor Sales Company, Incorporated, with offices, shops showrooms at Knight and Cushing streets. Since childhood he has been in almost constant touch with the affairs of this community, and since manhood has contributed liberally to its advancement, through endorsement of worthy projects aimed at the general welfare, or through active personal assistance in such movements. He is numbered among the foremost of the progressive figures of Auburn, and his talents, perseverance and integrity have been rewarded by a success that is above the average.

Born in Augusta, Maine, June 23, 1893, Mr. Cummings is a son of Charles S. and Addie F. (Larrabee) Cummings; the father a veteran of the Spanish-American War, operator in insurance, and a substantial citizen of his community.

In the public schools of Auburn, and in Edward Little High School, Auburn, Mr. Cummings acquired his elementary and secondary instruction in preparation for advanced studies. He matriculated at Bates College thereafter, and from it was graduated, in 1916, aged twenty-two years, with the degree of Bachelor of Arts. In the year of his graduation, he commenced his career in business, becoming identified with the Wade & Dunton Motor Car Company, of Lewiston, Maine, where he remained for six years, until 1922. In 1922, he became general manager and treasurer of the Auburn Motor Sales Corporation of Auburn, as noted, and in this connection has continued through the years succeeding to the present time (1928). The corporation distributes Ford and Lincoln automobiles, trucks and tractors. It deals in radio supplies, and gives full service in radio repair, together with the repair of automotive machines. Trade in sales and repairs is very large indeed, and requires the constant application of several men to the various branches.

While Mr. Cummings is thus busily engaged as manager and official of the company, his interests are not limited to it strictly, but are widespread. A Republican, he is loyal to the principles of government upheld by the party. Fraternally, he is affiliated with the Free and Accepted Masons, as member of the Blue Lodge, Royal Arch Chapter, Royal and Select Masters, Knights Templar, and Ancient Arabic Order Nobles of the Mystic Shrine. He also is a member of the Auburn Chamber of Commerce, the Commercial Travelers' Association, and the Young Men's Christian Association, in the workings of all of which he is active. In religious adherence he is a communicant of the Methodist church.

On September 15, 1925, Mr. Cummings was united in marriage, at Hallowell, Maine, with Jane Glenola Wright, who was born in Canada, and they are the parents of one child, Cynthia Wright, born in Auburn, July 30, 1926.

BRADFORD PECK—One of the pioneer merchants of Maine is Bradford Peck of Lewiston, founder and president of B. Peck Company, of this city, one of the largest department stores of the State. This splendid establishment has been built up by a steady adherence to the policy of quality and service, earning and holding the confidence and loyalty of its customers by reason of its thorough dependability and the courteous treatment accorded to all. Mr. Peck is also interested in the real estate development of his community, being the founder and president of the B. Peck Real Estate Company, with offices in Lewiston.

Bradford Peck was born in the Charlestown district of Boston, Massachusetts, on February 21, 1853. At an early age he came to see the need of assimilating knowledge when he could, for when he was twelve years old, he was obliged to leave school and go to work. His first job was that of cash boy with Jordan Marsh Company, Boston, and Mr. Peck remained with this concern for twelve years, advancing through the different grades until he became second man in the lace department. Determined to have at least a fundamental knowledge and training, Bradford Peck, in the meantime, had been attending night school in Boston, for he looked into the future and knew that he must overcome the handicap under which he had started. He felt there was a time coming when he would need the early education he had missed. He felt he was going to be the head of a big business some day, and indeed this dream has been fulfilled.

After twelve years with Jordan and Marsh, Mr. Peck entered the employ of Merrill, Disney & Thompkins, a famous lace-importing house of New York, as New England representative. In this new field, acting as intermediary between producer and distributor, he broadened his understanding of business relations and on the combined knowledge he had gathered in his years at both ends of business, he founded in 1880, the business which today is a household word throughout Central Maine.

Mr. Peck was married, in 1877, to Mathilda Harding (Stevens) Lombard of Somerville, Massachusetts, who was accidentally drowned in 1901. Surviving children are: Sumner S., Frank G., and Mrs. H. G. Brown, all of Lewiston. Lewis L., the oldest son, died in 1923.

It has been the lifelong ambition of Bradford Peck to benefit producer and consumer alike by eliminating waste and loss of energy in distribution, and to make business something a bit more in harmony with the golden rule. A merchant, a philosopher, a social dreamer if you will, yet the businesses founded by Mr. Peck stand as a concrete example that above all else, Bradford Peck is a doer and his community and the State have benefited by his having been a part of it.

WALTER TOZIER—Among the substantial citizens and merchants of Auburn, whose work has been of importance to the local commerce, Walter Tozier stands high. From his young manhood various enterprises engaged his attention in Fairfield, Lewiston and elsewhere, but ill health compelled him to temporarily retire. With returning strength his indomitable will to succeed brought its reward and today he is prosperous in the grain business and dairy farming, a substantial citizen of highest character and industrious nature.

He was born in Fairfield, Maine, May 14, 1868, a son of George W. and Ann R. (Tobey) Tozier, both of Fairfield, his father having been a miller and dealer in grain. The son was educated in the public schools of Fairfield and at the Augusta Business College, after which he began work in Fairfield for the American Express Company. He received promotion to be agent for that corporation at Lewiston and held that post from 1888 until 1907, when his health failed and he purchased a farm near Lewiston, where he went to live and to do what work he could. In 1917, he entered into association with E. P. Ham, grain dealer, and in 1925 with J. B. Ham & Company, in similar business. In connection with that business, in which he is still engaged, he operates his dairy farm in association with his only son, George D. Tozier. He is an Independent Republican in politics and has served as councilman of Auburn. He is a member of the Free and Accepted Masons and attends the Methodist Episcopal church of Auburn.

Mr. Tozier married, April 5, 1889, Sarah Stinchfield, of Danville, Maine, daughter of Jeremiah and Ruth (Piper) Stinchfield. Their only child is George D., born in Auburn, February 20, 1903.

WILLIAM T. MORAN—For twenty-three years previous to organizing the shoe manufacturing business of Moran-Herman-McManus, Incorporated, of Auburn, William T. Moran, president and treasurer of the corporation, was associated with the Lunn & Sweet Shoe Company. His success since the incorporation has been notable, his knowledge of the business having been gained by close attention to details under the guidance of experts with whom he was fortunate enough to be associated. He is a citizen of sterling character, untiring industry and high ideals in business ethics which have brought him the approbation of a large clientele, as well as of a multitude of friends in fraternal and social circles.

He was born in Titusville, Pennsylvania, July 2, 1880, a son of Nicholas Moran, born in Rochester, New York, December 2, 1846, died July 3, 1901, who was a locomotive engineer and held the rank of captain in the Eighteenth Regiment of Infantry, Pennsylvania National Guard. The mother was Mary (Mulqueen) Moran, born in Brooklyn, New York, September 22, 1845, died September 14, 1921. William T. Moran acquired his education in the public schools of Titusville and was graduated from high school. He then entered business, making the record noted. His present enterprise employs an average of two hundred and sixty-five people and is located at No. 140 Main Street, Auburn. He is a Republican in politics, a Roman Catholic in religion, and is vice-president and director of the First Auburn Trust Company. His organization memberships include the Martindale Country Club, Chamber of Commerce, Knights of Columbus and Benevolent and Protective Order of Elks.

Mr. Moran married, at Franklin, Pennsylvania, June 10, 1920, Cecelia Rieseman, of Franklin, daughter of Joseph and Cecelia Rieseman. They are the parents of the following children: 1. Rita, born in Auburn, Maine, May 3, 1923. 2. Jean, born in Auburn, Maine, December 23, 1925.

DWIGHT H. EDWARDS—In the commercial and financial life of Auburn there is no more prominent man than Dwight H. Edwards, who owns and operates the old-established enterprise for the buying and selling of horses, a business which has steadily increased and expanded despite the great influx of automobiles and the place that mechanical contrivances have taken in modern industrial and agricultural affairs. It is a strange, but nevertheless well-known fact, that the number of horses used for both work and pleasure has increased and statistics show that there are more employed at the present time than ever before. In the civic life of Auburn, Mr. Edwards exercises a prominent and influential part, being popularly identified with all the leading organizations and societies and anxious at all times to promote municipal progress and improvement.

Mr. Edwards was born in Auburn, April 26, 1878, son of Jonas Edwards, born in Casco, and of Lydia (Merrill) Edwards, born in Auburn. Jonas Edwards (q. v.) was the founder of the business which bears his name.

Dwight H. Edwards received his early education in the public schools of Auburn and after graduating from Auburn High School, entered Rankin's Business College where he completed a course of commercial study. Upon completing his school career, he became associated with his father in the latter's business, and since 1897 has continued in this connection, having been in full charge of its direction and management since 1916. In banking circles, Mr. Edwards is an active factor as a director of the First Auburn Trust Company. His political principles are those of the Republican party and his religious adherence is given to the Congregational church of Auburn. Esteemed and popular in fraternal affairs, he is a member of the Free and Accepted Masons including the Temple, Ancient Arabic Order Nobles of the Mystic Shrine. His social activities are confined to the Martindale Country Club.

Dwight H. Edwards married Ina Walls, who was born in Danford, and they are the parents of one son, Jonas Homer, born in Winthrop, August, 1914.

CLARENCE NATHAN PIERCE—For the past seventeen years Clarence Nathan Pierce has been identified with the banking business in Dexter, Maine, and since 1922 he has been manager of the bank. Mr. Pierce is prominent in the Independent Order of Odd Fellows and is also a member of the Masonic Order.

Clarence Nathan Pierce was born in Northwood, New Hampshire, May 20, 1890, son of Charles S., a native of Des Moines, Iowa, who was engaged in the shoe industry to the time of his death, and of Clara Nettie (Giles) Pierce, who was born in Epsom, New Hampshire, and is now deceased. After attending the public schools of Farmington, New Hampshire, and completing his course in the high school there, Mr. Pierce entered a business college in Dover, New Hampshire. When his commercial training was completed he remained in the Dover Business College as an assistant. In 1910 he came to Dexter, Maine, and entered the employ of the First National Bank in the capacity of clerk. One year later, in 1911, the First National Bank of Dexter and the Dexter Savings Bank were consolidated, the name being changed this time to the Dexter Trust and Banking Company, of which Mr. Pierce was made assistant treasurer. In this official capacity he served until 1919. The bank was then taken over by the Merrill Trust Company, of which Mr. Pierce was made assistant manager. In 1922 he was made manager of the bank, and in this capacity he has continued to give efficient service to the present time (1928). Mr. Pierce is a Republican in his political sympathies. He is serving as town treasurer, in which office he has served since 1917, completing now his tenth year. He is auditor of the Dexter Loan and Building Association. Fraternally, he is identified with Plymouth Lodge, Independent Order of Odd Fellows, of which he is a Past Grand; with Silver Lake Encampment, No. 30, of which he is a Past Chief Patriarch. He is also a member of Dexter Canton, No. 8; and a Lieutenant-Colonel in the Second Regiment, Department of Maine, of the Patriarchs Militant, of America; of the Mystic of Order of Samaritans; and of Martha Washington Lodge of Rebekahs. He also holds membership in Penobscot Lodge, Free and Accepted Masons; and in Dexter Grange, No. 155, Patrons of Husbandry, which he has served as secretary for several years. His clubs are the Dexter and the Masonic; and he is an active member of the Dexter Chamber of Commerce. His religious affiliation is with the First Baptist Church, which he serves as chairman of the building and grounds committee.

Clarence Nathan Pierce was married, in 1914, to Alma Morrison, who was born in Monticello, Maine. Mr. and Mrs. Pierce are the parents of three children: 1. Reynold Nathan. 2. Dean Sawyer. 3. Helen Beatrice.

ROBERT HALE was born in Portland, Maine, November 29, 1889, son of Clarence Hale, United States District Judge, and Margaret Hale. He acquired his education in the public schools of Portland, where he was graduated from high school in 1906. He then went to Bowdoin College, took the four-year course and followed it with two years at Oxford University, from which he received the degree of Bachelor of Arts in 1912 and that of Master of Arts in 1921. From 1913 to 1914 he attended the Law School of Harvard University. He then became associated with the law firm of Choate, Hall & Stewart, of No. 30 State Street, Boston, Massachusetts, where he remained in practice until 1917, when he came to Portland and entered into association with the firm of Verrill, Hale, Booth & Ives, of which he has been a member since 1920. He was with the American Expeditionary Forces during the World War, serving from 1917 to 1919. In 1923 he was elected to membership in the Lower House of the Maine Legislature and was Republican floor leader during 1927. He has been reëlected and in 1928 was still a member of the House from Portland. He is a director of the Fidelity Trust Company of Portland. He belongs to the college fraternities of Psi Upsilon and Phi Beta Kappa. His clubs include the Portland, Cumberland, Purpoodock and Yacht of Portland, and the Harvard of Boston.

Robert Hale married, in Morristown, New Jersey, April 20, 1922, Agnes Burke, daughter of Eugene S. and Margaret S. Burke.

RUSSELL S. TAYLOR is Superintendent of Schools at Greenville, Maine. His career to the present has been in the main devoted to the field of education. He has been principal of academies and high schools, and before occupying positions of responsibility in the educational system, he attended a series of schools as student. He has had the care of the schools in the Sixtieth District of Maine from 1914 to the present time (1928).

Russell S. Taylor was born at Philadelphia, Pennsylvania, September 20, 1886, son of Charles W. and Elizabeth (Joyce) Taylor, of whom the father, who was a farmer, is still living, having been born at Sidney, Maine, and of whom the mother was born

at Solon, Maine, and is now deceased. He attended the public school and high school at Skowhegan, Maine, and then went to Bowdoin College, from which he graduated with the degree of Bachelor of Arts, in 1908. After that he attended also the summer school at Harvard, and the University of Maine. He had then decided on the field of education for a career and became principal of Hartland Academy, a position which he held during 1908 and 1909. In 1909 he became principal of Freeport High School, and continued as such from that year till 1914. In this latter year he became Superintendent of Schools at Greenville, Maine, in the Sixtieth District, and has continued in that office up to the present. He is a Republican in politics. He belongs to the National Education Association, the Free and Accepted Masons, and the Eastern Star. He attends the Congregational church.

Mr. Taylor married, at Flagstaff, Maine, August 12, 1909, Carrie A. Davis, born at Skowhegan, Maine, daughter of Boardman and Ella M. (Keefe) Davis.

SAMUEL BIGNY is a prominent business man of Greenville, Maine. For a great many years, following the avocation of his father, he was a lumberman in the woods of the State of Maine, and had considerable success at that arduous labor. The occupation furnished him with an intimate knowledge of the wide open spaces of Maine, its flora, its woodcraft, its topography and its geology. There was great attraction in the work, but he has not continued in it. He made a change a few years ago and entered the grocery and meat business in Greenville, taking over a business that is now forty years old. He has taken this business and greatly developed it. It has now taken on the character of a general store, catering to almost every want of the community.

Samuel Bigny was born at Greenville, Maine, April 10, 1887, son of Fred D. and Alice (Rowe) Bigny, of whom the father was born at Greenville, Maine, and of whom the mother was born at Bangor, Maine, and both of whom are now living. The father was a lumberman and also the master of a ship, steamboating on Lake Moosehead. His father was a boat builder. Samuel Bigny attended the public school in Greenville, and also the high school. Then he went to Doew's Business School at Bangor, Maine, and was also a student for a year at the University of Maine. It was then that he entered the lumber business in which his father had built up a considerable business. Mr. Bigny remained at this work for a period of seventeen years. At the end of that time he entered the grocery and meat business in Greenville, taking a receivership of another company, the General Corporation Supply Company, a business which was established in 1887. In 1926, Mr. Bigny took over the business for himself, and he has run it ever since as a general store.

Mr. Bigny is a Republican in politics. He belongs to the Masonic Lodge, and Woodmen of America. He attends the Congregational church.

Mr. Bigny married, at St. Stephen, New Brunswick, June 7, 1913, Sarah Martin, born at Calais, Maine, daughter of James and Hannah Martin. Children: Carl, Samuel, Mabel, and Alice.

ISAAC AUGUSTUS HARRIS—Fidelity to a chosen profession, when associated with enterprise, ability, a pleasing personality and upstanding probity in all dealings, invariably brings its reward. The record of Isaac Augustus Harris, of Greenville, covers the foregoing, his drug business in the town having shown that success may come to those who remain within their native environment, as well as to the restless ones who seek wider fields in which to conquer. He has ever had the high regard of his fellow-citizens, a condition which is invariably accompanied by patronage of the one upon whom this courtesy has been bestowed. It makes for success and Mr. Harris has achieved that in high degree.

Isaac Augustus Harris was born in Union, Maine, July 7, 1865, a son of Herman, of Union, and Gustana (Stubbs) Harris, born in Appleton, Maine. The father was a house joiner and a man of rectitude and honor among all who knew him. Isaac was given a sound education in the public and high schools at Bath, after which he took the full course at the Massachusetts College of Pharmacy, from which he was graduated in the class of 1891, with his degree of Pharmaceutical Graduate. He at once began his life-work in the drug business, associating with the firm of Hallett & Company, of Bath, in 1892. He remained there for four years, when he established himself independently in Greenville, where he continues to direct his enterprise. He is a Democrat in politics and has been elected to office as Selectman of Greenville. He has held the rank of Hospital Steward in the Maine National Guard and is a member of the Maine Pharmaceutical Association. His fraternal affiliations include membership in the Modern Woodmen of America; Columbia Lodge, No. 200, Order of Free and Accepted Masons; New England Lodge, No. 125, Independent Order of Odd Fellows; Knights of Pythias. He is also a member of the Greenville Chamber of Commerce. His church is the Union Congregational.

Isaac A. Harris' first wife was Bessie Merry, of Bath, whom he married, August 18, 1896. His second he took in February, 1908. She was Nora B. Mathew, a native of Greenville. His children are: 1. Wilbur H. 2. Doris M. 3. Gustana N. 4. A. Goldsmith. 5. Woodrow Wilson. 6. Mary S. 7. Roberta M. 8. Rachel S., all born in Greenville.

GUY E. DORE, M. D.—Among the practicing physicians of Guilford, the professional standing of Guy E. Dore, is high. Establishing himself here, shortly following his medical education in various institutions, he has built up a large practice and won a host of friends by reason of his personality and intimate knowledge of his profession. His interest in the civic and social activities of the community has been ever acute, his assistance whenever he has been called upon in any capacity has ever been at the command of the people who have given him their confidence. In civil, social, fraternal, military or religious duties he has never failed to answer the call in the same broad and comprehending spirit that actuates his medical work.

Guy E. Dore was born in Monson, Maine, October 12, 1887, a son of Everlyn, a lumberman and native of Wellington, and Rose H. (Smith) Dore, also of Wellington, both of whom are deceased. Dr. Dore received his early education in the Monson public schools and at Monson Academy. He then attended the University of Vermont, from which he was graduated with the degree of Doctor of Medicine in 1911. Far from satisfied with his medical education up to this point, he took a full course at the Illinois Post Graduate Medical College, after which

he established himself in practice in Cambridge, Maine, where he remained for six months only. This was followed by his removal to Guilford, where he has been in practice ever since. During the participation of the United States in the World War, he served ten months as a first lieutenant and attending surgeon in the army, from which he was mustered out at the end of the conflict, He favors the political policies of the Republican party. In religion he is an attendant of the Methodist Episcopal church. For ten years he has been a member of the Guilford Board of Health and is school physician. He belongs to the State and County Medical societies and to the American Medical Association. He is a thirty-second degree member of the Order of Free and Accepted Masons, and is active as a participant in the functions of the Ancient Arabic Order Nobles of the Mystic Shrine. He also belongs to the Modern Woodmen of America and to the Piscataquis Country Club.

Dr. Guy E. Dore married, January 1, 1912, in Monson, Barbara Stewart, daughter of Seth W. and Mary (Coan) Stewart.

ARTHUR W. BROWN—Treasurer of the Brown Furniture Company, of Bar Harbor, Maine, which had been founded by his father, Arthur W. Brown is one of the successful business men of the State, with a keen interest in everything tending to promote the welfare of the community.

Son of Henry A. and Carrie Y. (Wooster) Brown, he comes of old Maine stock on both lines. His father, a native of Bangor, was a veteran of the Civil War, having served in the United States Navy, and establishing the furniture business in which he continued until his death, soon after the restoration of peace. His mother was born in Hancock, Maine.

Born October 29, 1876, he was educated in the public and high schools of Bar Harbor, and then took the courses of the Bangor Business College, and became associated with his father in the furniture business. In 1916 he was taken in as a partner, and has been treasurer since 1917. A Republican in politics, he served one term in the Maine Legislature, was for two years a member of the local Board of Selectmen, and is a member of the Town Republican Committee. He is Past Master of Bar Harbor Lodge, Free and Accepted Masons, is Past High Priest of Mount Kebo Chapter, and a member of Blanquefort Commandery, Knights Templar. He is a member of the Masonic Club, and of the Bar Harbor Board of Trade. With his family he attends the Congregational church, and is a member of its business committee. Fishing and hunting are his hobbies.

Arthur W. Brown married Ruby Hodgkins, of Lemoine, Maine, in 1900. Their children are: Carroll C., and Emeline J.

ROYAL J. GOODWIN—In the business life of Ellsworth, the career of Royal J. Goodwin stands out as that of a man who first mastered his trade thoroughly and then advanced steadily to the position of one of the leaders in the plumbing and heating business, and today, as secretary of the J. P. Eldridge Company, is an important factor in the commercial affairs of the town.

Mr. Goodwin was born in Ellsworth, October 2, 1875, the son of Samuel A., of Mariaville, and Louisa (Jordon) Goodwin, of Waltham, both of whom are deceased. Samuel A. Goodwin led an active life, being engaged as a sea captain until his death. During the Civil War, he served in the United States Navy, and was a member of the Grand Army of the Republic.

Royal J. Goodwin attended the local public schools, and after completing his formal education, learned the plumbing, heating and metal work trade. In this occupation, he remained for thirty years, building up a successful business and a reputation for thorough, dependable work. In 1921, he became a member of the J. P. Eldridge Company, of Ellsworth, occupying the position of secretary, and in this capacity he has since continued, and as a progressive business man is active in all projects for the betterment of the community. In fraternal and social circles, Mr. Goodwin is always active, being a member of Lejok Lodge, Independent Order of Odd Fellows; Wivurna Encampment; and Patriotic Order Sons of America. He is a member of the local Chamber of Commerce and of the Maine Master Plumbers' Association. In politics, he is a member of the Republican party, and his religious affiliations are with the Congregational church. For twenty years he has been chief of the Ellsworth Fire Department, and by his energy and example has built up an organization of which the town is proud.

Royal J. Goodwin married, on August 15, 1897, Alice M. Tripp, of Ellsworth. Their children are: Ella Louise, and Roy.

HARRISON M. HODGKINS—A pioneer in the automotive industry in Maine, Harrison M. Hodgkins, of Bar Harbor, has developed one of the largest selling agencies in Hancock County, and his service station in Bar Harbor has proved so popular that within the last few years he has established branches in Ellsworth and in Bucksport, and plans still further expansion.

Born in Lemoine, Maine, February 18, 1878, son of John Fairfield and Hannah Jane (Ball) Hodgkins, he had the advantage of sound business training from an early age. His father, also a native of Lemoine, was in the fish business, which he combined with wharf building until his death in 1916, and soon after Harrison M. Hodgkins had completed the course in the Bar Harbor High School, took him into the business, which he still continues as his father's successor. His mother, who was a native of New Brunswick, Canada, survived until 1916.

After having been his father's assistant and associate in the fish business from 1899 to 1915, Mr. Hodgkins began his own venture in a small way by taking the agency for the Studebaker motor cars for Hancock County. In 1922, he added to this business the agency in Hancock County for the Cadillac car, and in 1925 also became sales representative in that territory for the Chevrolet cars. His first place of business was on Cottage Street, and is still the scene of operations, both as a salesroom and service station.

Mr. Hodgkins is a member of Bar Harbor Lodge, Free and Accepted Masons; of Mount Kebo Chapter, Blanquefort Commandery, Anah Temple-Shrine; of Island Lodge of the Independent Order of Odd Fellows, Mount Desert Encampment and Unison Rebekah Lodge; and of the Masonic Club. He is also a member of the Ancient and Honorable Artillery Company of Massachusetts, of the Kebo Valley Club, the Maine State Automobile Dealers' Association, president of the Bar Harbor Automobile Dealers' Association, a director of the Board of Trade, and a direc-

tor of the Clark Coal Company. He is a Democrat, and has served on the Democratic Town Committee. He attends the Protestant Episcopal church, and finds his chief recreation in hunting, fishing, baseball, and golf.

In 1899, Harrison M. Hodgkins married Minnie Grindle Conners, of Bar Harbor. Their son, Gerald Conners Hodgkins, is now associated with his father in the automobile business.

CHARLES R. BURRILL—The oldest insurance business in Ellsworth is the C. C. Burrill and Son General Insurance Agency, headed by Charles R. Burrill, the genial proprietor and manager, who is successfully carrying on the business founded by his father in 1866. Under Mr. Burrill's direction, the organization has made rapid strides and today it is the oldest and one of the best-known institutions of its kind in Hancock County.

Mr. Burrill was born in Ellsworth, February 4, 1878, son of Charles C. Burrill of Corinna, who died in 1916, and Frances (Forsith) Burrill of Ellsworth, who died in 1917. Charles C. Burrill was one of the leading figures in the business and financial life of the community, having founded the Burrill National Bank of Ellsworth, the Hancock County Savings Bank, and the insurance agency mentioned before. He was a man of forceful character and great business ability and assisted greatly in the development of his town.

Charles R. Burrill received his education in the local public schools and in Kent's Hill Seminary, after which he attended Dartmouth College. After completing his course there, he entered the employ of the Burrill National Bank of Ellsworth in 1898, beginning his career as a clerk. His progress was rapid and he constantly advanced until he was appointed vice-president, in which capacity he served until the bank was amalgamated with the Liberty National Bank, in 1918. At that time, he assumed charge of the insurance company founded by his father many years before, and which his father had actively carried on until his death. Mr. Burrill has ever since continued in this business in a most successful manner, bringing to it the advantages gained in his long business experience. He takes an active part in all projects for local advancement, and as a director of the Liberty National Bank and member of the Chamber of Commerce, he is an enthusiastic supporter of all campaigns which best serve the interests of the town. In fraternal circles, Mr. Burrill is prominently active, being a member of Lygonia Lodge, Free and Accepted Masons; Esteric Chapter, Royal Arch Masons; Blanquefort Commandery, Knights Templar; Anah Temple, Ancient Arabic Order Nobles of the Mystic Shrine; a member of all bodies of the Ancient Accepted Scottish Rite, including Maine Consistory; Lejok Lodge, Independent Order of Odd Fellows, and the Improved Order of Red Men. In politics, Mr. Burrill is a member of the Democratic party, and his religious affiliations are with the Congregational church.

Charles R. Burrill married, in 1905, Mary Witham, of Ellsworth Falls.

CHARLES CARR MORRISON, Jr., M. D.—From the year 1925 Charles Carr Morrison, Jr., of Bar Harbor, Maine, has spent the winter months in Palm Beach, Florida, and has built up an extensive practice in medicine and surgery in both cities.

Son of Dr. Charles Carr and Lucy J. (Carr) Morrison, he was born in Bar Harbor, July 5, 1893, and his inclination for the medical profession may be said to have been inherited, for his father was among the most distinguished of Maine's physicians of an earlier generation. The elder Dr. Morrison, while in general practice, was an oculist of wide repute, spent much time in the European scientific centers, was for three years a member of the State Legislature, and was a member of the Governor's Council in 1909-1910.

Educated in the public and high schools of Bar Harbor, at Phillips-Andover Academy, and at Bowdoin College, where he was graduated in 1915 with the degree of Bachelor of Arts, Charles Carr Morrison, Jr., then entered the medical school of Harvard University, where he received his degree of Doctor of Medicine in 1918. He next spent a year in the Boston City Hospital as interne, and on the completion of this service, opened an office in Bar Harbor. During the World War he was in the Medical Reserve Corps of the United States Army, receiving degree of Fellow of the American College of Surgeons, in 1928.

Dr. Morrison is a member of the surgical staff of the Bar Harbor Hospital, and the surgical staff of the Good Samaritan Hospital of Palm Beach, Florida. He has been a director of the Maine Public Health Association since 1922, and is a member of the American Medical Society, the Maine State Medical Association, and the Hancock County Medical Association. He is a member of the Zeta Psi and Alpha Kappa Kappa fraternities; of the Free and Accepted Masons, Bar Harbor Lodge, Mt. Kebo Chapter, Royal Arch Masons; Blanquefort Commandery, Anah Temple-Shrine; of Island Lodge, Independent Order of Odd Fellows and Mt. Desert Encampment. His clubs are the Kebo Valley Club and the Masonic Club, of Bar Harbor; the Everglade Club, of Palm Beach. He is also a member of the American Heart Association, and of the Scientific Committee of the Hancock County Medical Association. He attends the Episcopal church, is a Republican, and finds his recreation in golf and hunting.

On November 22, 1919, he married Hazel R. Allen, a native of Bar Harbor, in that city. Their children are: Charlotte Allen, Marion Sherborne, Barbara Baker; and Charles C. (3), deceased.

CHARLES C. KNOWLTON, M. D.—Since 1903, Dr. Charles C. Knowlton has been known among the leading practicing physicians of Ellsworth and this vicinity. Dr. Knowlton's father was born in South Montville, Maine, and was clerk of the United States District Court at Portland, Maine. His mother, Jessie Merservy, was also born at South Montville, Maine.

Charles C. Knowlton was born at Bucksport, Maine, March 3, 1885. His boyhood school days were spent in the public schools of Ellsworth and here, too, he finished his high school work. After this, he attended Bowdoin College from where he graduated in 1906 with a degree of Bachelor of Arts. He then went to Harvard Medical School and obtained his degree of Doctor of Medicine in the class of 1911. He then served a term as interne at the Hartford Hospital of Hartford, Connecticut. A year and a half after entering the Hartford Hospital, he came to Ellsworth and began the general practice of medicine and surgery and has continued here ever since. He is a member of the American Medical Association, the Maine State Medical Society, and the Hancock County Medical Society. His fraternities are the Zeta Psi; Phi Beta Kappa; Boyleston Society of Har-

vard; Lygonia Lodge, Free and Accepted Masons; Arcadia Chapter, Royal Arch Masons; Blanquefort Commandery, Knights Templar; Lejok Lodge, Independent Order of Odd Fellows, also of the Wivurna Encampment; Dougua Lodge, Knights of Pythias; Modern Woodmen of America; Independent Order of Foresters. He is a director of the corporation of Morang, Robinson Company and since 1919 has been medical examiner of Hancock County. He is a Republican in politics and attends the Congregational church. His predominating hobby is golf.

In 1909, Dr. Charles C. Knowlton married Ella Morang of Ellsworth, Maine. They have one child: John F. (2).

WALTER M. SEELEY—Though a native of New Brunswick, Canada, Walter M. Seeley has been identified with the Presque Isle National Bank for a period of twenty-two years, and for many years now has been serving as its cashier. He had had a varied experience in New Brunswick, as telegrapher, railroad agent, and bookkeeper, and all of these connections furnished experience which has been valuable in his present position.

Walter M. Seeley was born in Kings County, New Brunswick, March 3, 1862, son of Robert Seeley, and received his education in the common schools of his native district. When school days were over, he came to Presque Isle in 1884. For several years he served as a railroad station agent and telegraph operator, and then became bookkeeper in the employ of a hardware company. After he had gained considerable experience and when the opportune time came, he was elected cashier of Presque Isle National Bank, and has continued to discharge the duties of that position to the present time (1928). He is known as an able man, faithful to his trust, and has fully the confidence and esteem of his associates. He is a member of the Episcopal church.

Walter M. Seeley was married to Frances Tweedie, and they became the parents of three children: 1. Laura, who married Ralph Shaw. 2. Charlotte, who lives at home. 3. Frank, who met his death in a railroad accident when he was seventeen years of age.

JOHN WATSON—Coming to America at the age of twenty, from England, John Watson spent more than thirty-five years of his life in Sanford, and during those years carved a place in the annals of this city's records that will survive for many generations to come. Descendant of William Watson, of Yorkshire, England, he was the third generation of this branch of the Watson family to devote his life to the fabric-dyeing industry, his father and grandfather having been similarly engaged. William Watson, already mentioned, married Nancy Chappell, and they were the parents of several children, among them Henry, father of John Watson.

John Watson was born June 8, 1869, son of Henry and Matilda (Scott) Watson, who had five other children, Lucinda, Annie, Harry, Frank, and William, all natives of England. Henry Watson, born in Leeds, Yorkshire, England, in 1833, had a common school education, but began working in a dyehouse when eight years of age. Twenty-eight years later he was made superintendent and manager of this same plant. He came to America in 1877, and for five years was superintendent of dyeing and finishing in the Pacific Mills, Lawrence, Massachu-

MAINE—A HISTORY

setts. Returning to England in 1882, he launched a dyeing and finishing establishment of his own, which he operated for ten years, after which he again came to America and became superintendent of the dyeing and finishing departments of the Goodall Woolen Company, Sanford. This position he held until 1899, when he retired and spent the remainder of his years at Lawrence. In English politics, he was a Conservative, and in this country adopted the principles of the Republican party. In Sowerby, Yorkshire, England, he became a member of the Free and Accepted Masons, and at the time of his death was a member of the Episcopal church. Matilda (Scott) Watson was born in 1833, at Dundee, Scotland, and she and Mr. Watson were married in England.

John Watson attended the public schools of his birthplace, Bolton, Leeds, England, and then entered the dyer's trade, wherein he was under the preceptorship of his father. In 1889, John Watson left England and for a year thereafter was an employee of the Stevens Mills, Lawrence, working in the dyeing department. In 1891, Mr. Watson removed to Sanford and entered the mills of the Goodall Woolen Company. Here his experience and training were quickly recognized by his superiors, and promotion followed promotion until 1899, when he stepped into the place vacated by his father's retirement. As boss dyer and overseer of the dyeing and finishing departments, Mr. Watson demonstrated his splendid qualifications for this post, and was retained therein until his death. He was recognized as second to none in dyeing and finishing, both through training and inheritance, and his keen judgment and powers of perception were most valuable to the conduct of his office. Recognizing that Mr. Watson knew every detail of his departmental duties, and impressed by his sense of justice and impartiality, the men under his supervision gave him loyal and faithful coöperation. His absolute lack of conceit added much to his popularity with subordinates and with his associates, and to most of these he was known as "Johnnie."

Mr. Watson enjoyed the contacts of fraternal and social life and many such organizations were blessed by having him as an active participant in their meetings and deeds. He was a Republican in politics, but by no means a blind partisan, rating the individual candidate oftentimes above the party. Among the fraternal bodies to which he attached himself were the Ancient Order of United Workmen; Benevolent and Protective Order of Elks, Dover, New Hampshire; and the Glover Chapter, Order of the Eastern Star. The Masonic organization, however, appears to have been his favorite, for in this Order he held the thirty-second degree and he was prominent throughout the State, belonging to Preble Lodge, Free and Accepted Masons, Sanford; White Rose Chapter, Royal Arch Masons; St. Armand Commandery, Knights Templar, a Past Commander thereof; Maine Council, Royal and Select Masters; and Kora Temple, Ancient Arabic Order Nobles of the Mystic Shrine. Later in life, Mr. Watson assisted in organizing Bethany Commandery, No. 24, Knights Templar, of Sanford, and transferred his membership to this local body, from St. Armand Commandery. His religious beliefs were those of the Episcopal faith, and he was a member of St. George's Episcopal Church.

John Watson married, June 23, 1894, Annie Eliza-

beth Young, born October 16, 1869, daughter of Charles Young of Leeds, England, and their only child is Alice Irene, born November 20, 1895; educated in the public schools of Sanford, and in Bradford Academy, Massachusetts; married Mason H. Dutton, an electrical contractor of Sanford, and they are the parents of two children: Elizabeth Jane, and John Mason.

Mr. Watson passed away November 22, 1927, at Sanford, and profound indeed was the sorrow and regret on the part of the members of his family and the hundreds of friends, who realized that in the loss of "Johnnie" Watson, the city and State had been deprived of a most worthy citizen. His many kindnesses and good deeds, however, will long keep his memory alive in this town.

WALTER JEAN HAMMOND, M. D.—In the general practice of medicine and surgery both at Enfield and Dexter, and as an official representative of his profession in camp and field in the World War, Dr. Walter Jean Hammond has the well-established repute of a skilled and well-equipped practitioner, and as one who has served his country and his community with devotion and loyalty. He is prominent in his professional associations, and is interested in whatsoever has to do with the general welfare and progress of Dexter.

Dr. Walter Jean Hammond was born May 22, 1881, at Paris, Maine, a son of Arthur Hammond, an agent for the International Paper Company, now deceased, both parents natives of Paris. After attending the public schools at both Paris, Maine, and Berlin, New Hampshire, Dr. Hammond was graduated at Hebron Academy with the class of 1901, and at Colby College with the degree of Bachelor of Arts in 1905. He prepared for his profession in the Medical School of Bowdoin College, where he was graduated in 1912, with the degree of Doctor of Medicine, and a year of internship followed in the Eastern Maine General Hospital.

Dr. Hammond first established himself in the practice of his profession at Enfield, so continuing until 1918, when he joined the United States Army Medical Corps in the World War; and after the war he was a member of the corps at the Bangor State Hospital for a year and a half. For a similar period, also, Dr. Hammond served in the Norristown State Hospital, Norristown, Pennsylvania; and in 1923 he came to Dexter, where he has continued with increasing success to practice medicine and surgery.

In January, 1918, Dr. Hammond received his commission as a captain in the United States Army Medical Corps, and he was in the service of his corps in France with the American Expeditionary Forces, for eleven months. With captain's rank he received his discharge, July 17, 1919. He is a member of the American Medical Society, Maine Medical Society, and Penobscot Medical Association.

In fraternal matters, Dr. Hammond is affiliated with Penobscot Lodge, Free and Accepted Masons; St. John's Chapter, Royal Arch Masons; St. John's Commandery, Knights Templar, with the Delta Epsilon and the Phi Chi College fraternities; and he is a member of the Masonic and Dexter clubs. He is a Republican in his political views; automobiling and fishing are his hobbies; and his religious faith is that of the Congregational church.

Dr. Walter Jean Hammond married, November 30,

1905, Maud Hooper, who was born in Haverhill, Massachusetts. They have one son, Elwood Jean.

LAWRENCE E. KELLEY, D. D. S.—Prominent in his professional associations, and both a skilled and popular dentist, Dr. Lawrence E. Kelley has an established position in his field and is regarded as one of the foremost practitioners in Dexter and its neighborhood.

Dr. Lawrence E. Kelley was born March 27, 1894, at Jonesport, a son of Eugene L. Kelley, also a native of Jonesport, and for the past thirty-five years superintendent of the plant of the William Underwood Company, at McKinley, and Delana (Ackley) Kelley, who was born at Whiting. Dr. Kelley attended the public and high schools at Jonesport, and preparing for his profession, he went to the Dental School of Tufts College, Boston, Massachusetts, for a year, completing the course at the Baltimore College of Dental Surgery, where he was graduated in 1918, with the degree of Doctor of Dental Surgery.

Dr. Kelley began the practice of dentistry at Island Falls, and he removed to Dexter in 1923, where he has continued in his profession to the present, with offices on Main Sreet. He is a member of the Penobscot County Dental Society, and the Harris Hayden Odontological Society.

During the World War, Dr. Kelley served at the Officers' Training Camp at Fort Oglethorpe, Georgia. Fraternally, he is affiliated with the Jonesport Lodge, Free and Accepted Masons; Daniel Randall Royal Arch Chapter; and St. Aldmar Commandery, Knights Templar; and the college fraternity, Xi Psi Chi; his hobbies being fishing and hunting. He attends the Congregational church.

Dr. Lawrence E. Kelley married, May 12, 1923, Elizabeth Rafford, who was born in Ashland.

ARTHUR HALE PARCHER, M. D.—Although widely known in the general practice of medicine and surgery, Dr. Arthur Hale Parcher, of Ellsworth, Maine, has been specializing for some years in orthopedic surgery, in which he took a course in 1924 at the New York Post Graduate Hospital and Medical School and was appointed assistant orthopedic surgeon at the Eastern Maine General Hospital.

Born in Ellsworth, Maine, July 4, 1889, he was the son of George A. and Lucy (Hale) Parcher, both deceased. His father, a native of Pittston, Maine, (now called Randolph), was engaged in business as a druggist until his death. His mother was a native of Ellsworth. Educated in the public and high schools of Ellsworth, and at Bowdoin College, where he received his degree of Bachelor of Arts in the class of 1912, he next entered the medical department of Bowdoin, where he was graduated in 1915 with the degree of Doctor of Medicine. After a year as interne in the Eastern Maine General Hospital at Bangor, he took up his residence in Ellsworth, where he has since been in active practice except for the interruption caused by the World War, in which he served overseas with the British Expeditionary Forces. Commissioned a first lieutenant in the United States Army Medical Corps, he remained in the service a year and half, was commissioned captain in February, 1919, being stationed at various British Orthopedic Hospitals in England, and was discharged in May, 1919, and now holds the rank of captain in the United States Medical Reserve Corps.

Dr. Parcher is a member of Maine State Medical Society, of the Hancock County Medical Society, and of the American Medical Society. He is also a member of the Beta Theta Pi and the Phi Chi fraternities; of Lygonia Lodge, Free and Accepted Masons; Arcadia Chapter, Blanquefort Commandery; of the American Legion, the Veterans of Foreign Wars, the Medical Officers of the World War, the Association of Military Surgeons, and of the Chamber of Commerce. He attends the Congregational church, is a Republican, and finds his chief recreation in hunting.

In 1919, Dr. Parcher married Winifred Hassall, daughter of Dr. Albert Hassall, of Baltimore, Maryland. They have one daughter, Joan M. Parcher.

SAMUEL L. SMALL—The proprietor of the oldest and largest flour and grain business in Dexter, Maine, Mr. Small has also the distinction of owning the only grist-mill run by water power in that community. Born on January 9, 1858, at Dexter, Mr. Small is a son of Samuel C. and Sophie (Williams) Small, both of whom are now deceased. Samuel C. Small, the father, who was born in Cherryfield, Maine, was engaged as a carpenter and builder until the time of his death. The mother, Sophie (Williams) Small, was born in Dexter.

Their son, Samuel L. Small, received his education in the public schools of Dexter, later attending and graduating from the Dexter High School. Upon the completion of these courses of study, he worked for about two years in the grain business. In 1880, he established a business for himself in grain and flour, in Dexter. His efforts met with increasing success, and today, Mr. Small has the distinction of owning, not only the oldest but also the largest grain and flour business in Dexter. He now carries a complete supply of the various kinds of feed, grain, and fertilizer, and his grist-mill is the only one in Dexter to be run by water power. Mr. Small is also a director of the Merrill Trust Company, and a director of the Dexter Building and Loan Association.

The building up of so extensive a business has undoubtedly made great demands on Mr. Small's time and attention, but nevertheless he has always taken a keen interest in the affairs of his community. In his political preferences he is a strong supporter of the Republican party. Prior to the Spanish American War he served for one enlistment in Company C of the Maine State Militia. He is fraternally affiliated with the Penobscot Lodge, Free and Accepted Masons, of which he has been secretary and treasurer for the past thirty years; the St. John's Chapter, Royal Arch Masons; the Council, Royal and Select Masters; the Consistory, Ancient Accepted Scottish Rite; the St. John's Commandery, Knights Templar; and the Anah Temple, Ancient Arabic Order Nobles of the Mystic Shrine; and the Knights of Pythias. He is also a member of the Dexter Chamber of Commerce and of the Dexter Club, of which he is one of the original members and past president.

Samuel L. Small married, in 1880, Lillian M. Maxfield, who was born in Corinna, Maine. Mr. and Mrs. Small are the parents of three children, two sons and a daughter: 1. Marion M. 2. Harold E. 3. Arthur, who died in his twenty-third year. Mr. Small and his family attend the Universalist church.

HAROLD A. ROBINSON—One of the most enterprising citizens of Ellsworth, Maine, is Harold A. Robinson, the son of William Merton and Susan M. (Atherton) Robinson. His father was born in Taunton, Massachusetts, and was engaged in the banking business. His mother was born at Dor-

MAINE—A HISTORY 335

chester, Massachusetts. Both parents are now deceased.

Harold A. Robinson was born at Lynn, Massachusetts, on February 5, 1890. He was educated in private schools of Massachusetts and finished his education at the Massachusetts Institute of Technology at Boston, in the class of 1912, when he was graduated with the degree of Bachelor of Science. He then went to Mexico where he remained for three years in the work of mining engineer. This experience enriched his practical knowledge and after he returned to the United States, he was in Chicago, Illinois, for a while associated with the Oxo Acetylene Welding Company. In 1917, he came to Ellsworth, Maine, and became an associate with Charles L. Morang in the automobile business acting as agents for automobiles under the name of Morang, Robinson Company. This business has been carried on with good success and in 1925 Mr. Robinson and Mr. Morang formed another enterprise for the purpose of giving Ellsworth a moving picture house. The firm name of this business is the Dirigo Amusement Company which conducts the only moving picture house in the town. Mr. Robinson is a member of the Lejok Lodge, Independent Order of Odd Fellows; Wivurna Encampment; Lygonia Lodge, Free and Accepted Masons; Arcadia Chapter, Royal Arch Masons; Blanquefort Commandery, Knights Templar; Anah Temple, Ancient Arabic Order Nobles of the Mystic Shrine. He is president of the Chamber of Commerce, a Republican in politics and a member of the Unitarian church. His especial hobby is golf.

In 1913, Harold A. Robinson married Carrie A. Morang of Ellsworth, Maine. They have three children: 1. Ella M. 2. Kent Thayer. 3. Harold A., Jr.

H. EDWARD WHALEN, M. D.—The medical profession has attracted to its ranks, H. Edward Whalen, a rising young physician of Dexter, Maine. Born on June 19, 1897, at Bangor, Maine, Dr. Whalen is a son of Henry B. and Mary (Angley) Whalen, both of whom are natives of Bangor. Henry B. Whalen, the father, is engaged in the grocery business in that city.

His son, H. Edward Whalen, received his preparatory education in the public and high schools of Bangor. He then studied at the University of Maine for two years, transferring at the end of that time to the Bowdoin Medical College where he remained for two years. He left there to enter the Jefferson Medical College, and he graduated from there with the class of 1922, when he received his degree as Doctor of Medicine. Upon the completion of these courses of study, he spent one year gaining practical experience as an interne at the Maine General Hospital, in Portland. In 1923 he removed to Dexter, Maine, where he began the practice of his profession. Dr. Whalen is engaged in the general practice of medicine and surgery, and in the few years he has been at work he has gained a reputation for his skill which gives great promise for his future efforts.

Although the career of a physician does not leave much leisure, Dr. Whalen has nevertheless found time to take an interest in many outside activities. In his political preferences he is a strong supporter of the Democratic party. During the World War he served in the United States Army Medical Reserve Corps. Among the learned organizations which pertain to his profession in which he holds membership are the American Medical Association, the Maine Medical Society, and the Penobscot County Medical

Society. He is fraternally affiliated with the Cardinal Mercier Council, Knights of Columbus, of which he is Past Grand Knight, and the college fraternities, Lamba Chi Alpha and Alpha Mu Pi Omega.

Dr. H. Edward Whalen married, in 1925, Floreda Mountain, who is a native of Dexter, Maine. Dr. and Mrs. Whalen are the parents of one child, a daughter, Barbara A. Dr. Whalen and his family attend St. Ann's Roman Catholic Church.

ELROY OSBORNE LA CASCE—A thorough believer in the adage, "A sound mind in a sound body," Elroy Osborne La Casce, of Fryeburg, is one of the leaders in the State of Maine in educational and recreational activities, having a deep and sincere interest in the proper training of the youth of the country. Mr. La Casce has been associated with various institutions of learning during his career as an educator, and he has officiated as headmaster of the Fryeburg Academy since accepting that office in 1922, and has served as treasurer of the Wawenock Camps, Incorporated, of South Casco, since 1920. His solicitous desire to provide proper vacation facilities for boys led him to purchase the camps, where the youths enjoy wholesome and constructive recreation, ably supervised by councilors especially chosen for this work.

Mr. La Casce was born in Skowhegan, February 6, 1891, son of Joseph H. and Etta A. (Pierce) La Casce. He was educated in the public schools of Skowhegan, and after graduating from high school, entered Bowdoin College, from which he received his degree of Bachelor of Arts with the class of 1914. He then entered the business world and was successful as a salesman for two years, but his desire to enter the field of education led him to give up his business career. He became a teacher at the Westbrook Seminary in 1917, remaining in that school until 1920. During the years, 1920-1921, he taught in Laconia, New Hampshire, and the next year, was spent at Melrose, Massachusetts, after which he came to Fryeburg to occupy his present position. Under his capable and inspiring administration, the affairs of this academy are in a most flourishing condition, and the institution holds a high place in educational circles, having a splendid reputation for scholastic attainments as well as the admirable provision made for its students to enjoy all the advantages of collegiate life. In his official connection with the Wawenock Camps, Mr. La Casce has been untiring in his enthusiasm and energy to build up an organization of the highest type, a summer camp of such attraction and completeness that will be an inspiration to the youths gathered there, and the esteem with which it is held by all is a consummate proof of his successful efforts. In fraternal circles, Mr. La Casce is a member of the Free and Accepted Masons, and the Zeta Psi Fraternity. His political affiliations are with the Republican party, while his religious adherence is given to the Congregational church.

Elroy Osborne La Casce married, September 3, 1918, at Lawrence, Massachusetts, Marion Steward, daughter of John W. and Nettie (Frost) Steward, and they have four children: Elroy, Jr., Charles R., Joseph H., and Marion.

WALTER D. THURBER—As an executive, organizer and manager of campaigns for important organizations, and as a social worker, Walter D. Thurber, of Augusta, Maine, is probably even more widely known elsewhere than in the State of his adoption.

Born in Judson, Indiana, July 30, 1881, son of Alonzo B. and Sarah B. (White) Thurber, he entered journalism soon after leaving school, where his progress was rapid, and in 1909 he was editor of the "Post" of Terre Haute, Indiana, a position he filled during the next two years. In 1910, however, he had also become editor of the "Public Officials' Magazine," and in 1911, he left the editorship of the "Post" to have more time for the new venture. His capacity for organization was soon to take a new direction. In 1911 he was secretary of the Vigo City Tuberculosis Association, and in 1911-1912 he served in the same capacity for the Terre Haute Booster Club. From 1912 to 1915 he was executive secretary of the Indiana Tuberculosis Association, and he was the originator of the Observance of Disease Prevention Day in the State of Indiana, and organized the first programme for the State-wide meetings on that occasion in 1914. From 1916 to 1921 he was manager and director of the Illinois Tuberculosis Prevention Society, and in 1918 he was associate director of the United States War Exposition, held in Chicago. In 1916 he had been president of the Mississippi Valley Conference on Tuberculosis Prevention, and from 1916 to 1918, was a director of the Illinois Red Cross. His first eastern engagement was as executive secretary of the Maine Public Health Association, to which he was appointed in 1921, and which he still holds. In 1926 he was president of the New England Conference on Tuberculosis, and the previous year he had originated and organized the Maine Three-Quarter Century Club.

Mr. Thurber is a member of the Maine Society of the Sons of the American Revolution, and of the Kiwanis Club and the Country Club of Augusta, Maine. He is also a member of the National Aeronautic Association, of the American Public Health Association, National Geographic Society, American Child Health Association, American Social Hygiene Association. He belongs to the Congregational church in Augusta.

Walter D. Thurber married Ruth Agnew, of Chicago, Illinois.

LEWIS HODGKINS, M. D.—Choosing the same profession as his father, the late Dr. Lewis W. Hodgkins, Dr. Lewis Hodgkins of Ellsworth, Maine, has inherited a talent and ability which he has improved during the many years he has practiced the profession of a physician. His genial disposition makes him a good companion in outdoor sports of which he is very fond, and also he is well known among those who play bridge whist, the card game that requires skill and intellect. His father, Lewis W. Hodgkins, M. D., who died in 1907, was a Civil War veteran, having served his country during that conflict as surgeon in the Sixty-eighth Regiment, Indiana Volunteers. He was taken prisoner three different times and after coming to Maine 'where he made his home at Ellsworth, he became a member of the Ellsworth Post, Grand Army of the Republic. His mother, Julia L. Thomas, was born at Pine Plains, New York. She died in 1902.

Lewis Hodgkins was born at Fairfield, Indiana, May 23, 1862. He came with his parents to Ellsworth, Maine, when a young child, and was educated first in the public schools of Ellsworth and then attended Dartmouth College, from where he was graduated with the degree of Bachelor of Arts in 1885. After this, he attended the University of New

York Medical School and obtained his degree of Doctor of Medicine in the class of 1888. After completing this work, he came back to Ellsworth and took up the practice of medicine. In 1905 and 1920, Dr. Hodgkins took post-graduate courses in the New York Post Graduate School. He is a member of the Maine State Medical Society, the Hancock County Medical Society and the American Medical Society. His college fraternities are Delta Kappa Epsilon and Phi Beta Kappa. He is a director in the Liberty National Bank, and during the World War, he was chief surgeon for the Hancock County Draft Board. In politics, he is an Independent and has served several years as chairman of the Ellsworth School Board. From 1924 to 1926 he was mayor of the city of Ellsworth.

In 1897, Dr. Lewis Hodgkins married Ida Mary Norris, of Ellsworth. They had one child, Norris L., who graduated at Dartmouth College in the class of 1919, with the degree of Bachelor of Arts. Mrs. Hodgkins died in 1910.

ARTHUR C. STROUT, M. D. — His general practice of medicine in both Massachusetts and Maine has established Dr. Arthur C. Strout in his present successful medical activities at Dexter, as a physician of recognized standing and well-proven reliability. As a local medical official, too, and as one of the professional advisers in the World War, Dr. Strout's services have received the merited commendation of his colleagues and constituency.

Dr. Arthur C. Strout was born April 7, 1881, at Sanford, Maine, a son of Greenleaf A. Strout, who was born at Limington, Maine, and was active in textile matters to the time of his death, which occurred in 1913, and Annie L. (Lowell) Strout, a native of Lowell, Massachusetts, who survives her husband. Dr. Strout's early education was obtained at the grammar and high schools of Springvale; and preparing for his profession at the College of Physicians and Surgeons in Boston, Massachusetts, he was graduated there in 1904, with the degree of Doctor of Medicine, a year of internship following at Ellis Hospital, Schenectady, New York.

Dr. Strout began the practice of his profession in 1905 in Boston, where he continued for a year, when he removed to Garland, Maine, where he settled as a physician and surgeon until 1922. He then came to Dexter, and here he has again proven his value to his profession, and with his offices centrally located on Main Street. He is a member in excellent standing of the Penobscot County Medical Association, Maine State Medical Association, and American Medical Association.

As a voter, Dr. Strout gives allegiance to the Republican party and its principles; and he has served for three years as school physician for Dexter.

In fraternal matters, Dr. Strout is affiliated with Penobscot Lodge, Free and Accepted Masons; St. John's Chapter, Royal Arch Masons; De Molay Commandery, Knights Templar; Plymouth Lodge, Independent Order of Odd Fellows; and the Order of Maccabees; he is a member of the Masonic Club; and his hobbies are fishing and outdoor life. He is a member of the board of trustees of the Free Baptist Church.

Dr. Arthur C. Strout married (first), in 1908, Grace Preble, who was born in Garland, Maine, and is now deceased. He married (second), in 1919, Mabel P. Ridley, who was born in Sanford. His children: Chester R.; Warren G.

JOHN OBED PIPER, M. D., of Waterville, Maine, is one of the younger physicians of this State who has had the experience of serving in the Medical Corps of the United States Army during the World War and supplementing that experience with post-graduate work before returning to resume his practice here. He is the son of Dr. Albert Augustus and Fannie (Pierce) Piper. His father was a practicing physician in Bingham, Maine, for a number of years, also active in taking part in civic affairs, holding the office of chairman of the School Board for a period of fourteen years.

John Obed Piper was born at Bingham, Maine, July 14, 1881, and has enjoyed the privileges of the best educational advantages beginning with the Bingham graded schools and after one year at the North Anson Academy, he entered the Maine Central Institute, from where he graduated in 1899. He then had four years at Bates College and graduated from there in 1903. This work was followed by work at McGill University, Montreal, Canada, where he finished in 1910, having received the degree of Doctor of Medicine. During the World War he was in the Medical Officers' Training Camp in Camp Greenleaf, Georgia. He was a first lieutenant in the United States Army from November 1, 1918, to January 1, 1919. After he was discharged from military service, he resumed his practice of medicine and in 1921 did some work in the New York Post Graduate School, and from 1924 to 1925 he did added study at the University of Pennsylvania Post Graduate School. He is a member of the Blue Lodge, Free and Accepted Masons; the Council; the Royal Arch Chapter; the Commandery of Knights Templar; and the Ancient Arabic Order Nobles of the Mystic Shrine, and also of the Eastern Star. Since October, 1925, Dr. Piper has been located at Waterville, Maine, where he is a specialist in internal medicine. He is a member of the Kennebec County Medical Society; the Maine Medical Association; and a Fellow of the American Medical Association. He is a member of the Kiwanis Club and the Waterville Country Club, and of the Congregational church. In his political views he is an adherent of the Republican party.

On July 26, 1910, Dr. John Obed Piper married Mary Esther Clark, daughter of Omar and Caroline (Baker) Clark, of Caratunk, Maine. Dr. and Mrs. Piper have two children: 1. Albert Omar, who was born December 8, 1913. 2. Caroline Fannie, born March 9, 1918. Dr. Piper is enjoying a constantly growing clientele and has before him the prospect of a brilliant career.

FRED S. SHERBURNE—To his native town of Sanford, the late Fred S. Sherburne, well-known lumber operator and realtor, had the distinction of having brought to the development of the community the first modern methods of building construction. He was the leader in a well concerted and sustained movement for adding to the assessable valuations of the town, through the erection of hundreds of homes and many commercial and other structures for various useful purposes. On all sides he was esteemed one of the greatest practical benefactors that the Sanford community has had in its midst.

Mr. Sherburne was eighth in direct descent from the founder of the family of this name in America, representatives of which have since become prominent in the professions and avocations in Maine and New Hampshire. The first or immigrant founder of the line was Henry S. Sherburne, who with his wife,

Rebecca (Gibbons) Sherburne, came from England, and settled at Strawbery (now Portsmouth), New Hampshire, as early as 1638. The line was continued through their son, Captain Samuel Sherburne, born at Portsmouth, in 1638, and settled at Hampton, New Hampshire, where he kept the ordinary. He married Love Hutchins, at Haverhill, Massachusetts, and among their children was John, so named after his older brother, who had died young. John Sherburne, born February 2, 1688, at Portsmouth, removed to Epping, New Hampshire, where he married, November 12, 1713, Jane, daughter of Abraham and Sarah (Hobbs) Drake. Among their children was John (2), born February 2, 1723, at Hampton; later lived at Northwood, and married, his wife's Christian name Sarah. To the latter couple was born at Northwood, about 1750, a son, Colonel John (3) Sherburne, who fought in the Revolutionary War. Benjamin Sherburne, as disclosed by family records, was of the sixth generation of Sherburnes in America, although vital statistics do not give the name of his mother and the date of her marriage. This Benjamin was born in Northwood, November 6, 1781, died November 25, 1837. He was a school teacher. His wife was Nancy Durgin, and they had children, of whom was Nathaniel S., of whom further.

Nathaniel S. Sherburne, seventh in the descending line of the family, and second son of Benjamin and Nancy (Durgin) Sherburne, was born June 3, 1823, and educated in the public schools of his native town. He was a carpenter and later a millwright. When he died, January 31, 1865, he owned a mill at North Berwick. He was a Democrat, and an attendant of the Baptist church. He married Lydia E. Thompson, born in Sanford, April 20, 1827. Of their children, was Fred S., of this review.

Fred S. Sherburne, the youngest of the five children of Nathaniel S. and Lydia E. (Thompson) Sherburne, was born in Sanford, April 5, 1859. At the age of six years, when most children are just beginning their education, his father died, and he was deprived of the advantages of schooling. Thus it came about that he was a self-made man, gaining his training for business through the hardships attending his struggle for existence. His first job was at the old Battley mill in Sanford, and for his labor received one dollar a day. He gave his best efforts in the interest of his employer while working at the Battley mill, and thence went, about 1890, to the newly-established Goodall Worsted Company in the capacity of master mechanic. For four years he remained with that concern, in the meanwhile having started, as a sideline, a little sawmill on High Street, Sanford, and from a small beginning his enterprise reached the point where he deemed it wise to devote all his time to its development. He opened an office on High Street, near the mill, and there both mill and office have remained. For many years Mr. Sherburne manufactured all the packing cases used by the Goodall Worsted Mills, and eventually he branched out in the manufacture of house finishing material. As time passed, he gradually entered into the lumber business, and expanded his interests in that direction by buying timber lots and operating in the lumber industry on a large scale.

His lumbering enterprise naturally led him to take up construction work, and finally to make an important entry in the real estate field. His first venture along this line comprised two houses which he built on North Avenue, then an undeveloped field. Encouraged by his first attempts, he soon had twelve houses constructed and streets laid out. As other real estate men entered the section and began operations, the town of Sanford witnessed the closely settled residential and business district of North Avenue arise to become an important part of the community. Mr. Sherburne conducted his operations more extensively and built houses on Sherburne Street, Sherburne Heights and Cottage Street Extension. As his interests rapidly expanded, he assumed the leadership in this line of endeavor in Sanford. He was responsible for the erection of many beautiful public buildings. The land on which the new Holy Family Church stands was given to that society by him, and a portion of the land as a site for the Henrietta Goodall Memorial Hospital was purchased of him. He was one of the originators in Sanford of the idea of permitting tenants to purchase homes on easy payments, much like rent; and practically all of the two hundred or more houses he built on the East Side were taken over by tenants under this plan. One of his last transactions involved the expenditure of more than one hundred thousand dollars, at High Street and North Avenue, in the erection of the Sanford Theater, an apartment house and stores on those corners.

Though Mr. Sherburne was never a politician and never aspired to the holding of public office, he was always an interested citizen and an acknowledged leader in the Republican policies of the town of Sanford, and more particularly as they affected the East Side. He held but one town office, that of road commissioner, 1916-17, and he only consented to be a candidate for that office, according to his intimates, because he earnestly desired to demonstrate to the townspeople that good roads could be built. Mr. Sherburne was a supporter of the First Baptist Church of Sanford, and affiliated with Portland Lodge, Benevolent and Protective Order of Elks, and Sagamore Tribe, Improved Order of Red Men.

Fred S. Sherburne married, November 9, 1915, Maude J. Harmon, born July 23, 1874, daughter of Hon. Cyril P. and Sarah G. (Elwell) Harmon. Mrs. Sherburne's father was treasurer of the Buxton Savings Bank, represented his town in the Legislature in 1883, and was advanced to the State Senate in 1887. He was prominent in fraternal organizations, a member of Buxton Lodge, Free and Accepted Masons, of which he was a Past Master; Eagle Chapter, Royal Arch Masons, of Westbrook; and St. Albans Commandery, Knights Templar, of Portland. Her mother was the daughter of Jane Wise (Vaughan) Elwell, and granddaughter of Eliot G. Vaughan, Esq., who was an influential figure in the affairs of Maine when it was a part of Massachusetts.

The death of Mr. Sherburne occurred February 21, 1928, at his home in Sanford. He was survived by his widow and a brother, Frank Sherburne, of Hawthorne, California. The regard in which he which he was held in Sanford was given attest through the following tribute in a local newspaper: "The removal of this man by death from active participation in community affairs is irreparable. His loss will be felt deeply in all parts of the town, and more especially on the East Side, which owes its inception and prosperity to him. There will be many who will mourn his passing, besides those near and close to him."

OSCAR CHARLES ROBBINS—One of the important adjuncts of successful conduct of commercial enterprises is the solidity of the financial institutions of the community in which they operate. In this respect the people of Harrison, Maine, have reason for congratulation in the possession of such establishments as the Fidelity Trust Company of Portland, whose careful methods may be comprehended by the selection of their officers. The instance in this case is Oscar Charles Robbins, with important posts in each, one of the leading citizens of the community, whose future seems secure for many years, since he has not yet reached the age when he can be termed near middle life.

Born in North Chesterville, Maine, May 9, 1895, a son of Charles W. and Bertha (Vaughan) Robbins, he received his early education in the public schools and later at Wilton Academy. At the conclusion of this foundation he became associated with the banking business with the Wilton Trust and Banking Company, of Wilton, where he was teller and assistant treasurer from 1913 to 1917. On April 30, 1917, he enlisted in the regular army, serving with the forces overseas until July, 1919. On demobilization he was secretary of Kineo Camps, Incorporated, at Harrison, for about one year, on completion of which he returned to the bank, May 22, 1921, when the Harrison branch was organized, and held the office of manager of the United States Trust Company of Harrison from 1921 to 1926. In 1926 the United States Trust Company was purchased by the Fidelity Trust Company of Portland, Mr. Robbins remaining as manager. He is also half owner of the Harrison Insurance Agency. He is a member of the Lodge, Free and Accepted Masons; Oriental Chapter, Royal Arch Masons, Bridgton; Oriental Commandery, Knights Templar; Kora Temple, Ancient Arabic Order Nobles of the Mystic Shrine, of Lewiston; a charter member of William R. Pembroke Post, No. 139, American Legion of Harrison, now serving as post adjutant. In politics, he is a Republican.

Mr. Robbins married, in Harrison, May 29, 1921, Dorothy Pitts. They have two children: Joseph P., and John R.

THE OGUNQUIT LIBRARY—This library is the gift to Ogunquit of Mrs. Nannie D. Conarroe, a Philadelphian with a summer residence in the town, who soon after the death of her husband, George M. Conarroe, decided upon the library as a memorial. A lot was purchased from W. B. Littlefield, plans were drawn by Charles M. Burns, a Philadelphia architect, and the contract was awarded to E. B. and C. H. Blaisdell, of York, Maine, and the building was completed and formally opened to the public in June, 1898. About fifteen hundred volumes were originally on its shelves and Miss Annie M. Norton was chosen as the first librarian. The library was conducted under Mrs. Conarroe's direction until her death. Miss Norton was succeeded by Miss Grace E. Weare, who held the librarianship for eight years, after which there were several changes, Miss Hazel Ramsdell being the present incumbent.

In 1914, Mrs. Conarroe decided that an enlarged building would best serve the community and the contract for the addition was awarded to Luther S. Weare, Henry McComb, of Philadelphia, being the architect.

At Mrs. Conarroe's death her will provided for a legacy of $20,000 for the support of the library, and

MAINE—A HISTORY 339

the institution has operated on the income from this sum without assistance from the local town authorities. At that time several improvements were made on the property, including the installation of electric lights, and a considerable quantity of books was purchased, the library generally being placed in excellent condition for public service. About four thousand volumes are now on the shelves, and to these residents of Ogunquit and the vicinity have free access, although a small fee is charged for its use by summer visitors. The following are the library trustees, named in the provisions of Mrs. Conarroe's will: Robert N. Simpers, of Philadelphia; Albert M. Bragdon, of York, Maine; Henry W. Weare and Luther S. Weare of Ogunquit. Mrs. Conarroe's generosity and foresight provided a valuable and much appreciated asset to the town.

DEXTER WATERMAN HODGDON, Jr.—Since 1919 Dexter W. Hodgdon, Jr., has been engaged in the real estate business in Boothbay Harbor, and since 1926 he has been conducting this business under his own name. Besides doing an extensive brokerage business he also represents locally the development of Appalachee Shores. In addition to being a successful business man, Mr. Hodgdon is an author who has had a considerable amount of historical work published.

Dexter Waterman Hodgdon, Jr., was born in Boothbay Harbor, Maine, June 13, 1895, son of Dexter W., a native of East Boothbay, who was formerly engaged in the ice business and also as a general merchant, now deceased, and of Clara E. (Sherman) Hodgdon, who was born in Edgecomb, Maine, and died in 1925. He received his education in the public schools, and after completing a course in the Boothbay Harbor high school continued his studies in Burdett College. When his commercial training was completed he became associated with the J. B. Hunter Company, of Boston, with whom he remained for a year and a half. He then made a change and identified himself with the New England Telephone and Telegraph Company of Boston as accountant, and that connection he maintained until 1917. His next position was with the National Canners' Association, inspecting canneries along the Maine coast, and as assistant in the main offices at Washington, District of Columbia, continuing in this line until 1919. He then assisted his brother-in-law, Mr. I. C. Kenniston, in the development of Sprucewald, and has been successfully engaged in real estate to the present time (1928). Mr. Hodgdon is a member of the Boothbay Harbor Chamber of Commerce and is one of the most active members. He is also president of the Boothbay Harbor Historical Society. In addition to his varied business responsibilites, Mr. Hodgdon is also interested in historical and literary matters, and has made for himself an enviable reputation as a writer of local history. He was for some years treasurer of the Commonwealth Art Colony of Boothbay Harbor, and one of his best-known historical writings is a work entitled "The Romance of Boothbay," which has just been published. Mr. Hodgdon also has a very valuable collection of Indian relics which he personally excavated, and his collection ranks among the best in the State. He is a member of the American Legion, a former Vice Commander, and his religious affiliation is with the Congregational church.

Mr. Hodgdon is unmarried and resides at No. Twenty-four Eastern Avenue, in Boothbay Harbor.

HARRY B. BROWN—For many years before his appointment as Postmaster of Farmington, Maine, Harry B. Brown had enjoyed the respect of its citizens as editor and part owner of the Farmington "Journal," which he helped to found. When he concluded his association with that newspaper and entered the service of the Post Office Department in 1919, this esteem became even more apparent and his appointment as head of the department in Farmington was generally approved.

Although Mr. Brown was born in Augusta, Maine, on July 6, 1869, his parents, Leonard and Annette (Higgins) Brown, moved to New Hampshire when he was a baby. Consequently, he was educated in the public schools of Concord, New Hampshire, and as soon as he could do so he entered the employ of a newspaper in Concord first, later in Dover, New Hampshire. His father, who had been a newspaper man in Augusta, Maine, for many years, came to Farmington to practice law and Harry B. Brown also came, to enter newspaper work there. He and Henry P. White helped to organize the Farmington "Journal," and Mr. Brown was its editor for seven years.

When he lived in New Hampshire, Mr. Brown served four years in the New Hampshire National Guard as a Captain, and was assigned to command Company E, of Concord. He is member of Blue Lodge, Free and Accepted Masons; and a communicant of the Congregational church. He married Gertrude M. Combs, and they have one child, Gladys A. Brown.

EDWARD F. SMALL—Having spent the whole of his business life in the service of what is now called the Liberty National Bank, of Ellsworth, Maine, Edward F. Small is probably known to every man, woman and child in the community, for he is a native of Ellsworth himself, and so were both his parents.

Born August 13, 1880, he was the son of William and Frances (Lee) Small. His father served in the United States Navy during the Civil War, and for fifteen years was commander of William H. H. Rice Post No. 55, Grand Army of the Republic. He was a machinist, and actively at work until his death in 1920. His mother survived until 1922. Educated in the public and high schools of Ellsworth, Maine, Edward F. Small found his first and only employment with the Burrill National Bank in 1899. At first a clerk, he was promoted to assistant cashier in 1908, and to cashier in 1911, in which capacity he still acts. During the World War he served on all the patriotic drives for raising funds and selling Liberty bonds, and made himself useful in other civic activities. It was not until 1919 that the Burrill National Bank changed its name to the Liberty National Bank, the present corporate title.

Mr. Small has always been independent in politics, but served four years as an alderman of Ellsworth. His principal recreation is gardening. He is a member of Bayside Grange, of the Improved Order of Red Men, and is vice-president of the Chamber of Commerce.

In 1913 he married Mollie Hamilton, of Ellsworth, their children being Edward F., Jr., and Elizabeth L. Small. Mrs. Small died in 1918, and he married (second) Frances Milliken, of Ellsworth Falls, Maine.

JONAS EDWARDS—A man who worked tirelessly to assist his fellow-men, the late Jonas Ed-

wards, whose death occurred June 7, 1916, as the
result of a runaway accident, was one of Auburn's
outstanding citizens of whom this entire community
was proud. Mr. Edwards was a fearless advocate
of the cause of right and championed every issue
which, in his opinion, provided for the public good
and the well-being of each individual, and he achieved
a position of prominence in the realm of religious
and temperance reform. In the business world, he
was a leader in aiding and developing Auburn's
progress and successful advance, having founded the
large and prosperous market for the buying and selling of horses which still bears his name.

Mr. Edwards was born in Casco and received his
education in the schools of this State. He started
his commercial career as a merchant on a small
scale and gradually progressed by reason of his
sturdy principles of absolute honesty and integrity.
He was one of the most popular residents of this
vicinity, as his lifelong occupation as a horse-dealer
gave him a wide acquaintance. In civic affairs, he
was prominent for his active participation in all
campaigns for reform and improvement, and as a
public speaker, he was recognized for his brilliant
eloquence all over the State, while his staunch support of prohibition bought him into political prominence. For many years, he was a lay preacher, having always been a deeply religious man, and conducted Sunday services in nearly every rural school
building in this district, while he also served as president of the Mechanics' Row Mission. Mr. Edwards
was a leading member of the Auburn Reform Club
and of the High Street Congregational Church. The
fatal runaway accident which caused his death occurred in the center of this city, when he was thrown
from a carriage on Spring Street. He was showing
one of his out-of-town customers a new horse and
as they were driving over Spring Street into Hampshire Street, toward Mr. Edwards' office, a shifting
engine crossed the track before them. This frightened
the animal, with the result that it bolted and Mr.
Edwards lost control, being thrown out upon the
roadway and rendered unconscious, from which condition he never rallied. Of the high opinion in which
he was held by his friends and fellow-citizens,
nothing speaks more highly than the following tribute in the pages of the Lewiston "Evening Journal," which reads, in part:

Of all the men with whom I have been associated in many
relations in Auburn in the last forty years, I know of none
who has taken finer advantage of opportunity when it was
supplied him. His great talent, however, is to have created
opportunity and to have grappled odds successfully with
what ordinary men would have regarded to be insuperable
or at least discouraging. . . . . The first time I saw Mr.
Edwards was forty years ago on a pedlar's cart whence my
own ancestors were graduated upwards of three generations
ago. In small mercantile beginnings, many a New Englander
has evolved skill in business and acquaintance with situations through better self-acquaintance, and thus has graduated successful students of human nature. Without such
culture, no business man can get a start on his own initiative, or maintain himself if he is unlucky enough to have
been boosted by someone else. Mr. Edwards was one of the
best and delightfully known men in Maine. He did more
business in an unostentatious way than any one of my acquaintance. In all good works he has ever been active, in
temperance, the religious and wayside fields.

JAMES B. PULSIFER—In the business development and progress of Auburn, there is none more
active than James B. Pulsifer, who operates an enterprising coal and wood concern in this city, in ad-

dition to which he also conducts a modern real estate business, with offices located at No. 50 Railroad
Street. Mr. Pulsifer has been active in the commercial affairs of this city since 1898, and since
venturing into the coal and wood trade in 1906, has
gradually built up a substantial and discriminating
patronage and a reputation for fuel of the finest
quality. His success is due mainly to the good will
of hundreds of satisfied customers, who recognize
and appreciate the splendid business ethics of his
organization.

Mr. Pulsifer was born in Auburn, October 7, 1875,
son of Fobes F. Pulsifer, born in Poland, Maine, and
Adelaide S. (Bucknam) Pulsifer, born in Boston,
Massachusetts. Fobes F. Pulsifer was active as a
harness-maker for many years.

James B. Pulsifer was educated in the public schools
of Minot, after which he attended Hebron Academy.
Upon completing his education, he entered upon
his business career and after engaging in various
occupations, started out on an independent venture
in the milk business, in 1898, here in Auburn, and he
continued in this activity with great prosperity until 1906, when he began his present well-known concern. In politics, he is a staunch supporter of the
principles of the Republican party, although he has
never desired public office, being content to support
to the best of his ability every civic project which
aims at municipal welfare and advancement. Thus he
has acquired the distinction of being a true public-
spirited citizen of the highest type. His fraternal
affiliations are with the Free and Accepted Masons,
Knights Templar, and Ancient Arabic Order Nobles
of the Mystic Shrine, and he is a member of the
Martindale Country Club. Mr. Pulsifer attends the
Congregational church.

James B. Pulsifer married, October 29, 1900, at
Auburn, Maine, Maidee Parsons, who was born in
Turner, January 7, 1877, daughter of Edward and
Mary (Allen) Parsons. both natives of Turner. Mr.
and Mrs. Pulsifer are the parents of one daughter,
Pauline Rebecca, born March 22, 1907.

HOWARD WALTER MANN, president of the
Maine School of Commerce, Incorporated, with
schools at Auburn, Augusta, Bangor, Portland and
Presque Isle, was born in Orange, Massachusetts,
November 3, 1891, a son of Walter L. and Irene L.
(Mattoon) Mann, and was educated in the elementary
public and high schools of that town and at the Bay
Path Institute, at Springfield, Massachusetts, from
which last-named institution he was graduated in
1912. After two years of post-graduate work in private schools he came to Maine and established the
Maine School of Commerce at Auburn which has
become one of the largest private commerical schools
in New England. He was chairman of the Department of Commercial Branches from 1917 until 1924
and has membership in the Maine Teachers' Association; New England Business College Association;
Eastern Commercial Teachers' Association; the
Young Men's Christian Association; the Kiwanis
Club; the Auburn Chamber of Commerce; the Free
and Accepted Masons; the Shrine, and the Benevolent and Protective Order of Elks.

Mr. Mann married, November 28, 1917, Hazel W.
Fitz, of Auburn, Maine. They have one child:
Josephine A.

FABIUS MAXIMUS RAY—Intimate with all phases of the law, active in a political way, a man thoroughly cultured and possessed of a wide general knowledge, especially of historical and literary matters, Fabius Maximus Ray was, during his lifetime, one of the outstanding citizens of Maine. In Westbrook, where he made his home, he had a host of friends, whom he won by his genial personality and splendid traits of character, all of whom realized that in his death the State had lost a more than ordinarily useful man. Not only were Mr. Ray's contributions of a broad, general interest, however, for he left among his intimate friends and those of his business associates who had the pleasure and privilege of knowing him well an influence for good. Especially in his professional work did he have a keen sense of his responsibility to his clients. And in his own family circle, he was loved and cherished as an excellent husband and father, whom death took away all too soon.

Mr. Ray was born in Windham, Maine, March 30, 1837, son of Colonel Caleb and Susan (Bickford) Ray and a descendant of Daniel Rhea, who came to Plymouth, Massachusetts, in 1630, removed to Danvers, Massachusetts, in the following year, and became a prominent pioneer settler there.

Fabius Maximus Ray received his early education in the Windham and Westbrook schools, and later became a student at Bowdoin College, from which he was graduated in the class of 1861 with the degree of Bachelor of Arts and from which he received, in 1864, the degree of Masters of Arts. In 1861 and 1862, after he had received his bachelor's degree, he studied privately at Heidelberg and Geneva. In Portland, he read law with the Hon. William H. Vinton, and was admitted to the bar in Maine, in 1865. In 1871 and 1872, he was a member of the Maine House of Representatives; and from 1885 until 1886, was a member of the State Senate. From 1883 to 1885, he was Judge of the Westbrook Municipal Court. He was a friend and colleague of Thomas B. Reed. A quite, modest man, his ideals were high and his knowledge of the law great; he was a diligent worker, made thorough preparation for each case, and was rewarded by a gratifying degree of success. Fond of studying the ways of former days, he made a careful study of history, especially the history of Maine, and of his hometown, Westbrook, and, possessing a retentive memory, he carried with him to the grave much knowledge of local history that never became publicly known. He was a trustee of Gorham Academy, a member of the Maine Historical Society, and a past president of the Maine Genealogical Society. He was a member of the Chi Psi, Elians Book-lovers' Club, and was author of "Christmas Tree and Other Poems," which he wrote in 1874; of "Translations, Imitations and a Few Originals," published in 1904; and other works. He edited the "Journal" of his great-grandfather, Dr. Caleb Rea, written from Dr. Rea's diary, 1758.

Fabius Maximus Ray married (first), in Lexington, Massachusetts, on August 28, 1863, Mary M. Marrett, of Westbrook, Maine, who died on January 27, 1877; and he married (second), on November 22, 1893, Isabel Tibbetts, daughter of Robert P. Tibbetts. The children by his first marriage were: 1. Sarah Adeline, who became the wife of Dr. Albert H. Burroughs, of Westbrook. 2. William Caleb Ray, born May 16,

1871, who married Mary A. Plumer, of Portland, and has a son, Roger B., of Portland.

The death of Fabius Maximus Ray occurred on November 23, 1915, and caused widespread grief among his many friends and acquaintances. It is only proper that his life should become an important part of the history of his community and his State; for not only was he deeply interested in the people and history of Maine and ever ready to assist in compiling historical and genealogical data, but actually, in his own professional and public career, did much to make that history.

DR. ALTON L. GRANT, Jr., was born in Lewiston, Maine, November 1, 1888, a son of Alton L. Grant, a native of Gardiner and a confectioner and caterer by profession, and of Margaret (Parrow) Grant, of Derby Line, Vermont. He acquired his preliminary education in the public schools of Lewiston and was graduated from the high school there. He then attended Bowdoin College and was graduated in the class of 1912 with the degree of Bachelor of Arts. This was followed by attendance at the Bowdoin Medical School, which institution graduated him in the class of 1916 with his degree of Doctor of Medicine.

In the Central Maine General Hospital, in Lewiston, he served during 1916 and 1917. This was followed by an experience as interne in the Boston City Hospital, where he confined himself to Aural and Ophthalmic practice, remaining there for twenty months. In August, 1921, he came to Auburn and opened an office for the treatment of the afflictions already noted, at No. 133 Court Street, continuing successfully in his specialty to the present time. In August, 1917, he was commissioned a lieutenant in the United States Naval Reserve and on January 18, 1918, was transferred to the regular Navy. In this he served until February 3, 1920, when he was honorably discharged. He is a member of the Free and Accepted Masons, of the Kiwanis Club, the American Legion Club, the Auburn Chamber of Commerce and the Martindale Country Club. He also belongs to the American Medical Association, and the State and the County Medical societies. His church is the St. Michael's Protestant Episcopal of Auburn.

Mr. Grant married, in Auburn, August 20, 1917, Beatrice Soutar, daughter of James Soutar, a native of Scotland, and of Annie (Fader) Soutar, born in Nova Scotia. Their children are: Barbara S., John E., and Peter O.

CHARLES BRIDGHAM DAY—Occupying a prominent place in the hotel circles of Maine, Charles Bridgham Day is one of Lewiston's best-known and progressive citizens in his position as manager of the DeWitt Hotel of this city. Mr. Day has held this responsible post since 1925, prior to that time having been active in the wholesale grocery business, in which he still maintains his interest. Since accepting his present appointment, he has administered the affairs of this splendid hotel to the eminent satisfaction of everyone concerned, taking particular care that all guests have the most comfortable and convenient surroundings, receive the most courteous and agreeable service and are accorded every consideration that not only impress them with the advantages and charm of this organization but give them pleasure to recommend this house to their friends. In the civic affairs of Lewiston, Mr. Day has always taken a constructive interest, being particularly popular in fraternal affairs, to which he gives much of his attention, while in forwarding the progress and welfare of his city, he is always to the fore in every project that is launched for municipal improvement.

Mr. Day was born in Whitneyville, December 7, 1867, son of Larkin Lawrence Day, born in Whitneyville, and of Belle B. (Looke) Day, born at Jonesboro. Larkin Lawrence Day was an active factor in the lumber business in this State for many years.

Charles Bridgham Day was educated in the public schools of North Stratford, New Hampshire, and later entered Portland High School, from which he was graduated with the class of 1889. After the completion of this formal education in 1891, he removed to Richmond, Maine, where he was salesman for C. A. Weston & Company of Portland until 1900, when he accepted a position as salesman with the Milliken, Tomlinson Company, of Portland, one of the leading wholesale grocery houses in the State, remaining with this company until 1928. Mr. Day was appointed manager of the DeWitt Hotel in 1926, in which position he has attracted considerable and favorable attention for his expert handling and brilliant management of this leading, modern hostelry. It can also be safely said that he is a great factor in promoting the progress and advancement of this city, for in so many cases, travelers and visitors judge the merits of a city by the treatment accorded them at the hotel in which they stay, and its comfort and convenience, and in the case of the DeWitt Hotel under Mr. Day's supervision, they can receive only the most favorable and pleasant impression of this splendid municipality. In 1928, he purchased an interest in the Rangeley Lake Hotel Company, at Rangeley Lakes, Maine, of which Mr. Day is managing director. In politics, Mr. Day has always been an Independent, although during 1911-12, he served on the staff of Governor Plaisted, of this State, having the rank of major. His fraternal connections are with the Free and Accepted Masons, Richmond Lodge, No. 63; the Chapter, Royal Arch Masons; Council, Royal and Select Masters; Maine Commandery, No. 1, Knights Templar, of which he is a Past Commander; Kora Temple, Ancient Arabic Order Nobles of the Mystic Shrine, and the Independent Order of Odd Fellows. He is prominently identified with the Rotary Club, the Martindale Country Club, the New England Hotel Association, and the Maine Hotel Association, and the Lewiston and Auburn Chambers of Commerce. His religious adherence is given to the Congregational church of Lewiston.

Charles Bridgham Day married (first) Maude B. Oakes, of Argyle, and he married (second) Marietta H. (Harriman) Pattée, born at Stockton Springs.

GEORGE ADELBERT BABB—It seems but natural that a boy born in Maine and near the sea, should turn to the ocean with expectant eye for adventure when he had finished school days, and also it is not amiss to think of him in the granite quarries of his native State. These were the first occupations of George Adelbert Babb, of Camden, but he swerved from the average course of the Maine boy for a few years, when he felt the urge of the West and went

to the Black Hills of Dakota, before that great territory was divided to make two States of the Union, where he worked in the mines. Both he and his State are to be congratulated that fate drew him back, for his business success here has been to the advantage of both.

George Adelbert Babb was born in South Thomaston, Maine, January 15, 1856, son of Harrison Patterson, and Harriett Ann (Newhall) Babb. His father was a ship's carpenter and operator of a granite quarry. He received his education in the public and high schools in South Thomaston, at the conclusion of this course going to sea. He next worked at granite cutting in Maine and then went West, where he stopped in the Black Hills and went to work as a miner. He spent three years there and then returned to Maine, in October, 1886, where he became superintendent of the Clark's Island Granite Works, remaining in that position for three years. July 1, 1890, he entered the employ of the Knox Woolen Company, of Camden, where he has continued to the present time, as boss weaver, assistant superintendent and assistant treasurer. For the past fourteen years he has sold the product of this concern, paper makers' felts, in the New England territory. He is in politics a Republican and has held the offices of selectman, treasurer of the town and collector of taxes. He is a director in the Camden National Bank and is affiliated with the order of Free and Accepted Masons, Royal Arch Masons and Knights Templar. He also belongs to the Masonic Club and the Camden Rotary Club. His church is the Congregational.

George A. Babb married, in South Thomaston, Maine, December 2, 1882, Emma Theresa Longfellow, daughter of Abram and Kate (O'Neil) Longfellow.

JUDGE FREEMAN DANIEL DEARTH—Not alone prominent as judge and successful politician, but Freeman Daniel Dearth of Dexter, Maine, is known as a baseball fan which gives added proof of true Americanism and general good fellowship among his friends and acquaintances. He is the son of Freeman Daniel and Mary B. (Spooner) Dearth, of Sangerville, Maine. His grandfather was Leonard Dearth, who was born October 30, 1791, at Sherborn, Massachusetts, and moved to Sangerville, Maine, when a young men, clearing land which he cultivated and on which he built his home and lived until his death in 1880.

It was here that Freeman Daniel Dearth, the first, was born May 19, 1831, and educated in the public schools, or as they were then called common schools, and at Foxcroft Academy. He was always engaged in farming and spent his entire life on the old home farm where he was born. He died in 1886. He was a member of the Methodist church and Republican in politics. About 1853, he married Mary B. Spooner, daughter of Daniel and Jemima (Knowlton) Spooner, of Sangerville, Maine. They had thirteen children including two sets of twins.

Freeman Daniel Dearth (2), the fifth child of Freeman Daniel and Mary B. (Spooner) Dearth, was born in Sangerville, Maine, April 16, 1861. He began school in the district school here and then went to Foxcroft Academy and Maine Central Institute. Finishing his preparatory work, he matriculated in Bowdoin College and in the class of 1887 was graduated with the degree of Bachelor of Arts. Continuing in the same college, he attained the degree of Master of Arts in 1890. After leaving college, he read law in the office of Crosby and Crosby at Dexter, Maine, but his whole time was not given to the study of law, for he was at this time filling a government position in railway mail service on the route between Bangor and Greenville, and between Bangor and Vanceboro. By diligence and industry, he completed his study of law and was admitted to the bar of the State of Maine in 1894 and has continued to practice law ever since. In 1909, he was admitted to the bar of the United States Supreme Court. For three years, he was Judge of the Municipal Court and resigned from this position to fill an appointment of postmaster which was awarded him in 1900. In December, 1919, he was appointed Reporter of Decisions of Supreme Judicial Court of the State of Maine and has continued in that position. He has held many political offices of responsibility which include the thirteen years as postmaster of Dexter; two years each in the House of Representatives and in the Maine Senate when he resigned to take the position as Reporter of Decisions. In civic and social affairs, he has always taken a keen and active interest.

Judge Dearth is a member of the board of trustees of the Abbott Memorial Library; a director in the First National Bank; was at one time chairman of the School Board; and is a member of the Bedivere Lodge, Knights of Pythias, of Dexter; and of the Penobscot Lodge, No. 39, Free and Accepted Masons, and the Eastern Star. During the World War, he served on the local advisory board of the town of Dexter and was one of the "four-minute" speakers. He is an ardent Republican and has been on the Republican Town Committee and on the Republican County Committee. He was president of the Dexter Club, and is a member of the Chamber of Commerce. He attends the Methodist church.

NELSON T. GORDON—Nelson T. Gordon, postmaster of Readfield Depot, and a well-known merchant of Readfield, was born on February 4, 1884, in Readfield, Maine. Mr. Gordon is a son of Nelson D. and Mary (Henry) Gordon. The father, Nelson D. Gordon, who was also born in Readfield, and who died in 1906, was a well-known dealer in general merchandise in that vicinity. A supporter of the Republican party, Mr. Gordon was very active in the service of the people and during his life he held at various times all the offices of the town and he was also a member of the State Legislature. The mother, Mary (Henry) Gordon, was born in Beverly, New Jersey, and she now resides in Readfield Depot.

Their son, Nelson T. Gordon, received his education in the public schools of Readfield, later attending the high school at Winthrop, Maine. Upon the completion of these courses of study, he went to work with his father. The elder Mr. Gordon had conducted a general merchandise and grain and feed business for over fifty years and Mr. Gordon carried on the business with his father until the time of the latter's death in 1906. For a short time thereafter, Mr. Gordon carried on the business in association with his brother. Since that time he has been sole proprietor of the large and prosperous business. In 1906 he was appointed postmaster at Readfield Depot, Maine, a position which he still holds.

Despite the many duties which the conducting of this extensive business entailed, Mr. Gordon has nevertheless found time in which to take a keen interest in civic affairs. In his political preferences he is a supporter of the Republican party and he served

on the School Board for three years. He is fraternally affiliated with all bodies of the Masonic Order up to and including the Shrine and is a thirty-second degree Mason. He is also a member of the Rotary Club of Augusta, Maine.

Nelson T. Gordon married, September 12, 1906, at Winthrop, Maine, Emma L. Pike, who was born in Winthrop, a daughter of George A. and Esther L. (Lawrence) Pike. Mr. and Mrs. Gordon are the parents of four children, one son and three daughters: 1. Nelson T., Jr. 2. Lawrence R. 3. Lucille. 4. Rachel. Mr. Gordon and his family attend the Friends' church at Winthrop Center.

HARRY C. STRATTON—After a varied experience in merchandising and banking, Harry C. Stratton, of Ellsworth, Maine, purchased the business of F. P. Aiken, which had been dealing in kitchen ware and stores for half a century, and has since developed it into a variety store, which has become one of the largest in its neighborhood.

Son of Purbot H. and Sophia J. (Hutchins) Stratton, he comes of Maine families on both lines, for his father, who was born in Hancock, and was a contractor and builder from early manhood until his death, was of pioneer origin; and his mother, who is still living, was born in West Franklin, Maine. Born January 7, 1876, Harry C. Stratton was educated in the public schools of Ellsworth, his native town, and entered business life in 1893 in the service of the Burrill National Bank of Ellsworth, where he remained until 1899. He then became associated with his father in the hardware business, and in 1900, bought his father's interest, and took into partnership Horace F. Westcott, the firm name being Stratton & Westcott. This association continued for seven years, at the end of which period Mr. Stratton sold his interest, and went on the road as the traveling representative of a paint house, in which employment he continued for the next ten years. He then began business on his account in Ellsworth.

Mr. Stratton is a member of Lygonia Lodge, Free and Accepted Masons, of Arcadia Chapter, Blanquefort Commandery, and Anah Temple, Ancient Arabic Order Nobles of the Mystic Shrine; Past Chancellor of Donaqua Lodge, Knights of Pythias, a member of the Modern Woodmen of the World, the Masonic Club, and has been secretary of the Chamber of Commerce. He is a Republican in politics, and has served three years as a member of the Ellsworth Board of Aldermen. With his family he attends the Baptist church. Always a lover of outdoor life, his chief recreations are fishing and gardening.

In 1897, Mr. Stratton married Annie Langley, of Ellsworth, Maine. Their one child is Harry L. Stratton.

BERT L. CALL—Photography has engaged Mr. Call's attention for many years, and in this pursuit he has become one of the best known scenic and wild life photographers in the State of Maine. Born on May 16, 1866, in Exeter, Maine, Mr. Call is a son of Edwin R. and Emma Jane (White) Call, both of whom are now deceased. Edwin R. Call, the father, who was born in Dresden, Maine, was one of the "forty-niners," and he was engaged in farming until the time of his death. The mother, Emma Jane (White) Call, was born in Exeter.

Their son, Bert L. Call, received his education in the public and high schools of Exeter. Upon the completion of these courses of study, in 1886, he re-

344 MAINE—A HISTORY

moved to Dexter to take a position with A. G. Fassett in the photography business. In November, 1886, he bought out this business and the name was changed to Call's Studio. Mr. Call has carried on this work since that time and he has been particularly successful in this exacting type of enterprise. The business was first located in the Parson Building on the corner of Grove and Main streets. In 1913, the business was moved to the top floor of the Waterville Trust Company Building, and in 1924, when it was burned out Mr. Call bought the building at No. 405 Main Street, where his studio now is. It was at this time that he bought the gift shop and jewelry store of J. W. Springall, which he now carries on as well as his photography work. In 1918 Mr. Call took his son, Edwin C. Call into partnership with him. Mr. Call is one of the best-known photographers of wild life and spots of scenic beauty in the State of Maine. He and his son are the official photographers of the Bangor & Aroostook Railroad and they have furnished numerous cuts for the various publications of the State of Maine.

Although his business is one which demands a great deal of close attention, Mr. Call has never been too busy to take an active interest in the affairs of his community. In his political preferences he is a strong supporter of the Republican party. He has served as a member of the Dexter School Board for nine years, and he was also a selectman for one year. He is fraternally affiliated with the Knights of Pythias, of which he is Past Chancellor. He is also a member of the New England Association of Photographers, of which he is past vice-president, the Dexter Chamber of Commerce, the Dexter Club, and the Elkinstown Club.

Bert L. Call married, in 1888, Carrie B. Safford, who was born in Dexter. Mr. and Mrs. Call are the parents of one child, a son, Edwin C., who was born on May 25, 1894, in Dexter, Maine. Edwin C. Call received his education in the public and high schools of the community in which he was born, later attending Bowdoin College from which he graduated in 1918 with the degree of Bachelor of Arts. That same year he became associated with his father, Bert L. Call, in photography business. Since that time he has continued as a partner in Call's Studio. During the World War Mr. Edwin C. Call was commissioned second lieutenant, Infantry Corps, United States Army on August 15, 1917. He was assigned to the Twenty-sixth Division and served overseas for ten months with the American Expeditionary Forces in France. He took part in most of the major conflicts, during which he was slightly gassed, and wounded. On August 24, 1918 he was promoted first lieutenant, and on March 17, 1919, he was made captain. Later, on August 3, 1923, he was commissioned major and he is now assigned to Regimental Headquarters, 386th Infantry, United States Army. In his political preferences he is a supporter of the Republican party. He is fraternally affiliated with the Penobscot Lodge, Free and Accepted Masons, the St. John's Chapter, Royal Arch Masons, of which he is Past High Priest, the Council, Royal and Select Masters; the Consistory, Ancient Accepted Scottish Rite; and the St. John's Commandery, Knights Templar; and he is a contributing member of the Wauskeage Chapter of the Eastern Star. He is also a member of the New England Association of Photographers, the Dexter Chamber of Commerce, of which he is a director, the Dexter Club, of which he is past president, and the

Masonic Club; and the college fraternity, Beta Theta Pi. Edwin C. Call married (first) Maybelle Haines, who was born in Dexter, and who died in 1924. By this union there was one child, a daughter, Mary Augusta. Mr. Call married (second) Buella Edes, who was born in Dexter. Mr. and Mrs. Bert L. Call, and Mr. Edwin C. Call and his family attend the Universalist church, of which Mr. Edwin C. Call is a trustee.

CORNELIUS J. RUSSELL—After an extended experience in the clothing business, Cornelius J. Russell became identified with the Maine and New Hampshire Theatres Company, and this connection has been maintained to the present time (1928). For the past four years he has been manager of the Bijou, Park, the Opera House, and the Graphic theatres of Bangor, and is giving to the residents of this city excellent service in the way of amusement. Mr. Russell has been active in public affairs both in Lewiston and in Bangor, and has served in the State Legislature.

Cornelius J. Russell, father of Mr. Russell, was born in Ireland. He came to this country at an early age and located in Lewiston, Maine. Here he engaged in the textile manufacturing business, and for forty-three years was foreman of the Androscoggin Mills of Lewiston, continuing in that position to the time of his death in 1920. He was a veteran of the Civil War, serving with the Nineteenth Massachusetts Volunteers, rank of sergeant, and was wounded in action in the second battle of Bull Run and in the battle of Gettysburg. He was a member of Lewiston Post, Grand Army of the Republic, and was active in its affairs to the time of his death. Cornelius J. Russell married Margaret Buckley, who was born in Ireland, and died in 1914.

Cornelius J. Russell, son of Cornelius J. and Margaret (Buckley) Russell, was born in Lewiston, Maine, October 27, 1880. He received his education in the public schools of Lewiston, and upon the completion of his course in the high school secured a position as clerk in a local clothing store, where he remained for ten years. At the end of that time, in 1908, he engaged in the clothing business for himself in Lewiston under the name of Russell and Geary, Men's Furnishing and Clothing Store. This enterprise was continued to be successfully conducted until 1915, when he sold out and associated himself with the Maine and New Hampshire Theatres Company in the capacity of field manager. Four years later, in 1919, he was made manager of the Empire theatre at Lewiston, Maine. Here he remained until 1923, rendering efficient service and acquiring valuable experience. In 1923 he was transferred to Bangor as manager of four of the theatres of this city, namely, the Bijou, Park, Opera House, and Graphic. As manager of these four well-known places of amusement Mr. Russell has fully demonstrated his ability, and he is giving to the public most satisfactory service. Along with his business responsibilities Mr. Russell has found time for a large amount of public service. He is a Republican, and was very active in local affairs in Lewiston. He served in 1912-13-14 as alderman of the city of Lewiston; was city treasurer of Lewiston in 1915-16, and resigned the last-named office after having been appointed recorder of Lewiston Municipal Court by Governor Curtis. In 1915-16 he served as a Representative in the State Legislature. In his fraternal affiliations, Mr. Russell is identified with Lewiston Lodge, Be-

nevolent and Protective Order of Elks, and with Lewiston Council, Knights of Columbus. His club is the
Rotary of Bangor. Mr. Russell is an active and interested member of the Bangor Chamber of Commerce, and one of the public-spirited citizens of the
city. He is fond of out-door sports, his favorite recreational activities being baseball and football. His
religious preference is with St. John's Roman Catholic
Church.
Cornelius J. Russell married, in 1904, Jane T.
Sullivan, who was born in Lewiston, Maine. Mr. and
Mrs. Russell are the parents of one son, Cornelius
J., Jr.

WESTON BRADFORD HASKELL was born
in Auburn, February 27, 1893, son of Robert and
Elsie A. (Day) Haskell. He was educated in the
public schools of Auburn, graduating from the Edward Little High School, after which he furthered
his education at the University of Maine, from
which institution he was graduated with the class
of 1917, receiving his degree of Bachelor of Science.
Coincidental with his graduation from the university, he enlisted in the United States Army as a
private. After a short period of training he was
sent to France, where he was promoted to the rank
of second lieutenant, later being made first lieutenant.
He saw active service on the battlefields of France,
and after the Armistice, remained in the war zone,
later going into Germany with the Army of Occupation, remaining there until 1919, having been commissioned captain. Upon returning to the United
States, he entered the dairy business and advanced
therein until he was appointed to his present position, in 1926, of general manager of the Turner Center System, one of the largest and most important
concerns engaged in the manufacture and distribution of dairy products in New England. He is a
member of the Chamber of Commerce of Auburn and
of the New England and National Ice Cream associations. His political views are Independent, while
his fraternal affiliations are with the Free and Accepted Masons, in which he has attained the thirty-
second degree; the Kiwanis Club, and the Young
Men's Christian Association, of which he is a director. He is a member of the Boston City Club,
and is commander of the local post of the American
Legion.
Weston Bradford Haskell married, November 17,
1917, at Plattsburg, New York, Pauline Derby, and
they have children: Weston B., Helen Y., and Richard D.

WILBUR R. BLODGETT—Since 1917 engaged
as cashier of the Searsport National Bank, at Searsport, Waldo County, Wilbur R. Blodgett is prominently identified with the commercial, fraternal and
public life of this community, and is known and respected throughout the county as a capable and understanding banker and financier, having the interest of Searsport and the countryside at heart.
Wilbur R. Blodgett was born at Belfast, Maine,
September 28, 1885, son of Alvan Blodgett, native
of Freedom, Maine, and of Mary Elizabeth (Calder-
wood) Blodgett, native of Northport, Maine; his
father having been for a number of years occupied
at Belfast as carpenter and building contractor. Wilbur R. Blodgett received his education in the public
schools of Belfast, there graduating from the high

school; and at the age of seventeen years, in 1902,
went to work in clerical capacity for the Belfast
Peoples National Bank. Later he became associated
with the City National Bank, of Belfast, and maintained this connection during five years, by which
time he had completely mastered the theories and
practices of banking. He next went with the Waldo
Trust Company, Belfast, and remained there two
years, as treasurer. Thus far he had become exceptionally well grounded in matters of town and
rural banking methods; but, desiring to expand this
knowledge to include a more comprehensive scope,
he left Belfast, and secured a position with the
National Rockland Bank, of Boston, Massachusetts.
Here he secured the broader understanding which he
desired, and in 1917, became identified with the
Searsport National Bank, as cashier, and as member
of the board of directors. Mr. Blodgett is outstanding among the public-spirited citizens of Searsport,
and, as a member of the Republican party, takes an
active part in the political affairs of town and county.
He is a member of the American Bankers' Associa-
tion and of Timothy Chase Lodge, No. 26, Free and
Accepted Masons; Royal Arch Masons, Royal and
Select Masters, Knights Templar, York Rite. He
is a communicant of the First Congregational Church,
and generous in his contributions to charity.
Wilbur R. Blodgett married, at Brooks, Maine,
Erma M. Barker, born at Brooks on February 20,
1885, daughter of Wilbur E. Barker, born at Troy,
Maine, and of Edith G. (Roberts) Barker, born at
Jackson, Maine.

WALTER G. HICKS—For more than twenty-
five years Walter G. Hicks has resided in Rumford,
and has here been engaged in the hardware business
all of that time, first as employee and later as proprietor and owner. He is accounted one of the foremost of Rumford's public-spirited citizens, and participates freely in movements calculated to benefit the
public-at-large, politically and otherwise.
Mr. Hicks was born at Colebrook, New Hampshire, February 1, 1879, son of Gilbert W. and Elizabeth (Williams) Hicks, both of whom are natives of
Colebrook. Gilbert W. Hicks has given his career
to agriculture, has attained to fair prosperity as
farmer, and is influential in the general movements
of Colebrook, where he now (1928) serves on the
Board of Selectmen.
Walter G. Hicks attended Colebrook Academy,
graduated with the class of 1895, and entered Gray's
Business College, at Portland, Maine, whence he
graduated in 1896. That same year he began his
career in business, securing a place with the Berlin
Mills Company, of Berlin, New Hampshire. He
continued with the plant in Berlin until 1901, then
accepted an offer of employment from Stanley Bisbee, proprietor and owner of a hardware store in
Rumford. As an assistant to Mr. Bisbee, Mr. Hicks
made himself invaluable, and when Mr. Bisbee wished
to retire from trade, in 1917, he purchased the store
and stock, for he had accumulated a fund of considerable proportion during the twenty-one years of
his service as employee in Berlin and Rumford. Mr.
Hicks has always been a man to manage his affairs
well, and with expedition, and forethought. Had
this not been the case he might never have become
a proprietor in his own right; but he realized at the
outset of his experience that success can be won in

commerce if proper method is used, and proceeded to use that method. His industry and purpose were rewarded on the day when he first took charge of the Bisbee store, then no longer the Bisbee store but the Hicks store. Materially, in 1917, at the age of thirty-seven years, he had attained to the success he sought; whereupon he set about the attainment of further progression. In that year, the first of his proprietorship, Mr. Hicks took a partner, S. R. Pennell, and they did business under the style of Hicks & Pennell, which style it still bears, though in 1920, Mr. Pennell withdrew from the firm, disposing of his holding to Mr. Hicks. Rumford is well acquainted with Mr. Hicks and with his store. A large proportion of the townspeople resort to him for supplies in hardware, and the store, at No. 136 Congress Street, has been much renovated and improved indeed, since 1901, when Mr. Hicks first entered its doors.

While he has of necessity confined himself closely to his commercial interests in Hicks & Pennell, Mr. Hicks has never failed to participate in community matters, political and fraternal. A Democrat, he is loyal to the principles of the party, and is influential in its workings locally, though never has he accepted the suggestion that he become a candidate for office. He is known for the readiness with which he contributes in time, money and direction to programs for the advancement of the community, and is accounted among the foremost of progressive citizens. Fraternally, he has strong connections: he is Past Grand Patriarch in the Independent Order of Odd Fellows, and a member of the Blue Lodge, Free and Accepted Masons, Royal Arch Masons, Royal and Select Masters, and Knights Templar. He is also a Deputy Grand Master of the Masonic fraternity. He is active in the workings of the Rumford Chamber of Commerce, and its secretary, which position he fills admirably, to the pleasure of business associates and the profit of the town. He is a communicant of the Baptist church, most benevolent in his attitude toward charity, generous in contributions, regardless of race or creed.

At Canaan, Vermont, September 30, 1901, Walter G. Hicks was united in marriage with Carrie Fuller, who was born at Canaan, January 15, 1876, daughter of Luther Fuller, native of Canaan, and of Fannie (Carlton) Fuller, native of Colebrook, New Hampshire. To this union was born one child, a daughter, Lucille F., in Rumford, July 12, 1906.

PERLEY CHASE DRESSER, well known in the real estate world of Portland, Maine, and a member of the realty firm of W. F. Dresser & Sons, was born on May 30, 1885, at Scarborough, Maine, a son of Wilbur F. and Sarah (McLaughlin) Dresser, both natives of Scarborough. Wilbur F. Dresser, the father, was particularly prominent in the realty field in and around Portland, having started the business of W. F. Dresser & Sons in 1890, later taking his two sons into the business with him. He died on January 5, 1924.

Perley Chase Dresser received his early education in the public schools of the community in which he was born, and attended Portland High School, graduating from there with the class of 1903. Immediately after the completion of these courses of study he entered the work in which he was to make his mark—the real estate business—in company with his father and brother. The head offices of this concern are located at No. 80 Exchange Street, Portland, and since the death of the elder Mr. Dresser, the concern is in the able hands of his two sons, Perley Chase Dresser and William W. Dresser. Both these men have come to hold positions of prominence in the commercial world of Portland, and both have contributed much toward the progressiveness of that community.

Despite the many exacting duties of the work in which he is engaged, Mr. Dresser has found time in which to take a keen interest in the civic and general affairs of Portland. In his political views he is a staunch supporter of the Democratic party, and is noted for the excellent manner in which he stands behind any movement designed for the welfare and advancement of his city. He is a member of the New Hampshire State Grange, and has been active in the good work of that organization. He has also taken a keen interest in the club and social life of the world in which he lives, for he is affiliated, fraternally, with Portland Lodge, No. 1, Free and Accepted Masons; Greenleaf Chapter, No. 13, Royal Arch Masons; the Portland Council, No. 4, Royal and Select Masters; the Consistory, Ancient Accepted Scottish Rite; St. Albans Commandery, No. 2, Knights Templar; Kora Temple, Ancient Arabic Order Nobles of the Mystic Shrine; Order of the Eastern Star. He is treasurer of the Masonic Trustees; member of Portland Lodge, No. 188, Benevolent and Protective Order of Elks, and president of the Portland Real Estate Association.

Perley Chase Dresser married, June 26, 1912, at Portland, Maine, Alice Barbour, who was born in Portland, a daughter of George L. Barbour, of Maine. Mr. and Mrs. Dresser maintain their residence in Portland, in which community they attend the Williston Church.

ALFRED AUGUSTUS KENDALL—Throughout his life a most conspicuous figure in the city of Portland, Maine, Alfred Augustus Kendall owed his high position entirely to his own ability and great personal worth. Utterly indifferent to notoriety and publicity, refusing to play what he called the "game of politics," he nevertheless achieved an eminence denied to most men, however much they may seek it. His death, on March 6, 1910, was a great loss and a severe shock to the whole community.

The Kendall family is an old and prominent one in Maine, Nathan Otis and Lydia (Emerson) Kendall, Mr. Kendall's paternal grandparents, being residents of the town of Alfred at the very beginning of the nineteenth century. Their son, Joseph Kendall, was born at Alfred on May 7, 1823, and passed his childhood there, but while still very young he made his way to Norway, in the same State, and there lived for a number of years. At this time the Hon. Mr. J. B. Brown was one of the most important men of the town, the proprietor of a store, and the operator of a six-horse coach between Norway and Portland, before the coming of the railroad. Joseph Kendall became associated with him in the management of the store, finally, however, removing to Portland where, with Mr. B. F. Chadbourn, he established the successful wholesale house dealing in woolen goods and tailors' trimmings, with which his son was connected for so many years, and which is today active and prosperous and the oldest partnership company in Portland. Chadbourn and Kendall were located originally in Middle Street, before the great Portland fire, and although forced to move three or four times, still occupy quarters in approximately the same position. Mr. Chadbourn died in 1889, the whole interest in the business devolving upon the other partner, who, at his own death, November 28, 1908, left to his son, Alfred A. Kendall, the large establishment.

Alfred Augustus Kendall was born on February 28, 1855, at Norway, Maine, where his father was at that time working with Mr. Brown. When he was only three months old, he came with his parents to Portland, where he later attended the excellent public schools and the Portland High School, from which he was graduated in 1871. During his course in the Park Street grammar school he was a pupil of the late Professor E. P. Wentworth, an educator of the very highest reputation. After his graduation from high school, he attended a business school to prepare himself for the mercantile career which he chose to pursue, graduating when only seventeen years old and then entering the business world.

He was given a minor position in his father's woolen company, it being his wise intention to become thoroughly familiar with all details of the business before attempting to share in its direction. It was not long, however, before his natural aptitude and his willingness to work won him rapid promotion. For a time he acted as a buyer of goods for the firm, in which capacity he first displayed the unusually keen judgment which later brought him such a wide reputation. After the death of Mr. Chadbourn he participated more and more in the active management of the company, so that before his father's death as a very old man in 1908, he was its virtual head. After 1908 the ownership as well as the management of affairs was vested in him personally, and upon his own death, passed solely to his wife. Mrs. Kendall conducts the business with the assistance of George H. Parsons, who, trained in the establishment, is now her general manager.

The prestige of Mr. Kendall's position did not rest entirely upon business success. He was an active participant in every movement designed to promote the welfare and progress of the community. He was interested in the State Militia and with the aid of the late John Anderson, of Portland, organized the body known as the "Portland Cadets," of which Mr. Anderson became captain. Mr. Kendall refused to accept the commission of lieutenant, but consented to serve as orderly sergeant. When his son Ralph joined this body, the older man had the distinction of being the only active member with a son also in the ranks. Mr. Kendall was a member of the Independent Order of Odd Fellows, and prominent in the affairs of that great fraternity, and he was also a member and lifelong attendant of the Universalist church in Portland, which his father had helped to organize.

On June 1, 1876, Alfred Augustus Kendall married Mary Buzzell, of Portland, a daughter of Dr. John Buzzell of that place, and of Susan M. (Whitmore) Buzzell. Her grandfather, John D. Buzzell, was a prominent physician and surgeon, a member for a time of the Maine Legislature, and otherwise active in the early history of Portland. His father, the Rev. John Buzzell, the pioneer member of the family in Maine, had been the founder of the Free Will Baptist Society. Mrs. Kendall is a clubwoman

of note in Maine, much in demand as a public speaker, and very active in the civic, political, and charitable affairs of her city and State. She is a former national vice-president-general of the Daughters of the American Revolution, and ex-Regent of the Elizabeth Wadsworth Chapter of that organization, the ancestor through whom she is eligible for membership being Captain Benjamin Bean, of her mother's family, who was one of the Governor's staff at Bennington, and was especially commended for bravery. Mrs. Kendall is a member of the Maine State Federation of Women's Clubs, a member of the Conklin Class, the Brush and Thimble Club, the Clifford Club, and many other organizations.

Mr. and Mrs. Kendall were the parents of one child, Ralph Talbot, who was graduated from Tufts College in 1900, with the degree of Electrical Engineer, and is now at Fort Monmouth, New Jersey, as chief engineer of the research department, radio division. He saw service during the World War, enlisting as a captain, and before his discharge, attained the rank of major. Ralph Talbot Kendall married Lucy Marble, a daughter of John B. and Ella Marble, of Rangeley Lakes, and they are the parents of two children: 1. Marguerite Whittemore. 2. Ralph Talbot, Jr.

Alfred Augustus Kendall was a man of forceful character, one who could not fail to impress himself upon all with whom he came in contact, yet there was nothing like unpleasant aggression in his dealings with other men, and his keen sense of humor, as quick to laugh at his own expense as at another's, made him a most delightful comrade. His tastes were many and varied, and he was especially fond of reading and travel, the latter of which he was able to gratify extensively, although his interest confined him for the most part to his own country, of which he saw many parts. He was possessed of the sterling virtues so typical in general of the best New England character, of sincerity, courage and industry, and all his talents were freely placed at the disposal of the community. Few men have exercised a greater or more wholesome influence in the life of the city of Portland.

HORACE G. WINTER—As head of the well-known novelty wood-cutting establishment, H. G. Winter and Son, and as bank president and leading citizen, Horace G. Winter is an outstanding factor in the progress of Kingfield, Maine. He was born in Freeman, Maine, June 1, 1873, son of Ira S. F. and Harriet (Williamson) Winter, both now deceased. The former, also native to Freeman, and a Republican in political faith, was a prosperous farmer.

After completing the course of studies in the Freeman public schools, Horace G. Winter worked in the general store of A. G. Winter for about three years, then learned the business of novelty woodturning and has remained in that department of production for thirty-one years. From 1893 to January, 1925, he was associated with Jenkins and Bogert, manufacturers. In that year Mr. Winter bought out the business which now operates under the title of H. G. Winter and Son. Since 1919 this able business man and executive has found time for the presidency of the bank, of which he is also a director.

His political alignment is with the Republican party, and his long service on the School Board has

348 MAINE—A HISTORY

greatly upheld the cause of improved educational facilities in the town. He is a member of all bodies of Masonry up to the thirty-third degree He belongs to the Associated Industries of Maine and for two years was president of the Association of Woodturners of New England. Since 1920 he has been president of the Kingfield Water Company. His relireligious affiliation is with the Baptist church in Kingfield.

Horace G. Winter married, in Kingfield, in 1900, Irma Josephine Hutchins, daughter of J. George and Josephine Hutchins, of New Portland. They are the parents of two sons: 1. Emil E., born 1902. 2. Harold S., born 1905. Both sons are now associated with the firm of H. G. Winter and Sons.

WILLIAM E. BREWSTER—For more than forty-four years William E. Brewster has been engaged in the grocery and provision business in Dexter, Maine. Mr. Brewster had had considerable experience before coming to Dexter, both in the meat business and in the restaurant business, and during the more than four decades in which he has been engaged in the retail grocery and provision business here, he has established a reputation for ability and for integrity.

William E. Brewster was born in Parkman, Maine, September 1, 1858, son of Abatha Brewster, who was born in Parkman, Maine, and was engaged as a farmer to the time of his death, and of Clara (Warren) Brewster, who was born in Hudson, Maine, and is now deceased. He received his education in the public schools of his birthplace, and when school days were over came to Dexter, Maine, where he worked for two years in the retail meat business. He then, in 1881, went to Boston, Massachusetts, where he was engaged in the restaurant business for himself for two years. In 1883 he returned to Dexter, Maine, and established the grocery and provision business on Main Street which he has successfully conducted now for a period of forty-four years. Mr. Brewster carries a full line of groceries and supplies, and he knows the wants and needs of his special trade so well that he carries, in addition to his general line, several side lines to meet the needs of his special custom. Politically, Mr. Brewster gives his support to the Republican party, and he takes an active part in local public affairs. He has served for three terms in the Maine State Legislature, and locally has been active on the School Board, serving as a member of that board for four years. He has served as a member of the Republican Town Committee for several terms, and is an active supporter of all the candidates of his party. In addition to the care of his general merchandise business Mr. Brewster is also a member of the board of directors of the Merrill Trust Company. Fraternally, he is identified with Penobscot Lodge, Free and Accepted Masons; St. John Chapter, Royal Arch Masons; Mt. Moriah Council, Royal and Select Masters; St. John's Commandery, Knights Templar; and Anah Temple, Ancient Arabic Order Nobles of the Mystic Shrine. He is also a member of Plymouth Lodge, Independent Order of Odd Fellows. His clubs are the Masonic and Dexter, and he is an active and interested member of the Dexter Chamber of Commerce. Mr. Brewster is fond of fishing and hunting, and his religious interest is with the Congregational church.

William E. Brewster was married, in 1883, to Carrie S. Bridges, who was born in Sangerville, Maine. Mr. and Mrs. Brewster are the parents of two sons:

1. Charles S., who served on the Mexican border with Company A, Second Infantry, Maine National Guard, and who is now a partner in the W. E. Brewster Company, of Dexter. 2. Ralph O., who is now Governor of the State of Maine.

EARLE POPE GREGORY, M. D.—Among the members of the noble profession of medicine in the State of Maine, Dr. Earle Pope Gregory, of Fryeburg, is well known as a physician who is untiring in his devotion to the cause of alleviating and banishing human suffering. He is one of the most popular doctors in this vicinity and has ever received the trust and confidence of all since he opened his present office here in 1920. From the first, the people have been attracted to him through his earnest and sincere interest in their welfare and to his patients he has been not only a physician but also a friend. His remarkable ability as a diagnostician coupled with splendid medical skill has brought him a large and ever-increasing practice, while in affairs relating to general civic health and improvements, his advice is often sought and utilized by the town authorities.

Dr. Gregory was born in Mount Upton, New York, September 29, 1877, son of George A. Gregory, a native of New York, and Lilly (Pope) Gregory, a native of Ottawa, Illinois. George A. Gregory was engaged for many years in the real estate business, and also was active as a buyer of horses in both Canada and the United States.

Earle Pope Gregory was educated in the public schools of Sidney, New York, graduating from the Sidney High School with the class of 1896. He at first desired to become an educator and accordingly entered the Oneonta Normal School, from which he was graduated as a qualified teacher in June, 1900. He taught in the schools of New York State for two years, but realizing that his life's vocation lay in the practice of medicine, he gave up his educational career and entered the University of Michigan, where he applied himself to the arduous studies of medicine, receiving his degree of Doctor of Medicine with the class of 1909. After serving his internship, he commenced the general practice of his profession at Arkport, New York, ministering to an extensive clientele from 1912 to 1920, in which year he came to Fryeburg and is now one of its most esteemed adopted sons. Dr. Gregory is a constant student of all things medical and is quick to take advantage of every modern discovery or invention that in his opinion will bring ease and comfort to the ill or aid in preserving the health of the community. He is a member of the American Medical Association, and is past medical examiner of Oxford County. His fraternal connections are with the Free and Accepted Masons, Blue Lodge, and his religious attendance is at the Congregational church. In politics, he is a follower of the principles of the Republican party. During the recent World War, he served as medical examiner for the United States Army at Arkport, New York.

Dr. Earle Pope Gregory married, October 22, 1912, at Hornell, New York, Edna Phelan, born in Cambridge, Massachusetts, January, 1877, daughter of Edward Phelan.

MARCELLUS CAIN—Among the widely known morticians of the Pine Tree State, Marcellus Cain, of Clinton, ranks high for leadership. He is president of the Maine Funeral Directors' Association, and is prominent also as a business man in his home town, where he conducts a house-furnishings store in connection with his funeral home. Mr. Cain has been one of the most active members of the Republican party in Kennebec County, and has served his town in public offices and his district as a member of the Maine House of Representatives. His political career has been attended with fruitful results along constructive lines for the respective constituencies that have honored him with election.

A native of Clinton, Marcellus Cain was born August 9, 1873. He attended the common schools and was graduated from Shaw's Business College at Portland. He is the son of Daniel and Betsy (Chase) Cain. On both sides of his house, he is descended from good old substantial Maine stock. His father operated one of the largest farms in Kennebec County. He was successful as an agriculturist and a man of unusual business ability and political acumen, holding a position high in the respect and confidence of the citizens. Having been sent to Augusta as the choice of his district for a seat in the Lower House of the Legislature, he achieved an enviable record for legislative ability, energy, initiative and resourcefulness.

Marcellus Cain purchased a farm of his own and for a number of years gave his attention to its cultivation. About that time he thought to pursue the career of journalist, and, having bought out the "Clinton Advertiser," he conducted that newspaper for some three years, when he disposed of the property. Mr. Cain having altered his projected line of endeavor, set himself to the task of learning the mortician's profession, in which he perceived an opportunity for a larger service in meeting the requirements of the families of his town when occasion should demand. He attended the Massachusetts College of Embalming, made an excellent student record, and was graduated in the class of 1904. With diploma in hand, he returned to Clinton and in the year of his graduation established his funeral home and the department of complete lines of house furnishings. He enjoys high standing in the associational interests of his profession, having been elected president of their State organization, known as the Maine Funeral Directors' Association.

Throughout the years of his majority, Mr. Cain has been a loyally registered Republican. His native town of Clinton long since recognized his capacity for public office, and the voters installed him as a member of the Board of Selectmen, of which he was chairman for three years. He also served the educational interests of the community as a member of the School Board for three years. Then he was made a member of the Kennebec County Republican Committee, in whose proceedings his presence and counsel were highly esteemed by his colleagues. The high point of his political career was reached with his election, in 1927, as a representative to the Maine Legislature, where as a lawmaker he gave further exhibition of constructive capacity. The State and his district benefited from his zeal, enthusiasm and unremitting attention to the duties of his high office.

His fraternal affiliations are with Sebasticook Lodge, No. 146, Free and Accepted Masons, of which he is a Past Master; Dunlap Chapter, Royal Arch Masons; St. Omar Commandery, No. 12, Knights Templar, of Waterville; Pine Tree Lodge, Independent Order of Odd Fellows; and the Patrons of Husbandry. He is a member of the Kiwanis Club, an attendant of the Clinton Methodist Episcopal Church, and a trustee of the Brown Memorial Church and the Greenlawn Rest Association, all of Clinton, and was chairman of Old Home Week, August, 1921.

Marcellus Cain married, June 13, 1900, at Clinton, Lottie S. Stewart, daughter of James and Octavia (Farrington) Stewart, and their children are: 1. Mrs. Olive (Cain) Simonson. 2. Stanley S., graduated, April, 1928, from the Massachusetts College of Embalming, and now associated with his father in the funeral director and house furnishings business.

LUMAN C. SHEPHERD—The oldest real estate and insurance business in Dexter, Maine, is conducted by Luman C. Shepherd, whose office is located on Main Street. Mr. Shepherd has been engaged in this line for more than twenty-two years, and does a general real estate and fire insurance business.

Abner Shepherd, father of Mr. Shepherd, was born in Fairfield, Maine. He received his education in his birthplace, and then was engaged as a lumberman and as a cattle dealer to the time of his death. He served in the Civil War with the Third Maine Battery, Heavy Artillery, and also with the Eighteenth Maine Infantry. He was a member and Past Commander of H. F. Safford Post, Grand Army of the Republic. Fraternally, he was identified with the Independent Order of Odd Fellows, of which he was a charter member and Past Noble Grand; and of Penobscot Lodge, Free and Accepted Masons. He married Clara Cleaves, who was born in Abbot, Maine, now deceased.

Luman C. Shepherd, son of Abner and Clara (Cleaves) Shepherd, was born in Dexter, Maine, June 10, 1871, and received his education in the public schools of Dexter, including the high school. When school days were over he found employment as a salesman, in which line of work he continued for a few years. He then entered Uncle Sam's employ in the Dexter post office, where he continued for three years, later becoming identified with the American Railway Express for another three years. In 1905 he engaged in the real estate and insurance business for himself in Dexter, and in this line of business activity he has been successfully engaged to the present time (1927). Being the oldest real estate and insurance agent in Dexter, he is very well known and he has a large and well-established patronage. He does a general real estate business, and is known as an expert in the appraisement of real estate values. He is also a keen judge of the possibilities of future increase in value and his opinion is frequently sought by those desiring to sell or buy real property. In the insurance line he carries only fire insurance. Mr. Shepherd is a Democrat in his political sympathies. Fraternally, he is identified with Penobscot Lodge, Free and Accepted Masons; with Bedevere Lodge, Knights of Pythias, of which he is a Past Chancellor; and with the American Order of Foresters.

Luman C. Shepherd was married, in 1908, to Grace B. Cushman, a native of Dexter, Maine, and they are the parents of one daughter, Ruth Burleigh, now Mrs. W. E. Slater, of Dexter.

WILLIS R. LEAVITT—A practical business man of an unusually varied experience, is Willis R. Leavitt, for the past ten years proprietor of a real estate and lumber business in Phillips, Maine, and since 1926 Sheriff of Franklin County, Maine. Mr. Leavitt, an ardent Republican, has served the county as Deputy Sheriff and Road Commissioner.

Mr. Leavitt was born in Phillips, Maine, on July 14, 1875, and was educated in the grammar and high schools there. His parents, William H. and Marcia J. (Gordon) Leavitt, also were natives of Maine, his father having come from Madrid, Maine. William H. Leavitt, a farmer, had served through the greater part of the Civil War in the Thirteenth and Seventeenth Regiments of Infantry. Willis R. Leavitt, upon leaving school, obtained employment in Phillips and managed to save enough to form a partnership, under the name of Leavitt and Jacobs, grocers and butchers. The business prospered and the partners expanded, including among their wares livestock, hay, apples, potatoes and other produce, which they bought and sold for ten years, until Mr. Leavitt retired to found the real estate and lumber business which he conducts at present in Phillips and Avon, Maine.

He became deeply interested in Republican politics and the work of his party in his native town. His diligent services were rewarded, as he became Deputy Sheriff of Franklin County, a position he held for ten years and also served as chairman of the Board of Assessors in Phillips and as Road Commissioner for three years. He is a member of the Free and Accepted Masons, of the Grange, the Knights of the Forest and the Masonic clubs of Farmington and Phillips.

Willis R. Leavitt married (first), in 1899, Nancy Mae Booker, daughter of Simon G. and Matilda E. Booker, and they were the parents of five children: 1. Helen R. 2. Louise R. 3. Laura M. 4. Doris W. 5. Reuel A., who died in 1925. Mrs. Leavitt died December 22, 1923. He married (second), July 6, 1927, Edith H. Wells, daughter of Thomas and Anastasia (Martin) Wells, of Kingsland.

LOUIS F. HIGGINS—After having spent a varied and interesting life, Louis F. Higgins, the present postmaster of Ellsworth, Maine, enjoys the satisfaction of serving both his country and his native town in the same office. He is the son of Josiah H. Higgins of Indian Point, Maine, who was a ship carpenter and boat builder by trade. His mother was Harriet F. Caswell, of West Rockport, Maine. Both parents are now deceased.

Louis F. Higgins was born at Ellsworth, Maine, on November 26, 1864. After finishing his education in the Ellsworth high school, he attended the Ellsworth Business College. He then went to work for the Isaac Grant Shipyards at Ellsworth where he worked for ten years. At the end of this time, he moved out to California and worked at the trade of a carpenter for four years when he returned to Ellsworth. In 1908, he became associated with the Ellsworth Post Office and was in the position of assistant postmaster. In 1924, he was made postmaster and has continued to hold this position. He is a member of the Lygonia Lodge, Free and Accepted Masons, of which he is a Past Master; and he is a member of the Eastern Star. He is also a member of the Chamber of Commerce. In politics he is a Republican. He is a member of the Unitarian church, of which he is one of the trustees and also a member of the Laymen's League. His hobby is antiques and in this hobby he is an interesting collector.

In 1888, Louis F. Higgins married Minerva A. Young, of South Surry, Maine.

ALBERT H. BURROUGHS, M. D.—For forty years Albert H. Burroughs practiced medicine in Westbrook. He was a man of fine dignity, a trusted friend and counselor in the many homes to which his profession brought him, and a ready supporter of any plan for the growth and welfare of the community. His large practice demanded most of his time and attention, and this he gave unreservedly, but he was also prominent in local Masonic circles and in the civic and social life of Westbrook.

Dr. Burroughs was born in Houlton, Maine, on October 16, 1842, a son of James and Elizabeth (Smith) Burroughs. While still very young he went with his parents to Portland, Maine, and attended the public schools of Portland and Buckfield. At the age of nineteen, he enlisted in Company D, Seventh Maine Volunteers, for service in the Civil War, was wounded severely, at the battle of Antietam and later honorably discharged. He then engaged in business for a few years in Boston and upon his return to Maine, began the study of medicine with Dr. Frederick H. Gerrish, of Portland, and subsequently was graduated from Bowdoin Medical College. In 1878, he began the practice of his profession in Westbrook, where he remained for forty years, until the time of his death in 1918.

He was affiliated, fraternally, with the Free and Accepted Masons, and in this organization he was a member of Temple Lodge, Westbrook Council, and Eagle Chapter, Royal Arch Masons. He was first Grand Patron of Mizpah Chapter of the Order of the Eastern Star; Past Commander of St. Albans Commandery of the Knights Templar, of Portland; Past Grand Commander of the Grand Commandery of Maine, and an Ancient Accepted Scottish Rite Mason. He was fond of fishing and other outdoor sports, and was especially devoted to horses. He was a member of Westbrook Congregational church.

In 1865, Albert H. Burroughs married (first) Fanny C. Gerrish, who died in June, 1907. On June 23, 1909, he married (second) Adeline S. Ray, a daughter of Fabius M. and Mary M. (Marrett) Ray.

When Dr. Burroughs' long life came to an end in September, 1918, he was sincerely mourned by the whole community, which only then, perhaps, came to realize the extent of its affection and esteem for him, and the constant value of his presence.

ALEXANDER SPEIRS—Prominent in Republican circles in Maine, Alexander Speirs was a political leader in his day, and one who was profoundly missed when he was taken away by death. He had a host of friends, was highly trusted, and was loved for his genial personality and eagerness to help his fellowmen. His passing, needless to say, caused widespread grief in this State and wherever he was known; for everyone recognized his contributions to the public life of his community and his State, and felt that not only a desirable and useful citizen, but a splendid man, had passed on.

He was born in Scotland in 1859, son of Archibald and Anna Speirs, and was brought to the United States when he was only one year of age. After a few years, he settled in Portland, where his father was a tinsmith, manufacturing various sorts of tinware. As a boy, Alexander Speirs attended the public schools in Portland, and also went to private schools there. Then, after he had been employed for a short time with the C. P. Kimball Company, carriage manufacturers, he went into the tinshop with his father. Later he established a tinware factory in Windham, Maine, and also conducted a mail order business and in later years was occupied with the building of houses and real estate development. He lived in Westbrook for a total of thirty-one years; was a member of the Republican town committee; became a representative of the Maine State Legislature on the Republican ticket in 1917; and was elected Senator in 1923. Holding the office of Senator in 1923, 1925 and 1927, he served on several important committees, including those on insurance, education and many other subjects. His greatest interest was in education, and he was chairman of the committee on education. In Westbrook, he also served as alderman and chairman of the city committee. One of his chief contributions during his period as Senator in the State Senate was the work of framing and sponsoring the law providing for more liberal pensions to the teachers of the State. He was strongly opposed to the increase of the gas tax, and warned his fellow senators in the winter of 1926-1927 that if the measure was passed he would see that a referendum was invoked on the law. Before the Legislature adjourned, he had his petitions prepared, and was ready to circulate them as soon as the tax bill was signed. Almost single-handed, he carried on the work of circulating the referendum petitions, and had the work finished and petitions completed and sent to Secretary of State at Augusta, when he became ill and forced to go to Boston for treatment.

In addition to his political and public interests, which at all times kept Mr. Speirs busy, he was active in civic and social affairs. He was a member of the Free and Accepted Masons, in which Order his affiliation was with the Windham Lodge and St. Albans Commandery; the Rotary Club, of Westbrook; and the Westbrook Congregational church. With service as the keynote of his life, he was quiet and temperate by nature and had many friends, both in public and private life. He was especially interested in the Pownal School for the Feeble-minded, introducing a bill to change the name to its present title, Pownal State School; and, while he was a State Senator and at other times as well, he was a champion of better education and finer schools. He was loved by the children, and they, in the school paper of the Westbrook High School, paid tribute to him after his death.

Alexander Speirs was married (first) to Charlotte Plummer; and (second) to Bessie Mains, daughter of Josiah and Lucretia Mains, of Windham, Maine.

After an illness of several months, Senator Speirs died on October 9, 1927, at St. Barnabas Hospital, in Woodfords, where an emergency operation had been performed two days earlier. He had returned to his home in Westbrook only a week before his death, from his summer residence at Torrington Point, Peaks Island, apparently much improved in health. Many noted men attended his funeral services, including Governor Ralph O. Brewster; ex-Governor Percival P. Baxter; Frank H. Holley, president of the Senate; Senator Arthur G. Spear; Senator Raymond S. Oakes, and Senator Paul F. Slocum. Interment was in Woodlawn Cemetery, Westbrook.

"The death of Senator Alexander Speirs, of Westbrook," said the Portland Sunday "Telegram," "re-

moves from the ranks of the Republican party in this county one of the ablest legislators of the county and one of the ablest of the party's leaders. . . . As a political leader, Senator Speirs had few if any equals in the county. He was chairman of the Republican city committee of Westbrook and it was largely through his instrumentality that the city elected Republican representatives a year ago September. Westbrook had got into the habit of sending Democrats to the Legislature, but Mr. Speirs confided to me (the writer was Fred Owen) the spring before that he was going to change all that. He made good his promise."

EDWIN L. BRADFORD—One of Maine's outstanding citizens, Edwin L. Bradford, of Turner Center, is a leading factor in the dairy industry of this State, having associated with the business of selling and distributing dairy products since 1882. Since 1925, Mr. Bradford has served as treasurer of the Turner Center System, of which organization he was one of the founders, it being one of the largest and most comprehensive concerns engaged in merchandising eggs, creamery products and ice cream, employing on an average of eight hundred people. The success of this new enterprise is largely due to Mr. Bradford's ability for concentration and his splendid foresight in commercial matters, the value of which has been thoroughly demonstrated by the rapidity with which the venture has grown and expanded.

Mr. Bradford was born in Turner Center, March 23, 1857, son of Alfred Bradford, a native of Maine, and of Flora (Leavitt) Bradford, born at Turner, both of whom are now deceased. Alfred Bradford was engaged in farming for many years.

Edwin L. Bradford was educated in the public schools of Turner Center, and in Hebron Academy, after which he entered Coburn Classical Institute, where he prepared for a career as an educator. At the conclusion of his academic studies, he became a teacher and for twenty terms taught in the schools of Turner and Hartford, achieving a splendid reputation for his high scholastic ability and erudition, while at the same time, giving to his pupils a splendid training to fit them for their future place in society. In 1882, Mr. Bradford resigned from the teaching profession, became identified with the Turner Center Dairying Association, and was occupied under general manager in the affairs of this organization until 1925. His experience and training as a disciplinarian and leader gained in his school work were of great value in his new position, and his wonderful facility for system and management assured his success in the business world. In his present capacity as treasurer of the Turner Center System, he is interested in the business life of the town, and is constantly active, both by influence and example. To advance the welfare of his community is another of his unselfish desires and he is ever to the fore in all campaigns for progress and improvement. In politics, he is an Independent, and has never aligned himself with any particular political party. His religious attendance is at the Universalist church.

Edwin L. Bradford married, at Turner Center, Mary Frances Ridley, born March 17, 1857, at Wayne, daughter of Hellett Ridley, born in Maine, and of Frances (Hood) Ridley, born at Turner Center.

To this union were born three children: Bertha B., Alfred, and Ada.

MILES WALTER TOBEY—Located in a district where manufacture of building material from the products of the forests that cover the State of Maine is one of the principal industries, Miles Walter Tobey, of Winslow, has made a high reputation in that business and earned the respect of his fellow-citizens. He is a man of energy, industry and vision, and possessed of a keen mind and an intelligent grasp of such matters as engage his attention, while his nature also calls him to fraternal association with his fellows and he easily makes friends. Honesty in all his dealings is as much a part of Mr. Tobey as is his physical make-up, and his code of morals is not confined to social affairs, but it is carried constantly in his business. He is possessed of civic virtues that urge him to lend his assistance in all matters that are of advantage to the general welfare, an able citizen, a valuable asset to the community.

He was born in the town of China, Maine, December 18, 1873, a son of William Sylvester and Mary Angelie (Northrup) Tobey, the father having been a lumberman and a veteran of the Civil War. Miles Walter Tobey was educated in the public schools and at business college, after which he engaged in the wholesale lumber business, operating a moulding mill and dealing in paint and hardware by retail, this work being located in Winslow. He is affiliated with the Modern Woodmen and attends the Advent church.

Miles Walter Tobey married, in the town of China, Lillie Belle Brown, daughter of John M. and Eliza Jane (Young) Brown.

PERCY ETHER WEYMOUTH—Following his graduation from high school, Percy Ether Weymouth, of Auburn, worked at various callings, not finding himself until he was twenty-three years of age, when he secured employment with the Lewiston, Augusta & Waterville Railroad Company. This was a fortunate event for the young man and for the corporation, inasmuch as he had found what he could do best and the company had discovered a most capable administrator of such offices as were given to his skill. Eight years of various posts with the company brought him to promotion to be superintendent of the Augusta Division, where he remained until the close of 1918, when he became superintendent of the Androscoggin Electric Company's railway department at Lewiston, which office he still fills (1928).

He was born in Hollis, Maine, June 1, 1886, a son of Luther Stillman and Lucy Marie (Edgecomb) Weymouth, the father a carpenter, deceased. His education was acquired in the public schools of Bridgton, Maine, and he was graduated from high school with the class of 1904. He is independent in politics and attends the Universalist church of Lewiston. He is a member of the Lewiston Chamber of Commerce, Portland Chamber of Commerce, and of the New England Street Railroad Club. His fraternal affiliations include the Lodge, Free and Accepted Masons; King Hiram Chapter, Royal Arch Masons; Dunlap Council, Royal and Select Masters; Lewiston Commandery, Knights Templar, and Kora

Temple, Ancient Arabic Order Nobles of the Mystic Shrine.

Mr. Weymouth married, in Portland, Maine, October 25, 1919, Vera Ruth Daicey, of Auburn, daughter of Pearl and Alice Tarr Daicey. They have one son by a previous marriage of his wife: Alfred Lawrence, born in Lewiston, in 1917.

WENDELL E. MAXWELL—Appreciation of the worth of a man may be shown by his selection for public office by his fellow-citizens, a case in point being that of Wendell E. Maxwell, of Sabattus, who has held the post of Road Commissioner for this town since 1908 and who has been the town clerk for eight successive years. Prospering in a business in which he has been engaged since early manhood, he has shown himself to be a man of vital interest in the welfare of the community, while his fraternal and religious inclinations are those of a sound citizen. Industry, honesty, a personality of attractive quality have had great weight in advancing his standing, which he has answered by an attention to duty that has been of constant benefit to the town and community.

He was born in Sabattus, Maine, January 27, 1876, a son of J. W. Maxwell, of Webster, and of Clara (Moulton) Maxwell, of Greene, Maine. His father was a farmer and a civic engineer and served in both the Upper and Lower Houses of the State Legislature.

Wendell E. Maxwell acquired his education in the public schools of Sabattus and at the Lewiston Business College. He entered the grain business when a young man and has since continued in that line. He is a Republican in politics and attends the Community church. He hold membership in the Free and Accepted Masons, Webster Lodge, No. 164; the Commandery, Knights Templar, and the Temple, Ancient Arabic Order Nobles of the Mystic Shrine.

Mr. Maxwell married, in Portsmouth, New Hampshire, Jennie Berry, who was born in New Brunswick, Canada, and who died February 4, 1927.

FREDERICK GREELY KINSMAN—One of the best known and best loved citizens of Augusta, Maine, was the late Frederick Greely Kinsman, whose death in October, 1926, in his sixty-fourth year, closed a life of successful business activity, of faithful public service, and of warm and helpful human contacts, a life of sincerity, strongly and courageously lived, busy and achieving, but always ready with a helping hand and a word of cheer for those with whom he came in contact. During the last thirty-five years of his life he was president of the Capital Drug Company, of Augusta, Maine, manufacturers of proprietary medicines, and he was also closely identified with the banking interests of Augusta.

Frederick Greely Kinsman was born in Augusta, Maine, August 10, 1862, son of Frank W. and Octavia (Greely) Kinsman, and after attending the local public schools began professional study in the Bowdoin Medical School. As time passed, however, his business capacity became apparent, and when he was twenty years of age he succeeded his father as proprietor of the well-known Kinsman Pharmacy. Later, in association with his brother, Frank W. Kinsman, he became a member of the firm of F. W. Kinsman and Company, druggists, of which his brother was the senior partner. In 1891 he established in Augusta, the Capital Drug Company, manufacturers of proprietary medicines, and of this concern he was president from the time of its incorporation to his death. An able business man, from the beginning of his career he made his business interests minister to the good of the community and to all with whom he was associated. Shrewd and resourceful, always willing to "lend a hand" he showed even in his benefactions that wisdom, mingled with human sympathy and understanding, which enabled him to achieve the difficult feat of giving wisely and with real benefit to those who received. He was actively interested in the political affairs of the city, State, and nation, and bore a generous share of the burdens of public office, serving for a period of four years as a member of the city government, respesenting his district in the State Legislature, and serving as a member of the Council of two governors, namely Governor Fernald and Governor Haines. In 1904 he was a member of the Electoral College, which cast the vote of the State of Maine for Theodore Roosevelt for President, and he was a generous supporter of all plans formed for the advancement of the general welfare of the city. He was, in addition to his other business responsibilities, closely identified with the banking interests of Augusta, serving for many years on the executive boards of the Kennebec Savings Bank and the State Trust Company. Fraternally, he was identified with the Free and Accepted Masons, being a member of the local Blue Lodge; of Trinity Commandery, Knights Templar; and of Kora Temple, Ancient Arabic Order Nobles of the Mystic Shrine. He was also a member of the Benevolent and Protective Order of Elks, the Abnaki Club and an honorary member of the Rotary Club. His religious affiliation was with the Penney Memorial United Baptist Church.

The following quotations from one of the local publications indicates something of the regard in which Mr. Kinsman was held by his associates. Of him it is recorded that "It probably can truly be said that living, none had more friends, and dying, none was ever more sincerely mourned." "He was an intensely human man; he entered into the lives of others and shared with them their joys and sorrows. He was thoughtful and generous; he learned the joy of giving, and he showered his benefactions with lavish hand, yet absolutely without show." "He was most companionable. He met life with a smile, however stern its aspect; he faced a decade of suffering with Spartan courage; he died as he has lived, with his face toward the morning."

Frederick Greely Kinsman was married, January 1, 1883, to Alice Hewett Penney, daughter of the late Charles F. Penney, of Augusta, and they became the parents of one son, Honorable Charles P. Kinsman, who survives him.

HON. CHARLES PENNEY KINSMAN—Charles Penney Kinsman, business man, drug manufacturer, public official, was born in Augusta, Maine, April 28, 1884, and has been identified with that city all his life. His father, Frederick G. Kinsman, was a member of the Maine Legislature, and both he and his wife, Alice H. Kinsman, were natives of Augusta.

After passing through the public schools of Augusta, including the Cony High School, Charles Penney Kinsman entered Bowdoin College, whence he was graduated in the class of 1907. His first business experience was obtained during a year's engagement with Mason & Lewis, dealers in stock

and bonds, in Boston, Massachusetts. Then he entered into partnership with his father, Frederick G. Kinsman, in the business he had founded in 1897 for the manufacture of proprietary medicines, and in due course became manager of the concern, which is known as the Capital Drug Company, and is located at No. 242 Water Street, Augusta. He is also a director of the State Trust Company.

A Republican in politics, Mr. Kinsman has been a member of the Augusta City Council four years, of the Board of Aldermen four years, and he represented Augusta in the Maine Legislature in 1924 and 1926. He is a member of the Free and Accepted Masons, and a Shriner, a member of the Benevolent and Protective Order of Elks, the Rotary Club, the Chamber of Commerce, of the Aknaki Club, the Augusta Country Club, and is on the board of governors of the National Aeronautic Association, and is also active in the affairs of the Proprietary Medicine Association, of the United States. He is a member of the Episcopal church.

He married Hortense Powers, daughter of Don A. H. and Frances (Shaw) Powers, at Houlton, Maine, December 6, 1906. Mrs. Kinsman was born in Newport, Maine, May 15, 1885, the birthplace also of her parents. Their children are: 1. Frances P., born June 27, 1909, in Augusta. 2. Charles P., Jr., born in Augusta, August 29, 1912.

ANSON AUGUSTUS COBB, M. D.—Descended from English stock, his earliest American ancestor having settled in Barnstable, Massachusetts, in 1632, Anson Augustus Cobb was a consistent supporter of the traditions of his patriot forefathers and had established in Auburn a reputation for excellence among the medical profession, in which he had membership, as well as among the laymen of the community he served. He was a man of fine personality and a practitioner who won the respect of all through his meritorious conduct in all circumstances, professional as well as civic and social. Serious in his work, he was a deep student from boyhood, ever ambitious to advance himself in knowledge, that he might be better equipped to serve his fellow-man, a characteristic that brought the respect and admiration of all with whom he came in contact. He made friends readily and held them steadfastly, leaving a legion to mourn his passing.

Mr. Cobb was born in Casco, Maine, January 31, 1868, a son of Albion Cobb, a native of Westbrook and a practicing physician of Webb's Mills, in the town of Casco, later removing to Mechanic Falls, where he died, about 1888. His wife, mother of Anson Augustus, was Louise Amelia (Stockman) Cobb, of Poland, Maine, daughter of Robert and Thankful Stockman. Her and her husband's other children were: Albion E., deceased; Carolus M., a physician of Lynn, Massachusetts, and Ernest O., deceased, two others having died in infancy. Dr. Albion Cobb, father of these children, was the eldest son of Asa and Nancy D. Cobb, whose eight children, with one exception, attained maturity and became noted for their scientific and literary achievements. Dr. Cobb's opportunities to acquire an education in his youth were extremely limited, attainable only by the most strenuous efforts and sacrifices. The district school was two miles from his home, the road poor and often blocked by snow, yet he attended it when he could and also took two terms of eleven weeks each at Westbrook Seminary, which constituted his entire student work, save such as he gained through independent reading. Under these handicaps he acquired a broad knowledge of ancient and modern languages, natural science and literature surpassed by few of his contemporaries who had had greater advantages. He began the study of medicine in 1847, and was graduated from the Medical School of Maine, at Bowdoin College, with the class of 1851, having in the meantime attended for one term the Medical School of the University of New York. He established himself in the practice of his profession at Bolster's Mills, in the town of Harrison, Maine, in May, 1852, and remained there in active practice for nearly eight years, when he removed to Webb's Mills. In 1862, he entered the army as assistant surgeon of the Fourth Maine Volunteers and had, for the greater part of his service, sole charge of the medical department of the regiment, from which he was honorably mustered out in July, 1864. In November, 1863, at Bristow Station, Virginia, he was severely wounded, which disabled him for life. From August, 1864, until June, 1865, he was acting assistant surgeon, United States Army, with station at Harewood Hospital, near Washington, District of Columbia.

His son, Anson Augustus Cobb, acquired his education in the public schools of Casco and later attended Bridgton Academy. He had determined to make medicine his life-work, but for seven years after leaving his studies he taught school in the higher grades of Oxford and Welchville, using his evenings to prepare for matriculation at the Medical School of the University of Vermont. He took the course there and was graduated in 1892 with the degree of Doctor of Medicine, then going to Europe, where he studied for half a year at the Royal Ophthalmic Hospital, in London, and at the private clinics of Edmund Donders, in Paris, on errors of refraction. Returning to the United States, he established himself in practice in Auburn, Maine. He was professor emeritus of Ophthalmic Surgery at the Central Maine General Hospital and oculist at Bates College. He belonged to the Sons of Veterans and to the Free and Accepted Masons. In his political work he had been interested as a good citizen, but never indulged in active participation to the detriment of his professional occupation. He was a man of quiet, domestic tastes, fond of motoring and the outdoors to the time of his final illness and death.

Anson Augustus Cobb married, in March, 1891, Annie L. Bailey, daughter of Hiram P. and Louise M. (Work) Bailey, of Mechanic Falls, Maine, both deceased. They were the parents of one child: Annie Louise, born May 28, 1910.

Dr. Cobb left a name that will be an inspiration to the rising doctors of his district. He was a man of exceptional erudition and scientific skill, a deep student of his craft and a citizen of devoted allegiance to the cause of sound government and community progress. His friends were limited only by the list of his acquaintances, which covered a great territory of this State, and which was ever growing. He was a fine citizen and a noble exponent of the science of medicine, a man whose niche it will be difficult to fill.

LUTHER C. SPILLER—Selection of postmasters for important offices is usually the result of careful consideration of the qualifications of the individual, regardless of political affiliation. Such a post must be administered by a man of the highest integrity, coupled with business ability and an aptitude for organization and efficient results. These points mark the postmaster of Mechanic Falls, Maine, Luther C. Spiller, first appointed in February, 1922, and reappointed, February, 1926, for a term of four years.

Mr. Spiller was born in Mechanic Falls, October 2, 1880, a son of Josiah S. Spiller, a farmer, of Casco, deceased in 1908, and of Margaret (Hall) Spiller, also a native of Casco, and who died there in 1898. Josiah was a veteran of the Civil War, during which he served with the Seventeenth Maine Infantry.

Luther C. Spiller received his education in the public schools of Mechanic Falls and at Hebron Academy. At the close of his scholastic period he worked at various occupations in Rumford, Lewiston, Auburn, and other places. For nearly three years he was a meat cutter, then engaging in the grocery business in Mechanic Falls, where he worked for G. O. Goodwin & Company until his appointment to be postmaster, in 1922. Prior to this he had served for six years as collector of taxes at Mechanic Falls and for three years he was deputy sheriff of Androscoggin County. He is a member of the Free and Accepted Masons, holding the thirty-second degree; is a member of the Temple, Ancient Arabic Order Nobles of the Mystic Shrine, and several other bodies of the Masonic organization. He is an attendant of the Federated Church.

Mr. Spiller married Harriett M. Cole, of Portland, Maine.

JOHN KENDRICK BANGS, the famous American humorist, editor, and lecturer, was for the last fifteen years of his life a citizen of Ogunquit, in the town of Wells, Maine. He was of old New England stock, a descendant of the eighth generation from Edward Banges, Pilgrim of Plymouth, who came to these shores in the ship "Anne," 1623. The descendants of Edward Banges have spread throughout the nation, and some came early to Maine. Commodore Edward Preble, whose mother was Mehetable Bangs of the fifth generation from Edward, was a native of Falmouth, now Portland, Maine. It is part of American history that Commodore Preble took charge of the frigate "Constitution" in 1803, and commanded the fleet sent against the Barbary powers and repeatedly attacked Tripoli with valor and success. Then there was Isaac Sparrow Bangs, of the eighth generation, resident of Waterville, Maine, who was brevetted brigadier-general, United States Volunteers, for "gallant and meritorious" service during the Civil War. It was while this member of the Bangs family was entering the service as a private in August, 1862, in response to the call of Lincoln for volunteers, that John Kendrick Bangs, born in Yonkers, New York, on May 27th of that year, was, to use his own words, "in arms in the infant-ry."

The line of the Bangs family to which John Kendrick belonged had branched off from Cape Cod in the eighteenth century and become New Yorkers; and John Kendrick's grandfather and father had become men of great distinction in their callings. The grandfather, Nathan Bangs, D. D., was an eminent Methodist Divine; the most prolific author of his church during the first half of the nineteenth century; its recognized historian; the editor successively of "The Christian Advocate," "The Methodist Magazine," and "The Quarterly Review;" and was for a time president of Wesleyan University, Middletown, Connecticut. The father, Francis N. Bangs, was for the decade before his comparatively early death in 1885 one of America's very eminent lawyers, and was in 1883-1884 president of the Bar Association of the City of New York.

John Kendrick Bangs was graduated from Columbia College, 1883, and although destined for the law by his father, quickly followed his natural gifts and joined the staff of the newly created comic weekly, "Life," writing more comic copy for it in its formative years than any other man. After four years on "Life" as associate editor, he was at the age of twenty-five invited to take charge of the Departments of Humor in the distinguished publishing house of Messrs. Harper & Brothers. The Harpers were at the time the periodical center of the United States, their "Weekly," their "Magazine," their "Bazar," and their "Young People," being in the forefront of American periodicals. Young Bangs found himself an associate editor of "Harper's Magazine" with such veteran writers as Charles Dudley Warner, George William Curtis, Henry Mills Alden, and William Dean Howells. He had charge of "The Editor's Drawer" in the "Magazine," and the "Facetiae" page in the "Bazar," and wrote extensively for the other periodicals as well. Subsequently in 1899 he became the editor-in-chief of "Harper's Weekly," and was a powerful supporter of the administration of Theodore Roosevelt, with whom, among other eminent men, he had many interesting contacts. Outside his editorial work he wielded a busy and prolific pen, contributing widely to practically all the leading journals of the time. His most famous book, out of the sixty-odd volumes of verse and prose which came from his pen, was "A House-Boat on the Styx," which in 1896 was one of the best sellers in America, and which soon went through a score of editions in London. Mr. Bangs, with Artemus Ward and Mark Twain, was one of the few Americans invited to contribute to London "Punch." His "Coffee and Repartee," 1893, was the first of his books to give him a wide reputation as a humorist, and the quality of its humor has been characterized as being a mixture of Oliver Wendell Holmes and Bill Nye (a native of Maine, by the way, as was also Artemus Ward). Biographically speaking, something of Mr. Bangs' experience when running for mayor of Yonkers on the Democratic ticket may be found in his little brochure "Three Weeks in Politics," 1894. As he himself felicitously puts it in contemplating his defeat, "he was by the grace of the electorate returned by a comfortable majority to the bosom of his family, unwept, unhonored, and unstung." The sale of "Three Weeks in Politics" covered all his campaign expenses, nicely!

Not long after the turn of the century, about 1905 to be exact, Mr. Bangs gave up active editorial work, and became a "free lance," still writing extensively for the magazines, but giving more and more time to lecturing. It was in 1906 that he first spent a summer at Ogunquit. He so liked the place and its inhabitants, that he and Mrs. Bangs bought a property of a dozen acres in Sea Pasture of that village, and built a home of substantial proportions on a beautiful rise of land over the Atlantic. In 1907 he transferred his citizenship from New York to Maine, and became an out and out "Mainiac and a son of o' gun-quit." His three boys, John Kendrick Bangs,

Jr., Howard Russell Bangs, and Francis Hyde Bangs, became at the same time sons of the same stripe, and the youngest of them, Francis Hyde, still maintains his citizenship there. At Ogunquit, with the sea and the piney hills for his neighbors, John Kendrick did his literary work for six months of the year, laying up the stores of physical strength needed to carry him through the strenuous efforts of the lecture platform. In the most recent book on American humor, "Sixty Years of American Humor," the editor characterizes Mr. Bangs as a lecturer as follows: "He was a genius as a lecturer and traveled this country to its boundaries during the last fifteen years of his life, and wherever he went he left a memorable personal mark. He was one of the few literary artists of his own—or any other—time, who delighted to express himself orally—even oratorically—and he became the most popular and notable humorous lecturer and after-dinner speaker this country has ever known." His most notable platform effort was "Salubrities I Have Met," a lively running talk about the more or less famous men and women he had known in the course of his career. It included gossipy anecdotes of statesmen, poets, novelists, philanthropists, and others, and closed with an exquisite presentation of the character of one of the greatest of Salubrities, his friend Mark Twain, in a vivid personal sketch of the great humorist which was profoundly appealing. Mr. Bangs' experiences as a lecturer throughout the country are delightfully told in his book "From Pillar to Post," 1916. Mr. Bangs as a brilliant speaker was called upon by the Maine Republicans in the Presidential election of 1908, when, in answer to the call, he stumped the State for Taft, Fernald, and the other party candidates, delighting and influencing audiences in towns large and small. He had opened the campaign at the York County seat of Alfred, and was generally considered the leading Republican speaker in that campaign, being always kept to the last to hold the crowd.

When the World War came, Mr. Bangs was too old to enlist, but he joined the American Red Cross, and as a director of the American Committee for Devastated France, did notable service. He twice visited the American Expeditionary Forces, and gave many talks to the boys in the Army; one of his talks was interrupted by an air-raid. In this country on his returns from France he gave two war lectures throughout the land, "Light and Shade in the Land of Valor" and "America Abroad." After the war he continued to render such aid as he could to the devastated regions, always bringing, where he legitimately could, his influence to bear toward helping the American Committee to carry on its work. When after-war propaganda against France began to assert itself, he vigorously attacked it, and what he said was reported in the leading papers of every community where his lecturing took him. Because of this work, Myron T. Herrick, Ambassador to France, stated that "what Mr. Bangs said here and there and everywhere, in his forceful way of stating, did more than any one thing" toward destroying that propaganda; and the French Government showed its appreciation of Mr. Bangs' work by making him Chevalier of the Legion of Honor.

John Kendrick Bangs died at Atlantic City, January 21, 1922, as the result of illness brought on by over-exertion. For the last three years of his life he had taken no rest. He had carried on his usual

356

MAINE—A HISTORY

business of lecturing during the autumn and winter months, and had in the summers of 1919 and 1920 continued to speak on behalf of devastated France along the Atlantic coast one year, and the Pacific, the other. The last summer of his life, 1921, he spent with Mrs. Bangs in the devastated districts, personally working on their behalf. And to over-work in this good cause is attributed the illness of which he died. During his last days, confined to his bed and unable to eat or drink, his mind turned often to the coast of Maine which he so dearly loved, and one of his last remarks was that he wished he could have a good drink of Maine water out of the garden hose.

JOHN K. FORHAN—Influenced by the career of his father, who was in the United States Navy during the Civil War and a sea captain during the remainder of his active life, John K. Forhan, upon leaving school, for a few years followed the sea as a vocation. Commercial life, however, made a stronger appeal to the young man, who entered business in Canton, Maine, where he is now one of the most prominent citizens. Upright, courageous, a man of keen mind and vigorous personality, he has advanced to a high plane in the civic and commercial activities of the community in which he resides, with further honors at the hands of his fellows a question only of his own choice.

John K. Forhan was born in Brooklin, Maine, October 6, 1862, a son of Michael H., a native of Boston, Massachusetts, and Margaret G. (Allen) Forhan, of Brooklin, Maine. He was educated in the public schools of Brooklin and at an early age went to sea, where he was occupied for a few years. In 1887, he became identified with the canning business at Canton, Maine, where he accepted the position of superintendent of the Canton Cannery, owned by the Portland Packing Company. He was a member of the Eighty-second and Eighty-third sessions of the Maine State Legislature. He attends the Universalist church, and belongs to the Free and Accepted Masons and to the Independent Order of Odd Fellows.

Mr. Forhan married (first) Minnie D. Nason, of Raymond, Maine; and (second) Lillian (Wentworth) Bicknell of Dummer, New Hampshire. He is the father of one son by his first marriage: Neil K., born November 25, 1886, at Sedgwick, Maine, now a physician, who served in the United States Army during the World War.

ARTHUR H. RAY—For nearly forty years Arthur H. Ray has been identified with the tanning industry, specializing in sheep and lamb skins and the manufacture of the leather into various articles of commerce, his headquarters being at Canton, Maine. During that period he has established for himself and his industry a name for honesty of effort and products of merit. Wherever he has found it commensurate with the best interests of all he has followed causes initiated by the citizenry and seen them carried on to successful conclusion. He is regarded as a citizen of unimpeachable integrity and of the highest character, worthy of the unqualified approval of all with whom he happens to become associated.

Arthur H. Ray was born in Elizabethport, New Jersey, September 14, 1866, and acquired his education in the public schools of that State. Soon after the Lyman W. Smith Company (organized at Canton) was incorporated, in 1901, as the Lyman W. Smith Company, Incorporated, Arthur H. Ray became associated with it as a stockholder and director. He was later elected president of the corporation, as well as its treasurer, positions he holds at present. The factory tans and prepares sheep and lamb skins and makes a product for roller coverings in textile mills. Mr. Ray is a director in the Manufacturers' National Bank of Lewiston, Maine.

He has one son, Charles A. Ray, who was in the Naval Aviation Service at Gulfport, Mississippi, now associated with his father, and is assistant treasurer of the company.

RAY DUTTON ROBINSON—Education in Maine is well cared for through the selection of the individuals who make up the personnel of its pedagogic organization, of which one of the most important members is Ray Dutton Robinson, superintendent of the Canton-Livermore school system since 1925. This educator reached his present position by the natural advances that come to teachers of conspicuous ability, who have founded their labors upon a comprehensive preparation at schools and colleges. There has been nothing haphazard about the rise of Superintendent Robinson. He has won by sheer merit the distinction to which he has risen in a comparatively brief space of time and, still a man barely at life's middle span, there are other heights to which he will undoubtedly climb, in which event his own good fortune will be diametric to that of the community which he now so well serves.

Ray Dutton Robinson was born in Warren, Maine, December 19, 1887, a son of Mansfield R. and Harriet (Luce) Robinson. He attained his early education in the public schools of Warren and was graduated from the high school there. He then attended Colby College, from which he obtained his degree of Bachelor of Arts in 1915. He also took the course at Bates College and in 1915, became district superintendent of the Winterport-Frankfort School Union, which he retained until 1918. He then became superintendent of the Millbridge-Harrington-Columbia schools, remaining in that position until 1925, when he assumed his present post. For one year he was president of the Washington County Teachers' Association. He is a Republican in politics and maintains his residence in Warren. During the vacation period Mr. Robinson is attending the Bates Summer School taking courses in Education.

ELFORD H. MORISON—Starting as a clerk in the Livermore Falls Trust & Banking Company at the age of sixteen, Elford H. Morison attained, in 1912, though rapid promotions, the post of treasurer of Wilton Trust & Banking Company which he still holds, a record far from usual in a business as conservative as banking, in Maine or elsewhere.

Son of Hollis A. and Jennie F. (Walton) Morison, he was born in Wilton, Maine, January 1, 1888, and was educated in the grammar and high schools of Livermore Falls. He entered the service of the Livermore Falls Trust & Banking Company immediately after his graduation, in 1904; became manager of the Wilton branch four years later, and was made treasurer of Wilton Trust & Banking Company, when it was started in 1912. He is a member of Wilton Lodge, Free and Accepted Masons, and has been its treasurer since 1914, and is also a member of Pilgrim Commandery. He is a thirty-second degree Mason in the Scottish Rite and a member of the Shrine. He attends the Universalist church, and is a Republican.

Mr. Morison married Florence Holmes, August 20, 1913, at Wilton. Their children are: Keene H., and Marjorie.

JOSEPH H. MURPHY, M. D.—The late Dr. Murphy, whose skill was well known throughout Dexter, Maine, was a man whose work during the World War, and unselfish service to the people of his community, won him the deep regard and affection of his fellow townsmen. Born on May 4, 1866, in Andover, New Brunswick, Dr. Murphy was a son of George Will and Nancy (Britt) Murphy, both of whom are now deceased. George Will Murphy, the father, who was born in Andover, was engaged as a hotel keeper until the time of his death. The mother, Nancy (Britt) Murphy, was born in Fredericton, New Brunswick.

Their son, Joseph H. Murphy, learned the drug business as a young man, and became a registered druggist, holding positions in stores in Calais and Auburn. This type of work, however, did not satisfy him and he determined to become a physician. He entered the Maine Medical School at Bowdoin College and he graduated from there with the class of 1891, when he received his degree as Doctor of Medicine. Soon after his graduation he began the practice of his profession in Fort Fairfield, Maine. After remaining there for a number of years, Dr. Murphy removed to St. Albans, where he built up a practice. In 1922, he established in Dexter the practice which he carried on so successfully until the time of his death on January 12, 1927. During the twenty-five years of his residence in Dexter, Dr. Murphy became noted for his skill as a physician and surgeon, and he enjoyed a large and aristocratic clientele. His gentle patience and kindly wisdom have made for him a place in the hearts of his fellow-townsmen that cannot readily be filled. During the World War, he gave unreservedly of his services to the Government. In 1916, when old Company A of the Second Maine Infantry was formed in Dexter, Dr. Murphy began his war work. At that time he was chosen to examine the recruits and on January 4, 1916, he was commissioned first lieutenant in the Maine Medical Reserve Corps. At the time of the Halifax disaster, he went with that unit to serve for a month in that city. Later when the Third Maine Infantry was formed he was assigned as examiner of recruits. After this he was made a captain in the Medical Reserve Corps and he was called into active service at Camp Wadsworth on February 9, 1918. On July 13, 1918, he was sent overseas. While in France, Dr. Murphy was cited for bravery under fire by General John F. O'Ryan of the Twenty-seventh Division, in which he served as first lieutenant in the Medical Corps, being assigned to the 107th Ambulance Company of the 102nd Sanitary Train. He returned to the United States on March 3, 1919, and received his discharge at Camp Devens in April of that year. Since the war Dr. Murphy was commissioned a major in the Medical Reserve Corps.

During his residence in Dexter, Dr. Murphy always took a keen and active interest in civic affairs. A strong supporter of the Republican party, he served for several years as school physician. He was also

town physician for Dexter many years, and chairman of the Dexter Board of Health. Among the learned organizations which pertain to his profession of which he was a member, are, the American Medical Association, the Maine Medical Society, the Penobscot County Medical Society, and the Association of Military Surgeons of the United States. He was fraternally affiliated with the Penobscot Lodge, Free and Accepted Masons; and the St. John's Chapter, Royal Arch Masons; and the Mt. Moriah Council, Princes of Jerusalem. He was also a member of the Edward I. Winslow, a daughter of Samuel A. and Sarah J. Poulliot Post of the American Legion, and the Dexter Club.

Dr. Joseph H. Murphy married, May 1, 1895, Annie I. Winslow, a daughter of Samuel A. and Sarah (Lane) Winslow, both of whom are now deceased. Mrs. Murphy's father, Samuel A. Winslow, who was born in New Gloucester, Maine, was engaged as a painter and decorator until the time of his death. Her mother, Sarah (Lane) Winslow, was born in Ripley, Maine. Dr. and Mrs. Murphy became the parents of one child, a daughter, Grace Minette Murphy, who married Charles Henry Ansell, president of the George Park Manufacturing Company, Incorporated, whose biography appears below. Dr. Murphy and his family attended the First Universalist Church of Dexter, of which they were members.

CHARLES HENRY ANSELL—As president of the George Park Manufacturing Company, Incorporated, Mr. Ansell is well known as one of the prominent business men of Dexter, Maine. Born on January 14, 1894, at Windsor Mills, Province of Quebec, Canada, Mr. Ansell is a son of Arthur Homer, and Elizabeth (Clark) Ansell. The father, Arthur Homer Ansell, is a machinist.

His son, Charles Henry Ansell, is a graduate of St. Catherines Collegiate Institute, at St. Catherines, Ontario, Canada. After the World War, during which he saw service overseas in the 224th Aero Service Squadron, American Expeditionary Forces, he returned to the United States where he began his business career. For six years he was engaged as superintendent of the Dumbarton Woolen Mills of Dexter, Maine. He then became president and superintendent of the George Park Manufacturing Company, Incorporated, at Dexter. This position he has held for the past two years, and his efforts have been marked with outstanding success.

Although Mr. Ansell has been deeply engrossed in his business affairs, he has nevertheless taken a keen and active interest in many outside activities. He is fraternally affiliated with the Penobscot Lodge, No. 39, Free and Accepted Masons; the St. John's Chapter, No. 25, Royal Arch Masons, of which he is Past High Priest; the Council, Royal and Select Masters; the St. John's Commandery, No. 3, Knights Templar; and the Anah Temple, Ancient Arabic Order Nobles of the Mystic Shrine. He is also a member of the American Legion, the Masonic Club of Dexter, the Dexter Club, the Piscataquis Country Club of Guilford, and the Penobscot Country Club of Bangor.

Charles Henry Ansell married, June 4, 1919, at Dexter, Maine, Grace Minette Murphy, a daughter of the late Major Joseph Harvey Murphy, Doctor of Medicine, and Annie (Winslow) Murphy. Mrs. Ansell's father, Major Joseph Harvey Murphy, whose biography appears in the preceding review, is the distinguished officer and physician whose recent death on January 12, 1927, was the cause of deep sorrow

358   MAINE—A HISTORY

throughout Dexter. Mr. and Mrs. Ansell are the
parents of three children, all of whom are daughters:
1. Elizabeth Clark, who was born on June 29, 1920.
2. Mary Isabel, who was born on February 12, 1923.
3. Dorothy Maybelle, who was born on October 28,
1926. Mr. Ansell and his family maintain their residence at No. 136 Spring Street, Dexter, Maine, in
which community they attend the Universalist
church, of which Mr. Ansell is a member of the
board of trustees.

HORACE F. WESCOTT—In the political and
business life of the city of Ellsworth, Horace F. Wescott stands out prominently as a man who has always upheld the best interests of the town. His value
in the opinions of his fellow-citizens is shown by the
many years he has served both the city and county
in political offices. In addition to his work in civil
affairs, Mr. Wescott has for many years conducted
the important hardware concern which bears his
name.

Mr. Wescott was born in Penobscot, September
24, 1861, son of Giles Wescott and Hester A. (Wardwell) Wescott, both of Penobscot, and who are now
deceased. Giles Wescott was engaged in farming
until his death.

Horace F. Wescott was educated in the local public schools and after completing his formal education, he learned the trade of carpenter, which occupation he followed for eighteen years, acquiring a
reputation for dependable and substantial work
throughout the vicinity. In 1900, he entered the
hardware business independently, as sole owner and
proprietor of the H. F. Wescott Hardware Company
of Ellsworth. In this line he has been highly successful and his organization is today one of the
important business houses of the town. Mr. Wescott
has always been known as a public-spirited citizen
ever willing to assist in town progress. In fraternal
circles, he takes a responsible part, being a member
of Lygonia Lodge, Free and Accepted Masons; a
member of Chapter and Blanquefort Commandery,
Knights Templar; Lejok Lodge, Independent Order
of Odd Fellows, in which he is Past Grand, and
Wivurna Encampment, in which he is Past Chief Patriarch, Patriotic Order Sons of America. He is
a member of the Dirigo Club and of the New
England Hardware Dealers' Association. In politics,
he is a Republican and has always been prominently
active, serving ten years as county treasurer in Hancock County, and four years as alderman for the city
of Ellsworth. Mr. Wescott, by his long years of
public service, proved to the people that they were
justified in electing him to positions of trust and confidence. In his religious affiliations, he is an attendant of the Baptist church, and for recreation, depends on the outdoor life afforded by hunting and
fishing.

Horace F. Wescott married Lillian Wardwell of
Penobscot, and they have one son, Percival L., who
served in the United States Army during the World
War, with rank of private, attached to the Three
Hundred and Forty-first Aero Squadron. For ten
months during his enlistment, he saw service in
France with the American Expeditionary Forces.

WALLACE A. PRICE—Since his return from
service in the World War, Wallace A. Price has been
identified with the Central Maine Power Company,
and since January 1, 1926, he has been division manager of the Central Division of this concern. He is
a veteran of the World War and well known as an
able business man and a good citizen.

Wallace A. Price was born in Augusta, Maine,
February 15, 1892, son of Charles A. Price, who was
born in Farmingdale, Maine, and died in August,
1897, and of Addie V. (Bagley) Price. Charles A.
Price was superintendent of the Gannett Publishing
Company, and was well known in the Masonic Order,
being a member of all the York Rite bodies and of the
Consistory, in which he held the thirty-second degree. Wallace A. Price received his education in the
public schools of his birthplace and, after completing his course in the Cony High School, engaged in
the retail shoe business as junior partner of the firm
of Turner and Price, which connection was maintained until after the close of the World War. The
partnership was formed in 1910, and in May, 1917,
Mr. Price was among the first to enlist for service.
He was assigned to the Coast Artillery of Maine,
being stationed first at Portland and later sent to
Florida, and then to Fort Worth, Texas, and San An-
tonio, Texas, where he was discharged October 31,
1919, as captain of the Quartermaster's Corps. Soon
after the close of the war he sold his share in the
retail shoe business and became identified with the
Central Maine Power Company, as salesman. That
was in May, 1920. On August 1, 1922, he was promoted to the position of district superintendent of the
Norway district. Ability and thorough knowledge
brought him further promotion, when, in August,
1925, he was made superintendent of the Augusta
district. About five months later he was again promoted, this time to the responsible position of division
manager in charge of the Central Division, which he
still holds (1928). Politically, Mr. Price is a supporter of the Republican party. He is a member
of the American Legion, Forty and Eight, and of
the United States Army Reserve Officers' Association, and fraternally he is identified with Bethlehem
Lodge, No. 35, Free and Accepted Masons. His religious interest is with the Congregational church
of Augusta, Maine.

Wallace A. Price was married, in Vassalboro,
Maine, February 15, 1914, to Marian B. Low, who
was born in Vassalboro, Maine, March 24, 1891,
daughter of Asa S. and Anna E. (Chamberlin) Low.
Mr. and Mrs. Price are the parents of one daughter,
Elizabeth, who was born in Augusta, Maine, April
15, 1920. The family home is located at No. 33 Jackson Street, in Augusta, Maine.

CYRUS NATHAN BLANCHARD—A descendant of Thomas Blanchard, who sailed from London,
England, in the good ship "Jonathan," in 1639, Cyrus
Nathan Blanchard, an attorney of Wilton, Maine, has
an undisputed claim to pure American stock. This
same Thomas Blanchard settled first at Braintree,
Massachusetts, where he purchased two hundred
acres of land with buildings, on the south and west
sides of the Mystic River. He was married three
times; two of his wives he married in England, and
the third he married after coming to this country.
His son Samuel was only ten years of age when
his father came to New England and he grew into
manhood here and became a prominent citizen in the
towns of Charlestown, Malden and Andover, Massachusetts. He held many public offices of trust
and died in Charlestown, Massachusetts, on April
22, 1707. His son, John, born in Andover, Massachusetts, married Mary, daughter of Simon Crosby.

He died April 10, 1750. His son, Samuel, born August 17, 1717, married Mary, daughter of William Brown. He died March 26, 1807. His son, Timothy, born October 16, 1755, was a soldier in the Revolution in Colonel Ebenezer Bridge's regiment, Captain Jonathan Stickney's company. He was wounded in the battle of Lexington, April 19, 1775. He enlisted in the Continental Army, from which he was honorably discharged in December, 1780. He married Mary Kidder and they had one child, Cyrus, who was born at Billerica, Massachusetts, April 29, 1783. He moved to Wilton, Maine, and there bought what has since been known as the Blanchard farm. He was married twice; his first wife was Chloe Fitch, of Wilton, and his second wife was Elizabeth Floyd of Augusta, Maine. He had five children by the first wife and four by the second. The children of the second wife were: 1. Died in infancy. 2. Jesse, mentioned below. 3. James. 4. John.

Jesse Blanchard was born at Wilton, Maine, April 12, 1819. He was educated in the public schools and always engaged in the business of farming, living on the old home place. He was a man whose influence for good in the community was greatly felt by all who came in contact with him. He was strong in his proclivities to the Republican party and a useful and active member of the Free Baptist Church of East Wilton. He married Phebe Holt of Weld, Maine, November 17, 1853. She died, May 7, 1896. They had five children: 1-2. twins; one died in infancy, and the other is Luetta. 3. Edgar F. 4. Albert E. 5. Cyrus Nathan, of whom further.

Cyrus Nathan Blanchard was born in Wilton, Maine, on October 6, 1869. He received his early education in the public schools of Wilton and attended the Normal School at Farmington, Maine. He graduated from the North Anson Academy in 1888, and entered Bates College, graduating in 1892. His education and the study of law were intermingled over a period of years when he found it necessary to divide his time between the practical and theoretical problems, learning and doing. He taught in the high school at Dexter, Maine, for two years and then began to read law with Hon. J. C. Holman of Farmington. After two years of application to the reading and study of law, he was admitted to the bar in 1896 and soon thereafter, he opened an office in Wilton where he has been a practicing attorney ever since. He is one of the leading lawyers in this vicinity and has held many public offices, testifying to the esteem with which he is held by his fellow-citizens. He was elected as State Representative for 1897 to 1898. And then elected State Senator in 1899 to 1900. He is a staunch Republican and served on the Republican State Committee from 1903 to 1907. He was a member of the Governor's council in 1906 and 1907. He was county attorney from 1907 to 1912. He has also held prominent offices in the town of Wilton. He is a member of the American Bar Association and the Maine State Bar Association, of which he has been president. He is a director in the Wilton Trust & Banking Company. He is a member of Wilton Lodge, Free and Accepted Masons; St. John's Chapter, Royal Arch Masons; of Jephthah Council, Royal and Select Masters, of Farmington; of Pilgrim Commandery, Knights Templar; and of Kora Temple, Ancient Arabic Order Nobles of the Mystic Shrine, of Lewiston, Maine.

He is a Past Grand Commander of its Grand Commandery of Maine. He is a member of Franklin Lodge, Knights of Pythias, No. 94, of North Jay, and of Farmington Grange, Patrons of Husbandry. He is also an attendant of the Congregational church.

On September 19, 1901, Cyrus Nathan Blanchard married Florence E. Noyes, daughter of Philander and Elvira (Small) Noyes of Wilton, Maine.

CHARLES EDWIN PURINTON, president of Purinton Brothers, Incorporated, of Augusta, who died in that city, February 9, 1924, is remembered not merely as a business man of uncommon probity and efficiency, but for his long continued services of a public character. He was mayor for a time, and his unselfish work in building up the various fraternal organizations with which he was associated gained him much renown. His family, long settled in New England, was of English origin, but the name is variously spelled in early records, sometimes appearing as Puddington, and these variations have continued among the several branches, widely separated in the course of centuries.

The first of the Purintons in America were George, who was a resident of York, Maine, as early as 1640, and his brother, Robert Purington, a landholder of Portsmouth, New Hampshire, from 1640 to 1647. He joined the church in Portsmouth in 1640; was made a freeman in 1672, and married Amy Davis. John, elder son of Robert and Amy Purinton, was born about 1635, lived in Exeter, New Hampshire, but removed to Salisbury, Massachusetts. His son, Deacon Hezekiah Purinton, born about 1674, was a soldier, farmer and fisherman, who finally settled at Truro, Massachusetts, where he was made a freeman in 1707, and subsequently filled several town offices, including that of selectman. The line was continued by his son, Humphrey, born about 1700, in Portsmouth, but whose children were born in Truro, eight having been baptized there; Humphrey, his son, born in Truro, and baptized there September 7, 1729, and settled in Bath, Maine; his son, the Rev. Humphrey, the first of the family to be converted to the Baptist faith, who, after an honorable army record from 1775 to 1777, was accused of being a Universalist, which led to his becoming one of the first Free Will Baptist ministers, and who served as chairman of the first Board of Selectmen in Bowdoin; Abiezer, son of the Rev. Humphrey and Thankful (Snow) Purinton, born in Bowdoin about 1780, who combined farming with shoemaking; Amos, son of Abiezer and Eunice (Thompson) Purinton, selectman, justice of the peace, schoolmaster, farmer and Universalist; Amos Edwin, son of Amos and Martha J. (Patterson) Purinton, born in Bowdoin, May 3, 1842, schoolmaster, merchant, brick manufacturer, selectman of Richmond, alderman of Waterville, and a prime mover in the establishment of the Free Baptist Church in Waterville. He married Sarah M. Moore, daughter of Fairfield Moore, December 1, 1866.

Of the six children of this union, the second, Charles Edwin Purinton, was born in Bowdoin, January 19, 1870. He was educated in the common schools of Bowdoin, and then joined his father, at that time in the contracting business, and was his assistant for four years. He entered Colby College, where he took a three years' special course. His one business venture was a partnership with his brother, Francis B. Purinton, under the firm name of Purinton Brothers, dealers in coal and wood, in Augusta. The enterprise prospered, and was later incorporated, with Charles Edwin Purinton as president and Francis B. Purinton as treasurer of the company.

A Republican in politics, Mr. Purinton was a member of the Augusta City Council for two years, of the Board of Aldermen for four years, and was acting mayor for a time. He belonged to Augusta Lodge, No. 141, Free and Accepted Masons; Cushnoc Chapter, Royal Arch Masons; Alpha Council, Royal and Select Masters; Trinity Commandery, Knights Templar; Kora Temple, Ancient Arabic Order Nobles of the Mystic Shrine, and Asylum Lodge, Independent Order of Odd Fellows. He was also a charter member and treasurer of the local lodge of the Benevolent and Protective Order of Elks.

Mr. Purinton married, on November 4, 1894, Carrie L. Ripley, born in North Appleton, Maine, October 24, 1873, daughter of Arthur L. Ripley. Their children were: 1. Frances L., born August 18, 1895. 2. Lawrence G., born April 17, 1897. 3. Lucille M., born January 4, 1902. 4. Irene A., born March 1, 1903. 5. Richmond M., born November 9, 1905.

A worthy member of a family which for ten generations has contributed to the upbuilding of the State as pioneer farmers, teachers, clergymen, and as patriotic soldiers, Mr. Purinton was mourned by a host of friends, relatives and business associates, and his memory is honored by the many organizations to whose well-being he made substantial contributions.

JAMES ALOYSIUS O'BRIEN—In bringing happiness, joy and romance into the lives of millions, the theatre is one of the most profound forces for good, providing a source of recreation for tired lives by its entertainment, with its comedies chasing dull care away, or its more serious productions teaching lessons which are touching and true. Prominent in amusement circles, James Aloysius O'Brien is the proprietor of the well-known Strand Theatre of Rumford, with a reputation for presenting only the finest type of amusement in a playhouse that is a credit to this great city. Mr. O'Brien expends great care in the successful selection of the dramas and comedies for presentation at his house, with the result that he has ever received the commendation of his patrons for his excellent judgment and for the efficient and courteous manner in which everything connected with his theatre is conducted. He has never been satisfied with anything less than the best, with the result that all his endeavors have been laudatory and his organization is a splendid influence and a credit to this city in the development and progress of which it is an indirect aid.

Mr. O'Brien was born in Portland and received his education in the public schools here, graduating from the North End High School. Completing his formal education, he entered upon his career in the professional world and became associated with the theatrical business, in which he advanced with considerable success from the very first, by reason of his great ability and determination to succeed; maintaining from the beginning the same high principles which have advanced him to his present prominent position in the entertainment realm. In the civic

life of his community he takes an active part and is an inspiring influence for improvement and advancement in his membership in the Rotary Club, while fraternally, he is popularly identified with the Benevolent and Protective Order of Elks. In his religious adherence, he is a member of the Roman Catholic church.

James Aloysius O'Brien married, at Portland, Mary E. McCann, and they are the parents of one daughter: Jane Meehan, now Mrs. J. W. E. Stearns of Springfield, Massachusetts. Mrs. O'Brien died in 1915.

GEORGE W. LANE, Jr.—Few business men are better known in Lewiston than is George W. Lane, Jr., president of the Lewiston Trust Company. Mr. Lane has been identified with this bank since he was eighteen years of age and has held practically every position in the institution. He is also president of the Auburn Wood Heel Company; president and a member of the board of directors of the Maine & New Hampshire Theatres Company.

George W. Lane, Jr., was born in Lewiston, November 15, 1880, son of George W. Lane, a native of Maine, who was engaged in business as a builder and a contractor, and whose death occurred October 25, 1924, and of Carrie (Gardner) Lane, who was born in Maine and died December 2, 1918. Mr. Lane attended the public schools of his birthplace, and when his school training was completed secured a position as clerk in the employ of the Lewiston Trust Company, beginning his connection there November 28, 1898. From that time to the present (1928) he has been continuously identified with that bank, rising from one position to another by successive promotions until he had filled every position except that of president. On June 1, he was made president of the Lewiston Trust Company, thus completing his rise from the modest position of clerk to the highest official position in the bank. He is known as an expert in banking affairs, and stands high in financial circles in this part of the State. But though his whole active career has been associated with this bank, this institution by no means represents the full scope of his business activities and interests. He has always been quick to recognize opportunity, and has invested in various enterprises, where his financial knowledge and his sound judgment have been of value to all concerned. He is president and member of the board of directors of the Maine & New Hampshire Theatres Company, and president of the Auburn Wood Heel Company. He also has taken an active part in local public affairs. He gives his support to the Democratic party, was a member of the first City Council of Auburn under the charter form of government, and at the present time (1928) is trustee of the Auburn Water District. He is a director of the Turner Center System, and has always been ready to aid in forwarding any project which seemed to him to be well planned for the advancement of the general welfare. Fraternally, he is identified with the Masonic Order, in which he is a member of all bodies and holds the thirty-second degree, and is a Past Potentate of Kora Temple, Ancient Arabic Order Nobles of the Mystic Shrine. He is a member and trustee of the Lewiston Lodge, Benevolent and Protective Order of Elks, and is also a member of the

Calumet Club and the Martindale Country Club. His religious affiliation is with Calvary Methodist Church of Lewiston.

George W. Lane, Jr., was married, November 18, 1924, to Una C. Fosdick, who was born in Lawrence, Massachusetts, foster daughter of J. Colquhoun. Mr. and Mrs. Lane make their home in Lewiston.

CHARLES A. RAITT—The first of the family of Raitt, well known in the Kittery and Eliot sections of the State, and to which the late Charles A. Raitt, prominent fruit-grower and brick manufacturer, belonged, was Alexander Raitt. He was a Scotchman, born about 1722, who came to America about 1745, settling in Kittery. He married, October 21, 1747, Miriam (Frost) Frost, widow of Eliot Frost, and daughter of Hon. John Frost, of Newcastle, New Hampshire. He was a seaman and made extensive journeys for his time. He died in the West Indies.

William Raitt, son of Alexander, the founder, and Miriam (Frost-Frost) Raitt, had a son, John B. Raitt, who married Anna Marsh, and their son, William Raitt, born November 23, 1825, married Louisa Frost, daughter of John and Mary Ann (Seavey) Frost, and they had a son, Charles A., of whom further.

Charles A. Raitt, son of William and Louisa (Frost) Raitt, was born in Kittery, February 5, 1861, and when he was seven years old his parents removed with him from his birthplace to Eliot, where he obtained his education in the public schools. From textbooks he turned his attention to learning the trade of brick-mason, which he followed, together with operation of the home farm until his death. He purchased the land for his farm, set out a large orchard of fruit trees, and built first a three-room house, afterwards erecting the large and beautiful house, where his family resides. About thirty years prior to his death he established a brickyard and developed a large and successful business. His fruit farm was his pride and pleasure, and he made it one of the model places of its kind in that region. He was a man of essentially home interests, and most of his time, away from business, was spent in his orchard planting trees and in the beautification of the grounds about the house.

Actively interested in the affairs of the town, Mr. Raitt always discouraged attempts on the part of the citizens to have him stand for public office. He gave his political allegiance undeviatingly to the Republican party, which was strengthened locally by his personal influence and loyalty. His fraternal relations were with St. John's Lodge, Free and Accepted Masons, of South Berwick; the Kittery Tribe, Improved Order of Red Men; and Eliot Grange, Patrons of Husbandry. His religious fellowship was with the East Eliot Methodist Episcopal Church.

Charles A. Raitt married Carrie L. Frye, daughter of Josiah and Mary Ellen (Brooks) Frye, of Eliot. Their children: 1. Arthur G., married Susie Shephard and they have four children: Charles S., Oscar E., Gordon M., and Daniel A. 2. Cora E., married A. Earle Hurd. 3. George W., married Elizabeth Hale; they have one child, Frances. 4. Marion L., married Raymond Andrews and had one child, Rae Philice. Mrs. Andrews died October, 1914. 5. Charles Clinton, married Alice Burchill, and they are the parents of two children: Deane B. and Harley R. 6. Norman J., married Blanche Cassidy. 7. Roland A., married Irma Spinney; their child is Arlene A. 8.

Florence E., married Vincent Trefethen. 9. Verna J. 10. Eleanor C., died April 27, 1907.

EVERETT VALENTINE PERKINS—Since 1923, Everett Valentine Perkins has been serving as principal of the Cony High School of Augusta, Maine, and in this capacity he is rendering very efficient service. Mr. Perkins had had thirteen years of experience in the teaching profession in Vermont and five years in Maine, before coming to Augusta, and in his present connection he is making the benefits of his long experience clearly felt. He is a graduate of the University of Vermont, and has done special work in Harvard University.

Everett Valentine Perkins was born in Bridgewater, Vermont, February 14, 1882, son of Elisha Paddock Perkins, a farmer of Bridgewater, who took an active part in public affairs and served as a member of the State Legislature, and of Adelaide E. (Abbott) Perkins. He received his early education in the public schools of Bridgewater, Vermont, graduating from the Woodstock High School in 1901, and then matriculated in the University of Vermont, from which he was graduated with the degree of Bachelor of Arts in 1905. From 1905 to 1907 he served as principal of the Lyndon, Vermont, high and grade school, and then, in the fall of 1907, he accepted the position of assistant principal of the Lyndon Institute, where he served during the year 1907-08. His next position was as principal of the Enosburg Falls, Vermont, schools, 1909-1911, after which he was appointed assistant in the Burlington (Vermont) High School, in which capacity he served from 1911-1912, resigning in order that he might accept appointment as principal of the Woodstock (Vermont) High School, 1912-1915. In 1915, he was appointed District Superintendent of Schools, Woodstock, in which responsible position he rendered most efficient service from 1915 to 1918. He then became principal of Presque Isle High School, in Maine, 1918-1919, after which experience he was made principal of the high school of Houlton, Maine, where he served from 1919 to 1923, when he came to Augusta, Maine, as principal of the Cony High School. Here he has, for the last four years, been rendering exceptionally valuable service, winning the warm appreciation of both pupils and teachers, and placing the school of which he has charge on a par with the best in the State. During the years of his active teaching and supervising career, Mr. Perkins has continued to be a student and has constantly improved his equipment for his work by study during the summer sessions of the University of Vermont and of Harvard University. Mr. Perkins gives his support to the principles and the candidates of the Republican party. He is a member of the local Grange, Patrons of Husbandry; of Sigma Nu College Fraternity; of the county, State, and national educational associations, and of the Rotary Club, of which last he is a past president, also president Augusta Young Men's Christian Association, 1927-8. His religious affiliation is with the Congregational church.

Everett Valentine Perkins was married, at Essex Junction, Vermont, June 18, 1907, to Eliza Belle Read, daughter of Alfred Eugene and Sarah (Johnson) Read. Mr. and Mrs. Perkins are the parents of five children: 1. Everett Paddock, born January 9,

1911. 2. Margaret Elizabeth, born July 2, 1915. 3.
Alfred Read, born March 15, 1918. 4. Priscilla Read,
born November 21, 1922. 5. Constançe Read, born
February 8, 1924.

ELDAR MARKSON—A resident of Portland
since his early childhood, Mr. Markson has been
engaged in that city in the men's and ladies' garment trade for a quarter of a çentury. From small
beginnings this business, conducted under the firm
name of Markson Brothers, has grown steadily, until today there are stores not only in Boston and
Portland, but also in many other New England States.
Each of these stores is a leader in these several
communities amongst establishments of a similar
type, and Mr. Markson today is considered one of
the most successful and progressive merchants of
Portland. In every other respect, too, he takes an
active part in the life of the community and every
movement tending to advançe its growth and welfare can always count on his liberal and loyal support.
Eldar Markson was born in Russia, November 15,
1874, a son of Abram and Rachel Markson. He came
to this country with his parents as a small child, the
family settling in Portland, in the public schools of
which city he received his early education. After
leaving school he gradually acquired a very thorough
business training, being successively connected with
various business enterprises. About 1903, together
with his brother, Morris Markson, he founded the
firm of Markson Brothers. At first there was only
one store, in Portland, selling men's and ladies'
garments. As a result of able management the firm
quickly established for itself a very high reputation
and before long began to expand. In 1928 branch
stores were maintained at Waterville, Augusta, Bath,
Biddeford and Sanford in Maine, Newburyport,
Worcester, Milford, Gardiner and Salem in Massachusetts, Nashua in New Hampshire, and Middletown,
New Britain, Waterbury, Bristol and Danbury in
Connecticut. Until early in 1928 the headquarters
and main offices were located at No. 504 Congress
Street, Portland, in connection with the Portland
store, but since then they have been moved to Boston, where the offices and a large store are located
at No. 694 Washington Street. The firm not only
engages in the retail business, but also manufactures
certain of its goods. In 1928, its officers were: Morris Markson, president; Eldar Markson, treasurer;
and Yoland D. Markson, secretary. Mr. Markson is
a member of the Masonic Order, the Independent
Order of B'nai B'rith, the Portland Young Men's
Hebrew Association, and several other Portland organizations. His religious affiliations are with the
Hebrew faith, and more particularly with Etz
Chaim Synagogue of Portland, and he is also active
in various Hebrew benevolent and other movements,
including the Maine and Portland Zionists' organizations, of which latter he is chairman.
Mr. Markson was married (first), in 1898, to Jennie Ida Ginsburg, a daughter of Bere and Anna
Ginsburg. Mrs. Markson died at Portland, March
13, 1925. He married (second), July 7, 1927, Mrs.
Lena (Wolfson) Marçus, a daughter of Rabbi Wolfson of Lowell, Massachusetts. By his first marriage Mr. Markson is the father of two sons: 1. Yol-
and D. Markson, born in Portland in 1900; associated

in business with his father and uncle, as secretary
of Markson Brothers; married at Portland in 1924,
to Annabelle Caplan, a daughter of Dr. Elias Caplan, a prominent physican of Portland, by which
marriage there is one daughter, Rhonda Markson,
born February 7, 1925. 2. Robert T. Markson, born
in Portland in 1905, and connected with "Women's
Wear," an important trade journal in New York
City. Mr. Markson makes his home at No. 29
Sherman Street, Portland, though in recent years
the continuous expansion of his business has made
it necessary for him to spend much of his time in
Boston and in the other cities, in which his stores
are located.

ARTHUR MARSHALL STANLEY—Substan-
tial and continuous development of a business enterprise has marked the commercial life in Maine of
Arthur Marshall Stanley, who, with his brother, C.
L. Stanley, conducts establishments at Dixfield and
Mexico. In the two stores are çarried men's and
boys' clothing, shoes, and a line of general merchandise at the Mexico center, while meats, groceries and provisions are handled at the Dixfield headquarters. The business was founded by the father,
Charles Stanley, but for nearly thirty years the sons
have continued it, enlarging from time to time as
occasion demanded. Mr. Stanley is a merchant of
the highest honor and industrious qualities, a citizen
of courageous devotion to civic advancement, a man
of unblemished character and most attractive personality, honored and respected by his fellow-citizens wherever he is known, with a prosperous business and a host of friends.
He was born in Dixfield, Maine, October 30, 1881,
a son of Charles and Alfreda Stanley, the father a
native of Dixfield, Maine, removing to Bloomington,
Illinois, where he conducted a flour and grain business for fifteen years before returning to Maine.
Settling in Dixfield, he established himself in the
same business, which he conducted for ten years.
He then entered the grocery business, and a disastrous fire in the Odd Fellows' Block in 1900, caused
him great loss, but he rose superior to the catas-
trophe, reëstablished himself, adding groceries and
men's furnishings to his line, and continued his merchandising until his death in 1914.
Arthur M. Stanley acquired his education in the
public schools of Dixfield, graduating from the high
school, and at Gray's Business College. When he
was fourteen years of age he was taken into his
father's store, where he continued as an employee
until he was twenty years of age, at which time he
became associated with his brother, Charles L. Stanley, and opened the store in Mexico, with the last-
named in charge. Since the death of the elder Stanley the brothers have conducted the business. Arthur
M. Stanley has served as selectman and as a member
of the School Board of Dixfield. His church is the
Congregational. He belongs to the Lodge, Free and
Accepted Masons; the Chapter, Royal Arch Masons;
the Commandery, Knights Templar, and to the Order of the Eastern Star, as well as to the Rebekahs
and the Independent Order of Odd Fellows.
Mr. Stanley married, in Cambridge, Massachusetts, October 20, 1908, Florence Ada Nutter, daughter of Fred and Lura Nutter. They have one child:
Lura, born January 14, 1912.

FRANK W. HAINES—For the past ten years Frank W. Haines has been identified with the Blaisdell Automobile Company, first as bookkeeper, and since 1922, as treasurer of the corporation. The concern carries the agency for Hudson and Essex Motor cars.

J. Willis Haines, father of Mr. Haines, was born in Dexter, Maine, April 7, 1856, and during the early years of his active career was engaged in the retail drug business. Later, he became associated with S. M. Leighton, with whom he formed a partnership under the name of Leighton and Haines, and engaged in the grocery and crockery business in Dexter. For a period of twenty-five years he was agent for the American Railway Express Company. At the present time (1928) he is devoting all his time to the duties of the office of town clerk of Dexter. He is a Republican in his political sympathies, and has been very active in local public affairs. He has served for one year as treasurer and collector of the town of Dexter, for three years on the School Board and for eight years on the Water Board. In 1895, he was elected town clerk, and he has been serving in this office ever since, a period of thirty-three years. During the earlier years of his incumbency in this office he attended to its duties while still engaged in business but he is now, as has been stated, giving all his time to this office. He is a member of Plymouth Lodge, No. 65, Independent Order of Odd Fellows, of which he is a Past Grand. He married Mary Augusta Roberts, who was born in Dexter, Maine. The father of J. Willis Haines was John Folsom Haines who was born in Bangor, Maine, and was engaged as a carpenter and builder to the time of his death. During the Civil War he worked in the Portsmouth Navy Yard.

Frank W. Haines, son of J. Willis and Mary Augusta (Roberts) Haines, was born in Dexter, Maine, October 8, 1889, and received his education in the public schools of his birthplace. After completing his high school course he attended the University of Maine, in the class of 1913, studying electrical engineering. He was then appointed assistant postmaster in Dexter and this position he filled for a period of five years, leaving the Post Office Department to enlist in the United States Navy during the World War, serving as third class electrician. On December 30, 1918, he became associated with the Blaisdell Automobile Company, as bookkeeper, in which capacity he served until 1922. In that year the business was incorporated and Mr. Haines was made treasurer of the corporation, which official position he has filled to the present time (1928). The corporation sells Hudson and Essex motor cars, and is conducting a prosperous and steadily growing business. Like his father, Frank W. Haines is an ardent Republican, and he has served as a member of the Penobscot County Republican Committee and of the Dexter Republican Town Committee. Fraternally, he is identified with Penobscot Lodge, Free and Accepted Masons; St. John's Chapter, Royal Arch Masons; Mt. Moriah Council, Royal and Select Masters; St. John's Commandery, Knights Templar. He is also a member of Beta Theta Pi College Fraternity. He is a member of the American Legion, of Dexter; of the Masonic Club, and of Dexter Chamber of Commerce. Mr. Haines finds his relaxation in fishing and hunting; he attends the Universalist church.

Frank W. Haines was married, in 1919, to Winifred Beverly, who is a native of Machias, Maine, and they are the parents of two sons: 1. Frank W., Jr. 2. John B.

CARLL N. FENDERSON—One of the youngest but none the less prominent of the public-spirited citizens of Farmington, Franklin County, now (1928) serving as county attorney, is Carll N. Fenderson, who was born in Farmington, June 11, 1900, son of Albion L. Fenderson, native of Scarboro, Maine, and Harriet N. Fenderson, native of Buxton, Maine. Albion L. Fenderson lived for many years in Farmington, and until the time of his death, in 1914, was accounted one of the town's most highly respected citizens. Attorney-at-law, he enjoyed an extensive practice, and served with justice and distinction as Judge of the Municipal Court and Register of Probate.

Carll N. Fenderson received his early education in the public schools of Farmington, and graduated from high school with the class of 1917. He matriculated at Bowdoin College, then, at the entrance of the United States into the World War, enlisted in the Army, and was stationed in an officers' training school. At the close of the war, Mr. Fenderson continued his studies, entering the Law School of Boston University, whence he graduated with the class of 1922, holding the degree of Bachelor of Laws. He passed the Maine State bar examination in February of the following year, and began practice of his profession in the place of his birth. Since that time he has figured more and more prominently in the public life of Farmington. Member of the Republican party, loyal to its principles and popular with leaders of other parties in the vicinity, Mr. Fenderson conducted his campaign for the office of county attorney, and was elected to it, in 1927, just four years after the commencement of his professional career. He took office in January, and the term of service is for two years. At the present writing (1928) Mr. Fenderson is achieving distinction and a popularity still more extensive through the ability with which he exercises his position of responsibility, and it is generally conceded that if he wishes to devote his entire career to public life he will go far indeed. Mr. Fenderson is one of the best-known members of the Franklin County Bar Association, and a member of the Maine State Bar Association. He is also active in Masonry, as member of the Blue Lodge, Chapter, Council, Knights Templar, and a member of the Farmington Chamber of Commerce, American Legion, and Forty and Eight. He contributes liberally to charitable causes, and is a communicant of the Congregational church.

Carll N. Fenderson married, at South Portland, Maine, Christmas Day, December 25, 1919, Irene S. Record, native of Portland, Maine, and daughter of W. C. Record, born at Jefferson Maine, and Edith Record. Mr. and Mrs. Fenderson are the parents of two children, sons: 1. Albion W., born at Winthrop, Massachusetts. 2. Carll, Jr., born at Farmington. Both Mr. and Mrs. Fenderson are active in matters pertaining to the church, and are numbered among the most popular of younger couples of the community.

CHARLES DRUMMOND BARTLETT—One of the able attorneys and progressive public officials of Bangor, Maine, is Charles Drummond Bartlett, who has been engaged in legal practice here, with offices at Nos. 313 and 314 in the building at No. 6

State Street, since 1914. Mr. Bartlett is active in public affairs and at the present time (1928) is serving in the State Legislature, this being the second year of his service there.

Charles Drummond Bartlett was born in Bangor, Maine, February 1, 1890, and received his earliest education in the local public schools, later attending Middlesex School, at Concord, Massachusetts. When his preparatory course was finished he became a student in Harvard College, at Cambridge, Massachusetts, where he completed his course with graduation in 1913. He had decided to enter the legal profession, and the following fall he began professional study in the Law School of the University of Maine, where he completed his course in 1914, receiving the degree of Bachelor of Laws. He was admitted to the bar that same year, and since his admission has been engaged in practice in Bangor. Along with his general practice he has specialized in corporation and probation work, and he has been admitted to practice in all of the State and Federal courts. He is a member of the Penobscot County Bar Association, the Maine State Bar Association, and the American Bar Association, and has established a reputation which is a valuable business asset. Politically, Mr. Bartlett supports the principles and the candidates of the Republican party, and he is active in local public affairs, as well as in the affairs of the State. He served as a member of the Board of Aldermen of the city of Bangor for one year, was city solicitor for Bangor in 1922, and since 1925 has been serving in the State Legislature, his term running until 1928. In October, 1918, Mr. Bartlett was commissioned a second lieutenant in the United States Army Air Service, and stationed at Kelly Field, Texas, where he remained until he received his discharge in January, 1919, rank of second lieutenant. In September, 1926, he was commissioned a captain in the adjutant-general's department of the State of Maine, National Guards, and he still holds that rank. Mr. Bartlett is one of the many busy men who find their recreation on the golf links. His religious interest is with the Unitarian church, of which he is an attendant.

Charles Drummond Bartlett was married, in 1917, to Margaret Wood, who was born in Bangor, Maine. Mr. and Mrs. Bartlett are the parents of one child, Charles D., Jr.

MOSES J. BYER, treasurer of the Byer Manufacturing Company, was born on July 4, 1892, in Bangor, Maine, son of Joseph A. and Ida (Kaplan) Byer. The father, Joseph A. Byer, who was born in 1866, in Russia, was educated in the public schools there, coming to the United States at the age of eighteen. In 1884, he came to Maine, where he worked several years as a pack peddler, selling dry-goods and tinware, until 1893. In that year he started the manufacture of lumbermen's clothes, a business which he carried on until 1920. Since that time he has been president of the Byer Manufacturing Company. The mother, Ida (Kaplan) Byer, who was born in Russia, died in 1911.

Their son, Moses J. Byer, received his education in the public and high schools of Bangor, Maine. Upon the completion of these courses of study, he went to work for his father, Joseph A. Byer, in the manufacture of lumbermen's clothes. In 1920, the Byer Manufacturing Company was established by Joseph A. Byer in Bangor, and in 1925 the factory

was moved to Orono, Maine. The concern manufactures camp furniture, such as cots, chairs, stools, knapsacks and various other sportsmen's baggage. The wood used comes from the hardwood forests of Maine and is handled in premises which occupy twenty thousand square feet of floor space; machinery mostly is used and thirty-five hands are employed. This company is the only concern of its kind in the State of Maine and one of the largest in the country. The officers of this company are Joseph A. Byer, president; Moses J. Byer, treasurer and manager; Louis W. Byer, M. R. Byer and Harry L. Byer, directors.

During the World War Mr. Byer served with the Forty-second Machine Gun Company of the Twelfth Division of the United States Army. In his political inclinations, he prefers to remain independent.

FREDERICK A. HOBBS—For many years one of the leading lawyers of Alfred, Frederick A. Hobbs has won the esteem and the confidence of his clients and of the citizens of the town and the community, as well as the respect of his colleagues in the legal profession. He is keenly interested in the civic, social and fraternal life of Alfred, and is Great Sachem in the Improved Order of Red Men, the highest office in that organization in Maine. Although he has been busy with his legal practice since 1900 and was a teacher before that time, he has served his country in two wars.

Mr. Hobbs was born in Hollis, Maine, July 26, 1875, the son of George H. Hobbs, of Waterboro, a carpenter, and of Lucy A. (Dudley) Hobbs, of Hollis. His father is now retired. Frederick A. Hobbs attended the public schools and high school, and subsequently became a student at the University of Maine, from which he was graduated in the class of 1896, with the degree of Bachelor of Arts. Then he was made sub-master of the Westbrook High School, where he served until the Spanish-American War in 1898, when he joined the military forces of the United States, in which he was second lieutenant in Company M, of the First Maine Regiment of Volunteers. At the end of the war he returned to his position as teacher in the Westbrook High School. Then he began to study law in the offices of John B. Donovan, in Alfred, and, in the May term of court in 1900 he was admitted to the bar in Maine. He practiced his profession first in South Berwick, where he remained until 1914, in which year he removed to Biddeford, where he was a successful lawyer at the time the United States entered the World War in 1917. Thereupon he volunteered his services, was assigned to duty in the Officers' Training Camp at Plattsburg, New York; was commissioned second lieutenant, assigned to the Quartermaster Corps, and finally was discharged as captain at Camp Devens. He now holds a commission as major of the Reserve Corps.

He is a member of the Free and Accepted Masons, in which Order he is affiliated with Fraternal Lodge, No. 55, and has passed through the Chapter and the Council. He is a member of the Independent Order of Odd Fellows and the Improved Order of Red Men, in the latter order holding the office of Great Sachem, the highest that can be bestowed upon a member of the Red Men in Maine. In his religious affiliation he is a Congregationalist.

MAINE—A HISTORY 365

Mr. Hobbs married, in 1902, Cassandra M. Aspinwall, of Salmon Falls, New Hampshire, the daughter of William H. and Eliza (Goodwin) Aspinwall. They are the parents of one daughter, Pauline Dudley Hobbs.

WALTER P. BANCROFT—CHARLES O. BANCROFT—One of the oldest families in this State is that of the Bancrofts, the pioneer ancestor having come to this country in 1647. This was Lieutenant Thomas Bancroft, who settled in Dedham, Massachusetts, in that year and thus founded the family which has given men of prominence to professional and business circles of Maine. Of the modern generation, Walter P. Bancroft and Charles O. Bancroft, both deceased, were prominent in, respectively, the mercantile and banking businesses in Portland, Cumberland County.

Walter P. Bancroft was born in Portland on May 1, 1846, the son of Jonathan O. and Lucinda (Corey) Bancroft, representatives of two of the oldest and most respected families of that city. The former was one of the pioneer merchants of Portland, dealing in furniture, and was also the eighth president of the Mechanics' Association. Mr. Bancroft received his early education in the Portland public schools, later graduating from the local high school. He commenced his business career as a traveling salesman for Woodman, True & Company, later, with Davis Percey, founding the business of Percey & Bancroft, in Bath, Sagadahoc County, where they operated very successfully as drygoods merchants. He later returned to Portland, where in association with Bricena Eastman, he organized the firm of Eastman Brothers & Bancroft, in which company he continued successfully until his death, which occurred on March 4, 1884. Mr. Bancroft was an energetic and progressive merchant and in the few years he was in business he impressed all with whom he came into contact with his ability and personality. His death at the comparatively early age of thirty-eight years was a distinct loss to his community. He was ever noted for his courtesy in all his dealings, and he acquired and retained the fullest measure of confidence of all with whom he came into contact.

On March 27, 1879, Mr. Bancroft married Lena T. Berry, daughter of Colonel Alfred Lee Berry and granddaughter of General Joseph Berry, both noted shipbuilders of Bath, who had each served their State in the Legislature, and their country in the Maine Militia during the Civil War.

Charles O. Bancroft, brother of Walter P. Bancroft, was born in Portland in 1843. Following his graduation from the Portland High School, he began his career as a banker in 1864, taking a position with the Merchants National Bank of Portland. During more than half a century of active business, Mr. Bancroft became one of the foremost financial experts of the State, whose sound and practical advice was sought by those of the highest standing. When the Merchants National Bank was merged with the Portland Trust Company, Mr. Bancroft was appointed vice-president of the latter institution. He later became president of the Maine Savings Bank, as well as president of the Portland Power and Electric Company. Mr. Bancroft passed away on September 16, 1918, his death being a source of much deep and sincere grief and regret

to the many friends he had gained in his long years of business in Portland and the vicinity.

RALPH R. LITTLEFIELD—Though a native of the State of Massachusetts, Ralph R. Littlefield has been identified with R. P. Hazzard Company, manufacturers of shoes, since 1911. In 1915, he was elected assistant treasurer, which official position he is still filling (1928). The company manufactures men's and boys' welt shoes and is known throughout the country for the excellent quality of its products. Mr. Littlefield is also president of the Gardiner Trust Company.

Ralph R. Littlefield was born in East Stoughton, Massachusetts, July 10, 1871, son of George F., a Civil War veteran and a member of the Masonic Order, who was born in Randolph, Massachusetts, May 27, 1846, and was engaged as a manufacturer of shoes to the time of his death, in May, 1921, and of Hetty R. (Austin) Littlefield, who was born in Holbrook, Massachusetts, June 1, 1844. He attended the public schools of Brockton, Massachusetts, graduating from Brockton High School in 1888, and then became a student in the Massachusetts Institute of Technology. Upon the completion of his technical course he became associated with his father in the shoe manufacturing business, and maintained that connection from 1890 to 1905. In 1911, he became identified with the R. P. Hazzard Company, manufacturers of shoes, at Gardiner, Maine, and this connection he has maintained to the present time. In 1915, he was elected assistant treasurer of the company, which official position he has filled most efficiently, giving to the company expert service. In addition to his responsibilities with the Hazzard Shoe Company, Mr. Littlefield is also president of the Gardiner Trust Company. He takes an active interest in the advancement of the welfare of the community, is an interested member of the Gardiner Board of Trade, and is also a generous supporter of all projects which seem to him to be wisely planned for the betterment of the community. He is well known in Masonic circles, being a member of all the York Rite bodies up to and including the Consistory, in which he holds the thirty-second degree. He is a member of the Benevolent and Protective Order of Elks, of Gardiner, also of the Augusta and Portland Country Club, and his religious affiliation is with the Universalist church.

Ralph R. Littlefield was married, in Gardiner, Maine, September 30, 1917, to Anna E. Sutherland, who was born in Augusta, Maine, December 19, 1885.

ROBERT PARKS HAZZARD is president of two major companies dealing in the manufacture and retailing of shoes on a nation-wide scale, being the maker of the famous Hazzard Shoe, known throughout the United States and foreign countries, maintaining factories in Augusta and Gardiner, where is located the larger manufacturing plant. Mr. Hazzard is president of the firm of R. P. Hazzard Company, which operates the factories aforementioned, and also president of Beck-Hazzard, Incorporated, which corporation conducts a chain of one hundred and eighty retail shoe stores throughout the East, the main offices of which are in New York City. He is among the foremost of public-spirited citizens, having the welfare and advancement of his community always at heart. Although his affairs in commerce are so widespread and require the diligent direction of noteworthy ability without lapse, Mr. Hazzard has this direction so skillfully organized that time is left him for contact with fraternal and civic activities tending toward the improvement of Gardiner, and for frequent camping trips and contact with nature, which he dearly enjoys. He is an ardent lover of outdoor beauty and enthusiastically appreciative of the lore of the State of Maine. In order to facilitate his close association with nature, for fishing, hunting and camping, he has built a number of log cabins. The one near his home at Gardiner, is said to be unequalled in rustic architecture and appointments by any in the State. In politics, he follows the principles of the Republican party and although he has never sought public office, his observations on national political movements and decisions are regarded as unusually sound by his associates, both for their bearing on national and international situations of statecraft and on the industrial life of the United States, particularly as pertaining to the leather and shoe industries. Always interested in the proper development and education of the youth of the country, he served with distinction for seven years as member of the Gardiner School Committee, and by his energy and influence was instrumental in erecting the new high school which was completed during his tenure of office. Mr. Hazzard is a director of the National Boot and Shoe Manufacturing Association, having previously served as vice-president of the organization; he is a member of the National Industrial Conference Board, and a life-member of the National Advisory Council. At one time, he was a member of the National Guard of the State of New York, and during the World War was a valuable member of the Public Safety Committee. His fraternal connections are with the Lodge, Free and Accepted Masons; Kora Temple, Ancient Arabic Order Nobles of the Mystic Shrine; the Commandery, Knights Templar; and Maine Consistory, Ancient Accepted Scottish Rite, having attained the thirty-second degree. He is a member of the Boston Athletic Association of Boston, while his religious adherence is given to the Episcopal church, in which he holds the office of vestryman.

Robert Parks Hazzard was born at Jamestown, New York, April 15, 1869, son of Robert T. and Mary E. (Parks) Hazzard. He received his education in New York State, and in 1887, in his nineteenth year, became identified with the Parks-Hazzard Shoe Company, of Jamestown, New York, a business conducted by his father and uncle, with whom he remained until 1895, acquiring a comprehensive knowledge of shoe manufacturing both as to organization and management. In 1895, he removed to Brockton, Massachusetts, center of the men's boot and shoe manufacturing industry and of allied industries, and there he organized the Field-Hazzard Company. This occupied his executive attention for seven years, and in 1902, he removed to Gardiner, accepting the position of superintendent of the Gardiner and Skowhegan plants of the Commonwealth Shoe & Leather Company. His enterprises thence onward followed one after another: In 1906, Mr. Hazzard founded the Snow-Hazzard Company, in which he was identified until 1910; in 1910, he bought out the Snow interests and founded the R. P. Haz-

zard Company, of which he is now (1928) president, and which during the years that have succeeded has been his principal industrial interest; in 1913, he purchased the controlling interest in the Beck Shoe Company, a large chain of retail shoe stores, and changing the name to that of Beck-Hazzard, Incorporated, became president of this immense enterprise. Without question Mr. Hazzard ranks among the foremost of gifted industrial leaders of New England, and his career is a remarkable example of indefatigable energy and rightly directed ambition coupled with a sincere respect for the rights of others.

Robert Parks Hazzard married, at Brockton, Massachusetts, January 10, 1899, Edna G. Littlefield, and they are the parents of five children: Robert P., Jr.; Ruth, (who died in infancy); Barbara, Katharine, and Elizabeth.

Mr. Hazzard, in 1926 and 1927, finished and equipped a beautiful summer home in Grand Beach near historic Old Orchard, Maine. The house, an ornate Spanish type, is large and occupies a commanding view of the sea, with a suitable ground area beautifully landscaped.

FRANK A. EMERY—President of a granite company at North Jay, Maine, having quarries both in Maine and New Hampshire, Frank A. Emery also is director and president of a trust company at Wilton, Maine. He takes an active interest in the politics of his State and has served one term each as Representative and Senator. He is, in short, an active, sagacious business man, with numerous connections, and occupies a prominent and influential position in his community and State.

Mr. Emery was born at Auburn, Maine, July 25, 1863, son of James H. and Mary A. (Edgecomb) Emery. The father, who was born at Portland, Maine, was in the granite business in Maine and New Hampshire, and the mother was born at Auburn, Maine.

Frank A. Emery was educated in the public school and high school at Auburn, Maine, and at the Commercial School at Lewiston, Maine. His first work was as a telegraph operator and bookkeeper. He started in the granite business in North Jay, Maine, in 1892, and continued in it, until now he is president of the Maine and New Hampshire Corporation, having quarries in both States. Mr. Emery is president of the Wilton Trust and Banking Company at Wilton, Maine, which was organized in 1912. He is a Republican in politics, and served as Representative in 1907, and Senator in 1909. He has also been active on the School Board and in similar civic organizations. He belongs to the Free and Accepted Masons, and the Knights of Pythias, and is a member of the Masonic Club at Wilton, Maine. He attends the Universalist church.

ORLANDO WILLIAM BROWN—Manufacturing, salesmanship, real estate, wholesale and retail hardware—all of these were encompassed in the works of the late Orlando William Brown, who, although a native of New Hampshire, came to Sanford, Maine, more than thirty years ago, and was a prime mover in the progress and development of this city. Fortunate possessor of that rare faculty of foresight so necessary in attaining success in any line of endeavor, Mr. Brown combined his natural talents with study and hard work, and as a consequence acquired a competence in business life that any man might envy. Not content with what he might accomplish in the span of his own life, he built for the future, and his son is now carrying on a manufacturing establishment which he founded in Sanford, the American Specialty Company, whose products are both numerous and widely distributed. One of the oldest business men in Sanford, in point of service, Mr. Brown's advice often was sought by younger men, and his wise counsel also was valued by financial and civic organizations of the community.

Mr. Brown was born September 7, 1859, at Wolfeboro, New Hampshire, son of Bradley N. and Lucillia (Mason) Brown, the father having been a farmer in that vicinity throughout his life. Orlando William Brown attended the public schools of Wolfeboro, and until he was eighteen years of age remained under the parental roof. He left his home at that time to accept a position as clerk in a hardware concern at Somersworth, New Hampshire, and found therein splendid opportunities to obtain the fundamentals of this business. However, he realized the limitations of this position, and as soon as he had familiarized himself with the details thereof, availed himself of an opportunity to enter the wholesale division of hardware. This connection was with the Baldwin Robbins Company, wholesale hardware merchants of Boston, and until 1890 Mr. Brown remained with this firm as a salesman. His territory extended over most of the New England States, and throughout this district he became one of the best known and most popular salesmen in the trade. Convinced that he had reached the heights as an employee, and that he was thoroughly equipped to conduct his own business, Mr. Brown, in 1890, cast about for a favorable location for his activities. His keen insight led him to select Sanford, and soon he was operating a hardware store here. His wholesale experience and early training proved of inestimable worth to the new concern, which expanded so rapidly that, in 1896, he was forced to seek larger quarters. He solved this housing problem by erecting a business block at the corner of Main and Kimball streets, and in the last-named year he occupied the new quarters, at the same time greatly enlarging his stock. This step brought him into contact with real estate operations and believing in the future of Sanford, Mr. Brown built a number of houses on the east side of the town. The wisdom of this move was proved later, when the land was sold at a handsome profit to the Goodall Manufacturing Company, who desired to erect textile mills thereon. The houses on this plot were removed to a section known as Palm Beach City. As his interests developed, Mr. Brown became interested in other enterprises, and organized the American Specialty Company, of which he was president. This establishment was created primarily for the manufacture of steel ladders, but other products were encompassed from time to time, and the American Specialty Company now makes hundreds of other articles. It is under the management of Mr. Brown's only son, and is an important contributor to the growth and welfare of Sanford.

Orlando William Brown married (first) Addie Avery, and they had one son: O. Wendall, who is now treasurer and manager of the American Specialty Company; he married Marguerite Howard, of West Montreal, Canada, and they are the parents of Howard William, born November 30, 1923. Addie

(Avery) Brown died in 1913, and Mr. Brown married (second) Alice Bean, daughter of Luke Bean, of Waterboro, Maine, who survives him.

Mr. Brown was so engrossed in business affairs and such a lover of home life, that he had little time for outside interests, his only exception being his membership in the Sanford Town Club, where he occasionally sought recreation. His death brought deep regret in the manufacturing and business circles of Sanford, and sorrow to his family and many friends and close associates, including the directors of the Sanford Trust Company, he having been a member of their board.

WALTER J. CLARK, Jr.—An ingenious ability that has enabled him to surmount all obstacles has brought Walter J. Clark, Jr., to the position of one of the leaders in the business life of Ellsworth. Mr. Clark operates the modern and efficient printing shop at No. 360 Water Street, conducting the business under the name of Clark, the Printer. His advance has been steady and sure ever since the early days in his business when the first printing press he owned was a crude, wooden affair made by himself.

Mr. Clark was born in Ellsworth, May 27, 1882, son of Walter J. Clark of Ellsworth, and Margaret (Hammond) Clark of Surry, both deceased in 1927. Walter J. Clark, Sr., spent the early part of his life following the sea, but later in life engaged in business, operating a general store, which proved successful during the many years he conducted it.

Walter J. Clark, Jr., received his education in the local public schools and after completing his schooling entered the printing business independently in 1903. His creative ability and a determination to succeed were his greatest assets. He carried on his trade with the aid of his personally constructed press until he prospered sufficiently to afford the purchase of a small Kelsey Press, which he installed and used for about a year. Business increased rapidly and he bought a small Liberty Press and later added a Gordon Press continuing to add new equipment and machinery to accommodate the ever-increasing demands for his work. Today, Mr. Clark heads one of the most modern printing plants in the State, using two automatic presses, small job press, power cutting machines, and other equipment necessary to a business of the higher type. He also operates a stationery store in connection with his printing. Mr. Clark takes an active part in the political, fraternal and social affairs of the town. As a prominent member of the Republican party, he has served one term as alderman in this city and one term on the Board of Assessors. In 1927, he was elected treasurer of Hancock County and previously served several years as justice of the peace and as member of the Republican City Committee. At present he is a member of the School Board. He is a musician of great ability and conducts the orchestra and fife and drum corps, both of which bear his name. He is always in demand for amateur theatricals because of his dramatic talent. In fraternal circles, Mr. Clark is a popular member of Lygonia Lodge, Free and Accepted Masons; Blanquefort Commandery, Knights Templar; Lejok Lodge, Independent Order of Odd Fellows; Wivurna Encampment; Rebekah; Eastern Star, Donaqua Lodge, Knights of Pythias, of which he is Past Chancellor and District Deputy; Bayside Grange; Hancock County Pomona; and Chamber of Commerce. In his

religious affiliation, he is a member of the Baptist
church. During the World War, Mr. Clark was an
energetic worker in every branch of patriotic service, and his drum corps played for the departure
of all the recruits who left this town to enter the
service. For recreation, he makes a hobby of theatricals and motoring.

Walter J. Clark, Jr., married, (first), on November
2, 1904, Marianna Joy Treworgg of Surry, who died
June 16, 1920. Their children are: Margaret Estella
and Velma Louise. Mr. Clark married (second),
on June 28, 1922, Iva A. Walls of Southwest Harbor.

SAMUEL CONY MANLEY—Samuel Cony Manley was born in Augusta, Maine, July 21, 1867, son
of Joseph Homan and Susan (Cony) Manley. Joseph Homan Manley was the seventh in the line
of direct descent from the first William Manley who
was a resident of Easton, Massachusetts, in the latter
part of the seventeenth century, having come originally from Weymouth. Joseph Homan Manley was
born in Bangor, October 13, 1842, and died in
Augusta, February 7, 1905; son of James Sullivan
and Caroline Gill (Sewall) Manley. He was an attorney of ability, active in public, railroad, and financial affairs of Maine, and a Republican member of the
House of Representatives and of the State Senate.
He married, October 4, 1866, Susan Cony, daughter
of Governor Cony, and she died in Augusta, February 17, 1896.

Samuel Cony Manley was educated in the Augusta
public schools and Phillips-Exeter Academy, graduating with the class of 1885, after which he entered
Harvard College, where he received the degree of
Bachelor of Arts with the class of 1889, with honorable mention in history. At the close of his college
career, he became associated with the Maine Central
Railroad Company, first as clerk, later being promoted to the position of chief clerk to superintendent,
and train master, resigning in 1899. Mr. Manley
then entered the public utilities field, in which his
executive offices have included the following: Vice-
president of the Sagadahock Light & Power Company; treasurer of the Kennebec Light and Heat
Company; president of the Small Point Water Company; treasurer of the Maine Farmer Publishing
Company; director of the Edwards Manufacturing
Company; director of the State Publishing Association, and a director of the Portland Publishing Company. At the present time, Mr. Manley is president
of the Calais Water & Power Company. He is
vice-president and a trustee of the Augusta Savings
Bank and a director of the First National Granite
Bank of Augusta.

As a Republican, Mr. Manley has been a member
of the Common Council and of the Board of Aldermen, in both of which bodies he served as president.
He is a trustee of the Cony Female Academy, and
has been a member of the Augusta Board of Education, and of the superintending school committee. His
fraternal connections are with the Free and Accepted
Masons, and the Patrons of Husbandry; and his clubs
are the Abnaki and the Augusta Country.

HARVEY LeROY HASKELL, D. M. D.—The
interests of the dental profession are maintained at
their high standard at Dexter through both the coöperation and the acknowledged leadership in practice of Dr. Harvey LeRoy Haskell. Together with
his war-time record, in which his ministrations benefited the contingent to which he was assigned, and in

the course of which he was given high official rank,
and his service to the community where he resides,
Dr. Haskell has presented ample proofs of his abilities.

Dr. Haskell was born January 12, 1894, at
Dexter, a son of Charles H. Haskell, also a native
of Dexter, who was active in the creamery business
to the time of his death in 1914, and Annie (Rounds)
Haskell, who was born in Exeter, Maine, and survives her husband. Dr. Haskell attended the grammar and high schools at Dexter, and prepared for his
profession in the Dental School of Tufts College,
where he was graduated in 1916 with the degree of
Doctor of Mechanical Dentistry. He started in practice at Malden, Massachusetts, and after a year in
that city, he entered the World War service. In 1919,
he returned to Dexter, where he has continued in
the practice of dentistry to the present.

At about the time that the United States entered
upon the World War, Dr. Haskell was commissioned
a first lieutenant in the United States Army Dental
Corps, July, 1917, and was assigned to the Seventy-
sixth Division. He was transferred in April, 1918,
to the Second Division, Twenty-third Regiment of
Infantry; and receiving promotion to captain, served
overseas with the American Expeditionary Forces in
France for a year, receiving his discharge in August,
1919, with captain's rank; and he now holds the commission of major in the United States Army Dental
Reserve Corps. He is a member of the Maine State
Dental Society, American Dental Association, and
Penobscot County Dental Society. In political matters, he is a Republican.

Fraternally, Dr. Haskell is affiliated with Penobscot
Lodge, Free and Accepted Masons, of which he is
a Past Master; St. John's Chapter, Royal Arch
Masons, of which he is a Past High Priest; Mt.
Moriah Council, Royal and Select Masters; De Molay
Commandery, Knights Templar; Anah Temple, An-
cient Arabic Order Nobles of the Mystic Shrine;
and Delta Sigma Delta College Fraternity. He is
also a member of the American Legion; and Dexter
Chamber of Commerce; and his hobby is fishing.
He is treasurer of the Methodist Episcopal church
in Dexter.

Dr. Harvey LeRoy Haskell married, August 23,
1923, Madeline Daggett, also a native of Dexter; and
they have two daughters: Hilda Caroline, and Elaine.

FRANK HEWINS—Not only is Frank Hewins
an active business man of Augusta, having established
a number of years ago together with the late Charles
Knowlton the undertaking firm of Knowlton and Hewins, but he also takes an important part in the general civic and social life of the city. Having been
a lifelong resident of Augusta and thus thoroughly
familiar with local people and conditions, Mr. Hewins
was chosen some years ago as a member of the city's
Board of Education, of which he was for two years
chairman.

He was born in Augusta on May 12, 1877, the son
of George E. Hewins, a native of Augusta, who died
in 1892, and of Adelaide V. (Pierce) Hewins, also a
native of Augusta. His father, George E. Hewins, who
was a leading Democrat in the community, was a
farmer by occupation. Frank Hewins, as a boy, attended the public schools of Augusta, and later went
to the Cony High School in Augusta. He first
worked in the undertaking business for Charles
Knowlton, in Augusta, in 1900. In 1903 he became a
partner in the firm, which thereafter was known as

Knowlton and Hewins. But Charles Knowlton, who was father-in-law to Mr. Hewins as well as partner in business, died September 7, 1926, since which time Mr. and Mrs. Hewins have been the owners of the business, which is the first funeral home established in Maine. Mr. Hewins has served the community in many ways, especially through his membership on the Board of Education for a period of nine years, during two of which he was chairman of the board. He participates in the work of the Free and Accepted Masons, in which order he is a member and a Knight Templar; and is actively affiliated with the Maine Funeral Directors' Association, Incorporated, of which he is a past president. He and his family are members of the Universalist church.

In Augusta, on October 3, 1900, he married Alice G. Knowlton, who was born in Augusta on October 18, 1876, the daughter of Charles Knowlton, born in Augusta, April 8, 1840, died September 7, 1926, and of Delaney Pratt (Merrill) Knowlton, born in Turner, Maine. The children of Frank and Alice G. (Knowlton) Hewins are: 1. Charles, born in Wakefield, Massachusetts, graduated in 1927 from the United States Naval Academy, of Annapolis, Maryland, who played the violin for three years in the Annapolis Academy Orchestra and was for two years a member of the Bugle Corps. 2. Frank, Jr., born in Augusta, who was graduated in 1927 from the Boston University College of Business Administration, who had taken a four-year course in three years. 3. Beverly, born in Augusta, who was graduated in 1927 from the Cony High School in Augusta, who is president of the Young People's Christian Union of the Universalist Church in Augusta, and who shows considerable talent as an artist.

HENRY PATTERSON WHITE—Editor of the "Franklin Journal and Farmington Chronicle," of Farmington, Franklin County, Maine, Henry Patterson White is a native of Belfast, in this State, born there on July 29, 1860, son of Robert and Eliza (Simonton) White, his father having been well known as a shipbuilder, in Belfast, and one of the founders of the "Republican Journal" of that city in 1829. The elder Mr. White, in association with Cyrus Rowe, established this last-named paper on February 26, 1829.

Henry Patterson White obtained his early education in the public schools of Belfast, and afterward attended the Abbott School, at Farmington, where he established a record as an alert and an industrious student. Upon completion of his studies he became apprenticed to a printer, and learned that trade; then, becoming interested in newspaper work, he went West, and for a number of years was employed as a reporter on the newspapers of Bay City, Michigan. Following this experience he returned to the East, and settled at Rockland, Maine, where, in 1881-82 he served on the "Courier-Gazette." In the fall of 1882 he returned to Farmington, to become an instructor in his old school; but in November of that year discontinued the connection to associate himself with the Knowlton & McLeary Company, in the publication of the "Franklin Journal," which was conducted with success until 1886, when fire destroyed the plant and the paper was therefore suspended. In 1887, Mr. White established himself in a book and stationery business, which he still owns and controls; having met at once with fortune in this line, he continued in its

active management until 1911, when the "Franklin Journal" was reëstablished. The popularity of the periodical in years succeeding, and at present (1928), has been and is due to his editorial direction. The journal fills a positive need in the community, and is read by the well educated and high class clientele to which it appeals through its excellence of comment and coverage of local news. As editor and manager, to his efforts and ability the success of the publication is due, unquestionably. Mr. White has not, however, confined his talent to one single outlet here, but has participated prominently in many different departments of the life of the community. He is one of the incorporators of the Franklin County Savings Bank, and has been conspicuous locally in civic affairs. Although he is affiliated with neither of the major political parties, and is in sympathy with the principles of the Independent, his personal following and the following which accords itself naturally to the editorial influence he wields in the "Franklin Journal and Farmington Chronicle" are such as to give him a considerable prestige in affairs. He has been a member of the Superintending School Committee of Farmington for two years, a trustee for the State Normal School for a similar period, and has served as clerk and treasurer of the Farmington Village Corporation. He was one of the founders of the Farmington Public Library Association, one of its trustees for many years, and its vice-president. In religious inclination, Mr. White and his family are Unitarian, and at Farmington attend the church of that denomination.

Henry Patterson White married, September 17, 1883, at Farmington, Grace Adelaide Gould, a daughter of Nelson and Hannah (Philbrick) Gould, old and highly respected residents of Farmington. Mr. and Mrs. White are the parents of three children, a son and two daughters: 1. Robert F., born March 18, 1885, a lieutenant in the United States Army. 2. Isabel Gould Trumbull, born September 14, 1886. 3. Florence Adams Thurston, born July 26, 1888.

JAMES WILSON BARKER—One of the prominent business men of Farmington, James Wilson Barker has been engaged there since 1914 as a dealer in automobiles, having taken the agency for the Dodge car in that year and having continued it until the present time. He is now in partnership with his brother, Walter Davis Barker (q. v.), in the firm which is known as J. W. and W. D. Barker. This company does repair work and handles automobile accessories and parts, and is one of the leaders among firms of its kind in this section.

James Wilson Barker was born on October 24, 1878, in Fryeburg, Maine, the son of Frank Barker. His father, who was a farmer, was a native of Fryeburg, Maine, while his mother was born in Wisconsin. As a boy, James Wilson Barker attended the public schools in Fryeburg; and when he completed his education, he worked for some years at different occupations, until he finally decided to come to Farmington. In 1914, he settled in this town, going into the automobile business for himself. Since its early days this company has met with success and has prospered, so that today it is considered an important firm in its community. Mr. Barker at all times has shown a keen interest in civic, political, and fraternal affairs in Farmington. He is identified politically with the Republican party. His chief fraternal affiliation is with the Free and Accepted Masons, in which Order he has been admitted to the Blue Lodge and is a member of the Masonic Club. He and his family are members of the Congregational church, of Farmington. In Winthrop, Maine, on June 27, 1906, he married Marie F. Fairbanks, a native of Winthrop. James Wilson and Marie F. (Fairbanks) Barker are the parents of the following two children: 1. Leila, who was born in Winthrop, Maine. 2. Meriam, who also was born in Winthrop, Maine.

WALTER DAVIS BARKER—Identified, as a partner of his brother, in the business of automobile parts and accessories, as well as local distributors of the Dodge machine, Walter Davis Barker, of Farmington, Maine, is one of the substantial younger citizens and merchants of the community.

Walter Davis Barker was born in Fryeburg, Maine, in 1895, a son of Frank Barker, a farmer and native of Fryeburg. He was educated in the public schools and at Fryeburg Academy, at the conclusion of which he became associated with his brother, James Wilson Barker (q. v.), who had founded an automobile accessory and repairing business in Farmington in 1914. The firm is now J. W. & W. D. Barker and does a thriving business, growing with the constant development of the automobile and motor truck, and one of the leaders in this section of the State. During the World War Walter Davis Barker served with the Fifty-sixth Pioneer Infantry.

Mr. Barker married, in Fryeburg, Maine, in 1920, Lulu Shirley, daughter of Arthur and Bessie Shirley. The couple have two children: 1. James Shirley, born in 1921. 2. Marie Elizabeth, born in 1925.

FRANK E. KNOWLTON—Since 1919 Frank E. Knowlton has been engaged in the insurance business in Farmington, where, since 1921, he has been in partnership with Kenneth E. Ramsay in an agency which handles insurance for about twenty-five different companies. In his years in Farmington, Mr. Knowlton has shown himself to be a thoroughly successful business man, and he is one of the citizens of this section whose acumen is highly regarded by his fellow townsmen and by those with whom he transacts business.

Frank E. Knowlton was born in Strong, Maine, January 3, 1892, son of Samuel Francis and Isabel Rhoda (Towle) Knowlton, the former of whom is a farmer by occupation and both of whom are natives of Strong, Maine. As a boy, Frank E. Knowlton attended the public schools of Strong; then went to the high school in Farmington, from which he was graduated in the class of 1911; and finally became a student in Bowdoin College, from which he was graduated in the class of 1915 with the degree of Bachelor of Arts. When he completed his college course, he taught school for a time in Strong, Maine. In 1916, he became engaged in the spring water business for himself under the name of the Knowlton Spring Water Company; but this business had been scarcely started when the World War began and Mr. Knowlton gave his services to his country. Enlisting in January, 1918, he became attached to the Thirtieth Division, Sanitary Squad, No. 28; served on the Ypres front in Belgium, as well as on the Somme front, and finally was discharged in April, 1919. After the war, he returned to Farmington,

where he became engaged in the selling of insurance. In April, 1921, he purchased a one-half interest in the Currier Insurance Agency, in Farmington; and since that time, in partnership with Kenneth E. Ramsay, he has conducted a general insurance business for about twenty-five companies. Keenly interested in civic and political matters of his community, State, and nation, Mr. Knowlton is a member of the local Chamber of Commerce and is affiliated with the Republican party. He also is active in the fraternal affairs of Farmington, being a member of the Free and Accepted Masons, in which Order he has gone through all the York and Scottish Rite bodies and holds the thirty-second degree. He also holds membership in the American Legion. His church affiliation is with the Congregational church.

In Farmington, on June 11, 1922, he married Mildred L. Hardy, who was born in New Vineyard, Maine, the daughter of Austin L. and Lena (Ramsdell) Hardy, both of whom were natives of New Vineyard.

JOHN EDWIN SARGENT—The people of Fryeburg are fortunate in having for their postmaster, a man of the sterling qualities and ability which John Edwin Sargent possesses. Although still a young man, Mr. Sargent has demonstrated to the entire community his remarkable executive capacity and efficiency in handling the affairs of the postal service to the satisfaction and admiration of all. He received his appointment to his present responsible place in the government employ in 1922, having previously served for a short time as acting postmaster here, and the progress and improvements achieved during his régime have justified to the fullest degree the wisdom of the President in appointing him to this high office. Mr. Sargent is popular in all affairs of the town and takes an active and constructive interest in everything pertaining to community advancement.

Mr. Sargent was born in Fryeburg, February 9, 1898, son of Edwin Sargent, a native of Maine, who died in 1906, and of Katherine V. (Bemis) Sargent, born at Conway, New Hampshire, who is still living (1928). Edwin Sargent was engaged all his life in an agricultural career.

John Edwin Sargent was educated in the public schools of Fryeburg and in Fryeburg Academy, from which institution he was graduated with the class of 1917. He joined the service during the World War, and after his return to his native town, entered the employ of Perkins and Pendexter, filling the duties of clerk in this concern from 1918 until 1922, when he received his postal appointment. In fraternal circles, he is a popular member of the Knights of Pythias; Pythagorean Lodge, Free and Accepted Masons; and the American Legion. He is a member of the Postmasters' Association, in connection with his postal work. His political principles are those of the Republican party, while his religious adherence is given to the Congregational church. During the World War, he enlisted in the United States Navy, and served from July 15, 1917, until January 16, 1918, when he was honorably discharged from the service.

John Edwin Sargent married, June 22, 1922, at Lovell, Theona Farrington, born in Lovell, July 29, 1900, daughter of William H. Farrington, a native of New York City, and of Edith D. (McAllister)

Farrington. They have two children: Edwin F., and Beverly Priscilla, both born at North Conway, New Hampshire.

FRANK PERLEY FREEMAN—When he was twenty-three years of age, Frank Perley Freeman established himself in the drug business in Harrison, Maine, which he still conducts with success. During his lifelong career in this district he has fixed himself on a firm basis as a citizen of the highest repute, a business man of integrity and of value to the community. His interests are identical with those of the leading class, ever looking to the general improvement, the happiness and the welfare of the whole population. His civic qualifications have been recognized by his selection for responsible office, while his fraternal affiliations have brought him a host of friends.

Frank Perley Freeman was born in Denmark, Maine, March 22, 1887, a son of William H. Freeman, a farmer, of Fryeburg, now deceased, and of Annie Josephine (Ordway) Freeman, of Gilead, Maine. He was educated in the public schools of Denmark and Harrison and attended for two years the Bridgton Academy. In 1910, he established his drug business in Harrison, which he still conducts. In July, 1923, he was appointed for a term of four years to be postmaster of Harrison and he served several years as Harrison Town Treasurer. He is a member of the Community Church, and belongs to the Free and Accepted Masons, with the thirty-second degree, and to many other Masonic bodies. He also holds membership in the Independent Order of Odd Fellows and in the Masonic Club.

Mr. Freeman married, in Manchester, New Hampshire, June, 1912, Hattie A. Tuttle, daughter of Horace Tuttle, of Raymond, New Hampshire. They have two children: 1. Frank Perley, Jr., born in Harrison, December 14, 1914. 2. Stanley Bennett, born in Harrison, August 23, 1921.

FRANK SHERMAN PIPER—Educators throughout the State of Maine and citizens who have had reason to note the work among the students of Frank Sherman Piper, principal of Parsonsfield Seminary since 1923, accord him a high position as an instructor and citizen. Strenuous though his school duties are, he has been able to avail himself of the citizen's privilege of taking an active interest in the operations of government and in all matters that tend to advance the welfare of the whole people. This interest and activity have brought to him the added work of administering public office, of which he has availed himself to the credit of the community and himself.

Frank Sherman Piper was born at North Parsonsfield, Maine, July 5, 1884, a son of Sherman E. and Minnie C. (Black) Piper. He was educated in the public schools in Parsonsfield and at Parsonsfield Seminary, afterward taking the course at Bowdoin College, from which he was graduated in 1907 with the degree of Bachelor of Arts. His first business was lumber, in which he remained until 1921, when he engaged as a teacher for two years, at the end of which period he became principal of Parsonsfield Seminary, a post he still holds. He was a member of the School Commission from 1916 to 1920 and chairman of the Board of Health from 1918 to 1920. Since 1916 he has been a member of the executive

committee of Parsonsfield Seminary. He is a Republican in politics and from 1923 to 1925 was a member of the Town Committee. His college fraternity is Delta Upsilon. His residence is at Kezar Falls, Maine.

Mr. Piper married, at Gray, Maine, June 26, 1926, Frances L. Cushing.

PARKER R. WAITE is now president and treasurer of the Bates Street Shirt Company, the largest industrial unit of its kind in the State, and which has been one of the established institutions of Lewiston since 1870. The business was founded by Mr. Waite's father, David S. Waite. Parker R. Waite first became associated with this organization in 1898 and since that time has been a decided factor in its expansion and development, which in its turn has had a notable effect upon the progress and prosperity of this community.

Parker R. Waite was born on Bates Street, Lewiston, May 27, 1875, son of David S. Waite (q. v.), who died March 17, 1917, and of Josephine Louisa (Stanton) Waite, daughter of John Turner Stanton, of Norwich, Connecticut.

Parker R. Waite was educated in the public schools of Lewiston and later attended Hebron Academy. He then spent four years in the wholesale drygoods trade in connection with the firm of Bradford Thomas & Company at Boston, Massachusetts, and in 1898, became associated with his father in operating the Bates Street Shirt Company, manufacturing wearing apparel for men and producing only the highest grade and quality of shirts and pajamas. After his father's death, Mr. Waite succeeded to the control of the enterprise as president and treasurer. He directs the affairs of this large organization, giving employment to several hundred workers in a necessary unit of the commercial prosperity of Lewiston, while the quality and high standard of the products which it manufactures and sends throughout the country is a valuable advertisement for the city of Lewiston. Mr. Waite has continued the same policy originated by his distinguished father in factory operation and the highest tribute to the harmony which has existed between him and his employees, is the fact that many of the workers have been associated with the company for more than forty years. Mr. Waite is identified with civic progress as a member of the Lewiston Chamber of Commerce, and in his political views, he follows the principles of the Republican party.

Parker R. Waite married Maude R. Richardson, who was born July 22, 1885, daughter of I. M. Richardson, of Clinton. Mrs. Maude R. Waite has acquired a reputation as a business woman of superior ability, having been associated with the Bates Street Shirt Company since 1908, and is at the present time (1928) secretary of the organization and in charge of the credit department, positions she has successfully filled for several years, and much of the concern's substantial advancement has been due to her keen business judgment and clear insight into financial matters.

DAVID SIMMONS WAITE—Foremost among the industrial pioneers of Maine was the late David S. Waite, of Lewiston, whose death occurred March 17, 1917, a man of vision and amazing enterprise, who founded and for forty-seven years directed the now famous Bates Street Shirt Company. Mr. Waite was closely identified with the business and social life of Lewiston as also was Mrs. Josephine L. Waite, and in all civic activities, his worthwhile contributions to municipal welfare received their deserved recognition and appreciation. He was in the fullest sense of the word, a self-made man, and after conceiving the idea of organizing a concern for the manufacture of men's wearing apparel, he let nothing interfere with the fulfillment of his ideal, giving to his new project all the energy and enthusiasm he possessed.

David S. Waite was born in 1846, son of Major Otis Frederick Read and Mary E. (Barker) Waite. His father was a distinguished journalist and an author of great ability, having at one time been associate editor of the Springfield "Republican" and in April, 1861, he was appointed by Governor Goodwin, recruiting officer for Sullivan County, New Hampshire; served in various military offices, and was actively and for a long time identified with the militia organizations of the State of New Hampshire, a member of the famous Keene Light Infantry, later its quartermaster, and still later, by successive promotions, adjutant and major of the Twentieth Regiment of New Hampshire Militia.

David Simmons Waite was educated in the public schools of Keene, New Hampshire, and emulated his father by learning the printer's trade, completing his apprenticeship when he was seventeen years old, after which he was employed on the "Boston Herald" and with the firm of Alfred Mudge & Son until 1867. In that year, he turned his attention to mercantile pursuits and continued thus until 1870, when he founded the enterprise since conducted under the name of the Bates Street Shirt Company at Lewiston, Maine. The company incorporated in 1906 with Mr. Waite as its president and treasurer. He made the first Bates Street shirt on Bates Street, Lewiston, Maine, and the model factory of today on Bates Street, is the outcome of the style, material and fit he put into that shirt. In 1870, the Bates Street Shirt was a local product seeking a market in New England, while today, it is a standard of men's apparel in nearly every section of the United States, a fit testimonial to its excellence. At the beginning of the business, the chief asset was Mr. Waite's faith in his ability to produce a quality shirt, for style, fit and comfort, and the later demand proved his confidence in himself, causing the firm to seek larger quarters, first in 1874, then in 1879, and again in 1885. In 1912, the business had outgrown all available space in the Lewiston Journal Building, its last location, and Mr. Waite decided it was time to build a home for his creation. The result is the splendid structure that is now a model factory, absolutely fireproof and abounding in sunlight and fresh air. The occasion of the opening of the new factory was celebrated by a banquet arranged by the Chamber of Commerce of Lewiston, Maine, in which prominent men of this city and Auburn participated, as a testimonial to Mr. Waite and to the organization that means so much to Lewiston's industrial progress.

Mr. Waite was actively and constructively interested in everything pertaining to civic well-being and was also a director in the Manufacturers' National Bank, this city, and in his fraternal allegiance was a Free and Accepted Mason and Knight Templar.

David Simmons Waite married, March 30, 1870, Josephine Louisa, daughter of John Turner Stanton, of Norwich, Connecticut, and to this union were born two sons: 1. Parker R., born May 27, 1875 (q. v.). 2. John Turner, born August 12, 1877, died June 11, 1913, who married Inez Gilman, daughter of A. W. Gilman, of New York City. and they were the parents of two daughters: Virginia G., born February 18, 1898, and Josephine Louise, born December 25, 1908. John Turner Waite was vice-president of the Bates Street Shirt Company for a number of years until his death.

CHARLES P. ROWE—A man who followed various vocations throughout his commercial career, was Charles P. Rowe of Springvale, who was best known for his work in the confectionery and candy manufacturing industry in that town. Active in political affairs, Mr. Rowe served his community in public offices at various times and to the satisfaction of his constituents.. He also was a factor in financial circles of Springvale and a conscientious worker in his church.

Mr. Rowe was born, January 8, 1859, in Ellsworth, Maine, son of Elijah and Caroline C. (Brown) Rowe, his father having been for many years engaged as a carpenter in that vicinity. Mr. Rowe was educated in the public schools of his native town, but at an early age began work in the Springvale Cotton Mills. Subsequently he became a clerk and was employed by Edmund Goodwin for six years in the general store. Having thoroughly versed himself in the practices and methods of this business, he believed himself qualified to conduct his own establishment, and thereupon purchased a store which he operated for twenty-five years. While thus employed he operated a confectionery, fruit, and ice cream retail store and meantime was engaged in the manufacture of ice cream and candy. In the last-mentioned endeavor he built up an extensive wholesale trade, among the best known of his products being "Rowe's Famous Peanut Butter Caramels." His productions included also some eighty-seven different varieties of candy. In 1915 Mr. Rowe gave up his large factory, but remodeled a smaller building near his home on Main Street, wherein he devoted himself solely to the manufacture of candy for the wholesale trade. For five years during this period he leased this concern to Cheeney & Turner, who have since conducted the business.

As his interests increased, Mr. Rowe became engaged in other institutions outside of his candy factory, among these being his post of director in the Springvale National Bank with which he was affiliated from the time of its organization until his demise. He was a believer in the principles of the Republican party and took prominent part in local politics. He served his town as Selectman in 1918, 1919, 1921, and 1924, and for three years was chairman of the Board. In this public office he served most creditably, as is attested by the following excerpt from the Town Report of 1924: "Mr. Rowe was a veteran in the office of Selectman of this town and was thoroughly conversant with the duties as well as the needs of the town in which he took an unselfish interest. He sought in every way to have each appropriation expended in the most economical and judicious manner. The regrading of Main Street between the two villages had long been his most cherished wish and he lived to see its completion." Mr. Rowe followed the faith of the Baptist denomination and was a valued member of the First Baptist Church of Springvale.

Charles P. Rowe married Julia A. Hosmer, daughter of Charles and Olive (Hanson) Hosmer of Wells, Maine, who survives him and resides at No. 27 Main Street, Springvale.

Mr. Rowe passed away on December 19, 1924, mourned by a large circle of friends and business associates who realized that in his passing they had lost a sincere friend and an upright and conscientious business associate. Always noted for his ready smile, always jovial, always genial and cheerful, his loss has left a vacancy that will be difficult to fill.

JAMES OTIS KALER—As author of many stories, James Otis Kaler, of Portland, made a valuable contribution to the literature of Maine, having turned out fiction for some of the most notable publishing houses in the United States, and having thereby exerted a healthful and beneficial influence upon his readers, especially the young people, of whom he was extremely fond. He became a writer in the face of great odds; for, over a period of many years, he worked as a newspaper man, writing stories in his spare time, a procedure that he followed somewhat against the wishes of his father, who, himself a hotel man, desired that his son should have a similar career. His death, needless to say, caused great sorrow among his numerous friends in social and literary circles—men, women and children who knew that Mr. Kaler's life had been worth while.

Born in Winterport, Maine, on March 19, 1848, he was a son of Otis and Maria (Thompson) Kaler. His father was a prominent business man in Maine, where he was engaged in the hotel business; while the mother, Maria (Thompson) Kaler, was a woman of sound intellect and good judgment, who bequeathed to her children a happy disposition and habits of industry which blessed them through their lives. As a boy, James Otis Kaler attended the public schools in Scarborough, Maine, but he acquired the greater part of his education through outside means. He had no liking for the hotel business, and, while still very young, went to Boston to find employment. There he worked in a dry-goods store, and spent his evenings in attendance at a night school, where he studied Latin and broadened his views of the world. At this night school, he received his training in journalism and fiction writing. Possessed of a retentive memory, a rapid and judicious reader, he made great progress in a short period; and when he was only seventeen years old, he became engaged in newspaper work with the Boston "Journal," with which he remained for several years. Subsequently, he removed to New York, where he became connected with the "Sun," and distinguished himself as author of "The Perkins Letters." In his newspaper work, he became acquainted with many newsboys and others who were struggling to make their way in life, forming contacts and interests that later had their fruits in his writings and books. It was this interest in the struggles and careers of such boys that prompted him to take an editorial position with Frank Leslie's "Boys and Girls." Before 1880, he wrote his famous "Toby Tyler," which was published in the earliest volume of Harper's "Young People" and subsequently was brought out in book form by Harper and Brothers. It was followed soon afterward by a companion volume, "Mr. Stubbs'

Brother." In 1912, the third book of the "Toby Tyler" series, "Old Ben," was published. An indication of the struggle that Mr. Kaler himself experienced is the tradition that his first book, "Toby Tyler," was rejected by nearly every publisher in the business before it was accepted by Harper and Brothers. An account of his work, written by his friend, R. Hitchcock, appeared in the issue of "Harper's Weekly," for January 4, 1913, part of which gives a notion of Mr. Kaler's work:

In the earlier years of Harper's "Young People," Mr. Kaler was closely associated with the old Franklin Square publishing house in company with artists like Reinhart and Rogers and other of the artistic and literary friends whose company he sought in New York. He wrote frequently for Harper's "Young People"—not only serials, but also stories in two or three parts. Three of these were published last year in a volume called "Wanted." . . . Of the books due to this association with Harper and Brothers—indeed, among all his books—the famous "Toby Tyler" easily takes precedence, but an enduring popularity was earned by other stories like "Raising the Pearl," "Silent Pete," "Left Behind, or Ten Days a Newsboy," and "Tim and Tip." Mr. Kaler was a contributor also to "St Nicholas" and other periodicals, and as time went on the number of his books for boys and girls rapidly increased, until they have reached a total of nearly one hundred and fifty. Nearly all were stories. Assuredly it was no light achievement to have devised so many plots and incidents and to have found such a variety of themes. A few years ago he wrote a series of stories of Colonial History intended for use in supplementary reading. His books dealt with American subjects. They were wholesome and they were interesting. Our juvenile literature is the richer and better because James Otis Kaler has lived. When the news came of the end of this productive life some of us thought of Uncle David's words in the closing pages of "Mr. Stubbs' Brother," and one could almost hear the author himself saying: "He will die here, Toby boy, but it is simply an awakening into a perfect, glorious life to which I pray that both you and I may be prepared to go when Our Father calls us."

Mr. Kaler often said: "Anybody can write a book who will apply himself to it." It is true that writing came naturally to him; and, as a matter of fact, he found so much pleasure in it that he possibly did not realize the greatness of his gift. After all, if his work may be laid to any cause, it can probably be credited to the richness of the life that he lived, characterized by fondness for outdoor pleasures, young people and enjoyable comradeship. A man who was in no way aloof from his fellows, he was sympathetic, agreeable, jovial, true to his friends, and his home life was ideal. For many years preceding his death, he lived in South Portland, Maine, and he had a home on the point of land that stretches out to the sea from that town. For several years he was superintendent of the South Portland and Cape Elizabeth schools, where he found the companionship that he loved and spent his vacation periods in writing.

On March 1, 1898, Mr. Kaler married Amy L. Scamman, daughter of Stephen and Ellen (Dyer) Scamman, of South Portland, Maine. They had two children: 1. Stephen, a graduate of the University of Maine. 2. Otis, a graduate of Bowdoin College. After the death of James Otis Kaler, which occurred at his home in Portland on December 11, 1912, his widow received many letters from prominent publishers characterizing him as one of their best writers. It was recognized that his stories were never sensational, and that many of them were just wholesome stories for boys and youths, pieces that had a strong influence for good in the lives of many citizens.

WILLIAM HOWARD GANNETT—An interesting record of early New England settlers is that of the Gannett family. This family was of England and three of its members came to this country in 1634. These were two brothers and one sister and were among the early settlers. But they do not seem to have come at the same time, for Judith Gannett, aged twenty-six, came in the ship "Francis" and landed at Ipswich, on April 30, 1634, where she lived in the family of John Coggeshall and was admitted to the Boston church on September 7, 1636. On September 20, 1636, she married Robert Shelley, the marriage taking place at Scituate. She was dismissed from the Boston church on July 14, 1644, and received into the church at Barnstable in the same year.

Thomas Gannett seems to have come from England about 1638, and settled with his brother Matthew at Hingham, Massachusetts, and in 1642, Thomas Gannett became one of the first settlers and proprietors of Duxbury, but in 1651, after receiving a grant of land in Bridgewater, he became one of the first settlers of that town where he remained until the time of his death in 1655. He married Sarah Jarmill, who after his death married (second), September 6, 1655, William Saville. After the death of this husband, she married a third time, July 5, 1670, Thomas Faxon. Both of these men were of Bridgewater. She died there in 1697. Thomas Gannett made his will, June 19, 1655. It was proved August 7, 1655, bequeathing his estate to his wife and his brother Matthew, as he had no children. A family of this name lived in England, in the town of Blandford, from 1580 to 1680. It is thought that the name is of French origin, although it has been known in England for many centuries.

Matthew Gannett, the immigrant ancestor of this family, who, as has been stated, came with his brother Thomas and settled at Hingham, Massachusetts, moved to Scituate in 1651 and there purchased a half share in the Conihasset lands of Anna Vinal. He lived in Scituate the rest of his life and died there in 1694, at the age of seventy-seven. His will dated August 23, 1694, was proved November 15, 1694. He bequeathed to his grandsons, Mathew and Joseph, the lands which he had inherited from his brother. These lands were located at Bridgewater, and to his son, Matthew, he bequeathed the homestead and land at Scituate and Hingham. He married Hannah Andrews, who died at Scituate, on July 10, 1700, at the age of seventy-eight years. She was the daughter of Joseph and Elizabeth Andrews. The children of Matthew and Hannah (Andrews) Gannett were: 1. Matthew, who had two sons, Matthew and Joseph. 2. Rehoboth, who settled in Morristown, New Jersey, and died without issue. 3. Hannah, who married an Adams. 4. Abigail, married Jonathan Dodson. 5. Elizabeth, who married a Leavitt. 6. Joseph, of whom further. 7. Benjamin.

Joseph Gannett, son of Matthew and Hannah (Andrews) Gannett, was born at Scituate, Massachusetts, about 1660 and died there August 14, 1693. He is buried on his farm. He married at Marblehead, Massachusetts, August 15, 1682, Deborah Sharp, widow, who was the daughter of Henry Coombs of Marblehead, who died in 1660, and of his wife Elizabeth, who died in 1709. His widow, Deborah, married (third), about 1702, Joseph Howes, of Scituate. She died September 19, 1728. The children of this union of Joseph and Deborah (Coombs) Gannett were: 1. Hannah, born in 1684. 2 Joseph, born in 1686. 3. Matthew, born in 1688, married, in 1702, Mary Bacon. 4. Deborah, born

in 1690. 5. Joseph, born in 1693, of whom further.

Joseph Gannett (2), son of Joseph Gannett (1), and Deborah (Coombs) Gannett, was born at Scituate, Massachusetts, on September 14, 1693. Under the will of his grandfather, Matthew Gannett, he inherited half of the lands of the immigrant ancestor, Thomas, such lands being located at Bridgewater, in 1713, where he settled with his brother Matthew, who had inherited from the same source, the other half of these lands. He died at Bridgewater on April 30, 1774. He married (first), at Braintree, November 21, 1717, Hannah Hayward, daughter of Jonathan and Sarah (Hobart) Hayward, of Braintree. She was born January 22, 1693, and died at East Braintree, September 9, 1731. Mr. Gannett married (second), in 1732, Hannah Brett, who died in 1777, at the age of seventy-eight years. She was the daughter of Nathaniel Brett. The children by his first wife were: 1. Joseph, born March 29, 1722, of whom further. 2. Hannah, born 1724, married Ichabod Cary. 3. Benjamin, born 1726. 4. Benjamin, born 1728. 5. Jonathan, born 1730. The children by the second wife were: 6. Seth, born 1734. 7. Thomas, born 1738.

Joseph Gannett (3), son of Joseph Gannett (2), and Hannah (Hayward) Gannett, who was born at East Bridgewater, March 29, 1722. He was a soldier in the Revolution in Captain Abram Washburn's company, Colonel John Cushing's regiment, in 1776. It is said that he held the rank of captain during the war. He married, June 7, 1744, Elizabeth Latham, born December 14, 1726, and died March 1, 1818. She was the daughter of Charles and Susanna (Woodward) Latham. The children were: 1. Caleb, born August 22, 1745. 2. Elizabeth (or Betty), born 1749, married Nathan Hudson. 3. Simeon, born 1752. 4. Deborah, born 1755, married Adam Porter and removed to Cummington, Massachusetts. 5. Joseph, born 1760. 6. Barzillai, of whom further.

Major Barzillai Gannett, son of Captain Joseph Gannett (3), and Elizabeth (Latham) Gannett, was born at East Bridgewater, June 17, 1765. He graduated from Harvard College in 1785, and preached in various places. He settled in Gardiner, Maine, which was then a part of Massachusetts, and became one of the leading citizens of the country, clerk of the court of sessions, county treasurer, representative to the Legislature, State Senator in 1807, and member of the Congress of the United States in 1809-1811. He was one of the most useful and honored citizens of the section, and held various offices in the Federal Government, and was also a prominent member of the Protestant Episcopal church. He had the utmost confidence in everyone and was popular to an unusual degree for a man in public life. He moved West where he spent his latter days, dying in 1835. On April 30, 1797, he married Elizabeth Farley, who was born at New Castle, Maine, July 7, 1774, and died September 18, 1845. She came of an honored and respected family, and was a woman of remarkably fine character, courage and integrity. The children of Major Barzillai and Elizabeth (Farley) Gannett were: 1. Edward F. born June 5, 1798, died June 26, 1826. 2. Elizabeth L., born February 21, 1800, died May 30, 1836. 3. Michael F., born March 9, 1802, died in 1889. 4. Catherine born August 4, 1804, died February 2, 1861. 5. Joseph Barzillai, born July 1, 1806, died April 6, 1807. 6. Joseph Farley, of whom further.

Joseph Farley Gannett, son of Major Barzillai and Elizabeth (Farley) Gannett, was born at Gardiner, Maine, July 31, 1810, and died January 4, 1888. He married, May 13, 1833, Mary E. Patterson, who died November 25, 1873. There were fourteen children born to this union; 1. Charles E., born January 18, 1836, died July 18, 1867. 2. Eben F., born May 5, 1837, died February 2, 1842. 3. Mary E., born October 27, 1838, died February 14, 1843. 4. George F., born February 8, 1840. 5. Sarah P., born September 15, 1841, died October 30, 1846. 6. Isabel, born September 13, 1843, died January 30, 1881. 7. Addie, born February 24, 1845, died May 1, 1903. 8. Emma, born December 8, 1846. 9. Joseph E., born September 17, 1848, died September 11, 1849. 10. Miland F., born March 23, 1850, died December 11, 1870. 11. Anna E., born March 23, 1852. 12. William H., of whom further. 13. Arthur H., born August 6, 1857. 14. Samuel S., born February 10, 1861.

William Howard Gannett, son of Joseph Farley and Mary E. (Patterson) Gannett, was born in Augusta, Maine, on February 10, 1854. His ancestors, on both sides, were distinguished persons, conspicuous for ability as leaders in different lines, enterprising citizens in their respective communities and prominent in public affairs. His grandfather, Major Barzillai Gannett, a graduate of Harvard College in the class of 1785, made his residence in Gardiner, Maine, and there became prominent in holding many public offices in county, State and in the Federal Government. He was State Senator and in 1807 a member of Congress. His great-grandfather was a captain in the Revolution. Through his mother, Mary E. (Patterson) Gannett, he is a descendant of the Patterson and Howard families, whose progenitors were distinguished among the very earliest settlers of Augusta, Maine. His maternal grandfather, Captain Samuel Patterson, commanded one of the old-time clipper ships and engaged in foreign commerce in the early days of the American merchant marine. Captain James Howard, Mr. Gannett's great-great-grandfather on his mother's side, was the first settler, and so to speak founder of Augusta, Maine, and as commander of Fort Weston in the Revolutionary days, he entertained Aaron Burr and Benedict Arnold when the latter halted his army at Augusta on his ill-fated expedition against Quebec. Captain Howard, leading citizen and successful business man also held the office of judge. Honorable Joseph W. Patterson, an uncle of Mr. Gannett, was a leading citizen and four times elected mayor of Augusta. His great-uncle, Joseph Tinkham, was harbor master of New York City. He is also related to the late Dr. George Gannett, of Boston, founder of the Gannett institution for the liberal education of women, and he is related to the Reverend W. C. Gannett and to Kate Gannett Wells, the talented writer, and also to Henry C. Gannett, of Washington, District of Columbia, chief topographer of the United States topographical survey. His youngest brother, Samuel S. Gannett, also holds a high position in the United States topographic survey. Mr. Gannett is a member of the Mayflower Society, having the distinction of being a descendant from two of the passengers on that historic ship. One was Peter Brown and the other Mary Chilton, famed as the first to step foot on the Plymouth Rock, later became the wife of John Winslow, brother of Governor Winslow.

The education of William Howard Gannett and his progress in business is a most interesting history. The straitened circumstances of his father made it necessary for him to quit school at the very early age of eight years and help to support the family of fourteen children, of which he was the twelfth. But,

while this discouraging condition would have broken the spirit of many a child, it did not deter the progress of William Howard Gannett. Self-reliant, cheerful, hopeful, ambitious, courageous, sympathetic, kind, and charitable, he has, by his own efforts, attained an uncommon measure of success and won a host of friends. He is a man of the keenest sense of refinement and has acquired a liberal education and an enjoyment of culture such as is usually attributed only to those who have had college training and travel. He began work when a young boy as a clerk in a toy and novelty store. Later, in partnership with W. W. Morse, he purchased a stock of goods of the same line and they carried on a business for several years. In 1887, this firm, though continuing the business, published a magazine called "Comfort," which was begun with very little capital but in three years, 1890, the circulation had reached the million mark and the paper was being printed on one of the largest web-perfecting presses. The business continued to grow, and the original plant on ground once owned by Mr. Gannett's great-great-grandfather, was too small to accommodate it. A large brick building was erected on an adjoining lot and later, a fireproof addition was made, and the circulation of "Comfort" reached the figure of one million, two hundred and fifty thousand. This splendid success is due to Mr. Gannett's talent and business foresight. The paper, "Comfort," was designed especially for the plain people and through intuition, Mr. Gannett seems to have known how to reach them in a different way from what had been done, and being a man of courage, he ventured into new fields where others have followed him. He conceived the idea of printing parts of his paper in colors, but, at that time there was no color press in the world that could turn out his paper within a month. So, to overcome this condition, in 1892, he commissioned Hoe and Company, at a cost of $50,000, to design and build especially for him, the first web-perfecting color press ever attempted. The circulation of this paper, "Comfort," extends to subscribers in every State in the Union and Mr. Gannett maintains offices in New York, Chicago, and London, England. While making the building up of the circulation and a business success of "Comfort," his life-work, Mr. Gannett has also found time to be active in civic affairs.

In politics, Mr. Gannett has always been a Republican and has served for two successive terms in the State Legislature. This was from 1903 to 1905. He is a member of the Universalist church, and chairman of its executive committee. He is a member of Bethlehem Lodge, Free and Accepted Masons; of Cushmore Chapter, Royal Arch Masons; of Alpha Council, Royal and Select Masters; of Trinity Commandery, Knights Templar; and of Kora Temple, Ancient Arabic Order Nobles of the Mystic Shrine. He is also a member of the Asylum Lodge, Independent Order of Odd Fellows; of Canton Augusta, Patriarchs Militant; and of the Abnaki Club, of Augusta. He is a director of the Augusta Trust Company, a trustee of the Kennebec Savings Bank, and president of the Augusta City Hall Association.

Mr. Gannett's residential estate is one of the finest places in Augusta. It is called Ganeston Park and comprises four hundred and sixty acres of land partly wooded. The house, situated on Betsy Howard Hill, commands a magnificent view of the city and surrounding country. The house is elegantly furnished throughout in exquisite taste, holding, as it does, beautiful pictures and rare collections of curios and objects of art. Howard Hall, an old barn which has stood on the premises for nearly one hundred years, has been transformed into a museum housing Colonial relics and family heirlooms. This interesting building is constructed of hewn pine timber and, being of the old type of durable construction, is good for another century or more. In it has been constructed a dance hall and a stage for private theatricals.

On October 20, 1878, William Howard Gannett married Sarah Neil Hill, daughter of James Hill of Showhegan, Maine. Mrs. Gannett was born July 19, 1858; she died September 17, 1919. Her great-grand-father, General James Hill, of Newmarket, New Hampshire, was one of the leading men in the New Hampshire colony. He built the first warship at Portsmouth for the Revolutionary patriots and he represented his district in the State Legislature for six terms. The children of William Howard and Sarah Neil (Hill) Gannett are: 1. Grace B. 2. Guy Patterson. 3. Florence L.

EDWIN MOORE PURINTON—A young man who is advancing rapidly in his chosen profession is Edwin Moore Purinton, an educator of prominence and principal of the Maine Central Institute of Pitts-field, Maine. Mr. Purinton was appointed to his present office in 1925, and he has ever since continued to assist the cause of education through his zeal and energy in behalf of this institution.

Mr. Purinton was born in Lewiston, July 6, 1897, son of Herbert R. and Carrie (Knowlton) Purinton. He received his education in Edward Little High School, Auburn, and Bates College. From the latter, he was awarded his degree of Bachelor of Arts, in 1919, and his degree of Master of Arts, in 1925. From 1919 to 1921, he was engaged as a teacher in the West Hartford High School, and also taught in the Wakefield High School in 1921. Mr. Purinton soon established a reputation as an instructor of great ability and thoroughness, and he was next chosen by the High School of Commerce, at Springfield, Massachusetts, to teach there, which he did from 1921 to 1925. In 1925, he was elected to his present position, and is becoming a leading factor in the educational progress of the State. He takes an active part as a member in the Maine Teachers' Association and the National Education Association. In politics, he follows the principles of the Republican party, and in his religious affiliations, he is a member of the Baptist church.

Edwin Moore Purinton married, on February 22, 1922, at Wakefield, Massachusetts, Margaret Anderson, and they have one daughter, Margaret Jean.

LEROY C. TAFT—Through all his business career, Leroy C. Taft has been connected with the woolen industry. Beginning with the Mayo Woolen Company, soon after completing his education, he has risen through several companies to his present position of superintendent of the Madison Woolen Mills of Madison, Maine. He has shown himself to be a man of great energy and constructive ideas.

His father, Arthur L. Taft, born at North Oxford, Massachusetts, has retired from active business. His mother, who was Nellie Dunham, was born at Dudley, Massachusetts.

Leroy C. Taft was born on August 22, 1890, at Quinnebaug, Massachusetts. He attended the public schools at Union, New Hampshire, and later entered Nichols Academy, at Dudley, Massachusetts, where

he was graduated in 1909. He entered Norwich University, remaining there for two years, and he also attended the Lowell Textile School.

In 1912, he entered the employ of the Mayo Woolen Company, at Dover-Foxcroft, Maine, remaining there until November, 1915. At that time he became associated with the Pioneer Mill, of Pittsfield, Maine, acting as assistant superintendent from 1915 until 1920. In 1920, he went to the Madison Woolen Mills, at Madison, Maine, in the capacity of assistant superintendent, and in November, 1923, he was appointed superintendent of the same mills. He has remained in this position since that time.

Politically, Mr. Taft is a member of the Republican party. He is affiliated with the Ancient Free and Accepted Masons, Blue Lodge and Chapter, and is also a member of the Kiwanis Club, and the local Board of Trade. He is a director of the Maine Association of Industries, and a member of the Congregational church.

On October 16, 1916, at Pittsfield, Maine, he married Ida May Randlett. She is the daughter of Charles and Fannie Woodbury Randlett, and was born on October 19, 1890, at Pittsfield, Maine.

ELMER R. BIGGERS—Qualifications of an unusual nature, set upon a foundation of solid educational training through all elementary, high school and university courses, may be termed the basic reasons for the success of Elmer R. Biggers as an educator. Before coming to Guilford he had had a broad practical experience in teaching in various sections of the State, in all of them having been accorded a high rank in his profession. It is with this background of success that he may confidently look into the future.

Elmer R. Biggers was born in Monson, Maine, August 24, 1892. Both his parents are natives of Prince Edward Island. His father is James R., and his mother, Margaret (McKay) Biggers, the first-named having been an engineer. Both parents are still living. Elmer R. Biggers received his early education in the public schools of Monson and was graduated from the Monson Academy there in 1910. He then attended the University of Maine, after which he did special work at the International Young Men's Christian Association College, which was followed by a special course at Columbia University, New York City. His active teaching began in the Moose River High School, where he was engaged for nearly two years. He then became principal of the Casco High School, where he remained two years, then accepting the position of sub-master at Lisbon Falls. He went to Mechanic Falls as principal for two terms, and then to the Rockland High School, as sub-master, where he remained for three years. This was followed by acceptance of the position of Physical Director of the Eastport City schools, and then to the Hartland Academy, where he was principal for four years. In 1926 he came to Guilford, to become principal of the high school and instructor of science. He is a member of the Free and Accepted Masons, of the Order of the Eastern Star, and of the Grange. He also holds membership in the New England Athletic Association, the Maine Teachers' Association, Maine Principals' Association, president of the Piscataquis County Principals' Association, and County Teachers' Association. He is a Republican in politics, and attends the Congregational church.

Elmer R. Biggers married, July 29, 1925, Selma Wilson, of Sangersville, daughter of Stephen and Ruth Wilson. They have one child, Elmer, Jr.

ARTHUR JOSEPH HENRY—Though still relatively young, Arthur Joseph Henry occupies an important place in the life of Rumford, Maine. Thoroughly trained in the profession of law, he quickly won the confidence of the community when he began his practice at Rumford, and to this work he has since devoted his time and attention with complete success. Mr. Henry is also active in the various phases of civic and social life.

Mr. Henry was born at Canton, Maine, on February 11, 1898, a son of Ephraim and Aurilla (Lovejoy) Henry of that place. His father, a business man for many years, is now retired.

Arthur J. Henry attended the public schools of Maine, and was graduated in 1918 from Stephens High School at Rumford. Later he undertook the course of study in Boston University Law School, and from this institution he was graduated in 1925, with the degree of Bachelor of Laws. In the same year he was admitted to the Maine bar and immediately began the practice of his profession at Rumford, gradually building up an extensive local practice.

When the United States entered the World War, Mr. Henry enlisted, serving until the conclusion of hostilities. Politically, he supports the principles and candidates of the Republican party, and at Rumford, where he makes his home, he is treasurer of the town committee. He is affiliated, fraternally, with the Benevolent and Protective Order of Elks, and the Knights of Columbus, and is also a member of the American Legion.

On September 17, 1926, at Rumford, Maine, Arthur Joseph Henry married Doris Cummings, daughter of Arthur D. and Nettie (Richards) Cummings, of Oxford, Maine. Mr. and Mrs. Henry are the parents of one child, Hildred Mae, born February 17, 1927.

CHARLES OSCAR TURNER—The public school system of Ellsworth, Maine, is fortunate in having at its head a Maine educator who has enjoyed a wide experience in the teaching profession, not only in Maine, but in other States. Charles Oscar Turner has been Superintendent of Schools there since 1923, and has brought primary education there to a high degree of efficiency.

Charles O. Turner was born in Phillips, Maine, July 29, 1876, son of the Rev. Oscar M. and Georgia Anna (Hackett) Turner, his parents both of old Maine stock. His father, a Baptist minister, was born in Franklin County, and his mother likewise. Both are still living. Educated in the public and high schools of Farmington, Maine, with graduation from the latter institution in 1896, Charles O. Turner passed to the State Normal School at Farmington, and completed his professional training at Bates College, where he was graduated with the degree of Bachelor of Arts in the class of 1907. His first professional engagement was as a teacher in the schools of Westbrook, where he was assigned to the high school. Two years later he went to Hampden Academy for one year as principal, then to Houlton High School, where he was principal for three years, and next to Warren, Massachusetts, where he taught in the high school two years. His next engagement was in Milton, Vermont, where he was Superintendent of Schools for five years, after which he returned to his native State as Superintendent of Schools at St.

George and Thomaston for one year. For the following two years Mr. Turner was principal of the high school at South Paris, Maine, and for the year prior to his engagement in Ellsworth, was at the Camden, Maine, high school. In 1923 he came to Ellsworth, Maine, where he has since continued to serve as superintendent.

Mr. Turner is a member of the Maine Teachers' Association, of the National Education Association, of the Hancock County Teachers' Association, the Association of the Superintendents of New England Schools, and of the Maine State Superintendents of Schools Association. He is also a member of the Chamber of Commerce, and in his fraternal affiliations is a member of Mystic Lodge, Free and Accepted Masons; Order of the Eastern Star; Lejok Lodge, Independent Order of Odd Fellows; and Arcana Lodge, Knights of Pythias. His club is the Masonic. In politics Mr. Turner has always been an Independent. He attends the Methodist Episcopal church, wherein he serves as a trustee.

Charles O. Turner married, June 28, 1899, in Durham, Maine, Frances Osgood Wright, born in Richmond, Maine, daughter of Dr. Lester Wright and Laurie (Osgood) Wright. Mr. and Mrs. Turner are the parents of four children: 1. Hollis Coates, born in 1900. 2. Barbara Osgood (Mattor), born in 1903. 3. J. Stanton, born in 1905. 4. Christine Hinkley, born in 1906.

DANA H. EDES—For more than seventy years the drygoods house of Edes has been in operation in Guilford, now the oldest establishment of its kind in the county. Three generations of the same family have conducted the business, since the grandfather of Dana H. Edes, the present active head, founded it in 1856. Dana H. Edes is a popular representative of the family, held by his fellow-citizens to be of inviolate business and social reputation. He always has been deeply interested in the promotion of all civic, commercial or other undertakings that appear to be of advantage to Guilford and its surrounding territory.

Dana H. Edes was born in Guilford, on Christmas Day, 1888, a son of Wallis W. Edes, native of Guilford, and Flora (Woodbury) Edes, born in Dover, Maine; both are still living. Wallis W. Edes, who is retiring from active participation in the conduct of the Guilford store, is a Republican in politics and a member of the Order of Free and Accepted Masons, with the thirty-second degree; of the Knights Templar; Knights of Pythias; and of the Ancient Arabic Order Nobles of the Mystic Shrine.

Dana H. Edes received his education in the public schools of Guilford and was graduated from the Guilford High School, after which he took the course at Eastman's Business College, at Poughkeepsie, New York. Returning to Guilford in 1908, he entered into association with his father in conducting the store. In 1893 another partner, in the person of Taylor Edes, an uncle of Dana, was received into the firm. Another store was opened in Dexter, Maine, in 1919, which is conducted by Taylor Edes, while Dana H. heads the Guilford establishment. In politics Dana H. Edes is a Republican, in religion a Universalist. He is affiliated with the Free and Accepted Masons, and holds membership in the Knights Templar and the Knights of Pythias. He also belongs to the Guilford Country Club.

Dana H. Edes married, in Bangor, November 7,

1916, Mabelle Sawyer, daughter of Andrew C. and Ella Pendleton. The children of the couple are: 1. James K., born June 24, 1921. 2. Edith E., born December 19, 1923.

E. DELMONT MERRILL, M. D.—Having a keen interest in many affairs other than his profession of medicine, especially in local and State politics and fraternal matters, Dr. E. Delmont Merrill, of Dover-Foxcroft, has risen high in the esteem of the community. Man of Maine by birth and ancestry, possessed of a fine heritage of patriotism and devotion to duty, he has been honored by his fellow-citizens with their highest expression of esteem, by his election to public office of trust and importance. In other important positions in the gift of the people which he has been called upon to administer he has displayed an ability in full proportion to the charge, his eminence in all of the obligations being unquestioned.

E. Delmont Merrill was born in Dexter, Maine, February 24, 1865, a son of Ithamar B. Merrill, a native of Mainstream, Maine, and Mary A. (Toward) Merrill, of Freedom. His father was in the boot and shoe repairing business in Dexter for many years and was a veteran of the Civil War, during which he served in the Twenty-second Maine Volunteers. The son received his early education in the public schools of Dexter, at the Coburn Classical Institute of Maine, and at the Hahnemann Medical College, of Philadelphia, from which he was graduated in 1886 with the degree of Doctor of Medicine. In July of that year he established himself in practice of his profession at Dover-Foxcroft. During the participation of the United States in the World War he was on the County Advisory Medical Board and a volunteer in the Medical Reserve Corps. In politics a Republican, he was elected to represent the district of Dover-Foxcroft in the State Legislature as Representative in 1926. For two years he served as chairman of the Republican Board, also serving on the School Board. He was for eight years president of the Maine Public Health Association and is now honorary president of that organization. He is a thirty-second degree member of the Free and Accepted Masons, a Knight Templar, member of the Ancient Arabic Order Nobles of the Mystic Shrine, and of the Knights of Pythias. He belongs to the Piscataquis Club, and the Tarratine Club, of Bangor. His church is the Congregational.

Dr. E. Delmont Merrill married, in Dover, November 27, 1888, Lora Dyer, of Dover-Foxcroft, daughter of Thomas F. and Frances (Clark) Dyer. They have one child, Marian, who has served as librarian of the State Normal College, at Danbury, Connecticut, and assistant librarian at Wheaton College, Massachusetts. She is a graduate of Wheaton College and took post-graduate years at Simmons and Columbia University, with the degree of Master of Arts.

FRED A. HEATH has been in business for himself in the town of Guilford, Maine, for thirty years. He has not only been well known as a general contractor, but has also been prominent in public affairs. He has held offices in the town, in the county, and in the State. He has been moderator of the town of Guilford for almost a quarter of a century, tax collector at Guilford for many years, deputy sheriff of Piscataquis County for four years and sheriff for another four. He has in recent years served in the Maine Legislature, and is doing so at the present time. He has also numerous fraternal connections, so that it is clear that he touches affairs at many angles and leads a full and active life.

Fred A. Heath was born at Penobscot, Maine, August 24, 1864, son of William R. and Harriett (Jordan) Heath; the father who was a sailor, was born at Penobscot, Maine, and the mother was born at Dices Head, Castine, Maine. Mr. Heath attended the public schools in his native town and also the East Maine Conference Seminary. After leaving school he worked at various avocations for a time and then started in business for himself. He has conducted his own business as a general contractor and painter in Guilford now for over thirty years. In addition to this, as already noted, he has held several responsible positions dealing with public affairs. He has been moderator of the town of Guilford for twenty-three years, and has accomplished the difficult task of attending all its meetings at which the moderator was required. He has been tax collector of Guilford for sixteen years; Republican deputy sheriff of Piscataquis County from 1907 to 1911, and sheriff from 1917 to 1921. He has been a representative in the Maine Legislature from 1926 to the present time. Mr. Heath belongs to the Free and Accepted Masons, Mount Kineo, No. 109, Blue Lodge, the Independent Order of Odd Fellows and the Knights of Pythias. He attends the Methodist Episcopal church.

Fred A. Heath married (first), at Oakland, Maine, July 6, 1892, Marion Briggs, born at Parkman, Maine, daughter of Philip and Rosetta (Thomas) Briggs. He married (second) Grace Gould, born at Sebec, Maine, daughter of Alman H. and Harriett (Ladd) Gould.

GEORGE H. NOWELL—A few months in excess of the "threescore years and ten" allotted by the Scriptures were given to George H. Nowell. Virtually all of those years were spent in Sanford, where he accomplished works of lasting benefit to the community and to mankind. Here his memory is retained in tender affection by persons young and old and in all classes.

George H. Nowell was born at Berwick, August 30, 1850, and was a son of Samuel and Emily (Hanson) Nowell. His paternal grandparents were Samuel and Sally (Oates) Nowell, and his maternal grandfather, Joshua Hanson. Both the families of Nowell and Hanson have long been well known in annals of Maine, their members having participated largely in general affairs of several centers of the commonwealth.

George H. Nowell's father was by trade a carriage builder, and by vocation a farmer. When the son was but six years of age the family removed from Berwick and established itself in Sanford, where the father continued his enterprises and the son attended the public schools, laying a sound academic basis for a successful career in later life. At the age of eighteen he went to work as clerk for the J. R. Dorman Company, grocers. He learned the business of retailing through experience, liked it, and in due course entered the business for himself, joining in association with Orville V. Libby. Together they controlled two stores, one for the distribution of drygoods and kindred items, and the other for commerce in groceries, under the name style of Nowell and Libby. It was in 1876, when Mr. Nowell was twenty-five, that he entered into this partnership and the conduct of the joint store venture, and he continued actively thus engaged until 1911. over a period of thirty-five years, or until the date of his retirement from the more vexatious problems of mercantile life. For many years Mr. Nowell was treasurer of the Sanford Building and Loan Association. From the time of its foundation he was a vice-president of the Sanford National Bank, and held office as treasurer of the Sanford Water Company, these affiliations comprising the major items of his continued responsibility. He served as chairman of the Oakdale Cemetery Association, and, fraternally identified with the Free and Accepted Masons, was for twenty-five years treasurer of Preble Lodge, holder of the thirty-second degree and member of all bodies of Masonry inclusive of the Temple, Ancient Arabic Order Nobles of the Mystic Shrine. Fraternally, also, he was identified with the Knights of Pythias, as member of Riverside Lodge, in which he was a founding figure. It might appear from the foregoing that Mr. Nowell had been too occupied with business and diversified affairs for religious pursuits, but such was contrary to fact. He was a leader within the First Baptist Church, and was a deacon from 1905 until the time of his demise. For more than thirty-three years, also, he was superintendent of the denomination's Sunday school, 1887 to 1921. Politically active, an influence for the best interests of town and its environs, Mr. Nowell served the town in Maine State Legislature in 1890. His term of office was marked for his attention to the welfare and advancement of Sanford and the farming area around it. Throughout York County he was known as an honorable and upright citizen, and was held in warm esteem as civic, economic and social sponsor of worthy acts, a man among men, fearlessly devoted to the right.

Mr. Nowell married, in 1872, Lizzie E. Spinney, daughter of Aaron and Eunice (Gowan) Spinney. Mrs. Howell survives her husband, and on June 10, 1928, as a gift from her in memory of Mr. Nowell, dedication services were held in the First Baptist Church in appreciation of a new organ and baptistry. She has always been a lover of music, and for years sang in the church choir.

Mr. Nowell's death occurred June 8, 1921. News of it was received in deep sorrow by legion friends. But though he is gone, that which he accomplished in the material, and in the souls of those around him in life, will live on forever, its influence never to be dissipated by aging time.

WILLIAM LEWIS ROBERTSON, civil engineer and public utility executive of Skowhegan, Maine, was born in West Upton, Massachusetts, June 27, 1886, the son of William and Alice (Safford) Robertson. His father was born in New Brunswick, Canada, but his mother, died in 1891, was born in Dexter, Maine.

Educated in the public schools of New Brunswick, Canada, and in the University of New Brunswick, and having qualified as a civil engineer, William Lewis Robertson spent thirteen years in municipal employment in the construction of highways, and then specialized in hydro-electric engineering. while continuing his work in general engineering He was associated with Green and Wilson, civil engineers of Waterville, Maine, in 1903, later with the Canada and Gulf Terminal Railroad Company, and then with the New Brunswick Hydro-Electric Company. On

November 2, 1915, he became identified with the engineering department of the Central Maine Power Company, and was assistant superintendent of the Bath district in 1919, where he served until September, 1923, when he was promoted to be superintendent of the Skowhegan district.

He is a thirty-second degree Free and Accepted Mason; and of all affiliated bodies, and is Past Commander of Dunlap Commandery, Knights Templar, of Bath, Maine, and is also a member of the Independent Order of Odd Fellows, and of the Rotary Club of Skowhegan.

William L. Robertson married Edith M. Leavitt, daughter of Josiah C. and Ellura Stinnaford Leavitt, at Waterville, Maine, November 11, 1914. Her parents were both born in Cambridge, Maine. Their children are: 1. Marguerite, born October 30, 1916, at Waterville, Maine. 2. Jeannette, born October 8, 1918, at Bath, Maine.

HARRY A. FURBISH—Some men, it seems, are born predestined to become leaders in business, regardless of environment; in their case the size of the community appears to have little to do with the size of the man. One such man is Harry A. Furbish, of Rangeley, Maine, born in Lewiston, Maine, March 15, 1867, son of Albert B. and Caroline H. (Young) Furbish, his father having been a native of Hallowell, Maine, a veteran of the Civil War, and his mother a native of Madrid, Maine. For many years Albert B. Furbish was engaged in business as contractor and builder in Lewiston, and there took an active part in affairs of the trade, respected by all who knew him.

Harry A. Furbish attended the public schools of Lewiston until 1880, when he was thirteen years of age. He removed to Rangeley, here to make his home and career; and his first situation was that of clerk in a country store. In this enterprise he applied himself so industriously that before he had reached his majority he owned an interest in it. Soon thereafter he purchased the balance of control, and operated the store successfully, organizing the firm of Furbish, Butler and Oakes, increasing the business until it ranked with the largest in the county. Thus he launched auspiciously into a commercial career, and at the age of thirty-eight, on May 1, 1906, completed organization of the Rangeley Trust Company, and the Rangeley Water Company in association with other parties as founders. Mr. Furbish is president of this large and growing banking establishment, president of the Rangeley Water Company, director of Fidelity Trust Company, Portland, Maine, and of Wilton Trust Company of Wilton, Maine, and manager of the Oquossoc Light and Power Company.

Rangeley is one of the most favored summer resorts in the State, and quite naturally, the hotel business here takes a prominent place among businesses of the community. Mr. Furbish is owner of a large stock in the Rangeley Lake House, the Rangeley Tavern, and Pickford's Camps, and is treasurer of the holding corporations. His principal commercial interest in recent years, however, has lain in timber-lands and lumbering. Land companies in which he is a member own many townships, and their annual cut of pulpwood averages in excess of 100,000 cords. These companies are: The Kennebec Land Company, the Franklin County Land Company, the Kennebago Land Company, the Rangeley Land Company, the Haley-Furbish Company, the Redington-Dallas Land Company, the Furbish Goodspeed Company, and the

H. A. Furbish Company. Mr. Furbish is treasurer of the association of two organizations in the manufacture of lumber; they are the Kempton Lumber Company of Rangeley, and the Stratton Manufacturing Company, of Eustis, Maine. The concerns listed above do not include the Furbish holdings in a number of companies in Rangeley and elsewhere, nor do the names indicate the many organizations who appeal to his judgment in grave questions of finance and commerce. Of Mr. Furbish it cannot well be said that he is one of the most prominent citizens of Rangeley, but rather, more happily, that Mr. Furbish resides in Rangeley and here centers his large commercial activities.

In politics Mr. Furbish has consistently been a Republican, loyal to the party's principles of government, and possessed of a wide authority and influence in the politics of county and State. For four years he served his district, comprising three counties, in the Maine State Legislature, as representative; for two years he served as State Senator. He has long been a member of the Republican County Committee, is now (1927) treasurer of the Republican State Committee, and in the month of January, 1927, was appointed to sit with the Governor's Council.

Mr. Furbish finds time, despite his extensive commercial and political demands, to maintain active membership in three fraternal societies: the Independent Order of Odd Fellows; Blue Lodge of the Free and Accepted Masons, Royal Arch Masons, Royal and Select Masters, Knights Templar, and Ancient Arabic Order Nobles of the Mystic Shrine, thirty-second degree; and the Benevolent and Protective Order of Elks. He is a member of the American Bankers' Association, and a communicant of the Episcopal church. In matters of charity Mr. Furbish deals with large heart; his contributions to charitable and kindred worthy causes whether or not sponsored by the church of his denomination are ever generous and readily forthcoming.

Harry A. Furbish married, at Rangeley, Christmas day, December 25, 1888, Elizabeth M. Porter, native of Madrid, Maine, daughter of Rufus B. Porter.

MAURICE H. GRAY—Since 1917 identified with the textile industry of Guilford, Piscataquis County, Maurice H. Gray was first agent in charge of the Guilford Woolen Company's plant operations and later became agent for the Old Town Woolen Company, Incorporated, when it took over the Guilford Woolen Company, and remained in charge of the plant under the new administration. Now, president of the Old Town Company, Mr. Gray has distinguished himself for the excellence of his direction and his thorough comprehension of the manufacturing problems of the industry. As a citizen of Guilford he is accorded prominence as one of the younger and more progressive men, and is constantly interested in projects for community development. Mr. Gray was born in Old Town, Maine, September 25, 1890, a son of Herbert and Hattie (Brown) Gray. Herbert Gray is a native of Old Town, there attended the public schools, and engaged for many years in textiles. He is identified in a number of civic enterprises, and is a member of the Independent Order of Odd Fellows. Hattie (Brown) Gray was born in Sebec, Maine, and like her husband is high in the estimation of all who know her in Old Town.

Maurice H. Gray attended the public schools of Old Town, graduated from high school in the class of 1908, at the age of seventeen years, and matricu-

lated in Bowdoin College, whence he graduated in 1912, with the degree of Bachelor of Arts, having fulfilled all of his requirements with honor. He became engaged in the textile industry without loss of time, first with the Old Town Woolen Company, of Old Town, and later with the Old Town Canoe Company. In 1915 he became agent of the Sangerville mill of the Old Town Woolen Company, and remained in this capacity for two years, leaving the position in 1917 to accept one similar with the Guilford Woolen Company, of Guilford. Then began his residence in Guilford, and from the first he took an active part in affairs of the town, becoming well and favorably known as a public-spirited citizen. In 1922 the Guilford plant was absorbed by the Old Town Company, and Mr. Gray continued as agent. In 1927 the F. W. Phelps and Sons, Incorporated, of Sangerville, was absorbed by the Old Town Woolen Company. The Guilford mill of Old Town Woolen Company deals principally in the manufacture of fine all-wool blankets; its main office and mill are located in Old Town, and its New York City sales offices are at No. 456 Fourth Avenue. Mr. Gray is president of the Old Town organization; Herbert Gray, his father, is treasurer. Each plant is capacious, and covers a large tract of ground. The Old Town Woolen Company employs from five hundred to six hundred hands the year round in three mills and managed to do so throughout the period of depression which was general in the textile industry of New England in 1926-1927. This reflects to the credit of the Old Town company's product as fully as to the credit of its officials. It is recalled that a number of mills saw fit to leave New England to locate in the South, where conditions of taxation and scales of wages made operation easier in the time of depression; those mills who remained in their strongholds were of necessity the strongest and best established. Mr. Gray has of course given the greater portion of his time to business, but has also participated in communal enterprises tending toward development of Guilford; indeed, his participation in such movements has been wholehearted, frequent and efficient. He is a Republican, is loyal to the principles upheld by the party, and retains a considerable influence in local matters of politics, which he exercises without fanfare, invariably in the best interests of the people at large and the commercial betterment of the town. He is an attendant of the Universalist church, and generous in contributions to charity and to kindred causes of merit, regardless of denomination, sponsoring the appeal, without thought of race or creed, in a spirit purely humanitarian.

On September 2, 1914, Maurice H. Gray was united in marriage with Marian D. Keith, who was born on April 7, 1891, in Old Town, a daughter of Alfred J. Keith, a native of Brooks, Maine, and Hattie (Ballard) Keith, native of Argyle, Maine. To this union were born children: 1. Harriet B., July 6, 1916. 2. Herbert, September 25, 1920. Mrs. Gray died September 21, 1926.

GEORGE H. VILES, of Madison, Maine, bank executive, was born in Anson, Maine, March 2, 1886, the son of Marcellus and Ella (Copp) Viles. The elder Viles was a prominent member of the Independent Order of Odd Fellows, and was janitor of the Anson High School. He was born in Anson, June 17, 1860, one day earlier than his future wife, who was born in Embden, June 18, 1860. George H. Viles received his education in the public schools of his home town, and was educated from the Anson High School in the class of 1904.

He started in the banking business at Madison, Maine, where he was employed by the First National Bank, and continued there until 1907. In that year he joined the staff of the Augusta Trust Company; became manager of its Madison branch in 1924, and still retains that post. He is active in all local commercial affairs, and was president of the Board of Trade from 1921 to 1926, and is a member of the Kiwanis Club. He is a member of the Congregational Church of Madison, and in politics is a Democrat.

He married Lucy M. Salisbury, daughter of Wilbur R. and Julia (Hamor) Salisbury, at Bar Harbor,. Maine, September 10, 1910. She was born November 6, 1885, in Bar Harbor, where both her parents were also born. Their children are: 1. Anita Louise, born March 17, 1912; 2. Wilbur Salisbury, born April 4, 1914; both in Anson, Maine.

JOHN HOUSTON—Learning the trade of dyeing and woolen weaving as did his father before him, John Houston, of Guilford, has been a worthy successor in that occupation, now holding a prominent post in the manufacturing activities of the community.

Born in Paisley, Scotland, August 4, 1862, he is a son of Robert C. and Elizabeth (Leitch) Houston, both natives of Scotland. His father was a color maker and dyer and came to the United States when hs son was an infant, establishing himself at Bridgton and its neighborhood, where he continued to follow his trade. The son was educated in the public schools of Bridgton and Hartland and learned the textile business in Bridgton, Skowhegan and Guilford. Rising steadily, he was appointed agent in Guilford of the Piscataquis Woolen Manufacturing Company, employing one hundred and thirty hands, a post he still continues to hold. A Republican in politics, he was elected to the State Senate, in which he served during 1907 and 1908. He is a director in the Guilford Trust Company and during the World War was Chairman of the Piscataquis County Draft Board. He attends the Universalist church and is a member of all bodies of the Free and Accepted Masons, having the thirty-second degree. He belongs to the Knights of Pythias, to the Independent Order of Odd Fellows and is Past Master of Mt. Kineo Lodge, No. 109, Free and Accepted Masons. He belongs to the Guilford Chamber of Commerce and to the Maine Associated Industries.

John Houston married, at Madison, December 24, 1885, Charlotte E. Taylor, of England, daughter of Humphrey and Ellen (Haigh) Taylor, both natives of England.

RALPH EDWARD PECK, Ped. D.—Veteran of the World War and possessor of two degrees of higher education, Ralph Edward Peck of Bucksport, Hancock County, Maine, was born in New York City on January 2, 1894, son of Edward L. and Emma Louise Peck, his father having spent the many active years of his career as electrical engineer, and his mother deceased.

Ralph Edward Peck received his preparatory education in the Pennington School, in Pennington, New Jersey, and matriculated in Wesleyan University, from whence he graduated with the degree of Bachelor of Arts. Later the Wesleyan Trustees

awarded him the Master of Arts degree in recognition of graduate work at New York University and war service. He was awarded the degree of Doctor of Pedagogy by Gooding College, at Gooding, Idaho, which was founded in 1917 with President Charles W. Tenney as governing official. This small institution then numbered a staff of fourteen instructors and ninety students. When the United States joined the Allies in the World War, Mr. Peck enlisted, in the month of April, 1917. His enlistment followed closely upon the declaration of a state of war with Germany, on April 6. Mr. Peck was captain of Company I of the One Hundred and Sixty-Fourth Infantry of the American Expeditionary Forces, and served with bravery and distinction in line of duty in Europe, being discharged in the month of February, 1919, with a most honorable record in the cause of his country. In Bucksport, where he established residence upon completion of his educational work at Gooding College, Mr. Peck occupies a large place in local affairs. He was a member of the Board of Education of the Methodist Episcopal Church, New York City, as working treasurer of the board for four years, resigning to accept position of headmaster of the East Maine Conference Seminary. He is secretary of the Republican Town Committee, and active in all enterprises, educational, political and purely communal, for the advancement of Bucksport and the good of its inhabitants. Though comparatively young and at the commencement of his career as teacher, Mr. Peck exercises a considerable influence in public matters, and is classed as a leader in Republican politics. Fraternally, he confines his participation to membership in the Twentieth Century Club, and to the membership in three college fraternities, Delta Kappa Epsilon, national social society, and Corpse and Coffin and Skull and Serpent, honorary societies. He is a communicant of the Methodist Episcopal church, temperate in his conduct and devout in the service of the denomination. His contributions to charitable causes and kindred worthy appeals are as substantial as his means permit, and are given in that spirit of sympathy and assistance that is the true humanitarian spirit.

Ralph Edward Peck married, August 23, 1917, at Hagerstown, Maryland, Evelyn Vanderlip Billmyer, native of Shepherdstown, West Virginia, born March 4, 1895, daughter of Jefferson Davis and Phoebe Anna (MacDaniel) Billmyer; and to this union has been born one child: Edward Jefferson, January 15, 1920.

JOHN ALBERT RAND—Serious attention to business, an interest in all affairs of his fellow-citizens and the administration of good government, although never seeking public office, have resulted in bringing to John Albert Rand, of Guilford, the substantial regard of the community and the reward of merit for achievement. His life has been one of pleasing intercourse in both business and social avenues, in which have accrued many strong friendships and a large clientele of customers for his wares.

John Albert Rand was born in Parkman, November 18, 1870, a son of Charles Nelson, of Bangor, and Lucy Howard (Lyon) Rand, of New Gloucester. The elder Rand was editor of the Guilford "Citizen," a member of the State Legislature from 1883 to 1885, Master of Mt. Kineo Lodge, No. 109, Free and Accepted Masons; member of the Knights of Pythias, and of Odd Fellows; of the Grand Army of the Republic; chairman of the

Board of Selectmen of Guilford, and Superintendent of Schools of Parkman The son was educated in the public schools of Parkman and entered business at an early age, in the grocery and provision business. He became treasurer and general manager of the French and Elliott Company, Incorporated, organized in 1910, at Guilford, the other stockholders being Albert F. Stevens, Clara M. Cowie and Edward S. Chase. This enterprise he continues to manage. He is a Republican in politics, member of Mt. Kineo Lodge, No. 109, Free and Accepted Masons. He is a member of the Knights of Pythias and is Past Commander of Syracuse Lodge, No. 89.

John A. Rand married, at Guilford, Stella Gertrude Hobart, daughter of Walter and Amanda A. (Haskell) Hobart.

OSCAR L. HAMLIN—One of Maine's prominent young men in the banking world, Oscar L. Hamlin, of Milo, has been manager of the Kineo Trust Company of this town since October, 1922, being an active factor in the business life of the town and successfully conducting the financial activities of this organization since his appointment. Mr. Hamlin takes a prominent part in civic affairs being particularly interested in educational matters, and in his zeal to enable the youth of this vicinity to receive the most modern and progressive training, has been an energetic and enthusiastic member of the School Board for five years.

Mr. Hamlin was born in Milo, February 6, 1896, son of Edwin M. Hamlin, born at Orneille, and Carrie B. (Livermore) Hamlin, born at Milo, both of whom are living. Edwin M. Hamlin is one of the most prominent men of this community, being an ardent supporter of the Republican party and active in its interests, serving as member of the Republican State Committee, while his business interests are with the American Thread Company of this town, in which concern he is manager of the local industry.

Oscar L. Hamlin was educated in the public schools of Milo, and after high school, entered Bowdoin College, from which he received his degree of Bachelor of Arts with the class of 1918. He then entered the employ of the American Thread Company and was engaged in this work for two years. Leaving the business field, he taught school for a year, being eminently successful by reason of his deep and sincere interest in scholastic work and his splendid ability as an educator and disciplinarian. In 1921, he entered the Kineo Trust Company in the capacity of assistant manager, and he served so successfully, advancing the interests of the organization and attracting new depositors and customers, that in 1922, he was appointed to his present position as manager. He has ever continued to handle the affairs of this strong and growing institution in the most efficient and progressive manner, giving to the citizens of this vicinity, a financial organization in which they can place their deepest trust and confidence. In local affairs, Mr. Hamlin displays an active interest, being always in the lead to advance the welfare of his community and to promote modern improvements which will benefit his fellow-townsmen. His political affiliations are with the Republican party, being treasurer of the County Committee, and he continues to serve faithfully and diligently on the local School Board. His fraternal connections are with the Free and Accepted Masons, and with the fraternities, Psi Upsilon and Phi Beta Kappa, both of Bowdoin College.

His religious adherence is given to the United Baptist Church.

Oscar L. Hamlin married, July 3, 1917, at Milo, Pearl J. Morrill, daughter of George W. Morrill, who is living, and Julia A. (Frye) Morrill, who is deceased. To this union were born three children: Carl M., Robert E., and George E.

JUDGE WILLIAM ALDEN BURGESS, born at Atkinson, May 11, 1874, is the son of Thomas S. and Ellen (Perkins) Burgess. Thomas S. Burgess was for many years engaged in agricultural pursuits, and for sixty years a blacksmith. During the Civil War he served in the Quartermaster's Department. He is a man of high character, industry and thrift, contained of temper, restrained of manner. His regard for the finer things of life is profound, and in them he takes lasting pleasure, never through the long and useful life that is his losing interest in what goes on about him. In the affairs of Atkinson he took a responsible part. Both he and his good wife, who passed away in 1910, early inculcated in their son right principles of conduct and thought, which have rested with him through manhood, and have assisted him to attain honorable prosperity.

In the public schools of Atkinson, William Alden Burgess secured his training in preparation for advanced study, then went to Charleston, Maine, where he attended Higgins Classical Institute, and from whence he graduated in 1894, at the age of twenty years. For several years while he taught school he read of the law, and on September 23, 1897, was admitted to the bar of Maine, Piscataquis County. From 1898 until 1912 Judge Burgess practiced to a general clientele at Sangerville, and in the latter-named year was admitted to the bar of Florida; then removed to Florida, to the town of Bartow, and there practiced eight years. In 1920 he came back to his native State and took residence and offices in Dover-Foxcroft, where he has since been engaged.

Judge Burgess is a Republican in politics. For ten years, at Sangerville, Maine, he was postmaster; also, in that community, for seven years he acted as town clerk, and for five years was chairman of the Board of Selectmen. He has moreover served on the School Board and as Superintendent of Schools. For four years he was County Attorney, Piscataquis County. It was in 1926 that he was elected Judge of the Probate Court for Piscataquis County. Fraternally, he retains membership in the Knights of Pythias, and in the Free and Accepted Masons. While he is a communicant of no church, Judge Burgess is president of the board of trustees in the Methodist Episcopal church, Dover-Foxcroft,. Of this denomination his family are members. Toward charity he is kindly and sympathetically disposed, giving generously to all worthy causes.

On May 4, 1898, at Atkinson, William Alden Burgess was united in marriage with Eva May Morrill, daughter of Elbridge C. and Mary (Smart) Morrill; and to this union have been born children: 1. Thomas Seldon, born March 7, 1900. 2. Wilma Marion, born June 24, 1902. 3. Margaret Morrill, born February 10, 1905. The family residence is on Paul Street.

ALBERT FRED STEVENS—Connected with the firm of French & Elliott, of Guilford, Piscataquis County, since 1911, and since 1925 as member and its president, Albert Fred Stevens has spent the whole of his business career to date in this community, and is closely identified with its many aspects of endeavor, commercial, political and fraternal. Mr. Stevens was born in Guilford, March 1, 1875, a son of George F. and Annette (Folsom) Stevens. George F. Stevens was born in Guilford; indeed the surname Stevens is old in local history. For a period of many years he was employed by the Piscataquis Woolen Company, of Guilford, and served the organization faithfully throughout. His wife, Annette (Folsom) Stevens, was born in Old Town, Maine.

Albert Fred Stevens received his academic education in the public schools of Guilford, and at the age of seventeen years went to work in the woolen mills of his native town. In all this first employment endured ten years, from 1892 until 1902, when Mr. Stevens left it to become associated with the grocery firm of Gelman & Trafton. In 1907 he retired from this connection, and went with T. H. Gilbert who operated a shop for sale of meats at retail; he had learned meat cutting while in the grocery store, and his knowledge of business methods had meanwhile increased, so that the undertaking was in no wise fraught with apprehensions as to its success. Trade in meats was flourishing, but in 1911 Mr. Stevens had an opportunity to enter the firm with which he is now (1928) associated as member and president. He has not regretted the transfer to this day, nor had reason to regret it. To French & Elliott, a corporation under the laws of the State of Maine, he made himself invaluable, soon demonstrating the business ability that then was his in full flower. For some time before actual reorganization of the firm in 1925 there was talk of admitting him to a share in it, and since his assumption to its presidency the business has flourished in a manner complimentary to his administration.

A Republican, Mr. Stevens is staunch in support of the principles of the party in all applications, National, State and communal. He owns a considerable voice in local political questions, and exercises it, but quietly, without ostentation, and always to the best effects favorable to Guilford and vicinity. He is a member of several secret orders, including Mt. Kineo Lodge of the Free and Accepted Masons, and the Knights of Pythias. He is also a member of Valley Grange, as he has been concerned in husbandry for several years and is equally concerned in agricultural problems; and of the Pythian Sisterhood. Although he was somewhat advanced in years for service in the military during the World War, Mr. Stevens did serve on the various local boards and committees in charge of prosecuting the war from within this country, and took part in the several Liberty Loan campaigns. He is a communicant of the Methodist church, is devout in its service, and generous in contributions to charity, regardless of race or creed whence the appeal may come. Of him it is said by those who know him well, that he is industrious, kind, firm in his opinions but ready to alter them when presented with evidence, honorable in all his dealings, and a valuable member of the Guilford community.

Albert Fred Stevens married (first), in Guilford, June 10, 1897, and (second), in Lisbon Falls, Maine, June 22, 1926. His marriage with Angie Lewis, born in Sangerville, Maine, December 31, 1879, daughter of Charles and Addie (Johnson) Lewis, both natives of Sangerville, came to an untimely close on July 19, 1924, with the death of his beloved wife. One child

was born to him by his first marriage, a daughter, Elva A., who is now Mrs. Elva A. Palmer.

GEORGE CLEMENT LORD (2)—In the marvelous strides made by the Pine Tree State in the past half-century, she owes much to the family of Lord, members of which have contributed in a marked manner to her industrial, political and agricultural advance. In this grouping is placed George Clement Lord, owner and operator of "Laudholm Farms," at Wells, a leading member of the State Senate, a former representative in the Lower House at Augusta, for a number of years a member of the Wells town government, and a widely known expert cattle breeder. Another distinguished representative of the family was the late George Clement Lord, grandfather of George Clement (2), who was one of the foremost transportation chiefs of New England in his day, president of the Boston & Maine Railroad corporation, executive of a leading fire insurance corporation, shipping head and manager of a fleet of vessels which found their way into waters of every sea.

Born in Kennebunk, February 27, 1823, a son of George and Olive (Jefferds) Lord, George Clement Lord (1) was a grandson of Lieutenant Tobias and Hephzibah Conant (the latter the daughter of Roger Conant, governor of the Massachusetts Colony) Lord. His father, George Lord, son of Lieutenant Tobias Lord, was master of the brig "Alliance." He retired from a seafaring life and settled in Kennebunk, and engaged in the shipping business in 1817 in association with Ivory Lord, under the style of G. & I. Lord. He married, April 22, 1816, Olive Jefferds. George Clement Lord (1), after his preliminary studies in the Kennebunk schools, entered Dummer Academy, Byfield, Massachusetts, from which he was graduated in 1838.

The year following his graduation from the academy, he began his business career, which was to eventuate in such close connection with the development of the natural resources and industrial enterprises of the State. His first essay in the business world was in the wholesale drygoods house of Holbrook, Bourgoyne & Company in Boston. In 1843 he transferred his interest to the wholesale grocery business, becoming a member of the firm of Dymond, Howe & Company, which in 1846 was changed to Howe & Lord. In the following year he formed a co-partnership with his brother, Charles H. Lord, naming the organization George C. Lord & Company, engaging in the shipping business and the building of a fleet of vessels which they managed. He continued to attain prominence in the business world. In 1865 he was elected president of the New England Mutual Fire and Marine Insurance Company. In 1866 he was made a director of the Boston & Maine Railroad Company, and in 1880 was advanced to vice-president. In 1880 he was elevated to president of the Boston & Maine system, and during his régime of eight years, and due to his able management, the trackage of the company increased from two hundred and two miles to 1,210 miles. It was during his term of office also that the extension of the Boston & Maine from South Berwick to Portland was accomplished, and that the Eastern and the Boston & Lowell railroads were merged with the Boston & Maine.

George Clement Lord (1) married, on September 22, 1846, Marion R. Waterson, and to them were born three children: 1. Robert Waterston. 2. Marion Ruthven. 3. Charles Edward, born at Newton, Massachusetts, March 29, 1858; married Effie Marion Rogers, daughter of Charles Frederick and Caroline Rogers, of Newton, and had a son, George Clement (2).

George Clement Lord (2), son of Charles Edward and Effie Marion (Rogers) Lord, was born in Newton, Massachusetts, June 12, 1889, and received his education at the grammar school of his native city, Dummer Academy at Byfield and Phillips-Andover Academy.

For five years Mr. Lord was connected with the Bates Manufacturing Company at Lewiston, but because of ill health he was compelled to abandon the idea of pursuing a strictly business career. He returned to the old homestead farm at Wells, and since 1916 he has given his attention to the specialty of breeding thoroughbred Guernsey cattle and to general farming. His "Laudholm Farms" are one of the showplaces of the countryside and a model of modern scientific agriculture.

The town of Wells in having a citizen of the progressive type as Mr. Lord in its midst has often availed itself of its good fortune. First it elected him a member of the Board of Selectmen, where it has retained his services for six years, and the town government has benefited in appreciable degree from his administrative ability and sound judgment. Then his district chose him as its representative in the Legislature for the session of 1923-1924. Further honors were accorded him by advancing him to the State Senate for the term of 1925-26 and reëlecting him for the term of 1927-28, where he was made chairman of the Committee on Publicity. He is the leading Republican of his community and holds the office of chairman of the Republican Town Committee, and is a trustee of the Wells Water Supply.

The organized interests of the cattle breeders of his district are carefully fostered and protected by Mr. Lord, who is president of the York County Breeders Association. He is one of the most enthusiastic farmers in the State, who gives much time and thought to the affairs of those similarly engaged. As a member of the Farm Bureau and the local Grange of the Patrons of Husbandry he finds agreeable channels for the direction of his energy to serve the farmers' interests. During the World War he rendered a fine patriotic service along the lines of civilian war work, and held the office of registrar under the Selective Service Act. Highly placed in the Masonic Order, he affiliates with the Portland Consistory, thirty-second degree Scottish Rite; High Pine Lodge, Free and Accepted Masons; Murray Chapter, Royal Arch Masons; Kennebunk Commandery, Knights Templar; and Korea Temple, Ancient Arabic Order Nobles of the Mystic Shrine.

George Clement Lord (2) married, January 27, 1912, Mary Adam Jones, daughter of Nathaniel N. and Jennie (Davis) Jones, her father a judge of the United States Circuit Court for Massachusetts. Mr. and Mrs. Lord are the parents of three children. 1. Charles Edward (2). 2. Nathaniel Nelson. 3. Mary Waterston.

BERT H. YOUNG—As a postmaster, Bert H. Young, of Bar Harbor has filled his position to the satisfaction of merchants and citizens. His father is John F. Young, of Southwest Harbor, Maine, and his mother Geneva (Robinson) Young, a native of Southwest Harbor, Maine. His father is by trade a blacksmith.

Bert H. Young was born at Millbridge, Maine, on February 1, 1884. His education began in the public schools of Southwest Harbor and then he attended high school in Bar Harbor and finished in the University of Maine. On the completion of his education, he went to work for W. H. Davis of Bar Harbor in the business of carriage building. He was in this position for eight years and in 1913, he bought out the business and changed its character to an automobile business, carrying it on under the name of Davis Bar Harbor Buckboard Company. He operated a garage in connection with his business and continued to handle it as a whole until 1922 when he was appointed postmaster of Bar Harbor, which office he continues to hold. His fraternities are the Bar Harbor Lodge, Independent Order of Odd Fellows; Mount Desert Encampment; he is a Past Master of the Bar Harbor Lodge of Free and Accepted Masons; Mount Kebo Chapter, Royal Arch Masons, of which he is a Past High Priest; Blanquefort Commandery, Knights Templar; and Anah Temple, Ancient Accepted Order Nobles of the Mystic Shrine. For three years he was a director of the Bar Harbor Board of Trade; he is a member of the Masonic Club and the Kebo Golf Club. He is a director of the Bar Harbor Banking and Trust Company and president of B. H. Young Company, Incorporated. He is a Republican in politics and served two years as a selectman of Bar Harbor and one year was chairman of the board. He was for several years a member of the Republican Town Committee. His pastime is spent in fishing or playing golf, of both of which sports he is very fond.

In 1905, Bert H. Young married Florence Davis of Bar Harbor, Maine. They attend the Unitarian church.

ELMER D. BENNETT—For more than twenty years, Elmer D. Bennett engaged as a contractor, plumber and steamfitter, at Sanford, Maine, and in this work his industry and skill brought him great success. But Mr. Bennett's place in the business world, important as it was, could not begin to measure the extent of his participation in the life of the community. It seemed almost as if no movement, civic or social, was entirely successful without his active support, while as a musician his services were constantly in demand in all parts of the State.

Mr. Bennett was born in Sanford, February 12, 1869, a son of Bradford S. and Etta (Emery) Bennett, and a grandson of Captain Horace Bennett, a pioneer farmer of South Sanford, and of Sally (Haslum) Bennett. Bradford D. Bennett was born in Sanford, March 25, 1844. A shoe worker by trade, he was also an accomplished musician, and extremely popular in the community which mourned his death at the early age of thirty-six, on June 25, 1880.

Elmer D. Bennett was educated in the local schools, after which he took up, and became proficient in, the plumbing trade. When he was only twenty-four years old, he established his own business on Mechanic Street, Sanford, continuing this enterprise until the time of his death, on April 12, 1915. The excellence of his work and the high quality of his materials gained him a large and prosperous business, as well as a wide reputation in Sanford. In addition to this work, he was superintendent of the Sanford Water Works Company for nearly twenty years.

Mr. Bennett inherited from his father great musical talent, and for thirty years he was actively connected with various musical organizations in Sanford. He had studied the trombone under Professor Collins, of Portland, Maine, and was considered to be the finest slide trombone player and soloist in the State. Mr. Bennett also played the bass viol and cello, and gave instruction in the playing of all band instruments. For many years he was a member of Chandler's band and orchestra of Portland, traveling with these organizations into all parts of the State.

Mr. Bennett served two enlistments in the Sixth Company, Coast Artillery Corps, of the State Militia. He was affiliated, fraternally, with the Independent Order of Odd Fellows, in which organization he was a member of Friendship Lodge and Moreh Encampment, and he was also a member of the Knights of Pythias, and of Mousam Lake Tent of the Knights of the Maccabees, and Red Men. He worshipped in the faith of the Congregational church.

Elmer D. Bennett married Georgie E. Clifford, daughter of George Henry Clifford of North Conway, New Hampshire, and he became the father of two children: 1. Lena, who married William A. Garnsey, employed in the Sanford plush mills. 2. Elmer Clifford, born in Sanford, August 12, 1906. He attended the public schools of his birthplace, and when he completed his education, entered the employ of the Cumberland County Light and Power Company. Industrious and affable, possessing great personal warmth and charm, he has proved himself already, a business man of the finest progressive type, rising in his company, solely through his own energy and ability, to positions of confidence and trust.

Mr. Bennett's death was the occasion of great sorrow in Sanford. It had seemed that he might be spared for many more years of usefulness and service, and it is impossible to speak with any adequacy of the desolate sense of loss wihch attended his passing. The memory of the man, however, and of his work, will long remain an inspiration in the hearts of those who knew him.

CARROLL S. DOUGLASS — Counted high among the substantial business men of Guilford, leading manufacturer, associated with its financial institutions, a good churchman and member of many fraternal organizations, Carroll S. Douglass has won success at an early period of life.

He is a son of Henry and Ellen (Ellis) Douglass, both natives of Guilford. The elder Douglass was himself a Mason of high degree and, in business, treasurer of the Piscataquis Woolen Manufacturing Company. He died in Guilford in 1907. Carroll S. Douglass was educated in the public schools of Guilford, at the high school of Guilford and at the Comers Commercial School, of Boston, from which he was graduated with the class of 1897. He became associated with the Piscataquis Woolen Company in 1908 as a director and in 1915 was elected treasurer of the company, a post he continues to administer. He attends the Universalist Church and is a Republican in politics. He is a member of the Guilford Chamber of Commerce and a thirty-second degree Mason, holding all badges. He is a member of the Ancient Arabic Order Nobles of the Mystic Shrine, a Knight Templar, Past Master of Mt. Kineo Lodge, No. 109, and Past Junior Grand Warden of the Grand Lodge

of Maine, Free and Accepted Masons. He also belongs to the Knights of Pythias and is a director in the Guilford Trust Company.

Carroll S. Douglass married, February 12, 1902, at Guilford, Annie L. French, of Parkman, daughter of John E., of Parkman, and Agnes (Cousins) French, of Guilford. Their children are: 1. George H., born October 16, 1905. 2. Louise C., born February 8, 1907.

WASHINGTON I. PARTRIDGE—A record of more than forty years of service to the pharmaceutical needs of the community is that of Washington I. Partridge, who owns and operates the only drug business in Blue Hill. A good, reliable pharmacy is not only a necessity but an asset to any locality, and Mr. Partridge's store has always received the trust and approbation of his fellow-citizens.

Mr. Partridge was born in Orland, August 9, 1858, son of Ellison L. Partridge, and Sarah Anne (Cotton) Partridge, both of Orland and who are now both deceased. Ellison L. Partridge was actively engaged in the livery business until his death. Washington I. Partridge received his education in the local public schools, and after high school, entered the Eastern Maine Conference Seminary. Upon the completion of his studies there, he entered the drug business in Blue Hill in 1879, where he worked for three years when he went to Boston with A. G. Wilbur for a year and a half, gaining much valuable experience in that time. Returning to Blue Hill in 1884, he associated himself with Benjamin Morrell in the pharmacy business and commenced a successful partnership which existed until 1889, when it was dissolved. After that time, Mr. Partridge continued in the business independently, winning the confidence and esteem of the people and a high reputation for the quality and careful preparation of his products, which has ever remained with him. Today, the only pharmacist in the town, he receives the respect of the entire community which appreciates his long career of service to the public. In fraternal circles, Mr. Partridge has always taken an active interest, and is a member of Ira Berry Lodge, Free and Accepted Masons, and a member of the Ancient Order of United Workmen. In his political views, he is a follower of the Republican party, and in religion, he is an attendant of the Congregational church.

Washington I. Partridge married, in 1880, Elizabeth L. Peters, of Blue Hill, and their children are: Abbie Elizabeth, who was the first lady to enlist in the Naval Reserve, serving all through the war at Bar Harbor and Great Lakes, was secretary of Commander at the Great Lakes; and Myrtle, who is deceased.

RALPH HEMENWAY MARSH, M. D., is a physician and surgeon practicing at Guilford, Maine. He has been in practice for something like thirty-four years, and of that time all but a year has been spent in Guilford. He is consequently one of the best-known physicians in the vicinity. His experience too has been varied. He held an official medical post during the World War. He received his training in two noted schools. His social connections are large from his connections with numerous organizations, fraternal, and professional. His family has grown into the third generation, so that he occupies an established position with a large clientele which has grown up around him as the result of years of

386MAINE—A HISTORY

effort and of help and counsel his skill and experience have enabled him to extend.

Ralph Hemenway Marsh was born at Greenville, Maine, February 3, 1863, son of Martin V. B. and Celia Paulina (Foss) Marsh, the father born at Cornville, Maine, and the mother at Brighton, Maine, and belonged to the Free and Accepted Masons, Lodge Star of the East. Dr. R. H. Marsh attended the public school at Bradley, Maine. He then went to the Maine State College, graduating in the class of 1888 with the degree of Bachelor of Science. After that he was a student of Bowdoin Medical School, receiving his degree of Doctor of Medicine in 1893. In that year he started medical practice at Lincoln, Maine. But he stayed at Lincoln only for about a year. In 1894 he started general practice and surgery at Guilford, Maine, and he has been settled in that town and has there continued in practice to the present time. During the war Dr. Marsh was on the Medical Advisory Board, District No. 10. He is a Republican in politics. He was formerly town treasurer for Guilford, and has always taken a keen interest in public affairs. He was a member of the School Board for a period of fifteen years. He is now county medical examiner for Piscataquis County, and special pension examiner for the same county. He belongs to the American, State and County Medical associations. He is past president of the Maine Medical Association. He belongs also to the Independent Order of Odd Fellows, and the Free and Accepted Masons, Mt. Kineo Lodge, No. 109, thirty-second degree, all bodies. He is a member also of the Piscataquis Valley Country Club. He is a member of the First Universalist Church.

Dr. Ralph H. Marsh married at Bradley, Maine, October 6, 1888, Myrtie Alice Holbrook, born at Bradley, Maine, June 5, 1866, daughter of Reuben and Mary Ann (Banks) Holbrook; the father was born at Plymouth, Maine, and the mother at Old Orchard, Maine. Children: 1. Helen Celia, born at Bradley, Maine, who married Bertram Arthur Loane, born in Canada, and they are the parents of two children: Marsh McBurney, born at Guilford, Maine; Ruth Ann, born at Fort Fairfield, Maine. 2. Alice Holbrook, born at Guilford, Maine.

NORMAN SHAW—The junior partner of the law firm of Wood and Shaw, of Bar Harbor, Maine, is Norman Shaw the son of Frank and Sarah F. (Allen) Shaw. His father, a native of Gouldsboro, Maine, has always been interested in farming and the hotel business, being proprietor of a hotel. His mother is a native of Maine.

Norman Shaw was born at Bar Harbor, Maine, on March 6, 1892, and had his early schooling in the public schools of his birthplace. He then attended Higgins Classical Institute and spent one year at Dartmouth College. From there he went to the University of Maine where he went in the law school for two years and then he transferred to the Boston University where he continued the study of law and graduated in the class of 1921. After finishing at the Boston University he went into the hotel business with his father and remained in this line of occupation until 1923 when he was admitted to the bar of the State of Maine. He then became a member of the firm of Wood and Shaw and has continued in the practice of law ever since. He is a member of the Hancock County Bar Association, the Maine State Bar Association, and the American Bar Association. He is a member of the Sigma Chi Fraternity, and the Phi Beta Phi Fraternity, the Bar Harbor Lodge, Free and Accepted Masons; the Mount Kebo Chapter, Royal Arch Masons; Island Lodge, Independent Order of Odd Fellows, Mount Desert Encampment; he is a Past Commander of the American Legion; a member of the Société 40 hommes et 8 chevaux; also a member of the Bar Harbor Board of Trade and the Masonic Club. He is a Republican in politics and a member of the Board of Selectman and the Republican Town Committee. During the World War he served with the Three Hundred and Third Field Artillery Corps and was nine months in France with the American Expeditionary Forces, being in the defensive center of the battles of the Marne and the Argonne. He is very fond of all outdoor sports and participates in such recreation whenever business admits. He attends the Congregational church.

In 1926, Norman Shaw married Erma V. Stafford, of Bar Harbor, Maine. They are the parents of one son, Norman P. Shaw, born April 20, 1928.

FRED RAY HUNTINGTON is a prominent business man of Guilford, Maine. He is at present the owner of an establishment including a garage and automobile repair shop, that deals also in radio supplies and automobile accessories. Back of this he has had a varied business experience. He was for three years in the lumber business. Then he was with a firm of electrical contractors and did other kinds of work. He had the management of a garage, which finally led him to the establishment of one of his own in Guilford, which he has steadily developed during the seven or eight years he has been managing it.

Fred Ray Huntington was born at Bradford, Maine, May 1, 1884, son of Fred W. and Nellie (Church) Huntington, the father born at Bradford, where he was a lumberman and worked in the mills. Fred Ray Huntington attended the public and high schools in his native town, and then went to work. He first went with his uncle, Ernest ·Huntington, in the lumber business at Bradford, and was engaged in that for three years. He then became an employee of the Amos Abbott Company at Dexter, Maine, and remained there for a period of two years. After that he was with the E. D. Blaisdell firm, electrical contractors, at Dexter, Maine, and acted as foreman there until 1917. Then for a year he worked and operated the garage of H. D. Simons at Madison, Maine. In 1919 he himself opened a garage and repair shop at Guilford, Maine, and in course of time added side lines to it, including auto accessories and radio supplies. This business is known as the Huntington Garage. Mr. Huntington is a Republican in politics. He belongs to the Free and Accepted Masons, Penobscot No. 29, Blue Lodge. He attends the Methodist church.

Fred R. Huntington married, at Bradford, Maine, Myrtle L. Cunningham, born at Prospect, Maine, daughter of Fred and Cora (Hobbs) Cunningham, of whom the father isnow deceased.

REV. FRANK C. POTTER — United with the Methodist Episcopal church while a young man, Frank C. Potter, of Portland, received the call to the pulpit in his youth and when only twenty years of age preached his first sermon to a small congregation in the suburbs of New Haven, Connecticut. He was by nature very intense and enthusiastic and he worked with a zeal that carried him beyond his strength and, finally, resulted in a breakdown. He served in many charges in this State and is lovingly remembered by those he aided and assisted by his kindly encouragement and advice in their times of trouble and distress.

Mr. Potter was born in North Bridgton, Cumberland County, April 25, 1868, the son of Elbridge and Mary H. (Newbegin) Potter, the former a son of Captain John Fowler, of fame in the days of the old Militia, and the latter a native of Parsonsfield, York County. The grandfather of Mr. Potter was one of the foremost residents of Bridgton, and occupied many offices of trust and responsibility in that town's civic offices. The education of Mr. Potter was received in the common schools of Bridgton and in Bridgton Academy, from which latter institution he graduated in 1885. After the close of his scholastic terms he spent some three years in mercantile pursuits and in the offices of the New York, New Haven & Hartford Railroad at New Haven, Connecticut. He received what he felt was a call to the work of the Church while sitting under the ministry of Rev. J. O. Peck, a noted Doctor of Divinity, who at that time occupied a pulpit in the Trinity Methodist Episcopal Church at New Haven. His earnestness made a deep impression on the officials of the Church and they finally waited upon Mr. Potter with the announcement that they felt he was fitted for the ministry and ought to take out his license as a local preacher. This license was issued to him during the pastorate of Rev. George H. Reed, Doctor of Divinity, and under the presiding eldership of Rev. John W. Beach, Doctor of Divinity, who afterwards became president of the Wesleyan University. After preaching his first sermon in the outskirts of New Haven, Mr. Potter returned to his home in Bridgton, and for several years supplied at Stowe. He joined the Maine Conference in 1889; was ordained Deacon by Bishop R. S. Foster in 1891, and Elder by Bishop W. N. Ninde in 1893. He continued the effective relation until 1906, when failing health compelled the supernumerary relation, and in 1921 he was forced to retire from active work. During his active work in the ministry his labors were ever crowned with true success. Enthusiastic and hopeful, he was a natural leader of the young people, and he was especially successful in interesting them in the work of the Church. Among the charges in which he worked and did great work were the following: Fryeburg and Stowe; West Cumberland, East Poland and Minot; West Durham and Pownal; Berlin; Eliot; Kezar Falls; Bethel; Wilton, Cornish; the People's Church of South Portland; Kent's Hill, and Trinity Church, South Portland.

In August, 1889, Rev. Mr. Potter married Florence Whitcomb, daughter of William C. Whitcomb, one of the leading citizens of Fryeburg, Oxford County. Mrs. Potter was a true and loyal helper during the years of his itinerant labors, and a most faithful companion and comforter during his years of bodily suffering and trial. Of this union there were four sons, as follows: 1. Clifford W. 2. Frederick E. 3. Frank E. 4. Herman W. A.

It was on December 21, 1927, that the host of friends acquired by Rev. Potter during his years of labor in the religious field were shocked to hear of his death that day. Much sympathy was expressed for his sorrowing wife and family, and all united in the declaration that with Rev. Potter had passed a man whose example was ever a criterion for others and who had left a world the better for his presence in it.

MRS. ALTHEA GOULD QUIMBY—A woman whose keen political sagacity brings public leaders to her for counsel and opinions, Mrs. Althea Gould Quimby holds a high place in the life of her native State, Maine, where for years she has studied temperance reform and other social and civic questions and has devoted her energies consistently to the advancement of all those causes which she believes to be for the general good. Always active in organizational work, she has made a special investigation of the temperance situation in every State in the Union with the exception of two, and has visited Great Britain, Belgium, France and Switzerland.

She was born in Norway, Maine, daughter of Daniel and Sarah Stuart (Collins) Coffin, a descendant in direct line from Tristram Coffin, of Nantucket, Massachusetts, founder of the family in America. Her paternal grandfather, James Coffin, guided by blazed trees, brought his wife from New Hampshire into the wilderness of Maine, where in Lovell a clearing had been made and a log cabin built. Later a frame house was erected, which for many years served as church for the circuit-riding pastors of this pioneer community. Daniel, the father of Mrs. Quimby and the youngest of James Coffin's eleven children, married Sarah S. Collins, of Portland, a woman of unusual intellectual ability and fine early educational advantages. She took a great love of education to her new home in the country, offering the parlor of her house in Norway as a schoolroom until a schoolhouse could be built. It was in this improvised schoolroom that the little girl received her first school training. The following year, Mr. Coffin donated land and timber, and a schoolhouse was erected—a small red structure that now stands as a monument to the builder and has been in constant use throughout its history.

Althea Gould Coffin attended the schools of Auburn, whither her parents removed in the period of her early childhood; and later she became a student in Hebron and Bridgton academies, having been graduated from Bridgton Academy in the class of 1880. She then became a teacher in her *alma mater* and in the public schools of Auburn, and continued as such until her marriage in 1884, to J. Frank Quimby, of Turner. In 1922, Bates College conferred upon Mrs. Quimby the honorary degree of Master of Arts as the "typical representative of the best in the modern feminist movement." In the same year, the Methodist Episcopal church licensed her as a local preacher, the highest honor then bestowed by this church upon women, and which carries with it the title of Reverend. The "Lewiston Journal" commented upon the two honors that had lately fallen to "a distinguished Maine woman" by saying that they had been "worthily bestowed."

Prominent always in the work of the Women's Christian Temperance Union, Mrs. Quimby was chosen in 1912 as vice-president-at-large to the State officiary board of the Maine Women's Christian Temperance Union. At that time, Mrs. Lillian M. N. Stevens, who had succeeded Frances E. Willard as president of the National Women's Christian Temperance Union, and was at the same time president of the Maine body and vice-president of the corresponding world-wide organization, had carried her burden of office a dozen years; and when it was recognized that the time had come when she should be given assistance, she chose Mrs. Quimby as the vice-president-at-large. Mrs. Quimby, who, up to 1912, was assistant recording secretary of the Maine organization, had been for years a familiar figure on the convention platform—a tall, auburn-haired woman of dignified bearing, whose cool, clear voice had occasionally been heard giving brief, firm expression to thoroughly sifted convictions. In 1914, she succeeded Mrs. Stevens as president of the Maine temperance body. Her election to this high office was of more than local interest, especially considering the close connection between the Maine Women's Christian Temperance Union and such world leaders as Neal Dow and Lillian Stevens. Mrs. Quimby's first legislative experience was her appearance in 1913 before the committee in behalf of a bill against white slavery, and after that time she led the Maine forces on behalf of suffrage measures and law enforcement bills. She is a member of the advisory board of the State Parent-Teachers' Association and of several child welfare associations, and during the World War she served on several important State committees. She represented her State at two international temperance conferences, and four times was a delegate to the world conventions of the Women's Christian Temperance Union. In London, in 1920, she was the speaker at the morning service of one of the churches.

Within a circle of a few miles' radius enclosing segments of three counties in the oldest and most beautiful part of Maine, Mrs. Quimby had her birthplace, her academic and collegiate training, and later her home as wife and mother on the many-acred Quimby farm, in Turner. Her husband, J. Frank Quimby, is a successful business man and farmer, active in town, county and general legislative affairs, a sound adviser and a loyal advocate of the principles for which the Women's Christian Temperance Union stands.

Of the three sons born to Mr. and Mrs. Quimby, one died in infancy. The two who are living are both Bates-Harvard men. Clarence Paul has served as principal of Cony High School, in Augusta, and president of Westbrook Seminary, in Portland, and, in 1928, became principal of the South Manchester High School, in Connecticut; while the other, Frank Brooks, is professor of argumentation at Bates College, and is considered one of the best coaches of debating in the State. In 1925, the family removed to Portland, where Mrs. Quimby now has her home and office, not far from the headquarters of the Maine Women's Christian Temperance Union.

JOSIAH SMITH MAXCY—Banker, railroad executive, and builder and operator of public utility companies, Josiah Smith Maxcy is known throughout the confines of Maine as one who has contributed more than his share to the development of the State and more especially to Gardiner, wherein he resides and maintains headquarters for his various activities. Since early manhood, Mr. Maxcy has been an important contributor to affairs of finance and public utilities; he has constructed, owned, and managed water companies; has presided over the destinies of railroads, and his wise counsel and sagacious business acumen have helped greatly in promoting the welfare of varied banking institutions. Attesting to the confidence and trust placed in Mr. Maxcy, are the honors that have been bestowed upon him by his election to the Maine Legislature, where he was a representative during 1897-1899, and his connection with numerous societies and fraternities in Gardiner. During the last few years of his life, Mr. Maxcy has

found that his connections with banking and finance require most of his attention, although he devotes time freely to the civic affairs of his city.

Mr. Maxcy was born September 13, 1854, at Gardiner, son of Josiah and Eliza Jane (Crane) Maxcy. Josiah Maxcy is best known for his organization work and management of corporations. Josiah Smith Maxcy attended the public schools of Gardiner, and graduated from high school there in 1872. Beginning in 1889, he entered upon his career as a builder and operator of water companies. He was one of the owners and general manager of the Sandy River and Rangeley Lakes Railroad until its sale to the Maine Central Railroad in 1911, and is now receiver for the Sandy River and Rangeley Lakes Railroad. In 1889, he was elected a trustee of a savings institution; in 1898, became a director of the Maine Trust and Banking Company of Gardiner, and in 1918, became president of this institution, an office he continues to occupy. Also, since 1908, he has occupied the post of president of the Gardiner Savings Institution. Notwithstanding the fact that these business connections have drawn greatly upon the time and talents of Mr. Maxcy, he has been most liberal in his support of outside interests. In 1908, he became a director of Hebron Academy, located at Hebron, Maine, and so serves in that capacity now. In 1897-1899, he was elected representative to the Maine Legislature, and in this law-making body gave most loyal and valuable service to his district. A student of history, Mr. Maxcy is a member of the Maine Historical Society, serving on the standing committee in that organization. He has been quite prominent in the Masonic Order, having attained the thirty-second degree, and is also a member of the Sons of the American Revolution. In relation to his historical interests, it should be noted that Mr. Maxcy is the author of historical addresses, one given in 1903 at the centennial celebration of the city of Gardiner, and one at Christ Church, Gardiner, in 1920. Mr. Maxcy and his family are attendants at the Episcopal church.

Josiah Smith Maxcy married, October 26, 1882, at Providence, Rhode Island, Louise Maria Allen, daughter of Daniel R. Allen, a soldier in the Civil War, serving in the Eleventh Regiment of Rhode Island throughout that conflict, and of Maria (Sweet) Allen. Mr. and Mrs. Maxcy have three children: Helen (Maxcy) Bates, Robert Farrington, and Josiah Richard. Mr. Maxcy resides in Gardiner, his office being located in the building of the Maine Bank and Trust Company, also in Gardiner.

IRVING C. MOULTON—Ever thoughtful of the best interests of his native community, of their appreciation of full details of the day's news, carefully edited, Irving C. Moulton, of Guilford, has made a success of his work as editor and manager of the "Guilford Register," now operated as a weekly journal. Young in years, he is old in editorial experience, careful and painstaking, with an appreciation of news values and a comprehensve method of placing these before his reading public.

Irving C. Moulton was born in Guilford, February 14, 1889, a son of William Otis, deceased, and Abbie (Cole) Moulton, both natives of Maine. His father was a carpenter and a staunch Republican in his political faith. Irving C. Moulton was educated in the public schools of Guilford and graduated from the high school here. His first work was with the "Register," when it was established in 1909 by Andrew Tibbetts, who conducted it for one year. In 1910 a stock company was organized, Irving C. Moulton being appointed editor and manager. He is still engaged in that work, the paper now being issued as a weekly. He, too, is of Republican faith, as well as a member of the Blue Lodge, Free and Accepted Masons, and of the Knights of Pythias. He belongs to the Guilford Country Club, and attends the Universalist church.

Irving C. Moulton married, October 17, 1917, in Guilford, Hazel Bonney, daughter of Edgar H., and Delta (Wilcox) Bonney. Their children are: 1. Grace E. 2. Irving, Jr. 3. Mary Bonney.

WYMAN P. WADLEIGH—The highly esteemed and eminently efficient town clerk of Bar Harbor, Maine, is the son of William W. Wadleigh and Hattie L. (Brown) Wadleigh, both natives of Exeter, Maine. His father was a carpenter by trade and followed that line of work until his death in 1925. His mother died in 1922.

Wyman P. Wadleigh was born in Exeter Mills, Maine, on August 18, 1877. He moved with his parents to Bangor, Maine, when he was only eight years of age and received his education in the public schools of Exeter and Bangor. After leaving school he engaged in the laundry business which he continued to be active in for a number of years when he found the work too confining and took a position as traveling salesman for the Hughes Piano Company of Foxcroft, Maine. In 1902, he resigned from this position and engaged in the insurance business in Dover-Foxcroft, and later was transferred to Bar Harbor. This was in 1907. In 1909, he accepted the position of manager of the Casino Theatre at Bar Harbor and in 1920 he was elected town clerk and resigned from the theatre management to fill that office which he still holds. He is secretary of the Board of Selectmen and town bookkeeper. He is treasurer of the Bar Harbor Board of Trade and was clerk of the Bar Harbor Medical and Surgical Hospital for about three years. He is a member of the Independent Order of Odd Fellows, of which he is now active in the service, being seventy-ninth Grand Master of the Grand Lodge of Maine. He has always been an active member of this body, serving as secretary, pianist for Island Lodge and for Mount Desert Encampment since his first becoming a member. He is also a member of the Unison Rebekah Lodge, No. 107, and is one of the charter members of Canton de Monts, No. 20, Patriarchs Militant, having been the third Captain of that organization, at present Major of Third Battalion, First Regiment; Patriarchs Militant, of Maine. He held an appointive office in the Grand Encampment until 1923 when he was elected Grand Warden of the Grand Lodge. He is also a member of the Bar Harbor Lodge, No. 185, Free and Accepted Masons; Mount Kebo Chapter, No. 50, Royal Arch Masons; Bangor Council, No. 5, Royal and Select Masters.

On April 13, 1902, Wyman P. Wadleigh married Sadie E. Everett, of Bangor, Maine. They have one son: Wyman Everett. Mr. and Mrs. Wadleigh are members of St. Saviour's Protestant Episcopal Church. In politics Mr. Wadleigh is a Republican.

CHARLES S. BENNETT—For upward of thirty years, Charles S. Bennett has succesfully conducted a profitable jewelry business in Guilford, where he has been known from his boyhood. He happens to be one of that interesting group of native-born New Englanders to have faith in the development of his birthplace. There is still a heavy percentage of these individuals here, all of whom have contributed their mite toward the general improvement of the

community. None of them is more worthy of the high regard of his fellows than Charles S. Bennett, who has, through the years, won their respect and admiration by his work for them as well as himself. His standing is high and undisputed, his friends countless, for they equal in number his acquaintances.

Charles S. Bennett was born in Guilford, October 2, 1867, a son of Charles B., and Sarah B. (Herring) Bennett. Both of his parents were also natives of Guilford, where his father, a lifelong Republican, was a practicing physician all of his active life. Both are now deceased. Charles, Jr., received his education in the Guilford public schools, at Kent's Hill and then took the course at the Bryant & Stratton Business College, in Boston, from which he was graduated in 1886. Returning to Guilford, he began his study of the jewelry business and in 1894 purchased the establishment of E. R. Forbush, who had been conducting a store of that description for several years. Deeply interested in all affairs associated with his locality and of the country, he engaged in work with the American Red Cross during the participation of the United States in the World War and acted as secretary for that organization for its Guilford branch. He was elected to the office of town clerk in 1899 and is still serving in that office. He is an attendant of the Universalist Church of Guilford and holds membership in the Order of Free and Accepted Masons, of which he is Past Master. He is also a member of the Independent Order of Odd Fellows, in which association he has held high office, and, since 1908, has been Master of the Exchequer of the local lodge of Knights of Pythias.

Mr. Bennett married twice, first, Clara E. Brown, June 29, 1900. She was a native of Foxcroft, Maine, and died February 25, 1911, leaving one child, Margaret B., born November 29, 1904. His second wife was Blanche M. Scales, of Guilford, whom he married, June 9, 1914.

RAYMOND WILLIS CLARKE, M. D.—When a man's hobby is hunting and fishing and his vocation and profession that of relieving human suffering, it is not hard to know that such an one is good friend and genial companion to all who are fortunate enough to know him. Such a man is Dr. Raymond Willis Clarke, of Ellsworth, Maine, who is the son of James W. Clarke, a contractor and builder of Franklin, Maine. His mother was Mabel L. Butler, also a native of Franklin, Maine.

Raymond Willis Clarke was born in Franklin, Maine, on June 23, 1888. As a small boy he went to the public schools of Franklin and then to the Maine Central Institute. He then attended Bowdoin College from where he was graduated in 1916 with the degree of Doctor of Medicine. After receiving his diploma in medicine, he spent one year in hospital practice at Eastern Maine General Hospital. In 1917, he went to Deer Isle, Maine, where he engaged in the practice of medicine and surgery until 1921. He then moved to Searsport, Maine, where he continued to practice his profession until 1924. In 1924, he moved to Ellsworth and has continued his residence there ever since. He is interested in the general welfare of the city and gives some of his time to public affairs. He is a member of the Chamber of Commerce; the Maine State Medical Association; the Hancock County Medical Society; the American Medical Society; and for three years he was on the staff of the Waldo County Hospital. During the World War, he was commissioned as a First Lieutenant in the United States Army Medical Corps on July 1, 1918, and was in service overseas until December 31, 1918, when he was given an honorable discharge. He is a member of the American Legion. His college fraternity is the Alpha Kappa Kappa; he is member of the Reliance Lodge, Free and Accepted Masons; Searsport Chapter, Royal Arch Masons. In politics, he is a Republican. He is a member of the Congregational church. In 1917, Raymond Willis Clarke, M. D., married Etta L. Young of Brooklin, Maine.

HARRY W. DAVIS—Courteous consideration for all with whom he is brought into contact, an integrity without flaw, an intimate knowledge of every detail of his profession and a studious regard for the best interests of those who have given him their confidence and trust, have carried Harry W. Davis, of Guilford, to a commanding position in the financial and commercial world. A lifelong resident, he has grown with the community about him, winning the respect and affection of his fellows, by both his rigorous adherence to the best traditions of his craft and his sympathetic understanding when faced with complex problems that confront his business associates. Harry W. Davis was born in Guilford in 1862 and was educated here, in the public schools, later finishing in the University of Maine. He is a Republican in politics and has served as town treasurer of Guilford for four years and two terms in the House and one term in the Senate in the Maine Legislature. He has risen in the service of the Guilford Trust Company, with which he has been for years associated, to become, first, cashier, which post he occupied until May, 1906, to treasurer of the Guilford Trust Company, which was a merger of the bank, to become president of the institution in 1910, which office he still fills with honor. His fraternal affiliations are limited, his chief association being with the local lodge of Free and Accepted Masons.

CHARLES H. SHAPLEIGH—Descendant of a Colonial pioneer, who was indirectly responsible for the naming of the town of Kittery, the late Charles H. Shapleigh, of Eliot, dignified the trade of carpenter and the business of manufacturing builders' finish by the excellence of his workmanship and his managerial ability. In the latter enterprise he rose to the position, first of superintendent and subsequently of general manager, for a large concern in a Massachusetts city. More recently his career had to do with filling a supervisory position in connection with his trade at the United States Navy Yard at Kittery, during the World War. Nor did he cease from his labors until retired by reason of having reached the prescribed legal age limit. He was a valued member of his community, whose citizenship qualities constituted a model for his fellows.

Alexander Shapleigh, the immigrant pioneer and founder of the family of that name in America, came from Devonshire, England, in 1640, and settled in what now is the town of Eliot, having first visited that locality in 1635. He was agent in New Hampshire and Maine for Sir Ferdinando Gorges, the founder of Maine and a most important factor in Plymouth Colony. He was a ship-owner and trader, and built on the present site of Kittery a log-cabin and garrison, in 1638. This combination of buildings was called the Kittery House. It was destroyed by fire and rebuilt, only again to be leveled by fire and later rebuilt, in 1800, by Captain Elisha Shapleigh, and occupied by the latter's descendants, this latter

Kittery House having given the community its town name.

Charles H. Shapleigh was born in South Berwick, November 14, 1859, the son of Albert and Lydia (Earle) Shapleigh, and when he was seven years of age, he removed with his parents from that town of Eliot. He finished his education at South Berwick Academy, and being desirous of becoming proficient in some craft, he chose the carpenter trade, which he learned while serving his apprenticeship at Dover, New Hampshire. After he had been rated a full-fledged journeyman he followed his trade for fifteen years in that section of the State. Then, a larger opportunity opening for him, he went to Massachusetts, and accepted the offer of the position of superintendent of the Otis Wood Working Company's plant at Somerville. Recognition of his ability was made with his advancement to the office of general manager. All told, he was with the Otis concern for fourteen years, and during that period he had been of invaluable assistance in the company's achievement of a widespread reputation, and financial success as manufacturers of high-grade builders' finish material.

Mr. Shapleigh returned in April, 1917, to the old homestead in Eliot to make it his permanent residence, where he had spent most of his summers when living in Massachusetts. It was the entry of the United States in the World War that called up the patriotic desire to serve his country in some capacity—preferably that of carpentry, which he knew best. He offered his services to the Federal Government and was assigned to the position of carpenter at the United States Navy Yard at Kittery. Here he performed a highly exemplary tour of duty, until by the operation of the age-limit law he was compelled to retire, much against his will. Thereafter he spent his days in peace and quietude at his ancestral home in Eliot.

In fraternal circles, Mr. Shapleigh reached high station and enjoyed a very wide acquaintance. He was a Past Noble Grand of Dover (New Hampshire) Lodge of the Independent Order of Odd Fellows, a Past High Chief of the Dover Tribe, Improved Order of Red Men, and affiliated with the Ancient Order of United Workmen. To the Republican party he gave long-maintained and enthusiastic support, although he would never allow himself to be brought forward for public office. His religious interest was in the Congregational Church, of Eliot, of which he was an attendant.

Charles H. Shapleigh married Annie Merrill, daughter of Charles C. Merrill, of South Berwick, and of this marriage there is a son, Dr. Harry Lee Shapleigh, a graduate of the Charlestown (Massachusetts) High School, of Tufts College and the School of Physicians and Surgeons at Boston. He married Edith Belle George of that city, where he has a large and desirable practice.

The death of Mr. Shapleigh, on March 21, 1928, was the occasion for deep regret throughout York County. By his estimable traits of character and gracious manner he had made friends almost without number, and his loss to the community cannot be measured in words. It was, indeed, a rich memory that he bequeathed to all who had become heirs of his extensive estate of friendship.

DANIEL E. HURLEY—Practically the whole of his life having been spent in Ellsworth, Maine, where he has been in continuous practice since his admission to the bar, Daniel E. Hurley has a wide acquaintance among the business men and officials of that region, by whom he is highly regarded in both his professional and personal capacities.

His father, Jeremiah Hurley, was born in St. John's, New Brunswick, Canada, and was a wheelwright and carriage builder in early life, was for several years street commissioner of Ellsworth, and was engaged in farming at the time of his death. He married Margaret Ford, of New Jersey, who died June 3, 1928. Born July 14, 1873, in Ellsworth, Maine, Daniel E. Hurley was educated there in the public and high schools, and then entered the Law School of Boston University. He was admitted to the bar in 1898, and began practice at once, and his office is now on State Street, Ellsworth. He is a lifelong Democrat, served several years on the board of registration, was chairman of the Democratic City Committee for a long time, as well as a member of the Democratic County Committee. He is a Past Grand Knight of Sheridan Council of the Knights of Columbus, and a communicant of St. Joseph's Roman Catholic Church. He is a member of the Hancock County Bar Association, and of the Maine State Bar Association. During the World War, he was a member of the legal advisory board for Hancock County, and was also a "four-minute" speaker. His car is his hobby.

In 1907, Daniel E. Hurley married Mary E. Mahoney, of Ellsworth, and they have one son, Charles J. Hurley.

STANFORD M. LEIGHTON—For nearly a quarter of a century Stanford M. Leighton was identified with the banking business in Newport and in Dexter. During the last years of his active career he was associated with the Dexter Trust and Banking Company as treasurer, and then with the Merrill Trust Company of Bangor, Maine, as manager of the Dexter branch.

Stanford M. Leighton was born in Dexter, Maine, September 10, 1853, son of Joshua W., who was born in Tuftonboro, New Hampshire, and was engaged in the meat and grocery business, having retired twenty years prior to the time of his death, and of Laura (Additon) Leighton, a native of Maine, now deceased. Mr. Leighton received a good practical education in the public schools of Dexter and then after completing his high school course, was engaged for twenty-five years in the grocery business, operating his own business. In 1898 he became associated with the Waterville Trust Company, as manager of the Dexter branch, and this connection he maintained until 1910. He then became identified with the Kenduskeag Trust Company of Newport, which connection he maintained for only one year. At the end of that time, in 1911, he became associated with the Dexter Trust and Banking Company as treasurer, which official position he continued to fill until the bank was taken over by the Merrill Trust Company of Bangor, Maine. He was then made manager of the bank, which position he filled until 1922, when he retired. Mr. Leighton is one of the active and public-spirited citizens of Dexter. He is a member of the board of directors and vice-president of the Dexter Loan and Building Association, and has for many years been known as a business man of marked ability. He has been a member of the town library board for a number of years and president for the past ten years. He is a Republican in his political

sympathies, and fraternally, is identified with Plymouth Lodge, Independent Order of Odd Fellows, of which he is a Past Grand. He finds his relaxation in hunting and fishing and in the study of birds, and his religious affiliation is with the Methodist church.

Stanford M. Leighton was married, November 8, 1885, to Laura Haskell, who was born in Garland, Maine.

AMOS A. SPRINGALL—One of the successful insurance men of Dexter is Amos A. Springall, who has been engaged in this line of business since 1906. Mr. Springall is one of the organizers of the Dexter Loan and Building Association, of which he has been secretary since 1886, and treasurer for more than fifteen years. He has also been treasurer of the Dexter Library for the past thirty years.

Amos A. Springall was born in Sangerville, Maine, November 17, 1856, son of John B., a native of England, who came to this country and graduated from Harvard Medical College, continuing as a physician to the time of his death, and of Emily J. (Abbott) Springall, who was born in Dexter, Maine, now deceased. Mr. Springall received a good practical education in the public schools of Dexter, Maine, and after completing his course in the high school found employment in a retail drugstore, where he continued for one year. In 1874 he engaged in the drug business for himself, in Dexter, and continued to operate this business successfully until 1906. In that year he engaged in the insurance business, and he has been taking charge of a large general insurance business since that time. Mr. Springall gives his support to the principles and the candidates of the Republican party. He is one of the active and public-spirited citizens of the town, and has always willingly borne his full share of the burdens of local public office. He served as town treasurer for five years, was collector of taxes for four years, and for one term was chairman of the Board of Selectmen. He has been most active in promoting organizations which would be of benefit to the residents of Dexter, and was one of the organizers of the Dexter Loan and Building Association, of which he has served as the official secretary since 1886, and as treasurer since 1912. As has already been stated, he has been treasurer of the Dexter Library Association for the past thirty years; and he is a member of the financial board of the Dexter branch of the Merrill Trust Company. He is a member of the Knights of Pythias, and of the Royal Arcanum, and is a charter member of the Dexter Club. Mr. Springall finds his recreation and relaxation in fishing and automobiling, and he is a member of the Universalist church.

Amos A. Springall was married, June 9, 1885, to Carrie J. Dustin, who was born in Providence, Rhode Island, and who died in 1925.

DR. ROSWELL E. HUBBARD—In contributing to the progressive development of humanity, the science of medicine has probably done more within the last few decades than any other in the discoveries it has made which have done so much to alleviate the sufferings and promote the health of the people, collectively. In the medical annals of the State of Maine, the name of Dr. Roswell E. Hubbard stands out prominently as that of a physician of great ability and skill. Dr. Hubbard has been engaged in the practice of his profession in Waterford since September, 1919, and since that time, he has built up a large and unswerving clientele, having won the confidence and coöperation of all his patients from the very beginning of his career in this city, due to the almost immediate recognition of his expert skill and ability. He maintains the deepest interest in everything relating to civic health and civic progress, his advice being sought on many matters which concern the welfare of the inhabitants of this community, while, personally, he has rendered invaluable service as health officer of Waterford, in which position he continues to guide the city's progress along this particular line.

Dr. Hubbard was born in Hatfield, Massachusetts, January 1, 1891, son of Roswell and Fannie L. (Graves) Hubbard, both natives of Hatfield. Roswell Hubbard, the father, is prominently identified with the agricultural industry and is active in politics, adhering to the policies of the Republican party. Roswell E. Hubbard was educated in the public schools of Hatfield, later attending Smith Academy, at Hatfield, from which he was graduated in 1909. Entering Bowdoin College, he received his degree of Bachelor of Arts with the class of 1914, after which he turned his attention to the study of medicine, attending the medical school of that same institution, and receiving his degree of Doctor of Medicine with the class of 1918. Immediately after the completion of his medical course, he entered the United States Navy and served until 1919, when he came to Waterford, where he has ever continued to be held in the highest esteem by his fellow-citizens, benig ready and willing at all times to aid and assist the sick and unfortunate, and so courteous and considerate are his attentions that his patients feel that he is not only their physician but also a true friend. In politics, he is an Independent, preferring to judge the merits of each particular candidate in the various elections rather than align himself with any particular political party, and he has never sought public office, although in the interests of the people's welfare, he ably and tirelessly fills all the requirements and qualifications demanded by his position as health officer for the city. Dr. Hubbard is prominent in professional organizations, being a member of the County and State Medical associations, and of the American Medical Association. During the World War, he enlisted in the United States Navy and was given the rank of junior lieutenant in the Medical Corps, being stationed first at Washington, District of Columbia, later at the Naval Hospital, Portsmouth, New Hampshire, and engaged in active duty aboard ship 1918-19. He was honorably discharged from the service at Hoboken, New Jersey, June, 1919.

Dr. Roswell E. Hubbard married, on December 28, 1918, at Portland, Amy Field, born at Whitefield, daughter of John and Mary (Welsh) Field, and to this union have been born three children: 1. John F., born May 23, 1920. 2. Roswell E., Jr., born August 13, 1923. 3. Mary A., born September 25, 1924.

GUY MAXWELL MONK—In the educational system of Maine there is no better equipped community of its population than Bridgton, nor is there an official head more worthy of such position than Guy Maxwell Monk, superintendent. Specializing in mathematics, this educator has had a broad experience in teaching that and science, as well as in the general work of the school curriculum where he has been engaged. For these and other reasons he is held to be one of the more valuable of the citizens of the district, interested as he is in every movement that is intended to advance

the position of the community in the general forward march of progress.

Guy Maxwell Monk was born in Norway, Maine, August 3, 1887, a son of Luther S. and Alice M. (Head) Monk. He received his early education in the public schools and later at Bridgton Academy, from which he was graduated in 1906. He attended Bates College for one year and then took the courses at the summer schools at Bates and Dartmouth colleges. He began his career by teaching at Gardiner, Maine, during 1910 and 1911, his subject mathematics. He was then called to the High School of Norway, where he taught mathematics and science during 1911 and 1912. He temporarily abandoned his educational work from 1912 to 1915, during which time he conducted a summer hotel, and in 1916 and 1917 he engaged in farming. The following year, however, he returned to teaching mathematics and science, being associated with Bridgton Academy until 1920. In that year he became Superintendent of School District No. 18, a position which he still holds. He is chairman of the executive committee of the board of trustees of Bridgton Academy, member of the board of managers of the Bridgton Chamber of Commerce, and a member of the Independent Order of Odd Fellows. In politics he is a Democrat.

Guy Maxwell Monk married, November 14, 1914, at North Bridgton, Blanche L. Meserve. They had five children: Fred M., deceased; M. Alice; Claude M.; Harry W.; and Janet Meserve.

GEORGE BENJAMIN GOODALL—A member of the grand triumvirate which made possible the mammoth development of the Sanford Mills and the Goodall Worsted Company, the principal industries of the town of Sanford, the late George Benjamin Goodall was regarded as a genius of the wool and mohair manufacturing trade in this country. Son of an accomplished father, who was one of the first producers of shaped horse blankets and carriage robes in the United States, he inherited marked ability as an inventor and an executive of great manufacturing interests. He was the first in this country to weave plush by hand on a wooden loom, and perfected the power loom for the weaving of mohair. He was the principal factor in the enlargement of the great industry which has given Sanford its highest station among the leading textile centers of the country. To the upbuilding, material and civic progress of the town, he, in association with his brothers, Hon. Louis Bertrand Goodall and the late Hon. Ernest Montrose Goodall, whose biographies accompany this sketch, contributed generously of his great wealth and cultural resources.

The Goodall family background is a most interesting one, especially as showing the marked industrial trend of a resourceful and industrious father. Thomas Goodall came from his native Yorkshire, England, to the United States, in 1846, possessing neither money nor influential friends, but a strong determination to make his fortune in the New World. He had an experience of eleven years as an apprentice in wool manfacture, followed by years of training and practice as manager and salesman of the mill's products. Following his marriage, in 1849, he settled in West Winchester, New Hampshire, in the Ashuelot Valley, where his sons, George Benjamin and Louis Bertrand (twins), were born. Perceiving an opportunity to establish himself in business on his own account, he removed, in 1852, to Troy,

New Hampshire, where he began the manufacture of overcoatings and horse blankets. He passed safely through the panic of 1857, made a great deal of money, for those times, during the Civil War, and, in 1865, disposed of his mill to Keene (New Hampshire) capitalists. Up to that time he had been the only manufacturer of shaped horse blankets in the United States. For twenty years he had given himself indefatigably to his business concerns, and then gave himself a "leave of absence."

Thomas Goodall took his vacation in England. He was convinced that carriage robes and plushes could be manufactured at a satisfactory profit in this country, and while in the mother country he conducted an investigation of the production of these goods, sending back to the United States for examination by a close friend and associate samples of the English products. Having returned to this country, in October, 1867, he came to Sanford and purchased there for fifteen thousand, five hundred dollars, the William Miller flannel factory, now the site of Mill No. 1, of the Sanford Mills, and the James O. Clark saw and grist-mill, now the site of Mill No. 2, and began the manufacture of horse blankets and carriage robes. This was the inception of the wool, plush, mohair and worsted industry, which father and sons saw well on its way to prosperity and magnitude ere he passed on.

Thomas Goodall married Ruth Waterhouse, daughter of Jeremiah Waterhouse, a prominent manufacturer of South Hadley, Massachusetts; they were the parents of three sons: 1. George Benjamin, of whom further. 2. Louis Bertrand, whose sketch accompanies this. These two sons, twins, were born September 23, 1851. 3. Ernest Montrose, whose biography also accompanies this. The father of this family achieved a notable record as the founder of a nationally known industry and an enviable reputation as a citizen. His memory is tenderly cherished by the family of his own and the present generations and in the archives of the business and the town he helped to develop.

George Benjamin Goodall, son of Thomas and Ruth (Waterhouse) Goodall, was born in Winchester, New Hampshire, September 23, 1851, receiving his common school training in Troy, New Hampshire, and private instruction at a select school in Thompson, Connecticut, 1862-63; attending the Vermont Episcopal Institute, a military school at Burlington, Vermont, 1863-66; and a private school in England, from 1866 until his return with his parents to this country in the fall of 1867. A pronounced talent for art was encouraged by his going to Europe, in 1872, and he was a pupil of Untemberger in Brussels, Belgium. The cultivation of his talent was turned to good account when he became a manufacturer, and took charge of the designing and coloring of the robes, in the making of which his father was engaged.

With his return to the United States, Mr. Goodall went to work in the Sanford mill, and under his father's preceptorship learned all the processes of manufacture, becoming as one of the operatives, whose problems and viewpoint he came to know thoroughly, this knowledge furnishing him with a valued point of contact during his years as an employer. Among other difficulties which beset the father in those early years of the business, and demanding solution if the mill was to be operated successfully, was the problem of satisfactory printing

of the product. A competent color-maker had been imported from England, but he became a liquor addict and while on his protracted debauches, the mill was often forced to stop for want of colors. Finally the colormaker had to abandon his work entirely through physical incapacity, but he taught his art to Louis Bertrand, who in turn acquainted his brother, George Benjamin, with its mysteries and applications. The latter supplemented his newly acquired knowledge of dyes. He soon became very proficient in the operation of the department on which the success of the business hinged. He would go to the mill at five o'clock in the morning, don overalls, lock himself in his room, and there, before he had eaten breakfast, prepare the dyes needed for the day. Those were the days when the mills started at six thirty a. m. and closed at six p. m.

To the perfection of the plush industry, George Benjamin Goodall gave of his best thought and energy during his early years. He worked many hours in the basement of his home in Sanford, toiling over the development of a power loom, which was to be the successor of his wooden hand loom from which had come the first piece of car plush woven in this country. His wife was a most loyal helpmeet, encouraging him in his prodigious toil by her presence and holding a kerosene lamp as a torch to furnish the light needed for his efforts.

With the perfection of the power loom for the production of mohair plush, this genius of the industry formed a copartnership consisting of himself and his brothers, Louis B. and Ernest M., and under the style of Goodall Brothers they began the manufacture of plush and pile fabrics October 1, 1881. All was not plain sailing, however, in those infant days of the budding industry, and it became necessary for the firm to employ the services of a finished inventor of weaving machinery before the perfectworking, wire-motion plush loom now in use in the mills was produced. But the three brothers were made of the stuff of which heroes are constituted, and they hung on tenaciously through bitter trials and disappointments until the day that a piece of perfect plush was produced.

The reward that honors perseverance eventually came to the house of Goodall, with the achievement of a reputation for the preëminence of the firm's products, which is now nation-wide. Since 1881, George Benjamin Goodall was, until his passing, the major figure in the expansion of the business and extension of the plant of the Sanford Mills Company. From the original forty thousand-dollar plant in 1867, it has been developed, much of it under the direction and on the initiative of George B. and Louis B. Goodall, to its present forty-eight acres of floor space of Sanford Mills and Goodall Worsted Company, representing a capital of $31,500,000, and Goodall Worsted Company, $7,500,000. The most extensive users of mohair in the United States, the Pullman Company, are furnished mohair plush by the Sanford Mills, as are a large percentage of the railroads of the country.

Mr. Goodall was president of the Sanford Mills Corporation and the Goodall Worsted Company, of Sanford, manufacturers of pile fabrics and Palm Beach cloth, and held these offices for many years. He had also been president of the Maine Alpaca Company before it was taken over by the Goodall Worsted Company; a director of the Holyoke Plush Company, Holyoke, Massachusetts, before it was liquidated; a former treasurer of the Sanford Power Company, and a director of the old Sanford & Cape Porpoise Railroad, the forerunner of the York Utilities Company. He was one of the founders of the Sanford Unitarian Society, the Sanford Town Club and the Bauneg Beg Country Club, to all of which he was a generous contributor. Goodall Park, a large athletic field in Sanford, was made possible through his gifts of money, as were the site and structure of the Town Hall. The Henrietta Bennett Goodall Hospital, named for his late wife and costing half a million dollars, was given by Mr. Goodall and his daughter, Mrs. William Marland, as a memorial. This institution was in process of building when Mr. Goodall died. In his will he made bequests of five thousand dollars each to the Unitarian, Congregational, Baptist, Methodist and Episcopal churches of Sanford.

George Benjamin Goodall married, October 28, 1872, Henrietta D. Bennett, of Sanford, who died in 1923. Their only daughter and child is the wife of William H. Marland, of Sanford and Brooklin. The death of Mr. Goodall occurred from a sudden seizure in his seventy-seventh year, on December 13, 1927, at Hollywood, California, where he was visiting his brother, Hon. Louis Bertrand Goodall (see a following biography), a winter resident of California for five years preceding the bereavement.

Home and the two mills of which he was president focused the affections and major attention of Mr. Goodall during his long and remarkable career. These he treasured to the point that he could never permit himself to affiliate with social or fraternal organizations. In those associations he had his chief delight and comfort—nothing could woo him from them. Yet there was glory a-plenty to clothe the name of this outstanding man and successful manufacturer. The textile industries of Sanford stand as a monument to his inventive and constructive genius. His memory will remain indefinitely as charged with the personal qualities of a splendid mind and a loving heart. His keenness of intellect and artistic temperament and culture never conspired to a feeling of loftiness above his fellows. He was a hard worker and an equally strenuous player, fairness to all being one of the fine traits fo his character. Simple in his tastes, democratic in his manner and contacts, he moved with the ease and grace becoming the perfect gentleman and four-square individual that he was.

HON. ERNEST MONTROSE GOODALL—

One of the principal figures in the building up of the great textile interests of Sanford and the town itself to proportions and standing that command countrywide attention was the late Hon. Ernest Montrose Goodall. He was scion of a remarkable family, comprising in addition to himself, the father-founder, Thomas Goodall, and the latter's sons, Hon. Louis Bertrand Goodall and the late George Benjamin Goodall, of each of whom there are to be found accompanying biographies. Ernest Montrose Goodall was gifted with unusual executive ability, and to him quite early in life were entrusted the chief responsibilities of management of the immense Sanford Mills Corporation's business and allied interests of the Goodall family, in addition to directorships in a number of various concerns in the textile and other industries in Maine and other States. Mr. Goodall had rendered a fine political service in different capacities

during his notable career, having been a selectman of Sanford, a State representative of his district and a State Senator. His life was one of continuous usefulness in the industrial, community and political life of his time.

Hon. Ernest Montrose Goodall, son of Thomas and Ruth (Waterhouse) Goodall, was born in the picturesque town of Troy, New Hampshire, August 15, 1853. He was the youngest of three sons, George Benjamin and Louis Bertrand being twins. From the pursuit of studies in the public schools of his native town, he went to Thompson, Connecticut, where he was a pupil in a private institution. Later he was a student at a military school in Burlington, Vermont, and while his parents were sojourning in Europe, he attended a select school in England, from 1866 to 1867.

As in the case of his two brothers, his father was of the same mind toward Ernest M.—he never regarded their education as completed until they had made the grades in the Sanford Mills. It was in line with this family policy, therefore, that Ernest Montrose Goodall, on his return to this country, entered his father's factories, in which he made a complete study of the textile manufacture in all its processes and departments, mingling with the employed force as one of them, acquiring the experience which comes to one in the ranks of the workers. He was thoroughly furnished in the knowledge of the trade and in the handling of the employees, when his father, having become convinced that he also possessed executive ability out of the ordinary, appointed him superintendent of the mills. In this capacity he was an important factor in getting out the production, maintaining the high standards of perfection established by the Goodall interests, and in every way at his command helping to build the business to the very large proportions which it realized as father and three sons bent all their energies in constructing and equipping a plant that could meet the demands for the company's offerings.

When Mr. Goodall's father retired from active direction of the business, in 1883, he was elected to the office of president as his successor. He was then thirty years old, and for something like thirty-five years he filled the post of chief executive of the Sanford Mills Corporation with that outstanding ability that reflected credit on the establishment and the fine old family name. Other concerns which were fortunate in availing themselves of Mr. Goodall's services in the capacity of president were the Sanford Light and Water Company, elected in 1886 on the organization of that utility; the Sanford & Cape Porpoise Railway Company, 1897; Mousam River Railway Company, November 9, 1893; Atlantic Shore Line Railroad Company, 1898; the Cape Porpoise Land Company, the Holyoke Plush Company, of Holyoke, Massachusetts, and the Oakdale Cemetery Association. He was a director of the Goodall Worsted Company and the Maine Alpaca Company.

The political career of Mr. Goodall was both comprehensive and of great value to the constituencies he so capably served. From 1879 to 1883, he was a member of the Board of Selectmen of the town of Sanford, and in the discharge of his duties helped effect many physical improvements and in different ways better the system of government by which the community rules itself. In 1880 he was elected by his fellow-Republicans to the Lower House of the

Maine Legislature, holding his seat in that body until 1882, when he was elected State Senator from his district. Further attestation of the value placed on the standing and influence of Mr. Goodall came with his appointment as a member of Governor Robie's Executive Council. In that position he was enabled to serve the interests of the State in an advisory capacity for which by training, temperament and preference he was admirably fitted.

Endowed with a friendly disposition, having a democratic spirit and manner, Mr. Goodall knew nothing of the distinctions of class and creed for himself. It was not, therefore, to be remarked as an extraordinary thing that he numbered his friends by the hundred. The whole town of Sanford, it seemed, could be placed in this category; in addition there were business and political associates without number, almost, who were included in this his loyal legion. By those who knew him best he was admired also for his true sportsmanship. He enjoyed the major recreational diversions, and to a number of them he gave of his time and support in a generous manner. His keen interest in sports was another link in the chain of friendship that bound him to his fellows. Hon. Ernest Montrose Goodall never married. Something of what he lacked in the charm and affection that exists in a properly ordered domestic circle was made up to him in the ties that bound him and the Sanford Mills force and the townspeople into a sort of community family. He loved the town and its people, its industries and institutions; and he derived great pleasure in helping to promote their various interests. He entered heartily into the program of the Goodall family for building up the town and its chief industries, and all who knew of his many years of sustained efforts in that direction recall how eminently successful and extremely happy he was in his work. His death, which occurred January 29, 1919, was the occasion for widespread mourning. A great captain of industry and a friend of the people, a truly loyal adopted son of Maine had fallen, but his memory ever remains bright in the hearts of those who revere it as a priceless treasure.

HON. LOUIS BERTRAND GOODALL—Under the auspices of a kindly fate it was both fitting and proper that the destiny of Hon. Louis Bertrand Goodall, former Congressman from the First Maine District, should have been worked out synchronously, from a business aspect, with that of his twin brother, the late George Benjamin Goodall, during the latter's lifetime, as a co-builder of Sanford's dominating industries, the Sanford Mills Corporation and the Goodall Worsted Company, whose principles and products have attained a reputation for integrity and quality that is country-wide. Appreciations of the lives, labors and successes of their late father and of the departed brothers—George Benjamin and Ernest Montrose—together with an account of the rise and progress of the great industry with which the name Goodall is inseparably associated are to be found accompanying this sketch.

Hon. Louis Bertrand Goodall was born in Winchester, New Hampshire, September 23, 1851, son of the late Thomas and Ruth (Waterhouse) Goodall. He also received his common school education in Troy, New Hampshire, and private instruction at a select school in Thompson, Connecticut, 1862-63; and at the famous Kimball Union Academy, Meriden, New Hampshire. After one

year in private school in England he entered on his career in the textile trade, beginning with the manufacture of wool at the Mousam River Mills, in 1874. He made a complete study of the processes, from the raw product to the finished material, and became one of the best-equipped men in the industry. Being of an inventive turn of mind, as was his gifted twin brother George, he devoted many long hours to the study of the power development of the mills with a view to improving the manufacturing processes, and thus produce a better quality of goods and with greater facility than was possible under the old hand-loom system.

Especially after locating in Sanford with his parents and brothers was he enabled to be of great assistance to his father in the establishment of the Sanford Mills on a modern basis of operation. After many years of experimentation, he conquered many obstacles and solved numerous problems. His brother George and he perfected the invention of the first power looms for the manufacture of mohair plush. It was largely through his brother's and his mechanical ingenuity and technical skill that the Sanford Mills were enabled to produce high-grade mohair, alpaca and other linings, which for a time constituted a large proportion of the products. Likewise in more recent years the Goodall interests have become the largest manufacturers of Palm Beach cloth and of high-grade mohair and velmo automobile upholstering. Plush automobile robes also are a considerable part of the mills' output, all these comparatively new lines having been made possible through Mr. Goodall and his brother's ability to keep step with the modern advance in textile production and designs.

In 1886, Mr. Goodall became a director of the Sanford Mills Corporation, which is a consolidation of various concerns, and has ever since been a moving spirit in the management of that huge concern. He is the last survivor of that splendid group of father and three sons who brought about the creation of the industry which ranks among the leading companies in the textile world. He is a fine exemplar of the family tradition which has had much to do with the making of the town of Sanford an ideal manufacturing center and a desirable place of residence. The religious, social and cultural environment of the community has been raised to a high level, the housing conditions rendered praiseworthy, and the general surroundings of the town and its local government put on a lofty plane with the powerful assistance of the Goodall family. In all this forward-looking work, Mr. Louis B. Goodall has played a part and continues to take a genuine and intimate interest in the maintenance of the high standards to which his father, his brothers and himself set their hearts and hands to attain many years ago.

In addition to the great Sanford Mills Corporation, of which he is a director, Mr. Goodall has numerous manufacturing and other industrial and financial interests, with which he is officially associated. He has served the Mousam River Railroad Company as treasurer since 1895; the Sanford National Bank as president since 1896; the Goodall Worsted Company, of Sanford, as treasurer and president since 1899, when he was one of the organizers of this important concern; the Harriman & Northeastern Railroad Company, of Tennessee, the Sanford & Cape Porpoise Railway, the Sanford Power Company and the Goodall Matting Company as treasurer. Mr. Goodall was one of the founders of the Sanford Unitarian Society, the Sanford Town Club and the Bauneg Beg Country Club, and gave generously to their needs.

Official recognition of Mr. Goodall's standing in the manufacturing world was accorded in 1904, when he was made a member and chairman of the Maine Commission to the St. Louis (Missouri) Exposition. In that capacity he did much to make the various exhibits of the Pine Tree State stand out with marked advantage and favor. The Republican party is most fortunate in having held the undivided political allegiance of Mr. Goodall throughout the years of his majority. He has been of valued assistance in his party councils for the success of its tickets and policies, and in 1909 was appointed a member of the staff of Governor Fernald with the rank of lieutenant-colonel. The highest point in his political career was reached with his election from the First Maine District to Congress, taking his seat in the 1917-19 session. He was still further honored by reëlection for the succeeding session, his term expiring in 1921. The many social, educational and civic enterprises of the Sanford community are given the cordial and generous support of Mr. Goodall, whose more immediate religious affiliation is with the Unitarian church.

Hon. Louis Bertrand Goodall married, July 21, 1877, Rose V. Goodwin, of Saco. She died April 15, 1894, survived by her husband and three children: 1. Lela Helen. 2. Mildred V., married William N. Campbell, and they are the parents of three children: Constance V., Barbara L. and William N., Jr. 3. Thomas Milton, married Marion W. Gray, and they have a daughter, Ruth Helen.

The success which Mr. Goodall has attained is not alone that which has come to a captain of industry and a leader of finance. That he has achieved in abundant and merited measure. But also in the moral values has he won distinction among his fellow-men in State and town. In the Sanford community he holds the respect and esteem, akin to affection, of the people for his unusual mental gifts, his friendly and helpful interest in their affairs, and the constant thoughtfulness and consideration in numerous individual cases that stand to his credit as it becomes a part of the brilliant and enduring family record. The perpetuation of an honored name is in safe-keeping in his hands.

CHARLES F. WOODARD, treasurer and vice-president of an important shipping company of Greenville, Maine, operating on Moosehead Lake, has been connected with the company for nearly a quarter of a century, rising from one responsible position to another more responsible, and seeing the company grow, while helping largely in its growth. He has taken a large interest in public affairs also and has held, important public positions.

Charles F. Woodard was born at Stacyville, Maine, January 15, 1881, son of Kit Clinton and Ruby Jane (Bragg) Woodard, of whom the father, who was a hotel proprietor and farmer and lumberman, now retired, was born at Patten, Maine, August 25, 1857, and of whom the mother was born at Stacyville, Maine. Charles F. Woodard attended the public schools at Sherman, Maine, and then the Sangerville High School. He worked as telegraph operator for the Bangor & Aroostook Railroad from 1899 to 1904. In this latter year he became connected with

the Coburn Steamship Company at Greenville Junction, Maine. The company operated boats on Moosehead Lake and he acted as general agent. He then served as general manager until 1915. He was elected vice-president and treasurer of the company in 1919 and has continued in that capacity until the present time. The firm operates four motor ships and two steamships and four barges.

Mr. Woodard is a member also of the Board of Selectmen. He has been on the School Board of Greenville for fifteen years. He belongs to the Free and Accepted Masons, thirty-second degree, all bodies, Lodge Columbia, No. 200, the Knights Templar, the Greenville Chamber of Commerce, of which he is also a director. He attends the Methodist church.

Mr. Woodard married, at Island Falls, Maine, Lyle E. Faulkner, born December 7, 1883, at Hartland, New Brunswick, daughter of Joseph Faulkner. Children: 1. Pearl Ruby, born at Greenville, Maine. 2. Ardis Josephine, born at Greenville, Maine. 3. Audrey Nathalie, born at Greenville, Maine.

FRANK EDWARDS McLEARY—The business career of Frank Edwards McLeary has been a long and successful one. A printer by trade, he established a publishing business which attained national reputation, and later organized the automobile business which operates under the name of the F. E. McLeary Company, in Farmington, Maine. The company are distributors of Ford products and under the management of Mr. McLeary abundant success has been the reward of careful planning and faithful work. Mr. McLeary is also vice-president of the First National Bank of Farmington.

Frank Edwards McLeary was born in Strong, Maine, May 10, 1859, son of Justin Edwards, a farmer and lumberman, and Harriet (Voter) McLeary. As a young boy he attended the public schools of Strong, but his later school training was received in the public schools of Farmington. When he left school he learned the printer's trade, and about 1880, when he was twenty-one years of age, he established a publishing company which attained national reputation as producers of supplementary reading for schools. The supplementary reading books won recognition because of the excellence of the material they contained and because of the first-class craftsmanship which went into their making, and for many years were used by public schools throughout the country. Being a man of administrative and executive ability, Mr. McLeary later, in 1899, organized the F. E. McLeary Company for the purpose of engaging in the automobile business. His entrance into this line of business at so early a stage in the development of the industry is conclusive evidence of the generally progressive and alert spirit of the man. In 1899 the automobile was still an object of curiosity and of annoyance to those who were upon the highways with the faithful horse. Traffic problems there were, for the autoist of those days was frequently obliged to stop his motor and allow some spirited and frightened horse to pass before he went on his triumphant way, and venomous, indeed, were some of the remarks directed to these noisy disturbers of the old order of transportation. Mr. McLeary, however, was one of those who understood the fact that the automobile had come to stay, and he acted accordingly. As distributors of the Ford products in Farmington, Maine, and vicinity, the F. E. McLeary Company has been very successful, and on the corner of Main and Church streets, in Farmington, their well-appointed establishment is taking care of a large and still growing business. Along with his other responsibilities, Mr. McLeary is vice-president of the First National Bank of Farmington. Fraternally, he holds membership in the Blue Lodge, Chapter, Council, and Commandery, Free and Accepted Masons; and his religious connection is with the Congregational church.

Frank Edwards McLeary was married (first), May 21, 1883, in Farmington, Maine, to Cornelia Jennie Woods, daughter of John French and Georgiana Payson (Burnham) Woods. She died in 1916, and he married (second), September 20, 1917, in Farmington, Maine, Emma Demuth, daughter of Gustav and Ida (Landert) Demuth. To the first marriage four children were born: 1. Anine W., February 9, 1884. 2. Frank Burnham, November 23, 1887. 3. Donald Hunter, June 28, 1891. 4. Louise Wentworth, December 21, 1895. To the second marriage two children have been born: 5. Barbara, born July 23, 1918. 6. Constance, born January 26, 1922. The family home is located at No. 40 Main Street, in Farmington.

FREDERICK JOHN PRITHAM, M. D., is a general practitioner at Greenville Junction, Maine. He has now practiced in that town and neighborhood for over twenty years and is one of its prominent figures. He occupies also a responsible county position. He has taken an active part in public affairs and has been active also in its fire brigade.

Frederick John Pritham was born at Freeport, Maine, July 6, 1880, son of Charles and Amelia (Merrell) Pritham, of whom the father, who was a farmer, was born at Old Orchard, Maine, and of whom the mother was born at Portland, Maine. Dr. Pritham received his preliminary education in the public schools at Freeport and attended also the high school, the course at which he completed in 1901. He then went to the Maine Medical School from which he graduated in the class of 1905, with the degree of Doctor of Medicine. He started general practice at Greenville Junction, Maine, and has continued practicing there to the present time. During the World War he was chairman of the Medical Advisory Board, No. 11, and a member of the Reserve Corps. Dr. Pritham is medical examiner for Piscataquis County. He has been health officer of the town of Greenville for eighteen years. He has been a member of the School Board for six years. He is treasurer of the Hose Company, No. 2, and one of the original hydrant men. He attends the Methodist Church of Greenville Junction, and has been treasurer for fifteen years.

Dr. Pritham married, June 20, 1906, at Freeport, Maine, Sadie Rose Ring, born at Charlestown, Massachusetts, May 3, 1883, daughter of John and Olive (Durgin) Ring, both of whom were born at Freeport, Maine. Children: 1. Carol Frederick, born at Greenville, Maine, November 22, 1907. 2. Howard Charles, born also at Greenville, June 11, 1914.

HOSEA WILLARD—Fewer citizens of Sanford have contributed more to the upbuilding of that community than did the late Hosea Willard, and the many fine residences and homes now existent here were of his conception and handiwork. A dignified, imposing man, Mr. Willard, nevertheless, was most democratic, and was deeply interested in encourag-

ing the ownership of homes, giving every assistance to would-be home owners. Popular and respected in many lines of endeavor in Sanford, Mr. Willard was extremely fond of horses and for a time maintained a stable for rental of horses. His keen mentality, public spirit, and conscientious performance of his duties as a citizen obtained for him a mark of repute during his residence in Sanford and in other sections of the State. He was conspicuous in political affairs, having at one time served as a member of the State Legislature, and many other offices of public trust and responsibility were held by him at one time or another.

Mr. Willard was born in South Sanford, Maine, his parents having been the late Captain Stephen and Lovica (Tripp) Willard. He was one of a family of ten children, consisting of seven girls and three boys. Hosea Willard obtained the elementary portion of his education in the public schools of Sanford, a training that was later enhanced by studies at Alfred Academy and at Limerick Academy. His school days at an end, he then joined with his father in the conduct of the latter's farm and lumber operations. After a few years Mr. Willard entered into the grocery business, forming a partnership with B. F. Hanson. As previously noted, he was extremely fond of horses and took great pleasure in his ownership of some of the finest stock in this section. For a time, also, he owned an establishment devoted to the rental of horses. In South Sanford, he carried on the previously mentioned enterprise, in addition to the conduct of a large lumber business. This naturally led to his becoming interested in construction work, and in 1868 he moved to Sanford, where he had erected a magnificent residence, located in the center of this town. Here, too, he was the owner of an extensive tract of land, extending from Main Street to Mousam River. It was not for profit alone that Mr. Willard encouraged building, for he realized the pleasure and content that one derives from ownership of a home, and he rendered every possible aid to people possessed of an ambition to own their own place of residence.

After his removal to Sanford, Mr. Willard became more and more interested in the activities of the Republican party, he having been a staunch supporter of that political division throughout his life. In 1870, his fellow-citizens prevailed upon him to accept membership on the Board of Selectmen, and for several years thereafter he functioned as tax collector and treasurer. As his abilities became better known and his circle of friends increased, Mr. Willard was chosen for the Legislature in 1877. During this period of service he was a member of many important committees, and did much to forward legislation beneficial to his district. A man of imposing appearance, with prematurely gray hair, he was dignified and unaffected, but close acquaintances soon recognized that under this outer reserve reposed capabilities and faculties equalled by few others. In each of the numerous functions of his public service he gave the very best that was possible to the welfare of his constituents, and many were the expressions of regret and sorrow heard at the time of his demise.

Hosea Willard married Carrie A. Ricker, daughter of Ebenezer and Mary (Abbott) Ricker. Ebenezer Ricker, born in Acton, Maine, was a successful and respected farmer. Mary (Abbott) Ricker was born in Andover, Massachusetts.

Having lived a life filled with good deeds and devotion to his friends and neighbors, Mr. Willard passed to his reward on March 18, 1910. While not having experienced what might be called a spectacular career, he had filled his span on this earth with good deeds and works that will long remain with those whom he benefited. Mr. Willard is survived by his widow, who resides at No. 202 Main Street, Sanford.

JOHN C. MORTON—As head of the Morton Motor Company, of Farmington, John C. Morton is one of the leading figures in the business life of that town. In addition to handling the Chevrolet automobiles, the company does repair work and automobile painting, and deals in all sorts of parts and accessories. Mr. Morton, who has been engaged for most of his life in different business enterprises in Maine, and who has been in the automobile business since 1912, is president and general manager of this company; while his son, Lloyd Morton, is the firm's secretary and treasurer.

John C. Morton was born October 19, 1874, in Washington, Maine, the son of John C. and Abbie L. (Wilson) Morton, the former of whom is a native of Union, Maine, and the latter of Washington, Maine. The father, all his life, was a merchant. The son, John C. Morton, attended as a boy the public schools of Washington, Maine, and later the Washington High School. His first work was in the barber's trade, in which he was engaged in Washington for nine years. In July, 1903, he entered the baking business in Farmington, Maine, in which he continued until 1920. In 1912 there was formed in Farmington a stock company known as the Metcalf Auto Company, and in 1920, Mr. Morton, who had owned a part of this auto firm's stock, purchased all the stock and changed the name to the Morton Motor Company, which he now operates with his son. He is president and general manager, while his son Lloyd is secretary and treasurer. John C. Morton has many interests in addition to his own business, including political, fraternal, and organizational affiliations. He shares the political beliefs of the Republican party; is a member of the Chamber of Commerce and the Maine State Auto Dealers' Association; and is a member of the Independent Order of Odd Fellows and the Free and Accepted Masons, in the latter of which orders he is a Knight Templar, and is connected with the Masonic Club. His religious affiliation is with the Methodist Episcopal church.

In Washington, on August 5, 1894, Mr. Morton married Lulu M. Glidden, who was born in Jefferson, Maine. Their children are: 1. Lloyd B., who was born in Washington, Maine. 2. Edith L., who was also born in Washington.

ERNEST L. DEAN, a prominent business man of Greenville, Maine, started in the lumber business at an early age and then became connected with a thriving company at Greenville, with which he worked in various capacities until he was appointed accountant. His interests and activities are wide. He is trustee of a leading hospital, director of a trust company, and in addition holds several responsible positions in the city government. His social and fraternal connections are wide, so that he is an active figure in many different spheres of interest.

Ernest L. Dean was born at Farmingdale, Maine,

August 20, 1879, son of Simeon P. and Addie B. (Peacock) Dean, of whom the father, who was a lumberman and mill operator, was born at Vassalboro, Maine, and of whom the mother was born at Litchfield, Maine. Ernest L. Dean attended the public schools at Farmingdale, Gardiner, and Hallowell, Maine. He worked for Elias Milliken in the lumber business at Hallowell, Maine, from 1890 to 1895. He then became connected with the Hollingsworth, Whitney Company, and from the year 1895 to the present has held various positions in that company. In 1921 he was appointed accountant and has since held that position. Mr. Dean is trustee and treasurer of the Charles A. Dean Hospital. He is a director of the Guilford Trust Company. He is a Republican in politics, and holds several public offices. He has been chief of the Fire Department for fifteen years. He has been chairman of the Greenville School Board for twelve years. He is also a selectman and chairman of the selectmen. He belongs to the Greenville Chamber of Commerce, the Free and Accepted Masons, Columbia No. 200, thirty-second degree all bodies, the Piscataquis Country Club, and the Tarratine Club of Bangor. He attends the Methodist church.

Mr. Dean married, at Revere, Massachusetts, June 13, 1899, Delia M. Snowdale, born at Weston, Maine, daughter of Fred and Delphine (Gellerson) Snowdale, of whom the father was born at Rockland, Maine, and of whom the mother was born at Weston, Maine, Children: 1. Elwin R., born August 11, 1903, at Island Falls, Maine. 2. Marion A., born August 19, 1904, at Island Falls, Maine. 3. Mildred S., born August 17, 1906, at Waterville, Maine. 4. Faye Ruth, born July 23, 1909, at Greenville, Maine. 5. Sarah May, born November 23, 1911, at Greenville, Maine. 6. Paul Simeon, born October 18, 1913, at Greenville, Maine. 7. Arthur Lanigan, born November 16, 1916, at Greenville, Maine. 8. Selia Delphine, born January 4, 1925, at Greenville, Maine.

OMA JOHN LOMBARD—After years of success as a merchant in Guilford, a good military record and with a high character for uprightness among his fellow-citizens, Oma John Lombard accepted the Postmastership of the town at the request of President Harding. His position in the community is secure, his friends legion, his future assured, for he is a man of action, judgment and engaging personality.

Oma John Lombard was born in Guilford, March 17, 1889, a son of Clarence C., and Jennie (Hammond) Lombard, both also natives of Guilford. Both are now deceased. Oma was educated in the public schools of Guilford and upon finishing entered the grocery business, in which he continued for ten years. Since then he has devoted himself to the public service. He is a Republican in politics, a member of the Free and Accepted Masons, of the Knights of Pythias and was the first commander of the local post of the American Legion. He served overseas during the World War in the Twenty-sixth Division, being attached to the 128th Infantry, Thirty-second Division in France. At the close of the war he returned to the United States and was honorably discharged at Camp Devens, Massachusetts. He is a member of the Guilford Country Club and of the Universalist church.

Mr. Lombard married, at Abbot, Maine, May 8, 1918, Cassie Marion Brown, daughter of the Hon.

C. W. Brown, who was a member of the National House of Representatives for two terms, and of Fannie (Goodwin) Brown. Their children are: Gloria Brown and Oma John, Jr.

EUGENE W. VAUGHAN—From a lumber camp in the Maine woods to the management of one of the most substantial financial institutions of this section, Eugene W. Vaughan has risen during a comparatively few years. He has done it on merit alone, although a solid business education was the foundation upon which he erected the edifice of his success. He has displayed a commendable sincerity in his interest in all affairs of importance to the citizenry of the locality, by which he has been honored by selection for public office. His work in his own line has shown a keen mind, coupled with a perfect comprehension of financial affairs, while his deep interest in matters of importance outside his zone of activity has created for him a host of friends in all walks.

Eugene W. Vaughan was born in Greenville, Maine, May 1, 1873, a son of Francis H., of Plymouth, Massachusetts, and Cordelia (Bardwell) Vaughan, also a native of Plymouth. The elder Vaughan was a veteran of the Civil War, in which he saw service with the Fifth Massachusetts Infantry, a worker in a cotton factory in Massachusetts and a guide in the Maine woods. The couple are both deceased. Eugene received his early education in the public schools of Greenville and was also graduated from the high school in that town. He then took the course at Shaw's Business College, in Portland, finishing which he returned to Greenville and began his life-work. Undecided as to just what avenue he should best select, he took a position as clerk for a lumbering concern. For two years this occupation kept him in the deep woods. Familiar with the lake region, he accepted a position on Moosehead Lake and for several years was captain of a steamboat on those inland waters. In off periods, when navigation was closed, he worked at surveying, never idle and unconsciously looking for what fate had chosen him to do. He became interested in the Greenville branch of the Guilford Trust Company. His careful education now stood him in good stead and he advanced in the work of that financial institution, in 1903 becoming manager of the Greenville branch. With the exception of six years, he has held that post ever since. He assisted in the organization of the Greenville Public Library and was elected town treasurer, a post which he took in 1922 and which, at this writing, he still conducts. He was also chosen a member of the Board of Selectmen and served for two years. He is a member of Columbia Lodge, No. 200, Free and Accepted Masons, has the thirty-second degree of that Order and belongs to the Scottish Rite of Portland. He is a member of the Guilford Country Club and attends the Congregational church, of the Sunday School of which he was formerly superintendent.

Eugene W. Vaughan married, in Farmington, Maine, January 10, 1899, Florence E. Holley, daughter of George and Emeline (Backus) Holley, both deceased.

REV. CHARLES I. BROWN—A clergyman of unusual popularity and influence in the little town of Farmington, Maine, is the Rev. Charles I. Brown, pastor of St. Joseph's Church, whose energy and personality have resulted in the steady growth of the church and its congregation since he assumed the pastorate six years ago.

The Rev. Father Brown was born in Woburn, Massachusetts, August 21, 1903, the son of Daniel J. and Elizabeth (Tonry) Brown. His father came to this country from Ireland when a boy and built up a substantial leather business in Boston, from which he retired to interest himself in Democratic politics and municipal affairs there. Mr. Brown's mother, the former Elizabeth Tonry, was a native of Boston and died at the family home there in 1926.

The Rev. Father Brown passed some of his boyhood in his native town, but later attended the public schools in Chelsea, Massachusetts, where the family had moved by the time he was of school age. Almost before he had completed his studies at the High School of Boston College he determined to become a priest and after his graduation he entered St. Mary's, where he studied for four years. He was graduated and then completed his studies at the Catholic University, in Washington, District of Columbia, and was ordained to the priesthood in 1918. His first charge was as assistant pastor of St. John's Church in Bangor, Maine, where he remained for two years, before being assigned to a church of his own, St. Mary's Church, Biddeford, Maine, and he served there as administrator for six months, coming to St. Joseph's Church in Farmington, Maine, in 1922.

The Rev. Father Brown is regarded as one of the most progressive young clergymen of the town and already has done much to further the development of his congregation. He is chaplain of the Knights of Columbus in Farmington and is particularly active in the affairs of that fraternity.

ARTHUR A. CRAFTS—Few migrate from the busy marts of metropolitan centers, where their antecedents have displayed unusual acumen in rapid barter on such intensive planes as stock and produce exchanges, to our Atlantic border States, where they settle. The reverse has been the usual condition, the lure of the West having taken many promising youths from the home nest. A most conspicuous instance in eastward migration is that of Arthur A. Crafts, of Greenville, Maine, who is a native of Ohio and came to this section from Chicago, Illinois, when a young man. That he has never regretted his choice is undoubted, for both fortune and happiness have been bestowed on him, his fellow-citizens have demonstrated their confidence and regard by electing him to important public office and he has risen to unusual heights in financial, fraternal and commercial affairs, in addition to his positions of political prominence. His business interests are widespread and successful, his friends as extensive as his acquaintances. His loyalty to his political party, which is Republican, is no greater than to his friends in all walks, who hold him to be a citizen of outstanding value to the community.

Arthur A. Crafts was born in Auburn, Ohio, June 21, 1867, a son of Miles B., of Auburn, and Julia F. (Gilbert) Crafts, of South Newbury, Ohio. Miles B. Crafts went to Chicago, Illinois, where he operated as a grain broker, and at the time of his death was the oldest active member of the Chicago Board of Trade. Arthur received his education in the Chicago public schools, was graduated from the high school in that city and afterward attended Oberlin College and graduated from the Commercial College, at Oberlin, Ohio. He came to Maine in 1890, where he became a general storekeeper and lumberman. He conducted a general store in Greenville for twenty-six years and in 1915 he opened the Squaw Mountain Inn, at Greenville. He also operates a sawmill at Shirley, and, in partnership with F. L. Huston, a native of Patten, Maine, manufactured diamond pointed tools, with a factory in Boston. He is a trustee of the Guilford Trust Company and is the only man ever elected to the Maine Senate to have served two terms from Piscataquis County. He was Town Clerk of Greenville and has served two terms as a member of the Lower House of the State Legislature. He is a Knight Templar and a member of the Order of Free and Accepted Masons, is a thirty-second member of the Ancient Accepted Scottish Rite; is also a member of the Order of the Eastern Star, and of the Improved Order of Red Men. Mr. Crafts is building the Masonic Temple in Greenville, which he is presenting to the local lodge. He holds membership in the Piscataquis Valley Country Club and attends the Union Church of Greenville.

AARON B. COLE—Law and the Legislature, the public interest, municipal advance and financial enterprise commanded the active and constructive participation of the late Aaron B. Cole, a distinguished son of Maine, who left a lasting impress of his career upon the statute books of the Commonwealth and in the annals of the county of York and the town of Kittery. Earlier in his life-work he had been an educator and legal practitioner in Massachusetts for some time, but his home State called him to resume his labors among his own people.

Aaron B. Cole was born in the town of Eliot, the son of John R. and Mary (Cottle) Cole. Passing through the schools of his birthplace, he took his preparatory training at Kents Hill Seminary, Kents Hill, and thence entered Boston University from whose Law School he was graduated with his degree of Bachelor of Laws. In Plainfield he filled the office of Superintendent of Schools, thereby contributing to the improvement of the educational department of that community. Those were the years when he was developing the latent powers with which he had been so generously endowed, and by which he was destined to serve in a large way his native beloved State. The days he spent in law practice and as an educator in the Bay State town served to give him polish and confidence in his own resources, so that when he concluded his services at Plainville, he was prepared to enter upon a more important sphere of his profession in the "land that gave him birth and opportunity."

Mr. Cole gave exhibition of his wisdom by making choice of the town of Kittery as the scene of his law practice on his return to Maine. He established his office there, and became one of the leading practitioners of York County, noted for his powers as a pleader of causes and for his ability as a counselor in office practice. Not only did he rise to the front rank of members of the bar, but he also became prominent in affairs of the community, the county, and the State. His abilities commanded the favorable attention of the citizenry, who saw in him a man to be preferred for public office.

Mr. Cole was honored with election to the State Senate for the session of 1913, and again was chosen for the same office for the 1916 session. In his last term he served as chairman of the special legislative committee to investigate the legislative expenditures. The report of his findings was most exhaustive, and was indicative of his thoroughness and reliability, outstanding qualifications for which he was well known. Nothing of great moment arose in York County during his lifetime that he did not have some connection with it, either in an official or an advisory capacity. The people of that jurisdiction came to repose every confidence in his ability and integrity.

For a term of several years, Mr. Cole was Judge of the Kittery Municipal Court, and his administration of justice furnished additional adornment to the proceedings of the bench. He was a director of the York County Trust Company, a trustee of the Eliot Public Library and served in a similar capacity for York Hospital. Always he gave freely of his time in the interests of the people, and was ever eager to coöperate in the achievement of civic advantage. He was a member and a Past Noble Grand of North Attleboro (Massachusetts) Lodge, Independent Order of Odd Fellows, and affiliated with the Kittery Tribe of the Improved Order of Red Men and with the Ancient Order of United Workmen.

Aaron B. Cole married Lilla B. Goodwin, daughter of Daniel and Mary (Lord) Goodwin, and their union was blessed with eight children: 1. Myra. 2. Marion. 3. Hollis B., who studied law at Boston University and is continuing his father's law business at Kittery. 4. Mildred. 5. Hosmer. 6. Hobart. 7. Lena. 8. Hoyt.

The death of Mr. Cole, on February 18, 1924, removed one of the substantial, stalwart citizens of Maine, whose loss was keenly felt in all those fine associations and constructive enterprises in which he had so notably figured. A tried and true son of the State had fallen, but his memory will survive the ravages of time.

JAMES LEONARD PACKARD—To the mercantile standing and success of Dexter, James Leonard Packard contributes through his own repute as a first-class plumber and as a dealer in hardware and crockery; while his directorship of corporations and his association with the general business life of the town have proven his value to the growth and activities of the community.

James Leonard Packard was born December 12, 1888, at Greenville, a son of Peter Packard, who was born in Presque Isle, where he was employed to the time of his death in 1891, and Mary (Brown) Packard), a native of Greenville. Mr. Packard attended the public and high schools at Greenville, and then learned both the plumbing and heating trade, so continuing for five years. In 1911, he became associated with Dana Crockett, as a partner in the Dana Crockett Company, this partnership existing until 1924, when he bought out Mr. Crockett's interest. In 1925, the firm name was changed to J. L. Packard Company, with Mr. Packard as sole owner; and he specializes in plumbing and heating, and carries a large line of hardware, crockery and glassware, with his store located on Main Street. He is also a member of the board of directors of the Exchange Hotel Corporation, and of the Waldheim Corporation.

In his political views a Republican, Mr. Packard with his vote and influence supports the principles of that party. Fraternally, he is affiliated with Penobscot Lodge, Free and Accepted Masons; St. John's Chapter, Royal Arch Masons; Mount Moriah Council, Royal and Select Masters; Order of the Eastern

Star; Plymouth Lodge, Independent Order of Odd Fellows; Silver Lake Encampment of Odd Fellowship; and the Rebekah Degree of that Order. He is a member of the Dexter 'Club; and the Dexter Chamber of Commerce; and his hobbies are hunting and fishing, and sports of all kinds. He attends the First Baptist Church.

James Leonard Packard married, June 10, 1914, Grace M. Smart, who was born in Dexter.

BRIGADIER-GENERAL MARK FERNALD WENTWORTH—No better synonym for patriotism, expressed in terms of military and civil service, has been found in the history of this State than that of Wentworth, an ancient and honorable surname, borne by many noted sons, among whom was Brigadier-General Mark Fernald Wentworth, Bvt., regimental commander in the Civil War and recipient of the Congressional Medal for meritorious and valorous service on the field of battle. General Wentworth was also a medical practitioner with a fine professional record, and served in various Federal and State offices of great responsibilities. He was an original Republican and helped nominate the Lincoln-Hamlin ticket in 1860.

The immigrant ancestor of this family was Elder William Wentworth, who came from England about 1639. General Wentworth's great-great-grandfather, John Wentworth, was Lieutenant-Governor of New Hampshire. The General came rightly by his pronounced patriotic strain, his forebears being good old fighting stock. His great-grandfather served as a captain in the French and Indian War and with the same rank in the Revolutionary War. His grandfather and two great-uncles were among the ardent patriots who took up arms in the Revolution.

Mark Fernald Wentworth was born in Kittery, March 14, 1820, the son of John Wentworth, an honest farmer and worthy citizen. From early childhood he gave evidence of student qualities as he attended the Kittery schools, and at the age of twelve years, when his father died, much was expected of him in making a career. At the age of seventeen he left high school, and taught school in the winter and operated the farm in the summer for four or five years. Already having made choice of the medical profession, he was twenty-one when he began the study of the science in the office of Dr. Trafton in South Berwick. In 1842-44 he attended lectures in the Dartmouth Medical School. From 1845 to 1849 he was chief clerk to the Naval Storekeeper at Kittery, and then served as clerk for York County to the State Valuation Commission at Augusta. By this time he had accumulated funds sufficient to warrant resumption of his medical studies, and he went to Philadelphia, Pennsylvania, and attended medical lectures at the University of Pennsylvania, from which institution he was graduated.

Dr. Wentworth began practice in South Boston, Massachusetts, and after two years returned to his native town of Kittery, where he built up a large and remunerative practice, to which he gave faithful and skillful attention for many years, until his death, which occurred in 1896. He was a physician of remarkable energy, genuine sympathy and versatile activity, a lover of his community and the State, its people and institutions.

The notable military record which Dr. Wentworth achieved dates back to 1854, when he organized a militia company known as the Kittery Artillery, and he was its commander until 1862. In 1857 he was appointed Chief-of-Staff to Governor Hannibal Hamlin, with the rank of lieutenant-colonel. Hardly had the repercussion of the first shot fired on Fort Sumter been felt in the North, than Colonel Wentworth and his Kittery Artillery enlisted to a man, eager to get to the front in defense of the Union. They were ordered to Fort McClary, where they were stationed for three months. In June, 1861, he was made Naval Storekeeper at Kittery at the behest of the Federal Government.

He soon proffered his services for action in the field and was commissioned lieutenant-colonel of the Twenty-seventh Maine Regiment. By vote of the line offices he was advanced to a full colonelcy, and went with his command on the call of President Lincoln for the "nine months' men." Near the expiration of their term of enlistment, Colonel Wentworth and his regiment, at the earnest request of President Lincoln and his Secretary of War, volunteered to remain for the defense of Washington, the North being at that time in one of its most critical exigencies of the war. Colonel Wentworth and his men from Maine held the Nation's Capital inviolate until General Lee and his army had been driven out of Pennsylvania and across the Potomac. After the crushing defeat of the Confederate forces at Gettysburg, Colonel Wentworth and his command were honorably mustered out of service, having been voted the coveted medals by special act of Congress in recognition of their heroism and patriotism in an hour of their country's greatest need. Their journey back home was a continuous ovation from Washington to Maine.

Colonel Wentworth had not the slightest idea of his war service being considered at an end. By the personal selection of Governor Samuel Cony, he was commissioned colonel of the Thirty-second Maine Regiment, which had been organized, officered and equipped under his supervision. This command was made a part of the Second Brigade, Second Division, Ninth Army Corps, and with the redoubtable colonel at its head, participated in the battles of the Wilderness, North Anna River, Bethesda Church, Cold Harbor, and Hanover Court House. Later they were active in the severest action of the siege of Petersburg. On July 30, 1864, Colonel Wentworth was severely wounded in the now historic "Mine Explosion" before Petersburg, and in November of that year was mustered out with honor. "For gallant and meritorious service during the war," he was brevetted brigadier-general by order of President Johnson.

No more enthusiastic and devoted member of the Grand Old Party has arisen in the rock-ribbed Republican State of Maine than General Wentworth. True as the steel of his trusty sword which he carried on many a field of glory, he was one of the first to espouse the Republican faith on the organization of that party. Thereafter, until the end of his days, he was intensely active in political affairs. In 1860 he was a delegate from the First Maine District to the Republican National Convention, and to him was given the marked distinction of casting the vote of the Pine Tree State for Abraham Lincoln for President and for Hannibal Hamlin—the Man from Maine—for Vice-President. In 1864, at the request of Washington, he again was made Naval Storekeeper at Kittery. He was elected Representative of his district to the State Legislature and served in the session of 1873-74. He was elected for a second term in 1880-81. In 1887 he was appointed a member of the Board of State Prison Inspectors and served four years. In 1891 he was named by President Harrison as Surveyor of Customs at Portland and Falmouth. As a delegate to the Republican National Convention of 1868 he assisted in the nomination of General Grant for President. He served as a member of the Electoral College in 1881.

General Mark Fernald Wentworth married (first), in 1843, Elizabeth Jane Wilson, daughter of Hon. Gowen Wilson, of Kittery. He married (second), in 1886, Hattie J. Phillips, who survived her husband at his death. Thus passed one of Maine's noblest of men—born to command, of compelling presence, prompt, energetic, thoughtful, resourceful. He was the soul of geniality, honor and hospitality, and nowhere were these happy traits to be better observed than in his home, which was ever open to his friends, to whom he remained as true as the geological structure of his beloved State. Public-spirited to the highest degree, he did all within his power for the welfare of his community. His entire life was punctuated with good deeds which with his memory will long live in the hearts of his countrymen.

JUDGE GEORGE WILLIAM HANSON—Having been appointed Judge of the Sanford Municipal Court in 1897, at the time it was established, Judge George William Hanson filled this office most satisfactorily for sixteen years. One of the leading legal lights of Maine, Judge Hanson was well versed in all details of the law, having followed this profession since 1886. During this period he practiced in various sections of the United States previous to coming to Sanford. He was a very prominent member of the bar in Sanford, and filled various other public offices during his residence here, including two years as a member of the School Board and seven years as chairman of the Board of Selectmen. The surname Hanson is of ancient origin and was handed down by the Flemings to the English-speaking people. The branch of this family in Maine, of which Judge Hanson was a descendant, has figured prominently in the affairs of the Pine Tree State, members thereof having been occupied in various walks of life and having filled positions requiring business sagacity, courage, tact, and integrity. They ever have been found in the foremost ranks. Hon. George William Hanson was the ninth generation of the family, established in America by Thomas Hanson, who, in 1658, had a grant of land near Salmon Falls, Province of New Hampshire.

(II) Thomas (2), son of the founder, Thomas H., was born about 1634. He married, and the line descends through his son.

(III) John Hanson, son of Thomas (2), was born about 1682, lived at Nock's Marsh, and is said to have been a Quaker. He had a son,

(IV) John (2), who resided near Nock's Marsh, and among his children was:

(V) William, born in 1730, at Waterboro, Maine.

(VI) Thomas (3) Hanson, son of William, was born in 1760, at Waterboro.

(VII) Joshua, son of Thomas (3), was born in 1790, at Waterboro, removed to Sanford, Maine, where he lived with his uncle. He married Philina Hobbs.

(VIII) Hon. Benjamin Forsythe Hanson, son of Joshua and Philina (Hobbs) Hanson, was born July

28, 1818, at Sanford, and was educated in the public schools there, learned blacksmithing, and then for several years was employed in the granite quarries at Quincy, Massachusetts. Then followed a period in Great Falls, New Hampshire, where he owned a livery business. He eventually returned to Sanford, farmed, conducted a general store, and became a leader in local affairs. He served as town treasurer, was a Republican, and represented his district in the Legislature during the year 1865; was promoted to the Senate in 1873-74. Senator Hanson was a member of the Republican County Committee, and of Springvale Lodge, Independent Order of Odd Fellows. He married Mary E. Libbey, a daughter of Elias and Mehitable Libbey of Sanford, in 1841, who died February 27, 1891. Their children were Luther L., Benjamin F., Charles H., and George W., of further mention.

Hon. George William Hanson, who was the ninth generation of this family in America, was born in Sanford, Maine, January 26, 1861. He attended the district schools, prepared for college at Coburn Classical Institute, and in 1883 he was graduated from Colby University. Then followed a two years' course of law under the direction of Hon. W. F. Lunt of Portland, Maine. Returning to his scholastic pursuits he entered Boston University and was graduated from the Law School there in 1886, with his degree. Mr. Hanson was one of the most prominent students in this university and at the time of his graduation stood fourth in a very large class. After practicing his profession in Boston for a time, he became a member of the editorial staff of the West Publishing Company of St. Paul, Minnesota, publishers of legal reports. Severing his connection with this firm, he proceeded to Sioux Falls, South Dakota, and there practiced law for three years. In 1891, he was called back to Sanford by the death of his father and at this time decided to remain here where he opened his office. He rapidly obtained the respect of his fellow practitioners and when, in 1897, the Sanford Municipal Court was established by an act of the Legislature, Mr. Hanson was appointed Judge. This appointment came as a result of a lengthy petition which was presented to the governor and council. Deeply public-spirited and possessing excellent qualities as a leader, Judge Hanson often was approached by his community for other positions of public trust. In 1892 he was appointed a member of the Board of Selectmen and filled this office with honor, having been chairman for seven years. His services also included two years as a member of the Sanford School Board, and one term in the Maine Legislature. Fraternally, he was a member of the Masonic Order and a member of the Grange. His religious affiliation was with the Baptist Church of Springvale, Maine, which he served as deacon and as superintendent of the Sunday school for many years.

In 1886, Judge Hanson married Maria H. Shaw, daughter of John H. Shaw of Sanford, and to this marriage were born three children: 1. Pauline, born September 17, 1891, a teacher in the high school at New Haven, Connecticut. 2. Mary, born January 28, 1895, married Alva W. McDougal, an electrician at the Sanford Mills, and a veteran of the World War, having served during this strife with a company recruited in New Mexico; they have four children: Marjorie Alice, born June 24, 1921; Alva Warren, Jr., born January 29, 1923; Robert Hanson, born

December 6, 1924; and Beverly Jane, born December 18, 1926. 3. Benjamin Shaw, born September 13, 1896, representing the tenth generation of the Hanson family in America. He married Emma Grimm, of Staunton, Virginia, and is a teacher in the Staunton Military Academy at Staunton, Virginia. They have one son, Benjamin Shaw, Jr., born on November 2, 1924, the eleventh generation in direct descent from the American founder of this family.

At the time of Judge Hanson's death, in November, 1922, there were many sincere expressions of sympathy and regret on the part of his confreres and numerous friends in this section of Maine. Through his long residence here and through his good works he had become one of the most popular men in Sanford. Well versed in the law, he tempered his decisions from the bench with mercy and leniency, although with habitual offenders he was stern and just. In this office he established a record that will be difficult for succeeding occupants to excel.

CLAIR A. RUNNALS—Born in Pittsfield, Maine, May 4, 1879, Clair A. Runnals is a son of William F. and Ida J. (Bowker) Runnals. William F. Runnals was born in Garland, Maine, and was by trade a machinist. In Pittsfield he pursued this calling for a number of years, and was highly regarded as an industrious and honorable man by all who knew him. He was active in affairs of the community, took part in political movements and belonged to the Free and Accepted Masons, Monson Lodge, Monson, Maine. His wife, Ida J. (Bowker) Runnals, was a native of Ellsworth, Maine; and she was a good mother to her son Clair.

Clair A. Runnals received his education in the public schools of Dover and Foxcroft, Caribou Academy (1893-94), and Monson Academy (1895-96). In 1897-98 he worked for the Willimantic Linen Company. Then from 1899 to 1900 he was employed by B. B. Merrill, druggist, brewer, and from 1900 until May 1, 1901, he worked for the New England Telephone & Telegraph Company. At that time he accepted an offer from the Dover-Foxcroft Light & Heat Company, which position he continued to hold until the company was absorbed through purchase by the Central Maine Power Company. For the four years following 1918 he was local superintendent in Foxcroft for the Dover-Foxcroft organization; from 1922 until 1926 he was district superintendent with supervision over all Central Maine Power Company's property in Piscataquis and West Penobscot counties. In 1926, on January 1, he was appointed by officials of the Central Maine Power Company to the position of division superintendent, with authority over the upper northern division of the company's territory.

In Foxcroft, where he makes his home, Mr. Runnals is known chiefly for his position of authority with the power organization, but at the same time he does concern himself freely with local affairs. A Republican, he is ardent in support of the party, and is possessed of a considerable influence, which he exerts without fanfare, always quietly, for the welfare of the community as a whole. Never once, however, has he accepted the suggestion that he run for public office, preferring to direct, as it were, from a position aside. He has been heartily interested in educational supervision and progress, and for six years was a member of the Dover School Board. For three years he has been a member of the

board of directors of the Dover-Foxcroft water district, and is past chairman of that body. Fraternally, his connections include membership in the National Electric Light Association, in which organization his acquaintance is of large proportion. He is a communicant of the Foxcroft Baptist Church, is devout in its service and generous in contributions to charitable and kinded appeals of worthy character, regardless of race or creed, giving readily and in a spirit truly humanitarian. During the World War, although he was somewhat advanced in years for service in the military overseas, he was on several boards and committees in charge of the prosecution of the war from within this country, and was instrumental in the solicitation of subscriptions in the several Liberty Loan campaigns. Of Mr. Runnals it is said by those who know him best, that he is a manly man, kindly, well disposed toward all persons until disqualification is evidenced, firm in opinion but open minded and ready to listen to opposite sides of questions when he feels he may be in error, honorable in his dealings, no matter how large or small, and a valuable citizen to community, State and nation.

In the month of March, 1899, Mr. Runnals was united in marriage with Charlotte L. Burgess, of Sebec, Maine, daughter of William E. and Lucy (Parsley) Burgess, her father a native of Sebec, her mother of Sangerville, Maine. The ceremony was performed in Sebec. To this union have been born children: 1. Doris C., born in Willimantic, Maine, September 3, 1900. 2. Margaret B., born in Foxcroft, October 15, 1907.

JOSEPH THOMPSON—A native of England, where he was educated and where he obtained his early training in the textile industry, Joseph Thompson came to America in early manhood. During the years of his long and useful life in this country, Mr. Thompson remained in the work he had chosen early for his career, and his many contributions to the advancement of textile manufacturing in Pennsylvania, Rhode Island and Maine will serve to keep his memory fresh in the minds of those who follow. Not only did Mr. Thompson become recognized as a valued factor in the production of woolen goods and allied products, but he also occupied a place of moment in the fraternal and social circles of his adopted country.

Mr. Thompson was born February 2, 1858, at Halifax, Yorkshire, England, his parents having been the late Samuel and Mary Ann (Green) Thompson. After having obtained his education in the public schools of his native district, he entered upon his apprenticeship in the textile mills there, where, under competent instructors, he soon gained a thorough knowledge of the industry which he was to follow until the end of his days. On his arrival in America, Mr. Thompson located in Philadelphia, Pennsylvania, and worked in the mills of that city for about a year. Thence he removed to Providence, Rhode Island, one of the largest centers of textile manufacturing in the United States, where he was employed in the mills of that city for a period of five years. At that time, he was possessed of a desire to return to England, but upon his arrival there, found conditions so unsatisfactory, that he soon returned to America and came to Sanford, Maine. The Goodall Worsted Company was being organized in Sanford at that time, and Mr. Thompson entered this

MAINE—A HISTORY

organization as foreman of the finishing department. For the remainder of his lifetime he devoted himself loyally to the interests of the Goodall Company in this capacity, while at the same time he gave much time and thought to possible betterments of manufacture. These efforts resulted in his perfecting the present method of putting a permanent finish on mohair, alpaca, and worsted linings, now in general use.

Popular among his fellow workers and neighbors, Mr. Thompson was selected for membership in numerous fraternal and social bodies, among them being the Preble Lodge, Free and Accepted Masons; White Rose Chapter, Royal Arch Masons; Sanford Lodge, Benevolent and Protective Order of Elks, and the Sanford Town Club. In all of these organizations Mr. Thompson was an enthusiastic and well-liked associate. He was a faithful and devoted worker in the church of his choice, the Unitarian, and his political allegiance was given to the Republican party, although he cared little for the emoluments of public office, and declined to enter contests therefor.

Joseph Thompson early in life assumed the responsibilities and joys of family life, having married Sophia Hudson before he had attained his twenty-first birthday, and this happy union endured for almost half a century, being broken only by his death in May, 1928, a short time before they would have celebrated their golden anniversary. Mr. and Mrs. Thompson became the parents of four sons, all of them holding positions of prominence and trust in the business affairs of Sanford: 1. Samuel Harry (see a following biography), married Alice A. Ashworth, and they have two children: Lenora A. and Joseph. 2. John W. (q. v.), married Milca Planche, and they also have two children: Lorina M. and Irene A. 3. Ernest (q. v.), married Lennie Horlor; they have one child, Ernestine. 4. Clarence (q. v.), married Florida Normandeau, and they are the parents of a daughter, Mildred E. Sophia (Hudson) Thompson, who survives her husband, resides at No. 23 Riverside Avenue, Sanford.

Mr. Thompson's death occasioned profound sorrow and regret in Sanford, for the entire community realized that his place would be difficult to fill in that town, wherein he had lived a life replete with good deeds, and where he passed his last days in a manner typical of that class of citizens who maintain the institutions and liberties of this nation, going peacefully to their reward in the Great Beyond.

SAMUEL HARRY THOMPSON—Although a native of England, Samuel Harry Thompson was brought to America by his parents early in life and since has made his home in Sanford, where he is employed in the work that was followed by his father, who was one of the outstanding figures for many years in the textile industry. Mr. Thompson now (1928) occupies the same position that at one time his father filled, overseer of the Goodall Worsted Company. He not only is an authority on the methods and practices used in the finishing of wool and other textiles, but also is considered a leader in many other spheres in Sanford—civic, social and fraternal.

Mr. Thompson was born January 21, 1878, at Bradford, Yorkshire, England, son of Joseph (see a preceding biography) and Sophia (Hudson) Thompson, both natives of England, and one of the four sons born to this couple. He was educated in the grammar schools of England and there also attended evening high school classes. He early in life chose to follow in the footsteps of his father, and after coming to Sanford became connected with the Goodall Company. He since has remained with this concern and through loyal and devoted service thereto has been steadily advanced until now (1928) he is serving as overseer, a post that his father at one time occupied. Mr. Thompson is held in high regard by his firm and is an acknowledged authority on the processes use by the Goodall Company, some of which were perfected by the senior Mr. Thompson. Mr. Thompson has become sincerely interested in many organizations of Sanford, being a member of the Lodge, Free and Accepted Masons; the Benevolent and Protective Order of Elks, and the Improved Order of Red Men. In this last-named Order he has at various times held every office in the local Tribe, being a Past Sachem thereof. His recreation is gained through membership in the Bauneg Beg Country Club, and in the Sanford Town Club, while his religious convictions are those of the Unitarian faith.

On November 10, 1900, at Sanford, Samuel Harry Thompson took as his bride Alice A. Ashworth, daughter of George Ashworth, now deceased, and of Elizabeth Ashworth. Mr. and Mrs. Thompson have two children: 1. Lenora Ann, born June 13, 1901. 2. Joseph, born July 30, 1911. Joseph, who is seventeen years old, was the only one of the four Maine boys appointed by Senator Gould to enter the Naval Academy at Annapolis who successfully passed the examinations, and he is the first Sanford youth to enter that Academy.

JOHN W. THOMPSON—In commercial circles, fraternal associations, club life and religious affairs, John W. Thompson has been a figure of note in Sanford for many years and probably enjoys the friendship and acquaintance of a majority of the people of this town because of his civic spirit and willingness to aid in every way possible the betterment and progress of his community. Mr. Thompson, while a native of England, came to this country in his boyhood and most of his life has been spent in Sanford. He is a son of the late Joseph Thompson (q. v.), who died in May, 1928, and of Sophia (Hudson) Thompson, who survives her husband and now (1928) resides at No. 23 Riverside Avenue, Sanford.

John W. Thompson was born in 1879, at Halifax, England. He resided in England for a time, attending the grade schools in Bradford, and then accompanied his parents to this city, where he completed his education in a private school. Since finishing his scholastic studies Mr. Thompson has been variously employed in Sanford, much of his career having been devoted to mercantile pursuits. He now (1928) holds the responsible position of manager of the Ladies' Department Store. In addition to zealous cooperation in proposals and projects designed for Sanford's best interests, Mr. Thompson has become a factor of note in fraternal societies, his principal affiliation being with the Masonic Order. He is a member of Preble Lodge, No. 143, Free and Accepted Masons; Chapter No. 54, Royal Arch Masons; Bethany Commandery, No. 24, Knights Templar; and Lodge No. 1470, Benevolent and Protective Order of Elks. He also popular in social circles as is attested by his membership in the Sanford Town Club.

John W. Thompson married, January 28, 1909, at Sanford, Milca Planche, and they have two children: 1. Lorina M., born January 15, 1915. 2. Irene Anita, born January 22, 1918. Mrs. Milca (Planche) Sanford's parents were Claude and Marceline (Gauthier) Planche, the father a native of France, the mother born in Canada.

ERNEST THOMPSON—Among the principal industrial concerns of Sanford is the Goodall Worsted Company, and since the organization of this corporation members of the Thompson family have been closely identified with it. Ernest Thompson's father, Joseph Thompson (q. v.), during his lifetime, was one of the most valuable employees of the Goodall Company, he having become associated with the firm at the time of its organization. Now (1928) two of his sons are following his footsteps, Ernest and Samuel Harry Thompson (q. v.), but it is with Ernest Thompson that we deal in this brief biography. He is now functioning as a finisher and overseer, carrying on many of the processes which were developed by his father for this work. Mr. Thompson, in addition to a splendid military record during the World War, enjoys a reputation of being an outstanding factor in social and fraternal circles of Sanford.

Mr. Thompson was born June 26, 1891, in Halifax, Yorkshire, England, and was an infant when brought to America by his parents, Joseph and Sophia (Hudson) Thompson, they also being natives of England. Mr. Thompson's paternal grandparents were Samuel and Mary Ann (Green) Thompson. Joseph Thompson first came to the United States, worked in various textile mills in this country, and then spent a period in his native land, returning to America and locating at Sanford when Ernest Thompson was about one year old. He was educated in the local schools here and completed his training when he was graduated from Sanford High School. Soon thereafter he entered the Goodall Worsted Company's mills, where, under the skillful guidance of his talented father, he soon became unusually well informed in the products manufactured by the Goodall Company and especially in that process perfected by his father and now in general use, through which a permanent finish is given to mohair, alpaca, and worsted linings. Thus it came about, eventually, that he was promoted to overseer and since has functioned in that office.

After the entrance of the United States into the World War, Mr. Thompson volunteered for service and was assigned to Company D, Thirty-fifth Machine Gun Battalion, Twelfth Division. He remained in the military forces until the cessation of hostilities, and after having been honorably discharged, returned to Sanford, where he resumed his duties in the mills. Mr. Thompson is a Republican, and while he has never agreed to the use of his name for public office, has been loyal in supporting the issues and candidates of his party. His fraternal affiliations, devoted in the main to the Masonic Order, include membership in Preble Lodge, No. 143, Free and Accepted Masons; White Rose Chapter, No. 54, Royal Arch Masons; Bethany Commandery, No. 24, Knights Templar; Maine Council, No. 7, Royal and Select Masters; Maine Consistory, Sublime Princes of the Royal Secret; thirty-second degree Ancient Accepted Scottish Rite, located at Portland, Maine; and Kora Temple, Ancient Arabic Order Nobles of the

Mystic Shrine. He is also a member of Sanford Lodge, No. 1470, Benevolent and Protective Order of Elks; the Sanford Town Club, and the Unitarian church. In all of these organizations Mr. Thompson is a devoted worker, as he is in community projects.

Ernest Thompson married, January 6, 1918, at Somersworth, New Hampshire, Lennie Horlor, and they have one child: Ernestine, born August 18, 1918. Mr. Thompson resides in Sanford, is popular in social circles, and enjoys the friendship of a large group of congenial people here.

CLARENCE THOMPSON—Among the four sons of the late Joseph Thompson, all of whom have attained positions of prominence and esteem in Sanford, is Clarence Thompson, the sole member of this family native of Sanford, the others having been born in England, and having been brought to this country by their parents. Clarence Thompson, the youngest of these brothers, is the only one who has not followed some branch of the textile or clothing business, in which the father was engaged. He chose the drug business as his career and now (1928) owns an establishment at No. 146 Main Street, Sanford.

Mr. Thompson is a son of the late Joseph Thompson (q. v.), who died in May, 1928, and of Sophia (Hudson) Thompson, who survives her husband. They had four sons, Samuel Harry, John W., Ernest (whose biographies are given at length preceding this), and Clarence, of further mention.

Clarence Thompson was born February 20, 1893, at Sanford, about one year after his father, mother and brothers came to this city, and after attending the public schools of Sanford, graduating from high school on June 14, 1911, entered the Massachusetts College of Pharmacy in order to perfect himself for this profession. He was graduated from this institution on May 14, 1914, and for three years thereafter was employed as a pharmacist, during which time he enhanced his theoretical training through practical experience. At the end of that time, through frugal habits and a systematic plan of saving, Mr. Thompson was enabled to launch his own enterprise, and on December 15, 1917, opened the drugstore he now conducts at No. 146 Main Street. Since the opening of this place of business Mr. Thompson has combined his thorough experience with a high code of ethics, and as a consequence his concern has prospered steadily, and now is one of the foremost establishments of its kind in Sanford. Only the highest grade drugs and merchandise are handled by Mr. Thompson, and due to the fact that most of the citizens of this city have known him throughout his life and are fully aware of his pharmaceutical knowledge, his patronage has grown to large proportions. Not only does he evidence a spirit of progressiveness in the conduct of his business, but these same methods have been utilized in his association with the civic development of Sanford. Mr. Thompson is a Republican, but not an office-seeker, and neither is he a blind partisan, often placing an issue or the personal qualifications of a candidate above party lines. He is a member of Sanford Lodge, No. 1470, Benevolent and Protective Order of Elks, and has been quite liberal in the support of the Unitarian church.

Clarence Thompson married, April 11, 1917, at Sanford, Florida Normandeau, and they have a daughter: Mildred Eleanor, born January 30, 1918.

PERCY EMERTON GILBERT, M. D.—As a physician, teacher, and director of medical research, Percy Emerton Gilbert, M. D., is known by educational and medical organizations throughout the State of Maine. Native of that State, his entire professional career has been concentrated there. Since 1923 his home has been in Madison.

Percy Emerton Gilbert was born at Greene, Maine, January 9, 1876, the son of Marcellus N. Gilbert and Rachel (Emerton) Gilbert. His early education was at the Coburn Classical Institute, after which he matriculated in Colby College, graduating there with the degree of Bachelor of Arts in 1900. His interests lay in scientific research while at Colby, and he felt a growing desire to undertake the practice of medicine. Accordingly, Dr. Gilbert entered the Bowdoin Medical School, graduating with the degree of Doctor of Medicine in 1906, meanwhile acting as instructor in the Ricker Classical Institute at Houlton, Maine, from 1900 until 1902 and as principal of the Bridgewater High School from then until 1904. Having graduated at Bowdoin he served his period of internship at the Maine General Hospital, at Portland, from 1906 until 1907, when he opened an office at Linneus and conducted a general practice until 1913. During the next ten years he removed to and practiced in Ashland, Maine, in 1923 taking his present (1928) residence in Madison. While at Ashland Dr. Gilbert was on the visiting staff of physicians in the Presque Isle General Hospital. This connection continued from 1917 until he left Ashland in 1923. He was school physician from 1921 until 1923, also part-time local Health Officer, at the same time, and among the several honors bestowed upon him was the presidency of the Aroostook County Medical Association, a position which he held for one term. Dr. Gilbert conducted a survey of health conditions of 23,000 school children in thirty-seven cities and towns, and after compiling the data thoroughly so as to indicate the real state of health existing together with remedies to counteract certain health problems he put the findings into a pamphlet entitled, "Medical Inspection of School Children." At the present time he is a member of the courtesy surgical staff of the Sisters' Hospital, Waterville, Maine. From time to time Dr. Gilbert has published articles of interest to his profession in the journal of the Maine Medical Association. While his time has been devoted almost exclusively to the pursuit of his profession in general practice and as applied to school research, Dr. Gilbert has taken a constructive part in the civic affairs of the towns in which he lived, and at Madison is a member of the Kiwanis Club, of which he was president in 1928. He is affiliated with the Free and Accepted Masons, and a member of the Baptist church.

Percy E. Gilbert married, June 28, 1906, Emily Carpenter, of the family name of Hodgdon. One child has been born of the union: Margaret R. Gilbert.

JOHN S. WILLIAMS—One of Maine's distinguished sons, John S. Williams, of Guilford, holds a high place in legal circles in the State, having been established in the practice of his profession for many years and taking an active and prominent part in the civil affairs of this town. Mr. Williams is one of the ablest lawyers of this vicinity, being a popular member of the bar whose brilliant ability and keen, intuitive sense in legal matters is recognized and ap-

preciated by his clients as well as by his fellow-citizens. He has served in various offices in the administration of local governmental policies and he has ever maintained a deep and sincere interest in the progress and welfare of his community, being always ready to assist by his influence and his energy in all projects for advancement and improvement.

Mr. Williams was born in Monson, July 24, 1864, a direct descendant of Richard Williams, who settled in Taunton, Massachusetts, having first come to America in 1633. The line of descent is as follows: (I) Richard Williams, son of William Williams, was born in England. He settled first in Dorchester, Massachusetts, in 1633, and later moved to Taunton. He married Frances Dighton, sister of the first wife of Governor Thomas Dudley, and to this union were born eight children. (II) Benjamin, son of Richard and Frances (Dighton) Williams, was born in Taunton, about 1645. He married, March 18, 1690, Rebecca, daughter of Captain George Macy, of Taunton, and to this union were born four children. (III) Benjamin (2), son of Benjamin (1) and Rebecca (Macy) Williams, was born in Taunton, July 3, 1695. He married, December 22, 1720, Susanna, daughter of Major John and Sarah (Dean) Howard, of Bridgewater. (IV) Rufus, only son of Benjamin (2) and Susanna (Howard) Williams, was born in Taunton, in 1723. He married, March 11, 1745-46, Mercy, daughter of Jonathan and Mercy (Mason) Shaw, of Raynham. (V) Oliver, son of Rufus and Mercy (Shaw) Williams, was born at Taunton, about 1750. He married and moved to Grafton, New Hampshire, signing the petition for the incorporation of that town in 1777 and again in 1778. (VI) Oliver (2), son of Oliver (1) Williams, was born about 1775, and married, at Canaan, New Hampshire, October 24, 1799, Jemima Barney, of Grafton. (VII) Norman Smith, son of Oliver (2) and Jemima (Barney) Williams, was born at Canaan, in 1817. He married, in May, 1844, Martha Ann Haynes, born in Canaan, in 1825, daughter of Josiah Porter and Sally (Atherton) Haynes. Norman Smith Williams was engaged in the agricultural industry for the greater part of his career, moving in 1840 to Dexter, and later settling in Monson, where he spent the remainder of his life. He was a prominent Republican, active in local political and church affairs, and was one of the most highly esteemed men of his community.

John S. Williams, son of Norman Smith and Martha Ann (Haynes) Williams, was educated in the public schools of Monson and at Monson Academy, after which he entered the University of Maine, where he graduated in 1887. He studied for the legal profession in the office of Henry Hudson, Jr., at Guilford, and in the Law School of Boston University, graduating in 1890, with the degree of Bachelor of Laws. He was admitted to the bar in 1889, before he was graduated, and while pursuing his studies, taught in the Guilford High School for three years. He commenced his practice of law in Guilford, in 1891, and soon attracted a large and distinguished clientele. In 1893, he was appointed by President Cleveland to the office of Collector of Internal Revenue for the Maine District, holding this responsible position until 1899, serving two years during President McKinley's administration. He is an ardent supporter of the principles of the Democratic party and takes an active part in politics, having served as a member of the Board of Selectmen of Guilford for several years and also as town agent and Superintendent of Schools. For eight years, he gave to the citizens of Guilford and vicinity, an efficient and progressive administration in his position of postmaster for this town, having the interests of the community ever in mind and inaugurating many modern and advanced methods to facilitate postal service. In 1908, he was presidential elector for the Fourth Congressional District. He is a member of the County and State Bar associations and of the United States Supreme Court Bar, the Piscataquis County Country Club, while his fraternal connections are with the Free and Accepted Masons, the Knights Templar, and the Knights of Pythias. His religious affiliations are with the Universalist church.

John S. Williams married, September 25, 1897, at Marblehead, Massachusetts, Helen K. Montgomery, daughter of Rev. Hugh and Anna E. (Roberts) Montgomery, and to this union have been born seven children: Hugh Montgomery, John H., Roger, Victor F., Matthew, Edwin R., and Helen A.

MOSES GERRISH FARMER—Distinguished as a pioneer in the realm of electricity, Professor Moses Gerrish Farmer, a native of New Hampshire and an adopted son of Maine, built, as far back as 1847, a model locomotive operated by electricity, which he used on a miniature railway on which he transported the first passengers ever so carried in the United States. He is credited also with having been the first to build a dynamo machine and the first to light a dwelling by electric light, with an automatic system of his own invention. He perfected the first electro-magnetic clock, and brought to light and perfected many other inventions. The organizer of the American Institute of Electrical Engineers, he was considered one of the most brilliant minds of his day.

Moses Gerrish Farmer was born in Boscawen, New Hampshire, February 9, 1820, and when a young boy removed to Eliot, where he finished his preparatory training. He was graduated from Dartmouth College in the class of 1844. For two years he taught school in Eliot and Dover, New Hampshire, and it was while located in the latter town that he devoted his leisure hours to the study of electricity and the possibility of its application to various uses as suggested to his keen mind. He invented several forms of electro-motors, one of which he used in his experimental workshop to drive a vertical lathe, and the other was used on a miniature railway. Both motors were originally designed to illustrate his lectures.

Professor Farmer demonstrated that the electrical current could be used for discharging torpedoes and in submarine blasting. In many other ways did he develop the practical use of electricity, and it is safe to say that he was the forerunner of the marvelous electrical epoch—especially in dynamics—in which the world is now moving.

Professor Farmer rendered a splendid service as principal of the old Eliot High School, having succeeded Israel Kimball, who was the first headmaster there. Thence he removed, in July, 1848, to Boston, Massachusetts, to take charge of the telegraph office. Already he had become acquainted with the preliminary details of telegraphy, and he continued to manifest the keenest interest in all things pertaining to electricity. Later in the year 1848 he con-

structed two new machines for the striking of fire alarms, and one of them was installed in the Court House at Boston. In 1849 he had the distinction of bringing out, under his own design and construction, the first electro-magnetic clock, made of three wheels, each having sixty teeth, for the operation of second, minute and hour hands, and for this he was granted patent rights in 1852. It was while living in Salem, in or about the year 1850, that he perfected a dynamo by which he lighted his house by electricity, being declared to have been the very first to have accomplished this feat. It is also claimed for him that he cooked a steak by electricity that same year. In 1880 he was issued a patent on an automatic electric-light system. Having removed some years previously from Salem to Newport, he kept steadily at work in the latter city on the perfection of his fire-alarm telegraph and other electrical devices. To his widespread reputation was added his discovery of the self-exciting power of the dynamo. In July, 1851, he was made superintendent of all electrical construction work for the city of Boston.

Professor Farmer was acclaimed far and wide for the success that attended his electrical inventions, and he was hailed as one of the earliest and greatest benefactors of the age. Certain it is that he was many years ahead of his time in the designing and completion of many remarkable machines operated by the electrical current, and that the principles he laid down have been employed in a very large degree, and in many cases in their entirety, by the electrical geniuses or "wizards" who have come after him. Recognition of his invaluable contributions to science and the field of mechanics was made with his election to membership in the American Association for the Advancement of Science. Here he was in notable company, and his fellowship with kindred spirits was most congenial to one of his keen intellect and profound learning. In 1884 he was instrumetal in bringing together a group of men who were thinking and acting along the lines in which he were already had become a national figure. Following his lead, these men adopted his organization plans for the formation of the American Institute of Electrical Engineers, which body has since come into prominent association with everything marking the almost phenomenal advance in the electrical world. Professor Farmer was made an honorary member of the institute, a distinction which he was the only American, up to the time of his death, to hold.

The city of Boston was extremely grateful to the former Salem and Newport telegraph operator, who, impelled by his genius for invention, had perfected, with the assistance of Edwin Rogers (see a following biography), a relative and also gifted with great ability for the construction of electrical machines, the fire-alarm telegraph, which marked a new era in the campaign of prevention of loss of life and property through fire. Following Professor Farmer's installation in office of superintendent of electrical construction work in Boston, he was made superintendent of the entire fire-alarm system of the city, his services in that office covering the term of 1851-55. In the second year after he took office the first Boston fire-alarm system plant was installed under his personal supervision.

Professor Moses Gerrish Farmer married Hannah Tobey Shapleigh, sister of Mrs. Sarah Frances (Shapleigh) Rogers, who is the mother of Marguerite B. Rogers, of York. Professor and Mrs. Farmer were blessed with a daughter, Sarah, a gifted woman, endowed with a remarkably pleasing personality—generous in all her ways and true in every fibre of her being—loving and loved by all who knew her best. Miss Farmer founded and gave the land and buildings and endowment for the Green Acres Fellowship, of which she was an inspiration during her lifetime. To her distinguished father she brought an intelligent assistance in his scientific research work, without which undoubtedly much of his splendid success in the electrical world would have been delayed or perhaps never even achieved.

The death of Professor Farmer in Chicago, Illinois, May 25, 1893, marked the passing of one of America's greatest—whose name deserves a place on the column of achievement whereon might be carved those of Franklin, Channing, Edison, De Forest and others, who have helped illuminate and generate the world's most advanced activities in the field of electrical science. Farmer will ever remain an historic figure; in the broadest sense he belongs to the world at large; in terms of America he was in his day a product of the new world and an exponent of its spirit of progress; in a more intimate way, in which the ties of home and the bonds of affection hold him in enduring and precious memory, he belonged to the commonwealth of United States of America, any histroy of which would be sadly incomplete without an appreciation of his contributions to the advancement of science.

EDWIN ROGERS—The name of Edwin Rogers will ever remain associated with a number of important perfections of first inventions of electrical apparatus, notably the fire-alarm telegraph and the automatic fire-alarm repeater signals. Mr. Rogers was one of the most distinguished of the natives of Eliot, and by reason of the remarkable results of his inventive ability he brought distinction to his home State, while he contributed vastly to the development of electro-mechanics for a variety of uses. Throughout his busy life, he continually kept before him his main purpose, the saving of life and property from fire.

Edwin Rogers was born in Eliot, July 8, 1829, died August 15, 1907, the son of John Pray and Elizabeth (Hammond) Rogers. Having completed his education in the public schools of his native town, he went to Dover, New Hampshire, and worked as a carpenter there for a few years. While in Dover he had his attention drawn to the practical application of electricity. In or about 1852, he transferred his activities to Salem, Massachusetts, and in April of that year, became an associate of Moses Gerrish Farmer (see a preceding biography), another inventive genius along electrical lines, and a relative. It was in April, 1852, that Mr. Rogers brought out his perfected invention of the fire-alarm telegraph, which revolutionized the calling of fire companies and apparatus to the scenes of fires, and resulted in the saving of many lives and a vast amount of property. In Boston, Mr. Rogers supervised the construction of the machinery which first made the application of his device practical.

Then it was that Mr. Farmer and his associate, Dr. W. F. Channing, were quick to perceive the advantage to be gained from Mr. Rogers' service, and they made him an important member of their staff. In this connection he acquired much additional knowledge of the science of electricity. He soon attained the status of an expert electrical mechanic, making a specialty of fire-alarm telegraphs. Still further development of his inventive powers was made possible through the aid rendered by Mr. Farmer. Subsequently he brought out for use by the Federal Government a device for the striking of the number of each lighthouse and perfected other beacon signals as well. Among his more important inventions in line with his specialty was his automatic repeater of alarm signals, from one to all other currents, this machine accomplishing a remarkable saving of time and labor.

When Mr. Farmer and Dr. Channing disposed of their patent rights to the Gamewell Fire-Alarm Telegraph Company, of New York, Mr. Rogers, in 1855, entered the employ of that concern in the capacity of electrical engineer and constructor, remaining with the company for half a century, engaged in the supervision of the installation of fire-alarm systems throughout the United States.

Wherever and whenever Mr. Rogers made an acquaintance, there and then he made a friend. Handicapped from early youth by a serious ailment, he was an example of uncomplaining and patient endeavor. He was kind, generous and loving, and ever ready to lend a helping hand. Honest and faithful in every relation of life, true and just in all his dealings, he bequeathed to those he loved a memory which is gratefully cherished. Among his many noble qualities, many recall another side of his make-up, in which a jolly disposition and a dry humor found happy expression.

Edwin Rogers married Sarah Frances Shapleigh, of an old and esteemed family of Maine, which has figured in its history and advance from early Colonial times. They were the parents of Marguerite B. Rogers, a social leader, prominent in the York Woman's Club, the Daughters of the American Revolution, and is active in the civic affairs of her community. She is a descendant of Joseph Pray of Berwick and Lieutenant James Shapleigh, both cf whom played an important part in the Revolutionary War as gallant soldiers.

FRANK U. WITHAM—Actuated by that spirit of determination to win that is a heritage from his forefather pioneers, who helped to make New England dominant in many of the commercial enterprises of the country, Frank U. Witham, of Guilford, set his hand to many tasks. His reward came with the confidence of his fellow-citizens, who saw in him a man worthy of respect and of leadership at their call. Growing from boyhood to man's estate in his native community, he has made a host of friends and enjoys a reputation for all that stands for successful activity in the affairs with which he has been engaged.

Frank U. Witham was born in Abbot, Maine, February 16, 1877, and educated in the public schools of that town. His father was John, born in Rome, Maine, and his mother, Mary (Hoyt) Witham, a native of Vienna, Kennebec County. The elder Witham was a farmer and a veteran of the Civil War. The son first worked as a clerk, then establishing himself in the tinning and plumbing business in 1906, when he bought out the Page-Spearing Company. The business grew under his management and he added to his enterprises an interest in pulp wood and lumber and machinery. All of these he continues to handle. He is a director in the Guilford Trust Company, a Republican by political affiliation and attends the Universalist church. He holds membership in the Blue Lodge, Free and Accepted Masons, and in the Knights of Pythias, as well as the Piscataquis Club.

Mr. Witham married, in June, 1905, at Greenville, Maude Drake, of Greenville, Maine, daughter of Herbert and Ida (Watson) Drake. They had three children: 1. Herbert Lloyd, born in October, 1906, died in 1924. 2. Constance, born in November, 1910. 3. Paul Francis, born in April, 1920, died in the winter of 1925.

HIRAM B. ROWE—Recalled as one of the foremost figures in the financial and civic life of Springvale, Hiram B. Rowe was a native of Lamoine, Hancock County, born November 13, 1866, son of Elijah and Catherine (Brown) Rowe. His father, a native of New Hampshire, came to Maine as a young man; and when Hiram B. Rowe was thirteen years of age the family residence was removed from Lamoine to Springvale. Here he made his career. Having completed courses in the public schools he entered the employ of W. A. Fogg, as clerk in Mr. Fogg's general store. In due course he went into the mercantile business for himself, and subsequently entered into partnership with T. H. Makin, 1895. In 1905 he was one of those most active in founding the Springvale National Bank, of which he was cashier for nearly twenty-one years, from its organization until his demise. Under his assistance, amounting to leadership, the financial house grew steadily, and today, on the basis of its solid foundation is among the most responsible of banking institutions in the State of Maine. Mr. Rowe was held to be a leader by his business associates—a man of foresight, aggressiveness and talent, having at all times a desire for the fulfillment of the best interests of Sanford and Springvale. A strong Republican, prominent in local politics, he served three years on the Board of Selectmen, at the time having been one of the youngest men ever inducted into the public service. For three terms he was deputy sheriff under Sheriff Usher B. Thompson, two terms under Newell T. Fogg, and one term under George O. Alhorn. In addition to the business connections before referred to, Mr. Rowe held others, one of which was directorship of the Springvale Shoe Shop. He was a trustee of the Nasson Institute, member of Bauneg Beg Country Club, Springvale Fish and Game Club, and had fraternal affiliations as follows: with the Free and Accepted Masons, as member of Springvale Lodge, of White Rose Chapter, Royal Arch Masons, and St. Armand Commandery, Knights Templar; with the Improved Order of Red Men, as member of Fluellen Tribe; and with the Knights of Pythias, Mousam River Lodge. He attended the Baptist church, which he supported liberally.

Mr. Rowe married, in 1891, Alberta M. Stimson, daughter of John and Elizabeth (Bradeen) Stimson, of Limerick. And of this union were born children: 1. Pauline, born August 21, 1894, died November 20, 1905. 2. Harland S., born in April, 1896; graduate of Hebron Academy; studied for two years at the University of Maine, then enlisted in the One Hundred and First Engineers Corps, Maine, for service in the World War. While overseas he was gassed, and, returned home in August, 1918, has

become assistant cashier of the Springvale National Bank. Harland S. Rowe married Helen Sanborn, and they have a son, Richard Sanborn, who was born October 15, 1926. 3. Bernard H., born February 26, 1903, graduate of Herbon Academy, now employed in Sanford Mills; married Pauline Burnham, and they have a son, Malcolm B., born February 29, 1924. 4. Mahlon C., born September 24, 1905, student at Bowdoin College. 5. Neva A., graduate of Sanford High School, Nasson Institute and Columbia University, of New York City; formerly a school teacher, now employed in the Springvale National Bank. Mrs. Alberta M. Rowe also survives her husband, and resides in Springvale, No. 21 Main Street.

Mr. Rowe's success in life was largely self-acquired. He was a man with a ready smile, a kindly word. His willingness to go forth for others endeared him to his fellow-men. His home reflected the kindly spirit by him borne, and was a haven of peace and rest. He set an example of honesty of purpose and love of humanity that those who recall him do well to emulate.

Mr. Rowe died on March 21, 1926.

ALLEN GARNER—Native of England and coming to the United States in 1856, Mr. Garner by unlimited perseverance and indomitable courage, became a powerful factor in the textile mills of the State of Maine, and particularly in the woolen mills at Kezar Falls, which he helped organize in 1881. Mr. Garner's success was no doubt due, in large measure, to his thorough knowledge of the undertaking, having begun as a bobbin-boy and step by step advanced to the position of treasurer and agent. Allen Garner was born in England, the son of William and Amelia (Ashton) Garner. His father was also a native of England, born in Huddersfield, and died when the son, Allen, was but six years of age. In 1856, Allen Garner came to America with his mother and located in Middlebury, Vermont. He aided in the establishment of the Kezar Falls Woolen Manufacturing Company, at Kezar Falls in 1881, and continued as treasurer and agent for this company from the time of its organization until his death in 1925. Of remarkable executive ability and with a high regard for business integrity, Mr. Garner obtained the good will of his employees, and with his associates he was held in high esteem.

Allen Garner married Mary D. Jordan, daughter of Captain James D. Jordan, of Sumner, Maine, and they were the parents of the following children: 1. Alice, now married to W. O. Merrifield. 2. Mary Evangeline, who married W. M. Chellis. 3. Florence R., who married W. T. Norton. 4. William Allen. 5. Allen. 6. Ethelbert, died in infancy.

Mr. Garner's death, which occurred in 1925, removed from the textile industry a dominating personality in that field, from the home of his adoption a powerful influence for good throughout the community, and from the home circle an influence for kindliness and gentleness.

ORRIN ROBERTS—There are many persons in Sanford who recall Orrin Roberts, beloved figure, around whose smithy forge used to congregate numbers of children who are now men and women of prominence in Maine and other commonwealths. A kindly man, given to thought and genial conversations with his neighbors, he was a true philosopher, much as we picture the village blacksmith immortalized by Longfellow. His name goes down for all time upon the rôles of Sanford's respected dead, and the works of good by him accomplished in a full life will live on through several generations, not to be dissipated until the souls of men with whom he came in contact have likewise perished along with the material of which man is composed.

Orrin Roberts was born at Lyman, September 3, 1847, and was a son of Thomas J. and Mahala (Cook) Roberts. He received his preliminary instruction in the public school of Lyman, put down the educational foundation upon which he was to build a privately acquired knowledge truly broad in later years through reading and reflection, and at the age of fifteen years went to work to learn the trade of blacksmith. This he continued, and in 1873, at the age of twenty-five, came to Sanford, here set up a forge and shop and went about his work quietly, making it his business until death left the leathern apron to grow dusty upon its peg. A staunch Republican, adherent of the principles of the party and ardent supporter of its candidates, he was much interested in political questions, particularly as they affected local conditions. He came to have a broad influence politically, for men around him respected his judgment in all things where the public weal might be the subject. This he employed wisely, with discretion, and to good effect, more for the advancement of conditions than for the limited profit of that party with which he had affiliation. In no sense was he himself a seeker after office, but he assisted numbers of worthy men to high position in town and county. He owned several valuable connections in business, chief of which, perhaps, was his directorship in the Sanford Loan and Building Association, and was a member of the Knights of Pythias. Strong physically through the years of middle age, his character increased in its strength unto the eventide of life, rounded and mellowed by goodness and charity.

Orrin Roberts married Abbie M. Cheney, of South Berwick, daughter of Jotham and Abbie L. (Roberts) Cheney, and this union was blessed in the birth of children: 1. Blanche Roberts, who survives her father. She is a graduate of Sanford High School, for several years taught in grammar schools, and married John Wright, son of James and Nannie Wright, of England. For more than twoscore years Mr. Wright has been an employee in Sanford Mills, now being assistant overseer of the wool and mohair sorting shifts in the plush department, Mill B. He is treasurer of the Sanford Loan and Building Association; is ex-Secretary, Preble Lodge, Free and Accepted Masons; Past High Priest and also Past Secretary of White Rose Chapter, Royal Arch Masons, and a member of Bethlehem Commandery, Knights Templar. Their son, Carl, is employed in the Methods and Standards bureau of Sanford Mills. He is a graduate of Sanford High School and of the General Electric course at Lynn, Massachusetts. He is now secretary of White Rose Royal Arch Masons. Carl Wright married Edith Mitchell, of Springvale. 2. Fred S. Roberts, who also survives his father, has worked for Sanford Mills through a number of years, now being overseer of the weaving room, Mill A. Fraternally, he is affiliated with the Knights of Pythias, and is prominent in divers affairs of Sanford. He married Ethel Richardson, who died

in 1913, leaving a daughter, Editha. Editha Roberts is at home with her father.

"Choose ye this day whom ye will serve" had no empty meaning to Orrin Roberts. In the ultimate analysis, he served mankind — and served well. Death came to him on August 7, 1908.

AUSTIN A. WILSON—Fewer men have overcome the handicaps of early life to attain prominence in a greater degree than did the late Austin A. Wilson of Springvale, who assumed the care of his mother at the age of nine years, at which time his father died. Although he followed agriculture during the early years of his life, Mr. Wilson became one of the outstanding factors in business circles at Springvale, where, at the time of his death he was the owner of the firm of W. H. Nason & Company, dealing in flour and grain. Mr. Wilson was the great-grandson of Daniel Wilson, one of the early pioneers of New England, who was born in Brentwood, New Hampshire, in 1730. He married Mary Wiggins, in 1770, who was born in Stratham, New Hampshire, in 1728. Soon after his marriage, Daniel Wilson came to Shapleigh, Maine, and here cleared the ground and erected the log cabin, which was the first structure built on the Wilson farm. This homestead has remained in the Wilson family for six generations. Daniel Wilson died in 1810. His son, Frederick, married Eunice Low, and they constructed the new and larger house on the farm and made extensive improvements thereon.

Austin A. Wilson was born in Shapleigh, Maine, November 23, 1851, son of Simeon and Hannah (Low) Wilson. Simeon Wilson was a prominent farmer in Shapleigh. Austin A. Wilson received his elementary education in the public schools of his native town, but when he was nine years of age his father died, and thereafter he cared for his mother and operated the Wilson homestead farm in Shapleigh until he was thirty-three years of age. In this year Mr. Wilson removed to Boston and in this city took up the trade of cabinetmaker, in which he attained great proficiency. An example of his excellent work is found today in the Science and Fine Arts Building in Boston. In 1884 he returned to Maine and formed a partnership which operated under the firm name of W. H. Nason & Company at Springvale. Some time later Mr. Wilson purchased the interests of his partner, assuming full control of the concern, which dealt in flour and grain, and through his efforts it became one of the leading business firms of Springvale. In all of his business dealings Mr. Wilson was fair and just, and as the years passed his reputation for square dealing spread throughout the surrounding country, bringing his patronage from points far distant.

Mr. Wilson was a public-spirited man, and all movements designed for the welfare of his town were given his full support. Fraternally, he was affiliated with Friendship Lodge, and the Independent Order of Odd Fellows. He was a member of the Baptist church, and in this denomination he was a zealous worker and liberal in his financial contributions.

Austin A. Wilson married, on June 17, 1886, Annie L. Rowe, daughter of Elijah and Caroline Rowe of Springvale, and they have one son, Maynard Rowe Wilson, who is now conducting the firm which was owned by his father. He also operates the old homestead farm at Shapleigh. Maynard Rowe Wilson was born in Springvale, March 3, 1892. He attended the public schools of Sanford; was graduated from Hebron Academy at Hebron, Maine, and immediately entered his father's firm, taking over the management after the latter's death. He married Ruth Brophy, daughter of Henry D. Brophy of Fairfield, Maine, and they have become the parents of three children: 1. Roberta Elizabeth, born January 1, 1918, died September 13, 1921. 2. Caroline Ruth, born July 9, 1920. 3. Robert Maynard, born September 29, 1921.

A man of sterling character, Austin A. Wilson was noted for his honesty and fair business ethics. Such were the characteristics of his mind and heart, his aptitude for making friends, his judicious management of business affairs, his clear perception of the truth, and his impressive manner of living the truth, that he had formed many valuable friendships throughout the State of Maine. He is survived by his widow, Annie L. Wilson, who resides at No. 59 Pleasant Street, Springvale, Maine, and by his son and grandchildren.

FRANCIS LAW SENIOR—In variety and range of talent, in scope and intrinsic quality of intellectual endowment, in amplitude of solid scientific attainment, in the breadth and diversity of his accomplishments, and in the wide extent of his reputation, the late Francis Law Senior, chief chemist of the Sanford Mills Corporation, stood out among his fellows as a genius of his time and profession. To be sure, he turned his profession to commercial advantage, but in doing so he served a great purpose, and the value of his contributions to the success of the mammoth textile industry at Sanford was incalculable. He was a mighty force in the upbuilding and maintenance of the success and prestige of that nationally known concern. An Englishman born, he transferred his allegiance to the American Republic and became an ardent citizen of the United States. His years of residence in the town of Sanford were filled with intense activity along political and community lines in addition to the performance of absorbing and exacting duties in his professional association. The town lost a strong, forceful and influential figure in his passing.

Francis Law Senior was born in Dewsbury, Yorkshire, England, December 14, 1849, a son of Robert and Mary (Law) Senior. He was a student in the local schools until he attained the age of fifteen, and then took employment in the Dewsbury woolen factory, where he remained for five years. At the age of twenty he came to Sanford to work in the Sanford Mills as an associate of the late George Benjamin Goodall, one of the three brothers Goodall and sons of the founder, Thomas Goodall. For three years he worked in the Sanford Mills, acquiring a practical knowledge of the various processes to which the plant was devoted. At the end of that time he returned to England and took charge of the cloth finishing department of the Ellis Mills in Birstall. For four of the five years that he was resident in that city he employed most of his time that he was not at his work in the study of organic, inorganic, theoretical and practical chemistry in the night school of the South Kensington Science and Arts Department of the British Government. His professional and technical equipment at that time

was about as complete as the textile trade could demand of a finished executive and chemist.

The year 1884 saw Mr. Senior again located at the Sanford Mills, this time as the holder of the high position of head chemist of the industry. He proved a strong right arm of the Goodall brothers in their operation of the great plant and in the production of the plush and other goods for which the business attained a very enviable reputation throughout the country. It might be said that, from a commercially professional point of view, he was the keystone of the arch which upheld the splendid structure of success for which the Sanford interests are so widely and favorably known. For some twenty-eight years, until his death, he remained at his important post, developing, strengthening and mellowing in wisdom and efficiency and fellowship as the years came and went.

A Republican to the core in his politics, none who did not have knowledge of the fact would have been able to guess that he once had been a subject of the British Crown. He was intensely loyal to his new allegiance, and served as a member of the Sanford Republican Town Committee for many years. He enjoyed actively participating in town meetings, where his wisdom and political sagacity were often expressed in powerful argument on the floor or in an advisory capacity in committee work. As a member of the Sanford Board of Trade he coveted earnestly the best that could be obtained or achieved for the town's interests. He was a director of the Sanford Loan and Building Association, and in many other endeavors his advice on matters of civic importance often sought. In his fraternal affiliations he was highly esteemed for his genuine worth and spirit of coöperation, a member of Preble Lodge, Free and Accepted Masons; White Rose Chapter, Royal Arch Masons; Kennebunk Commandery, Knights Templar; Pioneer Lodge, Knights of Pythias; and the Sons of St. George. His religious fellowship was with the Baptist church, and he was also a liberal supporter of all Protestant churches in Sanford.

Francis Law Senior married, in 1874, Sarah A. Dickson, of Dewsbury, England, a native of his own birthplace; she died about the year, 1903, survived by her husband and three children: 1. Wilfred, who became the successor of his distinguished father as head chemist of the Sanford Mills. He attended the Sanford schools, spent two years at Hebron Academy, and was graduated from the Philadelphia (Pennsylvania) Textile School as a chemist, having won honors for his standing in the course, maintaining an average of ninety-seven per cent. He is a member of Preble Lodge, Free and Accepted Masons. He married Millie A. Burgess, daughter of Horatio Gates Burgess, of Livermore, Maine, and their children are: i. Mildred Laura, born December 5, 1905, married M. Arthur Allen. ii. Ada Gertrude, born November 16, 1916. 2. John C., who is at the head of the coloring and printing departments of the Sanford Mills. He is prominent in Masonic circles, having received the thirty-second Scottish Rite degree. After he had held various chairs in the Grand Lodge of Knights of Pythias of Maine, he was elected Grand High Chancellor of the same jurisdiction, in which office he is still (1928) serving. He married Nellie Genthner, who died December 24, 1916, survived by her husband and three children: i. Sarah Louise, born September 19, 1905, married Carl Lambert, of Evanston, Illinois. ii. Robina Editha, born July 19, 1909. iii. Sybil, born August 31, 1914. 3. Ada, married Charles A. Bennitt, of Wollaston, Massachusetts, and their children are: i. Donald Senior Bennitt, born January 9, 1903. ii. Ansel G. Bennitt, born August 16, 1908.

The death of Francis Law Senior, on November 7, 1913, removed from the town of Sanford one of her finest citizens, from the practice of chemistry a master of his profession, which in his case amounted almost to a recreation. He was an ideal husband and father, and a member of the community who left an impress for good upon his fellows. The people of Sanford are proud to have had him as one of their own for so many years as he was spared to them.

AMOS GARNSEY—One of the original organizers and stockholders of the Sanford Mills, largely responsible for the establishment of this industry here, and with the Goodall Brothers, the late Amos Garnsey held a position of responsibility in manufacturing circles in this city, and others, was a citizen of prominence and attained material of worldly goods before his demise. He was a member of one of the oldest families in New England.

Garnsey, Garnsy, or Guernsey, as it was spelled interchangeably in the early records, is taken from the Isle of Guernsey; the family undoubtedly originating on the Isle of Guernsey. Henry Garnsey settled in Dorchester, Massachusetts, as early as 1635, and was admitted a Freeman in 1690. John and Joseph Garnsey settled in Milford, Connecticut, about 1639. Both seem to have had sons named Joseph. Joseph Garnsey removed to New Hampshire, where he was living in 1647, and finally to Stamford, where he and his descendants lived for many years. He or his son, Joseph, married, May 11, 1659, at Stamford, Rose Waterbury, and had Joseph, born June 30, 1662; settled at Stamford; John, born May 23, 1697, resided in Waterbury.

(I) Joseph, son of John Garnsey, was born about 1640-49, married at Milford, Hannah Cooley, daughter of Samuel Cooley, Sr., April 10, 1673. Children, born at Milford: 1. Joseph, born January 13, 1674; married (first) Elizabeth Disbrow, of Horseneck; and (second) Eleanor; removed to Woodbury, Connecticut, where his wife died September 15, 1753, aged seventy-seven, and he died September 15, 1764, aged eighty. Children: i. Joseph, born in 1700. ii. Ebenezer, born in 1703. iii. Jonathan, had grandsons, Amos, Jonathan, et al. iv. Peter, born April 6, 1709. v. John (twin), born April 6, 1709. vi. Betsy, married Joshua Baldwin. 2. Hannah (also given Sarah), born March 4, 1678.

(II) John (2), probably son of John Garnsey, and certainly of this family, born about 1660, died at Rehoboth, Massachusetts, March 31, 1722. His wife, Elizabeth, died April 11, 1714, at Rehoboth. He settled in Rehoboth, where he married (second), August 16, 1716, Sarah Titus. Among his children were: 1. John, of further mention. 2. Ebenezer, married, at Rehoboth, January 19, 1709-10, Mehitable West. 3. Elizabeth, married, May 6, 1703, James Bowen, at Rehoboth. 4. Mary, married, September 13, 1713, Samuel Hicks, at Rehoboth.

(III) John (3), son of John (2) Garnsey (or Garnzey, as spelled in Rehoboth records), was born about 1690. He married (first), October 14, 1714, at Rehoboth, Judith Ormsbee, who died August 27,

1715. He married (second), at Rehoboth, June 6, 1716, Elizabeth Titus, who died April 11, 1771. There was one child of the first marriage: Beriah, born in September, 1715. The children of the second marriage: 2. John, born February 7, 1718-19, died February 17, 1718-19. 3. John, born January 4, 1719-20, of further mention. 4. Oliver, born September 27, 1722. 5. Elizabeth, born April 17, 1725. 6. Solomon, born in 1727. 7. Mary, born February 22, 1731. 8. Sarah, born May 15, 1735.

(IV) John (4), son of John (3) Garnsey, born at Rehoboth, Massachusetts, January 4, 1719-20, married, May 13, 1742, Lydia Healey. Among their fourteen children was Amos, the first child, of whom further.

(V) Deacon Amos Garnsey, son of John (4) Garnsey, born at Rehoboth, March 31, 1743, died February 12, 1813, at Richmond, New Hampshire. He and his brothers removed to Richmond when young men, although his son, Amos, was born in Rehoboth in 1768. Deacon Garnsey was located in Richmond in 1766, probably bringing his family to settle after 1768. He was a soldier in the Revolution from Richmond, a private in Captain Humphrey's company in the Continental Army, in 1776. The name was spelled Guernsey in many cases. (New Hampshire Revolution Roles Vol. I, p. 356). He married, at Rehoboth, November 15, 1763, Miriam Hike, who died December 12, 1814. Among their six children was Amos (2), of further mention.

(VI) Amos (2), son of Amos (1) Garnsey, was born in Rehoboth, April 9, 1768. His uncle, Oliver Garnsey, a veteran of the Revolutionary War, settled in Westminster, Vermont, and died there January 30, 1737, aged eighty-five. Amos, John J., and Oliver, were all in the same company in the Revolution. The child of Amos (2), Amos (3), born at Richmond, and of further mention.

(VII) Amos (3), son of Amos (2 Garnsey, born at Richmond, New Hampshire, September 6, 1803, died March 9, 1886. He settled in his native town on the Benjamin Hees's place and removed to his late home in 1845. He was a farmer and well-known citizen. He married Clarissa Randall, born in Swanzey, New Hampshire, December 7, 1806, died April 15, 1875. Children, born at Richmond: 1. Amos, of further mention. 2. William, born Septemmber 27, 1739. 3. Watrous, born September 6, 1742.

(VIII) Amos (4) Garnsey, son of Amos (3) and Clarissa (Randall) Garnsey, was born in Richmond, December 26, 1831, and died in Sanford, Maine, March 9, 1898. He attended local public schools until he was seventeen years old, working during vacations on the farm. Later he learned the trade of wood-worker and blacksmith, and in 1866 went to Sanford to become a master mechanic in the Sanford Mills. In fact he was one of the original stockholders of the Sanford Mills, and is credited with having been largely responsible for its start and subsequent remarkable expansion, along with the Goodall Brothers. For thirty years, thereafter, with the exception of enterprises hereafter noted, he was closely allied with these mills, which have since become internationally known. Mr. Garnsey, for a period of ten years, was connected with the Mousam River Mills, being a large stockholder in that enterprise. His experience also included a few years at Troy, New Hampshire, where he was engaged in a similar enterprise. Amos Garnsey was interested in the progress and advance of his community, and worked unceasingly to upbuild Sanford.

Mr. Amos Garnsey married, June 15, 1854, Mary Jane Martin, born at Rochester, New York, September 2, 1835, daughter of Ezra and Irene (Dalmas) Martin. Ezra Martin was born in Richmond, New Hampshire. To Amos and Mary Jane (Martin) Garnsey two children were born: 1. Frederick Amos, born January 14, 1857, and of further mention. 2. Almon Ezra (see a following biography).

Frederick Amos, son of Amos (4) and Mary Jane (Martin) Garnsey, was born in Richmond, New Hampshire, January 14, 1857, and died in Sanford, Maine, May 29, 1899. He was educated in the public schools of Troy, New Hampshire; the high school in Sanford, Maine, and Gray's Business College, Portland. He learned the trade of weaver in the Sanford Mills and rose to the position of bossweaver. He was taken into the counting room and was connected with the management for a number of years. He engaged in business as superintendent for his father, and for Charles Frost, in the mills at Moultonville, and later at Cordaville, Massachusetts. These mills were engaged in the manufacture of blankets. Thoroughly conversant with every detail of his business, he made a very successful manager. He possessed an upright character and was gifted with great ability in various directions. Thus his early death was a profound loss to the manufacturing world and to a large circle of friends. He had the esteem of employees as well as of associates in commercial life. In politics he was a Republican.

Frederick Amos married, December 9, 1876, Julia A. Bennett, daughter of Nahum and Nancy (Hanson) Bennett. Mr. and Mrs. Amos Garnsey have one grandchild, Frederick, born in Cordaville, in the town of Southborough, Massachusetts, March 14, 1892.

ALMON EZRA GARNSEY — Having been the first jeweler and watchmaker in this town, Almon Ezra Garnsey has, from time to time, increased the scope of his activities, eventually becoming one of the principal members of business circles in Sanford. His vocations during his lifetime have been many and varied, including textile work, watchmaking and other enterprises such as the conduct of a shoe store and a jewelry establishment. Politics also occupied him to some extent, he having served in the State Legislature, and was a pioneer in organization of fire fighting facilities in Sanford. Mr. Garnsey's ancestry, which is given at length in a review of his late father's life, which precedes this, is most impressive. The first member of this family having settled in New England prior to the revolt of the colonies, several of the Garnseys served with honor and distinction during the Revolutionary War, in order that the present United States might be founded.

Mr. Garnsey was born March 11, 1863, at Richmond, New Hampshire, son of Amos and Mary Jane (Martin) Garnsey. At the time he was four years of age his parents removed to Sanford, and here he received his education. For an extended period, thereafter, he was employed in the Sanford Mills, obtaining the position of overseer in the weave room. Dissatisfied with this vocation he later attended Parson's School for Watchmakers, at LaPorte, Indiana, and was graduated from that institution in May, 1889. During that year he returned to Sanford

where he erected a building and opened a store on School Street. It was the first jewelry and watchmaking establishment in Sanford, where he has since continued in this business. In 1896 he added a line of shoes to his stock and occupied the Garnsey Block on Central Square, which at that time was one of the finest stores in the State of Maine. Seeking further knowledge in his favored calling, Mr. Garnsey went to New York City, studied in the Spencer Optical School there, until 1898, at which time he received his diploma. This, perhaps, has been his most successful pursuit in the years that have elapsed. A Republican in political beliefs, Mr. Garnsey was a vital factor in the counsels of that party, which led to his election in the State Legislature. Here he proved himself able to cope with many of the more experienced statesmen, and brought numerous benefits to his constituents while serving in that office. He has for a long period of years been interested in the Fire Department at Sanford, was a pioneer in obtaining more efficient fire fighting facilities for Sanford, and was head of the local fire department for many years, his connection therewith having been made more than twenty years ago. He was a thirty-second degree Mason; and a member of the Benevolent and Protective Order of Elks, Orange Lodge, of Sanford.

Almon Garnsey married (first) Minnie Stackpole, and they had one daughter: Alice E., born March 9, 1890; married George Field, an employee in the Sanford Mills, and they have one child, Jeannette. Mr. Garnsey married (second) Esther Lunt.

Mr. Garnsey now has practically retired from active commercial pursuits and resides at No. 224 Main Street, Sanford.

HON. GEORGE CAMPBELL YEATON—One of the foremost figures at the bar of the State of Maine is that of the Hon. George Campbell Yeaton. Legal advance in Maine for several years has felt his influence; his New England nativity and farseeing vision have combined to give his usefulness a lasting significance to any circle upon which his activities impinged. By birth and by the strong ties of early pioneering memories, the Yeaton family is closely knit into the history of a certain section of Maine, that of South Berwick of York County. It has grown to be a rich and prosperous community, created so through its splendid forests yielding immense returns from the lumber business. The Hon. George Campbell Yeaton was born at South Berwick, May 22, 1836, the son of Isaac and Frances (Gordon) Yeaton. George Campbell Yeaton received his preliminary education at Berwick Academy, graduating in 1852, entering Bowdoin College the following year, to graduate from there in 1856 with the degree of Bachelor of Arts. In 1909, Bowdoin bestowed the degree of Master of Arts upon its distinguished alumnus. He was admitted to the Suffolk County bar at Boston, Massachusetts, in 1859, and after three years of practice there, returned to his native town and was admitted to the Maine bar. He gave the best of his great powers to the State and was attorney for York County in 1871 to 1875 and admitted to the United States Supreme Court Bar in 1876. From 1871 until the time of his death, he was attorney for the Boston & Maine Railroad for York County. He lent his administrative skill and integrity of character to the South Berwick National Bank, acting as president of that institution

414 MAINE—A HISTORY

and also to the South Berwick Savings and Trust Company. He was a Mason in all its branches including the thirty-second degree, and a Republican in his politics, although he never accepted the various political honors that were offered him. His career at the bar was powerful, colorful; and his pleadings before the jury were masterpieces of erudition and force, yet simple and direct. A famous murder case in which he appeared as County Attorney, associated with Attorney-General Harris M. Plaisted, was that of Louis Wagner, tried for the murder of Anethe and Karem Christinson, in which Wagner was convicted and executed. Mr. Yeaton practiced law brilliantly for fifty years and was a picturesque figure of stately old-time dignity in his latter years, perhaps of the last of the cultivated, highly polished legal minds of the old school. He had been offered a seat on the bench many times but always declined, as his private and civic practice was too extensive to admit of an acceptance.

Mr. Yeaton married, November 9, 1859, Harriet M. Ramsdell of Newton, Massachusetts. Their only child, Jennie, was born in 1860 and died four years later. Mrs. Yeaton passed away several years before her husband, who died April 10, 1918, much honored, loved and mourned in his community.

ORRIN HALL BUTLER—Throughout a long life, Orrin Hall Butler was prominent in the life of Berwick, Maine. For many years he devoted his fine energy and ability to the operation of a soap factory, which he purchased at Berwick soon after the Civil War, and whose affairs he guided along the path of success. The sales record of this enterprise was one of constant expansion and growth. This work, however, by no means limited Mr. Butler's activity in Berwick, and he was prominent in many other phases of the community life.

Mr. Butler was born in Berwick, May 29, 1844, a son of James and Betsey (Hall) Butler. His father was a farmer at Berwick until the time of his death, and both parents were members of old Maine families.

Orrin Hall Butler received his education in the public schools of his birthplace, of which he was always a resident except for a short period spent at Lawrence, Massachusetts. In 1866 he purchased from Gould and Varney the soap factory which he operated successfully for so many years, finally disposing of his interest to Swift and Company in 1917. Mr. Butler was very fond of horses and kept a fine large herd of registered cattle. He also owned several farms which he operated, and dealt extensively in local real estate. His obvious business ability and sound judgment caused his advice to be sought frequently in important financial transactions, and he served as a member of the board of directors of the First National Bank of Somersworth, New Hampshire. Mr. Butler was affiliated, fraternally, with the Independent Order of Odd Fellows, and he worshipped in the faith of the Methodist Episcopal church. Vitally interested in the welfare of Berwick, he was a liberal supporter of all worthy civic and charitable enterprises.

On May 2, 1868, Orrin Hall Butler married Orianna Chellis, of Somersworth, New Hampshire, who died on April 9, 1885. Of this marriage seven children were born, five of whom are still living: 1. Clarence O., of Berwick. 2. Arthur C., also of Berwick. 3. Lillian, who married Edward G. Clark, of Lawrence, Massachusetts. 4. Jessie, married Charles L. Batchelder, of North Hampton, New Hampshire. 5. Effie, now Mrs. John F. Gleason, of Lynn, Massachusetts. In 1894 Mr. Butler married (second) Bessie Ricker, daughter of Edmund Ricker, an overseer in the Springvale, Maine, Mills, and in the Great Falls Mills, in Somersworth, New Hampshire. They became the parents of three children: Dean, Harry, and Ella.

Mr. Butler's death brought to a close a life of usefulness and service. His strict integrity in all his relations with others, together with his personal warmth and charm, brought him the affectionate esteem of all those with whom he came in contact. The community at Berwick recognized his sterling worth of character, and will long hold in grateful remembrance the inspiration which it derived from his life and work.

ABNER OAKES—The name of Abner Oakes is of outstanding interest to the State of Maine, and as a true native son, he impressed himself upon the educational life of the State in ways that made for development and growth along the best and most far-seeing lines. He was born in Sangerville, Maine, Piscataquis County, April 13, 1820, son of William and Mary (Weymouth) Oakes. His grandfather was Rev. William Oakes of Skowhegan, Maine, and that rugged State has produced others of this name who have been of importance along professional and authoritative lines. His father, William (2), was a man of much natural ability and took a keen part in county and town affairs, being high sheriff of the county and town treasurer and chairman of the Board of Selectmen of Sangerville for several years.

Abner Oakes was educated at the schools of Sangerville and graduated at Colby University with the class of 1847. He studied law with Charles P. Chandler of Foxcroft, Maine, and was admitted to the bar of the State and New York. He established his practice in South Berwick, a prosperous town in the heart of the important lumber interests that create so large a part in the commercial prosperity of this New England State. The school authorities early recognized in Mr. Oakes those marked qualities of leadership and administrative ability along educational lines and he was called upon to act in the important capacity of County Superintendent of Schools, a position that he held for many years, beginning in 1852. He sought to improve the educational methods then in vogue and did so with splendid and lasting success. He was also for many years, secretary and treasurer of the Berwick Academy and, later, served on its board of trustees in a very active way. In 1893 he was sent to the Maine Legislature as representative and for four years subsequently, he held the joint office of town clerk and town treasurer. He was a man of greatest probity and of highest mental and ethical culture. A close student of both books and men. A keen observer of life and a successful jurist.

Abner Oakes married, October, 1853, Susan M. Bennett, daughter of Dr. Gillman L. and Hannah (Merrill) Bennett. Dr. Bennett was an outstanding figure in the annals of the State. He was an excellent physician, a successful financier and a man of wide and brilliant social contacts. A graduate of Bowdoin College, class of 1827, a member of the State Legislature in 1838 and of the State Senate for

MAINE—A HISTORY   415

two terms. Also county treasurer and chairman of
the board of trustees of the Maine Hospital for the
Insane. He died December 10, 1872.
Mr. and Mrs. Abner Oakes were the parents of
six children, of whom two died in infancy: 1. Susan
Marcia Oakes, became a painter of international
note, one of the best of our American women artists. She married the well-known artist, Charles
H. Woodbury, whose seascapes have immortalized
the rough and rugged Maine coast. They had a
studio home in Boston but their summer home at
Ogunquit, Maine, was the nucleus of a group of successful and well-known painters, augmented by a
following of earnest art students. Susan Marcia
(Oakes) Woodbury died December 7, 1913. 2. Katharine, married Charles S. Adams of Wollaston, Massachusetts; she died at the age of twenty-eight. 3.
Charles W., born in South Berwick, was educated at
Dartmouth College, and at the Bellevue Hospital
Medical School at New York. He practiced medicine with splendid success in New York City for
forty years, retiring in 1926 to live in South Berwick. Dr. Oakes married Marcella Sheil of New
York, and has two children: i. Abner (2), a graduate
of Dartmouth, class of 1926, is now carrying on
the family traditions by preparing for a career in
medicine at the Dartmouth Medical School. ii. Marcia Oakes, bearing the name of her famous artist
aunt, is a student at the Berwick High School. 4.
Frederick, who also studied medicine but died in his
twenty-second year.

MRS. MARION E. (PRIME) NELSON—The
family of Kennard, one of the oldest in the Pine
Tree State, and from which Mrs. Marion E. (Prime)
Nelson, of Eliot, is descended, traces its line to
Benjamin Kennard as the first member to settle in
Maine. Having decided upon Eliot as the place of
his residence, he purchased the large house, built by
Dr. Pierpont about 1795, and in 1801 he began to
operate a tavern there. This enterprise he managed
for some time and developed a large patronage, it
becoming a well-known watering-place for travelers
in that section. Benjamin Kennard married, July
14, 1805, Mary Leighton, daughter of William and
Miriam (Fernald) Leighton. Their eldest son, William Leighton Kennard, born May 25, 1806, took
over the tavern-keeping business established by his
father, but devoted most of his attention to the
operation of the home farm. He married, June 6,
1832, Mary E. Frost, and his death occurred December 25, 1882. Their daughter, Emily Frances
Kennard, born February 21, 1835, married Oliver
Prime, a grocer and farmer, who died in 1904, leaving a daughter, Marion E., of whom further.
Marion E. Prime, daughter of Oliver and Emily
Frances (Kennard) Prime, married Fred S. Nelson,
who is operating the farm and occupying the old
Kennard homestead in Eliot, which descended from
the founder, Benjamin Kennard. Mr. Nelson is a
man of influence among the agricultural population
of the section, and a leading citizen of Eliot. To Mr.
and Mrs. Nelson have been born two sons: 1. Stanley Eliot, a wholesale produce merchant of Portsmouth, New Hampshire, married Carrie Trefethen,
and they have two daughters, Priscilla R. and
Marion L. 2. Howard B., married Donna L. Birch-
ard, and is associated in business with his brother
in Portsmouth.

GEORGE D. EMERSON, M. D.—In 1888 George
D. Emerson came to South Berwick, Maine, and here
began the practice of medicine which he was to continue so successfully for a period of twenty years.
Dr. Emerson was active at all times in the care of
the sick and injured in the community, counting his
own convenience and safety as nothing when opposed to his professional duties. He thought nothing
of traveling many miles at any time of day or night
to bring relief to the suffering, and it was this devotion to the finest ideals of his profession, together
with his own deep personal sympathy which won
for him so high a place in the affectionate esteem of
all those with whom he came in contact.
Dr. Emerson was born at Auburn, Maine, August 14, 1864, a son of Colonel Charles S. and Izan-
nah (Young) Emerson, of that place. His father
served in the Union Army during the period of the
Civil War, rising in the ranks as the result of distinguished service under difficult conditions. He
was promoted from captain to major of the Tenth
Maine Regiment, and was later appointed lieutenant-colonel in the Twenty-ninth Maine Volunteers.
George D. Emerson attended the Auburn public
schools, and later entered Burlington Medical School,
at Burlington, Vermont, from which he was graduated with high honors, receiving the degree of
Doctor of Medicine. Soon afterwards, he came to
South Berwick and began the practice of his profession. Rapidly winning the confidence of his patients, he built up a highly successful practice, his
reputation as a physician spreading throughout all
this part of the State.
Dr. Emerson was affiliated, fraternally, with the St.
John's Lodge of the Free and Accepted Masons,
and in the Masonic organization he was also a member of Unity Chapter, Royal Arch Masons, at South
Berwick; Bradford Commandery, Knights Templar at Biddeford; and a member of all bodies of the
Scottish Rite. He was also a member of the Knights
of Pythias, the Improved Order of Red Men, the
New England Order of Protection, the Ancient Order of United Workmen, and Olive Branch Lodge,
of the Independent Order of Odd Fellows, all at
South Berwick. He was a member of Emerson
Temple, which was named after him, of the Pythian Sisters. Dr. Emerson was always intensely interested in the developments in his profession, and
he was, for many years, a member of the York
County Medical Association. He was also very fond
of his flower gardens and his horses.
George D. Emerson married (first) Maud Jamison,
of Bridgewater, Maine, who died in February, 1901.
He married (second) June 10, 1903, Mrs. Myra
Parsons Ladd, and of this marriage one daughter,
Virginia, was born, and only recently died. She had
married Clifton Shorey, and they were the parents
of two children, Roger Emerson, and Jean Elizabeth.
Dr. Emerson died on May 23, 1908, at his home
in South Berwick, to the great sorrow of his many
friends and acquaintances. Aside from his professional work, he had always taken an active part in
promoting the growth and welfare of the community, which recognized his sterling worth and character, and loved him for his charm.

ELBERT H. RUSSELL—Although of a modest
and retiring disposition, Elbert H. Russell attained a
marked reputation in Sanford during his lifetime, as

a farmer and as an operator in lumber and timber-lands. The third generation of this family to carry on such dealings in Maine, Mr. Russell undoubtedly inherited his inclinations for this business, for both his father and grandfather were so occupied. His lumber interests brought material profit to Mr. Russell, but these rewards were not gained through taking advantage of business associates, for few men in Sanford were more highly esteemed and few held the confidence of fellow-citizens to the extent enjoyed by him.

Mr. Russell was born April 10, 1865, at Sanford, son of William and Dorcas (Allen) Russell, and grandson of William and Annie (Perkins) Russell. William Russell and his wife were natives of Wells, Maine, where the former was a prosperous and respected farmer and lumber man, as was his son, William, the father of Elbert H. Russell. Dorcas (Allen) Russell was a daughter of Thomas and Affa Allen.

Elbert H. Russell lived on his parents' farm until 1924. He was educated in the public schools of Sanford, whence he came after leaving the farm, and where he later erected his own home, on Grove Street. His schooling completed, Mr. Russell quite naturally followed the vocation that had attracted his father and grandfather, that of lumbering, and in this industry he remained until the end of his days. Mr. Russell kept apace with the progress of lumbering and applied every modern convenience and advanced idea thereto, when he believed them to be practical. Thus it was that his undertakings were universally successful and profitable. He was connected with many of the more important deals involving the transfer of farms and timberlands in the vicinity of Sanford, and his accurate judgment of values was often utilized on behalf of friends and associates who sought his counsel.

Elbert H. Russell married Jennie Chadbourne, daughter of Andrew and Mercy (Twombly) Chadbourne. Andrew Chadbourne, now deceased, was a prominent farmer of Alfred, and is survived by his wife, who now (1928) resides with her daughter, at No. 6 Grove Street, Sanford. Mrs. Russell is of Revolutionary stock and a direct descendant of Corporal Samuel Chadbourne, who was in Captain Noah M. Littlefield's company of minute-men, who marched away on April 19, 1775. He served throughout the entire period of the Revolution, with honor and distinction. Another Samuel Chadbourne, the great-grandfather of Mrs. Russell fought against the French and Indians in t' ; Louisburg Campaign, and later, in 1758, lost his life in the battle of Lake George. The first of the branch of the family to settle in Maine was Humphrey Chadbourne, who came from Devonshire, England, to Kittery, in 1631.

Elbert H. Russell passed away on March 23, 1928, in his sixty-third year, after a life replete with good works. A man of kindly thoughts and deeds, he had lived unostentatiously and quietly, finding his greatest interest in the simple things of this world, a loyal citizen and a loving and thoughtful husband. He was ever cheerful, and popular with the children of his neighborhood.

DAVID OSGOOD CAMPBELL—Prominently identified with the industrial life of Sangerville for many years, as was his father before him, David Osgood Campbell, in his retirement from active business, can look back upon a career with satisfaction

that during it he earned the respect and high regard of his associates and all with whom he was brought into contact. His family is one of the old Maine stock, early settlers of New England, with an inherited adaptation for large business enterprises. His father was for many years a successful manufacturer of woolen goods in this region.

David Osgood Campbell was born in Sangerville, July 28, 1874, a son of David Rae and Eleanor (Lovejoy) Campbell. During his youth he attended the public schools of his native town, later taking the course at the East Maine Conference Seminary, from which he was graduated in the class of 1891. He at once entered business, soon becoming treasurer of the woolen manufacturing house of D. R. Campbell & Sons, in Sangerville. This company was later reorganized as the Campbell Manufacturing Company, with the same treasurer for several years, the last two of which he acted as general manager. He was a director in the concern until it was sold to the Dumbarton Mills Company. He was elected a director in that company and for a few years served as its secretary. Becoming greatly interested in western development, he went to Seattle, Washington, where he assumed the position of assistant treasurer, and a director of the Seattle and Yukon Steamship Company. At the same time he performed the duties of manager of the company operating the steamship "Elishu Thompson," of San Francisco and Seattle. He remained in Seattle for two years, then returning to Sangerville, Maine, where he became a director in the Guilford Trust Company. Withdrawing from his active business interests he retired, to enjoy a well-earned leisure. In politics he is a Republican, deeply interested in the political affairs of the community and of the nation, but never seeking public office. He is very active in local fraternal and social circles and holds membership in many organizations. He has been through all the grades of the Knights of Pythias and is a Past Chancellor of Sir Godfrey Lodge, of Sangerville. He belongs to Abner Wade Lodge, Free and Accepted Masons, of Sangerville; to Piscataquis Chapter, Royal Arch Masons, of Dover; and to Court Kinhoe, Independent Order of Foresters, of Sangerville. He is also a member of the Tarratine Club, of Bangor, the National Geographic Society, Penobscot Valley Country Club of Bangor, and Piscataquis Valley Country Club of Guilford. He attends the Methodist Episcopal church and is liberal in its support.

David Osgood Campbell married twice, his first wife having been Virginia M. Ring, of Orono, Maine, whom he married September 25, 1900. She was a daughter of the late Charles B. and Abbie Ring. Mrs. Campbell passed away in 1912. His second wife was Mrs. Genevieve (West) Collins, daughter of Hon. Joseph H. and Mary (Brackett) West, of Franklin, Maine. By his first marriage there was born David Rae, November 7, 1901.

ALBION E. COBB, M. D.—During the many years in which he practiced medicine, Albion E. Cobb was always active in the care of the sick and injured of the community. Thoroughly trained in his profession, he gave freely of his time and energy and long experience in the work which he had chosen to perform. His large practice in the various Maine towns in which he lived was a tribute to his ability, and his many warm friendships a testimonial of his fine personal character and worth.

His father, Dr. Albion Cobb, a well-known and very popular physician of Westbrook, Maine, was the eldest son of Asa and Nancy A. Cobb, and a graduate of the Medical School of Maine, at Bowdoin, in 1851. During the Civil War, he served as assistant surgeon in charge of the Fourth Maine Volunteers, from 1862 to July, 1864, and during 1864 and 1865, as assistant surgeon of the United States Army at Harwood Hospital, near Washington, District of Columbia. He married Louise Stockman, and they were the parents of three sons: 1. Albion E., of whom further. 2. Carolus M., who lives at Lynn, Massachusetts. 3. Anson M., who lived at Auburn, Maine. All of these children became doctors.

Albion E. Cobb was born on July 10, 1854, in Westbrook, Maine. He attended the public schools of his birthplace, and Dartmouth Medical College, serving, after his graduation from this institution, as an interne in the Mary Fletcher Hospital in New York. He began the practice of his profession at North Windham, Maine, where he lived for three years, moving at the end of that time, to Biddeford, where he remained for about eight years. In 1891 he came to Westbrook and soon built up a successful practice to which he devoted himself until his death on February 25, 1914. He was a member of the Democratic party and of the Free and Accepted Masons. He was a well-known political worker, and held at various times several important local positions. Much of his leisure he devoted to the cultivation of his flowers and gardens, which were a source of constant pleasure to him.

Dr. Cobb married Flora M. Page, of Windham, Maine, a daughter of Stephen and Mary (Mayberry) Page, of that place.

Dr. Cobb's death was a severe loss to the community which had come to know him so well. But the memory of his life and work and the inspiration of his example will not soon be lost.

JOSEPH PITTS—For more than forty years successfully conducting one business, and that one the first essay of his life, is the unusual record of Joseph Pitts, of Harrison, Maine, whose timber and pulp enterprises are as well known as the town itself.

Mr. Pitts was born in Harrison, October 13, 1864. His parents were Samuel Farnsworth Pitts, born in 1818 and died in 1888, and Calista B. (Stewart) Pitts. He was educated in the public schools, and early in youth became associated with the timberland and pulp business. From that moment he has not departed from his first choice and still conducts the enterprise known far and wide as Joseph Pitts & Son, which owns more than 3,000 acres of timberland in the neighborhood. Joseph Pitts is a member of the Community Church and is vice-president of the Fidelity Trust Company, of Portland, Maine. He belongs to the Maine Lumbermen's Association, and to the Independent Order of Odd Fellows. His other affiliations with fraternal orders are with the Masons, in which he belongs to the Blue Lodge, Free and Accepted Masons; the Knights Templar; Royal Arch Masons; and the Temple, Ancient Arabic Order Nobles of the Mystic Shrine.

Mr. Pitts married, at Naples, Maine, January 1, 1886, Effie Robinson, born in Naples, July 10, 1868, daughter of John and Esther (Smith) Robinson, both

Maine—27

natives of Otisfield, Maine. The children of the couple were: 1-2. Joseph Harvey and Charles Hartley (twins), born in Harrison, Maine, May, 1896. 3. Samuel Lee, born in Harrison (see a following biography). 4. Dorothy Esther, born in Harrison, May 19, 1903.

SAMUEL LEE PITTS—Associated with his father in the pulpwood and timberlands business of Joseph Pitts & Son, located at Harrison, Maine, Samuel Lee Pitts also finds time and pleasure in his successful administration of a summer camp for boys, at Crystal Lake, near Harrison. Among the younger active business men of this section, his natural abilities have been augmented by a groundwork of sound education. His patriotism has been proven, his upstanding citizenship rewarded by his selection for public office, while his interest in fraternal affairs commends him to the public as a man of highest worth.

Mr. Pitts was born in Harrison, March 13, 1898, a son of Joseph Pitts, also of Harrison (see a preceding biography), and of Effie (Robinson) Pitts, a native of Naples, Maine. Joseph Pitts has been active in the business of pulpwood and timberlands for many years and is the owner of some 3,000 acres of timberland near Harrison.

Samuel Lee Pitts was educated in the public school of Harrison, at the Bridgton Academy, from which he was graduated with the class of 1915, and at the University of Maine, which graduated him in the class of 1919. He immediately became associated with his father in business and has since then continued as a member of the firm. In addition to this he operates "Camp Ha-Wa-Ya," at Crystal Lake, near Harrison, where he takes care of about eighty boys during the season. He is a Democrat in politics, and a member of the Harrison School Committee. During the participation of the United States in the World War he served in the navy and saw active service. In Harrison he attends the Calvary Community Church and has membership in the Free and Accepted Masons, Royal Arch Masons, Knights Templar, Independent Order of Odd Fellows, and the Masonic Club.

Mr. Pitts married, at Greenwood, Maine, July 14, 1919, Frances Witter, a native of Texas. They have two children: 1. Virginia, born in Harrison, September 12, 1922. 2. Samuel Lee, Jr., born in Harrison, July 21, 1926.

LISTON P. EVANS, ORA L. EVANS—Beginning his active business life in the profession of journalism, Ora L. Stevens, of Dover-Foxcroft, has been fortunate in being associated in that career with his father, Liston P. Evans, who conducts and edits the Dover-Foxcroft "Observer," a journal established in 1838 and in which the senior Evans has been actively interested for many years. The elder Evans is a native of Brownsville, while his son was born in Dover-Foxcroft. Liston P. is the president of the Dover-Foxcroft Trust Company, while his son is a trustee of the Dover-Foxcroft Savings Bank. The father and son are members of the Order of Free and Accepted Masons, the son of the American Legion, having served in the World War in the Quartermaster Corps. The younger man is a graduate of Bowdoin College, of the class of 1916, where he received the degree of Bachelor of Arts. They attend the Congregational church of Dover-Foxcroft.

HENRY F. LIBBY is a prominent banker of Pittsfield, Maine. He had been in business for himself in Pittsfield, which is his native town, for a quarter of a century before he became connected with the Pittsfield National Bank. He was postmaster for thirteen years in the "eighties" and "nineties." He has always taken an active interest in public affairs and was for a time town treasurer. He has also been head of bankers' associations and has held other official positions in which his ability has been found of great value.

Henry F. Libby was born at Pittsfield, Maine, December 2, 1862, son of Henry A. and Augusta J. (Farnham) Libby, of whom the father, who was a farmer and grocer in Pittsfield, was born at Belgrade, Maine, and of whom the mother was born at Island Pond, Vermont. He was educated in the public schools of Pittsfield, Maine, at the Maine Central Institute, and at Eastman's Business College at Poughkeepsie, New York. He was then in the drug business under his own name in Pittsfield for a period of twenty-five years, ending in 1903, and then became cashier of the Pittsfield National Bank. He has been with the bank ever since and in addition to his post as cashier is also a director.

Mr. Libby is a Democrat in politics. He was postmaster in Pittsfield from 1885 to 1898, and he is now town treasurer, and has been since March, 1898. He is on the executive council of the American Bankers' Association, and was president of the Maine Bankers' Association in 1917. He belongs to the Free and Accepted Masons, the Knights Templar, the Odd Fellows, and the Knights of Pythias. He attends the Universalist church, of which he is a moderator.

Henry F. Libby married, September 4, 1886, Minnie E. Mitchell.

FRED SHAPLEIGH—From Alexander Shapleigh, one of the earliest Colonial settlers of Maine, whose pioneering activities furnished enthusiasm and direction to the first inhabitants of the section now known as Eliot and Kittery, is descended Fred Shapleigh, who is a native of Eliot where he attended the public schools. He has been connected with the Boston & Maine Railroad for a quarter of a century. He first entered the service of the railroad in 1893, serving five years in engine work, after which he became connected with the train service which he followed for twenty years. He entered the Government service for one year during the World War, 1917-1918, in the ship-building department. Following this he served an apprenticeship at the carpentry trade, and then reëntered the Boston & Maine Railroad service on bridge building. He is much interested in the historic associations of the ancient community of Eliot and its environs, and to his own town he lends a coöperative sirit and a helpful influence in the promotion of all that is best in municipal and civic endeavor.

Fred Shapleigh married Annie M. (Downing) Small, a leader in social circles, and descendant of Colonel William Pepperell and Sir George Downing. She is the daughter of Benjamin Downing, of whom further.

Benjamin Downing was a direct descendant of Sir George Downing, for whom Downing Street, the seat of the British Ministry, in London, England, was named. He was born in Newington, New Hampshire, and when a young man removed to

Maine, settling in the town of Eliot. He married there, December 28, 1861, Elizabeth (Drew) Bartlett, a descendant of John Heard Bartlett, who was graduated from Harvard College, in 1747, and of Richard Bartlett, immigrant ancestor, who arrived in this country in 1635 and settled in Newbury, Massachusetts. John Heard Bartlett was a successful school teacher, who married, in 1747, Dorcas Moulton, of York, and they had children, of whom was Daniel. This Daniel Bartlett, born July 23, 1763, received a commission as captain. He married Sarah Cutts, and their son, Daniel, born December 9, 1791, married (first) Mary Yeaton, of Dover, New Hampshire. He married (second) Placentia Odiorne, and of their children was Elizabeth, born in 1837, who married Benjamin Downing, above-mentioned. The original ancestors of the Bartlett family were among the followers of William of Normandy, when the Conqueror invaded Britain and they fought with him at the battle of Hastings.

To Benjamin and Elizabeth (Bartlett) Downing were born eight children: 1. Annie M., born in 1865, married Fred Shapleigh, of this review. She occupies a prominent position in society, is president of the Pepperell Family Association, of which she is a member by right of descent from Colonel William Pepperell, eligible to the Daughters of the American Revolution, and other important organizations. 2. Henry Bartlett Downing, a painter and farmer, resides in Eliot. 3. Elizabeth Placentia, married Fernando W. Hartford, mayor of Portsmouth, New Hampshire, and editor of the "Portsmouth Herald." 4. Edward P., an engineer on the Hartford & New Haven Railroad and resides at Middleboro, Massachusetts. 5. Benjamin, died at the age of fifteen years. 6. Emma, died aged eighteen years. 7. Charles L., station agent and telegraph operator for the Boston & Maine Railroad at Williamstown, Massachusetts. 8. George, engaged in the general insurance business at Portsmouth.

EDWARD K. BENNETT—Early thrown upon his own resources, his father having died when he was but three years of age, Edward K. Bennett, during his life, attained a position of prominence in Sanford in the shoe industry, and also in the express business. Mr. Bennett had other commercial enterprises at various times, having been a successful dealer in coal and an agent for the American Express Company, in Sanford. In political affairs, too, he was also a notable character, having served his district in the Maine State Legislature. Fraternal organizations and his church also came in for their share of his abilities, and he was ever ready and willing to promote any proposition designed for the welfare of Sanford. The Bennett family has long been represented in the various occupations of life throughout Maine and other sections of New England, and members of this family have occupied positions of trust and responsibility almost since the very beginning of this country's government.

Mr. Bennett was born November 2, 1837, and died in 1902. He was the son of Nathaniel Bennett, the sixth generation of this branch of the family in America.

(I) Anthony Bennett, the first known member of the Bennett family in America, lived in Gloucester, previous to 1680. He married, and among his children was Peter, of whom further.

(II) Peter Bennett, son of Anthony Bennett, was born in Gloucester, about 1680; married, February, 1704, Hannah Eveluth. He removed to York County, Maine. It is recorded that he sold by deed, dated June 26, 1728, rights to his property in Falmouth (now Portland), Maine. He lived in Falmouth, York. He sold a lot in Georgetown in 1717 to John Cookson. His brother, John, sold leases of lands at Spruce Creek to Benjamin Weeks, April 17, 1732. His brother, Anthony, and his wife sold land they bought of Sarah Jamison, in Falmouth, to John Smith, March 7, 1721-22; Sarah was the daughter of William Jamison. Anthony Bennett (2) married Rebecca.

(III) Dr. David Bennett, son or nephew of Peter Bennett, was born about 1705, died in 1745. He lived in York, and thought one of the original of first four grantees of the town of Sanford, Maine. Removed thither. On one of his first house-lots, he built the first "proper" (frame) house built in Sanford, and in company with others was owner of the first mill erected in the town. In 1743 his house was occupied by Samuel Staples. He thence owned lots 26, 27, 28, in 1742, about the same, time that he built the house. The fact that one Staples, one Howard, and others lived in it is proved by three depositions of persons whose memory extended back to a time earlier than 1743. His widow, Alice, married Joseph Simpson. She gave her lands to William and Nathaniel Bennett, her sons, by deed and will. Children: 1. William, sold one-half of lot 27 to his son, William, Jr., in 1790. 2. Hannah. 3. David. 4. Lieutenant Nathaniel, of whom further mention. 5. John.

(IV) Lieutenant Nathaniel Bennett, son of Dr. David Bennett, was born at York, in 1741, and died January 23, 1804, in his sixty-third year, at Sanford. He came to Sanford about 1730 and settled in South Sanford, and became one of the leading citizens of that village. He was a lieutenant in the Revolution and captain of David Butterfield's and Colonel John Frost's regiment, in the Rhode Island company, in 1776. He was ensign in Captain Morgan Lewis's company at the Lexington Alarm, April 19, 1775. These were the minute-men of Sanford and Gloucester. He was sergeant later, in 1775, in Captain Moses Merrill's company, Colonel Edmund Phillaney's regiment, First, and later commissioned lieutenant in Captain Edward Harmon's company (Ninth of Sanford), Colonel Ebenezer Sawyer's regiment (First, York). He was in Captain Samuel Nasson's company at one time. He was a charter member of the Congregational church at Sanford; was a salesman in 1780-81. All the Bennett families in South Sanford are descended from him. Among his children were: 1. Rufus, of further mention. 2. Joseph, born February 11, 1786, died in August, 1846; married Abigail Batchelder, born April 4, 1792, died 1875; removed to Hiram, March 18, 1824, and thence to Denmark, in December, 1825.

(V) Rufus Bennett, son of Lieutenant Nathaniel Bennett, was born about 1780 at South Sanford, Maine. He was a farmer at South Sanford. He married Annie Batchelder. Children, born there: 1. Horace. 2. Mary. 3. Nahum. 4. Nathaniel, of whom further. 5. Son, lost at sea when a young man, unmarried.

(VI) Nathaniel Bennett, son of Rufus Bennett, was born in Sanford, where he resided until his death in 1840, at the early age of thirty-three years. He occupied a prominent place in Sanford, served as captain of

a militia company, filled the office of deputy sheriff in the county, and in addition he favorably discharged the duties of a good citizen. He was a farmer, as so many of his ancestors had been. He married Abigail Hanson, also a native of York County and they had children: 1. George, deceased. 2. Elizabeth. 3. Lucy, deceased. 4. Edward K., of whom further. 5. Abigail, married Charles O. Amory, of Sanford. 6. Nathaniel. Mrs. Bennett married (second) William B. Amory, of Sanford.

(VII) Edward K. Bennett, second son and fourth child of Nathaniel and Abigail (Hanson) Bennett, was but three years of age at the time of the death of his father, and he was only seven years old when he was placed in charge of Jotham Moulton, and at the end of one year returned to his mother. Several months later it became necessary to find a home for him where he might earn his own bread. This resulted in his being sent to the farm of Dr. Bennett where he received two dollars per month for the work he was able to accomplish. At the end of six months he began to work regularly on the farm of Calvin Bennett, with whom he found employment each summer, until he had reached his fourteenth year. His wages were increased from five dollars a month and board to nine dollars, he having proved himself industrious and reliable. He then entered the shoe shop of Eben Hobbs and here applied himself so steadily and earnestly to his work that at the end of a year he received thirty dollars and was presented with a set of shoemakers' tools. Now he was ready to begin in business for himself. His first venture was a modest one, and soon he was enabled to enlarge his business, until eventually he employed sixteen men. For twenty years, thereafter, he was engaged in this occupation, at the end of which time he removed to Sanford. Here he bought an interest in an express business, and his partner, Darling Ross, soon withdrew from the firm, disposing of his interests to Mr. Bennett, who thus became the sole proprietor. This concern steadily increased in importance, its activities combining hack and stage transportation, and was quite lucrative until the advent of the electric road in Sanford, with its much swifter mode of transportation, brought a decline in the express business. Various other interests engaged Mr. Bennett from time to time, he having been a successful dealer in coal, and also an agent of the American Express Company, in Sanford.

A firm believer in the tenets of the Republican party, throughout his mature years, Mr. Bennett was signally active in its affairs. He possessed inborn qualities of leadership which were soon recognized by his fellow-citizens, and a short time after the close of the Civil War he was chosen to represent his district in the Maine Legislature. Here he discharged the duties incidental to the position with credit to himself and the State, and won the esteem and appreciation of his constituents. A communicant of the Congregational church, he was also a member of Riverside Lodge, No. 12, Knights of Pythias, of Sanford.

Edward K. Bennett married Calista D. Willard, daughter of Stephen Willard. To Edward K. and Calista D. (Willard) Bennett were born three children: 1. Willard H. (see a following biography), proprietor of the Sanford Hotel. 2. A daughter, who died in infancy. 3. Myron Edward, born December 2, 1876, at Sanford. He was educated in the public schools of Sanford and Maine Wesleyan Seminary,

420   MAINE—A HISTORY

from which he graduated in 1896, and then took a course of two years in special work at Harvard University, then returning to Sanford to succeed his father as agent of the American Express Company, a position he resigned in 1900 in favor of that of Superintendent of Schools, which he filled very capably for seven years. He was a partner in a drugstore, known as C. G. Brown & Company, in 1906, and in 1907, he purchased the interest of his partner, and became sole proprietor. Later he assumed the duties of editor of the "Sanford Tribune"; this was in 1911, and he has since remained in that work. A Republican, he is affiliated with Washington Lodge, Free and Accepted Masons, of Boston; White Rose Chapter, Royal Arch Masons; Bethany Commandery, Knights Templar, of Sanford; Maine Council, Royal and Select Masters, of Saco; Portland Consistory, Ancient Accepted Scottish Rite; Kora Temple; Friendship Lodge, Independent Order of Odd Fellows, of Springvale; Portland Lodge, Benevolent and Protective Order of Elks. Mr. and Mrs. Bennett have a daughter, Doris.

Edward K. Bennett passed away in his sixty-fifth year, and while he did not quite attain the threescore and ten years commonly allotted to man, he did, during the period of his residence upon this earth, follow the dictates of his conscience and lived a clean and useful life, and attained the honor and respect of those with whom he had come into contact.

WILLARD H. BENNETT—A former operator
of stage lines, previous to the days of modern rapid transit, Willard H. Bennett later became proprietor of the Sanford Hotel, and during his conduct of this hostelry, it became one of the best-known establishments in this section of Maine. Mr. Bennett, although now practically retired from active commercial pursuits, retains his interests in out-door sports and of these, perhaps, motoring is his favorite. His career in Sanford, while it has not been spectacular, has comprised numerous good works and services to his fellow-men.

Mr. Bennett was born at Sanford, oldest of three children of Edward K. and Calista D. (Willard) Bennett. Edward K. Bennett (see a preceding biography), who was a son of Nathaniel and Abigail (Hanson) Bennett, was born November 2, 1837, at South Sanford, Maine, and died in 1902. He was variously occupied around Sanford during his lifetime, and established the stage lines which were operated by his son. Edward K. Bennett was a grandson of Rufus Bennett, who was the fifth generation of this family in America.

After completing his education in the public schools of Sanford, Willard H. Bennett was prevailed upon by his father to enter into the latter's concern, which at one time was operating several stage lines. As this mode of transportation became practically obsolete, he was forced to seek another calling and purchased the Sanford Hotel, which he has continued to operate. As years have passed Mr. Bennett has assumed other interests, and, as director of the Sanford National Bank, is esteemed and respected by his fellow-men and valued by the other officers of this financial institution, which has benefited from his business sagacity and wise counsel. The last few years he has practically abandoned the arduous duties connected with the operation of his hotel, and has devoted himself more to the enjoy-

ment of his well-earned success. Motoring especially has attracted him and he derives much pleasure therein. He maintains a shore house at Wells, Maine, wherein he spends many happy hours. Among his fraternal affiliations is the local Lodge, Benevolent and Protective Order of Elks. Mr. Bennett is a brother of Myron E. Bennett (a fuller account of whose life is found with his father's biography), who is editor of the "Sanford Tribune."

FREDRIC A. FOGG—The profession of life insurance, the postmastership of his town and the station agency of the railroad traversing the community claimed at different periods of the career of the late Fredric A. Fogg, of Eliot, his capable attention and driving force which made him a leading figure in his community for all too brief a lifetime.

Born in Saco, October 12, 1876, died November 8, 1915, Fredric A. Fogg was the son of Joseph R. and Emily (Billings) Fogg. His preparatory course was taken at Thornton Academy, whence he entered Bowdoin College, from which he was graduated in the class of 1899. For a few years after he left college he taught school. He then entered the service of the Metropolitan Life Insurance Company, of New York, in the capacity of local agent and was thus employed for twelve years. When the time came for making an appointment of postmaster at Eliot, he was selected for the office and filled the position with credit to himself and the Government for a four-year term. He was also station agent for the railroad at Eliot for four years, and his service was featured at Thornton Academy, while exercising uniform courtesy to the patrons of the railroad at that point.

Mr. Fogg was highly placed in the Masonic fraternity, and affiliated with the Nashua (New Hampshire) Consistory of the Scottish Rite (thirty-second degree); Rose Croix Chapter, Princes of Jerusalem, of Dover, New Hampshire; Biddeford (Maine) Commandery, Knights Templar; and he was also a member of the Independent Order of Odd Fellows.

Fredric A. Fogg married Edna Paul, daughter of Moses N. and Ida (Frost) Paul, her father a descendant of Daniel Paul, who figured in the early history of Maine as a Colonial pioneer.

The death of Mr. Fogg, on November 8, 1915, shortly after he had entered his fortieth year, removed from the Eliot community a fine type of citizen who had proved his worth through public and quasi-public service in a number of stations in which the people of the town had come to know him for his friendly, generous and coöperative spirit in all things that had for their objective the betterment of the common interests. His record is most properly included in this history of his native State.

CHARLES HAYWARD HAINES, D. D. S.—Among the professional men who have practiced in Dexter, Maine, and have been called away from their activities by death, but have left behind them cherished memories, is the late Dr. Charles Hayward Haines, whose death occurred in February, 1924. Dr. Haines assumed the practice of his father at the time of the death of the latter, and from that time to the time of his death took care of his own and what had been his father's practice. He was one of the prominent and public-spirited citizens of Dexter, and it is fitting that in this work some memorial of his life and professional career should be included.

Dr. Charles Hayward Haines was born in Dexter, Maine, November 21, 1858, son of Dr. George A. Haines, who was the first dentist to locate in Dexter, and of Martha A. (Severance) Haines. He received his early education in the public schools of Dexter, and then began professional study in the Boston Dental College (now known as Tufts College), from which he was graduated with the class of 1880, receiving the degree of Doctor of Dental Surgery. In that year he engaged in practice in Dexter, opening an office in the Buckman and Mountain Building, and there he was successfully engaged to the time of the death of his father. He then took over his father's practice, locating in his father's office, and taking care of both his own patrons and those of his father. He remained in his father's offices in the Titcomb Building for some time, and then removed to the Fish Block in Dexter. Finally, he located permanently in rooms over the Merrill Trust Company Bank, where he took care of a large practice to the time of his death, which occurred February 6, 1924. Dr. Haines was held in very high esteem among his associates, and professionally was known as one of the best. He was a member of the Knights of Pythias; the Independent Order of Odd Fellows; and was also a member of Penobscot Lodge, Free and Accepted Masons; of the local Chapter, Royal Arch Masons; and of St. John's Commandery, Knights Templar, of Bangor, Maine. He was identified with the Dexter Club and with the Elkinstown Club, and professionally, was a member of the Maine State Dental Association, of which he was a past president. Along with his professional and other activities, Dr. Haines was talented as a mimic and an impersonator, and was much interested in amateur theatricals. With the assistance of Charles R. Favor he organized the Favor and Haines Comedy Company, a club which is still (1928) in existence. A man of varied talents, and of versatile gifts, he endeared himself to all with whom he was associated, and his memory is still cherished by those who knew him best and by a host of those whose way in life touched his.

Charles Hayward Haines was married, in Dexter, Maine, January 6, 1898, to Susie M. Gove, daughter of Charles L. and Josephine E. Gove. Mr. and Mrs. Haines are the parents of two children: 1. Kenneth H., who was born April 10, 1902. 2. Charles Favor, born March 9, 1907.

ELMER E. WENTWORTH—A long, distinguished career was that of Elmer E. Wentworth, late of Springvale, where he is recalled with appreciative and affectionate regard to the memories of those legion persons who were his friends. Economic and civic factor of foremost importance, he was largely responsible for the advancements wrought in this community during the last decade of the nineteenth and first quarter of the twentieth centuries. His name goes down for all time on the rolls of the honored dead.

Elmer E. Wentworth was a native of North Rochester, New Hampshire, a son of Simon and Francis J. (Cook) Wentworth. In Rochester he attended the public schools, there laying down the groundwork for future studies to be carried on independently, through wide reading and reflection during later years of life. Having completed his course in high school he went to work as a traveling salesman, for a wholesale hardware firm, and it was in

this connection that he secured his initial valuable business experience, destined to serve him well and profitably at more secure posts. In 1890, coming to Springvale, he purchased the livery and sales stable owned by Captain E. G. Murray, conducted the stable with good fortune nine years, and in 1899 purchased the John Dennett and Stephen Goodwin farms in the Deering district. These he united, and the combined tract subsequently became known as the Dennett Stock Farm, upon which Mr. Wentworth kept numbers of highly blooded horses, together with other stock of value and pedigree. Meanwhile also he continued the stables, but with the advent of automobile travel and the consequent passing of horse-drawn vehicles he turned his attention to auto sales and service, having a large garage at Houlton and another at Bangor, while a third he maintained in Springvale, where so long his headquarters had been. He handled the Ford product, and later secured the State agency for the Overland. Mr. Wentworth was a charter member of the Portland Automobile Association, but he never took the interest in auto races that he had borne toward horses. He was noted through the State as a starter at horse races and as a judge of horses at county fairs, and was resorted to frequently to decide fine points pertaining thereto, for he was known for his fairness and strict judgment. Mr. Wentworth was a founder of the Springvale Shoe Manufacturing Company, and of the Springvale Realty Company. He built up an extensive coal and wood enterprise (which is now managed by his daughter expertly) and was identified in fine with a great number of endeavors of financial nature calculated to benefit the community in which he lived. For a time he was a member of the town Board of Selectmen, served as road surveyor, and finally as road commissioner of Springvale. During the period of our country's participation in the World War he was of service in securing funds for the campaigns of the Liberty Loan, War Savings Stamps and Red Cross, in addition to having contributed of time, effort and money in other directions for the prosecution of the common cause.

Mr. Wentworth married Hattie B. Lord, daughter of James Alvah Lord, and of this union was born a daughter, Marion Francis. Marion Francis Wentworth married John Donohue, and they have a daughter, Shirley Louise, who was born June 25, 1924.

Mr. Wentworth died on July 24, 1923. Leading citizen, talented man of affairs, loyal patriot, it seemed that the town of Springvale as one person was affected at his loss — the loss of a valued and beloved figure, the common loss of an entire community, and certainly a loss to mankind.

GEORGE A. FIELD—Sanford's citizenry will remember long the position in local affairs filled by George A. Field. In both public and private activities his influence was constructive, designed for the welfare and advancement of interests of the town. His was a life of charity, honor and service.

George A. Field was born at Augusta, March 18, 1870, son of Charles and Mary (Folsom) Field. He received his elementary and secondary academic instruction in the public schools, graduated from Cony High School of Augusta with markings significant of scholastic ability, and took further work in preparation for a business career, at Augusta Business

College. His first employment upon completion of school was as clerk in a store operated by his uncle, Albert Field, at Old Orchard, Maine. Then, for several years, he served as postmaster and express agent for the community, and came to Sanford in 1900, as agent for the American Express Company. In 1907 he entered the employ of Sanford Mills, as one of the office staff, soon afterward becoming head accountant over the company's plants. This position he retained until the time of his death, being largely responsible for the efficiency of production which marked the mills' course while he was chief of accountants.

Mr. Field took an active interest in the civic affairs of Sanford, and owned to a considerable influence in local political circles. Holder of public office, at the time of his death he was serving the community as auditor. He was interested also in matters pertaining to the State Militia, having been a lieutenant in the Sanford company. Excellent as marksman, he took many cups at target shooting. He enjoyed the out-of-doors, gunning and fishing, and was a true sportsman, fond of the pleasures of the chase. Fraternally, Mr. Field was identified with Preble Lodge, Free and Accepted Masons, White Rose Chapter of Royal Arch Masons, and Riverside Lodge of the Knights of Pythias. He belonged to the Sanford Town Club, and was a communicant of the Congregational church. During the World War he was of service in the campaigns of patriotic appeal.

Mr. Field married Jane Barrows, daughter of Daniel D. and Emily (Bradbury) Barrows, of Saco, and of this union was born a son, George A. Field, Jr. He graduated from Sanford High School and went into the Sanford Mills offices with his father, now being head accountant. A master electrician and mechanic, during the war he was kept in the United States, in cantonments, at Fort Williams and elsewhere, and sent to Europe for six months, stationed at Limoges, France. He married Alice Garnsey, of Sanford, and they have a daughter, Jeanette Field.

Throughout his lifetime, George A. Field made lasting friends; and at the time of his death these were numerous. From them came many tributes attesting to the position he had held in their hearts, as citizen and man. Few failed to realize the inherent goodness of the one departed. Mr. Field's death occurred in December, 1922, when he was but little more than fifty-two years of age. During the more than score of years that he lived in Sanford he had been connected with practically all worthy projects aimed at the town's development along substantial lines, and his name must be perpetuated among those honored dead who were benefactors of the community.

EBEN KEZAR BRADEEN, born at Limington, Maine, April 20, 1842, was the son of Martin and Sophronia (Kezar) Bradeen. He was of Scotch-English ancestry and a descendant of John Bradeen—or Bradwardine as the family name was then spelled—a Scotch Royalist who came to this country settling at Tri-Mountain (Boston) Massachusetts, after the confiscation of estates following the battle of Dunbar in 1651. Mr. Bradeen had traits and qualities of those people in a marked degree, and had the sturdiness of character that kept him steadfast in his principles of right living and right doing.

In the maternal line he is descended from George (1) Kezar, a pioneer settler of Massachusetts at Salem and Lynn. The men of this line were noted Indian fighters and bore an honored part in the early wars of the colonies. George (5) Kezar, the fifth in the line, came to Maine in the year 1768 and purchased lands, forming a settlement at what is now known as Kezar Falls, Maine. Ebenezer, son of George (5), married Hannah White of "Mayflower" descent, and they were the parents of eight children, their youngest daughter being Sophronia, who married Martin Bradeen, September 13, 1840, and were the parents of the subject of this sketch.

With but few exceptions, his forebears in every line were of the Massachusetts Bay Colony, including one who was an early Innholder, being proprietor of "The King's Arms Tavern," which formerly (to quote the old record) "Was the principal place of entertainment in the town." This ancestor was also a charter member of the Ancient and Honorable Artillery Company. Another ancestor was one of eleven pioneers who in 1634-5 cleared the forest and founded the present city of Haverhill, Massachusetts. Later generations in these lines removed to Kittery, Maine, and engaged in the business of shipbuilding. During the early childhood of Eben K. Bradeen, his parents removed to Beverly, Massachusetts, from which place they came to Berwick, Maine, to reside when he was ten years old. His home has ever since been in Berwick. Mr. Bradeen's business was that of stone mason and building moving contractor. He built many of the foundations for buildings in this section, his work always being done in a most faithful and intelligent manner; and moved many large buildings in this and surrounding towns. The thoroughness and care which characterized everything he did made him an expert at this work, and his services were in great demand.

In politics Mr. Bradeen was a life-long Democrat and a firm believer in the principles of his party. Despite this fact he served his town several terms as selectman and assessor, being elected by Republican votes, as the town for many years has been overwhelmingly Republican. This was due to the qualifications which he had and the regard with which he was held by his townsmen, irrespective of party views. Twice during this time he assisted in taking the revaluation of the whole town, as is done every ten years. His services have been in frequent demand in the appraising and settlement of estates. His absolute integrity and rare good judgment gave him an equipment for this work which was quick to be recognized by those who knew him.

He was a member of Washington Lodge, Independent Order of Odd Fellows of Somersworth, New Hampshire, for forty-eight years, in the work of which Order he took much interest.

Mr. Bradeen attended the First Congregational Church of Somersworth, as long as the condition of his health permitted. For two years prior to his death he suffered with valvular disease of the heart, during which time he gradually failed until the end came on June 29, 1921. Strong in his friendships as in his convictions, unyielding where he believed himself to be right, Mr. Bradeen was honest and upright in all his dealings. He was a man who could be depended upon and trusted absolutely. He was possessed of more than ordinary intelligence, and his excellent judgment made his opinion, as well as his work, of much value. He was a self-made man in the sense of having had to depend upon his own efforts and judgment from boyhood.

Mr. Bradeen married, on April 19, 1868, at North Berwick, Maine, Olive Anne Hurd, only daughter of Rufus and Anne Staples Hurd. Mrs. Bradeen is from a long line of Colonial and Revolutionary ancestry, being descended in every line from the early Founders of New England. Her family bore an honored part in the early struggles of this country from the earliest Colonial War, and at Louisburg, at Quebec, at Bunker Hill, the men of her family have served their country with distinction; not alone in the military, but also in civil affairs have her forebears borne an honored part; in her line of ancestry being two Colonial governors, a deputy governor, Chief Justice of Supreme Court, deputies to the "Great and General Court," president of the council, associate justice and judge; and also, the first physician and surgeon of Maine and New Hampshire.

In the paternal line she is eighth in descent from Captain John Hurd, pioneer settler at "Cocheco," (Dover) and one of the Historic Founders of New Hampshire, and his wife Elizabeth (Hull) Hurd. Captain John Hurd was a shipmaster and sailed his ships between London and New England as early as 1635. When trouble with the Indians came he built a fortified garrison under the "Great Hill" (from which fact it is now called Garrison Hill); this was the frontier post between that settlement and Canada, and therefore much exposed to attack from the enemy. Elizabeth (Hull) Hurd survived her husband and after his death commanded the Garrison through a ten-year Indian War.

In the early years of their married life, Mr. and Mrs. Bradeen established their home at No. 32 Rochester Street, Berwick, which has since been the family residence, and here the two daughters, Annie Margaret Staples Bradeen and Mary Marcella Bradeen were born.

Mrs. Bradeen is a member of the First Congregational Church of Somersworth, New Hampshire; a member of the Alumni Association of Berwick Academy, South Berwick, Maine; a charter member of the Somersworth Women's Christian Temperance Union; a member of Margery Sullivan Chapter, Daughters of the American Revolution, of Dover, New Hampshire; and of the Society of Piscataqua Pioneers. Though throughly interested in the religious and social life of her community it is in her intense devotion to her home and family that her true worth and character is shown.

HENRY W. WEARE—Prominent among the public-spirited men of Ogunquit is Henry W. Weare, proprietor of the Hill Crest Inn, who also operates extensively in the real estate market. The Hill Crest Inn, containing fifty rooms, and operating as a summer hotel, has sheltered beneath its roof many men and women of national reputation and fame.

Henry W. Weare, son of Stephen and Eunice (Parsons) Weare, was born March 19, 1869, at York, Maine, his father having been a farmer. Mr. Weare received his early education in the public schools of York, helping with the farm work after school and during vacations. He remained on the farm with his father for some years, later engaging in various commercial enterprises before establishing his residence in Ogunquit, where he built the Hill Crest Inn. His

charming personality, distinct integrity, and strict probity have won him the deep respect of hosts of friends, and he has been most successful in his hotel venture, and in his real estate dealings.

Henry W. Weare married, in 1894, Katherine Martin, of Jericho, Vermont, daughter of Michael and Sarah (Moore) Martin. Mr. and Mrs. Weare are the parents of two children; 1. George D., a graduate of Dartmouth College, Hanover, New Hampshire; married Helen F. Shum, and they are the parents of three children, two sons and one daughter. 2. Joseph A.

THOMAS STANLEY BRADY, asphalt expert, lumber, and investment banking, of Augusta, Maine, was born in New Rochelle, New York, October 21, 1887, the son of Thomas and Mary Brady.

After being graduated from the New Rochelle High School, he took a special course at Fordham University, and also special course at Columbia University. During the World War he served on the staff of the Chief Engineer, First Army of the American Expeditionary Forces, and was troop movement officer, as such seeing active fighting at St. Mihiel and in the Argonne. Traveled extensively and completed trip around the world. Returning to America he engaged in business in Augusta. He is a director of the Augusta Trust Company, director of Augusta Lumber Company, president of Brady-Hichborn & Company, president of First Maine Investment Company. He is president of Augusta General Hospital, and a member of the Augusta Country Club, of the Bonnie Briar Country Club of Larchmont, New York, and of the Benevolent and Protective Order of Elks.

Mr. Brady married Hope Manchester Haynes, daughter of Josiah Manchester and Elizabeth Sturgis Haynes, March 4, 1922, at St. Andrew's Cathedral, Sydney, Australia.

JUDGE WILLIAM ROBINSON PATTANGALL—With a legal career that fast is approaching the four-decade mark, William Robinson Pattangall, Justice of the Supreme Judicial Court of Maine, has devoted the largest portion of this to public service, and has bestowed upon the citizenship of his State the benefits of his keen, judicial mind, and his many years of study and training in the profession of law. For several years he published and edited a newspaper, but law and its departments have ever been the paramount interests of his life. Most of his public offices have been more or less closely allied with his profession, and included the attorney-generalship of the State.

Judge Pattangall is a native of Maine, and a son of the late Ezra Lincoln and Arethusa (Longfellow) Pattangall. Ezra Lincoln Pattangall attained success in various vocations during his lifetime, he having been a shipmaster, a shipbuilder, and a merchant. William Robinson Pattangall was born June 29, 1865, at Pembroke, Maine, and his preliminary education was obtained in the public schools. After his graduation from high school he matriculated at the University of Maine, and was graduated therefrom. Admitted to the bar soon thereafter, he launched into the practice of his profession, and began the climb that was to place him so high in legal circles of Maine. It was in 1893 that Judge Pattangall was admitted to the bar, and he since has continued a member of the Bar Association. In 1906 he became interested in journalism, and for three years thereafter edited and published a newspaper. While building up his private practice, Judge Pattangall was rapidly assuming a place of importance in politics and public affairs, and he eventually became one of the leaders in the Democratic party. For four years he was elected to the Maine State Legislature, in 1897, 1901, 1909, and 1911; was a candidate for Congress from the Fourth District, 1904; candidate for this same post from the Third District, 1913-14. He was a member of the Democratic State Committee in 1905, 1906, 1907, and chairman of that committee in 1916 and 1917. Judge Pattangall was appointed Attorney-General of the State of Maine on April 12, 1911, and elected to that office for 1915-1916; elected mayor of Waterville in 1911, and reëlected in 1912 and 1913. From 1912 until 1916 he served as a member of the board of trustees for the University of Maine, and in 1922 and 1924 was the Democratic candidate for Governor of his State. One of the outstanding characteristics of Judge Pattangall has been his honesty and his courage to follow the dictates of his convictions. This was demonstrated in the Presidential campaign of 1928, when he refused to support the issues of his party, with which he could not reconcile himself. His present post, that of Justice of the Supreme Judicial Court, came to him in 1926, and his record in this honored position has placed him high in the estimation of his confrères and the bar.

Judge Pattangall, while a member of the college fraternities, Beta Theta Pi and Phi Beta Kappa, has confined his fraternal associations in later life to one or two of the best-known secret societies. He is a member of the Lodge, Free and Accepted Masons; the Chapter, Royal Arch Masons; the Council, Royal and Select Masters, and of the Commandery, Knights Templar. He also is a member of the Knights of Pythias and of the Benevolent and Protective Order of Elks. His recreation is found through his affiliation with the Abnaki Club, of Augusta.

William R. Pattangall married (first), June 6, 1884, Jean M. Johnson, of Calais, Maine, daughter of George M. and Mary A. Johnson, and they had a daughter, now Mrs. Katherine P. Brown, who was born May 4, 1886. Jean M. (Johnson) Pattangall died in 1886, and on September 27, 1892, Mr. Pattangall married (second) Gertrude McKenzie, of Machias, daughter of Ella and Edward McKenzie. The children of the second marriage are: 1. Edith P. Gilman, born July 13, 1893. 2. Grace P. Fassett, born April 27, 1896. 3. Josephine L., born March 13, 1905. Judge Pattangall's offices are in the County Court House, at Augusta, and he and his family have their home at No. 1 Green Street.

ERNEST D. BLAISDELL—It is an open question with many business men as to whether what is called "service" really pays, but in the case of Ernest D. Blaisdell, of Dexter, Maine, there is no question at all. In building up an automobile business which is at once the largest and the oldest in his region, service has been the secret of success, and that doesn't mean operating a filling station and keeping spare parts.

Born in Oakland, Maine, August 4, 1882, son of Dennison A. and Nellie (Tibbetts) Blaisdell, he is of

Maine stock on both sides. His father, who was born in Oakland, Maine, was a merchant there until his death in 1907. His mother, a native of Rome, Maine, died in 1886. Ernest D. Blaisdell, after passing through the public schools of Oakland, and being graduated from the high school, entered the class of 1906 in the University of Maine, where he was graduated with the degree of electrical engineer. He then went into business for himself in Dexter, Maine, as an electrical contractor, but in 1910, took over the local agency for the Ford cars, adding the Maxwell, Overland and Buick lines. In 1915 he dropped the Maxwell and Overland agencies, and took over the representation of the Hudson and Essex cars, and in 1920, he discontinued the Ford agency, and took on the Chevrolet line. Since 1920 he has represented Hudson, Essex, and Chevrolet cars, and the business has expanded to a point which enables him to employ twenty-five salesmen, and all cars are serviced.

Mr. Blaisdell finds his recreations in hunting and fishing. He is a Republican, and a member of the Universalist church. He is prominent in the Free and Accepted Masons, being a member of Penobscot Lodge, St. John Chapter, De Molay Commandery, Mt. Moriah Council, Anah Temple of the Shrine. He is also a member of the Theta Epsilon Community. His clubs are the Masonic and the Dexter. He is also a member of the Maine Auto Dealers' Association, and past president of the Dexter Chamber of Commerce.

Mr. Blaisdell married Imogene M. Buneps, in 1917. She was born in Dexter, Maine.

WILLIAM RAY SPENCER, the treasurer of the Fay & Scott Company, is a well-known business man of Dexter, Maine. Born September 25, 1892, at Argyle, Maine, Mr. Spencer is a son of William W. and Inez (Dow) Spencer, both of whom are natives of Argyle, the father is engaged in farming, and he is also a noted lumberman of that vicinity.

His son, William Ray Spencer, received his preparatory education in the public schools of the community in which he was born, later attending and graduating from the Dexter High School. He then entered the Shaw's Business College of Bangor, Maine, and later studied at the National School of Accounting at Portland, Maine. Upon the completion of these courses of study he became associated with the firm of Fay & Scott Company, in the capacity of bookkeeper, in 1913. The following year, in 1914, he was made treasurer of this company. In 1919, Mr. Spencer received his certificate as Certified Public Accountant. He has held the office of treasurer of this company since 1914, and his integrity and sound judgment have made him a valued officer of the concern.

Mr. Spencer has always taken a keen interest in other affairs and in the welfare of his community. In his political preferences he is a strong supporter of the Republican party. He is fraternally affiliated with the Plymouth Lodge, Independent Order of Odd Fellows; Penobscot Lodge of Free and Accepted Masons; St. John's Chapter, Royal Arch Masons. He is also a member of the Dexter Club, and the Dexter Chamber of Commerce. In his recreation Mr. Spencer finds his greatest pleasure in fishing, tennis and golf.

William Ray Spencer married, in 1913, Hazel M.

Slater, who was born in Dexter, Maine. Mr. and Mrs. Spencer are the parents of one child, a daughter, Barbara E. Mr. Spencer and his family attend the Congregational church.

HARRY A. SANDERS is head of a company dealing in general merchandise at Greenville, Maine. The business is nearly three-quarters of a century old, and was established by the father of Mr. Sanders. For almost twenty years now, since the time of his father's death, Mr. Sanders has been at its head. He is also director of a leading bank and takes a keen interest in public affairs.

Harry A. Sanders was born at Greenville, Maine, September 14, 1859, son of David T. and Louise A. (Sawyer) Sanders, of whom the father, who was a general merchant, was born at Bath, Maine, and died April 11, 1909, and of whom the mother was born at Augusta, Maine. Harry A. Sanders attended the public school at Greenville, and then the Eaton School of Norridgewock, Maine, and then the Eastman Business College at Poughkeepsie, New York. After leaving college he went to work in his father's business, founded by David T. Sanders in 1857, and later known as D. T. Sanders & Son Company. When his father died in 1909 Harry A. Sanders took control, and has since developed the business, which deals in general merchandise. He is a director of the Guilford Trust Company. He belongs to the Tarratine Club of Bangor, Maine, and the Piscataquis Valley Club. He attends the Union Congregational Church.

Mr. Sanders married, at Chester, Pennsylvania, December 15, 1888, Octavia S. Dean, born at Philadelphia, daughter of Buel W. and Frances (Osborn) Dean, of whom the father was born at Vergennes, Vermont, and of whom the mother was born at Corinna, Maine. Children, all born at Greenville, Maine: 1. Harry A. 2. Paul D. 3. David T. 4. Louise A. 5. Robert W.

STILLMAN WHITE SAWYER is general manager of Coburn Steamboat Company at Greenville, Maine. He has been in the shipping business for many years, both actively as mariner and master, and on the business side as agent and manager. He likewise takes an interest in the municipal affairs of the town in which he works and in which he was born, and has held public positions.

Stillman White Sawyer was born at Greenville, Maine, February 28, 1880, son of Henry P. and Louisa Mary (Davis) Sawyer, of whom the father was a lumberman, who was also in the steamship business. Mr. Sawyer attended for the main part of his school education the Greenville public schools.

Mr. Sawyer is an Independent in politics, and he belongs to the Free and Accepted Masons, Columbia Lodge, No. 200; the Greenville Chamber of Commerce, and other organizations. He attends the Union church.

Mr. Sawyer married, at Greenville, Maine, Winnie Dunning, born at Clifton, Prince Edward Island. He married (second) Bertie M. Gould, born in Dixmont, Maine. Children, all born in Greenville: 1. Florence E. 2. Oliver Stillman. 3. Erma Leola. 4. Edward. 5. Virginia May. 6. Frances Ardis.

HERBERT R. WELCH—Throughout his life Herbert R. Welch occupied an important place in the life of Sanford, Maine. A typical son of his

State, he was a prosperous farmer and dairyman, possessed of all the sterling virtues characteristic of the people which, since Colonial times, have formed the backbone of the nation. Mr. Welch was always vitally interested in the growth and welfare of the community in which he made his home, contributing liberally to worthy civic and benevolent enterprises.

Mr. Welch was born September 1, 1862, in Sanford, a son of Rufus and Mary (Bennett) Welch, and grandson of Solomon Welch, one of the early settlers of the town. Rufus Welch, who achieved success entirely through his own efforts and ability, was a farmer for most of his life in Sanford, where he also was born. Of his children, four are still living: 1. Angeline, widow of Moses H. Libby, Jr. 2. Julia, the wife of Samuel Mitchell. 3. Mildred, the wife of Fred Perkins. 4. Mary, wife of Lewis T. Trafton.

Herbert R. Welch attended the public schools of his birthplace until he was seventeen years old, after which, for six years, he worked in' the Sanford Mills. At the end of this time, he decided to adopt an independent vocation, and acquired property near Sanford, where he engaged in general farming. Very successful in this work, he also added dairying to his activities and in 1887 started the milk route in Sanford, which his sons are now continuing, supplying the purest of milk and cream from a fine herd of Holstein and Jersey cattle. His strict attention to the task at hand, together with his foresight and sound judgment won him not only merited prosperity, but also the respect and esteem of his fellow-townsmen, who appreciated his fine integrity of character and valued his presence as a man.

Herbert R. Welch married Clara E. Libby, daughter of Mr. and Mrs. Otis R. Libby, of Sanford, and of this marriage three children were born: 1. Rufus L., who married Hattie Anders, daughter of Walter Anders, of Sanford, and they have five children, Walter, Carl, Pauline, Frances, and Beatrice. 2. Everett C., who married Fannie Towne, daughter of James H. Towne, of Sanford, and they are the parents of four children: Mildred and Marion (twins), Roger Everett, and Otis R. 3. Maurice H., died in infancy.

Everett C. Welch resides on the home farm, while his brother Rufus occupies an adjoining farm. They continue the dairy business, established by their father, in partnership, employing all modern machinery and limiting their stock strictly to pure-bred cows. Under their able guidance the volume of business is constantly increasing.

Herbert R. Welch died at his home in Sanford on October 25, 1921, to the great sorrow of his many friends and acquaintances in Sanford and the vicinity. The inspirational value of a life such as his extends through the years, while the memory of the man himself will always remain with his friends.

WILLIAM O. FULLER—Native of Rockland, Maine, and now (1927), in his seventy-second year, William O. Fuller has devoted his entire career to journalism. He was born February 3, 1856, the son of William O. Fuller, born at Warren, Maine, and Bethiah (Snow) Fuller, born at Thomaston, Maine, both deceased, his father having been active in public life, a Republican, and one of the founders of the department store firm of Fuller-Cobb-Davis, at Rockland.

William O. Fuller, the son, received his early education in the public schools of Rockland, then took courses at the Kent Hill Seminary. It was during the last years in school that Mr. Fuller became interested in newspapers, first through employment in a print shop, and when only eighteen years of age, he founded the Rockland "Courier" almost simultaneous with the completion of courses in secondary school. Although this enterprise would be well nigh impossible at the present time (1928), owing to the cost of a bed press, typesetting machines, and general equipment and payroll incurred, the undertaking was not so heavy in 1874; withal, it was sufficiently burdensome for a lad of eighteen. His enthusiasm, courage, hard work and imagination made the venture successful from the beginning. He proved himself thoroughly as capable as a business manager and advertising solicitor as he was an editor. It was not long before Mr. Fuller realized how wise had been his choice of a profession, and he saw his circulation increase along with the expansion of his plant. Still further growth was most natural, and with that growth there followed amalgamations. The Rockland "Gazette," established in 1846, was merged with the "Courier" in 1882. The "Free Press" was established in 1855, and in 1891 changed its name to the "Tribune"; in 1897 it was merged with the "Courier-Gazette" and the name, under the new amalgamation, remained unchanged. Mr. Fuller has been editor-in-chief of the "Courier-Gazette" and president of the Courier-Gazette Publishing Company since the date of consolidation. As a prominent editor during a period when an editor's personality and opinion were in truth the moulders of public opinion, it was not strange that he exerted a powerful influence on the history of Rockland. He did more than suggest reform and the method of executing public office, but himself held public office. For five years he was city clerk; for twelve years he was postmaster. An outstanding member of the Republican party, he has always, when he thought advisable, taken part in local and State and national campaigns. He is a member of the Rockland Rotary Club and of the Blue Lodge of the Free and Accepted Masons, and of the First Baptist Church of Rockland.

GEORGE H. BASS—One of the well-known manufacturers of Maine, George H. Bass has been engaged for more than half a century in the manufacture of shoes, the name of his firm being G. H. Bass and Company. In this company his son, Willard Streeter Bass, is now very active, having been engaged in it since 1908. The son has taken most of the burden of the business from his father's shoulders by this time, and is now president of the company, a position which he has held since 1925.

George H. Bass, whose show manufacturing business is now one of the leading enterprises of Milton, Maine, was born July 22, 1843, the member of an old and distinguished family, being the seventh generation descended from Samuel Bass, who was a citizen of the Massachusetts Bay Colony in 1630. He is a son of Seth and Nancy (Russell) Bass. His childhood, George H. Bass spent at the home of his father in Wilton, where he was educated in the public schools until he reached the age of seventeen years. Then he taught in the local schools for a year until he became engaged in business. In 1861,

when he was eighteen years old, he became apprenticed to Corydon Bacheller, the owner of the Wilton tannery, where he continued to work for two years and to grow familiar with that trade. His wages at that time amounted to fifty dollars per year. Mr. Bass then became associated with John Cummings, in whose plant he worked. This plant, the largest in Woburn, Massachusetts, gave him further experience in the tanning trade. When he returned home at the end of six months to cast his first vote for President, voting for Abraham Lincoln for a second term, he found that his father, Seth Bass, was preparing to buy the tannery of his former employer, Mr. Bacheller. Seth Bass thereupon leased the tannery to his son, George H., on December 5, 1865, and the latter began his business career with a capital of two hundred dollars. The products of his tannery—calf skin and wax upper leather for long leg boots—were used in the manufacture of the most famous boots in Maine: by Nathaniel Hardy, in New Sharon; by Ara Cushman, in Auburn; by C. A. Wing, in Winthrop; by Joshua Adams, in Wilton; and by I. C. Lombard and Company, in Auburn. During the latter part of this period he also sold much leather to Foster, Packard and Company. Deciding to manufacture boots and shoes himself he bought Mr. Foster's interest, and in association with E. P. Packard ran that company in 1876. At the end of that year he purchased Mr. Packard's interest, and became so successful in his new venture that he sold his tannery to devote his entire attention to shoe manufacturing. Knowing the requirements of farmers, Mr. Bass decided to specialize in a type of boot that would be especially adaptable to rough out-of-door use, calling his product the "Bass shoe for hard service." Consistently adopting the policy of making shoes of certain types for specific purposes, he developed a line of river drivers' shoes that has become standard in New England and known in all logging regions from Newfoundland to California; and in 1909 he began the manufacture of moccasins, which since that year have constituted an important part of the firm's business. In 1906, the business was incorporated, with Mr. Bass as president, and his two sons, J. R. Bass and W. S. Bass, treasurer and secretary of the company respectively.

Always having had many interests outside of his business, Mr. Bass has been a supporter of welfare movements; has been one of the leading members of the Congregational church; has been in politics a Republican; has been president of the Wilton Water Company since its inception, having been largely responsible for the construction of the present water works; has served for many years as trustee of the Wilton Academy and as president of the board of this institution. For twenty-three years he was town treasurer of Wilton and in the term of 1914-1915 he served his district in the State Legislature.

Mr. Bass has been twice married, first to Mary Louise Streeter, of Saybrook, Ohio, a daughter of Sereno Wright and Sarah Jane (Willard) Streeter, of that place, this marriage having taken place on November 10, 1874. She died on May 2, 1896, and Mr. Bass married (second), October 27, 1897, Mary Ella Barry, of Wollaston, Massachusetts. By his first marriage he was the father of the following children: 1. Willard Streeter, of whom further. 2. John Russell, born in 1878. 3. Elizabeth, born in 1881. 4. Anne Louise, born in 1888.

Willard Streeter Bass, the first son of George H. and Mary Louise (Streeter) Bass, was born in Wilton, July 27, 1876. He received his education in the public schools of Wilton, then at Wilton Academy; and finally he became a student at Bowdoin College, from which he was graduated in 1896 with the degree of Bachelor of Arts. Later he took work at Harvard University, from which he was graduated in the class of 1899 with the degree of Master of Arts. Before he went to Harvard he was a teacher in the Wilton Academy in 1896 and 1897; and later he continued his teaching work, having been a teacher at the Chicago Institute in 1900 and 1901, and at the Francis W. Parker School in Chicago from 1901 to 1908. In 1908 he became engaged with his father in the shoe manufacturing business, which had been incorporated under the name of G. H. Bass and Company, and since that year he has been continuously with this company. Since 1925 he has been its president. He is a member of the Delta Kappa Epsilon Fraternity. Active in the affairs of the Congregational church, he was president of the Congregational conference in Maine in 1917. His political affiliations are with the Republican party.

Willard Streeter Bass has been twice married: First, on August 2, 1904, to Elizabeth Adams, in Tower Hill, Wisconsin; and, second, on June 24, 1913, to Harriet Spencer Carson, at Greenville, Illinois. The children by his first marriage are: Mary L., and Willard Streeter, Jr.

NORMAN H. NICKERSON, M. D., was born in Red Beach, Maine, April 8, 1892, and attended the public schools. Following high school studies, he entered Bowdoin College, and after receiving his Bachelor of Arts degree, continued a student in the Bowdoin Medical School, whence he was graduated Doctor of Medicine, in 1919. From June 16, 1919, to August 1, 1920, he served an internship in the Eastern Maine General Hospital, and in 1920 came to Greenville, where he has since practiced continuously. Dr. Nickerson is a member of the County and State Medical associations, fraternizes with the Masonic Order, and is a Republican in political sympathy.

SELDEN D. RICE—One of the most substantial men of Guilford, Piscataquis County, is Selden D. Rice, who, through his industrial and commercial activities as well as through his service in offices of town and county, has accomplished incalculable good to his community, the community of his birth, and the community which has been the center of his development from boyhood to manhood, from farmer on the rolling acres of his father's land to industrialist employing an average of sixty workers from year to year. Mr. Rice was born on the family farm near Guilford, August 24, 1866, son of Daniel and Malinda (Cayford) Rice, his father having been for many years engaged in agriculture here, and his mother a native of Fairfield, Maine.

Selden D. Rice attended the public schools of Guilford, and went to work with his father upon the farm. In 1888, when his father died, however, he went into trade, opening a general store and grist-mill in North Guilford, which he operated successfully for two years, then sold. With the proceeds of the sale and with other moneys he had acquired Mr. Rice engaged

in the lumber business, and as building contractor in large lumber operations, branching out continually, until he attained the prosperity enjoyed of recent years. Mr. Rice had vision, and, although remuneration was large from lumber, he perceived greater opportunities still, and in 1907 he acquired control of large steam mills in Piscataquis and Somerset counties ,operating in Guilford, Bowerbank and Canaan. He manufactures crating and spool bars, and his products are known throughout New England. Also, in 1907, Mn. Rice commenced the construction of roads under State contract, and has engaged in this during every summer succeeding that year until he is one of the best-known road builders in this part of Maine. By nature of great modesty, Mr. Rice is reluctant to talk of his progress in business matters; his friends esteem him for this perhaps as much as for his success itself, and for the services he has performed in benefit to the town, through supplying means of existence to the many families dependent upon him for wages, through his generosity in those wages, and for his appreciation and promotion of men under him who present evidence of extraordinary ability. As a reader of character Mr. Rice has achieved no little proficiency. It is his pleasure to meet and talk with every man entering his employ, whether upon the very day of his hire or later; and he is able to foretell in almost every case just what the applicant or worker will be able to do for the organization, thus laying for him a suitable course of employment leading to advancement when merited. Through his observations early in an employee's period of service, so called square pegs are seldom put into round holes; and this is true in all of the organizations headed by Mr. Rice, in large part accounting for their excellence, and, accordingly, for Mr. Rice's success. His judgment in commercial questions is frequently sought out by men in parallel ventures, and is easily secured when their character is known to him as worthy.

Aside from his ramified business interests Mr. Rice has many others, chief of which are those pertaining to the conduct of Guilford. He is a Republican, loyal to the principles of government upheld by the party, and is owner of a considerable voice in affairs of town and county. Among the public offices which he has held are those of town selectman and road commissioner of Guilford, which latter post he held for fourteen years. He is now (1928) county commissioner of Piscataquis County, and in this office as in those of the town, has distinguished himself for the excellence of his direction in matters having to do with the county at large and Guilford in particular. Fraternally, Mr. Rice is active in two orders: the Free and Accepted Masons and the Independent Order of Odd Fellows. In the former he is a member of Mt. Kineo Lodge, No. 109, and is senior warden; in the latter he is member of Good Cheer Encampment, No. 37. He is a member of the Guilford Chamber of Commerce and active in its projects as they affect the commercial life of the town. He is a communicant of the Methodist church, is devout in its service, and generous in contributions to charity, without regard for race or creed. Although he was somewhat too advanced in years for service in the military during the World War, Mr. Rice did serve tirelessly on the various boards and committees in charge of the prosecution of the war from within this country, and was instru-

MAINE—A HISTORY

mental in securing subscriptions in Guilford and surrounding country for the several Liberty Loan campaigns. Those who know him well are pleased to say of him, that he is honorable in his dealings, large and small, that he is talented as a business man, and that he is a decided asset to his community, and worthy citizen of State and nation.

On July 4, 1893, in Guilford, Mr. Rice was united in marriage with Bertha M. Cobb, native of Bangor, Maine, a daughter of William and Sarah Rose Cobb, her father a native of Livermore, Maine, and her mother of Guilford. To this union were born children: 1. Ida M., now Mrs. Ida M. Nagle, November 30, 1895. 2. Dorothea W., now Mrs. Dorothea W. Ellis, born December 5, 1897. Mrs. Rice is a woman of charm and refinement.

EDWARD LEANDER HIGGINS, a member of the firm of Burnham & Higgins, well-known architects of Portland, Maine, and a member of an old and distinguished New England family, was born March 8, 1879, at Bar Harbor, Maine. Mr. Higgins is a son of Ambrose H. and Elizabeth A. (Ash) Higgins.

Their son, Edward Leander Higgins, received his early education in the public schools of the community in which he was born, later attending the Bar Harbor High School, from which he graduated with the class of 1898. He then entered the Massachusetts Institute of Technology at Boston, Massachusetts, and he graduated from there with the class of 1906. Immediately upon the completion of these courses of study he branched out for himself, and journeying to Portland, Maine, he started his work as an architect in partnership with Mr. Burnham, under the firm name of Burnham & Higgins. This partnership in which Mr. Higgins carried on the practice of his profession with eminent success, continued until 1915. In that year, Mr. Burnham retired from all further business pursuits. Mr. Higgins has carried on the work alone since that time with undiminished success. He maintains his offices at No. 95 Exchange Street, Portland, Maine.

Despite the many varied and exacting duties which his profession entails, Mr. Higgins has nevertheless found time in which to take an active interest in the life of his community. He is fraternally affiliated with the Ancient Landmark Lodge, Free and Accepted Masons, and the Mt. Vernon Chapter, Royal Arch Masons. He is also a member of the Society of the Mayflower Descendants, the Sons of the American Revolution, the Portland Club, and the Maine Chamber of Commerce.

Edward Leander Higgins married, December 12, 1906, at Wakefield, Massachusetts, Hortense L. Stevens, a daughter of Charles B. and Dove Blanche (Parks) Stevens. Mr. and Mrs. Higgins are the parents of two children, a son and a daughter: 1. Ambrose Stevens. 2. Blanche Elizabeth. Mr. Higgins and his family maintain their principal residence in Portland, Maine.

WINTHROP L. FAY—As president of the firm of Fay and Scott Company at Dexter, the only manufacturers of lathes in the State, Winthrop L. Fay is a son of one of the founders of this, one of the long-established industries of Maine, and carries along to increasing success the plans of a concern whose product has become vitally necessary to corporations and general users of special machine tools and machinery. His city, his State, and New England know Mr. Fay not only as a man of enterprise in' his own specific field, but as a broad-minded business factor and counsellor in general industry.

Winthrop L. Fay was born July 29, 1875, at Abbot, Maine, a son of Norman H. Fay, a native of Upton, Massachusetts, a founder of the firm of Fay and Scott Company, and its president until his death in 1919, and Ada (West) Fay, who was born in Gray, Maine, and survives her husband. Norman H. Fay had held several prominent public positions, both in city and State: at the time of his death, he was a member of the Governor's Council, and had served a prior full term in that office; and he represented his District two terms in the State Legislature. At the time of his death, he had served for twenty-three years as president of the Dexter Building and Loan Association; and he was also president of the Maine League of Loan and Building Associations, having held that position two terms.

Winthrop L. Fay attended the public and high schools at Dexter, and received special training at the Massachusetts Institute of Technology. Upon completing his education, he became associated with the firm of Fay and Scott Company, at first in the capacity of vice-president; and since 1919, he has been president and general manager of the company. The firm of Fay and Scott Company manufactures a line of lathes, such as engine and wood-turning lathes, the only plant thus engaged in the State; they also manufacture special machines on contract, producing a large amount of work for well-known concerns throughout the United States. The concern maintains its own foundry for grey iron and composition casting. The company has a three-year apprenticeship system; has group life insurance for its employees; and owns about thirty industrial houses for employees only. The history of this industry is as follows:

Norman H. Fay and Walter Scott formed a partnership in 1881 for the purpose of manufacturing wood-turning lathes, which they afterwards extended to machine tools and special machinery, at first leasing the building that is now occupied by the Enterprise Creamery Company. The equipment was moved in 1884 into a building located on the site of the present plant, when the concern had the following-named officials and machinists: Norman H. Fay, general manager, died in 1919; Walter Scott, superintendent, died in 1898; Dexter McKechnie, pattern maker; William Knox, foreman molder; A. H. Fassett (who was the first employee of the firm) W. S. Gould, W. E. Hill, C. H. Brown, G. Safford, E. Moore, machinists; Henry Marsh, blacksmith. At this time, the weekly payroll was approximately one hundred and fifty dollars; and the floor space of the plant did not exceed 10,000 square feet; but with the steady increase of the business, it became necessary in 1890 to extend the machine shop forty feet. Further extensions followed in 1891, 1892, 1893, 1902, 1906, 1911, 1913, 1915, 1917, and 1918, and now a floor space of two acres is utilized, the firm employing annually about two hundred and fifty men. The present officers are as follows: Winthrop L. Fay, president and general manager; Peter S. Plouff, vice-president and assistant general manager; R. W. Spencer, treasurer-accountant.

Among Mr. Fay's other business associations are

those of his directorship with the Merrill Trust; membership on the Committee on Machinery of the New England Shippers' Advisory Board; on the Advisory Committee of the Maine State Branch of the American Vocational Society; membership with the Associated Industries of the State of Maine; and directorship of the Dexter Building and Loan Association. In the political field, Mr. Fay is a Republican, and he has served as a member of the Republican Town Committee, also on the Republican County Committee.

In 1916, Mr. Fay was a second lieutenant of Company A, 103d Regiment Maine National Guard, and saw service on the Mexican border. During the World War, the firm of Fay and Scott Company was engaged in the manufacture of materials essential to winning the war.

Fraternally, Mr. Fay is affiliated with Penobscot Lodge, Free and Accepted Masons; St. John's Chapter, Royal Arch Masons; St. John's Commandery, Knights Templar; Anah Temple, Ancient Arabic Order, Nobles of the Mystic Shrine; and he is a past president of the Dexter Club; and a member of the Dexter Chamber of Commerce; and his hobbies are hunting and fishing. He attends the Universalist church.

Winthrop L. Fay married, May 20, 1915, Edith (Hale) Brewster, who was born in Dexter.

REV. MARCIAN L. BALLOU is pastor at the Catholic Church of St. Agnes, Pittsfield. He has had a remarkable record of charges as pastor both in Nebraska and Maine and has had an almost equal record in the number of colleges in which he has studied both in this country and abroad. He has had the pastorate in Pittsfield only a short time, having been put in charge in June, 1927.

Marcian L. Ballou was born June 17, 1888, at Quincy, Massachusetts, son of John C. and Ellen G. (Hurley) Ballou, of whom the father, who is still living, and was a granite manufacturer at Quincy for over fifty years, was born at Cambridge, Massachusetts, and of whom the mother, who is now deceased, was born at Quincy, Massachusetts. He attended the public schools at Quincy, and then high school and Boston College. After that he was a student at St. Francis College, Brooklyn, New York, from which he graduated with the degree of Bachelor of Arts in 1907. Later he went to the American College at Rome, Italy, and was there for three years. He was ordained priest at St. Paul's Seminary, St. Paul, Minnesota, in 1910.

The following is an account of his various pastorates up to the present time: Father Ballou was at Omaha, Nebraska, as pastor, for six years; at O'Neill, Nebraska, one year; at Grand Island, Nebraska, one and a half years; at Scotch Bluff, Nebraska, one year; at Hyams, Nebraska, two years; at Coleridge, Nebraska, one year and a half; at Elkhorn, Nebraska, five years; at Bellevue, Nebraska, two years; at Portland, Maine, three months; at Lewiston, Maine, one year; at the Sacred Heart Church at Portland, Maine, four months; at Biddeford, Maine, two years and a half; at Winthrop, Maine, four months; at Millinocket, Maine, eight months; at Ellsworth, Maine, five months; and at Pittsfield, his present location, since June, 1927. Father Ballou belongs to the Catholic Order of Foresters of Massachusetts.

BURLEIGH—The surname Burleigh is an ancient English family name. The most common spellings of this name in the early records are Burleigh, Burley, Burly, Birle, Birley, Birdley and Burdley. No less than nineteen branches of this family in England had or have coats-of-arms.

(I) Giles Burleigh, immigrant ancestor of the American family, was an inhabitant of Ipswich, Massachusetts, as early as 1648, and was born in England. He was a commoner at Ipswich in 1664. He was a planter, living eight years on what was later called Brooke Street, owning division lot No. 105, situated on Great Hill, Hogg Island. His name was spelled Birdley, Birdly, Burdley and Budly in the Ipswich records, and his name as signed by mark to his will is given Ghils Berdly. He bequeathed to his wife Elizabeth (called elsewhere Rebecca); his son Andrew; his son James; his son John, and an uncle whose name is not given. Theophilus Wilson was executor, Deacon Knowlton and Jacob Foster, overseers, Thomas Knowlton, and Jacob Foster, the witnesses. Soon after his death his widow was granted trees for a hundred rails and a hundred posts, June 13, 1668. She married (second), February 23, 1669, Abraham Fitts, of Ipswich. Children: 1. Andrew, born at Ipswich, September 5, 1657; married Mary, daughter of Governor Roger Conant. 2. James, mentioned below. 3. Giles, born July 13, 1662. 4. John, born July 13, 1662, died February 27, 1681.

(II) James, son of Giles Burleigh, was born in Ipswich, Massachusetts, February 10, 1659, died in Exeter, New Hampshire, about 1721. He married (first), May 25, 1685, Rebecca, daughter of Thomas and Susannah (Worcester) Stacy. She died October 21, 1686. Her mother was a daughter of Rev. William Worcester, of Salisbury, Massachusetts. His sons, Joseph, Giles, Josiah and James, made a written agreement in 1723. Children: 1. William, born in Ipswich, Massachusetts, February 27, 1692-93, was at Newmarket in 1746. 2. Joseph, born April 6, 1695. 3. Thomas, born April 5, 1697. 4. James, born in Exeter, in 1699. 5. Josiah, mentioned below. 6. Giles, born in 1703; married, December 9, 1725, Elizabeth Joy, of Salisbury, Massachusetts.

(III) Josiah, son of James Burleigh, was born in Ipswich in 1701, died in Newmarket, New Hampshire, in 1756. He married Hannah, daughter of Hon. Andrew (2) Wiggin and his wife, Hannah (Bradstreet) Wiggin. Thomas Wiggin, father of Andrew (2), was the immigrant, coming in 1631 as agent for the proprietors of New Hampshire. Hannah Bradstreet was a daughter of Governor Simon and Ann (Dudley) Bradstreet, and granddaughter of Governor Thomas Dudley. A tract of land at Exeter was set aside for him by the committee in 1718. He signed a petition for a bridge at Newmarket in 1746. Children: 1. Josiah, died at Newmarket; married Judith Tuttle. 2. Thomas, of whom further. 3. Samuel.

(IV) Thomas, son of Josiah Burleigh, was born about 1730. He was an inhabitant of Deerfield, New Hampshire, in 1766, and was appointed on a committee to locate the meeting-house. He married Mercy Norris. In 1775 he settled at Sandwich, New Hampshire, on what is now known as Burleigh Hill. He was a farmer. Children: 1. Deacon Thomas, married (first), April 6, 1779, Hannah Etheridge; (second) Susan, daughter of Benjamin and Lydia (Hanson) Watson, widow of Colonel Lewis Went-

430   MAINE—A HISTORY

worth, of Dover. 2. Mercy, married, March 5, 1784, Eliphalet Smith, son of Colonel Jacob and Dolly (Ladd) Smith. 3. Benjamin, of whom further. 4. Samuel, died at Sandwich, July 5, 1851; married, March 7, 1785, Ruth, daughter of Joshua and Ruth (Carr) Prescott. 5. Josiah, died at Sandwich, August 31, 1845; married, February, 27, 1788, Rosamond Watson, of Moultonborough, New Hampshire. 6. Dolly.

(V) Benjamin, son of Thomas Burleigh, was born about 1755, in Deerfield, New Hampshire. He was a merchant, having a general store at Sandwich, New Hampshire, the first in that town. He married, November 23, 1779, Priscilla Senter, of Centre Harbor, New Hampshire, born November 1, 1759, died January 1, 1819. She married (second) Colonel Parker Prescott, son of Lieutenant John and Molly (Carr) Prescott, born at Manchester, Massachusetts, April 4, 1767, died December 17, 1849. Children: 1. Colonel Moses, mentioned below. 2. Benjamin, born at Holderness, March 1, 1783, died at Oakfield, Maine; married Hannah Sanborn, of 'Centre Harbor. 3. Thomas, born March 1, 1783; married, April 21, 1808, Hannah, daughter of Thomas and Hannah (Etheridge) Burleigh. 4. Priscilla, born in 1785; married William Cox. 5. Polly, born at Sandwich in 1787, died May, 1831; married Captain Ezekiel Hoit, son of Joseph and Betsey Hoit. 6. Olive, born April 12, 1789. 7. Another child born in 1790.

(VI) Colonel Moses, son of Benjamin Burleigh, was born at Sandwich, New Hampshire, March 25, 1781; died at Linneus, Maine, February 13, 1860; married Nancy Spiller. He settled before 1812 in Palermo, Maine, where he lived until 1830, when he removed to Linneus, Aroostook County, where he resided until his death. At Palermo he was elected to various offices of trust and honor. He was captain of the militia company there when called into service in the War of 1812, and marched with his company to Belfast at the time that the British vessels entered the Penobscot River, to destroy the United States frigate "Adams." He was commissioned captain in the Fourth Regiment, Second Brigade, Eleventh Division, Massachusetts militia, in 1814, and promoted to lieutenant-colonel in 1816. He was a representative to the General Court of Massachusetts when Maine was a part of that State and afterward was in the Maine State Legislature. He was a delegate to the convention in 1816 at Brunswick, to frame the constitution for the State of Maine. He carried the first mail by carriage from Augusta to Bangor, it having been carried on horseback previously. At Linneus he was appointed by the marshal to take the census in the northern section of Washington County. When he was engaged in that service, the provincial warden, alleging that he was in disputed territory in violation of the provincial law, pursued with authority to arrest Colonel Burleigh, but the latter was successful in eluding the pursuit and completing his work. In 1831 he was appointed assistant land-agent, to guard that section of the public lands, and in that office drove various parties of Canadian squatters back to the provinces. He was for several years postmaster at Linneus. We are told by his biographer that he was a man of activity, energy and probity of character; his hospitality was particularly marked, the hungry were fed and the weary found rest beneath his roof.

His wife died January 2, 1850, aged sixty-four.

"She lived a life of usefulness, was kind and beneficent, beloved and respected by her numerous friends." Children of Colonel Moses and Nancy (Spiller) Burleigh: 1. Elvira Senter, born January 7, 1806, died October 27, 1829. 2. Benjamin, born March 6, 1809. 3. Benjamin, born February 21, 1811. 4. Hon. Parker Prescott, of whom further. 5. Nancy Spiller, married Jabez Young, of Houlton, Maine. 6. Moses Carlton, born at Palermo, May 15, 1818; married, in 1843, Caroline Elizabeth Frost, of Lubec, Maine. 7. Samuel Kelsey, born January 8, 1820; married Keziah Byron, of Linneus. 8. Olley Seaver, born September 11, 1822, died March 20, 1876; married Dudley Shields. 9. Rufus Burnham, born February 9, 1826, died at Fulton, Arkansas, April 30, 1864; married, at Belfast, Maine, September 21, 1857, Ann Sarah Flanders.

(VII) Hon. Parker Prescott, son of Moses Burleigh, was born in Palermo, Maine, May 16, 1812. He was educated at the Hampden Academy, in Maine, and the Hartford (Connecticut) grammar school, at that time one of the best-known schools of the country. At the same time he received instruction in military tactics from Colonel Seymour, afterwards governor of the State. He removed with his father from Palermo to Linneus in 1830, and devoted some time to obtaining instruction in land-surveying. His knowledge of timberlands in the Maine wilderness was excelled by none, and he invested extensively in this form of property. He followed the profession of civil engineering and surveying, in addition to farming. As State chairman in 1869 of the Maine commission on the settlement of the public lands of Maine, he contributed largely to the development and settlement of Aroostook County. He was elected State land-agent in 1868 and served in that office eight years. He himself was one of the pioneers there, in 1830, and at the incorporation of the town of Linneus in 1836 he was chosen town clerk, treasurer, collector of taxes and chairman of the school committee. Throughout his long life he held nearly all the time some office of trust and honor. In 1839 he was commissioned captain of Company M, Sixth Regiment, First Brigade, Third Division, of Maine militia, and in 1840 was elected lieutenant-colonel of the Seventh Regiment, a position he held for seven years. He was appointed county commissioner by Governor Kent in 1841, and was subsequently elected to that office; was county treasurer also, and postmaster at North Linneus for twenty-five years. He was a member of the House of Representatives in 1856-57, and a State Senator in 1864-65, 1877-78. He was chairman of the Board of Selectmen several years. He died April 29, 1899, in Houlton, Maine.

He married (first) Caroline Peabody, daughter of Jacob and Sally (Clark) Chick, of Bangor. She was born January 31, 1815, died April 6, 1861. He married (second) May 29, 1873, Charlotte Mehitable, daughter of Colonel James and Mehitable (Jones) Smith, of Bangor. Children of first marriage: 1. Hon. Albert Augustus, born at Linneus, October 12, 1841; married Lucinda G. Collins; enlisted in the Union Army in the Civil War in 1864; was wounded, taken prisoner and confined at Petersburg and Richmond; resided at Oakfield and Houlton, Maine; was commissioner of Aroostook County twelve years; surveyor of land by profession. Children: i. Everett Edwin, born November 9, 1862. ii. Albert Augustus, born January 8, 1864, died July 30, 1864. iii. Preston Newell, born at Oakfield, February 18, 1866. iv. Parker Prescott, born February 15, 1868. v. Frances Lucinda, born November 19, 1871. vi. Harry Ralph, born October 5, 1874. 2. Hon. Edwin Chick, mentioned below.

(VIII) Hon. Edwin Chick, son of Hon. Parker Prescott Burleigh, was born in Linneus, Maine, November 27, 1843, and died June 16, 1916. He was educated in the public schools of his native town and at the Houlton Academy, where he fitted for college. Following the example of his father, he educated himself as a land surveyor, a profession that offered excellent opportunities at that time to young men on account of the necessity of surveying timberlands. For a time after leaving the academy he taught school, but when the Civil War broke out he and his brother went to Augusta and enlisted in the District of Columbia cavalry, but he was rejected, on account of the state of his health, by the examining surgeon, Dr. George E. Brickett. Disappointed in his ambition to enter the service, he accepted a clerkship in the office of the adjutant general of Maine, and remained to the close of the war. He then followed his profession of surveyor and the business of farming until 1870, when he was appointed clerk in the State land office at Bangor, and two years later made his home in that city. In 1876-77-78 he was State land agent, and during the same years also assistant clerk of the House of Representatives. In 1880 he was appointed clerk in the office of the State treasurer and removed permanently to Augusta. In 1885 he was elected treasurer of the State, an office that he filled with conspicuous ability and success. He was reëlected in 1887, and in the year following was chosen governor of the State, with a plurality of 18,053 votes. In 1890 he was reëlected governor with a plurality of 18,899 votes. His administration of State affairs was preëminently constructive and progressive in character. His experience in public life, his executive ability and well-balanced character fitted him admirably for the office of governor. Democratic in his ways, indefatigable in his attention to the varied duties of his position, he strengthened himself in the hearts of the people during his term of office. He was popular and won the commendation of press and public alike. His appointments were satisfactory. His addresses to the Legislature and on public occasions marked him as a master of expression. Through his influence and action the plan to remove the State capitol from Augusta to Portland was defeated, and an appropriation of $150,000 made for the enlargement of the old State House. He was chairman of the commission in charge of the State House addition. Incidentally the State saved at least two million dollars by refusing to abandon the old capitol. In 1899 Governor Burleigh became chairman of a committee to locate and purchase a permanent muster field, and after something of a contest he secured the selection of historic Camp Keyes, in Augusta, an ideal field for the purpose, at a cost of $3,500. The value of the real estate has since then tripled and the wisdom of the choice has been applauded. During the winter of 1889 he called attention through the columns of his newspaper, the "Kennebec Journal," to the crowded condition of the State insane hospital, and the Legislature authorized the appointment of a commission to purchase grounds near Bangor for the erection of a new State hospital for the insane. At the suggestion of Governor Burleigh

the valuations for the purpose of taxation were investigated by a commission, and the State valuation, as a consequence, increased from $236,000,000 to $309,000,000, and a State Board of Assessors created. Taxes have since then been more justly and equitably levied in Maine. In funding the State debt Governor Burleigh effected a substantial saving to the taxpayers. At his suggestion the Legislature authorized an issue of bonds to take up the entire State debt, which was then bearing interest at the rate of six per cent. These three per cent bonds were sold at a premium of $79,900 and an annual saving of $71,520 effected at the same time. In 1891 he advocated the Australian ballot system in his address before the Legislature. The House of Representatives voted against the bill, but the governor fought hard, the popular support was given him, and in the end the bill was enacted. Since then, this system of voting has been adopted in almost every State in the Union. On the recommendation of Governor Burleigh, the secretary of the board of agriculture was given a larger salary and quarters in the State House, largely increasing the efficiency of the board. On his recommendation, the appropriation for State aid for soldiers, disabled veterans of the Civil War, was increased from $70,000 to $135,000. At the same time he effected great improvements in the National Guard of Maine. It was upon his recommendation that the law was passed providing heavy penalties for the careless setting of forest fires, making the land agent the forest commissioner of Maine, with wardens in every section. The results of this legislation have been very effectual and valuable. When the State library was to be moved to its new quarters in the State House extension in 1891, he advocated a modern card catalogue, the appropriation for which was made, and today the State library of Maine in convenience and usefulness is second to none in New England. During his administration, it should be added, the rate of taxation reached the lowest point in the history of the State, notwithstanding the progress and improvements mentioned.

When his four years as governor expired, Mr. Burleigh had aspirations to go to Congress, and in the campaign of 1892 he sought the nomination, against Hon. Seth L. Milliken, of Belfast, then member from the third district. Mr. Milliken won after a lively and close contest, and was given the cordial support of Mr. Burleigh. In 1897, when Mr. Milliken died, the nomination was given Governor Burleigh by acclamation. In Congress Mr. Burleigh's ability and usefulness were plainly conspicuous. His first important achievement in Congress was the apportionment bill in the Fifty-sixth Congress, when he served on the select committee on the census. Chairman Hopkins, of Illinois, had a bill for three hundred and fifty-seven members, based on a population of 208,868 for each member, while Governor Burleigh's bill provided for three hundred and eighty-six members, based on a population of 194,182 for a district, the smallest number that would allow Maine to retain four members of the House. The Hopkins bill was approved by the majority of the committee, but on the floor of the House the Burleigh bill was successful. As a legislator Mr. Burleigh was remarkably successful, having the tact and ability to persuade others to his way of thinking. After the custom of his State, he has been reëlected at each successive election to the present time. Upon the death of the late Congressman Boutelle, Governor Burleigh was Maine's member of the National Republican Congressional Committee.

Mr. Burleigh had large investments in timberlands, especially in Aroostook County. He was interested with his brother, Albert A., in constructing the Bangor & Aroostook Railroad into the Aroostook wilderness, an enterprise that has had a great influence in the development and upbuilding of that resourceful region. For a number of years his chief business interest was centered in his newspaper, "The Kennebec Journal." When Congress was not in session he would nearly always be found at his desk in the "Journal" building, or in the private office of his summer cottage on the shore of Lake Cobbosseecontee, where he spent part of the summer with his family. Congressman Burleigh was a frequent contributor to the newspaper, which has held its position and the high reputation it won under the management of Luther Severance, James G. Blaine and John L. Stevens as an organ of the Republican party, to which the growth and strength of that party were in no small degree due. He was a director of the First National Bank and of the Granite National Bank, and trustee of the Augusta Trust Company. He was a member of Augusta Lodge, Free and Accepted Masons.

Governor Burleigh married, June 28, 1863, Mary Jane, born in Linneus, Maine, November 9, 1841, daughter of Benjamin and Anna (Tyler) Bither. Her father was the son of Peter Bither, a native of England, who died in Freedom, Maine, and who served in the American army in the Revolution. Benjamin Bither was in the service in the War of 1812. Children: 1. Clarence Blendon, of further mention. 2. Caroline Frances, born at Linneus, July 23, 1866, married Robert J. Martin, M. D., of further mention, father, Dr. George W. Martin, was a leading physician of that city; Dr. Robert J. Martin was drowned June 16, 1901, while attempting to rescue a drowning girl; they had one child, Robert Burleigh Martin, born September 3, 1888. 3. Vallie Mary, born at Linneus, June 22, 1868; married Joseph Williamson, Jr., of Augusta, son of Hon. Joseph Williamson, of Belfast, Maine; children: i. William Burrill Williamson, born November 20, 1892. ii. Robert Byron Williamson, born August 23, 1899. 4. Lewis Albert, of further mention. 5. Lucy Emma, born in Bangor, February 9, 1874, married Hon. Byron Boyd, ex-secretary of State and now (1928) chairman of the Republican State Committee; son of Dr. Robert Boyd, of Linneus; children: i. Dorothy Boyd, born November 12, 1895. ii. Robert Boyd, 2d, born June 25, 1902. iii. Mary Edwina Boyd, born December 21, 1903. iv. Richard Byron Boyd, born December 10, 1904. v. Edwin Burleigh Boyd, born December 12, 1905. 6. Ethelyn Hope, born in Linneus, November 19, 1877, married, April 20, 1904, Dr. Richard H. Stubbs, son of Hon. P. H. Stubbs, of Strong, Maine.

(IX) Clarence Blendon, eldest child of Hon. Edwin Chick Burleigh, was born November 1, 1864, in Linneus, Maine, and educated in the common schools of Bangor and Linneus, and New Hampton Literary Institute, graduating in 1883. He then entered Bowdoin College, from which he graduated with the class of 1887, after which he became editor of the "Old Orchard Sea Shell," which was published by the Biddeford "Times" until the close of the beach season, when he returned to the city of Augusta,

where he purchased an interest in the "Kennebec Journal" in 1887. In 1896 he was elected State printer, which office he held until 1906. During the years 1896-97 he was president of the Maine Press Association. He has been president of the Augusta City Hospital since its establishment; was member of the Board of Assessors in 1897; president of the Augusta Board of Trade in 1899-1900; chairman Republican city committee since 1902. He is the author of the following works: "Bowdoin '87, a History of Undergraduate Days," "Camp On Letter K," "Raymond Benson at Krampton," "The Kenton Pines" and other works. He is a member of Augusta Lodge of Ancient Free and Accepted Masons, Chushuc Chapter, No. 43, Royal Arch Masons; Trinity Commandery, Knights Templar, Augusta, and the Maine Consistory, thirty-second degree, Portland, Maine; also is identified with the Independent Order of Odd Fellows, Knights of Pythias, and is a charter member of the Benevolent and Protective Order of Elks. In religious affiliations he is a member of the Congregational parish.

Mr. Burleigh was married, November 24, 1887, to Sarah P. Quimby, born May 22, 1864, in Sandwich, New Hampshire, daughter of Joseph H. and Nancy P. (Fogg) Quimby. Their children are: Edwin C., born December 9, 1891; Donald Q., born June 2, 1894.

(IX) Lewis Albert, son of Governor Burleigh, was born in Linneus, March 24, 1870, attended the schools in his native town, at Bangor and Augusta, was graduated from the Cony High School, in 1887, and from Bowdoin College in the class of 1891, with the Bachelor of Arts degree. He entered the Harvard Law School, after a short interval, received his degree of Bachelor of Laws in 1894, and was admitted to the bar of Kennebec County the same year. In October, 1894, he formed a partnership with his brother-in-law Joseph Williamson for the practice of law, and the firm took a leading position in corporation and general business. At the termination of the partnership in 1912 he took charge of the business interests of his father, and at the latter's death in 1916 succeeded him as president of the Kennebec Journal Company until the disposal of his interest in that concern in 1922. He is now the trustee of his father's estate.

A Republican like his father, Mr. Burleigh has been town clerk of Augusta, a member of the Maine House of Representatives, and a United States Commissioner. He was a director of the Augusta National Bank, until it was liquidated, and at present a vice-president and director of the First National Granite Bank of Augusta. He is a Past Master of Augusta Lodge, Free and Accepted Masons; member of Chushuc Chapter, Royal Arch Masons, of Council, Royal and Select Masters; of Trinity Commandery, Knights Templar; and has attained the thirty-second degree in Masonry. He is a member of Kora Temple, Ancient Arabic Order Nobles of the Mystic Shrine, Lewiston. In 1907 he was Master of the Lodge of Perfection. He is also a member of Augusta Lodge, Benevolent and Protective Order of Elks. He is a member of the Congregational church, and has served on its prudential committee. He served for nine years as city clerk of Augusta, and for several years upon its Board of Education.

Lewis Albert Burleigh married Caddie Hall Brown, daughter of Hon. S. S. Brown, of Waterville, Maine, October 18, 1894. She was born in Fairfield, Maine,

April 22, 1871. They have one child, Lewis Albert Burleigh, Jr., born July 20, 1897, now in the legal department of the New England Public Utilities Company, at Augusta.

CHARLES H. PERKINS occupies the responsible post of superintendent of school buildings of Portland. He is the builder of many schools throughout Cumberland County, as well as some similar structures in adjoining States.

Mr. Perkins was born in Ogunquit, York County, the son of Charles L. and Addie (Hitchins) Perkins. Following his early education in the local public schools, he served for a time as an apprentice at the carpenter trade. He then went to sea for two years, at the end of which time he returned to Portland and engaged in the business of builder and contractor. Among other large public buildings he superintended the South Portland High School and the York Grammar School. He also superintended the dormitory of the Nason Institute at Springvale, York County, and erected a very fine scholastic establishment at Kingston, New Hampshire. In 1924 Mr. Perkins was appointed superintendent of school buildings in Portland, which office he still holds (1928). He is affiliated with the Free and Accepted Masons and is a member of the Woodford Club. His religious affiliations are with the Elm Street Methodist Episcopal Church of Portland.

In 1903, Mr. Perkins married Gertrude Chalk, daughter of Richard Chalk, who for seven years was Factory Inspector of the State of Maine and was very prominent in political circles. Mr. and Mrs. Perkins are the parents of two children, as follows: 1. Charles Richard, who graduated from Deering High School, and who is now a registered embalmer in Portland. 2. Bernice, who at this time of writing (1928) is a student at the Boston Physical School of Education.

JOHN H. MACOMBER—One of the prominent men in the civil affairs of the State is John H. Macomber, of Ellsworth, who holds the office of High Sheriff of Hancock County, to which position he was elected in 1925. In the administration of his duties, Mr. Macomber has shown the same high qualities which induced the voters to choose him for this important work.

Mr. Macomber was born in Franklin, September 29, 1859, son of Henry E. Macomber of Ellsworth, and Julia M. (West) Macomber of Franklin, both of whom are now deceased. Henry E. Macomber was a prominent man in the lumber and shipbuilding trades until his death. John H. Macomber received his early education in the public schools of Franklin, and after high school, entered the Maine Central Institute. After finishing his formal education, he entered business in a clerical capacity, which he continued for ten years, when he engaged independently in the granite business at Sommes Sound, Mount Desert Island, carrying on a successful business there under the firm name of Campbell and Macomber for twenty-two years. He then relinquished this business and accepted a position with the State of Maine as Chief Game Warden of Hancock County, which office he performed with great efficiency for fourteen years, until 1925, when he was elected High Sheriff of Hancock County in which

capacity he continues to serve the citizens of this county. In politics, Mr. Macomber is an active member of the Republican party. He is a member of Lygonia Lodge, Free and Accepted Masons, and his religious affiliations are with the Congregational church. He finds great recreation from his public duties in making a hobby of farming.

John H. Macomber married, in 1885, Elizabeth Jordon of Ellsworth, who died in 1927. Their son, Ronald W., served in the United States Army during the World War, having the rank of first sergeant in the Fourth Evacuation Company of the Forty-second Division.

GEORGE ASHWORTH—In 1884 George Ashworth came to Sanford, Maine, which was to be his home thereafter for more than thirty years. An expert block printer, he was also a highly successful farmer and grower of prize fruits and vegetables, and to this latter interest he came to devote more and more time. At his death in 1917, he had acquired wide reputation throughout Maine for his agricultural, poultry and stock exhibits, while at Sanford he was highly esteemed as a public-spirited citizen.

Mr. Ashworth was born in Newchurch, near Manchester, England, June 23, 1856, a son of John R. and Alice Ashworth. His parents were people of broad culture, each having had the advantage of a liberal education. His father was an architect by profession, while his mother, before her marriage, was a school teacher. George Ashworth attended the national schools of his native town, and later served an apprenticeship as a carpet printer in the Barcroft woolen mills in Newchurch. A natural taste for the cultivation of flowers, however, caused him to devote his leisure time to gardening, and he acquired a high reputation as an exhibitor at different agricultural fairs, receiving many prizes for the high standard and perfection of his products. At a fair held in Lancashire, he won a silver loving cup as a special prize for the best exhibit of celery. In 1881 Mr. Ashworth came to the United States, and was first employed as a printer in the Brown Manufacturing Company Mills at Paterson, New Jersey. He then became head gardener for Dr. Kimball of Plainfield, New Jersey, where he remained for a period of eight months, after which he resumed his trade as a block printer in Brooklyn, New York. For five months he was employed in this capacity in Union, New Hampshire, and finally, in October, 1884, he came to Sanford, accepting a position in the Sanford Mills, where he soon became known as an expert and reliable workman in his special line. Shortly after his arrival in Sanford, he purchased the Hiram Witham farm, and began the raising of prize fruits and vegetables, and in 1892, he bought the Chadbourne farm adjoining. With this large estate he had ample scope to indulge his taste for gardening and fruit culture. He also gave considerable attention to stock and poultry breeding, and was successful in winning many prizes in the annual fairs of Sanford and Springvale.

Politically, Mr. Ashworth supported the principles and candidates of the Republican party, and he was affiliated, fraternally, with the Ancient Order of United Workmen. He was also a founder of the Society of the Sons of St. George, of Sanford, Maine. Mr. Ashworth was a stockholder of the Sanford Fair and Trotting Association, and for some time was a member of its board of directors. He and his family worshiped in the faith of the Unitarian church. On March 9, 1874, George Ashworth married Elizabeth A. Clark, who was born in Lancashire, England, a daughter of Henry and Ann Clark. Of this marriage children were born: 1. John R., of Baltimore. 2. Alice A., wife of Samuel H. Thompson, of Sanford, whose son, Joseph, will enter the United States Naval Academy, at Annapolis, Maryland, this fall. 3. Leona, who married Carlton K. Woodard, of Brockton, Massachusetts. 4. Sarah E., who lives with her mother at home. 5. Mary J., who married Charles H. Emery, of Haverhill, Massachusetts, and they are the parents of one child, Edith. 6. George, who married Ellen Brown, of Sanford, and they have one child, Elizabeth. 7. Lena E., who also lives at home with her mother. Mr. Ashworth died at his home on June 30, 1917.

ERNEST R. WOODBURY, principal of Thornton Academy, at Saco, Maine, a man whose broad mind and earnest spirit has done much to increase the progress of the Academy, was born July 3, 1871, at Farmington, Maine. Mr. Woodbury is a son of Roliston and Maria D. (Billings) Woodbury, both of whom are deceased. Roliston Woodbury, the father, who was born in Sweden, Maine, was a veteran of the Civil War, having served with the Fifth Maine Battery, and died in 1888. The mother, Maria D. (Billings) Woodbury, was born in Fayette, Maine, and she died in 1926.

Their son, Ernest R. Woodbury, received his preliminary education in the public schools of the community in which he was born. He later attended and was graduated from the Normal School at Castine, Maine, and from the Deering High School at Portland, Maine. Upon the completion of these courses of study he entered Bowdoin College, and was graduated from there with the class of 1895, when he received the degree of Bachelor of Arts. Some time later Mr. Woodbury received the degree of Master of Arts. For several years after this he taught school. In 1905 Mr. Woodbury accepted the position of principal of Thornton Academy, an office he is filling at the present time. A man of scholarly attainments and whole-hearted devotion to his charge, Mr. Woodbury may well be proud of the work that has been accomplished at the Thornton Academy under his leadership. During the World War he served as one of the "four-minute" speakers of his district, and was also a member of the Home Defense.

Despite the manifold duties which his work has entailed Mr. Woodbury has nevertheless found time in which to take an interest in other activities. He is fraternally affiliated with Saco Lodge, Free and Accepted Masons, of which he is a Past Master; Maine Council; Bradford Commandery, Knights Templar; Maine Consistory; and York Chapter, of which he is Past High Priest. Mr. Woodbury is also a member of the Kiwanis Club, of the Biddeford and Saco Country Club, and of the college fraternities, Theta Delta Chi and Phi Beta Kappa.

Ernest R. Woodbury married, in 1898, Fannie L. Gibson, a native of North Conway, Maine, the daughter of James L. and Addie L. (Dow) Gibson. Mr. and Mrs. Woodbury are the parents of three children; two sons and a daughter: 1. Roliston G.,

who served in the Naval Reserve during the World War. 2. Wendell DeWitt. 3. Darthea.

AMARIAH FROST—A descendant of one of the oldest families in New England, Amariah Frost for many years served as an inspector in the United States Custom House at Portland, Maine, before his retirement about the year 1882 to a small farm in Brooks, Maine, where he passed the remainder of his days. The immigrant ancestor of this branch of the Frost family was the Rev. John Frost. He was an English Non-Conformist, and his son Edmund, with his wife Thomasine, came from Ipswich, England, to New England in the ship "Great Hope" about 1635. The children of Edmund and Thomasine Frost were: 1. John. 2. Thomas. 3. Samuel. 4. Joseph. 5. James. 6. Mary. 7. Ephraim. 8. Sarah. Edmund Frost settled in Cambridge, was made a freeman in 1636, was a ruling elder in the church there and died July 12, 1672. His second child, Thomas, settled in Sudbury, Massachusetts, where he married Mary Goodridge, and they became the parents of four children: 1. Thomas. 2. John. 3. Samuel, of whom further. 4. Mary. Samuel, who resided in Framingham, on February 1, 1710, married Elizabeth Rice, and they were the parents of children, the fifth of whom was Rev. Amariah Frost, who was born October 4, 1720; graduated from Harvard College in 1740; was ordained to the ministry in Mendon, Massachusetts, on December 24, 1743; married Esther, daughter of Rev. Henry Messenger of Wrentham, on April 27, 1747. Rev. Amariah Frost died on March 14, 1792, after forty-nine years in the ministry at Mendon. He was a most honored and respected member of his community, it having been said of him: "Mr. Frost was reputed an excellent man and one of the most popular preachers of his age, for almost half a century a loved pastor with one church and society."

The second child of Rev. Amariah and Esther (Messenger) Frost was Amariah Frost, Jr., who also became a minister. He was born February 5, 1750; graduated from Harvard College in 1770, and married Esther Messenger, the daughter of John and Melatiah (Corbett) Messenger. Among their children was Deacon John Frost, who settled in Sanford, Maine. He was born in Milford, Massachusetts, February 20, 1787. Throughout his mature life he was a successful merchant and farmer and an influential member of the Congregational church, wherein he served as a deacon for many years. On May 21, 1812, he married Hannah, the daughter of Captain Nahum Morrill of Wells, Maine, and they had children, among them: 1. Hon. George A., born in Sanford, April 2, 1813. He was a general merchant of Springvale for thirty years; politically he was a Republican, and in 1861-62 served as a member of the Executive Council, and was a trustee of the Maine Insane Hospital for nine years. He took deep interest in all local enterprises, especially those having to do with the education of the rising generation and the prosperity of the people. Deeply religious, he was of a charitable nature and ever a friend of the poor. He married, April 14, 1835, Mary Lord, daughter of Moses Lord of Sanford. They had one child, born in 1836, who died in his sixth year. Mary (Lord) Frost passed away December 22, 1881. 2. Amariah Frost, of whom further. 3. Hon. Charles Henry Frost, born in Sanford, October 17, 1829, was a most successful merchant, and with his brother conducted one of the largest stores of its kind in Springvale. A Republican in politics, he was an active worker for that party's interests and represented the towns of Sanford and Lebanon in the Legislature of 1864, serving with credit to himself and to his party. He was one of the legislators to vote for the amendment to the State Constitution in 1865 which abolished slavery. In 1888 he was nominated for Senator without opposition and was elected by a very large majority. Mr. Frost married (first) Abbie A. Wilson, who died November 7, 1897, and he married (second) Eva Harris of Brockton, Massachusetts. He died on February 28, 1926, and having no heirs of his own, left all of his property to his sister-in-law, Elizabeth Frost, the widow of Amariah Frost.

Amariah Frost, the third son and fourth child of Deacon John and Hannah (Morrill) Frost, was born April 16, 1819, at Sanford, where he attended the public schools. After completing his education he was engaged as a farmer in Springvale, later moving to Jackson, Maine, where he conducted a general store for three years. After this period he returned to Sanford and here he entered the grocery business, but remained there only a very few years, going thence to Portland, Maine. In Portland he conducted a very successful grain business, but subsequently entered the Custom House service in that city as an inspector. About 1822 he retired to a small farm in Brooks, Maine, where he resided until the time of his death.

Mr. Frost married Elizabeth Wilson, who survives him and maintains her residence at No. 88 Main Street, Springvale, Maine. She is the daughter of the late Captain Robert and Nancy (Forbes) Wilson of Nova Scotia.

Amariah Frost passed away on June 13, 1886, mourned by his widow and a large circle of friends. His career, while not spectacular, was devoted to those pursuits which fall to the lot of what is commonly called "a good citizen," and he will long be remembered in the minds of those who knew him.

JOHN ELMER GOODWIN—Since his graduation from the University of Maine, in 1919, John Elmer Goodwin has been identified with various phases of engineering work, in various connections, and in 1923 he became associated with the Maine Public Utilities Commission, of which he is now chief engineer (1928). His ability and his skill are unquestioned, and the service which he is rendering is fully appreciated.

Stuart Hussey Goodwin, father of Mr. Goodwin, was born in St. Albans, Maine, and died in 1914. He was a man of more than average ability, and in addition to his successful farming operations, was a commercial traveler. He supported the principles of the Republican party, and was active in its affairs, serving in whatever capacity he could be of most use, and was elected to represent his district in the State Legislature. He married Myra Finson, who was born in Boston, Massachusetts, and among their children is John Elmer Goodwin, of further mention.

John Elmer Goodwin, son of Stuart Hussey and Myra (Finson) Goodwin, was born in St. Albans, Somerset County, Maine, March 5, 1896, and during his early boyhood years attended the public schools of St. Albans. Later, he was a student in the Hart-

land Academy at Hartland, Maine, for one year. Entering Maine Central Institute, at Pittsfield, Maine, as a second year student, he graduated with the class of 1915. Four years later, in 1919, he was graduated from the University of Maine, at Orono, Maine, with the degree of Bachelor of Science, and in October of that same year he became associated with the Brown Company, at Berlin, New Hampshire, with whom he remained until January 15, 1923, doing research work in the chemical engineering department. In January, 1923, he became associated with the Maine Public Utilities Commission, as assistant engineer, and later, he was made chief engineer of the commission, which responsible position he is still (1928) filling. Mr. Goodwin is a member of Maine Society of Engineers, and is an active and interested member of the Augusta Chamber of Commerce. Like his father, he gives his support to the Republican party. He is a member of the Free and Accepted Masons, and of the Royal Arch Masons, and his club is the Kiwanis. His religious membership is with the Episcopal church.

John Elmer Goodwin was married, in Augusta, Maine, August 24, 1923, to Gertrude Staples Trafton, who was born in Fort Fairfield, Maine, May 8, 1900, and died April 18, 1924. She was a daughter of Herbert W., a native of Fort Fairfield, Maine, and of Kate P. (Winslow) Trafton, who was born in Dexter, Maine. There are no children. Mr. Goodwin has his offices in the State House, in Augusta, and makes his home in Augusta.

JEROME BORDEN CLARK is a well-known lawyer at Milo, Maine. He has been a practicing lawyer in Maine for about a score of years, but for the last decade his work has in the main centered round the district in which Milo is located, and he has also held responsible legal positions in the county government.

Jerome Borden Clark was born at Steuben, Maine, April 15, 1878, son of Albert W. and Eunice H. (Cleaves) Clark. He attended the public schools of his native district, and then went to Cherryville Academy, Fryeburg Academy, and the University of Maine, receiving his Bachelor of Laws degree in 1907. He was in general law practice at Presque Isle, Maine, from 1908 to 1918. Then he was in practice at Dover-Foxcroft, Maine, from 1919 to 1922. Since 1922 he has been at Milo, not only practicing but taking an active part in public affairs and holding public positions at both. He has been county public administrator since 1922, and county attorney also from the same year, his term closing in 1928. He has been Superintendent of Schools at Gouldsboro. He is a Republican in politics and has been chairman of the Republican Committee in Milo since 1923. He belongs to the Free and Accepted Masons, thirty-second degree, Scottish Rite, and the Grange. He belongs also to the Sons of the American Revolution, the Mayflower Society, the Masonic Club, and the Country Club.

Jerome Borden Clark married, November 20, 1901, Miss Grace B. Wood of Gouldsboro.

ARTHUR A. COOK—Devoting tne better part of his life to a single purpose, advancing step by step, all the while making friends among all he met and silently setting up for himself a sturdy citizenship, Arthur A. Cook of Greenville, may be said to have tasted copiously of the rewards of faithful service. Not a native of this State, he came here as a young man and for twenty-eight years has worked in the trade of butter tub and plywood veneer manufacture.

Mr. Cook was born in Stockholm, New York, October 11, 1875, a son of Arthur, a farmer and still living, and Mary (Gandeau) Cook, now deceased, both of whom were natives of Stockholm. He was educated in the public schools of Stockholm and at the State Normal College at Potsdam, New York. He afterward attended the Burlington Business College, at Burlington, Vermont. He then came to Greenville and began his work in the woodenware manufacturing industry. In 1916 he was made superintendent of the Veneer Products Company, which is now the Atlas Plywood Corporation, a post he still fills with satisfaction to the owners. He is a Republican in politics and attends the Union church of Greenville. He is a member of the Scottish Rite 'Chapter of Free and Accepted Masons and of the Woodmen of the World.

Arthur A. Cook married, October 9, 1903, at St. Albans, Vermont, Sadie M. Shufelt, of Sutton, Quebec, Canada. Their children are: Arlene Grace, Florence Lee, and Arthur A., Jr.

GEORGE CALL—His ancestors owners of the land upon which Pittsfield now stands, tilling it prior to the War of the Revolution, himself born in Pittsfield and identified with its growth during his entire life, there was no more respected citizen of the community than George Call. For thirty years he had charge of the cemetery, abandoning that work in 1896 to engage in farming. His father was Samuel Call, as well and favorably known and respected in his day as was the son. The family is a representative of pioneer Americans who hewed their way into the virgin land and helped to bring it to its present commercial and agricultural position. George Call was a staunch Republican in politics, and a deacon of the Baptist church, a respected citizen and a valued friend. He died May 23, 1900.

LOUIS W. COHEN—With so broad acquaintanceship as Louis W. Cohen has secured in the general business world, he has also added thereto a host of friends who recognize his abilities in real estate dealings and in insurance in which he successfully engages at Bangor. He is one of the foremost of the realty men in this part of the State, as well as one of the best informed with regard to the finest localities and the general values of property; while his insurance activities are steadily on the increase.

Louis W. Cohen was born August 7, 1889, in Bangor, a son of Nathaniel Cohen, who was born in England, and was a well-known clothier throughout his career, and' Rose (Kramer) Cohen, also a native of England, and who survives her husband. Mr. Cohen attended the public schools, and was graduated at Shaw's Business 'College, and he then followed in his father's footsteps in the clothing business, his interests therein being in his own name, and with his headquarters in Bangor. He so continued for fifteen years, until in 1922 he established himself in his present real estate and insurance business, and with his offices at No. 4 Broad Street. He is well known as one of the most extensive real estate dealers in Bangor, and he is agent for eight different insurance companies, writing all kinds of insurance except life. In his real estate work Mr. Cohen carries all deals through with completeness and satisfactorily registering the deeds as well, and his listing of properties is inclusive of the entire State, while many sales are made to patrons in various sections of the country. For several years he was associated with his brother in New York Syndicate, a complete department store in Bangor.

Mr. Cohen is a Republican in his political views and, though he has not sought public office, he supports with his vote and influence the principles of that party. He served in the United' States Army during the World War, with the rank of sergeant in the Tenth Bath Infantry Corps. Fraternally, Mr. Cohen is affiliated with Bangor Lodge, Benevolent and Protective Order of Elks, in which he is very active, and with the Independent Order of B'nai B'rith; and he is a member of Veritans Service Club, Bangor 'Chamber of Commerce; and the American Legion. His hobbies are music, hunting and fishing; for twelve years, also, he played in the Bangor Symphony Orchestra.

JOSEPH H. LITTLEFIELD—Bonifaces of the Pine Tree State have spread their good cheer, famous hospitality and groaning tables with such genuine regard' for the good taste and tender feeling of their patrons that their reputation is the envy of hotelkeepers from coast to coast, from which extensive area are annually drawn thousands as much by the excellent cuisine, perhaps, as by the rugged coastline, invigorating air and interior scenic beauties. Among other things, the name Littlefield is a synonym for pioneering, modernizing and the last word in hotelkeeping in the village of Ogonquit and at Wells Beach. The first of the surname to be considered in this connection was Joseph H. Littlefield, who raised the profession of host to the highest point of excellence known to the Maine chain of resorts. His memory lingers with a fine fragrance that permeates the recollection of his genial, generous manner, his masterful hand in playing the rôle of purveyor of hospitality, and his superior public service in the offices of legislator and postmaster, and as builder and lumberman. One of his sons, Joseph Philip Littlefield, worthy of the name, is carrying on with Littlefield finesse as manager of the High Rock House, famous "from Maine to California."

Joseph H. Littlefield was born in Wells, January 3, 1856, the son of Joseph and Emma Littlefield. From the public schools of his native town he entered on his business career, which at the beginning gave little indication of the important place he was to fill as one of the most famous of Maine's providers of creature comforts for resident and transient guests. His initial position was that of clerk in Barak Maxwell's general store at Wells. He was ambitious, aggressive and' efficient, saved his money and one day bought his employer's business, thus early acting up to a native capacity for proprietorship. Disaster in the form of fire leveled the store buildings, but he was not discomfited—he went out and purchased the business that had' been conducted by Charles Littlefield, and soon again was riding atop the wave.

Some time later, Mr. Littlefield diverted his energies from the more prosaic channel of storekeeping to the (to him) more desirable avocation of hotel keeping. His soul and spirit animated a vigorous body and urged a compelling personality with such convincing effect that he made one of the most capable and popular managers that the Maxwell House has known. His success there was ample attest of the fact that he had made no mistake by entering upon that line of business.

Mr. Littlefield next built the "High Rock House," which became one of the most popular of Maine coast hotels. Year on end the same people, bringing new patrons, continued to journey from far and near to sit and eat at his tables and to bask in the sunshine of his smile. None went away at the end of short or season's stay but to return to receive the grasp of his cordial handshake and his cheery word, a tonic of life that rivaled the healthgiving qualities of air and sea which environed his house. Everybody deemed life worth while when lived within the atmosphere surcharged by the personality of Joseph Littlefield. Mr. Littlefield also built and managed a number of summer cottages at Ogonquit, and from the beginning these were highly popular with guests who sought a closer approach to the sea. Through his great activity in one direction and another, he did much for the advancement of the town of Wells, in whose affairs he was esteemed an indispensable counselor.

Mr. Littlefield served the town of Wells as postmaster for twenty years, and administered the office with his customary courtesy and businesslike ability. He was elected to the Legislature, sitting in the session of 1914-15, and in every way conducting himself as a faithful, sagacious legislator and a worthy representative of his constituency. A deacon of the Christian church, he carried his religion into everyday life. His fraternal affiliations were with Ocean Lodge, Free and Accepted Masons; Ogunquit Tribe of Red Men, of which he was a Past Sachem; and Wells Grange, Patrons of Husbandry.

Joseph H. Littlefield married Nellie F. Perkins, daughter of Captain Charles Perkins, shipbuilder, of Portland. Their children: 1. Grace, graduated from Wellesley College, travels extensively, and is a teacher of Spanish in the schools of Passaic, New Jersey. 2. Ocy L., resides at home with her mother. 3. Joseph Philip, a graduate of the University of Maine and of the General Electric Company, Lynn, Massachusetts, with the degree of Electrical Engineer; served in the World War as a lieutenant in the United States Marine Corps; now (1928) manager of the High Rock House at Wells, and has built a number of important buildings, including those housing the United States Post Office and the Publicity Bureau. He married Amanda Guptill, and they have a son, Joseph D. 4. Robie, a graduate of the University of Maine; a member of Phi Kappa Phi Fraternity; served as lieutenant in the World War, with eighteen months' service in France with the Seventy-seventh Division; gassed and invalided home. In his university days he was the winner of the quarter-mile run at several meets. Ill-health resulting from his war service has been somewhat improved by engaging in fruit-growing and poultry-keeping.

ROY M. HESCOCK—Active in all affairs relating to pharmacy in the State of Maine, Roy M. Hescock plays an especially important part in the life of the town in which he resides, Monson, Maine. Here he has lived for many years, and, in addition to his own work, has taken a prominent part in civic and social matters pertaining to the welfare of the people of Monson. A number of town offices have been bestowed, from time to time, upon him, while Mr. Hescock also takes a prominent part in the fraternal activities of several different organizations in Monson.

He was born in Abbot, Maine, November 8, 1875, a son of Enos T. and Mary (Greenleaf) Hescock. His father is now deceased. Roy M. Hescock attended the public schools in his native town of Abbot, and then studied for a time at Monson Academy before becoming a student at the University of Maine. Upon completion of his course at the university, he worked for a short time in Boston. Then he came to Monson and purchased the business of C. W. Folsom, which he has conducted since 1897 under his own name. In this work he was greeted from the start with success, and with the passing years acquired a host of friends and loyal customers, people who relied upon him and continue to do so for their needs in the way of drugs. At all times he has demonstrated the utmost skill and care in the preparation of medicines, and in turn has been rewarded with the trust and confidence of the people whom he has served.

In addition to his activity in his own business enterprise, Mr. Hescock is president of the Board of Commissioners of Pharmacy of the State of Maine, and is a member of the National Association of the Boards of Pharmacy and the Maine State Association of Pharmacy. Mr. Hescock also is keenly interested in political developments, being an active supporter of the Republican party and its policies and candidates. Both he and his wife are members of the town and county committees of the party. He has served as town clerk, selectman, for twelve years a member of the School Board, and is a trustee of Monson Academy, which he formerly attended. His fraternal affiliations are strong, he being a member of the Free and Accepted Masons, in which order he is identified with the Doric Lodge, the Piscataquis Chapter of Royal Arch Masons, St. John's Commandery of Knights Templar, and Anah Temple of the Ancient Arabic Order Nobles of the Mystic Shrine, and has taken all degrees in the Ancient Accepted Scottish Rite, in which he belongs to the Portland Consistory and holds the thirty-second degree. He is a member of the Masonic Club, the Piscataquis Valley Country Club, and the Congregational church. Mr. Hescock also is represented on the board of trustees of the charity fund of the local Masonic lodge.

On June 1, 1898, Mr. Hescock married, in Skowhegan, Maine, Blanche G. Humphrey, a daughter of David and Anna (Flint) Humphrey. By this union there has been born a son, Milton A., born August 2, 1900, who is now a chemical engineer, having been graduated from the University of Maine in the class of 1922, and is employed with the Brown Company, of Berlin, New Hampshire. Mrs. Hescock is a member of the Department of Public Welfare of State, and she is esteemed as one of the outstanding women engaged in public affairs.

NATHANIEL AUSTIN—That he was a man with a fine and true appreciation of his civic and social responsibilities is an outstanding characteristic one feels in reviewing the life of Nathaniel Austin. He was born and grew up in North Berwick, Maine, going through the graded schools there. He clerked in a store for a while and then opened a grocery and provision store of his own. He sold this later to take a position as bookkeeper with the Prescott Blacking Company, eventually going with them to New York. Later, he returned to North Berwick and, forsaking the purely commercial field, went into the North Berwick National Bank as cashier, continuing in this responsible post until his death. His genial presence and understanding sympathy won him many friends and it may be rightfully said that his influence for good was real and graciously achieved. Mr. Austin took an active interest in church matters and was affiliated with the Congregational church. As a member of the School Board for many years, he did much helpful and constructive work in developing a good school system. He was a staunch Republican in politics and served his town at one time as selectman. Aside from his work at the bank, he found time to foster a flourishing general insurance business; a business which is now being carried on most efficiently by his wife.

When quite a young man, Mr. Austin married Josephine Hall, and some time after her death, he married (second) Ethel Mills, daughter of a prominent citizen of Wells, Maine, Mr. Horace Mills.

NEHEMIAH SPINNEY—Having been connected with catering and allied pursuits for more than thirty-five years, the late Nehemiah Spinney was, perhaps, one of the most prominent figures in this department of business in the State of Maine. His various enterprises included the establishment of one of the first restaurants in Sanford, operation of a candy and fruit store, and catering at the various fairs throughout Maine and New Hampshire. His first enterprise is still in existence and is being managed most thoroughly by his widow. Mr. Spinney was especially prominent in Sanford, however, where he had held public office and was a member of many fraternal organizations.

Mr. Spinney was a native of Nova Scotia, having been born in that province on August 19, 1866, son of Miner and Elizabeth Spinney. Miner Spinney, who belonged to that hardy class which has given this section of America many of its sea captains, was a sailor, fisherman, and farmer. Nehemiah Spinney, in his early boyhood, was brought by his parents to Sanford, and here he received his education in the public schools. Thence he obtained his first employment, working in the Sanford Mills for a time. Soon, however, he operated a candy and fruit store, which gradually led him into the catering business. It was in 1893 that he established one of the first restaurants in this town. Attaining fair success in this establishment, Mr. Spinney later enlarged his sphere of activities, and soon became a familiar figure in the various fairs conducted throughout Maine and New Hampshire, where he provided eating facilities for large numbers of people. Recognizing the prospects for future success of the restaurant business at Wells Beach, in 1920, Mr. Spinney there founded the enterprise which was to occupy him until his death. This restaurant, under the conscientious management of Mrs. Spinney, is steadily increasing its patronage and proving the wisdom of Nehemiah Spinney's judgment. For several years Mr. Spinney served as a constable at San-

ford, and during his occupancy of this official position, gave a most creditable performance. It was, perhaps, in fraternal affairs that Mr. Spinney found greatest enjoyment, as is evidenced by his many affiliations in organizations of this kind. He was a member of Friendship Lodge, Independent Order of Odd Fellows; Sanford Lodge, Benevolent and Protective Order of Elks; Riverside Lodge, Knights of Pythias; Preble Lodge, Free and Accepted Masons, being most popular among his brothers and ever ready and anxious to bear his share in their good works. He was a member of the Congregational church, and to this denomination contributed materially, financially and otherwise.

Nehemiah Spinney married, December 17, 1890, Myrtie E. Rowe, daughter of Elijah and Caroline (Brown) Rowe. Elijah Rowe, who was born in Manchester, New Hampshire, came to Maine during the early years of his life. Three children were born to Nehemiah and Myrtie E. (Rowe) Spinney: 1. Carrie Bernice, born November 12, 1891; graduated from Sanford High School; married Charles Lord, of Portland, Maine, and they have three children: Henry, Donald, and Barbara. 2. Evelyn, born January 3, 1894; married Griffith Roberts, of Sanford, an employee of the Sanford Mills. 3. Lucille, born May 25, 1910, a graduate of Deering High School; now employed as a stenographer in the office of Herman Joy.

A man of excellent habits, sterling character, who loved above all things his home life, Nehemiah Spinney had one of the largest circles of friends in this town. He was an enthusiastic baseball fan, and always optimistic. Jolly and generous, he was adored by children and respected by adults. In addition to his children and grandchildren, Nehemiah Spinney is survived by his widow, who resides at Sanford, Maine.

HON. CHARLES BLANCHARD CARTER—In the annals of Maine history the records of men who have given themselves to the service of commonwealth and citizens, serving at all times without thought of self and having at heart only the best interests of the people, should prove an inspiration to all who follow, that they may, to some degree, emulate the worthy deeds of those who have gone before.

One of the commonwealth's most esteemed citizens, whose vision and high ideals in service to the public good greatly enriched his State, the Hon. Charles Blanchard Carter, State Senator, whose death occurred suddenly April 6, 1927, was a man of whom it could truly be said that he was a friend of all. His accomplishments bespoke constantly his sincere belief in the brotherhood of man; his entire life was a continued exemplification of the fact that it is better to give than to receive. The regret and sorrow occasioned by his demise is perhaps most fittingly expressed in the words of George C. Wing, Jr., State Representative of Auburn, a close personal and political friend of the deceased:

The passing of Senator Charles B. Carter removes from Maine life an outstanding personality. Young in years, ardent in spirit and wise in counsel, Mr. Carter loved Maine, believed in the destiny of the State, hoped that the future might be filled with much that would redound to the common good. He was of ample mold. Like his body, his mind and heart were large. He could not be small. He was generous in impulse, loyal in friendships, honest in convictions, determined in endeavors, but reasonable in willingness to meet and discuss the point of view and argument of such as opposed him. His services as a senator from Androscoggin County were particularly distinguished. He had a frank sense of his responsibility, of his position, and the dignity of the legislative body of which he was a member. The name Senator became him. His fellow-citizens trusted him. Such confidence touched his pride and spurred him to greater efforts to discharge the duties of his office.

The very evening of his death he spent in consultation with those charged with the financial problems of the State. To the end, he was generous of his time, his talent, and himself. He was to give, not to receive. Our community has lost a citizen of whom it could well be proud, of whom it could well hope that the future might reward with great honor.

The Hon. Charles Blanchard Carter was born in Auburn, May 10, 1880, son of Seth May Carter, deceased, and Mary A. (Crosby) Carter, who survives to the present time (1928). Seth May Carter was a prominent lawyer, a leading figure in the political, legal and business life of Maine, having for many years been general counsel to the Maine Central Railroad. Also, for many years, he was a partner in the firm of Frye, Cotton and White, which subsequently became known as White and Carter, barristers of outstanding prestige.

In the public schools of his native Auburn, the Hon. Charles Blanchard Carter secured his earliest academic instruction. He graduated from Edward Little High School, and thereafter, for two years, studied in Brown University, whence he transferred to the Law School of the University of Michigan, from which he received the degree of Bachelor of Laws. During his college years, he became famed as a football player, and was named to the All-American eleven. An outstanding athlete on the gridiron, he was known affectionately in collegiate circles as "Babe" Carter. Admitted to the bar of Maine in due course, he began to practice the profession of law, forming a partnership with Wallace H. White, Jr., who has since become Congressman from the Second District of Maine. He became general counsel to the Great Northern Paper Company, and at one or two sessions of the State Legislature represented that organization in Augusta. He acted as counsel to the Maine Central Railroad, being afterward retained by the road for a certain portion of its trials before jury. Having always maintained a deep interest in politics, in 1922 Mr. Carter became a candidate for the office of Senator from the West Side of Androscoggin. In that year there appeared but little hope of Republican success, but his integrity and talent, his forceful manner of speaking and his pleasing and gracious personality caused him to win, and in 1925 he went to the State Legislature as a member of the Upper House. His term was characterized throughout by his distinguished stand against exportation of hydro-electric power, and by his vigor of address. Returned to the Senate in 1927, he devoted himself to the people's interests, and probably would have been chosen Republican candidate for governor in 1928, though he himself had announced that he was not desirous of political preferment. His last important speech took place the day before his death, when he stood with Senator Foster and fought for passage of a bill which would make the purchaser of liquor equally guilty with the seller thereof. This measure was defeated. Just prior to this, Mr. Carter had aligned himself with the proponents of the Shepard-Towner bill—maternity legislation—

which was passed. His record at all times in the public's service was most admirable.

As a speaker, Mr. Carter was greatly appreciated, and addressed hundreds of gatherings in the Grange, the Rotary and other civic clubs and societies. He was fond of social life, and greatly loved all out-of-door activities. He enjoyed golf, played regularly, and was a member of the Augusta Golf Club. His fraternal affiliations were with Delta Phi and Delta Chi, and with the Free and Accepted Masons. He was likewise a member of several clubs, and concerned in business in diverse directions. A communicant of the Episcopal church, he was active in the parish in Auburn, to whose support he contributed of funds, personal attention and time.

The Hon. Charles Blanchard Carter married, December 15, 1911, in Chicago, Illinois, Claire Scanlon, of whom follows. In addition to his wife and mother, he is survived by a brother, Horace P. Carter, formerly agent of the Edwards Manufacturing Company, of Augusta, and more recently of Chicago, where he is general manager of the Buick Automobile Company.

Mrs. Claire (Scanlon) Carter's career has been of unusual interest, and in many matters, notably in politics, she has followed the precedent laid down in the life of her husband. She was born at Sault Ste. Marie, Michigan, received her education in the public schools there, and cast her first vote in 1911, at Tacoma, capital of the State of Washington. This was but a few months before her marriage, in Chicago, as noted, to the Hon. Charles Blanchard Carter, and was several years before the franchise was given to all women in the United States above the age of twenty-one years. From that time on, Mrs. Carter has participated, directly and indirectly, in political matters. Her first glimpse of national politics was in 1920, when she accompanied her husband to the Republican National Convention, Mr. Carter having been a leader of the Maine group which favored the nomination of General Leonard Wood. In 1924, she was chosen an alternate from the Second District to the Republican National Convention of that year, and served as chairman for Androscoggin County of the Women's Coolidge Clubs. Ever since her residence in Auburn, which began soon after her marriage, she has been in close contact with State politics, and was with Mr. Carter practically all of the time at Augusta during the legislative sessions of 1925 and 1927. When Mr. Carter died, she was elected to fill the senate vacancy occasioned by his death and said at that time: "The work which my husband had undertaken was interrupted, and I have felt from my knowledge of the policies in which he believed that I am qualified to go on with it, if called upon to do so." In January, 1928, she announced her candidacy for nomination for a full term, with the following announcement:

On October 18 last (1927) the citizens of Androscoggin County elected me to fill the unexpired term of my late husband, Senator Charles B. Carter. In view of this fact, it would seem logically proper that I be accorded the nomination and election for a full term in the Senate.

Having lived for five legislative sessions in close touch with the various problems concerning the progress of our State, I naturally would be familiar with questions involved. It is my desire to assist in such solution of the great issues as shall tend to the development of Maine industrially and agriculturally, and at the same time safeguard the interests of the people, as was the purpose of Senator Carter during his term as senator.

Although there has not been a session of the Legislature in the three short months since my election, I have been called upon and was glad to appear before the State Highway Commission on two occasions, once for the designation of a State highway between Lewiston and Rockland . . . and again for the designation of a truck line for snow removal between Augusta and Portland. . . .

I am very grateful for the support given me in the past, and, if elected, I shall devote myself conscientiously and earnestly to the benefit of Androscoggin County, to the best of my ability.

Regarded as a woman of brilliance, Mrs. Carter is a member of the Androscoggin County Republican Club, and has interested herself liberally in general affairs. She was the first president of the Women's Auxiliary of the Auburn Home for Aged Women, has been president of the Women's Hospital Association of the Central Maine Hospital, and was chairman of the 1927 drive for the Young Women's Christian Association. During the World War she was active in several campaigns of patriotic direction, and was an organizer of first aid classes.

Just as the life of the Hon. Charles Blanchard Carter inspired those about him in its living, and as that of Mrs. Carter continues to do, so may this record inspire still others, who may find in one career completed by death the essence of worthiness which made it notable, and in another career still extant being honorably unfolded, a true and intelligent reflection of that worthiness. Rightly it is said: the good men do lives after them.

ELLSWORTH CHANDLER BUZZELL—Having always been deeply interested in politics and public affairs, Ellsworth Chandler Buzzell, of Fryeburg, has served his community and State in various official capacities, and in addition to his activity in civic affairs, is one of the leaders in the farming and lumber industries in the State of Maine. Mr. Buzzell has ever taken a constructive interest in local events, receiving the coöperation and commendation of his fellow-citizens, and when he served in the Legislature as a representative elected from this district, he gained an enviable record as a statesman of sterling worth and unusual ability.

Mr. Buzzell was born in Fryeburg, November 3, 1869, son of Benjamin F. and Ruth J. (Wiley) Buzzell. He received his education at Fryeburg Academy, and after his graduation from that institution of learning, entered the business world and was soon a prominent factor in the agricultural and timber industries, steadily advancing through his indefatigable energy and thorough knowledge of the details of both these trades. An ardent supporter of the Republican party, he was a popular candidate in many elections to fill various town offices, and he has served as street commissioner, selectman, and State highway inspector, while in the service of the commonwealth he was a valuable member of the State Legislature for a number of years. His political policy has always been one of unselfish devotion to the interests of his constituents, having the welfare and progress of his district and State ever in mind and consistently striving to secure for his fellow-citizens the benefits of modern and intelligent legislation. Mr. Buzzell is prominently identified with the leading fraternal societies of the country, being active in the Free and Accepted Masons, the Independent Order of Odd Fellows, and the local Grange, being Past Master

in the first-named organization. His religious adherence is given to the Congregational church.

Ellsworth Chandler Buzzell married, June 4, 1902, at Fryeburg, Edith M. Andrews, and they have six children: Francis G., James C., Leonard A., Edward W., Mary E., and Donald W.

LAVELLA A. NORTON—Having been engaged since 1895 in the contracting and building business, Mr. Norton is one of the outstanding business men and a leading citizen of Kingfield, Maine, his native town. He takes an active interest in the public affairs of the town, and of the State, and is active in the fraternal life of his community.

Lavella A. Norton was born in Kingfield, February 16, 1860, the son of Tristram and Amanda (Durrell) Norton, both of whom were natives of Kingfield. He received his education in the public schools of Kingfield, and later became a student in the normal school in Farmington. After having been employed in different capacities for some time after he left school, he engaged in 1895 in the contracting and building business, in which he has continued since that year. Many of the beautiful homes and buildings in this section of Maine stand as monuments to his skill as a builder. His business activity, although it occupies a great deal of his time, is by no means his principal interest, for he takes time to participate freely in the civic and fraternal life of his community. Politically, he is identified with the Republican party, for whose candidates he casts his vote. He is a member of the Free and Accepted Masons, in which order he has been admitted to the Commandery; and of the Independent Order of Odd Fellows. His religious affiliation, as well as that of his family, is with the Universalist church.

On August 19, 1883, in New Portland, Maine, Mr. Norton married Imogene F. Parker, who was born October 30, 1857, in New Portland, Maine, the daughter of Joseph N. Parker, also a native of New Portland. Her mother's maiden name was Boynton. Lavella A. and Imogene F. (Parker) Norton became the parents of four children, two of whom are living: 1. Parker L., who was born in Kingfield, Maine. 2. Flora A., who was born in Vineland, New Jersey. 3. Stella, deceased, who was born in Kingfield, Maine. 4. Donald W., who was born in Kingfield, Maine, and met his death in the World War, having been killed in action on November 2, 1918, on the Hindenburg line in France. He held the rank of second lieutenant in the American Expeditionary Forces.

HORACE JEWETT COOK, born in Burnham, Maine, February 23, 1887, was a son of Emery W. and Nellie A. (Reed) Cook. His preliminary education was received in the public schools of Waterville, Maine, and he was graduated from the high school here. He then matriculated at the University of Maine, graduating therefrom in 1910 with the degree of Bachelor of Science.

Mr. Cook was engaged in miscellaneous engineering work from 1910 to 1914, in the latter year becoming associated with the Kennebec Water District and remaining with them four years, until 1918. In the following year he was appointed Superintendent of Streets of Auburn, Maine, holding this post for one year. During 1919 to 1922, he served as city manager of Auburn. He was appointed Superintendent of Auburn Water and Sewerage Districts in 1922, a position he continues to hold. In his political preference, Mr. Cook is a Republican. During the period of the World War he served in the United States Army with the rank of captain, 1918-19. He is a member of Alpha Tau Omega College Fraternity; Maine Association of Engineers, serving as president in 1926; Maine Water Utilities Association, in 1925 serving as secretary and treasurer; and a member of the American Legion. His club is the Lions Club, while his fraternal affiliation is with the Free and Accepted Masons. He is a member of the Universalist church.

Horace Jewett Cook married, June 1, 1915, Mary E. Parker, of Norridgewock, Maine.

W. LINWOOD FERNALD—Naturalist, writer and lecturer of note on ornithology, arboriculture and flowers, W. Linwood Fernald, through his very extensive practice as a landscape architect, properly belongs to that illustrious company which has added to the historic renown of the State of Maine. The town of Eliot claims this ardent and learned student of Nature as one of its first citizens, but in a larger sense he belongs to the nation, since he carries his professional services to a large area of the country in the execution of many and important commissions.

W. Linwood Fernald's first American ancestor was Dr. Renald Fernald, who came from England in 1631 and settled in New Castle, New Hampshire, now a part of the city of Portsmouth. Family tradition has it that he resigned his commission as surgeon in the English Army to join the Colonists in America. After his arrival he was made surgeon of Captain John Mason's company of militia. He was also elected the first Town Clerk of Portsmouth, an office which he filled with efficiency, a qualification for which he was well known. He had an eye to the future when he purchased a number of islands in Portsmouth Harbor, among them Great Island and Fernald's Island. These later were sold to the Federal Government and now are used for the United States Navy Yard and Naval Station.

Dr. Renald Fernald's son, Deacon John Fernald, married Mary Spinney, and their son, Deacon John (2) Fernald, married Sarah Hincks. The son of the last-named couple was James Fernald, who married Hannah Rogers, and their son, John (3) Fernald, married Sarah Wentworth, daughter of Captain William Wentworth. John and Sarah (Wentworth) Fernald's son, William Wentworth Fernald, married Waite Salisbury of Providence, Rhode Island, the former a prominent citizen and farmer of Eliot, and their son, William Salisbury Fernald, was a highly placed man and a well-known farmer; he married Sarah Hanscom, and to them was born a son, William Augustus Fernald, father of William Linwood, and of whom further.

William Augustus Fernald, son of William Salisbury and Sarah (Hanscom) Fernald, was one of the Federal Government's most skillful employees in the Navy Department, and was raised to foreman of naval construction, serving in this capacity at Kittery, in this State. His qualifications for public office did not pass unnoticed by the citizens of his home town of Eliot, in whose municipal and community affairs he rose to a station of prominence.

He served the town as a member of the Board of Selectmen and in the office of auditor, which positions he filled with rare dignity and integrity, and with that care for the niceties that featured his work for the Government. He married Margery Cutts, member of an old and esteemed family, and they were the parents of twin sons, William Linwood, of this review, and Dr. Walter Elmore Fernald, late noted psychiatrist (see a following biography).

W. Linwood Fernald, son of William Augustus and Margery (Cutts) Fernald, was born in Kittery, February 11, 1859. He was graduated from New Hampton Literary Institute, in 1879, and from Dartmouth College, class of 1884. For ten years he taught school in Kittery and Eliot, and subsequently served as principal of high schools in New Hampshire and Massachusetts. From the responsibilities of educator he turned his attention to a line of endeavor for which by endowment and temperament he was eminently fitted, and established the Eliot Nursery for the growing of ornamental trees and plants, giving himself in that connection to the practice of landscape architecture.

In process of time, through his artistry, Mr. Fernald developed a very extensive business, covering that area of the country, from Bar Harbor in this State, on the north, to Florida on the south, and in every State east of the Rocky Mountains. Soon his marked ability as a writer and lecturer on nature subjects brought him a wide and favorable reputation, and from his communion with birds, flowers and trees, both in domestic environment and in the wilds, he has gathered inspiration for his best lecture efforts, among those by which he is best known being "God in Nature," and "Nature, the Autograph of God." His works on nature subjects are considered as authorities, being written in a charming style that commands the interest of old and young alike. His platform presence is pleasing, and he is popularly known to select audiences, having a prepossessing personality, which gives point to his tall figure, a benign countenance with eyes that speak good humor, while his flowing gray hair and pointed beard add a commanding picturesqueness to the happy make-up which is himself. For many years he has spent his winters in Florida, passing the summer season among his own people in Eliot. From his earliest youth, Mr. Fernald has been an enthusiastic worker in the church, and for many years he has been prominent in this respect as senior deacon of the Eliot Congregational Church.

W. Linwood Fernald married, September 7, 1886, Lillian A. Brooks, whose union has been blessed with three children: 1. Winnifred Wilson, born May 29, 1887. 2. Norman Leighton, born July 15, 1889, died July 7, 1908. 3. Marjorie Gladys, born December 10, 1892; married Maynard Fred Douglass, who fought in the World War, serving from March, 1918, to March, 1919, eight months of that period in the battle area of France. They are the parents of three children: Priscilla Wilson, born July 29, 1921; Jean Brooks, born January 27, 1923; and Dwight Fernald, born June 11, 1924.

WALTER ELMORE FERNALD, M. D.—In the field of psychiatry, the late Dr. Walter Elmore Fernald won distinction throughout the United States for his constructive contributions to that department of medical science. He was a noted lecturer on the immediate subject of his professional practice, and as an alienist he figured in numerous cases of importance that came before the law courts for adjudication. Highly placed State authorities reposed every confidence in his ability, and his standing in the estimation of judges before whom his expert testimony was often adduced was second to none. As a son of Maine and member of an old and distinguished family, his career reflected honor upon the State of his birth, the ties of relationship and the associations in whose circles he moved. He is cordially remembered in the Bay State, where for many years he served brilliantly as the superintendent of the Massachusetts School for Feeble-minded Children at Waltham.

Walter Elmore Fernald was a twin-brother of W. Linwood Fernald, widely known naturalist (see a preceding biography), they the sons of William Augustus and Margery (Cutts) Fernald. His birth occurred in the town of Kittery, February 11, 1859, and his preparatory education at New Hampton Literary Institute was followed by training in the Medical School of Maine at Bowdoin College, from which he was graduated in the class of 1881, with the degree of Doctor of Medicine. His scholarship record showed that intelligent and meticulous attention to minute details such as featured his after-life in actual practice.

Dr. Fernald's degree had hardly been received than he accepted the appointment of assistant physician at the Mendota (Wisconsin) State Insane Asylum. He had early shown a preference for the study of mental diseases and their remedy, and while serving the institution at Mendota he achieved remarkable development, with every promise in his favor of becoming a finished psychiatrist. An important post even as the one he was filling so acceptably for the period of 1882 to 1887 could not hold a man of Dr. Fernald's gifts and attainments, and in the latter year he was called to the superintendency of the Massachusetts School for Feeble-minded Children at Waltham. In the administration of the government of the latter institution he rose to his greatest height in the department of psychiatry. By taste and temperament, plus a culture which left nothing to be desired, he fitted into the office wherein he was enabled, through a carefully supervised corps of assistants, to be of incalculable service to hundreds of unfortunates who had come into the world as mental defectives or had become so through disease or from other causes. Combining the tender expressions of a sympathizing heart with profound learning in the diagnosis and treatment of the diseases which was his specialty, he was the means of helping many afflicted souls to bear their lot with fortitude, and in some cases helping them to emerge from their condition which had isolated them from society. In public and private practice his counsel was rated at a high value. As an adviser in cases that did not require his attendance upon the courts his services were esteemed most highly. The same was true when called by one side or the other as an alienist in actions that came on before bench and jury for disposition. He was an extremely busy man, one who was in love with and at home in the practice of his profession, and his enviable reputation eventually became as wide as the country itself, in the sense that his fame had preceded him throughout the United States.

Further idea of the value of Dr. Fernald to the field of medical practice and especially to that department of psychiatry in which he shone so brilliantly is to be had from the honors bestowed upon him and the associations to which he was elected. He was made an honorary Master of Arts by Harvard University in 1913; appointed associate professor of Tufts College in the department of mental diseases; and held a lectureship on the mental diseases of children at the Harvard Graduate School of Education. He was a member of the Massachusetts Medical Society, American Association for Study of the Feeble-minded, American Academy of Medicine, American Psychiatric Association, American Institute of Criminal Law and Criminology, National Committee for Mental Hygiene, New England Society of Psychiatry, and Boston Society of Psychiatry and Neurology. His social organizations were the St. Botolph and City clubs, of Boston, and the Century Association, of New York.

Dr. Walter Elmore Fernald married, October 5, 1887, at Janesville, Wisconsin, Katherine M. Nolan, of Cambridge, Massachusetts. Their children are: 1. Thomas, born May 12, 1891, married Gwendolyn Moore, April 11, 1917, and they have a son, Bruce Wentworth Fernald. 2. Helen Louise, born June 2, 1895, graduated from Smith College, 1916; married, in June, 1924, Edward Lawrance Shaw.

The death of Dr. Fernald, November 27, 1924, removed from the special department of medicine wherein he had achieved so fine a record a practitioner and exponent who advanced the code of ethics beyond the high plane it already had reached when he came on the stage of action. He accomplished a splendid work in life, not only in the public view but also in the necessarily more restricted area of his intimate contact with many of the world's social derelicts. His record remains untarnished, and his memory will ever be fondly cherished by many in the State of his adoption and in Maine to which bonds of family and early associations bound him.

DEAN W. ROLLINS—The broad educational experience of Dean W. Rollins has made him a successful high school principal and superintendent of schools in many different parts of Maine. He has been engaged ever since he completed his school and university work in educational activity.

His parents are both of Maine: Frank H. Rollins, born at New Sharon, Maine, who was engaged as a carriage manager until his retirement; and Grace (Whittier) Rollins, born in Chesterville, Maine. Both of his parents are still living. Dean W. Rollins was born in Farmington Falls, Maine, September 25, 1882. He was educated in the public schools of Chesterville; Farmington High School; and University of Maine, from which he was graduated in the class of 1907 with the degree of Bachelor of Arts.

When he completed his education, he took a position in 1907 as principal of the Clinton, Maine, High School, where he remained until the following year, when he became principal of Stonington High School for three years. Afterward he served for three years as principal of the Madison High School. Then he served for five years as Superintendent of Schools for the union of towns of Deer Isle, Stonington, and Isle au Haute, after which he was for four years Superintendent of Schools of the union of towns of Castine, Brooksville, Islesboro, and Penobscot. Since 1922, he has served as Superintendent of Schools of the union of towns of Dexter, Ripley and Garland. While attending the University of Maine he taught one year in the rural schools.

Fraternally, he is a member of the Phi Gamma Delta; is Past Master of Hancock Lodge, No. 4, of the Free and Accepted Masons; Past High Priest of the Castine Royal Arch Chapter; a member of Mt. Moriah Council; St. John's Commandery; the S. K. Whiting Chapter; and the Eastern Star. He belongs to the Dexter Club, the Maine Teachers' Association, the Penobscot County Teachers' Association, and is a member of the National Education Association. Politically, he is a Republican. He is a trustee of the Abbott Memorial Library and a director of the Dexter Club. He attends the Universalist church.

In 1908, Dean W. Rollins married Margaret E. Carsley, who was born in South Paris, Maine. They are the parents of one child, Charline C.

ROGER S. BRAGDON—To the town of Wells and the county of York the name Bragdon has been one of prominence and intimate association with their community and material advance for three centuries. In this day and generation, Roger S. Bragdon, high sheriff of York County, is not one who rests behind his forebears as a promoter of civic progress and builder of physical values of his jurisdiction. Substantial farmer, a leading Republican in local and State councils, proprietor of a large cattle business, he is a typical son of the Pine Tree State and scion of a house to which it is a coveted honor to belong.

The founder of the family of Bragdon in America was Arthur Bragdon, who came from England to York, Maine, in 1634. Five years after his arrival Sir Ferdinando Gorges was appointed Governor-General of New England and the latter's son Thomas was sent as lieutenant to administer the laws in 1640. He established himself at Agamenticus (now York), when, in 1642, the city called "Gorgeana" was incorporated. There the first representative government in Maine was established (1640). Arthur Bragdon was a man of no little prominence in the affairs of the first municipality, being held in high esteem by his fellow-citizens, who elected him to the office of alderman.

Sewall Bragdon, grandfather of Sheriff Bragdon, about 1826 came to live on land in what now is the town of Wells that had been granted to an ancestor. He was prospered in his pioneering work and married Ann Littlefield, her surname for many generations that of a leading Maine family. They were the parents of a son, Daniel Wallace.

Daniel Wallace Bragdon, son of Sewall and Ann (Littlefield) Bragdon, was born in Wells, December 13, 1858, on the original farmstead, which he subsequently inherited from his father and continued to operate for the greater part of his life, finally bequeathing it to his son Roger. He made a success of his agricultural enterprise, accumulated large holdings of real property, and bought and sold real estate extensively. Above all, he was a public-spirited man, who did much for the benefit of his town, and the people looked up to him with high regard, esteeming him a leader in their affairs. They elected him as a member of the Board of Selectmen, and he

figured helpfully through a constructive administration lasting a number of terms. Among other activities, he was vice-president of the North Berwick Bank. He married Emma L. Perkins, and they were the parents of three children: 1. Roger S., of whom further. 2. Margaret, born November 27, 1889. 3. Elizabeth Ann, born August 8, 1892.

Roger S. Bragdon, eldest child and only son of Daniel Wallace and Emma L. (Perkins) Bragdon, was born on the old Bragdon homestead in Wells, November 5, 1887. Having received a good, practical education in the common schools of his native town, he was still quite young when he entered wholeheartedly into the business of farming. He has always been proud of the fact that he is the son of a farmer and the grandson of one, both of whom passed on to him a strong, vigorous strain, an affinity for the soil and a capacity for public service. Agriculture with him is a science, which he has raised to the standing of a profession, and while giving particular attention to the operations of his large farms, his chief commercial endeavor is buying and selling cattle. For this line, too, he has a fine example in his father's conduct of a similar business, which he established on a profit-returning basis. Also, in emulation of his worthy sire, he is moved by a public spirit to serve the interests of the community, county and State. Called to occupy the shrievalty of York County, he stands as the principal civil law enforcement officer of the jurisdiction, with the people of the county solidly supporting the administration of his high position. Throughout the State he is known in Republican circles for his helpful influence in behalf of his party. He has been a strong exponent of the principles and promoter of the policies of his organization, a former member of the Republican State Committee and the Republican Town Committee of Wells. He is a director of the North Berwick Bank, of which his father was an executive officer.

He has advanced to high station in the order of Freemasonry, affiliating with the Maine Consistory (thirty-second degree Scottish Rite), Ocean (Blue) Lodge, of Wells, of which he is a Past Master; Unity Chapter, Royal Arch Masons; Maine Council, Royal and Select Masters; and Bradford Commandery, Knights Templar.

Sheriff Bragdon married Elva L. Gray, daughter of Edmund Gray, of Wells, and they are the parents of four children 1. Dorothy. 2. Wallace. 3. Marjorie. 4. Robert.

GEORGE CLEMENT LORD, Jr.—In the marvelous strides made by the Pine Tree State in the past half-century, she owes much to the family of Lord, members of which have contributed in a marked manner to her industrial, political and agricultural advance. In this grouping is placed George Clement Lord, Jr., owner and operator of "Landholm Farms," at Wells, a leading member of the State Senate, a former Representative in the Lower House at Augusta, for a number of years a member of the Wells town government, and a widely known expert cattle breeder. Another distinguished representative of the family was the late George Clement Lord, grandfather of George Clement, Jr., who was one of the foremost road transportation chiefs of New England in his day, president of the Boston & Maine Railroad Company, executive of a leading fire insurance corporation, shipping head and builder of tugboats.

Born in Kennebunk, February 27, 1823, son of George and Olive (Jeffards) Lord, George Clement (1) Lord was a grandson of Lieutenant Tobias and Hephzibah (Conant) Lord, the latter the daughter of Governor Roger Conant of Maine. George Lord, son of Lieutenant Tobias Lord, was master of the brig "Alliance." He retired from a seafaring life and settled in Kennebunk, and engaged in the shipping business in 1817 in association with Ivory Lord, under the style of G. & I. Lord. He married, April 22, 1816, Olive Jeffards.

From his preliminary studies in the Kennebunk schools, George Clement (1) Lord entered Dummer Academy, Byfield, Massachusetts, from which he was graduated in 1838. The year following his graduation from the academy, he began his business career, which was to eventuate in such close connection with the development of the natural resources and industrial enterprises of the State. His first essay in the business world was in the wholesale drygoods house of Holbrook, Bourgoyne & Company in Boston. In 1843 he transferred his interest to the wholesale grocery business, becoming a member of the firm of Dymond, Howe & Company, which in 1846 was changed to Howe & Lord. In the following year he formed a co-partnership with his brother, Charles A. Lord, naming the organization George C. Lord & Company, engaging in the shipping business and the building of tugboats. He continued to attain prominence in the business world. In 1865 he was elected president of the New England Mutual Fire and Marine Insurance Company. In 1866 he was made a director of the Boston & Maine Railroad Company, and in 1880 was advanced to vice-president. In 1880 he was elevated to president of the Boston & Maine system, and during his régime of eight years, and due to his able management, the trackage of the company increased from two hundred and two miles to 1210 miles. It was during his term of office also that the extension of the Boston & Maine from South Berwick to Portland was accomplished, and the Eastern and the Boston & Lowell railroads were merged with the Boston & Maine.

George Clement (1) Lord married, September 22, 1846, Marion Ruthven Waterston, and to them were born three children: 1. Robert Waterston. 2. Charles Edward, born at Newton, Massachusetts, March 29, 1858; married Effie Marion Rogers, daughter of Charles Frederick and Caroline Rogers, of Newton, and has a son, George Clement, Jr., of whom further. 3. Marion Ruthven.

George Clement Lord, Jr., son of Charles Edward and Effie Marion (Rogers) Lord, was born in Newton, Massachusetts, June 12, 1889, and received his education at the grammar school of his native city, Dummer Academy at Byfield, and Phillips-Andover Academy.

For five years Mr. Lord was connected with the Bates Manufacturing Company at Lewiston, but because of ill health he was compelled to abandon the idea of pursuing a strictly business career. He returned to the old homestead farm at Wells, and since 1916 he has given his attention to the specialty of breeding thoroughbred Guernsey cattle and to general farming. His "Landholm Farms" are one of the showplaces of the countryside and a model of modern scientific agriculture.

The town of Wells in having a citizen of the progressive type as Mr. Lord in its midst has often availed itself of its good fortune. First it elected him a member of the Board of Selectmen, where it has retained his services for six years, and the town government has benefited in appreciable degree from his administrative ability and sound judgment. Then his district chose him as its representative in the Legislature for the session of 1923-24, where he was made chairman of the Committee on Publicity. Further honors were accorded him by advancing him to the State Senate for the term of 1925-26 and re-electing him for the term of 1927-28. He is the leading Republican of his community and holds the office of chairman of the Republican Town Committee, and is a trustee of the Wells Water Supply.

The organized interests of the cattle breeders of his district are carefully fostered and protected by Mr. Lord, who is president of the York County Breeders' Association. He is one of the most enthusiastic farmers in the State, who gives much time and thought to the affairs of those similarly engaged. As a member of the Farm Bureau and the Local Grange of the Patrons of Husbandry, he finds agreeable channels for the direction of his energy to serve the farmers' interests. During the World War he rendered a fine patriotic service along the line of civilian war work, and held the office of registrar under the Selective Service Act. Highly placed in the Masonic Order, he affiliates with the Portland Consistory thirty-second degree Scottish Rite; High Pine Lodge, Free and Accepted Masons; Murray Chapter, Royal Arch Masons; Kennebunk Commandery, Knights Templar; and Kora Temple, Ancient Arabic Order Nobles of the Mystic Shrine.

George Clement Lord, Jr., married, January 27, 1912, Mary Adam Jones, daughter of Nathaniel N. and Jennie (Davis) Jones, her father a former judge of the United States Circuit Court for Massachusetts. Mr. and Mrs. Lord are the parents of three children: 1. Charles Edward, Jr. 2. Nathaniel Nelson. 3. Mary Waterston.

HAROLD CLINTON MOUNTAIN — Coming from an ancestry combining English and Scotch, the industrious character of his forebears left its indelible strain in the blood of Harold Clinton Mountain, of Sangerville. Himself a native of the United States, he grew up amid the manufacturing industries of New England and early evinced a tendency in that direction of effort. His success has been the proof of his foresight.

Harold Clinton Mountain was born in Amesbury, Massachusetts, November 12, 1888. His father was William T., born in Danville, Quebec, and his mother Eunice (Park) Mountain, born in Galashields, Scotland. The elder Mountain was a maker of automobile bodies, employed by the Walker Body Company, of Amesbury, and had served in the English Army in Canada. Harold Clinton was educated in the elementary public schools and the high school, of Amesbury. He began work for the Riverside Woolen Mills, at Stafford, Connecticut, from 1906 until 1910, where he learned the textile business. He then took the position of assistant superintendent of the Dumbarton Mills, at Sangerville, where he remained until 1922, when he accepted the post of superintendent, his present position, having under his control more than one hundred employees. He is a member of the Methodist Episcopal church, and of

Abner Wade Lodge, No. 207, of which he is Past Master, Free and Accepted Masons. He also belongs to the Modern Woodmen of America and to the Overseers' Association.

Mr. Mountain married (first), at Sangerville, Maine, December 18, 1912, Marion Barrows, a daughter of George and Jennie (Whitemore) Barrows, of Sangerville. He married (second), April 9, 1919, Mabel Ames, of Blanchard, Maine. Children of the first marriage are: 1. Marjorie E., born May 5, 1914, in Sangerville. 2. Dorothy E., born in Sangerville. By the second marriage: 3. William H., born in Sangerville, March 11, 1921.

HENRY P. BARTLEY is proprietor of the Piscataquis Exchange Hotel, located at the gateway of Moosehead Lake, Greenville, Maine, which had been founded by his father. The hotel has ninety-one rooms. It employs twenty-eight employees during the summer months and a yearly average of about twenty-one employees. The Bartley family has been in the hotel business at Greenville for over forty years and is as a consequence known all over the country.

Henry P. Bartley was born at Greenville, Maine, July 27, 1895, son of Henry N. and Nellie L. (Dillon) Bartley, of whom the father was born at Jackman, Maine, and of whom the mother was born in Canada. Henry P. Bartley attended the public school in Greenville, and then the high school, graduating in the class of 1916. After leaving school he became associated with his father in the operation of the Piscataquis Exchange Hotel, and in 1917 he became proprietor. The hotel had been run by his father for many years, and when he died in September, 1925, he had been in the hotel business in Greenville for thirty-eight years, so that a sort of hereditary skill in hotel-keeping may be said to have descended to the present owner. Mr. Bartley was in the United States Navy during the World War. He enlisted July 7, 1918, and was discharged January 10, 1920. He was a first-class machinist's mate. He belongs to the Odd Fellows, the Greenville Chamber of Commerce, the Elks, and the American Legion. He attends the Congregational chapel at Greenville, Maine.

Mr. Bartley married, at Greenville, Maine, July 10, 1917, Mary E. Lord, born at Island Falls, Maine.

CHARLES L. PERKINS—The romantic element of the seafaring life was in the blood of one of Maine's most intrepid skippers, the late 'Charles L. Perkins, of Ogunquit—he was the son of an oldtype commander of vessels in the coastwise trade from his native town to Boston. Much of life afloat on the high seas in the capacity of pilot fell to his lot in his earlier young manhood years. With the inception of steam as the propelling power of ships, he became a pioneer in the building and operation of tugboats, and it may be said that his span of more than three-score years and ten witnessed one of the greatest of evolutions in water transportation—from the days of the old windjammers to the swifter and more efficient sidewheelers and then the stern propeller craft. As he lies becalmed in the peaceful acres where his fathers sleep, his memory is kept alive by his children and children's children by a review now and again of his exploits on the rolling main and his more prosaic, but none the less important, activities

as a builder of a line of sturdy craft that dotted the waters off his beloved shores.

Born in Ogunquit, August 3, 1848, Charles L. Perkins was the son of Moses and Nancy (Stevens) Perkins. Nurtured in Nature's lap at the cleavage line of a rockbound port and the broad Atlantic, he was a child of the sea from the cradle to the grave. The old home was a port in many a storm or state of calm, wherein his sturdy father recounted the perils and pleasures of his experience as master of vessels that plied with merchandise from that haven to "The Hub." By father's tales of the sea and the associations of a seaport town, the salt that ran with his blood preserved and kept alive the urge to be one of those brave and hardy men who go down to the sea in ships.

Having finished his course in the public schools of Ogunquit, the future skipper turned his attention to charts and compass, and through persistent study and application he became, even when a very young man, a navigator of remarkable ability. The sirens of rock and inlet with all their wiles and proffers of comfort could not hold him—Neptune called him to the deeps and with a glad heart he shipped aboard a seagoing vessel, manned by men of brawn and courage. He was then but twenty-two years of age, but he was rated as an expert seaman and classed as a navigator of the first grade, in which capacity he piloted the brig "Erie" from Dutch Guiana to Maine, a feat fraught with many a hazard of life and cargo, which he successfully accomplished amidst the plaudits of his superior officers, mates and the crew. This achievement, while perhaps the first and not the least of his acts of seamanship, is often the substance, key and score of the songs of the sea that are written into the archives of the heirs of this faithful navigator.

Then the advent of steam and its application as the chief means of power. With keenness of mind and power to embrace opportunity, Captain Perkins became a pioneer in the new order of things. The Piscataqua Navigation Company was organized and he was placed at its head. Under his direction the company did a thriving business at Portsmouth, New Hampshire, in the building and operation of tugboats. Here was a line of craft for which there arose an exceeding great demand, and Captain Perkins was quick to seize upon the offering of business from that quarter. Throughout his lifetime he had experienced many a variable wind, but for the greater part he had sailed before a favorable and spanking breeze—and thus it was with him in the shipbuilding enterprise; he steered his business craft with the cautiousness and precision of the skilled navigator that he was, and the volume of trade won and served by the company gave proof of the ability of the chief pilot on the office-bridge.

Captain Perkins married Addie M. Hutchins, daughter of Charles W. Hutchins, a native of Kennebunkport. Their children: 1. Adelbert, born in 1871, died in 1924. 2. Bertha, married Edward Theodore Weare, and they are the parents of a daughter, Eleanor Wakefield. 3. Adela E., married Charles E. Weare, manager of the Cliff House on Bald Head Rock, Ogunquit, and one of the most desirable hostelries on this coast. 4. Charles H., superintendent of school buildings of Portland, and a review of whom is to be found in this work. 5. Helen Louise, married Lucius Williams, manager of Pasconway Inn.

The death of Captain 'Charles L. Perkins, in November, 1925, at the age of seventy-seven, was deeply regretted by a great body of people to whom this exponent of expert seamanship and business builder had become endeared.

GEORGE E. ALLEN—This surname has been borne with honor, and long, in the village of Sanford. The family is old in the history of New England, its members having contributed liberally of thought, time and constructive effort to the advancement of several communities in the commonwealth of Maine. But it was in Sanford that George E. Allen, and his father before him, made his own career, devoting the gifts of his mind and integrity to the town's progress. And here he is recalled with affection, as citizen and man.

Native of Sanford, Mr. Allen was a son of Emilus and Sarah (Hanson) Allen. His father, who was born in this center June 19, 1811, and who died here December 23, 1855, was a mason by trade. He was considered one of the town's most completely informed men in matters of history, particularly as to the history of his community. To this end he wrote copiously, somewhat in diary form; and the compilations of his pen, together with his commentaries appended, form very interesting reading, indeed. It is of interest to note in this connection that the notes so carefully kept by the father were added to, multiplied profusely, by the son, George E. Allen having maintained a similar diary form of comment on the transpirations of time, within and without Sanford, and he was considered an historical authority. To this end he wrote concisely, to the point, and analyzed the current trends in a manner revelative of positive talent as a writer, though he never saw fit to prepare himself for that as a profession, simply having done the work for the love of it.

George E. Allen was born July 13, 1846, and was but nine years old at the time of his father's death. Thus, he came early to feel that responsibility which all young persons undergo at the loss of a parent. Having secured a sound academic instruction in the public schools of Sanford, he turned, at the age of sixteen, to the trade of shoemaker, as apprentice. He followed the trade until 1872, then, at the age of twenty-six years, entered the employ of Sanford Mills, which connection he continued comparatively brief, however, as in 1876 he learned the business and craft of block printing on carriage robes. This business was of even less duration, as in the course of events he became a public figure, and in 1887 was appointed to the office of trial justice, by Governor Bodwell, being reappointed in 1894 by Governor Cleaves. It was in 1897 that the Sanford Municipal Court was established. The Hon. George W. Hanson was named justice of the court, and Mr. Allen became recorder. For two years he served as auditor of Sanford. In 1887, the year of his appointment as trial justice, he was elected to the Board of Health, later being made secretary of the organization, and continuing as executive officer nearly thirty years, until the time of his demise. Also, for a number of years he was Superintendent of Schools, taking always a direct and personal interest in the town's educational welfare. Himself a natural student, he took pleasure in affording opportunities for liberal educations for others. It delighted him to fall into the company of persons capable of philosophical discussion, and in these discussions he was a most interesting participant.

Quite aside from the replete career as outlined, Mr. Allen had other diversified connections, prominent among which was his fraternal activity. He was a charter member of Preble Lodge, Free and Accepted Masons, under the lodge's restoration, and for six years held office as its Worshipful Master. He was a charter member of Friendship Lodge, Independent Order of Odd Fellows, and was its first Noble Grand. He was a charter member of Riverside Lodge, Knights of Pythias, filled every office in the lodge, and for three years served as District Deputy of the First Pythian District. In addition, Mr. Allen was a charter member of Harmony Council, Junior Order United American Mechanics; a member of Torsey Lodge, Independent Order of Good Templars; was District Templar of the York District Lodge one year, and Lodge Deputy, local lodge, eight years. During America's participation in the World War he was of great aid in the campaigns of patriotic appeal—but did not live to hear of the Armistice which ended that mighty conflict in favor of the cause which he supported as only a patriot could.

Mr. Allen married, August 22, 1865, Hannah M. Carpenter, and of this union were born sons: 1. Edward E., who died in 1919. 2. Frank L., graduate of Sanford High School, now employed in the Sanford Mills. For a number of years Frank L. Allen was leader of the local band, and has continuously participated as a loyal citizen of public spirit in affairs of the town. He married Clara E. Kenney, of New Brunswick, Canada, and their children are: Louis, who married Helen Turner; and Gertrude, who married Dr. Bertrand M. Stretch, of Sanford.

From the foregoing it is obvious that this writing concerns no man of mere average ability or force of character. Mr. Allen's own advancement from position to position of respect, in judicial rôle and others, could not have been the lot of the usual figure. Though his school training was curtailed, his actual education, both academic and in the broader sense of human knowledge, was of the greatest possible scope. His interest in history, already cited, was but one of his pleasures in cultural accomplishment. In essence, perhaps, he was a philosopher of the world. Men turned to him for all manner of things—and were not disappointed. His friends were numerous throughout a life so richly lived, and their sense of bereavement at his loss was profound. Death came to him in the month of January, 1918.

HOMER HORACE HOBBS was born in Berwick, April 22, 1853, the son of Charles W. and Lydia (Littlefield) Hobbs. He received his education in public and private schools in Berwick and South Berwick, and early engaged in farming. Some years before his death he gave up farming and moved to Somersworth, having purchased the attractive house on Rochester Street, built by the late George Moore. There Mr. Hobbs and his family afterward lived, going South or West to pass the winters for the last few years of his life.

On November 29, 1877, Mr. Hobbs was married to Ella B. Hill, of Eliot, a sister of the late Governor Hill of Maine.

Mr. Hobbs was a member of Berwick Grange, but withdrew from membership several years ago. He belonged to no other fraternal organizations. While he resided at the farm, he was a regular attendant at and a trustee of the Free Baptist Church at South

Berwick. Since moving to the village, however, he has attended the Congregational church in Somersworth. In early manhood he attended the Congregational church.

In politics, Mr. Hobbs was a Democrat. He had well-formed opinions on public affairs, and had courage enough to give voice to them. He never cared for and never held public office, content to live a quiet life, amid the pleasant environment of his home and the friends around about. He was a man of much intelligence and had quaint wit that was very amusing. He was a man of good ideals and a worthy citizen of the community of which he was a lifelong resident. His death occurred May 8, 1922.

HENRY A. SAUNDERS—There are many men who seek their fortunes in foreign fields, leaving their home towns perhaps never to return, but Henry A. Saunders, postmaster and prominent business man of Blue Hill, after a number of years spent in successful business ventures in other States, returned to his native town where he is now one of the prime movers in the business and social advancement of the community. Mr. Saunders is a prominent figure in the political activities of Hancock County, and takes a leading part in all local affairs.

Mr. Saunders was born in Blue Hill, June 11, 1877, son of Benjamin A. Saunders of Deer Isle, who died in 1881, and Mary E. (Curtis) Saunders, of Deer Isle, who is still living. Benjamin A. Saunders was a sea captain and was active in the maritime trade until his death.

Henry A. Saunders received his early education in the local public schools and later attended Blue Hill Academy. He then entered the University of Maine and upon the completion of his course, began his business career as a commercial traveler, which occupied him for nine years. He built up a splendid reputation for himself in his work during that time, after which he was engaged as manager of a retail shoe business in Providence, Rhode Island, in which capacity he served for one year. From there, he went to Boston, Massachusetts, where he spent six years in the same business, managing a number of retail shoe stores in that city. In 1914, he returned to Blue Hill, where he engaged in the shoe business independently, where the experience gained in his many years' engagement in this trade was of great value, and he continued in this business until 1919, when the character of the business was changed completely to that of a news and periodical store. Mr. Saunders has ever since continued to operate this business. In addition to his business affairs, he has been a leader in the civic life of the town, having served six years as the local town clerk and ten years as secretary of the Republican Town Committee. For a period of one year, he was a member of the Republican County Committee, and in 1922, he was appointed postmaster of Blue Hill, which office he continues to discharge to the satisfaction of the community, bringing to the position his experience gained in his many years of business. In fraternal circles, Mr. Saunders is particularly interested in the Knights of Pythias, having been first Chancellor of Kewaydin Lodge, and a member of the Grand Lodge, and for two years, Deputy Grand Chancellor of the State of Maine. He is also a member of the Sigma Chi and the Theta Nu Epsilon fraternities. Ever a public-spirited citizen, Mr. Saunders takes an active

part in the progressive development of the town and vicinity and has been secretary of the Blue Hill Community Club since its inception. For two years, he was secretary of the Hancock County Agricultural Society; he is a member of the Blue Hill Improvement Association, and holds membership in the State of Maine Club of Boston and the Pine Cone Club of Boston. During the World War, Mr. Saunders was engaged in different branches of war work, serving as a member of the Judiciary Board, a member of the Registration Board, and chairman of the War Savings Stamp Committee. His religious affiliations are with the Baptist church. For his recreation, Mr. Saunders prefers chess, checkers, whist and baseball.

Henry A. Saunders married, in 1911, Lena Maddox, of Blue Hill, and their children are: Paul M., Claire C., Elaine, Ruth H, and Wayne F.

WINFIELD BENJAMIN TRICKEY, M. D.—Prominent in the medical profession, Dr. Winfield Benjamin Trickey is known to his fellow-citizens of Pittsfield as a physician of great success and skill, who, in addition to caring for his large medical practice, takes an active interest in community activities and in Masonic circles. Dr. Trickey came here in 1914, and has since built up a reputation for thorough ability and unswerving devotion to his profession.

Dr. Trickey was born in East Corinth, November 19, 1881, son of George Myron Trickey of Exeter, and Anna Eliza (Jewell) Trickey, of Lisbon, New Hampshire, who is deceased. George Myron Trickey was the son of Benjamin Trickey, and has always been engaged in agricultural pursuits. The Trickey family is of English origin, the founder of the American branch having settled in New Hampshire.

Winfield Benjamin Trickey received his early education in the public schools of East Corinth, after which he attended the East Corinth Academy, graduating with the class of 1899. For a time, he studied in the school of the Young Men's Christian Association in Boston, eventually matriculating in Bowdoin Medical School of Bowdoin College, receiving his degree of Doctor of Medicine in 1913. After spending a year as interne in the Eastern Maine General Hospital, he settled in Pittsfield, December 1, 1914, and won the respect and confidence of the people from the start. He is a member of the Penobscot Medical Society, the State Medical Society, and the Phi Chi Medical Fraternity. In politics, Dr. Trickey follows the principles of the Republican party, although he has never identified himself actively with the affairs of the organization, showing no preference for public office, being engaged wholly in the work of his noble profession.

Dr. Winfield Benjamin Trickey married, January 23, 1915, in Portland, Florence Marcella Buck, born at Bath, daughter of William and Elizabeth (Cowley) Buck, both of Maine. Mrs. Buck is deceased. Mr. Buck was engaged for many years as a locomotive engineer. Dr. and Mrs. Trickey have one daughter, Ruth Elizabeth, born January 28, 1918.

E. LEROY PHELPS—Textile manufacture having been the father's occupation for many years, E. Leroy Phelps, of Sangerville, was a natural inheritor of that vocation. His success has been notable, his operations a gratifying addition to the local industries. Only in the prime of middle age, he is filled with the ambition of youth, while guarded against its mistakes by a long apprenticeship in the undertakings with which he is associated.

E. Leroy Phelps was born in Wilmot, New Hampshire, March 26, 1888. His father was Frank W., born in Andover, New Hampshire, and still living, his mother, Nettie (Hoyt) Phelps, born in Springfield, New Hampshire, now deceased. The father was general manager of the Old Town Woolen Company, of Old Town, Maine, with which he was associated for more than twenty years. He is a Republican, and served a term as mayor of Old Town. The son was educated in the Old Town public schools and at Eastman's Business College, Poughkeepsie, New York, from which he was graduated in 1907. He entered the textile business in Old Town, and remained there until 1926, when he purchased the Old Colony Mill at Sangerville, which he since has been operating. The mill manufactures woolens, and was established by the Carr family, afterward owned by L. Coburn. Mr. Phelps was a city councilman of Old Town. He is a Republican, and a member of the Free and Accepted Masons, also the Knights of Pythias. In religion, he is a Baptist.

HON. SCOTT WILSON—Chief Justice of the Supreme Judicial Court of Maine, Scott Wilson has builded up one of the most distinguished careers of bench and bar within the records of this State. He is descended in the ninth generation from Gowen Wilson, who, according to tradition, was born in Scotland in 1618, and took residence in Maine in 1635. It is known that Gowen Wilson was a member of the town of Kittery in 1647. From him to Judge Scott Wilson, the line is thus: (II) Sergeant Joseph. (III) Gowen (2). (IV) Gowen (3). (V) Nathaniel, a lieutenant in the Revolution. (VI) Nathaniel (2). (VII) Nathaniel (3). (VIII) Nathaniel Baker. (IX) Scott Wilson.

Nathaniel Baker Wilson, father of Judge Wilson, and named in part for his mother's family, was born on the old Wilson estate at Falmouth, July 25, 1827, and died in 1897. Of the home estate he made a model farm. At the outbreak of the Civil War, he enlisted in the Union Army, becoming a member of Company B, Twenty-fifth Regiment, Maine Volunteer Infantry, September 30, 1862. He was detailed with this regiment to defend the national capital, and here was engaged until April 1, 1863, when ordered to Chantilly for picket duty. Mustered out of the service July 17, 1863, he returned to the North, and spent the last thirteen years of his life at West Cumberland, where he engaged as trader, before the war having engaged as farmer, as noted, and as carpenter. He married, November 7, 1850, Loemma Pearson Leighton, native of Cumberland, Maine, born May 15, 1831, daughter of Moses and Hannah (Pearson) Leighton, and direct descendant of William Brewster and Governor Thomas Prince of the Plymouth Colony; Rev. John Cotton of the Massachusetts Bay Colony, the Rossiters, Sears, Pearsons, and Bradburys, leading Massachusetts families. Her death occurred in 1924, at the age of ninety-three. Of this union were born children: George N., Alnah L., Orman H., Herman M., and Scott, of whom we write.

Fifth child of Nathaniel Baker and Loemma Pearson (Leighton) Wilson, Judge Wilson was born at Falmouth, Maine, January 11, 1870. He spent thirteen years there, then went with his parents to Cum-

berland, where he continued his academic education in the schools for two years, afterward entering Greeley Institute, Cumberland, where he spent a year. He prepared for college at Nichols Latin School, of Lewiston, matriculated at Bates in 1888, and from it graduated as Phi Beta Kappa four years later. During this period, as his father's resources were not plentiful, he began to teach when aged seventeen, keeping up with this, supplementing the funds from home, until graduation. He also taught at Haverford School in Pennsylvania, two years. The law came more and more into his mind as a desirable career; he determined definitely upon it as such, and entered the law offices of Symonds, Snow and Cook, of Portland, where he studied the case books through summer months, alternating with his teaching at the Haverford School. Also, he took a special course at law in the University of Pennsylvania, and was admitted to the bar of Cumberland County, Maine, in April of 1895; and at once he engaged in practice at Portland. Five years later he formed a partnership with his brother-in-law, Eugene L. Bodge, an association which continued up to his appointment to the Supreme bench.

Resident in the Deering district of Portland, he had served Deering as city solicitor before it became a part of the greater city, and was then, 1899, elected to the city's Common Council, becoming president of the council in 1900. In 1901 and 1902, he served as assistant county attorney, Cumberland County, and from 1903 to 1905 as city solicitor of Portland. In 1913 he was elected attorney for the State of Maine, and served in that capacity until the close of 1915. His work as State's attorney was of lasting importance. From 1913 to 1919 he was a member of the School Board of the city of Portland. He was appointed an associate justice of the Supreme Judicial Court of Maine, August 4, 1918, and on March 1, 1925, became chief justice of the court.

Judge Wilson still continues his residence and has his official headquarters in Portland. He has several financial connections, was for many years a member of the board of overseers of Bates College, having been president of that board in 1905-06, and in 1926 was elected to the Board of Fellows; president of the board of trustees of Greeley Institute; member of the board of trustees of the Portland Public Library, the Portland Athletic, Economic and Fraternity clubs; lecturer on Legal Ethics at the Boston University Law School; and adheres to the principles of the Republican party.

Judge Wilson married, December 24, 1895, at Windham, Maine, Elizabeth M. Bodge, born April 1, 1871, daughter of John Jackson and Martha Maria (Webb) Bodge, of that town, both since deceased. Mrs. Wilson is a graduate of Bates College, class of 1891, a Phi Beta Kappa student, and pursued studies at Radcliffe after her course in Bates. Mrs. Wilson has always been interested in education and literary pursuits, having been a member of the School Board of the city of Portland for eight years, and a member of the leading clubs of the city and State. Judge and Mrs. Wilson have one son, Nathaniel Webb, born June 29, 1900; graduate of Amherst, 1922; member of the Amherst Students' Army Training Corps, September to December, 1918; Harvard Law School, and is now assistant counsel for the New England Public Securities Company, with offices at Augusta. The family residence is on Beacon Street, in Portland.

Honors in many have come to Judge Wilson through the course of his career. The degree of Doctor of Laws was conferred on him by the University of Maine in 1920, and by his *alma mater* three years later, and by Bowdoin in 1927. He is one of Maine's outstanding men.

HAROLD HOWARD SAMPSON — Rising to the distinction of a principalship of an important educational institution at the age of twenty-six years has proven the high worth as an educator of Harold Howard Sampson, of Bridgton, Maine. It may be said that even now he is scarcely at the beginning of a career in the profession of pedagogy that may lead to the greatest heights. Although all who have had the fortune to observe his work would wish him the best of opportunities, there is also a concensus of opinion that this district would be the loser by such advancement that might take him elsewhere.

Harold Howard Sampson was born in Garland, Maine, November 14, 1893, a son of Frank G. and Laura G. (Clark) Sampson. He received his early education in the public schools at Garland and at Dexter High School, from which he was graduated. He then attended Bowdoin College and was graduated therefrom in 1917 with the degree of Bachelor of Arts. From 1917 to 1919 he taught in the Biddeford High School, becoming principal of Bridgton Academy in 1919, a position he still holds. In politics he is a Republican, and his church is the Congregational. He belongs to the college fraternity of Beta Theta Pi, and is a member of the Order of Free and Accepted Masons.

Mr. Sampson married, at Deer Isle, Maine, March 31, 1918, Dorothy Lufkin. They have two children: Lufkin C., and Dorothy L.

BIOGRAPHICAL INDEX

TO VOLUME III ONLY

ADDENDA

*Pride, Byron G., pg. 198. Mr. Pride has passed away since his biography went to press.
*Ross, Dr. Frank M., pg. 307. Dr. Ross passed away August 31, 1927, after his biography had gone to press.

BIOGRAPHICAL INDEX

*Refers to Addenda.

*Refers to Addenda.

474   MAINE—A HISTORY

Sarah J., 19
Sophia, 104
Stanley B., 315
Susie M., 315
Thomas H., 67
Thomas S., 19
William G., 20
William H., 205
William W., Dr., 6
William W., Jr., 6
Wynifred, 301
Snow, Anna A., 13
Charles A., 27
Charles A. (2), 27
Clara, 27
Ella K., 13
John A., 13
John A., Jr., 14
John S., 13
Junita, 27
Kathleyne S., Dr., 14
Soroker, Anna, 140
Jacob, 140
Soule, Alice W., 293
Anna E., 293
Samuel D., 293
Silas M., 293
Southard, Charles H. T. J., 297
Edgar J., 282
Grace E., 297
Joshua N., 282
Julia B., 282
Olive S., 297
Ruth M., 297
Thomas J., 297
Speed, Alice M., 200
Frank H., 200
Lena, 201
Perley E., 200
Robert E. C., 201
Speirs, Alexander, Sen., 350
Anna, 350
Archibald, 350
Bessie, 351
Charlotte, 351
Spenard, Ernest, 185
Jean, 185
Julia, 185
Napoleon, 185
Spencer, Hazel M., 424
Inez, 424
William R., 424
William W., 424
Spiller, Harriett M., 354
Josiah S., 354
Luther C., 354
Margaret, 354
Spinney, Elizabeth, 438
Elvington P., Hon., 153
Grace E., 154
Leon L., 154
Mary J., 153
Miner, 438
Myrtie E., 438
Nehemiah, 438
Palmer O., 153
Sprince, Henry, Dr., 18
Morris, 18
Norma, 19
Rose, 18
Springall, Amos A., 391

Carrie J., 391
Emily J., 391
John B., 391
Stanley, Alfreda, 362
Arthur M., 362
C. L., 362
Charles, 362
Charles S., 362
Elizabeth M., 107
Florence A., 362
J. Malcolm, 107
Naomi, 106
Orman L., 106
Preston J., 106
Stetson, Elisha L., 287
Lewis, 287
Lucy L., 287
Martha, 287
Robert L., 287
Stevens, Albert F., 382, 383
Angie, 383
Annette, 383
Calvert S., 23
Carl H., Dr., 58
Clyde H., 23
Eleanor G., 59
Emma J., 58
George F., 383
Helen, 203
John C., 35
John F., Dr., 202, 203
John H., 35
John W., 59
Leander, 35
Maria J., 35
Martha L., 35
Mason I., 58
Samuel B., 203
Stewart, Albert, 323
Delbert M., Dr., 291
Duncan, 116
Georgia M., 324
John C., 116
Joseph L., 291
Margaret, 116
Mary E., 291
Samuel, 323
Sarah, 323
Stilphen, Annette, 55
Arthur, 55
Florence, 55
Ralph P., 55
Stacy W., 55
Stockwell, Carl V., 200
Carl V., Jr., 200
Edward D., 200
Fannie, 200
Freda, 200
Stone, Edwin, 249
Elizabeth, 60
George F., 60
Gertrude L., 249
Nellie, 249
Philip F., 60
William H., 249
Stratton, Annie, 343
Harry C., 343
Harry L., 343
Purbot H., 343
Sophia J., 343
Strout, Annie L., 336

Arthur C., Dr., 336
Chester R., 336
Frahk L., 142
Grace, 336
Greenleaf A., 336
Mabel P., 336
Rachel, 142
Raymond, 142
Roy M., 142
Stella M., 142
Thomas, Rev., 142
Warren G., 336
Stubbs, Ethelyn, 70
Julia A., 70
Philip H., 70
Richard H., Dr., 70
Richard H., Jr., 70
Sturtevant, Charlotte L., 19
Chester H., 19
Helen E., 19
Josiah H., 19
Norman G., 19
Reginald H., 19
Ronald W., 19
Sweet, Abel S., 225
Abigail, 225
Caldwell, 225
Caldwell, Jr., 226
Helen M., 226
Julia, 226
Nellie K., 226
Swett, Captola E., 279
Frank A., 279
Lucius B., 279
Margaret A., 279
Maria A., 279
Swift, Clara A., 68
George D., 68
Lillian, 68
Raymond W., 68
Willis E., 68
Taft, Arthur L., 376
Ida M., 376
Leroy C., 376
Nellie, 376
Tarbox, Abijah, 143
Alice, 143
Cora E., 143
Fred A., 143
Sophronia, 143
Taylor, Carrie A., 329
Charles E., 179
Charles S., 179
Charles W., 329
Charlotte E., 179
Edgar C., 179
Edward H., 312
Elizabeth, 329
Flossie, 311
Harold E., 311
John, 311
Lida M., 179
Nellie, 311
Russell S., 329
Teague, Carrie W., 47
Greenleaf, 46
Howard A., 46
Rebecca, 46
Thaxter, Julia S., 41
Marie P., 41
Sidney S., 41

476   MAINE—A HISTORY

Matilda, 332
Nancy, 332
Perley L., 260
William, 332
Willis E., 260
Willis L., 260
Watts, Clarissa B., 296
Joseph, 296
Mary J., 296
Samuel, 296
Sarah, 296
Weare, Eunice, 423
George D., 423
Grace E., 338
Henry W., 423
Joseph A., 423
Katherine, 423
Luther S., 338
Stephen, 423
Weatherbee, Albert A., 217
Albert W., 217
Alexander M., 169, 217
Artemus, 169, 217
Helen L., 217
Lucinda E., 217
Mary, 169
Mary J., 217
Randolph A., 217
Webb, Ann D., 107
Jason L., 107
Laura E., 107
Walter L., 107
Webster, Alice E., 189
Daniel, 189
Edwin P., 189
Edwin P., Jr., 189
Wilhelmina J., 189
Wedge, Amelia, 48
Israel, 48
Leland B., 48
Sophia, 48
William A., 47, 48
Weed, Albert W., 255
Chester A., 254
Chester A., Jr., 255
Emmerson G., 255
Hazel P., 255
Kenneth M., 255
Susie E., 254
William H., 254
Weeks, Alanson M., 26
De Forest, 140
Estelle F., 140
Eva J., 26
Fred A., 26
George W., Dr., 139
Ivory B., 139
Mary A., 139
Vesta E., 26
Welch, Clara E., 425
Everett C., 425
Herbert R., 425
Mary, 425
Rufus, 425
Rufus L., 425
Solomon, 425
Wentworth, Carroll H., 111
Charles, 273
Charles H., 22
Charles K., 22

Delia, 273
Elizabeth J., 402
Ellen, 22
Elmer E., 421
Florence E., 22
Francis J., 421
Hattie B., 421
Hattie J., 402
Herbert E., 111
Isa G., 111
John, 401
John, Lieut.-Gov., 401
Mark F., Brig.-Gen., 401
Mildred H., 111
Nellie, 273
Simon, 421
William, Elder, 401
William G., 272, 273
Wescott, Giles, 358
Hester A., 358
Horace F., 358
Lillian, 358
Percival L., 358
Weymouth, Lucy M., 352
Luther S., 352
Percy E., 352
Vera R., 352
Whalen, Floreda, 335
H. Edward, Dr., 335
Henry B., 335
Mary, 335
Wheaton, Calvin, 269
Fred B., Dr., 269
Grace C., 269
Josephine, 269
Wheeler, Alton C., 223
Dean E., 308
Edith H., 224
Eliza F., 308
Lucy E., 223
Pierce E., 223
White, Eliza, 369
Grace A., 369
Helen, 196
Henry P., 369
Martha H., 196
Robert, 369
Robert F., 369
Thomas C., 196
Thomas C., Jr., 196
Wallace H., 196
William F., 196
Wiggin, Albert J., 22
Alvin, 22
Margaret, 23
Mary, 22
Willard, Carrie A., 397
Christine M., 257
Elizabeth, 257
George S., 257
Hiram, 257
Hosea, 397
Lester H., 257
Lovica, 397
Samuel, 257
Stephen, Capt., 397
Willey, Caroline H., 177
Matthew K., 176
Matthew K. (2), 177

Melissa A., 176
Pearl G., 176
Williams, Benjamin, 406
Benjamin (2), 406
Frances E., 78
George S., 78
George S. (2), 78
Helen K., 407
Hugh M., 407
John H., 407
John S., 406
Leroy E., 288
Martha A., 406
Mary E., 78
Norman S., 406
Oliver, 406
Oliver (2), 406
Richard, 406
Roger, 407
Rufus, 406
William, 406
William H., 78
Williamson, Ida, 87
Joseph, 87
Joseph (2), 87
Vallie, 87
William B., 87
William B., Jr., 87
Wilson, Adeline F., 324
Alexander G., 128
Annie L., 410
Arthur E., 324
Austin A., 410
Clinton D., 115
Clinton W., 115
Daniel, 410
Edith M., 324
Elizabeth A., 128
Elizabeth M., 448
Emory C., 324
Francis A., 129
Frederick, 410
Gowen, 448
Hannah, 410
Julia, 128
Loemma P., 448
Mary D., 115
Maynard R., 410, 411
Nathaniel B., 448
Nathaniel W., 448
Ruth, 115, 411
Scott, Hon., 448
Simeon, 410
William, 128
William H., 129
Wing, Moses, Dr., 83
Winslow, Albert, 284
David, 284
Jennie, 284
Sarah F., 284
Winter, Emil E., 348
Harold S., 348
Harriet, 347
Horace G., 347
Ira S. F., 347
Irma J., 348
Wiseman, Armand J., 30
George A., 30
Mary, 30
Philip J., 30

www.ingramcontent.com/pod-product-compliance
Lightning Source LLC
Chambersburg PA
CBHW060127280326
41932CB00012B/1447